# NOSTRADAMUS

## COUNTDOWN TO APOCALYPSE

Jean-Charles de Fontbrune

*Translated by Alexis Lykiard*
*Preface by Liz Greene*

*An Owl Book*
HENRY HOLT AND COMPANY
New York

*To my father,*
*Max de Fontbrune*

Henry Holt and Company, Inc.
*Publishers since 1866*
115 West 18th Street
New York, New York 10011

Henry Holt ® is a registered
trademark of Henry Holt and Company, Inc.

Library of Congress Cataloging-in-Publication Data
Nostradamus, 1503–1566.
Nostradamus, countdown to Apocalypse.
Translation of Nostradamus, historien et prophète
Bibliography: p.
1. Prophecies (Occult sciences)   I. Fontbrune, Jean-Charles de,
1935–   .  II. Lykiard, Alexis, 1940–  .  III. Title.
BF1815.N8A22513   1983                 133.3'092'4        83-10846

ISBN 0-8050-1048-3 (An Owl Book: pbk.)


Henry Holt books are available for special promotions
and premiums. For details contact: Director, Special Markets.

Originally published in France under the title
*Nostradamus: Historien et Prophète.*

First American edition published by
Holt, Rinehart and Winston in 1983.

First Owl Book Edition—1985

Printed in the United States of America
All first editions are printed on acid-free paper.∞

9   11   13   15   14   12   10

# CONTENTS

# PREFACE

The prophecies of Nostradamus are as indestructible as the Revelation of St John, and equally obscure. Nowhere is man's fascination with the irrational as evident as in the matter of prophecy; and no prophet since biblical times has enjoyed as long a life in the popular imagination as Michel de Nostredame, the sixteenth-century Provençal physician turned seer. Since the Centuries of Nostradamus were first published at Lyon in 1555 they have not been out of print, nor has there been any dearth of interpretations in the intervening four centuries. It would seem that decoding the bizarre outpourings of prophets is as irresistible as decoding the unfathomable language of dreams.

The quality of interpretations of the Centuries has varied, and Nostradamus has been described as everything from a Rosicrucian initiate intimate with the secrets of God to a drunkard whose badly rhymed quatrains are a dubious alternative to the proverbial pink elephant. Yet however accurate and astute some of these interpretative efforts have undoubtedly been, there is something stubbornly elusive about Nostradamus' verses which, once again, suggests a similarity to the elusive dream-language that so fascinated Freud and Jung.

Jean de Fontbrune is alone among interpreters of Nostradamus in being wise enough to concede that he does not know it all, even though he has every right to be boastful because of the enormous labour involved in his impeccable historical research. It is possibly because of his humility that his work is unusually sane – too sane, perhaps, for the reader who expects wild, esoteric revelations. M. de Fontbrune is wise, too, in his use of documented history to validate the meanings he attaches to Nostradamus' verses. It is easy to forget that Nostradamus was very much a man of his time, and used the peculiar images and associations of Renaissance symbolism to describe events and persons within his own national and spiritual sphere. He is speaking not in the language of the twentieth century, but in that of the sixteenth, and M. de Fontbrune is the only interpreter I have read who seems to remember this.

The most unusual aspect of M. de Fontbrune's work, however, lies in its chronological approach. Nostradamus himself admitted that he had scrambled his quatrains, and this has made a dog's breakfast of most efforts to interpret them. The prophet leaps about from one time frame to another with no apparent order or continuity. Rather than simply plodding through the verses hoping for inspiration, which is the usual way interpreters have approached them, M. de Fontbrune has followed the unfolding of history through time, beginning with the events occurring around the publication of the Centuries and connecting them with the verses which seem to describe them. He then moves slowly forward through history, gathering verses as he goes.

The effect is magical: Nostradamus no longer sounds like a lunatic, but rather like a careful chronicler of the awesome unfolding of man's fate through world events. The patterns of history are suddenly apparent, and the prophet becomes disturbingly credible. It is only when M. de Fontbrune arrives at the present that he must, obviously, dispense with historical validation of his interpretations, and leave us to believe or disbelieve in the future that is presented. It remains for the reader to decide whether he or she can accept this grim vision. Perhaps it also remains for readers to decide whether there is anything they might do to contribute to or alter that vision.

The questions which the Centuries raise are profound ones, and even if only two or three of Nostradamus' peeps into the future were accurate we would still be confronted by them. The primary question is, of course, whether it is possible to predict the future. If it is, then what does this say about our treasured belief in free will, and in the possibility of a better world built upon conscious efforts toward understanding and good will? Some of Nostradamus' prophecies are so specific that they are impossible to contradict; it is hard to explain away how he managed to see that England's Parliament would behead its king a century after the prophet's own death. So, then, some of history at least *is* predictable. That is a frightening thought, and it is no wonder that so many people use scepticism as a shield to protect themselves from such a revelation.

Perhaps we ought to consider the perspective of Nostradamus himself, because he was after all working with beliefs and techniques which were perfectly appropriate in the context of the world view of his time. He was not unique in his utilization of astrology, magic and prophecy; he was simply better at it than his contemporaries. Prophecy was completely acceptable in the sixteenth century because the universe was viewed as a living organism, governed in its orderly development by the cyclical and inexorable patterns of the planets moving through the zodiac. And the patterns of astrology, as any sixteenth-century magus would have said, were considered the visible signatures of God's inscrutable will and

probable, in the light of trends which are observable now. But whether this *must* be, or *might* be, is a tricky question. To Nostradamus a king meant only one thing: the physical king of a physical country. We, however, are somewhat more sophisticated now. There are not many kings left these days, and though they rule they do not govern as they once did. Now we have presidents and prime ministers, juntas and governing committees. More fancifully, perhaps, there are also inner rulers: dominant ideas, governing our morals and values, little petty tyrants of our minds and souls, benign spiritual leaders that we call our good will or our higher principles. What if an inner king, rather than an outer one, retrieved his lost throne at the end of the millennium? What if the great war that Nostradamus foresees were a psychological battle-field, rather than a physical one? Like an image from a dream, the Great King ruling by right of heaven is open to many levels of interpretation, and they may all occur at once. The French monarchy may indeed be restored; but if there is a possibility of an inner restoration of some long-lost spiritual value, therein lies our possibility of free will in the midst of fate. If one took a dream about the Great King to a Freudian analyst, he might speak of the father problem and its resolution, and he would be perfectly right in his interpretation. If one took that dream to a Jungian analyst, he might speak of the inner King, the symbol of the Self, the Great Man within each individual who represents the essence of one's individual life meaning. And he, too, would be perfectly right.

M. de Fontbrune is concerned that we will make Nostradamus' proph-ecies come true because of our inability to deal with our own natures: our greed, aggression, blindness, intolerance. Perhaps the patterns of history of which Nostradamus speaks are the inevitable confrontations at which we are given the opportunity to handle these ancient issues in new ways; and our capacity to deal with them depends upon how aware we are that war can be an inner thing, and that an enemy can lie within one's own soul – that the old king ripe for dethronement may be an internal and highly individual matter. Perhaps we make prophecy real in concrete life because it is real in the dream world, and in our ignorance of the dream world we force it to enact itself outwardly as fate because it has nowhere else to go.

For many readers a perusal of M. de Fontbrune's marvellous study of the prophecies of Nostradamus may be a sobering and even a frightening experience. Perhaps it is not a bad thing if this is so. I do not believe that either Nostradamus or Jean de Fontbrune intended the reader's response to be one of helpless fatalism. The end of the world might be the end of *a* world, and as such this might be a *world view* rather than a concrete landscape. Any analyst worth his salt will inquire, when brought a dream in which various characters enact their dramas great

and small, what that dream has to do with the dreamer. I am inclined
to feel that Nostradamus' prophetic vision has very much to do with the
individual who explores it. Society is after all made up of individuals,
and wars and plagues and the vicissitudes of kings and popes are also
inner experiences encountered in the bedroom and over the breakfast
table as much as they are great events enacted on the world stage. Jung
once wrote that if there is something wrong with society, then there is
something wrong with the individual. Prophecy is about fate, but fate is
not always so solid and concrete as we imagine it to be. The panorama
of struggle and battle and catastrophe and redemption which Nostradamus unrolls before us may, in the end, be the inner responsibility of each
one of us.

Liz Greene, 1983

# TRANSLATOR'S NOTE

As Jean Charles de Fontbrune himself observes, it should be pointed out that this edition, although of considerable length, does not include *all* the Centuries, presages and sixains of Nostradamus. He hopes to complete this huge task with a second volume in due course. In fact there is currently no complete edition in English of Nostradamus, and most previous versions have been prone to wild error and dubiously Procrustean interpretation. What this edition does provide, unlike others erroneously claiming to be complete – and here it is both unique and impressive – is comprehensive, wide-ranging, impartial annotation drawn from an enormous variety of sources. It represents the fruits of almost fifty years of research by the de Fontbrunes, father and son, and their dedication, scholarship and finally even the services of a computer have shed considerable light on many of the intentional and unintentional obscurities of the prophecies.

By its very nature this is a compilation to be sampled and argued over, rather than a consecutive or 'easy' read; it will, I am sure, continue to exert considerable fascination. Like myself, readers, however sceptical initially, may well find themselves becoming uneasily convinced by a disturbing percentage of these predictions.

They may find, too, that Nostradamus' Letter to his son César, included here for the first time in an English-language edition, often remains obscure, odd or ambiguously phrased, important though it is. By the time he wrote it Nostradamus must have been more than a little apprehensive about the Inquisition; nor did he wish his son to decipher and disseminate his visions too readily or prematurely. One feels also that the seer wanted to impose a sort of extra, unofficial education upon the youth, for human beings possess a compulsive urge to explore and solve mysteries, and where the works of Nostradamus are concerned this twin process requires, as de Fontbrune notes, a considerable fund of learning, often specialized, and acquired slowly and with patience. 'Please do not understand me too quickly,' André Gide once wrote. One incomplete edition of the Centuries now available (and Nostradamus has never been out of print in some form or other since his own time), which includes what seem to be wilfully inaccur~   interpretations by contrast with de Fontbrune's sober and painstakir   approach, merely states that the Letter to César has been omitted 'br   ase of length and obscurity'! Readers must judge for themselves.

It should be stressed that the latter part of this edition deals with predictions for the future and such prophecies obviously cannot be precisely dated, verified by events or checked as yet, since they remain in the realm of speculation. De Fontbrune's interpretations of the prophecies, as a whole, have not been 'tidied up' or made to read more smoothly by this translator, but are set down as literally as possible. Readers should bear in mind that this is rhyming sixteenth-century French with a Provençal accent, employed by a polymath author virtually thinking in Latin and Greek and deliberately juggling with anagrams and all the other linguistic and riddling devices de Fontbrune describes more fully in his own preface. Inevitably the result is compression and obscurity: imagine, for instance, trying to send future generations a coded rhymed telegram in a mixture of high-flown yet colloquial language and in which, say, the destruction of London might be foretold in terms of 'The Great Wen lanced' or 'The Smoke dispersed', and then contemplate a hapless commentator's difficulty four hundred years later when attempting to break this sort of condensed, archaic, gnomic quatrain.

When the author wishes to emphasize a parallel between Nostradamus' work and the historical verification, he will sometimes repeat the word or phrase in brackets or place it in italics (for example, *sous la ramée*, CIV,Q62 where both these devices have been employed, or *naked* in CIII,Q30, which has simply been italicized). Similarly, if a quatrain strongly implies a crucial link, for instance '*le grand*' in CXII,Q36, de Fontbrune will sometimes include in his interpretative passage the 'missing' word – in this case 'armies', but place it in brackets. Other points regarded as particularly significant by de Fontbrune have been italicized in the histories following quatrains.

There are further complications. Imagine too Nostradamus' sixteenth-century frame of reference, and recall how he 'sees' and describes the furniture van into which Mussolini's body was flung. A metal box upon wheels – that certainly makes sense. And how, accordingly, would *you* yourself predict events revealed to you – very visually, sometimes specifically, but bewilderingly too – situated in the twenty-fifth century, without any real knowledge of how technology, politics or human biology had by then developed? Nostradamus' panoramic or cosmic viewpoint, almost from aloft like Hardy's in *The Dynasts*, represents a curious perspective of history, time and space, and whether or not readers agree with the interpretations offered here, they will find much to interest them.

Alexis Lykiard, 1983

# I

# ON METHOD

'The wise man will rule over planetary influences, which do not necessarily bring their properties to bear upon terrestrial bodies; but he only influences the latter, because it is possible to protect oneself through prudence and discretion.'

Ptolemy

Of all the famous men of the sixteenth century, Michel de Nostredame, known as Nostradamus, has probably prompted the most controversy. A considerable body of criticism and study has accumulated, especially in the twentieth century which is the main subject of his prophetic vision. All this interest suggests a work of unusual and considerable fascination. Excluding apocrypha and keeping to the 1568 edition, the *oeuvre* of Nostradamus consists of:

1. *The letter to his son César*. This text is really in the nature of a foreword to his future translator and is of prime importance in understanding his writings.

2. *Twelve books or 'Centuries'* containing a total of 965 quatrains, subdivided as follows:
Centuries I, II, III, IV, V, VI, IX, X, each of one hundred quatrains.
Century VII, of forty-six quatrains.
Century VIII, of one hundred quatrains, together with an additional eight quatrains.
Century IX, of two quatrains.
Century XII, of eleven quatrains.

3. *One quatrain in Latin*, at the end of Century VI and before Century VII, constituting a supplementary foreword.

4. *Portents (présages)* totalling 141.

5. *Sixains*: fifty-eight in all.

6. *The letter to Henri, Second King of France*: prose text at the end of Century VII, which constitutes a sort of synopsis of Nostradamus' vision.

In deciphering any of Nostradamus' writing, complete accuracy is essential – readers will be aware of how a subtle shift of emphasis can alter the whole meaning of a phrase. This letter just mentioned is introduced by a dedicatory greeting reproduced as follows in all the early editions of Nostradamus' work until that of Chevillot at Troyes in 1611:

'To the Invincible, Almighty and Christian Henri, the second King of France, Michel Nostradamus, his very humble and obedient servant and subject sends victory and happiness.'

In many editions after 1611, the following modification appears:

'To the Invincible, Almighty and Christian Henri II, King of France, Michel Nostradamus . . .'

The transformation of '*Henri Roy de France second*' to '*Henri II Roy de France*' changes both the sense of the letter and the identity of the addressee. If indeed it refers to Henri II, the description of him as invincible and all-powerful hardly applies since his reign was so brief and, moreover, he died somewhat ingloriously in a jousting accident on 11 July 1559. In the earlier editions, however, the word '*second*' is placed not directly after the name Henri, but where it refers specifically to 'King'. If we look at the word's Latin origin, *secundus* means favoured, propitious or fortunate. Now the letter refers not to Henri II but to a future king of France who will accede at a particularly crucial time in that country's history. Certain authors have assumed accordingly that Henri IV was intended. This hypothesis cannot be supported, since in several quatrains Nostradamus specifically states that he is referring to a king whose christian name is Henri, but associates the name with the number V: this letter must therefore be addressed to a person of exceptional qualities who has not yet played his role in history.

The verses of Nostradamus – 4772 lines – are in old French, a language still very close to its Latin and Greek roots. This explains the problems encountered by commentators lacking the literary background, first in translating the work into contemporary French and then in reconstituting the vast jigsaw puzzle of the quatrains. Consequently, innumerable linguistic errors appear in many editions, which has given rise to the opinion that Nostradamus' writings are obscure or incomprehensible, and to the frequently levelled criticism that virtually any meaning can be attributed to them.

Various attempts were made at expounding Nostradamus' Centuries before the twentieth century, but these were few compared to the many important studies published since 1938, the year in which my father, Dr

Max de Fontbrune, published the first complete critique of the *Works*. The first attempt to expound the work of Nostradamus dates back to 1594, and was made by a friend of Nostradamus, Jean Aimé de Chavigny.[1] Then came Guynaud[2] in 1693, and Bareste[3] in 1840, the latter inspired by his two predecessors. There followed Le Pelletier[4] in 1867, who in his turn drew upon these three earlier commentators, then the Abbé Torné-Chavigny[5] in 1870, who made use of all the forerunners. In 1929 P. V. Piobb,[6] taking no notice of Nostradamus' cautions, claimed to have found the key to the problem in occultism.

However all these writers translated only a few of the quatrains. Even the most important, Le Pelletier, only translated 194 out of 965 quatrains, four out of 141 portents and five out of fifty-eight sixains – a far from complete study. Perhaps Nostradamus' ultimate 'message' was intended for the twentieth century and the texts relating to earlier periods of history simply bear witness to the value and accuracy of his prophecy.

In 1934 my father was sent a 1605 edition; he slowly began translating Nostradamus' quatrains, and published the first major commentary in 1938. Apart from describing Nostradamus' prediction of the German army's advance through Belgium to invade France, he wrote of Germany's loss of the war and Hitler's wretched end. These grim prophecies resulted in his being hounded by the Gestapo and having his book confiscated and withdrawn from every bookshop in France; the type itself was broken up and melted down. The following article is from the *Journal Sud-Ouest* in September 1944:

LAVAL BANNED THE PROPHECIES OF NOSTRADAMUS
because they referred to an old man 'mocked by everyone' and
'a general who returned in triumph'.

Some time ago Pierre Laval personally intervened to withdraw from sale and ban Dr de Fontbrune's edition of *The Prophecies of Nostradamus*. Who could have expected this to have been a wise move?

Dr de Fontbrune lives quietly at Sarlat. This learned man, who has provided the best translation of the sayings of the great sage, now has something of a reputation as a soothsayer. In any case, during the war, with incredible generosity

---

[1] *La Première Face du Janus français extraite et colligée des centuries de Michel Nostradamus*, les héritiers de Pierre Roussin, Lyon, 1594.

[2] *Concordance des prophéties depuis Henri II jusqu'à Louis Le Grand*, Jacques Morel, Paris, 1693.

[3] Edition of *Centuries*, Maillet, Paris, 1840.

[4] *Les Oracles de Nostradamus, astrologue, médecin et conseiller ordinaire des rois Henry II, François II et Charles IX*. 2 vols, self-published by Le Pelletier (also printer and typographer), Paris, 1867.

[5] Several works published at the author's expense between 1860 and 1878.

[6] *Le Secret de Nostradamus*, Adyar, Paris, 1929.

he has actively resisted in his capacity as a doctor, saving many of our young compatriots.

In his Nostradamus book, Dr de Fontbrune predicted the war in North Africa; the future victors' invasion of Italy; aerial combat on the grand scale, followed by fighting on French soil (specifically at Poitiers and Belfort). Finally, too, France's misfortune 'under an old man who will subsequently be despised', and according to the ancient text, 'mocked by everyone'; and the glorious rescue by a general 'temporarily absent and who shall return in triumph'.

This last remark caused the book to be banned: its concluding chapter forecasts the defeat and partition of Germany. Not bad going, we must admit. Dr de Fontbrune and his friend Nostradamus have been avenged . . . and so have we!

Here is the censorship order, dated 13 November 1940, banning my father's book:

> From M. Nismes, Principal Censor, Cahors, to the Managers,
> Coueslant Press, Cahors.

This is to confirm that subsequent to a decision by the Vice-President of the Council, the work printed by your firm and entitled *The Prophecies of Master Michel Nostradamus* by Dr de Fontbrune, published by Michelet of Sarlat, has now had its permit revoked. Accordingly it is illegal to offer the work for sale and, should you yourselves be its distributors to local bookshops, you are requested to take the appropriate measures to call back all copies to your premises, such copies in due course to be forfeit whether on your premises or those of the publishers at Sarlat. The question of first, limited editions or reprints is irrelevant, given that in all versions of this work Dr de Fontbrune's commentary risks provoking severe reaction from the occupying authorities.

Born in 1935, I can almost say I was born and bred into Nostradamus studies, living with my father as I did until his death at Montpellier in 1959. So it is not surprising that after military service I took up my father's work in 1963. I found that there were a good many errors and obscurities in it. Starting from the nonetheless extraordinarily coherent vision he had of the work, I began a detailed analysis of the text. This involved my restoring to the past certain prophecies thought by my father to relate to the future, but I also translated and interpreted various texts never previously translated nor understood by any earlier commentator.

Since 1938 numerous books about Nostradamus have appeared, many inspired by my father's, but also some cases of blatant plagiarism. For instance, a 'reputable' astrologer, Maurice Privat, published a work on Nostradamus in 1938. Its title alone is nothing if not schematic: *1940,*

*Year of French Greatness*[1]. This was at a time when my father's book was warning that the Second World War would prove catastrophic for France – warnings based, of course, on centuries-old predictions.

Some authors did give my father his due:

Before the Second World War, Dr de Fontbrune published a profound study of the Prophecies.[2]

Dr de Fontbrune's interpretation seems the most generally accepted since Bareste in 1840 began the first attempts at decoding.[3]

In memory of Dr de Fontbrune, through whose work I came to know Nostradamus.[4]

Without a doubt, one of the most serious works is Dr de Fontbrune's.[5]

In a letter to my father, after meeting him in the Dordogne in 1953, Henry Miller wrote:

'Once again I must stress your gift for making everything clear in a very few words. It's a rare gift, believe me. One senses your unswerving integrity – which makes all you say seem lucid. You see, without your wanting to do so, you have become a sort of 'confessor' for me. What I could never tell a priest I can tell you quite freely. I like men who have won through to their own vision of the world and the life everlasting. The more I think about your creative work of interpretation, the more I admire you. The way in which you have gone into the prophecy always astounds me, despite the fact that it was the only, the inevitable way of undertaking this. It takes inspiration to make such a discovery.

*Labor omnia vincit improbus* [Persistent toil conquers everything] wrote Virgil in his *Georgics*. This is why I am now making public the fruits of a total of forty-four years' research by father and son. Readers will find here all those texts which history has already proved correct: they are presented as a virtually irrefutable demonstration of Nostradamus' authentic powers as a prophet, although he himself never claimed to be one.

To understand the hermetic nature of the work, one must read the Letter to César, included here in its entirety. The prefatory admonitions Nostradamus addressed to his future translators are essential in deciphering his message. In this way magic and occultism can be dismissed.

---

[1] Editions Médicis, Paris, 1938.
[2] Michel Touchard, *Nostradamus*, Grasset, 1972.
[3] Eric Muraise, *Saint-Rémy de Provence et les Secrets de Nostradamus*, Julliard, 1969.
[4] Jean Monterey, *Nostradamus, prophète du XXe Siècle*, la Nef de Paris, 1961.
[5] Camille Rouvier, *Nostradamus*, la Savoisienne, Marseille, 1964.

# Preface by
# M. Nostradamus to his Prophecies

*Greetings and Happiness to César Nostradamus my son*

Your late arrival, César Nostredame, my son, has made me spend much
time in constant nightly reflection so that I could communicate with you
by letter and leave you this reminder, after my death, for the benefit of
all men, of what the divine spirit has vouchsafed me to know by means
of astronomy. And since it was the Almighty's will that you were not
born here in this region [Provence] and I do not want to talk of years to
come but of the months during which you will struggle to grasp and
understand the work I shall be compelled to leave you after my death:
assuming that it will not be possible for me to leave you such [clearer]
writing as may be destroyed through the injustice of the age [1555]. The
key to the hidden prediction which you will inherit will be locked inside
my heart. Also bear in mind that the events here described have not yet
come to pass, and that all is ruled and governed by the power of Almighty
God, inspiring us not by bacchic frenzy nor by enchantments but by
astronomical assurances: predictions have been made through the inspiration of divine will alone and the spirit of prophecy in particular. On
numerous occasions and over a long period of time I have predicted
specific events far in advance, attributing all to the workings of divine
power and inspiration, together with other fortunate or unfortunate
happenings, foreseen in their full unexpectedness, which have already
come to pass in various regions of the earth. Yet I have wished to remain
silent and abandon my work because of the injustice not only of the
present time [the Inquisition] but also for most of the future. I will not
commit it to writing, since governments, sects and countries will undergo
such sweeping changes, diametrically opposed to what now obtains, that
were I to relate events to come, those in power now – monarchs, leaders
of sects and religions – would find these so different from their own
imaginings that they would be led to condemn what later centuries will
learn how to see and understand. Bear in mind also Our Saviour's words:
*Nolite sanctum dare canibus, nec mittatis margaritas ante porcos ne conculent
pedibus et conversi dirumpant vos* [Do not give anything holy to the dogs,
nor throw pearls in front of the pigs lest they trample them with their
feet and turn on you and tear you apart]. For this reason I withdrew my
pen from the paper, because I wished to amplify my statement touching
the Vulgar Advent (1), by means of ambiguous and enigmatic comments
about future causes, even those closest to us and those I have perceived,
so that some human change which may come to pass shall not unduly
scandalize delicate sensibilities. The whole work is thus written in a

nebulous rather than plainly prophetic form. So much so that, *Abscondisti haec a sapientibus et prudentibus, id est potentibus et regibus et eunuculeasti ea exiguis et tenuibus* [You have hidden these things from the wise and the circumspect, that is from the mighty and the rulers, and you have purified those things for the small and the poor], and through Almighty God's will, revealed unto those prophets with the power to perceive what is distant and thereby to foretell things to come. For nothing can be accomplished without this faculty, whose power and goodness work so strongly in those to whom it is given that, while they contemplate within themselves, these powers are subject to other influences arising from the force of good. This warmth and strength of prophecy invests us with its influence as the sun's rays affect both animate and inanimate entities. We human beings cannot through our natural consciousness and intelligence know anything of God the Creator's hidden secrets, *Quia non est nostrum noscere tempora nec momenta* [For it is not for us to know the times or the instants], etc. So much so that persons of future times may be seen in present ones, because God Almighty has wished to reveal them by means of images, together with various secrets of the future vouchsafed to orthodox astrology, as was the case in the past, so that a measure of power and divination passed through them, the flame of the spirit inspiring them to pronounce upon inspiration both human and divine. God may bring into being divine works, which are absolute; there is another level, that of angelic works; and a third way, that of the evildoers. But my son, I address you here a little too obscurely. As regards the occult prophecies one is vouchsafed through the subtle spirit of fire, which the understanding sometimes stirs through contemplation of the distant stars as if in vigil, likewise by means of pronouncements, one finds oneself surprised at producing writings without fear of being stricken for such impudent loquacity. The reason is that all this proceeds from the divine power of Almighty God from whom all bounty proceeds. And so once again, my son, if I have eschewed the word prophet, I do not wish to attribute to myself such a lofty title at the present time, for whoever *Propheta dicitur hodie, olim vocabatur videns*; since a prophet, my son, is properly speaking one who sees distant things through a natural knowledge of all creatures. And it can happen that the prophet bringing about the perfect light of prophecy may make manifest things both human and divine, because this cannot be done otherwise, given that the effects of predicting the future extend far off into time. God's mysteries are incomprehensible and the power to influence events is bound up with the great expanse of natural knowledge, having its nearest most immediate origin in free will and describing future events which cannot be understood simply through being revealed. Neither can they be grasped through men's interpretations nor through another mode of cognizance or occult power under the firmament, neither in the present nor in the total eternity to come. But bringing about such an indivisible eternity through Herculean efforts (2), things are revealed by the planetary movements. I am not saying, my son – mark me well, here – that knowledge of such things cannot be implanted in your deficient mind, or that events in the distant future may not be within the understanding of any reasoning being. Nevertheless, if these things current or distant are brought to the awareness of this reasoning and intelligent being they will be neither too obscure nor too clearly revealed. Perfect knowledge of such things cannot be acquired without divine inspiration, given that all prophetic inspiration derives its initial origin from God Almighty, then from chance and nature. Since all these portents are produced impartially, prophecy comes to pass partly as predicted. For understanding created by the intellect cannot be acquired by means of the occult, only by the aid of the zodiac, bringing forth that small flame by whose light part of the future may be discerned. Also, my son, I beseech you not to exercise your mind upon such reveries and vanities as drain the body and incur the soul's perdition, and which trouble our feeble frames. Above all avoid the vanity of that most execrable magic formerly reproved by the Holy Scriptures – only excepting the use of official astrology. For by the latter, with the help of inspiration and divine revelation, and continual calculations, I have set down my prophecies in writing. Fearing lest this occult philosophy be condemned, I did not therefore wish to make known its dire import; also fearful that several books which had lain hidden for long centuries might be discovered, and of what might become of them, after reading them I presented them to Vulcan [i.e. burned them]. And while he devoured them, the flame licking the air gave out such an unexpected light, clearer than that of an ordinary flame and resembling fire from some flashing cataclysm, and suddenly illumined the house as if it were caught in a furnace. Which is why I reduced them to ashes then, so that none might be tempted to use occult labours in searching for the perfect transmutation, whether lunar or solar, of incorruptible metals (3). But as to that discernment which can be achieved by the aid of planetary scrutiny, I should like to tell you this. Eschewing any fantastic imaginings, you may through good judgement have insight into the future if you keep to the specific names of places that accord with planetary configurations, and with inspiration places and aspects yield up hidden properties, namely that power in whose presence the three times [past, present, and future] are understood as Eternity whose unfolding contains them all: *quia omnia sunt nuda et aperta*, etc. That is why, my son, you can easily, despite your young brain, understand that events can be foretold naturally by the heavenly bodies and by the spirit of prophecy: I do not wish to ascribe to myself the title and role of prophet, but emphasize inspiration revealed to a mortal man whose perception is no further from heaven than the feet are from the earth. *Possum non errare, falli, decipi*: although I may be as great a sinner as anyone else upon this earth and subject to all human afflictions. But after being surprised sometimes by day while in a trance, and having long fallen into the habit of agreeable nocturnal studies, I have composed books of prophecies, each containing one hundred astronomical quatrains, which I wanted to condense somewhat obscurely. The work comprises prophecies from today to the year 3797. This may perturb some, when they see such a long timespan, and this will occur and be understood in all the fullness of the Republic (4); these things will be universally understood upon earth, my son. If you live the normal lifetime of man you will know upon your own soil, under your native sky, how future events are to turn out. For only Eternal God knows the eternity of His light which proceeds from Him, and I speak frankly to those to whom His immeasurable, immense and incomprehensible greatness has been disposed to grant revelations through long, melancholy inspiration, that with the aid of this hidden element manifested by God, there are two principal factors which make up the prophet's intelligence. The first is when the supernatural light fills and illuminates the person who predicts by astral science, while the second allows him to prophesy through inspired revelation, which is only a part of the divine eternity, whereby the prophet comes to assess what his divinatory power has given him through the grace of God and by a natural gift, namely, that what is foretold is true and ethereal in origin (5). And such a light and small flame is of great efficacy and scope, and nothing less than the clarity of nature itself. The light of human nature makes the philosophers so sure of themselves that with the principles of the first cause they reach the loftiest doctrines and the deepest abysses. But my son, lest I venture too far for your future perception, be aware that men of letters shall make grand and usually boastful claims about the way I interpreted the world, before the worldwide conflagration which is to bring so many catastrophes and such revolutions that scarcely any lands will not be covered by water (6), and this will last until all has perished save history and geography themselves. This is why, before and after these revolutions in various countries, the rains will be so diminished and such abundance of fire and fiery missiles shall fall from the heavens that nothing shall escape the holocaust. And this will occur before the last conflagration [1999]. For before war ends the [twentieth] century and in its final stages [1975–99] it will hold the century under its sway. Some countries will be in the grip of revolution (7) for several years, and others ruined for a still longer period. And now that we are in a republican era, with Almighty God's aid, and before completing its full cycle, the monarchy will return, then the Golden Age (8). For according to the celestial signs, the Golden Age shall return, and after all calculations, with the world near to an all-encompassing revolution – from the time of writing 177 years 3 months 11 days (9) – plague, long famine and wars, and still more floods from now until the stated time. Before and after these, humanity shall several times be so severely diminished that scarcely anyone shall be found who wishes to take over the fields, which shall become free where they had previously been tied. This will be after the visible judgement of heaven, before we reach the millennium which shall complete all. In the firmament of the eighth sphere, a dimension whereon Almighty God will complete the revolution, and where the constellations will resume their motion which will render the earth stable and firm, but only if *non inclinabitur in saeculum saeculi* [He will remain unchanged for ever] – until His will be done. This is in spite of all the ambiguous opinions surpassing all natural reason, expressed by Mahomet; which is why God the Creator, through the ministry of his fiery agents with their flames, will come to propose to our perceptions as well as our eyes the reasons for future predictions. Signs of events to come must be manifested to whomever prophesies. For prophecy which stems from exterior illumination is a part of that light and seeks to ally with it and bring it into being so that the part which seems to possess the faculty of understanding is not subject to a sickness of the mind. Reason is only too evident. Everything is predicted by divine afflatus (10) and thanks to an angelic spirit inspiring the one prophesying, consecrating his predictions through divine unction. It also divests him of all fantasies by means of various nocturnal apparitions, while with daily certainty he prophesies through the science of astronomy, with the aid of sacred prophecy, his only consideration being his courage in freedom. So come, my son, strive to understand what I have found out through my calculations which accord with revealed inspiration, because now the sword of death approaches us, with pestilence and war more horrible than there has ever been – because of three men's work – and with famine. And this sword shall smite the earth and return to it often, for the stars confirm this upheaval and it is also written: *Visitabo in virga ferrea iniquitates eorum, et in verberibus percutiam eos* [I shall punish their injustices with iron rods, and shall strike them with blows]. For God's mercy will be poured forth only for a certain time, my son, until the majority of my prophecies are fulfilled and this fulfilment is complete. Then several times in the course of the doleful tempests the Lord shall say: *Conteram ergo et confringam et non miserebor* [Therefore I shall crush and destroy and show no mercy]; and many other circumstances shall result from floods and continual rain (11) of which I have written more fully in my other prophecies, composed at some length, not in a chronological sequence, *in soluta oratione* [in prose], limiting the places and times and exact dates so that future generations will see, while experiencing these inevitable events, how I have listed others in clearer language, so that despite their obscurities these things shall be understood: *Sed quando submovenda erit ignorantia*, the matter will be clearer still. So in conclusion, my son, take this gift from your father M. Nostradamus, who hopes you will understand each prophecy in every quatrain herein. May Immortal God grant you a long life of good and prosperous happiness.

Salon, 1 March 1555

*Notes*

1. *le commun advènement*, the Vulgar Advent, or the accession of the people to power, is generally taken by commentators to refer first to republicanism (via the French Revolution), then to its development towards and change into communism. (*Tr.*)

2. Nostradamus here compares his work, the twelve Centuries, to the Twelve Labours of Hercules, in order to stress their difficulty and importance.

3. Moon and Sun are constant symbols in Nostradamus of the republic and the monarchy respectively, hence the alchemic imagery also has a political aspect here.

4. Reference to *toute la concavité de la lune*. Cf. note 3 above.

5. Ether: originally personified as a deity of the upper atmosphere, and later confused with Zeus. (DL 7V).

6. Water and flooding are often taken as a symbol of revolution in Nostradamus.

7. The French text refers to Aquarius, i.e. the water-bearer. Cf. note 6 above.

8. Golden Age: rule of Saturn, the happy, peaceful time, to commemorate which the Romans celebrated with Saturnalia.

9. 1555 + 177 = 1732, the exact date when Rousseau arrived in Paris, Nostradamus considered Rousseau the father of revolutionary and atheistic ideas.

10. Breath or inspiration, oracular possession.

11. Upheavals and revolution. Cf. notes 6 and 7 above.

---

The specifically 'scientific' side of Nostradamus' personality is in no way vitiated by his recourse to hermeticism so as not to be witch-hunted: when his fellow citizens of Salon burned him in effigy outside his house he went to the French court to seek protection from Queen Catherine de Médecis. She not only granted protection but visited him at Salon, which soon stopped the gossip in that small town.

Nostradamus also found out how the plague was transmitted, and discovered a form of asepsis four centuries before Pasteur. Indeed, sixteenth-century chronicles which describe the methods used by Nostradamus to control the plague epidemics at Aix-en-Provence, Marseille and Lyon make one realize that this Provençal doctor took quite sophisticated antiseptic precautions, though he had to invent a special powder to conceal his true scientific discovery, for had the extent of his knowledge been made known, he would have been burned at the stake for sorcery. At this time the Church still considered that sickness and plague were God's way of punishing man for his sins. The Inquisition's reign of terror was being enforced and Galileo, born in 1564, two years before the death of Nostradamus, would himself fall foul of this anti-scientific consensus for stating that the earth revolved.

It is thus all the more understandable that Nostradamus deliberately shrouded his prophecies in linguistic and even astrological mists, for had he openly expressed his vision of the future it would certainly not have survived. The religious authorities would very likely have destroyed it. My father's own misfortunes with his book in 1940 illustrate what can happen when a prophet's 'message' is expressed absolutely directly.

The prophecies of Nostradamus, then, were written in the sixteenth century in order to depict the twentieth, to which two-thirds of the work is devoted, for their author seemed to know that his text would be expounded and understood only in the century which was the focus of his vision. As for the fulfilment of his prophecy, writers have discovered or invented this either by resorting to astrological calculations, more or less arithmetical 'keys', or the Cabbala and so on. Actually the prophecies end with the seventh millennium, which according to biblical chronology is the conclusion of the Piscean Age, approximately 2000 AD. Here again, Nostradamus cunningly concealed this fact: the calculation can only be arrived at using the biblical reckoning he gives in the letter to 'Henry Roy de France Second', as follows:

| From Adam, the first man, to Noah | 1242 years |
|---|---|
| Noah to Abraham | 1080 years |
| From Abraham to Moses | 515 years |
| Moses to David | 570 years |
| David to Jesus Christ | 1350 years |

i.e. from Adam to Christ, a total of 4757 years.

In the letter to César, Nostradamus mentions prophecies from the year of writing until 3797. From the time of writing (the letter is dated 1555) until 3797 there is a difference of 2242 years. If one adds this length of time to the biblical chronology above the result is 6999, or in Christian (taking into account Christ's thirty-three years) chronology 1999, the date clearly given by Nostradamus as the starting point of the Wars of the Anti-Christ:

> L'an mil neuf cent nonante neuf sept mois
> Du ciel viendra un grand Roy d'effrayeur
> Ressusciter le grand Roy d'Angoulmois,[1]
> Avant après Mars regner par bonheur.

CX,Q72

## Interpretation

In July, the seventh month of 1999, a great and terrifying leader will come by air, reviving or recalling the great conqueror of Angoulême. Before and after, war will reign happily.

Nostradamus gives only a few specific dates. Other than 1999, he mentions in the letter to '*Henry Roy de France Second*' that the monarchy 'will last until the year 1792 which will be considered the start of a new age'. The way in which he wrote down his visions suggests that these two specific dates are more important if taken as points of departure and arrival rather than in isolation. 1792 (the year of the proclamation of the French Republic) represents the beginning of the end of the Christian Era (Piscean Age) and 1999 its actual end, which thus begins the Age of Aquarius with the pains of apocalyptic childbirth necessary in order for man to stop concentrating his efforts upon more and more horrifying means of destruction. This is the reason why Nostradamus completes his quatrain with this surprising line, 'Before and after Mars [War] will reign *happily*' [*par bonheur* = happily, or, as luck would have it].

A prophecy that comes true becomes history. For example, Nostradamus writes of Napoleon I:

> De la cité marine et tributaire,
> La teste raze prendra la Satrapie:[2]
> Chassez sordide qui puis sera contraire,
> Par quatorze ans tiendra la tyranie.

> CVII,QI3

## Interpretation

From the port under foreign domination the shaven-headed man will take power. He will drive out the squalid revolutionaries, the wind of history having changed, and will rule tyrannically for fourteen years.

---

[1] Angoulême was conquered by the Visigoths, then threatened by the Mongolian race of Huns led by Attila, 'the scourge of God'. Note the neat analogy in the fact that the Huns first occupied Pannonia so as to ravage France and Italy.

[2] Satraps were governors of provinces under Persian rule, filling the dual roles of administrators and tax collectors.

## History

From Alexandria, which had become a French dependency, Bonaparte organized Egypt into a sort of prefecture, then embarked for France, whose political situation was giving him cause for anxiety.[1] He helped to overthrow the Directorate and in the coup of 18 Brumaire assumed power, which was absolute until the Allies entered Paris on 31 March 1814, i.e. after fourteen years, four months and eleven days of his rule.

I have chosen this particular quatrain because like many others its message covers a span of time. The first part of the quatrain was accomplished on 18 Brumaire 1799, becoming history while the second part remained prophecy until 31 March 1814.

This 'stroll' across time and space which is the prophet's habit defies all rational chronological classification. Should a quatrain referring to the retreat from Moscow (CII,Q99) be placed before or after the one just quoted? The retreat occurred after the 1799 coup but preceded Napoleon's Fontainebleau abdication on 6 April 1814. Nostradamus' prophecy constitutes a vision of history which has nothing in common with the version taught in schools.

This quatrain leads me to formulate a useful principle for anyone interested in prophecies like those of Nostradamus and hence obliged to abandon preconceived ideas. Events in particular, and history in general, never unfold according to man's Cartesian pattern. I need only instance the eminent French economists of the 'Club of Rome' who in 1972 boldly forecast that France would be the third major world power by 1980. In September 1973 the Arab–Israeli war precipitated the world economic crisis and shook the West, reducing our economic pundits' fine promises to nothing.

To illustrate history's caprice let us return to Napoleonic times, to 2 December 1805, the date of Austerlitz, when the Emperor had the world at his feet. Imagine that a prophet were to announce Napoleon's ignominious end as a prisoner of the English on an island in the mid-Atlantic. He would have risked imprisonment, execution or internment in a psychiatric hospital. My father was ridiculed in much the same way in 1946 and later when he maintained that General de Gaulle – who had just withdrawn from the political arena for what might be termed a 'period in the wilderness' – would return to power in a coup d'état. Friends who had once mocked wrote politely to him after 13 May 1958, astonished by an event which twelve years earlier they had all thought impossible.

History, and events that lie ahead, almost always completely contradict

[1] LCH3

in both matter and manner the times which we are living through. This is why so few can aspire to the perception the prophet has tried to transmit to posterity. The obstacle to understanding the spirit of prophecy lies basically in the antagonism between vision and rationalism. Adherents of the latter cannot abandon their system of logic to enter into any other form of reasoning. The essential requirement for getting to grips with prophecy is a very open mind.

Continuing my father's work, I spent five years making an exhaustive study of Nostradamus' vocabulary. This enabled me to explicate the prophet's language, except for a few minor details, and to correct errors of translation made by the Centuries' innumerable previous commentators. Many errors perpetrated by Le Pelletier were repeated verbatim by other authors.

Take, for example, the most famous quatrain predicting the death of Henri II while jousting:

> Le Lyon jeune le vieux surmontera,
> En champ bellique par singulier duelle,
> Dans cage d'or les yeux lui crèvera
> Deux classes une, puis mourir mort cruelle.

CI,Q35

*Interpretation*

The young lion shall overcome the old in a tourney (single combat). Inside a golden cage his eyes will be put out in one of the two contests, then he shall die grievously.

Montgoméry, captain of the Scottish Guard, whose arms were 'or, with lion of Scotland passant, gules' jousted with Henri II. Montgoméry's lance splintered and penetrated the visor of the King's gilded helmet.

In this quatrain Le Pelletier and his followers derive *classes* from the Greek word χλασις (breakage or lopping of a branch) and translate: 'Here is the first of the two breakages.' What they fail to note is that Le Pelletier himself translates the word *classes* correctly in CII,Q99. It comes from the Latin and means 'fleet' or 'armed combat', and is always used in this way by Nostradamus. Le Pelletier, not understanding that the king was fatally injured in one of the two jousts he fought, conveniently dropped the *s* from *classis* so that the Greek word might be interpreted instead. Similar philological errors occur elsewhere. This begins to explain how one can ascribe virtually anything to Nostradamus, and why I have here tried to demonstrate that in fact the prophet wrote precisely.

Mistakes are inevitable if one assumes that the text is ambiguous where it is, in fact, specific.

Readers will find that, in order to follow the text as faithfully as possible and extract its full meaning, when translating the quatrain I have decided that the only possible 'key' is a linguistic one. The result was a Sherlock Holmesian investigation that left no detail unconsidered. It seemed clear to me that Nostradamus, playing with anagrams, puns and etymology, put the Latin language through an alchemic transmutation, 'gallicizing' it to conceal his prophetic message and bringing to his intellectual riddling an immense fund of classical learning which has discouraged many interpreters.

One of the first books to be written about Nostradamus' texts after Jean Aimé de Chavigné and Guynaud was the Curé de Louvicamp's *Key to Nostradamus or Introduction to the True Meaning of the Prophecies of this Celebrated Author* (Pierre Giffart, Paris, 1710). This writer is only rarely mentioned, although he was the first to understand Nostradamus' method of setting down his prophecies. (Le Pelletier was, however, deeply indebted to him.) 'I wish to state in conclusion,' writes de Louvicamp,

... that when France's oracle made his Gallic prophecies, he hardly ever departed from the Latins' usage, often writing Latin under the pretext of writing French, and not only etymologically, i.e. when he describes a Prince *Flagrand d'ardent libide* as if thinking *flagrans ardenti libidine*, rather than writing *burning with the horrid fire of lust*. Often he even employed a Latinate French, drawing attention and alluding to the Latin phraseology in word order and placement – what we call syntax ... The Latin poets often had recourse to metaplasm – the changing or transformation of words – by adding, dropping, changing or transposing letters and syllables to and from words so as to scan or embellish their verses. In the same way Nostradamus too sometimes metamorphosed or altered ordinary words in his verses, not just for the sake of keeping the rhythm and scansion but at the same time to divert unlettered persons from the real meaning of his prophecies. In this book examples may be found of aphesis, syncope, apocope, prothesis, epenthesis, antithesis, metathesis, anastrophe, etc, as in the Latin authors, with the exception of paragoge – the addition of a letter or syllable to the end of a word.

It will probably be helpful to readers to define these grammatical terms:

1. *Aphesis*. The omission of a letter or syllable at the beginning of a word: *bondance* for *abondance* (abundance); *verse* for *renverse* (reverse); *tendant* for *attendant* (waiting).

2. *Syncope*. Letter or syllable dropped from the middle of a word: *donra* for *donnera* (will give); *emprise* for *entreprise* (enterprise).

3. *Apocope.* Letter or syllable dropped from the ending of a word (i.e. *profond' colon'* for *profonde colonne*).

4. *Prothesis, epenthesis and paragoge.* Instead of dropping a letter or syllable, one is added to the beginning, middle or end of a word. Virgil took this to apply also to metathesis and even apocope, e.g. *Tymbre* for *Tiberis* (the Tiber). Nostradamus sometimes imitates him in this, using *Tymbre* for *Tibre* (Fr.).

Elsewhere, as he indicated in the Letter to his son César, Nostradamus 'condenses' his prophecies, either to obscure his text or to preserve the required number of feet in each line, since he wrote his Centuries in decasyllabic verse.

A modern translation can therefore only be achieved by attentive and close study of the words, phrases and constructions employed by Nostradamus.

Among his Latinisms he frequently uses the ablative absolute, that bane of schoolboys. He often omits prepositions, as if French were similar to Latin in possessing genitive, ablative and dative cases. This means that one must reassess a word in its context before discovering what its precise case is. Thus *'la voye auxelle'* (CVIII,Q27) is the equivalent of the Latin *'medium auxillio'* (the means by whose aid . . .). It is clear that though Nostradamus was writing in sixteenth-century French he was thinking in Latin, which accounts for the apparent obtuseness of most scholars in the face of such daunting difficulties.

To complicate matters still further and lead the 'common herd' astray, he gallicized Greek words too. This suggests that he wanted to prevent *all* commentators who were not classicists from understanding his prophecies. For example, he invented words like *oruche* and *genest*. The first derives from ὀρυχη, an excavation pit, while the second comes from γενέσθαι, aorist infinitive of the verb γιγνομαι, meaning 'to be born'. No reader without a knowledge of Greek, since the words *oruche* and *genest* will not be found in any French dictionary, nor even a Latin one, could make sense of the quatrains where these coinages appear.

The text I use here is that of the second edition of 1605 (Benoit Rigaud, Lyon), acquired by my father in 1934. This is a complete copy of the 1568 edition, considered the most reliable and containing the fewest misprints. Comparing it with more modern editions, it is evident at first glance that errors proliferate in the later works. Take the fourth line of CVIII,Q61:

Portant au coq don du TAG armifère

Many editions after Chevillot's (Troyes, 1610) give: 'TAO armifère', which enables wilfully esoteric commentators to introduce Taoism to the texts of Nostradamus! I deemed it important to assure readers that I have taken enormous pains to ensure the authenticity of my decodings.

I hoped, for the first time ever, to match history itself against the writings of Nostradamus. The most frequent criticism levelled at previous commentators is that they used Nostradamus' work to put across their personal ideologies. My approach on the other hand involved various history books by very different authors with completely opposed philosophical, political or religious viewpoints. I even drew for my documentation from school textbooks. Readers will realize from this that the prophecy of Nostradamus is history in its purest state, beyond the narrow vision of the historians themselves. They may be surprised, too, at some of the value judgements made by Nostradamus, e.g. 'the miserable, unfortunate Republic' (CI,Q61) or that Napoleon Bonaparte 'will be found to be less prince than butcher' (CI,Q60).

I had to consult numerous history books, too, because none was complete enough to contain Nostradamus' vision. This is why against one quatrain may be set extracts from several different works. It has often amused me to juxtapose and reunite in this way, say, two historians as different as Victor Duruy, a Republican and anti-clerical atheist, and the conservative Pierre Gaxotte, and thus observe that history transcends people's confined, partisan, ephemeral and above all presumptuous conceptions. This is especially true of the twentieth century in which Manicheanism has penetrated all realms of thought, setting son against father, country against country, one political party against another, and finally, worst of all, has created peoples or races internally divided by liberation movements of one kind or another, thus realizing this prophecy of Christ's:

And ye shall hear of wars and rumours of wars; see that ye be not troubled: for all these things must come to pass, but the end is not yet. For nation shall rise against nation, and kingdom against kingdom; and there shall be famines, and pestilences, and earthquakes, in divers places. All these are the beginning of sorrows.

Matthew 24, 6–8, Authorized Version.

As regards the choice of definition, and from which dictionary, in every instance that choice was influenced by the meaning of the line, itself set in the context of its whole quatrain. Indeed, if I found myself faced with particular words which, in their current meaning or in their original or specialized sense, rendered the text incomprehensible, I then felt it essential to examine the etymological aspects or the text's symbolic meaning. Take '*Par cinq cens un trahyr sera titré*' (CIX,Q34). Given that the verb *trahir* (betray) is here used as a noun, since it is preceded by the indefinite article, one cannot use *titrer* in its contemporary sense of 'to give a title to'; and 'a betrayal shall be given a title' is meaningless. But a dictionary eventually reveals that this verb can also mean 'to scheme' or 'to intrigue', so the text swiftly becomes very specific: a treacherous act will be plotted by five hundred persons. This is a good example of the linguistic traps Nostradamus set for his future translators.

My father fell into some of them, setting too much store by his own researches and not enough on the verbal mannerisms and gallicisms liberally employed by Nostradamus. My father's book *What Nostradamus Really Said* (Stock, 1976) includes only sixty-three quatrains covering the period 1555 to 1945; this seems to me very few, given the importance of the work and the profuse details lavished upon certain events. So I had to re-examine the whole work from A to Z, to advance step by step, doggedly reconstituting the puzzle by eliminating along the way various quatrains either without prophetic purpose or ambiguous, and which Nostradamus inserted to mislead commentators still further.

Matching up Nostradamus' work with historical events required considerable research. As he wrote in the Letter to César, Nostradamus did indeed supply a translator with very precise geographical guidelines. When the small town of Varennes is mentioned (CIX,Q20) it is easy to see the significance of the quatrain, for the capture there of Louis XVI is well known, which is why we find this quatrain, give or take an occasional error, commented upon in all the post-1792 books. However when a quatrain mentions Vitry-le-François, the commentator will be unable to see its significance unless he knows or finds out that in this town Kellermann reassembled the French army to surrender after the Battle of Valmy. Take another example: Nostradamus mentions the small Italian town of Buffalora (CVIII,Q12). Comparatively few people know that the Napoleonic General MacMahon's army was encamped there before launching the Italian campaign which led to the victories of Magenta and Solferino.

Nostradamus would conceal the names of towns destined to become famous or important by using instead those of small, neighbouring villages. Thus Aquinas, Italy will stand for nearby Naples; the village of Apameste indicates Calabria, of which it is a part; while Rimini or Prato indicate Mussolini's birthplace, equidistant as it is from these two towns. To necessitate still more research, Nostradamus vulgarized town names, disguising them by means of popular names or nicknames, transcribed of course, without capital letters. Hence Apameste in Calabria becomes *apamé*, its last syllable disappearing through apocope (CIX,Q95). But the most striking illustration of this method is the word *herbipolique* which

Nostradamus fabricated partly from Herbipolis, the Latin name for the town of Würzburg in Germany (CX,QI3).

Finally, Nostradamus gallicized foreign names while respecting the rules of phonetics or of letters which correspond in both languages. Thus the East German town of Ballenstedt becomes Ballènes, gallicized and by apocope; the town of Lunegiane, Lunage, through a combination of apocope and anagram, and Llanes, a small port in Asturia, Spain, becomes by gallicization Laigne.

Various typographical errors, mercifully rare, further complicate the decoding process. Some mistakes are simple to correct, i.e. 'Madric' for 'Madrid', but others are more difficult and can only be spotted if set against other quatrains referring to the same persons or events. Thus CVI,Q49 contains the word 'Mammer' which needs to be compared to 'Mammel' (CX,Q44), both words for the River Niemen, which until 1772, the year Poland was partitioned, ran through the centre of that country. In addition to all this, sixteenth-century printing commonly substituted 'y' for 'i', 'u' for 'v' as in Latin script, and 'z' for 's' and vice versa. Sometimes too the letter 'h' might be added to or removed from a word, as in Hébreux/Ebreu (for Hebrew).

For general poetic reasons, and metrical requirements in particular, Nostradamus was obliged to shorten words by using grammatical devices – as in 'd'mour' for 'Dumouriez' (CX,Q46), modified by both syncope and apocope. Like Latin authors Nostradamus frequently omits the auxiliaries 'be' and 'have', which must be read in to restore the modern construction. Parodying Tacitus, he leaves out nouns like 'person' or active verbs like 'go', 'return', 'attack', etc., omissions the context alone clarifies. All this will give the reader some idea of the immense effort required to decipher quatrains which the prophet has almost completely codified by using Latin constructions, etymology, figures of speech and rhetoric, obscure topography, and anagrams, the latter sometimes in combination with the rhetorical figures.

Many have speculated about the following passage from the Letter to his son César: 'Fearing lest various books which have been hidden for centuries be discovered, and dreading what might happen to them, I presented them to Vulcan.' This has been taken to mean that Nostradamus had a secret library upon which he drew for his prophecies, taking all the credit without acknowledging his debt to the occultists, magi, astrologers or cabbalists who preceded him. My own studies lead me to a far less esoteric or mysterious conclusion, which will doubtless disappoint enthusiasts of the occult.

Indeed, as I went into the linguistic and historical aspects of Nostradamus' text, I became more and more convinced of one thing. We know that the sixteenth-century classical scholars were immensely learned, especially in languages and ancient history. The longer my researches progressed, the less likely it seemed that a single mind could contain such a store of knowledge. I could imagine Nostradamus in his study consulting many erudite literary, historical and geographical works to codify the vision which had just been vouchsafed him. I became even more convinced of this when I was confronted with the huge mass of documentation and cross-reference which I myself needed, first to understand the meaning of the quatrains, then to collate them with the historical events they were describing.

The books used by Nostradamus must have been the key to the Centuries; since he knew what would happen to his message if it were understood immediately, he destroyed these books, simultaneously hurling into the fire both the code and the key to the treasure chest his work represents. To break into this coffer, one must first assemble a very comprehensive toolkit drawn from a variety of different disciplines.

All fanciful notions and personal theories had to be dispensed with, along with imagination, 'that mistress of error and falsehood, all the more of a cheat because she is not so always', as Pascal wrote in his *Pensées*. Nostradamus offered the same advice, but it was hardly ever followed. To César he wrote: '. . . eschewing any fantastic imaginings, you may through good judgement have insight into the future if you keep to the specific place-names. . . .' This constitutes a true appeal to reason and objectivity.

In this book I have given exhaustive references for everything – quotations, definitions, extracts from history books – so that readers can check, verify or expand whatever historical point is being made by a quatrain or sixain. I have also repeated various definitions of recurrent words so that readers may gradually memorize some of them and so facilitate their reading, for I am well aware that such a work cannot be read like a novel.

Both with quatrains already authenticated by history and with those which will be verified by future events, I have abstained from speculating, offering opinions or otherwise commenting. I wanted my attitude towards the work of Nostradamus to differ from that of previous 'interpreters' and to respect the caveat he left César: 'But, my son, lest I venture too far for your future perception, be aware that men of letters shall make such grand, unusually boastful claims about the way in which I interpreted the world. . . .' Nostradamus unequivocally, not prophetically, stated that numerous books about his prophecies would ultimately turn out to be no more than 'grand, unusually boastful claims', proof of which is provided by the lengthy bibliography at the end of this book. So I trust readers will excuse my lack of theorizing, for I feel that far too much of this sort of thing has already harmed Nostradamus' work and detracted from its seriousness.

The commentators' numerous, often glaring, errors have been the result of scanty research and a lack of attention to minutiae, but above all to excess – whether of subjectivity or of political, philosophical or religious commitment.

While decoding quatrains particularly specific about place-names, I realized that commentators had systematically ignored many of them in order to preserve only the ones which accorded with, or showed off, their peculiar convictions: historical events had been twisted or even invented at will so as to fit in with their theories. I also discovered that quite a few of these books contained definitions of words or translations from Latin not to be found in any dictionary, which leads one to conclude that the so-called definitions had been created by translators bent on bestowing particular meanings upon one word or another. Then again, Nostradamus writes in his letter to César that he has set down his quatrains in no special order, so I often wonder how some interpreters, obviously thinking they were on the right track, have written books describing a grid system or some concealed numerical pattern – but which, on reading and examining their results, has still led them to a dead end.

As for astrology, why is it no professional astrologer ever manages to predict an important historical event? If the position of the stars in the sky determined the history of mankind, all such events would have been programmed long ago, day by day, month upon month, year after year. Hence we should have known by the position of the stars on 1 September 1939 that the Second World War would begin, or that on 13 May 1958 Algeria would experience a convulsion which would lead to independence. One understands Nostradamus' stern warning: 'Let all astrologers, fools and barbarians keep away from my work.' Astrology would thus remove from man his free will and make him a robot programmed for an endless succession of catastrophes. The prophet only sees in advance the behaviour of men writing their history themselves, with their own wills, decisions, and above all their complete, heavy and inalienable responsibilities.


What was the purpose of Nostradamus' prophecy? What were the areas, countries and historical changes into which Nostradamus 'received' detailed insights? This is probably the most vexed question as far as interpreters are concerned. British and American writers in particular have tried to find in the Centuries as many events as possible concerning the USA. It must be remembered that Nostradamus was French and a devout Catholic. The Church to which he belonged and refers in his work is his only allegiance and his message accordingly centres upon France, the history of the Catholic Church, and that of the papacy itself as the backbone of Western Christian civilization. And when we know that the end of Western civilization coincides with the end of the Roman Catholic Church and the destruction of Rome, we can understand why the countries Nostradamus refers to most are, in order of frequency, France, Italy and Spain, the three upholders of Catholicism.

This also explains why many writers, fired by a violently emotional agnosticism and unable to rise above such bias, could not acknowledge the profundity of Nostradamus' message. Perhaps too this is the reason for the consistent and recurrent blindness of American leaders to the dangers threatening Catholic Europe – with the exception, perhaps, of John F. Kennedy, the first Catholic President of the USA. Concerned as he was by the destruction of the Church, Nostradamus looked closely at the period from 1792, the year of the beginning of the end of Western civilization, until 1999, its actual end.

One can appreciate too why he devoted a great many quatrains to Napoleon I, judging him sternly for his struggle against the Catholic Church. The anti-clericalism of the eighteenth-century philosophers was put into practice by the revolutionaries and pursued by the child of the Revolution, Napoleon himself. It also explains why Napoleon III and Garibaldi, whose common battle with the papacy ended the pope's temporal power, are given considerable attention. For Nostradamus the history of Christian civilization is closely linked with that of the people of Israel, for Christianity began in Palestine. Thus everything that concerns the Moslem world, especially during the second half of the twentieth century, so interested Nostradamus that he devoted many texts to it. He refers to the Moslem world with a multiplicity of names and adjectives: Barbarians (because of the Barbary Coast), Arabs, Crescent, Ishmaelites, Moors, Lunars, Persians, Tunis, Algeria, Byzantium, Turkey, Morocco, Fez, Mahomet, Hannibal and Punic (because of the Carthaginians' hatred of Rome), Syria, Judea, Palestine, Hebron, Soliman and Mesopotamia (Iraq). These words appear in no fewer than 110 quatrains. Nostradamus simultaneously foresaw the defeat of the expansionist Ottoman Empire at Lepanto in 1571 and the revival of Moslem power in the second half of the twentieth century.

If Nostradamus included a significant number of particularly precise quatrains such as those mentioning Varennes (CIX,Q20), Buffalora (CVIII,Q12) and Magnavacca (CIX,Q3), it was so that on the day these texts were at last understood the value of his work would be acknowledged. This he also predicted in his Letter to César:

. . . and the reasons shall be universally understood throughout the earth. . . .
For God's mercy will only be poured forth for a certain time, my son, until the
majority of my prophecies are fulfilled and this fulfilment be complete . . .
despite their obscurities, these things shall be understood, but when ignorance
has been dispersed, the meaning will be clearer still.

Aix-en-Provence
June 1980

# Abbreviations

| | |
|---|---|
| AE | *ALPHA Encyclopédie*, 17 vols. |
| AVL | *Atlas Vidal-Lablache.* |
| AU | *Atlas Universalis.* |
| CUCD | *Chronologie Universelle*, Ch. Dreyss, Hachette, 1873. |
| DAFL | *Dictionnaire d'Ancien Français Larousse.* |
| DDP | *Dictionnaire des Papes*, Hans Kuhner, Buchet-Chastel, 1958. |
| DENF | *Dictionnaire étymologique des noms de famille*, Albert Dauzat, Librairie Larousse, 1951. |
| DGF | *Dictionnaire Grec-Français*, A. Chassang. |
| DH3 | *Documents d'Histoire*, 3, Cours Chaulanges. |
| DH4 | *Documents d'Histoire*, 4, Cours Chaulanges. |
| DHB | *Dictionnaire d'Histoire*, N. M. Bouillet, Hachette, 1880. |
| DHCD | *Dictionnaire d'Histoire*, Ch. Dezobry, 2 vols. |
| DL | *Dictionnaire Littré*, 4 vols. |
| DLLB | *Dictionnaire Latin*, Le Bègue. |
| DL7V | *Dictionnaire Larousse*, 7 vol. |
| DP | *Dictionnaire de la Provence et du Comté Venaissin*, Jean Mossy, Marseille, 1785. |
| DSGM | *Dictionnaire de la Seconde Guerre mondiale*, Jean Dumont, Historama, 1971. |
| DSH | *Dossiers secrets de l'Histoire*, A. Decaux, Librairie académique Perrin, 1966. |
| EU | *Encyclopaedia Universalis*, 20 vols. |
| GP & MR | *Garibaldi*, Paolo et Monika Romani, Les géants de l'Histoire, Fayolle, 1978. |
| HAB | *Hitler*, Alan Bullock, Marabout University, 1963. |
| HC4 | *Histoire classe de 4ᵉ*, Fernand Nathan. |
| HDA | *Histoire de l'Allemagne*, André Maurois, Hachette, 1965. |
| HDCAE | 'Histoire de Chypre', Achille Emilianides, *Que sais-je?* no. 1909. |
| HDGM | 'Histoire de la Grèce moderne', Nicolas Svoronos. *Que sais-je?* no. 578. |
| HDMJG | 'Histoire de Malte', Jacques Grodechot, *Que sais-je?* no. 509. |
| HDVFT | 'Histoire de Venise', Freddy Thiriet, *Que sais-je?* no. 522. |

HEFDP — *Histoire d'Espagne*, Fernando Diaz Plaja, France-Loisirs.

HFA — *Histoire de France*, Anquetil, Paris. 1829

HFACAD — *Histoire de France et des Français*, André Castelot et Alain Decaux, 13 vols, Plon et Librairie académique Perrin, 1972.

HFAM — *Histoire de France*, Albert Malet.

HFJB — *Histoire de France*, Jacques Bainville.

HFPG — *Histoire des Français*, Pierre Gaxotte.

HFVD — *Histoire de France*, Victor Duruy.

HRU — *Histoire du Royaume-Uni*, Coll. Armand Colin, 1967.

HISR — *Histoire de l'Italie, du Risorgimento à nos jours*, Sergio Romano, Coll. Point, Le Seuil, 1977.

HLFRA — *Histoire de la Libération de la France*, R. Aron, Fayard.

HSF — *Histoire de la Société Française*, L. Alphan et R. Doucet.

LCH3 et 4 — *La Classe d'Histoire*, 3, 4.

LCI — *La campagne d'Italie*, Maréchal Juin, Ed. Guy Victor, 1962.

LDG — *La Dernière Guerre*, Éd. Alphée, Monaco.

LDR — *Le Dossier Romanov*, Anthony Summers, Tom Mangold, Albin Michel, 1980.

LFL XIV — *La France de Louis XIV*, Culture, Art, Loisirs.

LGESGM — *Les Grandes Enigmes de la Seconde Guerre mondiale*, Ed. St-Clair, Paris.

LGR — *Les Guerres de Religion*, Pierre Miquel, Fayard, 1980.

LGT — *La Grande Terreur*, Robert Conquest. Stock, 1970.

LMC — *Le Monde Contemporain*, Hatier.

LMSH — *Le Mémorial de Saint-Hélène*, Las Cases.

LRFPG — *La Révolution française*, Pierre Gaxotte, Fayard.

LSEOA — *Le Second Empire*, Octave Aubry, Fayard.

LTR — *Le Temps des Révolutions*, Louis Girard.

LXIVJR — *Louis XIV*, Jacques Roujon, Ed. du Livre Moderne, 1943.

MAB — *Mussolini, le Fascisme*, A. Brissaud, Cercle Européen du Livre, Robert Langeac, 1976.

MCH — *Mussolini*, Christopher Hibbert, R. Laffont, 1963.

MGR — *Mythologie grecque et romaine*, Classiques Garnier.

NEE — *Napoléon et l'Empire*, Hachette, 1968.

NELGI — *Napoléon et la Garde Impériale*, Commandant Henry Lachouque, Ed. Bloud et Gay.

NLM — *Napoléon*, Louis Madelin, Hachette.

PCHF — *Précis chronologique d'Histoire de France*, G. Dujarric, Albin Michel, 1977.

PGB — *Pétain*, Georges Blond, Presses de la Cité, 1966.

VCAHU — *Vingt-cinq ans d'Histoire Universelle*, Michel Mourre, Ed. Universitaires, 1971.

# 2

# NOSTRADAMUS AS HISTORIAN

## THE PREFATORY QUATRAINS

Estant assis de nuict secret[1] estude,
Seul, reposé sur la selle[2] d'aerain?
Flambe[3] exiguë sortant de sollitude,
Fait prospérer[4] qui n'est à croire vain.

CI,QI

*Interpretation*

At night, studying alone in a secluded place, and rested on a bronze chair, a small flame comes out of the solitude and brings things to pass [predictions] which should not be thought vain.

*History*

Some commentators have gone to great lengths to present Nostradamus as an 'initiate', working with some occultist group or sect. He denied this vehemently in his very first quatrain of the first century, twice repeating in two verses that he was inspired and worked alone in his study at Salon.

The bronze seat has been the subject of many rather fantastic and esoteric interpretations. Without falling over backwards to prove anything, it seems more obvious [knowing Nostradamus' preoccupation with obscure imagery. *Tr.*] to find parallels in Christian symbolism and opt for 'mortification of the flesh'. By sitting on a hard seat and working by night Nostradamus could both fight off drowsiness and keep the spirit pure and receptive. The little flame resembles the one which descended on the Apostles' heads at Pentecost, symbolizing the Holy Spirit and thus divine inspiration.

[1] Latin *secretum*: secluded spot, retreat. DLLB.
[2] Latin *sella*: seat, chair. DLLB.
[3] Old French *flamme*. DAFL.
[4] Latin *prospero*: I make succeed, favour. DLLB.

---

La verge[1] en mains mise au milieu de Branches,[2]
De l'onde[3] il moulle[4] et le limbe[5] et le pied,
Un peur[6] et voix fremissent par les manches,[7]
Splendeur divine le divin près s'assied.

                                        CI,Q2

## Interpretation

The magic wand [or his doctor's symbol, the caduceus of Mercury], placed in the hands of him who has the gift of prophecy. With a wave [of words] he shapes the fringes and feet [of his verses]; which makes the weak tremble with fear for divine splendour, divinity itself, sits beside him.

This quatrain too has prompted magical or hermetic interpretation, even though it follows on from the first quatrain in explaining the whys and wherefores of the ensuing prophecies. So that the reader does not dwell under any scurrilous misapprehensions as to his inspiration, Nostradamus (as in the preceding quatrain) twice repeats the most important word – divine – thus reaffirming what he wrote on the subject in his Letter to César.

[1] Latin *virga*: thin branch, magic wand, but also caduceus. DLLB.
[2] Branchus, priest of Apollo, who received from the latter the gift of prophecy. DLLB.
[3] Latin *unda*: water movement, wave. DLLB.
[4] Latin *mollire*: *modeler* or *modles* (old French) = to mould, model. DLLB.
[5] Latin *limbus*: fringe, border, edging. DLLB.
[6] Latin *pavor* (noun, m.): fear, fright. DLLB.
[7] Old French: weak, feeble-minded.

## Legis Cautio Contra Ineptos Criticos[1]
## (Precautionary Words against Foolish Critics)

Qui legent hosce versus nature censunto:
Prophanum vulgus et inscium ne attrectato:
Omnesque Astrologi, Blenni, Barbari procul sunto,
Qui aliter faxit, is, rite sacer esto.

*Interpretation*

Let those who read these verses judge them naturally:
Let the vulgar and stupid rabble not approach them:
And let all Astrologers, fools and barbarians keep away;
May whoever does otherwise be justly accursed.

Here we have a series of emphatic warnings, especially those concerning astrologers – classed here with fools and barbarians. It might be considered at variance with what Nostradamus wrote in his Letter to César when he said he had practised official astrology, but there is nothing contradictory here, for astrology in the sixteenth century was simply the study of the stars, and hence a synonym for astronomy. In the twentieth century, however, these two words define very different disciplines: it is thus clear that Nostradamus was addressing modern astrologers. This can be exemplified by citing a book written in 1938 by an 'eminent' astrologer applying his knowledge to Nostradamus: Maurice Privat's *1940 World Predictions, Year of French Glory*, which appeared some months after my father's book predicting the war with Germany.

[1] The only quatrain in Latin. Unnumbered, it is placed between CVI,Q100 and CVII,Q1, i.e. exactly in the middle of the twelve Centuries.

---

## The Duke of Alba's Revolt Against Pope Paul IV, 1557.
## The War between the Dukes of Alba and Guise, 1557

Le grand Duc d'Albe se viendra rebeller,[1]
A ses grandes pères fera le tradiment:[2]
Le grand de Guise le viendra debeller,[3]
Captif mené et dressé monnument.[4]

CVII,Q29

## Interpretation

The great Duke of Alba will rebel and betray the fathers [of the Church] and will end the war with a victory over the Duke of Guise, prisoners being taken. He will be remembered.

## History

'Paul IV intercepted letters from the Spanish minister to his court which informed the Duke of Alba of armed retainers kept by certain Roman noblemen, together with details of their possible disaffection or rebellion, in order that they might be taken over by him. Learning this, the Pope not only ruined some and excommunicated others but even had one of the Spanish envoys arrested. The Duke asked in vain for his release and suggested peace negotiations: the Pope was deaf to all such propositions. The Duke then ordered his troops to invade Church territory and seize a number of towns in the name of the Holy See and the future Pope. The Pope was already in dire need of French aid. The French Council's decision soon restored all his pride and he issued a fiery pronouncement that declared King Philip of Spain to be a rebel against his sovereign, and, this being so, he was relieved of his kingdom of Naples. Philip took every step to precipitate war with France. The exchange of prisoners, which had prompted the truce, was daily postponed. The Duke of Guise, at the head of an army, rapidly crossed the mountains and, hurrying towards Naples, got as far as Milan. The Vice-Regent, the Duke of Alba, did not have enough troops to match such a powerful army and was at first in difficulties. The Duke of Guise made no progress; the land army weakened itself by marches and counter-marches in order to tempt Alba to battle. The latter had grasped that he only had to remain on the defensive in order to wear down an enemy attempting an invasion. He could not be drawn from his tactics, and all the *honours* [*dressé monument*] of the campaign were his.'[5]

[1] Latin *rebello*: I revolt, rise up, begin fighting again. DLLB.
[2] Latin *trado*: I betray. DLLB.
[3] Latin *debello*: I end the war through a victory. DLLB.
[4] Latin *monumentum*: anything that recalls a memory. DLLB.
[5] HFA.

# The Death of Henri II, 10 July 1559

Le Lyon jeune le vieux surmontera,
En champ bellique[1] par singulier duelle,
Dans cage d'or les yeux lui crèvera,
deux classes[2] une puis mourir mort cruelle.

CI,Q35

## Interpretation

The young lion will triumph over the old, jousting in the lists. His eyes inside his golden helmet will be put out, in one of the two combats; then he will die a cruel death.

## History

'The third tourney is due to begin. The king is mounted on a steed belonging to Emmanuel-Philibert. Delighted by this spirited horse, he tells his brother-in-law so, but the latter asks him, on the Queen's behalf, "to toil no more", since it is already "late, and the weather exceeding hot". In fact it is just twelve noon, but Henri replies that he is *champion*, and because of this, as is the custom, he must joust thrice. His opponent is already in the saddle. It is Gabriel de Lorges, Comte de Montgoméry, Captain of the Scottish Guard. "Trumpets and bugles sound deafening fanfares." Then the two men take up positions and charge. The shock is fearful and both lances shatter, but neither combatant falls to the ground. The King could now stop, but wishes to tilt again [*deux classes une*]. "Sire," begs Vieilleville, "I swear by Almighty God that for more than three nights running I have dreamed that some misfortune will befall you today and that the end of June would be fatal for you. Make of this what you please." Montgoméry also argues for stopping the tournament, but the King wishes to continue. The champion and the challenger rush towards each other. Again the collision is frightful and both lances break, and riders and steeds have difficulty recovering their balance. Reaching the end of the lists, the two combatants execute a half-turn. Henri II takes a new lance but Montgoméry forgets to throw down the stump he still holds. Contrary to convention – no one knows why – the trumpets are silent. The mailclad horsemen set off again at full gallop and there is a deafening noise of clanging, clattering steel and hooves pounding the raked sand of the track. The spectators gasp, seeing that the Captain of the Scottish Guard has not flung aside his broken weapon but is still levelling it. The two men clash yet again and

Montgoméry's fragment of lance slips off the King's cuirass, lifting *the visor of the helmet* and piercing the King's head. The King is borne to Tournelles. His wound is appalling: the lance has entered his right *eye* and emerged through the ear. While the King lay in *agony* [*mort cruelle*], Diane remained cloistered at home. On the morning of 10 July, the King died.'[3]

[1] *champ bellique*: the lists, palisade enclosing the area marked out for the jousting. DAFL.
[2] Latin *classis*: army, fleet, combat; *classe depugnare*: to surrender a battle. DLLB.
[3] HFACAD.

---

# The Conspiracy of Amboise, March 1560

Un coronel[1] machine[2] ambition[3]
Se saisira de la plus grande armée:
Contre son prince feinte invention
Et descouvert sera sous la ramée.[4]

CIV,Q62

## Interpretation

Intrigues with a view to seizing the crown result in the seizure of the main armed forces of the country. A trick will be contrived against the King, which will be discovered under the branches.

## History

'The Protestants *plotted to abduct* the King from the castle of Amboise to remove him from the influence of the Guises. An obscure person called La Renaudie was the nominal arch-conspirator, but its real, secret organizer was the Prince of Condé. But the Conspiracy of Amboise was discovered: *surprised in the neighbouring forests* [*sous la ramée*], the plotters were drowned, decapitated, and hanged from the castle battlements.'[5]

'Once the first angry realization was over, it was hoped to lend an air of justice to the previous executions by legally sentencing some of the chief conspirators. One of the leading lights was Castelnau who had surrendered to Jacques de Savoie, the Duke of Nemours, whose superior forces had surrounded him in the castle of Noizai, *the army depot* of the plotters, and had parleyed with him. Nemours swore to give him safe conduct, and Castelnau followed him, but no sooner was he at Amboise than he was put in chains.'[6]

[1] Latin *coronalis*: of the crown. DLLB.
[2] Latin *machina*: (figurative) artifice, intrigue, ruse. DLLB.
[3] Latin *ambitio*: cabal, intrigues. DLLB.
[4] Latin *rami*: branches. DAFL.
[5] HFAM.
[6] HFA.

---

# The Guise War, 1560. The Condé War, 1562

Guerres, débats,[1] à Blois guerre et tumulte,
Divers aguets,[2] adveux inopinables:[3]
Entrer dedans Chasteau Trompette,[4] insulte,[5]
Chasteau du Ha,[6] qui en seront coupables.

CXII,Q52

## Interpretation

There will be wars and debates [parliaments] at Blois, as well as up-heavals, ambushes and incredible confessions. The *Chasteau Trompette* [Trumpet Castle] will be attacked by those seeking entry, but the guilty ones will be imprisoned.

## History

'To obtain Calvin's absolution, it was necessary to rally the royal princes. They were wary of taking sides, but clandestinely supported the opposition who thus appeared to be *conspirators*. Condé, who had least to lose, was boldest. Bourbon made no move. At last a gentleman in reduced circumstances, La Renaudie, was found to head a strong *conspiracy* that intended to accuse the Guises of peculation and lèse-majesté! Condé agreed to head the whole affair. When La Renaudie sent messengers into the provinces urging the King's supporters to rise and put a stop to the evil politicking of the Guises, thousands of men went on the march. In February 1560, an *immense tumult* occurred at the mouth of the Loire. The court, then at *Blois*, thought it safest to take refuge immediately in the castle of Amboise.

Condé, however, was recruiting troops. The coast was clear: Bourbon was Catherine's hostage. In the provinces the Huguenots mobilized and the uprising was general. But Condé hesitated at Paris. He was caught unawares by Guise, who had left the castle of Fontainebleau and led the King and Queen back to Paris. Condé believed that they were prisoners and said so. Yet Catherine continued to issue declarations favouring the Guises and denouncing the Huguenot plotters. The Guises must have let her do so: she assumed leadership of their party. From Meaux, Condé took Orleans, which he "liberated" with a handful of mounted troops. The whole of the Loire Valley fell into his hands. Towns surrendered to him, enthusiastically organizing reformed *assemblies* [*débats*], which were particularly well attended at Tours, *Blois* and Angers. This was a sort of revenge for the failed *tumult* or civil commotion. Since early April men had taken up arms throughout the provinces as if a fuse had been lit. In 1562 Duras failed to seize *Château Trompette*, on Condé's orders. Montluc had driven him out of the town. After this intervention the magistrates or "aldermen" *promised* "to spare neither their possessions nor their lives in the King's service and that of the righteous, ancient, Catholic and Roman religion". The persecution had disposed of the most prominent Calvinists. The rest lay low or returned to Catholicism."[7]

[1] The Parliament of Blois, 1576, was a triumph for the League. Its members asserted the state's rights to administer matters of public welfare and voted to continue *the struggle* against the Protestants. The second Parliament of Blois, 1588, was just as successful for the League's members, who were by then even more *violent* then in 1576. DL7V.

[2] Ambush.

[3] Latin *inopinabilis*: inconceivable, incredible, DLLB.

[4] Famous fortress in Bordeaux, beside the Garonne, demolished in 1785. DL7V.

[5] Latin *insulto*: I attack, defy. DLLB.

[6] Ha = Ham: chief town of the canton of the Somme, another famous fortress, built in 1470, and which served as *state prison*. DHB. Example of apocope.

[7] LGR.

---

# The King of Navarre, Antoine of Bourbon, Surrenders to the Triumvirate, 1561. His Death at the Siege of Rouen, 1562

Le grand Antoine[1] du nom de faict sordide,
De Phtyriase[2] à son dernier rongé:
Un qui de plomb[3] voudra estre cupide.
Passant le port d'esleu sera plongé.

CIV,Q88

## Interpretation

Great Antoine of the name [Bourbon] will give in/surrender to a sordid act. On his last [day] he will be gnawed by vermin, because he will be one who is greedy for lead; in the port he will be casually plunged [into the grave] by those who have chosen him.

## History

'To keep the King of Navarre on the side of the Triumvirate, the King of Spain, by way of indemnity for the part of Navarre he still retained, promised him the Kingdom of *Sardinia*. The most enticing and flattering descriptions of this island's fertility, *seaports* and towns were circulated. The weak *Antoine* was led to think that this was the only way to wrest from Spain lands equivalent to those which Spain was keeping and that if he sided with the Protestants he would never become rich. These considerations made up his mind for him: he openly allied with the Guises, coming out clearly in favour of the Catholics. He also broke with the Calvinists.

The siege of Rouen[4] is remembered for the death of the King of Navarre. He was wounded during it, and the surgeons were not at first unduly concerned, but in a few days his wound took him to his grave. He *sank into* it, along with the seductive promises that the King of Spain had given him – the possession of Sardinia, and the thought of the pleasant life he had counted upon leading on that island.'[5]

[1] Antoine of Bourbon, King of Navarre, Duke of Vendôme, b. 1518, became King of Navarre through his marriage to Jeanne d'Albret. Heading the Catholic army, he had to *fight his own brother*, Condé, who led the Protestants. Born a Protestant, he incurred their hatred by abandoning them, and was scarcely mourned even by the Catholics. DHB.

[2] Pediculosis, lice. DL7V.

[3] Sardinia: rich in minerals, mines sunk by the Romans yielded *lead*, silver, zinc and iron. DL7V.

[4] Rouen: *port* on the Seine, 120 km from the sea.

[5] HFA.

---

# The Death of Nostradamus, 2 July 1566

De retour d'Ambassade, don de Roy mis au lieu
Plus n'en fera: sera allé à Dieu
Parans plus proches, amis, frères du sang,
Trouvé tout mort près du lict et du banc.

Presage 141

*Interpretation*

Having returned from a visit and placed the gift given him by the King in safe keeping, he will do no more, being dead. With his family, kin and friends nearby, he will be found dead near his bed and by the bench.

*History*

This famous quatrain foretelling his own death is quoted by most commentators. In 1564 Nostradamus visited Charles IX, who gave him 300 gold crowns. His friends and family found him dead beside the bed, near the bench on which he usually sat. His work was done.

The quatrain is the last in Nostradamus' work, since it is followed by the 58 sixains which conclude it. In his letter to his son, on page xxiv of this book, Nostradamus was already talking of his own death.

---

## The Siege of Malta by the Turks, 1565.
## Maltese Participation in the Battle of Lepanto, 1571.
## The Christian Fleet Reunited at Messina,
## 24 August 1571

> La pille faite à la coste marine,
> Incita[1] nova[2] et parens amenez:
> Plusieurs de Malte par le fait de Messine,
> Estoit serrez seront mel[3] guerdonnez.[4]
>
> CIX,Q61

*Interpretation*

Pillage around the sea coasts, new raids and the abduction of families will cause several men of Malta to take part in the fighting at Messina. Those besieged will be rewarded with sweetness.

*History*

'In 1565, there could be no more doubt that old Suliman II was arming impressively at Constantinople. His objective remained a mystery, but *Malta* seemed most likely. At dawn on 18 May, lookouts spotted 38 Turkish galleys on the horizon. They were carrying an invasion force of more than 38,000 men and 50 cannon, under the command of Mustapha

Pasha. At last on 26 August the relief expedition left Syracuse. Without tempting providence further, the Turks re-embarked. On 12 September, the last Moslem vessels left Maltese waters. The great *siege* [*serrez*] was lifted. It had seemed that on Malta's fate hung that of the entire West. The victory at Malta marks the beginning of the decline of Turkish maritime power. This was not clear immediately, and during the succeeding years another Moslem offensive was still feared. But six years after the siege of Malta, the great victory of Lepanto, in the Gulf of Corinth, won by the Holy League assisted by four galleys of the *Maltese Order*, showed spectacularly that the Turks had lost control of the Mediterranean. There were 230 Turkish vessels captured or sunk; 30,000 killed or wounded; 3000 prisoners; 15,000 Christian slaves freed [*parens amenez*]. It was decided to build a new town surrounded by huge fortifications. All the Catholic sovereigns sent *gifts*, with the King of France subscribing the most – 140,000 livres [*mel guerdonnez*]).'[5]

'The Battle of Lepanto: the entire nobility of Italy and Spain flocked to the banner of Don John of Austria. The rendezvous was agreed – *Messina*. From Genoa 25 galleys raised anchor, commanded by the most illustrious nobles. Don John arrived at *Messina* on 24 August with 90 Spanish galleons and left on 16 September. He wrote to the King that he had decided to search for the Turkish fleet.'[6]

[1] Latin *incitus*: hurried, impetuous, violent. DLLB.
[2] Latin *novus*: new. DLLB.
[3] Latin *mel*: honey, sweet thing. DLLB.
[4] To recompense, reward. DAFL.
[5] HDMJG.
[6] 'Lepanto, a battle of the giants, to save the West.' André Thévenet in *Historama*.

---

## The Capture and Sack of Cyprus by the Turks, 1571

Assault farouche en Cypre se prépare,
La larme à l'oeil,[1] de ta ruine proche:
Bysance classe, Morisque si grand tare;
Deux différents le grand vast par la roche.

CXII,Q36

*Interpretation*

A savage attack is being directed against Cyprus, which begins to bewail its impending fate – sacking by the Turkish fleet. Islam will wreak havoc and two different [armies] will lay waste these rocky places.

## History

'The growing power of Turkey alarmed the Venetian Republic, which
in order to keep its territories wanted to preserve the strictest neutrality.
But it was impossible. In 1566 the Turks occupied the island of Chios;
in 1567 they seized Naxos. Sultan Selim II grew more and more arrogant
towards the Venetians, *no longer concealing his intention of occupying Cyprus*. In 1570 he sent an ambassador to Venice demanding the surrender
of Cyprus for reasons of security and its nearness to Turkey. The Venetian Senate scornfully rejected this demand and instructed the ambassador that Venice intended keeping Cyprus at all costs. Hostilities
commenced. The Sultan ordered Lala Mustafa, his army commander, to
prepare *an expedition against Cyprus*. Several months later, on 1 July
1570, the *Turkish fleet* disembarked at the port of Larnaca and occupied
it without resistance. But the Venetians concentrated their forces on
defending Nicosia, the capital, and Famagusta, the main port.

Despite continuous attacks the Turks did not succeed in defeating the
Venetians, so they proposed that their adversaries should voluntarily
surrender the town: the defenders at once rejected this suggestion. The
besiegers then renewed their attacks, reinforced by Piali Pasha's recently
disembarked army. In early September the Venetians' position became
more desperate, and Nicosia capitulated on the ninth. The crescent flag
waved above the ramparts. For three days *there was total carnage, and all
the Christians were massacred* and the Cathedral of St Sophia was turned
into a mosque.

In April 1571 Mustafa, whose army had been reinforced by troops
newly arrived from Syria and Asia Minor [*two different*], laid siege to the
last Venetian fortress on Cyprus. In the besieged town Bragadino, its
brave commander, and his 7000 defenders fought to the bitter end.

By early August they surrendered Famagusta honourably, on conditions that Mustafa had accepted. But Mustafa did not keep his promise:
he arrested Bragadino, put him in irons, forced him to watch his companions being tortured, and finally flayed him alive.'[2]

[1] To have tears in one's eyes, be about to weep. DL7V.
[2] HDCAE.

# The Battle of Lepanto, 7 October 1571

Le chef[1] de Perse remplira grands Olchades[2]
Classe trirème[3] contre gent mahométique
De Parthe et Mede,[4] et piller les Cyclades[5]
Repos longtemps au grand port Ionique.[6]

CIII,Q64

## Interpretation

The Persian *Shah* will fill up great ships, whereupon a Roman fleet will sail against the Moslems because of him who will resemble a Parthian or Mede, in order to pillage the Cyclades; all this will ensure peace for a long time in Ionia.

## History

'In the Gulf of Lepanto in 1571 a great sea battle took place, when the combined fleets of Venice, Spain and the Papacy, under Don John of Austria, defeated the Turks, who lost 200 galleys and 30,000 men, and because of this defeat had to *halt their invasion*.

Selim II, the Ottoman Sultan (1566–74), nicknamed the Drunkard, succeeded his father Suliman II, captured Cyprus from the Venetians, lost the Battle of Lepanto the same year and died of *dissipation*. He was the first of a series of effeminate and ignoble sultans. . . .

The pride, cruelty and capriciousness of the Parthians were proverbial. The King and nobility quickly adopted the ostentation, *vices and corruption* of oriental monarchs. . . .

*The weakness* of the Medes' princes encouraged insurrections.'[7]

[1] *Shah*: Persian = king, sovereign. DL7V.
[2] Ὀλκας/αδος: transport vessel and by extension any ship.
[3] Trireme: three-decker rowed warship, adopted by the Greeks. The Romans adapted this form of galley, giving it the name of *trireme*.
[4] Parthia, Medea and Persia were provinces of the Persian Empire which extended as far west as Turkey.
[5] Aegean islands.
[6] Ionia: an area of Asia Minor comprising roughly the Aegean coastline between the Gulf of Smyrna to the north and the Gulf of Mendelia to the south.
[7] DHCD.

# Don John of Austria
## Commands the Christian Fleet at Lepanto, 1571.
## Rebellion in the Low Countries, 1578

Le grand Pilot sera par Roy mandé,
Laisser la classe pour plus haut lieu attaindre:
Sept ans après sera contrebandé,
Barbare armée viendra Venise craindre.

CVI,Q75

## Interpretation

The great leader of the fleet will be named by the King. He will leave
to make for a more northerly place. Seven years later he will fight against
the rebels [contre des bandes]. The Moslem army will need to fear Venice.

## History

'The Holy League, formed on Pope Pius V's initiative, with *Venice* and
Spain, avenged the disaster of Cyprus, which fell to the Turks on 1
August 1571. Don John of *Austria* and Sebastian Venier fully succeeded
in blocking the Turkish fleets from the western approaches and destroying the Turks at Lepanto (7 October 1571).'[1]

'*Philip II*, son and successor of Charles V of Spain, in 1570 delegated
Don John of Austria, Charles V's natural son [*sera par Roy mandé*] to
suppress a revolt by the Moors in Granada. Chosen in 1571 by the
Christian princes to command *the fleet* [*le grand Pilot*] they were sending
against the Turks, he won the famous victory of Lepanto. In 1573 he
seized Tunis, but lost it again the following year. In 1576 he was sent by
Philip II to the rebellious Low Countries [*plus haut lieu*] and defeated
the rebels at Gembloux [January 1578].[2] He died of a malignant fever a
few months later near Namur.'[3]

[1] HDVFT.
[2] 1571–78 = 7 years.
[3] DHB.

# The Massacre of St Bartholomew, 24 August 1572

La grand Cité qui n'a pain qu'à demy
Encore un coup la Sainct Barthelemy
Engravera au profond de son âme
Nismes, Rochelle, Genève et Montpellier
Castres, Lyon; Mars[1] entrant au Bélier,[2]
S'entrebatront le tout pour une dame.

Sixain 52

## Interpretation

Paris, suffering from hardship, will at the second toll [of the bell] record St Bartholomew in her history. Nîmes, La Rochelle, Geneva, Montpellier, Castres and Lyon will be the scenes of battles because of a woman, war [of religion] breaking out [at the sound of] the bell.

## History

'Civil War enriches only the foreigner. Charles IX and his mother, short of funds, had already enlisted the aid of the King of Spain and the Duke of Savoy.'[3]

'Reconciliation seemed to have been agreed between the two parties. Protestant gentlefolk came to court in great numbers. Charles IX appointed Admiral Coligny to his Council. This favour shown Coligny proved fatal to the Protestants. *Catherine de Médicis*, whose influence was waning, feared loss of power. She had just signed in 1570 an edict similar to the Edict of Amboise whereby the Protestants were granted *four places of safety* where they could establish garrisons. She agreed with Henri, Duke of Guise to get rid of Coligny by murdering him. She then plotted with Guise to arrange a general massacre of Protestant leaders.'[4]

'The bell tower of St-Germain l'Auxerrois was to give the signal, at 3 a.m. on 24 August. It was not necessary to wait that long. *At two o'clock* [*encore un coup*] *the bell* began ringing and soon afterwards the tocsin *sounded* in reply from every church.'[4]

'The example set by Paris was followed in *many towns*. The total number of victims was about 8000.'[5]

---

[1] God of war, symbol of strife and massacre.
[2] Small bell (because the ram, leader of the herd, carries around its neck the bell that *rallies* its members). DL7V.
[3] HFPG.
[4] HFAM.
[5] HFVD.

## The Massacre of St Bartholomew's Day.
## Coligny's Assassination, 24 August 1572.
## The Defender of St Quentin, 1557

La grand Cité d'assaut prompt et repentin[1]
Surprins de nuict, gardes interrompus:[2]
Les excubies[3] et veilles Sainct Quintin
Trucidez[4] gardes et les portails rompus.

CIV,Q8

### Interpretation

Paris will be surprised by night. There will be a rapid unexpected attack,
the guards having been silenced and the city gates broken open.

### History

'Two things make his [Coligny's] name famous forever: his first action
– the defence of St-Quentin. . . .

St Bartholomew's Day: Paris was ready. The merchant provost, instructed by the Louvre, received the King's order to close the gates. The
bell of St-Germain l'Auxerrois was to give the signal at three o'clock
during the night of 24 August, St Bartholomew's Day. A German,
Besme, was the first to enter the room [and] plunged his sword into
Coligny's chest. . . .

Philibert-Emmanuel, Duke of Savoy, suddenly fell upon St-Quentin,
where 7000 English joined up with him. Admiral Coligny resisted with
700 men. Philibert-Emmanuel attacked him and was utterly defeated
. . . more than 10,000 dead or injured [10 August 1557].'[5]

'Coligny dug in at St-Quentin, besieged by the Spaniards, and his
brave defence gave the French time to take up arms.'[6]

---

[1] Latin repentinus: sudden, unexpected. DLLB.
[2] Latin interrumpere: intercept. DLLB.
[3] Latin excubiae: guards, factions.
[4] Latin trucidare: massacre, butcher.
[5] HFVD.
[6] DL7V.

# Assassination of Admiral Coligny,
## 24 August 1572

Celui qu'en luitte et fer au fait bellique
Aura porté plus grand que lui le pris:
De nuict dans lict six lui feront la picque,
Nud sans harnois[1] subit sera surpris.

CIII,Q30

## Interpretation

He who has fought in the war and has supported someone greater than himself shall be taken. By night six persons shall stab him in his bed, and he shall be taken by surprise, naked and unprotected.

## History

'Gaspard de Châtillon, lord of Coligny, admiral of France, after distinguishing himself in *several campaigns* was in 1552 made colonel-general and admiral by Henri II. He played a part in winning the *Battle* of Renty, defending St-Quentin against the Spanish. After the Treaty of St-Germain in 1570 he reappeared at court and was welcomed and flattered like all those of his party. But the Massacre of St Bartholomew was being arranged and the Admiral was one of its first victims.'[2]

'The vindictive Guise scarcely waited for the signal to go to the Admiral's house. Three colonels from the French army, together with Petrucci, from Sienna and Besme, a German, charged up the staircase. Besme plunged his sword into the Admiral's body: scores of blows followed and the Admiral fell, drenched in his own blood. At the frightful cries and yells which broke out on all sides as soon as the bell tolled, the Calvinists rushed *half naked* from their houses, still half asleep and *unarmed*.'[3]

---

[1] Military term: armour worn by most military men from the fifteenth to the seventeenth centuries. It was still worn in Charles IX's day and even in Henri III's – the *Huguenots* had worn it at the Battle of Coutras.
[2] DHB.
[3] HFA.

# The Struggle between Henri III and the Duke of Alençon, 1574–75

Des sept rameaux à trois seront reduicts,
Les plus aisnez seront surprins par morts,
Fratricider les deux seront séduicts,
Les conjurez en dormant[1] seront morts.

CVI,QII

### Interpretation

There will be only three of the seven branches [offspring] left. The eldest being dead, two [of the three] will engage in fratricidal combat; the plotters will die, ineffectual or inactive.

### History

Deaths of the four eldest children of Henri II: François II [d. 1560]; Elisabeth [d. 1568]; Claude [d. 1573]; Charles IX [d. 1574]. So there remained in 1574 three children: Henri III, Marguerite [Queen Margot], and the Duke of Alençon.

'Apart from the Catholic nobility and the fanatical Protestants, there emerged a new party, that of the "Politicals". The King's brother, the Duke of Alençon, was its leader. The new King was angered by his *brother's* intrigues and *thought of killing him.* . . .

*At the critical moment,* d'Alençon unmasked everything.'[2]

'La Mole, d'Alençon's favourite, and the Piedmontese Count Coconasso, another friend of the Duke's, were *condemned to death and executed.*'[3]

---

[1] *Latin:* (figurative) to be inactive, idle.
[2] HFVD.
[3] DL7V.

---

# The Fifth War of Religion, 1574–76

Deux Royals frères si fort guerroyeront,
Qu'entre eux sera la guerre si mortelle,
Qu'un chacun places fortes occuperont,
De règne[1] et vie sera leur grand querelle.

CIII,Q98

*Interpretation*

Two brothers of royal blood will wage war upon each other, with the result that both die. They are both in strong positions and will quarrel over power and life.

*History*

'The last son of Henri III, Henri Duke of Anjou, succeeded to the Crown. With such a king the kingdom soon lapsed into anarchy. The Huguenots began the *war* again from 1574; this time their allies were a group of titled Catholics, who supported religious tolerance, and were headed by the younger *brother* of Henry III, Alençon. This group was called "the politicals" or "the malcontents". With 30,000 men the Protestants and malcontents marched upon Paris and forced Henri III to sign the Edict of Beaulieu [1576].'[2]

'The Duke of Anjou, put in command of the Loire army, rested on his laurels after the capture of La Charité and Issoire. Henri III took advantage of these paltry successes to conclude the Peace of Bergerac, which allowed the Protestants eight *places of safety*.'[3]

[1] Latin *regnum*: monarchic government, absolute power. DLLB.
[2] HFAM.
[3] HFVD.

---

# The Origins of the League.
# The Assassination of the Duke of Guise –
# 23 December 1588

Paris conjure[1] un grand meurtre commettre
Blois le fera sortir en plein effect:
Ceux d'Orléans[2] voudront leur chef remettre,
Angiers, Troyes, Langres, leur feront grand forfait.

CIII,Q51

*Interpretation*

At Paris, a plot is hatched to commit a notorious murder which will take place at Blois; those who will hold Orleans [the Protestants] will want to restore their leader to the throne, [the Leaguers of] Angers, Troyes and Langres will make them pay dearly.

## History

The League was a Catholic association formed in France by Henri, Duke of Guise in 1568. Its aim was the defence of the Catholic religion against the Huguenots. There had been founded, though, since the beginning of the religious conflict, local unions of defence against the Reformation [1563 at Toulouse, 1565 at *Angers*, 1567 at Dijon, 1568 at *Troyes*, etc]. From the start Henri III had proclaimed himself head of the League, but it was the Duke of Guise, known as Scarface, who almost immediately took control, using it to aid his *schemes* for taking over the throne himself, especially after the death of the heir presumptive, the Duke of Anjou, who *promised this royal succession to the King of Navarre* [the future Henri IV]. The Day of the Barricades failed to achieve a change of dynasty. The coup failed because of a lack of determination by Guise; but the King, chased from his capital, could only resort to *assassinating* this formidable *troublemaker* and his cardinal brother [at the States General at Blois, 1588] as a remedy for the increasing unrest.

¹ To conspire, plot. DL7V.
² Henri I of Lorraine, Duke of Guise, Scarface, elder son of François de Guise, b. 1550, witnessed the murder of his father on the walls of *Orleans*, and from that moment vowed vengeance and hatred against the Protestants. He it was who started the *Massacre of St Bartholomew* by ordering the murder of the Admiral [1572].

---

## Henri III and the Murder of Henri of Guise, 23 December 1588

> En l'an qu'un oeil¹ en France régnera,
> La Cour sera en un bien fascheux trouble,
> Le Grand de Bloys son amy tuera,
> Le regne mis en mal et doubte double.
>
> CIII,Q55

## Interpretation

In the year when power is shared in France the court will be in great embarrassment and difficulty; the King will kill his friend at Blois, and power will be disputed because of a double doubt.

## History

'The *de facto* head of the League, Henri of Guise, set his *sights* higher. For him the League was the stepping stone to the throne. But the King's conduct spoiled his best efforts and satirical pamphlets exposed the corruption of that amoral and vicious court where murder and licence were the order of the day. The States General assembled in Blois on 6 December 1576 and showed Henri III the extent of the danger. Strangely in these appalling times some important legislative reforms were accomplished. The Statute of Blois [1579] laid down some liberal civil rights measures. . . .

The death of the Duke of Anjou, brother and heir to Henri III, had inflamed religious and political feeling yet again. Until then it was almost unimaginable that a Bourbon and apostate might become the heir of the Valois; but now this danger existed, since Henri III, the last surviving son of Henri II, *had no descendants.* . . .

Killing Guise did not kill off the League, however. Paris was momentarily stunned at the news of his death, then the city *erupted in anger.* The Sorbonne decreed that the French people were released from their oath of allegiance to Henri III. It was difficult to shake *the loyalty of Parliament to the monarch, though, and so there was a purge.* . . .

Henri III was no better off as a result of the violence at *Blois*, but he had saved the fortune of the King of Navarre, to whom he now had to resort. Before the final tragedy the Béarnais [Henry IV's nickname] had been in *dire straits.*[2]

[1] Power, as in 'keeping an eye on' or 'under his master's eye'.
[2] HFVD.

---

# The Assassination of Henri III, 2 August 1589, and of the Guises, 23 and 24 December 1588

Les sept enfants[1] en hostage laissez
Le tiers[2] viendra son enfant trucider,
Deux par son fils seront d'estoc[3] percez,
Gennes, Florence viendra enconder.[4]

CIV,Q60

*Interpretation*

The seven children left as hostages [by Henri II], someone from the Third Order will come and kill his child [Henri III]. Two [persons] will be pierced by swordthrusts by his son [Henri II's, i.e. Henri III], the towns near Genoa and Florence will no longer be preserved.

*History*

'When Mary Stuart appeared at the ceremony of her husband Francis II's coronation wearing the jewels taken from Diane, it was a sign that for a long time the real sovereign had been Catherine de Médicis.'[5]

'The morning before, a young friar from the *Dominican* monastery, Jacques Clément, left Paris and made for St-Cloud. Led to the King, the assassin pulled a knife from his sleeve and thrust it into his abdomen.'[5]

'Henri III's first actions showed what might be expected of him. At Turin he repaid the hospitality of the Duke of Savoy with prodigal generosity, returning to him the towns of *Pignerol and Savigliano* [near Genoa] and *Perugia* [near Florence].'[5]

'Henri distributed their daggers. One of the forty-five seized Guise's shoulder and sank his *poniard* into his breast. Then all the daggers were immediately drawn. The Cardinal cried out on hearing the noise, "They're killing my brother." Marshal d'Aumont had him taken away and the next morning he was killed with blows from a *halberd*.'[5]

---

[1] By his marriage with Catherine de Médicis, Henri II had ten children, including two stillborn and a boy who died soon after birth. The others were: Francis II, future husband of Mary Queen of Scots, b. 1544; Elizabeth, wife of Philip II, b. 1545; Claude, Duchess of Lorraine, b. 1547; Charles IX, b. 1549; Alexandre, to become Henri III, b. 1551; Marguerite, Queen Margot, wife of Henri IV, b. 1553; Hercule-François, Duke of Alençon, b. 1555. EU.

[2] Third Order: name given to secular clergy, even married men, attached to certain religious orders (Franciscan, Augustinians and *Dominicans*). They were also called *Tertiaries*. DHCD.

[3] *Estoc*: long, thin sword. DAFL.

[4] Latin *inconditus*: not held together, not preserved. DLLB.

[5] EU.

---

# Henri IV, King from 1589.
## Absolution from Pope Clement VIII, 1595

Le grand Lorrain fera place à Vendosme,[1]
Le haut mis bas et le bas mis en haut,
Le fils d'Hamon[2] sera esleu dans Rome
Et les deux grands seront mis en défaut.

CX,QI8

## Interpretation

Charles of Lorraine will give way to [Henri IV] Duke of Vendôme. The one who was high will be put low, he who was low will be king. The son of the Huguenot will be elected in Rome and the two great ones [of royal blood] will not reign.

## History

'Charles of *Lorraine*, Duke of Guise, was arrested after his father's murder, though aged only seventeen, and held prisoner at Tours. He managed to escape in 1591 and at first took arms against Henri IV, but soon afterwards made his *submission* and was given the governorship of Provence.'[3]

'Clement VIII swiftly dispatched a cardinal to persuade King Philip of Spain not to baulk at reconciliation with the King [Henri IV]. The Holy Father declared the matter important enough to warrant more serious discussion than most, and that the best way to do this would be to hear the views of each cardinal in secret. Thus the Pope controlled the *votes*. During these deliberations, public prayers were said in *Rome* on the Pope's orders. The King's request for absolution and its conditions were read out, with du Perron and d'Ossat, his proxies, promising to observe them. According to the prescribed formula they then abjured errors contrary to the Catholic Faith.'[4]

'Mayenne, Henri IV's cousin, attended the absolution ceremony to make his submission. His nephew, the Duke of Guise, did better still: he wrested back Provence and Marseille from the Duke of Savoy, Philip II's troops and the traitors.'[5]

---

[1] Duchy established in 1515 by François I for Charles of Bourbon, Henri IV's grandfather. He bestowed the title of Duke of Vendôme on one of his sons by Gabrielle d'Estrées. DHB.

[2] Amon, King of Judah, son of Manasseh, imitated the blasphemies of his father and was *assassinated* by his own servants. DL7V.

[3] DHB.

[4] HFA.

[5] HFVD.

## The Siege of Paris by Henri IV, 1589–94.
## His Coronation at Chartres, 27 February 1594,
## and Entry into Paris, 22 March 1594

Du bourg Lareyne parviendront droit à Chartres
Et feront près du pont Anthoni[1] pause:
Sept pour la paix cauteleux[2] comme martres[3]
Feront entrée d'armée à Paris clause.[4]

CIX,Q86

### Interpretation

From Bourg-la-Reine [Henri IV and his group] will go straight to
Chartres and take a rest near Anthony [at Etampes], then thanks to seven
[persons] ready to become martyrs, and who will conspire together to
restore peace, they will enter Paris, which had been closed.

### History

'On 1 November 1589, Henri IV was at *Montrouge*. He risked an attack
on the left bank. The gate of St-Germain resisted. The King did not
press the action. Then once again he abandoned the siege, this time
marching on the south. The capture of *Etampes* allowed him to surround
the capital completely. The King himself had occupied the Beauce region: the Parisians would no longer have any corn. . . .

In 1593 Henri IV, from the hill of *Montmartre*, could look out over
Paris at the privileged subjects of his kingdom who, impatient to regain
their comforts, had already surrendered the town to him. . . .

Orleans and Bourges threw in their lot with him and the towns of
Picardy were ready to do so. In order to hasten this Henri IV knew he
had to appeal to the imagination, to appear as the rightful king decked
out in coronation robes and regalia. Rheims was in the hands of the
Guises, so it was at Chartres, where his family had a chapel, that the
coronation would take place. The ancient ritual began on 27 February
1594. The unusual circumstances of the ceremony did him no harm:
henceforth the King of Navarre was the true King of France. The
Spanish could no longer oppose him. Paris had to surrender. On 22
March 1594, less than a month after his coronation, the king *entered
Paris*. By *conspiracy* the town was his. The conspirators were *Charles de
Cossé, Comte de Brissac*, the governor, *Jean L'Huillier*, merchant-prov-
ost, *Martin Langlois*, advocate to Parliament, and its first President, *Le
Maistre*. The *Duchess of Neumours*, mother of Neumours of Lyon and

Mayenne, was apprised of it also. "It seems clear," said Cazaux, "that *Mayenne* consented to the handover of the capital." During the night of the twenty-first to the twenty-second Brissac and L'Huillier themselves went to the Porte Neuve to get the soldiers to unblock it: it was *closed* up by means of steep ramps. The Porte St-Denis was also cleared. A detachment of a thousand men, led by *St-Luc* [*seven*] immediately entered.'[5]

[1] Bourg-la-Reine and Anthony are situated roughly on a line between Montrouge and Etampes.

[2] *Cauteler*: to scheme, hatch a plot. DAFL.

[3] Popular form of *martyrem*. Persists in *Montmartre* – hill of the martyrs. DAFL.

[4] Latin *clausum*: past participle of *claudo*, I close. DLLB.

[5] LGR.

---

# Henri IV's Power Contested.
## His Official Recognition by Henri III, 1 August 1589.
## Cambrai Captured by Henri III, 1581, and Lost by Henri IV, 1595

L'ombre[1] du règne de Navarre non vray,
Fera la vie de fort illégitime,
La veu promis incertain de Cambrai,
Roy Orléans[2] donra mur[3] légitime.

CX,Q45

### Interpretation

The illusory reign of [Henri] Navarre will be deceptive and render this strong man's activities illegitimate. What had been promised for Cambrai will be seen to be uncertain. [Henri III] Duke of Orleans will legitimize it by his support.

### History

'It was thought at first that Henri III's injury was not fatal; but soon he was seized by a severe fever which heralded his demise. Henri of *Navarre* came to see him. "My brother," said the King, "you see how your enemies and mine have treated me: you may be sure you will never be king if you do not become a Catholic." Then, turning to those with him, he said: "I beseech you as my friends and order you as your king to recognise my brother here as King, after my death; swear the oath of allegiance to him in my presence" [*donra mur legitime*]. All swore.

"You are the King of the *strong*," one of the Catholic nobles had said to Henri. Despite these loyal words, many Catholics defaulted; to keep the rest loyal, Henri solemnly undertook [in an assembly of the principal nobles] to uphold the Catholic faith. At Paris, everyone agreed on religion but not on personalities."[4]

'Cateau-Cambrésis: in 1559 a treaty was signed between Henri II, King of France, and Philip II, King of Spain, by which France regained St-Quentin and Ham, while her possession of Calais and the three bishoprics of Metz, Toul and Verdun were also guaranteed. In 1581 the French took *Cambrésis* [the Cambrai region]. The Spaniards recaptured it from them around 1595. Regained in 1677, it became French once and for all in 1678 by the Treaty of Nijmegen.'[5]

[1] Latin *umbra*: shadow, simulacrum, appearance. DLLB.
[2] Henri III was Duke of *Orleans* (1560), then Duke of Anjou (1566), before succeeding his brother Charles IX (d. 1574). EU.
[3] Symbolic: defence, support.
[4] HFVD.
[5] DHB.

---

## The Conversion of Henri IV, 23 July 1593. The Battle of Ivry, 14 March 1590. The Occupation of Savoy 1596. The Attempted Assassination of Henri IV by Châtel, 1595

Trop tard tous deux les fleurs[1] seront perdues
Contre la loi serpent[2] ne voudra faire,
Des ligueurs forces par gallots[3] confondus[4]
Savone, Albingue,[5] par monech[6] grand martyre.

CVI,Q62

*Interpretation*

Being too late, they will both lose the monarchy; the Protestant will not want to act against the [Catholic] law; the forces of the Leaguers will be routed by cavalry; the Duke of Savoy, after the monk [Leaguer] will be made a martyr.

## History

Henri III and Henri IV, the two last French kings bearing this Christian name, were both assassinated.

'Although it cost the son of Jeanne d'Albret dear to break with the Huguenots who had carried him on their shoulders across the River Loire, he took his counsellors' advice and on 23 July 1593, after a debate lasting several hours with the Catholic divines reassembled at Nantes, he declared himself converted. 'I swear,' he said, 'before Almighty God, *to live and die in the Catholic religion*; and to protect and defend it before and against all, *renouncing all heresies contrary to the said faith.*'

The King [Henri IV] besieged Dreux. To save the town, Mayenne joined battle on the plain of Saint-André, near Ivry, on 14 March 1590. *The Leaguers* had 15,000–16,000 men, 4000 of them *cavalry*, so that their van resembled a thick forest of lances; the Royalists were 8000 infantry and 3000 *horse* in strength. *Every company* charged at once, the King attacking the French lancers and the Walloons. After two hours, the Leaguers' whole army *was in flight.*

Spain might possibly have been implicated in an assassination attempt against the King. Jean Châtel[7] stabbed at his throat. Henri, bending to embrace a nobleman, avoided this blow and was struck only upon the lip. Châtel had studied under the *Jesuits*, and in the League these *priests* had shown themselves to be most zealous supporters of the Spanish claims. *One of them was executed after Châtel.*

'Mayenne perhaps saved the royal army before Amiens. His nephew the Duke of Guise did better still, for he recaptured Provence and Marseille from the *Duke of Savoy*,[8] thus extending the frontiers towards Savona and Albenga.'

---

[1] The three *fleurs de lis*, symbol of the French monarchy.

[2] The Protestants were accused by the Catholics of diabolism.

[3] Alternative orthography of '*galops*' (gallop).

[4] Latin *confundere*: to throw into disorder, overwhelm. DLLB.

[5] The states of Savoy then comprised Bresse and Bugey, Lake Geneva and the surrounding area, Nice and *various Piedmontese territories* whose capital was Turin. In the sixteenth century the House of Savoy suffered simultaneously from the Reformation, which took over its Swiss possessions, and from *French designs upon Italy*. It lost Bresse and Bugey, ceded to Henry IV in 1601, and saw its territory frequently reoccupied by French armies using *Piedmont* as a defensive fortress. DHCD.

[6] Latin *monachus*: monk, *priest*, hermit. DLLB.

[7] Jean Châtel: 'The *Jesuits*, accused of having incited him to this crime, were driven out of the kingdom. The famous Jean Boucher wrote an apologia for Jean Châtel and the Leaguers incorporated this assassin into their *martyrology*.' DHCD.

[8] HFVD.

# The Persecution of Astronomers in the Sixteenth and Seventeenth Centuries: Copernicus and Galileo

Des plus lettrez dessus les faits celestes,
Seront par princes ignorans reprouvez[1]
Punis d'Edit, chassez, comme scelestes,[2]
Et mis à mort la où seront trouvez.

CIV,QI8

## Interpretation

Some of the most learned men in astronomy will be condemned by ignorant rulers, punished by edicts, hounded like criminals and put to death wherever found.

[1] Latin *reprobo*: I reprove, condemn. DLLB.
[2] Latin *scelestus*: criminal (French = *scélérat. Tr.*). DLLB.

---

Croistra le nombre si grand des Astronomes
Chassez, bannis et livres censurez:
L'an mil six cens et sept par sacre glomes[1]
Que nul aux sacres ne seront assurés.

CVIII,Q7I

## Interpretation

The number of astronomers will so increase that they will be hounded, banished and have their books banned, in 1607, by bulls, so that they will not be safe from the Holy [Office].

## History

Astronomers revere Galileo for the two following reasons: first, as fore-runner and *martyr* in the fight by the spirit of Science against the forces of obscurantism which at that time were strongly entrenched in the Catholic Church; secondly, for introducing, in 1610, the telescope for astronomical observation. Though Galileo confined himself to insisting (with many reservations) upon the resemblances between the Earth and the Moon in their relationship to the Sun . . . it was the affirmation of the homogeneity of the planets and stars, including the Earth, which played a part in the *condemnation* of Giordano Bruno to the stake in 1604.

At the end of 1615 Galileo went back to Rome to try to contest a disturbing decision, and once there, openly spoke in favour of arguments which his observations supported, but in spite of his talent he did not convince enough people. On 3 March 1616 the *work* of Copernicus was *placed on the Index. Condemned* by the *Holy Office* [Inquisition] on 22 June 1633, Galileo remained under house arrest until his death.

[1] Latin *glomus*, from *globus*: globe, ball, sphere. DLLB. Since the late Byzantine Empire important acts of civil administration were authenticated by means of a seal attached to parchment. This round seal was called a *bulla* (bull); thereafter, acts thus sealed were habitually referred to as bulls. DL7V.

---

## From the Peace of Cateau-Cambrésis, 1559, to the Peace of Vervins, 1598. The Executions During the Papacy of Clement VIII

> Lors que celuy qu'à nul ne donne lieu,
> Abandonner viendra lieu prins non prins:
> Feu Nef par saignes,[1] Regiment[2] à Charlieu,[3]
> Seront Guines,[4] Calais, Oye[5] reprins.

CIX,Q29

### Interpretation

When he [Philip II of Spain] to whom no one wishes to yield any territory, abandons a territory captured and recaptured, the Church will use fire to shed blood, the Charolais will be occupied and Guines, Calais and Oye will be taken back [from the Spanish].

### History

'The Peace of Cateau-Cambrésis: Henri II was obliged to restore *Calais*, *Guines* and the county of *Oye*. Henri II, in exchange for the places Philip II had seized in Picardy, returned Luxembourg and the *Charolais*.'[6]

'Henri IV ended the religious war through the Edict of Nantes, 13 April 1598. This was the definitive breach with the Middle Ages. Nineteen days later the King's deputies signed a peace treaty with Spain at Vervins. Philip II had been defeated by England, the Dutch, and by the man he called the Prince of Béarn [Henri]; after so much striving he saw his ambitions disappointed everywhere [*nul lieu*] and his kingdoms, like himself, ruined. He wished at least to die in peace. The Treaty of

Vervins established between the two states the borders marked out forty years *earlier* by the Treaty of Cateau-Cambrésis. *Spain and France both seemed to have reverted to the same position [prins, non prins].*[7]

'The Treaty of Vervins: Spain returned Calais, Ardres, la Capelle, Doullens and the Catelet, i.e. all the Vermandois plus part of Picardy. France gave up Cambrai and the *Charolais*.'[8]

'Two tragedies still of interest today occurred in the papacy of Clement VIII: the execution of the famous heretic Giordano Bruno, and that of the patricide Beatrice Cenci. In both cases the Pope had been prevailed upon to take sides.'[9]

'Giordano Bruno was arrested at Venice by the Inquisition, taken to Rome and *burned alive*, as a heretic and violator of his vows, in 1600. Francesco Cenci had four sons and one daughter: he maltreated them or viciously used them for his illicit pleasures. Revolted by such horrors his daughter, together with two of her brothers and Lucrezia her mother, assassinated Cenci. Accused of patricide, all four died on the scaffold by order of Clement VIII.'[10]

---

[1] From *saignier*: to stain or cover with blood. DAFL.

[2] Latin *regimentum*: act of ruling. DLLB.

[3] Town in the Charolais, 45 km south of Charolles. DHB.

[4] Chief town of the canton of the port of Calais. DHB.

[5] Pays d'Oye: small area of ancient France (Lower Picardy), part of the *recaptured land*. Today part of the *département* of the Port of Calais. DHB.

[6] HFA.

[7] HFAM.

[8] DL7V and DHB.

[9] DDP.

[10] DHB.

---

## Biron's Treason with Spain, 1599, and His Execution, 1602

Quand de Robin[1] la traistreuse entreprise
Mettra Seigneurs et en peine[2] un grand Prince,
Sceu par La Fin, Chef on lui trenchera:
La plume au vent,[3] amye dans Espagne,
Poste attrapé estant dans la campagne
Et l'escrivain dans l'eau se jettera.[4]

Sixain 6

*Interpretation*

When Biron's treacherous plan embarrasses the nobility and a great prince, he will be discovered by La Fin and his head will be cut off, because of his deviation and his friendship with Spain; letters being seized in the countryside, he who wrote them will, avoiding one evil, fall into a worse.

*History*

'Charles de Gontaut, Duke Biron, was celebrated for Henri IV's friendship and notorious for his own *treason*. Henri had saved his life in battle at Fontaine-Française in 1595. Despite such beneficence, Biron, *led astray* by pride, ambition and greed, *conspired* against his King, negotiated with *Spain* and Savoy and agreed to take arms against his own country. *The plot* was revealed by *La Fin* who had been its instigator. Biron wanted to *deny everything* [*se jetter à l'eau*] but he was convicted by his *written words*. Henri IV tried in vain on several occasions to obtain his confession and repentance, so as to pardon him. He was *beheaded* in 1602.'[5]

'The degree of complicity of the Count of Auvergne and the Duke of Bouillon with Biron is not exactly known. Possibly the two *nobles* were not the only ones involved in this affair.'[6]

[1] Anagram of Biron.
[2] Difficulty, embarrassment, trouble. DL7V.
[3] *Mettre la plume au vent*: to be carried along, drift, with the wind. DL7V.
[4] *Se jeter, se mettre dans l'eau*: out of the frying pan into the fire; avoiding a lesser evil and falling into a greater one.
[5] DHB.
[6] HFA.

---

# Henri IV, 1589. The Edict of Nantes, 1598. Brittany, 1610

Le successeur vengera son beau-frère,
Occuper règne sous[1] ombre de vengeance:
Occis ostacle son sang mort vitupère,[2]
Longtemps Bretagne tiendra avec la France.

CX,Q26

## Interpretation

The successor will avenge his brother-in-law and hold power without the least thought of vengeance. He who was the obstacle [to power] having been killed, a bad omen for his blood, Brittany will be united with France for a long time.

## History

Henri IV, Henri III's brother-in-law, succeeded him; Henri IV had represented an obstacle to the reconciliation between Catholics and Protestants.

'*The Assassination of Henri III* by Jacques Clément was the culmination of a plan drawn up by Mayenne. Henri of Navarre went to see the dying King. "Brother," said the King, "you see how your enemies and mine have used me; rest assured that you will never be King if you do not turn Catholic.". . .

The victory of Ivry won, Henri remembered he was King. "*Quarter for the French!*" he cried. . . .

Mercoeur, Prince of Lorraine, who had *turned Brittany into a sort of dominion*, had been bargaining for four years for its surrender. Seeing the royal army on its way against him, he deemed it sensible to make peace before it reached his territory. He offered his daughter in marriage, *with her inheritance*, to César de Vendôme, son of the King and Gabrielle d'Estrées. Mercoeur abdicated in favour of his son-in-law; he was the last of the great Leaguer rulers. The civil war had ended. . . .

Shortly afterwards Henri ended *the religious war* through the Edict of Nantes, 13 April 1598. . . .

Henri embraced Mayenne and made him walk briskly through the gardens. Mayenne, who was grossly overweight, sweated and puffed. Henri finally stopped and offered him his hand. "That is the only harm that you will ever come to through me." Indeed, it was the only *revenge* he took upon the head of the League.'[3]

[1] *sous* for *sans*; probable printing error. '*Sans l'ombre de*' was a current phrase.

[2] Latin *Cur omen mihi vituperat?* (Why is it a bad omen for me?): Plautus. DLLB. Note the Latin construction of line 3.

[3] HFVD.

# The Siege of La Rochelle, 1625–28.
## The Prince of Rohan at the Blavet, Royan and La Rochelle

Le Prince hors de son terroir Celtique,
Sera trahy, deceu[1] par interprete:[2]
Roüan,[3] Rochelle par ceux de l'Armorique
Au port de blave deceus par moyne et prestre.

CVI,Q6o

*Interpretation*

The Prince [of Rohan] will leave France after being tricked and betrayed by a negotiator [Walter Montague]. Royan and La Rochelle will be attacked by Breton troops [the Duke of Vendôme's]. After the Blavet expedition they will be outwitted by one of the clergy.

*History*

'At *La Rochelle*, power politics were making the people uneasy. Opposite the town walls the king had built Fort Louis. The Duke of Guise had based the royal fleet on the island of Ré: thus the area's pirates were under surveillance. Although at peace, the people of La Rochelle were subjected to the threat of pirates. They summoned Rohan and Soubise. To relieve the town, Soubise planned an exceptionally bold expedition: with several lightly armed ships, crammed with secretly recruited soldiers from Poitiers, he took the island of Ré in a surprise attack in January 1625. At the mouth of the River *Blavet* [au port de Blave] he captured seven great ships of the royal fleet. He eluded the forces of the Duke of Vendôme, Governor of *Brittany* [*ceux de l'Armorique*] and seized the isle of Oléron. Richelieu was angry at not being able to mobilize and retaliate: his own troops were in Italy fighting the Spanish. Soubise's vessels attacked *Royan*, and advanced into the Gironde, threatening Bordeaux. . . .
On the Isle of Ré, the resisting royal forces came up against English invasion troops. At last the citizens of La Rochelle themselves declared war, after two months of hesitation. Richelieu at once blockaded all the land approaches. The fleet was entrusted to a churchman [*moine et prêtre*], Sourdis, Bishop of Maillezais, an extraordinarily resourceful leader. Thanks to his efforts, a convoy of thirty-five vessels landed on the island on 16 October. From October 1627 to January 1628 an army of stonemasons worked on the sea wall. Buckingham, who was preparing an expedition, was assassinated at the beginning of September. The

English fleet still took to sea, however, commanded by Lindsey. On 18 September this fleet, together with Soubise's 5000 troops, was opposite the town of St Martin-de-Ré. Facing fusillades and cannonades from the harbour batteries, they did not risk a landing. An ambassador [*interprète*], Walter Montague, was sent to propose peace on the English behalf, and the fleet put out to sea again. La Rochelle capitulated on condition that its inhabitants would retain freedom of both life and religion. [It had been for some years a Huguenot bastion. *Tr.*] Most of the survivors had to go into exile, and the town walls and defences were razed.'[4]

'Henri, Duke of Rohan, *prince* of Leon, b. 1579 a Protestant, became leader of the French Calvinists after Henri IV's death and waged three wars against the government of Louis XIII (1620–22, 1625–26 and 1627–29). The last of these was disastrous for him, since La Rochelle, which he was defending, was taken by Richelieu and he was *compelled to leave France* [*hors de son terroir Celtique*].'[5]

[1] *Decevoir*: to trick. DAFL.
[2] Latin *interpres pacis*: peace negotiator. DLLB.
[3] Note *ü* for *y*.
[4] LGR.
[5] DHB.

---

# The Revolt of Gaston of Orleans and the Duke of Montmorency against Richelieu, 1632. The Siege of Beaucaire and its Defence by Monsieur, the King's Brother

> Le petit coing,[1] Provinces mutinées,
> Par forts Chasteaux se verront dominées,
> Encore un coup par la gent militaire,
> Dans bref seront fortement assiegez,
> Mais ils seront d'un tres-grand soulagez,
> Qui aura fait entrée dans Beaucaire.

> Sixain 43

## Interpretation

A small area of Provence will revolt, but will be defeated by powerful fortresses and then by the strength of the army. The sieges will be short and they will be raised by a very powerful person who will enter Beaucaire.

## History

'Gaston, Duke of Orleans, halted in the Duchy of Montpensier, counting on considerable support from those wishing to join his ranks, but no one came forward. This delay gave the royal troops a chance to close on him; Gaston feared being surrounded and, despite the Duke of Montmorency's remonstrances, rushed into Languedoc. Two armies, commanded by Marshals de la Force and Schomberg, advanced into the *province* as soon as the court was sure of the Governor's defection, and waited for him there. The support of the provincial assembly, which the latter was relying upon, was not forthcoming since the government had arrested suspect members, while the rest were under such close surveillance that they could not help him. The Spanish, despite their promises, failed to send men or money. During his trial of Monsieur's[2] troops, the attack on the *Castle of Beaucaire*, he was forced to give up *the siege* and realized that he could rely neither on the bravery of his soldiers nor on the skill of their commanders. *The King's forces*, on the other hand, flourished: wherever they advanced, anyone found bearing arms paid for his *rebellion* with his head – a frightening omen for Montmorency. His position became critical. Although greatly liked by his administration he could not rely on any *town*, because they were all *held in check* [dominated or bested] by the King's forces who filled *the province*.'[3]

[1] Small area of some particular place. DL7V.

[2] *Monsieur*: title given to the French king's eldest brother, Orleans, i.e. exalted or very great person. (Tr.)

[3] HFA.

---

## The Siege of La Rochelle, 1627. The Execution of the Duke of Montmorency, 1632. Occupation of Lorraine, 1634. War against the House of Austria, 1636

Le Lys Dauffois[1] portera[2] dans Nansi
Jusques en Flandre Electeur de l'Empire,[3]
Neufve obturée[4] au grand Montmorency,[5]
Hors lieux[6] prouvez[7] délivre[8] a clere[9] peine.

CIX,QI8

## Interpretation

The Dauphin [become] king will carry [the war] into Lorraine, as far as
Flanders and Germany. The great [Admiral] Montmorency, having been
before the new closure [the sea-wall fortification of La Rochelle], will be
elsewhere [Castelnaudary] found guilty and delivered over to an exem-
plary fate.

## History

'The Duke of *Lorraine* paid for the war. Louis XIII avoided Bar-le-Duc
and his *military occupation of the duchy* [1634] meant that for many years
it remained in French hands.

The many treaties signed by Richelieu pointed towards the imminent
*extension of the war*. Richelieu *carried on* the war along all our frontiers:
to the *Low Countries*, to share them with Holland; along the Rhine to
protect Champagne and *Lorraine*; into *Germany* to ally with the Swedes
and destroy Austrian omnipotence.'[10]

'Henri de Montmorency, made Admiral by Louis XIII in 1612, in 1625
conquered the isles of Ré and Oléron. When *La Rochelle* was attacked
by Richelieu, he offered his services for a huge sum. Alienated from the
court because he had been refused the title of constable, he rebelled,
with the King's brother, Gaston of Orleans. He was defeated by Schomberg at Castelnaudary, *captured*, judged and beheaded at Toulouse.'[11]

'This *terrible example* [made of Montmorency] was worth ten years of
peace to Richelieu.'[12]

'On the land side, Richelieu surrounded the town with a 12-kilometre
entrenchment. In order to *close the harbour* and prevent any English
assistance from entering by sea, he organized in *six months* the building
of a stone dyke or wall, 1500 metres long and 8 metres tall.'[12]

---

[1] French Dauphins: Louis XII ascended to the throne without having been Dauphin.
He had two sons, both of whom died young and bore the title. Then the title passed to
François I's son. Henri II and François II succeeded, but Henri IV was not Dauphin.
Louis XIII was of his line. DL7V.

[2] *Porter*: to introduce, carry war into a country. DL7V.

[3] Elector of the German Empire. Title of prince or bishop having a vote in the election
of the Emperor of Germany. DL7V.

[4] Latin *obturo*: I close up, stop up. DLLB.

[5] Henri, 2nd Duke of Montmorency, b. Chantilly 1595, d. Toulouse, September 1632.

[6] Plural = precise spot where event occurs. DL7V.

[7] *Prouver*: to be found guilty, convicted, DAFL.

[8] *Délivrer, livrer*: to put something into someone else's hands, make over. DL7V.

[9] Latin *clarus, clara exempla*: famous examples. DLLB.

[10] HFVD.
[11] DHCD.
[12] HFAM.

---

## Louis XIII's Army Besieges Barcelona, 1640. The Occupation of the Duchy of Montferrat by Louis XIII's Forces, 1640. The Title of 'King of France and Navarre'

De Catones[1] trouvez en Barcelonne,
Mys descouvers lieu terrouers[2] et ruyne:
Le grand qui tient ne tient voudra Pamplonne,[3]
Par l'abbage de Montferrat[4] bruyne.

CVIII,Q26

### Interpretation

Licentious men, to be found at Barcelona, shall be exposed and the place will be stricken with fear and sacked. The King will not occupy Navarre but will want the title of 'King of Navarre', and will occupy the Duchy of Montferrat that autumn.

### History

'The Marquis of Léganez had besieged *Casal*, which a French garrison still *held*. Count Harcourt, with forces only half as strong, marched to relieve the place. The Marquis, instead of going to meet him, lost his numerical advantage and let himself be attacked in his positions. His lines were breached in three places. The Spaniards lost most of their artillery and a quarter of their troops and were obliged to raise the siege.

The huge funds required to maintain such an expensive war meant that there were rebellions in Spain as well as in France. The Duke of Olivares had a plan to make Catalonia contribute to the common defence: the Catalans thought this a violation of their privileges. Their discontent increased when they were compelled to do forced labour for the Castilian army sent to defend Roussillon, and they also particularly objected to the excesses committed by the undisciplined army. Some soldiers among the more unruly elements, those *abandoned to licence* [*Catones*], were *recognized* [discovered] in *Barcelona* one day by a mob of peasants and became targets for their wrath and indignation. There were further

disturbances because the peasants disagreed with the Governor's resistance: the latter's murder brought about the *revolt* [*ruyne*] centred on this
town which then solicited the aid of the French. Substantial aid was sent
to Catalonia as a result of the Catalan decision to renounce their original
plan for a republic and to cede to Louis XIII, which revived their
courage. In alliance with the French, they defied the Spanish beneath
the cannons of Mont-Joui, the citadel of *Barcelona*.'[5]

[1] Latin *Cato, Catonis*: Cato. DLLB. In the sixteenth century 'cato' had become a
mocking term for those outwardly serious or soft-spoken, who were in fact unruly and
*vicious*. Amyot. DL.
[2] Latin *terreo*: I frighten, shock. DLLB.
[3] Capital of Navarre. Henri III of Bourbon, son of Anthony, King of Navarre, ascended
the throne in 1589 as 'Henri IV', and his successors added the title 'King of Navarre' to
that of King of France. DHB.
[4] Ancient duchy in Italy, bordered in the north and west by Piedmont, to the south by
the Republic of Genoa and east by the Milanese; its capital was *Casal*. DHB.
[5] HFA.

---

## The Thirty Years' War. The French Fleet Sunk off Corsica, 1646. The Fronde Wars

Classe Gauloise n'approche de Corseigne,
Moins de Sardaigne tu t'en repentiras:
Trestous mourrez frustrez de l'aide grogne,[1]
Sang nagera, captif ne me croiras.

CIII,Q87

### Interpretation

French fleet, do not approach Corsica or Sardinia, or you will regret it:
you will all die, deprived of help because of the Fronde, the sea will
become bloodstained, and the prisoner will not believe me.

### History

'In 1646, Italy was the main theatre of war. Mazarin and de Lionne
considered making Prince Thomas of *Savoy-Carignan* King of Naples.
Pope Innocent X declared himself hostile to this plan. A *French fleet*
assembled at Toulon and was placed under the command of the Duke
of Brezé, Admiral of France. It sailed rapidly towards the Tuscan
coastline and disembarked French and Piedmontese troops who besieged

Orbetello (which faces Corsica and Sardinia). The siege dragged on. Prince Thomas showed little enthusiasm and the Duke of Brezé was *killed* in a naval engagement with the Spanish which he himself had blithely instigated. His death flung the French fleet and army into disarray. The effects of this unfortunate enterprise were far-reaching: in Paris the Prince of Condé seized the opportunity of demanding that the new admiral should be the Duke d'Enghien who had married the Duke of Brezé's sister.[2] Mazarin refused and the Condés immediately allied with Gaston of Orleans.'[3]

'Condé surrounded himself with all *the malcontents* and prepared for war: his party, like the war, was called the Fronde. Mazarin decided to have Condé arrested [*captif*], along with his brother-in-law the Duke of Longueville [18 January 1650]. Master of Paris, Condé instigated a reign of terror, arranging for the *massacre* of Mazarin's supporters.'[4]

---

[1] Discontent, manifested by grumbling [*grogne*]. DL7V.

[2] Hence the link Nostradamus establishes between Brezé and the Prince's group, the Fronde.

[3] Louis XIV. JR.

[4] DL7V.

---

# The Age of Louis XIV

De brique en marbre seront les murs réduicts,
Sept et cinquante années pacifiques,
Joye aux humains, renoué l'aqueduict,
Santé, grands fruits, joye et temps melifique.[1]

CX,Q89

## Interpretation

Brick walls shall be rebuilt in marble, fifty-seven years of peace, joy to men, the aqueduct renewed, health, great results, time of joy and gentleness.

## History

'Versailles is a compendium of architecture. At least three Versailles exist. The "House of Cards" Louis XIII had had constructed, beginning in 1631, is the earliest. Today this forms the main *"marble forecourt"*.

When Louis XIV decided to take the place on, in 1661, he limited himself to *beautifying* it . . . a terrace with *marble* flagstones and a fountain. . . .

On 24 November 1658, faced with Spanish indecision over the marriage of the Infanta to Louis XIV, Mazarin, at Lyon, feigned wedding negotiations involving Marguerite of Savoy. Immediately Philip IV, fearing that the *peace* might thus be lost, sent a secret messenger to Lyon, offering both *the peace and the marriage*, and this offer was at once accepted by Louis. On 7 November 1659 France and Spain signed the Treaty of the Pyrenees.'[2]

There are almost fifty-seven years between 1659 and 1715, the date of Louis XIV's death.

'If Louis XIV did not found the state, he left it far stronger still. *For fifty years* the Parliament had neither revoked any edicts nor challenged the ministers and the royal power. There was no more than a single ruling authority in France. Contemporaries were well aware that the strength of the *French nation*, which had enabled her to resist European attacks, stemmed from this. Versailles symbolized a civilization which *for many years was* European civilization, so that France was in the forefront, her political prestige helping to spread her language and art.'[3]

[1] From *miel* (honey). Nostradamus' symbol for sweetness and gentleness.
[2] LFLXIV.
[3] HFJB.

---

# The Execution of Charles I of England, 1649.
# The French Occupation of Belgium, 1658–1714.
# England's Problems

Gand et Bruceles marcheront contre Anvers,
Senat[1] de Londres mettront à mort leur Roy:
Le sel et vin luy seront à l'envers,
Pour eux avoir le règne en désarroy.

CIX,Q49

*Interpretation*

[The French] after Ghent and Brussels, will march against Anvers. The English Parliament will put its king to death. England will experience economic reverses for having overturned authority.

## History

'In August 1658 Turenne seized Gravelines, which was still part of France. Then he took Oudenarde and Ypres. He threatened *Ghent* and *Brussels*. Flanders was almost completely conquered. The English had designs on capturing Calais and Philip IV of Spain hoped that there would be discord between Cromwell and Mazarin. But Cromwell died and England suffered a fresh period of *difficulties*.

In February 1677 Louis XIV planned an impressive campaign so that he could negotiate from a position of strength. Heading an army of 120,000 he forged on towards Lorraine, which deceived the enemy; then he doubled back towards Flanders and on reaching *Ghent*, besieged the town, which surrendered after five days. The fortress fell three days after that. It was now *Anvers* which was threatened.

On 22 March 1701 England and Holland sent their list of conditions to the French ambassador at the Hague. They demanded the French evacuation of *Belgium*; a promise that no Spanish possession would be ceded to France; the occupation of ten frontier towns by the Dutch and of Ostend and Nieuport by the English. Louis XIV responded by proposing simply to confirm the Peace of Ryswick – which did not preclude his fortifying *Anvers* and the main Belgian towns under French occupation.'[2]

'The Revolution which began in 1642 ended on 30 January 1649 with the execution of Charles I and an Act by which the proclamation of his heir was forbidden. A week later the House of Lords was abolished, as was royalty itself [*règne en désarroy*]. On Cromwell's death his son Richard succeeded him, but proved unable to maintain a balance between a politicized Army and a Parliament whose members wanted the respect that came with legality. A new Parliament, formed in January 1659, had to be dissolved that April, and Richard resigned. In the grip of *anarchy*, England then went through several months of extreme uncertainty.'[3]

[1] Latin *senatus*: assembly, council. DLLB.
[2] HFACAD.
[3] HRU.

# The Glorious Revolution, 1688.
# The Conspiracy against James II. The Landing of William of Orange, 7 November 1688.
# The Bill of Rights.
# William and Mary, 1689

Trente de Londres secret conjureront,
Contre leur Roy, sur le pont[1] l'entreprise:
Luy fatalites la mort desgouteront
Un Roy esleu blonde, natif, de Frize.[2]

CIV,Q89

*Interpretation*

Thirty people in London will plot against their king; the enterprise will take place by sea. The fatalities of death [his father's] will disgust him, then a king, a native of Friesland, will be chosen with a blonde woman. [Mary].

*History*

'When he ascended to the throne in 1685 James II knew the dangers threatening him, and that his religion would cause as much hostility as his political views. This hostility reached a peak on 20 June 1688 when a Roman Catholic heir was born, Prince James Edward. This event (the King was then fifty-five) put paid to all hopes of a Protestant successor. Ten days after the birth Arthur Herbert, former Vice-Admiral, brought William of Orange [*native of Friesland*] an appeal for assistance signed by various [*trente de Londres*] great noblemen. William, the son-in-law of James II by his marriage to Mary, *had been having discussions for several months with opponents of the English King*, and was therefore invited to lead the second English revolution. The 1688 Revolution was remarkably short. On 7 November 1688 William landed at Torbay. On 25 December James II, persuaded to flee, landed on French soil. On 23 February 1689 the royal succession was settled. The blundering James II had been unable to make the necessary concessions rapidly, so that the question of who should be king had not been posed by William himself, whose personal popularity remained doubtful. *The memory of his father's execution* greatly influenced the King's attitude and made him too eager to concede defeat. On 13 February 1689 Parliament adopted a law setting out the rights and liberties of every citizen and determining *the succession to the Crown [Roy esleu]*, known as the Bill of Rights. This law legitimized

William and Mary as joint monarchs, established their succession and excluded Catholics from the throne in future. On 23 February the two new sovereigns were proclaimed, since they adhered to this Bill.'[3]

[1] Greek πόντος: the sea. DGF.
[2] One of the provinces of the Kingdom of Holland. DHB.
[3] HRU.

---

## Villars and the War of the League of Augsburg. The Liberation of Provence, 1707, after its Occupation by the Duke of Savoy. Villars and the Camisard Rebellion, 1702–5

La mer Tyrrhene, l'Occean par la garde,
Du grand Neptune[1] et ses tridens soldats:
Provence seure par la main du grand Tende,[2]
Plus Mars Narbon l'héroiq de Vilars.

Presage 2

### Interpretation

The Tyrrhenian Sea and the Ocean will be guarded by England and her sailors, Provence will be delivered from the Duke of Savoy, [the great one from Tende], and the heroic Duke of Villars will put an end to the war in Languedoc.

### History

'The greatest calamity was *at sea*. The King [of France] had still not given up hope of restoring James to the throne. A landing force of 20,000 men was to have been supported by a fleet totalling 65 vessels, when all the squadrons had joined up. One contingent was *in the Mediterranean*; winds and storms prevented its arriving on time. The success tasted by *Villars* meant that the original plan was expanded. He was deprived of several detachments which were then redirected to *Provence*, recently invaded by the *Duke of Savoy*. Despite prudence the invasion of *Provence* did not proceed as planned. *An English fleet* supported the land army and was given the task of transporting the heavy artillery which could not have been carried over the mountain route. The enemy pushed forward without difficulty deep into Provence and neared Toulon by the end of July 1707. The Allies [the English and the Duke of Savoy] were luckier at Naples [Tyrrhenian Sea], which they captured from Philip II of Spain. This expedition was *the salvation of Provence*, which might have succumbed had all the armies separately employed been reunited against it. The Elector of Bavaria, who could not play second fiddle to his nephew the Prince, was sent to the Rhine against Prince Eugène; Villars was destined for Dauphiné and *Provence*, still menaced by the Duke of Savoy [*the great one from Tende*].'[3]

'The Camisard Rebellion was one of the repercussions of the Revocation of the Edict of Nantes. For two years Louis XIV had been obliged to dispatch armies totalling 20,000 men against the rebels. Various marshals of France had led his forces: first de Broglie, then de Montrevel, and finally Villars, who showed himself to be both soldier [*Mars*] and diplomat. Assisted by Nicolas Lamoignon de Basville, Intendant of *Languedoc*, Villars negotiated with Cavalier, whom he persuaded to support the rebel cause no longer. Deprived of their main leader, the rebels were soon defeated.'[4]

---

[1] God of the Sea (DL7V). For Nostradamus, a symbol of English naval might.

[2] Name of a county belonging to the Lascaris of Ventimiglia, and which finally by marriage passed to the House of Savoy. DHB.

[3] HFA.

[4] DL7V.

---

# The Regency, 1715

Coeur, vigueur, gloire, le règne changera,
De tous points, contre ayant son adversaire!
Lors France enfance par mort subjuguera,
Le Grand Régent sera lors plus contraire.

CIII,QI5

## Interpretation

In spite of courage, strength, glory, power will change hands, having its adversary opposed in all areas: the childhood [of the King] will then put France under a deadly yoke, the Great Regent will be even more harmful to the country.

## History

'The throne of France reverted to Louis XV who was the Duke of Burgundy's son and hence great-grandson of Louis XIV, but this prince was still only *five years old*. Louis XIV had set out in his will the Council of Regency which was to govern until Louis XV's majority. But Louis XIV's nephew, Philippe, Duke of Orleans intervened. He had Parliament rescind Louis XIV's will and confer the Regency upon him unconditionally. He is generally only referred to in French history by the title of *Regent*, and the period for which he governed is simply called the Regency.

The Duke of Orleans was highly intelligent and renowned for his gallantry, but his fickleness, love of pleasure and lack of moral fibre led to *great misfortunes* for France.'[1]

[1] PCHF.

---

## The Marseille Plague, 1720

La grande peste de cité maritime
Ne cessera que mort ne soit vengée;
Du juste sang par pris damné sans crime,[1]
De la grand dame par feinte n'outragée.

CII,Q53

## Interpretation

The great plague of Marseille will cease only when death is avenged, the blood of the just shed by the damned without being accused for fear that the monarchy might be outraged by this crime.

## History

'The nationwide *mourning* after the *death* of the Dauphin began again in early 1712, in even sadder manner. People mourned the Duke of Burgundy, who had assumed the title of Dauphin, his wife the Princess of Savoy, and finally the Duke of Brittany, the eldest of their two surviving children. All three deaths occurred within a month of each other. *Such a heavy loss* in the royal family was *thought to be unnatural*; and the public thoughtlessly accused the Duke of Orleans, who had adopted a scornful attitude towards all virtue and was quite shamelessly immoral. Thus he prompted the mingled suspicion, grief and hatred of all.

In 1720 Marseille was in the grip of a frightful plague due to the negligence of its health officers in the quarantine station. Their carelessness at the end of May led to the premature clearance of a vessel from Syria infected with the plague. At the end of September a north wind began to clear the putrid effluvia hovering over the town, which had stricken almost half the population of 100,000. The main ravages of the plague ended about this time but the last traces only disappeared a year after the original epidemic.'[2]

[1] Latin *crimen*: accusation.
[2] HFA.

---

## The Republic of Letters, 1720.
## The Eighteenth-century Philosophers

Lors que Venus[1] du Sol sera couvert
Soubs l'esplendeur sera forme occulte:
Mercure[2] au feu les aura descouvert,
Par bruit bellique sera mis à l'insulte.[3]

CIV,Q28

*Interpretation*

When venomous words are under the monarchy's shelter, under its splendour the real idea will hide, the flame of eloquence will bring it to light, [the monarchy] will be attacked with warlike noise.

*History*

'In theory, men of letters are *under the surveillance* of authority, guardian of religion, morals and the social order. In reality, they do, *say* and publish what they please. In general, the eighteenth-century French literature of importance and influence was anti-Christian. It was a *militant*, ambitious and *aggressive* literature. Writers became philosophers. Writing stopped being a lofty diversion in which the spirit freely wandered, and sought instead to establish a mastery of ideas over and against the *Church, authority* and tradition.

For thirty years Voltaire, ever bolder, more powerful and more *outrageous*, would exert upon the thought of a whole age a dictatorship almost without precedent.

In 1720 the republic of letters was a dream; half a century later, it was a reality.'[4]

[1] Venom: in Latin, *venus, veneris*: sexual desire personified by Venus, goddess of love. DL7V.

[2] Son of Jupiter, the gods' messenger, himself god of eloquence. DL7V.
[3] Latin *insulto*: I taunt. DLLB.
[4] HFPG.

---

# Eighteenth-century Literature Paves the Way for the French Revolution, the Cause of the Great Wars of the Nineteenth and Twentieth Centuries

> La grande perte, las que feront les lettres,
> Avant le cicle de Latona[1] parfait,
> Feu grand déluge plus par ignares sceptres
> Que de long siècle ne se verra refait.

CI,Q62

## Interpretation

Literature will make great subversive inroads before the Republic has completed its cycle, then incompetent powers will cause great wars which will be prolonged throughout the nineteenth and twentieth centuries.

## History

'The philosophers and economists had an enormous influence, not simply on the uncultured and largely uneducated masses, but on literature too, especially amongst the bourgeoisie. In order to spread new ideas, and since large political newspapers did not yet exist, they used the theatre, books and anonymous pamphlets, with such success that closures and confiscations ordered by Parliament or the police were not effective. At the same time the publication of the Encyclopaedia powerfully assisted the propaganda of the philosophers and economists. Its publication was completed in 1772 and it consisted of twenty-eight volumes. It was an unwieldy but forceful war machine, destined to *shake the foundations* [*grande perte*] of the *ancien régime* and to disseminate, together with atheism, all the key ideas of the new philosophy.

From France the new ideas infiltrated the whole of Europe.'[2]

'War against Europe: since 1792 victory had produced its own problems. Was France to negotiate or *carry on waging war*? To revolutionize the conquered territories or to leave the old order intact? To make protectorates or annex them? The pacifism of 1789, the Girondin cosmopolitanism, plans for universal revolution, the old dream of natural frontiers, the fear of engaging in *an endless war* – everything was in a state of flux. The radical solution was not slow to present itself. Humanitarian in principle, the Revolution very soon became *bellicose. The Revolution was swept into continental war*; its *heir*, the Emperor Napoleon, was finally destroyed by it and *France paid for the struggle, to her cost.*'[3]

[1] Apollo's mother. Allusion to the First Republic, which would spawn Napoleon, the New Apollo. Cf. CI,Q76.
[2] HFAM.
[3] HFPG.

---

# France on the Eve of the Revolution, 1789.
## The Execution of Louis XVI and Marie-Antoinette

> Le trop bon temps, trop de bonté royale
> Faicts et déffaicts prompt, subit, négligence,
> Léger croira faux d'espouse loyale.
> Luy mis à mort par sa bénévolence.[1]

CX,Q43

## Interpretation

The age being too good, the king also too good, will be annihilated promptly and suddenly through negligence. The king's wife will be wrongly supposed to be licentious and she will be put to death because of his genial nature.

## History

'France at the end of the eighteenth century was the largest European state and *one of the richest* and most advanced. A general unrest, however, pervaded the whole country.'[2]

'Times were too good.

Poverty can cause riots. It never creates revolutions. These have deeper-rooted causes, and in 1789 the French were not badly off. On the contrary, documents show that *individual wealth had considerably increased* over the previous half-century and that most classes of society except the rural nobility were distinctly more affluent.'[3]

'Also, for centuries kings had been in the habit of borrowing; but part of the revenue was swallowed up by interest due [*par negligence.*]'[2]

'Queen Marie-Antoinette made herself unpopular by her trifling [*Léger*].'[4]

'Louis XVI, *full of good will*, had even appointed ministers capable of bringing about reforms: first Turgot, then Necker [*par sa bénévolence!*].'[2]

[1] Latin *benevolentia*: good will, kindness. DLLB.
[2] LCH3.
[3] LRFPG.
[4] *futilité* (Fr.). See also note 1.

---

## Promissory Notes and State Bankruptcy, 1789–96. The Persecution and Execution of Men of Letters. The Emigrés

Ceux qui estoient en regne pour scavoir,
Au Royal change[1] deviendront appovris:
Uns exilez sans appuy, or n'avoir,
Lettrez et lettres ne seront a grand pris.

CVI,Q8

### Interpretation

Those who were in power because of their learning [the nobility] will be impoverished by promissory notes. Some will be exiled without aid or fortune. Literary men and their works will be in low repute.

### History

'Promissory notes were paper money whose value was redeemable against so-called "national" assets [royal change]. The promissory note played a part in the dawn of the 1789 Revolution. The issues continued without reserve or limit. Depreciation would be rapid, almost instantaneous. The fall was halted by converting 558 million francs in cash into bills payable to bearer, by the suppression of cash discounts and the redemption of shares by promissory notes, and by a compulsory wealth tax of 1000 million francs as decreed by the Convention.

The Laws of 29 Messidor, 5 Thermidor Year IV and 16 Pluviose Year V abolished dealings between holders of promissory notes and the mandated territories. *The state [ceux qui estoient en règne*], after having declared itself *bankrupt [approvris*] organized a sort of receivership with individual holders of notes. The *paper money* experiment [royal change] was over. As a business scheme it had proved disastrous, ruining thousands of families.'

'*French emigration* began after 14 July 1789 and did not end until 1825, with the special Emigration Law. The week following the Storming of the Bastille saw the exodus of princes of royal descent (Count of Artois, Dukes of Angoulême and Berry, Prince de Broglie, Vandreuil, Lambesc-Conti) [*ceux qui etaient en règne*]. The Convention later sentenced the émigrés to perpetual banishment [23 October 1792].'[2]

'Madame Roland, Lavoisier the great chemist, Malesherbes, and a thousand others were executed.'[3]

'André Chénier, disgusted by revolutionary excesses, dared to criticize the Revolution openly in the *Letters* he had published in the *Journal de Paris*. Charged before the Revolutionary Tribunal, he was sentenced to death in 1794.'[4]

[1] *Lettre de change*: ancient term for paper money, *bonds or credits* issued by the state and repayable to the holder on demand. DL7V.
[2] DL7V.
[3] HVD.
[4] DHB.

---

# The Storming of the Bastille, 14 July 1789.
## War, 20 April 1792

> Avant conflit le grand mur tombera,
> Le Grand à mort, mort trop subite et plainte.
> Nef imparfait[1] la plus part nagera,[2]
> Auprès du fleuve de sang la terre teinte.

CII,Q57

## Interpretation

Before the war the great wall will fall, the King will be executed, his death too sudden and lamented. Most [of the guards] will swim in blood; near the Seine the soil shall be bloodstained.

## History

'Marat wrote in *The People's Friend* (14 April 1791): "When an extraordinary conjunction of circumstances caused the poorly defended Bastille *walls to fall*, the Parisians appeared before the fortress: curiosity alone brought them there." . . .

De Launay, Governor of the Bastille, and the *entire garrison* with the exception of the King's lieutenant du Puget, were *massacred* by the mob, as well as the invalids Ferrand and Bécarel.'[3]

'Since *June 1791* there had been talk of *war*. The spirit of aggression was also prevalent abroad. It took the advent of the Emperor Leopold's son, Francis II, to spark off this *war*. The King, for once in agreement with his ministers and the majority of the Legislative Assembly, *declared war* in response to Francis' demand that France should return Avignon to the Pope [20 April 1792]. . . .

The execution of Louis XVI prompted Royalist indignation and the *horrified censure* of foreign monarchs [*mort trop subite et plainte*] who now considered alliance against a Republican, aggressive France which had just declared war upon England (1 February 1793).'[4]

[1] i.e. unfinished, incomplete. DL7V.
[2] Different phrasing: to swim in blood, i.e. be covered in it. DL7V.
[3] DL7V.
[4] LCH3.

---

# The End of the Monarchy, 1792. Letter to Henry Roy de France Second

. . . Et durera ceste cy jusqu'à l'an mil sept cens
nonante deux que l'on cuidra estre une rénovation
de siècle . . .

## Interpretation

And the latter [the monarchy] will last until the year 1792 which will be thought to be a renewal of the century.

## History

The year 1792, not 1789, was specified by Nostradamus. The end of the *ancien régime* actually dates from 21 September 1792, the date when Year 1 of the Republic began.

Nostradamus makes a statement which might seem surprising when he mentions 'a renewal of the century'. In fact he knew that the monarchy would last thirteen centuries from the coronation of Clovis at Rheims in

496 to 1792, but he also knew that not one of the five subsequent republics would endure for a single century:

1st Republic, September 1792 to December 1799: 7 years, 3 months.
2nd Republic, February 1848 to December 1851: 3 years, 7 months.
3rd Republic, September 1870 to June 1940: 69 years, 9 months.
4th Republic, October 1946 to September 1958: 11 years, 11 months.
5th Republic, from September 1958.
Hence the phrase 'renewal of centuries'.

---

## The End of the Ancien Régime, 1792

Le teste bleue[1] fera la teste blanche,[2]
Autant de mal que France a faict leur bien,
Mort à l'Anthene,[3] grand pendu sus la branche,[4]
Quand pris des siens le roi dira combien.

CII,Q2

### Interpretation

Republican power will do as much harm to monarchical power as the monarchy has done [good] to France. Death to the fleur-de-lis, the King will hesitate greatly when he can say how many of his party have been arrested.

### History

'If Napoleon did not save the Republic, he saved whatever could be salvaged from the Revolution: its mystique, personalities, foreign policy, cosmopolitanism and social organization. Until then France could only conceive of the return to order in the form of *restoration of the monarchy*. In ten years the Revolution had confounded all expectations and disappointed all hopes. A stable and ordered government had been expected; solvency, wise laws, peace abroad and tranquillity at home. But *there had been anarchy, war, terror, bankruptcy, famine and failure*. The idealists of 1789 had wanted to regenerate mankind and reconstruct the world. To escape the Bourbons, they had been reduced to taking up the sword. . . .

Louis XVI and Marie-Antoinette had at first shown some spirit. They ended up panic-stricken. At the last minute the King still *hesitated*.

In ten days everything was ready: the lists of *proscriptions* were printed and the cut-throats chosen and enrolled. At Carmes, at the Abbey, the

Salpêtrière, the Châtelet, Bicêtre. In four days there were more than 1100 murders. Among the dead were the *former minister* Montmorin, the Archbishop of Arles, the bishops of Saintes and Beauvais, and the *Swiss* who had escaped the events of 10 August.'[5]

'The revolutionary Commune sentenced the royal family to internment in the Temple Prison, and *arrested numerous persons on suspicion.*'[6]

[1] A name that the inhabitants of the Vendée gave the *Republican* soldiers because of the colour of their uniform. DL7V.

[2] White, under the *ancien régime*, always represented the nation and French *royalty.* DL7V. Cf. CX,Q20: the white stone.

[3] Greek ἀνθίνος: flower. DGF. NB capital A.

[4] Cf. CX,Q20.

[5] LRFPG.

[6] LCH3.

---

# The Seven Years of the First Republic, 21 September 1792 to 15 December 1799

La Dame seule[1] au règne[2] demeurée,
L'unic[3] éteint premier au lict d'honneur,
Sept ans sera de douleur explorée,
Plus longue vie au règne par grand heur.

CVI,Q63

## Interpretation

The Republic having attained power, the King dead in the front rank of honours, it shall be known in sorrow for seven years, but will not have longer to rule happily.

## History

'The Convention reassembled on 20 September 1792 and abolished royalty. Next day it decreed that official Acts would thereafter be dated from Year I of the Republic.

By applying severe penalties, most often the death sentence, the government became known as the Terror. The law concerning suspects (17 September 1793) silenced all possible forms of opposition. At Paris, the Tribunal sent accused persons to the guillotine after *summary trials* (Marie-Antoinette, the Girondins, etc.). Robespierre obtained the death sentence upon the followers of Hébert in March, then on Danton's supporters in April 1794.

After this sort of apotheosis, Robespierre took one of his most merciless measures: the Law of Prairial (10 June 1794) which gave any accused person practically no chance of escaping the scaffold. During this *Great Terror* more than one thousand executions took place in forty-five days in Paris.

On 20 May 1795 an *impoverished, wretched rabble* aroused the Parisians with cries of "Bread and the 1793 Constitution!" The Thermidorians called out the troops against the rioters. From street brawls the Royalists progressed to organize massacres in the provinces. The *White Terror* claimed numerous victims in the south-east. The Chouans [or Royalists, *Tr.*] supported an English landing at Quiberon Bay which was soon foiled by General Hoche's troops. On 5 October 1795 the Royalists tried to instigate an insurrection in Paris. The Convention entrusted their defence forces to a young general named Bonaparte, who shot down the rebels.

On the steps of the Church of St-Roch the Directorate came up against the same enemies: the Royalists and the Jacobins. So it practised pendulum politics, swinging sometimes against the right (the execution in spring 1796 of the Chouan leaders Stofflet and Charette), sometimes against the left (destroying the Conspiracy of Equals instigated by Gracchus Babeuf).'[4]

During 1792–99 France suffered an unparalleled series of disturbances and massacres, unrivalled even by the darkest days of the Inquisition! [*Sept ans sera de douleur explorée.*]

'The businessmen and the contented, reassured bourgeoisie favoured Bonaparte, who had raised their spirits. He authorized the return of the émigrés to France and gained the support of many of them by giving them government posts. He offered the Chouans an amnesty.'

'The Constitution of Year VIII (15 December 1799) gave executive power to three Consuls elected for ten years, but the first Consul, Bonaparte, *had sole power of decision*; increasingly he initiated laws.'[4] The First Republic thus lasted seven years and almost two months' [*plus longue vie au règne par grand heur*].

---

[1] Marianne, the woman without a husband, was the symbol of the French Republic.
[2] Latin *regnum*: reign, power. DLLB.
[3] The king was unique in the exercise of monarchical power.
[4] LCH3.

# The Tuileries, 20 June 1792 and
# 10 August 1792

Le part[1] soluz[2] Mary sera mittré[3]
Retour conflict passera sur le thuille[4]
Par cinq cens un trahyr[5] sera tiltré,[6]
Narbon et Saulce par contaux[7] avons d'huille.[8]

CIX,Q34

## Interpretation

Having made up his mind alone the King shall wear the Phrygian cap, after his return [from Varennes] conflict will continue into the Tuileries, treason will be plotted by 500 persons. No force, because of the Count of Narbonne and Sauce.

## History

'The population of Paris, warned by the clubs, rose against the King. On 20 June a crowd of armed demonstrators invaded the *Tuileries*, surrounded the King by a window and demanded the *withdrawal of the veto*; the King had to don *the red cap*, but would *not relent*. On 10 August, Federates from Marseille and people from the Paris suburbs invaded the Tuileries and massacred the Swiss Guard.'[9]

'*Narbonne*: in 1791, after promotion to brigadier on his return to Paris, he became War Minister. Soon *suspected* however, by both the revolutionaries and the court, he resigned from office on 10 March 1792 and went back to the northern army. When he returned to Paris, three days before 10 August, *he tried to save the monarchy*.'[10]

'At last on 30 June the Marseille group arrived. There were 500 of them.'[11]

'When the coach arrived, it was suddenly surrounded by armed National Guardsmen commanded by the *procureur* of the commune, *Sauce*. Growing ever more embarrassed, Sauce had time to send word to Paris. Twenty hours later, in Sauce's bedroom, through power of attorney a warrant for Louis XVI's arrest was handed to the King, who cried out, "There is no longer a King in France!" '[12]

---

[1] Masculine noun: decision (DAFL); determination, resolution (DL7V). 'During the Revolution the Suspensive Veto was retained by the King.' DL7V.

[2] Latin *solus*: alone, solitary. DLLB.

[3] Mitre: 'For Latin and Greek authors this term signified headgear worn by men and women of India and Phrygia.' DL7V.

[4] Tuilerie: place where tiles (*tuiles*) are made.
[5] Verb used as noun.
[6] *Titrer*: (symbolic) to scheme or intrigue. DL7V.
[7] *Comtal, comtaux*: belonging to a count or counts. DL7V.
[8] Popular usage: strength. DL7V.
[9] LCH3.
[10] DL7V.
[11] A. Thiers, *History of the French Revolution*.
[12] LRFPG.

---

# The Year 1792: Revolts in the Provinces, the Royal Family in the Temple

Deux estendars[1] du costé de l'Auvergne,
Senestre[2] pris, pour un temps prison regne,
Et une Dame enfans voudra mener,
Au[3] Censuart[4] mais descouvert l'affaire,
Danger de mort murmure[5] sur la terre,
Germain,[6] Bastille[7] frère et soeur prisonnier.

Sixain 9

## Interpretation

When there are revolts in the Auvergne area, the left having taken power, imprisonment will prevail for some time and the Queen will wish to take her children away, but Sauce will unveil the affair; popular discontent will constitute mortal danger; brother and sister of the same parents will be imprisoned in a castle flanked by turrets [the Temple].

## History

'In February 1792 not a day passed without news of some alarming insurrection. There were pillage and massacres in the Yonne and Nièvre where the troublemakers this time were the inhabitants of the *Morvan*. In March and April 1792 the Cantal department was troubled by a peasant revolt which terrorized a score of communes: castles were burnt, properties were forcibly requisitioned, and the authorities were powerless or acquiescent.'[8]

'Amid the agitation after 10 August the civil powers, Assembly and Executive Council, had to come to terms with the Revolutionary authority, *the Paris Commune [senestre]*, which exercised virtual dictatorship. Despite the Assembly's decree that Louis XVI and the *royal family* should be interned in the Luxembourg Palace, the Commune had them *imprisoned* in the *tower* of the Temple. Soon thousands of "suspects" were *incarcerated*."[9]

For the flight to Varennes and the part played by Sauce, see CIX,Q34.

[1] To raise the *standard* or banner of revolt; to revolt. DL7V.
[2] Latin *sinister*: left.
[3] For the Latin preposition, *a* or *ab* = by.
[4] Anagram of Sauce. The letters N, R and T added by epenthesis and paragoge.
[5] Act of complaining; complaints of discontented persons; murmurs of dissatisfaction from the people. DL7V.
[6] Issue of the same father and the same mother; brother and sister german. DL7V.
[7] Castle flanked by turrets, and by extension any prison. DL7V.
[8] LRFPG.
[9] HFAM.

---

## The Battle of Valmy, 20 September 1792. The Triumvirate, 1790. Robespierre and Mirabeau. Mirabeau at the Pantheon

Au costé gauche[1] à l'endroit de Vitri,
Seront guettez les trois rouges de France:
Tous assoumez rouge,[2] noir[3] non meurdry:[4]
Par les Bretons remis en asseurance.

CIX,Q58

### Interpretation

Because of the left [there will be a battle] near Vitry. The three reds of France will be spied upon and killed by the red, the aristocrat [Mirabeau] will not be killed and will be placed in safety by the Jacobins.

### History

'On 17 September 1792 Kellermann climbed up from Vitry-le-François towards the north-east. All the Allies and all the French troops then faced each other. On 20 September the Battle of Valmy was won. . . .

On the *left* were many lawyers like Tronchet or Le Chapelier, who founded the *Breton* club which would become the Jacobin Club. Very soon the left split into sects and coteries. The most famous was the *Triumvirate* of Adrien du Port, Charles de Lameth and Barnave. They opposed La Fayette and Mirabeau. The important figure was Barnave.

When Mirabeau grew closer to the court party, Barnave violently opposed him. In 1791 he defended the Jacobin Club against the Monarchists' Club. After Varennes, Mirabeau became reconciled with the King and turned into a supporter of constitutional monarchy. He was to be arrested, condemned and executed.'[5]

'The decree of martial law followed: if any riotous assembly became threatening the alarm cannon would be fired, and *a red flag* would be hung from a window of the Hôtel de Ville as a signal for the populace to disperse. The decree was backed by Mirabeau and attacked by Robespierre,[6] whose *demagogy*, already demonstrated more than once, began to be even more marked.

The discussions and decisions of the *Jacobins* were growing increasingly extreme and heated. Almost all of one whole session was devoted to the fate of the church of St Genevieve, which had not yet been consecrated by the Catholics. It was solemnly decreed that it would be known as the *Panthéon*. *Count* Mirabeau was the *first* to receive funeral honours there.'[7]

---

[1] Political ref. In assembly, benches would be placed to the right or left of the President; the members who occupied such benches. DL7V.

[2] Latin *rubeus*. Name for the most extreme Republicans. DL7V.

[3] *Noirs*: name given to the deputies of the Constituent Assembly who sat to the right of the room. The name of 'Blacks' was given to the aristocrats as much by analogy as because most of them wore ecclesiastical garb. DL7V.

[4] *Meurtrir*: i.e. kill, cause to perish by murder. DL7V.

[5] HFACAD.

[6] Cf. CVIII,Q19 and CVIII,Q80. Robespierre = *la pierre rouge*, the red stone.

[7] HFA.

---

## The Trial of Louis XVI, 17 January 1793.
## The Affair of the Iron Cabinet

Lettres trouvées de la Royne les coffres,[1]
Point de subscrit[2] sans aucun nom d'autheur:
Par le police seront cachez les offres,[3]
Qu'on ne sçaura qui sera l'amateur.

CVIII,Q23

*Interpretation*

The letters found in the Queen's cupboards will be discovered, without signature or author's name. The police will conceal the payment offers [contract of defence] so well that the beneficiary [of the funds] will not be known.

## History

'A letter from Laporte was said to be in Louis's own hand and dated, but he maintained he recognized neither the letter nor its date. Two others from the same source, both annotated in the hand of Louis, 3 March and 3 April 1791. He denied all knowledge of them. An unsigned paper, containing a "defence contract": before questioning Louis about this, the President asked the following: "Did you cause to be built in one wall of the Tuileries Castle *a cabinet* with an iron door, and keep papers therein?" Louis: "I know nothing about that, nor about the *unsigned* paper." '[4]

'I observed that even with the official seals affixed to the papers of every accused person, no inventory had ever been made in the presence of the accused of the individual papers thus bound together. I should add that nothing would be easier for hostile or malicious persons than to slide under the seals papers which might compromise an accused person and to *remove those which might justify him*. Louis's domicile was invaded and his *cabinets* forced open. During the confusion pieces of paper could have been *lost* or *stolen*, especially the ones which might have explained those used against him. Septeuil, in a public statement, explained away such a speculation by maintaining that not only did it concern himself alone, but that a special register was kept for Louis' *accounts, about which no one has given us any information*, and that it listed the particulars of such funds.'[5]

'In his cross-examination Louis XVI tried nonetheless to deny all knowledge of the notorious *cabinet* and the *papers* inside it. Besides, the most important documents would have been taken away in a large satchel and entrusted to *Marie-Antoinette*'s lady-in-waiting, Madame Campan.'[6]

---

[1] The importance of chests or coffers declined in the mid-sixteenth century with the increased use of cupboards and cabinets. DL7V.

[2] Latin *subscriptio*: signature at the foot of a document. DLLB.

[3] Contract statement akin to an IOU setting out terms of obligation in order to prevent or halt a court action. DL7V.

[4] Cross-examination of Louis XVI. HFA.

[5] Defence of Louis by Citizen de Sèze. HFA.

[6] DL7V.

# The Flight to Varennes, 20 June 1792.
# The Vote to Pass the Death Sentence on the King.
# War, 1 February 1793

De nuict viendra par la forêt de Reines,[1]
Deux pars voltorte[2] Herne[3] la pierre blanche[4]
Le moine[5] noir[6] en gris dedans Varennes
Esleu cap[7] cause tempeste, feu, sang, tranche.

CIX,Q20

## Interpretation

He will arrive by night through the forest of Rheims, tortured by two parties in his willingness to be a devout monarch, the noble monk in grey, at Varennes. The head of Capet put to the vote will cause storm, war, blood, guillotine.

## History

'In France, an absolute king reigned [who governed *alone*] by *divine right* [*hernute*]. The King had been too weak to impose *his will* [*voltorte*]. Louis XVI in spite of his *private virtues* [*hernute*] had not the qualities of a sovereign.'[8]

'Louis XVI was deeply *pious*. *Troubled by his conscience*, he then decided to escape.'[9]

'The King was *guillotined* on 21 January 1793. This execution prompted Royalist indignation and the horrified censure of foreign monarchs who now considered alliance against the Republic. France had just declared war upon England [1 February 1793].'[10]

'By 683 *Votes*, Louis *Capet* was found guilty of conspiring against the security of the state.'[11]

---

[1] All old editions give 'Reines'. It can therefore be taken either as a typographical error or as a modification by Nostradamus to preserve the rhyme. The Forest of Rheims is near Varennes and was crossed by the royal coach.

[2] Composite word from two Latin words: *voluntas*, will, and *tortus*, twisted. Early commentators translated it as *short cut* or *diversion*, and later ones (Hutin, Guerin, Monterey, Colin de Larmor etc.) followed this reading. But Propertius uses the phrase *torta via*, i.e. *labyrinthine detours*. Editions after 1610 have *vaultorte* for *voltorte*.

[3] *Herne*: abbreviation of *Hernute*, a Christian sect distinguished for its purity of morals. DL7V.

[4] 'The white rock or stone' was a symbol of the establishment. White was the Royalist colour, the Rock was the Church (cf. Christ's words to St Peter). Cf. also CII,Q2.

[5] Greek μόνος: only, unique, single. DGF. Cf. CVI,63: '*L'unic*'. Also reiterates the idea of king-as-monk.

[6] *Noir*: see CIX,Q58, note 3.

[7] Cap. Abbreviated pun whereby Nostradamus suggests both Latin *caput*: head and a shortened form of *Capet*.

[8] LCH3.

[9] HFAM.

[10] HFDG.

---

# The Execution of Louis XVI, 21 January 1793

Par grand discord la trombe[1] tremblera
Accord rompu dressant la tête du Ciel
Bouche sanglante dans le sang nagera
Au sol la face oincte de laict et de miel.

CI,Q57

## Interpretation

Amid great discord the hunting horn shall sound, the agreement having been broken, [the executioner] lifting up the head [of the King] to heaven, the bloody mouth swimming in blood, his face anointed with milk and honey shall be on the ground.

## History

'The King had been imprisoned from 10 August 1792 (the taking of the Tuileries and the massacre of the Swiss Guard). The Montagnards demanded his trial, but the Girondins wanted to prevent it' [*Amid great discord*].

'Execution of Louis XVI: the executioner *displayed the King's head* to the people' [*Holding aloft the head*].[2] The King's head, which had been crowned at Rheims in 1774, fell to the ground, into the basket below the guillotine.

[1] Kind of trumpet, esp. hunting horn.

[2] LCH3.

## The Execution of Louis XVI. His Succession

> Devant le peuple sang sera respandu,
> Que du haut ciel ne viendra eslonger;[1]
> Mais d'un long temps ne sera entendu,
> L'esprit d'un seul le viendra témoigner.

CIV,Q49

### Interpretation

Blood will be shed before the people and he will not be far from heaven. For a long time he will no more be understood, until the spirit of one who comes one day to bear witness.

### History

'The King slowly descended from the tumbril, let his hands be tied, climbed the steps, and at the top of the platform cried out: "People! I die innocent!"

In his will, dated 25 December 1792, after forgiving his enemies and urging his son to set aside all hatred and resentment, he ended by declaring to God, as he was ready *to appear before Him*, that he was not guilty of any of the crimes of which he was accused.'[2]

'Abbé Edgeworth calmed the King's brief resistance with the now legendary words: "Son of St Louis, *climb up to heaven!*" '[3]

The last two lines of the quatrain suggest that Louis XVII would not die in the Temple and that one of his descendants would one day come to bear witness.

[1] Cf. CI,Q57: *'dressant la tête au Ciel.'*
[2] DHCD.
[3] HFAM.

---

## The Execution of Louis XVI. The Terror, 21 January 1793

> Le juste à tort à mort l'on viendra mettre
> Publiquement et du milieu estaint.[1]
> Si grande peste[2] en ce lieu viendra naistre
> Que les jugeans fouyr seront contraints.

CIX,Q11

## Interpretation

It will be wrong to put the just man to death, executed amid the people. It will bring upon this spot [Paris] such a great calamity [the Terror] that those who did not vote [for the King's death] will be compelled to flee.

## History

'Louis is not an accused man, you are not *judges*. You do not have to pronounce sentence for or against a man, but to take a measure of public safety. Victory and the people have decided that he alone was the rebel. Louis cannot therefore be *judged*, he is already condemned.'[3]

'The Montagnards took power and had to deal with the Vendée uprising backed by the Girondins against the dictatorship in Paris. They constituted a revolutionary government. This was the Reign of Terror. On 9 Thermidor (27 July 1794) Robespierre was accused. He *fled*, was recaptured and executed without trial.'[4]

'Robespierre was lying at my feet and I was told that Henriot *was escaping* by a concealed staircase. I still had a loaded pistol and ran after him. I hit a *fugitive* on that staircase – it was Couthon who was *running away*.'[5]

---

[1] Latin *exstinguo*: I put to death, execute. DLLB.
[2] Latin *pestis*: misfortune, plague, disaster, calamity. DLLB. Cf. CVI,Q63: '*Sept ans sera de douleur explorée*'.
[3] Robespierre's speech to the Convention (3 December 1792).
[4] DHC.
[5] Report by the gendarme sent to arrest Robespierre, who had just been outlawed by the Convention.

---

# Marie-Antoinette and the Duchess of Angoulême at the Temple, 1793

La Royne Ergaste[1] voyant sa fille blesme[2]
Par un regret dans l'estomach[3] enclos:
Crys lamentables seront lors d'Angoulesme,
Et au germain mariage forclos.[4]

CX,Q17

## Interpretation

The Queen detained like a slave, seeing her daughter waste away will regret within her womb that she had children, swayed by the lamentations of the Duchess of Angoulême, married to her first cousin in an unacceptable union.

## History

'Marie-Antoinette, imprisoned in the Temple until 1 August 1793, endured every outrage and agony, whether as queen, wife or *mother*, and her captivity was a true martyrdom.

The Duchess of Angoulême, daughter of Louis XVI and Marie-Antoinette, entered the Temple to share her family's captivity. She married her cousin the Duke of Angoulême, son of the Count of Artois (the future Charles X), third brother of Louis XVI.'[5]

[1] Latin *ergastulus*: slave, prisoner. DLLB.
[2] *Blesmer*: to waste away. DAFL.
[3] Womb. DL7V.
[4] Legal term: inadmissible. DAFL.
[5] DHCD.

---

# The Survival of the Bourbons after Thirty Generations

Peuple assemblé voir nouveau expectacle
Princes et Roys par plusieurs assistans,
Pilliers faillir, murs, mais comme miracle
Le Roy sauvé et trente des instans.[1]

CVI,Q51

## Interpretation

The people will assemble for a spectacle hitherto unseen [a king's execution in a public place], together with several princes and leaders of royal blood; the pillars and walls [of the Bastille] will be broken down but miraculously the blood royal will be preserved after thirty successors.

*History*

After the demolition of the Bastille, the public execution of Louis XVI took place. A prince of the royal blood, Philippe Egalité, had voted for his death.

There were indeed thirty generations of French monarchs between Robert the Strong, father of King Odo, and Louis XVII.

Most historians now accept the hypothesis that the Dauphin did escape from the Temple Prison.

¹ Latin *insto*: I follow, succeed. DLLB.

---

## Louis XVII's Escape from the Temple Prison

> Sans pied ne main¹ dent aiguë et forte
> Par globe² au fort du port³ et l'aisne nay,⁴
> Près du portail desloyal se transporte,
> Silène⁵ luit, petit grand emmené.

CII,Q58

*Interpretation*

Without trial and without force he who has a sarcastic and eloquent tongue will be carried to power by the masses, and the eldest having died soon after birth, one will be transported disloyally to the main gate [of the Temple]. The Republic rules, the little [young] great one [by birth] is led away.

*History*

'Robespierre's name was picked from the *electoral urn* in the open polls in Paris for the elections to the Convention. During Louis XVI's trial he played the most *hateful* role until the fatal climax on 21 January 1793. On 31 May the Girondins were defeated, in which he was instrumental. From then on his power was immense. He entered the Committee of Public Safety and imposed a yoke of force and terror, pitilessly sacrificing men's lives to his political machinations. Arrested in the great chamber of the Hôtel de Ville on 10 Thermidor, he perished on the scaffold.'⁶

'The Temple was actually a palace. Its layout was quite similar to that of the Hôtel Soubise, with a long courtyard surrounded by arcades

ending in a semi-circle at the *gate*. The procession bringing the prisoners
was considerably delayed.'[7]

[1] Latin *manus*: hand, strength. DLLB.
[2] Latin *globus*: group of men, crowd, mob. DLLB.
[3] Action of bearing away or carrying. DL7V.
[4] Louis XVII, b. 1785, first had the title of Duke of Normandy, and became Dauphin on the death of his elder brother Louis-Joseph (4 June 1789).
[5] Phrygian god. (DL7V). The Phrygian cap or bonnet was adopted as a symbol of the Republic.
[6] DHCD.
[7] *Louis XVII and the Temple Enigma*, G. Lenôtre, Flammarion, 1920.

## Louis XVII Escapes from the Temple Thanks to the Simons

Sur le palais[1] au rocher[2] des fenestres
Seront ravis les deux petits royaux,
Passer aurelle[3] Luthèce, Denis Cloistres[4]
Nonnain,[5] mollods[6] avaller verts noyaux.

CIX,Q24

### Interpretation

In the palace with the steeply sloping windows the two royal children
will be taken away, they will traverse Paris like a breeze, escaping from
the Cloisters of St-Denis, thanks to a monk,[7] the wicked wretched ones
will devour green kernels.

### History

'If Paris itself lived through that dark day of 21 January 1793 in a sort
of stupor, there *on the third floor* of the Temple Tower the Queen was
plunged into anguish and despair.'[8]

'Antoine Simon: keeper of Louis XVII in the Temple. A master
cobbler in Paris, he became member for his district and belonged to the
Jacobin Club.'[9]

'Another riddle adds to the mystery. Simon left the Temple on 19
January, grumbling loudly about Chaumette's and the Commune's in-
gratitude. The next morning he went to the poor lodgings of two old
ladies, recluses and former *nuns*, who sheltered a *priest* who like themselves had escaped the Terror. They were celebrating mass in their garret

and the sound of knocking on their door startled them greatly. Yet they opened it to a man they did not know. "Do not be afraid," he said. "I know you have a priest here, but I won't betray you. I am Simon." A number of the most fervent and sincere Republicans remained devoted to the old beliefs and respected past traditions. Until at least 1792 the great majority of the Convention, the *Jacobins* and the members of the Commune went to church services and performed their religious *devotions*. Surprising as it may seem, Simon was one of these. The representatives thus knew that Citizeness Simon (among others), who lived in a house close to the Temple, used this passage. What could the shoemaker's wife do?'[10]

[1] The Tower of the Temple, a square building with thick walls, flanked by turrets at its four corners. The Palais du Grand Prieuré was built in 1767. DL7V.

[2] Rock, i.e. great mass of hard stone, sloping or steep.

[3] *Aurelle*: from Latin *aura*, wind. Diminutive = breeze. DL7V.

[4] '. . . the Church of St-Denis had the privilege of being the Royal Sepulchre.' DL7V.

[5] Nun, or general term including priests. DL7V.

[6] Composite word, from *mol* (mal) = bad, evil and *lods* = miserable, wretched. DAFL.

[7] Jacobin: monk or nun of the Order of St Dominic; member of the Jacobin Club, founded in 1789. DL7V.

[8] *Louis XVII and the Temple Enigma*, G. Lenôtre, Flammarion, 1920.

[9] DL7V.

[10] *Louis XVII and the Temple Enigma*, G. Lenôtre, Flammarion, 1920.

---

# The Execution of Marie-Antoinette, 16 October 1793. Madame Royale at the Temple

Un peu devant ou après très grand Dame[1]
Son âme au Ciel[2] et son corps sous la lame,
De plusieurs gens regrettée sera,
Tous ses parents seront en grand'tristesse:
Pleurs et soupirs d'une Dame[3] en jeunesse
Et a deux grands[4] le deuil délaissera.

Sixaine 55

*Interpretation*

Before [the people] shortly after [the execution of Louis XVI] the Queen will be guillotined and her soul will go to heaven. She will be mourned by many. Her relatives will lament: tears and sighs from her daughter. She will leave her two [brothers-in-law] in mourning.

## History

'Marie-Antoinette, imprisoned in the Temple until 1 August 1793, endured every outrage and agony, whether as Queen, *wife* or *mother*, and her captivity was a true martyrdom. Tried before the Revolutionary Tribunal, she was *condemned to death*. She nevertheless possessed enough fine qualities to be *generally beloved* in more normal circumstances, when she could or would have been judged dispassionately. Led in a tumbril to her fate, she showed great courage and, like her husband, died *forgiving* her enemies.'[5]

[1] Superlative designating the Queen.
[2] Cf. CIV,Q49: '*Que du haut ciel ne viendra éloigner.*'
[3] The Duchess of Angoulême, daughter of Louis XVI and Marie-Antoinette, received at birth the title of *Madame* Royale. After 10 August 1792 she entered the Temple to share her family's imprisonment. DHCD.
[4] Louis, Dauphin of France, son of Louis XV and Marie-Leczinska, left three sons, *Louis XVI, Louis XVIII and Charles X*, and two daughters, Clotilde, Queen of Sardinia, and Elizabeth. DL7V.
[5] DHCD.

---

# The Trial of Marie-Antoinette, 14 October 1793. Her Execution, 16 October 1793

La grande Royne quand se verra vaincue,
Fera excez de masculin courage:
Sur cheval, fleuve passera toute nuë,[1]
Suite par fer, a foy fera outrage.

CI,Q86

## Interpretation

When the great Queen [Marie-Antoinette] sees herself lost, she will put on excessive manly courage. She will cross the river [Seine] drawn by a horse, ill-clad. Then she will die by the sword [guillotine], and it will outrage belief.

## History

'Since August the clubs, the deputies of the main assemblies, and the popular societies had been demanding the Queen's trial, which opened on 14 October before the Revolutionary Tribunal presided over by Herman. Fouquier-Tinville was Public Prosecutor. She was asked the most insidious questions. The accusations concerning the monarchy by pamphleteers hostile to her were again dug up and used against her. Simple and dignified, the Queen replied that she had only obeyed her husband. In order to set the debate ablaze, Hébert made the most *outrageous* accusations against her. The grief-stricken woman managed to answer these calumnies movingly. Despite the pleas of Tanson-Ducoudray and Chauveau-Lagarde, the Queen was condemned to death. On the morning of 16 October she climbed on to a wagon and sat with her back to the *horse: clad in a loose gown*, wearing a white bonnet, her hands tied behind her back, and her eyes half-closed, *erect and impassive [excès de masculin courage]*, this woman who had received such adulation heard the crowd hurling *insults* at her. Marie-Antoinette rapidly mounted the steps leading to the scaffold. A few moments later her *tortured* body [*suite par fer*] was on its way to rejoin the remains of Louis XVI, at the Madeleine Cemetery. . . .

On 14 October 1793 Marie-Antoinette appeared before the Revolutionary Tribunal, wearing a *shabby* black dress [*nue*] and a lawn bonnet trimmed with "widow's weeds".'[2]

'I have just been condemned, not to a shameful death, which is only for criminals, but to rejoin your brother: innocent like himself, I hope to show *the same steadfastness as he* in his last moments' [*manly courage*].[3]

[1] By exaggeration, ill-clad. DL7V.
[2] HFACAD.
[3] Will of Marie-Antoinette, in the form of a letter to her sister-in-law Elizabeth. HFA.

---

# The Alliance of Philippe of Orleans with the Revolution. His Death, 6 November 1793

> Celui du sang resperse[1] le visage,
> De la victime proche sacrifice,
> Venant en Leo[2] augure[3] par présage,
> Mis estre à mort lors pour la fiancée.
>
> CII,Q98

## Interpretation

He whose face is bespattered with the blood of the victim, his close [relative] sacrificed, the adoption of the Phrygian bonnet will be an evil omen for him and he will be put to death because of his alliance.

## History

'Louis-Philippe of Orleans, called Philippe-Egalité, initially *allied* with Mirabeau and was one of the first to commit himself to the Third Estate. His followers were certainly privy to the events which led to the storming of the Bastille. He secretly supported the republicans of the Champ du Mars (July 1791) and became a member of the Jacobin Club. He developed *closer links* with the Cordeliers, the Jacobins and the Paris Commune. Overshadowed by the Montagnards, he sought favour with their leaders who, seeing that he intended to be impartial in Louis XVI's trial, forced him by various threats to vote with them. *He therefore voted for the King's death sentence without reprieve*, without appeal to the people, and *thereby became just as suspect*, especially at the first signs of Dumouriez's plan for re-establishing the 1791 constitution and restoring the throne for a prince of Orleans. He was arrested on 7 April 1793, taken back to Paris, adjudged a Girondin by the Revolutionary Tribunal, sentenced and *executed*.'[4]

[1] Latin *respergo*: I sprinkle water. DLLB.
[2] Latin *Leo*, priest of Mithras, worshipped by the Persians in the form of a lion. DLLB. Mithras is represented by a young man wearing the *Phrygian cap*. DHCD.
[3] Latin *auguro*: I predict. DLLB.
[4] DHCD.

---

# The Execution of Philippe-Egalité, 6 November 1793

Le Grand Baillif[1] d'Orléans mis à mort,
Sera par un de sang vindicatif:
De mort merite ne mourra ne par fort,
Des pieds et mains mal le faisoit captif.

CIII,Q66

## Interpretation

The great representative from Orleans will be put to death by order of a bloodthirsty and vengeful person, he will die a deserved death but only by force, evil binding his hands and feet.

## History

'Defender of the rights of the Third Estate in the Assembly of Notables in 1787, and at the States-General in 1789, the people's protector. Declared enemy of the royal family, he was openly revolutionary. A member of the Convention, he sat on the extreme left. Although he had voted for the death of his kinsman, the King, and was always a Montagnard, he became suspect to his former friends. The same day he appeared before the Revolutionary Tribunal he died very bravely on the scaffold.'[2]

[1] Ancient form of *bailli*, bailiff-governor(s), later replaced by deputies. DAFL.
[2] DL7V.

---

## The Committee of Twelve, May 1793.
## Their Arrest, 2 June 1793

Celuy qu'aura couvert de[1] la grand cappe,
Sera induict à quelques cas[2] patrer[3]:
Les Douze rouges viendront fouiller[4] la nappe,[5]
Soubz meurtre, meurtre se viendra perpetrer.

CIV,QII

### Interpretation

He [Robespierre] who will have covered the great Capet [Louis XVI] with shame will be led to accomplish various falls: the twelve reds will come to look through the plans minutely, and under cover of murder he shall perpetrate their own murders.

### History

'Invested with great powers and composed of deputies whose names would reassure all honest persons, the *Committee of Twelve* could frustrate all subversion against the Convention or any of its members. It might have spoiled all the *plans* of the Jacobins and the Montagnards. Thus the *Twelve* were destined to be targets for *assassins* the moment they began functioning as a group, and the struggle against them became a struggle to the *death*. Information indicated that a plot was being hatched against the lives of twenty-six deputies, which prompted them to issue a warrant for Hébert's arrest. The Committee considered him to be involved in the plot, and that for better or worse his writings were provoking the *murder* of the people's representatives. Couthon reported to the Tribunal and combined irony with arrogance: "Citizens," he said, "every member of the Convention must be reassured of their liberties," and he demanded that the Convention should decree the house arrests of the twenty-six along with the Committee of Twelve.'[6]

'The *coup* of 2 June provoked insurrection in several regions. The Convention resolved to pursue the struggle against its enemies to the bitter end. It entrusted power to the most intransigent Montagnards: Robespierre and his friends Couthon and St-Just. By the end of 1794, *2596 persons had been executed* in Paris.'[7]

[1] To cover with either shame or infamy, or glory. DL7V.
[2] Latin *casus*: fall, end, decline, death. DLLB.
[3] Latin *patro*: I do, execute, accomplish. DLLB.
[4] Figurative: to scrutinize, study attentively, examine the ills of society. DL7V.
[5] By analogy, a flat surface. DL7V.
[6] HFA.
[7] HFAM.

---

# The Nantes Massacres, November 1793

Des principaux de cité rebellée
Qui tiendront fort pour liberté ravoir:
Destrencher[1] masles infelice[2] meslée
Cris, hurlemens à Nantes; piteux voir.

CV,Q33

### Interpretation

Of the main rebels of the town, who will fight to the end to preserve their freedom, the men shall be guillotined, the unfortunates being mixed together, cries and shrieks at Nantes, all constituting a dreadful spectacle.

### History

'At *Nantes* Carrier, a member of the Convention, ruled. He was present at Cholet, but fled from the battle, and thereafter, consumed by fear, had only one obsession: to *kill* in order not to be killed. This deep-seated mania, exacerbated by his drunkenness, degenerated into lunacy.

On the hulks at *Nantes* were a hundred elderly and ailing priests, whom it had not been possible to deport to Guyana. They were therefore taken from one prison to the next. On the night of 16 to 17 November, on the pretext of moving them once more to land, their captors made them climb aboard an old barge which had once plied the lower Loire and now, owing to the decline in trade, had fallen into disuse. *Tied up in pairs*, they showed no resistance, although at the outset their money and watches had been taken from them. Suddenly one of the prisoners noticed that the barge had been holed in several places below the water-line and that water was slowly seeping through these apertures. The priests fell to their knees and gave each other absolution. A quarter of an hour later the barge sank with all its passengers except four. Of these, three were recaptured and put to death. Only one, picked up by fishermen, managed to hide, and the little that is known of the last moments of the victims derives from him.

On 5 December arrived fifty-eight more helpless priests. "Fling all those buggers in the water," Carrier ordered. On the night of the ninth they were drowned at Indret Point. The Proconsul immediately announced this new "shipwreck" to the Convention and ended his dispatch with this cynical remark: "What a revolutionary torrent the Loire is!" *At least eleven other executions by drowning followed, some by night, some by day, which claimed 4800 victims.* To this must be added *guillotinings*: there were three travelling committees and the Paris tribunal eagerly fed on the rich pastures of Brittany. One historian assures us that in fact Carrier killed fewer people than the typhus and other epidemics which were rife in the prisons of Nantes, which must be some sort of consolation."[3]

---

[1] *Détrenchier* = to cut into pieces, slice. DAFL.
[2] Latin *infelix*: unhappy. DLLB.
[3] LRFPG.

---

# The Abbé Vaugeois, President of the Committee of Insurrection, August 1792. The Capture of Chalonnes-sur-Loire by the Vendéans, 22 March 1793. Massacres of Priests on the Loire, 17 November and 5 December 1793

Au temple[1] hault de Bloys Sacre[2] Salonne
Nuict pont de Loyre, Prelat, Roy pernicant:[3]
Cuiseur victoire aux marests de la Lone,[4]
D'ou prélature de blancs[5] abormeant.[6]

CIX,Q21

## Interpretation

The important personage of the Church of Blois will be cursed at Chalonnes-sur-Loire. A priest will be found by night on the bridge of the Loire, the King having been made light [dethroned], the people of Olonne will win sharp victories in the marshes; the royalist priests having been bound.

## History

'There was a concentration of Federates and a stir in the divisions. These were the two initial factors leading to the events of 10 August 1792. Everything was directed by a Committee of Insurrection presided over by the Abbé Vaugeois, Vicar-General of the *Bishopric of Blois*. It was Robespierre who drew up the Federates' petitions for the *dethronement of the King*.'[7]

'On 22 March 1793, the Vendéan army seized *Chalonnes*.'[8]

'There were a hundred or so elderly priests on the prison *hulks* [Fr: *ponton*] of Nantes. *On the night* of 16 November they were made to board an old barge. ["*Tied up in pairs*", etc. (Cf. *CV,Q33*).]

Carrier was recalled in February 1794. His departure marked the end of the drownings, but General Turreau, Marceau's successor in the Vendée, carried on the terror in his own way. Almost all the leaders of the Vendée uprising had been killed. Charette and Stofflet, the two survivors, had no option but to take up arms again, one in the *Marais* [marshlands], the other in the *forest areas*. This was a new, appalling and futile war. At the start of 1794 the Revolution had completely triumphed over its internal enemies.'[9]

[1] Poetic: the Catholic Church.

[2] Latin *sacro*: I vow to gods of vengeance, curse. DLLB.

[3] Latin *pernix*: light. DLLB.

[4] Contraction of *Olonne*: area of La Vendée 5 km from Sables-d'Olonne; the Vendéans had a headquarters there in 1793. DL7V.

[5] During the *ancien régime* white was always taken to represent the nation and royalty. DL7V.

[6] From *ormeger*: to bind or tie up. DAFL.

[7] LRFPG.

[8] HFACAD.

[9] LRFPG.

# Pitt the Younger against the French Revolution, 1793–96 British Aid to the Vendéans, 1795. The Return to Power of Pitt the Younger

Le jeune nay au regne Britannique,
Qu'aura le père mourant recommandé:
Iceluy mort LONOLE[1] donra topique[2]
Et à son fils le regne demandé.

CX,Q40

*Interpretation*

[Pitt] the Younger returned to power in England, and he will have received instructions from his dying father. After the latter's death, he will bring aid to the Vendéans [those of d'Olonne] and the son will be asked to take power again.

*History*

'From 1793 to 1802 the British war effort increased, urged on by Pitt *the Younger* until 1801. He had *inherited from his father* a definite distrust of France.'[3]

'In the western departments [of France] the Royalist party offered bold resistance, which was helped by intrigues in *England*. Charette and Larochejacquelin had reappeared at the head of the *Vendéans [ceux d'Olonne]*. After giving the British hope of a general uprising throughout the areas, if an invasion force of émigrés, arms and supplies could be landed, the Marquis de Puisaye allied with the Chouans and was confident of striking a deadly blow at the Republic. *The English minister*, disappointed by the coalition's lack of success against the French forces, espoused this cause fervently and undertook to supply *60,000 rifles*, as well as *complete equipment [topiques]* for an army of 40,000 men.'[4]

'To raise funds for the war Pitt had to subject England to a regime of emergency regulations, but managed to prevent neither French victories nor the ruin of British trade. He resigned in 1801. Addington, his successor, concluded the Peace of Amiens [1802]. War having begun again, *Pitt once more accepted office* [1804].'[5]

[1] Anagram of Ollone or Olonne: see CIX,Q21, note 4.
[2] Word for localized medications, acting on specific parts of the body.
[3] HRU.
[4] HFA.
[5] DL7V.

## Robespierre, His Friends and Enemies

A[1] soustenir la Grand Cappe troublée
Pour l'esclaircir les rouges marcheront
De mort famille sera presque accablée,
Les rouges rouges le rouge assomeront.

CVIII,Q19

*Interpretation*

Without support the great Capet family will be disturbed. The reds will start decimating it. The royal family will be almost overwhelmed by death. The red extremists will kill the red [Robespierre] and other reds.

*History*

With the execution of Louis XVI, Marie-Antoinette, and Louis' sister Elizabeth, also the presumed death of Louis XVII in the Temple Prison, the Capet family was certainly 'thinned out' [*éclaircie*].

'As for Robespierre, his undoubted virtues were, in his colleagues' eyes, eclipsed by his pride, fanaticism and intransigence: he inspired fear. His *enemies* banded together in order *to get rid of him*.'[2]

'The followers of Robespierre who had been outlawed by the Convention were arrested. Robespierre's jaw was shattered by a pistol bullet. The same evening, on 10 Thermidor, he was *guillotined along with twenty-two of his supporters*; the next day and the day after that, it was the turn of *eighty-three more*. Thus the Great Terror ended with a new slaughter.'[3]

[1] Privative prefix = without.
[2] LCH3
[3] LTR.

---

## Robespierre, the Bloodthirsty Red.
## The Fall of the Monarchy, 1792

Celuy qu'estoit bien avant dans le regne,
Ayant chef rouge proche à la hierarchie,
Aspre[1] et cruel et se fera tant craindre,
Succedera à sacrée[2] monarchie.

CVI,Q57

## Interpretation

He who had already had some power earlier, having a red head [ideas] will attain the summit of the hierarchy; intractable and cruel, he will make himself terribly feared and will succeed to the consecrated monarchy.

## History

'Maximilian Robespierre, b. 1759 at Arras, son of the advocate to the Council of Artois, himself held this post in 1789. Deputy for Arras in the States-General, he was filled with Rousseauist democratic ideas about the Social Contract, sat on the far left [*chef rouge*] and on every occasion displayed *his hatred of the monarchy*. In June 1791 he was appointed Public Prosecutor for the Criminal Tribunal of the Seine; he allied himself with the Jacobins and the Commune, and in 1792[3] was elected a member of the Convention. In association with Danton he conducted the trial of Louis XVI; he pleaded vehemently for the death sentence, thwarting Girondin efforts to save the King. After the execution Robespierre set up the Revolutionary Tribunal and established the Reign of Terror throughout France. Sitting almost continuously on the Committee of Public Safety, he authorized the most bloodthirsty measures. He had imposed upon France an extreme and odious tyranny and not spared his colleagues; those who survived, vexed by his arrogance or afraid of his threats, finally united against him.'[4]

[1] Latin *asper*: hard, savage, intractable. DLLB.

[2] Allusion to the coronation.

[3] The French Republic was proclaimed on 21 September 1792. The Convention succeeded the legislative Assembly and lasted from 21 September 1792 to 26 October 1795. It had been convened after the insurrection of 10 August 1792 and the overthrow of the monarchy, in order to form a new constitution. It proclaimed the Republic at its very first sitting. DHB.

[4] DHB.

---

# The Death of Louis XVI, 1793.
# Robespierre in Power

Quand le deffaut du Soleil lors sera,
Sur le plein jour le monstre sera veu:
Tout autrement on l'interprétera,
Cherté n'a garde, nul n'y aura pourveu.

CIII,Q34

## Interpretation

When the monarchy falls, the monster [Robespierre] will be seen clearly. He will be viewed quite differently. No one will know how to provide against the austerity for none will have foreseen it.

## History

'Between the King's execution (21 January 1793) and the Girondins' proscription (2 June) was less than five months. A plan of action prepared by Robespierre between 16 and 19 May revealed the secret of the machinery by which they in their turn would be purged. The Committee of Public Safety, instituted on 5 April 1793, was originally under Danton's control, and after 10 June under Robespierre's. He was called The Incorruptible, but this name soon acquired another meaning! He came to embody Jacobinism, with all its sinister delight in persecution [*monstre*]. Always following the party line, he knew with a *fanatic*'s instinct how to destroy any factions guilty of deviation from it.

The victories of 1793 and 1794 did not slacken the Jacobin dictatorship. On the contrary, the *Terror* grew even worse. There was agitation from a small group led by a former priest, Jacques Roux: taking advantage of poor harvests, it stirred up trouble in the provinces against the Convention, accusing it of reducing the people to *starvation*. After various demonstrations, the Convention formed a policy that brought all essential areas of the economy under the absolute control of the state. Then came the real problem: how to apply these impossible laws. As soon as the maximum rate was announced, the shops were emptied in minutes, with everybody rushing to buy at artifically low prices what *had cost three times as much the day before*; there were *shortages* in every town. Paris no longer had sugar, oil or candles, and the bread was inedible. Black market activities sprang up everywhere.'[1]

[1] HFPG.

---

# Robespierre, the Terror and the Festival of the Supreme Being, June 1794

> Des innocents le sang de veufve et vierge,
> Tant de maux faicts par moyen ce grand Roge,
> Saints simulachres trempez[1] en ardent cierge
> De frayeur crainte ne vera nul que boge.

CVIII,Q80

## Interpretation

The blood of innocents, widows and virgins will flow; so many misfortunes brought about by this great Red. A false religious cult arranged with blazing candles [bonfires]. Through panic and fear no one will move.

## History

'The Vendéans were overwhelmed at Le Mans, where they were surprised at nightfall on 12 December. After a savage battle lasting fourteen hours, they were *massacred*. There were bodies everywhere, *many of them women*: these were naked, for they had been raped by the soldiers before being killed. About 6000 men managed to escape, but they were overtaken, surrounded and shot down at Savenay.'[2]

'Robespierre[3] decreed that *a new religion* of a simple and lay character would be imposed upon everyone. He presided over the first great ceremony, the Festival of the Supreme Being, on 8 June 1794. After this sort of apotheosis he took one of his most ruthless measures, the Law of Prairial (10 June 1794) which gave any accused person practically no chance of escaping the scaffold. During this *Great Terror* there were more than 1000 executions in forty-five days in Paris.

The Revolutionary government: after the violent overthrow of the Girondins, *no opposition to the Convention dared show itself*, and there the Montagnards remained the masters.'[4]

[1] For *temprer*, ancient form of *tremper* = to arrange. DAFL.
[2] LRFPG.
[3] From Latin *robeus*, red. DLLB. Robespierre thus means 'red stone'. Cf. CIX,Q20, where Louis XVI is 'the white stone'.
[4] LCH3.

---

# The Montagnards. The White Terror, 1794

L'armée Celtique[1] contre les montaignars
Qui seront sceus et prins à la pipée:[2]
Paysans fresz[2] pulseront tost faugnars[4]
Précipitez tous au fil de l'espée.

CIV,Q63

*Interpretation*

The army of the Chouans [will rise up] against the Montagnards who, being warned, will trap it; they shall rapidly push back the peasants, forcing them into the marshes, and wiping them all out.

*History*

'The White Terror claimed many victims. *In Brittany* the Chouans supported a British landing at Quiberon, which was *swiftly surrounded and annihilated* by General Hoche's troops.'[5]

'To confront the victorious advance of the rebel Chouans, the Republic's standing army under Kleber and Marceau had to be mobilized. *Pushed back* before Granville and defeated at Le Mans, the Vendéans suffered a dreadful reverse during their second crossing of the Loire. They continued their resistance in the *marshlands* and the forests until 1795. The armed force of émigrés landed by the British was defeated at Quiberon Bay. The Convention had all the prisoners shot.'[6]

[1] The Chouans in Brittany, a Celtic country.
[2] Snares for catching birds, also 'loaded dice'.
[3] Latin *fressus*, from *frendo*: I crush, wipe out. DLLB.
[4] *faugnars* = *fangeux*, filthy, muddy. DAFL.
[5] LCH3.
[6] HFAM.

---

## The Birth of Napoleon Bonaparte, 15 August 1769

Un Empereur naistra près d'Italie
Qui à l'empire sera vendu bien cher,
Diront[1] avec quels[2] gens il se ralie
Qu'on trouvera moins Prince que boucher.

CI,Q60

*Interpretation*

An emperor will be born near Italy, who will cost the empire dear. The amount of people with whom he allies himself will be talked about and he will be thought of less as prince than as butcher.

## History

When Napoleon was born in 1769, Corsica had been bought by Louis XV only two years previously. It was thus no longer Italian, but it was still not yet French. Hence Nostradamus' phrase *'près d'Italie'*.

'The Congress of Vienna [September 1814–June 1815] claimed to have erased from the map of Europe the changes effected by the French Revolution and the Empire. . . . France, surrounded by buffer-states could no longer hope to attain "natural frontiers".'[3] Thus France had paid dearly in lives, defeats and all manner of disasters.

'Napoleon mobilized the Grand Army: 700,000 men *from every nation.*'[3]

The Battle of Eylau, called 'the *butchery* amid the snow', was one of the bloodiest ever fought by Napoleon.

'By the Treaty of Paris [1815], France lost all her conquests and found herself *even smaller* than she had been before the Revolutionary Wars.'[4]

[1] For *'on dira'* – Latinism.
[2] *'Quels'* in the sense of *'combien'*, how many.
[3] LCH3.
[4] DHC.

---

# The Predestined Name of Napoleon

D'un nom farouche tel proféré sera
Que des trois seurs[1] aura fato[2] le nom,
Puis grand peuple par langue et faicts dira[3]
Plus que nul autre aura bruict et renom.

CI,Q76

## Interpretation

He will come to the fore with such a grim name that this name will be, in predestined fashion, like that of the Three Fates. Then through his speeches and actions he will thin out many people, more than anyone he will be renowned by the noise he will make.

## History

The name of Napoleon derives from two Greek words: νεος (new) and ἀπολλύων, present participle of ἀπόλλυμι (exterminating). Taken as a noun, Napoleon thus means 'new exterminator'. The sense of this verse therefore perfectly matches the etymological meaning of the Emperor's name. Think of the slaughter of Eylau (of 'the butchery amid the snow'), the Retreat from Moscow, or the following description of Peninsular War atrocities: 'Whenever our injured, sick, stragglers and orderlies, were taken prisoner anywhere, the luckiest had their throats cut on the spot; many were hurled into vats of boiling water, while others were sawn up between planks or slowly roasted alive.'[4]

'The Spanish War was distinguished by its fanatical ferocity: constant ambushes whittled away [*thin out*] the French Army.'[5]

[1] The Three Fates: mythological sisters whose task was to cut the threads of men's destinies; destructive divinities.

[2] Latin, ablative of *fatum*: by or through fate.

[3] Latin *dirare*: to thin out, prune (of trees). DLLB. Beginning with Le Pelletier, commentators have changed this word to *duira* (for *conduira*).

[4] General de Ségur: *Memoirs of an Aide-de-Camp*.

[5] LCH.

---

# The Sardinian Army Surrenders to Napoleon at Cherasco, 29 April 1796. The Austrian Forces Defeated in Three Months. The Battle of Löwen, 18 April 1797

> Les sept en trois mois en concorde,
> Pour subjuguer les Alpes Apennines,[1]
> Mais la tempeste[2] et Ligure[3] couarde,
> Les profligent[4] en subites ruyne.

CIII,Q39

## Interpretation

The seven [armies] will be allied for three months in order to enslave the Apennines. But the quick action [by Napoleon's forces] and the cowardice of the Sardinian army will cause their defeat and sudden ruin.

## History

'During this time the French position in Italy became threatened by Austria's major preparations *to reconquer* this country.

Dejection spread through the armies of the coalition. There was concern in Piedmont; the French were only ten leagues from Turin and the

Austrians could think only of protecting Milan. Thus unsettled, the Sardinian court did not know whose side to take. The King, although warned against the French, did not want to agree to surrender his three main fortresses to his ambitious neighbour, Lombardy. He preferred to *throw himself into the arms of the conqueror* [cowardice] whom he could in any case not fight for very long. The truce was signed on 9 Floréal of Year IV (29 April 1796) at Cherasco. The terms were that the Sardinian king should leave the coalition; Sardinian troops should be sent back to their garrisons; the roads of Piedmont should remain open to the French army; and the fortresses of Ceva, Coni, Tortone or failing that, Alexandria, would at once be surrendered together with all their ammunition and artillery.[5]

The aim of these orders was to reunite on the Rivoli plains early on *14 January 1797* more than 20,000 men, including 1500 cavalry, and 30 cannon. Hoche and Moreau got under way at last and on *18 April 1797* the Austrians signed at Löwen the draft agreement proposed by Napoleon two days earlier. Thus ended this campaign, during which Napoleon *defeated seven armies* and triumphed over four generals sent in succession against him by Vienna.'[6]

'Bonaparte rapidly advanced across the Carinthian mountains, driving back the enemy vanguard. The soldiers of the Rhine, charging with fixed bayonets, flung themselves upon the Austrians with *an impetuousness* that broke their lines.'[7]

---

[1] Apennines: long mountain chain, the backbone of Italy, which separates from the Alps at Cassino, north of Genoa, traces a semicircle around the Gulf of Genoa and ends in Sicily. DHB.

[2] Figurative: impetuous action. DL7V.

[3] Region of ancient Italy that formed the south-west of Cisalpine Gaul. Liguria originally extended from the north coast to the River Po. DHB. Part of the Sardinian states.

[4] Latin *profligo*: I overturn, completely vanquish, ruin. DLLB.

[5] The Sardinian states consisted not only of the island itself but lands in northern Italy, both east and west of the Alps, between Switzerland to the north, France to the west, Lombardy to the east and the Mediterranean to the south.

[6] HFA.

[7] 14 January–18 April = three months, three days. Cf. line 1.

# The Italian Campaigns over the Alps, 1796–1800.
# The Annexation of Tuscany by Napoleon, 1801.
# The Expulsion of Ferdinand III, Grand Duke
# of Tuscany

Dela les Alpes grand'armée passera,
Un peu devant naistra monstre vapin:[1]
Prodigieux et subit tournera,[2]
Le grand Toscan à son lieu plus propin.[3]

CV,Q20

## Interpretation

The Grand Army will cross the Alps. Shortly before will be born the
monster of Gap, which in an extraordinary and sudden manner will
oblige the Grand Duke of Tuscany to return to a neighbouring place.

## History

'The first Italian campaign: *the Army of the Alps*, commanded by Kellermann, holds the heights from Mont Blanc as far as the Largentière Pass,
and the Italian army, commanded by Scherer, extends from the Tende
Pass to the Mediterranean.

Some hold Napoleon's Italian campaign to be *"his undisputed master-
piece"*. Napoleon himself seems to have thought as much, because he
stated: "War is a singular art; I assure you that I have fought sixty battles
and have learned nothing more than what I knew from the very first."

Despite serious difficulties, Napoleon's plans succeeded, since 40,000
reserves crossed the St Bernard with their artillery, 5000 men descended
the Little St Bernard Pass, 4000 emerged from Mont Cénis and the
Moncey corps descended through the St Gothard upon Milan [May
1800].'[4]

'Ferdinand III, *Grand Duke of Tuscany*, 1769–1824.[5] During the first
Revolutionary Wars he remained neutral, despite British threats, which
meant that he was not unkindly treated by Napoleon in 1796. But later,
after allowing himself to be drawn into the Second Coalition, he was
*driven out of his states by the French* [1799], although he was able to re-
enter them a few months later, only to be despoiled yet again after the
Battle of Marengo by the Treaty of Luneville. He withdrew to Vienna
[neighbouring place] while Louis of Parma and Elisa Bonaparte occupied
his throne.'[6]

---

[1] *Vapincuum*: modern name, Gap. DHB. Allusion to the 100 Days: 'Napoleon had only

passed Sisteron in order to *veer towards Gap* on 5 March, 1815.' NEE. Example of apocope.

[2] To direct or govern (of a person). DL7V.

[3] Latin *propinquus*: near, neighbouring, close. DLLB. Note the similarity of apocope between *vapincuum* and *propinquum*.

[4] NEE.

[5] Nostradamus establishes a relationship between Bonaparte and Ferdinand III, both born in 1769.

[6] DL7V.

---

# Bonaparte's Army Marches from Verona to Venice via Vicenza, 1797. General Lusignan's Defeat near Belluno, 10 March 1797. The Venetian Rulers' Surrender to Bonaparte, 14 May 1797

Peuple infiny[1] paroistre à Vicence,
Sans force feu bruler la basilique,[2]
Près de Lunage[3] deffait grand de Valence,[4]
Lorsque Vinise par morte prendra pique.

CVIII,QII

## Interpretation

The French will appear at Vicenza and without setting it on fire they will destroy the aristocracy. General Lusignan will be defeated near Belluno, when Venice takes up the quarrel to mete out death.

## History

'On 20 Ventose of Year V (10 March 1797), the *commander-in-chief* of the Italian Army mobilized his entire line. The intrepid Masséna hurled his troops against the centre, driving it back upon *Belluno*, and advanced into the Ponteba gorges by the Tarwis Pass. During this rapid march he took a thousand prisoners, among whom was *General Lusignan*.

Everything was in turmoil or *on fire* in upper Italy. The Slavonian regiments, landing from the *Lagoons*, advanced towards the rebel villages: meanwhile the peasants ransacked them. They *slaughtered and murdered* any patriots or Frenchmen they could find.

Like all worn-out bodies, the *Venetian* aristocracy had been divided. In addition the principal members of the government could not agree. They all dreaded a siege. The old *oligarchs* were compelled to offer

Napoleon the changes in their constitution that he had demanded some
time before. Satisfied at having scared the Venetians, Napoleon thought
it better to leave them *to surrender of their own accord rather than overpower
them*, and allowed them a few days' grace. He returned to Milan, and
the *plenipotentiaries* were quick to follow him.'[5]

'On 25 Floréal, Year V, *the Doge of Venice* was deposed and the
French entered the city.'[6]

---

[1] The expression '*peuple infini*' is always used by Nostradamus for the French, with the
dual meaning of their being eternal but also very numerous. Napoleonic France was the
most populous country in Europe. Cf. CI,Q98.

[2] Greek Βασιλικός: royal. DFG.

[3] Gallicization of Lunegiano, the region in which Belluno is situated.

[4] Lusignan: from this family sprang the noble houses of Lezé, Eu, La Rochefoucauld,
*Valence*, Marais etc. DL7V.

[5] HFA.

[6] HFACAD.

---

## Pius VI's Papacy, 1795–99. The Papal States' Resistance against the Abduction of Pius VI, 1798

> Quatre ans le siège[1] quelque peu bien tiendra,
> Un surviendra libidineux[2] de vie:
> Ravenne et Pyse Veronne soustiendront[3]
> Pour eslever[4] la croix de Pape envie.[5]
>
> CVI,Q26

### Interpretation

He will keep the Holy Seat well enough for four years. Then a licentious
person will intervene. Ravenna, Pisa and Verona will resist the one who
wishes to take away the cross [his power] from the Pope.

### History

'Pius VI, elected 1775, died at Valence, France, in 1799. The Directorate
*invaded papal territory*, and the Pope had to sign the Treaty of Tolentino
(1797) with Napoleon: this proved disastrous for the Pope. After the
murder in a Rome street of General Duphot, the French government's
representative, the Directorate *seized* the Pope and proclaimed the Republic in Rome. Arrested by General Berthier, Pius VI was taken to

Siena, Florence and Turin and finally *taken back* in April 1799 to France. He was moved from Grenoble to Valence where he died.'[6]

'On 8 January 1797 Napoleon, who from Bologna, where he had gone to *threaten* the Pope, had not relaxed his vigilance, learned that *an engagement* had occurred, involving all his advance posts. Immediately he recrossed the Po with 2000 men and went to *Verona* to anticipate Marshal Alvinzi's plans.

The Treaty of Tolentino was drawn up on 19 February 1797. The Pope gave up the legations of Bologna and Ferrara as well as the beautiful province of Romagna.'[7,8] Cf. CI,QI2, CIX,Q5, CVIII,Q33.

[1] Always used by Nostradamus in the sense of the Papal Seat.
[2] Latin *libidinosus*: licentious, debauched. DLLB.
[3] Latin *sustineo*: I resist. DLLB.
[4] Latin *elevo*: I bear off, take off. DLLB.
[5] To wish for oneself. DL7V.
[6] DL7V.
[7] Ancient province of the Papacy, its chief town is *Ravenna*. DHB.
[8] HFA.

---

# The Massacres of Verona and Venice, 1797.
# The Annexation of Venetia and the French Revenge.
# Napoleon's Capture by Captain Maitland, 15 July 1815

Le grand naistra[1] de Véronne et Vicence,[2]
Qui portera un surnom[3] bien indigne,
Qui à Venise voudra faire vengeance,
Lui-même pris homme du guet[4] et signe.[5]

CVIII,Q33

*Interpretation*

The greatness of him who bears a name to be despised will result from [the campaigns] of Verona and Venice. He will want to wreak vengeance at Venice and will himself be taken prisoner by a sentinel and a red flag.

*History*

'On 23 Nivôse, Year V [1797], General Alvinzi attacked Joubert and boxed him in beside Rivoli. The same day Provera pushed forward two advance columns, one aimed at *Verona*, the other at Legnago. Masséna,

who was at Verona, made a sortie, overcame this force and took 900
prisoners. *Bonaparte arrived at Verona* just after Masséna had driven
back the Austrians.

While there was rejoicing in France, Upper Italy was still in a state of
complete turmoil. The *Venetian* towns continued to be at war with the
rural population. At *Verona*, particularly, major events seemed to be
imminent. On 28 Germinal, Year V, peasant bands entered *Verona* crying
"Death to the Jacobins!" Balland retired with his troops into the fortress,
but all the French in the streets were butchered and flung into the river.
However the *time for vengeance* was not far off. From all sides troops
came to the aid of *Verona*. After a bloody fight against the Venetian
forces General Chabran surrounded Verona, which surrendered unconditionally. Some of the rebel leaders were shot. This incident, called the
*Veronese Easter*, was not the only opportunity the French had *for revenge*.
A French lugger which had taken refuge under the batteries of the Lido
at *Venice* was bombarded and its crew slaughtered by Slavonian sailors.
When Bonaparte learned of the massacres of Verona and the Lido killings
he no longer wanted to listen to the two envoys from *Venice*. He issued
a long manifesto listing French grievances *against the Venetians* and
declared war. The Lion of St Mark was overthrown throughout all the
provinces. Everywhere *the abolition of the Venetian Government* was proclaimed. Thus, without compromising himself, Bonaparte overturned
the absurd aristocracy which had betrayed him and placed Venice in the
same plight as Lombardy, Modena, Bologna and Ferrara. Every day the
Revolution made new inroads throughout Italy.'

'The British ship *Bellerophon*, under Captain Maitland, came to reconnoitre the roads. Another British frigate drew closer so as to keep the
other frigates' movements *under surveillance*, and afterwards their departure presented some difficulties. . . .

Another warship, the *Northumberland*, received the *great prisoner*.'[6]

---

[1] *Naître de*: result from. DL7V.

[2] Napoleon set up a Duchy of Vicenza for General Caulaincourt. DL7V.

[3] Allusion to the etymology of 'Napoleon'. Cf. CI,Q76.

[4] Night patrol during a war. DL7V.

[5] Latin *signum*: red flag hoisted when attacking. DLLB. The battle ensign of the Royal
Navy was a red cross on a white background. DL7V.

[6] HFA.

# Venice Annexed. Napoleon's Occupation of Venice, 1797. Venice and Austria, 1797, 1805 and 1849

La liberté ne sera recouvrée,
L'occupera noir,[1] fier, vilain, inique,
Quand la matière du pont[2] sera ouvrée,
D'Hister,[3] Venise faschée la république.

CV,Q29

## Interpretation

The freedom [of Venice] will not be recovered. A proud person [Napoleon] in [a] black [hat] will shamefully and unjustly occupy it when a maritime matter [the fleet] is set under way. Then the Republic of Venice will be troubled by those from the Danube [Austrians].

## History

'In 1797 Venice, although apparently neutral, was *occupied* by Napoleon who, under the Treaty of Campoformio, surrendered all his territory in *Austria* (keeping only the south-east islands) in return for the Duchy of Milan and the Rhine border. In 1805, by the Peace of Pressburg, Venice became part of the kingdom of Italy, but it reverted to *Austria* in 1814 and then formed the Lombardo-Venetian Kingdom. Under Austrian domination, Venice declined. In 1848 she heralded the *Republic*, but was *reduced* in 1849 after a long and celebrated siege and her prospects darkened. Venice was subsumed by the kingdom of Italy in 1866.'[4]

'Legislator, arbitrator, counsellor to the peoples of Italy, Napoleon took on still greater responsibilities. He had taken over *the Venetian fleet* and had summoned Admiral Brueys and 4000 French sailors to the Adriatic to seize possession of the Venetian-occupied Greek islands.

Malta was also the object of Napoleon's cupidity. "From these different positions," he wrote to the Directorate, "we shall dominate the Mediterranean." '[5]

---

[1] Allusion to Bonaparte's famous black hat. Cf. CI,Q74
[2] Greek πόντος: sea. DGF.
[3] Old name for the Danube. DHB.
[4] DHB.
[5] HFA.

# Charles-Emmanuel II, King of Sardinia, 1798–1802

> Dans la Sardaigne un noble Roy viendra,
> Qui ne tiendra que trois ans le royaume,
> Plusieurs couleurs[1] avec soy conjoindra,
> Luy mesme après soin sommeil marrit[2] scome.[3]

CVIII,Q88

## Interpretation

Into Sardinia will come a king of noble descent who will keep his kingdom only three years. He will reunite several other states with his kingdom, after taking care of himself [his succession] he will die united with the Society [of Jesus].

## History

'Charles-Emmanuel II, associated with the misfortunes of the Bourbons, his allies, was forced to cede *his continental states* to Napoleon and *to retire to Sardinia* in December 1798. *Three years* later, after fruitless attempts to curb rebellious elements, he abdicated in favour *of his brother* Victor-Emmanuel and went to live in Rome, where he died a Jesuit.'[4]

[1] *Couleurs:* flags = states.
[2] Latin *maritus:* united. DLLB.
[3] Anagram of the Latin *comes,* companion.
[4] HFAM.

---

# The End of the First Republic, 6 November 1799. Napoleon and the Civil Code

> La république, misérable infélice,
> Sera vastée[1] du nouveau Magistrat,
> Leur grand amas de l'exil malefice,
> Fera Suève[2] ravir leur grand contract.

CI,Q61

## Interpretation

The miserable, unfortunate Republic will be devastated by a new magistrate, the great number of exiles causing trouble will make the Germans withdraw their treaty of alliance.

*History*

'Shortly after the Brumaire coup, Bonaparte presented a new constitution under which he held the *casting vote*. Bonaparte as First Consul had *sole* power of decision, and furthermore held *the right to propose legislation*.

He took the glory for publishing the *Civil Code* (1804), begun by the Constituent Assembly.

The *Grand Empire* dominated Europe at least until 1812. Many states adopted a code of laws and an administration imitating those of France.'[3]

'Prussia was a doubtful ally in 1812, and was Russia's ally in 1813. Austria herself declared against Napoleon, and this example was followed, despite his victory at Dresden, by Bavaria, Würtemburg and Saxony – whose aged King tried vainly to remain within *the French alliance*.'[4]

'The discovery of a new Royalist plot allowed Bonaparte to re-establish the monarchy but to his own advantage: he claimed to believe that they wanted to assassinate him so as to replace him with a royal prince, the young Duke of Enghien. Napoleon had him abducted from *German territory* and shot in the moat of Vincennes Castle in March 1804.'[3]

[1] Latin *vastus*: desert, desolated. DLLB.
[2] Suève: Suevi (Swabians): powerful tribe of ancient Germany. DHCD.
[3] LCH3.
[4] DHCD.

---

# The War Brings about the Fall of the Monarchy, 1792. The Ruin of the Papal States and the Misfortunes of Pius VI. The Coup d'Etat of 18 Brumaire 1799

> Par Mars contraire sera la Monarchie,
> Du grand pescheur[1] en trouble ruyneux;
> Jeune noir[2] rouge prendra la hiérarchie,
> Les proditeurs[3] iront jour bruyneux.

> CVI,Q25

*Interpretation*

The war will be unfavourable for the monarchy. The Revolution will be ruinous for the Pope. A young 'black' will take the hierarchy from the reds and the conspirators will seize power one day of Brumaire.

## History

'On 20 April 1792 Dumouriez snatched from the King the declaration of a *war* which would cause terrible bloodshed for ten years, and whose results Europe could not have foreseen. The Assembly were not at all grateful to the King for his co-operation and, even more threatening and demanding, disbanded his bodyguard, sending its commander M. de Brissac to the court of Orleans, so depriving the luckless Louis of any protection from the attacks upon him then being prepared.'[4]

'The French Revolution rolled across the Roman sky like thunder. Rome was apprised of the danger but the revolutionary movement had supporters in Rome itself. It was 1796 before the Romans fully appreciated the danger, when the French army under Napoleon's command entered Italy. The Pope negotiated with the General, and had to pay contributions collected from the Papal States, together with 500 ancient manuscripts and 100 works of art. By the Treaty of Tolentino (19 February 1797) the Pope had to renounce forever all claims to Avignon, also to the Comtat Venaissin, and to pay out 46 million scudi. On 20 February the Pope was made prisoner. Napoleon removed as spoils of war priceless works of art and filled 500 wagons with them.'[5]

'The 18 *Brumaire* [= *jour bruyneux* = drizzly day] was the *day* chosen for the transfer of the Councils, and the nineteenth for the final session. Although the secret of the *conspiracy* had been well kept, everywhere an important event was expected.'[6]

---

[1] The Fisherman's Ring. When Napoleon forced Pius VII, a prisoner at Savona, to send him St Peter's ring (*pescheur* = fisherman. *Tr.*) the Pope only did so after breaking it. He replaced it with a metal seal depicting St Peter with his Keys. The Fisherman's Ring had been used since the fifteenth century to seal papal documents. DL7V.

[2] Allusion to the black hat worn by Napoleon, but also pejorative adjective. Cf. CV,Q29, CI,Q74, CIII,Q43.

[3] Latin *proditor*: traitor, one who breaks laws. DLLB.

[4] HFA.

[5] DDP.

[6] HFA.

# Napoleon against the Revolutionaries, 1799.
# The Occupation of Italy, 1797

Aux profligez[1] de paix les ennemis,
Après avoir l'Italie suppérée:[2]
Noir sanguinaire, rouge sera commis[3]
Feu, sang verser, eau de sang colorée.[4]

CVI,Q38

## Interpretation

The enemies of peace [revolutionaries] will be conquered [by Napoleon] after he has overcome Italy. This black and bloodthirsty person will compromise the reds. Then through war he will make blood flow, which shall colour the water.

## History

'The initiatives taken by the émigrés at foreign courts to influence French affairs had prompted a reaction of French national pride. There were *cries for war* from the Brissots, Vergnauds, Dantons and other firebrands, who had changed their tune and were known by the names of Cordeliers and Girondins ["enemies of peace"].

The elections of Year V proved that the French people were not contented and that they had little confidence in their rulers. Only 5 per cent of the deputies seeking re-election were successful. The citizens elected to the Assemblies not only the hard-line leaders of the regime but very moderate Republicans and even Royalists. The two Presidents of the Assemblies were enemies of the Revolution. While the results of these elections, which proved so disastrous for the Directorate's collective peace of mind, were awaited, the draft text of the Treaty of Löwen reached Paris. What was to be done? Napoleon made clear that he was negotiating, without authorization, in the name of France. The preamble of the treaty was approved. After this, the Directors were forced to let Napoleon do as he pleased and rule at will over Italy.'[5]

[1] Latin *profligo*: I conquer totally, annihilate, ruin. DLLB.
[2] Latin *supero*: I conquer, triumph over. DLLB.
[3] Compromise, expose. DL7V.
[4] Allusion to crossing the River Beresina.
[5] HFA.

# The Coup of 18 Brumaire, November 1799.
# Fourteen Years of Rule: 9 November 1799–6 April 1814

De la cité marine et tributaire,
La teste raze prendra la Satrapie:[1]
Chassez sordide qui puis sera contraire,
Par quatorze ans tiendra la tyranie.

CVII,QI3

## Interpretation

From the port which pays him tax [tribute, from war], the 'shaven-headed one' will take [civil] power. He will drive out the squalid men against whom he rebels, and will rule as tyrant for fourteen years.

## History

'Immensely energetic and active, Napoleon organized Egypt with a sort of *protectorate*. But he was impatient to return to France, whose political situation was giving him cause for anxiety, and he embarked secretly from Alexandria.'[2]

'Napoleon overthrew the Directorate's regime and made himself Consul. This last coup *put an end to the Revolutionary period*.

Reorganization of the country: Napoleon used the immense powers with which he had been invested to reorganize France. The administration centralized: he created prefects, government representatives in the regions. Finance: a new fixed administration, with new officials – controllers and *preceptors* [Satraps].'[3]

From 19 November 1799 until 6 April 1814, Napoleon held power for 14 years, 3 months, 27 days!

'I passed by on horseback an hour beforehand and my glance rested upon an inscription in huge black letters on the first pillar of the bridge: "*Down with the tyrant!*" I just had time to have it erased.'[4]

---

[1] Satraps were the governors of provinces (prefects) under Persian rule, filling the dual roles of administrators and tax-collectors (preceptors). DL7V.
[2] DHC.
[3] LCH3.
[4] The Emperor's unpopularity in 1814: *Mémoires* of Pasquier. Plon.

## The Annexation of Verona, 1805.
## The Death of Napoleon, 1821.
## The Congress of Verona, 1822

Dans peu dira[1] faulce[2] brute[3] fragile[4]
De bas en hault eslevé promptement:
Puis en istant[5] desloyale et labile[6]
Qui de Veronne aura gouvernement.

CI,QI2

### Interpretation

In a short time the scythe [of death] will cut down the mad and vulnerable man, namely he who will have been rapidly raised from low to high.[7] Then, being disloyal, the one with power over Verona will be broken.

### History

'In 1796 Napoleon manoeuvred around Verona to reinforce the blockade of Mantua against Austria. But on 17 April 1797, prompted by the Austrians, there was a general massacre of the French in the town. In 1805 the Treaty of Pressburg *gave Verona to the French*, who made it *the chief town* of the Adige district. In 1815 the town fell into Austrian hands again, and in 1822 Austria held the famous Congress there.'[8]

Nostradamus notes here that immediately after Napoleon's death a reunion of the Holy League will take place at Verona!

'The Republic took freedom everywhere, making free men of all those subjected to the petty tyrants it overthrew; the Empire, by contrast, made these free men in turn the subjects of new sovereigns. How greatly had the Revolution and the revolutionaries *degenerated* since the 18 Brumaire coup. The Senate could no longer flatter Napoleon enough, but it was the bishops who were most fulsome in their adulation. No wonder Bonaparte believed himself *the greatest of mortals* and the one chosen by God.'[9]

[1] Latin *dirare*: to thin out. DLLB.
[2] Latin *falcem*: sickle. DAFL.
[3] Latin *brutus*: dull, stupid. DLLB.
[4] Latin *fragilis*: fragile, weak. DLLB.
[5] *Istre*: form of *estre*, i.e. *être* = to be. DAFL.
[6] Latin *caduc*. DLLB. Referring to a broken man. DL7V.
[7] Cf. CVIII,Q57, CV,Q26 and CIX,Q5.
[8] DL7V.
[9] HFA.

# The Duke of Brunswick and the Orange Divisions. The Battle of Auerstadt, 1805. His Secret Agreement with Dumouriez, 1792

> Vie fort mort de l'OR[1] vilaine indigne,
> Sera de Saxe non nouveau électeur[2]
> De Brunsvic mandra d'mour[3] signe
> Faux le rendant au peuple séducteur.
>
> CX,Q46

## Interpretation

He will lose his life, by violent death, despite the unworthy and treacherous actions of the Orange [divisions]; Brunswick, whose signature Dumouriez will have demanded, will not be the new Elector of Saxony, his false spirit having seduced the people.

## History

'By 8 October Prussian troops had entered Saxony, ahead of the Grand Army. But Prussia did not take advantage of the diplomatic initiative she had taken. Her forces were scattered; only 140,000 men under Ruchel, *Brunswick* and Hohenlöhe, bewildered by orders and counterorders, defended the road to Thuringia.'[4]

'Auerstadt: *Brunswick* had been directing the attack of the *Orange* divisions, and of Wartensleben as well as part of Schmettau's infantry. The French troops were forced to abandon Hassenhausen, which General Morand then succeeded in recapturing. But Prince William of Prussia charged furiously against Morand's division, which was drawn up in squares. The Duke of Brunswick and General Schmettau were mortally wounded ["*vie fort mort*"].'[5]

'Charles William Ferdinand, Duke of Brunswick-Lüneburg and a general in the service of Prussia (who had been known as *hereditary prince*), was chosen in 1792 as commander-in-chief of the Coalition armies against France. After publishing a threatening manifesto he entered Champagne with a sizeable army but was defeated at Valmy and made peace with Dumouriez ["*d'mour signe*"]. After taking up command again in 1805, he was beaten at Jena and *fatally injured* by a bullet near Auerstadt.'[6]

---

[1] For 'orange' by apocope.
[2] Auerstadt, Prussian town ('*Saxe*'). Victory by Davout over the Prussians (14 October 1805). DHB.

³ Abbreviation of Dumouriez.
⁴ NELGI.
⁵ LEE.
⁶ DHB.

---

## Napoleon's First Marriage, 1796.
## His Coronation, 1804. His Divorce and
## Second Marriage, 1809

Peu après l'aliance faicte,
Avant solemniser la feste,
L'Empereur le tout troublera,
Et la nouvelle mariée,
Au franc pays par fort liée,
Dans peu de temps après mourra.

Sixain 57

### Interpretation

Shortly after being married and before a solemn rite, the Emperor will divorce, and the new bride will be strongly allied with France through this marriage; soon afterwards he will die.

### History

'On 8 Ventose (8 March 1796) Bonaparte was nominated general of the Italian army; on the sixteenth he married the beautiful Creole [Joséphine de Beauharnais]. The *coronation* was continually deferred, mainly because of Pope Pius VII who had delayed his journey to France, and did not take place until 2 December 1804. The *previous day* ["*avant*"] Napoleon and Joséphine had celebrated their *religious* wedding ceremony. The coronation took place on 2 December 1804 in Notre-Dame. Before leaving for the Cathedral the Emperor received Talleyrand, who left the following description of the audience: "But for the *solemnity* of the occasion, I would have been hard put to it to preserve my composure."

'In October 1809 he decided to *divorce* and *remarry*. Austria promptly put forward one of her Grand Duchesses, *Marie-Louise*. Napoleon agreed, and on 2 April in the Louvre Chapel, Cardinal Fesch, the Emperor's uncle, solemnized *the marriage* of Napoleon and Marie-Louise. . . .

On the night of 4 May 1821 all the servants stayed in attendance.

Then he stammered out some words of which the following alone could be distinguished: "France . . . my son . . . army . . . head of the army . . . *Joséphine*. . . ."

These were his last words and seemed a synopsis of his life. So died, aged fifty-one, the man who seemed to have lived 200 years.'[1]

[1] NLM.

---

# The Egyptian Campaign, 1799. The Proclamation of the Empire, December 1804

Après séjourné vogueront en Epire[1]
Le grand secours viendra vers Antioche[2],
Le noir poil[3] crespé[4] tendra fort à l'Empire
Barbe d'airain[5] le rostira en broche.

CI,Q74

## Interpretation

After a stay [in Egypt] his soldiers will sail towards another continent, they will seek assistance from Antioch or thereabouts, he who wears a black felt hat will aim at the Empire and roast the Republic on a spit.

## History

'The Egyptian campaign was planned with great secrecy and began successfully, escaping Nelson's squadrons which were cruising the Mediterranean. But on 1 August 1798 Nelson, he of the black hat, destroyed the French fleet at Aboukir Bay. The French expedition was thwarted as a result. Napoleon repulsed Turkish attacks in *Syria* and Egypt, but was *impatient* to return to France.'[6]

[1] Greek Ἤπειρος: continent, terra firma. DGF.
[2] Latin *Antiochia*: Antioch, capital of Syria. DLLB.
[3] *Noir poil*: felt is made from pressed hair. DL7V.
[4] *Crespe: crêpé, crépu.* DAFL.
[5] Aenobarbus (Latin *Aeneus* = bronze), husband of Agrippina, is shorthand in Nostradamus for the Republic, through a historical parallel. Their child was Nero, who had his mother assassinated, just as Napoleon 'executed' the Republic which raised him to power.
[6] LCH3.

## The First Italian Campaign, 1796–97.
## The Rise of Napoleon, 1796–1800

Tiers, doigt du pied, au premier semblera
A un nouveau monarque de bas en haut:
Qui Pyse et Luques[1] Tyran[2] occupera,
Du précédent corriger le deffault.

CIX,Q5

### Interpretation

The Third Estate, which is no more than a toe of the foot, will come to
the fore thanks to a new leader risen from low degree to the summit [of
the hierarchy] who will occupy Pisa and Lucca; thus he will compensate
for the lack [of power] of the preceding monarch [Louis XVI].

### History

'Society at the end of the eighteenth century was officially comprised of
three orders: nobility, clergy and the Third Estate.

In the Third Estate the greatest differences were noticeable: the rich
bourgeoisie who had made fortunes in shipping, industry or business
was most evident. These wealthy merchants bought themselves *titles*.

Although his own tastes were simple, Napoleon thought it expedient
to raise his personal prestige by surrounding himself with a sizeable *court*
– a sparkling group responsive to a rigorous etiquette imitating that of
Versailles.

The war and *the rise* of Napoleon: Napoleon, a general at twenty-
seven, was still the "Vendémiaire" General, as he was known after
putting down the 1795 uprising.

*The war taxes he imposed upon the vanquished* allowed Napoleon to
maintain his army and send the Directorate indispensable funds. Thus,
in the position of victor and overlord, he fixed the terms of the peace
signed with Austria at Campo Formio, October 1797: in northern Italy
he set up a *Cisalpine Republic*, allied to France.'[3]

The southernmost point of this Republic was formed by Tuscany,
including the towns of Pisa and Lucca.

'The French Republic which vowed enmity against *tyrants* also swore
fraternity with the people!'[4]

[1] Tuscan towns.
[2] Cf. CVII,Q13: '*Par quatorze ans tiendra sa tyrannie*'.
[3] LCH3.
[4] Napoleon: *Correspondence* (vol.1).

# The Plebiscite.
## Napoleon's Destructive Megalomania

Par teste rase viendra bien mal eslire
Plus que sa charge ne porte passera
Si grand fureur et rage fera dire,
Qu'à feu et sang tant sexe tranchera.

CV,Q60

### Interpretation

'The little shaven-headed one' will unfortunately be elected, he will carry
out more things than his power can manage, he will have said of him
that he is full of [warlike] fury and rage, and he will put everyone to fire
and the sword regardless of sex.

### History

'In practice Napoleon *designated* the Assembly's members: all derived
from and reverted to him. *The arranged plebiscite* brought him a stunning
vote of popular confidence, more than 3 million votes for to 1600
against.'[1]

Letter from a French officer, Moscow, 30 September 1812:

'The occupation of Moscow and *unfortunately* almost total destruction
by fire of this rich and marvellous city. . . . We live by *pillage* and
marauding. It is claimed that the Russian government set fire to this fine
capital so as to deprive us of the resources we could have had. I do not
know about that; but I can say that our soldiers added to the blaze: one
could see drunken soldiery firing wooden houses with candles, torches
and fuses, and this was the spectacle Moscow presented the day after
our arrival. *The fire* lasted three days. You never saw a more terrible or
heartbreaking sight! In my view, it was *the most dreadful catastrophe*
which our century, itself so full of disastrous occurrences, has so far
presented.'[2]

---

[1] LCH3.
[2] *'Textes Historiques'*, Collection M. Chaulanges.

# Wars against Italy, Spain and England. Marriage to Marie-Louise of Austria

Du nom qui oncques ne fut au Roy Gaulois,[1]
Jamais ne fut un fouldre[2] si craintif:
Tremblant l'Itale, l'Espagne et les Anglois
De femme estrange[3] grandement attentif.

CIV,Q54

## Interpretation

From a name never borne by a king of France [Napoleon], never would there be seen such a fearful captain [of war]. He shall make Italy, Spain and England tremble, and be very attentive towards a foreign woman.

## History

'By the decrees of Berlin and *Milan* (December 1807) Napoleon prohibited trade with *England* from most of the European ports. For the blockade to be effective it had to be enforced everywhere. The *Pope* and the King of Portugal refused to apply the embargo: Napoleon annexed *the Papal States*, imprisoned the Pope and decided to invade Portugal. A French army crossed *Spain* to attack Portugal.'[4]

Nostradamus, like history, links these three countries confronted with the same problem!

Divorced from Joséphine, Napoleon married Marie-Louise of Austria, a foreigner.

---

[1] Announcing the new dynasty.

[2] *Fouldre*, thunderbolt, used in a specialized symbolic sense in this particular phrase to denote an impetuous orator or warrior. DL7V.

[3] *Etrange* is usually taken by Nostradamus to stand for *étranger* (foreigner, alien).

[4] LCH3.

# The Battle of Trafalgar,[1] 21 October 1805.
# The Sieges of Pamplona. Navarre and Spain

Vaisseaux, gallères avec leur estendar,
S'entrebatteront près du mont Gibraltar
Et lors sera fort faict à Pampelonne,[2]
Qui pour son bien souffrira mille maux,
Par plusieurs fois soustiendra[3] les assaux.
Mais à la fin unie à la Couronne.

Sixain 41

## Interpretation

Fleets with their flags will confront each other near Gibraltar, then
reprisals will be taken against Pamplona, which will suffer a thousand
ills for its good. It will resist attacks several times but will finally be
reunited with the crown [Spain].

## History

'Trafalgar: *naval battle* won by the English *fleet* under Nelson over the
*combined fleets* of France and Spain under Admiral Villeneuve. The
French fleet played only an insignificant role in the wars of the First
Empire.'[4]

'The French entered Pamplona in 1808 and 1829. The town often
changed hands during the Spanish Civil Wars of 1831–42.'[5]

'Navarre, province of northern Spain, capital Pamplona. The history
of Spanish Navarre is associated with that of the kingdom of Navarre
until 1512. Since then, Navarre has been distinguished for its attachment
to its ancient rights, its *resistance* (from 1808 to 1814), to the French
troops, and in the nineteenth century by its devotion to Carlism' [united
to the crown].[6]

[1] Spanish Cape, near the Straits of Gibraltar. DHB.
[2] Pamplona, town in Navarre.
[3] Latin *sustineo*: I resist. DLLB.
[4] DL7V.
[5] DHB.
[6] DL7V.

# The Battle of Trafalgar, 1805.
# The Seven 'Three-Deckers' of the English Fleet.
# Admiral Gravina's Wounds.
# The French Vessels that Survived

Fustes[1] et gallères autour de sept navires,
Sera livrée une mortelle guerre:
Chef de Madric recevra coup de vires,[2]
Deux escchapez et cinq menés à terre.

CVII,Q26

## Interpretation

With corvettes and frigates around seven ships, a deadly battle will take place. The Spanish leader will be wounded. Two ships which shall escape will be led back to land by five others.

## History

'At 7 a.m. on 21 October, off Cape Trafalgar, the English were seen approaching from the north-west. The Franco-Spanish fleet consisted of 33 warships (18 French and 15 Spanish) and five frigates, 2856 guns in all. Nelson's fleet consisted of only 27 battleships (seven *3-deckers*, however, as opposed to four) and six frigates or corvettes totalling 3214 cannons. The battle ended before 6 p.m., but during that night two violent storms disposed of many disabled hulks: four ships from the Franco-Spanish fleet which had been captured were smashed against the rocky shoreline and the English scuttled or burned four others. But on 22 October Captain Cosmao did succeed in leaving harbour with *five ships* and managed to *recover two* prizes [*"Deux escchapez et cinq menés à terre"*]. Franco-Spanish losses: 14,000 [4408 of these *killed or drowned*]; 2549 wounded and 7000 or more taken prisoner [*"mortelle guerre"*]. Rear-Admiral Magon was killed and Gravina fatally wounded.'[3]

'Gravina: the Spanish admiral was, it was said, the natural son of Charles III. After peace was made with France he *commanded the Spanish fleet* [*"chef de Madrid"*] which joined the French under Admiral Villeneuve at Cadiz in 1805. *He was wounded* [*"recevra coup de vires"*] at Trafalgar and died in 1806, quite soon afterwards, from his injuries.'[4]

[1] Long, rather shallow vessel, employing both sails and oars. DL7V.
[2] Crossbow bolt with a sort of screw-thread, which would cause it to revolve. DAFL.
[3] NEE.
[4] DHB.

# Würzburg, Starting-point for
# Napoleonic Conquests, 1806. The Return from Elba.
# Disembarkation near Antibes

Soulz la pasture d'animaux ruminants,
Par eux conduicts au ventre herbipolique:[1]
Soldats cachez, les armes bruits menants,
Non loing temptez de cité Antipolique.[2]

CX,QI3

## Interpretation

After having grazed and ridden his horses as far as Würzburg, [Napoleon] with concealed soldiers which he will lead with martial noise, and will make an attempt [at disembarkation] not far from Antibes.

## History

'All the information Napoleon received indicated that war was imminent. On 21 September 1806 he informed Duroc and Caulaincourt that he intended to be at Mainz on the twenty-ninth. The Emperor left Paris on 25 September and arrived at Mainz on the morning of the twenty-eighth. On his arrival at the bank of the Rhine Napoleon could count upon 200,000 fighting men. . . . He arrived that evening at Würzburg where he made for the Grand Duke's Palace. He was welcomed by numerous German princes, whom he engaged in good-humoured conversation. At the same time a Prussian council of war at Erfurt was being attended by the King, the Duke of Brunswick, the Prince of Hohenlohe, Marshal Mollendorf and several ministers and generals. A note was prepared for Napoleon: France was accused of underhand behaviour towards Prussia and her troops were requested to evacuate Germany by 8 October.'[3]

'Würzburg was occupied by the French in 1806 and returned to Bavaria in 1814.'[4]

'On the evening of 26 February 1815 the Emperor boarded the *Inconstant* with his general staff and some of his *1100 men*. The others swarmed aboard six vessels of various types. On the morning of 1 March the flotilla passed the bay of Antibes, and shortly after noon it anchored. They bivouacked in an olive grove between the sea and the road *from Cannes to Antibes*.'[3]

[1] Herbipolis: Würzburg, Bavarian town. DHB. The word *'ventre'* (womb or belly) is used by Nostradamus to suggest the importance of this town in the light of subsequent events.

# The Annexation of Naples and Sicily, 1806. French Troops in Spain, 1807–8

Qui au Royaume Navarrois[1] parviendra
Quand la Sicile et Naples seront joincts,
Bigores[2] et Landes par Foix Loron[3] tiendra,
D'un qui d'Espagne sera par trop conjoinct.

CIII,Q25

## Interpretation

He who will come into the kingdom of Navarre, when Naples and Sicily are reunited, will occupy Bigorre and the heathlands near Foix and Oloron, because of a Spanish king too closely allied with him.

## History

'In 1805 the Infante Don Carlos, in exchange for Parma and Piacenza, secured from the Emperor *Naples and Sicily*, as well as the Tuscan ports, for himself and his descendants.

In 1806, the *King* of Spain called the Spaniards to arms. Napoleon was in no doubt that this was a provocation directed against France and was probably delighted to have a pretext for attacking the *Spanish Bourbons*, but he had to disguise his fleeting anxiety at having such a timid *ally*. From that moment he vowed the downfall of that monarchy and boasted that he would seize the crown of Spain from the Bourbons in Madrid, just as he had seized that of the two *Sicilies* from the Bourbons of *Naples*.

Napoleon ordered General Junot to head the army of observation from the *Gironde* and march on Lisbon. Junot reached *Bayonne* [across the heathlands] on 5 September and crossed the Pyrenees several days later.

While Junot's force occupied the central areas of Portugal, one new French army was forming near *Bayonne* and another in the *Roussillon* region. Spain put no more difficulties in the way of these troops and soon afterwards French forces invaded Catalonia and Navarre.'[4]

[1] The history of Spanish Navarre is associated with that of the kingdom of Navarre

until 1512. Since then, Navarre has been distinguished for its attachment to its ancient
rights, and its resistance from 1808 to 1814 to French troops. DL7V.

² In 1284 the marriage of Jeanne de Navarre and Philippe le Bel guaranteed France's
acquisition of this county, but it later passed on to the houses of *Foix* and d'Albret, and
was finally reunited on Henri IV's accession. DL7V.

³ Town in the Bigorre region.

⁴ HFA.

---

## The Negotiation of the Papal States, 1807.
## The Retreat from Russia, 1812

Terroir Romain qu'interprétait[1] augure,[2]
Par gent gauloise par trop sera vexée
Mais nation Celtique craindra l'heure
Boréas,[3] classe[4] trop loin l'avoir poussée.

CII,Q99

### Interpretation

The Roman territory negotiated by the Emperor will be too molested by
the French, but France will have everything to fear when the hour of
the cold strikes, because she will have pushed her army too far.

### History

'Following *Augustus'* example, Napoleon wanted to immortalize his
memory.'[5]

'The religious difficulties stemmed from Napoleon's having kept the
Pope prisoner (at Savona first, then at Fontainebleau, since 1812). The
Pope refused to enforce the blockade throughout his territories – so
Napoleon occupied them.'[5]

'On 14 September 1812 Napoleon entered Moscow, expecting to establish winter quarters there. In the night a fire destroyed the town and
its supplies. Napoleon hoped the Tsar would sue for peace, but there
was no question of this as the Russian leader had received reinforcements.
Realizing that he had made an error, Napoleon gave the order to retreat.
The return march was appalling. The devastated countryside had no
resources left and the Cossacks attacked incessantly. Hunger and *an early
and severe winter wore out* the soldiers.'[5]

'I asked Napoleon why he thought the expedition had failed. "*Because
of the unexpected cold* and the burning of Moscow," he replied. "I was

some days in advance; I had studied weather conditions for the past fifty years and the real cold never began until 20 December, three weeks later than in fact happened." [6]

[1] Latin *interpres pacis*: peace negotiator. DLLB.
[2] Latin *augur*, i.e. *augustus*: title of Roman Emperors. DLLB.
[3] Latin *Boreas*: north wind. DLLB.
[4] Latin *classis*: army, fleet. DLLB.
[5] LCH3.
[6] LMSH.

---

# Napoleon's Annexation of the Church

Du grand prophète[1] les lettres seront prinses
Entre les mains du tyran deviendront,
Frauder,[2] son Roy seront les entreprises
Mais ses rapines bien tost le troubleront.

CII,Q36

## Interpretation

The bulls will be seized from the Pope and be in the tyrant's hands, he will undertake to despoil and defraud his [spiritual] sovereign, but his rapine will soon trouble him.

## History

'No Swedish, English or Russian vessel must enter the Papal States on pain of *confiscation*. I do not intend that the court of Rome should involve itself any longer in politics. I shall protect its states against all comers. It is pointless for the court to show such regard for the enemies of religion. Have *the bulls sent off* to my bishops.'[3]

'If I had not laid hands upon the Papal States,' Napoleon said, 'and thought I could subdue a spiritual power through force, the rest of my misfortunes would not have occurred.'[4] But his 'rapine' was soon to trouble him!

[1] Latin *propheta*: priest. The great priest, i.e. the Pope. DLLB.
[2] Latin *fraudare*: to despoil by fraud, defraud. DLLB.
[3] Letter from Napoleon to his kinsman Cardinal Fesch, 13 October 1806. LCH3.
[4] LMSH.

## The Rise of Napoleon. Napoleon and the Church

De soldat simple parviendra en empire,
De robe courte[1] parviendra à la longue
Vaillant aux armes en église ou plus pyre,
Vexer les prêtres comme l'eau faict l'esponge.

CVIII,Q57

### Interpretation

From plain soldier he will become emperor, from military man he will
become magistrate, as valiant in war as harmful to the Church, and will
harass the priests much as a sponge absorbs water.

### History

'His relationship with the *Church* was apparently good until 1808. But
when his policy led him to occupy the Papal States and imprison the
Pope, who protested and excommunicated him, the *clergy* and Catholics
took the Pontiff's side: thus he lost Catholic support.'[2]

' "You have let yourself be led by the *priests* and nobles who want to
re-establish titles and fiscal laws. I'll deal with them. *I'll* string them
up!" '[2] (Napoleon to the crowds in 1815.)

'The conflict with Spain became daily more pronounced and diverted
the Emperor from his original aim, which was simply to bring the head
of the Roman states to heel. He was already showing that *hostility* to
various types of *priests* which alienated others.'[2]

'Historians were astonished that Pius VII, in order to make the break
final, picked upon what was by and large a political incident. In 1810
Pius VII said to Chabrol: "I have been pushed to the very limit. *The
water had reached my chin* by the time I cried out." '[3]

---

[1] Heraldic tunic: short skirt or kilt worn by heralds in the Middle Ages and which they
retained until the Revolution. DL7V.
[2] LCH3.
[3] NEE.

# Napoleon and the Persecution of the Clergy in Italy, 1809. Napoleon's Likeness on the Coinage. His End upon Foreign Soil, 1821

Aux temples saincts[1] seront faits grands scandales,
Comptez seront pour honneur et louanges
D'un que l'on grave d'argent, d'or les medales[2]
La fin sera en tourmens bien estranges.[3]

CVI,Q9

## Interpretation

Great scandals will be perpetuated concerning the holy persons of the Catholic Church, among which will be counted honours and flatteries, because of one whose effigy will be engraved upon gold and silver pieces, but who will end tormented by foreigners [the English].

## History

'On 10 June 1809 a proclamation signed by Miollis, Salicetti and high-ranking bureaucrats informed the Romans that their city had been annexed like the other domains within the Church's Empire. Opposition, until the *Pope*'s abduction from his palace on 6 July and his transfer to Savona, remained passive. With the Pope a prisoner, *the seven cardinals*, who in December 1809 still remained in Rome, were in their turn evicted. *The monks* then had to be dispersed: disbanded Dominicans, Franciscans, Cordeliers, Augustinians and even three Maronites were expelled from their monasteries. There were more serious problems with the general clergy and bishops, who had to swear an oath of allegiance to the Emperor which Pius VII, from Savona, had secretly forbidden. Canons and other priests resisted, but popular feeling against their evacuation was such that it was decided not to deport clergy over sixty years of age. These men were therefore returned from Piacenza, and were welcomed by the Romans with *veneration*.'[4] [*"honneurs et louanges"*]

---

[1] Priests, bishops, monks. Note Latin construction.
[2] Coinage of the Ancient Greeks and Romans. Under the First Empire, French money bore on one side Napoleon's effigy with the legend '*Napoléon Empéreur*', and on the reverse, '*République Française*'. DL7V.
[3] Cf. CIV,Q35 and CVIII,Q85.
[4] NEE.

# The Ravages of the Napoleonic Wars. Napoleon against the Catholic Church. Arrests of Priests, 1809. The Internment of Pius VII at Fontainebleau, 1810

Renfort de sièges manubis[1] et maniples[2]
Changez le sacre[3] et passe sur[4] le prosne,[5]
Prins et captifs n'arreste les preztriples,[6]
Plus par fonds[7] mis eslevé, mis au trosne.

CVII,Q73

## Interpretation

There will be still further acts of pillage and armies. The holy laws will be changed and religion no longer practised. Priests will be arrested and imprisoned. Even he who had been placed on the throne [of St Peter, i.e. the Pope] will be kept at Fontaine[bleau].

## History

'We have never had *so many* nor such good *troops*,' Napoleon wrote on 7 Fructidor, Year XIII (25 August 1805) to Duroc, Grand Marshal of the Palace. The number of Frenchmen serving under arms between 1802 and 1815 is estimated at 1,600,000.

For material about the priests' arrests, see CVI,Q9.

The application of the *ecclesiastical legislation issued by the Revolution* (changing of the rites etc.) was unacceptable to the Vatican and led to more determined resistance than in the Po Valley or Tuscany. The members of the extraordinary States Council wanted to alter or temper the actual policy, but Napoleon insisted upon the uniformity of *law* within his Empire. Thus the clergy had to be dispersed and secularized.

*The imperial annexation of the Church* reached its climax with the *Imperial Catechism*, published in 1806.

The Catholic Church, however privileged, had to rely upon herself alone when countering overt or covert hostility, and in order to *lead waverers back into the fold* ["*passe sur le prosne*"]. *Disbelief* increased, nourished by sarcasm and rational objections such as those supplied by Voltaire in particular.

On 6 July 1810 Pius VII was arrested at the Quirinal, and his captivity was to last more than four years, at Savona first, then *Fontainebleau*.'[8]

[1] Latin *manubiae*: money from the spoils captured from the enemy. DLLB.
[2] Latin *maniples*, syncope of *manipulus*: troop. DLLB.
[3] Latin *sacer*: sacred. DLLB.

[4] To pass by, have no regard for, pass over. DL7V.
[5] *Prône*: formal homily delivered by priest during service. DL7V.
[6] *Prestrerie*: priesthood, priest's life. DAFL. Example of paragoge for reasons of rhyme.
[7] Latin *fons* (from *fundo*): spring, *fountain*. DLLB.
[8] NEE.

---

# The Siege of Saragossa, 1808–09.
# After Italy, the Peninsular War

Pau, Véronne, Vincence, Saragosse,
De glaives[1] loings, terroirs de sang humides:
Peste si grand viendra a[2] la grande gousse,[3]
Proches secours, et bien loin les remèdes.

CIII,Q75

## Interpretation

After Verona and Vicenza the Army of the Pyrenees will take the war further afield, as far as Saragossa, and will fill these territories with blood. A great calamity will be provoked by a great siege and, despite help approaching, the remedies will be distant.

## History

'In 1808, anticipating the need for a rapid mobilization towards the *Pyrenean* frontier or even an incursion into *Spain*, Napoleon ordered the disposition of troops along the staging road [where Pau is situated]: cavalry and infantry supported by some guns. Murat, the Emperor's right-hand man, hurried towards *Bayonne*.'[4]

'Don José de Palafox, Governor of *Saragossa*, organized a stern resistance in this town: after *a siege* of sixty-one days, he forced the French to withdraw [14 August 1808]. But they returned, and Saragossa had to undergo a new *siege* ["*grande gousse*"] lasting two months [December 1808–February 1809] and more *vicious* than the first, with each house and each street fiercely disputed. *Deprived of all means of defence* ["*bien loin les remèdes*"], he had to surrender.'[5]

'The English Army, which in January 1809 had advanced *deep into Spain* ["*proche secours*"], ran into difficulties as a result of the Battle of Tudela. Napoleon had directed that the English should be blocked from the sea. Moore, worried that his retreat might be cut off, hurried towards the Galician coast in a series of forced marches. Just then St Cyr had control of Catalonia and Marshal Launes was occupying Aragon and trying to reduce *Saragossa*."[6]

¹ Symbolic of war and fighting. DL7V.
² Latin *a* or *ab*: through, by means of. DLLB.
³ Husk or pod. DL7V. Image to designate an 'enveloping' siege.
⁴ NELGI.
⁵ DHB.
⁶ HFA.

---

## The Peninsular War, 1808. Wellington Lands, 1808. His March to the Pyrenees, 1813. The Spanish Royal Family in France, 1808

> Par mort la France prendra voyage à faire,
> Classe par mer, marcher monts Pyrénées,
> Espagne en trouble, marcher gent militaire:
> De plus grand Dames en France emmenées.
>
> CIV,Q2

### Interpretation

France will undertake a deadly voyage; an army that has arrived by sea will march to the Pyrenees. Spain will revolt; armies will march there and the greatest one and his ladies [wife and daughter] will be led back to France.

### History

'On 24 March 1808 the new King, Ferdinand VII, entered his capital to the acclamation of the delighted populace. This was the first act in the great drama that would give the Spanish people the chance to escape from the apathy into which they had sunk, and to prove themselves both heroic and cruel in the long and bloody war for independence. This was was *disastrous for France*, who lost the flower of her forces there [*"voyage de mort"*].

The first Portuguese rebellion began at Oporto on 16 June, and spread so rapidly through the northern provinces that the French had to evacuate them. At the same time, at Leiria, *14,000 English* troops under Wellington *landed* [*"classe par mer"*], also 5000 more commanded by General Spencer.

In 1813 Wellington, after seizing San Sebastian, passed through Bidassoa [*"marcher monts Pyrénées"*] and with a sizeable force took up positions upon French territory.'[1]

'On 10 April 1808 Ferdinand set off. There was a French detachment at each stage: the beloved ruler of Spain was already virtually *a prisoner*. On 20 April he arrived at *Bayonne* [*"en France emmenés"*]. Charles IV, his father and *Marie-Louise* [*"Dame"*] submitted to entering a coach, which, escorted by General Exelmans, *headed for France*. On 30 April at Bayonne they were received with regal honours and Napoleon welcomed them warmly. On 6 May Charles and Marie-Louise were taken to the castle of Compiègne. Ferdinand was given a comfortable prison, the Château of Valençay which belonged to Talleyrand. "I handled that affair very badly," Napoleon declared on St Helena. "It was seen to be altogether too immoral, cynically unjust, and the whole business was a shabby one, once I succumbed to it." '[2] [*'voyage de mort'*]

[1] HFA.
[2] NEE.

---

## The Invention of Rockets, 1806.
## Napoleon and the Church, 1809.
## Massacres in Spain, 1809–10

Seront ouys au Ciel les armes batre:[1]
Celui an mesme les divins ennemis,
Voudront lois sainctes injustement debatre
Par foudre[2] et guerre bien croyants a mort mis.

CIV,Q43

*Interpretation*

The noise of aerial armaments will be heard; the very year the Church's laws will be overthrown, the Catholics will become enemies [of Napoleon]; the believers will be put to death by Napoleon and the war.

*History*

'Napoleon seemed scarcely concerned with perfecting armaments. The armourer Pauly, it seems, could have supplied the infantry with a breech-loading gun. In fact it was Prussia who profited by this inventor's researches. Various engineers and French officers suggested *rockets* to the Emperor: they were not encouraged, so it was in England that Congreve's efforts resulted in the creation of the Rocket Corps; these weapons being used at Leipzig and Waterloo by the Allies. Congreve's rockets were used for the first time in 1806 against Boulogne by the Royal Navy.

The quarrel between the two powers [Napoleon and the Papacy of Pius VII] was not primarily due to the complete occupation of the Papal States in 1808, nor to economic factors, but to *religious considerations* ["*lois sainctes*"] on the Pope's side and urgent political and military necessities on the Emperor's. These destroyed the concord between the two rulers in *1809* and *plunged the entire Roman Catholic church into dissension* ["*divine ennemis*"].

The Peninsular War: the Spanish leaders rebelled during 1809 and 1810. Some of them were of the nobility, but they were outnumbered by Churchmen ["*bien croyants*"]. The French resorted to extreme brutality. One sergeant stationed in Navarre related an order received by his unit: "The first village to fire on us *will be burned to the ground and everyone in it killed* ["*a mort mis*"], not excluding babes in arms.'[3]

[1] *Battre le fer*: noise or clash of arms. DL7V.
[2] Cf. CIV,Q54.
[3] NEE.

## The Zenith of the Empire, 1807.
## Embarking for St Helena, 1815

Entre deux mers[1] dressera promontoire[2]
Que puis, mourra par le mors du cheval,
Le sien Neptune[3] pliera voile noire
Par Calpte[4] et classe[5] auprès de Rocheval.[6]

CI,Q77

*Interpretation*

Between two seas he will reach his peak but will die as a result, champing on the bit; the sea-god will wind him in his shroud [St Helena] after the return of L. Capet and the [English] fleet near Rochefort.

## History

'Crowned by the Peace of Tilsit the *"Grand Empire"* appeared *formidable*. All the European powers gravitated around Napoleon, whether as allies or subjected by force [the zenith of his rule].

At that very moment 'Napoleon *annexed the Papal States* and imprisoned the Pope.'[7]

'The Chamber demanded Napoleon's abdication. He wanted to get to the United States, but *the Royal Navy* was blockading the coasts. He finally *gave himself up* to the *English*, who treated him as a prisoner of war and deported him to the small island of St Helena.'[8]

Near *Rochefort* he boarded the Bellerophon which was to take him from the Isle of Aix[9] to St Helena. ' "If I had not laid hands on the Papal States," said Napoleon, "and thought to conquer a spiritual power by force, all my subsequent misfortunes would not have happened." '[10]

[1] The Papal States were situated between the Adriatic and Tyrrhenian Seas.
[2] Latin *promontorium*: culminating point, apex. DLLB.
[3] Albion: name given by the Greeks to England, because of the whiteness of her cliffs or from Albion, son of Neptune. DL7V.
[4] Anagram of Louis Capet: Louis XVIII.
[5] Latin *classis*: fleet, army. DLLB.
[6] *Roche-val*: Latin: fort, fortification. Hence 'rocky fort', 'Rochefort', strong rock.
[7] LCH3.
[8] LCH3.
[9] Aix: fortified islet defending the mouth of the Charente, opposite which are the roads of the Isle of Aix, forming a huge outer habour for Rochefort. DL7V.
[10] LMSH.

---

# The Annexation of the Papal States, 1807.
# The Continental Blockade, 1806–7

Le tyran Sienne[1] occupera Savonne,[2]
Le fort gaigné tiendra classe[3] marine,[4]
Les deux armées par la marque d'Ancone,[5]
Par effrayeur le chef s'en examine.

CI,Q75

## Interpretation

The tyrant will occupy Siena and Savona, having won [the battles] through being strongest, he will contain the English fleet, and the two armies [beaten], will also occupy the borderland of Ancona. The chief will examine his own conscience concerning this dreadful act.

## History

'Without awaiting the arrival of his Russian allies, the King of Prussia began hostilities: that same day his *army* was defeated at Jena by Napoleon and at Auerstadt by Davout [14 October 1806]. They still had to conquer *the Russian army* [the two armies]: the bloody but indecisive Battle of Eylau [February 1807] did not settle the matter, but Friedland [14 June] was a clear victory for Napoleon and led to parleys – the Peace of Tilsit [9 July 1807]. Napoleon then thought of coming to grips with England, which was isolated but still *mistress of the sea*. The continental blockade followed. Napoleon annexed *the Papal States* and imprisoned the Pope at Savona.'[6]

[1] Tuscan town.
[2] Ligurian town.
[3] Latin *classis*: fleet, army. DLLB.
[4] Cf. CI,Q98: '*La marine Grange*'.
[5] In 1532 Ancona was reunited with the Papal States. The French captured it in 1797. In 1809 it became the main town of the Metauro department. DHCD.
[6] LCH3.

---

# Napoleon and the Papal States. The Civil Code. The Struggle against the Royalist Rebels

> Par sacrée pompe[1] viendra baisser les aisles,
> Par la venüe du grand Législateur:
> Humble haussera, vexera les rebelles
> Naistra sur terre aucun aemulateur.

CV,Q79

## Interpretation

The advent of the great legislator will lay low the power of the Catholic Church. He will raise up the humble and vex the rebels. He will have no equal upon earth.

## History

'The Consulate did not limit its legal reforms, but succeeded in unifying the whole range of the law, public and private, through the Civil Code.

In this collective endeavour Napoleon, who presided over 55 out of 107 Council sessions, intervened frequently ["*grand Législateur*"] and often to great effect.'[2]

'Pope Pius VII's refusal to participate in the blockade gave the Emperor an excuse *to confiscate the Papal Border States* and then to occupy Rome. Pope Pius VII, held in the Quirinal, threatened to excommunicate the violators of the Holy City, and just when Napoleon made the serious mistake of arousing the Spaniards' hostility he compounded it by confronting the Pope.'[3]

So that his throne, born of the Revolution, might still be surrounded with the trappings of royalty, the Emperor created an *imperial nobility*, adding to his civil and military collaborators *of humble origins* a great number of former nobles of the *ancien régime* who, though formerly Royalists, had gradually joined his ranks during his seven years in power.

On 11 Vendémiaire [3 October 1795], Parisian electors were illegally convoked *by royalist agitators* ["*rebelles*"] who were at the same time mustering an army. A military operation was mounted against the insurgents, who rallied about 25,000 National Guards. The Convention had only about 5000 regulars with whom to oppose them. Barras was given command. The new leader was decisive and vigorous: he surrounded himself with officers he trusted and who thus began illustrious careers – Brune, Murat and, of course, *Napoleon*.

[1] Solemn and sumptuous raiment, the 'pomp' of Catholicism. DL7V.
[2] NEE.
[3] NLM.

---

## Monuments Erected by Napoleon

Gens d'alentour de Tarn, Loth et Garonne
Gardez les monts Appennines passer
Votre tombeau près de Rome et d'Anconne
Le noir poil crespe[1] fera trophée[2] dresser.

CIII,Q43

*Interpretation*

People of different regions [Tarn, Lot and the Garonne], beware of crossing the Apennine Alps, your tomb shall be near Rome and Ancona, he who wears a black felt hat shall erect a triumphal monument.

## History

'Following the example of *Augustus*, Napoleon wanted to immortalize his own memory, by means of monuments, especially in Paris. There he *erected* grandiose memorials [the Arc de Triomphe, the Vendôme Column, the Temple of Glory – which became the Madeleine, the Stock Exchange, etc.] to commemorate his victorious campaigns.'[3]

[1] Cf. CI,Q74: '*Le noir poil crespe*'.
[2] Latin *tropaeum*: trophy, monument of victory. DLLB.
[3] LCH3.

---

# The Directorate's Territorial Acquisitions.
# The Abductions of Pius VI, 1798, and of Pius VII, 1808.
# The Annexation of the Papal States, and the
# Peninsular War, 1808

Les ieux nouveaux en Gaule redressez,
Après victoire de l'Insubre[1] campaigne:
Monts d'esperie, [2] les grands liez, troussez,[3]
De peur trembler la Romaigne[4] et l'Espaigne.

CIV,Q36

## Interpretation

New powers will be established in France after the victories of the Italian campaign. Near the Italian mountains the great will be made prisoners and taken away; the states of the Church and of Spain will tremble with fear.

## History

'Arriving at Tolentino, from where he planned to march on Rome if necessary, Napoleon stopped to see what effect his swift incursion might have. The Pope dispatched his nephew Duke Braschi and three other envoys to Tolentino to arrange a peace with the conqueror. The Treaty was signed on 1 Ventôse [19 February 1797]. The Pope renounced his claims to Avignon and surrendered the legations of Bologna and Ferrara, also the rich province of *Romagna*.'[5]

'The Directorate ordered the invasion into papal territory, and Pope Pius VI had to sign what was for him the *disastrous* Treaty of Tolentino.

After General Duphot's murder in a Rome street [1798], the Directorate *seized* the Pope and proclaimed the Republic in Rome. *Arrested* by General Berthier [1798], Pius VI was taken to Siena, to a monastery in Florence, and then *taken away* in April 1799 to France – first to Grenoble, then Valence where he died.'[6]

'Pius VII refused to enforce the continental blockade. So Napoleon seized Rome [1808] and confiscated the Papal States. Pius VII responded by excommunicating all those who had taken part in desecrating the Holy Seat. General Radet immediately *took him away*, along with Cardinal Pacca, transporting him first to Genoa, then Savona and finally Fontainebleau.'[7]

'Religious fanaticism, which in *Spain* at that time only accentuated nationalistic fervour, found further motivation in *the Pope's abduction*. Pius VII, held in the Quirinal, threatened to excommunicate the violators of the Holy City, and just when Napoleon made the serious mistake of arousing the Spaniards' hostility, he compounded it by confronting the Pope.'[8]

---

[1] Ancient term for Cisalpine Gaul, roughly corresponding to the present-day Milan region, with its chief town Mediolanum (Milan). DHB.

[2] *Hesperia*: ancient classical name for Italy. DHB.

[3] To pack up in a trunk, take away. DL7V.

[4] Romagna: ancient papal province, capital Ravenna. DHB.

[5] HFA.

[6] DL7V.

[7] DL7V.

[8] NLM.

---

# The Victory over the English at Anvers, 24 December 1809. Napoleon's Divorce, 12 January 1810. The Mediterranean Becomes the Focus of Running the Continental Blockade, 1811. The Death of the Archbishop of Paris and the Arrest of Pius VII

Victor naval à Houche,[1] Anvers divorce,
Né grand,[2] du ciel feu, tremblement haut brule:
Sardaigne bois, Malte, Palerme, Corse,
Prélat mourir, l'un frappe sur la Mule.[3]

Presage 17, June

## Interpretation

After a naval victory over the English at Houke, near Anvers, he will divorce. He who is great from birth will unleash thunderbolts from the sky and will be incensed because of provocation from the high-placed one [Napoleon]. Sardinia, Malta, Sicily and Corsica [will resist the block-ade], a prelate will die and one [Napoleon] will attack the Pope.

## History

'While the envoys of Napoleon and the Emperor Francis were busy working out peace terms, the English, who had been preparing an ex-pedition for some time, mustered at the mouth of the Escaut. Their plan was to capture the town of *Anvers* and the French fleet moored on the Escaut. The English, masters of Walcheren Island, were simultaneously threatening Belgium and Holland. Anvers was at considerable risk. Mar-shal Bernadotte left for Anvers and raised more than 12,000 men to defend the town. The squadron moored directly beneath the town walls. On 30 September Lord Chatham's powerful force abandoned its position in order to return to England. On 24 December the English demolished the Flushing arsenals and re-embarked [naval victory]. . . .

The dissolution of the marriage of Napoleon and Joséphine was pro-nounced on 12 January 1810. . . .

From 1810 English trade with the Continent was gradually blocked and smuggling decreased. In 1811 trade between England and northern and western Europe was drastically limited. By contrast, smuggling in the *Mediterranean* continued to flourish, from *Malta* to the Balkans and up to Austria.'[4]

'At the end of 1810 French troops invaded *Sicily*: the result, for the King of Naples, was huge expense and 1200 men killed on the beaches.'[5]

On 9 June 1808, Cardinal de Belloy ['*prélat mourir*'], the Archbishop of Paris, died. His successor was to have been Cardinal Fesch, but he refused and Napoleon named Maury archbishop on 5 October 1810.

On 6 July 1810 Pius VII was arrested, the start of over four years' captivity. ['*l'un frappe sur la Mule*']

[1] District of Anvers.
[2] Pius VII, as Count Chiaramonti, was of noble birth. HDP.
[3] Possible allusion to Pius VII's obstinacy of character.
[4] NEE.
[5] HFA.

## The Peninsular War and the Fall of the Eagle.
## Wellington in the Pyrenees, 1812

Bien contigue des grands monts Pyrénées,
Un contre l'Aigle grand copie[1] addresser:
Ouvertes veines,[2] forces exterminées,
Que jusqu'à Pau[3] le chef viendra chasser.

CIV,Q70

*Interpretation*

Very near the Pyrenees a [country] will amass many troops against the
Eagle [Napoleon]: after trenches have been opened and forces extermi-
nated, it will pursue him into the lower Pyrenees.

*History*

'1811 ended indecisively. The French had been *driven out of* Portugal.
Determined to attack Russia, Napoleon realized that communication
between France and Spain needed to be strengthened. He ordered Mar-
mont to attack Salamanca, and then to ensure that the major route from
Madrid to *Bayonne* was protected, which left the field open for the
English *commander-in-chief*, who took advantage of the opportunity to
dispose *the majority of his forces* around Badajoz. Following a fortnight of
*open trench warfare*, the town was attacked on 6 April. After a heroic
defence the French finally surrendered. *The excesses* of the Anglo-Por-
tuguese soldiery reached a *nadir of brutality* and even upset the taciturn
Wellington. On 21 June 1812 the Battle of Vittoria liberated almost all
of Spain as far as the Basque country and Navarre. The French flooded
back towards the frontier, retaining only Pamplona and San Sebastian in
*the region of the Pyrenees*. Ever methodical, Wellington wanted *to drive*
the French forces remaining in Spain out of the country altogether. But
the Cabinet insisted on his advance into France. Soult, who arrived in
*Bayonne* on 13 July, shifted to the offensive. At the end of August his
army began descending the south slopes of *the Pyrenees* towards Pamplona. Wellington pushed him back after a stern struggle. Thus unable
to relieve Pamplona, Soult tried to advance on San Sebastian. The English headed him off and forced him back over the frontier. On 8
September, San Sebastian capitulated and was *ransacked*. On 8 October
Wellington crossed the Bidassoa. Ten days later Napoleon, outnumbered, lost the Battle of the Nations at Leipzig. While the Allies crossed
the Rhine, Soult was forced to abandon the Nivelle line, then the Nive,

and to fall back on the entrenched camp of *Bayonne*. As for Wellington, he made his headquarters at *St-Jean-de-Luz*.'[4]

[1] Latin *copia*: army corps, troops, military forces. DLLB.
[2] Refers here to irrigation and trenches rather than blood-letting.
[3] Principal town of the Lower Pyrenees.
[4] NEE.

---

## Soult at Bayonne. Wellington at St Jean de Luz. Russia Enforces Napoleon's Abdication, 1814. The Death of Napoleon at St Helena, 1821

Entre Bayonne et à Saint Jean de Lux,
Sera posé de Mars le promontoire:[1]
Aux Hanix[2] d'Aquilon[3] Nanar[4] hostera lux,[5]
Puis suffoqué au lict[6] sans adjutoire.[7]

CVIII,Q85

*Interpretation*

The war will reach its peak between Bayonne and St-Jean-de-Luz. Russia's efforts will take away Napoleon's glory: he will suffocate in his bed without any help.

*History*

See the preceding quatrain (CIV,Q70) for references to Bayonne and St Jean-de-Luz.

'A few days later Mainz was in sight. A sapper is reported to have said, on seeing the town: "Damn it, we did well, looking for the *Russians* in Moscow, just to bring them back into France!" The garrisons left behind along the Vistula, the Oder and the Elbe were forced one after another to surrender. The disaster was total.'[8]

'*Tsar Alexander*, with no more to fear from Napoleon, immediately demanded Napoleon's abdication, which Caulincourt and his companions were directed to obtain.'[9]

'*The sufferings he endured at the end were appalling*: fighting the pain, worn out by quack remedies, harassed by flies and mosquitoes, and weakened by enemas, he struggled against *his annihilation*.'[8]

The end of the Peninsular War and the Battle of Leipzig were certainly the turning-points of the Napoleonic Wars.

[1] Latin *promontorium*: peak. DLLB.
[2] Latin *annixus*: effort. DLLB.
[3] Always denotes Russia, the Northern Empire.
[4] Abbreviation of *Napoleon Bonaparte*.
[5] Latin: light, glory (symbolic). DLLB.
[6] Die in one's bed, i.e. not unnaturally. DL7V.
[7] Latin *adjutorium*: help, succour. DLLB.
[8] NEE.
[9] NLM.

---

## The Defeat of the Grand Army, 1812–13. Treachery and the Emperor's Abdication

La grand copie[1] qui sera déchassée
Dans un moment fera besoin au Roy.[2]
La foy promise de loing sera faulsée,
Nud se verra en piteux désarroy.

CIV,Q22

### Interpretation

The Grand Army which will be tracked down, at a certain moment will fail the Emperor. The word given will be broken far away and he will find himself stripped and in pitiable disarray.

### History

'Davout's Army Corps was to become the nub of the new *Grand Army*. It was a composite army, in fact, for apart from the troops of the 130 departments of the Empire there were contingents from all the allied European countries.

On 3 June 1812 Napoleon rejoined his headquarters at Thorn on the Vistula: the core of his army was there, comprising about 400,000 men in three main groups.

"It was 6 November," Caulincourt wrote, "when the bad news arrived. The Emperor was already preoccupied with the information he had received concerning the retreat of his forces along the Dvina at the very time he most needed their success. He was very concerned when the first news came in about *the Malet conspiracy*. From that moment on his desire to return to Paris grew stronger." The Grand Army was now reduced to 24,000 fighting men, followed by another 25,000 stragglers.

On the night of 6 April Caulincourt heard the Tsar thank the Prince of Muscovy for the zeal he had shown in forcing the Emperor to abdicate. While false rumours swept Paris, where *cliques and intrigues* abounded, the Duke of Vicenza defended each clause of the treaty in detail. It is moving to read in his report to the Emperor of 8 April: "The Poles your Majesty exhorted me so firmly to protect will be well looked after." The last faithful allies, they ran through the streets of Fontainebleau with a band of the Old Guard crying: "Long Live the Emperor!" "Death to the traitors!"

Ney remained in Paris, having submitted to the new status quo. The Emperor, who knew him well, told Caulincourt: "He was against me yesterday and would die for me tomorrow." He also declared "Life is *unbearable* to me!" ["*piteux désarroy*"] and on the night of 12 April Napoleon tried unsuccessfully to commit suicide by means of some poison he had carried with him since the retreat from Russia."[3]

[1] Army corps, troops, military forces. DLLB.

[2] The word *king* is used by Nostradamus *passim* to denote heads of state, whatever their actual titles.

[3] NEE.

---

# The Fall of Napoleon, Waterloo, 1815.
## M. de St-Agnan Sent by Napoleon to Frankfurt, 1813.
## The Battle of Rheims, 13 March 1814

Le grand du fouldre tombe d'heure diurne,
Mal et prédict par porteur postulaire:[1]
Suivant présage, tombe d'heure nocturne,
Conflict Reims, Londres, Etrusques[2] pestifère.

CI,Q26

### Interpretation

The glory of the captain will begin to dwindle by daylight, misfortune being announced by the bearer of a request. Following this presage night will fall; after the combat at Rheims, Etruria, which has brought misery, will be defeated by the English.

### History

'On 2 November 1813 the French army, reduced to 70,000 men, crossed the Rhine. There this *bloody* campaign ended. No alternative remained but to try to parley with the Allies or to fight to the bitter end. Peace talks were resumed: M. de St-Agnan was called to Frankfurt by Metternich and on 9 November, in the presence of the ministers from Russia and *England*, the basis for a general peace treaty was laid down. The victors *demanded* that Napoleon abandon Spain, Italy, Germany and Holland. St-Agnan had the task of *conveying* these terms to Napoleon. The Allies stated that if they were met talks would begin in a town by the Rhine, but they also declared that such negotiations would not imply the cessation of hostilities. The French therefore had to prepare for battle.'

'On 13 March 1814 Napoleon reached some hills a mile or so from *Rheims*, which the Russian general St-Priest had just occupied. The Russians were spread out upon these heights just outside *Rheims*. General Krasinsky cut the Rheims road at Berry-au-Bac, and the Allies abandoned the town and withdrew in disorder. The French took 6000 prisoners in this battle. The Imperial Army stayed in the *Rheims* area until 16 March. During this time Napoleon received reports on the general situation of the Empire.'

'On *the morning* of 18 June 1815 Napoleon reconnoitred the entire English line and gave his battle orders to various commanders. Manoeuvring began. Napoleon bore down on Planchenoit to form a second position, making renewed efforts to steady some regiments. But rallying them became impossible *in the night* and this entire fine army was a confused mass amid which one heard cries of "Every man for himself!". *The losses* sustained by the French at Waterloo were *very severe*: 19,000 men lay on the battlefield. The Allies lost even more men, but their victory was decisive, nonetheless.'[3]

[1] Latin *postulo*: I demand, request, claim. DLLB.

[2] The Bonaparte family had two branches: one line became extinct at Treviso in 1447, the other established itself in Florence (capital of Tuscany, i.e. Etruria) and from this were descended the Bonapartes of Sarzane of whom Napoleon I was a member. DL7V.

[3] HFA.

---

# The Return from Elba, 1 March 1815

Le Captif Prince aux Itales[1] vaincu,
Passera Gennes par mer jusqu'à Marseille,
Par grand effort des forens[2] survaincu,[3]
Sauf coup de feu, barril liqueur d'abeille.[4]

CX,Q24

*Interpretation*

The vanquished prince, prisoner in Italy, will go past the Gulf of Genoa towards Marseille. By making great efforts [of war] the foreign [armies] will conquer him by their superiority. Safe and sound from shots, he will have barrels [of powder] instead of honey.

*History*

'On the island of Elba, Napoleon was informed that he still had the support of the French people. He *disembarked* at the Gulf of Juan on 1 March. *The Allies* were still gathered at the Congress of Vienna and their armies were encamped near the French frontiers. They declared Napoleon "outlawed from Europe". Obliged to carry on the war, Napoleon marched north with 125,000 men against 100,000 English and 250,000 Prussians ["*sur*vaincu"]. On the evening of 18 June panic and dismay spread through the French ranks. As for Napoleon, *who had tried to get himself killed* in the battle, ["*sauf coup de feu*"], he gave himself up to the English.'[5]

[1] Latin *Aethalis*: ancient name for the Island of Elba. DLLB.
[2] Foreign, strange. DAFL.
[3] *Sur*: implying superiority over and above.
[4] Honey symbolizing peace, tranquillity, Cf. cx,Q89.
[5] LCH3.

---

# The Return from Elba. Ney Rallies to Napoleon in Burgundy, 17 March 1815. The Declarations of Lyon. The Charter of 1815

Foudre[1] en Bourgogne[2] fera cas portenteux[3]
Que par engin[4] homme ne pourrait faire,
De leur Sénat[5] sacriste[6] fait boiteux
Fera scavoir aux ennemis l'affaire.

CII,Q76

*Interpretation*

Napoleon in Burgundy will make a deadly prophecy that man cannot triumph by means of his intelligence. Because of unsatisfactory things decreed by the very sacred Senate, he will make his intentions known to his enemies.

## History

'Napoleon thought it best to channel rather than confront this renewal of the revolutionary spirit. These tactics were reflected in the series of decrees Napoleon issued from *Lyon*, already couched in magisterial manner. The *Parliaments* were dissolved. The audacity and resolution of Marshal Ney were crucial. He had been given the command of the troops reassembled in the Franche-Comté; decisive action from this quarter could disrupt the advance of Napoleon's army, which was straggling along on the *Lyon–Auxerre* road near *Chalon* and *Autun*. "I'll take care of *Bonaparte*," Ney thundered. "We'll attack the wild beast." Emissaries from Lyon reached him at Lons-le-Saunier on the night of 13 March. They reported on what they had seen and brought a long letter from Bertrand and word from the Emperor himself. "Come and rejoin me at *Chalon*, and I shall receive you as I did the day after the Battle of the Moskva." On the morning of 14 Ney made up his mind, and he joined Napoleon again at *Auxerre* on 17 March.'[7]

'A few days after the signing of this celebrated treaty [20 May 1814] Louis XVIII's government reinstated a number of *senators* to the legislative assembly which Napoleon had dismissed on the preceding 31 December. Both these somewhat fraudulent assemblies ["*fait boiteux*"] were convened at the Palais Bourbon, during which session Louis XVIII gave notice of the treaty and presented the charter he was conferring.

The royal session took place on 16 March. Louis XVIII read a speech that ended thus: "He who would light the torch of civil war among us also brings the scourge of foreign war ['*cas portenteux*']; he comes to destroy this constitutional charter I have given you; this charter which every Frenchman *cherishes* ['*sacriste*'] and which I here swear to uphold." '[8]

---

[1] Cf. CI,Q26 and CIII,Q13, Napoleon '*foudre de guerre*'. DL7V.

[2] Burgundy was divided into various areas, including the Charolais, Macon, Auxerre etc. DL7V.

[3] Latin *portentum*: presage (usually ill-omen). DLLB.

[4] Latin *ingenium*: wit, intelligence. DLLB.

[5] Name given to the Upper or Senior House in certain states with two legislative assemblies, and not at all, or only indirectly, dependent upon popular election.

[6] Latin: superlative of *sacer*, i.e. very or most sacred.

[7] NEE.

[8] HFA.

# The Hundred Days. Waterloo, 18 June 1815.
## St Helena

Au mois troisième[1] se levant du Soleil[2]
Sanglier,[3] liépard[4] au champs Mars[5] pour combattre,
Liépard lassé au ciel[6] estend son oeil,[7]
Un aigle autour du Soleil voit s'esbattre.

CI,Q23

*Interpretation*

In March, having risen against the monarchy, near the Ardennes, England will fight upon the battlefield. Weary [of Napoleon], England will extend her surveillance upon him, even to a prison cell, after seeing the Emperor disport himself among the monarchists.

*History*

'Napoleon disembarked on *1 March; avoiding* the Rhône valley, which was *Royalist*-dominated, he took the Alpine route and reached Paris on *20 March*. His progress became a triumphal procession. The troops *sent against him by the King* acclaimed him. . . . *A furious battle* began on the plateau of Mont-St-Jean near Waterloo against the English led by Wellington. . . . Napoleon wanted to get to the United States but the *English* navy controlled the coastline. Finally he surrendered to the *English* who treated him as a prisoner of war and deported him to the small island of St Helena.'[8]

'There he lived for six years under strict *surveillance* in the *prison villa* of Longwood.'[9]

[1] March, third month.

[2] Sun: symbol of the Capets (Louis XIV, '*le roi soleil*').

[3] *Sanglier*: 'the Wild Boar of the Ardennes', name given to Count William de la Marck (1446–85). DL7V.

[4] Leopard: the heraldic leopard is a lion passant rather than rampant. *The Lion of Waterloo*, the victory of the Lion over the Eagle, was a half-symbolic, half-realistic painting by the Belgian artist Wiertz. At Waterloo the Allies erected a 50 ft pyramid topped by a huge cast-iron lion. DL7V.

[5] Mars, god of war.

[6] *Ciel*: Latin *cella*: small cell. DAFL.

[7] *Oeil*: look, and by extension, surveillance. DL7V.

[8] LCH3.

[9] HFAM.

# The Battle of Waterloo, 18 June 1815

Prest à combattre fera défection,
Chef adversaire obtiendra la victoire:
L'arrière-garde fera défension,[1]
Les défaillans[2] mort au blanc territoire.

CIV,Q75

## Interpretation

[The army], ready to fight, will be found wanting, the enemy leader will gain the victory; the rearguard will defend itself, those who died in the snowy territory will be missed.

## History

The army commanded by Grouchy was ordered by Napoleon to pursue Blücher's army. Not only did Grouchy allow Blücher to escape, but his troops were ineffective at Waterloo.

'Napoleon marched north with 125,000 men against 100,000 English and 250,000 Prussians. After a victory at Ligny [16 June], a bitter battle began on the plateau of Mont-St-Jean near Waterloo with the English under Wellington, soon supported by Blücher's Prussians [18 June]. That evening panic and dismay spread through the French ranks: *only the Old Guard* died without asking for quarter.'[3]

Napoleon had lost much of his army during the Russian campaign: 'Napoleon had mobilized the Grand Army: 700,000 men. Hunger and an unexpectedly early and bitter winter wore out the soldiers. The Grand Army, thus reduced to *30,000 men*, painfully crossed the Beresina ["*Mort au blanc térritoire*"].'[3]

[1] Action of defending oneself, defence, DAFL.
[2] *Défaillir: faire défaut*: to be found wanting, or to err. DAFL.
[3] LCH3.

# Napoleon on *The Bellerophon*. Fouché against Napoleon. The Second Abdication, 23 June 1815

Par foudre[1] en l'arche[2] or et argent fondu,[3]
De deux captifs l'un l'autre mangera:[4]
De la cité le plus grand estendu,
Quand submergé la classe[5] nagera.

CIII,QI3

## Interpretation

Because of the military leader [Napoleon] on a ship, wealth will melt away. One of two prisoners will rise against the other. The greater part of the town [Paris] will be overthrown when the French army is swamped and the [English] fleet forges on.

## History

'On 18 June 1815, after the Prussians had been driven back, the Emperor risked the final onslaught with the Old Guard. But at this critical moment a second Prussian corps came into action. The exhausted French army was overcome with panic and began *to flee, pursued and cut down* by the Prussians until almost 2 a.m.'[6]

'The enemy army was larger than ours, but the President of the Provisional Government, Fouché,[7] wanted the junior branch of the Bourbons to accede to the throne, or if that failed, to revert to the older branch of the family. When Napoleon offered to place himself at the head of the forces, Fouché refused and *compelled* the Emperor to leave Malmaison, where he had taken shelter.'[8]

'After his abdication he went to the port of Rochefort, hoping to sail to the United States. But an English cruiser blocked the harbour, so Napoleon decided to ask for asylum from the English government. He boarded the English *ship Bellerophon*, on which he was treated as a *prisoner* of war and transported to St Helena. . . .

England, *mistress of the seas*, kept Malta and the Ionian islands.'[9]

'The second restoration [of Napoleon] *cost France dear*. The Allies had first to be paid 100 million francs, then another indemnity of 700 million, followed by *300 million* special compensation. That was not all: 150,000 foreign soldiers remained for three years on French soil, maintained at French expense. France was *weakened* not only by her own losses, but also as a result of everything her enemies had won.'[10]

---

[1] Napoleon. Cf. CIV,Q54.

[2] Reference to Noah's ark, hence to a vessel providing refuge. DL7V.

[3] To disappear rapidly: money slipping through one's hands. DL7V.

[4] To eat someone: i.e. to attack, or fall upon. DL7V.

[5] Latin *classis*: army, fleet. DLLB. By elision Nostradamus uses the word in both its senses, thus avoiding repetition.

[6] HFAM.

[7] Joseph Fouché. Having returned to Paris he was elected president of the Jacobins and quarrelled with Robespierre, whom he helped overthrow. When the tide turned, a warrant was issued for his arrest. DL7V.

[8] HFVD.

[9] HFAM.

[10] HFVD.

---

# The Second Abdication, 21 June 1815

La prochain fils de l'aisnier[1] parviendra
Tant élevé jusqu'au règne des fors
Son aspre[2] gloire un chacun la craindra
Mais ses enfans du règne gettez hors.

CII,QII

## Interpretation

The son who succeeds the elder will manage to elevate himself to rule among the most powerful; everyone will fear his savage glory, but those near to him will cast him out of power.

## History

'Napoleon reached Lyon and then Paris, from where he counted on organizing once more the defence of the realm. But he was prevented from doing so. At the news of his defeat the deputies had only one thought: the Emperor was going to use even his defeat and the impending invasion in order to dissolve the Assembly and turn dictator on the pretext of the public's good. To forestall this, *it was necessary to make him abdicate. . . .*

He received Davout who immediately advised him to adjourn both chambers, adding that the chamber of representatives, *with its passionate hostility*, would paralyse all public-spiritedness. The deputies were *against him*. Napoleon gave Fouché himself, *whom he now saw through*, the task of conveying to the chamber his abdication.'[3]

[1] Charles-Marie Bonaparte married in 1767 Laetitia Ramolino, by whom he had five

sons and three daughters: Joseph, *Napoleon*, Marie-Ann-Eliza, Lucien, Louis, Marie Pauline, Marie-Annonciade-Caroline, and Jérôme. DHCD.

[2] Latin *asper*: of sentient beings, used to mean hard, savage, intractable, tough. DLLB. Cf. CI,Q76.

[3] NLM.

---

## Napoleon Betrayed by Women. Napoleon Prisoner of the English. His Agonizing Death, 1821

Le feu estaint, les vierges[1] trahiront,
La plus grand part de la bande nouvelle:
Fouldre[2] a fer, lance les seuls Roys garderont
Etrusque et Corse, de nuict gorge allumelle.

                                        CIV,Q35

### Interpretation

When the war ceases, women will betray [Napoleon] as well as the greater part of the new [monarchist] movement. Napoleon will be a captive, the ministers will want to keep the sword of him who originated from Tuscany and Corsica, then he will have fire in his throat at night.

### History

'General Belliard brought Napoleon the news of the capitulation of Paris, signed during the night. After this enemy troops were to occupy the capital. . . . At 6 a.m. he arrived at Fontainebleau where his Guard and the remainder of his army awaited him. Then began the series of salon intrigues which led to the restoration of the Bourbons. Some diplomats and a handful of Royalists and émigrés circulated busily everywhere while *their wives and womenfolk* flourished and waved white handkerchiefs [treason].

The way in which *the ministers* wanted Napoleon treated was somewhat shabby: they had even given orders that his sword be taken from him ["*garderont lance*"].'[3]

'The next day was appalling. On *the night* of 4 May 1821 all the servants remained in attendance on him. His last struggle began and his *death-rattle* was agonizing and dreadful.'[4]

[1] Latin *virgo*: young woman. DLLB.
[2] Cf. CIV,Q54, CI,Q26, CII,Q76, CIII,Q13.
[3] HFA.
[4] NLM.

# Napoleon at St Helena. Longwood House, 1815–21

Le chef qu'aura conduict peuple infiny
Loing de son Ciel, de meurs et langue estrange,
Cinq mil en Crète,[1] et Tessalie[2] finy,
Le chef fuyant sauvé[3] en la marine grange.

CI,Q98

## Interpretation

The leader who will have led the immortal people far from its own sky will end his life in the middle of the sea on a rocky island, with a population of 5000 whose customs and language are different. The leader who will want to escape will be kept in a barn in the middle of the sea.

## History

'When Napoleon returned to Paris, the Chamber demanded his abdication. *He wanted to get to the United States*, but the English navy was patrolling the coastline, and he finally gave himself up to the English, who treated him as a prisoner of war and deported him to the small island of St Helena.'[4]

'St Helena is only an African *rock* in the Atlantic, 1900 miles from land. Longwood House where the English installed the Emperor and his devoted retainers had been built to serve as *a barn* for a farm.'[5]

[1] Latin *creta*: rock. DLLB. St Helena, a rocky African island in the Atlantic, population 5000. DHCD.
[2] Greek: Θέσσαλη for Θάλασσα: the sea. DGF.
[3] Latin *salvo*: I keep. DLLB.
[4] LCH3.
[5] NLM.

---

# The Collapse of the Empire

Le divin mal surprendra le Grand Prince,
Un peu devant aura femme espousée
Son appuy et crédit à un coup viendra mince,
Conseil[1] mourra pour la teste rasée.

CI,Q88

## Interpretation

The divine curse will surprise the Great Prince, shortly after his marriage, and suddenly his allies and credit will be reduced, the good sense of the man with the cropped head will die out.

## History

'As soon as Napoleon married the Archduchess Marie-Louise of Austria, for whom he had divorced Joséphine Beauharnais, Fouché, Bernadotte and various others were more or less alienated from him. Pope Pius VII, whose states he wanted to ransack, excommunicated him, and the violent opposition to Napoleon created new problems for him. In spite of this, he did not hesitate in embarking upon a formidable conflict with Russia.'[2]

[1] Latin *consilium*: good sense. DLLB.
[2] DHCB.

---

# The First Italian Campaign 1796–97.
# The Return of the Bourbons. Louis XVIII
# and Charles X, 1815–30

Tranché le ventre[1] naistra avec deux testes,[2]
Et quatre bras: quelques ans entiers vivra
Jour qui Alquiloye[3] célebrera ses fetes
Fossen, Turin, chef Ferrare suivra.

CI,Q58

## Interpretation

When the mother has been decapitated [the monarchy], she will be reborn with two kings and four princes and will live for some years more, [meanwhile] the imperial eagle will celebrate its festivities [in France], then Fossano will follow, Turin, the Pope.

## History

In spite of the Queen Mother's execution the Bourbons are to return to the throne with two heads: Louis XVIII's and Charles X's. The four princes who will not reign are Louis Dauphin (Louis XVII), Charles

Ferdinand Duke of Berry, Louis Antoine Duke of Angoulême, Henri-Charles-Ferdinand Duke of Bordeaux and Count of Chambord.

'*Fossano*: fort with an arsenal seized by the French in 1796 (first Italian campaign).'[4]

'Napoleon was thus in control of the *Turin* road. But he did not stop there, savaging the Sardinian army and wiping it out at Mondovi. The Sardinians laid down their arms and had to sign the Armistice of Cherasco, ten leagues from *Turin* [18 April 1796], which was amended on 3 June to a peace treaty giving France Savoy, Nice, etc.

Pius VI signed the Peace of Tolentino with some trepidation; it cost him 30 millions. The Romagna [Ravenna, Rimini] was reunited, along with the legations of *Ferrara* and Bologna, to the Cispadane Republic and Ancona.'[5]

---

[1] The part here representing the whole: the genetrix. Cf. CX,Q17.
[2] Head: *caput = capet*. Cf. CIX,Q20.
[3] Latin *aquila*: eagle. DLLB.
[4] DHCB.
[5] HFVD.

---

# The Second Restoration of Louis XVIII, July 1815. The Proscriptions

Le blonds au nez forche[1] viendra commettre[2]
Par le duelle[3] et chassera dehors,
Les exilés dedans fera remettre.
Aux lieux marins commettant les plus forts.

CII,Q67

## Interpretation

The blond man with the aquiline nose [Louis XVIII] will come to head [the country] because of the mourning [for Louis XVI] and will drive out [the Bonapartists], he will reinstate the exiles [Royalists], sending out the strongest [the generals] beyond the seas.

## History

'The government was no sooner assured of the Loire army's adherence than the proscriptions began. Nineteen generals or officers, accused of having abandoned the King prior to 23 March and of having seized power, were immediately placed on reprisals lists and arrested and tried before military tribunals. Thirty-eight other *generals or administrators of the Empire* ["*les plus forts*"] were at the same time *sent far away from their homes*. In this way the minister tried to satisfy *the demands of the ultra-Royalist faction*. When death sentences were requested, there were gasps in the Assembly and Tribunals. *The Royalists* held their ground, seemingly quite confident of forcing the King's hand. Those who wanted severe sentences passed on the regicides had to be placated. The Commission's proposal of *banishment* was adopted. Exile was to be permanent and these declared enemies of France were ordered to leave French soil within a month. They were stripped of civil rights, possessions and titles. France was now *in the hands of the Royalists. The most experienced generals* had been purged, and the deputies, *all aristocrats*, did not hesitate to stiffen the tax laws at the very time when commerce was in the greatest difficulties.'[4]

[1] The celebrated profile of the Bourbon.
[2] Put foremost, at the head. DL7V.
[3] *deuil* (mourning), by transposition. DAFL.
[4] HFA.

---

# Charles-Ferdinand of Bourbon, Duke of Berry. His Marriage. Alliance with the Prince of Condé. His Assassination, 1820

> Et Ferdinand blonde[1] sera descorte,[2]
> Quitter la fleur, suyvre le Macédon:[3]
> Au grand besoin[4] défaillira sa routte,
> Et marchera contre le Myrmiden.[5]
>
> CIX,Q35

## Interpretation

Ferdinand will be in dissent [because of a woman]; he will abandon the monarchy to follow *Ma*[rshal] *Condé*; he will die in the road [causing] great privation and will march against the small man [Napoleon].

## History

'*In 1789 an émigré*, along with his parents, he served in *the army of Condé*, 1792–97, then in 1801 settled in England, where he married an

Englishwoman, Anna *Brown*. In 1814 Louis XVIII chose him to be commander-in-chief of the army *which was to oppose Napoleon* at the gates of Paris after his return from Elba. *His family, which had not wanted to recognize his first marriage*, made him marry Marie-Caroline-Ferdinande-Louise of Naples in 1816.'[6]

'On 13 February 1829 he was assassinated *at the entrance* of the Opéra, by Louvel, who wanted *to stamp out the Bourbon dynasty*.'[7]

[1] Play of words on Anna *Brown*.
[2] Latin *discors*: what is in dissension, different. DLLB. Nostradamus by a pun here mobilizes both senses of the word, discord and difference.
[3] Macédon: anagram of Ma(rshal) Condé.
[4] Privation. DL7V.
[5] Myrmidon: man of small stature. DL7V.
[6] DL7V.
[7] DHCD.

---

## The Duke of Berry's Assassination by Louvel, 13 February 1820

Par trahison de verges[1] à mort battu,
Puis surmonté sera par son désordre:[2]
Conseil frivole au grand captif sentu,
Nez par fureur quand Berich viendra mordre.[3]

CVI,Q32

*Interpretation*

Accused of treason he [Louvel] will be executed on the Place de Grèves, having been dominated by his mental disorder. He will be accused of asking for a futile audience with the great captive [Napoleon], when he will sink [his dagger] into the body of the Duke of Berry through hatred of those born [Bourbons].

*History*

'After more than three months' inquiries and investigation, and despite zealous efforts by the minister and various Royalists to discover in Louvel's crime some traces of *a conspiracy*, M. Bellart, the Public Prosecutor, had to admit in his indictment that he had found no accomplices. The Royalists were disappointed with this conclusion, for they wished to compromise the liberals. But it was only too clear that Louvel had acted

quite alone and without any motive but his *own deep hatred* [*"par fureur"*]
for the Bourbons. He admitted as much, confessed that the dagger he
had used was in fact his [*mordre*] and answered the questions put to him.
He had thought about his crime for six years; the Prince had done him
no harm, but the Bourbons had greatly harmed France. He had a grudge
against the royal family and wanted to kill the King himself, and he had
begun with the Prince because he was the hope of the Bourbons. He
confessed that he had been troubled by the presence of foreigners in
France and had journeyed to Elba in 1814. Yet he had returned *without
speaking to Napoleon nor discussing* his plans with anyone. [*"Conseil frivole"* etc. . . .] The court had nominated a celebrated advocate to defend
the accused, but M. Bonnet could only present Louvel as the prey of
monomania[4] [*"désordre"*]. He was condemned to death and led out the
next day to the Place de *Grèves* amid a silent crowd."[5]

[1] Anagram of Grèves.
[2] By analogy, a troubled or disturbed mind.
[3] Penetrate, enter, sink into. DL7V.
[4] Monomania: essentially characterized by partial madness, varying in its object, and
manifested in obsessions, compulsions and irresistible fears. DL7V.
[5] HFA.

---

# Bishop Kyprianos at Cyprus, 1810. The Massacre of Clergy and Prominent Greeks, 1821

> En ce temps-là sera frustrée Cyprie,[1]
> De son secours de ceux de mer Egée:
> Vieux trucidez, mais par mesles[2] et Lypres[3]
> Seduict leur Roy, Royne plus outragée.
>
> CIII,Q89

## Interpretation

At that very moment, Kyprianos will be thwarted at Cyprus in his
attempt to help the Greeks: the old [clergy] will be massacred by a dark
and wretched trick, their leader being seduced, the mother [Church] will
be offended still more.

## History

'From 1810 Cyprus was lucky to have as archbishop the young and energetic Kyprianos, who took a lively interest . . . in ecclesiastical affairs.

The Greek War of Independence found the island peaceful. But Kutchuk Mehmed, the governor, feared that the Greek Cypriots would take up arms against Turkey as the Greeks on *the Aegean* islands were doing, and asked Kyprianos for assurances of loyalty which the Archbishop willingly gave. But Kutchuk still had doubts and for security reasons requested 2000 Turkish soldiers to be posted to the island. He ordered all Greeks to be disarmed and as though this were not enough proceeded to arrest *prominent Greeks* and to *execute the Dragoman*. The distribution of several revolutionary tracts made him still more suspicious and he no longer believed the Archbishop's assurances. He wrote to the Sultan demanding the punishment of the rebels and their friends, but the Sultan at first refused to order such measures. Kutchuk Mehmed remained persistent until he received the Sultan's assent. Then, armed with the execution warrant, the governor *invited the priests to his Palace at Nicosia on the pretext* of their signing a "loyalty oath" [*"mesles et Lypres"*]. When, on the morning of 9 July 1821 the archbishop and bishops entered the Palace followed by other *Church dignitaries*, the governor ordered the gates to be closed and the Greeks to be chained. He then read them *their death sentences* and they were immediately executed in the main square of Nicosia. Afterwards Kutchuk ordered *the confiscation of Church property* and *the massacre of prominent Greeks* throughout all the towns of the island. More than 450 people perished; the only ones to escape managed to take refuge inside the French, English or Russian consulates and thence secretly leave the island.'[4]

---

[1] Nostradamus employs the double meanings of Cyprus and Kyprianos.
[2] Greek μέλας: black, dark. DGF.
[3] Greek λυπρός: wretched. DGF.
[4] HDCAE.

# Greek Independence, 1825–33.
# The Battle of Navarino, 1827

De l'Ambraxie[1] et du pays de Thrace,[2]
Peuple par mer, mal et secours Gaulois,
Perpétuelle en Provence la trace,
Avec vestiges de leurs coutumes et loix.

CIX,Q75

## Interpretation

From Arta to Thrace, the Greek people will be saved from misfortune
by France, by means of the sea. In Provence the reminders of this will
endure, along with traces of their costumes and laws.

## History

'In 1825 Ibrahim Pasha, son of Mohamed Ali, stamped out rebellions on
Kassos and Crete, then landed regular troops on the Peloponnese. From
1825 to 1827 he laid waste the region. Through the sack of Missolonghi
[1826], the *legendary* exodus from which revived *European Philhellenism*,
and the capture of the Acropolis, the Turks became masters of mainland
Greece and the rebellion seemed about to peter out.

In July 1827 Russia, England and *France* formed the Triple Alliance,
which undertook to mediate between rebel Greece and the Turkish
government, on the basis of an autonomous Greece under the overall
sovereignty of the Sultan, and which demanded an immediate truce
between both sides. The Turks' formal refusal to submit to the authority
of the Triple Alliance resulted in the naval *Battle of Navarino* [20 October
1827] in which the Turco-Egyptian fleet was annihilated.'

'Organization of the state: the national and liberal revolution of the
Greeks led to the formation of a monarchical state whose organization
was controlled by a foreign prince and government. King Otho, still a
minor, arrived on 25 January 1833 at Nauplia, provisional capital of the
new kingdom, which was composed of the Peloponnese, the Cyclades
and mainland Greece from *the demarcation line of* the *Gulf of Arta* to
Volos Bay in the north. He was accompanied by a Regency Council
under the Presidency of Count Armansperg.'[3]

'Military intervention in the Morea was accomplished without difficulty, agreement being reached with Mohamed Ali in November 1828.
Finally, the London Protocols established the borders of Greece. Russia
ratified these arrangements by the Treaty of Andrinopolis [a *Thracian*

town] on 14 September 1829. In February 1830, at the London conference, Greece was proclaimed independent.'⁴

[1] Ambracia: today Arta, a town in Epirus on the northern coast of a small gulf of the same name. DHB.
[2] District of the Ottoman Empire in 1827.
[3] HDGM.
[4] HDT.

---

# The End of the Ottoman Empire (1686–1829).
# The Capture of Buda by the Duke of Lorraine, 1686

Près de Sorbin[1] pour assaillir Ongrie.
L'héraut[2] de Brudes[3] les viendra advertir[4]
Chef Bizantin, Sallon[5] de Sclavonie[6]
A loy d'Arabes les viendra convertir.

CX,Q62

*Interpretation*

Near Serbia, in order to attack Hungary, the military leader will come to rage against [the Turks] at Buda; the Turkish chief having converted to Arab rule [territories] from Salonika to Russia.

*History*

'The Austro-Hungarian emperors had to deal with successive revolts by Bethlem-Gabor, Tekely and the Ragotskys. During these upheavals the *Turks* had invaded the greater part of the country. They were only finally *driven out* ["*advertir*"] in 1699, by the Peace of Carlowitz and the exploits of Prince Eugène, which led to the Peace of Passarowitz, 1718. The Hungarians thereafter remained loyal to the House of Austria.

Mohamed II took Constantinople [1453] and through this important conquest destroyed the Greek Empire [Salonika]. Turkey expanded under Selim I. Suliman II added parts of Europe – some of *Hungary*, Transylvania, *Slavonia*, Moldavia. The great war of 1682–99, which the Peace of Carlowitz ended, wrested almost all of Hungary from the Turks. The *Russians*, with whom they had been fighting since 1672, began to gain the upper hand. The war of 1790–92 took various Caucasian districts from the Turks. From 1809 to 1812 there was renewed warfare and the provinces between the Dnieper and the Danube were lost to *Russia* through the Peace of Bucharest. In 1819 Turkey lost the Ionian Islands; there followed in 1820–30 the loss of *Greece*, decisively liberated by the Battle of Navarino [1827], and the loss of part of Armenia, ceded to Russia in 1829; and under the Treaty of Andrinopolis [1829], Wallachia, Moldavia and Serbia also became free and under *Russian protection*.

*Buda*: capital of Hungary, occupied by the Turks from 1530 to 1686. *Recaptured in 1686 by the Duke of Lorraine* [*"héraut de Bude"*], it then remained under Austrian control.

After the Congress of Berlin [1878], a new problem arose in the Balkans. Austria, having become a Balkan power, was increasing her influence upon the Christians in those regions and simultaneously trying to gain Salonika, which led to furtive conflicts with Russia resulting in the First World War.'[7]

¹ Serbs or Sorabs, captive peoples who gave their name to Serbia. DHB.

² Public official who had the task of announcing a war, and whose person was sacrosanct.

³ Epenthesis and apocope: *Brudes* for *Bude* (Buda), the Hungarian capital.

⁴ Latin *adverso*: I rage against, punish. DLLB.

⁵ Epenthesis and paragoge: for *Salonica*, part of Roumelia (European Turkey at that time). DHB.

⁶ Slavonia owes its name to the Sarmatians. European Sarmatia, between the Vistula and the Tanais, is made up of all the countries that today form Poland and Russia. DHB.

⁷ DHB.

---

# Middle Eastern Problems, 1821–55. Greek Independence. The Massacres at Chios. The Crimean War, 1854–56

Dans les cyclades,¹ en perinthe² et larisse,³
Dedans Sparte⁴ font le Peloponnesse,⁵
Si grand famine, peste par faux coninsse⁶
Neuf mois tiendra et tout le cherronesse.⁷

CV,Q90

## Interpretation

In the Cyclades, Greece and the Morea there will be a great famine and a calamity as a result of false alliances, and the Crimea will be occupied for nine months [10 September 1855–June 1856].

## History

'In the *Morea*, Germanos, Archbishop of Patras, proclaimed the War of Independence [25 March 1821]; massacres of Greeks followed in Constantinople, and of Turks in Greece. On 12 January 1822 the Assembly of Greek Deputies declared Greek independence also. In April the infamous massacres of *Chios* took place and in May Joannina fell to the Turks. The Greeks waited in vain for help from the Tsar ["*faux coninsse*"], who remained faithful to the principles of the *Holy Alliance*. The Sultan was not slow to act, ordering Mohamed Ali to intervene in the Morea [February 1824], while Egyptian troops had already reconquered Crete [1822]. In 1825 Ibrahim, Mohamed Ali's son, recaptured *the main towns of the Morea*, but his policy of deportations to Egypt alienated French sympathies. The death of Alexander I and his replacement in December 1825 by Nicholas I, who favoured strong, direct methods, worried England. In March 1826 Nicholas gave the Turks an ultimatum, resulting in the Treaty of Akkerman, by which Russia obtained trading rights in all the seas of the Ottoman Empire. It was no longer simply a question of Greece. England, worried by this treaty, stepped in, but the three great powers, England, France and Russia, found their offer of mediation refused by the Sultan. The Allied Fleet attacked and destroyed the Turco-Egyptian navy at Navarino.[8] Finally the Protocols of London [November 1828 and March 1829] fixed the Greek borders. In February 1830, at the London conference, Greece was declared independent. . . .

New negotiations with Russia had broken down that winter, and in March 1854 France, England and Turkey signed an alliance; in June Austria and Turkey signed a treaty designed to get Austrian co-operation in driving the Russians from the Danube principalities. At the end of March 1854 English and French troops landed at Gallipoli [a Thracian town at the entrance of the Sea of Marmora], to proceed towards the Danube. But following the Russian evacuation it was resolved to carry the war into the *Crimea*. Sebastopol fell on 10 September 1855 and was to be evacuated by Anglo-French troops in June 1856 [nine months].'[9]

[1] Aegean archipelago, including Chios. AVL.
[2] Thracian town by the Sea of Marmora. AVL.
[3] Thessalian town. DHB.
[4] Morean town. DHB.
[5] Morea or Peloponnese, southern peninsula of Greece. DHB.
[6] Latin *connexus*: union, alliance. DLLB.
[7] The Chersonese of Tauris, i.e. the Crimea. DHB.
[8] Morean town.
[9] HDT.

# Weak Government in Italy and Spain, 1855.
## The Trap of Sebastopol, 1854–55

Peuple sans chef d'Espagne d'Italie,
Morts profligez dedans la Cheronese,[1]
Leur dict trahy par légère folie,
De sang nagez partout à la traverse.[2]

CIII,Q68

## Interpretation

The Spanish and Italian people will be deprived of a head of state just when Sebastopol is overwhelmed by death. The words [of the French] betray foolishness and blood will run everywhere over the fortifications.

## History

'From 1840 to 1875 there seemed to be little else in Spain except generals disputing power. During this time the generals were acting for Queen Isabella II, of whom even the kindest historians say that her natural benevolence was matched by an education so deplorable that one could scarcely wonder that *she completely lacked the capacity to govern*.'[3]

'In 1848 Sicily rose against the King of Naples and proclaimed its independence. Naples, Florence and Turin gave themselves constitutions. Rome called itself a republic. Parma and Modena *drove out their dukes*. The King of Sardinia headed these movements and defeated Austria on several occasions, but soon, weakened by his own supporters' quarrels, he was defeated at Novara [23 March 1849] and decided to *abdicate*.'[4]

'The London press, the cabinet and Prince Albert acclaimed the occupation of the Crimea and the attack on Sebastopol. It was a bold enterprise. Count Benedetti, French *chargé d'affaires* at Constantinople, wrote: "To throw 80,000 men and 200 guns upon an exposed shore, 700 leagues from a formidable fortress, was like stepping into the unknown. Nothing was known about either the terrain or the enemy's strength. Everything was at the whim of *chance* and accident [*légère folie*]."

The old *Chersonese* was only a grassy steppe and towns were few. Only Sebastopol had a large harbour, ill-protected on the land side, but with fortresses ["*traverse*"] on the Black Sea.

The Battle of Inkermann, so fiercely fought, cost the English 3000 men, the French 800, and the Russians more than 10,000 ["*de sang nagez partout*"]. It was a victory, but a hollow one, which proved to the Allies

how hazardous the expedition was. On 18 June 1855 the English marched
on the Great Redan [fortification] and the French on the Little Redan
and the Malakoff. Despite the soldiers' splendid bravery, the attack
failed because it had been so badly planned. . . . Pelissier sounded the
retreat. There were *so many dead* that a day's truce was called to bury
them.'[5]

---

[1] Sebastopol, the military port of the Crimea. Built in 1786 by Empress Catherine II
near the ruins of ancient Cherson. DHB.

[2] The fortifications were massive and steep. DL7V.

[3] HEFDP.

[4] DHB.

[5] LSEOA.

---

# The Fall of the Bourbons, 29 July 1830.
# King Louis-Philippe. The Tricolor

Le Roy Gaulois par la Celtique Dextre[1]
Voyant discorde de la Grand Monarchie
Sur les trois pars fera florir son sceptre,
Contre la cappe[2] de la Grande Hierarchie.

CII,Q69

*Interpretation*

The King of the French, because of the right wing and seeing the great
monarchy in discord, will make his sceptre flourish over the three parts
[of the flag] against the Capet hierarchy.

*History*

'The sovereign would henceforth rule by the will of the nation, the title
of King of France being replaced by that of *King of the French*. . . .

Only the bourgeoisie profited from the 1830 Revolution, for they were
Louis-Philippe's buttress, caught as he was between the hostility of the
masses whose illusions had been shattered and that of the *nobility* who
had remained almost completely loyal to the *Bourbon* family. . . .

Until 1835 the government was mainly concerned with fighting the
revolutionary, legitimist and republican groups. The legitimists were the
supports of the *Bourbons*. They recognized as *legitimate* king the Duke

of Bordeaux, in whose favour his grandfather Charles X had abdicated. They organized several absurd conspiracies, which were easily scotched.'[3]

'People of Paris, the deputies of France, presently reassembled in Paris, have asked me to fulfil here the duties of Lieutenant General of the Kingdom. Returning to the town of Paris, *I proudly bore the glorious colours* I have long worn and which you have now taken back. The chamber will sit and discuss the means by which to ensure the rule of law and the maintenance of the rights of the nation.'[4]

'The Prince was received at the Hôtel de Ville by General Dubourg, who thus addressed him: "Prince, the nation fondly sees you *wearing its colours*." '[5]

[1] Latin *dexter*, right. DLLB.
[2] Capet, the surname given to the King of France, is translated into Latin in the ancient chronicles by the word *Capatus*, referring to the regal cloak or cape. In time the surname was applied as a patronymic, and it is worth noting that it was the *ultra-royalist* right-wing authors who resurrected this ancient name. DL7V.
[3] HFAM.
[4] Proclamation by the Duke of Orleans, 1 August 1830. HFA.
[5] HFA.

---

# The Assassination of the Last of the Condés, 26 August 1830. The Second Empire Replaced by the Third Republic. The Château of St-Leu

De nuict dans lict supresme[1] estranglé,
Pour trop avoir seiourné blond esleu,
Par trois l'Empire subroge[2] exancle,[3]
A mort mettra carte, et paquet[4] ne leu.

CI,Q39

*Interpretation*

By night in his bed the last [Condé] will be strangled for having lived too long with a chosen blonde woman. The exhausted Empire will be replaced by the Third [Republic]. He will be put to death because of his will, with linen, at [St-] Leu.

*History*

'Louis-Henri-Joseph, Duke of Bourbon, Prince of Condé, the last of the Condés (1756–1830), lived with his small entourage at *St-Leu*, his only occupation being hunting. After the 1830 Revolution he quickly recognized his nephew as "King of the French". This weak, elderly man was completely *dominated by an Englishwoman*, Sophie Dawes, née Clarke, whose past was doubtful, and who had married one of the Prince's household, the Baron de Feuchères. She had cuckolded this loyal soldier for some time, which had been considered a scandal. Under her influence the Prince decided to draft *a will* by which he named the Duke of Aumale his sole beneficiary and which assured Baroness de Feuchères a legacy of 10 million, either in land or in cash. On 26 August 1830 the Prince *retired to bed* as usual at the Château of *St-Leu*. He was found hanged or rather attached to the hasp of the window by *two knotted handkerchiefs*. The circumstances seemed to discount suicide.'[5]

'He was found hanged in his apartment. It was then claimed, but without proof, that he had been *strangled* by his mistress, Mme de Feuchères. The family of Condé died out with him.'[6]

[1] Last: DL7V.
[2] Latin *subrogo:* I substitute. DLLB.
[3] Latin *exantlo*: I wear out, exhaust. DLLB.
[4] Several things strung or wrapped together – can refer to linen or leashes. DL7V.
[5] DL7V.
[6] DHB.

---

# Rebellion in the Rue St-Merri, 5 and 6 June 1832. The Bourbons Ousted by the Duke of Orleans

Par avarice,[1] par force et violence
Viendra vexer[2] les siens chef[3] d'Orléans
Près Sainct-Memire[4] assault et résistance,
Mort dans sa tente[5] diront qu'il dort léans.

CVIII,Q42

## Interpretation

Through greed, force and violence the Duke of Orleans will damage his interests. There will be an attack and resistance in the Rue St-Merri; having abandoned his cause [power] it will be said the King sleeps.

## History

'The President of the Council followed the same *energetic* internal policy he had determined upon. The legitimists were agitating in western

France, and troops had to crush *insurrection* there. The workers of Lyon
were disarmed after an appalling *riot*, and Grenoble too saw *bloodshed*.
There were conspiracies in Paris too, but Minister Perier did not waver
nor flinch in maintaining order. He dominated the Assembly, his colleagues and even the King himself.'[6]

'Rue *St-Merri* is famous in the history of Parisian revolution because
of *the fighting* that took place there after the funeral of General Lamarque.
*The resistance* lasted two days behind improvised barricades and claimed
many victims.'[7]

'A month after [22 July 1832], the death of Napoleon's son, the Duke
of Reichstadt, disposed of another formidable candidate for the *House of
Orleans*. Another pretender also failed: the *Duchess of Berry*[8] had started
a civil war in western France on behalf of *her son Henri V*. But the area
was full of troops, the movement was promptly put down, and the
Duchess, caught at Nantes on 7 November, was imprisoned at Blaye.'[9]

---

[1] Latin *avaritia*: greed, covetousness. DLLB.
[2] Latin *vexare*: stir up, shake, injure. DLLB.
[3] Latin *dux*: leader. DLLB.
[4] Possible typographical error, as the word *'memire'* is unknown.
[5] To retire into one's tent implies withdrawing, abandoning a party or cause. DL7V.
[6] HFVD.
[7] DL7V.
[8] Wife of Charles X, mother of the Duke of Bordeaux.
[9] HFVD.

---

# The Revolutions of 1830 and 1848.
# The Abdications of Charles X and Louis-Philippe

Deux révolts faits du malin falcigère[1]
De règne et siècles fait permutation[2]
Le mobil[3] signe[4] à son endroit s'ingère
Aux deux esgaux et d'inclination.[5]

CI,Q54

*Interpretation*

Two revolutions, inspired by the death-dealing spirit of evil, will completely change power and its secular laws: the red emblem of the flag
will install itself on the right and will lead to the weakening of two
[kings] in the same way.

## History

'The theories of Robert Owen in England and Fourier in France spawned dangerous notions of Utopia which themselves sparked off in 1830 and 1848 terrible *civil strife*. Men who were putting the whole of society and its laws and religion on trial were proposing to *overthrow it utterly*.'[6]

Charles X and the 1830 Revolution: 'On 26 July 1830 decrees were issued suppressing the freedom of the press, annulling the recent elections and creating a new electoral system. This represented a coup d'état against civil liberties, contrary to the conditions of the charter which had returned the Bourbons to the throne *of their ancestors*. Paris replied to the court's provocation by *the three days* [27–29 July] 1830. Charles X had lost. When *he abdicated in favour of his grandson* the Duke of Bordeaux and further revolution threatened it was already too late – 6000 men were *dead* or wounded. By taking back the *flag of 1789*, France also seemed to regain possession of liberties the Revolution had promised but not granted.'[6]

Louis-Philippe and the 1848 Revolution: 'Heated discussion in the Chamber of Deputies concerning the law of assembly. . . . The opposition mounted a vote of censure against the minister, and there was a new *revolution lasting three days. Abdication by the King in favour of his grandson*. The proposal that the Duchess of Orleans be Regent led to stormy scenes in the chamber but did not prevent *the fall of the dynasty* on 24 February. *A bloody battle* in front of the Palais-Royal.'[7]

[1] Latin *falciger*: one who carries a scythe. DLLB. Symbol of death.
[2] Latin *permutatio*: complete change, reversal, revolution. DLLB.
[3] Latin *mobilis*: capable of displacement. DLLB.
[4] Latin *signum*: red flag displayed as signal to attack. DLLB.
[5] Latin *inclino*: I abase, bring low, weaken. DLLB.
[6] HFVD.
[7] CUCD.

---

## The Junior Branch in Power, 1830. The Upheavals of 23 February. The Fall of Louis-Philippe, 24 February 1848

Le deffaillant[1] en habit de bourgeois,
Viendra tenter[2] le Roy de son offense:
Quinze soldats la plupart Ustagois,[3]
Vie dernière et chef de sa chevance.[4]

CIV,Q64

## Interpretation

The representative of the younger branch, dressed as a bourgeois, will occupy the kingdom through his offence: fifteen soldiers, the majority of the National Guard, will do what they can so that he will live for the last time as bourgeois leader.

## History

'La Fayette declared, presenting the Duke of Orleans to the people at the Hôtel de Ville: "This is the best of Republics." The private virtues of the Prince, his fine family, his previous links with the heads of the liberal party, carefully reawakened memories of Jemmapes and Valmy, *his bourgeois life style*, all gave good cause for encouragement. Louis-Philippe of Orleans, head of *the junior branch* of the Bourbons, was proclaimed king on 9 August. . . . Suppression of the article recognizing Catholicism as the official religion of the state, and of all the peerages created by *Charles X*.'[5]

'A law instituted a National Guard which should "defend the constitutional monarchy". Since the National Guard had *to equip itself at its own expense*, the Guard consisted only of affluent *bourgeois*. This regime favoured *the bourgeoisie* exclusively.'

On the night of 22 February 1848 barricades were erected. On the twenty-third the attitude of the *National Guard*, which prevented the cavalry from charging the demonstrators in the Place des Victoires, alarmed Louis-Philippe who decided to split with Guizot. But that same evening a bloody incident revived the struggle: a group of demonstrators arrived on the Boulevard des Capucines and fired on the troops. The soldiers fired back at point-blank range. *Fifteen* were killed and fifty more injured. On the morning of the twenty-fourth Paris was bristling with barricades, and shouts of "Long Live the Republic!" were heard everywhere.

---

[1] Lack or end (of a line). The senior branch *lacking*, the junior one would occupy the throne.

[2] Latin *teneo*: I hold, occupy, possess, control. DLLB.

[3] Seigneurial right paid for one's house. DL7V.

[4] Goods, fortune, what one possesses or acquires. DL7V.

[5] HFVD.

# The Accidental Death of Louis-Philippe's Eldest Son, 13 July 1842

L'aisné Royal sur coursier[1] voltigeant,
Picquer[2] viendra si rudement courir:
Gueule lipée,[3] pied dans l'estrein pleignant[4]
Trainé tiré, horriblement mourir.

CVII,Q38

*Interpretation*

The King's eldest son, on a runaway horse, will fall suddenly head-first in its rush, the horse's mouth being injured on the lip, with the rider's foot caught, groaning, dragged and pulled, he will die horribly.

*History*

'Ferdinand-Philippe-Louis-Charles-Henri-Rose of Orleans was the *eldest* son of Louis-Philippe and Marie-Aurélie of Bourbon-Sicily, and born in Palermo on 3 September 1810. In July 1842 he was about to leave to inspect the troops at St-Omer. He went to Neuilly to say goodbye to his father and *his horses bolted* on the road; he was flung out of the carriage and, *falling backwards on to the ground he broke his skull.*'[5]

[1] Poetic name for horse or thoroughbred. DL7V.
[2] *Piquer (une tête)*: to dive or fall headfirst. DL7V.
[3] *Lippe: lèvre* (lip). DAFL.
[4] To utter groans, cries. DL7V.
[5] DHCD.

---

# The Seven Years' Conquest of Algeria, 1840–47. The February Revolution, 1848

Sept ans sera PHILIP, fortune[1] prospère,
Rabaissera des BARBARES[2] l'effort:
Puis son midy perplex, rebours[3] affaire,
Jeune ogmion[4] abysmera son fort.

CIX,Q89

*Interpretation*

Fortune will smile on Louis-Philippe for seven years, and he will cut down the Barbarian [Algerian] forces, but will then be in trouble at noon because of a stubborn horse, and an eloquent young speaker will bring on his downfall.

## History

'The population of Algeria was composed of Algerians and *Berbers*. Since the sixteenth century the Algerian corsairs had terrorized merchant shipping in the Mediterranean. The fall of Charles X almost cost France Algeria. Louis-Philippe thought so little of conquest that he recalled all the French troops from Algeria except for one division of 8000 men. The idea was to limit France to a partial occupation. It was the native inhabitants who forced the French hand. By their incessant attacks they turned a partial occupation into a full-scale one and finally, *from 1840 on*, after ten years of hesitation, into a complete conquest. At the end of 1847, tracked down by eight columns and expelled from Morocco where he had gone a second time for asylum, Abd-el-Kader surrendered [23 December]. His submission ended the war. Charles X had retained the initiative; the conquest of Algeria remains the main *claim to fame* of the July monarchy. . . .

The round of banquets surprisingly culminated in the February 1848 Revolution. *Disconcerted* and vacillating, Louis-Philippe decided to recall the troops. At *noon* the King abdicated. His eldest son the Duke of Orleans, a very popular prince, had been killed at Neuilly while trying to jump out of *his carriage*. Louis-Philippe therefore abdicated in favour of his grandson the Count of Paris, a child of ten. The rebels surrounded the chamber, shouting for the King's overthrow. Ledru-Rollin and *Lamartine* proposed a provisional government, which was installed by popular acclaim. The democratic Republic succeeded the bourgeois monarchy of Louis-Philippe. On the steps of the Hôtel de Ville *Lamartine*, seated on a chair, made the speech in which he *eloquently* opposed the tricolor which had circled the globe to the red flag which had only gone round the Champs de Mars.'[5]

---

[1] Latin *fortuna*: fate, destiny, chance. DLLB

[2] Barbary: North African region including Tripoli, Tunis, *Algiers*, Morocco. DHB.

[3] *cheval rebours*: equestrian term denoting an erratic or obstinate steed apt to *bolt*. DL7V.

[4] God of *eloquence* and poetry revered by the Gauls. DHB.

[5] HFAM.

# Napoleon III's Accession to Power.
# The Empire Replaced by the Third Republic

De terre faible et pauvre parentele[1]
Par bout et paix parviendra dans l'Empire
Longtemps regner une jeune femelle[2]
Qu'oncques en regne n'en survint un si pire.

CIII,Q28

## Interpretation

Originating from a weak country [Corsica] and poor birth, [the country] at the end of its tether and wanting peace, he will succeed to the Empire. He will then rule a young republic. Such a disastrous person never succeeded to power.

## History

'A senate in council proposed the re-establishment of the Empire as personified by Louis-Napoleon Bonaparte, to be *hereditary* in relation to his direct adopted successors. Before his coronation Napoleon III stated: "The Empire means *Peace!*" – a happy formula had it been followed.'[3]

'Just like the bourgeoisie, the peasantry wanted a government which would ensure respect for property and internal peace. The Second Empire was to sweep away such views.

By virtue of the powers vested in him by the plebiscite Louis-Napoleon drafted a constitution on the lines of the *Constitution of Year VIII*. This was promulgated on 14 January 1852.'[4]

'For the first time for four centuries, *France actually shrank*. In 1815 she had at least more or less retained the frontiers established by the old monarchy. By the Treaty of Frankfurt on 10 May 1871 she lost Alsace-Lorraine.'[5]

[1] Parents as a group, parentage. DL7V.
[2] Allusion to Marianne, symbol of the Republic.
[3] HFVD.
[4] HFAM.
[5] HFVD.

# The Orsini Affair, 14 January 1858

Un chef Celtique dans les conflict blessé
Auprès de cave[1] voyant siens mort abbattre:
De sang et playes et d'ennemis pressé,
Et secourus par incogneux de quatre.

CV,QIO

## Interpretation

A French leader wounded in the conflict, seeing death overcome his
people near the theatre, hard pressed by his enemies amid the blood and
wounded, will be aided by the crowd [escaping] the four [bombs].

## History

'On Thursday 14 January 1858 the Emperor and Empress were due to
attend the Opéra. At 8.30 p.m. their landau arrived at the Rue le
Pelletier. There were three loud explosions, and cries of terror mingled
with agonized screams from soldiers, police and onlookers lying on the
ground. Napoleon left his carriage, his hat in tatters and his nose grazed,
and the Empress descended, her white dress and cape spattered with
*blood*. There were 156 *wounded*, eight of whom died.

Orsini had some mediocre accomplices – Simon Bernard, a neurotic
surgeon who provided the explosives; Pieri, an experienced criminal; and
two young men of good family, Gomez and Rudio. On 14 January their
preparations were complete. Of the *four bombs* they carried, three were
thrown.'[2]

[1] Latin *cavea*: part of a theatre or amphitheatre where the spectators sat; by extension,
theatre. DLLB.
[2] LSEOA.

---

# The Attempted Assassination of Napoleon III.
# The Congress of Paris, 25 February 1856.

Le nepveu grand par force prouvera
Le pache[1] fait du coeur pusillanime[2]
Ferrare[3] et Ast[4] le Duc[5] esprouvera,
Par lors qu'au soir sera le pantomime.[6]

CIV,Q73

## Interpretation

The great nephew will show off his strength, through a peace too prudently concluded, he who comes from Piedmont and the borderlands will test the sovereign the evening the play is presented.

## History

'*Peace* was to be arranged by a congress reunited in Paris. Talks began on 25 February 1856. On 30 March the peace was signed, which, though ending a hazardous enterprise, did not settle the Middle Eastern question so much as shelve it. However, France did derive something from it: *the valour of her soldiers* restored her to a leading place among European powers. Moreover, *Napoleon III's own situation was somewhat relieved.* Summoned to finish a war, *the Congress of Paris paved the way for another one.* It took only three years for this to break out. . . .

On 14 January 1858 the Emperor and Empress were due to attend the Opera. At 8.30 p.m. their landau arrived at the Rue le Pelletier. There were three loud explosions.

Felice Orsini had plotted the liberation of his country since his earliest youth. He stirred up the Italian *border country* against the Austrians, and returned to recruit accomplices with whom to murder Napoleon III. . . . While his trial was going on the Empire was enduring both internal and foreign crises. When on 16 January Napoleon received at the Tuileries numerous politicians who had come to congratulate him on his narrow escape, the pale and grave Emperor had to listen to harangues from some of them. Morny abandoned traditional courtesies and grew indignant: "The people want to know why neighbouring friendly governments are powerless to destroy actual laboratories of assassins." This was directed at Belgium, *Piedmont* and especially England, for offering asylum to all the exiles, leaving them free to conspire at will.'[7]

[1] Latin *pax, pacis*: peace. DLLB.
[2] Prudence or timidity stopping just short of cowardice. DL7V.
[3] Town on the Italian borders.
[4] Asti: town in Piedmont.
[5] Guide, prince, sovereign. DLLB.
[6] Theatrical representation. DL7V.
[7] LSEOA.

## Napoleon III near Buffalora, 3 June 1859.
## The Entry of Napoleon III and Victor Emmanuel
## into Milan, 6 June 1859. The Peace of Villafranca,
## 9 June 1859. The Dispersal of the Holy Alliance
## (Russia, Austria, Prussia, France and England)

Apparoistra auprès de Buffalore,
L'hault[1] et procere[2] entré dedans Milan,
L'Abbé[3] de Foix[4] avec ceux de Sainct Morre,[5]
Ferront la forbe[6] habillez en vilain.[7]

CVIII,QI2

### Interpretation

The Emperor will appear near Buffalora, the noble and first personage
[King of Italy] will make his entry into Milan, but the owner of Phoebus[8]
[Napoleon III] and those of the Holy Alliance will play a shameful trick.

### History

'The Holy Alliance: Tsar Alexander, the Emperor of Austria and the
King of Prussia signed the pact first, on 26 September 1815. Louis XVIII
and the Prince Regent of England followed suit.'[9]

'Napoleon, ensconced in an inn at San Martino, waited before starting
the battle to know that MacMahon had reached Magenta. On the stroke
of noon he heard the general's cannons in *the Buffalora direction*.'[10]

'The Battle of Magenta had opened up the whole of Lombardy for the
Allies, and the French army *entered Milan* to acclamation and rejoicing.
The Emperor Napoleon III and King Victor Emmanuel were on *horse-
back* at the head of the victorious troops.'[9]

'The Austrians continued retreating behind the Adigea and Prussia
hastened to mobilize. Tsar Alexander sent word to the Empress to urge
her to make peace quickly or be attacked on the Rhine. As for England,
her intervention could not be relied upon in the event of conflict with
Prussia so the Emperor decided to go directly to his adversary Franz-
Josef. He was going *to betray* Cavour. . . . Napoleon III went ahead to
Villafranca to meet the *young Emperor*. . . . When Napoleon in his turn
passed through *Milan*, the Piedmontese capital gave him a frosty reception. Italy never forgave him for *betraying* her hopes and on his return
to France he found public opinion surprised and strained. After the
much-vaunted victories, abandoning Venice was like sounding the
*retreat*.'[10]

<sup>1</sup> Latin *altus*: noble, elevated. DLLB.
<sup>2</sup> Latin *proceres*: the first citizens (by birth and rank). DLLB.
<sup>3</sup> Latin *abbas*: derived from Syrian *abba*, father. DL7V
<sup>4</sup> Gaston III, Comte de Foix, was nicknamed *Phoebus*. The name was perpetuated by several other members of the family. DL7V.
<sup>5</sup> Latin *mos*, *moris*: law, rule. *Pacis impossere morem*: to decide upon peace (Virgil). DLLB.
<sup>6</sup> Trickery. DAFL.
<sup>7</sup> Synonym: ugly, shameful, niggardly. DL7V.
<sup>8</sup> 'Napoleon III, mounted on his chestnut, *Phoebus*. . . .' LSEOA.
<sup>9</sup> HFAM.
<sup>10</sup> LSEOA.

---

## The Annexation of the Papal States, 1870. Victor Emmanuel and Clotilde of Savoy. The French at Turin and Novara, 1859

L'oeil¹ de Ravenne² sera destitué
Quand à ses pieds les aisles failliront:
Les deux de Bresse³ auront constitué,⁴
Turin, Versel⁵ que Gaulois fouleront.

CI,Q6

### Interpretation

The Pope's temporal power will be removed when the wings [of the eagle, Napoleon III] fall at his feet, when the two of Savoy [Victor Emmanuel II and his daughter Clotilde of Savoy] give [Italy] a constitution and when the French throng through Turin and Novara.

### History

'Victor Emmanuel II energetically defended the rights of the state against the Church, and reinforced his friendship with the Imperial French government by marrying his daughter Clotilde of Savoy to Prince Napoleon, the son of Napoleon III and Empress Eugénie. This friendship was maintained by France during the war against Austria. By this alliance he gained first Lombardy [June 1859], then Tuscany, Parma, Modena and the Romagna. The populations of the kingdom of Naples and *the Papal States* through universal suffrage voted for him by referendum and he became King of Italy ["*auront constitué*"] with his capital at Florence.

In September 1870 he entered Rome, which then became the capital of
the kingdom of Italy.'[6]

'The Austrian Field-Marshal Giulay crossed the Ticino and marched
upon *Turin* at the rate of 6 km a day. Near the Piedmontese capital he
halted to fall back upon Mortara, which presented an admirable opportunity for Napoleon to concentrate his forces and join up with the
Piedmontese. On 3 June *the French quartered* on a rather too dispersed
triangle between Turbigo, Trecato and *Novara*. They did not know
where the Austrians were: only by day was it certain that the latter had
bivouacked around Magenta.'[7]

---

[1] Nostradamus regularly uses *eye* or *eyes* to mean 'power'.

[2] Pepin the Short, son of Charlemagne, had originally made the Pope a gift of these
states centred upon the Ravenna area, and this formed the basis of the papal territories
which disappeared only in 1870. HFAM.

[3] Bresse was divided into small districts; the main one, Baugé, was subsumed into
Savoy in 1292. DHB.

[4] To give a constitution or organization. DL7V.

[5] Verceil: fortress town of Upper Italy, in the ancient Sardinian states (Novara). DHB.

[6] DHB.

[7] LSEOA.

---

# The Tower of Solferino, 24 June 1859.
# Savoy Returns to France. The Treaty of Turin, 1860.
# The Principle of Nationalities

> Mars eslevé à son plus haut beffroy,[1]
> Fera retraire[2] les Allobrox[3] de France:
> La gent Lombarde fera si grand effroy,
> A ceux de l'Aigle compris[4] sous la Balance.[5]

> CV,Q42

## Interpretation

The war will reach its climax with the Tower [of Solferino] and will force
Savoy to return to France. Lombardy will be greatly afraid because of
the Emperor's party and will be taken on a pretext of law.

## History

'The Lombard capital, where Bonaparte was still remembered by the
older folk, was decked out with French and Italian flags. From the

clocktower of the Castiglione church, his fieldglasses to his eyes, Napoleon III was intent upon cutting the enemy in two, and he issued orders for a cent.al attack. The *Tower* of Solferino[6] rose square and red atop a rocky crag. The battle went on for hours, *bitterly contested*. At the centre were the steep *heights* of Solferino, which after *furious fighting* were finally captured, along with the cemetery and the Tower itself.

*The horrible carnage* was *even worse* than that of Montebello and Magenta, when Napoleon III visited the battle area the next day.'[7]

'After numerous vicissitudes, Savoy was ceded to France in 1860 by the King of Sardinia – which was immediately approved by the *universal suffrage* of the inhabitants.'[8]

There appeared in Paris an anonymous pamphlet written by Councillor of State la Guéronnière and supervised by the Emperor himself. The work was entitled *Napoleon III and Italy* and boldly declared his views and intentions. It celebrated the *theory of nationalities* and ended with the hope of a federated Italy from which all foreign influences were excluded.

---

[1] From Middle High German *becvrit*: defensive tower. Watchtower in which troops are placed for surveillance. DL7V.

[2] Latin *retraho*: I force to come back. DLLB.

[3] Name that reappeared with the Revolution: the Allobrogian *départements* were those of Savoy. DL7V.

[4] Latin *comprehendo*: I take. DLLB.

[5] Political, implying balance or stability of the states in relation to alliances and territory. DL7V.

[6] Solferino: ruins of an old castle with a *tower*. DL7V.

[7] LSEOA.

[8] DHB.

---

# Victor Emmanuel II, King of Italy, 1860. Florence the Capital of Italy

Du vray rameau[1] des fleurs de lys yssu,
Mis et logé héritier d'Hetrurie:[2]
Son sang antique de longue main tyssu[3]
Fera Florence florir en l'armoirie.

CV,Q39

## Interpretation

Born from the true line of the fleurs de lis, situated and living in Etruria, his ancient blood long woven will make his coat of arms flourish in Florence.

## History

'Victor Emmanuel II, King of Italy [1820–78] was directly descended from Charles Emmanuel II [1634–75], Duke of Savoy and Piedmont, whose mother was Christine of France, daughter of Henri IV, and from her son Thomas-François, who married Marie de *Bourbon*, daughter of Charles, Comte de Soisson.'[4]

'Faced with Austrian intervention, Victor Emmanuel's father, Charles-Albert [1789–1849], was forced to stand down on 21 March 1821. Exiled in *Tuscany*, he was disgraced, but finally succeeded to the throne in 1831 since there was no direct *heir*, and effected some useful reforms. In 1817 he married Marie-Thérèse of Tuscany.'[5]

'Victor Emmanuel II was supported by France in the war against Austria, and through this alliance he gained first Lombardy [June 1859], then *Tuscany*, Parma, Modena and the Romagna. The populations of the kingdom of Naples and the Papal States [other than Rome], voted for him by referendum and he became *King of Italy* with *his capital at Florence*. He enjoyed great popularity during his reign, and adhered to the rules of parliamentary government established in Piedmont under Charles-Albert.'[6]

[1] The Bourbon arms were three fleurs de lis.
[2] Tuscany: Tuscia and Etruria to the ancients. DHB.
[3] Past participle of the verb *tistre* (*tisser*). DL7V.
[4] CUCD.
[5] DHB.
[6] DHB.

---

# Victor Emmanuel II and Cavour.
# Italian Unity, 1859–61. Victor Emmanuel II in Florence

Le successeur de la Duché viendra,
Beaucoup plus oultre que la mer de Toscane,
Gauloise branche la Florence tiendra[1]
Dans son giron d'accord nautique Rane.[2]

CV,Q3

## Interpretation

The successor to the duchy of Tuscany will occupy much more than the Tuscan coastline. A French branch will install itself at Florence with the consent of him whom England will have had in her lap.

*History*

'Instead of withdrawing behind his own borders and renouncing all ambition, Victor Emmanuel II, who *succeeded* the defeated Charles-Albert, began preparing for the return of Piedmontese troops to the plain of Lombardy.

Camillo Cavour had been at Victor Emmanuel's side since 1833. He was a Piedmontese who had lived for some time in *London*, Paris and Geneva. After an initial stay in Paris in 1835, he went to London where he conceived considerable admiration for the skill of the English in dealing with the problems of an industrial society, for their good sense and pragmatism.

In two years, from March 1859 to June 1861, a new state emerged in Europe – far beyond the Sea of Tuscany. It covered an area of 259,320 sq km and contained 24,770,000 inhabitants.'[3]

[1] For Victor Emmanuel's French origins and Florence as capital city, cf. cv,Q39.
[2] Latin *rana*: frog. DLLB. Frogs symbolize all the nations in history. DL7V.
[3] HISR.

---

# The Exceptional Pontificate of Pius IX, 1846–78. The Annexation of Bologna by Victor Emmanuel II, 1859

Dedans Bologne voudra laver ses fautes
Il ne pourra au temple[1] du Soleil:[2]
Il volera[3] faisant choses si hautes,
En hiérarchie n'en fut onq un pareil.

CVIII,Q53

*Interpretation*

He will want to make up for his errors in Bologna which he will not be able to retain for the Church because of the Bourbon [Victor Emmanuel II]. He will act alone to achieve such important things that there will never be such a pope in the Catholic hierarchy.

*History*

'In 1848 there was a nationalistic cry for war against Austria. Sardinia and Piedmont, as well as the occupied provinces of Venice and Lombardy, took up arms. Pius IX refused to wage war on Austria and thus betrayed the popular movement [*"ses fautes"*]. His minister Rossi was assassinated on 15 November 1848, the Quirinal was attacked and the Swiss Guard was disarmed. . . . Between 1857 and 1863 the Pope made journeys through his states including Bologna. Only the presence of the French expeditionary force maintained his temporal sovereignty. In 1860 the conflict with Piedmont began by the occupation of the north of the Papal States [Bologna]. The Pope excommunicated him, and Antonelli protested against the title of King of Italy assumed by Victor Emmanuel [*"le Soleil"*] on 26 February 1861.'[4]

'In 1859 the town and province of Bologna rejected papal authority and recognized the King of Sardinia, Victor Emmanuel. Pius IX *reserved* [*"volera"*] all religious issues for himself and was very active in settling them. *Three great acts* [*"choses si hautes"*] distinguished his papacy: the definition of the Immaculate Conception [December 1854]; the publication of the Encyclical Quanta Cura [December 1864], and its appendix known as the Syllabus. In 1869 the first ecumenical council held since the Council of Trent (1545–63) opened at the Vatican, during which, on 18 July 1870, Papal Infallibility was asserted. He died in 1878, and the news of his death aroused worldwide expressions of respect and veneration.'[5] In fact, a nonpareil.

[1] Poetic usage – the Catholic Church. DL7V.
[2] Reference to Victor-Emmanuel's descent from the Bourbons. Cf. cv,Q39.
[3] Fly with his own wings, act of his own accord. DL7V.
[4] DDP.
[5] DHB.

---

# The Ems Telegram, 13 July 1870
# From Bazaine at Metz,
# 18 August, to the Surrender, 27 October 1870

Le grand conflit qu'on appreste à Nancy,
L'Aémathien[1] dira tout je soubmets:
L'Ile Britanne par vin, sel en solcy,
Hem.[2] mi.[3] deux Phi.[4] longtemps ne tiendra Metz.

CX,Q7

*Interpretation*

The great war being prepared in Lorraine will say to the King: I surrender all, England will only be concerned for her trade; after the Ems dispatch, Metz will not hold out for long, despite twice 500,000 [soldiers].

## History

'King William I was taking the waters at Ems. Thanks to mutual concessions the King had declared himself wholeheartedly in favour of [Leopold
of Hohenzollern's] renunciation. Once again peace seemed assured. At
the same time Bismarck in Berlin was coolly *preparing* the catastrophe.
He received the King's telegram, which told him of the incidents of the
day, up to the dispatch of aides-de-camp to Benedetti. The text, doctored
by Bismarck, was immediately relayed to Prussian diplomats abroad.
Bismarck's calculations were correct; there was a furious German outcry
against France. On 19 July the official declaration of war was made in
Berlin. . . .

Having first comprised a single army under the sole command of
Napoleon III, the 200,000 men were split into two parts, the Alsace
army (67,000) and the *Lorraine* army (130,000) under Bazaine. . . .

The defeat of Froeschwiller hastened the loss of Alsace. MacMahon's
disorganized army recrossed the Vosges and fell back upon *Nancy*. The
same day as the Battle of Froeschwiller, the 1st German Army entered
*Lorraine* and defeated General Frossard's force at Forbach. Following
this double defeat, Bazaine, the commander-in-chief, led the army back
to *Metz*. . . .

Apart from Bazaine's army besieged inside *Metz*, France had 95,000
regular soldiers scattered between Paris and the provinces. On 19 September the Germans succeeding in surrounding Paris. Trochu had more
than 500,000 men with which to defend the city. In the provinces
Gambetta rallied troops with amazing speed and in several months he
had *600,000 men* in the field. These improvised armies, like the Paris
militia, were poor. Most of the German troops were static, at Paris and
*Metz*. Bazaine's stupid and criminal behaviour destroyed the last chance
of French success. On 27 October he surrendered Metz.

On 18 January 1871, in Versailles, German unity came about. The
South German princes joined the Federation, which received the title of
the German *Empire*.

France lost Alsace, except for Belfort, and north Lorraine including
*Metz*.'[5]

'British trade abroad outstripped that of all other countries. In *1872*
it exceeded 547 million pounds, more than all French, German and
Italian commerce put together.'[6]

[1] Macedonia was divided into numerous provinces or small counties: *Aemathia*, the cradle and centre of the monarchy, often referred to the whole territory. Philip II *reconquered the former provinces*, added new ones, and held all Greece under his sway. Alexander met with success but his Empire was dispersed after his death. DHB. Nostradamus establishes here a parallel between Macedonian and German history.

[2] Hems: ancient name for Ems. DL7V.

[3] Abbreviation of Latin word *missio*: act of dispatching, missive. DLLB.

[4] Twenty-first letter of the Greek alphabet. Numerically *Phi* = 500,000. DGF.

[5] HFAM.

[6] HRU.

---

## Gambetta's Departure by Balloon, 1870.<br>The Siege of Paris and its Surrender

La république de la grande cité,<br>
A grand rigueur[1] ne voudra consentir:<br>
Roy[2] sortir hors par trompette[3] cité,<br>
L'eschelle au mur, la cité repentir.

CIII,Q50

### Interpretation

The republic of Paris will not want to consent to the necessary austerity; the head of government will leave the city in great style, the city will be besieged and rue it.

### History

'A government of national defence was constituted, composed of eleven Parisian deputies, among whom was Gambetta. On 19 September 1870 the Germans completed the *investment of Paris*. Paris became the focus of the national defence effort and the next five months saw attempts from the provinces *to raise the siege*. There were hardly 25,000 men left in the provinces, and resistance seemed impossible, but while the government remained inside Paris Gambetta *escaped by balloon* to Tours to organize defence measures. He was the guiding light of the nation's defence.

Paris was doubly threatened, by famine and by revolution. Already on 31 October the national guards at Belleville had tried to topple the government, and there was a further insurrection on 22 January. Bismarck knew of this and when Jules Fabre came to Versailles to plead for an armistice so that Paris might revictual, the former demanded complete *capitulation*, disarmament of the fighting men, occupation of all the forts, and a 200 million franc payment. On 28 January these terms had to be accepted: *the fall of Paris* and the Versailles armistice marked the end of the war. [4]

[1] Extreme severity, rigour, austerity. DL7V.
[2] Latin *rego*: I govern. (DLLB). One who governs.
[3] Sound the trumpet, do something with verve, style. Reference to Roman triumphs. DL7V.
[4] HFAM.

---

## Garibaldi's Strength and His Wretched End

Le fort Nicene[1] ne sera combattu,
Vaincu sera par rutilant metal:
Son faict sera un long temps débatu,
Aux citadins[2] estrange[3] espouvantal.[4]

CVII,QI9

*Interpretation*

The powerful Nicean victor will not be defeated in battle but by money. His deeds will for a long time be cause for debate; this foreigner will strike terror among the bourgeoisie.

*History*

'Revolutionary Europe in the nineteenth century: the field was open for this young man from *Nice* ["*Nicene*"], Garibaldi, who dreamed of adventure, socialism and freedom. Garibaldi would have a hand in European affairs, and intransigently he pursued his policy, formed his army, conducted his campaigns and imposed his presence on the European scene.

The conservative [bourgeois] deputies continued to oppose him. It was a hate composed of a *fear and horror* of revolution, subversion and socialism.

"None of the European powers rose to defend France, which has so often embraced the cause of Europe (cheers from the left). Not a king, nor a state, nobody! Except *one* man. (Wry smiles on the right, cheers from the left.) The powers did not intervene, but one man did intervene and *this man is a power* ['*le fort Nicene*']. He came and *fought*. I do not wish to wound anyone but I speak only the truth in stating that *he alone* of all the generals who fought for France, *was never defeated.*" This tirade from Victor Hugo provoked an indescribable uproar. Leaping upon their benches, *the deputies of the right* shook their fists at him. . . .

In 1873 Garibaldi published a third novel, *The Thousand*, which met with only scant success. So he had to resign himself to selling the yacht his English admirers had given him, receiving a mere 80,000 lire for it. He entrusted this money to his ex-comrade in arms Antonio Bo, so that he could bank it in Genoa, but his old friend chose to run off to America with the *little nest egg* ["*rutilant metal*"]. The Italian newspapers got wind of his problems and published emotional articles headed: "Garibaldi in deep distress", and "Italians, help Garibaldi!". One special correspondent painted a picture of the old condottiere: "Every morning, sometimes using a stick and sometimes on his crutches, painfully pushing a barrow full of melons for which he might get at most five lire for the lot." "[5]

[1] Nicean: Greek mythology; name given to certain deities regarded as guaranteeing victory. DL7V. Nostradamus puns on 'victor' and 'born in Nice'.
[2] Strictly speaking, *bourgeois* referred not to all the inhabitants of a 'burgh' or town but to those involved in the administration and leadership of a *city*. DL7V.
[3] Nice was not French in 1804, Garibaldi's year of birth, and only became so by the Treaty of Turin in 1860.
[4] Symbolic: object inspiring vain terrors. DL7V.
[5] GP and MR.

---

## Garibaldi and the Thousand. The Conquest of Sicily and Naples, 1860. The Naples Campaign. Savoy's Cession to France, 1860

> De Languedoc, et Guienne plus de dix
> Mille voudront les Alpes repasser:
> Grans Allobroges[1] marcher contre Brundis[2]
> Aquin[3] et Bresse[4] les viendront recasser.[5]

CVII,Q31

*Interpretation*

With more than ten, coming from Languedoc and Guyenne, the Thousand would like to return, into Italy. The Duke of Savoy will march against the inhabitants of southern Italy [Brindisi]. They will come to recover Savoy and Naples.

## History

'Victor Emmanuel II was supported by France in the war against Austria. To this alliance he owed first Lombardy [June 1859], then Tuscany, Parma, Modena and the Romagna, which he annexed, ceding Nice and *Savoy* to France. After Garibaldi's expedition to Sicily and southern Italy [Aquina and Brindisi] in 1860, which he first secretly encouraged and then openly supported, the populations of the kingdom of Naples [Aquina] and the Papal States [except for Rome itself] by universal suffrage declared for him [*"recasser"*] and he became King of Italy.'[6]

'*The Thousand.* Since 1859 the kingdom of *Naples* had been troubled. Liberal ideas gained ground and led to the insurrection which broke out in Palermo on 3 April 1860. It was the opportunity Garibaldi was waiting for. The small army he reunited at Genoa [*"les Alpes"*] on 5 May 1860 was composed of *1085* men. The whole of Italy was represented, and various foreigners also joined; among the *French* were: Ulric de Fontvielle,[7] Cluseret,[8] Maxime du Camp,[9] Lockroy,[10] Henri Fouquier,[11] and de Flotte, commanding a French unit [*"more than ten"*]. He landed at Marsala with *1015* men. After three days of fighting the *Neapolitans* retreated. Garibaldi beat them again at Milazzo. Messina then capitulated. He reached Salerno, then Naples. At that moment the Piedmontese government [Victor Emmanuel, Duke of Savoy], which had secretly helped Garibaldi, intervened and began the military and diplomatic campaign which led to the annexation of Naples.'[12]

[1] Tribe of Transalpine Gaul – the larger area of Savoy. DHB. Victor Amédée II, at first Duke of Savoy, received in 1713 the title of King of Sicily. DHB.

[2] Brindisi: Latin *Brundisium*, Italian town on the Adriatic. DHB.

[3] Village in the kingdom of Naples.

[4] Bresse is divided into small seigniories, the main one, Baugé, being subsumed into the House of *Savoy*, 1292. By the Treaty of Lyon it was ceded to France in 1601. DHB.

[5] Latin *recedo*: I return, recover. DLLB.

[6] DHB.

[7] Toulouse family, Toulouse being capital of *Languedoc*. DL7V.

[8] Fermented revolution in Marseille and was deputy for Toulon. DL7V.

[9] Family from Bordeaux, capital of the *Guyenne* area. DL7V.

[10] Deputy from Bouches-du-Rhône (Aix). DL7V.

[11] Born in Marseille.

[12] DL7V.

# Reunion of the Thousand at Genoa, 1859

La cité franche[1] de liberté fait serve[2]
Des profligez[3] et resveurs fait Azyle:
Le Roy changé à eux non si proterve,[4]
De cent seront devenus plus de mille.

CIV,QI6

## Interpretation

The city whose freedom has been reduced by slavery, having become free will give asylum to the depraved and the dreamers [i.e. of revolution]. After boldly changing the king, they will go from a hundred to more than a thousand.

## History

'Garibaldi established his headquarters in a suburb of *Genoa*, at Quarto, in his old friend Augusto Vecchi's house. Arms were the greatest problem. The Ansaldo factory at *Genoa* was the biggest supplier and secretly assisted their operations. Cavour feared that foreign powers would accuse Piedmont [Genoa] of being too hospitable [*"fait Azyle"*] to the revolutionaries. On 5 May 1860 Garibaldi, standing on the Piedmont bridge, asked "How many of us are there?" *"More than a thousand*, including the sailors." In fact, his "Thousand" were *1049* strong. His men captured the telegraph office at Marsala [Sicily] from which they transmitted false messages to confuse the enemy. Garibaldi proclaimed himself dictator in the name of Victor Emmanuel, *"King of Italy."* '[5]

[1] In 1805 Genoa became part of the French Empire [*"de liberté fait serve"*], and in 1814 was given to the King of Sardinia through the Congress of Vienna. DHB.
[2] Latin *servus*: slave. DLLB.
[3] Latin *profligatus*: lost, depraved. DLLB.
[4] Latin *proterve*: boldly, impudently. DLLB.
[5] GP and MR.

# Garibaldi at Magnavacca and Ravenna.
# Pius IX and Temporal Power. German Unity through
# Two Major Wars, 1866 and 1870

Le magna vaqua[1] à Ravenne grand troubles,
Conduicts par quinze[2] enserres à Fornase:[3]
A Rome naistra deux monstres[4] à teste double,
Sang, feu, déluge, les plus grands à l'espase.

CIX,Q3

## Interpretation

He [Garibaldi] will experience great upsets at Magnavacca and Ravenna.
Borne by fifteen vessels they will take refuge at the farm of Zanetto
[FERme de ZANettO]; will then spawn two prodigies at Rome because
of a double power [the Pope's spiritual and temporal powers], then
blood, war, revolution will affect the great nations, because of space [i.e.
Lebensraum, expansionism].

## History

'Garibaldi asked the mayor of Cesenatico for thirteen vessels. An hour
later the Austrians entered the village. The thirteen ships made rapid
progress. The next night they skirted Ravenna. They were intercepted
in the bay of the Marches of Comacchio by an Austrian warship, whose
captain ordered them to surrender. They refused and were pursued.
Since the Austrians were gaining on them, they decided to head for the
coast. Coming under fire, they rounded the Cape of Magnavacca, but
only three got through. Finally no more than thirty of them landed,
among them Garibaldi, and the Austrians and papal police set up a
manhunt to round up the fugitives. It was impossible to get to Venice
since all northern roads were blocked or watched by the Austrians. They
decided to try their luck around Ravenna, where the patriots were numerous. He added that Anita should be left behind, for she would not
survive such a journey. He thought of taking her to Zanetto Farm.'[5]
'Few Popes have aroused more conflicting comments than Pius IX,
ranging from flattering adulation to open hostility. With hindsight, it
may be said that he lacked the energy to separate the spiritual and temporal
sides of the papal sovereignty.'[6]
'In Germany, as in Italy, the question of unity had been posed since
1815. But among the thirty-eight German states two, Austria and Prussia,
were major powers. By means of two full-scale wars brought about by

Bismarck, the war of 1866 against Austria and that of 1870 against France, German unity was achieved.'[7]

[1] Italian town at the mouth of the Po.
[2] Biographies of Garibaldi mention thirteen ships, while Nostradamus has fifteen.
[3] Anagram and abbreviation of Zanetto Farm where Garibaldi sought shelter.
[4] Latin *monstrum*: divine omen, prodigy. DLLB.
[5] GP and MR.
[6] DDP.
[7] HFAM.

---

# The War of 1870 and the End of Papal Temporal Power. Anti-clericalism

Mars nous manasse[1] par la force bellique,
Septente fois fera le sang espandre:
Auge[2] et ruyne de l'Ecclesiastique,[3]
Et plus ceux qui d'eux rien voudront entendre.

CI,QI5

## Interpretation

War menaces with its bellicose strength and will see bloodshed in [18]70. The Ecclesiastic will be scorned and ruined and all the more so shall be those who do not wish to reach understanding with him.

## History

'On 8 December 1869 Pius IX opened the Twentieth Ecumenical Council, during which Papal Infallibility was proclaimed [18 July 1870]. Next day France declared *war* on Prussia. The Pope, as a last hope, tried to mediate between William I and Napoleon III. On 2 September Napoleon surrendered at Sedan, following which Italy informed France of her intention of occupying Rome. Pius IX refused to relinquish the Vatican as requested, and Austria refused to give him the aid he sought against the invaders. Prussia too was on the side of the invaders. General Cadorna *bombarded* ["*ruyne*"] the Porta Pia, and after heroic defence by his troops the Pope had to surrender. The same day his temporal power was annulled at the Capitol. The Papal States had ceased to exist: the Pope was in fact a prisoner. The rulers and governments of the world were indifferent to the annexation of St Peter's estate. The measures directed against the Church continued, and atheistic satires against the Pope himself circulated in Rome.'[4]

[1] *Manasse*: form of '*menace*'. DAFL
[2] Proverb: 'One might as well carry a pig-trough.' Said with the sense of an expression of scorn for a job or particular work. DL7V.
[3] Note capital E to denote the Pope.
[4] DDP.

---

# Pius IX at the Head of the Church, 16 June 1846. His Alliance with France, 1848–70. His Temporal Power Annulled at the Capitol, 20 September 1870

Un dubieux[1] ne viendra loin du règne,
La plus grand part le voudra soustenir:
Un Capitole ne voudra poinct qu'il règne,
Sa grande charge ne pourra maintenir.

CVI,Q13

## Interpretation

A [pope] who will often be indecisive will come to power. The greater part [French Empire of Napoleon III] will want to support him. At the Capitol, his rule will not be wanted and he will be unable to maintain his great charge [temporal power].

## History

'Pius IX seemed to react emotionally to situations demanding reason and forcefulness. Thus the vacillation [*"dubieux"*] between his role of pontiff and that of benevolent despot plunged him into even deeper *confusion*, especially when a nationalistic war against Austria was demanded. By November 1848 he was treated like a prisoner, so he fled to Neapolitan territory. At Rome he was formally deprived of his temporal sovereignty and the Roman republic was proclaimed. When Pius IX asked the main powers to intervene France did so and captured Rome on 2 July 1849. On 12 April 1850 Pius IX re-entered the Holy City *by French invitation* [*"la plus grand part"*]. . . .

On 20 September 1870, the Pope's temporal sovereignty was annulled at the *Capitol*.'[2]

[1] Latin *dubius*: wavering between two parties, irresolute, uncertain. DLLB.
[2] DDP.

---

# The Vatican Council, 1870. Napoleon III at Milan, 1859. Bombardment of the Porta Pia at Rome, 20 September 1870

Avant l'assaut l'oraison prononcée,[1]
Milan prins d'Aigle par ambusche[2] déceus,
Muraille antique par canons enforcée,
Par feu et sang à mercy peu receus.

CIII,Q37

## Interpretation

Before the assault they will meditate upon doctrine, the eagle [Napoleon III], who had occupied Milan will be tricked by a plot. The old walls [of Rome] will be shattered by cannon. Because of the strife and bloodshed many will need the [papal] blessing.

## History

'The Lombard capital was draped in French and Italian flags. Napoleon III and Victor Emmanuel rode in side by side on 8 June 1859. *Milan* welcomed them wildly.'[3]

'The French military presence maintained Pius's temporal sovereignty. In 1860 conflict with Piedmont began: the north of the Papal States was occupied, and the Pope excommunicated Piedmont ["*à mercy peu receus*"]. By virtue of the September 1864 agreement, signed *without the Pope's knowledge* [plot] by which Piedmont undertook not to attack the papal territories, Napoleon withdrew from Rome, which was now left defenceless. Italian legislation grew more anti-clerical. Garibaldi's troops, which were laying waste the Papal States, were beaten at Mentana in 1866 by papal troops and the French who had returned to occupy Rome and protect the Pope.

On 8 December 1869 Pius IX opened the Twentieth Ecumenical Council ["*oraison prononcée*"] at which Papal Infallibility was *proclaimed* [July 1870]. On 2 September 1870 Napoleon surrendered at Sedan, after which Italy informed France that she intended to occupy Rome. General Cadorna *bombarded the Porta Pia* on 20 September 1870, and after heroic defence by his troops the Pope had to surrender. The same day his temporal power was annulled at the Capitol.'[4]

[1] *Faire oraison*, i.e. meditate upon Christian doctrine and duties. DL7V.
[2] Plot, machination, ruse, trap. DL7V.
[3] LSEOA.
[4] DDP.

## Bazaine's Treason. Metz and Sedan. Garibaldi, 1870

La garde étrange trahira forteresse
Espoir et umbre de plus hault mariage:
Garde déceuë, forte prinse dans la presse
Loire, Saone, Rosne, Gar à mort outrage.

CII,Q25

*Interpretation*

The guard of the fortress will indulge in strange treachery in the secret hope of a stronger alliance, the guard will be deceived, the strong town caught in a vice; the Loire, Saône and Rhône armies, and Garibaldi's, will be outrageously overcome by death.

*History*

'Bazaine was reluctant to leave the fortifications of Metz and did not move for two days. He used the Emperor's authority as an excuse, without giving any orders, not even destroying the four bridges of the Moselle over which the enemy had to advance. Moltke sought *to bottle him in between the Metz fortresses* – thus the Châlons camp was deprived of all defensive cover and MacMahon was forced to take a decision, willy-nilly. He gave the order to evacuate the camp and fall back upon Rheims, hoping to be able *to help out* Bazaine in due course. . . .

Eighty-three thousand prisoners: the Battle of Sedan cost *3000 dead* and 14,000 injured. German armies reached Paris, and the French could find no allies. Only *Garibaldi*, the enemy of Imperial France, came to the aid of Republican France. The improvised *provincial* forces had some successes. But Bazaine, negotiating secretly with Bismarck – an attempt at intrigue repulsed by the Empress – *surrendered*, handing over even his flags.'[1]

[1] LSEOA.

# Defeat at Sedan. The Third Republic

L'aigle poussée entour des pavillons,[1]
Par autres oyseaux d'entour sera chassée
Quand bruit des cymbres,[2] tubes[3] et sonnaillons[4]
Rendront le sens de la Dame insensée.

CII,Q44

## Interpretation

The Emperor, after advancing right to the battlefield, will be pursued
by other [Germanic] eagles nearby, when the noise of trumpets and
cavalry bugles from the Germans will turn his mind back to the Republic.

## History

'The King of Prussia thought Napoleon had left Sedan. When informed
he seemed astonished. *"The Emperor is here!"* he repeated.

It turned into a rout, every man for himself; there was total confusion
and different regiments mingled and swarmed back towards the banked
fortifications of Sedan. The Prussian infantry harassed them, taking
many prisoners. At two o'clock the battle was over, the whole army was
overwhelmed and *the Empire lost*.

The Empress, alone in the Tuileries, saw and heard the yelling crowds
in the Rue de Rivoli, their flags draped in mourning. Their shouts made
the windows rattle: "Down with the Empire! *Long Live the Republic!*"
The Republicans took their revenge: they had been waiting *eighteen years*
for it. The war and the manner in which it had been conducted were
alike unforgivable. The Empire stood condemned by its own acts. Pitilessly the Republicans saw to its downfall.'[5]

---

[1] Sort of portable, round or square construction formerly used in military encampments.
DL7V.
[2] Germanic tribe settled on the right bank of the Elbe. DL7V.
[3] Latin *tuba*: martial trumpet.
[4] *Sonnaille*: in the pl. meaning a group of bells attached to horses' harnesses.
[5] LSEOA.

# Napoleon III in the Ardennes. The Third Republic

Le grand Empire sera tost désolé,
Et translaté[1] près d'arduenne[2] silve[3]
Les deux batards[4] par l'aisné décollé,[5]
Et régnera Aenobarb,[6] nez de milve.[7]

CV,Q45

## Interpretation

The great Empire will soon be devastated, the Emperor being transported to the area of the Ardennes Forest. The two persons born from two opposed regimes [Empire and Republic] deprived of the monarchy by the elder [the legitimist pretender] will then rule the Republic, Marianne the harpy.

## History

'Napoleon seemed to want to trap himself from the very start: witness his bizarre message to Trochu asking whether the Italian troops should be directed towards Belfort or Munich! Trochu wanted to go back. The Emperor, then in *the Ardennes*, asked him to stay where he was. . . .

The consequences of *the catastrophe which engulfed the Second Empire* make it hardly possible for Frenchmen to consider this period dispassionately, even now.'[8]

'*Monarchist* originally, Thiers had reasoned his way towards *the Republic*, and the Assembly showed hostility to him. He resigned and Marshal MacMahon was immediately elected to replace him. Thereupon the monarchists agitated for restoration of the monarchy. The clergy led a vigorous campaign for the Count of Chambord who was already being called Henri V. But negotiations floundered and this idea was considered impossible.'[9]

[1] Latin *translatus*: transported. DLLB.
[2] Latin *Arduenna*: the Ardennes. DLLB.
[3] Latin *silva*: forest. DLLB.
[4] Illegitimate, i.e. irregular. DL7V.
[5] Latin *decollo*: I deprive of something. DLLB.
[6] Domitius Aenobarbus: Roman patrician family, its surname 'bronze beard' deriving from the story that the black beard of one of its members turned suddenly *red*. Domitius was Agrippina's husband and their child was Nero. Violent and debauched, Domitius said that Agrippina and himself could only breed a monster. DHCD. Nostradamus here establishes an analogy with the French Republic which added *red* to the national flag. From the 'socialistic' ideas of the eighteenth century which she spread through Europe, she finally spawned the 'monster' of Communism.

[7] Latin *milva*: female kite; harpy in symbolic and abusive sense.
[8] LSEOA.
[9] HFAM.

---

# The Rift between the Orleanists
# and the Legitimists, 1871. The Courts Martial
# after the Commune

Par detracteur calomnié a puisnay,[1]
Quand istront[2] faicts enormes et martiaux:
La moindre[3] part dubieuse[4] à l'aisné,
Et tost au règne seront faicts partiaux.

CVI,Q95

## Interpretation

The representative of the younger branch will be calumniated by a detractor, when the courts martial for atrocities are done with, the smaller faction [Orleanists] will have doubts about the elder one; so the parties will swiftly reach power.

## History

'The Republic proclaimed in Paris on 4 September 1870 had difficult beginnings. It could not prevent *defeat*. The Republicans were still few and disorganized, but they took advantage of the *rift* between the royalists, divided as they were into legitimists and Orleanists, to organize a provisional republic presided over by Thiers. The monarchists succeeded in ousting him from power: they reproached him for his defection to the Republican ranks. Under MacMahon's presidency they prepared for the restoration of the monarchy, but could not overcome their differences; this allowed the Republicans to pass the Constitution Laws of 1875 which definitively structured the Republic.'[5]

'The courts *martial* were kept incredibly busy in Paris. Since the morning [28 May 1871] a thick cordon stood around the Châtelet where a tribunal sat continuously. From time to time groups of fifteen or twenty would emerge, condemned to death.'[6]

'The first actions of the Republican government were to decide upon the return of Parliament to Paris. But the Republicans' victory did not put an end to *party* squabbles.'[7]

[1] *Puiné*: the second-born, younger of a family.DL7V.
[2] *Istre*, form of *issir*: to issue forth. DAFL.
[3] Smallest in quantity or dimension. DL7V.
[4] Latin *dubiosus*: doubtful. DLLB.
[5] DH3.
[6] Aimé Dupuy: *1870–1871, The War, the Commune and the Press*.
[7] HFAM.

---

## The Fall of Napoleon III, 4 September 1870. MacMahon at Versailles, 1871. His Seven-Year Presidency, 1873–79. The Constitution of 1875

En lieu du grand qui sera condamné,[1]
De prison hors, son amy en sa place:
L'espoir Troyen[2] en six mois joint,[3] mort né.
Le Sol à l'urne seront prins fleuves en glace.

CVI,Q52

### Interpretation

Instead of the great man [Emperor] who will be rejected once out of prison, his friend will take power in his place: monarchical power will be shackled in six months, stillborn, the monarchy will be abandoned because of a vote, after the rivers have been taken by ice.

### History

'The Emperor's surrender at Sedan meant the immediate overthrow of the Empire. . . .

From 5 January 1871 the Germans rained shells on the forts and barracks on the Left Bank of the Seine. Paris was to endure the threats of both famine and revolution. There was neither wood nor coal *through one of the severest winters of the century*, so cold that the wine froze in the barrel.'[4]

'Wounded at the start of the Battle of Sedan, MacMahon was sent off to Germany as a *prisoner of war*. After the Paris treaty he commanded the Versailles army which recaptured Paris from the Commune.'[5]

'On 27 October 1873 negotiations broke down and the Restoration, with the Count of Chambord, was declared impossible. The monarchists still did not renounce the *hope* of re-establishing the royal family. Mac-Mahon took on the presidency for seven years [19 November 1873]. At the end of 1894, after a sort of *plebiscite for or against the Republic*, it could not be doubted that France was largely Republican. Thus at the start of 1875 the Assembly decided to overhaul the laws of the constitution. It voted, in succession, three laws [February–July 1875].[6] These three laws became the basis of the 1875 Constitution which, with slight modification in 1884, is still adhered to in France. The 1875 Constitution *founded parliamentary rule* in France.'[7]

'The senate *elections* gave the monarchists a slim majority, but in the Chamber the Republican majority was 200. MacMahon, to comply with the constitution, took a Republican minister.'[7]

[1] Latin *damno*: I condemn, declare guilty, reject. DLLB.
[2] *The Franciad*: unfinished epic poem by Ronsard, whose central figure, Francus, is a Trojan prince, Hector's son. DL7V. Nostradamus here takes the Trojans as a symbol of the French monarchy.
[3] Latin *junctus*: assembled, linked. DLLB.
[4] HFAM.
[5] DL7V.
[6] Six months.
[7] HFAM.

---

## The Peace of Frankfurt, 10 May 1871.
## The Annexation of Alsace and Lorraine.
## Rome, Capital of Italy, 26 January 1871

L'élection faicte dans Francfort,
N'aura nul lieu[1], Milan s'opposera:
Le sien plus proche semblera si grand fort,
Qu'outre le Rhin es Marechs[2] chassera.

CVI,Q87

*Interpretation*

The choice made [France] will not be received at Frankfurt; Milan will be opposed [to Rome]; her neighbour will seem so great and powerful that he will push back the frontiers beyond the Rhine.

*History*

'The Peace of *Frankfurt*: during the armistice there was an *election* of a National Assembly which decided to negotiate the peace. The preliminaries were signed at *Versailles* on 26 February and ratified on 1 March at *Bordeaux*. France lost Alsace except for Belfort, and north *Lorraine* including Metz. These preliminaries became a definitive peace through the Treaty of Frankfurt, 10 May 1871. From this terrible war Germany thus emerged united, *powerful* and *dominant* in Europe.'[3]

From 25 January 1871 the heir apparent and Princess Marguerite took up residence in Rome. By 94 votes to 39 the Senate voted for the transfer of the capital. After long trials, said the King, Italy had been given back to herself and to Rome. After recognizing the absolute independence of the spiritual authority, he continued, they could be sure that Rome, capital of Italy, would continue to be the peaceful and respected throne of the papacy.

[1] To have no place, not to be received or admitted. DL7V.
[2] *Maresche* or *Maresc*: German, *Marsch*; English, *Marsh*. DAFL. 'Marches' thus often meant the military border of a state. DL7V.
[3] HFAM.

---

## The Annexation of Alsace-Lorraine, 1871. The Defeats of Chanzy at Le Mans, of Faidherbe at Cambrai, and of the Eastern Army on the Swiss Frontier

Des lieux plus bas du pays de Lorraine,
Seront des basses Allemagnes unies:
Par ceux du siège Picard, Normans, du Maisne,[1]
Et aux cantons[2] se seront réunis.

CX,Q51

### Interpretation

Territories situated lower than Lorraine [Alsace] will be reunited with Southern Germany because of the combatants [Germans] at the siege [of Paris], in Picardy, Normandy and as far as Maine, and the French troops which will be reassembled in Switzerland.

### History

'The final battles: without despairing, Gambetta organized a new initiative. Three armies took the field in December and January: the Northern Army under Faidherbe, the 2nd Loire Army under Chanzy, and the Eastern Army under Bourbaki. Chanzy clung on along the right bank of the Loire, trying to manoeuvre himself into position for a push towards Paris if he were successful. Defeated at *Le Mans*, he tried to reform his army on the Mayenne.

In the north Faidherbe showed the same tenacity. He was victorious at Bapaume on 3 January, but the defeat of St-Quentin [18 January] drove him back upon *Cambrai* [Picardy].

The Eastern Army tried to relieve Belfort. Pushed back upon Besançon, then to the Swiss frontier [*"aux cantons . . . réunis"*], and caught between two German armies, the Eastern Army only escaped surrender by *rushing into Switzerland* where it was disarmed [1 February 1871].

However, to hasten the capitulation of Paris [*"siège"*], the Germans began the bombardment of the town. . . .

The peace preliminaries negotiated by Thiers and Jules Faure were signed on 26 February and ratified on 1 March by the Assembly, reunited at Bordeaux. France lost Alsace except for Belfort [*"lieux plus bas"* etc.], and north Lorraine with Metz.'[3]

[1] Old French province bordered by Normandy in the north, Orleans to the east, Anjou and Touraine to the south and Brittany in the west. Its capital was Le Mans. DHB.

[2] In Switzerland, the term for each state of the Confederation. DL7V.

[3] HFAM.

---

## Bourbaki's Defeat, 1 February 1871.
## The Peace of Frankfurt, 10 May 1871

Au conclud pache hors de la forteresse
Ne sortira celui en désespoir mis:
Quand ceux d'Arbois[1] de Langres, contre Bresse[2]
Auront monts Dolle,[3] bouscade[4] d'ennemis.

CV,Q82

*Interpretation*

At the conclusion of the peace outside [Frank]furt, he who will have been reduced to despair will not be able to extricate himself, when those of Arbois, come from Langres against Bresse, will find in the Jura mountains an enemy ambush.

*History*

'The Eastern Army – 100,000 men concentrated around Bourges – had as their objective the relief of Belfort, which Denfert-Rochereau had held since 3 November. But like the Châlons army it moved so slowly that the Germans had time to organize. Victor of Villersexel [9 January 1871],[5] Bourbaki could not break the lines at *Héricourt* [15–17 January].[6] Pushed back upon Besançon, then to the Swiss frontier, and *caught between two German armies*, the Eastern Army only escaped surrender by rushing into Switzerland, where it was disarmed [1 February 1871].

The peace preliminaries negotiated by Thiers and Jules Faure were signed on 26 February and ratified on 1 March by the Assembly, reunited at *Bordeaux*. These were transformed into a definitive peace by the Treaty of *Frankfurt*, 10 May 1871.'[7]

[1] Chief town of the canton of Jura.

[2] Region on the left bank of the Saône, one of whose departments was the *Jura*. DL7V.

[3] Main town of the *Jura* district.

[4] Latin *boscum*: wood, ambush, i.e. place where the enemy can be unexpectedly attacked from a concealed position. DL7V.

[5] Chief town of the Upper Saône canton.

[6] Town in the Upper Saône canton. After the failure at Héricourt, the disastrous retreat of the Eastern Army across the *Jura* began. DL7V.

[7] HFAM.

---

## The Commune and the Civil War, 18 March–28 May 1871

Par arcs[1] feux, poix[2] et par feux repoussés,[3]
Crys, hurlements sur la minuict ouys:
Dedans sont mis par les remparts cassez,[4]
Par canicules les traditeurs[5] fuys.

CII,Q77

*Interpretation*

Through firing [curved trajectory], pushed back by the blazes caused by oil, cries and shouts shall be heard in the night; they will enter through empty ramparts and the traitors will flee because of the extreme heat.

*History*

'The murders of Generals Lecomte and Clément Thomas, shot down in the afternoon by rabble and *mutinous soldiers*, exacerbated feuds and made all conciliation impossible. It was the first episode in an atrocious two-month civil war. Thiers did not try to resist in Paris, but withdrew to Versailles and left the field wide open to the *insurgents*, abandoning even *the forts* to them. The Commune organized the fight against the Versailles government. The war was extraordinarily ferocious. When Thiers, together with the prisoners who had returned from Switzerland and Germany, had reconstituted an army of 150,000 men, he began a second siege of Paris, which lasted five weeks. On 21 May, at about 4 p.m., soldiers infiltrated the city by *an abandoned gate* at Auteuil.

The army entered Paris. In desperation the *Federates*, knowing themselves lost, used oil to set fire to the Tuileries, the Palais de Justice, the Gare de Lyon and innumerable houses. The Seine ran between two walls of *fire*. *Incendiary shells* fired from the high ground in the east rained down on the city centre. Hostages were assassinated [24–26 May]. Incensed by these atrocities, the troops gave no quarter. According to official accounts the battle cost 6500 dead in the fighting or executed. There were also 36,000 prisoners who were *prosecuted* by military courts; 13,000 people were condemned to deportation.'[6]

[1] Latin *arcus*: curves. DLLB.
[2] Mineralogy: name often given to bitumens, of which there are four varieties, among them naphtha, petroleum, etc. DL7V.
[3] Latin *repello*: I push back, drive back. DLLB.
[4] Latin *cassus*: empty. DLLB.
[5] Latin *traditor*: traitor.
[6] HFAM.

---

## Bazaine. Metz Abandoned, 1870. The Death of Napoleon III, 1873

Au deserteur de la Grand forteresse,
Après qu'aura son lieu abandonné:
Son adversaire fera grand prouësse
L'empereur tost mort sera condamné.

CIV,Q65

*Interpretation*

When the deserter of the great fortress has abandoned the place, the enemy will perform feats of great prowess and the Emperor will die soon afterwards.

*History*

'MacMahon was warned that Bazaine had not moved from Metz, and was inclined to leave him to his fate. On 14 August Napoleon left Metz, followed by his army. Bazaine was to follow on after the retreat. On 19 August the Marshal assured the Emperor that he had only directed a change in the front so as to guard against the enemy swinging round. He had always intended going north to Sedan and even Mézières in order to reach Châlons. He thus deliberately duped his master, and by persuading him that he still intended to rejoin him, led him to disaster. Sedan was actually named in his dispatch. Bazaine, by his *lie*, finally *undid Napoleon*. . . .

Against the advice of Gambetta, who was burning with patriotism and wanted to continue the fight, the government of national defence at last sought a truce and surrendered Paris. *The victorious Germans marched up the Champs Elysées.* Eighteen months later Napoleon III, ready to attempt another 'return from Elba', *succumbed* to his painful disease.'[1]

[1] LSEOA.

---

# The Belle Epoque, 1900. Rheims, Centre of the 1914–18 War

> Après la pluye de laict assez longuette,
> En plusieurs lieux de Reims[1] le ciel touché:[2]
> O quel conflit de sang près d'eux s'appreste,
> Peres et fils Roys n'oseront approché.

CIII,QI8

*Interpretation*

After a considerable period of easy living, several areas around Rheims will be smitten from the sky: O what a bloody conflict is being prepared near them; fathers and sons, governors, will not dare approach these places.

*History*

'Almost *forty-four years* to the day after Froeschwiller and St-Privat, the French and German armies clashed again. This war, the biggest and *bloodiest* ever, seemed like a universal cataclysm.'[3]

'The 1914 war, long and atrocious as it was, in hindsight made the turn of the century look like *a golden age*. The easy life of the bourgeoisie alone prompts one to refer to the *belle époque*. But it was the bourgeoisie which gave it its style.'[4]

*Preparations*, 1913: Germany was arming formidably, allotting huge sums of money to war materials. In 1913 France passed a law increasing military service to three years.

'In Flanders and Picardy Ludendorff's plans had been foiled, but on 27 May 1918, by a surprise offensive, the Germans shattered the French front between Soissons and *Rheims*. The effect on morale was enormous. Ludendorff decided to strike a decisive blow against Foch by attacking on a 90 km front on either side of *the Rheims salient*. For the second time, a victory on the *Marne* settled the outcome of the war.

France had deserved this triumph at the cost of frightful sacrifices. Of all the contenders she had lost most *blood*: more than 1,500,000 killed and nearly 3,000,000 wounded. Huge tracts of her richest land were no more than treeless, depopulated barren *deserts*. Great towns like *Rheims*, Arras, Soissons, Verdun and St-Quentin were little more than piles of rubble.'

---

[1] Chief town of the *Marne* department. Scene of numerous battles, *Rheims*, like the whole of eastern France, suffered greatly in the First World War.

[2] *Touche*: blow, act of striking. DL7V.

[3] LCH3.

[4] HFAM.

---

## The 1914–18 War. Spanish Flu, 1918

L'horrible guerre qu'en Occident s'appreste,
L'an ensuyvant viendra la pestilence[1]
Si fort terrible que jeune, vieil et beste,
Sang, feu, Mercur,[2] Mars, Jupiter,[3] en France.

                                        CIX,Q55

*Interpretation*

Horrible war brewing in the west; the year after will come an epidemic so terrible that it will strike young, old, animals, when fire, blood, pillage, war, aviation will be in France.

## History

'The epidemic of 1918 caused the deaths of almost 15 million people throughout the world.'[4]

'The conflict which began in 1914 was the culmination of the imperialism of the great *European* powers over half a century. The war spread all over the world, by sea, land and air, but the main fronts remained European ["*en Occident*"].[4] The Germans strove to annihilate the enemy, attacking the Verdun sector on 21 February 1916. This was the start of the bloodiest and most violent battle of the war, leaving more than 700,000 dead and wounded.

*Flame-throwers* and grenades gave the fighting a particularly horrific aspect. But the most feared weapon was poison gas, first used by the Germans in 1915. *Aeroplanes* at first were largely used for surveillance and observation, but soon their function was to gain control of air space.'[5]

[1] Plague, contagious disease in general. DL7V.

[2] Son of Jupiter, messenger of the Gods, and himself god of eloquence, trade and *thieves*. DL7V.

[3] Principal Roman god, sovereign of *the sky* and of the world. DL7V.

[4] EU.

[5] AE.

---

# The German Army, 1914–18. Peace Terms

Le camp[1] plus grand de route mis en fuite,
Guaires[2] plus outre ne sera pourchassé:
Ost[3] recampé et légion[4] réduicte
Puis hors de Gaule le tout sera chassé.

CIV,QI2

## Interpretation

The greatest army [German] put to flight and rout will not be pursued far beyond [the Rhine]. Because the troops will bivouac once more [after 1870], the army will be reduced. It will all be chased out of France.

## History

'Since the war was vital to their destiny and very existence, the protagonists flung all their resources into it. Almost 14 million Germans and more than 8 million Frenchmen were mobilized between 1914 and 1918.

From the Argonne to the North Sea the offensive continued relent-
lessly. By 1918 the Germans were weakening and were everywhere in
*retreat*. The November Armistice conditions demanded the evacuation in
a fortnight of occupied territories in France, Belgium and Alsace-
Lorraine; evacuation in one month of the *left bank of the Rhine*, which
would be occupied by the Allies, along with the bridgeheads on *the right
bank* at Mainz, Koblenz and Cologne.

Germany also had to abolish obligatory military service and *reduce its
army* to 100,000 men.

The most important condition from the French point of view was the
return of Alsace-Lorraine to the French nation.'[5]

[1] Terrain where an army lodges, and by extension an army in general. DL7V.
[2] *Guaires, gaires, guères*, i.e. not much. DAFL.
[3] Army, camp, troop. DAFL.
[4] Latin *legio*: legion, troops, army. DLLB.
[5] HFAM.

---

## The 1914–18 War. The Cost in Lives. The Collapse of the Currency

> Par guerre longue l'exercite[1] expuiser,
> Que pour soldats ne trouveront pecune:[2]
> Lieu d'or, d'argent, cuir on viendra cuser,[3]
> Gaulois aerain,[4] signe croissant de Lune.

> CVII,Q25

*Interpretation*

Because of a long war the army will be depleted to the point at which
money will not be found to pay the soldiers. They will have to mint
leather instead of gold and silver; French currency will be like a crescent
moon.

*History*

'The war endlessly demanded *more and more men and munitions*. The
protagonists had thought they would be waging a short and violent
struggle but found themselves in *a prolonged war*. Both sides experienced
from the outset critical shortages of *supplies and equipment*.

As for the financial consequences, they were difficult to estimate, but the respective national debts in 1919 for Britain and France were almost £8 billion and 219 billion francs. *Paper money* issued during the war was no longer *convertible into gold*. Should there be a reduction of the quantity in circulation [deflation]? Or, on the contrary, should inflation be maintained by devaluing the currency? Was there to be a return to *the gold standard*? Many problems had to be faced in the realm of finance.

France's new attitude was explained by the finances of a country whose coffers were empty and *currency* shaky.

The war lasted four years three months. France had 1,393,000 dead and 3 million injured (one casualty per twenty-nine inhabitants).'[5]

[1] Latin *excercitus*: army. DLLB.
[2] Latin *pecunia*: fortune, goods, riches, money. DLLB.
[3] Latin *cudere* argentum: to coin money. DLLB.
[4] Latin *aes*: bronze, money. DLLB.
[5] LMC.

---

# Ghent. Town of Alliances and Treaties: 1576, 1678, 1792, 1795 and 1918. The Capture of Anvers and the Floods, 8 October 1914

Au lieu ou LAYE et Scelde[1] se marient
Seront les nopces de longtemps maniées:
Au lieu d'Anvers ou la crappe[2] charient,
Jeune vieillesse conforte[3] intaminées.[4]

CX,Q52

*Interpretation*

At the junction of the Leie and the Escaut rivers [Ghent] many alliances will be signed. At Anvers the currents will wash away ordure [corpses]. Young and old not yet soiled will sustain [the combat].

*History*

'The famous Peace of Ghent in 1576 *united* the northern and central provinces of the Low Countries against Spain ["*alliances*"]. Ghent was captured by Louis XIV in 1678, by Lowendahl in 1745, and in 1792 and 1795 by the Republican armies. Under the Empire it became the chief town of the Escaut department ["*Scelde*"]. Louis XVIII retired there during the Hundred Days [1815]. In 1815 too, Britain and the USA signed a peace treaty there.'[5]

'On 11 November 1918, at 5 a.m., the Armistice was signed. The ceasefire sounded at 11 a.m. That morning the front line was near Ghent.'[6]

'British and French forces managed to help the Belgian army, which after abandoning *Anvers* [8 October 1914], made a hazardous retreat to the Yser. In nine days the Germans reduced the fortifications of *Anvers*: "the loaded pistol at England's heart" fell into dreadful hands. Von Falkenhayn's men were a motley collection of new recruits and dedicated soldiers, aged from sixteen to fifty ["*jeune vieillesse*"], who were *eager to strike the death blows* ["*conforte intaminées*"]. After merciless fighting at Dixmude on the Yser, a little coastal river, the battle got bogged down in *the muddy floods* ["*crappe charient*"] and torrential rain.'[7]

'When war was declared young Germans demonstrated their enthusiasm.'[8]

---

[1] Escaut, Scaldis (Scelde). Ghent is on the confluence of the Leie and the Escaut. DHB and AU.
[2] *Crappe*: ordure. DAFL.
[3] *Conforter*: sustain. DAFL.
[4] Latin *intaminatus*: pure, unsullied. DLLB.
[5] DHB.
[6] HFACAD.
[7] *Prologue to Our Century*: Universal History, vol. XI (Larousse 1968).
[8] EU.

---

# The Bolshevik Revolution, 1917.
## Foreign Intervention in Russia, 1917–22.
## The Proclamation of the USSR, 1922

> Courses[1] de LOIN, ne s'apprester conflits,
> Triste entreprise, l'air pestilent, hideux:
> De toutes parts les Grands seront afflits,
> Et dix et sept assaillir vint et deux.

> Presage 62

*Interpretation*

Hostile incursions from far away, people unprepared for conflict because of a sad enterprise [the Revolution] which will make the air unbreathable and hideous; from all sides the heads of states will be afflicted and will assail [the Russians] from 1917 to 1922.

## History

'The real face of the new regime did not appear in October *1917*. Twenty years of internal strife constituted *a tragic period* ["*triste entreprise*"] in Russian history, the former Empire which in *1922* became the USSR. Following the October Revolution the new government had to struggle against not only internal opposition but also *foreign intervention*. Russia had retired from the war after the Treaty of Brest-Litovsk [3 March 1918] and French, British, American and Japanese forces came to support the Civil War until November 1920, though it continued in the *Far East* until November 1922.'[2]

'The Russian Revolution began without violence but an assassination attempt against Lenin, and the Civil War sparked off the *Terror*. From 1919 to 1920 the victims of executions, famine ["*hideux*"], *epidemics* ["*l'air pestilent*"] numbered almost 7 million. Lenin's words set the tone: Death or Victory.'[3]

[1] Military term: hostile incursions. DL7V.
[2] EU.
[3] LMC.

---

# The October Revolution, 1917. The Mystery of the Romanov Massacre

Voici le mois par maux tant a doubter,[1]
Mors, tous seigner[2] peste, faim, quereller:
Ceux du rebours[3] d'exil viendront noter,[4]
Grands, secrets, morts, non de contreroller.[5]

Presage 89, October

## Interpretation

Here is the month [of October] redoubtable for the ills it will bring. All those of the red flag will bring death, sickness, famine and civil war. Opponents will be exiled, and it will not be possible to control the great ones' deaths, which will remain secret.

## History

'*In October 1917*, the home situation in Russia was *catastrophic*. Inflation and state debts made bankruptcy inevitable.

*The October Rising* [25 October–1 November]. While Kerensky left Petrograd to rally the troops he had recalled from the front, soldiers, sailors, workers and *red guards* took over the Winter Palace and arrested the members of the provisional government. The troops advancing on Petrograd did not want to fight and saw their way blocked, as it had been two months earlier; their commanders parleyed with the Bolsheviks; Kerensky escaped arrest. At Petrograd and then at Moscow attempts by young officers to restore the government failed. On a political level the Bolshevik Revolution triumphed on 1 November.'[6]

'While in the hands of the Communists, in July 1918, Tsar Nicholas II, his wife Alexandra and their five children ["*grands*"] disappeared, never to be seen again. Officially they were *killed* by shooting and bayoneting in the house where they were held prisoners. During the next forty-eight hours, however, the *mystery* and contradictions of this affair spread, masking the truth and creating a legend to add to the general confusion of the time. Although the story of the massacre has been questioned, researches into the truth of the Romanovs' fate have not progressed much further ["*non de contreroller*"].'[7]

[1] Example of aphesis.
[2] Latin *signum*: red flag. DLLB. From this, *seigniere*, band of material, sash. DAFL.
[3] Symbolic: opposite, contrary to what is required. DL7V.
[4] Latin *notare*: censure, condemn. DLLB.
[5] Ancient form of '*contrôler*'. DAFL.
[6] EU.
[7] LDR.

---

# The Internationale and Marxism in Russia.
# The Spread of Communist Ideas. Prisons

De gent esclave[1] chansons, chants et requestes,
Captifs par Princes et Seigneurs aux prisons:
A l'advenir par idiots sans testes,
Seront receus par divines oraisons.

CI,QI4

## Interpretation

The songs and demands of the Russians, whose heads of state will put people in prison, will be accepted as holy writ by the feeble-minded.

## History

'There were immense purges: while *arrests* for counter-revolutionary crimes multiplied between 1936 and 1937, the purges extended far beyond the party to include anyone who had any connection with the victims, however slight.

The great *prisons*: three of the five main prisons of Moscow were reserved for political prisoners, although some detainees were ordinary criminals. Work camps were set up almost everywhere. Kargopol camp, in the Archangel district, for instance, contained *almost 30,000 prisoners in 1940*. It had been founded in 1936 by 600 prisoners who had been simply flung off a train passing through the middle of the forest: of necessity, they themselves had to construct their shelter and enclosures.'[2]

[1] Esclavonia: Slavonia, ancient name for Russia, i.e. land of slaves or serfs. DHB.
[2] LGT.

---

# The Soviet Union Builds Itself up through Two World Wars. The Fall of the Tsar. Stalin in Power.

La gent[1] esclave par un heur[2] martial,
Viendra en haut degré tant eslevée:
Changeront prince, naistra un provincial,
Passer la mer, copie[3] aux monts levée.

CV,Q26

## Interpretation

Russia will derive such power through the war that she will change her prince for a provincial by birth, then his power will win the sea and will raise troops beyond the mountains.

## History

'Russia retired from the war after the Treaty of Brest-Litovsk [3 March 1918] and French, British, American and Japanese forces came to support the Civil War until November 1920, though it continued in the Far East until November 1922. Throwing out the foreign interventionist troops ["*heur martial*"] and the remnants of the White Armies, the Bolshevik government came to grips with its problems. The first three years of the Revolution have well been called the period of "militant communism".

Josef Vissarionovitch Djugashvili was born at Gori in *Georgia* in 1879. [Stalin, the provincial!]

Moving from a defensive to an aggressive position, the USSR entered the Second World War in September 1939 as an ally of Germany, having signed a non-aggression pact, in order to annexe certain areas of Poland inhabited by Byelorussians and Ukrainians. In November 1939 these became part of the USSR. Romania had to yield Bessarabia and northern Bukovina in June 1940, but on 22 June 1941, in the face of German invasion, Russia's war against Germany began. It was to be a turning-point in her history ["*haut degré*" etc.].[4]

[1] Latin *gens*: race, population. DLLB.
[2] Luck, happy outcome. DL7V.
[3] Latin *copia*: army corps, troops, military forces. DLLB.
[4] EU.

---

# War in the Balkans, 1908–19. Mustapha Kemal, 1920

Les Conseillers du premier monopole,[1]
Les conquérants séduits[2] par la Melite[3]
Rodes, Bisance pour leurs exposant[4] pole,[5]
Terre faudra[6] les poursuivants de fuite.

CII,Q49

## Interpretation

The first president's counsellors will be set aside at Malta by the conquerors [the Allies] because of the abandonment of the cities of Rhodes and Constantinople; then these places will be lost to their pursuers who will be put to flight.

## History

'In September 1911 Italy, eager to lay hands on Tripolitania, declared war on the Ottoman Empire and disembarked troops at Tripoli. At the same time her fleet conquered Rhodes and the Dodecanese. The fighting in Tripolitania was fierce and these were only the preludes to war in the Balkans which made Turkey *give way*. On 18 October 1912 war was declared by the Balkan states against Turkey. The Greek fleet seized the Aegean islands. . . .

Bulgaria's capitulation [29 September 1918] immediately brought on Turkey's. An armistice was signed on 30 October 1918 at Moudros Bay; its principal clauses were the freedom of the Straits and *occupation of Constantinople*.

On 4 September 1919 the National Congress of Sivas assembled and Mustapha Kemal was elected its first President; his position towards the Allied powers and the Istanbul government was clearly hostile. On 16 March 1920 the British arranged for Allied troops to take control of the War and Navy Ministries, the police and the Post Office, while *deputies* and *influential* people ["*conseillers*"] who were pro-Kemal were arrested and *deported to Malta*. . . .

The Conference of Lausanne, inaugurated on 21 November 1922, led to a peace signed on 24 July 1923. It was a victory for the Turks, who gained territory on the Thracian frontier and recovered the islands of Imbros and Tenedos. The Allies evacuated *Istanbul* six weeks after the ratification of the peace.'[7]

---

[1] Right possessed exclusively by one or a small number of persons. DL7V.
[2] Latin *seductus*: set aside, distanced. DLLB.
[3] Inhabitant of Malta.
[4] Latin *expositus*: abandoned. DLLB.
[5] Greek πόλις: town. DGF.
[6] Future of *faillir*: to lack. DAFL.
[7] HDT.

---

# The Turkish Revolution, 1920.
# The Ottoman Empire Loses Egypt. Its Dissolution

La trombe[1] fausse dissimulant folie,
Fera Bisance un changement de loix,
Hystra[2] d'Égypte, qui veut que l'on deslie
Edict changeant monnoye et alloi.[3]

CI,Q40

*Interpretation*

A false revolution disguising madness will make Turkey change laws. Egypt will leave [the Empire] which will be dismembered. Her edicts will change currencies and exchange rates.

*History*

'The Congress of Berlin [13 June 1878] was a new and serious stage in the dismemberment ["*deslie*"] of the Ottoman Empire. Though it had lost only *Egypt*, where Britain was increasingly imposing her authority, it possessed few European territories, and these were miserable relics of a dominion gradually being whittled away by the various local nationalist organizations supported by the great powers.

The *revolution* of Mustapha Kemal: by creating a single party and muzzling the opposition, Kemal succeeded in restoring the Turkish nation's confidence in itself [false revolution]. As for internal politics, the main achievements were abolition of polygamy, suppression of religious orders and the banning of the fez [August–November 1925]; new civil, criminal and commercial codes, established on the lines of the Italian, Swiss and German ones; and the enforcement of protective customs tariffs. In 1939 the Central Bank of the Republic was set up which succeeded the Ottoman Bank as the national bank and mint. ["*monnoye*"].'[4]

[1] Latin *tropa*: revolution. DLLB.
[2] Future of *issir*: to leave, go out of. DAFL.
[3] Alloy, general term for gold and silver. DL7V.
[4] HDT.

---

# The Lake of Geneva and the Towns of Geneva and Evian as Centre of International Conferences. The Red Cross

> Du Lac Leman les sermons fascheront,
> Des jours seront reduicts[1] par des semaines
> Puis mois, puis an, puis tous défailleront
> Les Magistrats damneront leurs lois vaines.

CI,Q47

## Interpretation

The speeches at the Lake of Geneva will cause ferment; days will be followed by weeks, then months and years, then everything will collapse and the legislators curse their vain laws.

## History

'The problem of protecting war's victims had taken on an unprecedented urgency by the end of the Second World War. Certain rulings of the *Geneva Conventions* of 1864, revised in 1905 and 1929, were no longer very relevant in the light of the total wars of 1914–18 and, above all, 1939–45. New terms ["*sermons*"] were needed. These were drafted at the International Red Cross Conference in 1948 and submitted to the Geneva Conference of 1949, all countries having agreed that revision was needed. On 12 August 1949 four conventions were signed: the *Geneva Convention* for improving the lot of the sick and injured on the field of battle; the *Geneva Convention* to improve the treatment of the sick, shipwrecked and wounded at sea; the *Geneva Convention* relating to prisoners of war; and the *Geneva Convention* concerning the protection of civilians during wartime. Certain guidelines were common to all four. At all times and in all places the following were forbidden: to take hostages[2] ["*lois vaines*"]; execution without proper trial; torture; and all cruel and dishonourable treatment. Despite some improvements applied to the rules of war, the 1949 Geneva Conventions run into numerous difficulties in the contemporary world. This is the result of the overlapping of concepts, previously clearly defined, about internal and international wars and the implications of revolutionary and guerrilla warfare.'[3]

[1] Latin *reducto*: I lead back. DLLB.
[2] Cf. the American hostages taken by Iran, which took place on the highest level, country v. country (4 November 1979).
[3] EU.

---

# England's Seven Changes of Alliance in 290 Years. The Franco-German Wars Cement Anglo-French Understanding

Sept fois changer verrez gens[1] Britannique
Taints en sang en deux cens nonante ans:
France non point par appui germanique
Ariès[2] doubte son pole[3] Bastarnan.[4]

CIII,Q57

*Interpretation*

The Britannic nation will be seen to change seven times in 290 blood-stained years, and change towards France which, when no longer supporting Germany, will be suspicious of the latter's guidance, because of German militarism.

*History*

1628: the siege of La Rochelle.
1. 1657: the alliance of France with Cromwell.
2. 1667: the War of the Spanish Succession. Turenne occupies Flanders.
3. England allies with Sweden and Holland against France in the Triple Alliance. The Peace of Aix-la-Chapelle (1668).
1670: the treaty with England against Holland.
4. 1688: the War of the League of Augsburg. William of Orange, King of England, grouped the League against Louis XIV; Spain, Sweden, Holland, Austria, the Duke of Savoy.
5. The Peace of Ryswick (1697).
6. 1716: the Abbé Dubois goes back to The Hague, his mission to aid the English to persuade the Dutch to resume the alliance against Spain: the Triple Alliance signed on 4 February 1717.
1744: Louis XV declares war on England and Austria.
7. 1914–18: the English fight beside the French against Germany.
1628–1918 = 290 years.

¹ Latin *nation*: a people or country. DLLB.
² Astrological sign of the ram: battering ram. DL7V.
³ Symbolic: that which guides, fixed like the Pole Star. DL.
⁴ The Bastarnes: a tribe, extant *circa* the second century AD, who occupied the area between the upper Vistula and the lower Danube. They were of German origin, according to Tacitus. DL7V.

---

# More than 300 Years of English Power, 1600–1945.
## The Occupation of Portugal by the English, 1703

Le grand empire sera par Angleterre
Le Pempotam¹ des ans plus de trois cens:
Grandes copies² passer par mer et terre
Les Lusitains³ n'en seront pas contens.

CX,QI00

## Interpretation

England will be a great empire and be all-powerful for more than 300 years. She will make great armies pass across the earth by land and sea, which will not please the Portuguese.

## History

'Elizabeth's cunning government engaged in trade. The chartered companies multiplied, the most prestigious being the East India Company founded in 1600. Comfort and luxury spread among the ruling classes. English *colonialism* in the seventeenth century, far from slowing down, expanded throughout the world. In Europe, by contrast, this century of revolution began a whole period of crises which, when overcome, enabled Great Britain to establish efficient political machinery and acquire *the durability* [300 years] of her moral and physical personality.'[4]

'The war ended in a Europe in which the British and Americans encamped facing the Soviets [1945]. The determination which enabled the British, while overcoming their pre-war troubles and controversies, to stand fast could not disguise the changes which beset *Great Britain's position in world affairs*. Compared with the new giants [USA, USSR and soon Mao's China] she was *weakened* in resources and economy.'[5] 1600–1945 = more than 300 years.

'Since the time of Pedro II, Portugal had favoured England, which in 1703 consolidated its position there through the Treaty of Methven. Soon the English predominated and reduced the Portuguese to a secondary role. Joseph Pombal wanted *to shake off this yoke*, but his efforts were fruitless. During his struggle with England Napoleon forced Portugal to close her ports to the English. Then, having agreed with Spain, in a secret treaty signed at Fontainebleau in 1807, to share Portugal with her, he tried to conquer that country. But England defended it as if it were its *province*. In the general peace of 1815 the Portuguese royal family had to remain in Brazil, and Beresford, the British ambassador, governed the country. In 1820 *a revolution* broke out in Oporto.'[6]

---

[1] Word partly invented from Greek: πας (all) and from Latin *potens*, powerful, i.e. omnipotent.

[2] Latin *copiae*: army corps, troops. DLLB.

[2] Portugal: part of ancient Lusitania. DHB.

[4] HRU.

[5] EU.

[6] DHB.

## Franco's Birth in Galicia. His Departure to Morocco and His Assumption of Power, 1936. The Asturian Revolt, October 1934

Du plus profond de l'Espagne enseigne,[1]
Sortant du bout et des fins de l'Europe:[2]
Trouble passant auprès du pont[3] de Laigne,[4]
Sera deffaicte par bande sa grande troppe.

CX,Q48

### Interpretation

From furthest Spain [the West][5] will come an officer who will go to the end of the confines of Europe [Gibraltar] at the moment the revolution arrives by the sea of Llanes; and the band of revolutionaries will be defeated by his great army.

### History

'Having failed to gain a place at the Naval Academy, at fifteen the *Galician* Francisco Franco entered the Infantry School at Toledo. From 1912 to 1926 he served almost continuously in *Morocco*. At thirty-three he became the youngest *general in Europe*. In October 1934 he *put down the revolt* of the left in *the Asturias*. After being chief of the general staff ["*enseigne*"] in 1935, he was sent to the Canaries following the victory of the Popular Front in the February 1936 elections. On 19 July he took command of the African army at Tetuan and immediately asked the Axis for aeroplanes which transported his troops to the urban areas ["*sortant du bout et des fins de l'Europe*"]. After his reverse of November 1936 outside Madrid, he *defeated* the Republican armies and entered Madrid on 1 April 1939.'[6]

[1] Name formerly given to the standard-bearing officer and certain officers of the king's bodyguards. DL7V.
[2] Straits of Gibraltar between the Hispanic peninsula and the kingdom of Morocco. DHB.
[3] Greek: ποντός the sea. DGF. The *Asturian* coastline has many fishing ports, among them is Llanes. AE.
[4] Gallicization of Llanes.
[5] Galicia: Spanish province situated at the north-west *corner* of the peninsula. DHB.
[6] EU.

# Franco is Named Head of Government at Burgos, 1 October 1936. Primo de Rivera Allied with Franco in Fascism

De castel[1] Franco sortira l'assemblée,[2]
L'ambassadeur[3] non plaisant fera scisme,
Ceux de Ribière[4] seront en la meslée:
Et au grand goulphre[5] desnieront l'entrée.

CIX,Q16

## Interpretation

Franco will emerge from a junta in a strong place in Castile. The representative who has not pleased will make [fa]scism, those with [Primo] de Rivera will be with him; they will refuse to enter into the great gulf of misfortunes [Germany].

## History

'A *junta* of generals named him Generalissimo at *Burgos* on 12 September, then head of government on 1 October. After being chief of the general staff he was sent to the Canaries following the Popular Front's victory in the elections of February 1936. . . . Caudillo, chief, concentrating in his person all power and responsible only before God and history [rule of the *caudillaje*, sometimes confused with *fascism*]. . . .

A Fascist despite himself yet an unwitting liberal, at Valladolid on 4 March 1934, Primo de *Rivera* managed to unite the Falange and the National Syndicalists, whose sole leader he became soon afterwards. The assassinations of which the Falangists were victims goaded him to authorize his partisans to carry out reprisals [Falangist terrorism] ["*en la meslée*"].[6]

'During the Second World War General Franco, in spite of his links with the Axis Powers, remained neutral and *refused to allow the German armies* to cross through Spain.'[7]

---

[1] Latin *castellum*: stronghold. DLLB. Burgos: Spanish town, main town of old *Castile*, stronghold. DHB. Pun by Nostradamus on Castile/castle.
[2] Junta: council, *assembly* in Spain and Portugal. DL7V.
[3] Diplomatic agent or envoy representing a sovereign or State. DL7V.
[4] Gallicization of Rivera. The *b* and *v* are two interchangeable labials, e.g. Lefèvre and Lefèbre.
[5] Said of misfortune or miseries into which one falls: to fall into a gulf of ills. DL7V.
[6] EU.
[7] AE.

# The Axis Powers Aid Franco. The Spanish Civil War, 1936–39. The French Maquis of the South-west against the Germans, June 1944

Les Cimbres[1] joints avec leurs voisins,
Depopuler viendront presque l'Espagne
Gens amassez,[2] Guienne[3] et Limosins
Seront en ligue, et leur feront campagne.[4]

CIII,Q8

## Interpretation

The Germans allied with their neighbours [Italians] will come and lay waste the land as far as Spain. People united in Guyenne and Limousin will form a league and take the field against them.

## History

'*Italy* sent Franco's *Spain* war materials and expeditionary troops; *Germany* sent technicians and planes [the Condor Legion]. . . . The number of those who died for their political beliefs on either side is difficult to assess, but must have been *very high*. Adding to them the fighting men killed, a rough estimate would be 750,000 dead. The Axis powers [*Germany* and *Italy*] had been great supporters of the Francoists.'[5]

'On 6 June 1944 the Liberation of France began at Normandy. The Germans pushed forward their reserves, among them an armoured SS Division stationed in the Toulouse area. This should have been able to reach the new front in three days at most, but it had not reckoned with the *French Resistance*. Two groups ["*ligue*"], the Hervé and Alsace-Lorraine brigades, waited for it as it crossed the *Dordogne*, the Charente and the *Haute-Vienne*. Fighting took place from 7 June in the *Lot* district, at the Souillac bridge and Cressensac. The SS deployed its infantry to open up a route through this *Dordogne* region which had just held it up for thirty hours. Then it turned east towards *Limoges*. Exasperated, and henceforth in dread of the 'terrorists', the SS became a menace to the local civilian populations, always ready to exact reprisals. On 10 June 1944, *near Limoges*, the massacre of Oradour-sur-Glane was perpetrated.'[6]

[1] Germanic tribe established on the Elbe's right bank. DL7V.

[2] To amass, reassemble, reunite. DL7V.

[3] Guyenne is today composed of seven departments: Gironde, Landes, *Dordogne*, *Lot*, Aveyron, Lot-et-Garonne, Tarn-et-Garonne. DL7V.

[4] The word employed to denote military action in time of war, as opposed to peace – to take the field, go into action. DL7V.

[5] HEFDP.

[6] *Historama*, no. 272.

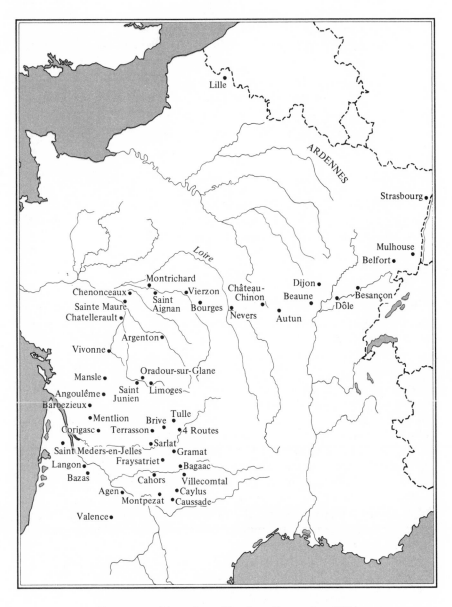

German positions from March to September 1944.
In each place marked on the map the SS carried out
executions and atrocious crimes. (Coll. Tallendier)
Extract from *Histoire pour tous*, no. 11
(March – April 1979)

# The End of the Spanish Republic, 1939.
## Massacres of the Clergy. The Capture of Seville, 1936

La vraye flamme engloutira la dame[1]
Que voudra mettre les Innocens[2] à feu,
Près de l'assaut l'exercite[3] s'enflamme,
Quand dans Seville monstre[4] en boeuf[5] sera veu.

CVI,QI9

## Interpretation

The real flame [of war] will engulf the Republic, which will want to put the Innocents to death. The assault forces will be inflamed when they have seen a disaster in the shape of a person at Seville.

## History

'The revolt began on 17 July 1936 at Melilla. Franco left the Canaries by air and took command of the Moroccan troops. . . . The coup succeeded quite easily at Saragossa in Old Castile and Galicia, the Republic ["*la dame*"] retaining the Cantabrian littoral. In Andalusia the military could only gain control of a few – though important – towns: *Seville* [with General Queipo de Llano], Cadiz, Cordova and Granada. All the Mediterranean side of Spain remained Republican. On the whole, the army and the Guardia Civil had favoured the coup, but not the *storm troops*, who were sent in against the workers' organizations. . . .

On the Republican side the Giral government could not prevent a real revolution. Except in the Basque country Catholicism was no longer respected and *thousands of clergy* ["*Innocens*"] perished. . . .

Taking the offensive on the Catalonian front at the end of December 1938, the Nationalists reached the frontier in six weeks. In the Madrid–Valencia zone, the partisans fought the war to the end, and it ended on 31 March 1939.

The victors of the Civil War built *a new state* around their leader, Francisco Franco ["*engloutira la dame*"].'[8]

---

[1] Customary use of feminine personage to denote Republic.
[2] Note capital I referring to priests.
[3] Latin *exercitus*: army. DLLB.
[4] Scourge, calamity. DLLB.
[5] Symbolic: coarse or brutal. DL7V.

# The Birth of Hitler in Austro-Bavaria, 1889. His Fight against the Soviet Union. The Mystery of His Death

Auprès du Rhin des montagnes Noriques[1]
Naistra un grand de gens trop tard venu,
Qui deffendra[2] Saurome[3] et Pannoniques.[4]
Qu'on ne sçaura qu'il sera devenu.

CIII,Q58

## Interpretation

Near the Rhine, a great leader of the people will be born in the Noric Alps, come too late; he will defend himself against Russia and Hungary; what becomes of him will be unknown.

## History

'Hitler, son of a customs official, born at Braunau-am-Inn, an *Austro-Bavarian* frontier town, in 1889.'[5]

'In this fight against *the USSR*, the Third Reich could count on the support of Romania, *Hungary* and Czechoslovakia. The role of the Regent, Horthy, was more modest, since *Budapest* had no quarrel with Moscow; only a minimal *Hungarian* force of two cavalry and one motorized brigade participated in this first phase of the campaign.'[6]

'At a press conference on 9 June Marshal Zhukov avoided the question uppermost in all our minds: that of Hitler's death. He did refer to it in surprising terms: "The circumstances were very *mysterious*," he said. "We have not identified the body of Hitler. I can say nothing definite about his fate. We found several bodies among which Hitler's might have been, but we cannot confirm that he is dead." On the tenth, the day after the press conference, Zhukov met Eisenhower at Frankfurt, who asked him point blank: "What do the Russians know about Hitler's corpse?" Zhukov replied no less bluntly: "Russian soldiers have found no trace of Hitler's body." '[7]

---

[1] Noricum, today part of *Bavaria* and Austria. The Noric Alps stretch across Carinthia, the Salzburg area and Austria as far as the Hungarian plains. DHB.

[2] Latin *defendo*: I push back, defend myself against. DLLB.

[3] Fr: Sauromates or Sarmates: those from Sarmathia, a vague name given by the ancients to a vast area west of Scythia, extending from Europe to Asia, between the Baltic and Caspian Seas. European Sarmathia, between the Vistula and the Tanais, including all the countries that today make up *Russia* and Poland. DHB.

[4] Ancient name for Hungary.
[5] DSGM.
[6] LDG.
[7] DSH.

---

# Hitler's Humble Origins, 1889.
# His Speeches. His Policies Towards Russia

Du plus profond de l'Occident d'Europe[1]
De pauvres gens un jeune enfant naistra,
Qui par sa langue séduira grande trouppe,
Son bruit au règne d'Orient plus croistra.

CIII,Q35

*Interpretation*

In the most easterly region of western Europe a child will be born to
poor parents. He will seduce great crowds with his oratory and will make
much more noise about the eastern power [USSR].

*History*

'Son of a customs official, born at Braunau, an Austro-Bavarian frontier
town in 1889. After an undistinguished school career, he began his life
not as a wastrel or wanderer but as a bourgeois bohemian living off *a
meagre inheritance from his parents.*'[2]

'Hitler, according to Alan Bullock, was the greatest *demagogue* in
history. It is no accident that these pages of *Mein Kampf* on *the conquest
of the masses* ["*séduira grand trouppe*"], winning them over to nationalism,
are among the most effective. Putting into practice such an efficient form
of *crowd*-rape suggests talents as an *orator* on the grand scale ["*langue*"],
with almost a sixth sense of their deepest needs. Hitler possessed these
qualities to an extraordinary degree.

The worst trap lay in the myth with which Hitler is finally identified,
that of the master race, kept pure at all costs, and which had to look *east*
for its expansion. Hence that obstinacy to stake all *upon Russia* and that
*fury* ["*bruit*"] with which he turned his murderous ideology into action
there.'[3]

[1] Austria is an easterly country of western Europe.
[2] DSGM.
[3] EU.

---

# Austria as a Breeding Ground for Nazi Ideology

Une nouvelle secte de Philosophes,
Méprisant mort, or, honneurs et richesses,
Des monts Germains ne[1] seront limitrophes,[2]
A les ensuyvre auront appuy et presses.

CIII,Q67

## Interpretation

A new sect of philosophers despising death, gold, honours and wealth will be born on the German borders and those who follow them will have support and audience.

## History

'The influence of *Vienna*: the hardest but most fruitful school of his life, Hitler said. He confirmed that he owed to it the foundations of his general view of society and a method of political analysis. In reality, the young Adolf had already formed his essential beliefs at Linz, during history classes run by Dr Poetsch, a pan-Germanist and anti-Semite. But in the capital of *Austro-Hungary*, daily life brought concrete justification for his odious theories ["*des monts Germains. . . limitrophes*"].'[3]

'Goering effectively took over command of the SA in spring 1923. He vetted each section, checking their loyalty, and made them sign a statement by which they had to be ready to risk their lives for the movement, to fight for its objectives and obey their superiors and the Führer utterly. Those who signed were utterly devoted to the cause and formed the hard core of the Nazi party. They were also the main force behind Hitler's political power.'[4]

'Hitler noticed Himmler, a twenty-five-year-old SS officer, very quickly and named him propaganda director in 1926, the year after his entry into the SS. This post was an excellent stepping-stone for a meteoric rise through the Nazi hierarchy ["*appuy et presses*"].'[5]

[1] Certain constructions, uncompleted by another negative, imply affirmative rather than negative. DL7V.

[2] Latin *limes*: limits, frontiers; placed on the limits of. DL7V.

[3] EU.

[4] *Histoire pour tous*, no. 9 (Nov.–Dec. 1978).

[5] *Histoire pour tous*, no. 9 (Nov.–Dec. 1978).

---

# Nazi Factions in Germany

En Germanie naistront diverses sectes,
S'approchant fort de l'heureux paganisme,
Le coeur captif et petites receptes[1]
Feront retour à payer le vray disme.[2]

CIII,Q76

## Interpretation

Various sects will spring up in Germany, greatly reminiscent of happy paganism, but their slavish aspects and slender resources will make them be despoiled in return.

## History

Factions: the SA, Youth Association of the Nazi party, the SS, the Hitler Youth, Thule Society, etc.

'Religious marriage was replaced by ancient wedding rites. The chief of the SS group presided, and when the couple exchanged rings he would offer bread and salt as a gift. It all diverted the couple away from the Church and towards a new cult, *a sort of Germanic neo-paganism*.

On 30 January, the anniversary of the seizure of power, the aspirant received a provisional SS identity card. On 20 April, Hitler's birthday, he received a full identity card, assumed the famous uniform and swore an oath of loyalty to the Führer: "I swear to you, Adolf Hitler, my leader, fidelity and bravery. I promise you and all those you designate to command me *obedience until death*." [3]

[1] Latin *recepta*: thing received. DLLB.

[2] *Dismer*: despoil, decimate. DAFL.

[3] Initiation rites of the Waffen SS: see *Histoire Pour Tous*, no. 9 (Nov.–Dec. 1978).

# Hitler in Power Thanks to the Weimar Republic, 1933. The First Volume of *Mein Kampf*, 1925

Sous ombre saincte d'oster de servitude,
Peuple et cité l'usurpera lui-mesme:
Pire fera par fraux[1] de jeune pute,[2]
Livre au champ[3] lisant le faux proësme.[4]

CV,Q5

## Interpretation

Under the saintly appearance of delivering people from servitude he will himself usurp the people's power and the town. He will wreak the worst by trickery with the aid of a new republic, using as text in the struggle the false ideas of the first part of his book.

## History

'At Munich, an ill-conceived and executed *putsch* [1923] led to the banning of the National Socialist Party and its Führer, who was condemned to five years' imprisonment [of which he served only thirteen months] in Landsberg Castle. This very comfortable captivity helped him write down his thoughts: *Mein Kampf*, Volume 1 ["*le faux proësme*"] appeared in 1925.

With their battle cadres the Communists in the doomed Weimar Republic ["*jeune pute*"] represented a force which contrived to weaken the regime and actually *assisted* the National Socialists. Hostility to the Treaty of Versailles, to the Weimar Republic, to bourgeois democracy and capitalism all resurfaced along with much else in the National Socialist ideology. At Munich in 1925 the "second founding" of the party took place under the recently freed Hitler's direction. In 1930 107 Nazi deputies were elected. This demonstrated the movement's strength and the success of *propaganda*, which found considerable assistance during the economic crisis and led to the 1933 triumph.'[5]

[1] Latin *fraus*: bad faith, trickery, ruse. DLLB.
[2] Latin *puta*: girl. DL7V. Cf. CV,Q12. Nostradamus designates by the term, often derogatory, a Republic.
[3] Said of any sort of struggle and the place where it occurs. DL7V.
[4] Proem: prologue, prelude to a work. DL7V.
[5] EU.

# Hitler Seizes Power, 1933. His Thirteen Years of Power, like the Emperor Claudius, 1933–45

> Celuy qu'en Sparte Claude ne peut régner,
> Il fera tant par voye séductive:
> Que du court long, le fera araigner,[1]
> Que contre Roy fera sa perspective.

CVI,Q84

## Interpretation

He who, like Claudius, does not have what is needed to rule Germany, achieves as much seduction by short speeches as long and will bring about a planned action against the government.

## History

Nostradamus establishes a parallel between Hitler and Claudius here, and Nazi Germany and Sparta elsewhere.

'Lycurgus built the Spartan state. He gave the state a military character, maintained by strict discipline, and communal education and meals. He held all executive power in his hands. *The Spartan state was organized upon conquest* and her history was an interminable series of wars. She sucked almost the whole of Greece into her battle with her rival, Athens. . . .

In his infancy the weak, sickly and timid Claudius was *given away to serfs. England* was conquered by Claudius in person. *The Rhine was liberated* and the right bank of the Danube [*Austria*] was conquered. Armenia was recaptured, Thrace [*the Balkans*] was overcome, while in *Africa* the conquest of Mauretania was accomplished. Domestically Claudius had to fight off *republican conspirators, whom he slaughtered.* Like Hitler, Claudius ruled *for thirteen years.*'[2]

'On 30 January 1933 Hitler agreed to form a government. He would become dictator in three stages. First, the Reichstag was dissolved and the new Reichstag voted Hitler, for four years, the full powers he requested. It was the end of the Weimar *Republic.* After a few months he was beset by critics and *opposition.* Hitler, anxious, began *the repression* with the Night of the Long Knives in 1934. Hitler held absolute power . . . he had known poverty, had lodged in doss-houses. . . . Unstable, with hysterical fits of temper and nervous crises, *an orator of extraordinary magnetism,* he carried audiences with him.'[3]

[1] *Paraisnier*: to discourse, speak. DAFL.
[2] DL7V.
[3] LMC.

# The Peace Declarations, 1938

L'oyseau de proye volant à la fenestre[1]
Avant conflit fait aux Français parure.[2]
L'un bon prendra, l'autre ambigu sinistre,[3]
La partie faible tiendra par bon augure.

CI,Q34

## Interpretation

The eagle, doing what he has decided to do, will honour the French before the war. One party will take him in good faith, the other, the left, will be ambivalent towards him. The weaker party will resist, luckily.

## History

'Peace overtures by Berlin and Moscow. The Reich and the USSR decided to consult each other upon necessary steps in case their peace proposals were not accepted by France and Britain. They claimed in this way to be establishing a lasting *peace* in central Europe, because they went on to partition Poland.

Communist propaganda: the Communist leaders only know one thing, how to translate Stalin's lies into French. The Bolsheviks must be credited with this – they do know their propaganda. But we who know about the finances of the newspaper industry can easily estimate the cost of such newspapers and magazines, which could explain why *the Communist leaders* find it impossible to sever their links with Moscow. Because it would be to their advantage, on French soil, to declare themselves *independent.*'[4]

[1] Come in or go out of the window: to do something no matter what. DL7V.
[2] Symbolic: that which embellishes, honours. DL7V.
[3] Latin *sinister*: left. DLLB.
[4] *L'Intransigeant*, 30 September 1939.

# The Munich Agreement, 1938. British Pacifism.
# The War, 1939

L'honnissement[1] puant abominable,
Apres le faict sera félicité:
Grand excusé,[2] pour n'estre favorable,[3]
Qu'à paix Neptune ne sera incité.

CVI,Q90

## Interpretation

Abominable and shameful infamy will follow the act on which they
congratulate themselves and which will only be a great pretext without
goodwill, to the point where Britain will not be incited to peace.

## History

'At the Quai d'Orsay on 6 December 1938 Ribbentrop and Georges
Bonnet signed the Franco–German declaration which seemed to end the
two nations' traditional hostility. The peace of Europe seemed assured.
Without actually declaring it specifically, Hitler seemed to be renouncing
forever, through Ribbentrop, any claims to Alsace or Lorraine. Particular
*congratulations* were voiced on the French side, in that various international agreements of theirs seemed to have been respected.'[4]

'In the Far East, as in Europe, Britain had long shown herself to be
anxious for *peace* and opposed to all direct action. But the most *pacifist*
of the heads of state, Neville Chamberlain, totally changed his attitudes
from 15 March 1939. The establishment of obligatory military service on
26 April, *in peacetime*, for the first time ever, was readily accepted by
public opinion. Though in August 1939 the government increased its
efforts to avoid war, it was without the least hesitation that it decided to
honour its obligation towards Poland. The British resolution in 1939 was
very different from the hesitation of 1914. The war which began for
Britain on 3 September 1939 was partly the result of short-sightedness
and a *pacifism* which did not know how to organize internationally where
the desire for peace was concerned. In 1939 a great dream of pacifism
crumbled ["*non incité*"] and Neville Chamberlain admitted this to
Parliament.'[5]

[1] Shame, infamy. DAFL.
[2] Latin *excuso*: I allege, make pretext for. DLLB.
[3] Latin *favorabilis*: benevolent. DLLB.
[4] LDG.
[5] HRU.

## The Death of Pius XI, 1939.
## The Pontificate of Pius XII, 1939–58

Par le décès du très vieillard pontife,
Sera esleu Romain de bon aage:
Qu'il sera dict que le Siège debiffe[1]
Et long tiendra et de picquant ouvrage.

CV,Q56

### Interpretation

After the very aged Pope's death, a middle-aged Pope will be elected.
He will be accused of harming the Holy See and will last a long time,
doing 'controversial' work.

### History

Pius XI, 1857–1939, was indeed elderly. 'Eugenio Pacelli, born in *Rome*
to an aristocratic *Roman* family, succeeded him in 1939 as Pius XII, *aged
sixty-three.* He was unquestionably a forceful personality whose *politics
and opinions have been criticized in various ways.* He had considerable
problems to face and did so vigorously, displaying *immense energy.* His
pontificate was also noteworthy for several acts or statements to which
he tried to lend great doctrinal significance. On some matters, Pius XII
remains a *controversial Pope.*'[2]
He died in 1958 after nineteen years as pontiff.

[1] *Debiffer*: put into a bad state. DL.
[2] EU.

---

## The Death of Pius XI, February 1939.
## Five Years of War, 1940–45. The Election of Pius XII

Après le Siège tenu dix et sept ans,
Cinq changeront en tel révolu terme:
Puis sera l'un esleu de même temps
Qui des Romains ne sera trop conforme.

CV,Q92

*Interpretation*

After a pontificate of seventeen years, five years will see changes that put an end to the revolution. Then at the same time will be elected one [a pope] who will be only too like the Romans.

*History*

Pius XI was elected Pope on 6 February 1922. He died on 10 February 1939 after a pontificate of seventeen years four days. 'Pius XII, born in *Rome* to an old aristocratic *Roman* family.'[1]

[1] EU.

In this cartoon of Churchill's face
the traditional determination of the British bulldog
is portrayed, symbolizing the spirit of endurance
shown in 1940
Extract from LDG

# Churchill Isolated in Politics, 1939.
# The German–Soviet Pact, 23 August 1939. War between Germany and Russia, 22 June 1941

Le gros mastin[1] de cité déchassé,
Sera fasché de l'estrange alliance,
Après avoir aux champs le cerf[2] chassé,
Le loup et l'Ours se donront défiance.

CV,Q4

## Interpretation

The great British bulldog [Churchill], after being isolated from the City, will be vexed by the strange alliance [the German–Soviet pact]. After chasing Poland from the field [of battle], Germany and Russia will defy each other.

## History

'All his life Churchill had a *powerfully* original personality. Everything about him was forceful and exaggerated [the big mastiff]. He was always a fighter who never admitted defeat. On the eve of the Second World War, despite a lively parliamentary and ministerial career, he seemed completely *isolated* from the Conservatives' decision-making bodies.

The Battle for Warsaw began on 9 September 1939 with the Wehrmacht attacking the Polish army. On 17 September, because of the *German–Soviet Pact*, the *Red Army* invaded eastern *Poland*. On 28 September the fifth partition of Poland occurred, this time involving Germany and the USSR ["*Ours*"/bear]. All hopes for her liberation now lay with Britain, who had remained alone in the fight. Hitler did not succeed in conquering her. . . . *Churchill's* resolve was unshakable.

Although the USSR kept to the letter of the economic clauses of the *German–Soviet Alliance*, to Germany's benefit, Hitler decided to drive her out of Europe before dealing with Britain. On 21 June 1941, without formal declaration of war, the Wehrmacht attacked the Red Army.'[3]

'German–Soviet relations, it was agreed, should be clarified before 26 August. The spectacular reconciliation of the Third Reich and Bolshevik Russia was timed to produce in London and Paris the effect of a real earthquake.'[4]

---

[1] The word *dogue* for bulldog appears only rarely in French before the seventeenth century. It was thus considered as a *large mastiff* coming from *England*. DL7V.

[2] Symbolic. In *Christian* legend and on monuments the deer features prominently. DL7V. Hence the deer used as a symbol for the devoutly Catholic Poland.
[3] EU.
[4] LDG.

---

# The Annexation of Czechoslovakia, 15 March 1939. German Landings in Tripolitania, February 1941

Foibles galeres seront unis ensemble,
Ennemis faux le plus fort en rempart:
Faible assaillies Vratislave[1] tremble,
Lubecq[2] et Mysne[3] tiendront barbare[4] part.

CIX,Q94

## Interpretation

When the weak warships are reunited the strongest country [the German Reich] will keep watch against false enemies [the Hungarians]. The weak will be attacked and Bratislava will tremble. Those of Lübeck and Misnen [Germans] will occupy part of North Africa.

## History

'*Weakness* of the German navy. Vice-Admiral Kurt Assmann, its historian, wrote: "The situation was the reverse of that of 1914. Then we possessed a powerful fleet but had no strategic position or proper base. Now we had such a strategic base, but not one fleet able to do anything to take any advantage from it."

On 9 March 1939 negotiations between Prague and *Bratislava* on Slovak autonomy reached a dead end, and President Hacha tried to act to unite the state. Shortly afterwards Hitler riposted by giving the Czech government a seven-point *ultimatum*. In this explosive atmosphere, on 14 March, and fearing Hungarian aggression [*"faux ennemis"*] *the Diet of Bratislava* proclaimed Czechoslovakia's independence, while asking the Chancellor–Führer to *guarantee* [*"le plus fort en rempart"*] the existence of the new state and take all necessary measures to *safeguard* its frontiers.

From 1 February to 30 June 1941 no fewer than 81,785 Axis troops disembarked at *Tripoli* with almost 450,000 tonnes of supplies, munitions and fuel. North Africa therefore contained divisions of the Italian army as well as the 5th Light Division which formed the forward unit of the German Afrika Korps [*"ceux de Lübeck"*].'[5]

[1] Bratislava, capital of Slovakia.
[2] Lübeck: German town 15 km from the Baltic.
[3] German town on the North Sea.
[4] Barbary: area of North Africa comprising Tripoli, Tunis, Algiers and Morocco. DHB.
[5] LDG.

# The Annexation of Poland, 1939.
# The Invasion of France via Holland and Belgium.
# The Restitution of Alsace-Lorraine to the
# French Republic, 1919

Quand le plus grand emportera le pris[1]
De Nuremberg, d'Ausbourg et ceux de Basle,[2]
Par Agrippine[3] chef[4] Frankfort repris.
Traverseront par Flamant jusqu'en Gale.

CIII,Q53

*Interpretation*

When the greatest [Hitler] takes the [country] prisoner [Poland] the Germans will cross Flanders [Holland and Belgium] as far as France, after the most important article of [the Treaty of] Frankfurt has been taken back by the Republic [annexation of Alsace-Lorraine by Germany].

*History*

'Having disposed of *Poland*, Hitler turned his attentions west, and revised his plan of attack on *Belgium* and *Holland*. The main force of German paratroops was scheduled to jump over or into the *Netherlands Redoubt* or *Vesting-Holland*. It was agreed not to transfer the main thrust of the attack to the south of Liège.'[5]

'The Treaty of Versailles was signed on 28 June 1919 in the same Hall of Mirrors which on 18 January 1871 had witnessed the proclamation of the German Empire by Bismarck. The signature of the peace was intended to have the character of a ceremony of expiry. From the territorial point of view, Germany *restored* Alsace-Lorraine to France.'[6]

[1] Used as prisoner, captured.
[2] Towns inhabited by Germanic peoples.
[3] Wife of Domitius Aenobarbus, always taken by Nostradamus as symbol of the Republic.
[4] Figurative: article, division, importance. DL7V.
[5] LDG.
[6] HFAM.

## The Maginot Line. The Rhine. Paris Occupied, 14 June 1940

Près du grand fleuve, grand fosse,[1] terre egeste[2]
En quinze pars sera l'eau divisée:
La cité prinse, feu, sang, cris, conflit mettre,
Et la plus part concerne[3] au collisée.[4]

CIV,Q80

*Interpretation*

Near the great river [Rhine] will be dug a great ditch, the drainage system will be divided into fifteen parts. The town [Paris] will be taken and the conflict will put all to fire and blood; and the majority of the French will be involved in the upheaval.

*History*

'The original plan of the offensive gave the principal role to the northern forces, Group B, under von Bock. He was to execute a wide sweep across the Netherlands, supported by Group A (von Rundstedt) which was the centre of the German disposition, facing the Ardennes, and by Group C (Leeb) on the left flank in front of the *Maginot Line*. It was a repetition of the 1914 German offensive, therefore unlikely to surprise the Allies; what was more, it meant sending armoured forces into a country criss-crossed by *innumerable canals and little rivers*.

Tanks and armoured vehicles formed a 160 km column extending 80 km beyond the other bank of the Rhine! The plan was an extraordinary success. Hitler wanted to avoid a stalemate such as happened after the Battle of the Marne in 1914. He sought at all costs to deploy his armoured troops in readiness for the second phase of the offensive, the battle for Paris and France. In eleven days it was all over, and on 14 June the Germans *entered Paris*.'[5]

---

[1] Latin *fossa*: ditch, trench. DLLB.
[2] Latin *egestu penitus cavare terras*: to dig out, throwing up earthworks. DLLB.
[3] Latin *concerno*: I mix. DLLB.
[4] Latin *collisio*: crash, shock. DLLB.
[5] HAB.

# The Invasion of the Netherlands and Belgium, 10 May 1940

Par l'apparence de faincte[1] saincteté,
Sera trahy aux ennemis le siège:
Nuict qu'on cuidait[2] dormir en seureté,
Près de Braban[3] marcheront ceux de Liège.

CVI,Q30

*Interpretation*

Under cover of feigned piety, the country will be besieged by enemies, through treachery, while the people thought they were sleeping safely. The troops who will be in Liège will march across Belgium.

*History*

'On 6 December 1938 Georges Bonnet, the French Foreign Minister, and his German counterpart, Ribbentrop, signed at the Quai d'Orsay *a joint declaration* which, based on the Munich agreement, *seemed* to put an end to the two countries' traditional hostility. It was thought in Paris that Hitler and Ribbentrop had vetoed any new recourse to aggression or unilateral measures which, three times in less than three years, had almost set Europe alight.'[4]

'The German Army invading *the Netherlands* and France on 10 May 1940 was eighty-nine divisions strong, with forty-seven more held in reserve. The first success was the destruction of the Dutch and Belgian defensive system, made possible because German commanders captured points vital for the offensive and also the famous fort of Eben-Emael on the *Albert Canal* [*Liège*]. The Wehrmacht armour swiftly crossed the Ardennes and the French frontier on 12 May. On 5 June the German Army resumed the offensive by crossing the Somme and advancing southwards. In eleven days it was all over and the Germans entered Paris.'[5]

[1] *Feinte*: sham, pretended. DAFL.
[2] *Croire*: believe. DAFL.
[3] Duchy of three provinces: (1) Noordbraband, comprising the largest province of the kingdom of the Netherlands; (2) Brabant, in Belgium; (3) Anvers, in Belgium. DL7V.
[4] LDG.
[5] HAB.

# The Vichy Government. The Occupation, 1940–44.
## General de Gaulle in London, 18 June 1940.
## The Landing: Rouen and Chartres

Règne[1] Gaulois tu seras bien changé,
En lieu estrange est translaté l'empire:
En autre moeurs et lois seras rangé,[2]
Roan, et Chartres te feront bien du pire.

CIII,Q49

*Interpretation*

French government, you will be much changed; the empire will be transferred into another country; you will be subjected to other ways and laws. Those who will come through Rouen and Chartres will wreak still further ill upon you.

*History*

'The fate of the *French Empire* was at stake. There was no one in France to inspire her to resist now that Pétain and a team of defeatists had taken office. If North Africa and the *French Empire* were to be saved it could only be from *London*. . . . I was going to return to England with de Gaulle and help him put his plans into practice. He was right: it was essential that without a moment's delay the call for resistance should come from *England*, as an immediate response to Pétain's demand for an armistice.'[3]

'Then the advance to the Seine, during which the Germans no longer resisted but evacuated as quickly as possible the country they had occupied for four years. Four Allied armies participated in this pursuit: the Canadian 1st Army advanced on *Rouen* and captured it on 27 August. The American 3rd Army thrust towards *Paris*: starting from Alençon and Le Mans, it reached Verneuil, Dreux and Mantes in the north, and *Chartres* and Rambouillet in the south, the final step. After the capture of Paris and the crossing of the Seine the campaign changed decisively.'[4]

---

[1] Latin *regnum*: government. DLLB.
[2] Figurative: to submit to a duty or be obedient.
[3] 'How I took General de Gaulle back to England' by Edward Spears. Dossier: *Historama* no. 23.
[4] HLFRA.

## Pétain, Hitler and Stalin.
## The Twenty Months of Absolute Occupation

Le vieux frustré du principal espoir,
Il parviendra au chef de son empire
Vingt mois tiendra le règne à grand pouvoir
Tiran cruel en délaissant un pire.

CVIII,Q65

*Interpretation*

The old [Marshal] frustrated in his principal hope, [Hitler] will reach the summit of his power and will hold power by force for twenty months, a cruel tyrant leaving a worse one behind him.

'The progress of the German-Russian collaboration.'
The two tyrants! (LDG)

*History*

'On 11 November 1942 Free France was occupied by the Germans. . . .
On 6 June 1944, the Allies landed in Normandy.'[1]
  From 11 November 1942 to 6 June 1944 = *nineteen months, twenty-five
days!*
  'From 1951 to 1955 the Russian regime grew more repressive. The
fight against internationalism was distinguished by persecutions of the
Jews in particular.
  The assassination of Kirov at Leningrad in 1936 was the signal for a
series of upheavals. The death penalty was the punishment for those out
of step with the regime. It even threatened the highest party officials.
The extent of the repression was only matched by the amazing compla-
cency with which the accused confessed ["*a worse. . .*"!].'[2]

[1] PCHF.
[2] LMC.

---

## Milestones in Hitler's Life:
### 1889, 1915, 1921, 1939 and 1945

Plusieurs mourront avant que Phoenix[1] meure,
Jusques six cents septante[2] est sa demeure,
Passé quinze ans, vingt et un, trente-neuf,
Le premier est subjet à maladie,
Et le second au fer[3] danger de vie,
Au feu[3] à l'eau[4] est subjet trente-neuf.

                                                    Sixain 53

*Interpretation*

Many will die before the Phoenix [Hitler] dies. After fifty-five years ten
months he will find his [last] home, when the years 1915, 1921 and 1939
have passed. In 1915 he will succumb to illness; in 1921 he will have an
armed force dangerous to his life; 1939 will be subject to a rain of fire.

*History*

'Adolf Hitler, born in 1889. Corporal, twice *wounded*, 1915.'[5]
  '*1921* was a successful one for the party, which now had 6000 or more

supporters, many of whom were in the SA, which the Munich papers dubbed *"Hitler's bodyguard"*.[6]

'While on a recruiting drive through Germany [they had 3000 supporters at the end of *1921*], Captain Roehm, his deputy, mobilized the *paramilitary* wing or assault squads of the SA. Hitler liquidated the right-wing opposition on the Night of the Long Knives [30 June 1934]. Several hundred were massacred, among them Schleicher, who tried to regroup those soldiers who had remained *lukewarm* towards Hitler, and Roehm, the all too powerful and independent leader of the SA.'[7]

'During the last weeks, in *March*–April 1945, the hunted Führer killed himself with a bullet through the mouth.'[5]

'They had news from the outside world of the capture and execution of Mussolini and Clara Petacci. The Duce and his mistress were hung upside-down in Milan. Eva Hitler cried out: "Will they do the same to us?" The Führer assured her that this would not happen and that their bodies would be *consumed* by fire until nothing remained, not even ashes.'[8]

[1] The legendary phoenix *lived for several centuries*. It was big as an *eagle*. When its end was approaching it *made itself a nest* of branches oozing sap or resin, exposed it to the sun's rays and was consumed therein. DL7V.

[2] April 1889–March 1945 = 670 months.

[3] Using fire and sword: violent means to attain one's end. Carrying the sword (iron) and flame into a country, meaning to ravage it with murder and war. DL7V.

[4] Biblical sense: deluge, flood. DL7V.

[5] EU.

[6] See *Histoire pour tous*, no. 9 (Nov.–Dec. 1978), about the SA.

[7] AE.

[8] LGESGM.

---

# The Liebensborn.[1] *Mein Kampf*

La voye auxelle[2] l'un sur l'autre fornix[3]
Du muy[4] de fer hor mis brave[5] et genest:[6]
L'escript d'empereur le fenix,
Veu en celuy ce qu'a nul autre n'est.

CVIII,Q27

## Interpretation

The means through which sexual relations were facilitated between one and another in the iron movement [SS], except for the wellborn. The book of the emperor phoenix in which one sees what is seen nowhere else.

## History

'In the *Liebensborn* or "love camps", where carefully chosen young women were at their disposal, the SS *procreated outside marriage* 6000–7000 children a year of "pure race", who were immediately abandoned to the care of the organization.

Coming as they did out of the Hitler Youth, the SS men had to conform to the Nazis' concept of a Germanic ideal: more than 1.75 m in height, with perfect health and teeth, "Aryan" looks, Nordic origin traceable back to 1750 for the leaders, *bravery* and absolute obedience.'[7]

'*No theoretician had been ready or able* to translate the myth into reality. Hitler the cold auto-didact, prompted by a coarse Darwinism which cheaply invoked "nature" and her cruelty, was ready and clever enough to take this step with implacable logic.'[8]

[1] Love-camps, concentration camps for breeding purposes.
[2] Latin *auxillium*: aid, help. DLLB.
[3] Fornication: sex between unmarried persons who are not tied by any vows. DL7V.
[4] Form of present and perfect of *mouvoir*, to move. DAFL.
[5] Intrepid, *courageous*, great, remarkable. DL7V.
[6] Greek γενέσθαι: aorist infinitive of γίγνομαι to be born. DGF.
[7] DSGM.
[8] EU.

---

# Hitler and the Third Reich.
# The Gas Chambers and Massacres. German Prosperity and Disaster

> Le tiers premier pis que ne fit Néron,[1]
> Vuider vaillant que sang humain répandre:
> Rédifier fera le forneron[2]
> Siècle d'or mort, nouveau Roy grand esclandre.
>
> CIX,QI7

## Interpretation

The first [person] of the Third [Reich] will do worse than Nero. He will be as valiant in draining as in shedding human blood: he will cause ovens to be built; prosperity will be at an end, and this new leader will cause great scandals.

## History

'Hitler, *Chancellor* ["*premier*"] of Germany in 1933, properly appointed by President Hindenburg, attained by plebiscite in 1934 absolute power as Chancellor–Führer of the new regime, the Third Reich. He succeeded in curbing the huge unemployment problem [6,200,000 out of work in 1932], in re-establishing *prosperity* ["*siècle d'or*"], and embarking upon housing and other building projects, social benefits schemes etc., which ensured him enormous popular support.'[3]

'Enraged by hatred for the Jews and against Christianity too [Nero!], the Germans also inflicted upon the Russian prisoners of war the worst slavery, by contrast with the *blissful* existence ["*siècle d'or*"] waiting for the German working man.

In 1945 books and films appeared entitled *Germany, Year Zero*, because the country seemed so totally *destroyed* ["*siècle d'or mort*"]. The mass graves and *crematoria* made people understand certain facts about 1945. Germany's unconditional surrender marked the end of *the huge massacre* planned and unleashed by Hitler. The towns were in ruins. *Dead*, prisoners, injured – *millions* of them. Into the chaos created by Hitler's total war millions of Germans were hurled, expelled from central European countries. Occupied Germany was in abject *misery*.'[4]

---

[1] Nero was present at a huge fire which consumed most of Rome. When accused of being its perpetrator, he rejected the Christians' accusation and massacred and tortured them cruelly. DHB. For Nostradamus, the Jews were to be Hitler's scapegoats as the Christians had been for Nero.

[2] Latin *fornus* or *furnus*: oven. DLLB.

[3] DSGM.

[4] EU.

---

# Hitler's Persecutions. The New Nero. The July Plot, 1944

Le Néron[1] jeune dans les trois cheminées,[2]
Fera de paiges[3] vifs pour ardoir[4] jetter,
Heureux qui loin sera de tels menées,
Trois de son sang le feront mort guetter.

CIX,Q53

## Interpretation

The new Nero will hurl into three ovens [Auschwitz, Dachau and Bir-
kenau] young people to burn them alive. Happy they who are far from
such acts. Three of his blood [Germans] will spy on him to kill him.

## History

'The extermination plan's outlines were laid down during a conference
near Berlin, on 20 January 1942, under the presidency of Heydrich:
"The final solution to the Jewish problem in Europe will be applied to
approximately 11 million persons."

Thereafter, under Eichmann's direction, Jews were methodically
hunted and rounded up to be sent mostly to Auschwitz for extermination.
According to the camp's director, 3 million deportees perished at Auschwitz. In all the camps the victims' bodies were *burned* in ovens
["*cheminées*"]. . . .

Towards the end of the war numerous opposition groups of very varied
natures and aims came into existence. The most important of these was
one which organized an assassination attempt upon Hitler. It was headed
by Karl Goerdeler, ex-burgomeister of Leipzig, and General Beck. Co-
lonel von Stauffenberg ["*trois de son sang*"] placed a bomb (that proved
not powerful enough) in Hitler's headquarters on 20 July 1944. The
attempt failed: Hitler was only slightly injured.'[5]

[1] Cf. CIX,Q17.
[2] Derived from *caminus*: oven. DL7V.
[3] Young boy. DAFL.
[4] To burn. DAFL.
[5] EU.

---

# Hitler in Power. Stauffenberg's Assassination Attempt on Hitler, 20 July 1944

> Avec le noir Rapax et sanguinaire
> Issu de peautre[1] de l'inhumain Néron:[2]
> Emmy[3] deux fleuves main gauche militaire,
> Sera meurtry[4] par joyne chaulveron.[5]

CIX,Q76

*Interpretation*

With the rapacious [eagle], black and bloody, spawned from the pallet of the inhuman Nero, caught between two rivers[6] because of the armed forces of the left [Russian troops], [Hitler] will be wounded by a young man [Stauffenberg] who will burn him.

> Au grand Empire parviendra tost un autre
> Bonté distant[7] plus de félicité:
> Regi par un yssu non loing du peautre,
> Corruer regnes grande infelicité.

CVI,Q67

*Interpretation*

In the great German Empire [the Reich] another leader will soon rise to power. But good fortune being distant there will be no more luck. Germany will be ruled by one spawned from the pallet [of Nero] who will hurl himself against countries causing them great miseries.

*History*

'Stauffenberg had only been gone one or two minutes when at 12.42 a violent blast wrecked the Conference Room, blew in the walls and roof and *set ablaze* the debris which rained upon the occupants. Amid the cries of the wounded and the guards running to the scene, Hitler staggered out from the smoke and confusion, supported by Keitel. The explosion had ripped one of his trouser legs and he was covered in dust and numerous cuts and *bruises* ["*meurtry*"]. His hair was *burned*, his right arm hung limp and stiff, one leg was *burned*: a falling beam had bruised his back and his eardrums had been affected by the explosion.'[8]

---

[1] *Peautre* or *peltre*: pallet, mean bed. DAFL.
[2] Cf. CIX,Q17.
[3] In the middle of. DAFL.
[4] *Meurtrir*: to wound or harm, bruise. DL7V.
[5] From *chalder*: to warm or heat up. DAFL.
[6] Rastenburg, scene of the assassination attempt, is between the Vistula and the Niemen, equidistant from these two rivers.
[7] Latin *distans*: removed, absent, distant. DLLB.
[8] HAB.

# Hitler's Power in October 1939

L'autheur des maux commencera régner[1]
En l'an six cens et sept[2] sans espargner
Tous les subjets qui sont à la sangsue,[3]
Et puis après s'en viendra peu à peu,
Au franc pays rallumer son feu,
S'en retournant d'où elle est issue.

Sixain 21

## Interpretation

He who will provoke great misfortunes will see the start of his power in
October 1939, without sparing the revolutionaries, and little by little will
come and make war in France, returning whence he came [Germany].

## History

'Having disposed of Poland, Hitler turned his attentions westwards. His
arguments were that the likely abandonment by Belgium of her neutrality
threatened the Rhineland and thus compelled Germany to *win space*, and
that as the British war effort was getting under way it was necessary to
prepare methods of launching an offensive. This was to take place between 20 and 25 October, through Holland and Belgium, and would lead
to the crushing of the Allied forces, gaining for Germany sufficient
territory in northern *France* from which to extend airborne and naval
operations. Generals von Brauchitsch and Halder presented, *on 19 October*, a first draft of the invasion plans, entitled the Yellow Plan.'[4]

'Hitler had a horror of Marxism, all the stronger for its being, in his
view, a Jewish doctrine, invented by a Marx and spread in Austria by
Austerlitzes, Davids and Adlers.'[5]

[1] Latin *regnum*: reign, empire, power. DLLB.
[2] April 1889–October 1939 = 607 months.
[3] Latin *sanguisuga*: bloodsucker. DLLB. Nostradamus uses this word for revolution,
the drinker of blood.
[4] LDG.
[5] EU.

# Ironies of War, from the Polish Defeat, September 1939, to the Invasion of France, January 1940

Au grand siège encore grands forfaits,
Recommençant plus que jamais
Six cens et cinq[1] sur la verdure,
La prise et reprise sera,
Soldats es[2] champs jusqu'en froidure
Puis après recommencera.

Sixain 14

## Interpretation

At the great siege [Warsaw] there will be great forfeits, and beginning again more than ever in September 1939 the army will be in the field ["*verdure*"]. The town will be taken and retaken; the soldiers will no longer be in the field until the cold, then war will begin again.

## History

'On 28 September 1939 Warsaw surrendered after two weeks of heroic resistance. The bombing had set fire to its flour mills, and over half its water supply and sewage system was destroyed.

The torrential rains of early autumn 1939 persuaded Hitler to delay till the last moment the offensive due to be launched on 12 November. Up to *16 January 1940* the *weather* caused no fewer than thirteen delays.

On 10 February 1940 the Führer met his generals and staff in his office at the new Chancellery. He informed them of his decision to launch the western offensive on the seventeenth at Aix-la-Chapelle, at dawn, 8.16 a.m. According to him, the meteorological situation prompted this sudden decision. A ridge of high pressure approaching from the east from the twelfth or thirteenth would mean settled, dry weather over Holland, though the temperature would drop *to 10–15° below zero*.'[3]

---

[1] April 1889–September 1939 = 605 months.
[2] Prefix expressing taking away, extraction. DAFL. Hence, literally, out of the field.
[3] LDG.

# Hitler on the Champs Elysées

Six cens et six, six cens et neuf,[1]
Un Chancelier gros comme un boeuf,[2]
Vieux comme le Phoenix du monde,
En ce terroir plus ne luyra,
De la nef[3] d'oubly passera,
Aux champs Elisiens faire ronde.

Sixain 25

## Interpretation

September 1939, January 1940, a coarse and brutal Chancellor, like the Phoenix in the world, will end by no longer shining in France, his power will pass into oblivion, when he has passed along the Champs Elysées.

## History

'*1st September 1939*: the Second World War begins.

Plans of German aggression unveiled. As the invasion on *12 January 1940* was imminent, Hitler addressed a new memorandum to certain factions of his command.'[4]

'On 14 June the first sections of the German 18th Army entered the French capital, declared an open city. At the start of the *Champs Elysées* German officers and an Italian army representative in civilian clothes awaited the arrival of a *column* of troops on to the Place de la Concorde.

The classical image of great politicians – Richelieu, Napoleon and Bismarck, say – is tied up with a certain charm or distinction. Hitler gave this image the lie. His personality was incurably vulgar, *coarse, cruel* [one discovers this from the books about the war period as well as from *Mein Kampf*], and disconcertingly brusque.'[5]

---

[1] From Hitler's birth (April 1889) to September 1939 = 606 months, i.e. fifty years six months; and to January 1940 = 609 months.

[2] Big, brutal. DL7V.

[3] Latin *navis*: ship. *Navis Reipublicae*: the Ship of State (Cicero). DLLB.

[4] LDG.

[5] EU.

# The Armistice of Villa Incisa, 22 June 1940.
# The Demarcation Line. The Occupation

D'un chef vieillard naistra sens hébété,[1]
Dégénérant[2] par scavoir et par armes,
Le chef de France par sa soeur redoubté,
Champs divisez, concedez aux gens d'armes.

CI,Q78

*Interpretation*

The good sense of an old leader will be rendered stupid, losing the glory
of his wisdom and feats of arms; the chief of France will be suspected
by his sister [Latin, i.e. Italy]. Then the land will be divided and
abandoned to the soldiers.

*History*

'Pétain's *senility* explained all. He was not aware of many things and
only half understood the rest. The defence counsel was obviously convinced that if he presented his client in this way, he would reinforce his
own well-organized defence. While he was speaking, Pétain seemed as
angry as the prosecution. "He's pleaded senility!" he said in irritation.'[3]

'The armistice of Villa Incisa: at Bordeaux no one of course knew
Mussolini's final conversion to Hitler's point of view about the neutral-
ization of the French fleet. This is why on 22 June, with *Marshal Pétain's
approval*, Admiral Darlan sent the other admirals the following telegram:
"If a Franco–German armistice is concluded, it must not be effected
until one with Italy is also signed, since blackmail is possible. If the
Italian conditions are unacceptable, I foresee putting the French fleet
into short-term action against military and sensitive areas on the Italian
coastline." The Italo–French armistice was signed at Villa Incisa in the
countryside near Rome on 22 June at 7.35 p.m.'[4]

[1] To render stupid, feeble-minded. DL7V.
[2] Figurative: to lose the brilliance of birth, nobility, merit.
[3] PGB.
[4] LDG.

# The Fall of the Third Republic, 22 June 1940

Six cens et quinze, vingt, grand Dame[1] mourra,
Et peu après un fort long temps plouvra[2]
Plusieurs pays, Flandres et l'Angleterre
Seront par feu et par fer affligez,
De leurs voisins longuement assiégés
Contraints seront de leur faire la guerre.

Sixain 54

## Interpretation

On the twentieth of the 615th month the Republic will die. Shortly afterwards war will rage for a long time. Several countries and especially Flanders and England will endure a rain of metal and flame; besieged by the Germans, they will have to wage war upon them.

## History

Taking our starting-point as 1889, if we add 615 months, we come to 20 June 1940.

'*The collapse of the Third Republic.* By the terms of the 22 June armistice, two-thirds of France was occupied by the Germans and the rest submitted to the authority of the Vichy government. Given full powers by Parliament, Pétain installed the *French state.*

The multiplication of fronts and the first setbacks, June 1940–early 1943: Hitler set out to make *Britain* surrender by means of *intensive bombing.* . . . New powers entered the war. . . .'[3]

The two cities that endured the worst ravages of the V1s and V2s were *London* and *Anvers* (England and Flanders).

---

[1] Grand Dame: Marianne, symbol of the French Republic.
[2] In the sense of troubled waters, agitation, also.
[3] *Third-Form History* (textbook, Editions Dunod).

# The Liberation of Italy by the Americans, British and French 1943–44

Milan, Ferrare, Turin et Aquilleye,[1]
Capue, Brundis[2] vexez par gent Celtique,
Par le Lyon et phalange aquilée,[3]
Quand Rome aura le chef vieux Britannique.

CV,Q99

*Interpretation*

Milan, Ferrara, Turin, Aquilia, Capua and Brindisi will be harassed by the French, the British lion and the army of the eagle [America], when the old British chief [Montgomery] will hold Rome.

*History*

'Seeing the risk the *American 5th Army* was running, Alexander called on *Montgomery* ["*le vieux chef Britannique*"] to ask him to ensure that he would surprise the attackers on the bridgehead. Some of the 8th Army had quietly landed in the well-equipped ports of Taranto and *Brindisi*. In spite of the evacuation of Naples on 1 October, they pushed on towards Rome via Cassino and Formia. On 22 November the French expeditionary force ["*gent Celtique*"] began disembarking in Italy.'[4]

On 4 June 1944, Allied Armies entered Rome.

[1] Aquilia: southern Italian town.
[2] Brundisium: Brindisi. DLLB.
[3] Latin *aquila*: eagle. DLLB.
[4] LDG.

---

# The French Expeditionary Force Lands in Italy, Winter 1944. Fierce Fighting at Monte Cassino and the Capture of Rome. Disagreements among Allied Commanders

De vaine emprinse[1] l'honneur indue plainte,
Galliots[2] errans[3] par latins, froid, faim, vagues.
Non loing du Tymbre de sang la terre tainte,
Et sur humains seront diverses plagues.[4]

CV,Q63

## Interpretation

A vain and futile enterprise undertaken for reasons of honour will be deplored, [landing] craft will make for the Italian coast, [assault] waves will take place in winter, with starvation; the land will be bloodstained near the Tiber and men will be stricken with different wounds.

## History

'General Clark kept us informed of the sad reverses of his landing at Salerno. He had been a hair's breadth away from being driven back into the sea by a German armoured corps. He had only held out thanks to *the support fleet* under Admiral Cunningham which fearlessly moved in nearer shore. . . . Next day, 1 October, we were at Pompeii. One could scarcely take risks in rough *wintry* countryside, yet it still cost us 65,000 men. The December 1943 operations had only gained control of the position we called *"Winter"* which covered the main line of resistance, called "Gustav", from which Marshal Kesselring, our opponent in Italy, hoped to stop all Allied progress towards Rome. In early January 1944 Anzio had allowed the French Expeditionary Force to breach the line for themselves. It was to cost numerous *futile* sacrifices [*"indue"*]. The road down to the Rapido, which had to be used for much of the way, was *quite murderous* [*"de sang la terre tainte"*] during the winter campaign. *Massive slaughter* took place there, only in order to force back the Gustav line to the Belvedere. For later operations and the push north, the French Expeditionary Force resumed its normal position *east of the Tiber* [*"non loin du Tymbre"*], in the mountains. At Carpinetto a French officer and his men, who had preferred to be billeted in a castle where they had been preceded by the Germans, were blown up by a booby-trap mine in the middle of the night and nearly all killed [*"diverses plagues"*].[5]

[1] For enterprise, by syncope.
[2] *Galliot*: small craft. DAFL.
[3] To voyage, wander. DAFL.
[4] Latin *plaga*: wound, bruise, contusion. DLLB.
[5] LCI.

# The Germans in Paris, 1940.
# The Attack on the Soviet Union, 22 June 1941.
# Allied Troops in Normandy and the Alps, 1944

En la cité où le loup entrera,
Bien près de là les ennemis seront:
Copie[1] estrange grand pays gastera,
Aux murs[2] et Alpes les amis passeront.

CIII,Q33

## Interpretation

In the town which the German enters [Paris], the enemies will be very close; foreign troops will injure a great country [Russia]. By the cliffs [of Normandy] and the Alps the Allies shall pass.

## History

'The French armistice with Germany was signed on 21 June 1940 at Rethondes, the one with Italy at Rome on 24 June. They came into force on 25 June. *Marching into Paris* and singing, the *German* troops crossed a Place de la Concorde empty of vehicles.

The Atlantic *Wall* was not a fiction, nor was it the seamless system of fortification described by Goebbels. Boulogne, Le Havre and Cherbourg were strongly fortified; some large forts were built at the port of Calais, but the rest was often just a sketch or blueprint.'[3]

'The Wehrmacht was then caught between two theatres; at the end of April, a month after the landing, there were fifty-two divisions in France, six in Holland, six in Belgium and twenty-four in *Italy [the Alps]* as opposed to 202 in *Russia ["grand pays gâtera"]*.'[4]

[1] Latin *copia*: troops. DLLB.
[2] Cliffs – defined as vertical natural walls, mostly limestone. DL7V.
[3] *Historama* no. 271: '*Overlord*' by Raymond Cartier.
[4] HLFRA.

# After Sicily, the Landing in Calabria, 3 September 1943

Le nouveau faict conduira l'exercite,[1]
Proche apamé[2] jusqu'auprès du rivage:
Tendant secours de Milannoise eslite
Duc yeux[3] privé à Milan fer de cage.

CIX,Q95

## Interpretation

A new feat of arms will lead the army near Apameste [in Calabria] right to the shore, despite an attempt at assistance by the military elite of Milan. Then the Duce, deprived of power, will go to Milan in a cage of iron [a lorry].

## History

'On 3 September, taking advantage of the covering fire provided by a naval division commanded by Vice-Admiral Willis, British infantry *landed on the Calabrian coast* north-west of Reggio.

Hitler transferred the 24th Panzer Division and the SS Division Leibstandarte to the eastern front. Kesselring allotted three infantry divisions to the 10th Army, and the remnant of the B armies *stationed in northern Italy* [elite of Milan] was made up into a 14th Army commanded by General von Mackenser.'[4]

'At 6 a.m. Geminazza set off again from Dongo where Audisio had directed the execution of the fifteen Fascists arrested at Rocca di Musso. The bodies of Mussolini and Claretta were put into Geminazza's car which drove off in the rain towards the Azzano road. *The removal van* ["*fer de cage*"] was waiting at the crossroads. The two corpses were thrown on top of the fifteen others. On 29 April 1945, early in the morning, the removal van arrived at *Milan* after passing through several American roadblocks. It stopped in front of the concrete shell of a garage under construction on the Piazzale Loreto.'[5]

[1] Latin *exercitus*: army, corps of troops. DLLB.
[2] Latin *Apamestini*: inhabitant of Apameste in *Calabria*. DLLB.
[3] In the sense of 'power', i.e. 'under his master's *eye*'.
[4] LDG.
[5] MCH.

# The Liberation of Corsica, September, 1943. The Italian Request to the Allies for an Armistice at Lisbon, August 1943. The Collapse of the Italian Republic. The Seventy-two Deaths during the Liberation of Corsica

Arrivera au port de Corsibonne,[1]
Près de Ravenne qui pillera la dame[2]
En mer profonde légat de la Vlisbonne,[3]
Sous roc cachez raviront septante ames.[4]

CIX,Q54

## Interpretation

[Germany] will arrive at the port of Bonifacio in Corsica, during which time the [Italian] Republic will be laid waste near Ravenna. The emissary sent to Lisbon will founder. Those who will be hidden in the mountains will kill seventy men.

## History

'The question of the Italians was thus settled, but there remained 10,000 Germans on the island, not counting those who when evacuating Sardinia reached *Corsica* through the Straits of *Bonifacio* so as to disembark from Bastia. On the eastern side, the Germans held *Bonifacio* and Porto Vecchio in the south, Ghisonnaccia in the centre, the airfield of Borgo and Bastia in the north. The first elements of the 90th Panzer Division *landed at Bonifacio*, coming from Sardinia. But how were the Allies to attack Bastia? By way of the mountains – during the night, the French advanced painfully across *rocks* and bushes. At dawn, while approaching the summit of the Secco, the French 47th Arab Unit fell into an ambush. In a few minutes it lost twenty-five NCOs and enlisted men. . . . So in twenty-seven days Corsica was liberated by the French. General Henry Martin executed his mission with minimum loss: *seventy-two killed* and 220 wounded. Far from the bloodbath some had claimed!'[5]

'Even when the Germans managed to regroup north of Florence and dig in for the winter on the Gothic Line between Rimini [40 km north of Ravenna] and La Spezia, the violence continued at almost the same level behind the front.'[6]

'On 17 July 1943 Bastiani tried an approach to the Vatican and received a favourable reception from Cardinal Maglione. The two men decided to send *an envoy to Lisbon* to contact the Allies. This man, a banker named

Fummi, granted special authority to speak for the Holy See, had to reach London via *Lisbon*. Unfortunately he waited some days in the Portuguese capital for his British visa, and the events in Rome *rendered his mission pointless* ["*en mer profonde*"].[7]

[1] Word coined by Nostradamus from Corsica and Bonifacio for rhyming purposes.
[2] Consistently used to denote Republic.
[3] Prothesis: letter *v* as prefix to Lisbon.
[4] Nostradamus can be allowed an approximation here: two persons too few dead!
[5] A. Goutard: *The Liberation of Corsica* (Historama).
[6] MCH.
[7] MAB.

---

# The Fight against Germany and Italy.
# Their Economic Ruin. The Ruin of the French State
# and the Third Reich. The Teheran Conference.
# The United Nations

Deux assiegez en ardante[1] fureur,
De soif[2] estaincts[3] pour deux plaines[4] tasses,[5]
Le fort limé,[6] et un vieillard resveur,
Aux genevoix de Nira[7] monstre trasse.

CIV,Q59

## Interpretation

Two beleaguered [countries: Germany and Italy] will be drained, because of their violent rage, both will have empty pockets [economic ruin]. The stronger [Germany] will be gnawed, as will the aged dreamer [Pétain]. At Geneva the repercussions [of the Treaty] of Teheran.

## History

'On 27 November 1943 the American President, the British Prime Minister and their entourage flew at dawn to *Teheran* where the Eureka Conference was to be held. The Conference's first session opened in a room of the Soviet Embassy on 28 November, at 4.30 p.m. A little earlier Stalin had privately met Roosevelt who told him his views on world reorganization. As regards the alteration of the map and institution of *a new international order*, discussions between Churchill, Stalin and Roosevelt were not so finely balanced for the very simple reason that the

British Prime Minister and the President of the USA ratified every whim of their Soviet ally. At his request, Roosevelt was allowed to set out his ideas about future world organization which, with peace restored, would carry on from *the former League of Nations*. It would be wrong to dissociate Teheran from Yalta and Potsdam.'[8]

'The Yalta Conference [4–11 February 1945] set out the basis for the future United Nations Organization.'[9]

[1] Latin *ardeus*: violent. DLLB.
[2] Burning desire. DL7V.
[3] Latin *extinguo*: I drain, exhaust. DLLB.
[4] From *planus*: flat. DAFL.
[5] Pocket. DAFL.
[6] Gnaw, upset. DAFL.
[7] Anagram of IRAN.
[8] LDG.
[9] VCAHU.

---

# The Normandy Landings, 6 June 1944

Quand le poisson terrestre et aquatique[1]
Par force vague au gravier[2] sera mis.
Sa forme[3] estrange suave et horrifique,
Par mer aux murs[4] bien tost les ennemis.

CI,Q29

*Interpretation*

When the amphibious contrivances, through the number of their waves of attacks, will land on the beach, their composition of strangers will be pleasing [to the French] and terrifying [to the Germans] and will soon strike the enemy, from the sea up to the cliffs.

*History*

'The defenders saw surging out of the sea, half-immersed, shapeless monsters which seemed to rear up: *amphibious* tanks! Rustling, they advanced across the *sand*. A second *wave* of tanks followed the first.'[5]

'On the beach at Ouistreham a monument commemorates the first landing of *Allied* troops on French soil. It bears the following inscription: On this beach, at dawn on 6 June 1944, Field-Marshal Montgomery's troops and Captain Kieffer's French commandos first set foot on French soil." [6]

'Part of the vanguard of the 5th *American* Army Corps [*estrange*] landed on Omaha Beach with the objective of crossing Grandcamp. The Pointe du Hoc is a salient of *chalky cliffs* that go right up to the sea, about 7 km east of Vierville. These cliffs are 30 m high, and sheer. Below is a shingle *beach* 20 m wide.' [7]

[1] Amphibian: something that lives and grows on both land and water. DL7V.
[2] Beach, shore. DAFL.
[3] Synonym: formation, configuration. DL7V.
[4] Cliffs. Cf. note 2 for CIII,Q33.
[5] *Histoire Pour Tous*, no. 7 (July–August 1978).
[6] HLFRA.
[7] *Histoire Pour Tous*, no. 7 (July–August 1978).

---

## The Landing in Provence, August 1944.
## Protests about the War, at Monaco

Au peuple ingrat[1] faictes les remonstrances,
Par lors l'armée se saisira d'Antibe:
Dans l'arc Monech[2] feront les doléances,[3]
Et à Frejus l'un l'autre prendra ribe.[4]

CX,Q23

### Interpretation

Remonstrations will be made by the discontented people when the army seizes Antibes. Complaints will be heard at Monaco and at Fréjus one will occupy the shore the other [the German] used to hold.

### History

'On the night of 10 August 1944 the concentration of the landing units began. The problem was how to make 2000 ships converge off the Provençal coast – the largest armada the Mediterranean had ever borne. In a speech General de Lattre hid neither the emotion the terrain inspired nor the problems it would pose: "It is a question of France, fighting in France, liberating France. I must *put you on your guard* ["*remonstrances*"] against your own sentiments. Justly proud of your efforts and the sacrifices of too many of your comrades, you might rest on your laurels."

Next day, 16 August, the commanders landed. Admiral Hewitt's account of the first *grounding* is as follows: "When we reached the beach ['*ribe*'], General Patch and myself held back to allow Admiral Lemonnier to take the first step on to his native soil."

On the coast, the French resistance consisted of 3000 men of the Lécuyer group, which fought mainly between Nice and Antibes.'[5]

'The concern for humanitarian actions was manifested by Albert I of *Monaco*, who founded the International Peace Institute in 1903. Thereafter Monegasque initiatives were tireless, spurred by the organization of international conferences (for example, that of 1934).'[6]

[1] Latin *ingratus*: discontent. DLLB.
[2] Latin *Monoeci arx*, fortress of the port of Monacus in Liguria, or Monaco.
[3] Piteous cries. DL7V.
[4] Provençal *rivo*, from Latin *riva* (riverside, bank, shoreline). DP.
[5] HLFRA.
[6] EU.

---

# The Retreat of Communism, 1942.
# The Abduction of Pétain, 20 August 1944

Es lieux et temps chair au poisson donra lieu[1]
La loi commune sera faite au contraire,[2]
Vieux tiendra fort puis osté du milieu,
Le Pantacoina Philon[3] mis fort en arrière.[4]

CIV,Q32

## Interpretation

In these times and places, there will be wavering between two opposed parties, out of weakness; democratic laws will be opposed. The old [Marshal] will hold power, then will be taken away from the place [Vichy], communism being strongly repulsed.

## History

'On 20 June 1940 Pétain met the ministers he had summoned to the Council that afternoon: there were two – the others were packing their bags, for the members of the government were due to embark from Port-Vendres. The men who had gone round in circles at Bordeaux *without being able to take a decision* were parliamentarians and there had been over 300 of them at Bordeaux. Not wanting to continue the fight was also to become a vexed issue later. What was to be done?

It was agreed that there should be a plan *different* from Laval's: *suspension of the constitutional powers of 1875,* until the peace was established, full powers to Pétain, more power over the state than Louis XIV. The state was himself and in fact *there was no longer any Parliament* capable of remonstrating against, or ratifying, what he did.'⁵

'On 20 August 1944 Pétain was taken away by the Germans and driven under military escort to Sigmaringen, without any opportunity to attempt an escape.'⁶

'*Soviet resistance routed*: in the north of the Pripet marshes Soviet resistance had been surprised and *overthrown* almost everywhere, as were the reinforcements coming forward to the front. The situation had *rapidly altered* ["*fort en arrière*"] between the Black Sea and the Baltic and not to the defence's advantage. Some days later the Soviet government and central administration left Moscow to establish itself at Kulbychev on the left bank of the Volga.'⁷

¹ One does not know whether it's fish or fowl. Said of a vacillator between two opposites. DL7V.
² To do the contrary, to oppose. DL7V.
³ Greek πάντα ἀοίγα φίλων: Everything held in common between friends.
⁴ Ablative absolute.
⁵ PGB.
⁶ HLFRA.
⁷ LDG.

---

## Pétain's Treason, 20 August 1944

> Le vieux mocqué et privé de sa place
> Par l'estranger qui le subornera¹
> Mains² de son fils mangées devant sa face
> Les frères à Chartres, Orléans, Rouen, trahira.

CIV,Q61

*Interpretation*

The old [Marshal] will be mocked and relieved of his post by the enemy, who will drive him to a bad action, the power he has created destroyed before his eyes, when the brothers in arms [the Allies] are at Chartres, Orleans and Rouen, he will betray.

## History

'The British 2nd Army reached the Seine south of *Rouen*. The American 3rd Army thrust towards Paris: starting from Alençon and Le Mans it reached in the south *Chartres* and Rambouillet, the final stepping-stones. On 15 and 16 August, according to plan, the 3rd Army entered *Orleans and Chartres*.

On 20 August Pétain was *taken away* by the *Germans* and driven under military escort to Sigmaringen, without any opportunity to attempt an escape.

The Marshal's enthusiastic welcome on his final visits to French cities [Paris, 26 April 1944, and St Etienne, 6 June 1944, in particular] showed his personal prestige undiminished despite *the failure of his policies*. But this high percentage of supporters *no longer constituted a political force* in 1944. All Laval's and Pétain's attempts to perpetuate the Vichy government ended in sheer fantasy.'[3]

'On 12 August 1945 the prosecutor, Mornet, made his speech. For four years, he said, to the actual day, France had been the victim of an equivocation which for want of a better word *was known as treason*.'[4]

[1] Latin *subornare*: win over, persuade, or secretly charge to do an evil or wicked action. DLLB.
[2] Latin *manus*: authority, strength, power. DLLB.
[3] HLFRA.
[4] PGB.

---

## The Occupation Zone from Rouen to Bordeaux. The Atlantic Wall. The Liberation. Rouen, 1944

Bordeaux, Rouen et La Rochelle joincts,
Tiendront autour la grand mer Océane,
Anglois Bretons et les Flaments conjoincts,
Les chasseront jusqu'auprès de Rouane.

CIII,Q9

## Interpretation

Bordeaux, Rouen and La Rochelle reunited [in the Occupation] will hold the French ocean coast [the Atlantic Wall], the Anglo-Americans, French and Belgians will push them back as far as Rouen.

---

## The Fall of the French State, 1944.
## Pétain's Departure for Sigmaringen.
## Pétain at the Ile d'Yeu, 1945

Le vieux monarque déchassé de son règne
Aux Orients son secours ira querre:[1]
Pour peur des croix ployera son enseigne
En Mitylène[2] ira par port[3] et par terre.

CIII,Q47

### Interpretation

The old head of state chased from power will go to seek help from the
east [Sigmaringen]: through fear of the [crooked] crosses [i.e. swastikas]
he will fold up his flag and end via port [Joinville] and by land, on the
Island of Mussels [Yeu].

### History

'Baron von Neubronn *threatened* that if the Marshal refused to comply,
the *Germans* would bombard Vichy. "I haven't the right to let the women
and children of Vichy be bombed," said Pétain. "I must give in, faced
with such threats."

On 16 November 1945 Pétain was looking obstinately towards the *Ile
d'Yeu*, which was to be his prison. The landing at Port-Joinville was not
going to be easy. Pétain had been transferred from the fort of *Port*alet
on 15 August, immediately after his sentence.'[4]

---

[1] Latin *quaero*: I seek. DLLB. From which comes *quérir*.
[2] Latin *mitylus*: mussel, shellfish. DLLB. The main activity of the island of Yeu is
mussel-gathering.
[3] Nostradamus suggests either Portalet or Port-Joinville for Pétain's landing.
[4] PGB.

## Mussolini's Birth between Rimini and Prato, 1883. Left-wing Opposition at Monte Aventino, 1924. The End of Mussolini and Fascism, Piazza Colonna, 1943. The Assassination of Fascists and of their Assassins, 1945

Du haut de mont Aventin[1] voix ouye,
Vuidez, vuidez de tous les deux costez:
Du sang des rouges sera l'ire assomie,[2]
D'Arimin,[3] Prato,[4] Columna[5] debotez.[6]

CIX,Q2

### Interpretation

Those who retreat upon Monte Aventino will make their voices heard; from two sides all will be annihilated; the anger of the reds will be swelled by the blood of the reds. He who originated from Rimini and Prato and those of the Piazza Colonna will be expelled.

### History

'Mussolini's autobiography: "I was born on 29 July 1883 at Varnano dei Costa, near the village of Dovia, itself near that of Predappio." '[7]

'On 10 June 1924, the *Socialist* deputy Matteoti was kidnapped in Rome by a Fascist group. His body was recovered on 16 August from some waste land about 20 km from the town. In protest, the *opposition* deputies left the Chamber and *withdrew to Aventino*. . . .

After vainly awaiting a message from Mussolini, Scorza desperately went back to party headquarters on Piazza *Colonna* where he ordered the mobilization of all Fascists in Rome – there were not even fifty Fascists to answer his call. The crowd began invading the homes of the main party militants and burned the offices of various Fascist organizations. A band of demonstrators rushed into the Venetian Palace to lay hands on their country's oppressor for twenty years, but nobody could force the gate and they left waving *red* flags. On the Piazza *Colonna* and elsewhere the crowd sang and danced with joy, crying "Fascism is dead!" '[8]

'On 27 April 1945 the main resistance leaders met in Milan, notably Longo, the fanatical Communist, and Walter Audisio, an ex-volunteer from the International Brigade in Spain. The order for Mussolini's execution had already been given by Togliatti, acting head of the Communist party. Moretti and Cavali were fervent Communists. Less than ten

minutes after Bellini's departure Audisio, Lampredi and Moretti hur-
riedly left Dongo. Their respective fates are interesting. Michele Moretti
was supposed to have died, according to some authors. Frangi talked
after the death of Mussolini and died under strange circumstances. Luigi
Cavali disappeared. His mistress Giuseppina Tuissi resigned herself to
his disappearance, and in her turn disappeared. Her friend Anna Bianchi,
distressed by this, was found floating in Lake Como: she had been beaten
to death. Anna's father swore to find and kill her murderers, but he too
was murdered.'[9]

'The first shot fired by Audisio from Moretti's gun killed Claretta.
The next hit Mussolini. Six hours later Germi again left Dongo, where
Audisio had led the execution of the fifteen Fascists arrested at Rocca di
Musso. The removal van was waiting at the crossroads. The two corpses
were thrown on top of the fifteen others.'[10]

[1] Retreat or withdrawal to Monte Aventino: vexed by Patrician tyranny, the Plebeians
emigrated en masse to the Monte Aventino. This historical episode gave rise to the
expression 'withdrawing to Aventino', i.e. severing all relations abruptly until satisfaction
is obtained.
[2] Fill up, overload. DAFL.
[3] Latin *Ariminum*: Rimini, town in Umbria. DLLB.
[4] Prato: Tuscan town. Predappio and Prato are quite near one another.
[5] Latin for Italian *colonna*: column. NB capital C.
[6] To expel. DAFL.
[7] MCH.
[8] HISR.
[9] MCH.
[10] HISR.

---

## Mussolini and Cardinal Schuster, 1945. Executions at Piazzale Loreto in Milan

Roy trouvera ce qu'il désiroit tant,
Quand le Prelat sera reprins[1] à tort,
Response au Duc le rendra mal content,
Qui dans Milan mettra plusieurs à mort.

CVI,Q31

*Interpretation*

The leader will find the one he so wants [arresting Mussolini] when the
Cardinal will be wrongly blamed for his answer, with which the Duce
will be displeased; and several will be put to death in Milan.

*History*

'On 13 March 1945 Mussolini's son Vittorio took to *Cardinal* Schuster, Archbishop of *Milan*, a letter requesting certain guarantees for the civilian population in case the Germans evacuated Italy and the Fascist forces took up positions in the Alps. Cardinal Schuster thought this gesture quite futile but transmitted the message to the Allies via the Papal Nuncio at Berne. As soon as it reached general headquarters at Caserta the Allies *answered* it with a dismissal assuming that the Germans had already accepted such a capitulation, but Mussolini refused to take into consideration the Allies' demands.'[2]

'Valerio stopped at Milan in the Piazzale Loreto, the same spot where on 9 August 1944 the Germans had taken reprisals and shot fifteen Italian political prisoners. The dead bodies had been dumped there. At 11 a.m. six corpses were strung up by ropes in the forecourt of a filling station, among them Mussolini and Clara Petacci. Shortly afterwards the former secretary of the party, Achille Starace, was shot in the back there by six partisans and strung up alongside the other dangling corpses.'[3]

[1] To blame. DL7V.
[2] HCH.
[3] MAB.

---

## Massacres at Milan and Florence.
## The Duce at Milan, His Capital, 19 April 1945.
## The Fall of Fascism in Rome in the Piazza Colonna,
## September 1944

> Pleure Milan, pleure Lucques, Florence,
> Que ton grand Duc sur le char[1] montera:
> Changer le Siege pres de Venise s'advance,
> Lorsque Colonne a Rome changera.

CX,Q64

*Interpretation*

There will be tears at Milan, Lucca, Florence, because your great Duce will leave by van. The seat of government will change when there is an advance near the Venice [Palace], when there will be a change at the Piazza Colonna.

*History*

'The *brigate nere* [Fascist blackshirts] did not take reprisals as frequently as the Germans, but they were often no less savage. It was the SS, for instance, who executed almost 700 people at Marzabotto.[2] The Fascist groups contained a criminal element far more dangerous than the least disciplined partisans. Even when the Germans managed to regroup north of *Florence* and winter along the Gothic Line between Rimini and Spezia[3] the atrocities continued at almost the same level behind the front.

On 16 April 1945 he had confided to Mellini: "Now Rome is lost, the Italian Republic can have only *one capital, Milan*." He prepared to leave for Milan on the tenth, escorted by German soldiers. His headquarters was the Monforte Palace, the Milan police department. . . .

Demonstrators rushed into the *Venice* Palace to lay hold of the country's oppressor for twenty years. On the *Piazza Colonna*, the party meeting-place, the crowd sang and danced as if at a carnival: "Fascism is dead!" That night in *Rome*, you would have supported Mussolini only at risk of life and limb. . . .

On 29 April 1945 the removal van reached *Milan* after negotiating several American road blocks. It stopped on the Piazzale Loreto. The bodies were hurled off the truck and a passer-by took the trouble to range them up neatly; he placed Mussolini a little apart. Then two young men appeared who proceeded to kick the body violently in the face. An authoritative voice yelled: "String them up!" '[4]

---

[1] Four-wheeled vehicle. DL7V.
[2] Village north of Florence.
[3] Line passing through Lucca and Florence.
[4] MCH.

---

# The Fall of the Reich, 1945. The Soviet Counter-offensive. Landings in Sicily, 10 July 1943

> Le neuf empire en desolation
> Sera changé du pôle aquilonnaire[1]
> De la Sicile viendra l'émotion[2]
> Troubler l'emprise[3] à Philip tributaire.

CVIII,Q81

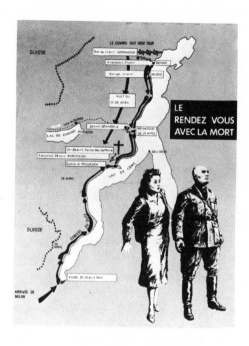

Extract from MAB

## Interpretation

The new [German] empire will be in desolation and undergo changes because of the north [USSR]. From Sicily they [Germans] will be chased and Philip's [Pétain's] enterprise of paying tribute will be disturbed.

## History

'For the two years following the invasion of *Russia* Hitler was almost entirely absorbed by the progress of the war on the Eastern Front. But in 1943 the loss of North Africa and collapse of *Italy* reminded him that he was at war with a world alliance.

On 30 April 1945 Goebbels and Bormann tried vainly to negotiate with the *Russians*. The answer was: "Unconditional *surrender*." '[4]

'German demands: the victors disposed of millions of prisoners and Vichy France, virtually blackmailed, had already *paid* 631,886 million francs for the occupying forces. . . .

The Allied attack then took shape. In July 1943, Operation Husky gave them *Sicily* and 200,000 prisoners.'[5]

[1] Aquilon: violent and impetuous north wind. DL7V. Symbol of the Russian Empire of the North.
[2] Latin *emoveo*: I take away, disperse, chase. DLLB.
[3] i.e. *entreprise* = enterprise. DL7V.
[4] HAB.
[5] LMC.

---

# The Nuremberg Trials, 1945–46.
# The Cold War

Des condamnez sera fait un grand nombre,
Quand les monarques seront conciliez:
Mais l'un d'eux viendra si mal encombre[1]
Que guerre ensemble ne seront raliez.

CII,Q38

## Interpretation

There will be a great number of condemned persons when the heads of state are reconciled. But one of them will make so many difficulties that those who waged war together will not be allies.

## History

'On 20 November 1945 the first hearing of the International Military Tribunal at Nuremberg took place, to try German leaders considered to be war criminals. Composed of representatives from the four *Allied* powers [USA, USSR, Great Britain and France], it was to judge twenty-four major political, economic and military leaders of Hitler's Germany and six groups and organizations of the Third Reich. The hearings went on until 1 October 1946. *Numerous* other trials of less notorious war criminals took place in Germany.

The *condemned men* were executed on 16 October 1946 between 1 and 3 a.m.; those sentenced to prison terms were interned at Spandau Prison near Berlin. . . .

On 2 February 1953, in his first speech on the State of the Union, Eisenhower announced that he had settled the neutrality of Formosa; he also envisaged denouncing the Yalta agreement concluded by Roosevelt. The American attitude aroused much anxiety.'[2]

[1] *Encombrier*: obstacle, embarrassment, damage. DAFL.
[2] VCAHU.

# Franco-German Friendship after the 1870, 1914 and 1939 Wars. Milestones of This Friendship: 1950, 1962, 1963 and 1967

Las quelle fureur! hélas quelle pitié,
Il y aura entre beaucoup de gens:
On ne vit onc une telle amitié,
Qu'auront les loups à courir diligens.[1]

CVIII,Q3a

*Interpretation*

Alas, what savagery and pity there will be between many people! Never will one see such a friendship as the Germans will make.

*History*

'Adenauer proposed to France a *Franco-German union* with a single parliament, one economy and a common nationality. . . .

During 4–12 August 1962 General de Gaulle made an official visit to West Germany. It was a triumph: he won the hearts of a people which despite economic recovery was seared by the guilt complex of 1945. . . .

The Franco–German treaty, foreseeing periodic summit consultations and cooperation in areas of defence, the economy and the arts, was signed on 22 January 1963. . . .

On 12 and 13 July 1967 de Gaulle and Kiesinger met at Bonn and decided to set up two joint commissions, one for economic, the other for political, cooperation.'[2]

[1] Latin *diligens*: attached to, liking. DLLB.
[2] VCAHU.

---

# The Return of the Jews to Palestine, 1939–48. The Arab–Israeli Wars

Nouveaux venus lieu basty sans défence,
Occuper la place par lors inhabitable,
Prez, maisons, champs, villes, prendre à plaisance[1]
Faim, peste, guerre, arpen long labourable.

CII,QI9

## Interpretation

Newcomers will build towns without defence and occupy hitherto un-inhabitable places. They will take with pleasure fields, houses, land and towns. Then famine, sickness and war will be on this land tilled for a long time [since 1939].

## History

'When the Second World War broke out the Jewish population of Israel had risen from 85,000 [11 per cent of the total] to 416,000 [29 per cent], the number of Jewish *settlements* from 79 to 200. *Agriculture* was developing considerably; the area of orange groves had increased from 1000 to 15,000 *hectares*.

Apart from an Arab minority of about 10 per cent, almost all the population was composed of Jewish *immigrants* who had been there less than a century. . . .

Whatever the immediate causes of the June 1967 *war*, it had a profound effect on the psychology of both Arabs and Israelis.'[2]

This quatrain of Nostradamus should be compared to the Book of Ezekiel: 'After many days thou shalt be visited; in the latter years thou shalt come into the land that is brought back from the sword, and is *gathered out of many people*, against the mountains of Israel, which have been always *waste*: but it is brought forth out of the nations, and *they shall dwell safely* all of them. And thou shalt say, I will go up to the land of *unwalled villages* [kibbutzes] I will go to them that are at rest . . . to place thine hand upon the desolate places that are now inhabited.'[3]

[1] Pleasure, joy. DL7V.
[2] EU.
[3] Ezekiel, 38: 8, 11 and 12. AV.

---

# The Hungarian Rising at Budapest, 23 October 1956. Crushed by Soviet Troops, 4 November 1956

Par vie et mort changé regne d'Ongrie,
La loy sera plus aspre que service:[1]
Leur grand cité d'urlements pleincts et crie,
Castor et polux[2] ennemis dans la lice.[3]

CII,Q90

## Interpretation

Power will be changed by life and death in Hungary; the law will be more pitiless than customs. The great town [Budapest] will be filled with screams and cries. Brothers will be enemies in this theatre of struggle [the capital].

## History

'In Hungary rebellion broke out in *Budapest* on 23 October 1956 and gathered momentum so fast that even the return of Imre Nagy [Castor] did not calm things down. Under pressure from Nagy, who had formed a coalition government, it was announced on 1 November that Hungary was leaving the Warsaw Pact and requested the UN formally to recognize her neutral status. The very next day Budapest was completely surrounded [*"lice"*] by Soviet tanks, which went into action on the fourth while a puppet government, loyal to Moscow, was formed by Janos Kadar [Pollux]. There was further fighting in Budapest where the rebels, despite fierce resistance, were quickly crushed. The number of deaths throughout the uprising exceeded 25,000. Imre Nagy, who had sought shelter in the Yugoslav embassy, was taken away by police and deported to Romania. More than 15,000 people were deported by the Russians, and another 150,000 managed to get to the West [*"lieu changé"*]. Budapest showed that to seek different versions of socialism only meant, to the Kremlin, a break of the ties [*"loi"*] imposed on eastern European countries since 1945. Continuing agitation obliged the Kadar government to proclaim *martial law* on 8 December; all the revolutionary workers' councils were dissolved.'[4]

---

[1] Usage, utility, derived from certain things. DL7V.

[2] Two brothers, sons of Jupiter.

[3] Lists: enclosed field for jousting and by extension the scene of some struggle or combat. DL7V.

[4] VCAHU.

## The Conquest of North Africa by the
## Third Republic, 1881–1911. The Fall of the
## Fourth Republic, 13 May 1958

Barbare empire[1] par le tiers[2] usurpé,[3]
La plus grand part de son sang mettra à mort:
Par mort sénile par luy le quart[4] frappé,
Pour peur que sang par le sang[5] ne soit mort.

                                        CIII,Q59

*Interpretation*

The Third [Republic] will appropriate the Barbarian Empire and put to
death most of its inhabitants. Because of senility the Fourth [Republic]
will be beaten to death by it [the Barbarian Empire] for fear that those
who have shed their blood might die in vain.

*History*

'Africa was the main area of French colonial expansion. Since the July
monarchy *France* had *possessed Algeria*, but Algeria is only the central
part of the Atlas mountains, which continue eastwards through Tunisia
and west through Morocco. The *three countries* are so closely bound that
one can only be complete master of Algeria by *dominating* the two neighbouring countries. This explains the importance of the Tunisian question, then that of Morocco, in French policy. The incessant *raids* carried
out upon Algerian territory by the Tunisian mountain fighters, the Krou-
mirs, were a pretext for a French army to enter Tunisia in 1881. Tunisia
seemed subdued and the troops were recalled. There was an immediate
general uprising centred on Kairouan, one of the Moslem holy villages.
Repression was swift. . . .
    The Act of Algeciras could not definitively settle the Moroccan ques-
tion. There were new incidents from 1907. The French were massacred
by the natives and France *occupied* Casablanca [1907–08]. In 1911 French
troops penetrated as far as Fez. . . .
    *Algeria, Tunisia and Morocco*, henceforth closely united, formed a new
France in Africa. . . .
    The Algerian crisis worsened because Guy Mollet, faced with the
hostility of the French in Algeria, renounced on 5 February 1956 the
reforms he had promised, and because the President of Council approved
a misguided initiative by an irresponsible officer who at Algiers took it
upon himself to try to ground the *Moroccan* aircraft carrying the FLN

chiefs. This futile act involved the French with the King of *Morocco* and with *Tunisia*. Mollet was defeated on 21 May 1957, but his successor Félix Gaillard did no better, and the French Republic had proved its *ineffectiveness*. . . . *Instability* and *weakness* led to impotence. . . . General de Gaulle accepted investiture and on 1 June 1958 he obtained full powers. The Fourth Republic lived.'[7]

[1] Barbary: Barbary States, region of North Africa consisting of the states of Tripoli, Tunis, Algiers and Morocco. DHB.
[2] Third in line, succeeding two others. DL7V.
[3] Latin *usurpo*: I pretend to, appropriate for myself. DLLB.
[4] For '*quatrième*', fourth. DL7V.
[5] *Sanguine barbarorum modico* (Tacitus): the barbarians having lost few men. DLLB.
[6] HFAM.
[7] LMC.

# The Six Days' War, 5–10 June 1967.
# The Occupation by Israel of Gaza, Transjordan and the Golan Heights

Nouvelle loy terre neuve occuper,
Vers la Syrie, Iudée et Palestine:
Le grand Empire barbare corruer,[1]
Avant que Phebes[2] son siècle détermine.

CIII,Q97

*Interpretation*

By a new law new territories will be occupied, towards Syria, Jordan and Palestine. Arab power will crumble before the Summer Solstice [21 June].

*History*

'Arab–Israeli War, 5–10 June 1967: in a campaign directed against Egypt, Jordan and Syria, Israeli armies *occupied* the whole of the Sinai Peninsula[3] as far as the Suez Canal, Transjordan[4] and the Golan Heights.[5]
At dawn on the fifth, Israeli planes attacked Egyptian airports and wiped out most of her aircraft. The Egyptian army was in *disarray* ["*corruer*"] from the first few hours of the fighting; masters of *Gaza* and El-Arich, the Israelis struck across the Sinai Desert, and from the seventh

occupied the port of Sharm-el-Sheikh and reached the Suez Canal. On the Jordanian side they encountered more resistance, but the old town of Jerusalem and all the *Transjordanian* part [Judea] of Jordan were *conquered*. *The Arab world* was overwhelmed by the scope and speed of the Israeli successes. The USSR accused Israel of aggression and at her request the General Assembly of the United Nations met on the nineteenth ["*avant que Phebes*"]. The main problem now was that of the occupied Arab territories. On the eleventh General Dayan declared that Israel would keep Gaza, Sharm-el-Sheikh, the Old City of Jerusalem and Transjordan. The Israelis maintained that it was no longer a question of returning to the pre-5 June frontiers, since it was a question not of frontiers but of demarcation lines traced by the 1949 armistices, and never *legally* ["*nouvelle loy*"] recognized by the Arab states. On 27 June the Knesset adopted a "fundamental law" for the protection of the holy places. The government decided to annexe the Old City of Jerusalem."[6]

[1] Latin *corruer*: to fall, collapse. DLLB.
[2] Phoebus: the sun. DLLB.
[3] Including the town of Gaza, in south *Palestine*. EU.
[4] Judea: southern area of *Palestine*, situated between the Dead Sea and the Mediterranean, the greatest part of which today constitutes the southern part of *Transjordan*, the territory Israel seized from Jordan in the Six Days' War of 1967. AE.
[5] Syrian territory.
[6] VCHAU.

---

# The Return of the Jews to Palestine, 1948. Golda Meir and Zionism. The Resignation of Golda Meir, 1974

La Synagogue[1] stérile sans nul fruit,
Sera receuë entre les infidèles:[2]
De Babylon[3] la fille[4] du poursuit,
Misère et triste, lui tranchera les aisles.

CVIII,Q96

*Interpretation*

Sterile Zionism,[5] with no fruit, will be received among the Arabs. Come from New York [Babylone] the woman [leader] of the pursued ones [Golda Meir] will lose power through ill-luck and sadness.

## History

'Golda Meir: born Kiev (Ukraine), emigrated to the USA with her family in 1906. She made a name for herself as a militant, responsible for the local section of the Zionist Labour Party. In 1924 she rejoined the Histadrut and in 1928 was named secretary of its female organization. In the course of the Second World War she was active alongside Ben Gurion to assure *the return of the Jews* to Zion. In 1946 when Moshe Sharett, head of the political department of the Jewish Agency, was arrested by the British with other activists, she [*"la fille du poursuite"*] replaced him temporarily and fought to get interned activists and immigrant Jews released. Shortly before Ben Gurion proclaimed the creation of the State of Israel she was sent to the UN to make a final plea for the recognition of a *Jewish State of Palestine*. In October 1973 Israel had to face a murderous war with Egyptian and Syrian forces, assisted by various contingents from other Arab states. Golda Meir's government *underwent attack* from the Israeli right wing and criticisms from leading military figures because the country was unprepared. The elections of 31 December were soon to return Golda Meir and her party to power. In March 1974 *the criticisms* of Golda Meir and General Dayan became stronger and the Israeli Prime Minister had to hand in her *resignation* a month later. [*"misère et triste"*].'[6]

NB. Nostradamus establishes a parallel between the first return of the Jews, in captivity in Babylon, and the second, from the modern Babylons: London, Paris and New York.

[1] The synagogue seems to have originated with the Jews exiled in Babylon, when far from the Temple and needing to worship together. On their return from exile the first synagogue was built in Jerusalem in the precincts of the Temple. DL7V.

[2] Those not of the true faith. DL7V. The Arabs here as opposed to the Jews.

[3] The great Babylon, the modern Babylon: denotes contemporary big cities such as London, Paris etc. DL7V.

[4] Poetic/symbolic terms: i.e. women of Israel = Daughters of Zion, etc. DL7V.

[5] Politico-religious movement founded by Theodor Herzl at the end of the nineteenth century with the aim of reuniting in Palestine and in their own state Jews dispersed throughout the world. AE.

[6] EU.

# The Yom Kippur War, October 1973.
## The Surprise Attack by Egypt upon Israel

Celuy qui a les hazards surmonté,
Qui fer, feu, eau, n'a jamais redouté,
Et du pays bien proche du Basacle,[1]
D'un coup de fer tout le monde estouné,
Par Crocodil[2] estrangement donné,
Peuple ravi de voir un tel spectacle.

Sixain 31

## Interpretation

The race which has overcome hazards, which has never feared war or
revolution, in the country very close to Christianity's point of departure,
will be astonished by an act strangely committed by Egypt whose population will rejoice at such a spectacle.

## History

'On 6 October 1973 at 1.50 p.m. the Council of Ministers was busy
ratifying the decisions taken by Golda Meir, Dayan and Eleazar that
morning, when General Lior opened the door to announce that the
enemy had just attacked. *The surprise was thus total*: simultaneous attack
by the *Egyptians* in the south and Syrians in the north. Five Egyptian
divisions, Soviet-trained and -equipped, overcame the forts of the Bar-
Lev Line and under missile cover struck 5–10 km deep into Sinai. The
Israeli tanks were decimated by the missiles [with their 3 km range],
whose extensive use by the Egyptians called into question, at a stroke,
the whole art of modern warfare. Were tanks in fact superior to infantry?
*1200 Egyptian tanks were used in the attack.*'[3]

'The Rais talked of Egypt, a peaceful society for thousands of years,
forced to war, by injustice and occupation. He added: "If we were not
good fighters it was because we had never liked fighting. This time was
different. We had a humiliation to avenge." '[4]

[1] Receptacle used to keep live fish in. DL7V. For the early Christians the fish was their
private symbol par excellence. DL7V.

[2] The oldest species known is the Nile variety, which the ancient *Egyptians* worshipped.
DL7V.

[3] *L'Express* (13–19 January 1975). *Israel la mort en face:* J. Derogy and J. N. Gurgand
(Laffont).

[4] *Le Point*, no. 60 (12 November 1973).

# The Yom Kippur War, 6 October 1973.
## The Egyptians' Surprise Attack

Dame par mort grandement attristée,
Mère et tutrice au sang qui l'a quittée,
Dame et seigneurs, faicts enfants orphelins,
Par les aspics¹ et par les Crocodiles,
Seront surpris forts, Bourgs, Chasteaux, Villes,
Dieu tout-puissant les garde des malins.

Sixain 35

### Interpretation

The lady [Golda Meir] will be greatly saddened by the death [of Israeli soldiers]; the mother and teacher [of the Jewish state] will abandon power because of the bloodshed. With her ministers she will be responsible for the orphans; because of the Egyptians who will attack the fortifications [the Bar-Lev Line] by surprise, also villages and towns. May God Almighty protect them from harm.

### History

'On 6 October Israel was in the synagogues for Yom Kippur. At noon, sirens sounded. Israel had been simultaneously attacked north and south by Syria and Egypt. During the first few hours the Golan lines were over-run and Syrian tanks almost reached Galilee, while on the Suez Canal 3000 soldiers had to hold *tens of thousands of Egyptians* [asps and crocodiles]. Far from congratulating themselves, the Israelis wondered: "How was the carelessness of Yom Kippur possible?" Some added with black humour: "We were lucky the Arabs attacked on the Day of Atonement. *God could not refuse us a miracle*" ["*Dieu tout-puissant les garde des malins*"].

The government scornfully rejected repeated warnings from the Pentagon's secret services. A major-general slept behind the *Bar-Lev Line* just as the French in 1939 did behind the Maginot Line ["*forts*"]. At Jerusalem and Tel Aviv 2000 dead were *mourned* ["*attristée*"], a considerable number for a country of only 3 million people, while 3000 wounded lay in hospitals, and on the front more than 150,080 reservists stood guard. On 10 April 1974, in the middle of the Passover, Mrs Meir, saddened and exhausted, handed in her resignation ["*quittée*"] to the President of the State.'²

[1] Cleopatra's serpent or asp. DL7V. The allusion to Cleopatra also terms the Egyptians
'crocodiles'.
[2] *Le Spectacle du Monde*, no. 147, June 1974.

## Revolutions, Wars and Famine in Iran, 1979. The Fall of the Shah, 1978–79. Ayatollah Khomeini at Neauphle-le-Château

Pluye,[1] faim, guerre en Perse non cessée,
La foy trop grande[2] trahira le Monarque:[3]
Par la finie en Gaule commencée,
Secret[4] augure[5] pour à un estre parque.

CI,Q70

### Interpretation

Revolution, famine, war will not cease in Iran; religious fanaticism will betray the Shah whose end will begin in France, because of a prophet who will be confined in a withdrawn place [Neauphle-le-Château].

### History

'With her *fanatical* demonstrators, brandishing the banners of their *faith* and confronting the weapons of the Shah's soldiers with chests bared, Iran last week furnished the most spectacular example of the astonishing Moslem revival. Meched and Qom in Iran and Al Nadjat and Karbala in Iraq are the sanctuaries of the Shi'ite Moslems. One may add for the present, though it has no mosques or golden minarets or turquoise domes, a third holy city amazed by the turn of events – Neauphle-le-Château. For a *medersa* [Koranic seminary] it has only an ordinary suburban house, but there squats or prays the Ayatollah Khomeini.[6]

On the eve of the Moharran this year, the call from Ayatollah Khomeini inviting the faithful to launch into a sort of *holy rebellion* succeeded in bringing passions to the boil. Do not hesitate to shed your blood to protect Islam and overthrow tyranny, *this exiled prophet* of the Shi'ites requested from his *retreat* at Neauphle-le-Château.'[7]

'Iran is heading for a fanatical *war*, predicted the revolutionary General Hadavi. The religious leader of the Iranian Arabs, Ayatollah Khafani, predicted *bitter tragedies*. General Rahini was indignant: it was shameful to see parts of Iran bathed in fire and blood when the army remained in its barracks.'[8]

[1] As with the words *onde* and *eau*, Nostradamus uses 'rain' to denote revolutionary troubles.

[2] Religious fanaticism is a blind, irrational faith: *excessive* zeal in support of a religious doctrine. DL7V.

[3] Persian *Shah*: king, sovereign. DL7V.

[4] Latin *secretum*: retired spot, retreat. DLLB.

[5] Latin *augur*: priest who forecasts the future, *prophet*. DLLB.

[6] Meaning 'sign of God'.

[7] *Le Point*, no. 325 (11 December 1978).

[8] *Le Spectacle du Monde*, no. 209 (August 1978).

---

# The Fall of the Shah of Iran, 16 January 1979.
# The Military Government, 6 November 1978.
# Seizure of Power by the Mullahs, 3 February 1979

Par le despit[1] du Roy soustenant[2] moindre;
Sera meurdry[3] lui presentant[4] les bagues:[5]
Le père au fils voulant noblesse poindre,[6]
Fait comme a Perse jadis feirent les Magues.[7]

CX,Q21

## Interpretation

Because of his contempt the Shah, in a state of least resistance, will be harmed when showing off his army, the father wanting to display the power of his son. Then will be done in Iran what the holy men did of old [taking power].

## History

'On 6 November 1978 General Azhari, commander-in-chief of the army, was named head of government. The army's intervention threw a completely new light on the problem. Only yesterday it had remained a shadowy presence in the background, intervening merely in order to contain the wave of discontent. From now on *the Army* would *take the main role* [*"presentant"*].'[8]

'In 1967, as he was preparing to have himself and Farah crowned Emperor and Empress, Mohammed Reza claimed: "*I shall leave my son* a young, developing, proud, completely modern and stable nation, looking ever to the future and to cooperation with the peoples of the entire world." In these last years, his father entrusted him with various representative missions which he performed ably. Even in 1971, at the

Persepolis celebrations, the Shah had let it be understood that he would one day hand over *power to his son.*'[9]

'16 January 1979: the Shah's departure for Egypt.

21 January 1979: the resignation of Tehrani, President of the Regency Council.

1 February 1979: the return of Ayatollah Khomeini to Teheran.

3 February 1979: Ayatollah Khomeini announces the creation of a "National Islamic Council."

Iran: 200,000 *mullahs* on the warpath.'[10]

[1] Scorn, contempt. DAFL.
[2] Latin *sustineo*: I resist. DLLB.
[3] Wound, harm, injure. DL7V.
[4] Exhibit, show off. DL7V.
[5] Weapons. DAFL.
[6] Demonstrate. DL7V.
[7] Greek μαγος: mage, priest among the Persians. DGF. In Persia the magi led a hard, austere life. The virtues they possessed or were attributed with gave them limitless authority over the minds of the people and the *nobility*. The king himself boasted of being their pupil and would consult them. DL7V. Nostradamus denotes *the ayatollahs* when using the word in this context.
[8] *Le Spectacle du Monde*, no. 201, 'Revolution of the Ayatollahs' by R. Faucon.
[9] *Le Spectacle du Monde*, no. 203, 'The Common Front against the dynasty.'
[10] Article in *Figaro-Magazine* (19 January 1980).

---

# Ayatollah Khomeini in Iraq, 1963–78. The Islamic Republic, 1979

Il entrera vilain, meschant, infâme,
Tyrannisant la Mésopotamie:[1]
Tous amis faict d'adulterine[2] dame,[3]
Terre horrible noire[4] de phisionomie.

CVIII,Q70

*Interpretation*

The frightful, wicked and infamous person will enter Iraq in order to impose his tyranny. They will all be friends of a false republic [the Islamic Republic]; the world will be horrified by this hateful physiognomy.

## History

'The *mullahs* called the faithful to revolt against the *impious* tyranny. The Shah in person was their target. "Shah, we will kill you!" chanted the fanatical crowds, who had formed processions after hearing speeches in the mosques. Even in 1963, at the time of the first great wave of upheavals in Iran unleashed by Ayatollah Khomeini, since then exiled in Iraq, the rebellion never took on such a widespread fervour.'[5]

'The Islamic Republic, as Ayatollah Khomeini conceived it, demonstrated its inability to rule Iran. Unpopular throughout the country as a whole, the regime only kept going through the fanaticism [*tyrannie*] of the lowest level of the population, which was completely subservient to the power of the "akhonds", the priesthood.'[6]

[1] Present-day Iraq: region between the Tigris and Euphrates. DHB.

[2] Latin *adulterinus*: falsified, false. DLLB.

[3] Frequently used word in Nostradamus, signifying the Republic, personified as a woman.

[4] Figurative: atrocious, perverse, odious. DL7V.

[5] *Le Spectacle du Monde*, no. 199, '*Iran, two worlds face to face*'.

[6] DHB.

# 3

# NOSTRADAMUS
# AS PROPHET

## THE PRE-WAR CLIMATE

### The Conflicts of the Twentieth Century between East and West: 1914–18, 1939–45, and the Third World War, 1999

> Par deux fois hault, par deux fois mis a bas,
> L'Orient aussi l'Occident faiblira,
> Son adversaire après plusieurs combats,
> Par mer chassé au besoing faillira.
>
> CVIII,Q59

*Interpretation*

Twice raised high to power, twice laid low, the West like the East will be weakened. Its adversary, after several battles, will be chased off by sea and will fall through penury.

---

### The Search for Peace and War. The War in France

> La paix s'approche d'un côté et la guerre
> Oncques ne fust la poursuite si grande,
> Plaindre homme, femme, sang innocent par terre
> Et ce sera de France à toute bande.
>
> CIX,Q52

*Interpretation*

They get ready to sign the peace with one hand and make war with the other. The two were never so much pursued. Then they will mourn men, women; innocent blood will flow upon the earth and particularly in all areas of France.

---

# Peace Negotiations: USA–USSR

Plusieurs viendront et parleront de paix,
Entre Monarques et Seigneurs bien puissants;
Mais ne sera accordé de si près,
Que ne se rendent plus qu'autres obéissants.

CVIII,Q2a

*Interpretation*

There will be talk of peace between very powerful heads of states [USA–USSR]; but peace will not be agreed, for the heads of state will be no wiser than any others.

---

# The False Peace Declarations.
# The Ignoring of Treaties. The War as far as Barcelona

On ne tiendra pache[1] aucun arresté,
Tous recevans iront par tromperie:
De paix et tresve, terre et mer protesté,
Par Barcelone classe prins d'industrie.[2]

CVI,Q64

*Interpretation*

They will take no notice of the decisions of the peace treaties. The men of state will receive each other in trickery. By land and sea peace proclamations will be made. The army will be active as far as Barcelona.

[1] Latin *pax*: peace treaty. DLLB.
[2] Latin *industria*: activity. DLLB.

## The Smaller Powers Confronted by the Greater

Beaucoup de gens voudront parlementer,
Aux grands Seigneurs qui leur feront la guerre:
On ne voudra en rien les écouter,
Hélas! si Dieu n'envoye paix en terre!

CVIII,Q4a

*Interpretation*

Many [little] people will want to engage in [peace] discussions with the
great powers which will wage war upon them. But they will not be heard,
alas, if God does not send peace upon earth.

---

## Pacifist Myths, Causes of Wars

Les Dieux feront aux humains apparences,
Ce qu'ils seront autheurs de grand conflict,
Avant ciel veu serein, espée et lance,
Que vers main[1] gauche sera plus grand afflict.

CI,Q91

*Interpretation*

Myths will mislead men because they will cause great wars, before which
men will see the sky serene, then land weapons ["*espée*"] and aerial ones
["*lance*"] will be even more distressing towards the forces of the left.

[1] Latin *manus*: force. DLLB.

---

## From the Second to the Third World War.
## Great Naval Battles

Un peu après non point long intervalle:
Par terre et mer sera faict grand tumulte:
Beaucoup plus grande sera pugne[1] navalle,
Feux, animaux, qui plus feront l'insulte.

CII,Q40

*Interpretation*

After a not very long interval a great war will break out on land and sea. The naval combats will be the most important. The ferocity [of men] will be worse than the war itself.

[1] Latin *pugnum*: combat. DLLB.

---

## The Third World War follows the Second. The Use of Nuclear Missiles

Après grand troche[1] humain plus grand s'appreste,
Le grand moteur[2] les siècles renouvelle;
Pluye, sang laict, famine fer et peste,
Au ciel vu feu, courant longue étincelle.[3]

CII,Q46

*Interpretation*

After a great muster of men [soldiers] another, bigger one is being prepared; God will renew the ages. Revolution and bloodshed will bring famine, war and pestilence; then fire will be seen in the sky and great rockets traversing it.

[1] Batch, bundle, assembly. DAFL.
[2] By analogy, governor, ruler. 'God is the First Principle and Prime Mover of all creatures' (Bossuet). DL7V.
[3] Spark, small particle of matter in combustion which becomes detached from a body. DL7V. Allusion to multiple warhead rockets.

---

## The Revolutionary Climate in Provincial France. The War in France

Roy contre Roy et le Duc contre Prince,
Haine entre iceux, dissenssion horrible:
Rage et fureur sera toute province,[1]
France grand guerre et changement terrible.

CXII,Q56

*Interpretation*

A head of state will rise up against another ruler. There will be dissension and strife between them. Rage and fury will spread throughout the provinces, then a great war will cause terrible changes in France [one of which is a change of the capital].

[1] Revolutionary movements in Corsica, Brittany and the Basque country.

---

# Shortage of Gold and Silver. Life Becomes Expensive

> Près loing defaut de deux grands luminaires,[1]
> Qui surviendra entre l'Avril et Mars:
> O quel cherté! Mais deux grands débonnaires[2]
> Par terre et mer secourront toutes pars.

CIII,Q5

*Interpretation*

Shortly after the shortage of the two metals [gold and silver] which will occur between April and March, how expensive life will become! But two heads of state of noble birth will bring help by land and sea.

[1] Latin *lumen*: lustre of a metal. DLLB.
[2] Of good stock, noble. DAFL.

---

# The Economic Crises. The End of the Monetary System

> Les simulachres[1] d'or et d'argent enflez,
> Qu'après le rapt lac[2] au feu furent[3] jettez,
> Au descouvert[4] estaincts[5] tous et troublez,
> Au marbre[6] escripts, perscripts[7] interjettez.

CVIII,Q28

*Interpretation*

Images produced in gold and silver, victims of inflation, after the theft of prosperity, will be thrown into the fire in anger; exhausted and disturbed by the public debt paper and coin will be pulped.

[1] Latin *simulacrum*: image, representation. DLLB.
[2] Latin *lac, lactis*: milk. DLLB. Symbol of prosperity.
[3] Latin *furens, -entis*: furious. DLLB.
[4] Now known as the balance of payments deficit.
[5] *Estanc*: worn out, exhausted. DAFL.
[6] Mortar, made of *marble* or similar substance in which materials are crushed, pounded or pulped with a pestle.
[7] Latin *perscribo*: I pay by ticket or form. DLLB.

---

# Decadence of Power Due to Inflation.
# The Corruption of Morals. Paris in Great Confusion

Despit[1] de règne nunismes[2] descriés,[3]
Et seront peuples esmeus contre leur Roy:
Paix, fait nouveau, sainctes loix empirées[4]
RAPIS[5] onc fut en si tresdur arroy.[6]

CVI,Q23

## Interpretation

Power will be despised because of the currency devaluation and the people will rebel against the head of state. Peace will be proclaimed; through a new fact, sacred laws will be corrupted. Never was Paris in such dire disarray.

[1] Contempt. DAFL.
[2] Latin *numisma*: small coin (gold or silver). DLLB.
[3] Depreciate. DAFL.
[4] *Empirier* = spoil, corrupt, deteriorate. DAFL.
[5] Anagram of Paris.
[6] For *désarroi* by aphesis.

---

# The Abundance of Money. The Deception of Power

Le grand crédit, d'or d'argent l'abondance
Aveuglera par libide[1] l'honneur:
Cogneu sera l'adultère l'offence,
Qui parviendra à son grand deshoneur.

CVIII,Q14

*Interpretation*

The importance of credit and the abundance of gold and silver will blind men greedy for honour. The offence of deception will be known by him who attains his own great dishonour.

[1] Latin *libido*: desire, corruption. DLLB.

---

# The Economic Crisis and the Negligence of the Politicians

La grande poche[1] viendra plaindre pleurer,
D'avoir esleu: trompez seront en l'aage.[2]
Guière avec eux ne voudra demeurer,
Deceu sera par ceux de son langage.

CVII,Q35

*Interpretation*

They will complain of lost wealth and weep over choosing [responsible politicians] who will make mistakes from time to time. Very few men will want to follow them, deceived as they will be by their speeches.

[1] Empty pockets: to have no money. DL7V.
[2] Latin *in aetate*: from time to time. DLLB.

---

# The End of the Consumer Society. Inflation and Violence. The Prophecies of Nostradamus Fulfilled

Des Roys et princes dresseront simulachres,[1]
Augures, creux eslevez aruspices:[2]
Corne[3] victime dorée, et d'azur,[4] d'acres[5]
Interpretez[6] seront les exstipices.[7]

CIII,Q26

*Interpretation*

The heads of states and governments will fabricate imitations [of gold: excess of paper money]; prophets will make forecasts devoid of sense [speeches of politicians and economists]. The horn of plenty [consumer society] will fall victim to them and violence will follow peace. The prophecies will be fulfilled.

[1] Latin *simulacrum*: imitation. DLLB.
[2] Latin *haruspex*: seer, prophet. DLLB.
[3] Abundance, or plenty, an allegorical divinity who had no temple, but symbolized health and prosperity, via her *horn* filled with flowers and fruits, which she is shown holding. DL7V.
[4] Symbolic: innocence, calm, peace, 'sky blue'. DL7V.
[5] Latin *acer*: sharp, hard, violent. DLLB.
[6] Latin *interpretor*: to comment on (an author), translate, explain. DLLB.
[7] Latin *extipex*: soothsayer who examines entrails of sacrifices. DLLB.

---

# Declarations of Peace and War.
# The Execution of 300,000 Prisoners

Sous un la paix partout sera clamée,
Mais non long temps pille et rebellion,
Par refus ville,[1] terre et mer entamée,
Mort et captifs le tiers d'un million.

CI,Q92

*Interpretation*

Under one [person] peace will be proclaimed everywhere, but shortly afterwards there will be pillage and revolution. Because of the resistance of Paris, land and sea will be invaded and 300,000 prisoners executed.

[1] Nostradamus' use of 'town' with no adjective always refers to Paris, also 'the great city'.

---

# The Revolution in Italy

Au lieu que HIERON[1] fait sa nef fabriquer,
Si grand déluge sera et si subite,
Qu'on n'aura lieu ne terres s'ataquer,
L'onde monter Fesulan[2] Olympique.

CVIII,QI6

*Interpretation*

In the place where God has built his Church [Rome] there will be so great and sudden a revolution that no areas or lands will escape attack. The revolution will reach Tuscany [Florence] after the Olympic Games.

¹ Greek ἱερός: holy, sacred, divine. DGF. Allusion to Christ's words to Peter: '. . . on this rock', etc.
² Faesula = Fiesole, town in Etruria (Tuscany). DLLB.

---

## Moral Ruin and the Bloody Collapse of Rome. Subversive Literature. Outrages

O vaste Rome ta ruine s'approche
Non de tes murs de ton sang et substance:
L'aspre par lettres fera si horrible coche,
Fer pointu mis à tous jusqu'au manche.

CX,Q65

*Interpretation*

O vast Rome your ruin is approaching, not that of your walls but of your lifeblood and substance. Wickedness will work such a horrible attack through writings that all will be persecuted.

---

## Discord among the French. Internal Strife at Marseille

L'accord et pache sera du tout rompuë:
Les amitiés polluées par discorde,
L'haine envieillie, toute foy¹ corrompuë,
Et l'espérance, Marseille sans concorde.

CXII,Q59

*Interpretation*

The peace agreement will be completely broken. Alliances will be destroyed by discord. The old hatred will corrupt all confidence and hope. There will not be concord at Marseille.

¹ Latin *fides*: confidence. DLLB.

# Common Market Europe and China. Weakness in International Relations

Predons[1] pillez chaleur, grand seicheresse,
Par trop non estre cas non veu, inoui:
A l'estranger la trop grande caresse,
Neuf pays Roy. L'Orient esblouy.

*Presage 41, July*

## Interpretation

Bandits go on the rampage in a great drought, which will scarcely be an unheard-of event. There will be too much amity towards foreign countries [the East]. The heads of government of 'the Nine' will be seduced by the Orient [China].

[1] Or *préon* (from *préder* or *préer*): bandit, pillager. DAFL.

---

# John-Paul II Flees from the Russian Invasion. Resistance to the Invaders

Vent[1] Aquilon[2] fera partir le siège,
Par mur jetter cendres, platras chaulx et poussière:
Par pluye après qui leur fera bien piège,
Dernier secours encontre leur frontière.

CIX,Q99

## Interpretation

Russian troop movements force the Pope to leave Rome. Plaster, chalk and dust will be reduced to ashes: but the revolution which will follow will be a trap for them, final aid opposed to their border.

[1] Symbolic: impulse, something which sweeps along or produces a general effect. DL7V.
[2] North wind, violent and impetuous; the north. DL7V. Symbol of Russia, the Northern Empire from the Baltic Sea to Vladivostok.

---

# John-Paul II by the Rhône.
# The Alliance of the Cock (France) and the Eagle (USA)

> Pol[1] mensolée[2] mourra à trois lieues du Rosne,
> Fuis les deux prochains tarasc détroits:
> Car Mars fera le plus horrible trosne,
> De Coq et d'Aigle[3] de France frères trois.

CVIII,Q46

## Interpretation

[John]-Paul II, the travail of the sun, will die near the Rhône, having fled near the passes of Tarascon [and Beaucaire]; for the war will do terrible things to the throne [of St Peter]; then in France there will be three allies of the King of France and the United States.

[1] Nostradamus often invests the word *Pol* with dual significance: John-Paul II's Christian name and the start of the word Poland, denoting his birthplace.

[2] The word appears twice elsewhere (CIX,Q85 and CX,Q29) spelt with an *a*. Invented by Nostradamus from two Latin words: *manus*: man's work, travail, industry, labour, and *sol*: sun. This corresponds with John-Paul's epithet in Malachi's prophecy: *'de labore solis'*, the work of the sun.

[3] Cf. CV,Q99: *'Phalange aquilée'*.

---

# The Bombing of Towns in South-West France

> Condom et Aux et autour de Mirande,
> Je vois du ciel feu qui les environne:
> Sol,[1] Mars conjoint au Lyon, puis Marmande,
> Foudre grand gresle, mur tombe dans Garonne.

CVIII,Q2

## Interpretation

I see the towns of Condom, Auch and Mirande and the neighbouring area surrounded by fire from heaven, the Pope at Lyon caught up again by the war, then bombing over Marmande and blocks of houses collapsing in the Garonne.

[1] Malachi's prophecy *'de labore solis'*. Cf. CVIII,Q46 above.

---

## The Bombing of the Gers Area. The Earthquake

Tout aupres d'Aux, de Lestore et Mirande,
Grand feu du ciel en trois nuits tombera:
Cause adviendra bien stupende[1] et mirande,[2]
Bien peu après la terre tremblera.

CI,Q46

*Interpretation*

Quite near Auch, Lectoure and Mirande heavy incendiary bombing will
be carried out for three nights. The cause of it will be astonishing and
amazing and shortly afterwards there will be an earthquake.

[1]Latin *stupendus*: astonishing, marvellous. DLLB
[2]Latin *mirandus:* worthy of and causing astonishment and wonder. Marvellous. DLLB.

---

## John-Paul II near Tarascon. Liberation from Salon to Monaco

Salon, Mansol,[1] Tarascon[2] de SEX,[3] l'arc[4]
Où est debout encore la piramide[5]
Viendront livrer[6] le Prince Dannemarc,
Rachat[7] honny au temple d'Artémide.[8]

CIV,Q27

*Interpretation*

Near Salon, 'the work of the sun' [John-Paul II] is at Tarascon, since
from Aix-en-Provence to Monaco, where the rock still stands, [the
French] will come to deliver the Prince of Denmark. The saviour will be
honoured in Turkey.

[1] Cf. CVIII,Q46.
[2] Cf. CVIII,Q46.
[3] Cf. CV,Q57.
[4] Arx Monoeci: Monaco. DLLB.
[5] By extension, hill or mountain taking on pyramidal shape. DLLB.
[6] Example of aphesis.
[7] *Rachatere*: redeemer. DAFL.
[8] The goddess Diana (Greek: Artemis), whose most famous temple was undoubtedly
that at Ephesus. MGR. Ephesus was situated in Asia Minor, present-day Turkey. AVL.

# The Invasion in the Gironde, in the South-West.
## The Conflict Reaches Marseille.
## The Vatican Occupied

Passer Guienne, Languedoc et le Rosne,
D'Agen tenans de Marmande et la Roole:[1]
D'ouvrir par foy[2] parroy[3] Phocen tiendra son trosne,
Conflit aupres sainct pol de Manseole.[4]

CIX,Q85

*Interpretation*

[The invasion] will pass through Guyenne and the Languedoc as far as
the Rhône. From Agen, the occupiers having arrived from Marmande
and La Réole will bring horror to the coast of Marseille, for they will
occupy the throne [of St Peter] and the conflict will get close to the spot
where [John]-Paul II – 'the work of the sun' – is taking refuge.

[1] Town on the Garonne, 67 km south-east of Bordeaux and 18 km from Langon. AVL.
Cf. CI,Q90 and CXII,Q65.
[2] From Celtic *fouy* (for *foui*): term expressing horror at a disgusting thing or event. DP.
[3] Shingle shore or gravel. DAFL.
[4] Cf. CVIII,Q46.

---

# John-Paul's Supporters Arrested and
## Imprisoned in Bigorre

De Pol MANSOL[1] dans caverne caprine,[2]
Caché et pris extrait hors par la barbe:[3]
Captif mené comme beste mastine,[4]
Par Begourdans[5] amenée près de Tarbe.

CX,Q29

*Interpretation*

[The entourage] of [John]-Paul, 'the work of the Sun', sheltering on the
Isle of Capri, will be taken prisoners and led away by the revolutionaries.
They will be taken to prison like animals, across the Bigorre near Tarbes
[Lourdes?]

[1] Cf. CVIII,Q46.
[2] Capri: island in the Gulf of Naples, noteworthy for its steepness and Blue *Grotto*. DL7V.
[3] Abbreviation of Aenobarbus, i.e. representative for Nostradamus of the revolutionary forces of destruction. Cf. Note, CV,Q45.
[4] Breed of domestic dog. DL7V.
[5] Inhabitants of the Bigorre; chief town, Tarbes. DL7V.

---

## The Pope at Lyon.
## His Journey to Capri and Monaco. His Death

Dans deux logis de nuict le feu prendra
Plusieurs dedans estouffez et rostis:
Près de deux fleuves pour seul il adviendra,
Sol,[1] l'Arq[2], et Caper,[3] tous seront amortis.[4]

CII,Q35

*Interpretation*

In the night fire will spread through two [ministerial?] blocks where some will be burned and suffocated. The Pope will arrive alone near two rivers [Lyon]; after his journey to Capri and Monaco, all will be put to death.

[1] Allusion to John-Paul's epithet '*de labore solis*'.
[2] Arx Monoeci: Monaco. DLLB.
[3] Capri.
[4] *Amortir*: to muffle, deaden. DAFL.

---

## The Pope Leaves Rome and Italy.
## The End of His Reign

Istra du mont Gaulsier[1], et Aventin,[2]
Qui par le trou advertira[3] l'armée,
Entre deux rocs[4] sera prins le butin,
De SEXT[5] mansol[6] faillir la renommée.

CV,Q57

*Interpretation*

He will leave Rome and cross the north Italian mountains because of him
who will lead his army towards a tunnel [Switzerland]. Between two
rocks [Beaucaire and Tarascon] his possessions will be seized. After
Aix-en-Provence the renown of 'the sun's work' [John-Paul II] will fail.

¹ Cisalpine Gaul, northern Italy. DHB.
² Aventine: one of the Seven Hills of Rome. DL7V.
³ Latin *adverto*: I turn, direct an object towards. DLLB.
⁴ Cf. CVIII,Q46, '*les deux tarasc détroits*'.
⁵ Aquae Sextiae: Aix-en-Provence. DLLB.
⁶ Cf. CVIII,Q46.

---

# Fighting in the Jura and Alps.
# The Death of John-Paul II at Lyon

Après victoire du Lyon¹ au Lyon,
Sus la montagne de JURA secatombe,²
Delues³ et brodes⁴ septiesme million,
Lyon, Ulme⁵ a Mausol⁶ mort et tombe.

CVIII,Q34

*Interpretation*

After the victory of the violent leader at Lyon, there will be a hecatomb
on the Jura Mountains, a seventh of a million soldiers will be annihilated
in the Alps. 'The work of the sun' [John-Paul II] will find death and
burial at Lyon.

¹ Violent, raging person. DL7V.
² Greek ἐχατόμβη: hecatomb. *S* replaces aspirate *h* at the beginning.
³ Latin *deleo, delui:* annihilate, destroy. DLLB.
⁴ Latin Brodiontii, Brodiontes, tribe of the Alps. DLLB.
⁵ Anagram of *mule*: Papal white slipper. DL7V.
⁶ Cf. CVIII,Q46.

# The Death of the Pope at Lyon.
# The Left in Power in France

Romain Pontife garde de t'approcher
De la cité que deux fleuves arrose:[1]
Ton sang viendra auprès de là cracher,
Toy et les tiens quand fleurira la Rose.[2]

CII,Q97

*Interpretation*

Roman Pope, do not approach the town which two rivers water [Lyon].
Your blood and that of your followers will flow near this spot, when the
left gets into power.

[1] Lyon, whose two rivers are the Rhône and Saône.
[2] Emblem of the French Socialist party.

---

# John-Paul's Assassination by Night.
# A Good, Gentle, Enterprising and Prudent Pope

Esleu en Pape d'esleu sera mocqué,
Subit soudain esmeu[1] prompt[2] et timide:[3]
Par trop bon doux a mourir provoqué,
Crainte estreinte la nuit de sa mort guide.

CX,QI2

*Interpretation*

The one elected Pope will be mocked by his electors. This enterprising
and prudent person will suddenly be reduced to silence. They will
instigate his death because of his too great goodness and mildness.
Stricken by fear, they will lead him to his death in the night.

[1] *Esmuir*: to become mute, dumb. DAFL.
[2] Latin *promptus*: (of persons) active, resolute, enterprising. DLLB.
[3] Latin *timidus*: prudent, circumspect. DLLB.

# The Death of John-Paul II at Lyon, 13 December.
# His Journey to Montélimar

Du mont Aymar[1] sera noble[2] obscurcie,
Le mal viendra au joinct de Saone et Rosne,
Dans bois cachez soldats jour de Lucie[3],
Qui ne fut onc un si horrible throsne.

CIX,Q68

*Interpretation*

From Montélimar the Pope will lose his fame. His misfortune will come
at the confluence of the Saône and Rhône [Lyon] because of soldiers
hidden in the woods on 13 December. Nothing so horrible will ever have
happened to the throne [of St Peter].

[1] Montélimar (by syncope).
[2] The popes, because of their coats of arms, could be considered as nobles. Nostradamus
here alludes to nobility of spirit.
[3] St Lucy's Day, i.e.13 December.

---

# The Left in Power. Revolutionary Upheavals.

Sur le milieu du grand monde[1] la rose,[2]
Pour nouveaux faicts sang public espandu:
A dire vray, on aura bouche close:[3]
Lors au besoing tard viendra l'attendu.

CV,Q96

*Interpretation*

When socialism is in power amid the bourgeoisie, the people's blood will
flow because of new acts. To tell the truth, freedom of expression will
disappear. Then the awaited [helper] will arrive late because of penury.

[1] *Grand monde*: expression for important, affluent, influential people as a whole or a
class. DL7V.
[2] Emblem of Socialist party in France.
[3] To silence someone, i.e. make them keep their mouths shut. DL7V.

# The Pope's Flight West. Religious Persecution

Flora,[1] fuis, fuis le plus proche Romain,
Au Fesulan[2] sera conflict donné:
Sang espandu, les plus grands prins à main,
Temple ne sexe ne sera pardonné.

CVII,Q8

*Interpretation*

You, the nearest Roman [the Pope], flee, flee westwards, the conflict will reach Fiesole: blood will be shed and the greatest will be captured. Neither churches nor sexes will be spared.

[1] Flora, wife of Zephyrus, the west wind.
[2] Latin Faesulae: today Fiesole, Tuscan town. DHB.

---

# The Polish Pope's Flight from Rome

En après cinq troupeau[1] ne mettra hors,
Un fuytif[2] pour Penelon[3] laschera:[4]
Faux murmurer secours venir par lors,
Le chef, le siège lors abandonnera.

CX,Q3

*Interpretation*

After five [days or months][5] the Church will be expelled; a person will flee, abandoning the Pope: false rumours of help will circulate, the Head [of the Church] will then abandon the Holy See.

[1] Flock, i.e. Christ's: the Church. DL7V.
[2] *fuytif*, i.e. fugitive, often with pejorative sense. DAFL.
[3] *Penelon*, anagram of Polenne – itself an old French word used as collective term denoting the countries which comprised Poland. DHB.
[4] Let go, abandon. DAFL.
[5] Probably five months after the start of the Third World War.

# A Comet Visible for Seven Days.
# An Appeal for Help from the British Head of State.
# The Pope Leaves Rome

La grande estoille par sept jours bruslera
Nuë fera deux soleils apparoir
Le gros mastin[1] toute nuict hurlera
Quand grand Pontife changera de terroir.

CII,Q41

*Interpretation*

The Comet will blaze for seven days. The sky will display two suns; the British leader will howl all night when the Pope changes countries.

[1] Symbol already used by Nostradamus for an English leader, i.e. Churchill. Cf. CV,Q4

---

# The Capture of the Pope during a Journey.
# The Assassination of His Favourite

En navigant captif prins grand pontife;
Grand après faillir les clercs tumultuez;
Second[1] esleu absent son bien debife,[2]
Son favori[3] bastard a mort tué.

CV,Q15

*Interpretation*

The great pontiff will be taken prisoner in the course of a journey. The Pope will die after that and the clergy will set up a tumult. He who will have been elected second, being absent [from the Vatican], will see his goodness weakened and his favoured friend of humble birth will be killed.

[1] John-Paul II, after John-Paul I.
[2] To weaken, reduce (*debiffer*). DAFL. Cf. CV,Q56.
[3] Perhaps the Secretary of State.

# Quarrels between Three Leaders at the Time of the Comet. The Basque Country and Rome in the Grip of Revolution

Durant l'estoille chevelue apparante,
Les trois grands princes seront faits ennemis
Frappez du ciel paix terre trémulent,[1]
Pau, Timbre[2] undans,[3] serpent sur le bort mis.

CII,Q43

*Interpretation*

While the Comet is seen, the three great leaders will become enemies; they will be hit from the sky and the earth will tremble. The Lower Pyrenees and Tiber will experience upheaval. Satan will install himself on the latter's banks.

[1] Latin *tremo*: I tremble. DLLB.
[2] The Vatican is by the Tiber.
[3] Latin, present participle of *undo*: I am agitated, seethe.

---

# Iraq against the West. The Pope on the Banks of the Rhône. Italy Occupied

Les Citoyens de Mésopotamie[1]
Irez encontre amis de Tarragone:[2]
Jeux, ritz, banquets, toute gent endormie,
Vicaire[3] au Rosne, prins cité, ceux d'Ausone.[4]

CVII,Q22

*Interpretation*

The Iraqis will march against the allies of Spain while people amuse themselves, laugh, banquet and everyone sleeps; the Pope fleeing beside the Rhône, the Vatican City will be occupied as well as Italy.

[1] Mesopotamia, region between the Tigris and Euphrates, now Iraq. DHB.
[2] Town in Spain (Catalonia). DHB.
[3] Vicar of Christ, i.e. the Pope. DL7V.
[4] Ausonia: ancient region of Italy, by extension all Italy. DLLB.

# The Ransack of the Vatican.
# The Pope by the Rhône

Lorsqu'on verra expiler[1] le sainct temple,
Plus grand du Rhosne et sacres prophanes:
Par eux naistra pestilence si ample,
Roy faict injuste[2] ne fera condamner.

CVIII,Q62

## Interpretation

When the Vatican is seen ransacked, the greatest [the Pope] beside the Rhône, and sacred things profaned [by enemies] who will cause a great calamity, the head of the government can only condemn these cruel acts.

[1] Latin *expilo*: I pillage, steal, sack. DLLB.
[2] Latin *injustus*: hard, wicked. DLLB.

---

# The Death by Poisoning of an
# Enemy Head of State. A Rain of Meteorites

L'ennemy grand vieil dueil[1] meurt de poyson,
Les souverains par infinis subjuguez:
Pierres pleuvoir, cachez, soubs la toison,
Par mort articles en vain sont alleguez.

CII,Q47

## Interpretation

When the great and old enemy who brings misfortune is poisoned, the sovereigns will be subjugated by innumerable [troops]. The meteorites hidden in the comet's hair will rain down upon the earth, when the articles [Geneva agreements] will be invoked in vain, concerning the rights of war [death].

[1] *Duel*, changed here to *deuil*: sorrow, misfortune, affliction. DAFL.

# The Fall of the Invaders. The Comet

Mabus[1] puis tost alors mourra, viendra,
De gens et bestes une horrible défaite,
Puis tout à coup la vengeance on verra,
Cent,[2] main, soif, faim, quand courra la comète.

CII,Q62

*Interpretation*

The wicked invader will soon die, after provoking a horrible hecatomb of men and animals. Then suddenly vengeance will come. Because of endless speeches, force will rule; they will know thirst and hunger, when the comet crosses the sky.

[1] Some editions have *malus*: wicked, evil, harmful. DLLB.

[2] Latin *cento*: incoherent speech, nonsense. DLLB. Allusion to International Conventions of Geneva.

---

# The Appearance of a Comet near Ursa Minor in June. War in Italy, Greece and the Red Sea. The Pope's Death

Apparoistra vers le Septentrion[1]
Non loing de Cancer[2] l'estoille cheveluë:
Suse,[3] Sienne,[4] Boëce,[5] Eretrion[6],
Moura de Rome grand, la nuit disparuë.

CVI,Q6

*Interpretation*

The comet will appear towards Ursa Minor around 21 June. Suse and Tuscany, Greece and the Red Sea will tremble. The Pope of Rome will die, the night the comet disappears.

[1] Latin *septentrio*: constellation of seven stars, near the Pole Star: Ursa Minor. DLLB.

[2] Sun enters the Sign of Cancer on 21 June. DL7V.

[3] Situated at the junction of the two great Mount Cenis and Mount Geneva approaches, Suse can thus be considered a key to Italy. DHB.

[4] Powerful Tuscan town. DHB.

[5] Boeotia: region of Greece. DLLB.

[6] Erythraeum mare: the Red Sea. DLLB.

## The Death of the Pope. The Comet.
## Economic Ruin. Italy's Restricted Areas

Un peu devant monarque trucidé,
Castor Pollux[1] en nef, astre crinite,[2]
L'erain[3] public par terre et mer vuidé,
Pise, Ast, Ferrare, Turin,[4] terre interdite.

CII,QI5

*Interpretation*

A little before the Pope is killed, the Church will have had two brothers [John-Paul I and II], and the comet will be seen; public money will be squandered by land and sea, and Pisa, Asti, Ferrara and Turin will be forbidden areas.

[1] Two brothers, sons of Jupiter.
[2] Latin *crinita stella*: fiery star with tail, comet. DLLB.
[3] Latin *aes, aeris*: silver, money. DLLB.
[4] Tuscany, Piedmont and the Romagna. AVL.

---

# THE FALL OF THE FIFTH REPUBLIC

## The Flight of the Head of Government.
## Enemies Overwhelmed by Death

Par conflit Roy, règne abandonnera
Le plus grand chef faillira au besoing
Morts profligez, peu en reschappera
Tous destrangez, un en sera tesmoing.

CIV,Q45

*Interpretation*

Because of the conflict the leader will abandon power. The greatest head of government [Russia] will succumb through lack of funds and her people will be overwhelmed by death from which few will escape. They will all be massacred; one person will bear witness to it.

---

# The Tyrant Executed in a Moslem Country. The War of Revenge against the West. The Fall of the French Republic

Au port Selin[1] le tyran mis à mort,
La liberté non pourtant recouvrée:
Le nouveau Mars par vindicte et remort,
Dame[2] par force de frayeur honorée.

CI,Q94

*Interpretation*

The tyrant will be put to death in the Moslem port, but that does not bring back freedom. A new war breaks out, through spite and vengeance; the French Republic will be paid in fear, through force.

[1] Greek Σελήνη: the moon, i.e. Moslem crescent.
[2] Constant reference to French Republic (Marianne).

---

# The Fall of the French Republic. Moslem Troops in Italy. The Occupation Government in Italy

A[1] Logmyon[2] sera laissé le regne,
Du Grand Selyn[3] qui plus fera de faict:
Par les Itales estendra son enseigne
Sera régi par prudent[4] contrefaict.

CVI,Q42

*Interpretation*

Power will be abandoned by the French Republic because of Moslem forces which will engage in many actions and extend their power to Italy, which will be ruled by a person who will pretend to be intelligent.

[1] Latin *a* or *ab*: by. DLLB. Often used thus by Nostradamus, hence one of the chief linguistic traps in the Centuries.
[2] Ogmius or Ogmios, Gallic God of Eloquence. DHB. For Nostradamus, denotes the French Republican system.
[3] Greek: Selene. Cf. CI,Q94, note. 1.
[4] Latin *prudens*: clear-sighted, intelligent. DLLB.

## The End of the Fifth Republic. The Quarrel Between the Russians and Their Moslem Allies

Quand la lictière du tourbillon[1] versée,
Et seront faces de leurs manteaux couverts[2]
La république par gens nouveaux vexée[3]
Lors blancs et rouges jugeront à l'envers.

CI,Q3

*Interpretation*

When the bed of revolution is overthrown and [the revolutionaries] resign themselves to their misfortune, the Republic will be injured the moment the whites [the Moslems] and the reds [Eastern Bloc] disagree.

[1] Latin *turbo*: revolution. DLLB.
[2] To envelop oneself in one's cloak, i.e. be resigned, stoically accept the misfortune with which one is threatened. DL7V.
[3] Latin *vexo*: I shake up, damage, injure. DLLB.

---

# THE MIDDLE EAST AND THE THIRD WORLD WAR

## Wars in Palestine. Arab–Israeli Conflicts

Les lieux peuplez seront inhabitables,
Pour champs avoir grande division:
Regnes livrez à prudens incapables,
Entre les frères mort et dissention.

CII,Q95

*Interpretation*

Peopled areas will be made uninhabitable [nuclear fallout?] for very divided territories [Palestine]. The powers will be given over to incapable governments. Death and dissension will reign between brothers [Arab and Jew].

# The Eastern Origin of the Third World War

De l'Orient viendra le coeur Punique[1]
Fascher Hadrie et les hoirs[2] Romulides,
Accompagné de la classe Libique,
Tremblez Mellites[3] et proches isles vuides.

CI,Q9

*Interpretation*

From the East will come the treacherous act which will strike the Adriatic
Sea and the heirs of Romulus [Italians], with the Libyan fleet; tremble,
inhabitants of Malta and its archipelago.

[1] *Foi punique*: bad faith. DL.
[2] Legal term for an heir. DL7V.
[3] Latin Melita: Malta. DLLB.

---

# Colonel Gaddafy Stirs up the Arab World against the West. The Great King: a Man of Culture against the Arabs

Prince libinique puissant en Occident,
François d'Arabe viendra tant enflammer
Scavant aux lettres sera condescendent,
La langue Arabe en François translater.

CIII,Q27

*Interpretation*

A Libyan chief of state, powerful in the west, will come to inflame so
many Arabs against the French, then comes an educated and well-inten-
tioned man who will translate the Arab language into French.

---

# Moslem Anti-Christian Forces in
# Iraq and Syria

La grande bande et secte crucigère,[1]
Se dressera en Mésopotamie:[2]
Du proche fleuve compagnie lege,
Que telle loy tiendra pour ennemie.

CIII,Q61

*Interpretation*

The great band and anti-Christian sect of Moslems will rise up in Iraq
and Syria near the Euphrates[3] with a tank force and will hold the [Christ-
ian] law to be its enemy.

[1] For *crucifigere*: Latin: to crucify, put on the cross. DLLB. Example of syncope.
[2] I.e. Iraq and northern Syria. AU.
[3] The Euphrates runs through both countries.

---

# Persecution in the Moslem Countries of Asia,
# Especially in Turkey

Par toute Asie grande proscription,[1]
Mesme en Mysie, Lysie et Pamphylie:[2]
Sang versera par absolution,[3]
D'un jeune noir[4] remply de felonnie.

CIII,Q60

*Interpretation*

There will be great confiscations [of Christian property] throughout Asia
and especially in Turkey where blood will be shed in the name of freedom
by a young Moslem leader full of treachery.

[1] Latin *proscriptio*: confiscation, putting outside the law. DLLB.
[2] Regions of Turkey. AVL.
[3] Latin *absolutio*: deliverance. DLLB.
[4] Name given to the Moslem dynasty of the Abassids, because it adopted the colour
black for its clothing and flags. DL7V.

## The Conference between Arabs and Jews

L'ire insensée du combat furieux
Fera à table par frères le fer luyre,
Les départir mort blessé curieux,
Le fier duelle viendra en France nuyre.

CII,Q34

*Interpretation*

The mad rage of furious battle will make swords shine even among brothers seated at the same table; in order to decide between them, one of them will have to be fatally injured in a curious way; their proud duel will extend to harming France.

---

## Italy Occupied. Spain in the Conflict. The Libyan Head of State

Saturne et Mars en Leo[1] Espagne captive,
Par chef libyque au conflict attrapé,
Proche de Malte, Heredde[2] prinse vive,
Et Romain sceptre sera par coq[3] frappé.

CV,Q14

*Interpretation*

At the time the war reaches Léon, captive Spain will be engaged in battle by the Libyan leader, Italy having been suddenly taken. Then the [red] power installed in Rome will be smitten by the French king.

[1] For Léon: one of the fifteen ancient areas of Spain. DHB. Example of apocope.
[2] Latin *heres, -edis*; heir. DLLB. The Italians. Cf. CI,Q9. *'les hoirs Romulides'*: the heirs of Romulus.
[3] Emblem of France, but also of the junior branch, the family of Orleans.

# The Russo–Moslem Invasion of the Rhine and Danube. Fighting at Malta and the Gulf of Genoa

En l'an bien proche esloingné de Vénus,
Les deux plus grands de l'Asie et d'Affrique:
Du Ryn et Hister[1] qu'on dira sont Venus,
Cris, pleurs à Malte et costé Lygustique.[2]

CIV,Q68

## Interpretation

The year people are ready to abandon treachery, the two greatest powers of Asia [USSR] and Africa [Arab countries] will come as far as the Rhine and the Danube. Then there will be cries and weeping at Malta and the Gulf of Genoa.

[1] Ancient name for the Danube. DHB.
[2] Latin Ligusticus sinus: Gulf of Genoa. DHB.

---

# The Invasion of Italy and the Mediterranean Coast. The Earthquakes

Je pleure Nisse, Mannego, Pize, Gennes,
Savone, Sienne, Capue, Modene, Malte
Le dessus sang et glaive par estrennes,[1]
Feu, trembler terre, eau, malheureuse nolte.[2]

CX,Q60

## Interpretation

I bewail Nice, Monaco, Pisa, Genoa, Savona, Siena, Capua, Modena and Malta, which will be covered in blood in the grip of fighting. The war, the earthquakes and the revolution will cause an undesired unhappiness.

[1] Grip, grasp, compression. DAFL.
[2] Latin noltis: archaic for 'non vultis': we do not wish. DLLB.

## Peace Breaks Down in the Middle East. France and Portugal Hit by the Conflict

La foy Punique en Orient rompue,
Grand Iud,[1] et Rosne Loire, et Tag changeront
Quand du mulet[2] la faim sera repue,
Classe espargie, sang et corps nageront.

CII,Q60

### Interpretation

Moslem duplicity will provoke a split in the Middle East. Because of a great person on the Jewish side, the Rhône, Loire and Tagus will see changes when the greed for gold has died down, the fleet will be engulfed, blood and sailors' bodies will be floating.

[1] Latin Judaei: the Jews. DLLB.
[2] Historical allusion: Philip, King of Macedon, used to say there was no impregnable fortress wherever a mule laden with gold could ascend. An expression of the irresistible power of gold. DL7V.

## From Israel the War Extends to Western Europe

Par la tumeur[1] de Heb, Po, Tag Timbre et Rome,
Et par l'estang Leman et Aretin:[2]
Les deux grands chefs et citez de Garonne,
Prins, morts, noyez. Partir humain butin.

CIII,Q12

### Interpretation

The troubles of Hebron [Israel] will reach the Po, Tagus, Tiber, Rome, Lake of Geneva and Tuscany. The two leaders in the towns of the Garonne [Bordeaux and Toulouse] will be taken prisoner, put to death and drowned. The human spoils will be shared.

[1] Latin tumor: trouble, agitation. DLLB.
[2] Inhabitant of Arezzo, Tuscany (Italy). DL7V.

## Conflict in the Adriatic Sea.
## Egypt in the War

Naufrage à classe près d'onde Hadriatique,
La terre tremble, esmuë sus l'air en terre mis,
Egypte tremble augment Mahométique,
L'Héraut[1] soy rendre à crier est commis.

CII,Q86

*Interpretation*

A fleet will be wrecked near the Adriatic Sea, the earth will tremble
when an airborne force is defeated. Egypt, augmented by Moslem troops,
will tremble. The commander-in-chief will be asked to give himself up.

[1] Public official, formerly entrusted with the task of proclaiming war, whose person
was sacrosanct. DL7V.

---

# MONSIGNOR LEFÈVRE AND THE
# TRADITIONALIST (TONSURED) PRIESTS

## Monsignor Lefève Suspended 'A Divinis'.
## The Traditionalist Seminary of Albano

Privés seront Razes[1] de leurs harnois,[2]
Augmentera leur plus grande querelle,
Père Liber[3] deceu fulg.[4] Albonois,
Seront rongés sectes à la moelle.

Presage 54, September

*Interpretation*

The tonsured ones will be deprived of their vestments, which will increase their quarrelsome spirit even more. He who has become independent from the Pope will be mistaken and those from Albano will be the
subject of wrath [from the Vatican]. The sects will be gnawed to the very
marrow.

[1] Tonsure: circular space on shaved heads of monks. DL7V.
[2] Vestments. DL7V.

³ Latin *liber a patre*, free from the paternal power. DLLB. Hence, freed from the Pope's authority.
⁴ Latin *fulgor*: lightning. DLLB.

# The Traditionalist Movement.
# The Comet and the War

Longue crinite¹ le fer le Gouverneur
Faim, fièvre ardente, feu et de sang fumée:
A tous estats Joviaux² grand honneur,³
Seditions par Razes allumée.

Presage 52

*Interpretation*

When the great comet is seen the leader of the government will be stricken by war; famine, plague, smoke of war and blood will be seen in all western countries with all their external signs, when a rebellion will be sparked off by the tonsured ones [traditionalists].

¹ Latin *crinitus*: long-haired. DLLB. Cf. CII,QI5, '*astre crinite*'.
² Latin *Jovialis*, pertaining to Jove (Jupiter). The planet Jupiter was regarded by astrologers as a source of good fortune. DL7V. Nostradamus thus denotes the West and its wellbeing.
³ Latin *honor*: ornaments, trappings, externals. DLLB.

# The Ecône Seminary and Monsignor Lefèvre

Du lieu esleu Razes n'estre contens,
Du Lac Leman¹ conduite non prouvée:
Renouveller on fera le vieil temps,
Espeuillera la trame² tant couvée.³

Presage 50, April

*Interpretation*

The traditionalists will not be content with the election at the Vatican. The conduct of those from Lake Geneva will not be approved of because they will renew the customs of former times,[4] the intrigue so secretly hatched will cause them to be ruined.

[1] The Seminary of Ecône is at Riddes, in Switzerland, on the banks of the Rhône, 30 km from Lake Geneva.
[2] Plot, intrigue.
[3] To develop secretly, hatch.
[4] The traditionalists reject the Second Vatican Council's reforms and will accept only the Mass of Pius V, Pope 1566–72.

---

## The Traditionalists against the Council

En péril monde et Rois féliciter,
Razes esmeu[1] par conseil[2] ce qu'estoit
L'Eglise Rois pour eux peuple irriter[3]
Un montrera après ce qu'il n'estoit.

Presage 99, July

*Interpretation*

The world will be in danger despite the heads of state, who will congratulate each other.[4] The traditionalists will rebel against what the Council will have decided. The cardinals will excite the people against them. And one of them will then show his true face.

[1] Latin *movere*: to rise up, revolt. DLLB.
[2] Latin *consilium*: deliberating assembly. DLLB.
[3] Latin *irritare*: to excite, provoke, anger. DLLB.
[4] Allusion to the Camp David agreement between Begin, Sadat and Carter.

---

## The Big Mistakes Made by Monsignor Lefèvre. His Supporters Deprived of All Power

De bien en mal le temps se changera
Le pache[1] d'Aust[2] des plus Grands esperance:
Des Grands deul[3] LVIS[4] trop plus trebuchera,
Cognus Razez pouvoir ni cognoissance.

Presage 88, September

*Interpretation*

The good times will change to ill-fortune, although the peace of the south will give rise to the greatest hopes. The great ones [the cardinals] will deplore Monsignor Lefèvre's acts which will make too many errors. His supporters will no longer have power or understanding.

[1] Latin *pax*: peace. DLLB.
[2] *Auster*: Latin word for south wind. DL7V. Nostradamus here refers to the Camp David agreement signed by two 'southern' countries by contrast with the USSR, the Empire of the North Wind (*Aquila*).
[3] From vb. *doloir*: to suffer, deplore, bewail. DAFL.
[4] Abbreviation of *LefeVre*.

---

# The Deaths of Monsignor Lefèvre and the Pope

> Les deuils laissez, supremes alliances,
> Raze Grand mort refus fait en à l'entrée:
> De retour estre bien fait en oubliance,
> La mort du juste à banquet[1] perpétrée.

> Presage 57, December

*Interpretation*

Sadness abandoned, great alliances having been made, the great tonsured one will die, not having been allowed to return to the fold of the Church. In return, he will end up forgotten; the death of the just man [the Pope] will be commemorated by communion [masses].

[1] The Sacred Banquet: Holy Communion. DL7V.

---

# The End of the Secession of the Traditionalist Movement. An End to Their Ecclesiastical Raiment

> Tout innonder[1] à la Razée perte,
> Vol de mur, mort de tous biens abondance:
> Eschappera[2] par manteau[3] de couverte,
> Des neufs et vieux sera tournée chance.

> Presage 101

*Interpretation*

The revolution will cause the loss of the traditionalist movement when the funds are stolen and the consumer society ends. The traditionalist movement will disappear when deprived of ecclesiastical vestments; the novices' luck, like that of the old, will change.

[1] Water or wave, taken as symbols of revolutionary movements.
[2] To vanish, disappear. DL7V.
[3] Bishop's mantle (*Bischofsmantel*); this vestment, in use in the Middle Ages and which the Germans wore until *c.* 1530, was a cloak of chainmail. DL7V.

---

# The Exodus Brought About by the War.
# Vatican Outbursts Against the Traditionalists

Au lieu mis la peste et fuite naistre,
Temps variant vent. La mort des trois Grands:
Du ciel grand foudres estat[1] des Razes paistre.[2]
Vieil[3] près de mort bois peu dedans vergans.[4]

Presage 98

*Interpretation*

They will begin to flee from the places stricken by war and sickness. The wind of history will change the course of the times and the three great heads of state will die. The great pastor will direct the wrath of heaven against the tonsured ones. The archaic system, near to death, will decline a little more.

[1] Latin *exstare*: to show oneself, be visible. DLLB.
[2] Latin *pastor*. DLLB. Like 'the great prophet' (Cf. CII,Q36), the great pastor signifies the Pope.
[3] Cf. CI,Q7: '*Par le Rousseau sennez les entreprises*'.
[4] Latin *vergo*: I decline, am in decline. DLLB.

## Certain Traditionalists Rejoin the Church

Remis seront en leur pleine puissance,
D'un point d'accord conjoints, non accordez:
Tous defiez plus aux Razes fiance,
Plusieurs d'entre eux à bande debordez.

*Presage 75, September*

*Interpretation*

The traditionalists will be rehabilitated and rejoin the Church through
an agreement. Those who do not come to terms will be challenged. No
longer will there be any confidence in the Traditionalists, several of
whom will be removed from the confraternity.

---

## The Schism in the Catholic Church.
## Prince Charles Murdered in London

Dedans la terre du grand temple Celique,[1]
Neveu[2] à Londres par paix fainte[3] meurtry,
La barque alors deviendra schismatique
Liberté fainte sera au corn[4] et cry.

**CVI,Q22**

*Interpretation*

In Vatican territory, when the grandson is murdered in London during
a false peace, the vessel [of St Peter] will become schismatic, and a
feigned freedom will be trumpeted and proclaimed.

[1] Celestial. DAFL. Poetic phrase for 'the Catholic Church'. DL7V.
[2] Formerly meaning 'grandson'. DAFL. Prince Charles of England is the grandson of
the last King of England, George VI.
[3] From *feindre*, to feign or pretend. DAFL.
[4] *Cor*, as in cor anglais. DAFL

# Schism during the War

Les forteresses des assiégez serrez,
Par poudre à feu profondes en abysme
Les prodireurs[1] seront tous vifs serrez,[2]
Onc aux Sacristes n'advint si piteux scisme.

CIV,Q40

*Interpretation*

The besieged will be shut inside fortresses which will be engulfed by incendiary weapons, the traitors will be shut away alive. Never will there be such a miserable schism in the Church.

[1] Latin *proditor*: traitor, perfidious man. DLLB.
[2] Enclosed spot, but also a bar for closing something up, a lock. DAFL.

---

# The Schism and the Anti-Pope.
# The Peace Treaty Signed near Venice

Sept mois sans plus obtiendra prélature[1]
Par son décez grand schisme fera naistre:
Sept mois tiendra un autre la préture,
Près de Venise paix, union renaistre.

CVIII,Q93

*Interpretation*

He will only obtain the prelature [the throne of St Peter] for seven months and will cause a great schism by dying. Someone other than the Pope will occupy the throne of St Peter for seven months, and then peace will be signed near Venice and the unity of the Church will be restored.

[1] Body of Roman prelates or officers in the Pope's house. DL7V.

# The Schism and the Foreign Pope

Par chapeaux rouges querelles et nouveaux scismes
Quand on aura esleu le Sabinois[1]
On produira contre lui grands sophismes
Et sera Rome lésée par Albannois.

CV,Q46

*Interpretation*

Because of the cardinals there will be quarrels and a new schism, during which the foreigner will have been elected. Great sophisms will be uttered against him and the Vatican will be harmed by the men from Albano.

[1] The Sabines were 'the foreigners' to the Romans.

---

# The Traditionalists and Spain

Devant le lac où plus cher fut jetté
De sept mois et son ost[1] tout déconfit,
Seront Hispans par Albannois gastez
Par délay perte en donnant le conflit.

CVIII,Q94

*Interpretation*

Near Lake Geneva, where a more cherished [heresy: i.e. Calvinism] was launched, his supporters will be discomfited at the end of seven months. The Spaniards will be corrupted by the men of Albano [the traditionalists] and the conflict will be the reason for their loss.

[1] Crowd, troop. DAFL.

## The Failure of Monsignor Lefèvre's Attempts.
## His Death in a Slum House

Pour Razes Chef ne parviendra à bout,
Edicts changez, les serrez mis au large:
Mort Grand trouvé moins de foy, bas dedo[1]
Dissimulé, transi frappé à bauge.[2]

Presage 68, February

*Interpretation*

The leader of the tonsured ones will not attain his ends; rules having
been changed [by the Council], those who were beset [by the Pope] will
be given latitude. The leader [of the traditionalists] found dead at the
moment when, laid low by circumstances, he will be propped up, hidden,
chilled, stricken in a wretched hovel.

[1] For *'debout'*, as in some editions.
[2] Miserable dwelling. DL7V.

---

# THE INVASION. MILITARY OPERATIONS

*Key definitions*

*USSR:* the Bear, Slavonia, Aquila (the North Wind), the North or Pole
   Star, the Normans, the Boristhenes, the Reds.
*The Warsaw Pact*: the Gryphon, the goshawk, the seven countries.
*John-Paul II*: Memel (the Niemen), Pol Mansol, the Great Pontiff, the
   noble, Penelon (Polenne), Vicar, the Lamb, Sol.
*The Moslem world*: the Barbarians, Punic, Hannibal.
*The Moslem countries cited*: Algeria, Tunisia, Morocco, Libya, Persia
   (Iran), Mesopotamia (Iraq), Carmania (Afghanistan), Byzantium
   (Turkey).

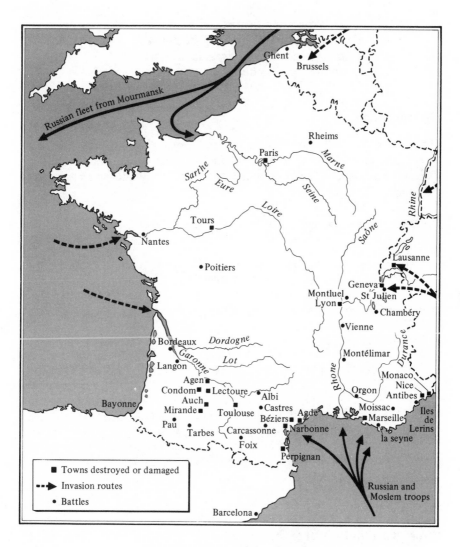

The Third World War – Invasion

# The Axis of the War. The 45th Parallel.
# Bordeaux, Geneva and Baku. The Destruction of Geneva

Cinq et quarante degrez ciel bruslera,
Feu approcher de la grand'cité neuve:[1]
Instant grand flamme esparse[2] sautera,
Quand on voudra des Normans[3] faire preuve.[4]

CVI,Q97

*Interpretation*

The fire of war will spread along the 45th Parallel and will approach the
great new city [Geneva]. In an instant the great divided flame will leap
[above the seas], when they will want to take up the war against the
Russians.

[1] Geneva means 'new land' and is situated on the 46th Parallel.
[2] Disseminated, separated, divided. DL7V. Probably an allusion to multiple-warhead
missiles.
[3] The men of the north. DHB. The Russians, Empire of Aquilon.
[4] To test: to cause to suffer, to subject to painful tests. DL7V.

---

# The War from the 48th Parallel
# to the Tropic of Cancer. Water Pollution

A quarante huict degré climaterique,[1]
A fin de Cancer[2] si grand sèeheresse,
Poisson en mer, fleuve, lac cuit hectique,[3]
Bearn, Bigorre par feu ciel en détresse.

CV,Q98

*Interpretation*

From the 48th Parallel to the lines of the Tropic of Cancer, there will be
a great drought. The fish will die in the sea, in the rivers, in the lakes
scorched by continual heat. The Béarn and Bigorre areas will know
distress because of incendiary bombing.

[1] Greek χλιματήρ: rank, degree. DGF. The 48th Parallel marks out the frontier
between China and USSR, while Paris and Kiev are also on it.

[2] Tropic of Cancer: crosses what was the Spanish Sahara, Mauretania, Algeria, Libya, Egypt, Saudi Arabia, and the Gulf of Oman where it meets the Persian Gulf.
[3] Continuous. Used of gradual or wasting fever, or degenerative illness.

## The Defeat of the West. The Pope's Warnings.
## The Message of Nostradamus Mocked
## by the Left and by Germany.
## The Return of the Monarchy

Le pourvoyeur mettra toute en desroutte
Sangsuë[1] et loup, en mon dire n'escoutte
Quand Mars sera au signe du Mouton[2]
Joint à Saturne, et Saturne à la Lune,
Alors sera ta plus grande infortune,
Le Soleil lors en exaltation.

Sixain 46

*Interpretation*

The procurer [Russia] will set the West in retreat. Neither the people born of revolution [left-wingers] nor the Germans will listen to my message when the dangers of war are mentioned by the Pope during his pontificate, and under the Republic, then, France, you will know your greatest misfortune. Then the monarchy will return.

[1] Revolution, the drinker of blood, i.e. leech.
[2] Cf. the lamb as symbol in Christian art, as referring to Christ, and hence here to the *Good Shepherd*, i.e. the Pope. DL7V.

## The Defection of Two Warsaw Pact Countries.
## The Pope, Paris and Provence Attacked despite Poland

Le circuit du grand fait ruyneux,
Au nom septiesme du cinquiesme sera:
D'un tiers[1] plus grand l'estrange belliqueux
Mouton,[2] Lutèce, Aix ne garantira.

CII,Q88

*Interpretation*

The course of the great war which will bring ruin ensures that what one calls the seven [Warsaw Pact countries] will only be five. The foreign country captured in the war, the largest, and representing one third [of the whole] will not be able to guarantee the safety of the Pope, Paris or Aix-en-Provence.

¹ Respective surface areas of Warsaw Pact countries: GDR 108,178 sq. km; Czechoslovakia 127,876 sq. km; Romania 237,500 sq. km; Bulgaria 110,912 sq.km; Hungary 93,032 sq. km; *Poland 312,677 sq. km*. Total 990,175 sq. km. Hence Poland represents a third of the total land area of the USSR's satellites.
² Cf. Sixain 46.

---

# The Use of Chemical Weapons. The Discovery of New Oil Deposits. The Declarations of John-Paul II at St-Denis. The Attack of the Moslem Fleet

Par pestilence et feu fruits d'arbres périront,
Signe¹ d'huile² abonder. Père Denys non guères:³
Des grands mourir. Mais peu d'éstrangers failliront,
Insult,⁴ marin Barbare, et dangers de frontières.

Presage 125, July

*Interpretation*

By fire and pestilence the fruits of the trees are destroyed, then signs of oil in abundance will be discovered. The [Holy] Father will hardly be heard at [St]-Denis. Heads of state will die,⁵ although few strangers will do so. The Moslem fleet will jeopardize frontiers by its attack.

¹ Latin *signum*: indication, trace. DLLB.
² Mineral oils – the general term for various hydrocarbon liquids, a group comprising shale oil, naphtha, petroleum etc. DL7V.
³ At St-Denis Pope John-Paul addressed a large gathering of workers and warned them of the perils of nuclear war. (See *Le Monde*, no. 10,992, 3 June 1980.)
⁴ Latin *insulto*: I attack. DLLB.
⁵ Tito, Brezhnev, Ayatollah Khomeini and others.

## The Preparations and Wiles of the Moslem Forces. John-Paul II at St-Denis. The West's Lack of Concern

Pleurer le ciel ail[1] cela fait faire,
La mer s'appreste. Annibal[2] fait ses ruses:
Denys[3] mouille[4] classe[5] tarde ne taire,[6]
N'a sceu secret et à quoy tu t'amuses.

Presage 11, September

*Interpretation*

To see the sky weep prompts a wail of sorrow. The war fleets prepare. The Moslem leader plans his tricks. [The Pope] swirls up at [St]-Denis.[7] The army will delay mobilizing because no one will know what is secretly brewing, and during that time people will be enjoying themselves.

[1] For *aie*: cry of pain, usually repeated. DL7V.
[2] Hannibal: Carthaginian general, son of Hamilcar. In his childhood his father made him swear unremitting hatred of the Romans. DHB. Nostradamus uses the words Carthaginian, Punic or Hannibal among others to denote the Moslem world. Cf. CIII,Q93.
[3] Nostradamus uses the word Denis three times, always in the sense of St-Denis. Cf. CIX,Q24.
[4] Reference to John-Paul II's helicopter journeys, also to the wet weather.
[5] Latin *classis*: fleet, army. DLLB.
[6] Not to show or display oneself. DL7V.
[7] 'At St-Denis . . . he met the world of the workers. . . . A huge, patient, orderly crowd. It was 4.30 p.m. Two hours more to wait, footsore, with every so often hard gusts of rain *soaking* their faces and making several thousand umbrellas open simultaneously. . . .' (*Le Monde*, no. 10,992, 3 June 1980.)

---

## Two Countries Unite and Quarrel. Egypt Tried by the War.

Les deux contens[1] seront unis ensemble,
Quand la plupart à Mars seront conjoint:
Le grand d'Affrique en effrayeur et tremble,
Duumvirat[2] par la chasse[3] desioinct.[4]

CV,Q23

*Interpretation*

The two countries which were quarrelling will unite when most countries are dragged into war. The great country of Africa [Egypt] will tremble and this duumvirate will fall out because of their defeat.

[1] Latin *contendere*: to quarrel. DLLB. Iraq and Iran?

[2] Latin *duumviratus*: duumvirs, the name for the two magistrates making up a tribunal. DLLB.

[3] Used ordinarily to signify pursuit, chasing, rushing at. DL7V.

[4] Latin *disjunctus*: disunited, split, separated. DLLB.

---

# Missiles Used against the West and Japan.
# The Third World War. The Reign of the Reds

Celeste feu du costé d'Occident,
Et du midy, courir jusqu'au Levant,[1]
Vers demy morts sans poinct trouver racine[2]
Troisième aage, à Mars le belliqueux,
Des Escarboucles on verra briller feux,
Aage Escarboucle,[3] et à la fin famine.

Sixain 27

*Interpretation*

Fire come from the sky [missiles] will strike the West and then the South [the Moslem world] will rush upon Japan. Worms will die of hunger without even finding a root to feed upon. This will be the third world war, which will light the warlike fires of the Reds, who will rule, and at the end there will be famine.

[1] Empire of the Rising Sun (*soleil levant*): Japan.
[2] Image to symbolize (and stigmatize) the scarcity.
[3] The carbuncle or garnet is poppy- or blood-red. DL7V.

---

# Religious Persecution in Poland

Persécutée de Dieu sera l'Eglise,
Et les saincts temples seront expoliez,
L'enfant, la mère mettra nud en chemise,
Seront Arabes aux Polons ralliéz.

CV,Q73

*Interpretation*

The Catholic Church will be persecuted in Poland and the churches will be expropriated. The mother [Church] will be stripped naked by her children, and the Arabs will ally with the Poles [Warsaw Pact].

---

## The Economic Crisis.
## War against the West and the Catholic Church

Le parc[1] enclin[2] grande calamité,
Par l'Hesperie[3] et Insubre[4] fera,
Le feu en nef, peste et captivité,
Mercure[5] en l'Arc[6] Saturne fenera.[7]

CII,Q65

*Interpretation*

The economy in decline, there will be a great calamity in the West and Italy, war, disaster, and captivity will affect the Church. The time of pillage will ruin Monaco.

[1] Latin *parcus*: economy. DLLB.
[2] Latin *inclino*: to lower, decline. DLLB.
[3] Greek 'Εσπερις: the West. DGF.
[4] The Milan region. DHB.
[5] Son of Jupiter, messenger of the gods, himself the god of eloquence, trade and *thieves*. DL7V.
[6] Latin Monoeci Arx: Monaco. DLLB.
[7] Latin *feneror*: to ruin. DLLB.

---

## Debauchery in England.
## The Conflict Spreads to the United Kingdom

Jupiter[1] joinct plus Venus qu'à la Lune,
Apparoissant de plenitude blanche:
Venus cachée sous la blancheur Neptune,
De Mars frappée par la gravée[2] branche.[3]

CIV,Q33

## Interpretation

The world will be even more in the grip of venomous speech and lust than under the influence of the Republican [i.e. Radical] theories which appear during times of extreme candour. Debauchery will be disguised as frankness in England, which will be hit by the grave spread of the conflict.

[1] God of the sky and of the world. DL7V.
[2] Latin *gravis*: heavy, weighty, grave. DLLB.
[3] Figurative: for 'spread', 'extension'.

---

## The Sapping of English Society.
## Great Britain Surprised by the War.

Venus, Neptune poursuivra l'entreprise,
Serrez[1] pensifs. troublez les opposans:
Classe en Adrie. citez[2] vers la Tamise,
Le quart bruit[3] blesse de nuict les reposans.

Presage 12, October

## Interpretation

Virulent words and debauchery will carry out their purpose in Great Britain. Intellectuals will be imprisoned and opponents tortured. A fleet in the Adriatic will move towards the Thames. The noise [of war] will wake a quarter of the inhabitants from their sleep.

[1] *Serre*: prison. DAFL.
[2] Latin *cito*: I put into motion. DLLB.
[3] Quarrel, dispute. DL7V.

---

## The Attack on England after the Invasion of Germany.
## War and Revolution

Un peu devant ou après l'Angleterre
Par mort de loup mise aussi bas que terre,
Verra le feu resister[1] contre l'eau,
Le ralumant avec telle force
Du sang humain, dessus l'humaine escorce[2]
Faute de pain, bondance de couteau.[3]

Sixain 50

*Interpretation*

A little before or after, England will be ruined because of the fall of Germany and will see war put an end to revolution; the war being revived with such force that human blood will be spilt all over the earth, so that food will be lacking and weapons abound.

[1] Latin *resisto*: I stop. DLLB.
[2] The earth's crust.
[3] Poetic: dagger. DL7V.

---

# Revolutionary Movements in Great Britain and Italy

> La Grande Bretagne comprise l'Angleterre,
> Viendra par eaux[1] si haut inonder,
> La ligne neusve d'Ausonne[2] fera guerre,
> Que contre eux ils se viendront bander.[3]

CIII,Q70

*Interpretation*

Great Britain, including England, will be very thoroughly submerged by revolution. The new Italian league will wage war and the Italians will make an effort to resist it.

[1] Symbolizing revolution.
[2] The Ausonii were a tribe in Italy and the name was often extended to mean the whole of Italy. DHB.
[3] To make an effort to resist. DL7V.

---

# The Invasion of Great Britain by the Russians

> De l'Aquilon les efforts seront grands,
> Sur l'Océan sera la porte ouverte:
> Le regne en l'Isle sera réintégrand,
> Tremblera Londres par voille descouverte.

CII,Q68

*Interpretation*

The [war] efforts of Russia will be great; she will have access to the Atlantic Ocean. The government will be re-established in England and London, covered with boats, will tremble.

---

# The British Isles Besieged. Famine

Ceux dans les Isles de long temps assiegez:
Prendront vigueur force contre ennemis,
Ceux par dehors morts de faim profligez
En plus grand faim que jamais seront mis.

CIII,Q71

*Interpretation*

The inhabitants of the British Isles will be besieged for a long time; they will strongly resist the enemy. The latter will die of hunger because of those come from outside and they will know greater famine than ever.

---

# The Attack on the British Isles. Combat between the French and the Moslems

Le grand Neptune du profond de la mer,
De gent Punique et sang Gaulois meslé:
Les Isles à sang pour le tardif ramer,[1]
Plus luy nuira que l'occult mal celé.

CII,Q78

*Interpretation*

England will be attacked from the bottom of the sea [submarine attack]; French and Moslem blood will mingle. The British Isles will be bloodied because of taking pains too late, this will be far more harmful than hiding the misfortune [from the people].

[1] To take considerable pains, trouble. DL7V.

---

# The Invasion of Aquitaine and England by Moslem Troops

Vers Aquitaine par insuls Britanniques,
De par eux mesmes grandes incursions:
Pluyes, gelées feront terroirs iniques,[1]
Port Selyn[2] fortes fera invasions.

CII,QI

*Interpretation*

Around Aquitaine and the British Isles there will be great troop landings. Revolutionary movements and a hard winter will render these territories wretched for they will have endured strong invasions from a Moslem port.

[1] Latin *iniquus*: unfortunate, wretched. DLLB.
[2] Greek Σελήνη: the moon. DGF. Denotes the Moslem crescent. The name of the Moslem port involved remains uncertain.

---

# The Siege of London.
# The Capture of the British Head of State

La forteresse auprès de la Tamise,
Cherra[1] par lors, le Roy dedans serré,
Auprès du pont[2] sera veu en chemise,
Un devant mort, puis dans le fort barré.[3]

CVIII,Q37

*Interpretation*

The fortifications near the Thames will collapse then, the leader of the government besieged inside. He will be seen in reduced circumstances by the sea, one having died beforehand, then he will be locked up inside the fort.

[1] Future of *cheoir*: to fall. DAFL.
[2] Greek ποντός: sea. DGF.
[3] To close by means of bars. DL7V.

# The War in the Rhône Valley.
# The Occupation of England

Sur les rochers sang on verra plouvoir.
Sol Orient, Saturne Occidental:
Pres d'Orgon[1] guerre, à Rome grand mal voir,
Nefs parfondrées et prins le Tridental.[2]

CV,Q62

## Interpretation

Blood will be seen raining down upon the mountain ranges when the king comes from the East to re-establish the West. The war will reach Orgon, the Pope will be disgraced in Rome, ships having been sunk and England occupied.

[1] Main town of the canton of Bouches-du-Rhône, on the left bank of the Durance. DHB.
[2] Symbolically, 'Neptune's trident' denotes the empire of the sea. DL7V. Symbol for England.

---

# The Invasion of West Germany and Italy
# by the Russians. Yugoslavia Delivered up to Massacre

Laict,[1] sang grenouilles[2] escoudre[3] en Dalmatie,[4]
Conflict donné, peste près de Balennes,[5]
Cry sera grand par toute Esclavonie,[6]
Lors naistra monstre[7] pres et dedans Ravenne.

CII,Q32

## Interpretation

After the milk of wellbeing, the blood of the people will flow in Yugoslavia, when war breaks out, as well as a calamity near Ballenstedt. The [war] cry will be loud throughout Russia. Thus, then, a scourge will be born near and in Ravenna.

[1] Milk = biblical symbol. Nostradamus uses it to denote easy living and wellbeing.
[2] Swarms of frogs symbolize all the races of history, and also all people not content with their lot. DL7V.
[3] For escorre: flow, rush. DAFL.

[4] Region of Europe situated between the Adriatic on the west and the Dinaric Alps on the east. Part of the general area of Illyria. DHB.

[5] Gallicization of Ballenstedt: town of the Duchy of Anhalt, on the Gretel, several kilometres from the border of West Germany and the GDR. DHB.

[6] Slavonia: under the Romans, made up part of Pannonia (Hungary). Owes its name to the Slavi, Sarmatian tribe which settled there in the seventh century. DHB. Denotes Russia.

[7] Latin *monstrum*: scourge. DLLB.

## The Invasion of Italy and Yugoslavia.
## Petrol Shortage

Entre Campagne,[1] Sienne,[2] Flora, Tustie,[3]
Six mois neuf jours ne pleuvra une goute,
L'estrange langue en terre Dalmatie,
Courira sus, vastant la terre toute.

CII,Q84

*Interpretation*

Between the provinces of Campania, Siena, Umbria, there will be six months and nine days of total penury [petrol?]. A strange language will be heard in Dalmatia [Russian or Arabic?] which will run through and devastate the whole earth.

[1] Campania: province of Italy, main town Naples; made up of Naples, Salerno, Avellino etc. DL7V.

[2] Province of Italy (Tuscany). DL7V.

[3] Tuscia: comprising Etruria and Umbria. DHB.

## Moslem War in the Black Sea and Yugoslavia.
## Help from Portugal: American Landings?

Conflict Barbar en la Cornere noire,
Sang espandu trembler la Dalmatie
Grand Ismael mettra son promontoire[1]
Ranes[2] trembler, secours Lusitanie.[3]

CIX,Q60

## Interpretation

The Moslems will take the war into the Black Sea and the blood they will shed will make Yugoslavia tremble, where the Moslem leader will reach his zenith. The people will tremble, then help comes from Portugal.

[1] Latin *promontorium*: culminating point. DLLB.
[2] Latin *rana*: frog. DLLB. See CII,Q32, note 2.
[3] Ancient name for Portugal.

---

# The Russian Attack on Yugoslavia and in the Adriatic. The Turkish Head of State. Help Comes from Spain and Her King

Au port de PUOLA[1] et de Saint Nicolas,[2]
Péril Normande[3] au goulfre Phanatique[4]
Cap.[5] de Bisance rues crier hélas.
Secours de Gaddes[6] et du grand Philippique.[7]

CIX,Q30

## Interpretation

At Pola, come from Russia [6 December?], the peril of the men of the North [Russians] will reach the Yugoslav coast. The ruler of Turkey will cry for quarter, then help will come from Spain with the descendant of Philip V.

[1] For Pola or Pula, by epenthesis: Yugoslav town on the Adriatic, south of Trieste. Good military *port*. DHB and AU.
[2] Patron saint of Russia, Saint's Day 6 December.
[3] Or North-men, i.e. men of the north. DHB.
[4] Flanatic Gulf, part of the Adriatic between Istria and Illyria, in Yugoslavia, today the Gulf of Kvarner. DHB. Nostradamus drops the *l* by syncope. Pola is situated at the entrance to this gulf.
[5] Latin *caput*: chief, leader. DLLB.
[6] Ancient name for Cadiz, Spain. DHB.
[7] Philip V, head of the Spanish House of Bourbon. DHB. Nostradamus here signifies the King of Spain.

## Turkey Ransacked from Yugoslavia

Le plus grand voile[1] hors du port de Zara[2]
Près de Bisance fera son entreprise:
D'ennemi perte et l'amy ne sera,
Le tiers à deux fera grand pille et prise.

CVII,Q83

*Interpretation*

The greatest airborne force will leave from the port of Zara to make a
warlike enterprise in Turkey. It will make a huge slaughter and will not
be allied [to the Turks]; it will devastate and ransack two-thirds of the
country.

[1] Used by Nostradamus to denote planes (the first planes were partly built of canvas).
[2] Port of Dalmatia, Yugoslavia, on the Adriatic. DHB.

---

## The Moslem Invasion

Le temps purge,[1] pestilence, tempeste,
Barbare insult. Fureur, invasion:
Maux infinis par ce mois nous appreste,
Et les plus Grands, deux moins, d'irrision.[2]

Presage 60, April

*Interpretation*

The time will be filthy, pestilential and violent because of a furious
Moslem attack and invasion. Great calamities are prepared in April and
great persons will be ridiculed except for two among them.

[1] Latin *purgamen*: filth, ordure. DLLB.
[2] Latin *irrisio*: mockery. DLLB.

# The End of the Good Times.
# Devastation Wrought by the Moslems

Triremes pleins tout aage captifs,
Temps bon à mal, le doux pour amertume:
Proye à Barbares trop tost seront bastifs,[1]
Cupide de voir plaindre au vent la plume.[2]

CX,Q97

## Interpretation

Ships will lead away prisoners of all ages. Good times will become times
of misfortune; bitterness replace sweetness: the Moslems will get hold of
the booty all too soon, eager to see [France] and the French complain
and float in the wind.

[1] To dispose of, procure for oneself. DAFL.
[2] To be carried by, or float in the wind, as the wind directs. DL7V.

---

# The Battle Fought by German and Spanish Forces
# against the Moslems

Guerre, tonnerre, maints champs depopulez,
Frayeur et bruit, assault à la frontière:
Grand Grand failli. pardon aux Exilez,
Germains, Hispans par mer Barba. bannière.

Presage 29

## Interpretation

War and bombing will devastate many territories in dread and noise:
frontiers will be attacked. The great leader having fallen, exiles having
been pardoned. The Germans and Spaniards will attack the Moslem
forces by sea.

# The Mediterranean Coast Surrendered to Looting

Depuis Monach jusqu'auprès de Sicile,
Toute la plage demourra désolée,
Il n'y aura fauxbourg, cité ne ville,
Que par Barbares pillée soit et volée.

CII,Q4

*Interpretation*

From Monaco to Sicily, the coastline will be ransacked. Not a town or district will escape the looting of the Moslem troops.

---

# The Invasion of West Germany, the Mediterranean and Atlantic Coasts. Recognition of the Inefficacy of the Geneva Conventions

Par les Sueves[1] et lieux circonvoisins,
Seront en guerre pour cause des nuées:[2]
Camp marins locustes[3] et cousins,[4]
Du Leman fautes seront bien desnuées.[5]

CV,Q85

*Interpretation*

West Germany and her neighbours [Switzerland, the Netherlands, France and Belgium] will be at war because of the vast hordes [of Russian troops]. The ports of war will be full of planes and ships and the mistakes of Lake Geneva [treaties and conventions of Geneva] will be exposed.

[1] Name given by the Romans to tribes of the German area. The principal seat of the Suevic League, formed in the third century, was south-west Germany, from the Rhine to the Main, the Saale and the Danube. DHB. Today, West German territory.
[2] Innumerable multitude. DL7V.
[3] Latin *locusta*: locust. DHB. Nostradamus refers to aeroplanes by this word. Cf. Revelations: IX.
[4] Genus of Diptera – insects whose origins are aquatic. DL7V. i.e. warships.
[5] Expose, despoil, denude. DAFL.

# Bombings in Italy

Planure,[1] Ausonne[2] fertille, spacieuse,
Produira[3] taons si tant de sauterelle,
Clarté solaire deviendra nubileuse,
Ronger[4] le tout, grand peste venir d'elles.

                                                            CIV,Q48

## Interpretation

So many planes will advance over the fertile and spacious soil of the Po
that the sun will be obscured. These aircraft will bring destruction and
calamity.

[1] Latin *planura*: plain. DLLB.
[2] Latin Ausonia: ancient region of Italy, and by extension all Italy. DLLB.
[3] Latin *produco*: I cause to advance, push forward. DLLB.
[4] Attack, then destroy. DL7V.

---

# The Pillage and Ransack of the
# Mediterranean Coast

Erins,[1] Antibor, villes autour de Nice
Seront vastées, fort par mer et par terre
Les sauterelles[2] terre et mer vent propice,
Prins, morts, troussez, pillez, sans loy de guerre.

                                                            CIII,Q82

## Interpretation

The Lerin islands, Antibes and the towns near Nice will be devastated
by sea and land forces, with tanks borne by sea and land, and the wind
[of history] being favourable to them. The inhabitants will be taken
prisoner, massacred, dispatched, ravished, without respecting the rules
of war.

[1] The Lerin islands (example of aphesis), French Mediterranean islands off the coast
of the Var. DHB.
[2] Cf. Revelations: IX, 3 and 7. 'And there came out of the smoke locusts upon the
earth . . . And the shapes of the locusts were like unto horses prepared unto battle' . . .
Cavalry, i.e. tanks.

---

# Moslem Ravages in the Mediterranean, Corsica, Sardinia and Italy

Naples, Palerme, et toute la Cecile,
Par main barbare sera inhabitée,
Corsique, Salerne[1] et de Sardeigne l'Isle,
Faim, peste, guerre, fin des maux intemptée.[2]

CVII,Q6

## Interpretation

Naples, Palermo and all Sicily will be laid waste by the Moslem troops, as will Corsica, Sardinia and Salerno, where famine will reign, and sickness and war, then the end of the misfortunes will be reached.

[1] Italian town in ancient Kingdom of Naples.
[2] Latin *intento*: I direct, tend towards. DLLB.

---

# Invasion by Sea at Agde. The Landing of an Army a Million Strong. Western Naval Defeat in the Mediterranean

Au port d'Agde trois fustes[1] entreront,
Portant l'infect[2] non foy et pestilence.
Passant le pont[3] mil milles[4] embleront,[5]
Et le pont rompre à tierce résistance.

CVIII,Q21

## Interpretation

Three warships will enter the port of Agde, bringing with them lawless, faithless invasion and pestilence. A million soldiers will assemble to cross the sea and the resistance by sea will thrice be broken.

[1] Low-draught vessel with sails and oars. DAFL.
[2] Latin *inficio*: I mix, impregnate, penetrate. DLLB.
[3] Greek πουτός: sea. DGF.
[4] *Mil fois mille*: i.e. a million.
[5] Aphesis.

# The Defeat of a Franco–Spanish Army in the Pyrenees. The War in Switzerland and Germany. The Rhône and Languedoc Hit by the Conflict

Deux grands frères seront chassez d'Espagne
L'aisné vaincu sous les monts Pyrénées,
Rougir mer, Rosne, sang Léman d'Alemagne,
Narbon, Blyterres,[1] d'Agath contaminées.[2]

CIV,Q94

*Interpretation*

Two great allies will be driven out of Spain. The elder of the two [Juan Carlos I] will be defeated at the foot of the Pyrenees. The sea will be occupied by the red fleet and blood will flow beside the Rhône, on Lake Geneva, and in Germany. Narbonne, Béziers and Agde will be contaminated.

[1] Béziers, conquered *c.* 120 BC by the Romans, colonized by Julius Caesar, who named it Julia Biterra. DHB. Letter *l* added by epenthesis.
[2] Latin *contamino*: I soil, infect. DLLB.

---

# The War in Languedoc. The Defeat of the French Army

Chassez seront sans faire long combat,
Par le pays seront plus fort grevez:[1]
Bourg et cité auront plus grand débat,[2]
Carcas. Narbonne auront coeur esprouvez.

CI,Q5

*Interpretation*

The French army will be beaten without fighting long. The most powerful will be overwhelmed across the country. Towns and villages will be beset by still greater battles. The centres of the towns of Carcassonne and Narbonne will be hard pressed.

[1] Overwhelm, torment, oppress. DAFL.
[2] Resistance, struggle. DAFL.

# The Invasion from Switzerland to the Paris Area. The Defeat of the Germans, Swiss and Italians

Du lac Lyman et ceux de Brannonices,[1]
Tous assemblez contre ceux d'Aquitaine,
Germains beaucoup, encore plus Souisses,
Seront defaicts avec ceux d'humaine.[2]

CIV,Q74

*Interpretation*

From Switzerland to the Eure, troops will gather to march upon south-west France. The [West] Germans and even more of the Swiss will be wiped out with the originators of humanism [the Italians].

[1] Brannovices, a Gallic tribe who inhabited the area between the Sarthe and the Eure. DLLB.

[2] Florence was the first centre of humanism. From Italy humanism (the classics) spread throughout western Europe from the end of the fifteenth century. DL7V.

---

# Power Transferred to Savoy. The Occupation of Languedoc by Warsaw Pact Troops

Le monde proche du dernier période,[1]
Saturne encor tard sera de retour:
Translat empire devers[2] nations Brode,[3]
L'oeil[4] arraché à Narbon par Autour.[5]

CIII,Q92

*Interpretation*

The western world is nearing its end; the epoch of renewal is still slow to come. Power will be transferred to the Savoy area, having been taken from Narbonne by the Warsaw Pact.

[1] The last period, the end. The power of this empire entering its last phase. DL.

[2] Beside, near. DL7V.

[3] 'After the Allobroges, whom the Provençal people by corruption and syncope call Brodes, were conquered by Fabius Maximus near Isère . . .' (César Nostradamus: *History of Provence*, Lyon 1614). Savoy. DHB.

[4] Power, in sense of surveillance and right of survey.
[5] Genus of predatory bird. DL7V. Has same significance as the gryphon, meaning the Warsaw Pact countries.

---

# The Abandonment of Perpignan by its Inhabitants. The Western Counter-attack in the Mediterranean

La crainte armée de l'ennemy Narbon,
Effroyera si fort les Hespériques:[1]
Parpignan vuidé par l'aveugle darbon,[2]
Lors Barcelon par mer donra les piques.[3]

CVI,Q56

## Interpretation

Fear of the enemy army at Narbonne will greatly perturb the westerners [Americans]. Perpignan will be abandoned because of the loss of power at Narbonne; then, near Barcelona, rockets will be launched by sea [nuclear submarines].

[1] Greek Ἑσπερίς: West.
[2] For *De Narbo* (or Narbonne): anagram. Cf. CIII,Q92.
[3] Allusion to the pointed ends of the missiles.

---

# War in the Pyrenees and Languedoc

Plainctes et pleurs, cris et grands hurlements,
Pres de Narbon à Bayonne et en Foix:
O quels horribles calamitez changemens,
Avant que Mars revolu quelques fois.

CIX,Q63

## Interpretation

Laments, tears, cries and loud screams will be heard near Narbonne and the Basses-Pyrénées as far as Ariège. O the changes will be horrible before the time of war has run its course.

# The East German Military Leader
# in the Pyrenees and Languedoc. The Capet King
# in Difficulty

L'Æmathion[1] passer mont Pyrénées,
En Mars Narbon ne fera résistance:
Par mer et terre fera si grand menée,
Cap n'ayant terre seure pour demeurance.

CIX,Q64

## Interpretation

The East German leader will pass through the Pyrenees; Narbonne will
not resist during the war. There will be such great actions by land and
sea that the Capetian will not have anywhere to go in safety.

[1] Cf. cx,Q7.

# Attack by Portugal as far as
# the Pyrenees

Proche del duero[1] par mer Cyrenne[2] close,
Viendra percer les grands monts Pyrénées.
La main plus courte et sa percée gloze,[3]
A Carcassonne conduira ses menées.

CIII,Q62

## Interpretation

Near the Douro, by the Libyan coast, which will have been closed, it
will cross the Pyrenees. With inferior forces and by guerrilla action it
will drive on as far as Carcassonne.

[1] For Douro, river of Spain and Portugal, which crosses Portugal from east to west.
DHB.
[2] Cyrenia, capital of Cyrenaica, today Curin or Grennah, town in Libya. DHB and AU.
[3] *Gloz, glos*, derived from *glot* and *gloton*: ruffian, brigand, rabble. DAFL.

## The Treason of a Politician. His Death.
## Assault in Languedoc

La Cité prise par tromperie et fraude,
Par le moyen d'un beau jeune attrapé,
Assaut donné, Raubine[1] près de l'AUDE,
Luy et tous morts pour avoir bien trompé.

                                        CIII,Q85

*Interpretation*

Paris will be occupied thanks to a trick and betrayal through a handsome
young [politician] who will be caught. The region of the Robines of
Narbonne will be attacked; this politician and his supporters will die for
their treachery.

[1] Name given in the Midi to small canals, and which now applies to a group of
navigation canals: the *Robines* of Narbonne, Vic, and Aigues-Mortes. (Also, *Roubine*.)
DL7V.

---

## Moslem Troops in Italy

La faction cruelle à robe longue
Viendra cacher souz les pointus poignards:
Saisir Florence le duc et lieu diphlongue,[1]
Sa descouverte[2] par immeurs[3] et flangnards.[4]

                                        CX,Q33

*Interpretation*

The cruel sect of Moslems will come, hiding weapons under their long
robes. Their leader will seize Florence and burn the place twice, sending
in advance cunning men without laws [spies].

[1] From Greek δίς: twice; and φλογόω: set on fire. DGF.
[2] Military term: movement of a reconnaissance patrol. DL7V.
[3] Latin *im* and *mos, moris*: law, hence *lawless*.
[4] From *flasnier*: to trick. DAFL.

## The Invasion of Italy by Moslem Troops

Un qui les dieux d'Annibal[1] infernaux,
Fera renaistre, effrayeur des humains:
Oncq'plus d'horreur ne plus dire iournaulx,
Qu'avint viendra par Babel[2] aux Romains.

CII,Q30

*Interpretation*

A person who will revive the terrifying gods of the Carthaginians will frighten men. The newspapers could never say that more horror had afflicted the Romans, because of their confusion.

[1] Carthaginian general. He recommenced war with the Romans in the middle of a peace, and breaking all treaties, by taking and sacking Saguntum, a town allied with Rome (219 BC). Thinking the Romans could only be defeated at home, he crossed the Alps and invaded Italy. DHB. A parallel between ancient and modern Rome is established here by Nostradamus.

[2] Signifying confusion. DL7V.

---

## The Invasion of Moslem Troops at Port-de-Bouc. The Arrival of a Western Fleet

La tour de Boucq[1] craindra fuste Barbare,
Un temps, longtemps, après barque hespérique.
Bestail, gens, meubles, tous deux feront grand tare
Taurus[2] et Libra, quelle mortelle picque.

CI,Q28

*Interpretation*

Port-de-Bouc will fear the Moslem fleet for a while; long afterwards a western fleet will arrive. Animals, men and their possessions will be injured by the two [fleets]. What a deadly blow for fecundity and justice.

[1] Port-de-Bouc, town at the Gulf of Fos. DL7V.

[2] Astrological: second sign of the zodiac, ruled horoscopically by Venus; symbolizing creative forces and fecundity. DL7V.

# The Warsaw Pact and the Russians.
# The Invasion of France

Comme un gryphon[1] viendra le Roy d'Europe.
Accompagné de ceux de l'Aquilon:
De rouges et blancs[2] conduira grande troppe
Et iront contre le Roy de Babylone.[3]

cx,Q86

*Interpretation*

The chief of [eastern] Europe will come like a vulture, accompanied by
the Russians. He will lead a great force of soldiers from the Communist
and Moslem countries which will go against the government of Paris.

[1] Gryphon: from Latin, *gryphus*: vulture. General name for different birds of prey.
DL7V. Poland's coat of arms consists of a bird of prey.
[2] Reference to the white burnous worn by Moslems.
[3] Great Babylon, the modern Babylon: ref. to the great centres such as London, Paris.
DL7V.

---

# The Turkish Army Lands in Spain.
# West Germany Occupied

Le Bizantin faisant oblation,[1]
Après avoir Cordube[2] à foy reprinse:
Son chemin long repos pamplation,[3]
Mer passant proy[4] par Colongna[5] prinse.

CVIII,Q51

*Interpretation*

The Turkish leader will make a [peace] offer after taking Cordova for
the Moslem faith, will halt his expansion after a long journey, when by
sea West Germany will be occupied by the Warsaw Pact.

[1] Latin *oblatio*: offer. DLLB.
[2] Latin Corduba: Cordova. DLLB.
[3] Neologism from παν (all) and *ampliatio*, growth, expansion. DLLB.
[4] Reference to griffin, bird of prey denoting Warsaw Pact. Cf. cx,Q86.
[5] Agrippinensis Colonia: colony of Agrippina on the Rhine (Cologne). DLLB. West
Germany.

# The Russian Invasion of Western Europe

Vers Aquilon grands efforts par hommasse,
Presque l'Europe et l'univers vexer,[1]
Les deux eclipses mettra en telle chasse[2]
Et aux Pannons[3] vie et mort renforcer.

CVIII,QI5

## Interpretation

Around Russia great [war] efforts will be made by a mass of men who will come to stir up [western] Europe and almost the whole universe. Between two eclipses, this mass of men will put [the western troops] to such a flight that the Hungarians will receive life and death reinforcements.

[1] Latin *vexo*: I agitate forcibly, stir, shake up. DLLB.
[2] Running away, flight. DL7V.
[3] Pannonia: ancient name for Hungary.

---

# The Leader of Iran's Present to the West.
# The Attack on France and Italy Launched
# from Afghanistan

Le grand Satyre[1] et Tigre[2] d'Hircanie,[3]
Don présenté à ceux de l'Occean,
Un chef de classe istra[4] de Carmanie[5]
Qui prendra terre au Tyrren[6] Phocean.[7]

CIII,Q90

## Interpretation

The great cynical person from the Tigris and Iran will make a gift to those of the Atlantic Alliance; then a military leader will leave from Afghanistan to land in the Tyrrhenian Sea and Marseille.

[1] Cynical or impudent person. DL7V.
[2] River in Asia, running into the Persian Gulf, in Iran.
[3] Hyrcania: region of ancient Asia extending along the south-east coast of the Caspian Sea, belonging to the Persian Empire. DHB. Today Iranian territory.
[4] *Istre*, form of *issir*: to go out, forth. DAFL.

[5] Province of the old Persian Empire, now part of Afghanistan. DL7V.

[6] Naples, important NATO base.

[7] Nostradamus adds *an* to the word *Phocée*, by paragoge and for the rhyme's sake.

---

## The Russian Invasion of Afghanistan. Afghan Resistance. Its Extermination

Le sainct empire[1] viendra en Germanie,
Ismaëlites trouveront lieux ouverts:
Anes[2] voudront aussi la Carmanie,
Les soustenans[3] de terre tous couverts.

CX,Q31

*Interpretation*

The Russians will come into Afghanistan; the Moslems will find these places open. The Afghans would like to keep Afghanistan; but the resistance will be buried.

[1] Russian Empire, the largest state in the world. Orthodox religion dominated Russia and the Tsar was its head since Peter the Great; the *Holy* Synod supported him in the administration of ecclesiastical affairs. DHB. 'Holy Russia' is a well-known expression.

[2] Certain Carmanian tribes, according to Strabo, led donkeys into battle. DL7V. Nostradamus refers to the Afghan resisters of the Soviet invasion.

[3] Latin *sustineo*: I resist. DLLB.

---

## The Use of Nuclear Arms against Russia

Soleil levant un grand feu on verra,
Bruit et clarté[1] vers Aquilon tendans,[2]
Dedans le rond[3] mort et cris l'on orra,[4]
Par glaive[5] feu, faim, morts les attendans.

CII,Q91

*Interpretation*

In the East a great fire will be seen, noise and flames [of war] will extend across Russia. There will be deaths within a circle [nuclear bombs] and cries will be heard. By war, fire, famine, men will wait for death.

¹ Light, torch. DL7V.
² Latin *tendo*: I hold, extend.
³ Circle, circular line. DL7V.
⁴ Future of *oïr* (*ouir*), to hear. DAFL.
⁵ Sword: symbol of war and battle. DL7V.

---

## The Russo–Moslem Alliance

Le fait luysant de neuf vieux eslevé,
Seront si grands par midy Aquilon:
De sa seur¹ propre² grandes alles³ levé
Fuyant meurtry au buisson⁴ d'ambellon.⁵

cx,q69

*Interpretation*

The remarkable fact of the rise [to power] of a new leader [after the disappearance] of an old one, [efforts] by the Moslems and Russia will be so great that he will muster huge aerial forces [wings] in the neighbouring city [Warsaw Pact] and when hurt will manage, despite weakness, to make shift.

¹ Latin *soror* adj. *soror civitas*: sister city, ally. DLLB.
² Latin *proprior*: very close, neighbouring. DLLB.
³ Latin *ales*: winged, having wings. DLLB.
⁴ *Se sauver à travers les buissons* = to shirk the issue, run away from. DL7V.
⁵ Latin *imbellis*: weak, unwarlike, defenceless. DLLB.

---

## The Revolution in Paris.
## Turkey Agitated by Iran to Revolt
## against the West

Par les deux testes, et trois bras¹ séparés,
La grand cité sera par eaux vexée:²
Des Grands d'entre eux par exil esgarés,
Par teste Perse Bysance fort pressée.

cx,q86

*Interpretation*

Because of two leaders separated from their three executives, Paris will be shaken by revolution. A certain number of its leaders [ministers] will be distanced by exile at the moment when Turkey is spurred [against the West] by the Iranian leader.

¹ As in 'right-hand man'. DL7V.
² Latin *vexo*: I stir up, shake. DLLB.

---

# The French Fleet in the Mediterranean.
# Moslem Troops in the Adriatic: Their Defeat

Si France passe outre mer Lygustique,
Tu te verras en isles et mers enclos:
Mahommet contraire, plus mer Hadriatique,
Chevaux et Asnes¹ tu rongeras les os.²

CIII,Q23

*Interpretation*

If the French fleet goes beyond the Ligurian coast, it will find itself caught between islands [Sardinia, Corsica, Sicily] and the sea. The Moslem troops will oppose it and still more so in the Adriatic. It will finish with the complete ruin of the Moslem forces.

¹ Cf. CX,Q31.
² To gnaw something to the bone, i.e. ruin completely and thoroughly, bit by bit. DL7V.

---

# Sounds of War in Russia

Par la discorde effaillir au défaut,
Un tout à coup le remettra au sus:¹
Vers l'Aquilon seront les bruits si haut,
Lesions,² pointes³ à travers, par dessus.

Presage 26

*Interpretation*

Through discord [the French] will collapse by default. A [person] will suddenly raise them up. In Russia there will be such great noises [of war] that there will be damage done by rockets across the sky.

[1] Above. DAFL.
[2] Damage, wrong. DAFL.
[3] Thin, tapered end. DL7V. Allusion to the noses of missiles.

---

# The Breaking off of Diplomatic Relations with Iran

Un peu devant l'ouvert commerce,
Ambassadeur viendra de Perse,
Nouvelle au franc pays porter,
Mais non receu, vaine espérance,
A son grand Dieu sera l'offence,
Feignant de le vouloir quitter.

Sixain 8

*Interpretation*

A little before signing some trade agreements, an ambassador will come from Iran to bring some news to France. But he will not be received and his hope will be vain. He will take it as an offence to his status and will pretend to want to leave the country.

---

# The Hexagon Attacked on Five Sides. Tunisia and Algeria Incited by Iran. The Attack on Spain

France a cinq pars[1] par neglect assaillie,
Tunis, Argal esmeuz[2] par Persiens:
Léon, Seville, Barcelonne faillie,
N'aura la classe[3] par les Vénitiens.

CI,Q73

*Interpretation*

France will be attacked on five sides because of her negligence. Tunisia and Algeria will be incited against her by the Iranians. León, Seville and Barcelona will succumb and cannot be saved by the Italian army.

[1] Five sides of the hexagon's six, excluding the Pyrenees.
[2] Latin *emovere*: to displace, stir up, move about. DLLB.
[3] Latin *classis*: fleet, army. DLLB.

---

## A Notable Briton and Six Well-known Germans Captured by the Moslems. Spain Invaded from Gibraltar. The New and Redoubtable Iranian Leader

Le chef d'Escosse, avec six d'Allemagne,
Par gens de mer Orientaux captif:
Traverseron le Calpre[1] et Espagne,
Present en Perse au nouveau Roy craintif.

CIII,Q78

*Interpretation*

The British leader and the six German notables will be captured at sea by the Orientals who will cross Gibraltar and Spain after giving a present to the new, formidable Iranian.

[1] Latin Calpe: Betic mountain: Gibraltar. DLLB. Example of epenthesis.

---

## The Landing of Moslem Troops at Toulon and Marseille

Par la discorde negligence Gauloise,
Sera passage à Mahomet ouvert:
De sang trempez la terre et mer Senoise,
Le port Phocen[1] de voiles et nefs couvert.

CI,Q18

*Interpretation*

Because of the discord and negligence of the French, the way will be clear for the Moslem troops. The land and sea of the Seine will be bloodsoaked. Marseille will be covered by planes and ships.

[1] Phocée: ancient name for Marseille.

---

## Russian Invasion. Desolation in Italy

Amas s'approche venant d'Esclavonie[1]
L'Olestant[2] vieux cité ruynera:
Fort désolée verra sa Romainie,
Puis la grand flamme estaindre ne sçaura.

CIV,Q82

*Interpretation*

Massed troops will approach coming from Russia. The destroyer will ruin the old city [Paris]. Italy will be laid waste and no one will know how to extinguish the great fire [of war] which will have been lit.

[1] Cf. CII,Q32, note.
[2] Greek: Aorist inf. of ἄλλυμι, ἀλεσθαι, to cause to perish. DGF. Nostradamus has coined, partly from the Greek verb, a present participle he uses as a noun.

---

## The Destruction of Tours.
## Fighting from Nantes to Rheims.
## The End of the War in November

Bien defendu le faict par excellence,
Garde toy Tours de ta prochaine ruine,
Londres et Nantes par Reims fera deffence,
Ne passe outre au temps de la bruyne.

CIV,Q46

*Interpretation*

The act [of war] will be forbidden on the highest level. Beware, Tours, of your approaching ruin! England and France will defend themselves in the Rheims area, and [the war] will not go on past November.

---

## The Invasion of West Germany and Austria. The European Assembly

Quand les colonnes de bois grande[1] tremblée,
D'Austere[2] conduicte, couverte de rubriche,[3]
Tant vuidera dehors grande assemblée,
Trembler Vienne et le pays d'Autriche.

CI,Q82

*Interpretation*

When the great forests [of the Warsaw Pact countries] tremble [armoured divisions], the army will be led into West Germany which will be covered by the Red Army; the great [European] assembly will be expelled, Vienna and Austria will be invaded.

[1] The Polish forests are the last primeval forests in Europe.
[2] Latin Austerania: island off coast of Germany. DLLB.
[3] Latin *ruber*: red. DLLB. Cf. *'classe rubre'*, CIV,Q37.

---

## The Red Army on the Rhine. The Invasion of Germany, Austria and Italy

Translatera en la Grand Germanie,[1]
Brabant et Flandres, Gand, Bruges et Bologne;[2]
La trefve feint,[3] le grand Duc d'Arménie[4]
Assaillira Vienne et la Cologne.[5]

CV,Q94

*Interpretation*

The great Armenian general will cross West Germany, Brabant, Flanders, Ghent, Bruges and Bologna, after feigning peace, and he will attack Austria and the Cologne area.

[1] West Germany is larger than East Germany (248,744 sq. km as opposed to 108,178 sq. km). AU.

[2] Italian town, the most important of the Romagna. DHB.

[3] Ablative absolute.

[4] Probably a Red Army leader of Armenian origin.

[5] West German town on the Rhine.

---

# The Invasion of West Germany, Switzerland and France. The Occupation of Paris

Auprès du Lac Leman sera conduite,
Par garse[1] estrange cité voulant trahir,[2]
Avant son meurtre[3] a Augsbourg la grande fuite,
Et ceux du Rhin la viendront invahir.

CV,QI2

*Interpretation*

[The Army] will be led near Lake Geneva by a foreign republic [Soviet] wanting to take Paris by force. Before committing this great injury, the inhabitants of Bavaria will flee and those who will have struck at the Rhine [the Russians] will come and invade Paris.

[1] As usual Nostradamus refers to the French Republic in the feminine. Cf. *dame*.

[2] Latin *traho*: I take away by force, steal. DLLB.

[3] Great damage. DL7V.

---

# The Invasion of Marseille, Northern Italy, Yugoslavia and the Persian Gulf. Bases for These Invasions

Voille Symacle[1] port Massiliolique,[2]
Dans Venise port marcher aux Pannons:[3]
Partir du goulfre[4] et Synus Illyrique[5]
Vast à Socille, Lygurs[6] coups de canons.

CIX,Q28

*Interpretation*

Allied fleets will enter Marseille, the army will enter Venice to leave for Hungary. Troops will leave from the [Persian] Gulf and the Yugoslav coast to devastate Sicily and northern Italy with artillery.

¹ Greek σύμμαχος: ally. DFG.
² Latin Massilia: ancient name for Marseille. DHB.
³ Pannonia: ancient name for Hungary. DHB.
⁴ i.e. the Gulf par excellence, the Persian Gulf. DHB.
⁵ Illyria: Dalmatia, port of Yugoslavia on the Adriatic Sea. DHB.
⁶ Tribe of northern Italy. DHB.

---

# The Destruction of Istanbul by France.
# The Deliverance of the Moslems' Prisoners
# by Portugal

La grande cité de Tharse¹ par Gaulois
Sera destruite: captifs tous a Turban²
Secours par mer du grand Portugalois,
Premier d'esté le jour du sacre Urban.³

CVI,Q85

*Interpretation*

Istanbul will be destroyed by the French: all those captured by the Moslems will be helped by the great Portuguese leader between 25 May and 21 June [summer solstice].

¹ Anagram of *Tharse* [Thrace]. The largest town of Thrace is Istanbul.
² Habitual head-dress of many Moslem peoples. DL7V.
³ St Urban, Pope from AD 222 to 230. Saint's Day 25 May. DL7V.

---

# The War between Greece and Turkey.
# Turkey's Defeat

Pendant que Duc,¹ Roy, Royne² occupera,
Chef Bizantin captif en Samothrace:³
Avant l'assaut l'un l'autre mangera,
Rebours ferre⁴ suyvra de sang la trace,

CIV,Q38

*Interpretation*

While the King, commander-in-chief of the army, occupies the place of the French Republic, the leader of Turkey will be prisoner in Greece, for before the attack one will beat the other and, pushed back, he will be discovered through his trail of blood.

[1] Latin *dux*: leader of an army. DLLB.
[2] *Reine*, queen, like *dame*, is often used by Nostradamus to personify the French Republic.
[3] Aegean island off Thrace. DHB.
[4] Latin *fero*: I bring. DLLB.

---

## Catastrophe in the Black Sea. Shortages in Greece and Italy

Pour la chaleur solaire[1] sus la mer,
De Negrepont[2] les poissons demy cuits,
Les habitans les viendront entamer,[3]
Quand Rhod[4] et Gennes leur faudra le biscuit.

CII,Q3

*Interpretation*

Because of a heat like the sun's, the fish in the Black Sea will be half cooked, and its inhabitants will come to destroy them, when the Greeks and Italians will need food.

[1] Perhaps an atomic explosion.
[2] Latin *niger*: black; and πουτός: sea.
[3] To destroy. DL7V.
[4] Rhodes: Greek possession since 1947. AE.

---

## The War in the Eastern Mediterranean

A son hault pris plus la lerme[1] sabée[2]
D'humaine chair par mort en cendre mettre,
A l'Isle Pharos[3] par Croisars perturbée,
Alors qu'à Rhodes paroistra dur espectre.[4]

CV,Q16

*Interpretation*

Because of its very high price [life] will have a taste of tears, because human flesh will be reduced to ash. The Isle of Pharos [Egypt] will be perturbed by the Christians, then in Greece the spectre of war will appear.

[1] Ancient form of *larme*, tear. DAFL.
[2] Latin *sapio*: I taste of. DLLB.
[3] Small island off Egyptian coast, near the port of Alexandria. AVL
[4] Symbolizing dread: the spectre of war. DL7V.

---

## Arabia, Turkey, Greece and Hungary in Conflict

Le grand Arabe marchera bien avant,
Trahy sera par le Bisantinois:
L'antique Rodes lui viendra au devant,
Et plus grand mal par autre Pannonois.

CV,Q47

*Interpretation*

The great Arab leader will set out well before, and be betrayed by the Turkish leader; ancient Greece will anticipate him and he will sustain greater harm from the Hungarians [Warsaw Pact].

---

## The King of Blois, the Liberator. Alliance with the Pope, Spain and Yugoslavia. The Fall of the Seven Eastern Countries

Par lors qu'un Roy sera contre les siens,
Natif de Blois subjuguera Ligures:[1]
Mammel,[2] Cordube[3] et les Dalmatiens,
Des sept[4] puis l'ombre à Roy estrennes[5] et lémures.[6]

CX,Q44

## Interpretation

When the government is divided, the one who comes from Blois will subjugate the inhabitants of northern Italy, with the aid of the Pole [the Pope], Spain and the Yugoslavs, then he will return providentially and put the seven [countries] in the shade.

[1] Liguria: region of ancient Italy, forming the south-western areas of Cisalpine Gaul. DHB.

[2] Memel or Niemen. DHB. The River Niemen, until the eighteenth century, was at the centre of Poland.

[3] Latin *Cordoba*, Spanish town.

[4] The seven countries of the Eastern Bloc: USSR, Romania, Poland, GDR, Bulgaria, Hungary, Czechoslovakia.

[5] Chance, fortune. DAFL.

[6] Latin *lemures*: shadows of the dead, ghosts. DLLB.

# The Fall of the Seven Eastern Countries in Turkey. Religious Persecutions Conducted by the Turks

> Dieu, le ciel tout le divin verbe à l'onde,
> Porté par rouges sept razes[1] à Bisance:
> Contre les vingts trois cents de Trebisconde,[2]
> Deux loix mettront, et horreur, puis crédence.[3]

CVII,Q36

## Interpretation

God, the sacred word, delivered over to revolution and carried by the reds of the seven countries to Turkey, where they will be defeated. Three hundred Turks will issue two laws against the cardinals and make them experience horror, then faith will be re-established.

[1] To demolish, raze to the ground. DL7V.
[2] Trebizond, Turkish port on the Black Sea. DHB.
[3] *Croyance*. DAFL.

---

# The Campaigns of Liberation against the Reds. The Polish Pope

> De la partie de Mammer[1] grand Pontife,
> Subjuguera les confins du Danube:
> Chasser les croix, par fer raffe[2] ne riffe,[3]
> Captifs, or, bagues plus de cent mille rubes.[4]

CVI,Q49

## Interpretation

Of Polish origin, the great Pope will push back to the limits of the Danube [Black Sea] those who will harass the Christians and who have ransacked and stolen from them in war; he will recover their wealth and take 100,000 Reds prisoner.

[1] For Memel, other name for the Niemen. DHB. Until the eighteenth century the River Niemen was at the centre of Poland.
[2] Ancient form of *rafler*. DAFL.
[3] Ancient form of *rifler*: to pillage, rifle, loot. DAFL.
[4] Latin *rubeus*: red. DLLB.

---

## The USSR Makes the Orient Tremble.
## John-Paul II and the Catholic Church.
## Battles in Turkey

Quand ceux du pole artic[1] unis ensemble,
En Orient grand effrayeur et crainte:
Esleu nouveau, soustenu le grand temple,[2]
Rodes, Bizance de sang barbare teinte.

CVI,Q21

*Interpretation*

When the Arctic territories are united [Soviet *Union*] there will be great
fear and dread in the Orient. When a new Pope is elected to sustain the
Catholic Church, Rhodes and Turkey will be stained with Moslem blood.

[1] Empire of Aquila: USSR and all territories it occupies from the Baltic to Vladivostok.
[2] Poetic: the Roman Catholic Church. DL7V.

## The Invasion of Italy at Perugia
## and Ravenna

Champ perusin ô l'énorme deffaicte,
Et le conflit tout auprès de Ravenne:
Passage[1] sacre lors qu'on fera la feste,
Vainceur vaincu cheval manger l'avenne.

CVIII,Q72

*Interpretation*

O enormous defeat in the countryside of Perugia and the war near
Ravenna: what is sacred will experience ills when the victor celebrates
his victory and his horse eats the hay of the vanquished.

[1] Latin *passare*: to undergo. DLLB.

## The Defeat of the French Army in Italy.
## The Flight of the People of Rome. French Defeat.
## Battles in the Swiss Alps and the Adriatic

Armée Celtique en Italie vexée,
De toutes parts conflit et grande perte,
Romains fuis, ô Gaule repoussée,[1]
Près de Thesin, Rubicon[2] pugne incerte.

CII,Q72

*Interpretation*

The French army will be beaten in Italy. The conflict will extend on all sides and cause great havoc. Flee, Romans; France will be struck when there is an indecisive battle near Ticino [Switzerland] and in the Adriatic.

[1] Latin *repello*: I smite, strike. DLLB.
[2] Small Italian river flowing into Adriatic. DHB.

---

## The Invasion of Italy by Moslem Troops.

Pluye, vent, classe Barbare Ister.[1] Tyrrhene,
Passer holcades[2] Ceres,[3] soldats munies:
Reduits bien faicts par Flor, franchie Sienne,
Les deux seront morts, amitiez unies.

Presage 31

*Interpretation*

Revolution, storm, the Moslem army from the Tyrrhenian Sea to the Danube will bring well-equipped troops by boat to Ceres. Contentment will be reduced throughout the West by those who will cross the seas as far as Siena, when the two leaders allied in friendship have died.

[1] European river, today the Danube. DHB.
[2] Greek ὀλκάς,-άδος: transport vessel, any ship. DGF.
[3] Town in Piedmont, Italy, in the Turin area. DL7V.

## Chemical Warfare. The Soviet Government in France. Italy Laid Waste

Soleil ardant dans le gosier coller,
De sang humain arrouser en terre Etrusque:
Chef seille[1] d'eau, mener son fils filer,[2]
Captive dame conduite en terre Turque.

CIV,Q58

*Interpretation*

Burns stick in the throat. Italy awash with human blood. The leader of the revolutionary sickle [Russia] will prepare to head his regime. The French leaders will be led in captivity to Turkey.

[1] Contraction of *sëeille*, i.e. *faucille* = sickle. DAFL.
[2] To prepare (with reference to future). DL7V.

## Invasion from Marseille as far as Lyon. Invasion through the Gironde and Aquitaine.

Du tout Marseille les habitans changéz,
Course et poursuite aupres de Lyon,
Narbon, Toloze, par Bourdeaux outragée,
Tuez captifs presque d'un million.

CI,Q72

*Interpretation*

Throughout Marseille the inhabitants will be changed, they will be pursued almost to Lyon. Narbonne and Toulouse will be damaged by the invasion coming from Bordeaux. Nearly a million prisoners will be executed.

## The Invasion of Marseille by Sea

Pieds et cheval à la seconde veille,[1]
Feront entrée vastant tout par la mer.
Dedans le port entrera de Marseille,
Pleurs, crys, et sang, onc nul temps si amer.

CX,Q88

*Interpretation*

Infantry and tanks [cavalry] will enter Marseille between 9 p.m. and
midnight, laying all waste, by sea. There will be such tears, cries and
blood, such a bitter time was never seen.

[1] Latin *vigilie*: one of the four watches of the night. First watch 6–9 p.m. Second watch
9 p.m.–midnight. DLLB.

---

## The Invasion of the Mediterranean Coast from Barcelona to Marseille. The Occupation of the Islands

De Barcelonne par mer si grande armée,
Tout Marseille de frayeur tremblera,
Isles saisies, de mer ayde fermée,
Ton traditeur[1] en terre nagera.[2]

CIII,Q88

*Interpretation*

From Barcelona to Marseille there will be seen a great armada at sea
which will fill all with dread. The islands [Balearic, Corsica, Sardinia,
Sicily] will be occupied. A possibility of help coming by sea will be
blocked [Gibraltar]. He who has betrayed you will be buried.

[1] Latin *traditor*: traitor. DLLB.
[2] Fate of those guilty of treason.

# Three Allied Countries Start a War

Les bien aisez subit seront desmis[1],
Le monde mis par les trois frères en trouble.
Cité marine saisiront ennemis,
Faim, feu, sang, peste, et de tous maux le double.

CVIII,QI7

*Interpretation*

The rich will be easily brought low. The world will be plunged into revolution by three allies. Enemies will seize Marseille, which will know great famine, arson, killing and plague.

[1] Latin *demissus*: sunk, lowered, brought low. DLLB.

---

# The Invasion of Western France and Provence

Bourdeaux, Poitiers au son de la campagne,[1]
A grande classe[2] ira jusqu'à l'Angon,[3]
Contre Gaulois sera leur tramontane,[4]
Quand monstre[5] hideux naistra[6] près de Orgon.

CI,Q90

*Interpretation*

The tocsin will be heard at Bordeaux and Poitiers; the great army will go as far as Langon; the Empire of Aquila will march against the French, when a frightful thing happens near Orgon.

[1] Latin *campana*: bell. DLLB.
[2] Latin *classis*: fleet, army. DLLB.
[3] Port on the Garonne, formerly Alingo. DHB.
[4] From Italian *tramontana*: north, then the North Wind; called this in the Mediterranean because for Italy the north lies beyond the Alps. DL7V.
[5] Latin *monstrum*: divine omen, strange thing, scourge. DLLB.
[6] Latin *nascor*: to be born, begin, start. DLLB.

## Invasion in the South-West

A tenir fort par fureur contraindra,
Tout coeur trembler. Langon advent[1] terrible:
Le coup de pied mille pieds se rendra;[2]
Guirond, Guaron, ne furent plus horribles.

CXII,Q65

### Interpretation

Its fury compels one to resist and makes all hearts anxious. At Langon
a terrible invasion takes place which covers a lot of ground. There were
never such horrible events in the Gironde and Garonne areas.

[1] Latin *adventus*: arrival, presence; *adventus gallicus* = the invasion of the Gauls. DLLB.
[2] To make haste, pick one's feet up. DL7V.

---

## The Invasion of South-West France
## from Italy through Toulouse and Bayonne

Par arnani[1] Tholoser Ville Franque,
Bande infinie par le mont Adrian,[2]
Passe riviere, Hutin[3] par pont[4] la planque,[5]
Bayonne entrer tous Bichoro criant.

CVIII,Q86

### Interpretation

From Umbria up to Toulouse and Villefranche, a huge army will pass
through the mountains bordering the Adriatic and will cross rivers after
fighting at sea, so as to enter Bayonne, with all the inhabitants of the
Bigorre crying out with fear.

[1] Anagram of Narnia, Umbrian town on the Nar. DLLB. Today, Narni.
[2] The mountains of Yugoslavia and Italy.
[3] For *hustin*: dispute, struggle. DAFL.
[4] Greek ποντός: the sea. DGF.
[5] Place, spot, house. DL7V.

# The War in Burgundy in August.
# Massacres and Executions, March–June

De la sixieme claire splendeur celeste,[1]
Viendra tonnerre si fort en la Bourgongne,
Puis naistra monstre de tres hideuse beste
Mars, Avril, Mai, Juin grand charpin[2] et rongne.[3]

CI,Q80

*Interpretation*

Towards the end of August the thunder of war will be intense in Burgundy, then an appalling thing will happen because of a horrible and brutal person who will instigate a great massacre and executions.

[1] Virgo: the sixth zodiac sign, which the sun, leaving Leo, enters on 22 August. Followed by Libra, it is known as the Sign of Virgo. DL7V.
[2] From *charpir: écharper* = to hack to pieces. DAFL.
[3] To cut off a head. DAFL.

---

# Great Naval Battles in the Atlantic

Après combat et bataille navalle,
Le grand Neptune[1] à son plus haut befroy[2]
Rouge adversaire de peur deviendra pasle
Mettant le Grand Occean en effroy.

CIII,QI

*Interpretation*

After a naval combat, England will know her greatest alarm. Then the Soviet adversary will pale with fear, having sown terror in the Atlantic [or the Atlantic Alliance].

[1] God of the sea. Always symbolizes England.
[2] Belfry: tower with a bell for sounding the alarm. DL.

# France Allied with England. The Invasion of Provence and Languedoc

Classe Gauloise par appuy de grande garde,
Du grand Neptune et ses tridens soldats,
Rongée Provence pour soustenir grande bande,
Plus Mars Narbon par javelots et dards.

CII,Q59

*Interpretation*

The French army with the help of the English Guards and soldiers will see Provence wrecked defending itself against a large force, and the war will be still fiercer at Narbonne, hit by rockets and shells.

---

# The Occupation of Paris by the Russians

Poeur, glas grand pille passer mer, croistre eregne,[1]
Sectes, sacrez outre mer plus polis:
Peste, chant,[2] feu, Roy d'Aquilon l'enseigne,
Dresser trophée[3] cité d'HENRIPOLIS.[4]

Presage 34, 1559

*Interpretation*

Fear, alarms when [the enemy] comes by sea to wreak great destruction; the 'throneless one' will begin to grow stronger and despite factions will be crowned overseas by more civilized people: epidemics, wails of lamentation, fire, the Russian leader will rejoice at his victory over the town of Henri IV [Paris].

[1] *Esregner*: to dethrone, deprive of a throne. DAFL.
[2] Songs of grief, victory, joy etc. DL7V.
[3] Victory, success. DL7V.
[4] Neologism by Nostradamus: *Henri* and the Greek πόλις: town. Henri IV's famous phrase was: 'Paris is worth a mass'.

# The Attack on Paris and its Siege.
# Communism Brings the Fall of the French Republic

Siège à Cité et de nuict assaillie,
Peu eschappez, non loin de mer conflit,
Femme de joie retour fils deffaillie,
Poison es lettres caché dedans le plic.

CI,Q41

*Interpretation*

Paris will be besieged and attacked by night and few will be able to escape. Not far from there, there will be a naval engagement. On the return of her son [Communism] the Republic will collapse because of dangerously compromising documents which had been hidden.

---

# The Attack on Paris and the Occupation of Rome.
# Great Naval Battles

Tout à l'entour de la grande Cité,
Seront soldats logez par champs et ville,
Donner l'assaut Paris, Rome incité[1]
Sur le pont[2] lors sera faict grand pille.

CV,Q30

*Interpretation*

All around Paris soldiers will be lodged in the town and countryside, and inside the town when Paris is besieged and Rome invaded, there will then be great havoc caused at sea.

[1] Latin *incito*: I throw myself upon. DLLB.
[2] Greek ποντός: sea. DGF.

# The French Army of Liberation Fights
# the Red Army in Italy

Gaulois par sauts monts viendra penetrer,
Occupera le grand lieu de l'Insubre,[1]
Au plus profond de son ost[2] fera entrer,
Gennes, Monech pousseront classe rubre.[3]

CIV,Q37

## Interpretation

The French cross the mountains in quick stages and occupy the Milan
area. They will invade in depth and from Genoa and Monaco will drive
back the Red Army.

[1] The Milanese. DHB.
[2] Army, camp. DAFL.
[3] Latin *ruber*: red. DLLB.

---

# The Flight from France of a Leading Cleric.
# The Turco–Tunisian Alliance

Le grand Prelat Celtique à Roy suspect,
De nuict par cours sortira hors du regne:
Par Duc fertile à son grand Roy Bretagne,
Bisance à Cypres et Tunes insuspect.[1]

CVI,Q53

## Interpretation

The great French prelate will be suspected by the head of state and will
leave the country by night. Prosperity will be restored to Brittany by the
great soldier king. Turkey will not be suspected by Cyprus and Tunisia.

[1] Latin *insuspecte*: without suspicion. DLLB.

# Algeria's Important Role in the Conflict. The Russian Landing. Invasion of Switzerland through the Grisons

Amoura legre[1] non loin pose le siege,
Au saint barbare[2] seront les garnisons:
Ursins Hadrie pour Gaulois feront plaige,
Pour peur rendus de l'armée aux Grisons.[3]

CX,Q38

*Interpretation*

The headquarters will be established not far from Amoura and Algiers, where the garrisons of Mohammed's soldiers will be. Then the young Russian soldiers will land in France from the Adriatic, when they will go into Switzerland, via the Grisons, to terrorize the army.

[1] Nostradamus here juxtaposes Amoura, a town in southern Algeria in the Ouled-Nail range, and the town of Algiers. AVL.
[2] The prophet Mohammed.
[3] One of the Swiss cantons, containing five great valleys: upper and lower Rhine, the Engadine, Albula and Prettigau. DHB.

---

# The Attack by Air on Marseille and Geneva. The Invasion of Greece by Iran

Flambeau ardant au ciel soir sera veu,
Pres de la fin et principe[1] du Rosne,
Famine, glaive, tard le secours pourveu,
La Perse tourne envahi Macedoine.[2]

CII,Q96

*Interpretation*

A missile will be seen in the evening sky near the mouth and source of the Rhône. Famine, war, will reign and help will be too late, when Iran mobilizes to invade Macedonia.

[1] The Rhône begins in the Valais, Switzerland, near Mont St Gothard, running westwards to Lake Geneva which it joins and from where it flows to Geneva. DHB.
[2] Kingdom of ancient Greece. DHB.

# The Invasion of Switzerland
## through Tunnels

Jardin[1] du monde auprès de cité neuve,[2]
Dans le chemin des montagnes cavées,[3]
Sera saisi et plongé dans le cuve,
Beuvant par force eaux soulphre envenimées.

CX,Q49

*Interpretation*

The richest country of the West, near Neufchâtel will be seized and overwhelmed by means of the mountain tunnels, and its population will be forced to drink polluted water.

[1] Figurative, for 'fertile': DL. 'Garden of the world' in that it constitutes the strongbox of the West.
[2] Neufchâtel, Neuenburg (German), Novisburgum (Latin) = new city. Swiss town at the foot of the Jura. DHB.
[3] Latin *cavo*: I hollow out or pierce. DLLB.

---

# Invasion through Northern Italy
## and Switzerland. Famine and Shortages

Les deux copies aux murs ne pourront joindre,
Dans cet instant trembler Milan, Ticin:[1]
Faim, soif, doutance si fort les viendra poindre
Chair, pain, ne vivres n'auront un seul boucin.[2]

CIV,Q90

*Interpretation*

The two Western armies could not join up as far as the defences. At that moment Milan will be in dread and in Ticino famine, thirst and anxiety will afflict the inhabitants who will have neither meat, bread nor even scraps to eat.

[1] Latin Ticinus. DLLB.
[2] Provençal *boucoun*: scrap, morsel. DP.

# The Invasion of France via Switzerland

Pres du Tesin les habitans de Loyre
Garonne et Saone, Seine, Tain et Gironde
Outre les monts dresseront promontoire,
Conflict donné, Pau granci,[1] submergé onde.

CVI,Q79

## Interpretation

Near Ticino [Switzerland] the enemies will cross the mountains where they will set up strategic bases so as to attack the inhabitants of the Loire, the Saône, the Seine, the Tain and the Gironde. War will break out, the town of Pau will be protected, revolution will submerge all.

[1] *Garance*: protection, guarantee. DAFL. Example of syncope.

# Invasion from Switzerland to the Basses-Pyrénées

Pour la faveur que la cité fera,
Au grand qui tost perdra camp de bataille
Puis le rang[1] Pau Thesin versera,[2]
De sang, feux mors[3] noyez[4] de coups de taille.[5]

CII,Q26

## Interpretation

Because of the favour Paris will do the great country [USA] which will leave the field of battle at the start of the war, the [Russian] army from Ticino will drive towards the Basses-Pyrénées where blood will flow and the inhabitants will undergo the bite of fire and be killed by weapons.

[1] Military formation, *rank*. DL7V.
[2] Latin *verto*: I go towards, take a direction. DL7V.
[3] *Morsure*. DAFL.
[4] Latin *necare*: to kill. DL7V.
[5] Cutting edge or blade of a weapon. DL7V.

# The Invasion and Sack of Switzerland

Le chef du camp au milieu de la presse,
D'un coup de flesche sera blessé aux cuisses,[1]
Lors que Genève en larmes et en detresse
Sera trahy[2] par Lozan et par Soysses.

CIV,Q9

*Interpretation*

The head of the besieged army will be wounded through his protection,
while the inhabitants of Geneva will be in distress and will weep and be
ravaged by an invasion across Switzerland and through Lausanne.

[1] *Cuissel*: armour covering the thigh. DAFL.
[2] Take by force, ravish, steal. Latin *Trahere pagos* = to pillage the villages. DLLB.

---

# Property Ransacked in France
# and Switzerland

Geneve et Langres par ceux de Chartres et Dole[1]
Et par Grenoble captif au Montlimard,
Seysset,[2] Losanne, par frauduleuse dole,[3]
Les trahiront[4] par or soixante marc.

CIV,Q42

*Interpretation*

Geneva and Langres, attacked by those who will occupy Chartres and
the Swiss Jura and who, arriving from Grenoble, will take Montélimar
as well as Seyssel and Lausanne, will be despoiled of their gold by a
piece of trickery.

[1] Mountain of the Swiss Jura in the canton of Vaud on the French border. DL7V.
[2] Seyssel: principal town of the canton of Ain, but also another town in the canton of
Haute-Savoie. DHB.
[3] *Dol*: fraudulent manoeuvre, trickery. DL7V. Deception or fraud. DAFL.
[4] Cf. CIV,Q9.

# The War in Lyon and Roussillon

Clarté fulgure[1] à Lyon apparante,
Luysant,[2] print Malte, subit sera estainte,
Sardon,[3] Mauris[4] traitera décevante,[5]
Genève à Londes[6] a Coq trahison fainte.

CVIII,Q6

*Interpretation*

The light of the blaze to be seen at Lyon, after Malte has been quickly captured, will suddenly be extinguished. A deceptive treaty will be signed in Roussillon with the Moslems, because of treachery against the [French] King by Switzerland and England.

[1] Latin *fulgur*: lightning flash. DLLB.
[2] Figurative: to appear brilliantly, swiftly. DL7V.
[3] Sardones: tribe of the Narbonne area. Their country once formed Roussillon and is today the department of Pyrénées-Orientales. DHB.
[4] Latin *maurus*: Moor. DLLB.
[5] Latin *decipere*: to trick, deceive. DLLB.
[6] Lond[r]es: London. DHB.

---

# The War Conducted in Switzerland, England and Italy, the Countries Most Affected

Pleurs, cris et plaincts, hurlements, effrayeurs,
Coeur inhumain, cruel noir,[1] et transy:[2]
Léman, les Isles, de Gennes les majeurs,
Sang espancher, frofaim,[3] à nul mercy.

CVI,Q81

*Interpretation*

Because of an inhuman person – cruel, odious and terrifying – weeping, cries, complaints and screams of fear will be heard in Switzerland and the British Isles, and from the Italian leaders. Blood will flow there. Cold and hunger will reign: there will be no mercy for anyone.

[1] Symbolic: perverse, evil, hateful. DL7V.
[2] *Transir*: to make one shudder with fear. DL7V.
[3] *Miséricorde*, i.e. mercy. DAFL.

## Fear in Switzerland

Près du Leman la frayeur sera grande,
Par le conseil, cela ne peut faillir:
Le nouveau Roy fait apprester sa bande,
Le jeune meurt faim, poeur fera faillir.

Presage 4, February

*Interpretation*

Fear will be great near Lake Geneva, because of a [United Nations] resolution, and this is inevitable. The new leader prepares his army, and when the young leader dies of hunger, people will give way to fear.

---

## The Flight of the Inhabitants of Switzerland and Savoy

EIOVAS proche esloigner, lac Léman,
Fort grands apprest, retour, confusion:
Loin les nepveux,[1] de feu grand Supelman,[2]
Tous de leur fuyte.

CXII,Q69

*Interpretation*

It will be necessary to escape from the environs of Savoy and Lake Geneva. Great preparations [for war] will be made, which will bring back confusion. One must keep away from the Germans and from the great war upon Geneva, whence all the inhabitants will flee.

[1] Title given by German Emperors to the Secular Electors of the Empire. DL7V.
[2] For *super Leman*: on Lake Geneva. (Fr. *Lac Léman*.)

# The People of Geneva and Their Leader Put to Death

Devant le pere l'enfant sera tué,
Le pere apres entre cordes de jonc:
Genevois peuple sera esvertué,[1]
Gisant le chef au milieu comme un tronc.[2]

CX,Q92

*Interpretation*

The child will be killed in front of its father, who will be imprisoned thereafter. The inhabitants of Geneva will be destroyed, their leader to die by decapitation.

[1] Latin *everto*: I destroy, ruin, overthrow. DLLB.
[2] Latin *truncus*: mutilated body, headless trunk. DLLB.

# The Destruction of Geneva. Switzerland and Iran

Migrés, migrés de Genève trestous,
Saturne[1] d'or en fer se changera:
Le contre RAYPOZ[2] exterminera tous
Avant l'advent le ciel signes fera.

CIX,Q44

*Interpretation*

All you inhabitants of Geneva, leave your town! Your golden age will change into an age of war. He who will rise up against the Iranian leader will exterminate you all. Before this event there will be signs in the sky.

[1] God of time.
[2] Anagram of Zopyra: one of the seven Persian nobles who assassinated the pseudo-Smerdis and made Darius I king. DL7V.

## The Destruction of Paris and Geneva.
## The Exodus of their Populations

Auprès des portes et dedans deux citez
Seront deux fléaux onc n'aperceu un tel,
Faim, dedans peste, de fer hors gens boutez,
Crier secours au Grand Dieu immortel.

                                        CII,Q6

*Interpretation*

In the suburbs and within two cities [Paris and Geneva] there will be
two scourges the like of which have never been seen. Hunger and plague
shall reign in these cities, people will be driven out of them, beseeching
Almighty God for aid.

---

## The Destruction of Geneva.
## The Defeat of the Moslem Troops

Seicher de faim, de soif, gent Genevoise,
Espoir prochain viendra au defaillir,
Sur point tremblant sera loy Gebenoise,[1]
Classe au grand port ne se peut accueillir.

                                        CII,Q64

*Interpretation*

The inhabitants of Geneva will die of hunger and thirst, [Switzerland]
will succumb with no hope near. At this point in the war the Moslem
law will be shaken. Marseille will not be able to welcome the army.

[1] Latin Gebanitae: Gebanites, tribe of ancient Arabia. DLLB.

# Catastrophe at Lausanne

Puanteur grande sortira de Lausanne
Qu'on ne sçaura l'origine du faict,
L'on mettra hors toute la gent lointaine
Feu veu au ciel, peuple estranger deffaict.

CVIII,QIO

*Interpretation*

From Lausanne there will issue a foul stench whose origin will be unknown. The population will be evacuated, when fire will be seen in the sky [missiles] and a foreign country [Germany or Italy] will be defeated.

---

# The Invasion from Switzerland to Paris. The Fall of the Head of State

Verseil, Milan donra intelligence,
Dedans Tycin sera faicte la playe:[1]
Courir par Seine, eau, sang, feu par Florence,
Unique cheoir d'hault en bas faisant maye.[2]

CVIII,Q7

*Interpretation*

There will be secret agreements with the enemy in northern Italy. The army breakthrough will occur in Ticino and continue on to the Seine, where revolution will reign, blood and war having struck Florence. The head of state will fall while celebrating.

[1] Poetic, for 'breech' or 'gap'. DL7V.
[2] Maye: Maya, mother of Mercury, whose festival is celebrated in early May. DP. May also represents rejoicing, fine weather. DAFL.

# Battles near Orgon and the Albion Plateau. The Defeat of Iraq in France

Aux champs herbeux d'Alein[1] et du Varneigue.[2]
Du mont Lebron[3] proche de la Durance,
Camp des deux parts conflit sera si aigre,
Mesopotamie[4] defaillira[5] en la France.

CIII,Q99

*Interpretation*

On the plain of Alleins and Vernègues and the Albion plateau, near the Durance, the battle will be very fierce for both sides and Iraq will lose her forces in France.

[1] Alleins, near Orgon, small town in Bouches-du-Rhône. DL7V.
[2] Vernègues, small town off N7, in Bouches-du-Rhône.
[3] Lubéron or Léberon: mountain in southern France (Basses-Alpes et Vaucluse), above the valley of the Durance. DL7V. The Albion plateau is part of the Lubéron range.
[4] Region between the Tigris and Euphrates, today Iraq. DHB.
[5] To lose one's strength. DL7V.

---

# The Transportation of Gold along the Rhône

Par la fureur d'un qui attendra[1] l'eau,
Par la grand rage tout l'exercite esmeu:
Chargé des nobles[2] à dix-sept bateaux
Au long du Rosne, tard messager venu.

CV,Q71

*Interpretation*

Through the zeal of one person the revolution will spread. With great fury the whole army will be mobilized. A fleet of seventeen ships laden with gold will go up the Rhône, the messenger arriving too late.

[1] Latin *attendo*: I tend, drive towards. DLLB.
[2] Numismatic term. In 1344 Edward III of England coined gold 'nobles' whose weight was later modified. One pound of gold went into forty-five nobles. DL7V.

## The Invasion of Lyon Distinguished by Satellite

Le ciel (de Plencus[1] la cité) nous présage
Par clers[2] insignes et par estoilles fixes,[3]
Que de son change subit s'approche l'aage,
Ne pour son bien ne pour les malefices.

CIII,Q46

*Interpretation*

The sky announces to us by luminous signals and satellites that the moment of a change experienced at Lyon is approaching, neither for the town's good nor for its ill.

[1] Munatius Plancus, orator and Roman general. He founded, or at least discovered, Lugdunum (Lyon) while proconsul in Gaul. DHB.
[2] Early form of *clair*, clear. DAFL.
[3] Stars thus termed have their own fixed, or apparently fixed, positions in space. DL7V.

---

# THE DESTRUCTION OF PARIS

## The Occupation of Paris by the Red Army. Its Destruction: Great Loss of Life

Grand Cité à soldats abandonnée,
Onc n'y eust mortel tumult si proche,
O qu'elle hideuse mortalité s'approche,
Fors une offense ny sera pardonnée.

CVI,Q96

*Interpretation*

Paris will be abandoned to the [enemy] soldiers. Such a conflict so close to the town was never seen. What a fearful mortality there will be. An offence will not be forgiven.

---

## Paris Burned

Sera laissé le feu vif, mort caché,
Dedans les globes[1] horrible espovantable,
De nuict a classe cité en poudre[2] lasché,
La cité à feu, l'ennemy favorable.

CV,Q8

*Interpretation*

He who hides will be burned alive in horrible and dreadful whirlwinds
of flame. The town will be reduced to dust by night, by the [aerial] fleet.
The town in flames will be favourable to the enemy.

[1] Latin *globus*: mass, heap. *Globi flammarum* (Virgil) = whirlwinds of flames. DLLB.
[2] Latin *pulvis*: dust. DLLB.

---

## Paris saved in 1945.
## Paris Destroyed in the Third World War

La ville sens dessus dessous
Et renversée de mille coups
De canon: et fort dessous terre:
Cinq ans tiendra: le tout remis,
Et laschée à ses ennemis,
L'eau leur fera après la guerre.

Sixain 3

*Interpretation*

The town turned upside down by a thousand cannon blasts, and strong
below the ground [the métro]. It will resist for five years [1940–45],
everything will be restored to its place, then the town will be abandoned
to its enemies, against whom the revolution will wage war.

# A Missile against Paris.
# Revolutionary Troubles in the City

De feu volant la machination,[1]
Viendra troubler au grand chef assiegez;
Dedans sera telle sedition,
Qu'en desespoir seront les profligez.

CVI,Q34

*Interpretation*

An incendiary, flying war machine will come to trouble the leader of those who are besieged. Within, there will be such sedition that the unfortunate people will be desperate.

[1] Latin *machinatio*: mechanical apparatus, machine. DLLB.

---

# The Destruction of Paris

Le Celtique fleuve changera de rivage,
Plus ne tiendra la cité d'Aggrippine[1]
Tout transmué, hormis le vieil langage,
Saturn, Leo, Mars, Cancer en rapine.[2]

CVI,Q4

*Interpretation*

The banks of the French river [the Seine] will change their appearance. Paris will no longer last. All will be transformed except the French language, for it will be a time of totalitarianism, war and misery caused by looting.

[1] Nostradamus calls Paris by this name, comparing the Revolutionary French Republic of 1789 to Agrippina, and Communism, the Revolution's child, to Nero. And as Agrippina was killed by her son Nero, so the Republic will be put to death by her child: Communism will burn Paris just as Nero burned Rome.
[2] Theft, accompanied by violence, committed by a band of armed men.

# The Destruction of Paris

La grand Cité sera bien désolée,
Des habitants un seul n'y demourra,
Mur sexe, temple et vierge violée,
Par fer, feu, peste, canon peuple mourra.

CIII,Q84

*Interpretation*

Paris will be badly devastated. Not a single one of its inhabitants will remain there. Buildings, churches will be destroyed, women and young girls raped. By the sword of war, fire, sickness and artillery the people of Paris will die.

# The Paris Region Made Uninhabitable. The Invasion of England

Long temps sera sans estre habitée,
Où Seine et Marne[1] autour vient arrouser,
De la Tamise et martiaux temptée,[2]
De ceux les guardes en cuidant repousser.

CVI,Q43

*Interpretation*

The confluence of the Seine and Marne will remain for a long time uninhabited when the warriors attacking England will think about driving back her defences.

[1] Paris is at the confluence of the Seine and Marne.
[2] Latin *tempto*: I attack. DLLB.

# The King against the Occupier of Paris.
# A Missile Will Burn Paris. The Hated Military
# Governor of the Occupation

Prince sera de beauté tant venuste,[1]
Au chef menée, le second faict trahy:
La cité au glaive de poudre face[2] aduste,[3]
Par trop grand meurtre le chef du Roy haï.

CVI,Q92

## Interpretation

The prince will be handsome and charming and intrigue against the
leader of the government; also the second [government] will be betrayed.
The city [Paris] given over to massacre will burn because of an incendiary
rocket. The [red] head of government will be hated for his too blatant
murders.

[1] Latin *venustus*: charming, agreeable. DLLB.
[2] Latin *fax*: firebrand. DLLB.
[3] Latin *adustus*: burnt. DLLB.

---

# THE CONSPIRACY

## The Moslem Attack

Soldat Barbare le grand Roy frappera,
Injustement non esloigné de mort,
L'avare[1] mère du faict cause sera
Conjurateur et regne en grand remort.

CVIII,Q73

## Interpretation

The Moslem troops will smite the great Leader, whose death, unjustly,
will not be far off; the avarice of the mother [the French Republic] will
be the cause of this event. Conspirator and seat of power alike will be
greatly stricken.

[1] Latin *avarus*: greedy, miserly. DLLB.

# The Three Years and Seventy Days
# of the Red Regime. The Conspiracy

La déchassée[1] au regne tournera,
Ses ennemis trouvez des conjurés:
Plus que jamais son temps triomphera
Trois et septante à mort trop asseurés.

CVI,Q74

*Interpretation*

The left will be in power. It will be discovered that its enemies have
been plotting. More than ever, its time will triumph, but it is certain to
die after three years and seventy days.

[1] Dance step towards the *left*, as opposed to the chassé, in the other direction. DL7V.

---

# The End of the Republican System
# by means of a Conspiracy. The Senility
# of Rousseau's Ideas

Tard arrivé l'exécution faite,
Le vent contraire, lettres au chemin prises:
Les conjurez XIIII d'une secte,
Par le Rousseau senez les entreprises.

CI,Q7

*Interpretation*

[The saviour] having arrived late, the execution [of the regime] will be
accomplished, the wind [of history] having changed and documents being
seized. Fourteen conspirators of one party will render the enterprises
begun by Jean-Jacques Rousseau outdated.

---

## The End of the Red Leader.
## The Conspirators

De nuict passant le Roy près d'une Androne,[1]
Celui de Cypres[2] et principal guette,
Le Roy failly, la main fuit long du Rosne,
Les conjurez l'iront à la mort mettre.

CV,QI7

*Interpretation*

Passing through straits [the Bosphorus?] by night which are watched by
the Cypriot leader, the [enemy] leader will be ruined when his forces
flee along the Rhine; the plotters will then go and put him to death.

[1] Provençal *androuno*: narrow passage, alleyway. DP.
[2] Old French for Chypres, i.e. Cyprus.

---

# THE VICTORY OF THE WEST

## The Fifth Republic: Just over Twenty Years.
## The Return of the Monarchy until 1999. The End and
## Fulfilment of the Prophecy of Nostradamus, 1999

Vingt ans du règne de la Lune passéz,[1]
Sept mille ans autre tiendra sa Monarchie
Quand le soleil prendra ses jours lasséz,[2]
Lors accomplir et mine[3] ma prophétie.

CI,Q48

*Interpretation*

After twenty years of republican power, another will establish the monarchy until the seventh millennium [1999]. When the Bourbon knows
misfortune then shall my prophecy be accomplished and terminated.

[1] Beginning of the Fifth Republic: September 1959; end: September 1984 at latest.
[2] Latin *lassae res*: ill fortune. DLLB.
[3] For *terminer*: to end. Aphesis.

# Portugal, Departure Base for the Liberation of France. Fighting in the South-West and Languedoc

Albi et Castres feront nouvelle ligue,
Neur[1] Arriens[2] Libon et Portugues:
Carcas. Tholose consumeront leur brique,
Quand chef neuf monstre[3] de Lauragues.[4]

CX,Q5

## Interpretation

A new party will be set up in the Tarn, then a new Arrian, from Lisbon in Portugal, will destroy its manoeuvres as far as Carcassonne and Toulouse, when the new leader will bring about a calamity in the Lauragues.

[1] For *neuf*, new. DAFL.
[2] Arrian, Greek historian, statesman and soldier. He was made consul in return for his military services. DHB. Nostradamus establishes a parallel between Arrian and the French leader who will drive back the East German army of occupation. DHB.
[3] Latin *monstrum*: scourge, calamity. DLLB.
[4] Region including the departments of Haute-Garonne and the Aude. DHB.

---

# The Collapse of the Russo–Moslem Bloc

La loy Moricque[1] on verre déffaillir,
Après une autre beaucoup plus séductive:
Boristhènes[2] premier viendra faillir,
Par dons et langue une plus attractive.

CIII,Q95

## Interpretation

The Moslem law will be seen to collapse, following another far more seductive law [Communist]. Russia will collapse first and be drawn by the benefits and language [of the French].

[1] Mores or Maures: Moors, i.e. Moslems.
[2] Ancient name of the Dnieper, river of European Russia. DHB.

# The Naval Defeat of the Russo–Moslem Troops. The Defence of the Great Pope

Par mer, le rouge sera prins de pyrates,
La paix sera par son moyen troublée:
L'ire et l'avare[1] commettra[2] par sainct acte,
Au Grand Pontife sera l'armée doublée.

CV,Q44

## Interpretation

At sea the Soviet forces will be caught with the Moslems who will have troubled the peace. Anger and greed will unite against the Church's actions. Measures by the army for the great Pope's protection will be doubled.

[1] Latin *avaritia*: greed. DLLB.
[2] Latin *committo*: I assemble, join, reunite. DLLB.

# Great Battles in the Black Sea. Iranian Troops in Turkey. Arab Naval Defeat in the Adriatic

Par feu et armes non loin de la marnegro,[1]
Viendra de Perse occuper Trebisonde:[2]
Trembler Phato,[3] Methelin,[4] sol alegro,
De sang Arabe d'Adrie couvert onde.

CV,Q27

## Interpretation

By fire and weapons of war not far from the Black Sea, Iranian troops will come to occupy Trebizond. The mouth of the Nile, and Greece, will tremble because of the skill of the Bourbon, who will cover the Adriatic with Arab blood.

[1] Latin *mar[e]*: sea, plus *negro* (from *niger*), black. DLLB.
[2] Turkish town on the Black Sea. DHB.
[3] Phatnitique: an ancient tributary of the Nile, today the Damietta. DHB.
[4] Mytilene, ancient capital of the island of Lesbos; one of the main Greek towns of Asia. DHB.

# Fighting between England and East Germany. The War in France. The Occupation of Marseille. The Victory of the West

> Au temps du deuil que le félin monarque[1]
> Guerroyera le jeune Aemathien[2]
> Gaule bransler pérecliter la barque.
> Tenter[3] Phossens[4] au Ponant[5] entretien,[6]
>
> CX,Q58

## Interpretation

The moment the English leader wages war on the young German commander, France will be shaken, the Church will be in jeopardy. Marseille will be occupied, then the West will endure [suffering].

[1] Allusion to the leopard on the English coat-of-arms.
[2] Symbolizes the German spirit of conquest and war. Cf. CX,Q7.
[3] Latin *teneo*: I hold, occupy. DLLB.
[4] Phocéens: the inhabitants of Marseille.
[5] Word once used in the Mediterranean to denote the Ocean or the West, as opposed to the Levant. DL7V.
[6] To keep in a good state, render durable. DL7V.

---

# The Victory of the West

> Loin près de l'Urne[1] le malin[2] tourne arrière,
> Qu'au grand Mars feu donra empeschement:
> Vers l'Aquilon au midy le grand fiersl,[3]
> FLORA[4] tiendra la porte en pensement.[5]
>
> Presage 8, June

## Interpretation

At the approach of the Aquarian Age, the devil will turn back, and he will be given obstacles where the fire of the great war is concerned. From Russia to the Moslem countries the great proud one will rule, and the West will maintain freedom of thought.

[1] Latin Urna: attribute of Aquarius. DLLB.
[2] Devil or demon. DL7V.

' Proud, haughty. DL7V.

[4] Zephyr, the west wind, celebrated by the classical poets for the freshness it brought to the hot lands they inhabited. Its mild yet powerful breath brought life to nature. The Greeks gave it a 'wife', Chloris, the Roman goddess Flora. MGR.

[5] Action of thinking. DL7V.

---

## The Decadence of the West. The War

Venus[1] la belle entrera dedans FLORE,
Les exilez secrets[2] lairront[3] la place:
Vesves beaucoup, mort de Grand on déplore,
Oster du regne, le Grand Grand ne menace.

Presage 32, November

*Interpretation*

When sexual licence enters the West, exiled ones will leave the place seeking retreats. There will be many widows and the death will be deplored of a great person who has given up power; the greatness of this person threatened none.

[1] Sexual desire personified by Venus, goddess of love. DL7V.
[2] Latin *secretum*: retreat, quiet or secluded spot. DLLB.
[3] Future of *laier* = to leave. DAFL.

---

## The Liberation of France via Nantes. The Great Navy Sunk in the Red Sea. A Scourge in Germany Provoked by Russia and Turkey

De nuict par Nantes Lyris apparoistra,
Des arts marins susciteront la pluye:
Arabiq goulfre[1] grand classe parfondra,
Un monstre en Saxe naistra d'ours et de truye.[2]

CVI,Q44

*Interpretation*

Peace will be glimpsed by night, starting from Nantes when [the French] will start naval bombardments. A great fleet will be sunk in the Red Sea, when a scourge is born, because of Russia and Turkey, in Germany.

[1] Red Sea, or Arabian Gulf.
[2] Latin Troja, Troy. DL7V. Nostradamus refers here to Turkey, for Troy is in Asia Minor.

---

# The Franco–Belgian Armies against the Moslem Troops. The Death of the Moslem Leader in the Red Sea

Satur[1] au boeuf[2] iove[3] en l'eau, Mars en fleiche,
Six de Fevrier mortalité donra:
Ceux de Tardaigne[4] à Bruge[5] si grand breche,[6]
Qu'à Ponterose[7] chef Barbarin mourra.

CVIII,Q49

## Interpretation

When the time comes for violence and the atmosphere is of revolution, the war will spread. On 6 February there will be fatality. The French and Belgians will make such a breach in the enemy troops that the Moslem commander will die in the Red Sea.

[1] Saturn, in Greek Kronos: time.
[2] Poetic: brutal. DL7V.
[3] Jupiter, Jovis: air, sky, atmosphere. DLLB.
[4] Tardenois: ancient minor region of France, in the Soissons area, today subsumed under the Aisne department. DHB.
[5] Belgian town, the main town of west Flanders. DHB.
[6] By analogy, hole made in a group of men. DL7V.
[7] Neologism from ποντός sea, and rose (pink, red).

---

# The Victory of the West. Battles against the Moslem Troops

Les Rhodiens[1] demanderont secours,
Par le neglet de ses hoyrs delaissée,
L'Empire Arabe ravalera[2] son cours[3]
Par Hespéries[4] la cause redressée.

CIV,Q39

*Interpretation*

The Greeks will ask for help because of the negligence of their heirs, who will have abandoned them. The expansion of the Arab Empire will be halted and the West will redress the situation.

[1] Rhodes: Aegean Island returned to Greece in 1947.
[2] To lower, beat down, check. DL7V.
[3] March, progression, expansion. DL7V.
[4] Greek 'Εσπερις: West. DGF.

---

# The Victory of the West.
# The Fall of the Seven Eastern Bloc Countries

Libra verra regner les Hesperies,
Du ciel et terre tenir la Monarchie,
D'Asie forces nul ne verra peries
Que sept ne tiennent par rang la hiérarchie.[1]

CIV,Q50

*Interpretation*

Justice will see the Westerners reign, the Monarchy will maintain heaven and earth, but the forces of Asia will not be destroyed as long as seven countries are grouped together.

[1] The seven Warsaw Pact countries: USSR, GDR, Poland, Romania, Hungary, Czechoslovakia and Bulgaria.

---

# Revolution in the Eastern Bloc.
# A Rain of Meteorites on Land and Sea.
# The Fall of the Seven Warsaw Pact Countries

Nouvelle pluye[1] subite, impétueuse,
Empeschera subit deux exercites:
Pierres, ciel, feux faire la mer pierreuse,
La mort de sept terre et marins subite.

CII,Q18

*Interpretation*

A new, sudden and violent revolution will swiftly hinder [in their advance] two armies. Blazing meteorites falling from the sky will bombard the sea and provoke the sudden fall of the seven countries [Warsaw Pact] by land and sea.

¹ Constant symbol in Nostradamus of the revolution.

---

# The Burning of Paris. The Invasion of Sardinia by the Moslems. The Victory of the West

Par le feu du ciel la cité presque aduste,¹
L'urne² menace encore Ceucalion,³
Vexée Sardaigne par la Punique fuste,⁴
Après le Libra⁵ lairra⁶ son Phaëton.⁷

CII,Q81

*Interpretation*

By the fire fallen from heaven the city burns almost totally; revolution and death still threaten the upright man. Sardinia will be ravaged by a Moslem fleet, after which war will give way to justice.

¹ Latin *adustus*: burnt. DLLB.
² Vase for water carrying, collecting votes, or containing the ashes of the dead in ancient times. DL7V. Taken here by Nostradamus to symbolize revolution (water) and death.
³ Typographical error for Deucalion (cf. CX,Q6 and Presage 90). Son of Prometheus, in whose reign the famous flood was sent by Jupiter, who, seeing men's wickedness increase, determined to drown the human race. The surface of the earth was submerged except for one mountain on which the boat carrying Deucalion, the most upright of men, ran aground. MGR.
⁴ Italian *fusta*: long shallow-draught boat which had both sails and oars. DL7V.
⁵ Latin *libra*: scales, the zodiacal sign. DLLB. Also symbol of justice.
⁶ Future of *laier, laisser* = to leave. DAFL.
⁷ Greek name for the planet Jupiter. The Cyclops gave Jupiter thunder and lightning, Pluto a helmet, and Neptune a trident. With these weapons the three brothers conquered Saturn. MGR. Used as symbol for war. [Phaethon: son of Helios, the sun god and Clymene, was killed by Jupiter (Zeus) while driving the chariot of the sun. Tr]

# The King of Spain against the Moslems

Dans les Espagnes viendra Roy très puissant
Par mer et terre subjugant le midy:
Ce mal fera, rabaissant le croissant,
Baisser les aesles à ceux du vendredy.[1]

CX,Q95

## Interpretation

A very powerful King will come to Spain, subjugating the countries of
the south [North Africa] by sea and land; this he will do to reduce the
power of the crescent [Arabs] and make the worshippers of Friday lower
their wings.

[1] Holy day for the Moslems.

---

# The Defeat of the Moslems

Logmion[1] grande Bisance approchera,
Chassée sera la barbarique ligue:[2]
Des deux loix l'une l'estinique[3] lachera,
Barbare et franche en perpétuelle brigue.[4]

CV,Q80

## Interpretation

The eloquent person will approach great Turkey, the Moslem alliance
will be beaten: of the two Moslem laws one [Shi'ite] will be abandoned;
there will be continual upheavals between Moslems and French.

[1] Ogmios or Ogmius, the Gauls' god of eloquence and poetry depicted as an old man,
armed with bow and club, attracting to himself a variety of people by means of nets of
amber and gold coming out of his mouth. DHB.
[2] Alliance, confederation of several states: offensive and defensive league. DL7V. Cf.
'And the barbaric sect will be greatly afflicted and driven out by all the Nations.' (Letter
to Henri, Second King of France).
[3] Latin ethnicus: pagan. DLLB. The Sunnites, a Moslem sect derived from the Arab
word sunnah (tradition), because its adherents claimed to be preserving the true tradition.
The Shi'ites, a Moslem sect opposed to the Sunnites, derived their name (meaning
heretics, schismatics) from the Sunnites who called themselves the only orthodox believers.
(The two Moslem laws). DHB.
[4] Tumult, brawl. DAFL.

# The King of France in Italy.
## Fighting in the Alps

L'an que les frères du lys seront en l'aage,
L'un d'eux tiendra la Grande Romanie,
Trembler les monts, ouvert latin passage,[1]
Pache marcher[2] contre fort d'Arménie.

CV,Q50

*Interpretation*

The year the Bourbon brothers [kings of France and Spain] arrive, one
of them [the King of France] will occupy Italy, the mountains [Alps]
will shake, the passage into Italy will be open. Peace will be delayed
because of armies in Armenia.

[1] Col of Mont-Cenis, Tende or Mont Blanc.
[2] Latin *marcens pax*: sluggish peace. DLLB.

---

# The Movements of Large Forces in Iran and
## Armenia. The Defeat of the Moslem Troops

Aux chands de Mede,[1] d'Arabe et d'Arménie,
Deux grands copies[2] trois fois s'assembleront:
Près du rivage d'Araxes[3] la mesgnie[4]
Du grand Soliman en terre tomberont.

CIII,Q31

*Interpretation*

In the territories of Iran, Arabia and Armenia, two great armies will
reassemble; they will be concentrated on the Iran–Armenia border, then
the soldiers of the great Moslem commander will fall.

[1] Medea: part of Asia Minor. The plain, well irrigated at the foot of some mountains,
becomes infertile towards the east and south-east, and ends by forming, at the centre of
the Iranian plateau, what is called the great Medean Desert. DL7V.
[2] Latin *copiae*: army, troops. DLLB.
[3] River border between Russian Armenia and Iran, which flows out into the Caspian
Sea.
[4] Or *maisnie*: troop, force. DAFL.

# The Duration of the Third World War:
# Three Years and Seven Months. The Revolt of Two
# Socialist Republics. Victory in Armenia

Le règne a deux laissé bien peu tiendront,
Trois ans sept mois passés[1] feront la guerre:
Les deux vestales[2] contre rebelleront
Victor[3] puisnay[4] en Armonique terre.

CIV,Q95

## Interpretation

The two persons to whom power has been abandoned will keep it only a short time. The war will last a little more than three years and seven months. Two of the Warsaw Pact Republics will rebel against [the USSR], and the younger [the King of France in relation to the King of Spain] will be victor in Armenia.

[1] Cf. *Revelations*: 13: 'And I stood upon the sand of the sea, and saw a beast rise up out of the sea, having seven heads and ten horns . . . [seven Warsaw Pact countries] . . . the beast which I saw was like unto a leopard, and his feet were as the feet of a bear [USSR] and his mouth as the mouth of a lion . . . and power was given unto him to continue *forty and two months* . . . .'

[2] Name given to priestesses of Vesta. Their clothing consisted of a tunic of grey and white linen, covered by a big *purple* cloak. DL7V. Nostradamus always personifies republics as feminine.

[3] Latin *victor*: conqueror. DLLB.

[4] *Puîné*: person born after another (i.e. younger of two children). DL7V.

---

# The Two Years of Soviet Occupation.
# The End of the Soviet Empire

Le grand empire chacun an devait estre,
Un sur les autres le viendra obtenir:
Mais peu de temps sera son regne et estre
Deux ans aux naves[1] se pourra soustenir.

CX,Q32

*Interpretation*

The great [Soviet] empire, which seems set to survive, will gradually obtain countries one after the other, but its power and existence will not be very prolonged. It will be able to keep going only two years thanks to its navy.

¹ Latin *navis*: vessel, ship. DLLB.

---

## Great Changes in International Relations. The Liberation of Marseille

L'ordre fatal¹ sempiternel par chaine,
Viendra tourner par ordre conséquent:
Du port Phocen² sera rompuë la chaine³
La cité prinse, l'ennemy quant et quant.⁴

CIII,Q79

*Interpretation*

The universal order obtaining everywhere will be changed by the order succeeding it. The occupation of Marseille will be thrown off, after the city has been occupied by so many enemies.

¹ Universal order: according to Malebranche, the law governing all God's decisions, as it must also rule ours. DL7V.
² Phocéen: Marseillais. Phocea was the ancient Greek name for Marseille.
³ Dependence, servitude. DL7V.
⁴ Latin *quantum*: a great quantity. DLLB.

---

## The Anglo–American Landing at Bordeaux. The Liberation of South-west France. The Proclamation of an Occitanian Republic

Par la Guyenne infinité d'Anglois,
Occuperont par nom d'Anglaquitaine:
Du Languedoc I. palme¹ Bourdelois,
Qu'ils nommeront après Barboxitaine.²

CIX,Q6

*Interpretation*

A huge number of Anglo-Saxons and Americans will land at Guyenne, which they will occupy, calling it Anglo-American Aquitania. After winning victory from the Languedoc to the Bordeaux area, they will name this region the 'Republic of Occitania'.

[1] Symbolic: sign of victory. DL7V.

[2] Word made up of *Barbe* (Aenobarbe, i.e. Domitius Aeonobarbus, husband of Agrippina, symbolizing 'Republic'), and *Occitan*.

---

# The Landing on the Coast of Guyenne. The Battles of Poitiers, Lyon, Montluel and Vienne

Le grand secours venu de la Guyenne
S'arrestera tout auprès de Poitiers:
Lyon rendu par Mont Luel[1] et Vienne,[2]
Et saccagez par tous gens des mestiers.[3]

CXII,Q24

*Interpretation*

The great aid coming from Guyenne will stop close to Poitiers. The liberation army will go back to Lyon via Montluel and Vienne, which will be ransacked by the soldiers.

[1] Montluel: main town of the canton of Ain. DHB.

[2] Main town of the district of the Isère, at the confluence of the Gère and the Rhône. DHB.

[3] The *métier* of arms, i.e. the profession of war, soldiering.

---

# The Occupation of Toulouse. The Desecration of Its Cathedral

Les cinq estranges entrez dedans le Temple,
Leur sang viendra la terre prophaner,
Aux Thoulousains sera bien dur exemple,
D'un qui viendra ses lois exterminer.

CIII,Q45

*Interpretation*

The five foreign leaders will enter the cathedral where their blood will profane the soil; this will be a fearful example to the inhabitants of Toulouse because of him who will come to annihilate their laws.

---

## Revolutionary Movements in the South-west of France. The Republic of Occitania

> Bazar,[1] Lestore, Condon, Auch, Agine,
> Esmeus par loix, querelle et monopole:
> Car Bourd, Tholose Bay mettra en ruyne,
> Renouveler voulant leur tauropole.[2]

CI,Q79

*Interpretation*

Bazas, Lectoure, Condom, Auch and Agen will rebel against the laws and political quarrels of Paris, for the war will ruin Bordeaux, Toulouse and Bayonne which will want to reconstitute a republic.

[1] For Bazas, main town of the Gironde district.
[2] Greek ταυροπόλος: worshipped or adored in Tauris, i.e. Diana or Hecate. DGF. The moon, symbol of the Republic.

---

## Communist Forces Crushed at Toulouse

> Vuydez, fuyez de Tholose les rouges,
> Du sacrifice faire expiation:
> Le chef du mal dessous l'ombre[1] des courges[2]
> Mort estrangler carne[3] omination.[4]

CIX,Q46

*Interpretation*

Abandon and flee from Toulouse, Communists! You will pay for your extortions. The leader who has brought misfortune under the appearance of foolishness will be put to death according to a human prophecy.

[1] *Sous ombre de*: i.e. under the pretext or appearance of. DL7V.
[2] Provençal *coucoureou*: imbecile, fool. DP.
[3] Latin *carnea lex*: law of human origin. DLLB.
[4] Latin *ominatio*: prophecy, presage. DLLB.

---

## The Crushing of the Revolutionary Forces at Nîmes and Toulouse

Quand lampe[1] ardente[2] de feu inextinguible,
Sera trouvée au temple des Vestales:[3]
Enfant[4] trouvé, feu, eau[5] passant par crible,[6]
Nismes eau périr, Tholose cheoir les hales.[7]

CIX,Q9

*Interpretation*

When an incendiary missile which provokes an inextinguishable fire will be found in Rome, something considered abominable, the war will be at its height, the revolutionaries will be overwhelmed and perish at Nîmes; the churches of Toulouse will crumble.

[1] Latin *lampas*: meteor, light in the sky. DLLB.
[2] Latin *ardens*: flaming, blazing. DLLB.
[3] At Rome the house of the Vestals was between the Forum and the Palatine, near the small temple of Vesta. DL7V.
[4] Latin *infans*: abominable. DLLB.
[5] Symbol of revolution, along with words like wave, rain and whirlwind.
[6] To overwhelm. DL7V.
[7] From Anglo-Saxon *halla*: palace, temple. DL7V.

---

## Destruction in the Aude by Missiles or Meteors. Internecine Struggles among Perpignan and Toulouse Revolutionaries. The Death of the Revolutionary Leader

Gorsan,[1] Narbonne, par le sel[2] advertir,[3]
Tucham,[4] la grâce Parpignan trahie,[5]
La ville rouge n'y voudra consentir,
Par haulte[6] voldrap[7] gris[8] vie faillie.

CVIII,Q22

*Interpretation*

Coursan and Narbonne will be damaged by a missile, because of revolutionaries, Perpignan will want to claim the honour [of the revolutionary movement] but Toulouse will oppose this, and the bloody one will be put to death by him who will bear a noble standard [the King of France, the liberator].

¹ Coursan: town in the Aude, 7 km from Narbonne on the N113.
² Greek σέλας: sort of meteor, blaze, light. DGF.
³ Latin *adverto*: I rage against, punish. DLLB.
⁴ The Revolt of the Tuchins: a peasant rebellion, 1382–84, in southern France (including *Toulouse*), during which chateaux were destroyed and many nobles and priests were massacred. DL7V. Nostradamus establishes parallel between the Tuchins and the revolutionary movements of south-west France.
⁵ Latin *rei sibi gratiam trahere*: to take the honour or credit for something. DLLB.
⁶ Latin *altus*: noble. DLLB.
⁷ Neologism from *volt*: image, idol, and *drapeau*, flag. DAFL.
⁸ Allusion to Robespierre's donkey: Robespierre's donkey, it was said, was the guillotine, drunk with the blood it had swallowed. DL7V.

---

# The Revolutionary Movements in South-west France. Their Pillage and Extortion. Revolt against Them

Encore seront les saincts temples pollus¹
Et expillez par Senat Tholosain:
Saturne deux trois² siècles revollus;³
Dans Avril, May, gens de nouveau levain.

CIX,Q72

*Interpretation*

The churches will be desecrated and ransacked again by the members of a Toulouse group. The era [of pillage] will return six centuries later [1982], then in April and May new people will rise up [to resist].

¹ Latin *polluo*: I profane. DLLB.
² For twice three, i.e. six.
³ Tuchin Revolt, 1382 + six centuries = 1982. Cf. CVIII,Q22.

---

# Organized Groups against the Communists

Contre les rouges sectes se banderont[1]
Feu, eau, fer, corde[2] par paix se minera[3]
Au point mourir ceux qui machineront,
Fors un que monde sur tout ruynera.

CIX,Q51

## Interpretation

Various groups will resist the Communist forces during the war and the revolution; the spirit of peace will weaken. The traitors will die except for one of them, who will bring ruin to the world.

[1] Make an effort to resist. DL7V.
[2] Latin cor, cordis: intelligence, wit, good sense. DLLB.
[3] To consume, deteriorate, progressively weaken. DL7V.

---

# The Revolution and the Sack of Toulouse

Pont et molins[1] en Decembre versez,
En si hault lieu montera la Garonne:[2]
Murs, édifices, Tholose renversez,
Qu'on ne saura son lieu autant matronne.

CIX,Q37

## Interpretation

The bridges and mills of Toulouse will be destroyed in December; the revolution will be so strong on the banks of the Garonne that the houses and public buildings will be destroyed so that even mothers of families will not recognize their homes.

[1] Ancient form of moulins, mills. DAFL.
[2] Flood, rain, water, waves, always symbolizing revolution.

---

# The Occupation of Carcassonne
# by the Russians

Aux lieux sacrez animaux veu à trixe,[1]
Avec celui qui n'osera le jour:
A Carcassonne pour disgrace propice,
Sera posé pour plus ample séjour.

CIX,Q71

## Interpretation

The Russians will be seen in the churches with the person who will not be bold enough to show himself in broad daylight. After a propitious disgrace he will establish himself for a greater period of time at Carcassonne.

[1] Greek θρίς, τρίχος: hair, fleece, pelt. DGF. Bears are heavy, large animals covered with *thick fur*. DL7V.

---

# The Alliance of Romania, England, Poland
# and East Germany. Their Struggle with the Moslems
# in the Mediterranean

La gent de Dace,[1] d'Angleterre, et Polonne,
Et de Boësme[2] feront nouvelle ligue:
Pour passer outre d'Hercules la colonne,[3]
Barcins,[4] Tyrrans dresser cruelle brigue.[5]

CV,Q51

## Interpretation

Romania, England, Poland and East Germany will form a new alliance, in order to go beyond Gibraltar [into the Mediterranean] and against the Moslems who will have instigated a cruel tumult so as to impose their tyranny.

[1] Dacia: ancient name for Romania. DHB.
[2] Bohemia: today part of Czechoslovakia. AVL.
[3] Pillars of Hercules: Gibraltar. DHB.
[4] Barcinus: powerful Carthaginian family whose leader was Hamilcar Barca, and other

members of which were Hannibal and Hasdrubal. Always sworn enemies of Rome. DHB.
As with the words 'Hannibal' and 'Punic', Nostradamus here refers to the Moslems.
⁵ Tumult. DAFL.

## The End of the War. Misery in Italy.
## Moslem Troops Arrive from the Danube and Malta.
## Their Setback in the Drôme Region

L'indigne¹ orné² craindra la grande fornaise,
L'esleu premier, des captifs n'en retourne:
Grand bas du monde, l'Itale non alaise³
Barb. Ister,⁴ Malte. Et le Buy⁵ ne retourne.

Presage 15, January

*Interpretation*

The notorious military leader will fear the great furnace. The first choice
will not be among the returning prisoners. The great power [USSR] will
be low in world status, Italy will undergo misfortune because of the
Moslems who come via the Danube and Malta. They will retreat in the
Drôme area.

¹ Latin *indignus*: infamous. DLLB.
² Latin *orno*: I equip, arm. DLLB.
³ Greek αἴσιος: happy. DGF.
⁴ Hister: ancient name for the Danube. DHB.
⁵ Le Buis: main town of the canton of the Drôme.

## The USSR and the War in Europe.
## The USSR and Turkey

Des régions subjectes à la Balance¹
Feront troubler les monts par grande guerre,
Captif tout sexe deu² et tout Bisance,
Qu'on criera à l'aube terre à terre.

CV,Q70

*Interpretation*

The regions subject to the USSR will come to trouble the mountains
[the Alps] with a major war and will take prisoners of both sexes through-

out Turkey, so that at dawn there will be cries from one country to another.

[1] Seventh sign of the Zodiac: the Egyptians consecrated Libra and Scorpio to the god of evil, Typhon (or Set) who, not content with this astronomical homage, also required the sacrifice of red-haired men. DL7V. There is thus a triple allusion to the seven Eastern Bloc countries; to the revolution (Typhon/Typhoon); and to the Reds.

[2] Contraction of *de le*. DAFL.

---

## Negotiations for the Entry of England into the Common Market, July 1970

La soeur aisnée de l'Isle Britannique,
Quinze ans[1] devant le frère aura naissance,
Par son promis moyennant verrifique,
Succedera au regne de balance.[2]

CIV,Q96

### Interpretation

The elder sister of Britain [USA] will succeed to Soviet power. Fifteen years earlier, the British brother will be born [in Europe] on condition of verifiable promises.

[1] 1–12 December 1969: the European Summit of the 'Six' at The Hague. The principle of British entry into the Common Market established, negotiations began in July 1970. On his return to Paris President Pompidou stated that this reunion had contributed to dispel *unjustified distrust* ('*promis verrifique*'). VCAHU. 1969 + 15 years = 1984, which is thus the turning point in the war and fall of the USSR.

[2] Cf. CV,Q70 and CV,Q61

---

## The War between the King of France and the USSR

L'enfant du Grand n'estant à sa naissance
Subjuguera les hauts monts Appenis,[1]
Fera trembler tous ceux de la balance,[2]
Et des monts feux jusques à Mont-Senis.

CV,Q61

## Interpretation

The heir of the great [monarchical power], being only at the beginning of his rule, will subjugate Italy, make all those in the USSR tremble, and will take the war as far as Mont-Cenis.

[1] Nostradamus by syncope removes one letter from '*Appenins*' (the Apennines) to make a rhyme with Mont-Cenis.

[2] Cf. CV,Q70 and CV,Q46.

---

# The Russian Army Beaten at Chambéry and in the Maurienne Area

Grande assemblée près du lac du Borget,[1]
Se raillieront près de Montmelian:[2]
Passant plus oultre pensifs feront projet,
Chambry, Moriane[3] combat Saint-Julian.[4]

CX,Q37

## Interpretation

Great armies will assemble near Lake Bourget and will regroup near Montmélian. Not being able to go further, the baffled military leaders will make plans and be beaten at Chambéry and St-Julien-de-Maurienne.

[1] Lake in Savoie, not far from Chambéry and Aix-les-Bains. DL7V.

[2] Town in Savoie, 15 km from Chambéry. DHB.

[3] Valley of the Maurienne: commands access to Italy by the Mont-Cenis pass.

[4] Village near St-Jean-de-Maurienne.

---

# Reconquest from Barcelona to Venice. The Defeat of the Moslem Troops. Their Retreat to Tunisia

De Barcelonne, de Gennes et Venise,
De la Secille peste Monet[1] unis:
Contre Barbare classe prendront la vise,[2]
Barbar poulsé bien loing jusqu'à Thunis.

CIX,Q42

*Interpretation*

From Barcelona and Genoa to Venice, from Sicily to Monaco, the pestilence will reign, and will reconnoitre the Moslem army and push it back as far as Tunisia.

[1] Monoeci Arx: Monaco. DLLB.
[2] *Visere copias hostium*: to reconnoitre the enemy army. DLLB.

---

# The Defeat of the Western Navy by the Russians. The Persecution of Clergy. The Victory of the West, in November

Navalle pugne[1] nuict[2] sera supérée,[3]
Le feu, aux naves à l'Occident ruine:
Rubriche[4] neusve, la grand nef,[5] colorée,
Ire a vaincu, et victoire, en bruine.[6]

CIX,QIOO

*Interpretation*

A naval battle will occur at night and the war will ruin the Western [US] Navy. A new Red Army will cause bloodshed at the Vatican, the vanquished will be overwhelmed, but will end by gaining victory in November.

[1] Latin *pugna*: fight between two armies, battle. DLLB.
[2] This quatrain has been attributed by commentators to the Battle of Trafalgar, which lasted from 11 a.m. to 5 p.m.! DL7V.
[3] Latin *supero*: I have the advantage (in war), I conquer. DLLB.
[4] Latin *ruber*: red. DLLB. Cf. CI,Q82 and CIV,Q37.
[5] Refers to the ship of the Catholic Church.
[6] Cf. CVI,Q25, the coup d'état of 18 Brumaire.

---

# THE LAST AND GREATEST OF THE KINGS OF FRANCE, 1983/6–1999

Nostradamus gives this king several names, titles or attributes which all suggest the idea of legitimacy:

1. *CHIREN*, anagram of HENRIC, from Latin Henricus, for Henri.
2. *The King of Blois*: Counts of Blois were descended from the family of Hugues Capet.[1]
3. *Le Coq*: the first medal upon which a rooster appears was minted in 1601, the year of Louis XIII's birth.[2]
4. *Hercule*: frequently Hercules is an exemplar of strength and courage.[3]

[1] DHB.
[2] L. A. de Gremilly: *The Cock*, Flammarion, 1958.
[3] DL7V.

---

# The King of France Enters Rome.
# The Alliance between the Pope and the King of France.

Le Grand Celtique entra dedans Rome
Menant amas d'exilez et bannis:
Le grand pasteur mettra à port[1] tout homme
Qui pour le Coq estoyent aux Alpes unis.

CVI,Q28

*Interpretation*

The great Frenchman will enter Rome leading many exiles and banished persons. The great Pope will shelter every man who helped the King of France in the Alps.

[1] Latin *portes*: shelter, retreat. *In portu esse*: to be out of danger. DLLB.

---

# The War of the King of France against Libya.
# The Latter Driven out from Hungary to Gibraltar

Par grand fureur le Roy Romain Belgique
Vexer voudra par phalange barbare:
Fureur grinssant[1] chassera gent Libyque,
Depuis Pannons[2] jusques Hercules[3] la hare.[4]

CV,Q13

*Interpretation*

Driven by great wrath, the King arrived from Rome will enter Belgium harassed by Moslem troops. In fury and anger he will pursue the Libyans and track them down from Hungary as far as Gibraltar.

[1] Figurative: to be angry. DL7V.
[2] Pannonia: ancient name for Hungary.
[3] The Pillars of Hercules: name given by the Ancients to the African and European sides of the Straits of Gibraltar.
[4] *Harer*: to track down, harass. DAFL.

---

## The King against the Revolutionaries. His Arrival in Provence

> Ce qu'en vivant le père n'avait sceu,
> Il acquerra ou par guerre ou par feu,
> Et combattra la sangsue[1] irritée,[2]
> Ou jouyra de son bien paternel
> Et favory du grand Dieu Eternel,
> Aura bien tost sa Province héritée.

Sixain 40

*Interpretation*

What his father never knew in his lifetime, war and fire will enable him to acquire, and he will combat sterile revolution. He will benefit from his father's property and, favourite of the Almighty, will soon inherit Provence.

[1] Revolution: the leech or bloodsucker.
[2] Latin *irritus*: useless, vain, sterile. DLLB.

---

## War in Norway, Romania and England. The French Leader's Role in Italy

> Norneigre[1] et Dace,[2] et l'isle Britannique,
> Par les unis frères seront vexées:[3]
> Le chef Romain issu du sang Gallique,
> Et les copies[4] aux forêts repoussées.

CVI,Q7

*Interpretation*

Norway, Romania and Great Britain will be damaged by the united allies [Soviet Union and the Warsaw Pact].[5] Then the Roman commander of French origin will drive back their troops through the forests.

[1] Anagram of NERIGON, to which Nostradamus adds *re* (by paragoge) – ancient name for Norway. DHB.

[2] Traces of Roman domination are still to be found there: the Wallachians and Moldavians call themselves Romanians. DHB. Romania.

[3] Latin *vexo*: I trouble, ill-treat. DLLB.

[4] Latin *copiae*: troops, army. DLLB.

[5] 'On 14 May 1955, the treaty of friendship, cooperation and mutual assistance, the Warsaw Pact, was concluded between the USSR, Albania, Hungary, Bulgaria, Poland, the GDR, Romania and Czechoslovakia. A *single* military command was instituted.' VCAHU. Note that Albania withdrew from the pact and that Romania is the most controversial of these.

---

# The Role of the Saudi 'TAG' Society in France's Liberation

Jamais par le découvrement[1] du jour,[2]
Ne parviendra au signe sceptrifère,
Que tous ses sièges ne soient en séjour,
Portant au Coq don du TAG[3] armifère.

CVIII,Q61

*Interpretation*

He will never attain monarchical power through the exposure [of his origins] as long as all the cities are not liberated when the TAG will offer its armaments to the King.

[1] Action of uncovering, exposure. DL.

[2] Figurative: what enlightens, serves to make one understand. DL7V.

[3] The Society of the Saudi Akkram Ojjeh, a good friend to France, is called the TAG and has its headquarters at Geneva.

# The King of France against the Russians.
# The Sack of the Balearics

Par le grand Prince limitrophe du Mans,[1]
Preux et vaillant chef de grand exercite:[2]
Par mer et terre de Gallois et Normans,[3]
Caspre[4] passer Barcelonne pillé Isle.

CVII,QIO

*Interpretation*

The great prince originating from Blois, who will be the valiant and
courageous leader of a great army, [will lead the war] by land and sea
between French and Russians, who since Barcelona will have reached
the Balearics in order to ransack them.

[1] The Loir-et-Cher, where Blois is situated, borders the Sarthe.
[2] Latin *exercitus*: army. DLLB.
[3] Or Northmen, men of the North. DHB. Nostradamus refers to the Russians, inhabiting the country of Aquila, the North Wind.
[4] Capraria: Cabrera, one of the Balearics, south of Majorca.

---

# Henri V Established at Avignon

Le Roy de Blois[1] en Avignon régner,
Une autre fois le peuple en monopole,
Dedans le Rosne par murs fera baigner
Jusques à cinq[2] le dernier près de Nole.[3]

CVIII,Q38

*Interpretation*

The King of Blois will govern in Avignon, which will serve as the French
people's capital; the Rhône will bathe the walls of his dwelling place.
He will be the last of five [Henri V] and will go almost as far as Nole.

[1] The Counts of Blois were descended from the family of *Hugues Capet*. DHB. Nostradamus thus stresses the Capetian connection of this king.
[2] Cf. '*Le Lorrain V*', Presage 76.
[3] Town in Italy, 37 km south-east of Capua. DHB.

# The Occupation of West Germany
# by the Warsaw Pact. Invasion via the Loire Valley

Le Roy de Bloys dans Avignon regner,
D'Amboise et seme[1] viendra le long de Lyndre:
Ongle à Poitiers, sainctes aisles ruyner,
Devant Boni.[2]

CVIII,Q52

### Interpretation

The King of Blois will rule in Avignon. The seven countries will come along the Indre as far as Amboise: [the Russian bear] will show his claws at Poitiers and will ruin the West's airforce, but before that he will have occupied Bonn.

[1] Sedme: from Latin *septimum*: seventh. DAFL. Russia and the six other Warsaw Pact countries.
[2] Latin *Bonna*: Bonn. DLLB. Capital of West Germany.

---

# Avignon, Capital of France

Le grand empire sera tost translaté
En lieu petit qui bientost viendra croistre
Lieu bien infime d'exiguë comté[1]
Où au milieu viendra poser son sceptre.

CI,Q32

### Interpretation

The great empire [French] will be transferred to a small place which will soon grow. A place as small as a *comté* where [the King] will come and establish his power.

[1] Comtat Venaissin. This area is sometimes (wrongly) called the *comtat* of Avignon. DHB.

# Avignon, Capital of France

Dans Avignon tout le chef de l'Empire
Fera arrest pour Paris désolé:
Tricast[1] tiendra l'Annibalique[2] ire,
Lyon par change sera mal consolé.

CIII,Q93

## Interpretation

The capital will be moved to Avignon because Paris will be destroyed.
The Tricastin will be the cause of Moslem anger. Lyon will be very
upset by the change of capital.

[1] Tricastin: in the Bas-Dauphiné area, redivided between the departments of the
Drôme (cantons of St Paul-Trois Châteaux, Grignan and Pierrelatte) and the Vaucluse
(canton of Bollène). DL7V. This is where the uranium plant, financed by Iran, is
situated.
[2] Hannibal, Carthaginian general, son of Hamilcar. His father made him swear undying
enmity to Rome from his childhood days. DHB. Nostradamus uses Carthaginian, Hannibal or Punic to denote the Moslem world.

---

# Great Change in France.
# The Capital in Provence

Le changement sera fort difficile,
Cité, province au change gain sera:
Coeur haut, prudent mis, chassé luy habile,
Mer, terre, peuple son estat changera.

CIV,Q21

## Interpretation

Change will be very painful. The province [or Provence] will gain by the
change of capital. The [King] with noble and wise heart will attain power
after driving off [the enemy] through his skill; he will change the condition of people upon land and sea.

# The Installation of the King in Avignon.
# Offers from Other Cities Declined

En lieu libere[1] tendra son pavillon[2]
Et ne voudra en citez prendre place:
Aix, Carpen, l'Isle[3] volce,[4] mont Cavaillon,
Par tout ces lieux abolira sa trasse.

CV,Q76

## Interpretation

In a liberated place he will establish residence and will not wish to install himself in the following towns: Aix, Carpentras, L'Isle-sur-Sorgue, Cavaillon, nor to be any longer in the Languedoc, where he will suppress all traces of his passing.

[1] Avignon remained a possession of the Holy See until 1791 when it was reunited with France at the same time as the Comtat Venaissin. This reunion was confirmed by the Treaty of Tolentino, 1797. DHB.

[2] Portable tentlike dwelling, round or square, once used by campaigning troops. DL7V.

[3] L'Isle-sur-Sorgue: main town of the canton of Vaucluse, 22 km east of Avignon. DHB.

[4] Volces: Gallic tribe from the Narbonne area, which used to occupy the greater part of the Languedoc. DHB.

---

# Henri V Brings Victory and Reigns
# over France and Italy

Premier en Gaule, premier en Romanie,
Par mer et terre aux Anglais et Paris
Merveilleux faits par celle grand mesnie[1]
Violant,[2] terax[3] perdra le NORLARIS

CVIII,Q60

## Interpretation

[Henri V] will be the first person in France and Italy. By land and sea, for the English and Parisians, exceptional deeds will be accomplished by this great house [the Bourbons] and the man from Lorraine will dispose of the monster [the Russian bear] by attacking it.

¹ From *mansionem: maison* (house). The group inhabiting the house, family. DAFL.
² Latin *violo*: I do violence to, attack someone. DLLB.
³ Greek τέρας: prodigy, monster. DGF.

# Henri V, Descendant of the Capets and Guises. His Military Exploits on the Black Sea

L'ensevely sortira du tombeau,
Fera de chaînes lier le fort du pont,[1]
Empoisonné avec oeufs du Barbeau,[2]
Grand de Lorraine par le Marquis[3] du Pont.[4]

CVII,Q24

## Interpretation

The descendant of the buried Capet [Louis XVI] will come out of the shadow and put an end to the maritime power [of the Russians] which will be poisoned by this descendant of the Guises. The great Lorrainian will be the guarantor of the borders of the Black Sea.

¹ Greek ποντός: sea. DGF.
² Bar-le-Duc, the Duke of Guise's home ground. The town's coat of arms consisted of two barbels (mullet). DL7V.
³ Nobleman entrusted to guard the marches or frontier areas, originally a form of warlord.
⁴ Kingdom of Pontus: in southern part of Asia Minor, on the edge of the Euxine (Black Sea). DL7V. Now Armenia.

# The Lorrainian V Puts an End to Dissensions

Par le legat[1] du terrestre et marin,
La grande Cape a tout s'accomoder:[2]
Estre à l'escoute tacite LORVARIN,[3]
Qu'à son advis ne voudra accorder.

Presage 76, October

## Interpretation

Because of the ambassador of the land and sea power, the great Capetian will be reconciled with everyone: he will know how to listen to them without saying anything, the Lorrainian, so that they will be only too ready to agree with his view.

[1] Latin *legatus*: envoy, deputy, ambassador. DLLB.
[2] To come to agreement, reconcile. DL7V.
[3] Duchy of Lorraine: the first Duke was Frederick of Alsace, related to Hugues Capet. DHB. Nostradamus calls Henri V by this epithet to stress his Capetian antecedents. LORVARIN = anagram of LORRAIN V.

## The Liberation of the Vatican by Henri V

Par le[1] cinquiesme et un grand Herculès,
Viendront le temple[2] ouvrir de main bellique:
Un Clément, Jule[3] et Ascans[4] reculés,
Lespe,[5] clef[6] aigle, n'eurent onc si grand picque.

CX,Q27

*Interpretation*

Through the fifth [Henri] who will also be a great and strong person, the Vatican will be opened again by military means. A pope named Clement will be elected, the two Germanys having retreated. Spain and the papacy will never have had so great an attack by a military force [eagle].

[1] Some editions have *Carle* instead of *Par le*.
[2] Poetic term for the Catholic Church. DL7V.
[3] Jülich: town now in West Germany.
[4] One of the oldest German families, branch of the Anhalts, who provided Brandenburg and Saxe with rulers. DHB. Now part of East Germany.
[5] Some editions give *L'Espagne* instead of Lespe.
[6] Keys: attributes of the papacy, and gifts bestowed by popes upon other sovereigns on certain ceremonial or festive occasions.

## The King of France, Italy and Denmark. The Liberation of Italy and the Adriatic

Hercules[1] Roy de Rome et d'Annemarc,
De Gaule trois le Guion[2] surnommé:
Trembler l'Itale et l'unde de Sainct Marc.[3]
Premier sur tous Monarque renommé.

CIX,Q33

## Interpretation

Hercules [the King of France] will be King of Rome and Denmark. He will be given the name 'Leader of France' by three rulers [military or party]. Italy and the Adriatic Sea will tremble. First among all heads of state, he will be a renowned monarch.

[1] Nostradamus dubs the last King Hercules to signify his strength and the 'labours' he must accomplish.

[2] Guide, leader. DAFL.

[3] Lion of St Mark: winged lion, symbol of the Venetian Republic, whose patron is St Mark. DHB.

---

# The Reconquest of France.
# The Defeat of a Warsaw Pact Leader.
# The Role of the Tank Divisions

Les ennemis du fort bien esloignez,
Par chariots conduict le bastion:
Par sur les murs de Bourges esgrongnez[1]
Quand Hercules battra l'Haemathion.[2]

CIX,Q93

## Interpretation

Enemies will be driven back and the defence assured because of tanks; they will be cut to pieces at Bourges when the King of France defeats the [East] German commander.

[1] *Esgruignier*: to reduce to pieces, cut apart. DAFL.
[2] Word which always denotes a German leader. Cf. CX,Q7.

---

# The King of France Acknowledged.
# His Victory over the German Leader.
# The Submission of the Moslem World

Roy salué Victeur, Imperateur,[1]
La foy faussée le Royal faict cogneu:
Sang Mathien. Roy faict superateur[2]
De gent superbe[3] humble par pleurs venu.

Presage 38, April

*Interpretation*

The king will be hailed as conqueror and leader, after a piece of treachery his royal origin will be known. He will be victor through the blood of a German leader. The Moslems will become humble because of their misfortunes.

[1] Latin *imperator:* commander, chief. DLLB.
[2] Latin *superator:* victor. DLLB.
[3] Latin *superbes:* violent, tyrannical, proud. DLLB. Cf. CII,Q79: '*La gent cruelle et fière.*'

---

# The War in Greece. The Burning of Istanbul by the King of France

La legion[1] dans la marine classe
Calcine,[2] Magne,[3] souphre et poix[4] bruslera,
Le long repos de l'asseurée place,
Port Selin,[5] Hercle feu les consumera.

CIV,Q23

*Interpretation*

A seaborne army will set fire to Thrace and the Morea, after long peace in these areas, Hercule [the King of France] will set the Moslem port [Istanbul] ablaze.

[1] Latin *legio:* troops, army. DLLB.
[2] Chalcedon: town in Bithynia, on the Thracian Bosphorus facing Byzantium (Istanbul). DHB.
[3] Magnia: area of the Morea, Greece. DHB.
[4] Mineralogy: bitumens etc. DL7V. Probably reference to napalm.
[5] Greek Σελήνη:the moon. DGF. The Moslem crescent.

# The Restoration of a Bourbon.
# The End of the Revolutionary System

D'un rond,[1] d'un lis[2] naistra un si grand Prince,
Bien tost, et tard venu dans sa Province,[3]
Saturne en Libra en exaltation:[4]
Maison de Venus en decroissante force,
Dame en apres masculin soubs l'escorce,[5]
Pour maintenir, l'heureux sang de Bourbon.

Sixain 4

*Interpretation*

From a Capet, from a lily [of the Bourbons] a very great Prince will be
born, coming early and late into his Provence, the time of justice having
risen again: the established rule of lies and lust seeing its strength decrease after the reign of the Republic under its masculine exterior, in
order to maintain the fortunate blood of the Bourbon.

[1] Latin *rota*: the chariot of the sun. DLLB. Symbol of the Capets.
[2] The royal emblem. DL7V.
[3] The Roman province: Provence. DLLB.
[4] Latin *exalto*: I raise up again, exalt. DLLB.
[5] Appearance, exterior. DL7V.

---

# The Death of the Head of State.
# His Replacement by a Young Prince

La mort subite du premier personnage
Aura changé et mis un autre au règne:
Tost, tard venu à si haut et bas aage,
Que terre et mer faudra qu'on le craingne.

CIV,QI4

*Interpretation*

The sudden death of the chief of state will cause a change and put
another in power, one who has come both early and late, so young
despite his ancient descent that he must be feared by land and sea.

# Henri V – a World Leader

Un chef du monde le grand CHIREN[1] sera:
PLUS OULTRE apres aymé craint redoubté:
Son bruit et los les cieux surpassera,
Et du seul titre Victeur fort contenté.

CVI,Q70

*Interpretation*

The great Henri will be a world leader. More and more he will be loved, feared and dreaded. His renown and praise will reach the skies and he will be well content with the single title of Victor.

[1] Anagram of HENRIC, from Latin Henricus: Henri.

---

# Henri V, King of France

Le grand CHYREN soy saisir d'Avignon,[1]
De Rome lettres en miel plein d'amertume
Lettre ambassade partir de Chanignon,[2]
Carpentras pris par duc noir rouge plume.

CIX,Q41

*Interpretation*

Great Henri will seize Avignon when he receives bitter letters from Rome; a diplomatic mission will leave from Canino, when Carpentras is taken by a black general of the red persuasion.

[1] Cf. *'En Avignon tout le chef de l'Empire.'*
[2] Gallicization of the Italian town of Canino.

# The Defeat of the Red Army in Italy.
# The Enemy Leader a Prisoner of King Henri

Le grand mené captif d'estrange terre,
D'or enchaîné au Roy CHYREN offert:
Qui dans Ausone[1] Milan perdra la guerre,
Et tout son ost[2] mis a feu et a fer.

CIV,Q34

## Interpretation

The great head of a foreign country [Russia?] will be taken prisoner and presented with his gold to King Henri. In Italy, at Milan, this man will lose the war and all his army will be surrendered to war's fire and iron.

[1] Latin Ausonia: ancient district of Italy, by extension Italy. DLLB.
[2] Army, camp. DAFL.

---

# The Invasion of Austria, Germany and France.
# The Defeat of the Russo–Moslem Troops in the Alps

Dans le Dannube et du Rhin viendra boire,
Le grand Chameau[1] ne s'en repentira:
Trembler du Rosne, et plus fort ceux de Loire,
Et pres des Alpes Coq le ruinera.

CV,Q68

## Interpretation

The great Russo–Moslem commander will come to drink from the Danube and Rhine. Those who dwell beside the Rhône will tremble and those by the Loire still more so. Then, near the Alps, the French King will ruin him.

[1] Camels seem to have originated in central Asia. The most useful transport animal of central Asia (Turkestan, Afghanistan, Mongolia, southern Siberia, northern Persia). DL7V. Nostradamus indicates here a Russo–Moslem commander. Cf. CX,Q37.

# The End of the Revolution.
# The King Received at Aix and Crowned at Rheims

L'an que Saturne en eau sera conjoinct,
Avecques Sol, le Roy fort et puissant,
A Reims et Aix sera receu et oingt,
Après conquestes meurtrira innocens.

CIV,Q86

*Interpretation*

The year the Revolution and the monarchy are joined, the strong and powerful King will be received at Aix and anointed at Rheims, after rendering his enemies inoffensive by killing them.

---

# The King of France Ends the War.
# He Liberates the South-west

Le grand puisnay fera fin de la guerre,
Aux dieux assemble les excusez:[1]
Cahors, Moissac iront loin de la serre[2]
Refus[3] Lectore, les Agenois razez.

CVII,Q12

*Interpretation*

The younger [Henri V born after Juan Carlos I] will end the war and by God's grace reassemble those who had been exiled. These latter will liberate Cahors and Moissac. The occupiers of Lectoure will be driven back and Agen will be razed.

[1] Latin *excussus*: banished, exiled, rejected. DLLB.
[2] Action of grasping, submitting to pressure. DL7V.
[3] Latin *refusus*: pushing or driving back. DLLB.

# The Great King Raises a Liberation Army.
## Fighting in the Languedoc

Le Grand Monarque que fera compagnie
Avec deux Roys unis par amitié:
O quel souspir fera la grand mesgnie[1]
Enfans Narbon à l'entour, quelle pitié!

CI,Q99

*Interpretation*

The great King will raise an army. The two Kings [France and Spain] will be united by friendship. O what a sigh [of relief] the great army will utter. Pity the children in the Narbonne area!

[1] Troop. DAFL.

---

# The King of France's Headquarters
## in the Ariège

Moyne moynesse d'enfant[1] mort exposé,
Mourir par ourse et ravy par verrier[2]
Par Fois et Pamyes le camp sera posé,
Contre Tholose Carcass dresser forrier.[3]

CIX,Q10

*Interpretation*

A monk and a nun will see a child threatened with death. It will be put to death by the Russians after being captured by an Italian leader. The liberation army's camp will be set up in the Ariège and an officer sent by the King will rise up against [occupied] Toulouse and Carcassonne.

[1] Only events will reveal the identity of the child in question.
[2] The great glassworks flourished first under the Romans, then in medieval Italy. EU.
[3] Officer who preceded a travelling ruler; his duties involved arranging lodging for the retinue. DL7V.

# The King of France Arrives in the Pyrenees.
## The Monarchy and the End of Universal Suffrage

Dans Fois[1] entrez Roy cerulée[2] Turban,
Et régnera moins evolu[3] Saturne:
Roy Turban blanc Bisance coeur ban,[4]
Sol, Mars, Mercure[5] près la hurne.[6]

CIX,Q73

*Interpretation*

The King of France, with the blue emblem, will reign a short time. The Turkish leader in the white turban will be banished from his heart; the monarchy will rule after the war and the disappearance of universal suffrage.

[1] Principal town of Navarre.
[2] Azure, blue. DAFL. Colour of the dukes of France. DL7V.
[3] Latin *evolutus*: elapsed, passed. DLLB.
[4] Noun from bannir, to banish, ban. DL7V.
[5] God of thieves. DL7V.
[6] The urn, symbol of universal suffrage.

---

## Liberation from the Pyrenees to Rome

Autour des Monts Pyrénées grand amas,
De gent estrange secourir Roy nouveau:
Près de Garonne du grand temple du Mas[1]
Un Romain chef le craindra dedans l'eau.

CVI,QI

*Interpretation*

Large numbers of foreign [American] troops will be massed around the Pyrenees and will come to the new King's aid, near Mas-d'Agenais in the Garonne, which a leader in Rome ought to fear during the revolution.

[1] Mas-d'Agenais: main town of the canton of Lot-et-Garonne, on the Garonne. In this neighbourhood the Gallo-Roman temple of Vernemet is thought to lie. DL7V.

# The Reconquest from Spain to Italy

Dessus Jonchère[1] du dangereux passage,
Fera passer le posthume[2] sa bande,[3]
Les monts Pyrens passer hors son bagage,[4]
De parpignan courira[5] Duc[6] à Tende.[7]

CX,QII

## Interpretation

Over the dangerous pass of Junquera, the last [of the Bourbons] will lead his troops and will cross the Pyrenees with his armaments and pursue the [enemy] general as far as the Tende Pass.

[1] Gallicization of Junquera: town in Spain (Catalonia) at the southern foot of the Alberas. DL7V.
[2] Latin *posthumus*: the last, born after his father's death. DLLB.
[3] Army organized to fight under a single flag. DL7V.
[4] For *bague* (ring, weapon). DAFL.
[5] To pursue, try to catch up with and seize.
[6] Latin *dux*: commander of an army, general. DLLB.
[7] One of the passes in the Alpes-Maritimes, between Nice and Coni. DHB.

---

# The Young Prince Restores Peace.
# His Coronation

Le jeune prince accusé faussement,
Mettra en trouble le camp[1] et en querelles:
Meurtry le chef pour le soustenement[2]
Sceptre appaiser: puis guerir escrouëlles.[3]

CIV,QIO

## Interpretation

The young prince will be wrongly accused, and will bring controversy and dismay upon the territory. He will kill the [enemy] commander courageously, will bring back peace through his power, and will then heal the scrofula [he will be crowned.]

[1] Latin *campus*: territory. DLLB.
[2] Latin, *sustinentia*: patience, courage. DLLB.
[3] Kings of France (and England) were supposed to be able to heal scrofula ('the King's

evil'). In France the king, after the coronation ceremony, would for the first time touch sufferers from scrofula. Laying hands upon them he would say: 'The King touches you, may God cure you.' This custom continued until Louis XIV, who touched almost 2000 sufferers. DL7V.

---

## The King Crowned by the Pope.
## His Struggle against the Left-wing Forces in Italy

Au Roy l'Augur[1] sur le chef la main mettre,
Viendra prier pour la paix Italique:
A la main gauche viendra changer de sceptre,[2]
De Roy viendra Empereur pacifique.

CV,Q6

*Interpretation*

The Pope will come to lay his hand on the King's head [to crown him] and to beg him to restore peace in Italy. He will change the power in the hands of the left and this King will become a peaceful sovereign.

[1] Latin for prophet. DLLB. Note capital A. Used by Nostradamus to denote the Pope. Cf. CII,Q36. '*Du grand prophète . . .*'
[2] Absolute authority. DL7V.

---

## The Death of the French Republic in the War.
## The End of the Great Republics: the USSR

Au menu peuple par débats et querelles,
Et par les femmes et défunts grande guerre:
Mort d'une Grande. Celebrer escrouëlles.
Plus grandes Dames expulsées de la terre.

Presage 10, May

*Interpretation*

The little people [proletariat] will be agitated by debates and quarrels because of the womenfolk and the deaths in the great war. The Republic ['*une grande*' = Marianne, French Republican symbol] will die. The coronation will be celebrated and the greatest Republics [e.g. the USSR] will be driven from the earth.

---

## The End of the Bolshevik Revolution

De FLORE[1] issuë de sa mort sera cause,
Un temps devant par jeusne et vieille bueyre[2]
Car les trois Lys luy feront telle pause,
Par son fruit sauve comme chair cruë mueyre.[3]

CVIII,QI8

*Interpretation*

Its Western origin will cause its [the Revolution's] death, due just previously to a renewed yet old confusion, for the three lilies [of the Bourbons] will halt it so that its rescued child [Louis XVII] will be transmuted into living flesh.

[1] Wife of Zephyrus, the West Wind.
[2] Provençal: mixture, confusion. DP.
[3] *Muer:* to change. DAFL.

---

## The Capetian Origin of the King.
## The King Drives out the Moslems. The King Returns the Church to its Original State

De sang Troyen naistra coeur Germanique,
Qui deviendra en si haute puissance:
Hors chassera gent estrange Arabique,
Tournant l'Eglise en pristine prééminence.

CV,Q74

*Interpretation*

Of Capetian blood, the king will be born with pro-German sentiments and will become so powerful that he will chase the Moslems from France and restore the Catholic Church to its former eminence.

---

# The Liberation of the Arabs' Christian Prisoners by Henri V

La barbe crespe et noire par engin[1]
Subjuguera la gent cruelle et fière:
Un grand Chyren ostera du longin[2]
Tous les captifs par Seline bannière.

CII,Q79

## Interpretation

He will subdue by his intelligence the proud and cruel race with the curly black beards. The great Henri will free from afar all the prisoners of the Crescent banner.

[1] Latin *ingenium*: intelligence, wit. DLLB.
[2] Latin *longinque*: from far off. DLLB.

---

# The King of Monaco. The Fall of the Warsaw Pact

Dedans Monech[1] le Coq sera receu,
Le Cardinal de France apparoistra:
Par Logarion[2] Romain sera deceu?
Foiblesse à l'Aigle, et force au Coq naistra.

CVIII,Q4

## Interpretation

The king will be received at Monaco; a French cardinal will appear. The Roman leader [the Pope] will be disappointed by the speeches of the British leader, the Eagle [Warsaw Pact] will weaken and the king's power begin to show itself.

[1] Monaco. DHB.
[2] Neologism from two Greek words λογος: speech, word, and Αριων: Arion, the name of the horse Neptune with his trident caused to leap from the earth. DL7V. Nostradamus always refers to England via Neptune and his trident.

## The King's Landing at Monaco.
## He Installs His Chief of Staff at Antibes,
## and he Drives off the Moslem Troops

Grand roy viendra prendre port près de Nisse
Le grand empire de la mort si en fera
Aux Antipolles[1] posera son genisse[2]
Par mer la Pille[3] tout esvanouyra.

CX,Q87

*Interpretation*

The great king will disembark near Nice [Monaco] and will act against
the great [Soviet] empire, he will reveal his spirit at Antibes and drive
out the ravagers of the sea.

[1] Antipolis: Antibes. DHB.
[2] For *génie*, by paragoge, for the rhyme.
[3] Cf. CII,Q4.

---

## The Reconquest as far as Israel

Dans peu de temps Medecin du grand mal,
Et la Sangsuë[1] d'ordre et rang inégal,
Mettront le feu à la branche d'Olive,[2]
Poste[3] courir,[4] d'un et d'autre costé,
Et par tel feu leur Empire accosté
Se ralumant du franc finy salive.[5]

Sixain 30

*Interpretation*

In a short time he will bring the remedy for the great catastrophe [the
Third World War], and the countries of the Revolution [Eastern Bloc],
unequal in nature and rank, will carry the war into Israel; then he will
pursue them from their positions on all sides and the [Soviet] Empire
will be hit by the fire of war, which when lit will end the regime of
political speeches in France.

[1] Leech, drinker of blood.
[2] Mount of Olives, i.e. Jerusalem, and Israel by extension. DL7V.

³ Position. DAFL.
⁴ To pursue, chase out. DL7V.
⁵ Allusion to electoral campaign speeches.

# Great Henri and the Moslems.
## A Spanish Army Aids Israel

Soubs la couleur du traicté mariage,
Fait magnanime par grand Chyren[1] selin:[2]
Quintin, Arras recouvrez au voyage,
D'Espagnols faict second banc[3] macelin.[4]

CVIII,Q54

*Interpretation*

Under the pretext of an alliance treaty, great Henri will take a magnanimous attitude towards the Moslems. St-Quentin and Arras will be liberated in the course of his journeying. And a second exploit of war will be accomplished by the Spanish in Israel.

¹ Anagram of HENRICUS, Henri.
² Greek Σελήνη: the moon. DGF. The Moslem crescent.
³ Latin *bancus*: fish of uncertain species. DLLB.
⁴ Latin *macellum*: market (where one sells *fish* etc.) DLLB. Allusion to the Holy City, Christianity's starting point. Cf. Le Basacle, Sixain 31.

# Rivalry between the Kings of France and Spain.
## The Fall of the Moslem Forces. The Liberation of England and Italy

Entre les deux monarques eslongnez,
Lorsque le Sol par Selin[1] clair perdue:
Simulte[2] grande entre deux indignez,
Qu'aux Isles et Sienne la liberté, rendue.

CVI,Q58

*Interpretation*

Between the two kings [France and Spain] who will be far away from each other, when the Bourbon makes the Crescent's forces lose their lustre [power], there will be a great rivalry, unworthy of them, when the British Isles and Italy will be liberated.

[1] Greek Σελήνη: moon, moonlight. DGF.
[2] Latin *simultas*: rivalry. DLLB.

---

## The Liberation of Italy by the King of France. His Fight against the Moslem Forces

SELIN[1] Monarque l'Italie pacifique,
Regnes unis, Roy Chrestien du monde:
Mourant voudra coucher en terre blésique,[2]
Après pyrates avoir chassé de l'onde.

CIV,Q77

*Interpretation*

The King of France will bring back peace to Italy by defeating the Moslems; the countries will unite. He will be a Christian world ruler, and ask to be buried at Blois, after chasing the Moslem fleets from the seas.

[1] Greek Σελήνη: the moon. DGF. Denotes Moslem crescent.
[2] For Blaisois or Blésois: small region with Blois as its capital. DHB.

---

## Secession in Italy. The King of France's Assistance

Crier victoire du grand Selin[1] Croissant,
Par les Romains sera l'Aigle clamé,
Ticcin, Milan, et Gennes ny consent,
Puis par eux mesmes Basil[2] grand réclamé.

CVI,Q78

*Interpretation*

Victory over the Moslems will be announced with jubilation. The Romans will call the Eagle [Americans] to their aid. Ticino and northern

Italy will refuse this assistance, then they will call back the great king [of France].

¹ Greek Σελήνη: the moon. DGF. Denotes Moslem crescent.
² Greek βασιλεύς: king. DGF.

---

# John-Paul II's Successor.
## The Alliance between the Pope and the King of France

> Nouveau esleu patron du grand vaisseau,¹
> Verra long temps briller le cler flambeau
> Qui sert de lampe² à ce grand territoire,
> Et auquel temps armez sous son nom,
> Joinctes à celles de l'heureux de Bourbon
> Levant, Ponant, et Couchant sa mémoire.
>
> Sixain 15

### Interpretation

When a new commander of the great vessel of the Church is elected, this bright torch which will serve as symbol of life on earth will be seen shining for a long time. At this period armies will be reunited under his name and allied to those of the King of France, whose memory will remain in the Eastern countries, the Arab and African countries and in America.

¹ St Peter's boat.
² Metaphorical, source of light or of life. DL7V.

---

# The Quarrel between the Three Great Ones
## (USA, USSR and China). The End of the Reign
## of the King of France

> Icy dedans se parachevera
> Les trois Grands hors¹ le BON BOURG sera loing:
> Encontre d'eux l'un d'eux conspirera,
> Au bout du mois on verra le besoin.²
>
> Presage 44, October

## Interpretation

Here [in France] his reign will end. The three great powers [USA, USSR and China] will hatch plots and the Bourbon will be far away. One of the three [China] will conspire against the two others and, at the end of October, her work will be seen.

[1] For *horde*: machination, ruse. DAFL.
[2] *Besogne* (fem. form of *besoin*) = work, labour. DL7V.

---

# The End of Protestantism in Europe.
# The Death of the Great King

Apparoistra temple[1] luisant orné[2]
La lampe et cierge[3] à Borne[4] et Breteuil:[5]
Pour la Lucerne[6] le canton destorné,[7]
Quand on verra le grand Coq au cercueil.

CVIII,Q5

## Interpretation

The Catholic Church will be seen shining and honoured; masses will be said in Holland and Picardy. In Switzerland religion will change when the great king dies.

[1] Poetic term for the Catholic Church. DL7V.
[2] Latin *ornatus*: distinguished, honoured. DLLB.
[3] Allusion to the lamp and candles lit on the altar during mass.
[4] Village in the Netherlands. DL7V. A country with a Protestant majority.
[5] Main town of the Oise canton, near the source of the *Noye*. DL7V. In Picardy.
[6] Swiss town 94 km south-east of *Basle*. DHB.
[7] To change direction. DL7V. Nostradamus here describes the end of the Protestant 'heresy', by mentioning the precise geographical areas connected directly with the life of Calvin. 'John Calvin, founder of Protestantism in France, was born at *Noyon* in Picardy in 1509 and died at Geneva in 1564. In 1534 he retired to Strasbourg, then to *Basle*. In this town he finished his book in 1535. At the same time he occupied himself with propagating his doctrine; he corresponded with France, the *Netherlands*, Scotland, England, Poland.' DL7V.

# The King of France Welcomed in Cairo

Les vieux chemins seront tous embellis.
L'on passera à Memphis[1] somentrées:[2]
Le Grand Mercure[2] d'Hercules fleur de lys,
Faisant trembler terre, mer et contrées.

CX,Q79

*Interpretation*

The old roads will be decorated for the journey to Cairo[4] whose population will have been told about the powerful king of the fleur de lis, who will make several countries tremble by land and sea.

[1] Town of ancient Egypt, on left bank of the Nile, south of the famous Gizeh pyramids. When all of Egypt was reunited into a single kingdom, it was for a while the capital. DHB.

[2] *Somondre* or *semondre*: to warn. DAFL.

[3] Represented as a handsome young man. DHB.

[4] Cf. cv,Q81.

---

# The King of France in Egypt.
# The Fall of the Berlin Wall. The Russians in Paris in Seven Days

L'oyseau Royal sur la cité solaire[1]
Sept mois devant fera nocturne augure:
Mur d'Orient cherra tonnerre esclaire,
Sept jours aux portes les ennemis à l'heure.

CV,Q81

*Interpretation*

The king, in Cairo, will give a gloomy warning, seven months before [the end of the war]. The wall of East [Berlin] will fall under the thunder and fire of war, as will the enemies who had reached Paris in seven days.

[1] Latin Solis Urbs: Heliopolis. DLLB. Heliopolis, i.e. town of the sun, is 11 km north-east of Cairo. DHB.

# THE IMPORTANT ROLE OF SOUTH AFRICA
# IN THE THIRD WORLD WAR

## The USSR and the Warsaw Pact against South Africa.
## Fighting in Palestine

Tost l'Éléphant[1] de toutes parts verra
Quand pourvoyeur au Griffon[2] se joindra,
Sa ruine proche, et Mars qui toujours gronde:
Fera grands faits auprès de terre saincte,
Grands estendars[3] sur la terre et sur l'onde,
Si[4] la nef a esté de deux frères enceinte.

Sixain 56

*Interpretation*

South Africa will see [things happen] on all sides when the supplier
[Russia] joins up with the Warsaw Pact. Her ruin approaches and the
war which always rumbles will cause great upheavals near the Holy Land
[Israel]. By land and sea there will be great military forces when the
Church has given birth to two brothers. [John-Paul I and John-Paul II.]

---

[1] Olifant (from Latin *elephantus*: elephant). Name given to several mountains and rivers
in southern Africa, after the elephants the first Europeans encountered there. The Olifant
mountains are in the western part of Cape Colony, near a little river, the Olifant, which
flows into the Atlantic. DL7V.
[2] Cf. CX,Q86 '*Comme un gryphon viendra le Roi d'Europe*'.
[3] Battle flag. DL7V.
[4] Latin: when, at such time as. DLLB.

---

# Eastern Europe and the South African Army

Le Griffon[1] se peut apprester
Pour à l'ennemy resister,
Et renforcer bien son armée,
Autrement l'Elephant[2] viendra
Qui d'un abord le surprendra,
Six cens et huict, mer enflammée.

Sixain 29

*Interpretation*

Eastern Europe [Warsaw Pact] can prepare itself to resist the enemy and reinforce its army well, for the troops from South Africa will come and surprise it.

[1] Cf. CX,Q86 and Sixain 56.
[2] Cf. Sixain 56.

---

## The Defeat of the Eastern Bloc

> Le pourvoyeur du monstre sans pareil,
> Se fera voir ainsi que le Soleil,
> Montant le long la ligne Méridienne,
> En poursuivant l'Éléphant et le loup,[1]
> Nul Empereur ne fit jamais tel coup,
> Et rien plus pis à ce Prince n'advienne.
>
> Sixain 39

*Interpretation*

The supplier [Russia] of a scourge without equal will come to the fore at the same time as the Bourbon, following along the meridian, pursuing South Africa and Germany. No Emperor [e.g. Hitler] ever succeeded in such a coup, but nothing worse could happen to this leader.

[1] South Africa (the Cape) and Germany are on the same meridian.

---

# THE END OF WESTERN CIVILIZATION AND THE WARS OF THE ANTICHRIST

## The Holy See Moves

> Par la puissance des trois Roys temporels,
> En autre lieu sera mis le saint-siège:
> Où la substance de l'esprit corporel,[1]
> Sera remis et reçu pour vray siège.
>
> CVIII,Q99

*Interpretation*

Because of the power of three leaders, the Holy See will be installed in another place [than the Vatican] and mass will be celebrated once again there.

[1] *Corporal*: piece of sacred linen the priest lays upon the altar and on which the chalice and host are placed during mass. Originally represented Christ's shroud, and thus was far larger than today's version. DL7V.

---

# John-Paul's Successor Is Installed and Dies on Monte Aventino

Le penultième du surnom de prophète,[1]
Prendra Diane[2] pour son jour et repos:
Loing vaguera[3] par frenetique teste,[4]
En delivrant un grand peuple d'impos.

CII,Q28

*Interpretation*

The penultimate pope will establish himself upon Monte Aventino and die there, the throne of St Peter will be vacant because of a mad leader come from afar, who will have delivered a great people [the Chinese] from taxation.

[1] Latin *propheta*: priest who predicts the future. DLLB. The Pope is a priest too. Cf. CII,Q36.
[2] The Temple of Diana in Rome is situated on Monte Aventino. DL7V.
[3] *Vaguer*: old form of *vaquer*. DAFL. To be vacant, idle. DL7V.
[4] Stricken by wild madness. DL7V.

---

# The Antichrist, Son of a Buddhist Monk. The Antichrist a Twin

Devant moustier[1] trouvé enfant besson,[2]
D'héroicq[3] sang de moyne vetustique,[4]
Son bruit par secte, langue et puissance son,
Qu'on dira soit eslevé le vopisque.[5]

CI,Q95

*Interpretation*

A twin will be found in front of a monastery, the child of the noble blood of an aged monk. Through his party, his language and the power of his voice, his noise will be such that they will demand the surviving twin to be elevated to power.

¹ Popular form for *monastère*, monastery. DENF.
² Twin. DAFL.
³ Noble, elevated, epic. DL7V.
⁴ Latin *vetustico*: I age, grow old. DLLB.
⁵ Latin *vopiscus*: surviving twin. DLLB.

---

## The Birth of the Antichrist in Asia
## His Invasion as Far as France

Naistra du gouphre et cité immesurée.
Nay de parents obscurs et ténébreux:¹
Quand la puissance du grand Roy reverée,
Voudra destruire par Rouen et Evreux.

CV,Q84

*Interpretation*

He will be born in misfortune, in an immeasurable city [Chinese or Japanese] and of obscure and secretive parentage: when the great king of France's power has been honoured, he will want to destroy [the West] right up to Rouen and Evreux.

¹ Secret, perfidious. DL7V.

---

## The Invasion from Asia into Italy
## and France

L'Oriental sortira de son siège
Passer les monts Apennins voir la Gaule:
Transpercera le ciel les eaux les neiges
Et un chacun frappera de sa gaule.¹

CII,Q29

*Interpretation*

The Asiatic leader will leave his country to cross the Apennines and enter France. He will cross the sky [airborne invasion], the rivers and the mountains, and strike each country with his tax.

[1] Levy, toll or tax. DL7V.

---

# Aerial Attack on the King of France's Base.
# Seven Months of Fierce Fighting. Invasion at Rouen
# and Evreux, and the Fall of the King

Du feu celeste au Royal édifice
Quand la lumière de Mars deffaillera:
Sept mois grand guerre, mort gent de maléfice,
Rouën, Evreux au Roy ne faillira.

CIV,Q100

*Interpretation*

The king's palace will be destroyed by a rocket when the flashing lights of war die down. The war will be large-scale for seven months, and its calamities will be responsible for loss of life. The invasion at Rouen and Evreux will bring the king's downfall.

---

# The Birth of the Antichrist.
# Famine on Earth

L'enfant naistra à deux dents en la gorge,
Pierre en Tuscie[1] par pluy tomberont,
Peu d'ans après ne sera bled ni orge,
Pour saouler ceux qui de faim failliront.

CIII,Q42

*Interpretation*

The child will be born with two teeth in his throat [*sic*], there will be a rain of stones [bombs?] in Italy [Tuscany]. Some years later there will be neither corn nor barley to satisfy men, who will die of hunger.

[1] One of the seventeen diocesan provinces of Italy in the fourth century, comprised of Etruria and Umbria, with Florence as its principal town. DHB.

# The Antichrist: the Greatest Enemy
# of the Human Race

Tasche de murdre[1] enormes adultères,[2]
Grand ennemy de tout le genre humain:
Que sera pire qu'ayeuls, oncles ne pères,[3]
En fer, feu, eau, sanguin et inhumain.

CX,Q10

*Interpretation*

Soiled by murders and abominable crimes, the great enemy of the human race will be worse than all his predecessors. By the sword and flame of war he will shed blood in inhuman fashion.

[1] Early form of *meurtre*, murder. DAFL.
[2] Latin *adulterium*: criminal activity. DLLB.
[3] Hitler included!

# The Birth of the Antichrist.
# The Use of Defoliants. Starvation. Deportations in Asia
# (Cambodia, Vietnam)

Entre plusieurs aux isles desportez,
L'un estre nay a deux dents en la gorge:
Mourront de faim les arbres esbrotez,[1]
Pour eux neuf Roy, nouvel edict leur forge.

CII,Q7

*Interpretation*

Several men having been deported on to islands, one of them will be born with two teeth in his throat. Men will die because of defoliants. A new leader will impose new laws upon them.

[1] Provençal *esbroutar* = *ébourgeonner*, i.e. to disband, trim (of trees).

# The Election of the Antichrist.
# He Conquers the Greatest States

Esleu sera Renard[1] ne sonnant mot,[2]
Faisant le sainct public vivant pain d'orge,[3]
Tyrannizer apres tant a un cop?
Mettant à pied des plus grands sur la gorge.[4]

CVIII,Q41

## Interpretation

A wily man will be elected without saying anything; he will play the
saint, living in simple fashion. Then he will suddenly exercise his
tyranny, putting the greatest countries in a state of utter coercion.

[1] Figurative: cunning or wily (as a fox). DL7V.

[2] *Ne sonner mot* = *ne dire mot*: to say nothing, be silent. DL7V.

[3] *Grossier comme du pain d'orge*: to be very coarse, rustic. DL7V.

[4] To put one's foot on an enemy's throat, i.e. hold him absolutely at one's mercy.
DL7V.

---

# The Antichrist. The Asian Communist Countries
# Dragged into the War, 1999

Le chef de Londres par regne l'Americh,
L'isle d'Escosse t'empiera par gelée:[1]
Roy Reb[2] auront un si faux Antechrist,
Que les mettra trestous dans la meslée.

CX,Q66

## Interpretation

The head of the British government will be supported by the power of
the United States, when the cold will make Scotland hard as stone: the
red leaders will have at their head an Antichrist so false that he will drag
them all into war.

[1] Allusion to a particularly severe winter.

[2] Latin *robeus*: red. DLLB.

# The Twenty-seven Years of the War of the Antichrist, 1999–2026

L'antechrist trois bien tost annichilez,
Vingt et sept ans sang durera sa guerre:
Les heretiques[1] morts, captifs exilez,
Sang corps humain eau rougie greler terre.

CVIII,Q77

*Interpretation*

The Antichrist will soon annihilate three countries. The war he will wage will last twenty-seven years. Opponents will be put to death and prisoners deported. Blood from bodies will redden the water, the land will be riddled with blows [missiles, bombardments].

[1] By extension, whoever professes opinions contrary to those generally held. DL7V.

---

# The Alliance between the Moslems and the Yellow Races. The Invasion of Europe. The Persecution of the Christians

De Fez le regne parviendra à ceux d'Europe,
Feu leur cité, et lame tranchera:
Le grand d'Asie terre et mer à grand troupe,
Que bleux,[1] pers,[2] croix à mort déchassera.

CVI,Q80

*Interpretation*

The power of Morocco will reach into Europe, set its towns on fire and massacre its inhabitants. The great Asiatic leader will launch new armies by land and sea; the Yellow People, of cadaverous or livid hue, will hunt down the Christians to kill them.

[1] No particular or clearly defined colour; wan, pallid, from Latin *flavus*: yellow. DAFL.
[2] Cadaverous, wild. DAFL.

# Great Changes with the End
# of the French Republic. Airborne Invasion

Vous verrez tard et tost faire grand change,
Horreurs extrêmes et vindications.
Que si la Lune conduicte par son ange,
Le ciel[1] s'approche des inclinations.[2]

CI,Q56

*Interpretation*

You will see, sooner or later, great changes, appalling horrors and acts
of revenge, until the Republic is dead, and from the sky these changes
will approach.

[1] Allusion to CX,Q72: '*Du ciel viendra un grand roi d'effrayeur*'.
[2] Latin *inclinatio*: change, variation, vicissitude. DLLB.

---

# The Yellow Invasion across Russia
# and Turkey

Du pont Euxine,[1] et la grand Tartarie,[2]
Un Roy sera qui viendra voir la Gaule,
Transpercera Alane[3] et l'Arménie,
Et dans Bizance lairra[4] sanglante Gaule.[5]

CV,Q54

*Interpretation*

From the Black Sea and China, a leader will come as far as France, after
crossing Russia and Armenia and leaving his bloody standard in Turkey.

[1] Euxinus: ancient name for the Black Sea.
[2] Asiatic Tartary was divided into Chinese Tartary (Mongolia, Manchuria, etc.) in the
east, and independent Tartary (or Turkestan) in the west. DHB.
[3] Latin Alani, tribe of Sarmatia (ancient name for Russia). DLLB.
[4] Future of *laier, laisser* = to leave. DAFL.
[5] Marine term for a flagstaff or flagpole. DL7V.

# The End of the King of France.
# The Asiatic Leader's Power

Tant attendu ne reviendra jamais,
Dedans l'Europe, en Asie apparoistra:
Un de la ligue yssu du grand Hermes[1]
Et sur tous Roys des Orients croistra.

CX,Q75

*Interpretation*

[The Bourbon King] so long awaited will never come back to Europe. In Asia someone appears who will thieve and loot and hold power over all the Asian countries.

[1] In Latin Mercury, the god of thieves. Ambassador of the gods, he was present at the signing of treaties, alliances, and declarations of war between cities and nations. MGR.

---

# The Antichrist against Henri V. The Recession
# of Communist Power. New Moslem Terror

MENDOSUS[1] tost viendra a son haut regne,
Mettant arrière un peu le Norlaris:
Le Rouge blesme[2] le masle à l'interegne[3]
La jeune crainte et frayeur Barbaris.

CIX,Q50

*Interpretation*

The deceiver will soon reach the height of his power, giving the Lorrainian a setback. Communist power is weakened between the two conflicts, and once again it will be the Moslems who should be dreaded and feared.

[1] Latin *mendosus*: one who has defects or faults, vicious, false. DLLB.
[2] To weaken. DL7V.
[3] Third World War and Wars of the Antichrist, 1999.

# The End of the Bourbon.
# Israel's Economic Ruin

Princes et Seigneurs tous se feront la guerre,
Cousin germain le frère avec le frère,
Finy l'Arby[1] de l'heureux de Bourbon,
De Hierusalem les Princes tant aymables,
Du fait commis enorme et execrable
Se ressentiront sur la bourse sans fond.

Sixain 34

## Interpretation

All the heads of states and governments will be warring, there will be
fighting between brothers and cousins. The supreme arbitration of the
fortunate Prince of Bourbon will be ended. The friendly rulers of Israel,
because of a monstrous and execrable act, will experience economic ruin.

[1] Latin *arbiter*: master, supreme arbiter. DLLB.

---

# The Conquest of Spain by Moslem Troops

De la Felice[1] Arabie contrade,[2]
Naistra puissant de la Loy Mahométique,
Vexer l'Espagne conquester la Grenade,
Et plus par mer à la gent Ligustique.

CV,Q55

## Interpretation

From the territory of rich Arabia will be born a powerful Moslem ruler
who will harass Spain by the conquest of Granada, and Italy still more,
by sea.

[1] Latin *felix*: fecund, rich, opulent. DLLB. Oil.
[2] Early form for *contrée*, country or region. DAFL.

# The Last War of the Twentieth Century, 1999

Chefs d'Aries,[1] Jupiter[2] et Saturne,[3]
Dieu éternel quelles mutations,
Puis par long siècle son maling temps retourne
Gaule et Italie, quelles émotions.

CI,Q51

*Interpretation*

What changes will be provoked by the military leaders before the return to light and the Golden Age; then after a long century [twentieth] the time of the evil one [destruction] will return. What troubles in France and Italy.

[1] Latin name for the constellation of the ram: itself a machine of war used by the ancients to batter down walls. DL7V.

[2] Jupiter was worshipped by all the Latins, for whom he personified light and celestial phenomena. DL7V.

[3] Or Cronos: symbol of time. In mythology, the time of Saturn and Rhea, the Golden age, will last as long as Saturn governs the universe.

---

# Asiatic Communism against Europe and Black Africa

Un peu de temps les temples des couleurs,
De blanc et noir des deux entremeslée:
Rouges et Jaunes leur embleront les leurs
Sang, terre, peste, faim, feu d'eau affollée.

CVI,Q10

*Interpretation*

For a short while the Churches will recover their influence. The Whites and Blacks will unite with each other. The Reds and Chinese will ally and the earth will be maddened by blood, plague, starvation, war and revolution.

---

## The Invasion of Europe by China

De maison sept par mort mortelle suite,
Gresle, tempeste, pestilent mal, fureurs:
Roy d'Orient d'Occident tous en fuite,
Subjuguera ses jadis conquereurs.[1]

Presage 40, June

*Interpretation*

For having sown death, the seven Eastern European countries will know
a fatal consequence. They will be overwhelmed by bombing, tempest,
epidemic and their enemies' savagery. The leader of Asia will put all the
Westerners to flight and will subjugate his former conquerors.

[1] 'In 1839, China having seized cases of Indian opium, *England* embarked upon the
"Opium Wars". The Treaty of Nanking gave England Hong Kong and opened five
Chinese ports for her trade. These ports, by the Treaty of Whampoa (1884), were open
to trade with the *United States, France*, then other *Western Countries*. Under Hien-Foung
(1851–62), the murders of Christian missionaries led to *Anglo–French* intervention, the
capture of Canton (1857) and Tientsin (1858). The treaty was annulled, *Peking occupied*
(1860) and China forced to sign the second Treaty of Tientsin. In the north, China had
to give up territory to Russia. In 1871 Russia occupied Kouldja and the Illi Valley. From
1882 to 1885 China was at war with France over Tonkin, but had to renounce her claims
and make trade agreements with France. China was finally eroded not only by Japan but
by *Russia, Germany, England* and *France*.' DL7V. ('*ses jadis conquereurs*'!)

---

## The Airborne Invasion of France
## in July 1999

L'an mil neuf cent nonante neuf sept mois,
Du ciel[1] viendra un grand Roy d'effrayeur
Ressusciter le grand Roy d'Angoulmois,[2]
Avant apres Mars regner par bonheur.

CX,Q72

*Interpretation*

In July 1999 a great, terrifying leader will come through the skies to
revive [the memory of] the great conqueror of Angoulême. Before and
after war will rule luckily.

[1] Cf. the locusts of the Book of Revelation.

[2] The people of Angoulême (Angoulmois) were conquered by the Visigoths and soon invaded by the Huns, a Mongol race under the command of Attila.

---

# The End of Henri V's Reign.
# The End of the Catholic Church

Par l'univers sera fait un Monarque,
Qu'en paix et vie ne sera longuement.
Lors se perdra la piscature barque,[1]
Sera régie en plus grand détriment.[2]

CI,Q4

## Interpretation

A monarch will be revered by the world but he will not live for long in peace. Thus the Church will collapse, ruled in the greatest disaster.

[1] Barque of St Peter, or ship of the Church, symbols adopted by the early church. DL7V. Allusion to Christ referring to Peter as a 'fisher of men'.

[2] Disaster. DL7V.

---

# The Invasion from Asia Reaches Turkey
# and Egypt. The End of the Catholic Church

Le prince Arabe, Mars, Sol, Venus, Lyon,[1]
Regne d'Eglise par mer succombera:
Devers la Perse bien près d'un million,
Bizance, Egypte, ver. serp.[2] invadera.[3]

CV,Q25

## Interpretation

The Arab leader will launch war and subversion against monarchical power, and the Church's power will succumb through a naval invasion. Almost a million soldiers will be in Iran and Satan will invade Turkey and Egypt.

[1] Emblem of sovereignty. DL7V.

[2] Latin *versus serpens*: serpent coiled back upon itself. Allusion to Revelations XII, v.9: 'And the great dragon was cast out, that old serpent called the Devil, and Satan, which deceiveth the whole world: he was cast out into the earth, and his angels were cast out with him.'

[3] Latin: to attack, cross, invade. DLLB.

---

# The Fall of the Western European Countries

La fin le loup, le lyon, boeuf[1] et l'asne,[2]
Timide dama[3] seront avec mastins[4]
Plus ne cherra[5] à eux la douce manne,
Plus vigilance et custode[6] aux mastins.

CX,Q99

*Interpretation*

When the ends of Germany, England, South Africa and the Moslem troops are to be seen, timid Poland will be allied with England. They will no longer have an easy life and the English will no longer be under surveillance and guard.

[1] Lucanian ox, the name given to the elephant by the Romans. DL7V. The elephant represents South Africa (cf. Sixains 26, 39 and 56).

[2] Cf. CIII,Q23 and CX,Q31.

[3] Latin *dama*, French *daim*: deer. DLLB. Cf. CV,Q4.

[4] Cf. CV,Q4. Nostradamus certainly does not reunite the deer (Poland) and the bulldog (England) yet again in a quatrain by accident.

[5] From *cheoir*: to fall. DAFL.

[6] Latin *custos*: guard, sentry. DLLB.

---

# The Persecution of the Clergy.
# Life Grows Expensive

En bref seront de retour sacrifices,
Contrevenans seront mis à martyre,
Plus ne seront moines, abbés, novices,
Le miel sera beaucoup plus cher que cire.

CI,Q44

*Interpretation*

Sacrifices of believers recommence; those who oppose authority will be martyred. There will no longer be monks, priests, or novices, and there will be a rise in the cost of living.

---

## The Burning of Rome. A Cardinal Expelled by the Pope. Scandals Perpetrated by the Clergy

Mont Aventin[1] brusler nuict sera veu,
Le ciel obscur tout à un coup en Flandres,
Quand le Monarque chassera son neveu,[2]
Leurs gens d'Eglise commettront les esclandres.

CIII,Q17

*Interpretation*

Rome will be seen burning at night. The sky will darken abruptly in Belgium when the Pope will drive out a cardinal, and the clergy will commit scandals.

[1] One of the hills of Rome. DL7V.
[2] *Cardinal neveu*: a cardinal is the 'nephew' of the current pope. DL7V.

---

## The Pope's Assassination. The Death of the Capetian. The Landing on the Var Coast

Dix envoyez, chef de nef mettre à mort,
D'un adverty,[1] en classe guerre ouverte:
Confusion chef. l'un se picque et mord,[2]
Leryn,[3] Stecades[4] nefs, cap[5] dedans la nerte.[6]

CVII,Q37

*Interpretation*

Ten men will be sent to murder the Pope but one of them will be opposed to it; war will be started by the army. In the confusion the leader [of the group] will commit suicide and die, ships will disembark on the Var coastline, the Capetian will then be buried.

¹ Latin *adversor*: I am opposed to, go against. DLLB.
² From *mordrir*: to murder, kill.
³ French islands in the Mediterranean, off the coast of the Var *département*, facing the gulf of La Napoule. DHB.
⁴ Staechades: the Iles D'Hyères, the four islands off the Var coast – Porquerolles, Port-Cros, Bagneaux and the Isle of Levant. DHB.
⁵ The Capetian: cf. Louis XVI and Varennes, CIX,Q20.
⁶ Or Hertha, the Earth, German goddess. DLLB.

---

## The Ruin of Rome and the Vatican

La grand montagne ronde de sept stades,¹
Après paix, guerre, faim, inondation,
Roulera loing, abismant grand contrades,²
Mesmes antiques, et grand fondation.

CI,Q69

### Interpretation

The great town with the seven hills, after a period of peace, will know war, famine and revolution which will be widespread, ruining great countries and even ancient ruins and the great foundation [the Vatican].

¹ Step. DL7V. 'No town in the world offers so many *ancient* and modern monuments accumulated in so small a space. At first built upon *seven* hills, it gradually appropriated several others and ended by including in its environs twelve *mountains*.' DHB.
² *Contrede*: early form of *contrée*, country, region. DAFL.

---

## The Ruin of Rome and the Vatican.
## The Capture of the Pope

Bien pres du Tymbre presse la Lybitine,¹
Un peu devant grande inondation:
Le chef du nef prins, mis à la sentine,²
Chasteau,³ palais en conflagration.

CII,Q93

*Interpretation*

Very near the Tiber death threatens. There will have been a great
revolution shortly before. The head of the church will be taken prisoner
and rejected. The castle [Sant'Angelo] and the Palace [of the Vatican]
will be in flames.

[1] Latin *Libitina*: goddess presiding at funerals, and by extension death. DLLB.
[2] Latin *sentina*: dregs, reject. DLLB.
[3] The Castle faces the Vatican. DL7V.

---

# The End of the Monarchy and the Ruin
# of the Catholic Church

> Les mal'heureuses nopces celebreront,
> En grande joye mais la fin mal'heureuse:
> Mary et mere nore[1] desdaigneront,
> Le Phybe[2] mort, et nore plus piteuse.

CX,Q55

*Interpretation*

Men will congratulate themselves upon unfortunate alliances which will
please them, but in the long run will bring unhappiness. They will scorn
the Virgin Mary and the Church. The monarchy will end and the Church
will be in an even more pitiful state.

[1] *Nora* for *nurus*. DAFL. Daughter-in-law, wife of the son. DLLB. Bride of Christ,
the Church of Christ. DL7V.
[2] Phoebus, Apollo, the Sun God. DL7V. As usual, Nostradamus here refers to the
monarchy.

# EPILOGUE

'Man is a reed, the weakest in
nature, but he is a thinking reed.'

Pascal

If we consider the breadth of knowledge necessary for complete comprehension of a work like that of Nostradamus, we must conclude that no human could be capable of such understanding. Faced with such monumental learning, we can only feel humble. The more I continued with my work and the more the quatrains accumulated in meaning, the more certain I became of the authenticity and seriousness of the Centuries. Increasingly it seemed to me that I held the key to the riddle, and yet I felt even more ignorant and inadequately equipped to grasp the amazing intelligence demonstrated throughout Nostradamus' work.

If, from the letter he wrote on 1 March 1555 to his son and translator, I dare apply a particular passage to myself, it would undoubtedly be this one: '. . . and I do not want to talk here of the years which have not yet transpired, but of your months of struggle during which you will not be capable in your deficient understanding of comprehending what I shall be constrained, after my death, to leave you.' I do not claim, unlike certain others, to have definitively decoded Nostradamus' message. I feel I have made only a modest contribution, undertaken with the utmost sincerity and an intellectual honesty which I hope will not be doubted. Despite the twenty years I have spent on this book, preparing and accumulating documentation, reading numerous historical works, and committing to memory the vocabulary of Nostradamus and a great many quatrains and sixains, I feel a sense of imperfection. I am only too aware of the risk of errors and subjective comment or digression. It is quite possible, for instance, that I have attributed certain quatrains to the Third World War when they actually refer to the War of the Antichrist beginning in 1999. This kind of mistake is easy to make since the

Moslems appear to be the allies of the Russians in the Third World War, and the Chinese during the War of the Apocalypse. For this reason quatrains referring to the Moslem world are difficult to date – precisely, at any rate.

This book includes about half of the 1160 quatrains and sixains Nostradamus wrote: the remaining verses will be the subject of a second book. The texts translated here are generally the most specific ones and give some idea of the overall design, from the linguistic point of view as much as the philosophical one. I selected quatrains and sixains precise enough to convey a good grasp of past and future events as prophesied by Nostradamus.

After translating and matching up against historical facts over two hundred quatrains dealing with past events, I wondered for some time why Nostradamus had included details that are unverifiable at first glance. There are probably three reasons. First, Nostradamus wanted to impose considerable work on his translator to show that there are no short cuts to learning. Secondly, he was obliged to make his message obscure because of the religious background of the sixteenth century, and historical details had little chance of being understood or recognized; this guaranteed for four hundred years the necessary obscurity, so that his message might reach the twentieth-century reader. Finally – and this is probably the main reason – the abundance of astonishingly precise information found in the quatrains brings almost irrefutable proof of the authenticity, value and correctness of his prophecies. Examples such as the French army with MacMahon at Buffalora; Garibaldi landing at Magnavacca; the flight to Varennes; the number of Nelson's great three-deckers at Trafalgar; and the exact length of Hitler's life all make the Centuries difficult to gainsay.

Nostradamus' opponents are mostly people who do not really know the work but contest it because the little they do know of it upsets their personal convictions or beliefs. There are other sceptics (and they are more excusable), who have read translations that are as inaccurate as the original text (once the indispensable philological and historical research is done) is accurate. When I recall my work in supplying half the text, with all the imperfections of which I am aware, I wonder how so many people can allow themselves to discuss, criticize and challenge the prophecy of Nostradamus. The widespread twentieth-century tendency in the West, where whatever one does is criticized and disputed even before its value is assessed, acts as a curb on the creative spirit. Two principal defects are responsible for man's destructive instincts: pride and jealousy. If the individual did not always think himself superior to his neighbour, on whatever pretext – class, education, breeding, race etc. – he would open the gates of knowledge. In fact, through his pretension, he closes his mind.

The message revealed here will certainly not be to everyone's taste, for man's history appears in Nostradamus independent of political, philosophical, ideological or religious commitment. In 1938 my father wrote about the Franco-German war, Germany's loss of that war and Hitler's miserable end. He was subsequently accused of Germanophobia, which led to the seizure and destruction of his book. Similarly today I risk accusations of Russophobia or entrenched anti-Communism, whereas Sovietism is only a relatively brief episode in the history of Russia compared to the ten consecutive centuries of tsarist rule. The French Republican system, to take another example, adds up to only about 115 years compared to the thirteen centuries of the monarchy.

I should like the reader, whatever his race, religion or politics, to try to wipe the slate clean of everything formerly considered as the truth, which is only ever a subjective view, and to open his mind to a transcendental vision of history which perhaps prophecy alone can help him acquire. To attain an awareness uncluttered by prejudice, one should reflect on the analysis made about 441 BC by the Greek historian Thucydides, writing about the Peloponnesian War:

Thucydides showed what war was, why it happened, what it did and must continue doing, at least until men learn better conduct. Athenians and Spartans fought for only one reason . . . because they were powerful and through this fact were obliged (in Thucydides' own words) to seek to increase their power. The two adversaries fought not because they were different – Athens a democracy, Sparta an oligarchy – but because they were alike. The war had nothing to do with divergences of opinion or conceptions of good and evil. Is democracy good and oligarchy bad? To ask this question would have been, for Thucydides, to move away from the problem. There was no power representing the good. *Power*, whoever exercised it, was the demon, the corruptor of men . . . Thucydides was probably the first to grasp (and in any case to express in words) this new doctrine which would become that of the entire world.[1]

Don't we talk today of the two superpowers, the USA and USSR, as Sparta and Athens were in their day? And since Thucydides examples of the rivalry of powers have multiplied: antagonisms hidden for most of the time behind differences of religion or ideology.

To come down on the side of one of the two great powers or the other would be to come down on the side of war. Letting oneself be hoaxed

[1] Edith Hamilton: *The Great Age of Greek Literature*, New York, 1942.

by the political or ideological aspect of the problem allows the heads of states – consumed by ambition and the desire for power – to mass their armies in order to satisfy their supremacist lunacy. Ordinary people kill each other, when their deepest aspirations are in all probability exclusively peaceable.

When will the French stop glorifying victories like Austerlitz, Jena and Eylau which for their enemies were defeats, just as the English victories at Trafalgar and Waterloo were defeats for the French? Both sides, after all, inflicted or suffered rape, massacre and all the other nauseating fruits of war. When will we stop erecting monuments to the dead? The Arc de Triomphe commemorates Napoleon's victories, but is something obtained through thousands of deaths and indescribable suffering really a triumph? When will we decide to glorify life with all the potential it embodies for man's happiness?

The philosopher Montesquieu wrote in his *Persian Letters*: 'You say you fear that someone will invent a method of destruction crueller than the existing one. No. If a deadly invention came to be discovered, it would soon be prohibited by the law of man.' This is the archetypal anti-prophecy which Cartesianism made the eighteenth-century thinkers proclaim – at their head Jean-Jacques Rousseau, the man largely responsible, according to Nostradamus, for the dramas of the twentieth century. His Utopias were taken up again by the nineteenth- and twentieth-century philosophers such as Proudhon, St-Simon and Karl Marx, 'refurbished' by ambitious politicians and used ruthlessly as weapons with which to achieve their ambitions. In Germany Adolf Hitler created a National *Socialist* regime. Socialism? What crimes have been committed and go on being committed in that name!

My concern is for the ordinary people, basically good, and believers in a kind of socialism not far removed from Christ's teaching, which was intended to overthrow the powerful men of society and to make them face the responsibilities they bear for the misery of nations. Is it mere chance that whatever party politicians belong to, their speeches tend to show not the slightest sincerity? Power and love of one's neighbour cannot co-exist. Hence, perhaps, the profound meaning of Christ's words: 'Render unto Caesar that which is Caesar's, and unto God that which is God's.' Caesar is power, God is love.

In 1937 my father, deep in decoding the quatrains, wrote:

For sixty years more man will recklessly strive over the whole surface of the wretched speck of dust we inhabit within the infinite circle of the sky, to accumulate and perfect engines of destruction and death, to a rhythm here and now begun, and the massacres will be such that the earth will be depopulated, corroborating not only the Old Testament prophets' words but those of Nostradamus too, who tells us here that 'of the three parts of the world, more than two will be lacking'.[1]

The atomic bomb did not then exist, but soon the destruction of Hiroshima started the fulfilment of this 'prophetic vision'. The research, development and testing of nuclear, chemical and bacteriological weapons continued to accelerate, even though the countries possessing these weapons had all signed the 1925 Geneva Convention prohibiting them.

On 14 July 1790 the goddess Reason was consecrated on the altar of atheism, and by exporting the ideas of the French Revolution would inspire many countries who were gradually to regroup in the League of Nations and then in the United Nations Organization. However, all the countries fighting each other since the Second World War – the USA against North Korea, the USA against Vietnam, Turkey against Cyprus, the USSR and Cuba against Angola and Ethiopia – are members of this organization.

Hitler began his expansionist war by rushing to the aid of the German minorities in Europe. Whether wars are waged by monarchies, dictatorships or republics, they all have the same aim, power, and the same result, the people's misfortune. One might wonder why the Nostradamus prophecy centres mainly on man-made catastrophes. Indeed, the number of quatrains and sixains attributed to any event is proportional to its destructive and terrifying aspect. Louis XIV's France, much smaller than the present-day country, and with a mere 20 million inhabitants and a 300,000-strong army, interested Nostradamus less than twentieth-century France. In 1914 France had a population of 41 million: on the battlefields of the Marne she left 1,400,000 dead. Germany, with a population of 58 million, lost 2 million. Total losses in the 1914–18 War were 8,700,000; the Second World War claimed 36 million. To these figures should be added millions of 'survivors', mutilated, crippled, handicapped, gassed, burned, driven mad and unable to adapt to a normal life. And what can one say about the massive destruction of civilian populations: Hiroshima – 160,000 dead; Dresden – 300,000; and death camps saw the extermination of millions of Jews, gipsies, Armenians, Vietnamese, Cambodians and so on.

On the threshold of the twenty-first century the race towards ever larger scales of destruction still does not cease to burden humanity with the threat of annihilation. The twentieth century has seen so much of mankind coerced into power struggles even harsher and more dangerous than in preceding ages. Doubtless this explains why the vision of Nos-

---

[1] Letter to 'Henry, Roy de France Second', Adyar, 1937.

tradamus is so preoccupied with much based upon this period, when leaders, along with their fearful and apocalyptic weapons, have confronted each other with a destructive fury hitherto unparalleled. From the crossbow to the neutron bomb there is a terrible constant, representing an acceleration towards the perfection of death-dealing instruments.

The fundamental question is whether man, after millennia of scientific progress, has made any progress in the human sphere. It seems unlikely. If man, in his materialism, is left to his own devices, he rushes towards destruction.

However, we must not despair. If we had only the analyses of politicians, doomwatchers, demographers, sociologists and economists to go by, man's horizon would be completely blocked. Absolute and irreversible pessimism would be the rule. The only remaining hope is the prophetic message brought to man. Whether the prophets are those of the Old or the New Testaments, Christ or Nostradamus, they all announce the realization of the 'Kingdom' when universal peace shall at last reign among men.

For then shall be great tribulation, such as was not since the beginning of the world to this time, no, nor ever shall be.

And except those days should be shortened, there should no flesh be saved: but for the elect's sake those days shall be shortened. . . .

For there shall arise false Christs, and false prophets, and shall shew great signs and wonders; insomuch that, if it were possible, they shall *deceive the very elect*. . . .

For as the lightning cometh out of the east, and shineth even unto the west; so shall also the coming of the Son of man be.[1]

The Prophet Malachi[2] confirms this, attributing to the last Pope the following Latin commentary:

*In persecutione extrema sacrae Romanae Ecclesiae, sedebit Petrus Romanus qui pascet oves in multis tribulationibus; quibus transactis, civitas septicollis diruetur, et Judex tremendus judicabit populum.* (In the final persecution of the Holy Roman Church, Peter the Roman will occupy the See, who will guide his flock through numerous tribulations. These tribulations past, the town of seven hills [Rome] will be destroyed and the terrible Judge shall judge the people).[3]

In other words, Christ will come at the appointed time as prophesied, to chastise the arms vendors as He did the moneylenders in the Temple.

Nostradamus' prophecies centre upon the history of Israel, bearer of the Old Testament, and that of the Catholic Church, bearer of the New.

[1] Matthew XXIV, vv. 21, 22, 24, 27. AV.
[2] Author of the famous prophecy on the popes.
[3] Abbé Joseph Maître: *Les Papes et la Papauté*, Paris, 1902.

The emblem of Israel is a six-pointed star, and modern France is referred to as a hexagon (in which the six-pointed star can be drawn). Israel's flag is blue and white; the national flag of France before 1790 was a blue escutcheon with three fleurs de lis on a white ground.

At the end of the twentieth century the planetary significance of these two countries, around which the most important international problems revolve, is disproportionate compared to their material and economic power. Three cities receive more attention than any others: Jerusalem, with its Holy Places; Rome, with its Pope; and Paris, whoever governed France. These three towns constitute the three pillars of western Judeo–Christian civilization, whose first six millennia have elapsed. In fifty years the seventh millennium will begin, the Age of Aquarius, which will bring man universal peace and spiritual as well as material prosperity.

The importance of the message for man is this positive aspect, which Nostradamus noted in his Letter to César: 'For according to the signs in the sky[1], the Golden Age will return, after a revolutionary period which will turn all upside down, and which from the present moment of writing will begin in 177 years 3 months 11 days, bringing in its wake corruption of ideas and morals, wars and a long famine. . . .' The period of time indicated by the prophet, from March 1555 when he wrote the letter, corresponds with the arrival of Rousseau in Paris in 1732.

We are living through the end of *a* world, not the end of *the* world, as some exploiters of the morbid are claiming. This death of one civilization among so many others will herald the birth of a new civilization freed from the aberrations of its predecessor. This is what Henry Miller sensed, when he wrote in 1945:

A new world is being born, a new kind of man is springing up today. The great mass of mankind, destined in our time to suffer more cruelly than ever before, ends by being paralysed with fear, becoming introspective, shaken to the very core, and does not hear, see or feel anything more than everyday physical needs. It is thus that worlds die. First and foremost, the flesh dies. But although few clearly recognize it, the flesh would not have died if the spirit had not been killed already.

Every civilization thinks itself immortal: I am certain that the Romans of AD 200–250 could not imagine, according to their own prophets, that a few centuries later the ruins of their once immense and brilliant empire would be visited by tourists.

In conclusion, the prophecies of Nostradamus, like those of the great Old Testament prophets, Christ or the Revelation of St John are therefore not morbid speculation on uninterrupted catastrophes, nor imprecations

---

[1] The sun passing from Pisces into Aquarius, represented by a horn of plenty, fish living in water, symbol of revolution.

directed against man, but a message of hope. What would man's future be without this divine message? Man without God, but worshipper of the goddess Reason, should, we were promised, establish the rule of the Rights of Man upon earth. After two centuries of this so-called new world order it would require considerable disingenuousness to claim that man, his reason, and above all his pride, had bettered the lot of nations.

I learned history at school from mediocre textbooks, which mainly proved to be effective soporifics. When I left, only a little of what I had been taught remained with me; what was more serious was that these were false ideas, for the historians of right and left had distorted historic facts in order to accommodate them within their ideologies. I hope that this book will give younger readers a passion for history comparable to that which the prophecy of Nostradamus has instilled in me.

Despite the tribulations predicted by the prophets, I want to believe in man and his perfectibility, particularly at the time of writing (1980) when the clouds seem to be gathering before the storm. Let me end by quoting some words Shakespeare makes Hamlet speak:

What a piece of work is a man! How noble in reason! how infinite in faculty! in form, in moving, how express and admirable! in action how like an angel! in apprehension . . . how like a god! the beauty of the world! . . .

> What is a man,
> If his chief good and market of his time
> Be but to sleep and feed? A beast, no more.
> Sure he that made us with such large discourse,
> Looking before and after, gave us not
> That capability and godlike reason
> To fust in us unus'd.

# BIBLIOGRAPHY

*Abbreviations*

BN: Bibliothèque Nationale
BMA: Bibl. Municipale Aix-en-Provence
BML: Bibl. Municipale Lyon


Allaines, Henri d' : *Actualité de l'Apocalypse*, La Colombe, Paris, 1963.
Alleau, René : 'Nostradamus le plus grand prophète de l'histoire', *Sallonensa* Salon, 1957.
Alliaume, Maurice: *Magnus Rex de Nostradamus et son drapeau*, publ. at author's expense at Chartres, 1948.
   *Predictions vraies de Nostradamus et Mandragore*, publ. at author's expense at Chartres, 1949.
Amadou, Robert : 'Le Devin et son Art', *Le Crapouillot*, no. 18, 1952.
Amiaux : *Nostradamus*, Sorlot, Paris.
Anon. : *La Première Invective du Seigneur Hercules, Le François, contre Nostradamus*, Michel Jove, Lyon, 1558.
   *Huictain contre Nostradamus*, Roux, Lyon, 1557.
   *Déclaration des abus, ignorances, séditions de Michel Nostradamus*, Pierre Roux et Jean Tremblay, Avignon, 1558.
Anquetil, Georges : *L'Anti-Nostradamus*, Ed. de la Maison des Ecrivains, Paris, 1940.
Artigny, Abbé d' : *Nouveaux mémoires d'histoire, de critique et de littérature*, 1794.
Astruc, Jean : *Mémoires pour servir à l'histoire de la faculté de Montpellier*, 1767.
Auclair, Raoul : *Les Centuries de Nostradamus*, Deux Rives, Paris, 1958.
   *Le Crépuscule des Nations*, La Colombe, Paris.
   *Les Centuries de Nostradamus ou le dixième livre sibyllin*, Nouvelles Editions Latines, 1957.
Barbarin, Georges : *Les Derniers Temps du Monde, de l'Antéchrist au Jugement dernier*, 'History & Tradition' series, Ed. Dervy, Paris, 1951.
Bareste, Eugène : Editions des Centuries, Maillet, Paris, 1840–42. (BMA)
Bartoshek, Norbert : *Nostradamus und Seine berühmte Prophezeiungen*, 1946.

Belland, Dr : *Napoléon, premier empereur des français, prédit par Nostradamus*, Paris, 1806.

Beltikhine, G. : 'Un document chiffré : Le Secret des Centuries', *Inconnues*, no. 12, Lausanne, 1956.

Bertrand, Michel : 'Histoire secréte de la Provence', *Histoire secrète des provinces françaises*, Albin Michel, Paris, 1978.

Bjorndahl-Veggerby, Paul : *Nostradamus et les ruines gallo-romaines à Martres-Tolosane*, Ed. Leisner, Copenhagen, 1976.

Blanchard and Reynaud-Plense : *La Vie et l'Œuvre de Michel Nostradamus*, Imp. Léon Guillaumichon, Salon, 1933. (BMA)
*Histoire de Salon*, Salon, 1935.

Boniface, A. : *Buonaparte prédit par des prophètes et peint par des historiens, des orateurs et des poètes ou morceaux en prose et en vers sur les circonstances actuelles, recueillis par A. Boniface*, d'Hautel, Paris, 1814.

Bonnelier, Hippolyte : *Nostradamus, roman historico-cabalistique*, A. Ledoux, Paris, 1833, 2 vol.

Bonnet, Jean : *Résumé des prophéties de Nostradamus. Les événements et les symboles*, followed by : *Commentaires de la Bible par Nostradamus et de détermination des dates dans Nostradamus*, Jean Bonnet, Paris, 1973.

Bonnot Jean de : *Les Oracles de Michel de Nostredame dit Nostradamus*, annotated by Anatole le Pelletier and Serge Hutin, Paris, 1976, 2 vol.

Boroch, Erick Karl : *Der Prophet Nostradamus*, 1912.

Boswell, Rolfe : *Nostradamus speaks*, 1941.

Bouche, Honoré : *La Chorographie et l'Histoire de Provence*, Charles David, Aix-en-Provence, 1664.

Bouchet, Marguerite : *Les Oracles de Michel de Nostredame*, Les Livres Nouveaux, Paris, 1939.

Boulenger, Jacques : *Nostradamus*, Excelsior, Paris, 1933.

Bousquet, Raoul : *Nostradamus, sa famille et son secret*, Fournier-Valdes, Paris, 1950.
'La Maladie et la Mort de Nostradamus', *Aesculape*, November 1950.

Boutin, André : *Michel de Nostre-Dame, astrologue et médecin*, MD thesis, Librarie Le François, Paris, 1941.

Bouys, Théodore : *Nouvelles considérations sur les Oracles et particulièrement sur Nostradamus*, Paris, 1806, Desenne, Debray.

Boyer, Jean : 'Deux peintres oubliés du XVIIe siècle, Etienne Martellange et César Nostradamus', *Bulletin de la Société de l'histoire de l'Art Français*, 1971, pp. 13–20.

Bricaud, Joanny : *La Guerre et les Prophéties célèbres*, Paris, 1916.

Buget, P. F. : 'Etude sur Nostradamus', *Bulletin du bibliophile*, Librairie Techner, Paris, 1860.

Buset, Claude : *Nostradamus et autres prophètes du Père et de l'Esprit*, La Pensée Universelle, Paris, 1974.

Cadres, Geoffroy : *L'Etrange docteur Nostradamus*, La Pensée Universelle, Paris, 1978.

Candolle, comte de : *Armorial de César de Nostredame*, Arles, 1899. (BMA)

Cavanagh, John : *Michel de Nostradamus*, 1923.

Cave, Térence C. : 'Peinture et émotion dans la poésie religieuse de César de Nostredame', *Gazette des Beaux-Arts*, vol. LXXV, Jan. 1970. (BMA)

Centurio, N. : *Nostradamus, der Prophet der Welgeschichte*, Richar Schikowski, Berlin, 1955.

Chabauty, abbé E. A. : *Lettres sur les Prophéties modernes et concordance de toutes les prédictions jusqu'au règne de Henry V*, Ed. Henri Houdin, Poitiers, 1872.

Chavigny, A. de : *Les Pléiades du Sieur de Chavigny, Beaunois, divisées en VII livres, prises et tirées des anciennes prophéties et conférées avec les oracles du tant célèbre et renommé Michel de Nostradame, jadis conseiller et médecins de trois Rois très chrestiens. Où est traité du renouvellement des siècles, changement de l'Empire et advancement du nom Chrestien*, Lyon, Pierre Rigaud, 1604.

Chavigny, J. A. de : *Commentaires du Sieur de Chavigny sur les Centuries et Prognostications de feu Michel de Nostredame du Breuil*, Paris, 1596.
*La première Face du Janus français extraite et colligée des Centuries de Michel Nostradamus, par les héritiers de Pierre Roussin*, Lyon, 1594. (BML)
*Vie et testament de Michel Nostradamus*, Paris, 1789.
'Bref discours sur la Vie de Michel de Nostredame', *Revue de l'Agenois*, 1876.

Cheetham, Erika : *The Prophecies of Nostradamus*, Capricorn Books, Putnam's, New York, 1973.

Chollier, Antoine : *Les Prophecies de maistre Michel Nostradamus*, Imp. Allier, Grenoble, 1940.

Chomorat, Michel : *Nostradamus entre Rhône et Saône*, Ed. Ger, Lyon, 1971.
*Supplément à la bibliographie Lyonnaise des Nostradamus*. Centre culturel de Buenc, Lyon, 1976. 100 numbered copies.
'New research on the prophecies of M. N.', *Revue française d'histoire du livre*, no.22, spring 1979.
*Bibliographie lyonnaise de Nostradamus*, followed by a checklist of MSS relating to the Nostradamus family, Centre Culturel de Buenc, Lyon, 1973.

Colin de Larmor : *La Guerre de 1914–1918 vue en 1555 par Nostradamus*, La Roche-sur-Yon, 1922.
*Merveilleux Quatrains de Nostradamus*, Nantes, 1925. (BMA)

Colin-Simard : 'Rois et Reines au rendez-vous des astrologues', *Historia*, no. 157, 1959.

Corvaja, Mireille : *Les Prophéties de Nostradamus*, Vecchi, Paris, 1975.

Couillard, Antoine : *Les Contredits aux prophéties de Nostradamus*, Charles l'Angelier, Paris, 1560.

Crescimbeni, Giovanni-Mario : *Istoria della volgar poesia-TII : Le vite de'piu celebri poeti provenzali, seritte in lingua francese da G.M. Crescimbeni*. B.U. Montepellier (see Jean de Nostredame).

Cristiani, Chanoine : *Nostradamus, Malachie et Cie*, Le Centurion, 1955.
'Un Curieux Homme : Nostradamus', *Ecclesia*, no. 73, 1955.

Crouzet, François : 'Nostradamus, Poète français', *Idée Fixe*, Julliard, Paris, 1973.

Daudet, L. : 'Nostradamus', *Revue universelle*, 1925, vol. I. (BMA)

David-Marescot, Yves and Yvonne : *Prédictions et Prophéties*, Ed. Idégraf et Vernoy, Geneva, 1979.

D. D. : *The Prophecies of Nostradamus concerning the kings and queens of Great Britain*, London, 1715.

Delcourt, Marie : *L'Oracle de Delphes*, 1954.

Demar-Latour : *Nostradamus et les Evénements de 1914–1916*, Paris, 1916. (BN)

Deperlas, Félix : *L'Avenir ou les Grands Personnages et les Grands Evénements de ce temps*, Paris, 1885.

*Révélations de la Providence*, Paris, 1885.

Dupont-Fournieux, Y. : *Les Derniers Jours des Derniers Temps* (Preface by Dr Fontbrune), La Colombe, Paris, 1959.

Edouard, P. : *Texte original et complet des Prophéties de Michel Nostradamus*, Les Belles Editions, Paris, 1939.

Edouard and Mezerette : *Texte original des Prophéties de Nostradamus de 1600 à 1948 et de 1948 à l'an 2000*, Les Belles Editions, Paris, 1947.

Erlanger, Ph. : 'La Reine du Massacre', Historia, no. 340, March 1975.

Fervan, Jean : *La Fin des temps*, Ed. La Bourdonnais, Paris, 1937.

Fontbrune, Dr de : *Les Prophéties de Nostradamus dévoilées. Lettres à Henry Second*, Adyar, 1937.

*Les prophéties de Maistre Michel Nostradamus expliquées et commentées*, Ed. Michelet, Sarlat, 1938, 1939, 1940, 1946, 1958 & 1975, J.-Ch. de Fontbrune, Aix-en-Provence, distributed by le Groupe des Presses de la Cité.

Fontbrune, Dr Max de : *Ce que Nostradamus a vraiment dit*, Preface by Henry Miller, Ed. Stock, 1976.

Fontbrune, Dr de : *La Prédiction mystérieuse de Prémol*, Michelet, Sarlat, 1939, o.p.

*La divine Tragédie de Louis XVII*, Michelet, Sarlat, 1949, available from J.-Ch. de Fontbrune, 3, cours Gambetta, Aix-en-Provence.

Fontbrune, Dr de : *L'Etrange XXᵉ siècle vu par Nostradamus*, Michelet, Sarlat, 1950, o.p.

'Pourquoi je crois en Nostradamus', *Ecclesia*, no. 82, 1956.

'Le docteur Nostradamus vous parle,' *Les Cahiers de Marottes et Violons d'Ingres*, no. 10, Paris, 1953.

'Nostradamus', *Synthèses*, no. 3, August 1955.

Foretich, Rodolphe : *La Prophétie des Papes, analysée à la lumière des prédictions de Nostradamus*, Salvador, 1961. (BN)

Forman, Henry-James : *Les Prophéties à travers les siècles*, Payot, 1938.

Frontenac, Roger : *La Clé secrète de Nostradamus*, Denoël, Paris, 1950.

Fulke : *Contra inutiles Astrologorum praedictiones, Nostradamus*, Cunningham, 1560. (British Museum)

Garçon, Maurice : 'Il y a 450 ans Nostradamus naissait', *Historia*, no. 85, 1953.

Garencieres, Theophilus : *The True Prophecies of Prognostications of Michael Nostradamus*, London, 1672.

Gauquelin, Michel : 'Les Astres ont-ils changé le cours de l'histoire?', *Historia*, no. 203, 1963.

Gay-Rosset, Claude : 'Michel de Nostredame, une rencontre du quatrième type,' *Midi-Mutualité*, no. 12, Jan.-Feb. 1979. (Marseille)

Gimon, Louis : *Chroniques de la ville de Salon depuis son origine jusqu'en 1792*, Aix-en-Provence, 1882.

Girard, Samuel : *Histoire généalogique de la Maison de Savoie*, 1660.

Gravelaine, Joëlle de : *Prédictions et Prophéties*, Hachette, Paris, 1965.

Guérin, Pierre : *Le Véritable secret de Nostradamus*, Payot, Paris, 1971.

Guichardan, S. : *La Chasse aux prophéties*, Bonne Presse, Limoges, 1941.

Guichenou, Joseph : *Catalogue de tableaux au musée Calvet*, Avignon, 1909.

Guynaud, Balthazard : *Concordance des prophéties depuis Henri II jusqu'à Louis le Grand*, Jacques Morel, Paris, 1693.

Hades : *Que sera demain?*, La Table Ronde, Paris, 1966.

Haitze, Pierre Joseph de : *La Vie de Nostradamus*, Aix-en-Provence, David, 1712.

*Vie et Testament de Nostradamus*, 1789.

Haitze, Pierre Joseph de : *La Vie de Nostradamus*, Aix-en-Provence, 1911.

Harold, R. A. : *Les Prophètes et les Prophéties de l'Apocalypse à nos jours*, Ed. La Caravelle, Brussels; l'Avenir, Paris, 1948.

Hildebrand, Jakob : *Nostradamus sueddeutsche monatshefte*, 1932.

Holtzauer, Jean-Louis : *Nostradamus, un praticien sous la Renaissance*, Laboratoires S.O.B.I.O., Ed. Labo, 92 – Levallois, 1975.

Hutin, Serge : *Les Prophéties de Nostradamus avec présages et sixains*, Pierre Bellefond, Paris, 1962, 1972, 1978, Poche-Club, Paris, 1966; Hachette, Paris, 1975.

*Les Prophéties de Nostradamus*, Club Géant Historique, Les éditions de la Renaissance, Paris, 1966.

Iacchia, U. : *La Tunisie vue par Nostradamus*, Imp. d'Art, Tunis.

IAF : *Le Substrat mathématique de l'Œuvre de Nostradamus*, Ed. de Psyché, Paris, 1949.

I.M. : *Le vrayes centuries de Me Michel Nostradamus expliquées sur les affaires de ce temps*, I. Boucher, 1652.

Ionescu, Vlaicu : *Le Message de Nostradamus sur l'Ere Prolétaire*, publ. at author's expense, distributed by Dervy Books, Paris, 1976.

'Nostradamus et la gnose', *Atlantis*, no. 301, Jan.-Feb. 1979, 30, rue de la Marseillaise 94300 – Vincennes.

Jacquemin, Suzanne : *Les Prophéties des Derniers Temps*, La Colombe, Paris, 1958.

Jant, chevalier de : *Prédictions tirées des Centuries de Nostradamus qui, vraisemblablement peuvent s'expliquer à la guerre entre la France et l'Angleterre contre les provinces unies*, 1673.

*Prophéties de Nostradamus sur la longueur des jours et la félicité du règne de Louis XIV*, 1673.

Jaubert, Etienne : *Eclaircissement des véritables quatrains de Nostradamus et Vie de M. Nostradamus*, Amsterdam, 1656.

Kerdeland, Jean de : *De Nostradamus à Cagliostro*, Ed. Self, Paris, 1945.

Klinckowstroem, G. C. Von : *Die ältesten Ausgaben des Prophéties des Nostradamus*, March 1913.

Kniepf, Albert : *Die Weisagungen des alt Französischen Sehers Michel Nostradamus und der Weltkrieg*, Hamburg, 1915.

Krafft, Karl E. : *Nostradamus prezice viitorul Européi*, Bucharest, 1941.

Labadie, Jean : *Peut-on dire l'avenir?* Aubanel, Avignon, 1941.

Lamont, André : *Nostradamus sees all*, 1942.

Lamotte, Pierre : *De Gaulle révélé par Nostradamus il y a quatre siècles*, Le Scorpion, Paris, 1961. (BN)

Langlois, Charles : *Les Contradictions de Nostradamus*, 1560.

Laurent : *Prédictions jusqu'à l'an 2000. Prophéties du Christ, de Nostradamus, des Papes St Malachie*, Laurent, 91 Brunoy.

Laver, James : *Nostradamus*, Penguin Books, 1942.

*Nostradamus, the future foretold*, George Mann, Maidstone, 1973.

Legrand, Jean René : 'Pronostics pour l'an 1959', *Initiation et science*, no. 47, Jan.-March 1959, Omnium littéraire, Paris.

Leoni, Edgar : *Nostradamus, life and literature*, 1961.

Le Pelletier, Anatole : *Les Oracles de Nostradamus, astrologue, médecin et conseiller ordinaire des rois Henry II, François II et Charles IX*, Le Pelletier, 40, rue d'Aboukir, Paris, 1867, 2 vol.

Le Roux, Jean : *La Clé de Nostradamus, Isagoge ou Introduction au véritable sens des Prophéties de ce fameux auteur*, Pierre Giffard, rue Saint-Jacques-près-les-Maturins, Paris, 1710. (Musée d'Arbaud, Aix-en-Provence)

Leroy, Dr Edgar : 'Les origines de Nostradamus', *Mémoires de l'Institut historique de Provence*, vol. 18, Marseille, 1941.

*Sur un quatrain de Nostradamus.*

'Jaume de Nostredame et la Tour de Canillac', *Mémoires de l'Institut historique de Provence*, vol. 19, Marseille, 1942.

'Pierre de Nostredame de Carpentras', communication à l'Institut historique de Provence, 1948.

'Nostradamus et le curé d'Argœuvres', *Cahier de Pratique Médiocochirurgicale*, Avignon, 1939, no. 5.

*Saint-Paul de Mausole à Saint-Rémy de Provence*, Imp. générale du Sud-Ouest, Bergerac, 1948.

*Nostradamus, ses origines, sa vie, son œuvre*, Imp. Trillaud, Bergerac, 1972.

*Romanin, les cours d'amour de Jehan de Nostredame*, Avignon, 1933. (BMA)

*Saint-Rémy de Reims*, Marseille, 1937. (BMA)

*Nostradamus, détective avant la lettre*, Avignon, 1949. (BN)

*Le Latin du tabellion provençal Jaume de Nostredame, notaire à Saint-Rémy-de-Provence dans les actes de 1501 à 1513*, Avignon, 1961.

'Saint-Paul-Tricastin et Saint-Paul-de-Mausole, Contribution à l'histoire d'une légende', *Bull. Philologique et Historique*, 1959.

Ligeoix-de-la-Combe : *La Troisième Guerre Mondiale d'après les prédictions de Nostradamus*, Bordeaux, 1961.

Loog, C. L. : *Die Weisagungen des Nostradamus*, 1921.

Loriot, Louis : 'Entretien de Rabelais et de Nostradamus', Nogent-Le-Rotrou, 1960 & Paris, 1907, *Revue des Etudes rabelaisiennes*, vol. 5, pp. 176–84.

Mabille, Pierre : 'Nostradamus, ses prophéties, son temps', *Inconnues*, Lausanne, 1955.

Maby, Pascale : 'Le Dossier des Prophètes, voyants et astrologues', *Les Chemins de l'Impossible*, Albin Michel, Paris, 1977.

MacCann, Lee, *Nostradamus, the man who saw through time*, 1941.

MacNeice, Louis : *L'Astrologie*, Tallandier, Paris, 1966.

Madeleine, Georges : *La Prochaine Guerre Mondiale vue par Nostradamus*, Toulon, 1952, Ed. Proventia.

Maidy, Léon-Germain de : *Sur une inscription liminaire attribuée à Nostradamus*, Nancy, 1917.

Marques da Cruz : *Profecias de Nostradamus*, Ed. Cultrix, Sao Paulo.

Marteau, Pierre : *Entretiens de Rabelais et de Nostradamus*, 1690.

Menestrier, François : *La Philosophie des images énigmatiques*, Lyon, 1694.

Mericourt, M. J. : *Gesta Dei per Francos*, Paris, 1937.
*Nostradamus et la crise actuelle*, Paris, 1937.

Mondovi, Pierre : 'Un Provençal hors du commun : Nostradamus', *Racines*, no. 4, May 1979, Aix-en-Provence.

Monnier : *Résurrection merveilleuse en 1877 de Michel de Nostredame*, various pamphlets from 1889 to 1896.

Monterey, Jean : *Nostradamus, prophète du XXᵉ siècle*, La Nef, Paris, 1963.

Motret : *Essai d'explication de deux quatrains de Nostradamus*, Nevers, 1806.

Mouan, L. : 'Aperçus littéraires sur César Nostradamus et ses lettres inédites à Peiresc', Mémoires de l'Académie, vol. 10, Aix, 1873. (BMA)

Moult, Thomas-Joseph : *Prophéties perpétuelles, très anciennes et très certaines*, seventeenth-century almanac.
*Prophéties perpétuelles*, Ed. des Cahiers astrologiques, Nice, 1941.

Moura, Jean, and Louvet, Paul : *La vie de Nostradamus*, Gallimard, Paris, 1930.

Muraise, Eric: *Du Roy perdu à Louis XVII*, Julliard, Paris.
*Saint-Rémy de Provence et les secrets de Nostradamus*, Julliard, Paris, 1969.
*Histoire et Légende du grand Monarque*, 'Les Chemins de l'Impossible', Albin Michel, Paris, 1975.

Necroman, Don : *Comment lire les Prophéties de Nostradamus*, Ed. Maurice d'Hartoy, Paris, 1933.

Neyral, Georges : *La Vraie Vie de Michel de Nostredame*, Thesis, Toulouse, 1951.

Nicoullaud, Charles : *Nostradamus, ses prophéties*, Perrin et Cⁱᵉ, Paris, 1914.

Nostradamus, César : *Poésies*, Colomiez, Toulouse, 1606–8.
*L'Entrée de la reine Marie de Médicis en sa ville de Salon*, Jean Tholosan, Aix-en-Provence, 1602.
*Histoire et Chroniques de Provence*, Simon Rigaud, Lyon, 1614.

Nostradamus, Michel : *Les Prophéties de M. Michel Nostradamus :* Principal Editions :
    Macé Bonhomme, Lyon, 1555;
    Antoine du Rosne, Lyon, 1557–58;
    Barbe Régnault, Paris, 1560;
    Pierre Rigaud, Lyon, 1566;
    Benoist Rigaud, Lyon, 1568; in 8. *B.U. Montepellier*, no. 48340.

Charles Roger, Paris, 1569;
Pierre Meunier, Paris, 1589;
Jean Poyet, Lyon, 1600 (BN);
Benoist Rigaud, Lyon, 1605;
Pierre Rigaud, Lyon, 1605 (BN);
Pierre Rigaud, Lyon, 1610 (BN), 1649;
Claude La Rivière, Lyon, 1611;
Vincent Sève, Beaucaire, 1610;
Pierre Chevillot, Troyes, 1611;
Simon Rigaud, Lyon, 1644;
Pierre de Ruau, Troyes, 1649 (BN);
Winckermans, Amsterdam, 1657;
Jean Balam, Lyon, 1665;
Jean Ribon, vis-à-vis la Sainte Chapelle à l'image saint Louis, Paris, 1669;
Jean Huguetan, Lyon (17th century);
Jean Ianson, Amsterdam, 1668;
Jean Besongne, Rouen, 1681;
Besson, Lyon, 1691;
Jean Viret, Lyon, 1697 (BML);
Lambert-Gentot, *Nouvelles et Curieuses prédictions de M. Nostradamus, pour sept ans depuis l'année 1818 jusqu'à l'année 1824*, Lyon, 1818.

Landriot, Riom, no date (19th century);
Facsimiles of the 1611 Chevillot edition by Delarue, Paris, and of the 1668 Amsterdam edition by Ed. Adyar, Paris 1936.

*Prognostication nouvelle et prédiction portenteuse pour l'an 1555 composées par Maistre M. Nostradamus*, Jean Brotot, Lyon.

*Démonstration d'une comette*, Jean Marcorelle, Lyon, 1571 (BN)

*Prognostication et prédiction des quatre temps pour 1572*, Melchior Arnoullet, Lyon, 1572. (BN)

*Prophéties par l'Astrologue du Très Chrétien Roy de France et de Madame la Duchesse de Savoye*, F. Arnoullet, Lyon, 1572. (BN)

Nostradamus, Michel : *Lettre de Maistre Michel Nostradamus de Salon-de-Craux-en-Provence à la Royne, mère du Roy*, Benoist Rigaud, Lyon, 1566

*Almanach pour l'an 1573 avec les présages*, Pierre Roux, Avignon, 1562.

*Prophétie ou Révolution merveilleuse des 4 saisons de l'an*, Michel Jove, Lyon, 1567.

*Traité de fardements et confitures*, Antoine Volant, Lyon, 1555.

*Paraphrase de C. Galen*, trans. by Nostradamus, Antoine du Rosne, Lyon, 1557.

*Excellent et très utile opuscule de plusieurs exquises receptes*, Benoist Rigaud, Lyon, 1572.

*Almanach pour l'an 1567*, Benoist Odo, Lyon.

*La Grant Pronostication nouvelle avec la déclaration ample de 1559*, Jean Brotot, Lyon, 1558.

*Prophéties sur Lyon, La France et le monde entier dans les premières années du XXᵉ siècle*, 5 booklets, Lyon, P. Bousset & M. Paquet, 1907, 1909.

*Almanach des prophéties*, P. N. Jausserand, Lyon, 1871–72.

*Les Merveilleuses Centuries et Prophéties de Nostradamus*, colour illustrations by Jean Gradassi, Ed. André Virel, Ed. Artisanales SEFER, 880 copies, Nice, 1961.

*Les Prophéties de Nostradamus* (complete), Club des Champs Elysées, Ed. Baudelaire, Paris, 1967.

*Prophéties nouvelles de Michel Nostradamus trouvées dans sa tombe au moment de l'ouverture dans l'église des Cordeliers de Salon pour 1820, 1821, 1822, 1823, 1824, 1825 et 1826*, A Toulon de l'Imprimerie de Calmen, imprimeur du Roi, 11, rue d'Angoulême.

*Les Prophéties de Nostradamus* (complete), Les Cent un chefs d'œuvre du Génie Humain, Prodifu, 5, rue du Coq Héron, 75001 – Paris.

*Les Prophéties de Nostradamus*, pub. by the author, Marc Billerey, Mallefougasse (Alpes de Provence), 1973.

Undated edns (16th and 17th centuries) : Antoine Baudraud et Pierre André, Lyon.

Nostredame, Jean de : *Les Vies des plus célèbres et anciens poètes provençaux qui ont fleuri du temps des comtes de Provence*, Basile Bouquet, Lyon, 1575.

Novaye, Baron de : *Aujourd'hui et demain*, Paris, 1905.

Pagliani, Coraddo : 'Di Nostradamus e idi sue una poco nota iscrizione Liminare torinen', *Della Rassegna mensile Muncipale*, no. 1, Turin, 1934.

Parisot, F. : *Le Grand Avènement précédé d'un grand prodige*, typographie des Célestins, Bar-le-Duc, 1873.

Parker, Eugène : *La Légende de Nostradamus et sa vie réelle*, Paris, 1923.

Patrian, Carlo : *Nostradamus, le Profezie*, Edizioni Méditerranée, Via Flaminia, Rome, 1978.

Pelaprat, Jean Marie : 'Varennes et 1792, sauvent Nostradamus', *Historia*, no. 397(2), *Voyance et Prophéties*, Ed. Tallendier, Paris.

Pichon, Jean-Charles : *Nostradamus et le Secret des temps*, les productions de Paris, 1959.

*Nostradamus en clair*, R. Laffont, Paris, 1970.

*Le Royaume et les Prophètes*, R. Laffont, 1963.

Piobb, P. V. : Facsimile of Amsterdam edn, Adyar, Paris, 1936.

*Le Sort de l'Europe d'après la célèbre Prophétie des papes de Saint-Malachie, accompagnée de la Prophétie d'Orval et de toutes dernières indications de Nostradamus*, Dangles, Paris, 1939.

Privat, Maurice : *1938, année de relèvement*.

*1938, année d'échéance*.

*1939, année de reprise*, Editions Médicis, Paris, 1938.

*Demain, la guerre*.

*1940, prédictions mondiales, année de grandeur française*, Editions Médicis, Paris.

Putzien, Rudolf : *Friede unter volkern? Die Weisagungen des M. Nostradamus und ihre Bedeutung fur Atomzeitaler*, Drei eichen Verlag, H. Kissener, München, 1958.

Reed, Clarence : *Great Prophecies about the war*, Faber & Faber, London, 1941.

Reynaud, Jean-Lucien : *Nostradamus n'a pas menti*, lecture, ville d'Avray, 1948. *Nostradamus délié*, ville d'Avray, 1949.

Reynaud-Plense : *Les Vraies Prophéties de Nostradamus*, Salon, 1939.

Robb, Steward : *Nostradamus on Napoleon*, Oracle Press, New York, 1961. *Nostradamus on Napoleon, Hitler and the present crisis*, Scribner's, New York, 1941. *Prophecies on world events by Nostradamus*, New York, 1961.

Robert, Henry : *The Complete Prophecies of Nostradamus*, Ed. H. Robert, Great Neck, New York, 1971. Japanese trans. by Kasuko Daijyo with Hidéo Uchida, Ed. Tama, Tokyo, 1975.

Rochetaille, P. : *Prophéties de Nostradamus. The key to the 'Centuries', with special reference to the history of Third Republic*, Adyar, 1939.

Roisin, Michel de : 'Ulrich de Mayence, maître de Nostradamus', *Aesculape*, no. 5, 1969, 52nd year. 'Plus forte que Nostradamus : Ulrich de Mayence', *Constellation*, no. 199, November 1964.

Rollet, Pierre : *Interprétation des Hiéroglyphes de Horapollo*, Ramoun Béren-guié, Aix-en-Provence, 1968.

Roudene, Alex : *Les Prophéties, vérité ou mensonge*, 'Mondes Magiques series', Ed. de l'Athanor, Paris, 1976.

Rouellond de la Rouellondière de Chollet : *La Prophétie de Rouellond, Manuscrit du XVIᵉ siècle*, Victor Pipeau, Beauvais, 1861.

Rouvier, Camille : *Nostradamus*, Marseille, La Savoisienne, 1964.

Ruir, Emile : *Le Grand Carnage d'après les prophéties de Nostradamus de 1938 à 1947*, Ed. Médicis, Paris, 1938. *L'Ecroulement de l'Europe, d'après les prophéties de Nostradamus*, Paris. 1939.

Ruir, Emile : *Nostradamus, ses Prophéties, 1948–2023*, Paris, 1948. *Nostradamus. Les Proches et Derniers Evénements*, Ed. Médicis, Paris, 1953.

Ruzo, Daniel : *Les Derniers Jours de l'Apocalypse*, Payot, 1973. *Los ultimos dias del apocalipsis*, Michel Shultz, Mexico.

Sede, Gérard de : *Les Secrets de Nostradamus*, Julliard, Paris, 1969.

Spica-Capella : *La Clef des prédictions nostradamiques*, Ed. des soirées astrolo-giques, 1941.

Tamizey de Larroque : *Les Correspondants de Pieresc, César Nostradamus*, un-published letters from Salon to Peiresc, 1628–29, Typographie Marius Olive, Marseille, 1880.

Tarade, Guy : 'La Clef des centuries de Nostradamus', *Pégase*, no. 3, 1974. *Les Dernières Prophéties pour l'Occident*, 'Les Enigmes de l'Univers' series, Robert Laffont, Paris, 1979.

Torne-Chavigny, H. : Reissue of the *Prophecies of Nostradamus*, 1862 edition, enlarged in 1872. *Prospectus : interprétation de 30 quatrains*, 1860. L'Histoire prédite et jugée par Nostradamus, 3 vol., Bordeaux, 1860. Affiches : tableau de l'histoire prédite et jugée, 1862. *Prospectus des lettres du grande prophète : interprétation de 20 quatrains*. *Les lettres du grand prophète*.

*Henri V à Anvers.*
*Nostradamus et l'astrologie.*
*Les Blancs et les rouges.*
*La Salette et Lourdes.*
*La mort de Napoléon III.*
*MacMahon et Napoléon IV.*
*Le roy blanc et la fusion.*
*Portraits prophétiques d'après Nostradamus.*
*Prophéties dites d'Olivarius et d'Orval.*
*L'Apocalypse interprétée par Nostradamus,* 1872.
Almanach du grand prophète Nostradamus pour 1873.
Nostradamus éclairci ou Nostradamus devant monseigneur Dupanloup, Saint-Denis-du-Pin, 1874.
*Ce qui sera d'après le grand prophète Nostradamus,* followed by *Almanach pour 1878.*
*Influence de Nostradamus dans le gouvernement de la France,* 1878.
*Concordance de Nostradamus avec l'Apocalypse,* Veuve Dupuy, Bordeaux, 1861.

Touchard, Michel : *Nostradamus,* Grasset, 1972
'Histoire des personnages mystérieux et des sociétés secrètes' series, Ed. Celt, Paris, 1972.

Touchard, Michel : 'Les Prophéties de Michel Nostradamus. Le rêve fou', *Historia,* no. 34, 1974.

Tronc de Condoulet : *Abrégé de la vie de Nostradamus,* followed by *Nouvelle découverte de ses quatrains,* J. Adibert, Aix-en-Provence. (BMA)

Van Gerdinge, René : 'Le Nez de Cléopâtre', *Messidor,* no. 29, Montfavet, Vaucluse.

Verdier, du : *Les Vertus de notre maistre Nostradamus,* Geneva, 1562.

Viaud, Jean : '1999, Un tournant dans l'histoire des hommes', *Constellation,* no. 166, Feb. 1962.

Vidél, Laurent : *Déclaration des abus, ignorances et séditions de Michel Nostradamus,* Avignon, 1558.

Vignois, Élisée du : *Notre Histoire racontée à l'avance par Nostradamus,* Paris, 1910.

*L'Apocalypse, interprète de la Révolution, d'après Nostradamus,* Noyon, 1911.

Vogel, Cyrille : *Saint Césaire d'Arles,* 1937.

Voldben, A. : *After Nostradamus,* Neville Spearman, London, 1973.

Ward, Charles A. : *Oracles of Nostradamus,* London, 1891.

Willoquet, Gaston : *La Vérité sur Nostradamus,* Ed. Traditionnelles, Paris, 1967.

Winckermans : *Editions des Centuries,* Amsterdam, 1657.

Woolf, H. I. : *Nostradamus,* London, 1944.

Yram : *Prophéties connues et prédictions inédites,* Preface by Papus, l'Edition d'Art, Paris.

Zevaco, Michel : *Nostradamus* (novel), Fayard, 1909, Livre de Poche, no. 3306.

3/8/24

THEODOSIUS DOBZHANSKY

# *Genetics*

## OF THE

# *Evolutionary Process*

COLUMBIA UNIVERSITY PRESS

*New York and London*

Copyright © 1970 Columbia University Press
Library of Congress Catalog Card Number: 72-127363

Printed in the United States of America
ISBN: 0-231-02837-7 *Clothbound*
ISBN: 0-231-08306-8 *Paperback*

9 8 7 6 5 4

*To the Memory of My Mother*

〰〰

This book was started as a fourth edition of my "Genetics and the Origin of Species" (three previous editions: 1937, 1941, and 1951). It soon became apparent that so much has happened in evolutionary biology during the years since 1951 that no revision of the old book can be satisfactory. This does not exactly mean that everything in it is wrong. On the contrary, most of it is valid. Something more interesting has occurred: new problems have replaced the old at the forefront of our attention. Many things that had to be argued and documented in 1937, and even in 1951, now seem almost trite. For example, does one need nowadays to convince the reader that mutants are not mere laboratory products but occur as well in natural populations? Or that the differences between subspecies of wild animals and plants are mostly genetic? Or that species differences are compounded of the same building blocks as intraspecific and individual differences? On the other hand, it is now more clearly realized than it was in the past that natural selection is a common name for a complex of processes of rather diverse kinds and different biological significance. The discoveries of molecular geneticists have advanced our understanding of the origin of the evolutionary raw materials, and are throwing new light on the dynamics of the evolutionary process itself.

Some troublesome (and even painful) decisions had to be made in selecting the topics to be included in the book. The plain fact is that the relevant literature is now overwhelmingly vast. In the nineteen twenties, at the beginning of my career as a geneticist, I could truthfully claim to have at least glanced through a majority of the articles on genetics published until then in major European languages. I doubt whether anybody could make this claim at present, and I certainly cannot do so. An attempt to summarize all the available literature (even if this could be done) would not only make this book unduly long, but would also transform it into a kind of annotated bibliography. My intention is, rather, to present ideas with necessary examples, and not a miscellany of literature references. To this end, I have selected some illustrative references and, of necessity, left the rest aside. The choice could hardly be other than arbitrary. Many excellent contributions are not mentioned, and I can only beg forgiveness of their authors.

A whole field of mathematical genetics has developed in recent years. I am not at home in this field and must forbear from explaining it in detail. Yet no evolutionist can ignore the achievements of genetical mathematicians. My only recourse is to try to understand their assumptions and conclusions, and to hope that what comes in between is valid. Although much of the current research in genetics employs micro-organisms as experimental materials, higher organisms get more attention in the book than lower ones, diploids more than haploids, sexually reproducing more than asexual ones. Drosophila is no longer the queen of genetics, as at one time it was. It remains, however, probably the best material for studies on evolutionary and population genetics, and I happen to be most familiar with it. Hence it will figure prominently in the following pages.

Evolutionary genetics is at present in an exciting period of development. Discoveries currently being made upset some classical theories that have acquired a status almost of dogmata. Clashes of opinion and polemics abound; new theories are being put forward that may or may not gain acceptance. No matter how much one tries to keep a stance of objectivity, some persons will find their views not given sufficient prominence, or presented in ways not conforming to their tastes. Moreover, a book attempting to describe a rapidly developing field will inevitably soon be out of date. The bibliography was completed in November 1969, which means that only a few more recent papers with which I was familiar in manuscript are referred to. I regret most of all the non-inclusion of the collection of essays edited by Drs. M. K. Hecht and W. C. Steere (Appleton-Century-Crofts, New York, 1970), since all of these essays are most relevant to the topics discussed in this book.

When there is a choice between discussing older or newer works dealing with the same topic, the newer ones are generally chosen. Of course, I have not done this because new works are always better than the old. My rationale is rather that recent articles usually contain references to the older ones, while the converse is not true. For the same reason, reviews and secondary sources are sometimes cited, even when I am familiar with the primary ones. Problems of priority have often been given short shrift. And yet, to trace the evolution of ideas about evolution one often has to go back to Morgan, Mendel, Darwin, and even Aristotle and Plato.

In writing this book the help of several colleagues and friends was invaluable. It is a great pleasure to acknowledge my obligations to Drs. F. Ayala and Lee Ehrman, who read the entire text; and to V. C. Allfrey, Verne Grant, I. M. Lerner, R. C. Lewontin, R. C. Richmond, Bruce Wallace, and L. J. Wangh, each of whom read one or more chapters. None of them is responsible for mistakes which will doubtless be found in the book, especially since their advice was not always heeded. But who can produce a book entirely free of mistakes? Finally, I am grateful to Mr. Andrea Palestrina, who patiently typed and retyped the entire book.

Theodosius Dobzhansky

*July 20, 1970*
*New York City*

# CONTENTS

❧

# GENETICS OF THE EVOLUTIONARY PROCESS

# THE UNITY AND DIVERSITY OF LIFE

∾∾

## Life and Evolution

A man consists of some seven octillion ($7 \times 10^{27}$) atoms, grouped in about ten trillion ($10^{13}$) cells. This agglomeration of cells and atoms has some astounding properties; it is alive, feels joy and suffering, discriminates between beauty and ugliness, and distinguishes good from evil. There are many other living agglomerations of atoms, belonging to at least two million, possibly twice that many, biological species. What is most remarkable is that the individuals of every one of these species are so designed that they are able to live and reproduce in some existing environments. In other words, each species is adapted to a certain way of life. How has this come about? How can agglomerations of atoms accomplish any of these things?

Two kinds of answers have been proposed. Vitalists assume that living bodies are formed through the intervention of occult forces, variously called entelechy (Aristotle, Driesch), *vis essentialis* (C. F. Wolff), psyche, or inherent directiveness (Sinnott). Mechanists, on the other hand, claim that all biological structures and processes are only highly elaborate patterns of physical and chemical phenomena. Life can be understood without recourse to the assumption of any transcendental powers.

Vitalism goes often, though not always, together with creationism, that is, with the belief that the world as a whole, and the living species in particular, were created a few thousand years ago and have remained essentially unchanged since then. Lamarck, Darwin, and others after them expounded a different view: the living world that we observe at present has been shaped during billions of years of evolutionary history. The organisms now living have evolved gradually from ancestors that were generally more and more different from their descendants as one looks progressively farther back in time. Some vitalists do not deny evolution, but claim that it is guided toward predestined ends by inscrutable forces. Darwin thought otherwise. He posited natural selection as a process that impels and directs evolutionary changes. Subsequent research has on the whole vindicated his view.

Natural selection is a strictly biological phenomenon, in the sense that it is a sequel to life, and it exists solely in the living world. The essence of natural selection is the differential reproduction of the carriers of different hereditary endowments (see Chapters 4-7 for further discussion). Reproduction is the most important, or at any rate one of the most important, functions of life. Therefore, natural selection could not have begun before life appeared. (See, however, Spiegelman's work, discussed in Chapter 3.) Speaking of prebiological natural selection represents either a loose metaphor or a misapplication of a fundamental biological concept. On the other hand, reproduction, in conjunction with hereditary variation, makes natural selection inevitable. Natural selection is a pattern of physical events, and a pattern that is contingent upon and is restricted to life. Living bodies that have evolved under the control of natural selection can be described as machines, though machines of a very special sort. (For a contrary view, see Polanyi 1968.)

### Cartesian and Darwinian Biology

The mechanist hypothesis was enunciated by Descartes in the seventeenth century. "The body of a living man," he wrote, "differs from that of a dead man just as does a watch or other automation (i.e., a machine that moves of itself), when it is wound up and contains in itself the corporeal principle of those movements for which it is designed, along with all that is requisite for its action, from the same watch or other machine when it is broken and when the principle of its movement ceases to act."

Any living organism, even the "simplest," is a machine of prodigious complexity. To understand how a machine works one should examine it in two different but complementary ways. It is necessary both to know the components of the machine and to comprehend how they fit together. Also, the more complex is a machine, the more critical become its structure and the interrelationships of its parts. The Cartesian reductionist method calls for a description of life in terms of the chemical and physical components and processes in living bodies. Some of the major triumphs of biology have been achieved with the aid of the Cartesian method. The discovery of the role of nucleic acids in the transmission and realization of heredity is an outstanding recent example.

The Cartesian approach has as its goal the reduction of biology to the status of a specialized branch of chemistry and physics. Some "molecular biologists" proclaim aggressively that the only worthwhile way to study life is in terms of its chemical and physical components and processes. They are confident that, in the fullness of time, when this study has advanced far enough, all the more complex biological phenomena will be seen clearly, or even predicted, as patterns of simple physicochemical ones. The interest and importance of molecular biology are, of course, unquestionable. The self-sufficiency of the reductionist program is, however, quite another matter. Reduction is "the explanation of a theory or a set of experimental laws established in one area of inquiry, by a theory usually though not invariably formulated in some other domain" (Nagel 1961).

It may well be doubted that all biological explanations and laws can be deduced from the more "powerful" physicochemical laws. This does not imply any kind of attenuated vitalism. Biological laws, such as Mendel's laws, deal with particular patterns of physical and chemical processes that occur only in living bodies. They are simply irrelevant, not contrary, to physics and chemistry. Nagel has written:

There are sectors of biological inquiry in which physicochemical explanations play little or no role at present, and a number of biological theories have been successfully exploited which are not physicochemical in character. . . . Thus, there is a genuine alternative in biology to both vitalism and mechanism—namely, the development of systems of explanation that employ concepts and assert relations neither defined in nor derived from the physical sciences.

Biology is faced with several hierarchically superimposed levels of integration of structures and functions: molecular, cellular, individual, populational, ecosystemic. Discoveries have certainly been made on all these levels. Far more often, however, findings on higher levels point to the need of investigations of underlying levels than vice versa. Mendelian inheritance was not deduced from studies on the chemistry of DNA; these studies derive their significance in part from their bearing on Mendelian inheritance. Embryonic development was studied before the processes of transcription and translation in the DNA-RNA-protein codes were discovered. These findings suggest research strategies for further advances of embryology.

It is convenient to distinguish the molecular level from the organismic (cellular + individual + populational + ecosystemic) levels of integration. Explanations of the type termed by Simpson (1964a) as compositionist are important in biology, particularly on organismic levels. In this connection Simpson wrote:

> In biology, then, a second kind of explanation must be added to the first or reductionist explanation made in terms of physical, chemical, and mechanical principles. This second form of explanation, which can be called compositionist in contrast to reductionist, is in terms of adaptive usefulness of structures and processes to the whole organism and to the species of which it is a part, and still further, in terms of ecological function in the communities in which the species occurs.

### Adaptedness

Explanations in terms of adaptedness or teleology are not only appropriate but indeed necessary in biology, whereas they are meaningless in the nonliving world. The often misunderstood concept of teleology has been analyzed by Ayala (1968). The structures and functions of living bodies are said to exhibit adaptedness, or end-directedness, when they are shown to contribute to individual survival or to reproduction, which makes possible the survival of the species. Now, end-directedness may be due to external teleology, imposed by man for his purposes. Man-made tools, machines, and regulatory mechanisms are examples of such external teleology. The end-directedness of living bodies is of a different kind; it is internal teleology. The purposefulness of the components and of their configurations in living bodies that constitutes this internal teleology is a fact of observation. Such adaptedness makes survival and reproduction possible.

To understand and explain this internal teleology is the foremost, or at any rate one of the foremost, problems of compositionist, or Darwinian, biology. Satisfactory explanation of internal teleology eluded philosophers and biologists for a long time. Creationists believe that living bodies are engineered by a wise Creator; according to this view, organisms, like human contrivances, exhibit external teleology. To vitalists, teleology is an elemental property immanent in life. It cannot and need not be analyzed any further. To most biologists since Darwin, internal teleology is a product of evolutionary development. The adaptedness is neither devised nor planned by any external conscious agent; it is not guaranteed by a providential ability of living matter to act purposefully. Rather, it has evolved and is being maintained and often improved by natural selection.

Cartesian biology deals with organisms as they are today; Darwinian biology asks also how they got to be what they are. The "arrow of time" is most important in Darwinian biology. An individual organism develops from a fertilized egg or from a bud to an embryo, a juvenile, an adult, a senescent, a corpse. The development is directional and, except for minor details, irreversible. The directionality of individual development has always been recognized; the development of the living world as a whole, and of the Universe as a whole, is a relatively recent discovery.

The world images of Oriental philosophers and the philosophers of classical Greece were dominated by static or cyclic conceptions of time. Parmenides thought that changes which one observes happening in the world are illusions of the senses. Others believed that changes are cyclic and repeat themselves without end, as day becomes night and night changes to day. The most subtle synthesis of these speculations was given in the fourth century B.C. by Plato. What we observe in the world are only shadows of the eternal archetypes or ideas (*Eidos*). An individual man is only a distorted image of the unimaginably perfect and beautiful Man. All horses are warped replicas of the ideal Horse, and all dogs of the ideal Dog. The earthly replicas can perhaps be improved to reflect their archetypes more faithfully, but they cannot equal, much less exceed, the perfection of their celestial models. In what follows we shall have several occasions to criticize the application of this typological mode of thought to biological problems.

The evolutionary world view assumes a linear, instead of a cyclic, concept of time. Things, especially living things, were different in the past and will be different in the future. History is not an illusion, not a tedious return of past states. It is evolution, which has brought about the present state and will usher in the future states of the world. Because of an egregious miscomprehension, some Christians have fought Darwin's evolutionary interpretation of the living world, and eventually of the universe as a whole, though a linear concept of time is basic to Christian religious thought. At any rate, in biology nothing makes sense except in the light of evolution. It is possible to describe living beings without asking questions about their origins. The descriptions acquire meaning and coherence, however, only when viewed in the perspective of evolutionary development.

### Chemical Composition

Living bodies are composed of the same chemical elements as are found also in the inorganic world. Data on the composition of living matter are summarized in Table 1.1. The three most abundant elements, oxygen, carbon, and hydrogen, constitute about 98.5 percent of organic matter. Oxygen and hydrogen are also among the elements most abundant in nonliving things. Carbon, on the other hand, is conspicuously more abundant in living bodies or in their remains and derivatives than elsewhere.

More than a century ago (in 1848 and 1860) Pasteur discovered another characteristic of living matter that proved to be remarkably general. Many chemical substances exist in two dissymmetric molecular forms, the right (D) and the left (L) isomers. This leads to optical activity, manifested in a rotation of the plane of polarized light either to the right or to the left. Compounds synthesized in the laboratory, on the other hand, are usually racemic, that is, optically inactive. The

**TABLE 1.1**

Average composition of living matter in percentages of the chemical elements by weight (After Vernadsky 1965)

| Element | % | Element | % | Element | % |
|---------|------|---------|-----------------|---------|-----------------|
| O | 70 | Fe | 0.01 | Cr | $2 \times 10^{-4}$ |
| C | 18 | Al | 0.005 | Br | $1.5 \times 10^{-4}$ |
| H | 10.5 | Ba | 0.003 | Ge | $1 \times 10^{-4}$ |
| Ca | 0.5 | Sr | 0.002 | Ni | $5 \times 10^{-5}$ |
| K | 0.3 | Mn | 0.001 | Pb | $5 \times 10^{-5}$ |
| N | 0.3 | B | 0.001 | St | $5 \times 10^{-5}$ |
| Si | 0.2 | Th | 0.001 | As | $3 \times 10^{-5}$ |
| Mg | 0.04 | Ti | $8 \times 10^{-4}$ | Co | $2 \times 10^{-5}$ |
| P | 0.04 | F | $5 \times 10^{-4}$ | Li | $1 \times 10^{-5}$ |
| S | 0.05 | Zn | $5 \times 10^{-4}$ | Mo | $1 \times 10^{-5}$ |
| Na | 0.02 | Rb | $5 \times 10^{-4}$ | Y | $1 \times 10^{-5}$ |
| Cl | 0.02 | Cu | $2 \times 10^{-4}$ | Cs | $1 \times 10^{-5}$ |
|  |  | V | $2 \times 10^{-4}$ |  |  |

famous experiments of Pasteur demonstrated that such artificially prepared racemic substances consist of equal amounts of D and L isomers and that the isomers can be artificially separated.

What is notable is that in most organisms the principal constituents of protoplasm, particularly the amino acids, are represented exclusively by L isomers. Why this should be so is conjectural at present. This phenomenon may be evidence of life having arisen monophyletically (from a common stem), with L optically active constituents (Gause 1941 and Lederberg 1965). Certain bacteria contain also D amino acids, but these are mostly components of antimetabolites, toxic to competing organisms, whereas the essential proteins of the bacteria still contain L amino acids. In addition, D isomers are found in some relatively advanced forms, among earthworms and insects (Cloud 1968 and Corrigan 1969). This should not be taken as evidence that life is polyphyletic, having arisen independently two or more times. The many similarities in the key constituents of most diverse organisms (e.g., the two varieties of nucleic acids, DNA and RNA, and energy-storing compounds such as adenosine triphosphate) argue against a polyphyletic origin.

Much greater diversity of chemical compounds is found in living bodies than in nonliving ones. Nevertheless the distinction between organic and inorganic chemistry is not sharp. In 1829, Wöhler synthesized in the laboratory an organic compound, namely, urea. So many organic substances have subsequently been synthesized that additions to the list are important only if some particularly interesting or useful substance is involved. Although the progress of biochemistry has been impressive, it hardly warrants flights of fancy like that of Pollard (1965), who proposes, apparently in all seriousness, to construct not only the chemical components but actually a living bacterial cell!

How did life originate in the first place? It has been one of the biological certitudes since the days of Redi (seventeenth century), Spallanzani (eighteenth), and Pasteur (nineteenth) that life arises only from other life—*omne vivum ex vivo*. An impressive amount of research and an even greater amount of speculation have been devoted to this problem in recent years. It would be out of place here to attempt to review this large topic in detail, especially since technical as well as popular accounts are available (e.g., Oparin 1964, Sullivan 1964, and Bernal 1967).

Very briefly, the following scheme is proposed. Some chemical compounds were formed under the conditions of the primitive, lifeless earth that are now obtained only, or at least mainly, from living bodies. Experiments are therefore contrived to simulate the conditions supposed to have existed on the primitive earth. Several amino acids and even peptides and nucleotides have been thus obtained. Primordial oceans may, then, have contained a very dilute "broth" of organic compounds. But even if such a "broth" existed, the origin in it of the first self-reproducing, and hence living, systems remains an unsolved problem. Some writers have bravely, but not very convincingly, declared that, given the basic chemical properties of matter, the origin of life was inevitable. Since life has in fact appeared, its origin was indeed inevitable. Yet the problem cannot be resolved by a fiat; nobody really knows just how great an order of improbability this "inevitable" event involved. Hence we cannot be sure that, if there exist a million million planets more or less resembling the earth, any of them had extraterrestrial life originate and evolve.

### The Carriers of Genetic Information

Perhaps the most impressive demonstration of the unity of life is that in all organisms the genetic information is coded in two related groups of substances—the deoxyribonucleic (DNA) and ribonucleic (RNA) acids. Yet this method of coding is so versatile that the number of possible genetic "messages" is virtually infinite. Here, then, is the basis of the diversity as well as the unity of life.

A new era in understanding the physical basis of heredity, and hence of evolution, began in 1953 with the publication by Watson and Crick of the double-helix model of the structure of DNA. In the unbelievably short period since then, the model not only was shown to correspond to reality but also led to novel insights into the processes of gene and chromosome replication, gene mutation, and gene action in protein synthesis, and to a beginning of an understanding of the regulation of gene action in development. This explosive growth of biochemical and biological knowledge resulted from both independent and joint efforts of thousands of investigators. Although a detailed account of this success story, the greatest in the history of biology, cannot be given in this book, many accounts, ranging all the way from highly technical to popular ones (Watson 1965 and G. W. Beadle and M. Beadle 1966, to name only two examples from opposite ends of the spectrum), are now available. The brief description that follows is intended merely as a base line for the references to molecular genetics found elsewhere in this book. Only a sampling of the bibliography is given.

All nucleic acids are basically uniform in structure. Can the various genes in the same and in different organisms be so similar in composition? Most biologists held this impossible until Watson and Crick proposed their double-helix model of DNA. Nucleic acids are chainlike molecules; DNA molecules are paired chains, wound helically around a common axis. The backbone of each chain is made up of alternating deoxyribose sugars and phosphate groups; the links between the chains involve the nucleotide bases. Four nucleotide bases are commonly found—two purines (adenine, A, and guanine, G) and two pyrimidines (thymine, T, and cytosine, C). The paired chains are held together by weak hydrogen bonds between the nucleotides, in such a way that an A in one chain is always linked to a T in the other, and vice versa. Similarly, each G is linked with a C, and vice versa. As a consequence, the DNA's of quite diverse organisms have as many A as T bases, and as many C's and G's (in other words, the A : T and C : G ratios equal unity). By contrast, the proportions of $(A + T) : (C + G)$ bases vary rather widely.

The important variables are, however, the sequences of the bases in the chains. A particular sequence of specific letters of the English alphabet can make up any word of the English language; it can also convey information or a message. So can the sequence of the four genetic "letters" in DNA; genetic "messages" are composed of different linear sequences of the genetic letters. Four letters taken two at a time can give 16, and taken three at a time, 64 different combinations. If a gene is a genetic message consisting of $n$ letters, $4^n$ variant messages are possible. The numbers of nucleotide pairs in a gene may range in the hundreds or even the thousands. The possible variety of genes is enormous.

The double-helix model makes it possible to envisage how the genes direct their own precise replication. One has to suppose that the hydrogen bonds between the nucleotides in the paired chains break, and the chains unwind; each A attracts a T, each T an A, each C a G, and each G a C. The new bases are linked by a new sugar-phosphate backbone. The outcome is a pair of double helices similar to each other and to the parental one.

Meselson and Stahl (1958) submitted this scheme of the replication of DNA to a test. *Escherichia coli* were grown first in a medium containing $N^{15}$, a heavy isotope of nitrogen, and subsequently on ordinary nitrogen, $N^{14}$. The bacterium has no nucleus but a single circular chromosome; when grown on $N^{15}$, both strands of the DNA helix have this isotope. After the transfer to $N^{14}$ and a single division, one strand of the helix has $N^{15}$ and the other $N^{14}$. After two divisions one-half of the cells have no heavy nitrogen, and the other half have one heavy and one light strand. The replication of the chromosomes is therefore "semi-conservative;" both strands of the DNA in a helix serve as templates for the synthesis of new strands, but the integrity of the old and the new strands is conserved. The replication of the chromosomes in higher organisms may also be semiconservative (Taylor 1969).

The near universality of the four genetic letters, A, T, C, and G, indicates that evolution of life has taken place by means of the composition of ever new "messages," not of new "letters." The existence of some exceptions must nevertheless be noted. Methyl cytosine, hydroxy methyl cytosine, and methyl adenine replace cytosine and adenine in some bacteria and bacteriophages (Jukes 1966 and Vanyushin, Belozersky, et al. 1968). It is conceivable that among the primordial forms of life there may have existed a greater diversity of genetic "letters," and that the four now used proved more convenient and hence replaced the others. Sinsheimer (1959) showed that the tiny bacteriophage $\phi$ X 174 has a molecule of single-stranded, instead of double-stranded, DNA as its hereditary material. It probably becomes double-stranded while replicating, and reverts to the single-stranded condition later.

Some plant viruses, of which the tobacco mosaic virus is the best-known representative, and also some bacteriophages have RNA instead of DNA as the carrier of genetic information. However, RNA is present in all organisms, since it is involved in the translation of the information stored in the DNA into protein structure (see below). RNA differs from DNA in having a ribose, instead of a deoxyribose, sugar and in having thymine (T) replaced by uracil (U). A tobacco mosaic virus particle has a core of a single strand of RNA containing about 6000 nucleotides, surrounded by a protein coat. When the virus infects a cell of a tobacco plant, it sheds its protein coat, and its RNA subverts the metabolic machinery of the host cell to form virus proteins instead of tobacco proteins. Ingenious experiments of Schramm (1956) and of Fraenkel-Conrat and Singer (1957) demonstrated that it is, indeed, the RNA and not the protein that directs the formation of the virus. They separated the RNA of the virus from the protein, and showed that new complete virus particles are formed on infection of tobacco leaves by the RNA alone. An analogous feat was achieved by Guthrie and Sinsheimer (1960), who infected the protoplasts (i.e., cells stripped of the surface cuticle) of *Escherichia coli* with purified DNA obtained from the $\phi$ X 174 bacteriophage.

The brilliant work of Kornberg and his students has demonstrated that DNA may serve as a template for self-replication *in vitro* as well as in a living cell (Kornberg 1962 and other works). The key to their success was the discovery of an enzyme, DNA polymerase, which catalyzes the synthesis (or repair) of DNA chains replicating those of a given "primer" DNA. A cell-free system is made containing this enzyme isolated from *Escherichia coli*, the four deoxynucleoside triphosphates, A, T, G, and C, and magnesium ions. To such a system are added as primers small amounts of DNA isolated from *E. coli* or from some other organism. Not only is new DNA synthesized, but also —and more significant—this new DNA resembles in composition that of the organism furnishing the primer, rather than that furnishing the enzyme. If self-replication is considered the fundamental manifestation of life, in these experiments we come close to a reproduction of a life process. This is true even though the materials involved are isolated chemically from other living beings.

### The Genetic Code

Presumably every gene has at least two functions. It makes more of itself, serving as a template for the production of its facsimiles. It also forwards the genetic information stored in its DNA to direct the metabolic processes in the cell, and eventually in the body that carries it. The double-helix model has not only successfully explained the first function but also pointed the way toward elucidation of the second. S. Brenner, F. H. C. Crick, H. G. Khorana, M. Nirenberg, S. Ochoa, C. Yanofsky, and others have made major contributions in this field.

Although the basic understanding of heredity has come from studies on higher organisms, most of the current work uses prokaryotes (organisms lacking discrete nuclei) as materials. Bacteria, especially *Escherichia coli*, and bacteriophages are the predilect objects of molecular genetics. Caution is called for in extrapolation of the findings to the eukaryotes (the higher organisms having organized nuclei) and indeed to the entire living world. Unfortunately, such caution has not always been exercised.

Many, perhaps most, genes are structural genes, specifying the sequences of amino acids in proteins. Like nucleic acid, proteins are chain molecules. The backbone of a protein consists of so-called peptide linkages between successive amino acids. Many proteins (e.g., hemoglobins) are composed of two or more chains, coded by different genes, bent and folded in various ways. Although at least 170 different amino acids are known, only 20 are the common constituents of proteins. These 20 "letters" of the protein "alphabet" stand in a remarkable relationship to the 5 letters of the DNA and RNA alphabets.

Two processes, transcription and translation, intervene between the gene and the protein. At least three different kinds of RNA are involved—messenger, transfer, and ribosomal. The specificity of a gene resides in the order of the genetic letters in a certain section of the DNA helix. This order is transcribed, with the aid of the enzyme RNA polymerase, in a corresponding sequence of letters in a single-stranded messenger RNA. The latter is then translated into a specific sequence of amino acids in a polypeptide chain of a protein. Thus the DNA of a chromosome serves as a template, the sequence of the genetic letters in it dictating that in the messenger RNA (see, however, Bell 1969). The process is similar in principle to the synthesis of new DNA strands, except that in RNA uridine (U) corresponds to thymidine (T) in DNA, and that, for reasons not yet understood, only one of the two strands of the DNA helix is transcribed.

The translation is an even more complex process, which takes place on the cytoplasmic organelles known as ribosomes. There probably exist at least 60 different varieties of transfer RNA, corresponding to the triplets of the genetic code (see the next paragraph), and at least 20 activating enzymes that attach the different amino acids to the transfer RNA's. The ribosomes contain additional RNA's peculiar to them. Messenger RNA becomes associated with the ribosomes. The various amino acids, "activated" by the attachment to their transfer RNA's, are then added one by one to the growing polypeptide chain, in the order specified by the sequence of the code letters in the messenger. The translation of the nucleotide sequence in the messenger begins at a fixed end of the RNA strand and proceeds to the opposite end. Every three consecutive letters specify a certain amino acid.

The genetic code is a triplet and nonoverlapping code. This means that the translation proceeds by a "reading frame," which moves by three nucleotides in the messenger RNA and by a single amino acid in the protein at a time. One of the splendid achievements started in 1961 by the work of Nirenberg and Matthei was "breaking" the genetic code. Table 1.2 shows the correspondence between the 64 possible triplets, the 20 amino acids, and the protein chain initiation and termination.

The genetic code is said to be "degenerate." This refers to the fact that the same amino acid can be coded, at least *in vitro*, by more than a single triplet. Indeed, there are six triplets each coding for leucine, arginine, and serine. When a given amino acid is coded by different triplets in the same or in different organisms, these different triplets and the corresponding transfer RNA's need not be equally abundant in all cells. We shall return to this problem in Chapter 8. Three triplets, namely, UAA, UAG, and UGA, code for no known amino acids. They have been dubbed "nonsense" codons, a name hardly deserved since they appear to serve the important function of terminating the translation of the RN codons into polypeptide chains.

Nirenberg and Matthei (1961) have demonstrated that the same triplet code is "recognized" in protein synthesis in quite diverse organisms. For example, RNA of the tobacco mosaic virus induces protein synthesis in cell-free extracts that contain ribosomes of *Escherichia coli*. More recently Marshall, Caskey, and Nirenberg (1967) obtained even more remarkable results. They worked with cell-free systems including ribosomes, the necessary enzymes, messenger RNA of *E. coli*, and transfer RNA of either *E. coli*, a toad (Xenopus), or a mammal (guinea pig). As many as 50 codons were "recognized" in these systems by the transfer RNA's of the very different organisms just named, but considerable differences in the efficiency of certain codons were also noted. Hence, although these data are usually interpreted to mean that the genetic code is universal (or nearly so) in the living world, some skeptics (e.g., Commoner 1964) are impressed by the differences as well as by the similarities.

Conclusive evidence of the "colinearity" of the sequences of the nucleotides in a gene, and of the amino acids in a protein that this

**TABLE 1.2**

The genetic code of RNA nucleotide triplets, specifying the amino acids in protein chains: U, uracil; A, adenine; C, cytosine; G, guanine

| Triplet | Amino Acid | Triplet | Amino Acid |
|---------|-----------|---------|-----------|
| UUA UUG CUU CUC CUA CUG | Leucine (Leu) | ACU ACC ACA ACG | Threonine (Thr) |
| UCU UCC UCA UCG AGU AGC | Serine (Ser) | GGU GGC GGA GGG | Glycine (Gly) |
| | | AUU AUC AUA | Isoleucine (Ile) |
| CGU CGC CGA CGG AGA AGG | Arginine (Arg) | UUU UUC | Phenylalanine (Phe) |
| | | UGU UGC | Cysteine (Cys) |
| GUU GUC GUA GUG | Valine (Val) | UAU UAC | Tyrosine (Tyr) |
| | | CAU CAC | Histidine (His) |
| CCU CCC CCA CCG | Proline (Pro) | CAA CAG | Glutamine (Gln) |
| | | AAU AAC | Asparagine (Asn) |
| GCU GCC GCA GCG | Alanine (Ala) | AAA AAG | Lysine (Lys) |
| | | GAU GAC | Aspartic acid (Asp) |
| UAA UAG UGA | Chain termination | GAA GAG | Glutamic acid (Glu) |
| AUG | Methionine (Met) | UGG | Tryptophan (Trp) |

gene makes, has been provided by Yanofsky and his colleagues (Yanofsky, Drapeau, et al. 1967 and other works). A collection of mutants of *Escherichia coli* is available with different variant forms of the enzyme tryptophan synthetase. The sequences of the amino acids in these variant enzymes have been determined, pin-pointing the amino acids that have been substituted because of the mutations (see Chapter 2). The locations of the mutational changes in the chromosome of the bacterium were determined by genetic recombination studies. The linear arrangements of the changes in the chromosome and in the protein are similar.

### Organic Diversity

The apparent simplicity, uniformity, and universality of the genetic code make even more impressive the prodigious diversity of the organisms found on earth. The virus of the foot-and-mouth disease is an approximately spherical body 8–12 millimicrons (a millimicron is $10^{-6}$ millimeter) in diameter. This is the order of magnitude of large protein molecules. Tobacco mosaic virus is a rod some 15 millimicrons in diameter and 300 millimicrons long. The psittacosis virus is a sphere with a diameter of about 450 millimicrons. Perhaps the smallest forms of cellular life are the pleuropneumonia-like organisms, 100–250 millimicrons in diameter. The pigmy shrew, weighing about 2.3 grams, is the smallest mammal. At the opposite extreme, the blue whale (*Balaenoptera musculus*) reaches 100 feet in length and 150 tons in weight. The weight of the largest *Sequoia gigantea* tree is estimated at 6167 tons.

The variability in the duration of an individual's life is also impressive. Colon bacteria divide under favorable conditions once in about 20 minutes. A bacteriophage particle infecting a bacterium gives 200–300 new particles within about 30 minutes. The oldest being now living is a bristlecone pine, *Pinus aristata,* about 4900 years old (Ferguson 1968). There are, however, many species of trees that can perpetuate themselves by stump-sprouting; among them is the redwood, *Sequoia sempervirens.* The life of an individual of this type is limited only by climatic and other environmental changes that exceed the tolerance of the species concerned.

Some algae, such as *Sphaerella nivalis,* grow and multiply on the surface of alpine snows, that is, at temperatures close to 0°C, while *Bacillus megaterium* and the fungus Sporobolomyces grow in Antarctica in saline pools at −23°C, the lowest temperature at which active life has been recorded. Some algae living in the outflow from the hot springs in Yellowstone Park have an optimal temperature range of 50–55°C but can still grow at 73–75°; some bacteria grow there at 80–85°C and can tolerate a temperature of 91°C, which is only 2° below the boiling point of water at the elevation where they live. The bacterium *Thiobacillus thiooxidans* grows in strongly acid media, whereas the alga *Plectonema nostrocorum* tolerates an alkalinity of pH 13 (Skinner 1968). A species of Delphinium (larkspur) grows on Mt. Everest at 20,340 feet, and some spiders even exist at 22,000 feet, feeding apparently on springtails and other insects, also living there or blown in by winds.

The ways of obtaining nutrition, and hence sources of energy for life, are likewise diversified. Autotrophic organisms are independent of external supplies of organic materials. By far the most widespread and successful autotrophs are green plants, which need only water, carbon dioxide and some inorganic substances, plus energy derived from solar radiation. Chemosynthetic bacteria derive their energy not from sunlight but from the oxidation of certain inorganic compounds. Thus, sulfur bacteria (Thiobacteriaceae) oxidize hydrogen sulfide ($H_2S$) and certain other sulfur compounds to sulfates ($SO_4$). Nitrifying bacteria (Nitrobacteriaceae) oxidize ammonia ($NH_3$) to nitrites ($NO_2$), and nitrites to nitrates ($NO_3$). Iron bacteria (Siderocapsaceae) use the oxidation of ferrous to ferric ions as the source of energy in the assimilation of carbon dioxide. Heterotrophic organisms utilize as energy sources a wide range of organic compounds, derived ultimately from autotrophs.

Some heterotrophs are specialized to an astonishingly narrow degree (monophagous), while others feed on many substances (polyphagous). Thus, at least 78 species of food plants are used by the gypsy moth (*Lymantria dispar*), whereas some other moth and butterfly species occur on a single kind of food plant only. Some parasites occur on just one host species, while others feed on many hosts. Perhaps the most extraordinary food source, or at least feeding place, is that of the petroleum fly, *Psilopa petrolei* (Thorpe 1930 and Oldroyd 1964). Its larvae live in pools of crude oil in California oil fields and, as far as is known, nowhere else. Its food consists of corpses of other insects caught and killed by the oil. The larva of *Psilopa petrolei* is the only known insect that can live in the oil, and even the adults of the same species can walk on the surface unharmed as long as only the tarsi of their legs are in contact with the oil. If any other part of the body touches the oil, the fly is trapped, killed, and devoured by the larvae.

The diversity of organisms must be somehow inscribed in the DNA of their cell nuclei. Yet the differences most readily detectable in the various DNA's are merely quantitative. One kind of difference concerns the relative prevalence of the four kinds of nucleotides. As stated previously, each A(denine) in one chain of the double helix corresponds to a T(hymine) in the other, and each G(uanine) is linked to a C(ytosine). The two purines together $(A + G)$ are, then, equally as numerous as the two pyrimidines $(T + C)$. The ratios of $(A + T)$ : $(C + G)$ are, however, variable, especially in microorganisms. In higher organisms, both animals and plants, the proportions of $C + G$ are usually above 30 but less than 50 percent. In the bacteria *Micrococcus lysodeikticus* and *Streptomyces griseus* the amount of $C + G$ reaches between 70 and 80 percent, whereas in *Clostridium perfringens* and *C. tetani* it is only 30–32 percent (cited after Jukes 1966). The diversity of living beings is evidently based not on the proportions but on the arrangements of the genetic "letters."

The amounts of DNA per cell are, as a rule, uniform in different tissues and individuals of the same species. Sex cells carry one-half as much DNA as do body cells. The amounts vary, however, in different organisms, as shown in Table 1.3. More complex organisms generally have more DNA per cell than do simpler ones, but this rule has conspicuous exceptions. Man is nowhere near the top of the list, being exceeded by Amphiuma (an amphibian), Protopterus (a lungfish), and

**TABLE 1.3**

Estimated amounts of DNA (in $10^{-12}$ gram) per haploid chromosome complement (After Mirsky and Ris 1951 and other sources)

| | | | |
|---|---|---|---|
| Amphiuma | 84 | Duck | 1.3 |
| Protopterus | 50 | Chicken | 1.3 |
| Frog | 7.5 | Sea urchin | 0.90 |
| Toad | 3.7 | Snail | 0.67 |
| Man | 3.2 | Yeast | 0.07 |
| Cattle | 2.8 | Colon bacteria | 0.004,7 |
| Green turtle | 2.6 | Bacteriophage T2 | 0.000,2 |
| Carp | 1.6 | Bacteriophage $\phi$ X 174 | 0.000,003,6 |

even ordinary frogs and toads. Why this should be so has long been a puzzle. It seems unreasonable that Amphiuma needs twenty-six times as many genes as man does. The amounts of DNA in *Escherichia coli*, in man, and in Amphiuma correspond to some $4.5 \times 10^6$, $2.9 \times 10^9$, and $8 \times 10^{10}$ nucleotide pairs, respectively. If it is assumed that a protein coded by one gene has on the average 200 amino acids, or 600 nucleotides, *E. coli* has enough DNA for 7500, and man for 5,000,000, genes. Yet the variety of enzymes and proteins in higher organisms does not seem to be greater by three orders of magnitude than that in the lower ones.

A lead to the solution of this puzzle has perhaps been found by Britten and Kohne (1968). Heating DNA causes its "denaturation," since the paired strands of the double helix come apart; lowering the temperature leads to "renaturation," that is, to reassociation of the strands with complementary nucleotide sequences. For purposes of experiment, the DNA is broken by shearing into fragments some 400–500 nucleotides in length, heated to dissociate the paired strands, and cooled again to observe the rate at which the strand fragments are reassociated. To become reassociated, the fragments with similar nucleotide sequences must by chance come into contact; the more different fragments there are in a solution, the slower will be the reassociation of the fragments present in only two or another small number of copies. Conversely, if there are many similar fragments, their reassociation will be rapid.

Britten and Kohne found a most interesting difference between the lower and the higher organisms. A large fraction of the DNA in eukaryotes consists of segments with similar or even identical sequences, some of them repeated thousands and even as many as a million times. This redundancy of genetic materials is absent or at least is inconspicuous, however, in the prokaryotes, such as *Escherichia coli*. The following results were obtained with mouse DNA: about 10 percent of it consists of nucleotide sequences repeated close to one million times, some 20 percent of sequences repeated 1000–100,000 times, and 70 percent of unique sequences. About 40 percent of calf DNA consists of sequences repeated 10,000–100,000 times; a small percentage shows a slight degree of repetition, and 60 percent is made up of unique sequences. Redundancy has been found even in some unicellular algae (Euglena); whether or not redundancy increases systematically from the less complex to the more complex organisms remains to be seen.

## The Discontinuity of Individuals

The diversity of living matter as it exists on earth shows two fundamental properties: the diversity is discontinuous, and the discontinuity is hierarchically organized. Some pioneer biologists (Bonnet) and philosophers (Leibnitz) thought that the "order of nature" cannot be incomplete, and consequently missing links between all existing living creatures must eventually be discovered. This may have been true of the past but is certainly not of the present. Provided that the evolutionary process occurred by gradual modifications, rather than by sudden jumps, different organisms now living have evolved from common ancestors, and the lines of descent had no major gaps or interruptions. But such gaps are certainly found between existing organisms.

Life occurs in discrete quanta, in individuals. The boundaries between individuals are as a rule evident. Multicellular individuals may, in one aspect, be viewed as colonies of cells. The cells of a body are, however, so thoroughly integrated and interdependent that they are constituent parts of individuals rather than autonomous individuals themselves. If some cells excised from my body are propagated in a tissue culture, they will no longer be parts of me. Individuality becomes seriously ambiguous only in some colonial forms, such as siphonophores, certain hydroids, corals, and tapeworms. Here the colony acts as a functionally effective individual, while its components may be specialized in nutrition (gastrozooids), reproduction (gonozooids), perception of external stimuli (dactylozooids), etc. Boundaries between individuals may also be lost in plants that reproduce asexually by runners, stolons, bulbs, or sprouts. Interesting situations present themselves among colonial insects, such as ants and termites. The bodily separateness of the individual members of a colony is here unmistakable; nevertheless, a vast majority of these individuals are sterile workers, and the functionally and genetically effective unit is a colony that includes individuals of the reproductive caste.

The bodily discontinuity of individuals may or may not be accompanied by genetic diversification, depending on the reproductive biology of a given form of life. Among higher organisms, especially animals, including man, sexual reproduction and outbreeding are prevalent. Every individual is then likely to possess a genetic endowment, a genotype, that is unique and different from the genotypes of all other individuals who live now, who lived in the past, and, probably, who will live in the future. This genetic uniqueness is a corollary to the Mendelian mechanism of inheritance. The matter is basically simple. A diploid individual heterozygous for $n$ genes has a potentiality of producing $2^n$ kinds of sex cells with different gene complements. Two parents heterozygous for the same $n$ genes may produce $3^n$ kinds of progeny with different gene constellations. With two parents each heterozygous for $n$ different genes the potentiality rises to $4^n$. In Chapter 8 evidence will be presented which suggests that, among higher animals and plants, $n$ is of the order of hundreds or thousands.

The Mendelian mechanism of inheritance appears to be capable of generating a genetic diversity of individuals vastly greater than can actually be realized, because the number of individuals of any biological species is minuscule in relation to the diversity potentially possible. For example, the world population of human beings consists of somewhat more than 3 billion individuals, that is, between $2^{31}$ and $2^{32}$, or $3 \times 10^9$. With only 100 variable gene loci in the human species (a patent underestimate), a vast majority of the possible genotypes will not be materialized. Similarly, Williams (1960) estimates that the world population of all species of insects combined is of the order of $10^{18}$ living individuals. He assumes that there may be as many as 3 million living species of insects, and estimates the median number of individuals per species as about $1.2 \times 10^8$. One or two most abundant insect species may consist of between $3 \times 10^{16}$ and $5 \times 10^{16}$ living individuals. Even these figures are diminutive compared to the genetic variety potentially possible. Most of this variety has never been realized and probably never will be.

The numbers of individuals of microorganisms are certainly greater than those of insects. No estimates seem to be available, and it happens that such estimates would be of limited interest in the present connection. The reason is that asexual reproduction is much more prevalent among the simpler than among the more complex forms of life, and fission and other modes of asexual reproduction, as well as certain kinds of parthenogenesis or apogamy (see Chapter 12), yield progenies that consist of individuals genetically similar to the mother and to each other. Unless mutations intervene, there may arise aggregations, clones, of genotypically identical individuals. Stebbins (1950) gives examples of clones of several species of flowering plants that have perpetuated themselves apparently without change for thousands of years, and that

are represented by numerous individuals growing over extensive territories.

In many normally asexual species the asexual reproduction may
from time to time be interrupted by a sexual generation or by other
forms of gene exchange (Chapter 11). Conversely, in many normally
sexual forms, including man, there occur from time to time monozygotic twins and other multiple births. Monozygotic co-twins are
members of a clone, and they are, barring mutation, genetically identical. The biological meaning of individuality is, thus, not the same in
sexual and in asexual organisms. In the former, the genetic uniqueness
of every individual makes him a separate "experiment," testing a novel
kind of being. In the latter, what is being tested is not a unique individual, but an array of individuals with similar or identical genotypes.
Johannsen (1909) termed such arrays biotypes. In contrast to Johannsen's genotype and phenotype concepts, which have played important
and constructive roles in the development of genetics (Chapter 2),
the concept of biotypes has sometimes been misconstrued. It is not
really useful in outbreeding sexual species; every man or fly or corn
plant represents a biotype of its own. In asexual species a biotype is
usually (barring mutation) equivalent to a clone.

### The Discontinuity of Arrays
### of Individuals

Suppose that we make a fairly large collection, say some 10,000
specimens, of birds or butterflies or flowering plants in a small territory, perhaps 100 square kilometers. No two individuals will be exactly
alike. Let us, however, consider the entire collection. The variations
that we find in size, in color, or in other traits among our specimens
do not form continuous distributions. Instead, arrays of discrete distributions are found. The distributions are separated by gaps, that is,
by the absence of specimens with intermediate characteristics. We
soon learn to distinguish the arrays of specimens to which the vernacular names English sparrow, chickadee, bluejay, blackbird, cardinal,
and the like, are applied. Our collection of specimens, like the living
world at large, is not a single array in which any two variants are

connected by a series of intergrading variants. It is instead an array of discontinuous arrays, intermediates between which are absent. The small arrays, like those named above, are clustered into larger ones—passerine birds, the crow family, hummingbirds, birds of prey, etc. Still larger arrays are birds, mammals, reptiles, and fishes.

Biologists have exploited the discontinuity of variation as an aid in the construction of a classification of the living world. The hierarchical nature of the clusters and of the discontinuities lends itself admirably to this purpose. The small clusters are designated species, larger ones genera, still larger ones subfamilies, families, and orders. The classification thus obtained is natural, inasmuch as it reflects the objectively ascertainable discontinuities and the hierarchical order of the organic variations. The dividing lines between the species, genera, subfamilies, etc., are drawn to correspond to the gaps between the discrete clusters of the living forms. Biological classification is a man-made system of pigeonholes, serving the pragmatic purpose of recording observations in a convenient manner; it is also a reflection and an acknowledgment of the ubiquity of discontinuities in the living world.

The classification is also artificial, to the extent that it is a matter of convenience and convention which clusters are to be called genera or subfamilies or families. There have always been skeptics who contend that it is equally arbitrary which clusters we choose to call species. A great majority of biologists are convinced, however, that there are clusters which have, in at least the sexually reproducing organisms, biologically significant qualities which other clusters do not have, and that it is convenient to call these particular clusters species. Moreover, the vernacular names of animals and plants are most frequently attached to the clusters that biologists call species. The reality of species has apparently been perceived by biologically untrained people. This problem will be discussed in Chapter 11. Since we shall use the numbers of described species of organisms as measures of organic diversity, we may consider a single example as an illustration of what biological species really are.

Any two cats are individually distinguishable, as probably are any two lions. No individual has ever been seen about which there could be a doubt as to whether he was a cat or a lion. The species of cats (*Felis domestica*) and of lions (*Felis leo*) are discrete, because intermediates between them are absent. Difficulties that may arise in defining the two species will not be due to any artificiality of these species; however, the words cat and lion are sometimes used to refer neither to individual animals nor to all existing representatives of these species, but to some modal, average cat and lion. This is not far from Platonic "ideas" of these species. No matter how difficult it may be to define such ideal cats and lions, the discreteness of the species is not thereby impaired.

In sexually reproducing organisms, the existence of species could, in principle, be demonstrated without reference to the discontinuities in their bodily structures, by observing the pairing and procreation of the creatures concerned. Species are more or less discrete reproductive communities. Members of these communities are united by the bonds of sexual unions, of common descent, and of common parenthood. It will easily be discovered that there is a reproductive community of cats, and a separate reproductive community of lions. No lion cub was ever born to a pair of cats, or any kitten to a pair of lions. Members of different reproductive communities usually show no sexual interest in each other, or if they do, the results of their matings are inviable, sterile, or less fit than the progenies of mating within a community. A species, like a race or a genus or a family, is a group concept and a category of classification. A species is, however, also something else: a supraindividual biological system, the perpetuation of which from generation to generation depends on the reproductive bonds between its members.

The total number of species now living on earth is not known with precision. One reason is that many species have not yet been found, studied, described, and named. Aristotle knew approximately 500 species of animals, and Theophrastus 450 species of plants. Linnaeus listed 4235 animal species in 1758, and 5250 and 7000 species of plants in 1753 and 1774, respectively (see Zavadsky 1968). The available modern estimates, shown in Table 1.4, add up to some 1,594,565 species. Moreover, this number will quite probably be doubled or tripled by future studies. Another, though less important, reason for the inadequacy of the information concerning the numbers of species is that not all species are so clearly discrete as the cat and the lion. Darwin's crucial argument in favor of the origin of species by evolution was that all intergradations between distinct species and "varieties" (we would say at present races or subspecies) can be observed. This

**TABLE 1.4**

Estimated numbers of described species (After Grant 1963, Zavadsky 1968, and Mayr 1969)

| Animals | | Plants | |
|---|---|---|---|
| Vertebrates | 41,700 | Flowering Plants | 286,000 |
| Tunicata and Prochordata | 1,300 | Gymnosperms | 640 |
| Echinoderms | 6,000 | Ferns and allies | 10,000 |
| Molluscs | 107,000 | Bryophytes | 23,000 |
| Arthropods | 838,000 | Green algae | 5,275 |
| Annelids | 8,500 | Red algae | 2,500 |
| Bryozoans | 3,750 | Brown algae | 900 |
| Nematodes | 11,000 | Fungi | 40,000 |
| Rotifers | 1,500 | Slime molds | 400 |
| Nemertines | 800 | | |
| Flatworms | 12,700 | Total plants | 368,715 |
| Coelenterates | 5,300 | Monerans | |
| Sponges | 4,800 | Blue-green algae | 1,400 |
| Minor phyla | 800 | Bacteria | 1,630 |
| Protozoans | 28,350 | Viruses | 200 |
| Total animals | 1,071,500 | Total monerans | 3,230 |

argument fully conserves its validity. Moreover, the nature of the species differences varies in organisms with different reproductive biologies. This will be discussed in more detail in Chapter 11.

It is evident that the numbers of species in the different phyla of the animal and plant kingdoms listed in Table 1.4 are grossly unequal. The arthropods have about 82 percent of all animal species; among the arthropods some 92 percent of the species are insects; among the insects about 40 percent of the species are beetles, 16 percent moths and butterflies, 15 percent hymenopterans, 12 percent flies, etc. (Sabrosky 1952). By contrast, the very ancient and distinctive phylum Brachiopoda (lamp shells), abundantly represented in Paleozoic seas, is reduced to at most 260 species, and the phylum Phoronida to a mere 15 species. Inequalities almost as striking are found among the plant phyla in Table 1.4.

## Adaptive Peaks

Organic diversity is impressive, wonderful, fascinating, or exasperating, according to one's tastes and temperament. Does it have some biological function and meaning? Is it merely a product of the creative exuberance of a deity or of some forces of nature? Or does it fulfill specific needs? The answer was already implicit in Darwin's and even in Lamarck's writings. It was fully articulated by the creators of the modern biological theory of evolution, S. Tshetverikov (1926), R. A. Fisher (1930), J. B. S. Haldane (1932), and Sewall Wright (1931). Organic diversity is a response of living matter to the diversity of environments, and of opportunities for different modes of life on our planet.

One can imagine a planet having just one kind of living beings, capable of surviving in some specially protected and lenient environment. Perhaps primordial life was thus uniform and sheltered. Life has, however, a propensity ever to expand in numbers and in mass, and to spread, invade, and assimilate ever new environments. We may envisage two strategies with the aid of which such expansion could be achieved. One is a strategy of environmental adaptability; an extraordinarily versatile genotype would evolve, the carriers of which could survive and perpetuate themselves in all kinds of environments. The same form of life could then live everywhere. The second is a strategy of diversification and environmental specialization, whereby multitudes of genotypes, each of them ideally suited to live in one and only one environment, would be formed. These two strategies are the conceivable limiting cases. In reality both strategies have been used in the evolution of the living world, but in different proportions in different lines of descent.

There are no fewer than two million species, and possibly twice or more than twice that number. Here, then, is the most general result of the application of the strategy of diversification. On the other hand, no species is specialized to live in just a single environment. Since any environment constantly changes, such a species would not endure for long. Really successful species are masters of a variety of environments, including some that occur over large parts of our planet. This is an accomplishment of the first strategy, environmental versatility. The human species, mankind, is perhaps most adept at this strategy: it is capable not only of choosing but also of artificially contriving environments to suit its needs and tastes.

Reference has already been made to the prodigious powers of the Mendelian mechanism of inheritance to generate ever-new gene constellations. Suppose there are only 1000 kinds of genes in the world, each gene existing in 10 different variants or alleles. Both figures are patent underestimates. Even so, the number of gametes with different combinations of genes potentially possible with these alleles would be $10^{1000}$. This is fantastic, since the number of subatomic particles in the universe is estimated as a mere $10^{78}$. The question that presents itself is whether it is a matter of chance which of these potentially possible gene combinations are realized. Clearly, it is not chance alone that operates here. Some gene combinations, indeed a vast majority of them, would be discordant and inviable in any environment. Other combinations, perhaps a tiny minority of the potentially possible ones, are suitable for life in some environments.

This situation can be envisaged with the aid of a symbolic picture of adaptive "peaks" and "valleys" first contrived by Wright (1932). With two gene loci each having 10 alleles, 100 combinations are possible. They can be diagramed as a two-dimensional grid, on which each combination will be represented by a point. Now, some of the combinations will have a higher and others a lower Darwinian fitness or adaptive value (see Chapter 4). The fitness may be depicted as a third dimension, giving the diagram the appearance of a topographic map (Fig. 1.1). This representation is evidently an oversimplification; with $n$ variable genes a complete picture would require every gene combination and its fitness to be represented by a point in an $(n + 1)$. dimensional space. Nevertheless, Wright's diagram is very helpful. The contours in the figure symbolize the adaptive values of the gene combinations. Groups of related gene combinations that make their possessors able to inhabit certain environments are represented by adaptive peaks (plus signs in Fig. 1.1). Unfavorable gene combinations that make their carriers unfit to live in these environments are symbolized by adaptive valleys (minus signs in Fig. 1.1).

The diversity of living forms may then be envisaged as a multitude of adaptive peaks, corresponding to the multitude of ways of living that are possible on our planet. The variety of these possible ways of living—ecological niches—is, however, not only great; it is also discontinuous. One species of insect may feed, for example, on oak leaves, and another species on pine needles; an insect that required food intermediate between oak and pine would probably starve to death. Hence, the living world is not a formless mass of randomly combining genes and traits, but a great array of families of related gene combinations, which are clustered on a large but finite number of adaptive peaks. Each living species may be thought of as occupying one of the

**FIGURE 1.1**

"Adaptive peaks" and "adaptive valleys" in the field of gene combinations. The contour lines symbolize the adaptive values of the carriers of various genotypes. (After Wright)

available peaks in the field of gene combinations. The adaptive valleys are deserted and empty.

Furthermore, the adaptive peaks and valleys are not interspersed at random. "Adjacent" adaptive peaks are arranged in groups, which may be likened to mountain ranges in which the separate pinnacles are divided by relatively shallow notches. Thus, the ecological niche occupied by the species lion is relatively much closer to the niches occupied by tiger, puma, and leopard than to those occupied by wolf, coyote, and jackal. The feline adaptive peaks form a group different from the group of canine peaks. But the feline, canine, ursine, musteline, and certain other groups of peaks form together the adaptive "range" of carnivores, which is separated by deep adaptive valleys from the ranges of rodents, bats, ungulates, primates, and others. In turn, these ranges are again members of the adaptive system of mammals, which are ecologically and biologically segregated, as a group, from the adaptive

systems of birds, reptiles, etc. The hierarchic nature of biological classification reflects the objectively ascertainable discontinuity of adaptive
niches—in other words, the discontinuity of ways and means by which
organisms that inhabit the world derive their livelihood from their
environments.

## Evolution

The classical theory of evolution, as formulated by Darwin and
his immediate followers, can be summed up in four assertions: (1) the
beings now living have descended from very different beings that
lived in the past; (2) the evolutionary changes were more or less
gradual, so that if all the past as well as present inhabitants of the
earth could be assembled, a fairly continuous array of forms would
emerge; (3) some changes were divergent, and many species now
living are descended from fewer and fewer ancestral species as one
goes farther and farther back in the past; (4) all the changes were
products of causes that now continue in operation and therefore can
be studied experimentally.

Evolutionists of the nineteenth century were interested primarily in
demonstrating that evolution had in fact taken place. They succeeded;
evolution as a process that has occurred in the history of the earth is
no longer questioned either by scientists or by the informed public.
As the study of evolution proceeded, two main approaches were
employed. The first concentrated on unraveling actual evolutionary
histories, that is, phylogenies of various groups of animals and plants.
The methods used are those of systematics, comparative anatomy,
comparative embryology, and especially paleontology, the study of
fossils. The second approach emphasized studies of the mechanisms
that bring evolution about, of causal rather than historical aspects.
Genetics, especially population genetics and ecological genetics, has
supplied the basic concepts and the experimental as well as observa-
tional methods.

In the nineteen twenties and thirties, the foundations of the modern
biological theory of evolution were laid by Tshetverikov, Fisher,
Wright, and Haldane, as stated above. These four pioneers were
brilliant theoreticians; they leaned heavily on mathematical deduction
from a few fundamental postulates, especially those of Mendelian

inheritance. In the late nineteen thirties, the forties, and the fifties, a number of biologists of various specialities, working in different countries, showed that the theory made good sense in their respective fields. The resulting synthesis is, therefore, truly a biological, not only a genetical or ecological or paleontological, theory.

This book presents an outline of the biological theory of evolution, with special emphasis on its genetic aspects. The general principles of the biological theory are widely, but not universally, accepted among present-day biologists. A stridently dissenting voice is, for example, that of Koestler (1967). Though not himself a biologist, this author lists, as the first of the "monumental superstitions" on which "the citadel of orthodoxy" in modern science is built, the view "that biological evolution is the result of random mutations preserved by natural selection." I shall endeavor to show that Koestler's view and similar ones result from a monumental miscomprehension of what the biological theory of evolution really is.

# CHAPTER TWO

# GENETIC CONTINUITY AND CHANGE

*The Conservatism of Heredity*

Heredity is a conservative force: the genes function as templates for the production of their exact copies; by making the offspring resemble their parents, heredity confers stability upon biological systems. Evolution is the antithesis of permanence; the most general definition of evolution maintains, "The current state of a system is the result of a more or less continual change from its original state" (Lewontin 1968). If heredity were always perfectly exact, evolution could not occur.

The precision of heredity is tempered, however, by occasional instability. The counterpart of heredity is variation. Variation has two aspects, a static and a dynamic one. Variation as a status (variability) is the observable diversity between individuals or groups within a species, or the diversity between species. Variation as a process means that the development of individuals may be modified by environmental influences, and the hereditary endowment may be changed by gene recombination or mutation (Philiptschenko 1927). Changes of the latter type are the ultimate source of all genetic variability. If all life is monophyletic, derived from a single kind of primordial life, then all organic diversity must be the outcome of the accumulation and ordering of mutational changes. Not all mutations are conserved, however; as we shall see in Chapter 3, most of them are cast out by natural selection.

All living beings grow and reproduce. Growth occurs by the assimilation of materials taken up from the environment, and their transformation into body constitutents. The organism reproduces itself, in its progeny, from the food that it consumes. The processes whereby self-reproduction is accomplished are the essence of heredity. The basic discovery of genetics is that the units of self-replication are molecular-level systems called genes. The self-replication normally occurs within larger systems—chromosomes, nuclei, cells, organisms. Nevertheless, some components of the body are self-reproducing, whereas others are not. The former constitute both what early precursors of genetics (e.g., Weismann) called the germplasm or idioplasm and what we call genes, irrespective of whether they are located in the chromosomes (chromosomal genes) or in some cytoplasmic organelles, such as plastids or mitochondria (plasmagenes).

The distinction between self-reproducing and non-self-reproducing systems has proved incomprehensible to some people, such as Lysenko in Russia. The evidence of the actuality of self-reproduction seems, however, secure enough at present. A single example will be sufficient here.

The now classical work of Kornberg, mentioned in Chapter 1 (a review in Kornberg 1962), on the *in vitro* synthesis of DNA became possible because of the isolation of an enzyme DNA polymerase from *Escherichia coli*. A mixture is prepared containing this enzyme, the four kinds of nucleotides (in the form of deoxyribonucleoside triphosphates), and magnesium ions. After several hours of incubation, short chains of nucleotides are formed. The reaction is greatly accelerated by adding to the system "templates," that is, small amounts of DNA extracted from some organisms. Not only are DNA chains synthesized, but also—and this is crucial—the DNA that is formed is like the primer in composition. Kornberg and his colleagues used as primers DNA's from organisms as different as cattle, the bacteria *E. coli* and *Mycobacterium phlei*, and bacteriophage T2. The DNA's from the two bacteria differ in the proportions of the genetic "letters"; in *E. coli* the percentages of A, T, G, and C are 25, 24, 24, and 26, and in *M. phlei* 16, 16, 34, and 34, respectively. When the primers act as templates for the *in vitro* synthesis, the resulting DNA's have percentages of A, T, G, and C of about 26, 25, 24, and 25 with the *E. coli* templates, and of about 16, 16, 33, and 34 with those of *M. phlei* (the small differences are expected experimental imprecisions).

## Phenotype and Genotype

The concepts of phenotype and genotype were introduced by Johanssen (1909) and they remain basic for clear thinking about genetic and evolutionary problems. They can at present be defined as follows. The phenotype of an individual is what is perceived by observation: the organism's structures and functions—in short, what a living being appears to be to our sense organs, unaided or assisted by various devices. The genotype is the sum total of the hereditary materials received by an individual from its parents and other ancestors. The phenotype of an individual changes continuously from birth to death. Barring somatic mutation, the genotype, however, remains stable. This stability is due to the genes reproducing themselves, not to the genes being chemically inert materials or being somehow isolated from the environment.

The error of the Lamarckian belief in the inheritance of acquired characters lay in its failure to recognize that the phenotype is a by-product of gene activity, while the genes reproduce by serving as templates in the copying process. A very brief description of the present status of the problem of the translation of genetic information encoded in the DNA of genes into the sequences of amino acids in the proteins was given in Chapter 1. As pointed out by many authors (e.g., Crick 1967), the process is unidirectional: DNA $\rightarrow$ RNA $\rightarrow$ protein. The replication of the genetic material, DNA, requires, of course, the presence of certain enzymes, which are proteins. The protein, the composition of which is specified by a given gene and hence by a certain section of the DNA chain, does not, however, serve as a template for the synthesis of a new gene. In other words, genetic information is transferred from a section of DNA to the corresponding protein, but not in the reverse direction, that is, not from the protein to the DNA.

This conclusion is sometimes referred to as the "central dogma" of molecular genetics. How felicitous this designation is may well be questioned; at any rate, the basic idea was clearly present in the minds of those, beginning with Weismann, who discounted the hypothesis of inheritance of acquired traits. Consider such an acquired trait as big muscles strengthened by exercise. Its inheritance would require that some product secreted by the muscles changed the nucleotide sequence or number in the DNA chains of some genes. Such changes are unknown and seem quite improbable.

The statement that the genotype does not change during an individual's lifetime must be clarified to stave off ambiguity. The amount of DNA in a cell is doubled in the interval between successive cell divisions. New DNA chains are synthesized on the old ones. Does an adult person have the same genes that he had as an infant, an embryo, and a fertilized egg cell? The answer is that he has true copies of these genes. Even more liable to misunderstanding is the statement that genes go without change through many generations of individuals. An individual has copies of some of the genes of his ancestors. The lack of change means only that the gene-copying process is as a rule scrupulously exact.

## Genetic Programming of Potential Phenotypes

A gene, or a cistron according to Benzer's (1957) terminology, is a functional unit; it usually corresponds to a section of the DNA chain coding for an amino acid sequence in a protein. If this description of the action of structural genes is valid, then any gene can yield one and only one primary product, if it functions at all. Actually, however, the process of development is more complex. Between the genes and their messenger RNA's at one end, and the adult phenotypes at the other, there intervenes a set of developmental processes, which, particularly in complex organisms, may be exceedingly long and elaborate. This leaves ample opportunity for the uniform primary action of a gene to yield a variety of manifestations in the developing phenotypes. The genotype does not, therefore, determine the phenotype; it determines a range of potentially possible phenotypes. The range of phenotypes that can develop with a given genotype is technically known as the norm of reaction of that genotype. Which potentialities of the norm of reaction will in fact be realized in a given individual at a certain stage of his development is decided by the sequence of the environments in which the development takes place.

It used to be regarded as not implausible that gene action is a by-product of gene synthesis, and that all genes act hand in hand with cell division. The evidence is now overwhelmingly against these possibilities. Transcription of the genetic information in the DNA may occur independently of its replication, for example, in nondividing cells such as neurones. Cells in different tissues of a multicellular body carry probably identical sets of genes. Nevertheless, different batteries of genes are active in different tissues. It has been shown, particularly by Mirsky and his colleagues (Allfrey, Littau, and Mirsky 1963 and other publications), that a majority of genes are silent in cells of a given tissue at a given stage of body development. Only a minority of the genes are being transcribed in messenger RNA and are translated into proteins. Cell and tissue differentiation during the development of multicellular organisms can be envisaged as a succession of reactions between the genes in different cells of the embryo and the processes going on in neighboring cells. Some genes are switched on and others off in different tissues and at different stages of development (Bonner 1965 and Davidson 1968).

The processes that control the gene action in different cells are not fully understood, despite much research in this important and fascinating field. The already classical work of Jacob and Monod (1961) on the enzyme beta-galactosidase in *Escherichia coli* has led to the recognition of functional groups of genes, constituting operons. An operon is composed of several structural genes and of an operator gene, located in the chromosome in close proximity to the structural genes it controls. Other kinds of controlling elements are the regulator genes, which may have their chromosomal locations far from the operons they control. When the bacteria are grown on a medium lacking a lactose sugar, the enzyme is usually absent (although there are strains in which the enzyme is "constitutive," i.e., present regardless of whether the medium contains lactose). In the absence of lactose, the regulator produces a repressor substance, which combines with the operator and prevents transcription of the structural genes in the operon. Lactose acts as an inducer by rendering the repressor inactive and thus permitting the operon to produce its messenger RNA; the latter initiates the formation of the enzyme.

Evidence is rapidly accumulating that regulator genes are very important in the developmental processes in higher organisms (see Zuckerkandl 1964, Welshons 1965, and Britten and Davidson 1969). We saw in Chapter 1 that the amounts of DNA vary greatly in the nuclei of different organisms. It is a plausible hypothesis that these variations are due to the fact that higher organisms possess greater numbers of regulator genes than of structural genes. According to Britten and Davidson, "The principal difference between a poriferan and a mammal could be in the degree of integrated cellular activity, and thus in vastly increased complexity of regulation rather than a vastly increased number of producer [structural] genes." A much larger quantity of DNA may therefore represent the regulators rather than the structural genes. The evolutionary importance of regulator genes was stressed first by Wallace (1963a) and by Stebbins (1969).

## Genes and Characters

A hypothesis once widely accepted among geneticists postulated that each gene is responsible for the production of one and only one enzyme. This one-gene-one-enzyme hypothesis is now modified to state that each structural gene is transcribed into a single messenger RNA, and the latter is translated into a single polypeptide chain of a protein. It by no means follows that every gene produces just a single character or trait. This is a misconception refuted by the striking manifold (pleiotropic) effects of many genes (see below). The process of the development of an organism should not be misinterpreted as a gradual accumulation and superposition of independent contributions of its genes. Actually, the development is a complex network of processes. In these processes the gene products play, of course, the leading roles; taken all together, these processes are, however, integrated into harmonious systems capable of being alive. In other words, the genetic materials are aggregations of particulate or atomistic genes; the development is a unified network of interrelated events.

The phenotypic manifestation of a gene varies, depending on which other genes it is associated with—in other words, on the internal genetic environment. Textbook examples of such "epistatic" interactions are the arrays of genes controlling the coat colors of various mammals. A cat or a rabbit homozygous for the albino allele is an albino regardless of what other color genes it contains; in the presence of the pigment allele the animal can be yellow, black, tortoise-shell, tabby (in cats), or agouti (in rodents) according to its genotypic constitution. Perhaps the most dramatic epistatic interactions cause the synthetic lethals, abundantly represented in natural populations of some Drosophila (Chapter 3). Either one of two genes, $a$ or $b$, permits the viability to be normal, but the combination $a + b$ is a synthetic lethal that causes death.

The phenotypic manifestation of the genes can be modified by environmental agencies of various sorts, physical, chemical, and biological. Such modifications may spell the difference between life and death. Many mutants, especially in microorganisms, are inviable on culture media on which the ancestral forms grow easily. This inviability is often caused by the lack in the mutants of certain enzymes needed to catalyze essential metabolic reactions; however, additions to the culture medium of the substances that these reactions produce enable the

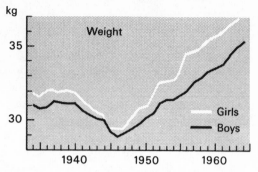

**FIGURE 2.1**

Changes in height and weight of 12-year-old children
in Sendai, Japan. (After Takahashi)

mutants to survive and to grow vigorously. Quite similar situations are
known in higher organisms. According to Walles (1963) and Boynton
(1966), mutants unable to synthesize their own vitamin $B_1$ are known
in the molds *Penicillium notatum, Neurospora sitophila,* and *N. crassa*;
in the bacteria *Escherichia coli, Aerobacter aerogenes,* and *Bacillus
subtilis*; in the algae *Chlamydomonas moewusei* and *Ch. reinhardi*;
and in the flowering plants *Arabidopsis thaliana,* barley, and tomato.
The mutants are lethals, except when vitamin $B_1$ is supplied in the
experimental environment.

## Modification, Morphoses, Homeostasis,
## and Canalization

A phenotype is a biological system constructed by successive
interactions of the individual's genotype with the environments in
which the development takes place. What the genotype determines is
the norm of reaction of the organism to its environments. The word
norm does not imply, in this context, that some reactions are intrinsi-
cally normal and others abnormal. The norm of reaction is the entire
range, the whole repertoire, of the variant paths of development that
may occur in the carriers of a given genotype in all environments,
favorable and unfavorable, natural and artificial. It is fully known for
no genotype. To experiment with the carriers of a genotype by exposing

cm

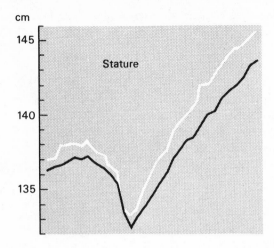

them to every existing or obtainable environment is patently impossible, since the number of environments is virtually infinite. And yet it is of the greatest importance to acquire information as complete as possible about the norms of reaction of human genotypes, and about those of agricultural animals and plants. Medical and educational studies, and much agronomic research, are directed toward this end.

Biological evolution is genetic change; environmental modifications of phenotypes do not constitute evolution. Increases of average stature over time have been recorded in diverse human populations (Fig. 2.1), wherever relevant statistical data are available (for an introduction to the extensive literature dealing with these increases, see Tanner 1962, Takahashi 1966). One would hesitate to call this evolutionary change if, as seems probable, most of the increases in stature are caused by nutritional and general hygienic improvements, rather than by genetic changes. This statement implies no underestimate of the evolutionary importance of the phenotype. Some paths of development bring about phenotypes that are adaptive in some environments and not in others. These phenotypes decide survival or death, the leaving or the not leaving of progeny. By and large, phenotypes that develop in wild species, in response to environmental stimuli that recur regularly in the habitats of these species, are conducive to survival and to reproductive success. Conversely, responses to unusual or artificially created environments are adaptively ambiguous and often even unfavorable. Schmalhausen (1949) has termed the former modifications and the latter morphoses. Modifications are forged in the evolutionary history of a species; morphoses are "new reactions which have not yet attained a historical basis."

Modifications take two outwardly different but closely related forms: physiological homeostasis or the "wisdom of the body" (Cannon 1932 and Dubos 1965), and developmental homeostasis or phenotypic flexibility (Thoday 1953 and Lerner 1954). Familiar examples of physiological homeostasis in man are the maintenance of constant body temperature despite fluctuating temperatures in the environment; constant ionic, glucose, and water concentrations in the blood; and antibody response to infections. Physiological homeostasis maintains constant the *milieu interieur,* to use Claude Bernard's famous phrase. This should not be misconstrued, however, as a kind of biological stubbornness. What is maintained constant is a complex of functions essential for the continuation of life, though this constancy is achieved by means of changes in the operation of physiological mechanisms that serve as regulatory devices. For example, constancy of blood composition is achieved through changes in the work done by the kidneys and the liver.

When adaptive changes are conspicuous and not easily reversible within an individual's lifetime, we are dealing with developmental rather than physiological homeostasis. An obviously intermediate case is the tanning reaction of human skin. This protection against sunburn requires some time to develop or to regress. Striking examples of developmental homeostasis are found among plants (Bradshaw 1965) and in lower animals. If the food available remains within a certain critical amount, starving larvae of Drosophila and many other insects do not die but metamorphose into adults of dwarf size. The coloration of some insects is modifiable to match that of the background. On the other hand, there is good evidence (Ergene 1951) that some grasshoppers choose, if available, surroundings matching their own coloration, thus achieving a protective camouflage by behavioral means. The rotifer *Brachionus calyciflorus* develops no spines unless its predator *Asplanchna sieboldi* lives in the same medium. The spines have a protective function; the most remarkable fact is that the effects of the Asplanchna-conditioned medium are exerted on the Brachionus eggs and seem to be irreversible thereafter (Gilbert 1966).

In higher animals, including man, the most interesting phenotypic flexibility occurs in the development of behavioral characteristics. The old "nature-nurture" problem is dead, in the sense that no serious investigator tries to dichotomize human or animal characteristics into those due to "nature" and to "nurture." All traits are products of the interactions of heredity with environment. Nevertheless, heritability studies, partitioning the observed variance into genetic and environmental components, are needed for many traits, especially those of social, medical, or economic interest. An account of the present status of this field is outside the purview of this book. A point worthy of emphasis is, however, the overwhelming importance of the early environment and experience in the formation of many behavioral characteristics (studies on man reviewed in Berelson and Steiner, 1964, Bloom 1964, and Edwards and Cauley 1964; on animals in Eibesfeldt 1965, Thorpe 1963, and Marler and Hamilton 1966). The adult phenotype, though never absolutely fixed, is nevertheless powerfully circumscribed by what happened in infancy.

Most fascinating are experimental studies of the socialization and training of dogs (Scott and Fuller 1965), wolves (Woolpy and Ginsburg 1967), and chimpanzees (Hayes 1951). A wolf cub can be brought up not only to have no fear of man but in fact to seek human companionship; a chimpanzee child can be taught many behavior patterns of a human child, with the notable exception of spoken symbolic language. Indeed, these experiments have revealed hitherto quite unsuspected potentialities of the norms of reaction of such "wild" species as wolves and chimpanzees.

A still different kind of phenotypic flexibility is found in some insects, particularly locusts and other orthopterans (Uvarov 1928, Uvarov and Thomas 1942, Gunn and Hunter-Jones 1952, and Key 1950, 1957). Some species of locusts occur in two "phases," so distinct in appearance and behavior that they were originally believed to be different species. One phase is solitary and the other gregarious in its habits. In some years the gregarious phase makes spectacular outbreaks; multitudes of these insects engage in distant migrations and become "plagues," recorded even in the Bible. Although important details of the causation of these phenomena are in dispute, it appears that the species involved have bimodal or even plurimodal norms of reaction. Their development turns toward either the solitary or the gregarious phase, as dictated by the degrees of crowding and other environmental conditions. Of course, the possibility that the populations of locusts have also a variety of genotypes, some of which can be turned toward the gregarious phase more easily than others, is not ruled out.

Rigidity or flexibility of development in the carriers of a genotype is a factor of major importance in determining the adaptive value of the genotype. A theoretically imaginable ideal genotype would so stabilize the course of development that vitally important organs and functions would appear in all environments, while the modifications arising in other characters would always be adaptive in the environments that evoked them. The reality is, in varying degrees, short of the ideal. However, especially in higher organisms, physiological and developmental homeostasis provides a buffering of the developmental path against environmental shocks. According to Waddington (1957), the development is "canalized." Under most or all conditions that the species encounters regularly in its habitats, and with most genotypes comprising the adaptive norm of the species population, development leads to generally similar results. Hence canalization can be symbolized by a landscape, in which the topography is such that the waters flow usually into the same valley or canal.

The development of the female and male sexes provides an excellent example of canalization. The female and male genotypes, usually determined by the X and Y chromosomes, give, under most circumstances, either functional females or males. Intersexes that are sterile or suffer various impairments occur rarely if at all in natural populations. They can, however, be produced by drastic environmental or genetic changes. Brust and Horsfall (1965) find that thermal stresses applied to larvae of the mosquito *Aedes communis* suppress the development of masculine traits in genetic males, but leave genetic females unaffected. The sexual traits in triploid intersexes of *Drosophila melanogaster* are greatly modified by temperature and other environmental variations that are without effect on normal diploid females and males. Sexual development of females and males is evidently canalized, whereas that of intersexes is not (Laugé 1966).

### Phenocopies

The concept of phenocopy was developed by Goldschmidt (1938). His assumption was that any alteration of the phenotype caused by a genetic change, a mutation, should be reproducible as a purely phenotypic modification if a suitable environmental agency is discovered. By employing temperature shocks or treatment with ether and other chemicals, Goldschmidt (1938), Rapoport (1939), Schatz (1951), Hadorn (1961), and others have obtained phenocopies mimicking some well-known wing, thorax, and pigmentation mutants in Drosophila. The treatments are administered during sensitive stages of development, specific for each phenocopy. Extensive and detailed studies of phenocopy induction in poultry have been made by Landauer and his colleagues (Landauer 1948, and a review in Hadorn 1961).

The degree of similarity between a phenocopy and the genetically determined change that it resembles varies from case to case. The curly-haired and blond-haired phenocopies induced by beauticians are usually recognized as such. In any case, the untreated progeny of a phenocopy are normal, whereas at least some of the progeny of a mutant inherit the mutant genes or chromosomes.

The phenocopy concept is also applicable in reverse—genetic mutants made by environmental treatments to resemble the ancestral type. Under this rubric belongs the "cure" of hereditary diseases and malformations by environmental treatments. Mutant plants and microorganisms unable to synthesize vitamin $B_1$ have been mentioned previously; they are lethal without treatment but viable when the vitamin is supplied. Some of the inborn errors of metabolism in man can be at least partly corrected by excluding from the diet substances that the affected individuals cannot metabolize, or by including substances that are needed. To the first category belong restrictions of phenylalanine intake in phenylketonuria, of galactose in galactosemia, and of phytanic acid in Refsum's disease; the second category is represented by the supplying of vitamins in hereditary vitamin deficiencies (Scriver 1967 and Larson 1961) and of insulin to diabetics. Learning how to induce phenocopies of vigorous health in carriers of deleterious genes is one of the central problems of human engineering (Neel, Fajans, et al. 1965).

## A Brief History of the Mutation Concept

The ultimate source of organic diversity is mutation. The mutation concept has had a tortuous history. The paleontologist Waagen (1869) designated as mutations the smallest perceptible changes in the temporal series of forms in a species of ammonites. Around the turn of the century, Bateson (1894) in England and Korzhinsky (1899) in Russia stressed the importance of the sudden origin of discontinuous variations as a source of evolutionary change. But it was de Vries (1901) who wrote, "As the theory of mutation I designate the statement that the properties of organisms are built from sharply distinct units. . . . Intergrades, which are so numerous between the external forms of plants and animals, exist between these units no more than between the molecules of chemistry." A mutation is, then, a change in one or more genes. Thus far, de Vries's statements have a decidedly modern ring. De Vries contrasts, however, his mutation theory and Darwin's selectionism:

The latter [selectionism] assumes that the usual or the so-called individual variability is the starting point of the origin of new species. According to the mutation theory the two [individual and mutational variabilities] are completely independent. As I hope to show, the usual variability cannot lead to a real overstepping of the species limits even with a most intense steady selection. . . .

On the other hand, each mutation "sharply and completely separates the new form, as an independent species, from the species from which it arose."

De Vries's "species" are evidently not identical with the usual Linnaean ones. Attempts were made to introduce the terms elementary species or Jordanons or biotypes for the former. These attempts met with little sympathy; the word species was here used in a new sense, and in sexually reproducing organisms one would have to consider almost every individual an elementary species. Individual variability, in so far as it is hereditary at all, is due to the populations of most species being mixtures of genotypes differing from each other in one gene or in several. Finally, the mutants obtained by de Vries in his classical investigations with Oenothera proved to be an assemblage of diverse changes, including gene alterations, segregation products due to hybridity of the initial material, and chromosomal aberrations.

Studies by Morgan and his colleagues of mutability in the fly *Drosophila melanogaster* (Morgan 1911, 1919, and Morgan, Sturtevant, et al. 1915) showed that the distinction which de Vries attempted to draw between individual and mutational variability was spurious. The changes produced by mutations range all the way from ones so drastic that they are lethal, through moderate, to barely detectable. Mutants that are easily recognizable to an untrained eye are most useful for genetic experimentation; they are preserved, while the slight ones are generally discarded. This has created a false impression that all Drosophila mutants show strikingly visible alterations, although Morgan (1919) repeatedly emphasized that slight mutants commonly occur in Drosophila. Slight mutants were observed as early as 1909 by Johannsen in beans, and Baur (1924) found them to be very common in the snapdragon (*Antirrhinum majus*). In the nineteen forties, fifties, and sixties, molds, bacteria, and viruses became favorite materials for mutation studies. The Drosophila story was re-enacted: clear-cut mutants were selected for experimental convenience, but ones with minor effects proved to be quite common.

Another turning point in mutation studies came with Muller's discoveries (1927, 1928a,b). Before this time mutations were said to arise spontaneously. A natural phenomenon is "spontaneous" when it is not brought about by man-made causes, and usually when we are, in fact, ignorant of its causes. Working with Drosophila, Muller showed that the frequencies of certain classes of mutations can be accurately measured. He also demonstrated that these frequencies are greatly increased in the progeny of parents treated with X-rays. This work opened the doors to later discoveries of other mutagenic radiations and of chemical mutagens. Of course, some mutations still arise spontaneously, in cultures not known to be treated with any mutagen. It is possible, however, to increase the mutation frequencies at will, and in some instances to promote the occurrence of particular kinds of mutations (see below). The most recent breakthrough followed the elucidation of the chemical structure of nucleic acids. It became possible, at least in some favorable materials and situations, to determine the chemical nature and mechanisms of the changes that on the biological level manifest themselves as mutations.

### A Classification of Mutations

The term mutation subsumes a variety of phenomena. In the inclusive sense, any change in the genotype not due to gene recombination is a mutation. Chromosomes, as well as self-reproducing cytoplasmic organelles, undergo mutational changes. Gene mutations are caused by alterations within genetic materials; chromosomal aberrations involve loss, multiplication, or rearrangement of genes in the chromosomes. A synopsis of the kinds of mutations may be as follows:

I. *Gene Mutations,* or point mutations in older genetic literature—changes caused by substitution, addition, or deletion of nucleotides within a section of the DNA or the RNA of a gene.

II. *Structural Chromosomal Changes,* affecting the arrangement of genes in the chromosomes.

   A. Changes due to loss or reduplication of some of the genes.

   a. *Deficiency* (deletion). A section containing one gene or a block of genes is lost from one of the chromosomes. If a normal chromosome carries genes *ABCDEFG,* the deficient chromosome may contain only *ABEFG.*

   b. *Duplication.* A section of a chromosome may be present at its normal location in addition to being present elsewhere. If a normal chromosome has genes *ABCDEFG,* the duplication may be *ABCDCDEFG* or the equivalent. Studies of chromosomes in the salivary gland cells of certain flies have shown that in the "normal" chromosomes certain sections are represented two or more times in the haploid set. Such "repeats" are duplications that have become established in the phylogeny of these flies.

   B. Changes due to an alteration in the arrangement of the genes.

   a. *Translocation.* Two chromosomes, with genes *ABCDEFG* and *HIJK,* may exchange parts, giving rise to "new" chromosomes having *ABCDJK* and *HIEFG.*

   b. *Inversion.* The location of a block of genes within a chromosome may be changed by rotation through 180°. The resulting chromosome carries the same genes as the original one, but their arrangement is modified, for instance, from *ABCDEFG* to *AEDCBFG.*

   c. *Transposition.* A block of genes is moved to a new position within a chromosome, for instance, *ABCDEFG* to *ADEFBCG.*

III. *Numerical Changes,* affecting the number of chromosomes.

   A. *Aneuploidy.* One or more chromosomes of the normal set may be lacking (monosomics, nullosomics) or present in excess (trisomics, tetrasomics, etc.).

B. *Haploidy.* Higher organisms are mostly diploid during a major part of the life cycle, that is, they possess two chromosomes of each kind in the nuclei of most cells. Gametes, as well as gametophytes in plants, are haploid and carry one chromosome of each kind. Under experimental conditions some diploid organisms have produced haploid aberrants, which have a single set of chromosomes in the tissues that are normally diploid.

C. *Polyploidy.* Normally diploid organisms may give rise to forms with more than two sets of homologous chromosomes. Such forms are known as polyploids.

Discrimination between point mutations and chromosomal aberrations is often difficult. Numerical chromosomal changes are most readily detectable by cytological examination. Only in more favorable materials, particularly in the giant chromosomes of the larval salivary glands of Drosophila and other flies, can structural changes, down to those involving very small portions of the chromosome, be seen under the microscope. Very small structural changes may conceivably be overlooked even under the most favorable circumstances. Stadler argued in several closely reasoned papers (see Stadler 1954 for further references) that what we call point mutations are merely the residue of mutational changes for which no structural basis in the chromosomes is detectable under the microscope. Goldschmidt (1938, 1940) went even further—all mutations, he said, are due to rearrangements in the chromosomes, whether or not one can see these rearrangements. The development of molecular genetics has made these views obsolete.

### The Molecular Basis of Gene Mutations

The effects of genetic changes are most often detected in higher organisms through the morphological or physiological alterations that they produce in the adults. Developmental geneticists used to believe that, if one could patiently unravel the development of a mutational difference backward from the adult to the early stages, it might be possible eventually to discover the nature of the alteration that took place in the gene structure. Things did not go as these early workers

| | | | | | | | | | | |
|---|---|---|---|---|---|---|---|---|---|---|
| Human Beta | VAL | HIS | LEU | THR | PRO | GLU | GLU | LYS | SER | ALA | VAL |
| Horse Beta | VAL | GLN | LEU | SER | GLY | GLU | GLU | LYS | ALA | ALA | VAL |
| Human Alpha | VAL | — | LEU | SER | PRO | ALA | ASP | LYS | THR | ASN | VAL |
| Whale Myoglobin | VAL | — | LEU | SER | GLU | GLY | GLU | TRY | GLN | LEU | VAL |

| | | | | | | | | | | |
|---|---|---|---|---|---|---|---|---|---|---|
| Human Beta | GLY | GLY | GLU | ALA | LEU | GLY | ARG | LEU | LEU | VAL | VAL |
| Horse Beta | GLY | GLY | GLU | ALA | LEU | GLY | ARG | LEU | LEU | VAL | VAL |
| Human Alpha | GLY | ALA | GLU | ALA | LEU | GLU | ARG | MET | PHE | LEU | SER |
| Whale Myoglobin | GLY | GLN | ASP | ILEU | LEU | ILEU | ARG | LEU | PHE | LYS | SER |

| | | | | | | | | | | |
|---|---|---|---|---|---|---|---|---|---|---|
| Human Beta | SER | THR | PRO | ASP | ALA | VAL | MET | GLY | ASN | PRO | LYS |
| Horse Beta | SER | ASP | PRO | GLY | ALA | VAL | MET | GLY | ASN | PRO | LYS |
| Human Alpha | SER | HIS | GLY | SER | — | — | — | — | — | ALA | GLN |
| Whale Myoglobin | LYS | THR | GLU | ALA | GLU | MET | LYS | ALA | SER | GLU | ASP |

| | | | | | | | | | | |
|---|---|---|---|---|---|---|---|---|---|---|
| Human Beta | GLY | LEU | ALA | HIS | LEU | ASP | ASN | LEU | LYS | GLY | THR |
| Horse Beta | GLY | VAL | HIS | HIS | LEU | ASP | ASP | LEU | LYS | GLY | THR |
| Human Alpha | ALA | VAL | ALA | HIS | VAL | ASP | ASP | MET | PRO | ASN | ALA |
| Whale Myoglobin | ILEU | LEU | LYS | LYS | LYS | GLY | HIS | HIS | GLU | ALA | GLU |

| | | | | | | | | | | |
|---|---|---|---|---|---|---|---|---|---|---|
| Human Beta | ASP | PRO | GLU | ASN | PHE | ARG | LEU | LEU | GLY | ASN | VAL |
| Horse Beta | ASP | PRO | GLU | ASN | PHE | ARG | LEU | LEU | GLY | ASN | VAL |
| Human Alpha | ASP | PRO | VAL | ASN | PHE | LYS | LEU | LEU | SER | HIS | CYS |
| Whale Myoglobin | PRO | ILEU | LYS | TYR | LEU | GLU | PHE | ILEU | SER | GLU | ALA |

| | | | | | | | | | | |
|---|---|---|---|---|---|---|---|---|---|---|
| Human Beta | PRO | PRO | VAL | GLN | ALA | ALA | TYR | GLN | LYS | VAL | VAL |
| Horse Beta | PRO | GLU | LEU | GLN | ALA | SER | TYR | GLN | LYS | VAL | VAL |
| Human Alpha | PRO | ALA | VAL | HIS | ALA | SER | LEU | ASP | LYS | PHE | LEU |
| Whale Myoglobin | ALA | ASP | ALA | GLN | GLY | ALA | MET | ASN | LYS | ALA | LEU |

■ Indicates amino acid common to the four proteins

▨ Indicates amino acid common to the three hemoglobins

□ Indicates amino acid common to the two beta hemoglobins

| | | | | | | | | | | | | | |
|---|---|---|---|---|---|---|---|---|---|---|---|---|---|
| THR | ALA | LEU | TRY | GLY | LYS | VAL | ASN | — | — | VAL | ASP | GLU | VAL |
| LEU | ALA | LEU | TRY | ASP | LYS | VAL | ASN | — | — | GLU | GLU | GLU | VAL |
| LYS | ALA | ALA | TRY | GLY | LYS | VAL | GLY | ALA | HIS | ALA | GLY | GLU | TYR |
| LEU | HIS | VAL | TRY | ALA | LYS | VAL | GLU | ALA | ASP | VAL | ALA | GLY | HIS |

| | | | | | | | | | | | | | |
|---|---|---|---|---|---|---|---|---|---|---|---|---|---|
| TYR | PRO | TRY | THR | GLN | ARG | PHE | PHE | GLU | SER | PHE | GLY | ASP | LEU |
| TYR | PRO | TRY | THR | GLN | ARG | PHE | PHE | ASP | SER | PHE | GLY | ASP | LEU |
| PHE | PRO | THR | THR | LYS | THR | TYR | PHE | PRO | HIS | PHE | — | ASP | LEU |
| HIS | PRO | GLU | THR | LEU | GLU | LYS | PHE | ASP | ARG | PHE | LYS | HIS | LEU |

| | | | | | | | | | | | | | |
|---|---|---|---|---|---|---|---|---|---|---|---|---|---|
| VAL | LYS | ALA | HIS | GLY | LYS | LYS | VAL | LEU | GLY | ALA | PHE | SER | ASP |
| VAL | LYS | ALA | HIS | GLY | LYS | LYS | VAL | LEU | HIS | SER | PHE | GLY | GLU |
| VAL | LYS | GLY | HIS | GLY | LYS | LYS | VAL | ALA | ASP | ALA | LEU | THR | ASN |
| LEU | LYS | LYS | HIS | GLY | VAL | THR | VAL | LEU | THR | ALA | LEU | GLY | ALA |

| | | | | | | | | | | | | | |
|---|---|---|---|---|---|---|---|---|---|---|---|---|---|
| PHE | ALA | THR | LEU | SER | GLU | LEU | HIS | CYS | ASP | LYS | LEU | HIS | VAL |
| PHE | ALA | ALA | LEU | SER | GLU | LEU | HIS | CYS | ASP | LYS | LEU | HIS | VAL |
| LEU | SER | ALA | LEU | SER | ASP | LEU | HIS | ALA | HIS | LYS | LEU | ARG | VAL |
| LEU | LYS | PRO | LEU | ALA | GLN | SER | HIS | ALA | THR | LYS | HIS | LYS | ILEU |

| | | | | | | | | | | | | | |
|---|---|---|---|---|---|---|---|---|---|---|---|---|---|
| LEU | VAL | CYS | VAL | LEU | ALA | HIS | HIS | PHE | GLY | LYS | GLU | PHE | THR |
| LEU | ALA | VAL | VAL | LEU | ALA | ARG | HIS | PHE | GLY | LYS | ASP | PHE | THR |
| LEU | LEU | VAL | THR | LEU | ALA | ALA | HIS | LEU | PRO | ALA | GLU | PHE | THR |
| ILEU | ILEU | HIS | VAL | LEU | HIS | SER | ARG | HIS | PRO | GLY | ASN | PHE | GLY |

| | | | | | | | | | | | | | |
|---|---|---|---|---|---|---|---|---|---|---|---|---|---|
| ALA | GLY | VAL | ALA | ASN | ALA | LEU | ALA | HIS | LYS | TYR | HIS | — | — |
| ALA | GLY | VAL | ALA | ASN | ALA | LEU | ALA | HIS | LYS | TYR | HIS | — | — |
| ALA | SER | VAL | SER | THR | VAL | LEU | THR | SER | LYS | TYR | ARG | — | — |
| GLU | LEU | PHE | ARG | LYS | ASP | ILEU | ALA | ALA | LYS | TYR | LYS | GLU | LEU |

| | | | |
|---|---|---|---|
| — | — | — | — |
| — | — | — | — |
| — | — | — | — |
| GLY | TYR | GLN | GLY |

**FIGURE 2.2** The sequences of amino acids in alpha and beta chains of the human adult hemoglobins, in the beta chain of horse hemoglobin, and in whale myoglobin. The sequences are arranged from left to right across both pages, starting from the upper left corner (position No. 1, valine) to the lower right (No. 153, Glycine, in the myoglobin). Empty spaces are gaps in the sequences in some of the chains. (After Dayhoff and Eck)

expected; the gene structure and primary gene action are at present understood far better than development and differentiation.

More and more mutational changes are being shown to produce specific changes in single proteins. For example, Pauling, Itano, et al. (1949) found sickle-cell anemia to be a "molecular disease." This ailment, widespread in some human populations native to Africa, is inherited as a single Mendelian recessive gene. The homozygote dies, usually before adolescence, of severe anemia; the heterozygote survives and in point of fact enjoys an advantage over the normal homozygote, being relatively resistant to certain malarial fevers (see Chapter 6). Pauling and his colleagues discovered that the hemoglobins of normal, heterozygous, and anemic individuals are distinguishable by electrophoresis, because these hemoglobins move at different rates in an electric field. Moreover, while normal homozygotes have a hemoglobin called A, and anemic homozygotes have hemoglobin S, heterozygotes have both A and S in approximately equal amounts.

A great amount of work has been done in recent years on the structure of normal hemoglobin and of its genetic variants in man (excellent reviews in Ingram 1963, Baglioni 1967, and Dayhoff and Eck 1968). A hemoglobin molecule consists of four protein (polypeptide) chains, two of them called alpha and two beta chains, and two iron-containing heme groups. An alpha chain has 141 amino acids and a beta chain 146, the sequences of which are shown in Fig. 2.2. Although the alpha and beta chains are encoded by different genes, their amino acid sequences are more similar than could reasonably be ascribed to chance (the similar portions are outlined in Fig. 2.2). The genes responsible for the formation of alpha and beta chains are probably the modified descendants of a single ancestral gene that underwent a duplication and a gradual divergence in evolution.

Hemoglobin S, found in carriers of the sickle-cell gene, has proved to differ from ordinary hemoglobin A in the substitution of a single amino acid: it has a valine (Val) instead of the normal glutamic acid (Glu) at position 6 in the beta chain. This change could be effected by substitution of a single letter of the genetic alphabet in the DNA and RNA produced at the gene coding for the beta chain of hemoglobin. Reference to Table 1.2 shows that the triplets for glutamic acid are GAA and GAG; substitution of U for A gives the triplets GUA and GUG for valine. Here, then, is a change in a single molecule, which is so amplified in the process of development that the individual who inherits this molecule from both parents dies of sickle-cell anemia.

Table 2.1 lists some of the variants of alpha and beta chains of human hemoglobins which have been found to differ in substitutions of single amino acids. Mutation evidently hits many spots in the nucleotide sequences of the genes coding for these chains. Only a few of these mutant hemoglobins (especially S and C in the beta chain) are common in populations of certain geographic regions. Others have been encountered mostly in single families or persons. Some of these "private" hemoglobins have, however, been discovered by different investigators in places remote from each other; this almost certainly means that similar mutations occurred independently in different populations (Konigsberg, Huntsman, et al. 1965). The carriers of variant hemoglobins are often, though not always, found to be suffering from diverse forms of ill health. Some have appeared, however, to be healthy; taken at face value, this seems to mean that certain changes in the hemoglobin molecule make it neither more nor less serviceable. The decided predominance of "normal" hemoglobin in man suggests, however, that this particular molecular species has proved itself advantageous.

The variant hemoglobins listed in Table 2.1 differ from the common one in single amino acid replacements, and the corresponding genes presumably by single nucleotide replacements. Most of the nucleotide replacements appear to be transitions, that is, replacements of one purine by another or of one pyrimidine by another (thymine by cytosine or vice versa, and adenine by guanine or vice versa). Less frequent are transversions, that is, replacements of a purine by a pyrimidine or vice versa. Hemoglobin C Harlem differs from the common one not by a single replacement but by two amino acids—substitution of valine for glutamic at position 6, and of asparagine for aspartic at position 73 in the beta chain. Still more complex are the changes in Lepore hemoglobins; here two normal alpha chains are combined with chains each of which consists of a part of the normal beta and a part of the delta chain. The latter is a normal constituent of hemoglobin $A_2$, which is present in small amounts in the blood of normal persons. The mutation that produced the Lepore hemoglobin chain probably involved crossing over between the partially homologous genes coding for the beta and the delta chains.

The mechanics of the origin of rearrangements of genic materials within chromosomes are far from completely understood. Deletions, duplications, inversions, and translocations of chromosome sections involve one or two chromosomes being broken in one or more places, and the resulting chromosome fragments being recombined in new ways. The basic event in all these changes is, then, chromosome fracture. This may be a process analogous to gene mutation, though it disrupts the nucleic acid backbone in one or more places in the chromosomes, instead of substituting one nucleotide "letter" for another. The fracture points in the chromosomes are said to be "sticky,' because

## TABLE 2.1

Variant human hemoglobins, caused by point mutations substituting single amino acids at certain positions (After Dayhoff and Eck 1968)

| Variant | Position | Amino Acid | |
|---|---|---|---|
| | | Old | New |
| Alpha Chain | | | |
| J Toronto | 5 | Ala | Asp |
| J Oxford, I Interlaken | 15 | Gly | Asp |
| I, I Texas | 16 | Lys | Glu |
| J Medellin | 22 | Gly | Asp |
| G Audhali | 23 | Glu | Val |
| G Honolulu, G Singapore, G Hong Kong | 30 | Glu | Gln |
| Umi, Kokura, L Ferrara | 47 | Asp | Gly |
| Sealy, Hasharan | 47 | Asp | His |
| Russ | 51 | Gly | Arg |
| Shimonoseki | 54 | Gln | Arg |
| Mexico | 54 | Gln | Glu |
| Norfolk, G Ibadan | 57 | Gly | Asp |
| M Boston, M Osaka | 58 | His | Tyr |
| G Philadelphia, G Bristol, G ST 1, D alpha St. Louis, Stanleyville 1 | 68 | Asn | Lys |
| Stanleyville 2 | 78 | Asn | Lys |
| Etobicoke | 84 | Ser | Arg |
| M Kankakee, M Shibata, M Iwate | 87 | His | Tyr |
| Chesapeake | 92 | Arg | Leu |
| J Cape Town | 92 | Arg | Gln |
| J Tongariki | 115 | Ala | Asp |
| O Indonesia | 116 | Glu | Lys |

**TABLE 2.1** (continued)

| Variant | Position | Amino Acid | |
|---|---|---|---|
| | | Old | New |
| Beta Chain | | | |
| Tokuchi | 2 | His | Tyr |
| S, X | 6 | Glu | Val |
| C | 6 | Glu | Lys |
| C Georgetown, Siriraj | 7 | Glu | Lys |
| G | 7 | Glu | Gly |
| Porto Alegre | 9 | Ser | Cys |
| Sogst | 14 | Leu | Arg |
| D Bushman | 16 | Gly | Arg |
| J Baltimore, J Trinidad, J Ireland, J New Haven | 16 | Gly | Asp |
| G Saskatoon | 22 | Glu | Lys |
| E | 26 | Glu | Lys |
| Genova | 28 | Leu | Pro |
| Hammersmith | 42 | Phe | Ser |
| G Galveston, G Texas, G Port Arthur | 43 | Glu | Ala |
| K Ibadan | 46 | Gly | Glu |
| G Copenhagen | 47 | Asp | Asn |
| J Bangkok, J Meinung, J Korat | 56 | Gly | Asp |
| Hikari | 61 | Lys | Asn |
| M Saskatoon, M Emory, M Kurume, M Chicago, M Hamburg | 63 | His | Tyr |
| Zurich | 63 | His | Arg |
| M Milwaukee 1 | 67 | Val | Glu |
| Sydney | 67 | Val | Ala |
| J Cambridge | 69 | Gly | Asp |
| J Iran | 77 | His | Asp |
| G Accra | 79 | Asp | Asn |
| D Ibadan | 87 | Thr | Lys |
| Agenogi | 90 | Glu | Lys |
| Oak Ridge | 94 | Asp | Asn |
| Hopkins, N Jenkins, N Baltimore | 95 | Lys | Glu |
| Köln | 98 | Val | Met |
| Kansas | 102 | Asn | Thr |
| New York | 113 | Val | Glu |
| D Los Angeles, D Punjab, D Cyprus D Conley, D Chicago, D Portugal | 121 | Glu | Glu |
| O Arabia | 121 | Glu | Lys |
| K Woolwich | 132 | Lys | Gln |
| Hope | 136 | Gly | Asp |
| Kenwood | 143 | His | Asp |

they tend to rejoin with other fractures. The reunion may either restore
the original gene arrangements or create new ones.

## *Mutagenic Radiations and Temperature*

Reference has been made to Muller's discovery (1927, 1928a,b)
that the frequencies of both point mutations and chromosomal changes
are increased in the offspring of X-rayed Drosophila. The large and still
rapidly growing literature on radiation genetics has been reviewed in
the books by D. E. Lea (1955), Purdom (1963), and Dubinin (1964).
Muller's findings were soon confirmed and extended by Stadler,
Timofeeff-Ressovsky, Oliver, Demerec, Gowen, and others, working
with animals and plants and with simple and complex organisms. All
so-called ionizing radiations, from soft X-rays to gamma rays, neutron
beams, and presumably cosmic rays, are mutagenic. Very important is
the fact that the frequencies of induced gene mutations are directly
proportional to the amounts of radiation administered, as measured by
the ionizations produced in the living tissue (r or rem units). This
direct proportionality rules out the possibility that "spontaneous" mutations might be accounted for by the small amounts of ionizing radiations omnipresent in nature; the radiation "background" is far too weak
to account for the observed spontaneous mutation frequency. At the
same time, no amount of radiation exposure can be regarded as safe
or innocuous, since it will inevitably produce some genetic damage.
This fact is fundamental for a reasoned evaluation of possible radiation
damage to human populations.

Ultraviolet light is also mutagenic. Its action is different, however,
from that of ionizing radiations (Witkin 1966 and references therein):
its penetration and absorption in living tissue depend on the wave-
length employed; the numbers of mutations induced are not in general
directly proportional to the amounts used in treatment; ultraviolet
light induces mainly point mutations and few or no chromosomal
aberrations. It is probably of little consequence as a natural mutagen,
in at least the higher animals and plants, because their reproductive
cells are generally too well protected for the ultraviolet part of the
light spectrum to penetrate.

The effects of temperature on mutation rates were studied by Muller
(1928b), Timofeeff-Ressovsky (1935), and others. Timofeeff-Ressovsky

gives the following data for the frequencies of origin of sex-linked lethal mutations in *Drosophila melanogaster* at three temperatures:

| Temperature, °C | Number of Chromosomes Examined | Number of Lethals Found | Percentage of Lethals |
|---|---|---|---|
| 14 | 6871 | 6 | $0.087 \pm 0.035$ |
| 22 | 3708 | 7 | $0.188 \pm 0.071$ |
| 28 | 6158 | 20 | $0.325 \pm 0.072$ |

Notwithstanding the large experimental errors, it seems certain that the mutation rate is doubled or trebled with a 10°C rise in temperature. Timofeeff-Ressovsky points out, however, that the development of the fly is more rapid at high than at low temperatures; he also finds that mutation is proportional to time, since the frequency of sex-linked lethals is higher in the spermatozoa of old males than in that of young ones. Taking this factor into consideration, he estimates that the temperature coefficient of the mutation process (i.e., the ratio of increase per 10°C) is in the neighborhood of 5.

### Chemical Mutagens

Over the years, many geneticists have been inclined to believe that mutational changes in the genes are produced by chemical agencies. Nevertheless, for a long time attempts to find chemical mutagens met with little success, and mutations were artificially induced first by radiations. In the nineteen thirties, a group of Russian investigators obtained suggestive results in *Drosophila melanogaster*, increasing the mutation rates by treatments with iodine and potassium iodide (Sacharov 1936, Samjatina and Popova 1934, and Kondakova 1935), with copper sulfate (Law 1938 and Magrzhikovskaja 1938), with ammonia (Lobashov and Smirnov 1934), with potassium permangate (Naumenko 1936), with sublimate (Kosiupa 1936), with lead salts (Ponomarev 1937–1938), and with asphyxia (Lobashov 1935). Later Rapoport (1946), Kaplan (1948), Herskowitz (1949b), and Vogt (1950) increased the mutation frequency by feeding Drosophila larvae on media with sublethal doses of formalin or urethane.

It remained, however, for Auerbach and her collaborators (Auerbach

1949, 1965; see Auerbach and Ramsay 1968 for references) to discover the first really powerful chemical mutagen, namely, mustard gas $(Cl \cdot CH_2 \cdot CH_2)_2 S$. Under the most favorable conditions, about as high a proportion (up to 25 percent) of the X chromosomes of *Drosophila melanogaster* acquire sex-linked lethals when treated with mustard gas as is observed after treatments with the highest doses of X-rays that the insect can stand without being completely sterilized. Hadorn and his colleagues (Hadorn and Niggli 1946, and Hadorn, Rosin, and Bertani 1949) treated ovaries of *D. melanogaster in vitro* with phenol solutions. In some experiments striking increases of mutation rates were obtained, whereas other experiments were negative.

Development of the genetics of microorganisms and of molecular genetics led to rapid advances in the studies of chemical mutagenesis. As materials for such studies microorganisms have an evident advantage—one can experiment with numbers of individuals several orders of magnitude greater than is possible with higher animals or plants. Even rare mutations are thus detected without undue amount of work.

In respect to the modes of action of chemical mutagens, some apparently operate by substitution of genetic "letters," the bases in the DNA chains; others cause deletion of some of the letters normally present, or insertion of additional letters (Brenner, Barnett, et al. 1961, Strauss 1964, and Freese 1965). Base substitutions may occur through formation of so-called tautomeric shifts in the nucleotides of DNA or RNA. These are occasional shifts in the positions of the hydrogen atoms responsible for bonding the purines, adenine and guanine, to the pyrimidines, thymine and cytosine, respectively. The tautomeric shifts cause alterations in the process of replication of the DNA strands. A modified adenine may now pair with a cytosine instead of with a thymine, or vice versa; and a modified guanine with a thymine, or vice versa. The tautomeric shifts are unstable, and at the next chromosome replication the normal bonding is restored. The nucleotide introduced into the altered chain of the helix will, however, be linked to its proper partner, thus making a permanent alteration of one genetic letter in the sequence. This may result in a triplet that contains the modified letter coding for a different amino acid, and hence in a modified protein.

Mutational changes that replace one purine in the sequence of genetic letters by another, or one pyrimidine by another, are called transitions. Replacements of a purine by a pyrimidine, or vice versa, are transversions. Transitions seem to occur more often than transversions; the frequency of transitions is greatly increased in bacteria, bacteriophages, and yeasts by treatments with 5-bromouracil, 2-aminopurine, and nitrous acid. The first two substances are chemical analogues of the nucleotide bases and presumably act by being occasionally incorporated in the DNA in place of some normal bases, thus increasing the frequency of mispairing to a value above the spontaneous rate. Nitrous acid is believed to act in a different manner—by replacing the amino groups in some of the bases with hydroxyl groups. The mutations induced by treatments with these substances are reversible, and the frequency of the reverse mutations is increased by treatments with the same substances.

Ethyl ethanesulfonate, nitrogen mustard, and other so-called alkylating agents act as powerful mutagens. Carlson, Sederoff, and Cogan (1967) and Jenkins (1967) have studied the induction of mutants in Drosophila by ethyl ethanesulfonate. Close to one-third of the mutants produced by this substance in the bacteriophage T4 appear to be transversions.

A different kind of mutation is induced by the acridine dyes proflavin and acridine orange. These substances are believed to become inserted between the normal bases in the DNA chains, pushing these bases apart. This results in addition or deletion of one or several bases during the process of DNA replication, and in the appearance of the so-called frameshift mutations (Freese 1965, Brenner, Barnett, et al. 1961, and Streisinger, Okada, et al. 1966). Briefly, their nature is as follows. The genetic code is a nonoverlapping triplet code (cf. Chapter 1). The sequence of three succeeding nucleotides is transcribed and translated into one of the twenty amino acids in a protein chain. The transcription process begins at a fixed point in the sequence of the nucleotides and proceeds in a definite direction, as though a "reading frame" were applied to transcribe the consecutive triplets of the nucleotides in the sequence. Insertion into or deletion from the sequence of one or two nucleotides causes a more drastic change in the gene product than substitution of one nucleotide for another, or than insertion or deletion of three nucleotides constituting a triplet. Indeed, substitutions, insertions, or deletions of single triplets permit the remainder of the series of triplets to be transcribed and translated correctly. On the contrary, in frameshift mutations, the "reading frame" will now be transcribing triplets different from those it transcribed in the ancestral gene. Moreover, there may be formed triplets UAA, UAG, or UGA, which, it will be recalled, are "nonsense" or chain-termination triplets (see Table 1.2). If a frameshift mutation produces such triplets, the result may be premature termination of a protein chain (Garen 1968).

### The Quest for Directed Mutation

Geneticists have always been on the lookout for means to control and direct the mutation process. Theoretically, it should be possible to change chosen genes in a predetermined direction. Thus far the quest has proved elusive. Ionizing radiations increase the frequencies of all kinds of mutations. Ultraviolet light, as pointed out above, induces relatively more point mutations than chromosome breaks. Of course, the frequencies of mutations that arise depend not only on the mutagen used but also on the organism treated. Thus, Witkin (1947, 1966) and Greenberg (1964) selected strains of colon bacteria both with increased and with decreased resistance to ultraviolet and to X-rays. Glass (1955) and Thomas and Roberts (1966) found that chromosomal aberrations induced by similar X-ray exposures are more frequent in male than in female sex cells of Drosophila. There seems to be little if any difference in the frequencies of radiation-induced gene mutations in female and in male sex cells, although more data on this subject are to be desired.

A greater differentiation of the mutation spectra is found with chemical mutagens. Working with bacteria, Demerec (1955) compared the mutabilities of certain genes after treatments with manganese salts and with X-rays; some of these genes responded more strongly to the manganese and others to the radiation. As mentioned above, some chemical mutagens induce base-pair substitutions and others frameshift mutations. De Serres (1964) found in the mold *Neurospora crassa* clear-cut differences between the mutation spectra induced by X-rays, nitrous acid, 2-aminopurine, and the spontaneous mutants.

Transformation is a genetic phenomenon really distinct from mutation. It leads, however, to a directed genetic change and should logically be discussed in this chapter (it will be mentioned in another context in Chapter 12). It was discovered and studied by Griffith, Dawson, Avery, MacLeod, McCarthy, Hotchkiss, and others. An account of this classical work can be found in any modern textbook on genetics; very briefly, the story is as follows. Some forms of pneumonia in man and in animals are caused by bacteria belonging to the species *Diplococcus pneumoniae*. The ability of the bacteria to cause infection (their virulence) depends on the presence on their cell surfaces of an envelope composed of polysaccharides. When grown on a laboratory medium, virulent pneumococci give colonies with a smooth, glistening surface. If, however, they are maintained for a long time by repeated transfers on laboratory media, the bacteria undergo a characteristic change. They lose their polysaccharide envelopes and their virulence; the colonies become small with rough outlines. The change from smooth to rough is reversible. Griffith showed in 1928 that mice inoculated with a mixture of living rough pneumococci and of heat-killed smooth ones became infected. Moreover, pneumococci that form smooth colonies when cultured on laboratory media can be isolated from such infected mice. The change from rough to smooth is conditioned by the presence of dead smooth bacteria.

The changes from smooth to rough, and vice versa, may be due to selection of spontaneous mutations adapted to one or the other of these conditions. The smooth phase is able to invade susceptible hosts, while the rough one is superior to the smooth on laboratory culture media. One or the other genotype is selected by the environment in which the strain is placed. Such transformations, involving differential survival of spontaneous mutants, are well known in many microorganisms. Dawson found, however, that the transformation from rough to smooth can be induced in a test tube by killed smooth cells. Avery, MacLeod, and McCarthy proved that the material responsible for the transformation in DNA was derived from dead smooth cells.

Furthermore, the transformation is remarkably specific. There are many variants or "types" of pneumococci, distinguishable by immunological tests and also by the kinds of polysaccharides in their envelopes. Suppose now that a smooth strain of type I loses its envelope and becomes a rough strain. Suppose further that it is transformed back to smooth with the aid of killed cells of type III. Will the new smooth strain belong to type I or to type III? It belongs to the latter; in other words the transformation depends on the strain that furnishes the DNA "transforming principle." Most or all known types of pneumococci can be transformed into other variants by using the dead cells of the desired types. Moreover, the transformed strains retain the induced-type characteristics after cultivation on laboratory media or after passage through animal hosts. They have acquired not merely a temporary polysaccharide envelope of a kind different from that which their ancestors had, but also the ability to synthesize the new polysaccharide indefinitely.

The "transforming principle" isolated by Avery and his associates is a viscous colorless substance, which proves to be a highly polymerized deoxyribonucleic acid with little or no impurities. The transforming power of this substance is so great that it is capable of causing transformation in a dilution of 1 : 600,000,000. Subsequent studies by Hotchkiss and others have revealed important details of the transformation process. The DNA of the donor type penetrates into the recipient cell; sections of this transforming DNA are then incorporated into the chromosome of the recipient cell. The genes located near each other in the transforming DNA are acquired by the transformed cells more often than are genes located far apart.

Genetic transformations first discovered in the pneumococci were subsequently achieved in several other genera of bacteria. Can they occur also in higher organisms? More than a decade ago, Benoit, Leroy et al. (1960) reported that they had induced transformations in the progeny of Pekin ducks injected with DNA extracted from ducks of the Khaki-Campbell breed. This claim has not been confirmed. Fox and Yoon (1966) reported carefully conducted experiments, treating dechorionated eggs of *Drosophila melanogaster* with DNA prepared from several classical mutants (yellow body, white eyes, singed bristles, etc.). When the adult flies obtained from the treated eggs were inspected, some of them showed patches of tissue seemingly altered in the direction of the mutants that were the DNA donors. These results are a suggestive and perhaps promising beginning, but as yet no more than that.

The potential importance of transformation, if it could be achieved in higher organisms, especially man, is enormous. It would open possibilities for genetic engineering, or "genetic surgery" as Muller (1965, 1967) called it, that stagger the imagination. One could envisage such operations as implanting desired genes or removing undesirable ones. Almost unlimited potentialities for eugenic betterment, as well as the improvement of domesticated animals and plants, would be within grasp. For the time being, however, one can say only that transformation may be an important evolutionary force in some microorganisms, especially those in which true sexual union and gene recombination does not occur (see Chapter 12).

## Mutational Changes in the Cytoplasm

Correns, one of the rediscoverers of Mendel's laws, studied the inheritance of a green and white variegation in *Mirabilis jalapa* and in some other plants as early as 1909. The inheritance was simple— seeds formed in the flowers on green branches gave green progeny those on white branches gave plants without chlorophyll, and those on variegated branches gave variegated, green or white plants. Crosses showed that the inheritance was through the mother only, the color of the progeny depending on the ovule and not on the pollen. The obvious explanation was that the difference between the green and the white tissues depends in this case not on nuclear genes but on some self-reproducing entities in the cytoplasm, most likely the chloroplasts, which are transmitted only through the female line. Subsequently such extra-chromosomal or cytoplasmic inheritance was found in several species of higher plants and in microorganisms (Paramecium, Neurospora, yeasts, Chlamydomonas; there is a review in Jinks 1964). It appears to be rare in animals, although a case has been established in mosquitoes (Laven 1967).

In recent years interest in cytoplasmic inheritance has been enhanced by the utilization of cytoplasmic male sterility in agricultural practice, especially in the production of hybrid corn and hybrid wheat (Kihara 1967). Moreover, both chloroplasts and mitochondria have been shown to contain DNA and thus to possess an unqualified genetic continuity. This does not mean that the chromosomal and the extrachromosomal carriers of genetic information are independent of each other. One of the commonest kinds of Mendelian recessive mutant in higher plants shows reduction or total absence of chlorophyll in the chloroplasts. On the other hand, Rhoades (1946) described a nuclear gene in corn, which induces irreversible mutational changes in the chloroplasts, subsequently inherited according to the classical Correns scheme just described. Very little is known about the mutational origin of other cytoplasmic variants, although chemical induction of such variants in yeasts has been recorded. Maly (1951) induced plastid variants by irradiation in fern prothallia.

## Pleiotropism or Manifold Effects

Early theorists of genetics, particularly Weismann, envisaged the germ plasm as a mosaic of particles, each representing an anatomically defined part of the body. This idea harks back to the preformistic notions that led some early microscopists to imagine a tiny image of man, a homunculus, in the head of the human spermatozoon. Darwin's provisional hypothesis of pangenesis followed the same tradition, since it postulated that the hereditary materials in the sex cells are compounded of particles, gemmules, secreted by the cells of each part of the body. Preformistic ideas became, largely by indirection, attached to the gene concept as well. Pioneers of Mendelian genetics in the early years of the current century imagined the organism to be a mosaic of "unit characters," each determined by a special gene.

The method of naming mutant genes and, by extension, their ancestral gene alleles reinforces these ideas. In Drosophila, mutations of the gene white turn the eye color from red to white, the mutation vestigial produces vestigial wings, etc. The names are convenient, but they can be misleading if taken for descriptions of the total range of effects of a particular gene. In point of fact, the mutation white changes not only the color of the eyes but also that of the testicular sheath, the shape of the spermatheca, the longevity, and the viability. Vestigial not only reduces wing size but also modifies the balancers, makes certain bristles erect instead of horizontal, and changes wing muscles, spermatheca shape, development rate, longevity, fecundity, and viability. Under favorable environmental conditions vestigial decreases the number of ovarioles relative to the long-winged form; under unfavorable culture conditions the wild type has fewer ovarioles than does the vestigial. The mutant split in *Drosophila melanogaster* makes the eye surface rough and the bristles on the thorax split or doubled. Stern and Tokunaga (1968) studied mosaic flies that have most of the body wild type, but have spots showing the mutant trait. Such spots show the roughness if they include parts of the eyes, and changed bristles if they occur on the thorax. The two manifestations of the gene split are autonomous in development.

Genes that change more than one character are said to be pleiotropic or to have manifold effects. The more detailed a comparison of a mutant with the ancestral form, the more differences are detected. For instance, most classical mutants in Drosophila reduce the viability of their carriers, in addition to whatever changes they produce in the appearance of the insects. The reduced viability may be evident in crowded but not in uncrowded cultures. Dobzhansky (1927) attempted to estimate the prevalence of manifold effects by examining a sample of mutants in *Drosophila melanogaster* for changes in an arbitrarily selected organ, namely, the spermatheca. In ten of the twelve mutants, differences in the spermatecae were detected, although these mutants were known as eye-color, body-color, and wing-shape mutants and were not suspected to differ in the internal anatomy in general or in spermatheca shape in particular. It remained uncertain whether the differences in spermatheca shape were due to polygenes lying in the chromosome in the vicinity of the gene loci responsible for the externally visible changes, or to the latter genes themselves (Schwab 1940).

In a subsequent study Dobzhansky and Holz (1943) obtained several mutations of the genes white and yellow in an inbred strain of *Drosophila melanogaster,* and showed that the mutants differed from the parent strain in spermatheca shape as well as in the colors of the eyes and of the body. It is unlikely that mutations of the genes modifying the shape of the spermatheca arise by chance every time the genes white and yellow undergo mutation; the changes in spermatheca shape must be ascribed to pleiotropic effects of these genes. Parsons and Green (1959) have likewise shown that the decreased fitness of vermilion-eyed flies is caused by the vermilion locus and not by associated linked genes.

Because of the importance of pleiotropism for understanding evolutionary mechanisms, we shall examine the following random examples that show how widespread it is. Varieties of garden onions may have white, cream-colored, red, or purple bulbs. The color variations are determined chiefly by alleles of a single Mendelian gene. Jones, Walker, et al. (1946) and Walker (1951) found that this gene also determines the resistance to the smudge fungus, Colletotrichum. White bulbs are easily infected with the fungus; cream-colored bulbs are slightly susceptible; red or purple bulbs are resistant. The resistance is due to the presence in the colored bulbs of catechol and protocatechuic acids, which are poisonous to the spores of the fungus. Ali (1950) found a parallel case in varieties of beans, some of which are susceptible and others resistant to the bean mosaic virus.

Hereditary diseases in man and higher animals are often complicated "syndromes," composed of changes in many body parts, organ systems, and physiological functions. A mutation in the rat causes thickened ribs, narrowed lumen of the trachea, emphysema of the lungs, hypertrophy of the heart, blocked nostrils, blunt snout, and low viability. Grüneberg (1938) found that the whole syndrome stems from a single primary change, an anomaly of the cartilage.

Homozygotes for the gene lozenge-clawless in *Drosophila melanogaster* differ from the ancestral form in the following syndrome of traits: size and shape of the eyes, structure of the ommatidia, distribution of the pigment in the eyes, reduction in size of the third segment of the antenna, reduction of the basiconic sensilia on the antennae and the palpi, reduction of the tarsal claws, lack of the spermathecae and parovaria in the female reproductive organs, tendency of the sperm to congeal in a mass in the vagina, failure of most of the eggs deposited by these females to hatch (Anders 1955). Anders believes that this syndrome may also be reduced to a single primary change.

Hadorn (1956 and other works) studied what he describes as biochemical pleiotropy in the fly Drosophila and the moth Ephestia. Figure 2.3 shows the relative amounts of the substances detected by

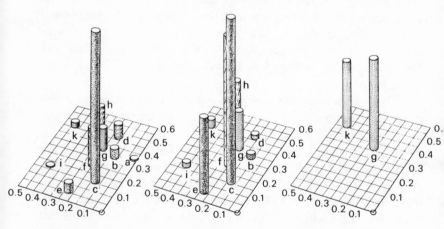

**FIGURE 2.3**

> Relative amounts of the fluorescent substances detected in normal (left) and mutant (center and right) moths Ephestia kühniella. The heights of the columns symbolize the amounts of the substances, and their positions on the grids show their locations on two-dimensional chromatograms. (After Hadorn and Kühn)

ultraviolet fluorescence on chromatograms of the wild-type and two mutants of *Ephestia kühniella*.

Rothe (1951) and Stebbins and Yagil (1966) have described complex syndromes produced by mutants in the snapdragon and in barley, respectively. These are due to single genes that alter "the course of development at an early primordial stage, and initiate an entirely new epigenetic sequence of development."

Particularly interesting are pleiotropic syndromes that combine morphological traits with specific changes in behavior. The mutant yellow in *Drosophila melanogaster* changes the body color and also the courtship pattern; yellow males are less successful than normal ones in mating with normal females, and Bastock (1956) found that the difference is not due to discrimination based on the yellow coloration. Cotter (1967) found the following effects of a single locus mutation in the moth *Ephestia kühniella*: change in eye color, reduced mean rate of development, decreased oxygen consumption, higher preadult mortality, increased variance in rate of development, and changes in the antennae; in addition, mutant males initiate the courting of females earlier but are less successful in copulation than wild-type males, and mutant females have increased mean progeny production. Belyaev and Evsikov (1967) have ascertained that the recessive genes modifying the coat color in mink (*Lutreola vison*) reduce the fertility of the animals when homozygous, though some of them increase the fertility when heterozygous. Rather less well established is the association claimed by Cattell, Young, and Hindleby (1964) between the classical ABO blood system in man, intelligence, and tender-mindedness versus tough-mindedness. The same judgment can be applied to the alleged association between eye and hair colors and susceptibility to poliomyelitis (D. E. Lea 1955).

The strikingly pleiotropic and apparently nonpleiotropic genes are certainly not two different classes of genes. Suppose that an ancestral gene, A, produces a certain phenotype in cooperation with all the other genes that the organism has; a mutant gene, a, gives rise to a different phenotype, but again in cooperation with the same residual genotype. The differences between the phenotypes of the ancestral type and the mutant are indicative of the effects of the change $A \rightarrow a$, not of the sum total of the effects of either A or a. More information about the total effects of a gene can be obtained by observation of what a physical removal, a deletion, of this gene does to the organism. In nonpolyploid organisms, such as Drosophila, most homozygous deficiencies act as lethals. As Demerec had already shown in 1936, most deficiencies in Drosophila are cell lethals, that is, the absence of a gene is fatal not only to the whole organism but also to a patch of cells surrounded by tissues in which this gene is present.

Furthermore, the gene may appear pleiotropic or nonpleiotropic, according to the level on which its action is studied. A "dogma" of molecular genetics is that each structural gene specifies one and only one polypeptide chain in a protein. On the molecular level, then, we would find no "genuine pleiotropism"; all pleiotropisms are "spurious pleiotropisms" in Grüneberg's (1943) terminology. This in no way diminishes their biological interest and evolutionary significance. In immunogenetics and enzyme genetics the phenomenon of codominance is most frequently observed: a heterozygote for two alleles coding for two variant enzymes or antigens shows both of these enzymes or antigens present. Formation of "hybrid substances" or interaction products is rather an exception.

As the traits studied are further and further removed from the primary gene action, the possibilities of epistatic interactions of different genes, as well as modifications due to environmental influence, increase. Contrary to the views of early geneticists, the organism is not an aggregate of "unit" traits or characters or qualities. Traits, characters, and qualities are not biological units; they are abstractions, words, semantic devices that a student needs in order to describe and communicate the results of his observations. A trait has no adaptive significance in isolation from the whole developmental pattern that an organism exhibits at a certain stage of its life cycle; one may define a trait only as an aspect of the path of development of the organism (Dobzhansky 1956a). Talking about traits as though they were independent entities is responsible for much confusion in biological, and particularly in evolutionary, thought.

# CHAPTER THREE

# MUTATION AND GENETIC VARIABILITY

## *The Building Blocks of Evolution*

Reference was made in Chapter 2 to the distinction drawn by de Vries between mutations creating new species and Darwinian "fluctuating" variability. This distinction is invalid. In point of fact, only chromosome doubling in interspecific hybrids (allopolyploidy) is a special kind of mutation that may lead directly to the emergence of new species (see Chapter 11). The process of mutation supplies only the building blocks, the raw materials, from which evolutionary changes, including species differences, are compounded by natural selection. Mutation is, then, the ultimate source of evolution, but there is more to evolution than mutation. It will be shown in the concluding pages of the present chapter that mutation is a random process with respect to the adaptive needs of the species. Therefore, mutation alone, uncontrolled by natural selection, would result in the breakdown and eventual extinction of life, not in adaptive or progressive evolution.

All genetic changes, except those due to gene recombination, are mutations by definition. Only the phenomena of transformation (see Chapters 2 and 12) are, in a sense, bridging the gap between mutational and recombinational variability. The synopsis on pp. 44-45 shows that a collection of diverse phenomena is subsumed under the name mutation. Attempts have been made repeatedly to hypothesize that different kinds of mutations produce changes of different taxonomic value. Goldschmidt (1940) contended that not only new species but also new genera, families, and orders arise by means of special "systemic" mutations. Singleton (1951) supposed that the "corn grass" mutation, derived from cultivated maize, may be a "macromutation" of possible significance as an "ancestral type," but neither Singleton himself nor Goldschmidt claimed it to be a systemic mutation. Lamprecht argued in a series of papers (summary in Lamprecht 1964) that there are two categories of genes and of mutations, some distinguishing species and others only varieties. Böcher (1951) believed that there are two kinds of mutations, some responsible for adaptation to the environment and others for progressive evolution. These views have very few adherents at present.

## The Types of Changes Produced by Mutation

Mutations change all sorts of characteristics—structural, physiological, biochemical, and behavioral. The classical mutants in *Drosophila melanogaster,* it will be recalled from Chapter 2, were hand picked for unambiguous recognition by inspection of the external characteristics of the fly. These "visibles" alter the eye and body colors; the numbers and shapes of the bristles; the size, shape, and venation of the wings; the manner in which the fly holds its wings in relation to the body; the antennae and the legs, etc. Mutants that can be distinguished from wild-type flies under some but not under all environments in which the flies are cultivated in laboratories were considered inferior, and usually discarded.

As early as 1912, the first recessive sex-linked lethal gene, which caused no visible changes in heterozygous females but killed hemizygous males, was identified. Recessive lethals, sex-linked and autosomal, eventually proved to be considerably more frequent than conveniently usable visibles; therefore, lethals rather than visibles were used for quantitative studies of the mutation process, with and without radiation, starting with the classical work of Muller (1928a,b). The nature of the changes that cause the lethality is largely unknown, although several studies have been directed specifically at detecting the manner of action of lethals (Hadorn 1951, Rizki 1952, Lindsley, Edington, and von Halle 1960, and summary in Lindsley and Grell 1968).

Lethals may cause death at any stage of the development, from early to late embryogenesis, any one of three larval instars, early or late pupa, or newly emerged adult. Hadorn and Rizki found indications that certain developmental stages are more sensitive than others. Different lethals harm different organ systems—digestive tract, Malpighian tubes, gonads, fat bodies, mouth parts, tracheal tubes, musculature, etc. The imaginal discs may fail to form, be underdeveloped, or fail to evert. Tumors, though mostly benign and rarely invasive, may develop. Physiological and biochemical changes were described in some lethal genotypes.

Mutants that modify the sex-determination mechanisms are also known. A dominant mutant in *Drosophila pseudoobscura* transforms females into intersexes without changing either the sexual traits or the fertility of males (Dobzhansky and Spassky 1941). The recessive gene double sex in *D. melanogaster* changes both females and males into almost similar intersexes (Hildreth 1965). Another recessive gene makes the females intersexual but does not change the males. A mutant strain in which the males evinced homosexual behavior was found in *D. melanogaster* by Gill (1963) and in the stickleback fish (*Pygosteus pungitius*) by Morris (1952).

Homeotic mutants produce quite spectacular transformations of some organs into others. A single pair of wings, a pair of balancers, and antennae and mouth parts built in certain ways are diagnostic characteristics of the order Diptera (flies). The mutant aristapedia has antennae replaced by leglike organs; in proboscipedia the proboscis becomes antennalike or leglike; bithorax and tetraptera transform the balancers into a second pair of wings; hexaptera adds a pair of winglike appendages on the prothorax, etc. (Herskowitz 1949a). Of course, all these mutants continue to belong not only to the order of flies but also to the genus and species *Drosophila melanogaster*.

The kinds of mutants found in a given organism depend in part on the methods used for their detection. The classical mutants in Drosophila, as mentioned previously, were discovered by visual inspection. Mutants in bacteria and other microorganisms change mostly biochemical traits, such as the ability or inability to metabolize certain substances, or to synthesize some vitamins and amino acids. However, a considerable number and variety of morphologically visible mutants, in addition to the biochemical type, are known in the bread mold *Neurospora crassa* (Garnjobst and Tatum 1967). Studies in higher organisms have in recent years disclosed a tremendous amount of genetic variability in enzyme, hemoglobin, and serum polymorphisms.

## The Numbers of Genes and Mutations

The existence of genes was inferred by Mendel from observations on the distribution of traits in progenies of hybrids between varieties of peas differing in clear-cut characteristics. If all members of a species were genetically alike, Mendelian genetics would be thwarted. One discovers the genes in man that control the blood groups, the eye colors, and other traits because people vary in these respects. Mendelian segregation of blood groups and of eye colors can be observed in families and in pedigrees. Only genes that have mutated and are represented by two or several allelic forms in the same species can be discovered by Mendelian methods. This is why geneticists are always on the lookout for genetic diversity. Genetically, highly variable species are predilect materials for investigation.

The number of genes is not known with precision in any species. The 56 genes in the bacteriophage T4 (Watson 1967) constitute probably the greatest fraction of the genes present in any organism that have been detected or studied. Since DNA is the carrier of genetic information, attempts have been made to estimate the numbers of genes through measurement of the DNA contents of cell nuclei. We saw in Chapter 1 that the haploid chromosome set in man contains approximately $3.2 \times 10^{-12}$ gram of DNA, which corresponds to some $2.9 \times 10^9$ nucleotide pairs. On the assumption of 600 nucleotides per gene, this is enough for more than 5 million genes. This number seems altogether excessive, and McKusick (1966) gives 100,000 as a reasonable estimate of the number of different genes in man. The amount of DNA in a haploid chromosome set in Drosophila suffices for at least 300,000 genes. This is again at least one order of magnitude greater than the number estimated by the pioneers of genetics. Their estimates were based on the assumption (which was admitted to be an oversimplification) that all genes mutate equally frequently, and that the genes which have been observed to mutate are a random sample of all the genes in a given species.

Several possible explanations for the above discrepancies can be offered. Perhaps not the whole mass of DNA consists of genes; a great majority of the genes have never been observed to mutate; mutations in most genes may be altogether inviable; most genes may be regulators rather than structural genes; mutations in most genes may produce slight and not easily detectable changes in the phenotypes of their carriers. The recent discovery of high redundancy of some genetic materials in higher organisms (Britten and Kohne 1968; see Chapter 2) affords at least a partial explanation. Unless the redundant gene loci are periodically derived from a single gene (which is unlikely), mutations will not be easily detected. They may be mutationally "silent" genes.

*Drosophila melanogaster* and man are the two species in which the greatest numbers of genes are known. A painstaking review of the mutants in the first of these species has been published by Lindsley and Grell (1968). They list 483 gene loci in the X chromosome, 279 in the second, 214 in the third, and 16 in the fourth—a total of 992 genes located with varying degrees of precision. McKusick (1966) catalogues 793 presumed autosomal dominants, 629 presumed autosomal recessive, and 123 sex-linked traits in man. However, among these only some 344 autosomal dominants, 280 autosomal recessives, and 68 sex-linked traits have their inheritances reasonably well established. Drosophila and man are higher organisms best studied genetically. Among microorganisms, bacteriophages T4 and lambda are also genetically well explored; about 56 genes in the former and 20 in the latter are known.

## The Mutation Rates of Different Genes

The difficulty of obtaining accurate data on the mutation pressure is apparent. Either one tries to determine the total frequency of mutations for all the genes that the organism possesses, or else a particular gene is selected and its mutability measured. In the former case, mutations that produce slight changes present an obstacle, for no known experimental procedure permits the detection of all such mutations, and yet they probably constitute the most frequent class. On the other hand, if a single gene is selected, the mutation frequency is usually so low that accumulation of accurate data on higher organisms is difficult, slight mutations may be overlooked, and there is no assurance that all mutations of the gene in question (because of its manifold effects) produce changes in the same character. Conversely, the same character may be modified in similar ways by mutations in different genes ("mimics"), so that the mutation rate ascribed to a single gene locus may be an overestimate. The techniques of estimation of the mutation rates in human genes and the sources of error encountered in such estimation are well described in Stern (1960).

A sampling of the recorded spontaneous mutation rates is shown in Table 3.1. The so-called unstable or mutable genes, some of which cause piebald, mottled, or dotted color patterns in animals and plants,

**TABLE 3.1**

Spontaneous mutation rates of specific genes in various organisms (After Strickberger 1968, modified)

| Species and Traits | Mutations per 100,000 Cells or Gametes | Species and Traits | Mutations per 100,000 Cells or Gametes |
|---|---|---|---|
| Escherichia coli (K12) | | Zea mays | |
| Streptomycin resistance | 0.00004 | Shrunken seed | 0.12 |
| Resistance to phage T1 | 0.003 | Colorless | 0.23 |
| Leucine independence | 0.00007 | Sugary seed | 0.24 |
| Arginine independence | 0.0004 | Pr to pr | 1.10 |
| Tryptophan independence | 0.006 | I to i | 10.60 |
| | | R$^r$ to r$^r$ | |
| Salmonella typhimurium | | Mus musculus | |
| Tryptophan independence | 0.005 | Brown | 0.85 |
| | | Pinkeye | 0.85 |
| Diplococcus pneumoniae | | Piebald | 1.70 |
| Penicillin resistance | 0.01 | Dilute | 3.40 |
| Neurospora crassa | | Homo sapiens | |
| Adenine independence | 0.0008-0.029 | Epiloia | 0.4-0.8 |
| Inositol independence | 0.001-0.010 | Retinoblastoma | 1.2-2.3 |
| | | Aniridia | 0.5 |
| Drosophila melanogaster | | Achondroplasia | 4.2-14.3 |
| Yellow body | 12 | Pelger's anomaly | 1.7-2.7 |
| Brown eyes | 3 | Neurofibromatosis | 13.0-25.0 |
| Ebony body | 2 | Microphthalmos-anophthalmos | 0.5 |
| Eyeless | 6 | Huntington's chorea | 0.5 |

are not included, because they may represent phenomena of a different nature. Even so, calculated in frequencies per generation (or cell division in unicellular organisms), the rates range over several orders of magnitude ($10^{-10}$ to $10^{-4}$). These differences would, of course, be much less pronounced if the mutation rates were calculated per unit time, since the generation lengths in the organisms mentioned in Table 3.1 differ by factors up to $10^6$. It should be noted, however, that genes in the same species may have mutabilities differing by at least two orders of magnitude, and data like those in Table 3.1 are necessarily a biased sample, since very rare mutations are likely not to be observed at all.

The mutation rates in varieties of a single species, and presumably in different species as well, are under genetic control. It has been known for at least two decades that some strains of *Drosophila melanogaster* have higher mutation rates than others, and that these differences may be caused by mutability enhancer genes, which can be located in one or another linkage group (see Ives 1950 and Thompson 1962 for further references). Abundant data have been accumulated on the frequency of origin of recessive lethal mutations in the X chromosomes of *D. melanogaster*. Dubinin (1966) has summarized the data on the frequencies of such mutations in 71 strains from different parts of the world. The total 385,207 chromosomes analyzed had 719 lethal mutants; this means that $0.187 \pm 0.007$ percent of X chromosomes acquire such mutants per generation. The mutation rates in different strains varied, however, from 0.05 to $1.09 \pm 0.15$ percent per generation. Similar variations are found also in the second chromosome, although here the information is considerably less extensive.

Table 3.2 summarizes the results of a comparative study of muta-

**TABLE 3.2**

Frequencies (in percentages) of recessive lethal and semilethal mutations in homologous chromosomes of four species of Drosophila (CL = 95 percent confidence limits)

| Species and Population | Frequency | CL |
|---|---|---|
| Pesudoobscura | 0.999 | 0.733–1.340 |
| Persimilis | 1.783 | 1.403–2.264 |
| Prosaltans | 0.638 | 0.467–0.869 |
| Willistoni, São Paulo | 1.714 | 1.203–2.438 |
| Willistoni, São Paulo | 0.762 | 0.472–1.231 |
| Willistoni, Belem | 0.568 | 0.317–1.016 |
| Willistoni, Total | 0.894 | 0.678–1.179 |

tion rates in four species of Drosophila (Dobzhansky, B. Spassky, and N. Spassky 1952, 1954). All experiments were made at the same temperature, 24°C. *Drosophila persimilis,* a species living in cool and humid parts of the western United States, has a mutation rate higher than that of the more widespread *D. pseudoobscura. Drosophila willistoni* is a common and widespread, and *D. prosaltans* a rare and specialized, tropical species. The last-named has the lowest mutation rate of the four species. Among the three populations of *D. willistoni* studied, the one from equatorial Brazil (Belem) has the lowest mutation rate; the populations from southern Brazil (São Paulo) have higher rates. The mutation rates seem to be adjusted to the climatic and ecological conditions of the habitats in which these insects live.

Many, and perhaps all, genes may be changed in various ways and may produce series of multiple alleles. The frequencies of different kinds of mutations depend on the structure of the gene itself and on the genotype as a whole. The classical work of Timofeeff-Ressovsky (1937 and earlier) showed that the gene $W$ (for the normal red eye color) in *Drosophila melanogaster* changes to the extreme allele $w$ (for white eye color) more frequently than to intermediate alleles, such as $w^e$ (eosin color) or $w^a$ (apricot color). The "normal" $W$, allele of this gene is, however, different in different strains. A strain of American origin, and another of Russian, were given identical X-ray treatments. In the former, 55 mutations at the white locus were observed among 59,200 chromosomes; in the latter, 40 mutations among 75,000 chromosomes. The "Russian" allele changed mostly to white, and the "American" one to white and to intermediates (eosin) with about equal frequency. Through further experiments Timofeeff-Ressovsky proved that the difference in the behavior of the Russian and the American strains was due to different mutabilities of the white gene itself, and not to modifying genes in other chromosomes.

Gene mutation is, in principle, a reversible process. Most mutations are caused by substitution of a single amino acid in a protein, and of a single nucleotide in the DNA chain coding for this protein. With such mutations, the reverse substitutions may also occur. Unfortunately, the experimental approach to the problem of mutation reversibility meets with complications. Suppose that a mutation changes the eye color in Drosophila from red to vermilion; a reverse mutation should change vermilion back to red. Study of such reversals shows, however, that some of them are due, not to mutations in the vermilion gene, but to mutations in other genes that suppress the phenotypic manifestation of vermilion. Be that as it may, the observable frequencies of "forward" and "reverse" mutations are often sharply unequal.

Schlager and Dickie (1966) summarize the data on spontaneous mutations in five genes in the house mouse, based on a study of approximately 1.5 million mice. The frequencies of forward and back mutations for 1 million gametes are as follows:

| Gene Locus | Forward | Reverse |
|---|---|---|
| a | 71 | 4.7 |
| b | 0 | 0 |
| c | 9.7 | 0 |
| d | 19.2 | 0.4 |
| ln | 15.1 | 0 |

An even more detailed study of forward and reverse mutations was made by Yanofsky and his colleagues (Yanofsky, Berger, and Brammar 1969, and other works) in *Escherichia coli*. Mutants that changed the gene coding for the enzyme tryptophan synthetase were collected, and the amino acids substituted in the different mutants were determined. Reverse mutations, which restored the original phenotype, that is, the normal physiological function of the enzyme, were also observed. Most of the reverse mutations did not, however, restore the original amino acids (and, hence, the original nucleotide sequence in the gene); in point of fact, some of the phenotypic reversions differed from the original enzyme in having more amino acid substitutions than did the mutants.

## Lethal and Subvital Mutations
## Induced by Radiation

Mutations form a spectrum, ranging from drastic changes that cause death, or dramatic alterations of the external appearance, to barely perceptible, and perhaps even imperceptible, modifications of body structures or of viability (subvital mutants). Drastic or easily visible changes are, of course, advantageous for study. In organisms such as Drosophila, the detection of lethals is easy and accurate. In contrast, some observers detect small changes in the external traits of the fly that are overlooked by others. With lethals such "personal equation" is unimportant. And yet it is possible that slight mutants outnumber drastic ones. Moreover, the drastic and spectacular mutants may really be only pathological by-products of the evolutionary changes, which are compounded of many small mutations.

Timofeeff-Ressovsky (1935) and Kerkis (1938) did the pioneering work in comparing the frequencies of large and small mutations in *Drosophila melanogaster*. Males from an inbred strain were treated with X-rays, and crossed to ClB females which previously had been crossed repeatedly to the same inbred strain. ClB females have in one of their X chromosomes a gene marker, Bar (*B*), making narrow eyes, a recessive lethal gene (*l*), and an inversion (*C*) which suppresses the recombination between the ClB chromosome and the other X chromosome present in the same female. In the $F_1$ generation, females with narrow eyes, which carry the ClB chromosomes, were selected and outcrossed to untreated wild-type males. In the progeny of such matings, some of the sons receive the ClB chromosome and die of the lethal contained in it; the sons receiving the other X chromosome survive, provided no lethal mutation has been induced in this chromosome by the treatment. The expected sex ratio is, therefore, 2 females : 1 male. If a lethal mutation is induced, the offspring are females only.

If a mutation that is not lethal but decreases the viability arises in the X chromosome, the resulting sex ratio falls between 2♀ : 1♂ and 2♀ : 0♂, depending on the degree of the deleterious effect produced by the mutation. For technical reasons it is preferable to record only the daughters that do *not* carry the X chromosome (ClB); they form about half of all females and can be recognized by round instead of Bar eyes. The frequencies of such females and males turn out to be 1♀ : 0.95♂ if no mutation has been induced in the treated chromosome, and 1♀ : 0♂ if a lethal mutation has been induced. Table 3.3 gives the sex ratios produced by individual females. The control series shows the ratios obtained in the progeny of males that have not been treated with X-rays.

## TABLE 3.3

Percentages of cultures giving various sex ratios obtained by Timofeeff-Ressovsky (1935) in his experiments on mutations affecting viability

| Culture | | | | | | | Ratio | | | | | | |
|---|---|---|---|---|---|---|---|---|---|---|---|---|---|
| | 1: 1.15 | 1: 1.05 | 1: 0.95 | 1: 0.85 | 1: 0.75 | 1: 0.65 | 1: 0.55 | 1: 0.45 | 1: 0.35 | 1: 0.25 | 1: 0.15 | 1: 0.05 | 1: 0.00 |
| Control | 2.1 | 14.1 | 77.1 | 5.5 | 0.7 | ... | ... | 0.5 | ... | ... | ... | ... | ... |
| Treated | 0.7 | 10.1 | 44.9 | 8.8 | 7.2 | 5.3 | 4.2 | 1.8 | 1.1 | 0.7 | 1.4 | 0.9 | 13.0 |

In the treated series, 13 percent of the cultures had no males at all, and about 3 percent produced less than one-third as many males as females; these cultures contained newly arisen lethal and semilethal mutants. Many cultures—no fewer than 20 percent of the total—gave appreciably fewer males than were observed in most cultures of the control experiment. These male-deficient cultures contained subvital mutants, which cause viability losses not drastic enough to be classed as semilethal. Although it is difficult to identify every culture that carries a subvital mutant, both Timofeeff-Ressovsky and Kerkis concluded that subvital mutants are more frequent than lethal and semilethal ones, and by extrapolation that mutations with small effects are generally more frequent than those with large effects. This was questioned by Käfer (1952), Bonnier and Jonsson (1957), Paxman (1957), and Friedman (1964). These authors found lethals the most numerous class of mutations, at least in the progenies of X-ray-treated flies. However, the well-designed and large-scale experiments of Mukai (1964, 1969) established conclusively the prevalence of small mutations.

## The Techniques of Chromosome Assay and of Accumulation of Mutants

At this point we must review certain techniques developed for Drosophila, which are being used in many experiments. There is a laboratory strain of *Drosophila melanogaster* that carries the dominant genes Curly wing ($Cy$) and Lobe eye ($L$) in one of its second chromosomes, and Plum-colored eyes ($Pm$) in the other second chromosome. Both chromosomes have also inverted sections to suppress the recombination in the second chromosomes. Analogous strains, with different mutant markers, exist in other Drosophila species.

Suppose that we wish to determine the proportion of the sex cells that contain newly arisen second-chromosome mutants, or the proportion of the second chromosomes in a natural population of *Drosophila melanogaster* carrying recessive lethal, semilethal, subvital, or any other recessive mutant genes. Following the scheme in Fig. 3.1, we cross a fly to be tested to $Cy$ $L/Pm$ flies. A single Curly-Lobe male is taken in the $F_1$ generation, and crossed further as shown in the figure. In the third generation, one quarter, i.e., 25 percent of the flies, carry in duplicate (in homozygous condition) the chromosomes $+_2$ or $+_3$,

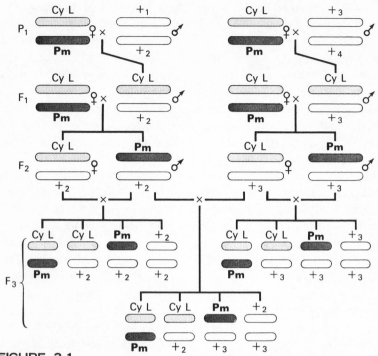

**FIGURE 3.1**

Technique of chromosome assay for recessive genetic variants in Drosophila melanogaster. The chromosomes with the dominant marker genes Cy, L, and Pm are shown shaded; wild-type chromosomes ($+_1$, $+_2$, $+_3$, and $+_4$) are white.

the effects of which in double dose we wish to test. These flies are recognizable by inspection, because they do not carry the marker genes Curly, Lobe, or Plum. Suppose now that the tested chromosome contains a recessive lethal gene or genes; the wild-type flies will then be absent in the test culture. A recessive condition that gives a proportion of wild-type flies more than zero but less than 12.5 percent is a semilethal; a subvital will make the wild-type class frequency more than 12.5 but less than 25 percent, and a supervital significantly more than 25 percent.

Another variant of the same technique involves intercrossing in the $F_2$ generation (Fig. 3.1) females and males that carry one Curly-Lobe and one wild-type chromosome ($Cy\ L/+_1$ or $Cy\ L/+_2$). One quarter of the zygotes in the $F_2$ will now die on account of homozygosis for the lethal genes Curly and Lobe. Two-thirds of the surviving zygotes carry one Curly-Lobe chromosome, and a chromosome the genetic contents of which are to be tested, represented as white in Fig. 3.1; one-third of the zygotes will have the chromosome to be tested in double dose (in homozygous condition). Now, if these homozygotes are equal in viability to the Curly-Lobe heterozygotes, the frequencies of the two classes will be 33.3 percent nonmutant (wild-type) and 66.7 percent Curly-Lobe flies, respectively. Suppose, however, that the tested chromosome contains a recessive lethal gene; no wild-type flies will then be found in the culture. A recessive condition that gives a proportion of wild-type flies of more than zero but less than 16 or 17 percent is conventionally called semilethal; a subvital will make the wild-type class more frequent than 17 but less than 33 percent. A recessive sterility gene will make the homozygous flies sterile, a recessive visible mutant will render them morphologically abnormal, etc. If large enough numbers of the flies are counted, the method is sufficiently sensitive to detect slight mutational changes.

Mukai's experiment (1964) was started by crossing a single male, carrying one wild-type second chromosome known to give homozygotes of good viability, and also a Plum second chromosome, to $Cy\ L/Pm$ females (see Fig. 3.1). In the progeny, 104 lines were established, by outcrossing in every generation a single $Pm$/wild-type male to $Cy\ L/Pm$ females. The purpose of this technique is to "accumulate" mutations in the 104 wild-type second chromosomes transmitted generation after generation from the $Pm$/wild-type fathers to their sons. Any completely recessive mutant will be protected from elimination by natural selection in the heterozygous state, even if it is completely lethal when homozygous. However, in the 10th, 15th, 20th, and 25th generations, tests were made, by means of crosses like those diagramed in Fig. 3.1, to examine the viability of flies homozygous for each of the 104 second chromosomes. By the 25th generation, 15 chromosomes had acquired recessive lethal, and 2 chromosomes semilethal, mutants. The remaining lines were "quasi-normal" when homozygous, but their mean viability gradually declined because in some of them recessive subvital mutations accumulated. This was manifested by the average percentage of the wild-type class declining from the theoretical value of 33.3 percent to 31.60 in the 10th generation, 30.93 in the 20th, and 28.35 in the 25th.

Hand in hand with the decline in average viability, the variance

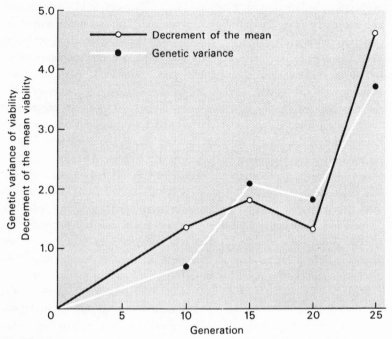

**FIGURE 3.2**

Relationship of the decrement of mean viability and the variance of viability in different generations in an experiment with Drosophila melanogaster. (After Mukai)

in the viabilities of the quasi-normal chromosomes increased, as shown in Fig. 3.2. The chromosomes that were originally similar descendants of the chromosome with which the experiments were started became more and more diversified, because many of them acquired mutations changing (usually decreasing) their viability. To analyze the data, Mukai has made a reasonable assumption: that spontaneous mutations occur among the chromosomes by chance, following a Poisson distribution. This permits computation of the average proportion of the chromosomes that acquire new mutations per generation. It can be shown that this average should be approximately equal to the squared regression coefficient of the decrement of the mean viability, divided by the regression coefficient of the increment of variance. The value found by Mukai was close to 0.15. In other words, about 15 percent of the second chromosomes of *Drosophila melanogaster* acquire new spontaneous mutants in each generation. Only about one-twentieth of the mutations are lethal or semilethal; a majority involve small, subvital changes.

In classical genetics, mutation was believed to be a rare phenomenon. And so it is, if changes of individual genes are considered. However, when the whole genotype is taken into account, mutations are seen to be quite frequent. Since the second chromosome of *Drosophila melanogaster* contains about two-fifths of the total chromosomal materials, one may conservatively estimate that at least 30 percent of the sex cells transport one or several newly arisen mutations affecting the viability in every generation. High rates of occurrence of small mutations are suggested also by observations on the genetic divergence of inbred strains in mice (Bailey 1959; see also Wallace 1965), and by the studies of Sprague, Russell, and Penny (1960) on maize. These findings have important practical as well as theoretical consequences. Inbred strains of experimental animals and plants are widely used in medical, physiological, and other research, in the belief that individuals of such strains are all alike genetically. This confidence is often misplaced because of high mutation frequencies. The decided predominance of small mutations over drastic ones is a fact of major significance to the evolutionist; some of the classical models of the evolutionary process were built on the implied assumptions that mutations are rather infrequent, but that those which do occur may be individually recorded and studied. A multitude of small mutations requires different approaches.

## *Mutation and Adaptedness to External Environments*

Most biologists were skeptical, and justifiably so, of the mutation theory of de Vries, who claimed that new species arise by sudden mutations. Likewise, when Morgan and his associates described mutant Drosophilae, many biologists remained skeptical, because these mutants looked like a collection of freaks rather than changes fit to serve as raw materials of evolution. Some biologists continue, though no longer justifiably, to be skeptical. The reason is that most mutations, large as well as small, are more or less deleterious to their carriers. Mutation appears to be a destructive, rather than a constructive, process. One should not forget, however, that a mutation is neither useful nor harmful in the abstract; it can be so only in some environment. If the environment is not specified, the statement that a mutation is useful or harmful is meaningless. A mutant that is harmful when its carrier is placed in one environment may be neutral in another, and useful in still other environments. Furthermore, a mutant gene does not exert its effects on adaptedness regardless of what other genes an individual carries; a changed gene may be harmful on some genetic backgrounds but useful on others.

One must be careful, of course, not to overstate the argument just presented. It does not mean that some environment, external or genetic, can be found to make every mutant gene useful. To be sure, it is rash to declare that a given mutant can never be useful. For example, scaleless chickens may appear to be hopelessly inferior, and yet Abbott, Asmundson, and Shortridge (1962) found that these mutants can grow with less methionine and cysteine in their diet than can normal chickens. Yet the fact remains that mutational changes are genetic accidents. They can be compared to random knocks on some delicate mechanism, such as a watch; such knocks will very rarely improve the functioning of the mechanism. If most mutations are substitutions of single nucleotides in the DNA of a gene, and of single amino acids in the protein that this gene produces, the chances of improvement are still small. The genes and proteins that a species has are products of selection in the evolutionary process; at least the frequently occurring changes have had time to be incorporated into the genotype. Another way of saying the same thing is that the level of adaptedness of every existing species is fairly close to the maximum achievable in its present environment. Therefore it is not surprising that most mutations are not clear-cut improvements in external and genetic environments in which the species normally exists.

To maximize the chances of observing favorable mutations, the experimental organisms should be placed in novel environments. Examples are plentiful, particularly in microbiology. It was known for a long time that, confronted with adverse environmental conditions or unusual food sources, bacterial cultures may quickly give rise to new genetically stable lines able to cope with these conditions successfully. In point of fact, it was precisely the ease with which such "adaptation" or "training" takes place that inclined bacteriologists to believe that these changes do not arise by mutation regardless of their usefulness, but are directly induced by specific environmental needs.

It took the brilliant work of Luria and Delbrück (1943) and Demerec and Fano (1945) to show that spontaneous mutation is involved. The bacteria *Escherichia coli* are attacked by bacteriophages, which reproduce in the bacterial cells and cause their breakdown, or lysis. If bacteriophages are added to a culture of bacteria, the latter are destroyed within minutes or hours, whereupon the medium contains great numbers of bacteriophages capable of infecting other bacterial cells. However, a few cells may survive and form colonies of bacteria that are henceforward resistant to the bacteriophage strain in the presence of which they appeared. Luria and Delbrück showed that this resistance arises by mutation, at the rate of about $2 \times 10^{-8}$ cell generation. The bacteriophage does not produce resistant bacteria; its role is that of a selective agent which destroys all nonmutant cells. In the presence of bacteriophages normal bacteria are killed and only the mutants survive and reproduce.

Several bacteriophage strains are known, and a bacterial strain that is resistant to one bacteriophage may not be resistant to others: the resistance is specific. Demerec and Fano (1945) found in *Escherichia coli* at least eight different kinds of mutants, each resistant to one or more of the seven bacteriophage strains used by these authors. If the bacteria are exposed to the proper bacteriophage, each kind of mutant can easily be obtained. Hence, by exposing bacteria to a succession of bacteriophages, it is possible to build up strains resistant to several or even to all phage strains. The rates of mutation to resistance to a given phage strain are independent of what other mutations have occurred previously.

The discovery and the widespread use of chemotherapeutic drugs and antibiotics were followed by the appearance and spread of bacterial mutants resistant to these drugs and antibiotics (a review, no longer up to date, in Wolstenholme and O'Connor 1957). Some diagramatically clear examples of adaptive mutations have been encountered. Demerec (1948) exposed cultures of *Escherichia coli* to streptomycin, which kills all the bacteria except streptomycin-resistant mutants. Some of these mutants are, however, not only genetically resistant to streptomycin but also streptomycin-dependent, that is, unable to grow without the presence in the nutrient medium of this substance, fatal to their ancestors. Reverse mutations, which remove the streptomycin dependence, also occur; by placing a large inoculum of streptomycin-dependent bacteria on streptomycin-free medium, independent strains of the bacteria can be selected. Some of these strains continue to be resistant to streptomycin, whereas others lose the resistance.

The question then presents itself: Since streptomycin-resistant mutants arise from time to time in cultures not exposed to this antibiotic, why have all the bacteria in nature not become resistant? This is easily answered for mutants that are streptomycin-resistant as well as dependent: they evidently could not exist in streptomycin-free environments. The answer is not so obvious for the resistant but independent mutants. One must suppose that they too are for some reason at a disadvantage in media free of streptomycin. The mutation to resistance, as well as the reverse mutation, is favored and discriminated against in different environments.

Domestic animals and cultivated plants are, next to microorganisms, the most favorable materials for the detection of useful mutants. The environments provided for them by cultivators, though permissive and sheltered in many ways, are quite different from the environments of their wild ancestors and hence demand genetic adaptation. The pioneer experiments of Gustafsson and his colleagues (Gustafsson 1941, 1963a,b, Gustafsson and Nybom 1950, and Gustafsson, Nybom, and Wettstein 1950) showed that even genetically so "destructive" an agent as X-radiation may induce some mutants in barley that are agriculturally useful. This lead has been followed by numerous other workers seeking useful mutants (e.g., Bandlow 1951, in wheat; Scholz and Lehmann 1962, in barley; and Stubbe 1950, in snapdragon). The Food and Agricultural Organization (FAO) of the United Nations has held a symposium at which many successful experiments were reported (Anonymous 1965 and Russian works reviewed in Shkvarnikov 1966).

## Extracellular Selection of Mutants

As stated in Chapter 1, natural selection is a function of differential reproduction; it could not have begun before there was life. Yet we have seen that DNA and RNA extracted from living organisms can "reproduce" *in vitro*, that is, act as templates for the synthesis of their replicas. Spiegelman and his collaborators (Spiegelman, Pace, et al. 1969, Levisohn and Spiegelman 1969, and references therein) have utilized this fact to make most elegant "extracellular Darwinian experiments with replicating RNA molecules."

They have isolated from *Escherichia coli* infected with RNA bacteriophages MS-2 and Q-beta replicase enzymes, which catalyze the *in vitro* synthesis of RNA chains. A fact of importance is that these replicases are specific in their action; the replicase extracted from the bacteria infected with MS-2 "recognizes" the RNA from that bacteriophage, while the replicase coming from Q-beta-infected bacteria is active only with RNA templates from that phage. A standard reaction mixture is used which contains the replicase enzyme, the four triphosphate nucleotides (A, U, G, and C), magnesium ions, and an RNA template. If the replicase and the template are of the same origin (i.e., both MS-2 or both Q-beta), new RNA chains are synthesized by copying the template. The new RNA can in turn serve as a template, and by making serial transfers to fresh reaction mixtures this reproduction can continue, presumably indefinitely.

Spiegelman et al. utilized a temperature-sensitive mutant of the Q-beta phage; the mutant grows poorly at 41°C, whereas the original phage thrives at this temperature. The RNA of the temperature-sensitive variant has replicated its mutant characteristic *in vitro*, that is, the new RNA synthesized is also temperature sensitive. Clones descended from single RNA strands, which reproduce their kind, can be obtained.

Spiegelman and his colleagues have now turned to selection for mutant RNA's arising *in vitro*, in their reaction mixtures. When multiplying in living bacterial hosts, the RNA of the bacteriophage must not only replicate itself but also induce the synthesis of the protein coat of the phage particle. The latter requirement is no longer binding on RNA's that replicate *in vitro*. Their V-1 mutant is a chain 83 percent shorter than the original or wild-type RNA chain. Yet the loss of the now dispensable parts permits the mutant to replicate appreciably faster in the standard mixture. Levisohn and Spiegelman (1969) selected also what they call "nutritional" mutants V-2, V-4 and V-6. These RNA templates can replicate more and more successfully in mixtures with less cytosine (cytidylic acid) than the standard mixture. Another mutant is resistant to tubercidine, an analogue of adenosine, which inhibits the replication of the original form. All this is quite properly described as Darwinian natural selection, though selection on a postbiological rather than a prebiological level.

### Mutation and Adaptedness
### to Genetic Environments

As early as 1934, Timofeeff-Ressovsky showed that the viabilities of some mutants of *Drosophila funebris* depend on both external and genetic environments (Table 3.4). Thus, the mutant eversae is, at 15–16°C and 28–30°C, inferior to the wild type, whereas at 24–25°C it is superior. The viability of venae abnormes and miniature mutants is only slightly inferior to that of the wild type at 15–16° but is much inferior at 28–30°C. On the contrary, the viability of the bobbed mutant is low at 15–16°C but approaches normal at 28–30°C. Overpopulation of the cultures decreases relative viability in the mutations eversae, venae abnormes, and miniature, but has an opposite effect on bobbed. Combination of venae abnormes and lozenge, each of which decreases viability, produces a summation of the individual deleterious effects; combination of miniature and bobbed gives a compound that is more viable than either mutation by itself.

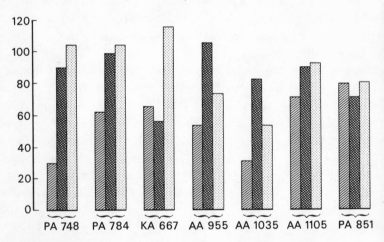

**FIGURE 3.3**

Fifty generations of natural selection for viability in laboratory cultures of seven strains of Drosophila pseudoobscura. Ordinates—percents of "normal" viability; left (crosshatched)—the viability at the beginning of the experiment; middle and right (light and dark stippled)—after fifty generations with and without exposure to low doses of X-rays. (After Dobzhansky and Spassky)

**TABLE 3.4**

Viabilities of some mutations and their combinations in Drosophila funebris, expressed in percentages of the viability of the wild type (After Timofeeff-Ressovsky)

| Mutation | Temperature, °C | | | Combination | Temperature, 24–25 °C |
|---|---|---|---|---|---|
| | 15–16 | 24–25 | 28–30 | | |
| Eversae | 98.3 | 104.0 | 98.5 | Eversae signed | 103.1 |
| Singed | | 79.0 | | Eversae abnormes | 83.7 |
| Abnormes | 96.2 | 88.9 | 80.7 | Eversae bobbed | 85.5 |
| Miniature | 91.3 | 69.0 | 63.7 | Singed abnormes | 76.6 |
| Bobbed | 75.3 | 85.1 | 93.7 | Singed miniature | 67.1 |
| Lozenge | | 73.8 | | Abnormes miniature | 82.7 |
| | | | | Abnormes lozenge | 59.3 |
| | | | | Abnormes bobbed | 78.7 |
| | | | | Miniature bobbed | 96.6 |
| | | | | Lozenge bobbed | 69.2 |

Dobzhansky and Spassky (1947) took a different approach. Many chromosomes in natural populations of *Drosophila pseudoobscura* and other species carry gene complexes that make them lethal, semilethal, or subvital in double dose (for more details, see Chapter 4). Three second and four fourth chromosomes were chosen which, as shown by the cross-hatched columns in Fig. 3.3, reduced the viability of their homozygous carrier to between 30 and 80 percent of the normal value. The average viability of individuals carrying two chromosomes of each pair, taken at random from a given population, is defined as "normal" (see Chapter 4). Populations of flies homozygous for each of the seven chromosomes were bred in cultures that were deliberately made grossly overpopulated. The experiment extended for fifty consecutive generations. The rationale of this experiment was that mutations might arise which would compensate for the loss of viability caused by the chromosomes subvital or semilethal in the homozygous condition. In a population living in a stringent environment, caused by crowding, such favorable mutants should survive and gradually enhance the adaptedness of the whole population. Furthermore, each population was subdivided into two sections, one of which received in every generation 1000 r of X-rays. It was hoped that the irradiation would increase the frequencies of mutations, including the favorable ones.

From time to time during the course of the experiments, as well as after the fifty generations were completed, the viability of the homozygotes for each of the seven chromosomes was tested by a series of crosses analogous to those diagramed in Fig. 3.1. The light-stippled columns in Fig. 3.3 show the viabilities of the populations not treated with X-rays, and the dark-stippled columns the viabilities of the irradiated ones. Every one of the chromosomes, except that designated PA-851, showed improvement of the viability either in the X-ray-treated or in the untreated population, or in both lines. It can be seen in Fig. 3.3 that at least six of the fourteen experimental lines attained fully "normal" viabilities, within the limits of experimental errors. The irradiated and the unirradiated lines did not differ significantly in the viability levels attained.

The results of the experiments in Fig. 3.3 do not show that all, or even most, mutations arising in the cultures were favorable. In addition to the cultures homozygous for each of the seven experimental chromosomes, there were kept also cultures in which these chromosomes were transmitted, from one generation to the next, always in the heterozygous condition. This was effected by means of a technique analogous to that previously described in connection with Mukai's experiments (see above). Lines treated with X-rays and untreated ones were kept. When, after fifty generations, the chromosomes were finally tested for viability in the homozygous condition, the results contrasted sharply with those shown in Fig. 3.3. Of the fourteen lines, seven became lethal when homozygous; in five there were no changes or slight deteriorations; and only in two cases were ostensible improvements observed. The irradiated and the unirradiated lines were not conspicuously different. It may be concluded that when mutations are allowed to accumulate indiscriminately they result in deterioration of the viability; there also appear, however, some favorable mutants, which improve the viability when conditions are propitious for their selection.

In the experiments of Ayala (1966, 1967, 1969b), irradiated populations of two closely related species, *Drosophila serrata* and *D. birchii*, outstripped the unirradiated ones in the pace of genetic adaptation to the experimental environments. The male progenitors of the experimental populations were treated with 2000 r of X-rays for three generations, and crossed to unirradiated sisters in uncrowded cultures. Experiments were then started with large numbers of flies, faced with rigorous competition for food and space in crowded cultures. Control populations were set up in the same way, except that the flies were not irradiated. At the beginning of the experiments the average number of flies per culture was smaller in the populations with radiation histories than in the unirradiated controls for several generations. Some deleterious mutants were evidently induced, and it took time to purge the populations of the excess of these mutants. Thereafter, however, the irradiated populations became more flourishing than the controls. Over a period of 1 year, the average sizes of the two irradiated populations of *D. serrata* were 493 and 972 flies greater than those of the control, and in *D. birchii* the irradiated cultures averaged 621 and 587 flies more than the unirradiated populations. The conclusion is inevitable that, although the average effect of newly induced mutations was deleterious, a minority of the induced mutations proved favorable, in the sense that they permitted the populations to exploit more efficiently their stringently limited environments.

## Genetic Techniques of Pest Control

Although geneticists and evolutionists are most interested in detecting the minority of mutants that are beneficial, in some situations the more numerous deleterious mutations can also be utilized. More than 40 years ago Muller (1927) observed the high mortalities of eggs deposited by untreated Drosophila females mated to males subjected to X-rays. This unusual mortality is due to dominant lethal mutations, many of them chromosome breaks that cause inviability, induced in the spermatozoa by the treatment. After a heavy dose of irradiation, a male may be as active as an unirradiated male in mating with females, but all eggs fertilized by his spermatozoa will be inviable. Bushland and Hopkins (1951) and Knipling (1955) saw here a possible method of combating insect pests, by releasing large numbers of sterilized males to compete with their normal counterparts for the available females, thus destroying the progeny of the latter. Much work has been done to develop this method to the point of practical applicability (reviews and bibliographies in Knipling 1967 and LaChance 1967).

Suppose that the population of some insect consists of 1,000,000 fertile females and 1,000,000 males, and that we release an additional 9,000,000 males sterilized by irradiation or by a chemical mutagen (of which several suitable for this purpose have been found). Fertile and sterile males will then be present in the ratio 1 : 9. If they are equally active, and each female mates only once, only 100,000 females will produce progeny. Suppose further that a fertile female can leave on the average 5 daughters and 5 sons. In the next generation the population will consist of 500,000 females and 500,000 fertile males. If then another 9,000,000 sterile males are released, they will outnumber the fertile ones in the ratio 18 : 1. Only some 26,316 females will produce fertile progeny, which, granting the same assumptions as above, will number about 131,625 females and males. Two additional releases of 9,000,000 sterile males will, theoretically, reduce the fertile populations to 9535, 50, and 0.

The most successful application of this method was made on the 170-square-mile island of Curaçao in the Caribbean, to control the population of the screw-worm fly (*Cochliomyia hominivorax*), the larvae of which develop in abscesses in the flesh of living mammals. A technique has been devised, however, to grow them on mass scale in shallow pans with a mixture of ground horse meat, water, blood, and a small amount of formaldehyde. The female of the species is monogamous. Releases of sterile males have destroyed the population on the island. A campaign to control the screw-worm fly in the southeastern United States in 1958 and 1959 was also effective, but another in Texas and New Mexico met with only partial success. Programs for the control of other insect pests, among them the true fruit flies (*Dacus dorsalis, Anastrepha ludens, Ceratitis capitata*) and tsetse flies (Glossina), are in the experimental stage.

## Recombination and Interaction of Genes

As mentioned above and discussed in detail in the next chapter, many chromosomes found in natural populations are lethal or otherwise deleterious in double dose. But some chromosomes, often only a minority, give homozygotes equal, or even superior (supervital), in viability to the natural population average. The question naturally arises, Are these the elusive "normal," typical, optimal chromosomes, unspoiled by mutation? One way to approach this problem is to find out whether these apparent "normals" are alike in their gene contents, carrying only the optimal gene alleles.

Dobzhansky (1946) in *Drosophila pseudoobscura* and Wallace, King, et al. (1953) in *D. melanogaster* have shown that, when pairs of chromosomes, both of which produce normally viable homozygotes, are allowed to undergo crossing over, some of the recombination products are semilethal or lethal when homozygous. Such lethals arisen by recombination are called synthetic lethals. A considerable literature has accumulated on synthetic lethals, chiefly in species of Drosophila but also in Tribolium (Sokoloff 1964). Most of the synthetic lethals are recessive, but Gibson and Thoday (1962) found also a dominant synthetic lethal in *D. melanogaster*.

It is hardly surprising that not all chromosomes, and not all populations, produce synthetic lethals (Hildreth 1956 and Spiess and Allen 1961). A systematic search for them has been carried out in *Drosophila pseudoobscura* (B. Spassky, N. Spassky, et al. 1958), *D. persimilis* (Spiess 1959), *D. prosaltans* (Dobzhansky, Levene, et al. 1959) and *D. willistoni* (Krimbas 1961). In each case samples of 10 chromosomes were chosen from one or two natural populations of a species, by methods analogous to that shown in Fig. 3.1. The chromosomes selected were those that produced homozygotes of nearly normal, and sometimes even superior, viability. Females containing all possible combinations of the 10 chromosomes (45 combinations) were obtained, and 10 chromosomes from each progeny (i.e., 450 chromosomes) were tested, again with the aid of techniques analogous to that represented in Fig. 3.1, for viability in the homozygous condition. Since crossing over occurs in Drosophila females, at least a part of the 10 chromosomes derived from each cross represented recombination products of the chromosomes that the mother carried. An example of the results obtained is as follows. Eleven of the 45 combinations of second chromosomes of *D. pseudoobscura* from a Texas population produced from 1 to 4 synthetic lethals in the groups of 10 chromosomes tested; 8 of the 45 combinations of the chromosomes from California gave from 1 to 7 lethals; and 19 of the 100 combinations in which 1 chromosome was of Texas and the other of California origin gave from 1 to 5 lethals. In sum, 77 out of 1900 recombination chromosomes tested, or about 4 percent, were lethal.

It should be noted that the chromosomes yielding lethal recombination products were often among the most viable ones in the homozygous condition. They evidently carried internally well-balanced gene complexes (Mather 1941), the components of which interacted favorably to produce viable homozygotes. Recombination, however, caused breakdowns of the internal balance; the epistatic interactions of the new combinations of the genes then resulted in lethality (Lucchesi 1968). Changes in traits other than viability may evidently arise by similar mechanisms; Krimbas (1960) obtained in *Drosophila willistoni* some recombination products of chromosomes making the flies fertile that caused "synthetic" sterility.

How frequent synthetic lethals are in natural populations of Drosophila and of other organisms remains to be ascertained. Magalhães and his colleagues (Magalhães, de Toledo, and da Cunha 1965 and Magalhães, da Cunha, et al. 1965) found that in experimental populations of *Drosophila willistoni* more than 20 percent of the second chromosomes were lethal in double dose after seven generations of breeding. Conversely, chromosomes previously known to be lethal had this effect expunged by "suppressors" found in natural populations. Evidently, synthesis and suppression of lethals by epistatic interactions with other genes are the two sides of the same coin. A lethal can be "synthesized" by combining in a chromosome genes that are not lethal separately, but that interact to produce a lethal in double dose; the lethal can be "suppressed" or "desynthesized" by breaking up this combination. A proof of this has been given by Dobzhansky and Spassky (1960); they obtained some synthetic lethals in *D. pseudoobscura* and then broke them up by subjecting the lethal chromosomes to crossing over.

Synthetic lethals are evidently the most spectacular products of gene recombination and of epistasis. More important still is the fact that crossing over between ostensibly similar chromosomes generates an enormous amount of genetic variation, ranging all the way from lethality and semilethality through subvitality and ostensible "normality" to supervitality. Dobzhansky, Levene, et al. (1959) measured this release of genetic variability by comparing the variance of the homozygous viabilities of the chromosomes found in natural populations of a given species (see Chapter 4 for more detail), with the variance observed among the recombination products of similar chromosomes. The results are collated in Table 3.5. It can be seen that the recombination in a single generation produces between 24 percent (*Drosophila persimilis*) and 43 percent (*D. pseudoobscura*) of the total variance in viability in the homozygous condition. If lethal chromosomes (both natural and synthetic) are disregarded, the remaining quasi-normal chromosomes

**TABLE 3.5**

Mean viabilities and variances of homozygotes for chromosomes of three species. "Natural" refers to mean viabilities and variances for samples of wild chromosomes obtained directly from natural populations. "Recombination" refers to mean viabilities and variances for chromosomes that were recombination products of pairs of quasi-normal original chromosomes obtained from nature.

| Species and Chromosomes | Mean Viability | | Variance | | Recombination Variance % Natural Variance | |
|---|---|---|---|---|---|---|
| | All Chromosomes | Quasi-normal | All Chromosomes | Quasi-normal | All Chromosomes | Quasi-normal |
| D. pseudoobscura | | | | | | |
| Natural | 20.29 | 24.26 | 140 | 65 | 43 | 74 |
| Recombination | 22.92 | 23.93 | 60 | 48 | | |
| D. persimilis | | | | | | |
| Natural | 23.54 | 28.00 | 110 | 60 | 24 | 27 |
| Recombination | 28.16 | 28.76 | 26 | 16 | | |
| D. prosaltans | | | | | | |
| Natural | 21.17 | 25.98 | 200 | 85 | 25 | 28 |
| Recombination | 28.14 | 29.72 | 50 | 24 | | |

show at least as great a recombination effect—from 27 percent in *D. persimilis* to 74 percent in *D. pseudoobscura.*

These observations throw some light on one of the basic problems of evolutionary genetics, that of the maintenance of the genetic diversity found in natural populations of sexually reproducing species. The simplistic view, adhered to by some geneticists, is that most genes are identical in most individuals comprising a population, and whatever genetic diversity is observed is due to the presence of rather recently arisen deleterious mutants, not yet eliminated by natural selection. This view is hardly tenable any longer. Overt genetic diversity is evidently far exceeded by concealed or potential variability. The latter is stored in the gene combinations found in naturally occurring chromosomes, and it can be released by recombination (Mather 1953 and Thoday, Gibson, and Spickett 1964).

The variance released in one generation by recombination of parts of chromosomes selected for a relative uniformity amounts to at least one-quarter of the total expressed variance. The fact that some of the recombination products are semilethal or lethal when homozygous is particularly illuminating. The frequency of such synthetic lethals will be maintained in a population not by newly arising mutations, but rather by an equilibrium between the frequencies of their being "synthesized" and "desynthesized." Genetic diversity is maintained primarily not by new mutants, but by the advantages of heterozygosis for gene alleles and gene complexes that are kept up by natural selection, and also by environmental fluctuations in space and in time that alter the signs and the magnitudes of selective advantages and disadvantages. With a population structure of this sort, a total suppression of the mutation process would probably fail to change the evolutionary plasticity of the species for many generations.

## The Randomness of Mutations

Random mutations are the raw materials of the evolutionary process. Natural selection orders them in functionally coherent, adaptive systems. Mutations are often described as accidental, random, undirected, chance events. Just what do these epithets mean? Mutations are accidents, because the transmission of hereditary information normally involves precise copying. A mutant gene is, then, an imperfect copy of the ancestral gene. It would be absurd, however, to say that human genes are only distorted copies of the primeval genetic materials. The serviceability of human genes, or of those of any existing species, has been validated by natural selection. Mutations are undirected with respect to the adaptive needs of the species. They arise regardless of their actual or potential usefulness. It may seem a deplorable imperfection of nature that mutability is not restricted to changes that enhance the adaptedness of their carriers. However, only a vitalist Pangloss could imagine that the genes know how and when it is good for them to mutate.

The frequencies of spontaneous mutations of some genes have been ascertained in genetically well-studied organisms. Yet where, when, and in which individual a particular mutation will appear is unpredictable. Even the rather more specific chemical mutagens discussed in Chapter 2 rarely change 100 percent of the genes exposed to treatment. The mutational repertoire of the gene is great but not infinite; it is limited by the composition of the gene. Consider only mutations due to single nucleotide pair substitution in a gene that codes for a protein chain 150 amino acids long, and has 150 triplet codons or

450 nucleotide base pairs. Since each base in a triplet can be substituted in three ways, a codon can be changed in nine ways. For 150 codons this means 1350 possible mutational changes. Because of the so-called degeneracy of the genetic code, about one-fourth of the single nucleotide substitutions will be to synonymous codons, that is, those coding for the same amino acid (see Chapter 1).

Approaching the matter from another angle, we note that there are 61 different codons specifying amino acids (Table 1.2); this gives $61 \times 9 = 549$ possible substitutions, of which 134 will be to synonymous codons (King and Jukes 1969). These figures do not, of course, include frameshift mutants and mutants substituting more than a single nucleotide. Frameshifts are likely, however, to give "nonsense" mutations, many of which may be lethal, and multiple substitutions are probably rare. The variety of possible mutations in a gene is impressively large.

Mutations cannot be said to change the development in random directions because a single nucleotide substitution is rarely if ever sufficient for a gene to change its function radically. The hundred or more mutant hemoglobins known in man (Table 2.1, and Perutz and Lehman 1968) produce variant hemoglobins rather than entirely different proteins. Although some of these variants are more or less deleterious to their carriers, others seem to be functionally equivalent to the ancestral condition. Accumulation of mutational changes may, of course, change a gene more radically. Wittmann-Liebold and Wittmann (1963) found that chemically induced mutants in the tobacco mosaic virus usually differ from the original kind in single, and rarely in two, amino acid replacements. Naturally occurring strains of the virus, however, differ from each other in as many as 30 of the 158 amino acids. The successive mutational gene changes acquire a direction because natural selection controls the fitness of the resulting phenotypes and thus indirectly imposes a restriction on the randomness of the mutational events. If it is assumed that life on earth arose only once, all existing genes have a common descent, and they are now different because of this long series of nucleotide substitutions that have taken place.

Hemoglobins and myoglobins are animal proteins of interest in connection with this discussion. There are good reasons to think that the genes coding for hemoglobins and myoglobins are modified descendants of a common ancestral gene. Human alpha differs from human beta hemoglobin in 84 amino acids (out of 141 and 146, respectively). Myoglobin (of sperm whale) has 153 amino acid residues; it differs in 115 amino acids from human alpha, and in 117 from beta, hemoglobins (Dayhoff and Eck 1968). Transformation of the gene coding for hemoglobin into that coding for myoglobin, or of the hemoglobin alpha gene into the hemoglobin beta gene or vice versa, has a zero probability of occurring by a single mutation. Yet these transformations have in fact taken place in evolutionary history, by way of a sequence of mutations, presumably controlled by natural selection. While each mutation in this sequence was, if considered on the molecular level, an accident, the sequence as a whole is in no sense accidental or random. Although we do not know the physiological functions served by the proteins intermediate between the modern hemoglobins and myoglobins, the alterations through which they passed were far from random.

The following illustration of the nonhaphazard nature of mutations is flippant but apt. Suppose that one wishes to transform, by selective breeding, the human race into a race of angels. We can be virtually certain that it would be much easier to breed for angelic disposition than for a pair of wings because there is available in human populations a variance in disposition, and it is not implausible to suppose that part of this variance is genetic. If so, selection may accentuate the dispositions that can be called angelic, and more variance may arise by mutation. There is much less chance of encountering variants on the basis of which the development of wings may be started, and to expect mutations providing such a basis seems rather farfetched. And yet birds and mammals, or bats and primates, have had a common, albeit remote, ancestry. There is no possibility, however, of reversing and repeating the evolutionary process that gave rise to these winged and wingless creatures.

# CHAPTER FOUR

# NORMALIZING NATURAL SELECTION

## *A Historical Sketch*

Charles Darwin relates that the idea of evolutionary changes being brought about by natural selection came to him in a flash of insight as he was riding in a carriage on a country road. The same idea came to A. R. Wallace with equal suddenness during a paroxysm of malarial fever. Empedocles in ancient Greece, Lucretius in ancient Rome, Maupertuis and Buffon in the Age of Enlightenment, and Erasmus Darwin, grandfather of Charles, all had germs of the same idea. That so many people arrived at this same idea independently is not strange; the idea is quite simple and even obvious. The most poignant discovery in science comes when one suddenly sees a truth that was open to view all the time.

Eiseley (1959) brought to light the forgotten writings of Blyth, published between 1835 and 1837, in which natural selection (of course, not so named) was quite clearly discussed. Darwin was probably familiar with Blyth's articles, yet nowhere acknowledged this. The reason is, I believe, quite simple. Blyth argued that natural selection keeps species constant; Darwin declared that it changes them and forms new species. Darwin was an evolutionist; Blyth, an antievolutionist.

That natural selection is a common name for several cognate but distinct processes has been realized only within relatively recent years. Schmalhausen (1949) distinguished dynamic (directional) and stabilizing selection. The first changes the adaptive norm of the population; the second tends to keep it constant. A natural population is adapted to a certain range of environments. Environmental change is likely to cause a decline in this adaptedness; some formerly favorable genetic variants become disadvantageous and are replaced by new ones. Conversely, in a population that has achieved a high degree of adaptedness in a certain range of environments, the genetic endowment is advantageous, and deviations from it are inopportune. Stabilizing selection eliminates such deviations and promotes, in Schmalhausen's words, "more stable mechanisms of normal morphogenesis."

Waddington (1957) distinguishes two kinds of stabilizing selection, normalizing and canalizing. The former protects the adaptive norm by the elimination of harmful mutants, malformations, and weaknesses of various sorts. It was normalizing selection that Blyth wrote about. Canalizing selection, Waddington states, favors "genotypes which control developmental systems which are highly canalized and therefore not very responsive either to abnormalities in the environment or to new gene mutations of minor character." Canalization refers to the "limited responsiveness of a developing system." Human development is a familiar example. It is so canalized that all human beings are fundamentally similar and recognizably human, despite manifold variations in environments and in individual genotypes. Only major mutations and drastic environmental stresses deflect the development from its regular course (or creode, in Waddington's terminology); the result is usually death or teratological changes (morphoses in Schmalhausen's terminology; see Chapter 2).

Several kinds of selective processes are subsumed under the name of balancing selection (Dobzhansky 1964b). Their common feature is that they maintain genetic heterogeneity or polymorphisms, that is, the continued presence in a population of two or several alleles of some genes or of variant chromosome structures, the frequencies of which are more or less fixed by selection.

Directional selection enhances the frequencies of some gene alleles or gene combinations, and depresses the frequencies of others. Usually it acts in response to environmental changes. If novel and favorable gene mutations or gene combinations appear, however, directional selection may come into action without environmental change. In either case it is an agency of innovation, with which Darwin was mainly concerned (Lerner 1958 and Dobzhansky 1964a,b). The fact that Darwin's natural selection was adumbrated by several predecessors does not in the least diminish his greatness. No one else has stated this as clearly as Wilkie (1959):

The theory of evolution must be considered as a scientific theory, a theory, that is, proposed to explain or systematize a set of facts, and no one has any claim to be considered as a serious rival of Darwin in the "discovery" of this theory who did not conduct his evolutionary studies upon a reasonably wide basis of fact. To have ideas, *aperçus,* is not enough, and it is the overvaluation of such clever but uncontrolled guesses which is apt to produce the ludicrous . . . fallacy of combination, in which fragments of the final theory are collected from widely scattered sources and are combined in such a way as to impugn the originality of him who was the first to see how such a synthesis is possible.

## *Selection, Struggle, Mortality, and Fitness*

Recognition of the diversity of selectional processes should not obscure the fact that all forms of natural and artificial selection have a common denominator. Lerner (1958) defines selection as nonrandom differential reproduction of genotypes; this can also be paraphrased as differential perpetuation of gene alleles and gene complexes.

Darwin and Wallace deduced natural selection from Malthus' principle that any population tends to increase in numbers in a geometric progression, and consequently will sooner or later collide with the limited resources on which it subsists. Only a part, often a small part, of the progeny survive; a majority die out. The carriers of better-adapted genotypes survive more often than do progeny inferior in this respect. The incidence of the former will increase and of the latter decrease from generation to generation. Yet natural selection may occasionally occur even if all the progeny survive in some generations. Consider a species that gives several generations per year; if food and other resources are not limiting during the warm season, the population may increase geometrically with no mortality among the progeny. Selection will nevertheless take place if the carriers of different genotypes have produced different numbers of offspring or have developed to sexual maturity at varying rates. A winter season may reduce the numbers of individuals drastically but unselectively; exponential growth and selection may be resumed the following year. Differential fecundity is, in principle, as powerful a selective agent as differential survival or mortality. This does not mean that the modern version of the theory of natural selection substitutes fecundity for survival as the principal method. Living beings must survive to reproduce, and must reproduce to survive in the following generation.

Darwin accepted, not without hesitation, Herbert Spencer's slogan "survival of the fittest in the struggle for life" as an alternative description of natural selection. At present this term seems inappropriate. Not only the fittest but also the tolerably fit survive and reproduce. Under flexible or soft selection (see Chapter 7) all the carriers of the same array of genotypes may survive when the population is increasing in size, and may be eliminated when it is shrinking. Moreover, as will be explained in more detail below, the fit are not necessarily the brawniest, the toughest, or the most aggressive. They are simply those who produce the largest numbers of viable and fertile progeny.

Selection does not create the materials that it selects. It operates effectively only as long as the population contains two or more genotypes, which perpetuate themselves at different rates (with natural selection), or among which a breeder can choose the parents of the next generation (with artificial selection). The crucial problem is, then, the source of the genetic raw materials, of the genetic diversity with which selection works. Darwin realized the importance of this problem, as well as the lack in his time of data adequate for its solution.

Early in the current century, Johannsen was making experiments, as simple as they were ingenious, on pure lines of beans. Beans are normally self-pollinating, that is, the seeds are produced by fertilization of the ovules by the pollen of the same plant. Commercial "varieties" usually contain mixtures of genotypes. By keeping the progenies of individual large-seeded and small-seeded plants separate, Johannsen easily isolated from these mixtures lines with large and with small seeds. On the contrary, selection failed to work in pure lines obtained by self-pollination from single individuals. The progenies of large and of small seeds from the same pure line were similar on the average.

In retrospect it seems strange that Johannsen's experiments, in the opinion of many of his contemporaries, demolished Darwin's theory of evolution by natural selection. Approximately between 1900 and 1925, the reputation of the selection theory was at its lowest ebb. The turn of the tide started with the work of T. H. Morgan and his school on mutations in Drosophila. It became evident that the process of mutation supplies the genetic raw materials on which selection may work. It remained, however, for Tshetverikov (1926), Fisher (1930), Wright (1931), and Haldane (1932) to lay the foundations of a modern version of the theory of natural selection. In the following decades, this theory expanded by inclusion of the results of other biological disciplines; it became the biological or synthetic theory of evolution (see Chapter 1).

## The Hardy-Weinberg Law

The difference between the concept of heredity on which Darwin had to rely, and the one that serves as a basis of modern views, is the antithesis between the blending and the particulate theories of inheritance. The corollaries of the two theories are strikingly different. If the heredities of the parents blend in the progeny as a water-soluble dye commingles with water, the genetic variance in a sexually reproducing, Mendelian population will be halved in every generation. No matter how large a genetic diversity may be present at the start, there will be a rapid decay of the variability, and eventual homogeneity. No such difficulty is encountered with gene heredity. The different alleles of a gene present in a heterozygote do not contaminate each other; at meiosis they segregate, uninfluenced by their temporary sojourn in the same body and the same cell.

Suppose that two strains of a sexual and cross-fertilizing species are introduced into a previously unoccupied territory, in which they are equally adapted to live. Suppose further that they differ in a single gene, one strain being $AA$ and the other $aa$, interbreed at random, and are introduced in the proportions $p$ of $AA$ individuals and $q = (1 - p)$ of $aa$ individuals. We assume that the individuals composing the population contribute equal numbers of gametes, some carrying the gene $A$ and others its allele $a$, to the gene pool of this population. What, then, will be the frequencies of $A$ and of $a$ in the gene pool, and what will be the proportions of the homozygotes, $AA$ and $aa$, and of the heterozygotes, $Aa$, in this Mendelian population in the next generation and in the following ones? The solution of this problem was given by Hardy and by Weinberg independently in the same year, 1908. The frequencies $p$ and $q$ in the gene pool will remain constant generation after generation. The distribution of the genotypes among the zygotes will be:

$$p^2 \, AA + 2pq \, Aa + q^2 \, aa = 1$$

This expression, known as the Hardy-Weinberg equilibrium, describes the situation in a randomly breeding Mendelian population. There may, however, be assortative mating, such as some preference for mating of likes (homogamy) or of unlikes (heterogamy), or inbreeding or self-pollination (in plants). The relative frequencies of the homozygotes (*AA* and *aa*) and the heterozygotes (*Aa*) will then be modified, but the frequencies, *p* and *q*, in the gene pool will remain constant.

Maintenance of constant gene frequencies is evidently a conservative factor. Evolution is change in the frequencies of some genes. We shall proceed now to discuss the agencies that modify gene frequencies. It is interesting that each of these agencies is counteracted by another, opposite in sign, which tends to conserve the status quo. Hence a living population is constantly under the stress of opposing forces; evolution results when one group gains the upper hand over the other.

### *Mutation and Genetic Equilibrium*

The value of *q*, the frequency of a gene or a chromosome structure in a population, can be modified by mutation pressure, that is, by gene mutations and chromosomal changes. If the change from *A* to *a* takes place, the frequencies *p* and *q* must also change. Let the mutation in the direction $A \rightarrow a$ have a rate of *u* per generation; the change in the frequency of *A* in the population per generation will be $\Delta p = -up$, where *p* is the frequency of *A*. If the mutation in the direction of $A \rightarrow a$ is unopposed by any other factor, the population will eventually reach uniformity for *a*. If the frequency of gene *A* in a certain generation is $p_o$, its frequency *n* generations later, $p_n$, will be:

$$p_n = p_o(1 - u)^n$$

Since the mutation rates, *u*, of most genes are small, of the orders of $10^{-4}$ to $10^{-7}$, many generations are required to bring about considerable changes in gene frequencies in a gene pool by mutation pressure alone.

When the mutation is reversible, the change in the direction $A \rightarrow a$ is opposed by the change $a \rightarrow A$. With the rate of reverse mutation equal to *v*, the frequency of *A* will change as $\Delta p = -up + vq$. An equilibrium will be reached when the change per generation is $\Delta p = 0$.

The equilibrium value of $p$ determined by the two mutually opposed mutation rates is therefore $p = v / (u + v)$. If, for example, the rate of mutation $A \rightarrow a$ is taken to be 1 in a million gametes per generation ($u = 0.000,001$), and the rate of mutation $a \rightarrow A$ to be $v = 0.000,000,5$, the equilibrium value for $p$ will be 0.33, which means that 33 percent of the gametes in the gene pool will carry gene $A$ and 67 percent gene $a$. If the mutation rates to and from a given allele are alike ($v = u$), the equilibrium values for $q$ and $p$ will be equal, 0.5.

Starting from an initially homogenous population, the mutation pressure will tend to increase the variability until the equilibrium values determined by the opposing mutation rates are reached. The process of mutation may, accordingly, make the population polymorphic, that is, composed of a variety of genotypes occurring with fixed frequencies in the same population. Whether polymorphisms due to opposing mutation rates are in fact widespread in nature is an open question. This is not improbable in microorganisms, where the generation time is short; in higher organisms, however, the numbers of generations and the time intervals required are so great that the adaptive values of the genotypes are not likely to remain equal. In this case, changes in gene frequencies will be determined more by selection than by mutation rates.

## Darwinian Fitness and the Selection Coefficient

The Hardy-Weinberg formula assumes that the carriers of genotypes $AA$, $Aa$, and $aa$ contribute, on the average, equal numbers of gametes to the gene pool of the next generation. The carriers of some genotypes may, however, be more viable and may reach the reproductive stage more often than the carriers of other genotypes. Or the carriers of different genotypes may vary in fecundity (numbers of eggs or seeds produced), in sexual activity, or in time of maturity or cessation of the reproductive period. All these variables influence the contribution that the carriers of a given genotype make to the gene pool. This contribution, relative to the contributions of other genotypes in the same population, is a measure of the Darwinian fitness of a given genotype. ("Adaptive value" and "selective value" are terms often used synonymously with "Darwinian fitness.") Thus, if the carriers of genotypes $AA$ and $Aa$ contribute on the average 100 gametes to the gene pool of the next generation, whereas the $aa$ carriers contribute only 90 gametes, the Darwinian fitness of the former is $W_1 = 1$, and of the latter $W_2 = (1 - s) = 0.9$. The value of $s$ is the selection coefficient. It is merely conventional to give the value of unity to the fittest genotype; one might just as well make the values of $W_1$ and $W_2$ equal $(1 + s)$ and 1, respectively.

If the Darwinian fitness of genotypes $AA$ and $Aa$ is 1, and that of $aa$ is $(1 - s)$, the frequencies of these genotypes in the population before and after selection will be as follows:

| Genotypes | $AA$ | $Aa$ | $aa$ | Total Population |
|---|---|---|---|---|
| Darwinian fitness | 1 | 1 | $(1 - s)$ | $\overline{W}$ |
| Initial frequency | $p^2$ | $2pq$ | $q^2$ | 1 |
| Frequency after selection | $p^2$ | $2pq$ | $(1 - s)q^2$ | $1 - sq^2$ |

The frequency, $p_1$, of gene $A$ in the next generation will be:

$$p_1 = (p^2 + pq)/(1 - sq^2) = p/(1 - sq^2)$$

The increment, $\Delta p$, of the frequency of gene $A$ in one generation will be:

$$\Delta p = spq^2/(1 - sq^2)$$

Let, for example, genes $A$ and $a$ be equally frequent in the original population, so that $p = q = 0.5$. Also, let the fitness value of the dominants $(AA$ and $Aa)$ be unity, and suppose that the recessives $(aa)$ have a fitness of 0 (a recessive lethal), 0.4 (a semilethal), 0.9, 0.99 (subvital), or 1.5 (supervital). The frequencies, $p_1$, of gene $A$ in the next generation, and the increments of the gene frequency, will then be as follows:

| Darwinian fitness | 0 | 0.4 | 0.9 | 0.99 | 1.5 |
|---|---|---|---|---|---|
| Selection coefficient $(s)$ | 1.0 | 0.6 | 0.1 | 0.01 | $-0.5$ |
| Frequency after one generation of selection $(p_1)$ | 0.67 | 0.59 | 0.5128 | 0.5012 | 0.444 |
| Increment of gene frequency $(\Delta p)$ | $+0.17$ | $+0.09$ | $+0.0128$ | $+0.0012$ | $-0.056$ |

For small selection coefficients, an approximate formula for the number of generations $(n)$ necessary to change the frequency of a deleterious recessive gene from $q_0$ to $q_n$ is derived from the equation:

$$ns = \frac{q_0 - q_n}{q_0 q_n} + \log_e \left( \frac{q_n}{1 - q_0} \cdot \frac{1 - q_n}{q_n} \right)$$

For the special case of complete selection, $s = 1.0$, against a recessive (i.e., selection against a recessive lethal), the formula becomes:

$$n = (q_0 - q_n)/q_0 q_n$$

The efficiency of selection depends on the gene frequency. Suppose that a recessive gene for some undesirable trait starts with a frequency of 0.5, and that the homozygous recessives are sterilized or otherwise eliminated from the population in every generation $(s = 1)$. The frequency of this gene will then change as follows:

| Generation | Frequency | Generation | Frequency | Generation | Frequency |
|---|---|---|---|---|---|
| 0 | 0.500 | 8 | 0.100 | 50 | 0.020 |
| 1 | 0.333 | 10 | 0.083 | 100 | 0.010 |
| 2 | 0.250 | 20 | 0.045 | 200 | 0.005 |
| 3 | 0.200 | 30 | 0.031 | 1000 | 0.001 |
| 4 | 0.167 | 40 | 0.024 | | |

The progress of selection is rapid at first, while the gene is frequent enough for an appreciable number of recessive homozygotes to be produced in the population, but it becomes slow as the gene frequency declines. It takes two generations to halve the frequency of a recessive lethal from 0.5 to 0.25, five generations from 0.20 to 0.10, fifty generations from 0.02 to 0.01, etc.

Very important in natural populations is normalizing selection against incompletely recessive genes or genes without dominance. Let the fitness of one of the homozygotes be $(1 - s)$, and of the heterozygote $(1 - hs)$, $h$ being the coefficient of dominance (where the heterozygote is exactly intermediate in fitness, $h$ is 0.5). We then have:

| Genotype | $A_1A_1$ | $A_1A_2$ | $A_2A_2$ |
|---|---|---|---|
| Darwinian fitness | 1 | $1 - hs$ | $1 - s$ |
| Initial frequency | $p^2$ | $2pq$ | $q^2$ |
| Frequency after selection | $p^2$ | $2pq(1 - hs)$ | $(1 - s)q^2$ |

The frequency of $A_1$ will increase, and of $A_2$ decrease, in the next generation by:

$$\Delta p = hspq/(1 - hsq)$$

Selection acting against both the homozygous and the heterozygous carriers of a deleterious gene is decidedly more efficient than that acting against a completely recessive gene, especially if the frequency of the latter in the gene pool is low. Consider a selection of $s = 0.01$ (1 percent disadvantage) against a complete recessive, and $hs = 0.01$ ($s = 0.02$) against a gene without dominance ($h = 0.5$). The numbers of generations needed to effect a reduction in the frequencies of deleterious genes for the intervals specified are as follows:

| From → To | Recessive | No Dominance |
|---|---|---|
| 0.25 → 0.10 | 710 | 110 |
| 0.10 → 0.01 | 9,240 | 240 |
| 0.01 → 0.001 | 90,231 | 231 |
| 0.001 → 0.0001 | 900,230 | 230 |

For other forms of selection, such as selection in haploid organisms, gametic selection, and sex-linked genes, see Li (1955a), Lerner (1958), and Falconer (1960).

### Experimental Models of Normalizing Selection in Drosophila

Natural selection in the laboratory is not a contradiction of terms. When man chooses individuals to be preserved and bred, and others to be eliminated or prevented from reproducing, he practices artificial selection. If an experimental population in the laboratory is placed in an environment in which some genotypes have an advantage over others, no discrimination by man toward producers and nonproducers is involved. Natural selection operates in the laboratory as well as in the wild.

Many investigators have contrived experimental populations of Drosophila in which selection could be studied. L'Héritier and Teissier (1934) constructed "population cages," in which containers of culture medium can be introduced or withdrawn without permitting the flies to escape. A mixture with known proportions of flies of desired kinds is introduced into the cage; samples of the population are taken at desired intervals, and the changing proportions of different phenotypes and genotypes are recorded. The experiments of Polivanov

(1964) with population cages containing the mutant Stubble and wild-type *Drosophila melanogaster* may serve as examples. They show very clearly the progress of the selection against Stubble, and at the same time display interesting deviations from the predicted course of the selection. Heterozygous Stubble flies ($Sb/+$) have short bristles, and wild-type flies ($+/+$) have long ones. Homozygous Stubble ($Sb/Sb$), is lethal. Polivanov set up four populations, the founders of which were $Sb/+$ heterozygotes. Thus the initial frequencies of $Sb$ and $+$ were equal, $p = q = 0.5$. The frequencies of $Sb$ observed in different generations are shown in Fig. 4.1.

Assume for simplicity that the heterozygotes $Sb/+$ and the homozygotes $+/+$ are equal in fitness. Since homozygous $Sb/Sb$ is lethal, one can predict the frequencies of $Sb$ generation after generation with the aid of the formula given above: $n = (q_0 - q_n)/q_0 q_n$. The decreasing frequencies predicted are indicated in Fig. 4.1 by black squares. The observed frequencies also show decreases of $Sb$ in all four popu-

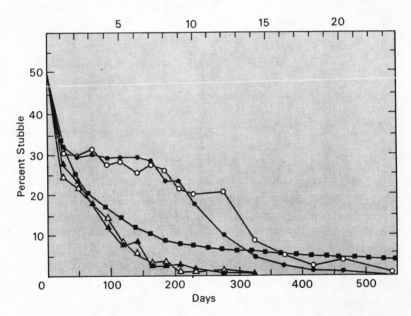

**FIGURE 4.1**

Selection against the mutant Stubble in experimental populations of Drosophila melanogaster. Circles—"monochromosomal" populations; and triangles—"polychromosomal" populations; squares—theoretically expected values. (From Polivanov)

lations. In two populations, however, symbolized in the Figure by triangles, *Sb* dwindled more rapidly than predicted. In the other two populations, symbolized by circles, *Sb* was for some generations more frequent than predicted.

These deviations are not accidental. The populations symbolized by triangles were polychromosomal, that is, they contained + chromosomes from several wild progenitors. The populations represented by circles were monochromosomal: their chromosomes with the + allele of *Sb* descended from a single progenitor. Why should this make any difference? We shall see that many "quasi-normal" chromosomes in natural populations are actually subvital, that is, cause slight but perceptible diminutions of fitness in double dose. In the monochromosomal populations the +/+ flies were actually less fit than the *Sb*/+ flies. Taking the fitness of *Sb*/+ to be unity, Polivanov estimated the fitness of +/+ flies during the first seven generations as 0.62. In polychromosomal populations +/+ flies were, on the contrary, more fit than their *Sb*/+ counterparts. This is not surprising, since *Sb* is a rather sharp mutant. Polivanov estimates the relative fitness of *Sb*/+ and +/+ in these populations as 1 : 1.25 to 1 : 1.44. Thus an ostensibly simple selective system reveals interesting complications.

## *Mutation Favored and Opposed by Selection*

Biologically very important is the interaction of mutation with selection. Little needs to be said about a mutation that is increasing the fitness and is accordingly favored by selection. A favorable mutant allele will increase in frequency and eventually will displace and supplant the original allele. The initial increase will be more rapid for a dominant than for a recessive favorable allele, but the situation will be exactly reversed during the final stages of replacement.

Unfavorable mutants are discriminated against by normalizing selection. However, if a mutation arises at a rate *u* per generation, and is counteracted by a selection coefficient *s*, a state of genetic equilibrium will eventually be established, and both the original and the mutant alleles will continue to be present with certain frequencies. The equilibrium frequencies will be determined not only by the mutation and selection rates, but also by which, if either, allele is dominant or recessive. If the deleterious mutant allele is completely recessive—that is, if the fitness of the heterozygote, $Aa$, equals that of $AA$, the mutant allele will reach an equilibrium frequency at

$$q_a = \sqrt{u/s}$$

The mutant allele may be partially or completely dominant, that is, the fitness of the heterozygote may be between $(1 - hs)$ and 1 (where $h$ is the coefficient of dominance). The equilibrium frequencies will then be reached at $p_A = u/hs$ (partial dominance) or $p_A = u/s$ (complete dominance).

What this means biologically is that a deleterious recessive mutant will reach a much higher equilibrium frequency in the gene pool than a dominant mutant. Let the mutation rate, $u$, be $10^{-5}$ (0.00001), and the selection coefficient, $s$, equal 0.1. A recessive mutant gene will then reach a frequency of 1 percent ($q = 0.01$), and a dominant mutant of only one-hundredth of 1 percent ($p = 0.0001$). These are, of course, the equilibrium frequencies of genes in the gene pool, and not of individuals in which these genes are manifested. Individuals heterozygous for a completely recessive mutant do not show its effects in their phenotype, whereas the opposite is true of heterozygotes for a dominant mutant.

The consequences of this are interesting. The smaller are the frequencies of recessive genes, the greater proportion will be concealed in heterozygotes ($2pq$), rather than manifested in homozygotes ($q^2$). For example, if a recessive and a dominant allele are equally frequent ($q = p = 0.5$), the heterozygotes are twice as common as either one of the homozygotes (0.50 and 0.25, respectively). Rare recessives, $q = 0.1$, 0.01, and 0.001, will be heterozygous with frequencies $2pq = 0.18$, 0.0198, and 0.001,998, and homozygous with frequencies of only $q^2 = 0.01$, 0.0001, and 0.000,001; hence, the heterozygotes will be 18 to almost 2000 times more frequent than the homozygotes.

On the other hand, if the mutation rates and the selection pressures opposing the mutants are equal, the dominants will be encountered and recognized more often than the recessives. Consider again what happens if $u$ is 0.00001 and $s$ is 0.1. Because the equilibrium frequency of a recessive mutant is $q = 0.01$, it will manifest itself in homozygous individuals with a frequency that will be $q^2 = 0.0001$, or 1 in 10,000. The equilibrium frequency of an equally deleterious dominant will be $p = 0.0001$, and the frequency of a heterozygous mutant individual, $2pq$, will be 0.0002, or 2 in 10,000, twice that of a recessive.

The matter can be approached from a different angle. Only dominant mutants whose Darwinian fitness is zero—that is, they are completely lethal or sterile—are extinguished by normalizing selection in the same generation in which they arise. In each generation a population will have only newly arisen completely dominant lethal or sterile mutants; no such mutants will be inherited from previous generations. With deleterious mutants whose fitness is greater than zero (semilethal or subvital), a population will contain some newly arisen and some inherited mutants. A variant allele arisen by mutation will persist in the population for a certain number of generations before its elimination. The persistence will be a function of fitness; it will be longer on the average for mildly deleterious mutants, and shorter for drastic ones. Fitness being equal, recessive mutants will persist longer than semidominant ones, and the latter longer than dominant ones, because the recessives, regardless of how drastic their effects may be when homozygous, are sheltered from normalizing selection when they are concealed in heterozygotes.

Populations of presumably all living species are said to carry genetic loads (Muller 1950). We shall see in the following chapters that the concept of genetic load, or genetic burden, is not easily definable in biologically meaningful and operationally useful ways. Not all mutants are deleterious, and the effects of some on the fitness of populations carrying them are ambivalent. Although a part of the genetic load may be said to exist because normalizing selection is not ideally efficient, other parts are maintained by various forms of balancing selection (see Chapter 5). Provisionally, we shall designate as genetic load simply the presence in populations of genetic variants that have deleterious effects on their carriers under some or under all conditions. Overt and concealed genetic loads will be distinguished; the former are detected by examination of individual members of a population, and the latter by study of their progenies.

*Mutants in Natural Populations*
*of Drosophila*

The pioneer experimental work on what was later called genetic load or genetic burden in Drosophila was done by Tshetverikov (1926), H. Timofeeff-Ressovsky and N. W. Timofeeff-Ressovsky (1927), and Dubinin and his colleagues (Dubinin and fourteen collaborators 1934 and Dubinin, Romashov, et al. 1937) on populations of several species, mainly *Drosophila melanogaster*. Although Drosophila flies are, if anything, overtly less variable in nature than many other insect species, aberrant individuals do occur, and some of them are identical with mutants observed to arise in laboratories. No matter how carefully one examines the specimens collected in nature, however, recessive mutants that may be carried in the heterozygous condition will go undetected. Tshetverikov (1926) pointed out that a genetic analysis is needed to reveal such concealed variability. The simplest technique is to study the progenies of Drosophila females collected in nature. In their offspring one may discover the autosomal dominant mutants that these females and their mates carried, and also the sex-linked mutant genes. Inbreeding the $F_1$ individuals will permit detection in $F_2$ and $F_3$ generations of the recessive autosomal mutants. When practical, more refined methods, of the type described in Chapter 3 (Fig. 3.1), are used. They permit detection of concealed recessive mutants, such as lethals, semilethals, and all kinds of physiological as well as morphological variations.

The older work on mutants found in nature, or obtained by inbreeding Drosophilae collected in natural habitats, was ably summarized by Spencer (1947b). Spencer himself found a population of *Drosophila hydei* in which 6.5 percent of the males were vermilion-eyed. This sex-linked recessive mutant continued to occur in this population for at least 6 years. Some populations of this species contained several percent of the mutant bobbed. A variety of bobbed alleles was discovered; their frequencies varied from locality to locality.

Dubinin, Romashov, et al. (1937) examined some 130,000 wild *D. melanogaster* from several localities in southern Russia and found about 2800 "aberrant" individuals. A part of the latter had noninheritable

**TABLE 4.1**

Numbers of Drosophila melanogaster and D. subobscura females collected in their natural habitats that carried from 0 to 12 mutants (After Boesiger 1962 and Pentzos, Boesiger, and Kanellis 1967)

| Species and Population | Number of Mutants | | | | | | | | | | | Average Number of Mutants per Fly |
|---|---|---|---|---|---|---|---|---|---|---|---|---|
| | 0 | 1 | 2 | 3 | 4 | 5 | 6 | 7 | 8 | 9 | 10–12 | |
| Melanogaster | | | | | | | | | | | | |
| Banyuls 52A | 7 | 24 | 59 | 38 | 20 | 4 | 6 | 2 | ... | ... | ... | 2.54 |
| 52B | 14 | 30 | 47 | 37 | 16 | 7 | 2 | 1 | ... | ... | ... | 2.29 |
| 53A | 5 | 7 | 20 | 30 | 55 | 41 | 27 | 21 | 9 | 2 | 1 | 4.45 |
| 53B | 1 | 1 | 7 | 18 | 27 | 32 | 13 | 8 | 9 | 3 | 2 | 4.88 |
| 53C | ... | 5 | 13 | 12 | 8 | 10 | 7 | 4 | 3 | 1 | ... | 4.00 |
| Domme 57 | ... | 6 | 15 | 17 | 18 | 13 | 9 | 9 | 3 | 1 | 4 | 4.36 |
| Subobscura | | | | | | | | | | | | |
| Litochoron | ... | 2 | 8 | 15 | 3 | 4 | 2 | 4 | 5 | ... | 4 | 4.6 |
| Samothraki | ... | 3 | 3 | 12 | 10 | 8 | 5 | 3 | 2 | 1 | 1 | 4.4 |
| Thassos | ... | 5 | 30 | 59 | 62 | 25 | 4 | 2 | 1 | 1 | ... | 3.5 |

abnormalities, but others were mutants, for the most part identical with well-known laboratory ones (extra bristles, ebony, sepia, yellow). The frequencies of the mutants varied from locality to locality and from year to year. Most mutants were recessives, although some semidominants were recorded; mutants that showed slight changes were more common than drastic and deleterious variants. At one collecting station—a pit with decomposing fruit—many individuals were homozygous for the gene divergent, which makes its carriers flightless.

Among the newer studies, those of Boesiger (1962) on *D. melanogaster* and of Pentzos, Boesiger, and Kanellis (1967) on *D. subobscura* are most carefully executed. In some populations of the former species in France, from 2.8 to 8.2 percent of individuals carry visibly detectable abnormalities; the corresponding percentages for the latter species in Greece are 6.3–9.5. After two generations of inbreeding, the females collected in their natural habitats were shown to have carried from none to as many as twelve mutants (Table 4.1).

Some comparable data exist for the housefly, *Musca domestica* (Milani 1967), and the mosquito *Aedes aegypti* (Craig and Hickey 1967). In the former, inbreeding reveals from zero to six mutants per progeny of a fertilized female; in the latter, the average number of mutants per female ranges in different samples from 0.72 to 2.96.

## Overt Genetic Loads in Human Populations

Although a complete bibliography of this subject would contain hundreds or even thousands of entries, the genetic load in the human species is far from adequately known. Stevenson, Johnston, Stewart, and Golding (1966) and Kennedy (1967) have compiled data on the incidence of congenital malformations, a short summary of which is presented in Table 4.2. The incidence in different countries seems to be variable, but this may be largely spurious, depending on the criteria and the reliability of the procedures used. More intensive investigations show an average frequency more than five times as high as that derived from official records. What proportion of congenital defects is of genetic origin is also not well known. Neel (1958), who records 3.1 percent of "major congenital defect" in Japanese populations, considers that "a significant fraction of human

**TABLE 4.2**

Incidence of congenital defects in human populations (After Kennedy)

| Source of Data | Number of Births Surveyed | Percentage of Malformations |
|---|---|---|
| I. Official records, birth certificates, retrospective questionnaires | | |
| Belgium | 740,956 | 0.67 |
| Italy | 2,660,990 | 0.15 |
| United States and Canada | 8,784,188 | 1.05 |
| Total | 12,186,134 | 0.83 |
| II. Hospital and clinic records | | |
| Britain and Ireland | 640,413 | 1.18 |
| Europe (excluding Germany) | 2,560,937 | 1.37 |
| Germany | 2,154,964 | 0.97 |
| United States and Canada | 876,835 | 1.95 |
| Other countries | 652,462 | 0.99 |
| Total | 6,885,611 | 1.26 |
| III. More intensive investigations | | |
| Britain | 170,224 | 2.88 |
| Europe (excluding Germany) | 78,610 | 2.96 |
| Germany | 8,516 | 2.20 |
| United States | 144,769 | 8.76 |
| Other countries | 121,264 | 2.85 |
| Total | 523,383 | 4.50 |

congenital defects are the segregants (phenodeviants) resulting from the existence and functioning of complex (multi-local) genetic homeostatic systems, of the type particularly discussed by Lerner (1954)."

McKusick (1966) lists 837 dominant, 531 recessive, and 119 sex-linked "phenotypes" in man, a great majority of which represent mild or serious genetic defects or diseases. Stevenson (1959, 1961) finds that, in Britain, 12–15 percent of all pregnancies that continue longer than 4 or 5 weeks end in abortions before the end of the twenty-seventh week, and more than 2 percent result in stillbirths. About 2.5 percent of all children are born with a "malformation detectable by the naked eye," and about the same proportion is recognized by 5 years of age. A considerable number of these are genetic. In Northern Ireland, about 26.5 percent of hospital beds are occupied by genetically handicapped persons, and 7.9 percent of consultations with medical specialists and 6.4 percent of those with general practitioners involve such persons. Genetic predisposition is involved in the etiology of many mental diseases, the incidence of which in human populations is considerable. The very careful study of Böök (1953) of an isolated population in northern Sweden showed the frequency of schizophrenia to be $2.63 \pm 0.27$, of oligophrenia $1.14 \pm 0.13$, and of epilepsy $0.35 \pm 0.08$ percent. The genetics of these nervous disorders is, however, far from clear. For reviews and bibliography see Pratt (1967), Petras and Curtis (1968), Erlenmeyer-Kimling and Paradowski (1966), and Shields (1968).

It was as recently as 1956 that Tjio and Levan established the correct chromosome number in man (46). Three years later, Lejeune, Turpin, and Gautier discovered the first chromosomal aberration. Individuals with the congenital malformation known under the misleading name of Mongolism (it has no relation to the Mongolian race) usually have 47 chromosomes. They are aneuploid mutants, trisomics, the extra chromosome being that designated No. 21 in the normal set. In little more than a decade since then, the study of chromosomal variations in man has burgeoned into a field with hundreds of publications and at least one special journal (reviews in Turpin and Lejeune 1965, Bartolos and Baramki 1967, Court-Brown 1967, and Reitalu 1968).

The fitness of aneuploid mutants in man is generally very low or even nonexistent. According to Stevenson, Johnston, et al. (1966), the frequency of trisomy-21 is at birth between 1 and 2 for 1000, ranging from between 0.3 and 0.5 per 1000 mothers 15–24 years old, to 6.34 for those aged 40–44 years, and as high as 16.65 for those older than 45. The frequency in the adult population is appreciably lower, owing to differential mortality, and since the affected persons seldom reproduce, their Darwinian fitness is close to zero.

Nondisjunction of the sex chromosomes gives rise to individuals with Turner's syndrome (45 chromosomes, a single X and no Y chromosome), Klinefelter's syndrome (47 chromosomes, two X's and a Y), and also XXX and XYY individuals (47 chromosomes). Court-Brown (1967) states that about 0.2 percent of the male baby population have a so-called Barr body in the nuclei of their buccal epithelial cells, and that a great majority of these are XXY Klinefelter individuals, while some are XXYY, XXXY, or even XXXXY in at least a fraction of their body cells. Persons with Turner's syndrome are probably always sterile, and those with Klinefelter's usually so. The relationship between abnormal sex chromosomes and mental disorder in man has been reviewed by Polani (1969).

Chromosomal aberrations in human individuals are more frequent than the above figures suggest. Failures of meiotic disjunction of the sex chromosomes and of chromosome 21 give rise to aneuploids at least some of which are viable, though usually more or less severely handicapped. The other chromosomes probably also undergo occasional nondisjunction, giving rise to aneuploid zygotes (trisomics and monosomics) that do not survive to birth. What proportion of spontaneous abortions results from this cause cannot be estimated with any degree of assurance. Persons heterozygous for translocations between chromosomes may enjoy normal health and have the normal number, 46, of chromosomes in their cells. A part of their progeny, however, will have some genes in excess (duplication) and some deficient, and will be malformed. This is the origin of the very severe abnormality called the *cri du chat* syndrome, which results from a deficiency for part of chromosome 5. Translocation heterozygosis is, thus, a part of the concealed genetic load (Lejeune 1969).

## Concealed Genetic Loads
## in Human Populations

Incest, the mating of close relatives, is interdicted by law or custom almost universally in human societies. Only a minority of anthropologists believes the injunction to have arisen because the progenies of incestual unions were observed to be weak or malformed. Though this is indeed true in a statistical sense, to ascribe this discovery to primitive man would be to credit him with rather improbable acuity of discernment. Many individuals in human populations are heterozygous carriers of deleterious recessive variants. These variants have a greater probability of becoming homozygous in families in which the parents are relatives than in the progenies of mates not closely related. The homozygotes will only be a part of the progeny, however; in their siblings the recessives will be concealed in the heterozygous condition. To genetically untrained observers this is likely to make the causal relationship between inbreeding and the manifestation of deleterious genes far from evident. Only when the simple rules of Mendelian heredity are understood does it become comprehensible why rare recessive traits, such as albinism, occur particularly often in the progenies of those who have married cousins or other relatives.

Marriages of first cousins are common enough in at least some populations to make the collection of statistically meaningful data practicable. Aunt-nephew and uncle-niece marriages are generally infrequent, even where legally permitted. Marriages between second or third cousins are common, but the probability of homozygosis in the resulting children is much lower than in first-cousin marriages. In recent years, studies of progenies of marriages between relatives, as compared to those of unrelated parents, have been made in several countries. Despite heterogeneities in the results, due in large part to differences in the criteria used, the greater frequencies of stillbirths, infant deaths, and malformations among children of relatives are manifest. The review by Stevenson et al. (1966) records 12,779 stillbirths and infant deaths among 335,710 children of parents not known to be related, compared to 855 among 13,763 offspring of relatives. The frequencies are, consequently, 35.9 and 62.1 per 1000 births, respectively. The same review gives frequencies of 12.1 and 16.9 per 1000 births for congenital malformation among children of unrelated and of related parents, respectively.

Probably the most careful and detailed studies on the effects of inbreedings are those made by Schull and Neel (1962) in Japan. In addition to increased frequencies of malformations and neonatal deaths, they found "the average child of inbreeding" to differ slightly though significantly from the offspring of unrelated parents on a series of anthropometric traits, neuromuscular tests, and even school performance. In the populations of the cities of Hiroshima and Nagasaki slight but statistically significant differences were recorded in the following criteria, the "child of inbreeding" scoring less favorably than the control child:

| | |
|---|---|
| Age when walked | Tapping rate |
| Weight | Color trail test score |
| Height | Maze tests score |
| Head girth | Verbal score |
| Chest girth | Performance score |
| | School performance |
| Calf girth | Language |
| Head length | Social studies |
| Head breadth | Mathematics |
| Head height | Science |
| Sitting height | Music |
| Knee height | Fine arts |
| Dynamometer grip | Musical education |

Great care was taken to evaluate a possible inflation of differences between the inbred and the control children by socioeconomic factors. Yet, even when due allowances are made for the effects of such factors, the differences remain statistically meaningful. It is interesting that the study by the same authors (Schull and Neel 1966) of the semi-isolated population of the island of Kure, Japan, failed to disclose a significant effect of inbreeding (chiefly first-cousin marriages) on mortality during the first 15 years of life. A further discussion of attempts to measure the concealed genetic loads in human populations will be found in Chapter 5.

## Genetic Loads in Maize and Other Plants

Many monoecious plants, though mostly cross-pollinated in nature, can produce seed also by spontaneous or artificial self-pollination. Selfing uncovers the concealed recessive mutants, because each mutant carried in heterozygous condition becomes homozygous in one-quarter of the progeny obtained by selfing. Crumpacker (1967) has published an excellent review and a summary of the extensive but scattered literature. Technically, the most easily detectable mutants are those that produce chlorophyll deficiencies, because they can be recorded in young seedlings from seeds obtained by selfing. In two species of rye grass (*Lolium perenne* and *L. multiflorum*), in timothy (*Phleum pratense*), orchard grass (*Dactylis glomerata*), *Festuca rubra,* clover (*Trifolium repens*), and cherry (*Prunus avium*) between 12 and 67 percent of the individuals tested were heterozygous for chlorophyll deficiencies or other seedling defects. Eiche (1955) examined 1,769,000 seedlings grown from seeds of 2031 Scotch pine trees (*Pinus sylvestris*) from 86 localities, mostly in Sweden. Some of these seeds came from cross-pollination, and others from selfing in nature. A total of 1368 mutant seedlings, or 0.077 percent, was recorded, but the incidence varied greatly among individual trees.

By far the most abundant data are available for Indian corn, *Zea mays.* Crumpacker (1967) summarizes 66 separate reports on the frequencies of recessive genes that give, when homozygous, defective and inviable seeds. Among 12,338 plants from field varieties tested, 11.0 percent were found heterozygous for such genes. A total of 106 reports describes tests of 18,697 plants for genes giving, in the homozygous condition, chlorophyll-deficient seedlings. The overall frequency of heterozygotes for such genes is 21.3 percent; in other words, about every fifth plant carries in its genotype such mutants, which are lethal or semilethal in double dose. In different samples, the frequencies varied from 0 to 64 percent. Chlorophyll deficiencies are of several different kinds and are produced by mutations of a number of different, nonallelic genes. About 180 such genes are known in maize. Crumpacker gives the following breakdown of the data (in percentages) according to the type of chlorophyll-deficient mutation:

| White seedlings | 5.5 | Striped seedlings | 3.1 |
| Yellow seedlings | 3.9 | Pale green seedlings | 3.3 |
| Yellow and green seedlings | 0.3 | Virescent seedlings | 2.6 |

The frequencies of the mutant alleles at any one locus are usually so low that in progenies of cross-pollinated plants chlorophyll-deficient seedlings are rarely found.

## Assays of Viability Modifiers Concealed in Natural Populations

A technique for quantitative studies of recessive genetic variants concealed in apparently normal individuals in Drosophila populations has been described in Chapter 3 and illustrated in Fig. 3.1. Variations of this technique are available and have been used for the analysis of natural populations, in five species of Drosophila (*Drosophila melanogaster, pseudoobscura, persimilis, prosaltans,* and *willistoni*). All the techniques are similar in principle: by means of a series of crosses to laboratory stocks with suitable mutant gene markers in certain chromosomes, a class of flies is obtained carrying in duplicate (i.e., in the homozygous condition) a chromosome that was carried singly in an individual collected in a natural habitat of the species. This class of flies develops in cultures together with siblings that carry the chromosome under test in single dose (heterozygote) or do not carry it at all. The frequencies of these classes are theoretically predictable from the nature of the crosses made.

Thus, with the procedure diagramed in Fig. 3.1, one-quarter of the zygotes in the $F_3$ generation will carry the markers $Cy$, $L$, and $Pm$, two-quarters either $Cy$ and $L$ or $Pm$, and one-quarter will be flies without mutant markers, homozygous for the "wild" chromosomes tested. These frequencies are expected, of course, only if the homozygous class is equal in viability to the classes carrying mutant markers. Suppose, however, that the wild chromosome carries a recessive lethal; a culture will then contain no wild-type flies. If the wild chromosome is semilethal (viability less than one-half normal), the wild-type class will appear with a frequency between 0 and 12.5 percent; a subvital chromosome will result in a frequency above 12.5 but below 25.0; and, finally, a supervital chromosome will raise the frequency above 25.0 percent.

For many purposes, it is more convenient to express the results of experiments in percentages, not of wild-type flies in the cultures, but of the average (or "normal") viability of flies heterozygous for pairs of chromosomes taken at random from the gene pool of the population. Such a "normal" viability standard is arrived at by making intercrosses of flies that carry the $Cy$ $L$ marker chromosomes and also chromosomes derived from different individuals sampled in the population. Because the mutant markers generally reduce, at least slightly, the viabilities of their carriers, the average normal viability corresponds to somewhat more than 25.0 percent of wild-type flies in the cultures (Fig. 3.1).

All species of Drosophila examined with the aid of the technique just described have yielded qualitatively, though not quantitatively, similar results. Figure 4.2 shows a sharply bimodal distribution of the

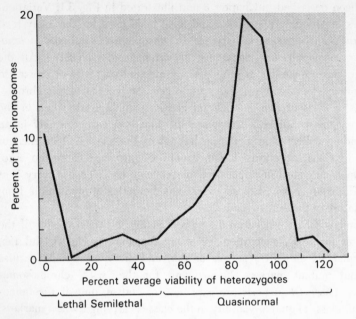

**FIGURE 4.2**

Viabilities in double dose of second chromosomes of Drosophila
pseudoobscura from natural populations. (After Dobzhansky and
Spassky)

viabilities in 284 second chromosomes of *Drosophila pseudoobscura*
from Texas and California. Many chromosomes (17 percent in the
experiment diagramed in Fig. 4.2) are lethal in double dose and produce only an occasional homozygous survivor, or none at all. Quasi-
normal chromosomes, with viabilities between 50 and 125 percent of
the normal average, are most frequent. The concavity between the two
peaks corresponds to the semilethal range—between 0 and 50 percent
of normal viability; only about 7 percent of the chromosomes are found
in this range.

A summary of the data on the frequencies of lethal and semilethal
second chromosomes in populations of *Drosophila melanogaster* is
given in Table 4.3. The frequencies vary from 11 to 62 percent—almost
a sixfold difference. Some of these variations are probably due to differences in experimental techniques; others reflect the ecological situ-

**TABLE 4.3**

Percentages of second chromosomes in natural populations of Drosophila melanogaster that are lethal or semilethal in double dose

| Population | Chromosomes Studied | Percentage Lethal or Semilethal | Authority |
|---|---|---|---|
| Caucasus, U.S.S.R. | 2971 | 15.6 | Dubinin et al. (1932-1936) |
| Caucasus, U.S.S.R. | 1040 | 25.4 | Berg (1939) |
| Uman, U.S.S.R. | 2700 | 24.3 | Olenov et al. (1937, 1938) |
| Crimea, U.S.S.R. | 1630 | 24.8 | Dubinin (1938, 1939) |
| Amherst, U.S.A. | 2352 | 35.8 | Ives and Band (1945-1959) |
| Maine, U.S.A. | 226 | 42.9 | Ives (1945) |
| Wisconsin, U.S.A. | 231 | 34.2 | Greenberg and Crow (1960) |
| Ohio, U.S.A. | 177 | 49.7 | Ives (1945) |
| Florida, U.S.A. | 468 | 61.3 | Ives (1945, 1951) |
| New Mexico, U.S.A. | 203 | 62.1 | Ives (1945) |
| Korea | 611 | 11.2 | Paik (1960) |
| Hiroshima, Japan | 1901 | 11.6 | Minamori and Saito (1964) |
| Kofu and Katsunuma, Japan | 2457 | 16.6 | Oshima (1967) |
| Kofu and Katsunuma, Japan | 2773 | 21.5 | Watanabe (1969b) |
| Egypt | 301 | 29.4 | Dawood (1961) |
| Lipari, Italy | 215 | 34.1 | Karlik and Sperlich (1962) |
| Israel | 1222 | 34.7 | Goldschmidt et al. (1955) |

ations in which the populations live, which cause some of these populations to dwindle periodically to very few individuals and permit others to maintain relatively high densities. The incidence of lethals and semilethals in the third chromosomes of the same species is less well known; Wallace, Zouros, and Krimbas (1966) found in a South American population about equal frequencies (55 percent) of second and of third chromosomes being lethal or semilethal in double dose, and Band and Ives (1963) also found the frequencies in the two chromosomes to be about equal in the population of Amherst, Massachusetts. Even the tiny fourth chromosome has a 3 percent frequency of lethals (Hochman 1961). This means that in many, probably most, natural populations almost every individual fly carries one or more recessive lethal or semilethal variant in its genotype.

As seen in Fig. 4.2, chromosomes with quasi-normal viability in double dose are most frequent. The percentage of wild-type flies observed in test cultures for a given chromosome is, of course, subject to sampling errors; therefore, part of the variation in the viability scores among quasi-normal chromosomes comes from sampling errors, part from unavoidable environmental variations in different cultures,

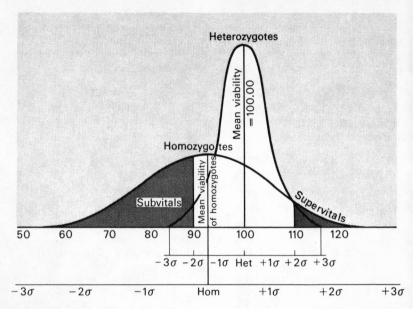

**FIGURE 4.3**

Technique of estimation of the frequencies of chromosomes which are subvital or supervital in double dose. Further explanation in text. (After Wallace and Madden)

and part from genetic differences between the chromosomes. Wallace and Madden (1953) developed a simple but ingenious method for analysis of the data (see Fig. 4.3). As stated above, the "normal" viability (or normal fecundity, or development rate, etc.) is defined as the average observed in an array of individuals with random combinations of the chromosomes from a given population in a specific environment. This is not an arbitrary but a biologically and operationally meaningful definition. In nature, "normal" Drosophila flies or butterflies or mice or men are not imaginary ideal types with perfect viability, optimum fertility, and fastest development, but arrays of genotypically as well as phenotypically diverse individuals, which arise by drawing sets of genes from the population's gene pool. Such arrays are obtained in laboratory experiments, as indicated above, by intercrossing females and males with a marker chromosomes and different wild chromosomes. The experiments are made by raising flies with each chromosome combination, and with each homozygous chromosome, in several replicate cultures. The numbers of the flies and the percentage variations observed in different cultures provide estimates of the variances due to sampling and to environmental fluctuations. By subtracting these from the total observed variance, we obtain an estimate of the genetic or "real" variance.

At this point, we must decide what ranges of viabilities we shall consider subvital, normal, and supervital. Since the frequencies of quasi-normal chromosomes with different viabilities form an approximately normal bell-shaped curve (Fig. 4.3), the choice of boundary points is rather arbitrary. Wallace and Madden (1953 and Wallace 1968) have proposed the following ingenious method. We have defined the mean "normal" viability as the average viability of random heterozygous combinations of chromosomes from a given population. Wallace also includes in the "normal" range all variants within two standard deviations (calculated from the genetic variance) above and below the average viability of the heterozygotes. Thus, about 95 percent of the heterozygous combinations are included among "normals." Now it is easy to calculate what proportion of the quasi-normal homozygotes fall below this "normal" range; these are considered subvital. Similarly, the ones above the "normal" range are supervital.

Table 4.4 shows the frequencies of chromosomes with different viabilities in double dose in populations of two species of Drosophila in a certain locality in California (estimates of Dobzhansky and Spassky 1953, corrected by Sankaranarayanan 1965). The most frequent class consists of the subvitals, followed by lethals, semilethals, and normals; supervitals are least frequent. Very few individuals in nature carry

**TABLE 4.4**

Percentages of chromosomes in natural populations of Drosophila pseudoobscura and D. persimilis with different effects in double dose

| Species and Effect | Chromosome Second | Third | Fourth | Species and Effect | Chromosome Second | Third | Fourth |
|---|---|---|---|---|---|---|---|
| Pseudoobscura | | | | Persimilis | | | |
| Lethal and semilethal | 33.0 | 25.0 | 22.7 | Lethal and semilethal | 25.5 | 22.7 | 28.1 |
| Subvital | 62.6 | 58.7 | 51.8 | Subvital | 49.8 | 61.7 | 70.7 |
| Normal | 4.3 | 16.3 | 22.3 | Normal | 24.5 | 13.5 | 0.9 |
| Supervital | <0.1 | <0.1 | <0.1 | Supervital | 0.2 | 2.1 | 0.3 |
| Female sterile | 10.6 | 13.6 | 4.3 | Female sterile | 18.3 | 14.3 | 18.3 |
| Male sterile | 8.3 | 10.5 | 11.8 | Male sterile | 13.2 | 15.7 | 8.4 |

only "normal" and supervital chromosomes. The properties of these rare chromosomes will be discussed further in the next chapter.

Table 4.4 does not mention the "first," that is, the X chromosome. Because Drosophila males carry only a single X, and most of the genes in this chromosome are not present in the Y chromosome, X chromosomes represent a special situation as far as accumulation of deleterious genetic variants is concerned. A recessive lethal mutant may be harmless in the heterozygous condition in females, but it will kill one-half of their sons. In hymenopteran insects, females are diploid whereas males are haploid; a deleterious recessive in any chromosome may be harmless in heterozygous females but will manifest itself in males. Normalizing natural selection will accordingly operate differently on the two-thirds of the gene pool carried in females and the one-third carried in males. If the mutation rate is $u$ and the selection coefficient against a mutant that is recessive in females is $s$, the equilibrium frequency of the deleterious allele will be approximately $3u/s$. Deleterious sex-linked recessives are expected to be found in nature only three times as frequently as equally deleterious dominants. And yet, Laidlaw, Gomes, and Kerr (1956) discovered that honey-bee females are frequently heterozygous for genes that are lethal in double dose. These genes have sex-limited manifestations, that is, they do not affect the two sexes in the same way. For example, Kerr and Kerr (1952) and Drescher (1964) found in natural populations of *Drosophila melanogaster* some X chromosomes that are decidedly subvital or even semilethal in homozygous females but do not appreciably harm the males.

## Assays of Fertility Modifiers in Natural Populations

The techniques used for assays of concealed recessive viability modifiers are applicable to the detection of other genetic variants as well. As shown in Fig. 3.1, one-quarter of the zygotes obtained in the $F_3$ generation carry in double dose a chromosome present singly in an individual in nature. Provided that these zygotes are not lethal, one can examine their morphological and physiological characters for possible genetic differences. The simplest tests distinguish completely sterile genotypes from fertile ones. Females or males from the test cultures are placed together with individuals of the opposite sex known to be fertile, and the numbers of cultures that do and do not produce progenies are noted. Table 4.4 shows, for natural populations of *Drosophila pseudoobscura* and *D. persimilis*, the frequencies of chromosomes that, though giving quasi-normal viability in homozygotes, make these homozygotes completely sterile as females or as males, but rarely have this effect in both sexes.

Temin (1966) in *Drosophila melanogaster* and Marinkovic (1967) in *D. pseudoobscura* made studies of the fecundity and fertility modifiers carried in natural populations. In the latter species, the average egg-laying capacity of heterozygous females, between the sixth and the twelfth day after emergence from the pupae, is 207.5 ± 5.9 eggs, and that of females homozygous for second chromosomes permitting quasi-normal viability is 161.5 ± 5.7 eggs. Furthermore, only 44.9 ± 2.2 percent of the eggs of homozygous females develop to adult stage, compared to 69.9 ± 1.8 percent in the control; 5.1 percent of the homozygous females studied were completely sterile, owing to the combination of drastically lowered fecundity and low viability of the few eggs deposited.

One of the frequent effects of homozygosis for chromosomes extracted from natural populations of Drosophila is deceleration of development. In extreme cases the time required for egg-to-adult development is more than twice as long in homozygotes as in an average heterozygote. So great a retardation would probably be fatal in nature. Accelerations of development are relatively rare, though Marien (1958) was more successful in selecting for faster than for slower development. Among the less common variations are homozyogtes of giant and of dwarf body size. One homozygote in *Drosophila pseudoobscura* was so sensitive to ether that it died before its heterozygous siblings were anesthetized.

## The Classical Model of the Genetic Population Structure

It has been pointed out above that normalizing natural selection is a conservative force. It perpetuates what has successfully passed the scrutiny of the environment and eliminates changes that impair Darwinian fitness. Although mutants presumably arise in all living species, most of them reduce the fitness of their carriers. However, a number of generations may intervene between the origin of a mutant and its elimination. This number is, on the average, smaller for more deleterious than for less deleterious mutants, and smaller for dominants than for recessives. This process of genetic elimination was termed "genetic death" by Muller (1950). This designation is acceptable if one keeps in mind that a "genetic death" does not always produce a cadaver. This should be remembered, for example, in estimating the "genetic deaths" expected in human populations over many generations as a result of radiation exposures. Weak or abnormal sexual drive, delay in sexual maturity, shorter reproductive period, lowered fecundity or complete sterility, and similar factors, cause genetic elimination just as effectively as differential mortality.

Muller (1950) and Haldane before him (1933, 1937) emphasized an important, and at first sight paradoxical, fact. Completely lethal or sterile mutants and mutants only mildly subvital cause the same amounts of genetic elimination, if the mutation rates that give rise to these variants are the same. The reason is that the inflow of a given kind of mutant into the gene pool must sooner or later match the outflow of the same mutant. We have seen above that the equilibrium frequency of a deleterious mutant in a population depends both on its fitness and on the mutation rate. The average number of generations that intervene between the appearance and the elimination of a mutant is a function of fitness. The number of eliminations (genetic deaths) is equal to the mutation rate for recessives and is double the mutation rate for dominants. Many mutants are incompletely recessive or—what amounts to the same thing—incompletely dominant. The rate of elimination will accordingly be between $u$ and $2u$, where $u$ is the mutation rate.

There are many gene loci that undergo mutation, and the aggregate mutation rate is quite considerable, $n\bar{u}$, where $n$ is the number of loci and $\bar{u}$ the average mutation rate. Hence, mutation imposes a heavy genetic burden. Muller and Kaplan (1966) have given a most explicit statement of the classical model:

Since even such tiny steps, so slightly and to the ordinary view imperceptibly altering the effectiveness of an individual gene, can affect fitness enough to become established, it follows that in the great majority of cases it is after all valid to speak of a "normal gene" and a "normal type". . . . The greatest part of the continuing genetic variation observed within a genetically united population must usually have been caused by multiple genes each of which, mutating separately, has given rise to its own small mutational load before the mutants are eliminated by selection. . . . Of course, this variation is in evolution a very necessary "evil," since it allows natural selection a grasp by which in time of changed needs or opportunities the constitution of the population may be altered adaptively.

# CHAPTER FIVE

# BALANCING SELECTION AND CHROMOSOMAL POLYMORPHISMS

## *The Maintenance of Genetic Variability*

Imagine a universe in which the environment is absolutely constant and uniform. In such a universe, evolution might culminate in an ideal adaptedness. Populations of every species would consist of genetically identical individuals, homozygous for all normal or wild-type genes, and free of what the classical model of genetic population structure regarded as "a very necessary evil" of genetic variability. Suppression of all mutability would be the climax of such evolution. It would have realized the *eidos,* the ideal types of human and other species, postulated more than two thousand years ago in Plato's philosophy. At least implicitly, the classical model conjures such perfect types as genetic ideals for each living species. Yet, as Mayr (1963) has rightly said, "The replacement of typological by population thinking is perhaps the greatest conceptual revolution that has taken place in biology." At any rate, there is hope that it is taking place.

In the world as it really is, the environment is neither constant nor uniform, and no genotype is a paragon of adaptedness in all environments. At any one time level, diverse genotypes are needed to exploit the environments varying in space. They are also needed to maintain the adaptedness to environments varying in time. Some genetic changes arising by mutation seem to be unconditionally harmful, that is, deleterious in all existing external and genetic environments. Such variability is an unavoidable evil. Other variability is necessary but not evil. As we have seen, normalizing selection keeps the level of "evil" variability as low as possible. Balancing selection is a complex of several selective processes that maintain, enhance, or regulate genetic variability, most of which is adaptively beneficial.

There are, then, two major kinds of genetic variability in natural populations: first, that maintained by mutation pressure and kept within bounds by normalizing selection; and, second, that maintained by balancing selection, though arising ultimately also by mutation. The latter variability, when sharply marked and discontinuous, is termed genetic polymorphism, defined as "the occurrence together in the same locality of two or more discontinuous forms of a species in such proportions that the rarest of them cannot be maintained merely by recurrent mutation" (Ford 1964, 1965).

There are several kinds of balancing selection. Of the two most important types, the relatively better known and more often discussed is heterotic balance, which is due to heterozygotes for certain gene alleles or gene complexes having fitness superior to that of the respective homozygotes. A less familiar form of balancing selection that is possibly even more important in nature than the heterotic type is diversifying (also called disruptive) selection. Most living species face a variety of environments, feed on different foods, grow in different soils, avoid or resist different enemies and parasites, etc. Diversifying selection favors different genotypes in different subenvironments or ecological niches; it occurs in experiments "when we maintain a single population by choosing more than one class of individuals to provide parents of each generation" (Thoday 1953, 1959).

Some diversifying selection is frequency-dependent. A genotype may be favored when rare and discriminated against when it becomes common or prevalent. The result will be a stable polymorphism. A frequency-dependent selection favoring the common and disfavoring the rare genotypes would, of course, lead to fixation of the favored genes and not to polymorphism. Diversifying and frequency-dependent natural selection will be discussed in Chapter 6.

## Heterotic Balance

The life cycle of sexually reproducing organisms consists of alternating phases. One phase (diplophase, zygote) has twice as many chromosomes as the others (haplophase, gamete, sex cell). Many mutants are more or less deleterious both in the homozygous and in the heterozygous condition, that is, when present in double dose as well as in single dose, in the diplophase. Yet some, though only a minority, of genetic variants give rise to hybrid vigor, heterosis, high Darwinian fitness in the heterozygous condition, although the same variants reduce fitness when homozygous. The behavior of such variants in cross-fertilizing populations is very different from that of variants neutral or deleterious in heterozygotes and hence subject to normalizing selection.

Let the fitness of the heterozygote $A_1A_2$ be unity and of the two homozygotes less than unity. The operation of the heterotic balancing selection will then be as follows:

| Genotype | $A_1A_1$ | $A_1A_2$ | $A_2A_2$ | Total Population |
|---|---|---|---|---|
| Darwinian fitness | $1 - s$ | 1 | $1 - t$ | $W$ |
| Initial frequency | $p^2$ | $2pq$ | $q^2$ | 1 |
| Frequency after selection | $p^2 - sp^2$ | $2pq$ | $q^2 - tq^2$ | $1 - sp^2 - tq^2$ |

The outcome of the selection will be, not fixation or elimination of either $A_1$ or $A_2$, but a genetic equilibrium at which both will occur in the population with predictable frequencies. Indeed, the rate of the gene frequency change per generation will be:

$$\Delta q = (q - tq^2)/(1 - sp^2 - tq^2) - q = pq(sp - tq)/(1 - sp^2 + tq^2)$$

At equilibrium no changes occur, the frequencies are constant, and $\Delta p$ and $\Delta q$ are zero. From the equation one obtains, then, $ps = qt$, and $p = t/(s + t)$ and $q = s/(s + t)$. When these frequencies of $A_1$ and $A_2$ are reached, a stable polymorphism is established. It should be noted that this form of natural selection will have some consequences that appear, at first sight, peculiar. It will cause retention in the population of all kinds of harmful genes, including those for crippling and even lethal hereditary diseases, provided only that the heterozygotes are at least slightly superior in fitness to the homozygotes. For example, suppose that $A_2A_2$ is lethal, and $A_1A_1$ is 95 percent as fit as the heterozygote $A_1A_2$. We have, then, $t = 1$ and $s = 0.05$. Equilibrium is reached when the lethal $A_2$ has the frequency $q = 0.05/(1 + 0.05) = 0.0476$. At equilibrium, the population will produce $q^2$, or 0.0023, that is, 23 per 10,000 lethal homozygotes.

The equilibrium frequencies of $p$ and $q$ depend only on the relative fitness of the two homozygotes, and not on the degree of heterosis. Thus, if both homozygotes are equally fit, the polymorphism is established at $p = q = 0.5$, regardless of whether the heterozygote is only slightly or is greatly superior to the homozygotes. The degree of heterotic superiority influences, not the equilibrium frequencies, but the number of generations needed to attain a stable equilibrium after the first appearance of a heterotic mutant or some environmental disturbance. It should also be noted that to possess a high Darwinian fitness the heterozygote need not be superior in all components of the adaptive value. Suppose, for example, that a heterozygote $A_1A_2$ is less viable but more fecund than $A_1A_1$, and more viable but less fecund than $A_2A_2$. If the product of relative viability and relative fecundity is higher in $A_1A_2$ than in $A_1A_1$ and $A_2A_2$, heterotic balanced polymorphism will be established and maintained.

## Chromosomal Inversion Polymorphism in Drosophila

In natural populations of outbreeding sexual species, polymorphisms abound in all kinds of externally visible morphological, physiological, and biochemical traits. We choose as a paradigm a rather recondite trait, chromosomal inversions in Drosophila flies, because these polymorphisms have been extensively studied both in nature and in experiment.

Very early in the work of the T. H. Morgan school on *Drosophila melanogaster*, inversions, or C-factors as they were then called, were detected as suppressors of crossing over. Sturtevant (1926) first showed that one of the C-factors had the gene arrangement in a part of the genetic linkage map of a certain chromosome inverted. With the introduction in the early nineteen thirties of the technique of examination of the giant chromosomes in the larval salivary glands, detection and description of inversions and other chromosomal aberrations in Drosophila became easy and accurate.

Suppose that an individual has the gene arrangements *ABCDEFGHI* and *AEDCBFGHI* in two homologous chromosomes; when these chromosomes pair, they must form a loop, shown in the upper right corner of Fig. 5.1. A second inversion may occur in the same chromosome. The location of the second inversion may be outside the limits of the first: *AEDCBFGHI* → *AEDCBFHGI*. Such inversions are called independent. An individual heterozygous for *ABCDEFGHI* and *AEDCBFHGI* will have a double loop, shown second from the top in Fig. 5.1. The

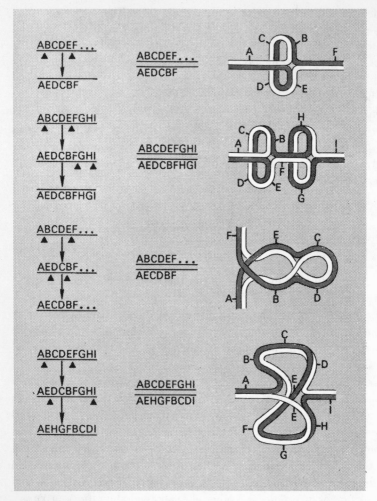

**FIGURE 5.1**

Chromosome pairing in the salivary gland cells of individuals heterozygous for inversions. Upper row—a single inversion; second from the top—two independent inversions; third from the top—two included inversions; lower row—overlapping inversions.

second inversion may occur inside the first, forming included inversions: *ABCDEFGHI → AEDCBFGHI → AECDBFGHI* (second from the bottom in Fig. 5.1). Finally, the second inversion may have one end inside and the other end outside the limits of the first; such inversions are overlapping: $ABCDEFGHI \rightarrow AEDCBFGHI \rightarrow AEHGFBCDI$ (the lower right corner in Fig. 5.1).

Overlapping inversions have interesting properties. Suppose we observe in different strains the arrangements $ABCDEFGHI$, $AEDCBFGHI$, and $AEHGFBCDI$. The first can arise from the second or give rise to the second through a single inversion. The same is true for the second and the third. But the third can arise from the first, or vice versa, only through the second arrangement as the probable intermediate step in the line of descent. If only the first and the third gene arrangements are found in some species, it is probable that the second remains to be discovered or that it existed in the past. If all three are found, the phylogenetic relationships are $1 \rightarrow 2 \rightarrow 3$ or $3 \rightarrow 2 \rightarrow 1$ or $1 \leftarrow 2 \rightarrow 3$, but not $1 \rightleftharpoons 3$. The existence of previously unknown gene arrangements was predicted in two different species, *Drosophila pseudoobscura* and *D. azteca*, and the predictions were verified by subsequent findings in nature (Dobzhansky and Sturtevant 1938 and Dobzhansky 1941).

Figure 5.2 shows a phylogenetic chart of gene arrangements found in one of the chromosomes (the third) in natural populations of two closely related species, *D. pseudoobscura* and *D. persimilis*. Only one of the gene arrangements, the Standard, occurs in both species, and only one, the Hypothetical, has been predicted as a necessary "missing link" but not yet actually found. Any two arrangements connected in Fig. 5.2 by a single arrow give a single inversion loop in the giant chromosomes of the salivary glands of heterozygous larvae. The four gene arrangements in the central portion of the diagram, the Standard, the Hypothetical, the Tree Line, and the Santa Cruz, may plausibly be supposed to be the ancestral ones, and the remainder to be derived from them as shown by the arrows.

None of the gene arrangements occurs over the entire distribution area of its species; and in no natural population is the complete collection of arrangements found. The geographic distribution of the gene arrangements will be discussed in Chapter 9. In some localities as many as eight arrangements occur together, and structural inversion homozygotes (flies having two chromosomes with the same gene arrangements) and inversion heterozygotes (flies with two chromosomes of a pair having different gene arrangements) are encountered in nature. The chromosomal inversions thus give rise to a remarkable polymorphism in fly populations (Dobzhansky and Epling 1944).

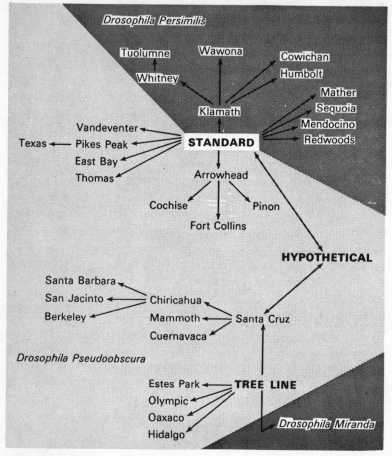

**FIGURE 5.2**

Phylogenetic relationships of the gene arrangements in the third chromosomes of Drosophila pseudoobscura, D. persimilis, and D. miranda.

Chromosomal inversion polymorphisms have been observed in natural populations of many species of Drosophila. Carson (personal communications) finds that, of the 68 species endemic to the Hawaiian archipelago and studied by him, about one-third have at least one polymorphic inversion. The proportion is higher among continental species, especially in the subgenus Sophophora, in which chromosomally monomorphic species are exceptional. The fairly extensive older literature has been reviewed by da Cunha (1955), Dobzhansky (1961), and Carson (1965). Among the most significant recent additions are the studies of Brncic and Koref-Santibañez (1964, 1965) on species of the *mesophragmatica* group; of Brncic (1966) on *Drosophila flavopilosa*, which is specialized to live in the flowers of a solanaceous plant, *Cestrum parqui*; of Prevosti (1964), Krimbas (1964), and Sperlich and Feuerbach (1966) on *D. subobscura*; of Stalker (1960, 1964a,b, 1965) on species of the *melanica* group; of Miller and Voelker (1968) on species of the *affinis* group; and of Carson, Clayton, and Stalker (1967) on species endemic to the Hawaiian Islands.

The polymorphism assumes quite different characters in different species of Drosophila; these variations are as yet not adequately understood, and many intriguing problems await investigation. Some species of Drosophila have become widespread geographically, owing to their association with man, and particularly with the fruit and vegetable trades. In most of such "domestic" species (*D. melanogaster, ananassae, immigrans, hydei, busckii*) the chromsomal polymorphism is little differentiated geographically, so that populations from remote and climatically unlike countries carry the same chromosomal variants, often with similar frequencies. In three domestic species (*D. simulans, virilis, repleta*) chromosomal polymorphisms are absent, and the populations everywhere are chromosomally monomorphic.

What the causal connections are between the uniformity or lack of chromosomal polymorphism and the ability of a species to adapt to man-made environments is a matter of speculation. Perhaps these chromosomally monomorphic species have reached some kind of "general-purpose genotypes" (Baker 1965), which confer upon them wide ranges of environmental tolerance. "Wild" species of Drosophila, which are not associated with man, show again a variety of conditions. Many, though not all of them, are chromosomally highly polymorphic, and the polymorphism is notably differentiated geographically (Chapter 9). In *Drosophila willistoni, paulistorum, robusta, subobscura,* and some others, inverted sections occur in every chromosome of the set, longer chromosomes having more inversions, approximately in proportion to their length, than shorter chromosomes. In other species, both wild and domestic, of which *D. pseudoobscura, persimilis, nebulosa,* and *busckii* are examples, the inversions are concentrated mostly in a single chromosome, which may or may not be the longest in the chromosomal set. The possibility that the variable chromosomes are especially prone to undergo breakage was ruled out for *D. pseudoobscura* long ago by Helfer (1941). Other conjectures have also been advanced, but none of them is supported by compelling evidence.

### Inversion Polymorphism as an Adaptive Trait

Individuals of chromosomally polymorphic species of Drosophila look outwardly identical, regardless of the gene arrangements in their chromosomes. Inversion heterozygosis can be detected in two ways. First, it causes a suppression, partial or complete, of the detectable gene recombination in the chromosomes involved. The second—and the easier—way of detection is to examine the gene arrangement cytologically by looking at the chromosomes under the microscope. The absence of visible changes in the external appearance of a fly with this trait led originally to the belief that inversions are adaptively neutral, a misinterpretation found in the second edition of the ancestor of this book (Dobzhansky 1941). The following facts have resulted in abandonment of this view.

If samples of a population of a species are taken repeatedly in the same locality, the relative frequencies of some chromosomes with different gene arrangements can be seen to undergo cyclic seasonal changes. Figure 5.3 summarizes the observations on populations of *Drosophila pseudoobscura* in a locality on Mount San Jacinto in California. These studies were conducted from 1939 to 1946, but later observations in the same and in other localities disclosed similar situations (Dobzhansky, Anderson, and Pavlovsky 1966 and references therein). The three commonest gene arrangements in this population are Standard (ST), Arrowhead (AR), and Chiricahua (CH). The frequency of ST decreases, and that of CH increases, from March to June; the opposite change takes place during the hot season, from June to August. Dubinin and Tiniakov (1945) and Borisov (1969) observed seasonal changes in the incidence of inversions also in populations of *D. funebris* near Moscow, Russia. We are witnessing here changes in the gene pool of populations; they are evolutionary changes by definition.

The seasonal genetic changes seemed startling at the time of their discovery, because their rapidity necessitated the assumption of very high

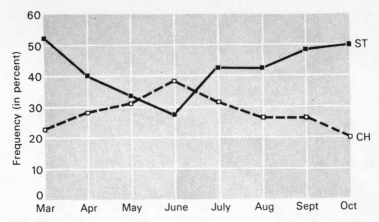

**FIGURE 5.3**

Seasonal changes in the frequencies of third chromosomes with
two different gene arrangement (ST and CH) in a population of
Drosophila pseudoobscura from a certain locality in California.

selection pressures. As Ford (1964) rightly remarked, "Their magnitude
would indeed be far beyond that envisaged twenty or twenty-five years
ago, but quite in keeping with that now being recognized as usual in
wild populations." Except for normalizing selection, which counter-
acts the spread of hereditary malformations, natural selection was
believed to act too slowly to be noticeable within a human lifetime.
Evidence of strong selection was obtained, however, in experimental
populations, maintained for several to many generations in population
cages (see Chapter 4). As described previously, a mixture of flies with
known proportions of chromosomal or genic variants is introduced into
the cage. The population reaches a maximum size consistent with the
amount of food given, usually within a single generation, and samples
of the population are taken from time to time for study.

An example of the results obtained in experimental populations of
*Drosophila pseudoobscura* appears in Fig. 5.4. Four populations were
started with about 10 percent Standard (ST) and 90 percent Chiricahua
(CH) third chromosomes derived from the population of a certain
locality in California. Within four months, a period that corresponds
under the conditions of the experiment to about four generations, the
frequency of ST approximately trebled. Thereafter it rose more slowly,
and reached an apparently stable equilibrium at close to 70 percent ST
and 30 percent CH. Making certain simplifying assumptions, the most

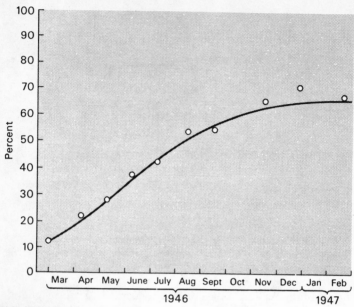

**FIGURE 5.4**

Frequency changes of third chromosomes with different gene arrangements in an experimental laboratory population of Drosophila pseudoobscura. The curve shows the frequencies of chromosomes with ST, competing with those with CH gene arrangements.

questionable of which is that the fitness of a genotype is independent of its frequency in the population, we can estimate from the slopes of the selection curves in Fig. 5.4 the fitnesses of the inversion homo- and heterozygotes (Wright and Dobzhansky 1946 and Dobzhansky and Pavlovsky 1953). The estimates turn out, averaging the results in the four experimental populations, as follows:

| Chromosome | Fitness (W) | Selection Coefficient (s) |
|---|---|---|
| ST/CH | 1 | 0 |
| ST/ST | 0.89 | 0.11 |
| CH/CH | 0.41 | 0.59 |

The differences between the selective values of the naturally occurring chromosomal variants are often quite striking. For example, Anderson, Oshima, et al. (1968) experimented with populations of *D. pseudoobscura* that contained third chromosomes with five different gene arrangements: ST, AR, CH, TL, and PP. The estimates of fitness obtained in one of the populations turned out as follows:

| *Heterokaryotypes* | | | | *Homokaryotypes* | |
|---|---|---|---|---|---|
| ST/AR | 1.00 | AR/PP | 0.33 | AR/AR | 0.58 |
| ST/CH | 0.76 | TL/PP | 0.27 | PP/PP | 0.45 |
| ST/PP | 0.61 | AR/CH | 0.26 | ST/ST | 0.35 |
| ST/TL | 0.51 | CH/PP | 0.26 | TL/TL | 0.35 |
| AR/TL | 0.45 | CH/TL | 0.19 | CH/CH | 0.26 |

Although these estimates are subject to large experimental and sampling errors, it is notable that the three fittest combinations are heterozygotes. All but one homozygote, and six out of ten heterozygotes, are less than half as fit as the fittest heterozygote (ST/AR). The selective forces acting on these populations are powerful indeed.

## The Superior Fitness of Heterokaryotypes

Although the evidence is unequivocal that at least some heterokaryotypes are superior in fitness to homokaryotypes, comparatively little is known about the physiological and ecological sources of this superiority. Several possibilities come to mind: differential survival between the egg and the adult stage, higher fecundity, greater sexual activity, superior longevity, or any combination of these. For the ST and CH gene arrangements in *Drosophila pseudoobscura*, experiments in population cages indicate the fitness sequence, ST/CH > ST/ST > CH/CH. Moos (1955) found the preadult viability to be ST/CH = ST/ST > CH/CH; the development rate ST/CH > ST/ST = CH/CH; the fecundity at 25°C ST/CH = ST/ST > CH/CH, and at 16°C ST/CH > ST/ST > CH/CH; and the longevity ST/CH > ST/ST = CH/CH. The overall fitness, computed from Moos's observations, taking ST/CH to be unity, is ST/ST = 1.08 and CH/CH = 0.44. Estimates from the changes observed in the frequencies of the chromosomes in the population cages are ST/CH = 1, ST/ST = 0.90, CH/CH = 0.41. The agreement between the two sets of estimates is probably about as close as could be expected. Brncic, Koref-Santibañez, et al. (1969) found that the rate of development of inversion heterozygotes in *D. pavani* is faster than that of homozygotes.

Spiess and his colleagues (Spiess and Langer 1964a,b, Spiess, Langer, and Spiess 1966, and E. B. Spiess and L. D. Spiess 1967) and Kaul and Parsons (1965) have made careful studies of the mating propensity of the carriers of different karyotypes in *Drosophila pseudoobscura* and *D. persimilis*. The picture revealed is quite complex: relative mating speeds are different for males and for females, they are not the same at different temperatures, they depend on the age of the flies, etc. Certain facts, however, stand out. Male heterozygotes are consistently superior in mating speed when compared to male homozygotes, whereas in females a corresponding superiority is less consistent or is absent. Males seem to play more active and females more passive roles in courtship, although it is up to the female to accept or reject a courting male. As an illustration, consider the differences in the mating propensity index for karyotypes of *D. pseudoobscura*:

| Karyotypes | Males | Females |
|---|---|---|
| AR/ST − AR/AR | +17.3 | + 3.7 |
| AR/TL − AR/AR | +17.6 | − 7.2 |
| AR/CH − AR/AR | + 1.3 | +11.7 |
| AP/PP − AR/AR | + 2.9 | −14.8 |
| ST/TL − ST/ST | +24.2 | − 3.8 |
| ST/CH − ST/ST | + 5.1 | + 6.7 |
| ST/PP − ST/ST | +10.6 | + 5.2 |
| Average | +11.3 | + 0.2 |

Differential mortality between the egg and the adult stage may change the proportion of karyotypes among the eggs compared to that among adult flies. To test this possibility, samples of eggs deposited by the flies in the population cages are removed and raised under optimal conditions, to enable all or most of them to develop into grown-up larvae and adults. Examination of the chromosomes reveals the karyotypes to be present in proportions demanded by the binomial square rule, $p^2$ ST/ST : $2pq$ ST/CH : $q^2$ CH/CH. The flies mate at random with respect to the chromosomal type. Now, samples are taken of the adult flies developed in the population cages, where there is stringent competition of larvae for a limited food supply, and the chromosomal constitution of these flies is determined. Among the adult flies, the heterozygotes are more, and the homozygotes are less, numerous than they should be according to the binomial square rule (Dobzhansky 1947).

In nature, as in experimental populations, differential mortality favoring the heterozygotes could maintain the polymorphism. Dobzhansky and Levene (1948) collected females of *Drosophila pseudoobscura* inseminated by males in their natural habitats and allowed them to produce offspring in the laboratory, under optimal conditions. In these offspring, the inversion homozygotes and heterozygotes were present with frequencies conforming to the binomial square rule. A small but significant excess of heterozygotes, and a corresponding deficiency of homozygotes, were found, however, among the adult male flies captured outdoors. This is not an invariable rule, and other polymorphic populations show no evidence of differential mortality.

The color polymorphism in the marine copepod *Tisbe reticulata*, though not known to be connected with chromosomal rearrangements, may be considered here. The studies of Battaglia (1958, 1964; Battaglia, Lazzaretto, and Malesani-Tajoli 1966, and references therein) have disclosed a situation remarkably paralleling that in Drosophila. Four color forms, determined by three alleles of a gene, occur in the lagoon of Venice. They are the recessive *trifasciata* ($vv$), the dominants *violacea* ($V^VV^V$ or $V^Vv$) and *maculata* ($V^MV^M$ or $V^Mv$), and the double dominant *violacea-maculata* ($V^VV^M$). The heterozygotes are superior in viability to the homozygotes. This is particularly clear in the progenies of *violacea-maculata*, which should theoretically produce 1 : 2 : 1 ratios of the homo- and heterozygotes. They actually produce, depending on the degree of crowding in the cultures, ratios from which the following viability estimates are derived:

| Crowding | $V^VV^V$ | $V^VV^M$ | $V^MV^M$ |
|----------|----------|----------|----------|
| Low | 0.89 | 1 | 0.90 |
| Intermediate | 0.67 | 1 | 0.76 |
| High | 0.66 | 1 | 0.62 |

If the viability of *violacea-maculata* is taken to be unity, the viabilities of the heterozygotes and the homozygotes for the recessive allele are:

$$V^Vv = 0.94, \qquad V^Mv = 0.92, \qquad vv = 0.85$$

The relative frequencies of the color forms differ in different parts of the lagoon of Venice, and Battaglia adduces evidence that these variations are responses to different salinities of the water. In experimental cultures only *violacea* survives at low salinity of 0.15 percent; at 0.25 percent the viability sequence is *maculata* > *violacea* > *trifasciata*, whereas at 0.45 percent it is *trifasciata* > *maculata* > *violacea*.

## Adaptedness of Polymorphic and Monomorphic Populations

Consider again a population of *Drosophila pseudoobscura* polymorphic for ST and CH third chromosomes. The estimates of the Darwinian fitness of the three karyotypes obtained above are ST/CH = 1, ST/ST = 0.89, and CH/CH = 0.41. Note that these estimates were obtained in populations kept at 25°C, whereas at 16°C the three karyotypes were not detectably different in fitness. The average fitness of a population, $\overline{W}$, would be greatest, 1.00, if it consisted of heterokaryotypes only. With sexual reproduction this situation cannot endure for more than a single generation, since homokaryotypes will inevitably appear. (Populations consisting only of heterozygotes are, however, possible with asexual reproduction or parthenogenesis; see Chapter 12.) It is easy to show that $\overline{W}$ is maximized when ST and CH reach equilibrium values of 0.84 and 0.16, respectively, by calculating the frequencies of the three karyotypes for different values of $p$ and $q$, multiplying them by fitness, and computing the average:

| Chromosome Frequency | Karyotype Frequency | | | Mean Fitness |
|---|---|---|---|---|
| ST = $p$, CH = $q$ | ST/CH | ST/ST | CH/CH | ($\overline{W}$) |
| $p = 0.99, q = 0.01$ | 0.020 | 0.980 | >0.000 | 0.892 |
| $p = 0.10, q = 0.90$ | 0.180 | 0.010 | 0.810 | 0.521 |
| $p = 0.84, q = 0.16$ | 0.269 | 0.706 | 0.026 | 0.908 |

The question that logically arises is, in what way is a population with a higher $\overline{W}$ better off than one with a lower $\overline{W}$ value? Apparently flourishing populations homozygous (monomorphic) for CH can easily be maintained in population cages. Beardmore, Dobzhansky, and Pavlovsky (1960) compared the productivity of monomorphic AR and CH and of polymorphic AR + CH populations kept in laboratory population cages. These cages have fifteen cups with culture medium, a fresh cup being inserted on alternate days or at other desired intervals. A polymorphic AR + CH population produced, on the average, 327 flies per cup, monomorphic AR 230 flies, and monomorphic CH only 202 flies. In terms of weight (biomass) the productivities were 261 milligrams for the polymorphic and 190 and 164 milligrams, respectively, for the two comparable monomorphic populations. An individual fly was, if anything, slightly smaller and lighter in the polymorphic than in the monomorphic populations. Nevertheless, the conclusion is inevitable that polymorphic populations can generate more flies and a greater biomass than monomorphic ones for the same amount of food.

The experiments just described were made at a temperature of 25°C. Battaglia and Smith (1961) obtained the same results at 16°C. Far from being a confirmation of the earlier work, their results were rather unexpected; as stated previously, if one judges by the lack of changes in the relative frequencies of the chromosomal types at 16°, the Darwinian fitnesses of the karyotypes at that temperature are at least not very different from each other.

A statistic, $r_m$, the innate capacity for increase or the intrinsic rate of natural increase (Andrewartha and Birch 1954), has been used by Dobzhansky, Lewontin, and Pavlovsky (1964) and by Ohba (1967) to estimate the adaptedness of polymorphic and monomorphic populations of *Drosophila pseudoobscura*. What this statistic measures (to oversimplify the matter considerably) is the rate of growth of a population when the quantities of food, space, and other resources are not limiting, and predators and parasites are excluded. Realistically, such a situation may occur in Drosophila when a small number of overwintering individuals encounter amounts of food that become limiting only after the population increases manifold. Other examples are readily imaginable. The value $r_m$ is obtained from equation:

$$\int_0^\infty e^{-r_m x} l_x m_x \, \sigma x = 1$$

where $e$ is the base of natural logarithms, $l_x$ the probability at birth of being alive at age $x$, and $m_x$ the number of female offspring produced in unit time by a female aged $x$. With an animal like Drosophila, one finds out the proportion of eggs that survive to become adults, the time the development takes, the adult longevity, and the numbers of eggs deposited by a female per day at different ages. In the experiments of Dobzhansky, Lewontin, and Pavlovsky, the tests were made deliberately in a rather stringent environment, since the adults tested developed in crowded population cages. The parameters $r_m$, at 25°C, were found for two polymorphic and four monomorphic populations:

| AR + CH | Polymorphic | 0.220 |
| AR + PP | Polymorphic | 0.214 |
| AR | Monomorphic | 0.207 |
| AR | Monomorphic | 0.205 |
| CH | Monomorphic | 0.192 |
| PP | Monomorphic | 0.170 |

In Ohba's experiments (1967) the environment was made as close as possible to the optimal state. The $r_m$ values were higher, but the polymorphic populations were no longer superior:

| AR + CH | Polymorphic | 0.269 and 0.266 |
| AR | Monomorphic | 0.275 |
| CH | Monomorphic | 0.263 |

Darwinian fitness is a measure of the reproductive success of the carriers of a given genotype in relation to that of the carriers of other genotypes. It is a comparative measure; the fitness of a population is meaningful if this population competes with others. The innate capacity for increase, on the other hand, is an absolute measure of one aspect of the adaptedness of a population under a given set of environmental conditions. It is not surprising that Darwinian fitness and adaptedness tend to be correlated, and yet it should be realized that they measure different qualities or properties of life (Dobzhansky 1968a,b).

A knowledge of the adaptedness of populations monomorphic for certain genotypes or karyotypes may or may not predict the Darwinian fitness of the genotypes in a polymorphic population, or vice versa. Ayala (1969a) has estimated the abilities of populations of *D. pseudoobscura* monomorphic and polymorphic for AR and CH gene arrangements in the third chromosome to compete with another species, *D. serrata*. A serial transfer technique has been used. Known numbers of adults of both species are placed in a culture bottle, allowed to deposit eggs, and transferred to fresh cultures at weekly intervals. When young adults emerge in the cultures where the eggs were deposited, the flies are etherized, counted, and added to the bottle with the adult and ovipositing individuals. The numbers and proportions of the two species are determined weekly. *Drosophila serrata* is a stronger competitor, and its proportions gradually increase. The fitness of *D. serrata* relative to monomorphic and polymorphic populations of *D. pseudoobscura* was found to be as follows:

| | |
|---|---|
| Monomorphic AR | 1.74 |
| Polymorphic  AR + CH | 1.62 |
| Monomorphic CH | 1.95 |

## Polymorphic Inversions as Supergenes

Despite their outward uniformity, representatives of the same species of Drosophila with different gene arrangements in their chromosomes may be perceptibly, even strikingly, different in their adaptive properties. The nature and the origin of these differences pose challenging questions. As pointed out above, the most prominent genetic effect of heterozygosis for inversions is suppression of gene recombination in the chromosomes that carry them. If the inverted and the noninverted chromosomes differed in a single gene, the suppression of recombination would be neither useful nor harmful. The suppression is beneficial, however, if the chromosomes carry supergenes, that is, complexes of linked genes that are favorable in some particular combinations but not in others. Suppose that the chromosomes $A_1B_1C_1D_1$ and $A_2B_2C_2D_2$ yield a highly fit heterozygote, but the recombination products, such as $A_1B_1C_2D_2$ and others, are inferior in fitness. Such mutually concordant gene complexes are *coadapted* to each other. Inversions binding together coadapted gene complexes will be favored by natural selection.

Experimental validation of the coadapted supergene hypothesis was achieved through studies of chromosomes of *Drosophila pseudoobscura* of different geographic origins. It will be shown in Chapter 7 that some of the gene arrangements are geographically widely distributed. Experimental populations may, then, be planned in two ways: the competing chromosomes may be derived from flies collected either in the same locality or in more or less remote localities. With chromosomes of geographically uniform origin, experiments like the one depicted in Fig. 8.4A give repeatable results; provided that the environment is adequately controlled, the slope of the selection curve, the equilibrium level, and the fitness estimates are nearly the same.

With chromosomes of geographically unlike derivations, however, the outcome becomes strangely unpredictable. Figure 8.4B shows the results for four experimental populations, all started simultaneously with the four the results of which are depicted in Fig. 8.4A. The initial frequencies were again 20 percent ST chromosomes from California, and 80 percent CH chromosomes, but this time from Mexican localities. Only one of the populations, that symbolized by triangles, achieved equilibrium. The three others followed erratic courses, tending toward fixation of ST and elimination of CH chromosomes. Calculations of the fitness of the three karyotypes give irregular results, the heterozygote (heterokaryotype) ST/CH no longer being the fittest. The CH chromosomes from California and from Mexico look identical under the microscope, and yet the experiment shows that they must carry different complexes of genes.

Wallace (1954) made the observation that "triads" of overlapping inversions rarely occur with high frequencies in the same population of *Drosophila pseudoobscura*. The following gene arrangements would constitute a triad: $A_1B_1C_1D_1E_1F_1G_1H_1$, $A_2E_2D_2C_2B_2F_2G_2H_2$, and $A_3E_3D_3G_3F_3B_3C_3H_3$. Suppose now that the heterokaryotype $B_1C_1D_1E_1/E_2D_2C_2B_2$ has a high fitness, and so does $C_2B_2F_2G_2/G_3F_3B_3C_3$. The part of the chromosome $F_1G_1H_1/F_2G_2H_2$ is, however, free to combine in the first heterozygote, and the part $A_2E_2D_2/A_3E_3D_3$ can undergo free crossing over in the second, thus disrupting the coadaptation. No such disruption will occur in the heterokaryotype with a double inversion (the first and the third of the gene arrangements above). Although Levitan, Carson, and Stalker (1954) found the rule of avoidance of triads inapplicable to *D. robusta*, it seems to fit the situation in several other species.

A more direct demonstration of coadapted supergenes carried in inversions was made in *Drosophila willistoni* and *D. paulistorum* (Dobzhansky and Pavlovsky 1958). In some South American populations of these species, more than half of the individuals found in nature are heterozygous for certain inversions. High frequencies of the inversion heterozygotes are maintained also in experimental populations set up in the laboratory with strains from any natural locality. Quite different is the behavior of populations started with hybrids between strains derived from localities some hundreds of kilometers apart. In such populations the inversion heterozygotes become much less frequent than in the parental populations. The interpretation of these findings is simple. In each locality, the chromosomes with different gene arrangements are coadapted to yield highly fit heterozygotes. The chromosomes of the inhabitants of geographically remote localities need not be coadapted, since they do not form heterozygotes, except in contrived laboratory populations. In these artificial populations, chromosomes with the same gene arrangements but with different complexes of genes can undergo recombination freely, thus disrupting the coadapted supergenes.

There is no way to tell in how many loci the coadapted supergenes, such as those locked in the ST and CH chromosomes of *Drosophila pseudoobscura*, may differ. An inversion, to be retained in a population in which it first arises and then to spread to other populations of a species, should presumably possess some adaptive advantage. One possible source of such an advantage is position effect (Sperlich 1958, 1966a,b). The action of a gene in the development may depend not only on its own structure but also on its neighbors in the linear series of genes in a chromosome (see Lewis 1967 for a review). It has been known for a long time that inversions and translocations that arise by mutation in laboratory experiments are often accompanied by lethal or visible effects resembling gene mutations. Hence it is conceivable that the inversions found in nature are selectively favorable because of the changes induced by position effects. The difficulty is that this hypothesis demands a coincidence of at least two rare events—mutational origin of an inversion and of adaptively valuable position effects.

A more plausible hypothesis is that a newly arisen inversion may be favored by natural selection if it causes an adaptively valuable linkage disequilibrium, that is, if it binds together two or more genes in the same chromosome that give fit heterozygotes with other chromosomes present in the same breeding population. Variant genes present in natural populations do produce positive or negative fitness effects, depending on the other genes with which they are associated in the same chromosome—this has been demonstrated, for example, by the experiments in synthetic lethals and the release of genetic variability by recombination (Chapter 3). Crossing over and recombination of linked genes are undesirable when they break up favorable gene associations.

Prakash and Lewontin (1968) have given most direct evidence of coadaptation and linkage disequilibrium in third-chromosome inversions in *Drosophila pseudoobscura*. It can be seen in Fig 5.2 that the gene arrangements in this chromosome belong to two groups or "phylads," those descended from Standard and those derived from Santa Cruz. Two genes, one responsible for the larval protein Pt-10 and the other for the enzyme alpha-amylase, are each represented by different alleles in the two phylads. The geological age of the phylads is not known, but Prakash and Lewontin are on safe ground in concluding that "different inversions are genetically differentiated and the differentiation has been maintained over several million generations by natural selection."

Vann (1966) and Sperlich (1966a) submitted the coadaptation hypothesis to different tests. Homozygous lines of *Drosophila melanogaster* and *D. pseudoobscura* were obtained by inbreeding or by special crosses with marker genes. Inversions and translocations were then induced by X-ray treatment. Most of these chromosomal aberrations were lost within a small number of generations in experimental populations. They were retained for longer periods, or established balanced polymorphisms, when the homozygous lines carrying them were outcrossed to various more or less unrelated lines of the same species. The heterozygotes for an inverted chromosome and one with the original gene arrangement were then also heterozygotes for some, presumably fairly numerous, genes. Such heterozygotes had, at least in some instances, heterotic properties.

The problems of the adaptive consequences of linkage disequilibrium, and particularly of the origin of inversion polymorphisms, have also been studied by mathematical analysis and by computer simulation. Papers of Lewontin (1967b), Fraser and Burnell (1967), and Bodmer and Felsenstein (1967) give critical summaries and further references to the pertinent literature.

### *Inversion Polymorphism in Organisms Other than Drosophila*

Inversion polymorphisms are particularly frequent in natural populations of Drosophilidae and related families of the order of flies (Diptera). This is probably not accidental. Male meiosis in these insects does not involve the formation of chiasmata between paired homologous chromosomes, there is no crossing over, and blocks of genes in the same chromosome are completely linked. Chiasmata and recombination of linked genes do occur at meiosis in females. The consequences of chiasma formation are different for paracentric inversions (inversions of chromosome sections not including the centromere) and for pericentric inversions (sections including the centromere). The situation with a paracentric inversion is shown schematically in Fig. 5.5. Of the four chromosomes resulting from the meiotic divisions, one has two centromeres, one has none, and two are normal non-cross-over chromosomes. It happens that one of the normal chromosomes is always included in the egg nucleus, while the other three are eliminated into the polar bodies. The fertility of females, as well as of males heterozygous for paracentric inversions, is consequently undiminished in comparison to that of individuals free of inversions. Inversion heterozygosis being per se a neutral trait, a small amount of hybrid vigor suffices to maintain the polymorphism.

The situation is different with pericentric inversions. Here chiasmata inside these inversions give rise to chromosomes lacking some genes and carrying other genes in excess, and consequently to a partial sterility of heterozygous females (Fig. 5.6).

Inversion polymorphism is, nevertheless, not restricted to forms lacking chiasmata in male meiosis. Giant chromosomes of larval salivary gland cells were discovered originally, not in Drosophila, but in midges of the family Chironomidae. Many species of this family are highly polymorphic for inversions (Keyl 1962, Martin 1965, Blaylock 1966, and references therein). Yet chiasmata are formed in male meiosis in Chironomus. Beerman (1956) found the solution to this puzzle—the fertility of male inversion heterozygotes in Chironomus is not reduced, presumably because the sperms containing abnormal chromatids fail to function. Inversion polymorphisms have also been observed in natural populations of mosquitoes (Kitzmiller 1967, and Kitzmiller, Frizzi, and Baker 1967), of simuliids or black flies (Rothfels 1956, Pasternak 1964, and Grinchuk 1967), of cecidomyids (Kraczkiewicz 1950), of Liriomyza (Mainx, Fiala, and Kogerer 1956), of *Phryne cincta* (Wolf 1968), and of other flies.

In organisms that lack giant chromosomes in the salivary glands, the detection of inversions is difficult and may be impossible. Crossing over within a paracentric inversion gives, as shown in Fig. 5.5, a dicentric and an acentric chromatid, which appear at the anaphase of the first meiotic division as a "bridge" and as an acentric fragment lagging between the disjoining groups of chromosomes. Although chromosome bridges and fragments may arise also because of abnormal "stickiness" of the chromosomes (Newman 1966), their formation is usually a reliable indicator of inversion heterozygosity. Such heterozygosity has been detected in populations of many species of plants; classical examples are *Paris quadrifolia* (Geitler 1938) and species of

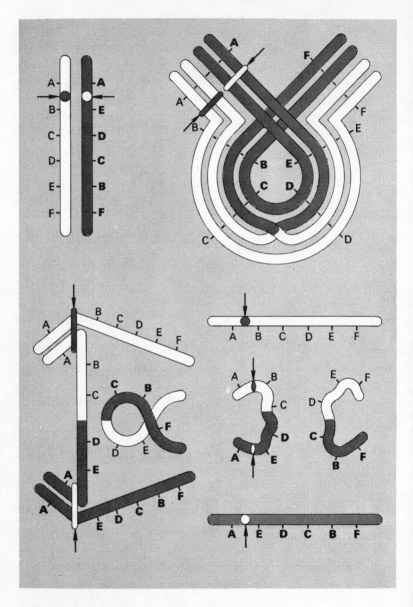

**FIGURE 5.5**

Crossing over in a heterozygote for a paracentric inversion. The centromeres are marked by arrows.

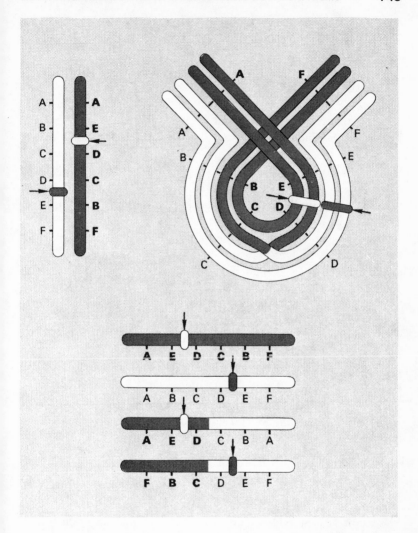

**FIGURE 5.6**

Crossing over in a heterozygote for a pericentric inversion. The centromeres are marked by arrows.

Paeonia (Stebbins 1939, Walters 1942, and Marquardt 1952), of Polygonatum (Suomalainen 1947b), and of Trillium (Haga and Kurabayashi 1954, and Haga 1956).

On the other hand, the absence of anaphase bridges and fragments at meiosis is not valid evidence of lack of inversion heterozygosity. This is true simply because chiasmata in the chromosome parts outside the inverted segments do not result in chromosome bridges and fragments; inversion heterozygosity, which suppresses chiasma formation within the inversions, will be undetectable by observations on meiotic division figures. Hence, although no instances of bridges and fragments in human meiosis have been securely established as yet, it is by no means certain that inversion polymorphism is absent or even rare in human populations.

Although chromosomal polymorphisms in natural populations of several species of grasshoppers have long been known, our understanding of them is due to the masterly studies of White and his collaborators (White 1949, 1954, 1957, 1968; White and Nickerson 1951; Lewontin and White 1960; White, Cheney, and Key 1963; White, Lewontin, and Andrew 1963; and White, Carson, and Cheney 1964). The polymorphisms manifest themselves mainly in the presence at meiosis of unequal bivalents, which consist of chromosome partners having the centromeres in different positions, one of them more or less median (metacentric) and the other subterminal (acrocentric). Such centromere shifts are best interpreted as due to pericentric inversions, in which the two breaks in the chromosome occur at different distances from the centromere. A possible alternative explanation is that the centromeres themselves are transposed to different locations in the chromosome.

At any rate, no chiasmata occur in the sections between the centromeres, and therefore the fertility of the heterozygotes is not reduced. In some instances, evidence has been obtained that inversion heterozygotes are in fact more viable than the corresponding homozygotes. Furthermore, in the Australian grasshopper species *Moraba scurra* the inversions in different chromosomes interact to produce a series of viability values (Lewontin and White 1960). With the two variants of one chromosome denoted as A1 and A2, and those of another chromosome as B1 and B2, the population of a certain locality showed the following relative viabilities (the most viable type being taken as unity):

|       | A1A1 | A1A2 | A2A2 |
|-------|------|------|------|
| B1B1  | 0.84 | 1.00 | 0.81 |
| B1B2  | 0.64 | 1.00 | 0.97 |
| B2B2  | 0.39 | 0.68 | 0.92 |

Unequal bivalents, interpretable most plausibly as due to pericentric inversions, have been found in natural populations of the beetle Pissodes (Manna and Smith 1959), of mice Leggada and Mastomys (Matthey 1964a, 1966a, b), and of the black rat, *Rattus rattus* (Yosida, Nakamura, and Fukaya 1965). They have also been found in laboratory colonies of Norway rats, *Rattus norvegicus* (Yosida and Amano 1965, and Bianchi and Molina 1966), and of *Peromyscus maniculatus* (Ohno, Weiler, et al. 1966). Whether these inversions originated in nature or in captivity is not wholly clear.

## Translocations and Other Chromosomal Polymorphisms

Let two nonhomologous chromosomes be symbolized as AB and CD. A translocation, that is, an interchange of blocks of genes, transforms them into AD and BC. The translocation heterozygote will form at meiosis a ring of chromosomes:

AB–BC–CD–DA

Six kinds of gametes may be formed, depending on whether alternate or adjacent chromosomes go to the same pole at meiotic divisions:

1. AB, CD    3. AB, DA    5. CD, BC
2. BC, DA    4. AB, BC    6. DA, CD

Gametes 1 and 2 are regular or euploid, since they contain all the chromosome parts once and only once; the remainder (3–6) are exceptional (or aneuploid), carrying some chromosome parts in duplicate and being deficient for other parts. In plants, pollen grains and ovules with duplications and deficiencies are usually aborted, unless the duplicated and deficient parts are very short or the plant is a polyploid. Animal gametes may function regardless of whether they carry normal or abnormal chromosome sets, but the zygote formed by the union of an euploid and an aneuploid gamete will die or develop into a malformed or weak individual. Translocation heterozygotes are accordingly semisterile, or a part of their progeny is of low fitness. Gametes, especially male ones, are produced in most organisms in so great an abundance that the loss of a fraction of them is more easily tolerable than the elimination of many zygotes.

By and large, a greater amount of heterosis is needed for balancing selection to maintain translocation than inversion polymorphisms. And yet some of the genetic systems in the living world are versatile enough for this handicap of translocation polymorphisms to be overcome. Indeed, the disjunction of chromosomes at meiosis is under genetic control, and translocation heterozygotes can be selected to produce a majority of the euploid (1 and 2 in the above scheme) and few or no aneuploid gametes (3–6). An elegant demonstration of this has been obtained in some plants. In rye (Thompson 1956, Hrishi and Müntzing 1960, and Rees 1961) and also in Chrysanthemum (Rana 1965, and Rana and Jain 1965), translocation heterozygotes occur in populations, and the proportions of regular and exceptional gametes vary from strain to strain. By artificial selection Sun and Rees (1967) have achieved in rye, which is normally a cross-fertilizing plant, striking reductions of the frequencies of aneuploid gametes.

In most animal populations translocation heterozygotes occur only as rare mutants, presumably to be eliminated by normalizing selection. Among many thousands of chromosome complements of several species of Drosophila examined in salivary gland cells by the present writer, only two translocation heterozygotes were seen: one in *Drosophila ananassae* from Brazil and the other in *D. pseudoobscura* from Arizona. Translocation heterozygotes in isolated individuals were found in the grasshoppers *Gesonula punctifrons* (Sarkar 1955) and *Chorthippus brunneus* (Lewis and John 1964). In man, healthy members of some families are translocation heterozygotes; grossly abnormal births occur, however, in such families because of the formation of duplication-deficiency gametes (Hauschteck, Mürset, et al. 1966, Court-Brown 1967, and Aya, Kuroti, et al. 1967). John and Lewis (1958, 1959) found translocation heterozygotes quite abundant in some colonies of the cockroach *Periplaneta americana* and in *Blaberus doscoidalis,* and adduced good evidence that these heterozygotes are superior in fitness to the homozygotes.

In Chapter 12 we shall discuss briefly the bizzare genetic systems evolved in some evening primroses (Oenothera), which are founded on translocation heterozygosis. Translocation polymorphisms have been found in natural populations of many plants. They were known for a long time in Jimson weed, *Datura stramonium* (Blakeslee, Bergner, and Avery 1937) and *D. meteloides* (Snow and Dunford 1961), in Paeonia (Walters 1942), in Trillium (Haga and Kurabayashi 1954), and in Clarkia (Håkansson 1942 and Mooring 1958, 1961). In at least some of these translocations the distribution of the chromosomes at meiosis is so regular that few pollen grains and ovules are aborted because of the duplications and deficiencies in their gene complements; other translocation heterozygotes do cause such abortion, but the fitness of the heterozygotes appears to be high enough to more than compensate for this loss.

An interesting kind of translocation involves the union of two rod-shaped chromosomes into a single V-shaped body, or vice versa. If each of two chromosomes has a subterminal centromere, breaks in the vicinity of the centromeres, followed by reunions of fragments, may result in one chromosome with a median centromere, and another centromere with only a little chromosomal material, which is subsequently lost. Some cytologists accept the existence of chromosomes with terminal centromeres; unions of two such chromosomes may occur because of centric fusions, while chromosomes with median centromeres may give rise by centric fission to two chromosomes with terminal centromeres. Finally, some groups of animals have diffuse instead of localized centromeres, removing most of the constraints on the fragmentations and unions of the chromosomes. In any event, increases and reductions of the chromosome numbers in related species are fairly ubiquitious in the animal as well as in the plant kingdom.

Consider, however, what happens to new chromosomes formed by centric fusion or separation. Let a chromosome with a median centromere be AB, and the two semihomologous chromosomes with terminal centromeres be A and B, respectively. Heterozygous individuals will be formed, in which the AB chromosome will pair at meiosis with A and with B. If this trivalent association disjoins so that some gametes receive AB and others A + B, the fertility of the heterozygote will not be affected. On the other hand, formation of gametes AB +A, AB + B, A, and B alone will lead to inviable or abnormal zygotes.

It appears that such trivalents give viable disjunction products often enough for them to occur in natural populations of some species. Staiger (1954, 1955) showed that about 1 percent of individuals of the snail *Purpura lapillus* near Roscoff, France, are translocation heterozygotes. In the isopode *Jaera albifrons* the chromosome numbers vary from 19 to 29 (Lécher 1967). In African mice of the subgenus Leggada, Matthey (1963, 1964a, 1966a) found individuals with 31, 32, 33, and 34 chromosomes in the populations of one species, and with 20, 21, and 22 chromosomes in populations of another species. White, Carson, and Cheney (1964) made a detailed study of the chromosomal races of the grasshopper *Moraba viatica* having 17 and 19 chromosomes, respectively; the distribution areas of the two overlap in a narrow belt, and there individuals with trivalent associations are found. The fertility of the heterozygotes is reduced, a fact that, according to the authors, explains the narrowness of the overlap. Manna and Smith (1959) found numerical chromosomal polymorphisms in bark weevils, Pissodes, and Smith (1962, 1966) in the ladybird beetle *Chilocorus stigma* and closely related species. The populations of the latter are monomorphic (26 chromosomes) in the eastern United States, but in Canada there is a gradient from east to west, with chromosome numbers dwindling to 22, 20, and 14.

Duplication and deficiencies for chromosome sections are rarely involved in polymorphisms in natural populations, and there is no proven case of such polymorphism being maintained by balancing selection. Five kinds of Y chromosomes have long been known in *Drosophila pseudoobscura,* and three in *D. persimilis* (Dobzhansky 1937). The differences in length between these Y chromosomes are due to greater or lesser amounts of heterochromatic materials. Variations in the size of the Y chromosomes have also been recorded in healthy individuals in human populations (Gripenberg 1964; Makino, Sasaki, et al. 1963; Makino and Takagi 1965, and Cohen, Shaw, and MacCluer 1966). If the average length of chromosomes 17-20 in the normal set is taken as unity, the Y chromosome common in Japanese populations has a length of 0.87, but some individuals have Y's measuring more than 1.0 on such a scale.

### From Intraspecific Polymorphism
### to Species Differential

No two species have the same genes, and present indications are that the numbers of genes that differentiate even closely related species are, in general, fairly large (Chapter 11). By contrast, species may have either the same or different numbers of chromosomes, and the gene arrangements in these chromosomes may be either similar or strikingly different. Speciation is usually, but not necessarily, accompanied by chromosomal differentiation. Carson, Clayton, and Stalker (1967) have called species with identical gene arrangements homosequential. These authors examined the disc patterns in the salivary gland chromosomes in many species of Drosophila endemic in the Hawaiian Islands. Four groups of homosequential species, with 3, 2, 2, and 2 species, respectively, were found. Kastritsis (1969) found the neotropical species *Drosophila guaramunu* and *D. griseolineata* to be also homosequential.

Among some 17,138 plant species examined cytologically up to 1955, the haploid numbers range from 2 (in *Haplopappus gracilis* and some molds) and 3 (in several species of Crepis), to more than 250 in a species of fern. The most frequent numbers are 9, 8, 11, 12, 7, 14, and 13, in that order (Grant 1963). Among 3317 animal species studied up to 1951, the numbers range from 2 pairs in some flatworms and scale insects (Icerya) to 127 in the crab Eupagurus (Makino 1951 and White 1954). It is frequently stated that the nematode worm *Ascaris megalocephala* has 2 or even a single chromosome in its sex cells; however, these chromosomes are compound and fall apart into more numerous elements in the somatic cells.

More important than changes in chromosome numbers are changes in the internal organization of the chromosomes, that is, in the gene arrangement. Such changes are brought about mainly by inversions and translocations of chromosome segments. We have seen above that the former are more likely to establish balanced polymorphisms in outbreeding populations than are the latter. A higher degree of heterozygous advantage is needed to compensate for the loss of fertility in translocation than in inversion heterozygotes. At least in Drosophila, species differences are due far more often to inversion than to translocation of blocks of genes. Nevertheless, translocations have played a not insignificant role in chromosome repatterning. If polyploidy is temporarily omitted from consideration, it can be said that changes in chromosome numbers are brought about by various kinds of translocations. Multiplications and deletions of whole chromosomes are even less likely than translocations to be retained in populations, except in polyploids which reproduce asexually or by parthenogenesis (see Chapter 12).

## Gene Arrangements in Drosophila Species Hybrids

If species of Drosophila can be hybridized, the giant chromosomes in the salivary gland cells permit more precise comparison of the chromosome structures in the species crossed than is attainable by any other method. All degrees of differentiation are found. As stated in the preceding section, some pairs of species are homosequential, that is, show no recognizable differences in the gene arrangement. Sturtevant (1929) found the genetic maps of the chromosomes of *Drosophila melanogaster* and *D. simulans* to be similar, except for a long inversion in the third chromosome. Pätau (1935), Kerkis (1936), and Horton (1939) studied the salivary gland chromosomes in the hybrids. Aside from the inversion in the third chromosome, these authors found 24 short sections, each involving a few stainable discs, that differ in the two species. Among these, 6 sections seem to be minute inversions. The remainder are undefined changes that may be minute inversions, translocations, or qualitative changes in the chromosomal materials.

*Drosophila pseudoobscura* and *D. persimilis* differ in two moderately long inversions in the X and in the second chromosome. Usually there is also a second inversion in the X, and an inversion in the third chromosome, that is, a total of four inversions. The variations in the numbers of the inversions that distinguish the species are due to differences between the strains of the parental species. No small undefined differences, like those in the hybrids between *D. melanogaster* and *D. simulans,* are present (Tan 1935, and Dobzhansky and Epling 1944).

The morphological resemblance between *D. pseudoobscura* and *D. persimilis,* on one hand, and *D. miranda,* on the other, is at least as close as that between *D. melanogaster* and *D. simulans.* Their metaphase chromosomes are identical, except that one of the autosomes of *D. pseudoobscura* is present only once in the chromosome group of the *D. miranda* male; *D. pseudoobscura* is XX and XY in the female and the male, respectively, whereas the *D. miranda* female is $X^1X^1X^2X^2$ and the male $X^1X^2Y$. The Y chromosome of *D. miranda* harbors some material homologous to that in the $X^2$ of the same species and in the corresponding autosomal pair of *D. pseudoobscura*. The origin of *D. miranda* must have involved a translocation of that autosome onto the Y chromosome, with subsequent rearrangement of the autosomal material by repeated inversions.

Dobzhansky and Tan (1936) have compared the gene arrangements in the *D. pseudoobscura* and *D. miranda* chromosomes in the salivary glands of hybrid larvae. The differences are so profound that the chromosomes either fail to pair entirely or else form extremely complex pairing configurations. Genes that in one species lie adjacent may, in the other species, be far apart in the same chromosome. Some small blocks of genes that are located in the same chromosome in one species have apparently been translocated to different chromosomes in the other. Finally, homologues of certain sections in *D. pseudoobscura* have not been detected in *D. miranda,* and vice versa. It seems, then, that some chromosome sections have been so thoroughly rebuilt by repeated inversions or translocations that their disc patterns in the salivary gland chromosomes no longer resemble each other, and pairing of the homologous genes does not take place.

A comparison of the chromosomes of *D. pseudoobscura* and *D. miranda* is shown in Fig. 5.7. If the chromosome sections that seem to be present in one species only are disregarded, the differences between the two species are due chiefly to repeated inversions and to a lesser extent to translocation of blocks of genes. To derive the gene arrangement in the chromosomes of one species from that in the other, a minimum of 49 breakage points (and perhaps twice as many) is necessary.

Patterson, Stone, and their colleagues have done excellent analysis of the evolution of the chromosomes in 12 species and subspecies of the *virilis* group of Drosophila (reviews in Patterson and Stone 1952, and Stone, Guest, and Wilson 1960). At least 92, and possibly as many as 120, inversions have occurred in the phylogeny of this group. If the gene arrangements in the chromosomes of the Oriental species *Drosophilia virilis* are used as the standard, the probable phylogeny of the group can be traced as shown in Fig. 5.8. Three of the 15 chromosome complements in this figure are hypothetical—Primitive I, II, and III. They are reconstructed with the aid of the overlapping inversions analysis described above and illustrated in Figs. 5.1 and 5.2. Primitive I differs from the existing *D. virilis* in a single inversion in the second chromosome. This is the ancestral gene arrangement of the whole group. Two more inversions, A and B in the X chromosome, transform Primitive I into Primitive II, which is the ancestor of the closely knit triplet of North American species *D. texana, D. novamexicana,* and *D. americana.* These species differ in, respectively, 6, 7, and 9 inversions from the Primitive II ancestors. Primitive III differs from Primitive I by 6 inversions in the autosomes, plus several rearrangements in the X chromosome that defied analysis because of their complexity. Primitive III is the ancestor of the Japanese *D.*

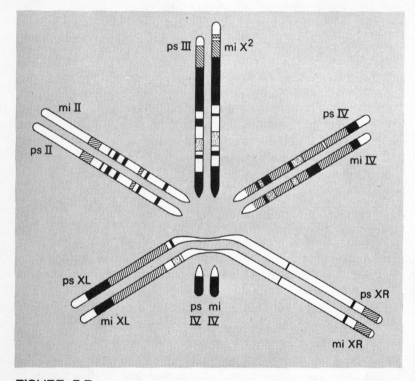

**FIGURE 5.7**

The gene arrangements in the homologous chromosomes of Drosophila pseudoobscura and D. miranda. Sections with similar gene arrangements are shown white, inverted sections crosshatched, translocations stippled, and those of obscure homologies black.

On facing page: Phylogenetic relationships of the gene arrangements in species of the virilis group of the genus Drosophila. The chromosomes of Drosophila virilis are taken as the standard; the inverted sections in various lines of descent are marked by letters. (After Stone, Guest, and Wilson)

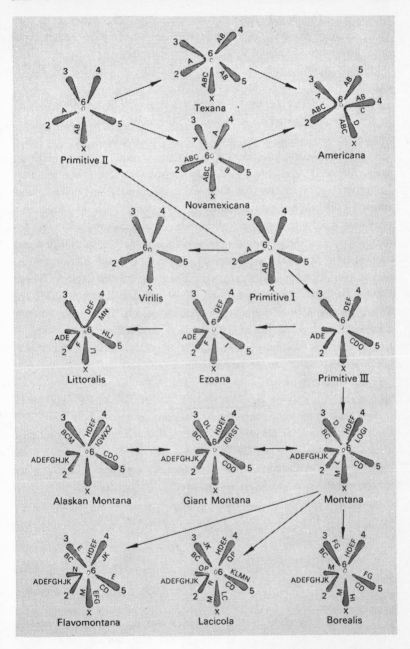

**FIGURE 5.8**

*ezoana* and the North American *D. montana.* The latter is in turn the presumed ancestor of 5 more species, which have accumulated more and more inversions as their evolution progressed. Some descent relationships that are uncertain are indicated in Fig. 5.8 by double arrows.

A great majority of the inversions in the phylogeny of the *virilis* group are paracentric, not including the centromere. This is as it should be, because crossing over within pericentric inversions, which include the centromere, results in partial sterility of the heterozygotes for such inversions (see above). And yet, the transition from Primitive I to Primitive III involved a pericentric inversion, which transformed the ancestral rodlike chromosome with a subterminal centromere into a V-shaped chromosome with a submedian centromere. This V-shaped chromosome was then passed to all the descendants of Primitive III, as shown in Fig. 5.8. For the same reason— partial sterility of heterozygotes—translocations are infrequent. Nevertheless, a translocation transformed the rod-shaped chromosomes 2 and 3 of Primitive II into a V-shaped chromosome in *D. texana.* Another translocation formed the X chromosome and chromosome 4 of *D. texana* into a V-shaped complex in *D. americana.* Still another translocation effected the union of chromosomes 3 and 4 of *D. ezoana* into a single chromosome in *D. littoralis* (Fig. 5.8).

A series of studies by Wasserman (1960, 1963, and references therein) on gene arrangements in the chromosomes of 46 species of the *repleta* group of Drosophila has revealed a slightly different situation. Although as many as 144 paracentric inversions have participated in the evolution of the chromosome complements, the gene arrangements in related species are generally less differentiated than those in the species of the *virilis* group, and therefore in turn have diverged less than those in *D. pseudoobscura* and *D. miranda.*

### *Gene Arrangements in Drosophila Species That Cannot be Crossed*

In the preceding section reference was made to the pioneering work of Sturtevant (1929) on linkage maps of the chromosomes of *Drosophila melanogaster* and *D. simulans.* Though very laborious, this method of comparison is applicable to species that cannot be crossed. Mutants that arise in different species frequently produce similar phenotypic changes. The inference is that the genes that produce similar mutations are homologous. The reliability of this method is limited, because phenotypically similar ("mimic") mutants are often produced at different gene loci in the same species.

Nevertheless, Sturtevant and Novitski (1941) were able to homologize the linkage maps of several species of Drosophila. They concluded that a chromosome complement of five pairs of rod-shaped (acrocentric) and one pair of dotlike chromosomes is the ancestral condition in the genus Drosophila (Primitive I in Fig. 5.8). This karyotype recurs in many unrelated species of different subgenera and species groups. Other karyotypes in Drosophila arose from this primitive one through translocations that combined in various ways the six chromosome limbs or "elements." Although the "elements" are retained quite tenaciously, the genes within them are found in rather different

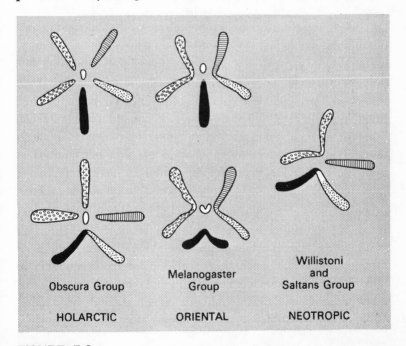

Obscura Group

Melanogaster Group

Willistoni and Saltans Group

HOLARCTIC   ORIENTAL   NEOTROPIC

**FIGURE 5.9**

Homologies of the chromosome sets in the subgroups of the subgenus Sophophora of the genus Drosophila.

linear orders in different species. This is a consequence of the prevalence of paracentric inversions and the relative rarity of pericentric ones and of translocations (see above).

Figure 5.9 shows chromosome complements (represented as haploid) in species of the subgenus Sophophora of the genus Drosophila. One of the species of the Holarctic *obscura* group, namely, the European *Drosophila subobscura,* has the ancestral karyotype of five rods and a dot. Other species in this group, including the American *D. pseudoobscura, D. persimilis,* and *D. miranda,* have a new X chromosome, which corresponds to the X and one of the autosomes of *D. subobscura.* (The X chromosome of the ancestral set is shown in Fig. 5.9 in black.) In the *melanogaster* species group, native apparently in the Oriental region, the four pairs of acrocentric autosomes are fused into two pairs of V-shaped metacentric ones. In some species, such as *D. ananassae,* a pericentric inversion has transformed the acrocentric X chromosome into a small metacentric. Finally, in the *willistoni* and *saltans* species groups, native in tropical America, only three pairs of chromosomes are left, the dotlike "element" of the ancestral set being translocated to the X chromosome.

Stalker (1965) introduced a method of comparative study of the gene arrangements, by painstaking matching of the disc patterns in photographs of sections of the giant chromosomes in the salivary gland cells. In the hands of a cytological virtuoso, this method gives results hardly less dependable than comparing the chromosomes in the cells of a hybrid. By such photographic comparison, supplemented where possible by study of hybrids, Stalker (1965, 1966), Kastritsis (1966, 1969a), and Carson and Stalker (1968) succeeded in tracing the phylogenies of the gene arrangements in the *melanica* (6 species), *tripunctata* (11 species), *guarani* (7 species), and *grimshawi* (29 species) groups of Drosophila.

Beerman (1955a,b) and Keyl (1961, 1962, 1965) discovered a variety of chromosomal differences between species of Chironomus, midges, and Kitzmiller, Frizzi, and Baker (1967) between species of Anopheles mosquitoes. Comparisons of disc patterns in the salivary glands of pure species and also, where possible, of interspecific hybrids were made. As in Drosophila, paracentric inversions are the principal agents of change in the gene arrangements. Thus, *Chironomus tentans* and *Ch. pallidivittatus* have similar gene arrangements in the right limbs of chromosome 1 and differ in one inversion each in the left limbs of chromosomes 1 and 3, and in two inversions each in the right limbs of chromosomes 2 and 3; the gene arrangements in the left limb of chromosome 2 and in chromosome 4 are too different to make analysis possible. The X and Y chromosomes have homologous banding but differ in several inversions; in *Ch. tentans* it is sometimes chromosome 1 and sometimes chromosome 2 that serves as the sex-determining pair. Among 20 species of Chironomus, Keyl (1962) found 4 translocations and numerous inversion differences, as well as differences in the appearance of homologous bands in salivary gland chromosomes, apparently resembling the differences found between *Drosophila melanogaster* and *D. simulans* (see above).

## Changes in Chromosome Structure in Speciation

There are several mechanisms whereby evolutionary changes in the chromosome numbers can be effected. Polyploidy makes the numbers in related species multiples of some basic haploid number, $n$. Among classical examples of polyploid series of species are wheats and related grasses with $2_n = 14, 28$, and 42, and Chrysanthemum with $2_n = 18, 36, 54, 70$, and 90. Polyploidy is frequent among plants and relatively rare in animals (Chapter 11); it is a one-way street, moving toward higher but rarely if ever toward lower numbers.

In most organisms every chromosome has one and only one centromere, and this organelle cannot arise *de novo*. Yet some groups, both among animals (lepidopterans, trichopterans, homopterans, heteropterans and some insects, some scorpions, and, as mentioned above, nematodes) and among plants (the family Juncaceae, some algae), have chromosomes with multiple or diffuse centromeres (a review in White 1954, Suomalainen 1966). This makes possible large differences in chromosome numbers among related species. For example, the butterfly genus Erebia has species with haploid numbers 11, 14, 17, 19, 21, 22, 28, 29, and 40, and the saturnid moths with 13, 14, 19, 29, 30, 31, 33, and 49 (Makino 1951). Such differences can be mistaken for polyploidy, but, as far as is known, they involve little reconstruction of the chromosomal apparatus and no increase or decrease in the amount of genic materials.

When the chromosomes have a single centromere each, the freedom of changes in the chromosome number and in gene alignment is more limited. The requirement is that each chromosome has one and only one centromere. In the elegant study of Gerassimova (1939) two translocations were obtained in the progeny of irradiated *Crepis tectorum*. This species has four pairs of chromosomes, denoted A, B, C, and D. One of the translocations exchanged sections of chromosomes A and D, and the other of B and C. Translocation heterozygotes are semisterile, because of the formation of aneuploid gametes (see above), but translocation homozygotes are fertile. By intercrossing the two translocation strains, a double-translocation heterozygote, involving all four chromosomes, was obtained. The fertility of this heterozygote was quite low. Among its progeny, however, there were individuals homozygous for both translocations. They were not only viable and fertile with each other, but also formed semisterile hybrids when crossed with the parental form. Gerassimova rightly considered her double-translocation homozygote deserving of a new species name, *Crepis nova*. A similar synthetic species was obtained by Stebbins (1957b) in the progeny of highly sterile hybrids between the grasses *Elymus glaucus* and *Sitanion jubatum*. Even earlier (1936) Kozhevnikov combined two translocations in *Drosophila melanogaster* to produce a "*Drosophila artificialis*." The latter, when crossed to the chromosomally normal *D. melanogaster*, produces no viable offspring at all. Unfortunately, only one-quarter of the eggs produced by intercrossing *D. artificialis* females and males are viable. As Grant (1963) has said, "The chromosome structural arrangement is the umbilical cord of the species."

# BALANCING SELECTION AND GENETIC LOAD

∽∿∽

## Heterogeneity of Environment

Mathematical models usually assume, and experimental studies endeavor to provide, uniform and constant environments in which the process of selection can take place. This convention is convenient, because the Darwinian fitness of a genotype in a constant environment is also constant. Unfortunately, it is also an oversimplification. Not only a species or a population but even a single individual faces a variety of environments in its lifetime.

We have seen in Chapter 2 that the genotype determines, not a single phenotype, but a norm of reaction, a repertoire of phenotypes that can arise in different environments or successions of environments. Within a certain range of environments these phenotypes are generally adaptive (adaptive modifications), whereas outside this range they are adaptively ambiguous or maladapted (morphoses in the terminology of Schmalhausen 1949). The range of environments may be greater or smaller than that to which the genotypes available in a population react by adaptive modifications. Environments often occur in "patches" succeeding each other in space or in time. If the patches are large or prolonged enough so that an average individual member of the population is likely to spend its lifetime in a single patch, the environment is coarse-grained; if an individual encounters many patches, it is fine-grained. In his perceptive theoretical study, Levins (1968 and references therein) has pointed out that coarse-grained and fine-grained environments call for different evolutionary strategies for adaptation.

The coarseness or fineness depends on the mobility of the organism, and on the topography and many other features of the environment itself. If the range of environments is smaller than the tolerance of individuals with a given phenotype, then the optimal strategy is a single phenotype, monomorphism. This phenotype probably has its highest adaptedness near the middle of its environmental range, and does at least moderately well in other environments. The range of environments may, however, be so great that a phenotype will do well in some of them and poorly in others. In a fine-grained environment the optimum strategy may still be a single phenotype, specialized for some of the subenvironments, especially those most frequently encountered. In a coarse-grained environment the optimum is sometimes a "mixed" strategy, that is, a multiplicity of phenotypes. Several phenotypes and genotypes may be called for, with frequencies dependent on those of the environments. This will usually, though not always, mean genetic polymorphism. Even in coarse-grained environments, however, there are also conditions in which a single phenotype is optimal.

## *Adaptive Norm and Stabilizing Selection*

An evolutionary strategy that favors phenotypic monomorphism need not rest on genetic uniformity. Classical geneticists assumed that "normal" or "wild-type" representatives of a species are similar in appearance because they are also similar genetically. Discovery of the concealed genetic variability in natural populations of Drosophila has shown how far off the mark this assumption was. Experiments in which different "normal" chromosomes from the same population were allowed to undergo gene recombination gave products some of which were subvital, semilethal, and even lethal. These chromsomes evidently carried different genes. Ford (1964) made an elegant study on phenotypically indistinguishable populations of the moth *Triphaena comes* from certain islands off the coast of Scotland. Since they proved to be quite distinct genetically, their phenotypic similarity evidently is reached by different genetic means.

Phenotypically monomorphic species or populations have single adaptive norms. An adaptive norm is, however, not a single genotype but usually a great array of genotypes. The common property of this array is that the constituent genotypes and the phenotypes engendered by them enable their carriers to survive and to reproduce in the environments that the species inhabits. Normalizing selection (Chapter 4) protects the adaptive norm by trimming off ill-adapted variants, the expressed genetic load of the population. As stated in Chapter 4, Schmalhausen (1949), Mather (1955), and Waddington (1957) distinguish also stabilizing (or canalizing) and diversifying (or disruptive) selections. Consider a character, such as stature or growth rate or fertility, the variation of which follows a bell-shaped probability curve. Stabilizing selection favors the modal phenotype and discriminates against both extremes. Diversifying selection, on the other hand, favors the extremes and discriminates against the intermediates. (I prefer the name diversifying to "disruptive" because, far from being disruptive, this form of selection is a constructive factor in adaptive evolution!)

The phenotypic repertoires of genotypes are of at least three kinds. First, homeostatic buffering or canalization (cf. Chapter 2) may give the same phenotype within the entire range of the environments in which the genotype is viable. Thus, almost all human genotypes ensure the development of a four-chambered heart, a suckling instinct in the infant, a capacity to think in symbols and to learn a language, etc. Second, a continuous range of phenotypes may develop, depending on the state of the environment. Weight, muscular development, educational achievement in man, and body size in many animals and plants are examples. Third, there may be an environmental threshold below which one phenotype and above which another phenotype develop, or a "stochastic switch" when an environment determines only the probability of the development of certain phenotypes (Levins 1968). Thus, the castes (workers, soldiers, queens) of some social insects are genetically similar and are determined by the quality or quantity of the food given to the larvae. Flowering in many plants and diapause in many insects (Andrewartha 1952) are induced by the length of daylight and darkness (photoperiod). In the marine worm Bonellia sex is determined by the environment—larvae growing on the mother's proboscis become males, and free-living larvae females.

## Diversifying Selection: Theoretical

A theoretical model of polymorphism due to heterosis, that is, superior fitness of heterozygotes over the corresponding homozygotes, was discussed in Chapter 5. A stable equilibrium can be maintained by balancing selection even in uniform environments. If the fitness of the three genotypes $A_1A_1$, $A_1A_2$, and $A_2A_2$ is $1 - s$, $1$, and $1 - t$, respectively, selection will drive the alleles $A_1$ and $A_2$ to equilibrium frequencies of $t/(s + t)$ and $s/(s + t)$, respectively. The mean fitness of the population, $\overline{W}$, is maximized when the equilibrium frequencies are reached. It remains, nevertheless, below that of the fittest genotype, $A_1A_2$.

Although the diversifying form of balancing natural selection may be widespread and important in nature, it is much less well understood and documented than the heterotic form. Ludwig (1950), Mather (1955), and Ford (1964) have discussed the possible role of diversifying selection in evolution. Levene (1953), Li (1955a,b), Prout (1968), and Levins and MacArthur (1966) constructed mathematical models of some special cases; a general treatment is yet to be made. Levene assumes a panmictic, random mating population that has available to it two or more environments. An insect whose larvae feed on different plants growing in the same locality presents such a situation. Now suppose that genotypes $A_1A_1$, $A_1A_2$, and $A_2A_2$ survive at different rates in the different environments. Levene has shown that a sufficient, though not necessary, condition for a stable polymorphism of $A_1$ and $A_2$ is that the harmonic mean of the viabilities of the heterozygotes be greater than that of the homozygotes. He gives an example in which this condition is not satisfied, but an equilibrium is nevertheless achieved. Let the fitness, $W$, of the genotypes in two environments be:

| Environment | $A_1A_1$ | $A_1A_2$ | $A_2A_2$ |
|---|---|---|---|
| I | 2 | 1 | 1.1 |
| II | 0.5 | 1 | 1.1 |

In neither environment is the heterozygote superior. If the two environments are equally frequent, and the initial frequency of $A_2$ is less than 0.65 (65 percent), a stable equilibrium will be established at frequencies of $A_2$ and $A_1$ equal to 0.4 and 0.6. The frequency 0.65 of $A_2$ is the point of unstable equilibrium; above this point no balanced polymorphism is established, $A_2$ reaches fixation (frequency 1.0), and $A_1$ is eliminated. Here, then, is a situation in which the outcome of the selection depends not only on the Darwinian fitness of the competing genotypes and the environment but also on the gene frequencies at which the selection starts operating.

Li (1955a) considered an instance of what Wallace (1968a) has later called marginal overdominance. A heterozygote may have an average advantage over a range of environments, even though it is not superior to the homozygotes in any one of them. Assume a panmictic population, in which 20, 30, and 50 percent of individuals live in environments I, II, and III, in which the viabilities of the three genotypes are as follows:

| Environment | $A_1A_1$ | $A_1A_2$ | $A_2A_2$ |
|---|---|---|---|
| I | 1.2 | 1 | 0.9 |
| II | 0.6 | 1 | 0.8 |
| III | 0.7 | 1 | 1.1 |

The heterozygote is superior in only one niche, and this is not the most frequent one. Li finds, however, that in the population as a whole a stable polymorphism is established at the frequencies 0.158 of $A_1$ and 0.842 of $A_2$.

An important constraint in Levene's and Li's models is that, though the selection takes place in different environments, the survivors meet and mate at random regardless of the environment in which they developed. In coarse-grained environments this constraint is relaxed. Most individuals that develop in a given patch (e.g., on a certain food plant) mate and produce progeny in the same patch. Or the carriers of different genotypes may preferentially seek the environments most favorable to themselves. This makes stable polymorphism more likely to be achieved than in Levene's model. Levins and MacArthur (1966) and Levins (1968) have made some headway in analyzing such situations.

Dempster (1955) and Haldane and Jayakar (1963a,b) found that stable polymorphism is possible if a regular cyclic variation in the selection favors one or the other allele in successive generations, or if the arithmetic mean of fitnesses of recessive homozygotes in different generations is higher, while the geometric mean is lower, than unity. As an illustration of this situation, Haldane and Jayakar state, "An occasional severe epidemic of *falciparum* malaria might suffice to keep the gene for hemoglobin S from disappearing, even if for generations on end heterozygotes for sickling were at a disadvantage compared with persons homozygous for hemoglobin A." Merrell and Rodell (1968) have described a "seasonal selection" in the frog *Rana pipiens*. Its color variant *burnsi* is due to a dominant gene. No evidence of heterozygous advantage is found, but *burnsi* survives winter better than the prevalent, wild-type *pipiens*. The frequency of *burnsi* is greater in spring, and decreases toward fall.

## Experiments and Observations on
## Diversifying Selection

A series of brilliant studies on diversifying selection (which the authors called disruptive) has been carried out on *Drosophila melanogaster* by Thoday and his colleagues (Thoday and Boam 1959, Millicent and Thoday 1961, and Gibson and Thoday 1962, 1963). The trait used in their experiments was the number of sternopleural bristles on the sides of the thorax. The selection procedure adopted in one of their experiments was as follows. In two populations, 1(H) and 2(H), males with the highest bristle numbers were mated in each generation to females that also had the highest bristle numbers but were derived from two other populations, 3(L) and 4(L). At the same time, males with the lowest numbers of bristles in 3(L) and 4(L) were mated to females with the lowest bristle numbers for 1(H) and 2(H). The populations were all started from a common source; 1(H) and 2(H) were selected for more bristles, and 3(L) and 4(L) for fewer bristles. The critical circumstance was that in each generation there was a

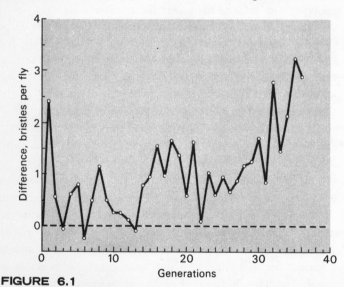

**FIGURE 6.1**

Diversifying selection for bristle numbers in Drosophila melanogaster. The diagram shows the differences between the mean bristle numbers per fly in the "high" and "low" lines. (After Thoday)

50 percent gene exchange between the H and the L populations. In effect, the selection was carried in a single population, in which individuals with extreme bristle numbers were selected, and those with modal numbers were discarded.

Figure 6.1 summarizes the results of one of the experiments. The difference between the mean numbers of bristles in the H and the L lines gradually increased. Further analysis showed that the variation in the bristle numbers was due mainly to only two genes on the second chromosome. A combination of alleles of both genes decreasing the bristle number acted as a recessive synthetic lethal, while two plus alleles of both genes on the same chromosome functioned as a dominant synthetic lethal (see Chapter 4).

Prout (1962), Scharloo (1964), Druger (1967), and others showed that both diversifying and stabilizing selection can modify very appreciably the manifestation of certain mutants in Drosophila, increasing or decreasing the variability. The most convincing evidence of the operation of diversifying selection in nature comes, however, from studies on mimicry in the swallowtail butterflies *Papilio dardanus* and *P. memnon* (Clarke and Sheppard 1960, 1962, Clarke, Sheppard, and Thornton 1968 and Sheppard 1969; see also a masterful summary in Ford 1964). The females of these butterflies mimic in shape and coloration butterflies of different genera and families, which are protected by being distasteful to predators. Furthermore, in different parts of Africa (*P. dardanus*) and of tropical Asia (*P. memnon*) they mimic different models. To be successful, a mimetic resemblance must be as close as possible to the model; accordingly the females have very different color patterns in different parts of the species distribution area. Males are nonmimetic, geographically relatively uniform, and quite different from the females, except in territories (Madagascar, Ethiopia) where the females are also nonmimetic and resemble the males in color patterns. In addition, in many places the females are polymorphic, mimicking different models.

Genetic analysis showed that the variety of female forms is determined by what at first sight appears to be a series of multiple alleles of a single gene locus, the manifestation of which is sex-controlled, being different in females but not in males. More detailed study disclosed a more complex and interesting situation. In the first place, instead of there being a single locus, the variety of mimetic forms is due to supergenes, closely linked alleles of several loci. Moreover, although the forms that are found in the population show clear-cut dominance and recessiveness, intercrosses of different populations give incomplete dominance. The products of such interpopulational hybridization have their mimicry disrupted by the breakdown of the gene patterns characteristic of separate populations. One may wonder why the mimicry is restricted to the females and the males are left unprotected; at any rate, natural selection has acted to diversify the females and to make them resemble butterflies of quite different species, rather than to be like the males of their own species.

## Frequency-Dependent Selection

An interesting suggestion of a possible mechanism maintaining the polymorphism of shell colors and patterns in the land snail Cepaea has been made by Clarke (1962). Bird predators learn to search for prey of a certain appearance, and therefore kill a disproportionately high percentage of the common varieties of the snail and a low percentage of the rare ones. Fitness is therefore decreasing as a color type becomes frequent. This is, then, a frequency-dependent selection.

Many plants (e.g., some Nicotiana, Petunia, Oenothera, and Trifolium) and also some animals (the ascidian Ciona) have evolved self-incompatibility mechanisms that enforce outcrossing and prevent close inbreeding. The key feature of these mechanisms is a series of multiple alleles of a gene, which make the pollen carrying a given allele fail to germinate and to grow on the stigma of a plant with the same allele. Since the stigma tissue is diploid and pollen grains are haploid, a minimum of three alleles is needed to make the mechanism operative. Even if the three alleles are equally frequent in a population, however, many of the pollinations will fail to effect fertilization. A fourth, a fifth, etc., allele appearing by mutation will therefore have selective advantages; furthermore, the advantages will be greatest when a new allele is rare because pollen carrying this allele will function on almost every plant in the population. Conversely, as an allele grows in frequency, its advantage will diminish and eventually disappear. This process was analyzed by Wright (1964b), using the observations of Emerson (1939) on *Oenothera organensis*. The total number of individuals of this curious species is only of the order of 500, growing in some canyons of the Organ Mountains in New Mexico. Yet

Emerson found 47 self-incompatibility alleles in the subpopulations of this species.

Petit (1958) and Ehrman (in Ehrman, Spassky, et al. 1965) independently discovered, in *Drosophila melanogaster* and *D. pseudoobscura* respectively, that when two kinds of males are present in a confined space the rare type has an advantage in mating. This Petit-Ehrman effect has since been found by these and other authors, in several species of Drosophila and under a variety of circumstances (Ehrman 1967, Petit and Ehrman 1969, Spiess 1968, Spiess and Spiess 1969, and references therein). An example of the results obtained is presented in Table 6.1. Equal numbers of females and males of two chromosomal types, CH and AR, of *D. pseudoobscura* are introduced into observation chambers, and the matings occurring during 3–4 hours after introduction are recorded. During this time no female copulates more than once, but a male can do so repeatedly. The chi squares ($\chi^2$) in the table serve to evaluate the probability of the observed deviations from random mating being due to errors of sampling; a chi square of 3.84 corresponds to a 5 percent, and of 6.64 to a 1 percent, probability level. It can be seen that CH and AR females mate very nearly in proportion to their numbers, regardless of their relative frequencies. This is not true of the males. Each type is very successful in mating when it is rare; when the two kinds of males are nearly equally numerous, neither kind has an advantage.

In laboratory experiments, rare males have mating advantages when

**TABLE 6.1**

Numbers of matings recorded in observation chambers with twenty females and twenty males of Drosophila pseudoobscura, among which individuals of two strains, CH and AR, were present in different proportions (After Ehrman)

| Proportions | Males Mated | | | Females Mated | | |
|---|---|---|---|---|---|---|
| CH:AR | CH | AR | $\chi^2$ | CH | AR | $\chi^2$ |
| 18 : 2 | 78 | 27 | 28.81 | 93 | 12 | 0.24 |
| 16 : 4 | 75 | 43 | 19.93 | 94 | 24 | 0.01 |
| 14 : 6 | 63 | 46 | 7.73 | 72 | 37 | 0.81 |
| 12 : 8 | 42 | 75 | 28.32 | 69 | 48 | 0.05 |
| 10 : 10 | 49 | 66 | 2.51 | 56 | 59 | 0.08 |
| 8 : 12 | 57 | 63 | 2.81 | 58 | 62 | 3.47 |
| 6 : 14 | 37 | 71 | 0.93 | 42 | 66 | 4.06 |
| 4 : 16 | 46 | 64 | 32.73 | 32 | 78 | 5.68 |
| 2 : 18 | 33 | 80 | 46.30 | 12 | 101 | 0.05 |

the two competing kinds differ in chromosomal inversions (see Chapter 5), in geographic origins, or in mutant genes, and even when they belong to the same strain but were raised in different environments. The nature of the stimuli responsible for this behavior is as yet obscure. Ehrman experimented with two superimposed observation chambers, of which the upper contained many males of one kind and a minority of a second kind; the lower chamber had many males of the type that was rare in the upper chamber. The matings were scored in the upper chamber. When the two chambers were separated only by a layer of cheesecloth, the "rare" males in the upper chamber no longer had the mating advantage. In such an arrangement, when a current of air is passed from one chamber to the other, the "rare" males lose their advantage if the air comes from the chamber that has their kind in excess, but not in the opposite case.

Nothing is known about possible mating advantages of rare genotypes in natural environments. If they exist in the natural habitats of the flies, the resulting frequency-dependent selection may be a potent instrumentality for maintaining the polymorphic equilibria of gene alleles without heterosis. Even mildly deleterious alleles could be maintained in natural populations by these means. Rare alleles will grow in frequencies until the mating advantages of their carriers decrease and disappear. More research in this field is evidently needed.

Frequency-dependent selection operates, at least in laboratory populations, for the beetle *Tribolium castaneum* (Sokal and Huber 1963), *Drosophila ananassae* polymorphic for certain inversions (Tobari 1966 and Tobari and Kojima 1967), and perhaps *D. melanogaster* polymorphic for variants of the esterase-6 enzyme (Yarbrough and Kojima 1967). Indications of frequency dependence are found also for inversions in *D. persimilis* (Spiess 1957) and *D. pseudoobscura* (Pavlovsky and Dobzhansky 1966). By and large, the fitness is higher when a genotype (or a karyotype) is rare than when it is common. When equilibrium is reached, the fitnesses of the polymorphs become uniform. Sokal and Huber (1963) found, however, more complex relations in Tribolium populations containing the mutant sooty ($s$) and its wild-type allele. When the frequency of sooty is $q = 0.25$, the viabilities of the three genotypes follow the sequence $+/+ > s/s > +/s$; at $q = 0.5$ they become $+/+ > +/s > s/s$; and at $q = 0.75$ the sequence is $+/s > +/+ > s/s$.

Little is known about the ecological and physiological factors that make the fitnesses of some genotypes frequency dependent. These factors may well be different in different cases. Carriers of one genotype may injure those of another in various ways. Dramatic examples of such hostile interactions, resulting in "xenocide" and "suicide" of one or both competitors, are described by Sokoloff, Lerner, and Ho (1965) and by Sokoloff and Lerner (1967) in mixed cultures of two species of flour beetles, *Tribolium castaneum* and *T. confusum*. These beetles engage in cannibalism, the egg and pupal stages being most liable to be devoured. When fed on corn flour, *T. confusum* is superior to *T. castaneum*, apparently because the latter requires some nutrient that is in short supply in corn. Nevertheless, *T. castaneum* can maintain itself on corn medium by cannibalizing *T. confusum* and thus gaining the otherwise deficient nutrient. When a mixture of the two species is placed on corn, *T. castaneum* eliminates *T. confusum* (xenocide). Yet, having done so, the winner is deprived of necessary nutrition, and its population approaches extinction (suicide). Some plants excrete into the soil substances that are toxic to other species, and even to individuals of the same species (Bonner 1950).

Mutual facilitation appears to be at least as common as mutual damage, and is of particular interest to us as a mechanism that can maintain genetic variability. If two or several genotypes are at their most efficient when exploring somewhat different environmental resources, a genetically mixed population may be better off than a genetically uniform one. Although the physiological reasons are difficult to pin-point, mixed plantings of varieties of barley (Gustafsson 1953), rice (Roy 1960), and oats (Jensen 1965) often give appreciably higher yields than plantings of any one of the component varieties.

Lewontin (1955) in *Drosophila melanogaster* and Lewontin and Matsuo (1963) in *D. busckii* studied the proportions of larvae surviving in limited amounts of culture medium. The same numbers of larvae were introduced into all cultures, but in some cultures all the larvae were of the same strain and in others they were mixtures of two different strains. For several genetic mixtures, the average survival was higher than that in pure cultures. This is, of course, not an invariable rule. Dawood and Strickberger (1964) and Weisbrot (1966) studied the influence of the presence in the culture medium of metabolic waste products, or of killed larvae, of some strains of *D. melanogaster* on the survival of larvae of the same and of different strains. In some combinations the survival of larvae exposed to the waste products of a foreign strain was very significantly reduced. Levene, Pavlovsky, and Dobzhansky (1958) compared the adaptive values of the homo- and heterokaryotypes for ST, AR, and CH inversions in the third chromosome of *D. pseudoobscura*. The values for populations that have pairs of these chromosome types (i.e., ST + AR, ST + CH, and AR + CH) are appreciably different from those for populations having all three. In other words, the fitness of a karyotype depends on what other karyotypes are present in the same medium, and in what frequencies they occur.

## Overdominance and Heterosis

We must now return to consideration of the genetic variability maintained in populations by the heterotic form of balancing selection. The paradigm of this kind of genetic variability discussed in Chapter 5 was rather complex—inversions and translocations found in natural populations of many animals and plants. Such chromosomal variants, though inherited as if they were alleles of one gene, actually represent supergenes. They are maintained in populations because the heterozygotes (heterokaryotypes) for the supergenes are superior in fitness to the homozygotes (homokaryotypes).

Superior fitness of heterozygotes may arise also through interaction of alleles at a single locus. A heterozygote can be similar in phenotype to one of the homozygotes (complete dominance), intermediate between the homozygotes (incomplete or lack of dominance), or outside the range of the homozygotes (overdominance). If the phenotype trait is viability or fitness, overdominance may mean that the heterozygote is heterotic and superior to both homozygotes. The fact that "overdominance" is properly applied only to phenotypes produced by the interaction of alleles of a single gene makes the term operationally of limited value. What we ordinarily observe are hybrids, not between gene alleles, but between strains, varieties, or populations that differ in many genes. The phenotypic effects of each gene are embedded in the matrix of the genotype as a whole. It is at least difficult, and usually impossible, to distinguish between a heterotic gene allele and a complex of linked genes, a supergene, in a chromosome that causes the heterozygote to be superior in fitness. In the following discussion we shall use the term heterosis in preference to "overdominance."

*Heterozygous Effects of Newly*
*Arisen Mutants*

A simple but essential distinction must be made in appraising the effects of a genetic variant on fitness. The array of variants newly arisen by mutation will inevitably be different from the variants that have persisted in a population for many generations. The former have not passed the winnowing process of normalizing natural selection, whereas the latter are the survivors of this force. The carriers of new variants are therefore likely to be, on the average, less fit than the carriers of long-persisting variants. The evidence is overwhelming that most mutations arising in any living species are deleterious (cf. Chapters 3 and 4). The problem here at issue has a narrower focus: Do the recessive genes that are deleterious or lethal when homozygous cause a reduction of fitness also in the heterozygous condition? As we saw in Chapter 4, normalizing natural selection is far more effective in lowering the incidence in the gene pool of variants that incapacitate the heterozygotes than in reducing the frequencies of those that harm only the homozygotes. In contrast, superior fitness in heterozygotes maintains a heterotic allele in the population even if the homozygote is lethal.

Stern, Carson, et al. (1952) examined the viability effects in the heterozygous condition of 75 sex-linked lethals in *Drosophila melanogaster*. Males with these lethals in their single X chromosomes do not survive. Tests were made to compare the viability in crowded cultures of two classes of females: one class carried a lethal X chromosome and an X with a visible gene marker, and the other class had a nonlethal X and an X with the same marker. On the average, the survival rate of the females heterozygous for lethals was 2.5 percent lower than that of females free of lethals. Stern and his collaborators pointed out, however, that not all lethals in this sample were deleterious in heterozygotes. Wallace (1968a) analyzed their data further and showed that about 29 percent of the lethals may have been not only neutral but also slightly heterotic. Wallace's own observations (1965, 1968) on lethals in the second chromosome of *D. melanogaster* disclosed a similar situation; of 32 lethals tested, 2 were semidominant and markedly deleterious in the heterozygous conditions, whereas the others resulted in an average lowering of the viability.

That some newly arisen mutants, including those that are lethal when homozygous, may increase fitness in the heterozygous condition is nevertheless certain. Gustafsson and his colleagues (Gustafsson 1946, 1951, 1963a,b, Gustafsson, Nybom, and Wettstein 1950, and references therein) have discovered several examples of this kind. Thus, some chlorophyll-deficient mutants in barley, though lethal when homozygous, are superior in the heterozygous condition to noncarriers in respect to productivity and to competitive ability in dense stands.

Mukai and Burdick (1959, 1961) and Tano and Burdick (1965) established, by most careful and extensive tests, the heterotic effects of one particular lethal in the second chromosome of *Drosophila melanogaster*. In the same species, Torroja (1966) found three sex-linked lethals that appeared to be heterotic. In all these cases, the evidence really shows the lethals to be heterotic in a particular genetic system and in a particular environment. An unconditionally heterotic gene is probably a will-o'-the-wisp.

## Newly Arisen Mutants in Relation to the Genetic Background

Most individuals in populations of sexually reproducing, diploid or polyploid, and outbreeding species are heterozygous for alleles at many gene loci. The proportion of heterozygous genes can be reduced by inbreeding or by means of more sophisticated genetic techniques described in Chapters 3 and 4. An entirely homozygous individual is, however, a freak, if found at all in natural populations. As will be shown in this section, heterozygosis exists even in self-fertilizing species, that is, under most rigorous inbreeding. High heterozygosity is the state of the genetic systems in most organisms, established during the eons of their evolutionary development. It is reasonable that for newly arisen mutants the effects of heterozygosis on fitness may well be different, depending on the degree of heterozygosity prevailing in the genotype into which they are introduced.

The trail-blazing work on this problem was done by Wallace (1958, 1965). Strains of *Drosophila melanogaster* homozygous for second chromosomes were obtained by means of a technique similar to that diagramed in Fig. 3.1. The chromosomes chosen for the experiments had homozygotes of quasi-normal viability. Males homozygous for these chromosomes were given a dose of 500 r of X-rays and crossed to unirradiated females with marker genes $Cy$ and $L$ (Curly and Lobe) in one second chromosome and $Pm$ (Plum) in the other. Unirradiated control males with the same chromosomes were similarly crossed. By means of a series of crosses, again similar in principle to those in Fig. 3.1, cultures were obtained segregating four classes of flies, theoretically in equal numbers: Curly-Lobe Plum, Curly-Lobe, Plum, and wild type. In the experimental series, however, the Curly-Lobe and wild-type classes carried one irradiated wild-type chromosome, whereas in the control series both chromosomes were unirradiated. Denoting a given wild-type chromosome as $+_1$ when unirradiated and as $+_1^{*}$ when irradiated, we have:

| | | | | |
|---|---|---|---|---|
| Experimental: | $Cy\ L/Pm$ | $Cy\ L/+_1^{*}$ | $Pm/+_1$ | $+_1/+_1^{*}$ |
| Control: | $Cy\ L/Pm$ | $Cy\ L/+_1$ | $Pm/+_1$ | $+_1/+_1$ |

Since the mutant gene markers depress slightly the survival rates of their carriers, the meaningful way to compare the irradiated and control cultures is to measure the viabilities of the different classes relative to that of the $Cy\ L/Pm$ flies, taken as 1.000. The choice of the $Cy\ L/Pm$ class as the viability standard is valid because it has exactly the same second chromosomes in the experimentals and in the controls. In one experiment the average ratios found in 764 experimental and 766 control cultures were as follows:

| *Experimental* | | *Control* | |
|---|---|---|---|
| $Cy\ L/+^{*}$ | 1.115 | $Cy\ L/+$ | 1.094 |
| $Pm/+$ | 1.137 | $Pm/+$ | 1.146 |
| $+/+^{*}$ | 1.033 | $+/+$ | 1.008 |

The viabilities of the wild-type and the Curly-Lobe classes carrying one irradiated second chromosome exceed the viabilities of the corresponding classes in the unirradiated controls. The difference may seem slight, but, because of the large numbers of flies counted, it is significant at the 4 percent probability level for the Curly-Lobe class, and at the 2 percent level for the wild-type class. It follows that the average effect of newly induced mutations in the heterozygous condition is a viability increase. With the total count of flies in seven experiments exceeding 3.25 million, the probability of the observed result being due to chance has been reduced for the wild-type class to 0.2 percent (Wallace 1968a). On the other hand, when irradiated second chromosomes were introduced in a heterozygous genetic background (hybrids of different strains of the same species), no heterotic effects were observed (Wallace 1963a).

Two working hypotheses suggest themselves. First, a degree of heterozygosity above a certain minimum level may be requisite for high fitness in normally outbreeding species. This idea was advanced by Lerner (1954) before Wallace's work was published, and supported by Lerner's analysis of selection for high productivity in poultry and other animals. Second, since only a part of the newly arising mutations may be heterotic, there is a better chance of such mutations improving highly inbred or homozygous strains than strains already having a heterozygosity that has accumulated under the control of balancing selection.

The findings of Wallace met with some disbelief and even hostility. Falk (1961), who used a quite different experimental design, interpreted his results at first as contradicting Wallace's findings but later (Falk and Ben-Zeev 1966) as confirming them. Crenshaw (1965b) obtained concordant evidence in *Tribolium confusum*. The best supporting evidence came, however, from the ingenious experiments, on spontaneous rather than radiation-induced mutants, carried out by Mukai and his colleagues (Mukai and Yamazaki 1964, 1968, Mukai, Chigusa, and Yoshikawa 1964, 1965, and Mukai, Yoshikawa, and Sano 1966).

The experiments of Mukai (1964) on the accumulation of mutations that modify the viability of *Drosophila melanogaster* were described in Chapter 3. He used a variant of the $Cy \, L/Pm$ technique, shown in Fig. 3.1 for the second chromosome, and concluded that as many as 15 percent of these chromosomes acquire a new mutation in every generation. In agreement with Wallace, Mukai found that the mutants are, on the average, deleterious in the homozygous condition. The more generations over which the mutations are allowed to accumulate, the lower becomes the average viability of the homozygotes.

The central question is, then, what effects these mutants have in heterozygotes. Mukai and his colleagues had 104 separate lines that initially contained the same second chromosome; this chromosome was "normal" in the sense that its homozygous carriers had good viability. Generation after generation, single males from each of the 104 lines, carrying the descendants of the "normal" chromosome and chromosomes with the mutant $Pm$, were outcrossed to $Cy \, L/Pm$ females. From time to time the viability of the homozygotes for each of the 104 chromosomes was tested as shown in Fig. 3.1. The viability in the homozygous condition of some of the chromosomes declined more or less conspicuously, whereas others remained "normal." Mukai believes that the latter escaped mutations affecting their viability.

The next step in the experiment was to test the viability of heterozygotes for a collection of chromosomes on (1) homozygous genetic backgrounds, (2) heterozygous genetic backgrounds from the same population, and (3) heterozygous genetic backgrounds from different populations. Heterozygotes (1) carried a supposedly "normal" chromosome and chromosomes changed by mutations; series (2) and (3) carried different chromosomes from the same population or from different populations. Figure 6.2 gives a concise summary of the results. The curve for the homozygous genetic backgrounds lies above that for the intrapopulational heterozygotes, and above its control. Not only are the newly arisen mutations heterotic when placed together with "normal" chromosomes, but also the lower the viability in the homo-

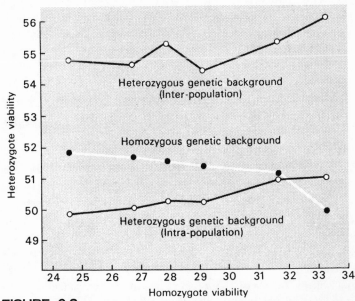

**FIGURE 6.2**

Relationships between the viabilities of homozygous and heterozygous carriers of certain chromosomes of Drosophila melanogaster, depending on the genetic background. (After Mukai et al.)

zygous condition the better are the heterozygotes. The opposite occurs in the interpopulational series—here the viability of the homozygous carriers of the respective chromosomes decreases. The viability of the interpopulational heterozygotes (3) is superior to the viabilities in series (1) and (2); this is the expected heterosis.

The earlier work of Wallace (1958) indicated that the $Cy$ $L/+$° class was slightly more viable than the $Cy$ $L/+$. This finding was unexpected, since the flies of both classes were heterozygous for many genes. A follow-up test by Wallace (1963b), however, showed no viability difference.

The work of Mukai and his colleagues (see especially Mukai 1969b) leaves an important question unanswered. Why should series (1) in their experiments show heterosis, and series (2) deleterious effects of the mutant genes (Mukai and his colleagues call these *cis-* and *trans-*heterozygotes, respectively)? It is certainly a misconception to regard the "normal" chromosome in Mukai's experiments as somehow mutation-free; any genotype has a history of origin from mutational elements. Why, therefore, should there be heterosis in combinations of this chromosome with its mutant derivatives but not in combinations of these mutant derivatives with each other? There is an obvious need for more work in this field.

## *Deleterious and Heterotic Mutants in Experimental Populations*

We saw in Chapter 4 that normalizing selection is far more efficient in eliminating mutants with deleterious effects in heterozygotes than completely recessive mutants. Heterotic mutants, unless they are lost by chance soon after their origin, are multiplied by heterotic balancing selection. Even if heterotic mutants are a small minority in the mutation spectrum, they are expected to increase in frequencies as selection does its work. Wallace (1962) found that newly arisen lethals in the second chromosome of *Drosophila melanogaster* had an average coefficient of dominance of about 0.07, while in his experimental populations maintained for several years the coefficient became reduced to about 0.02. Some of the lethals in such old populations must have been newly arisen, whereas others originated several, and still others arose many, generations before the tests; one may surmise that the lethals that persisted longest were least deleterious, neutral, or heterotic. Most convincing evidence in this connection has been obtained by Wills (1968) in populations of the yeast *Saccharomyces cerevisiae*. Mutants induced by frameshift mutagens (cf. Chapter 2) tend to be completely

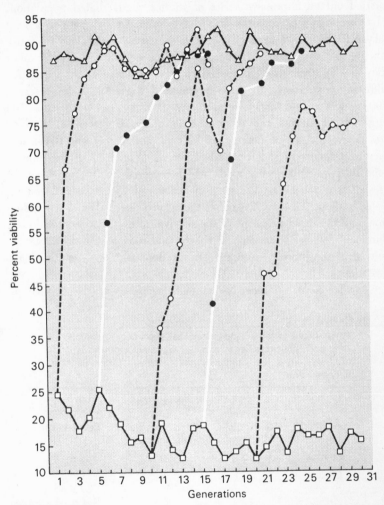

**FIGURE 6.3**

Egg-to-adult survival in the control (triangles) and irradiated (squares) populations of Drosophila melanogaster. Circles—populations with radiation histories that were gradually recovering normal viabilities after the irradiation was discontinued. (After Sankaranarayanan)

recessive in diploid heterozygotes. Base-substitution mutagens give mutants that are deleterious under some environmental conditions and heterotic under others.

Sankaranarayanan (1964, 1965, 1966) and Salceda (1967) have carried out an impressive series of studies on irradiated populations of *Drosophila melanogaster*. In order to minimize competition among larvae for food and space, the populations were maintained by introducing into each culture bottle only enough eggs to yield 50–70 adult flies; the numbers of eggs needed to produce these adults varied for different populations. In three populations the adult males received 2000 r, 4000 r, and 6000 r, respectively, of X-rays per generation. The egg-to-adult survival rate dropped from about 90 percent in the control down to about 50 percent, 28 percent, and 16 percent, depending on the amounts of radiation administered (Fig. 6.3). From time to time subpopulations were made which received no further radiation; as shown in the figure, the viability recovered within several generations, without, however, reaching the control level. The sharp reduction, and the rapid recovery, of the survival rates are accounted for by dominant lethals, chromosomal aberrations such as translocations resulting in semisterility, and deleterious dominant and semidominant mutants.

Consider now the recessive mutants induced by the irradiation.

**TABLE 6.2**

Percentages of lethal and semilethal second chromosomes of Drosophila melanogaster in populations having received 120,000 r of X-rays after the irradiation was stopped (After Sankaranaryanan 1966)

| Population | X-rays per Generation ( r units) | Generations after Irradiation Was Discontinued | Lethals and Semilethals |
|---|---|---|---|
| Control | 0 | 0 | $11.6 \pm 1.5$ |
| ER-20 | 6000 | 0 | $87.9 \pm 3.1$ |
|  |  | 19 | $75.9 \pm 3.6$ |
|  |  | 45 | $40.1 \pm 4.1$ |
| ER-30 | 4000 | 0 | $90.3 \pm 2.9$ |
|  |  | 19 | $59.8 \pm 4.6$ |
|  |  | 45 | $46.0 \pm 4.3$ |
| ER-60 | 2000 | 0 | $57.0 \pm 4.8$ |
|  |  | 19 | $40.9 \pm 4.7$ |

Table 6.2 shows the proportions of second chromosomes that were lethal or semilethal in the generation in which the radiation was discontinued and 19 and 45 generations thereafter. Except for the control, all populations received an aggregate dose of 120,000 r of X-rays, but at different rates per generation. At the time of relaxation (generation 0), as many as 90 percent of the chromosomes were lethal or semilethal. Thereafter the percentage fell sharply, but even 45 generations later it was still almost 4 times greater than in the control. At the same time, the frequency of allelic lethals increased instead of decreasing. What does this mean? The most reasonable inference is that, out of a variety of lethal genes induced by the irradiation, many were eliminated but some were not only preserved but even increased in frequencies. This inference has been upheld by Salceda (1967); out of 50 lethals from each population tested, some lethals were found as many as 8, 9, 10, and even 15 times in the same population. Since Salceda's material came from populations of thousands of individuals kept in population cages (see Chapter 5), these high frequencies can hardly be explained by random genetic drift (see Chapter 8).

Similar conclusions were reached by Mourad (1964) and Torroja (1964), who studied irradiated populations of *Drosophila pseudoobscura*. Wallace and Madden (1965) obtained evidence suggesting that some genes which in the homozygous condition cause sterility have positive selective values when heterozygous.

## Deleterious and Heterotic Mutants in Natural Populations

In Chapter 4 we saw that natural populations of Drosophila and other outbreeding species carry great accumulations of lethals and other deleterious variants concealed in the heterozygous state. What effects may these variants have on the viability and fitness of the heterozygotes? For about two decades this has been a bone of contention in population genetics.

Muller (1950) insisted that complete recessivity is very rare, and that the heterozygous carriers of deleterious "recessives" are really handicapped compared to noncarriers. He did not completely reject the existence of overdominant heterotic heterozygotes. However, since heterotic balanced polymorphisms make some individuals in the population less fit than the fittest heterozygote, Muller regarded polymorphism as a temporary miscarriage of natural selection, bound to be corrected when a mutant allele appears that yields a fitness at least as high as that of the formerly heterotic heterozygote. This conception was the keystone of Muller's evolutionary views, and particularly of his eugenic ideals. The evidence he used in his arguments pertained almost exclusively to newly arisen mutants, rather than those recovered from natural populations.

Cordeiro (1952) in *Drosophila willistoni,* as well as Greenberg and Crow (1960), Hiraizumi and Crow (1960), and Morton, Chung, and Friedman (1968) in *D. melanogaster,* found an average reduction of viability, and Temin (1966) a reduction of fertility, in heterozygotes for lethal, semilethal, subvital, and sterility factors. Furthermore, these authors argued that the degree of dominance (the $h$ coefficient; see Chapter 4) is greater for subvital than for completely lethal chromosomes. Morton and his colleagues (Morton 1964, Morton and Chung 1959, and Morton, Krieger, and Mi 1966) found no evidence of heterotic balancing selection maintaining polymorphisms in human populations, such as blood group polymorphisms (see, however, Morton and Chung 1959).

In contrast to the above, Wallace and Dobzhansky (1962) and Dobzhansky and Spassky (1963) found in *Drosophila pseudoobscura* no correlation between the viabilities of the homozygotes for a sample of chromosomes extracted from natural populations and of the heterozygotes for these same chromosomes. Marinkovic (1967) obtained similar results for fecundity and fertility. Band and Ives (1963, 1968), Band (1963, 1964), and Tobari (1966) found in *D. melanogaster* that the same chromosome may be deleterious in some but heterotic in other natural or experimental environments. Oshima and Hiroyoshi (1967) and Watanabe (1969a,b) discovered in some localities in Japan that certain lethals persist in the populations year after year. Magalhães, de Toledo, and Cunha 1965 and Magalhães, J. S. de Toledo, et al. 1965 observed what appeared to be a semidominance of lethals in *D. willistoni* at certain seasons; later they found the situation to be more complex, because a surprisingly high proportion of the lethal chromosomes contain synthetic lethals (see Chapter 3). Among eight lethals in the fly *Coelopa frigida* tested by Burnet (1962), one was deleterious, at least one and probably two heterotic, and the remainder apparently neutral when heterozygous. Müntzing (1963) studied in detail a chromosome in rye that was lethal in double dose but heterotic in single dose. For reviews of other pertinent literature, see Dobzhansky (1964a,b) and Wallace (1968a).

Crow and Temin (1964) used a different approach to detect the average deleterious effects of lethal chromosomes in the heterozygous condition in Drosophila populations. Most of the lethal chromosomes extracted from a natural population are not allelic, their lethal effects being due to mutations in different genes. Flies with two lethal chromosomes are viable if the lethals are not allelic, but they die if they have two allelic lethals. If one knew the incidence in a population of chromosomes lethal in double dose $(Q)$, and the proportion of such chromosomes with allelic lethals $(A)$, then the rate of elimination of the lethals because of homozygosis, $QA$, should be equal to the frequency of origin of lethals per chromosome, $U$. Now, the data available for populations of several species agree in showing that the mutation rate, $U$, is larger than $QA$. This is expected if most lethals have at least mildly deleterious effects in heterozygotes; since the heterozygotes for rare genes far outnumber the homozygotes, a slight depression of the fitness of heterozygotes makes elimination more effective in the heterozygous condition than in the homozygotes. Crow and Temin calculate the average deleterious effect of lethals in the heterozygous condition $(h)$ for different species to be between 0.015 and 0.018.

Unfortunately, this approach is not free of serious pitfalls. Not only does it ignore the existence of synthetic lethals, but also it assumes that all the lethals in a sample from the same "locality" came from one panmictic population. Yet Dobzhansky and Wright (1943) and Wallace (1966a, 1968a) have shown that the mobility of the flies in their natural habitats is so limited that local inbreeding doubtless takes place. The effects ascribed to semidominance of the lethals may well be due to such inbreeding.

A weakness of most experimental studies on the manifestation of near recessives in the heterozygous condition is that the experimental environments deviate, often grossly, from natural ones. To make matters worse, in many studies the chromosomes to be tested are placed on the genetic background of quite unrelated laboratory strains. This ignores the fact that natural selection operates, not with genes in a vacuum, but with genes and chromosomes in the external environments in which a population lives, and in genetic environments that are, in their turn, products of natural selection.

Dobzhansky and Spassky (1968) have made an attempt to overcome at least the second of these disabilities. Using a technique analogous to that diagramed in Fig. 3.1, they extracted 20 second chromosomes that were lethal and 25 that were quasi-normal when homozygous from a population of *Drosophila pseudoobscura* from a certain locality in California. Similarly, 25 lethal and 25 quasi-normal chromosomes were obtained from a population in Arizona. By means of a series of crosses, six kinds of strains were obtained with (1) California chromosomes on the genetic background of the California population, (2) California chromosomes on the Arizona background, (3) California chromosomes on the background of a mixture of strains of Mexico and Guatemala, (4) Arizona chromosomes on the Arizona background, (5) Arizona chromosomes on the California background, and (6) Arizona chromosomes on the Mexico-Guatemala background.

Six pairs of test crosses were then made. One cross in each pair involved a lethal and the other a quasi-normal second chromosome of the same geographic origin and genetic background. In all crosses the males had one wild-type second chromosome and one second chromosome with a mutant marker. The females were from populations of California, Arizona, and of mixed Mexico + Guatemala origin. The progeny of each cross should, theoretically, segregate in the ratio 1 : 1 of flies with and without the mutant marker. The marker-free flies have all their chromosomes of known geographic origin.

More than half a million flies were classified and counted. The results can best be summarized in the following tabulation, where asterisks indicate the differences significant at the 5 percent probability level or better:

| Second Chromosomes | Genetic Background | Viability in Heterozygotes |
|---|---|---|
| California | California | Lethals > Quasi-normals* |
| | Arizona | Quasi-normals > Lethals |
| | Mexico | Quasi-normals > Lethals* |
| Arizona | Arizona | Quasi-normals = Lethals |
| | California | Quasi-normals > Lethals* |
| | Mexico | Quasi-normals > Lethals |

Lethal chromosomes are, on the average, neutral or slightly heterotic on the genetic background of the population in which they were found; they are, on the average, slightly deleterious on foreign geographic backgrounds.

Results similar in principle have been obtained by Golubovsky (1969) and Watanabe (1969b). Watanabe tested 2773 second chromosomes of *Drosophila melanogaster* from a population in Japan on their native genetic background, and 1638 chromosomes from the same population on a foreign genetic background. The frequencies (in percentages) of lethal and semilethal chromosomes found were as follows:

|  | Native Background | Foreign Background |
|---|---|---|
| Lethals | 14.9 | 17.4 |
| Semilethals | 6.6 | 18.6 |

The deleterious effects of these chromosomes are, on the average, stronger on the foreign than on the native background.

The most securely established and, according to some, the only example of heterotic polymorphism in man is that of hemoglobin S-hemoglobin A (see Chapter 2). The gene allele responsible for hemoglobin S is quite frequent in populations that live in, or are descended from, the tropical lowlands of Africa. Homozygosis for this allele causes a severe sickle-cell anemia, and the homozygotes rarely survive adolescence. The heterozygotes have both hemoglobins, A and S, and not only enjoy nearly normal health but also are to some extent protected against *falciparum* malaria. Their adaptive value is accordingly superior to normal (A) homozygotes in lands where *falciparum* malaria is pandemic (Allison 1955, 1964, and Livingstone 1964, 1967).

Similarly, Mediterranean anemia (thalassemia) is due to homozygosis of a gene allele that makes hemoglobin C. This gene has a high incidence in populations of the Mediterranean lands and of some parts of southern Asia. Although the homozygote is lethal, the heterozygote enjoys protection against malaria (Montalenti 1965 and references therein).

The etiology of schizophrenia is a subject of unceasing polemics. Although its precise mode of inheritance is still obscure, the involvement of genetic factors is established beyond reasonable doubt. The incidence of this grave psychiatric disability in human populations is so high that the possibility must be seriously considered that at least some of the genetic factors enjoy heterozygous advantage (Erlenmeyer-Kimling and Paradowski 1966, Gottesman 1968, and references therein). The same hypothesis is applicable to a very common metabolic disorder, *diabetes mellitus* (Steinberg 1959). Also, the data of Myrianthopulos and Aronson (1966) strongly suggest that Tay-Sachs disease, a grave neurological disorder, is maintained by a reproductive advantage of the heterozygous carriers despite lethality in the homozygous condition.

## Shifting Concepts of Genetic Loads

Haldane pointed out in an insightful article (1937) that deleterious mutations impair the well-being of a population, not in proportion to the reduction of the viability or fitness of their individual carriers, but rather in proportion to the frequency of their origin. This paradox is easily explained. We saw in Chapter 4 that deleterious mutations opposed by normalizing selection eventually reach equilibrium states. At equilibrium the numbers of mutations that arise per generation are, on the average, equal to the numbers eliminated by selection. Consider, for example, a deleterious recessive that arises at a rate $u$ and is opposed by a selection $s$. Its equilibrium frequency in the population will be $q = \sqrt{u/s}$, and the frequency of homozygotes will be $q^2$. If the fitness of a homozygote is impaired to the extent $s$, the population suffers impairment $sq^2 = su/s$ or $u$, the mutation rate.

In 1950, Muller went further. "Our load of mutations," he said, consists of accumulated deleterious genetic variants arising by mutation; all such variants are eliminated eventually by "genetic death." The aggregate genetic death that "our" (i.e., the human) population suffers approximately equals the total mutation rate for all deleterious recessives, and is approximately double the mutation rate for the dominants because the latter are eliminated mainly in heterozygotes.

Since mutation rates are increasing (because, e.g., of radiation exposures), so are the genetic loads and genetic deaths. Calculations have predicted that mankind will suffer ghastly numbers of genetic deaths from its increasing genetic load. It has not always been made clear in such calculations that, as pointed out in Chapter 4, a genetic death does not necessarily produce a cadaver; if the carrier of a certain genotype gives birth to one child fewer than the carrier of another geno-type, we are witnessing a genetic death.

A formal definition given by Crow (1958) states, 'The genetic load of a population is . . . the proportion by which the population fitness (or whatever trait is being considered) is decreased in comparison with an optimum genotype." Later Crow and Kimura (1963) amended this as follows: "the proportion by which the fitness of the average genotype in the population is reduced in comparison with the best genotype." An obvious difficulty is that the operational usefulness of the "optimum" or "best" genotype as a yardstick is doubtful at best. At least in sexual outbreeding species, any two individuals, identical twins excepted, have different genotypes. How does one find, then, the individual who possesses the optimum genotype? Even supposing that this individual could be found, in the next generation there will be another single individual with another optimal genotype. It is also questionable whether this best genotype will conserve its matchless qualities in all environments in which the species lives.

The genetic load, defined as a departure from the optimal geno-type, is part and parcel of the typological thinking that is the basis of the classical model of genetic population structure (cf. Chapter 5). As Wright (1960) pointed out in his penetrating critique of this model,

If we assume that there is one best genotype and that this is homozygous for all type genes, it follows that all mutational changes from this are injurious and selected against. For each mutation there will be on the average one elimination ("genetic death") to restore the status quo. . . . If we define damage in terms of number of genetic deaths, it follows that all mutations produce equal damage in the long run and it merely becomes necessary to estimate the number of mutations produced by a given amount of radiation to appraise the damage.

The inadequacy of this model is never more apparent than when it is applied to man. Here the genetic load in a technical sense is too easily equated with its social repercussions. The "genetic death" of a child or an adult who succumbs to an agonizing hereditary disease is not at all equivalent in human terms to an early abortion or to a semisterility or sterility that interferes with childbearing. Genetic variation in man can be evaluated only in terms of the balance between the contribution that a carrier of a genotype makes to society and his social cost.

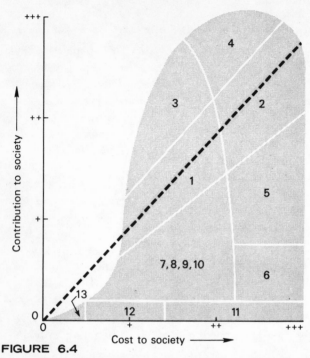

**FIGURE 6.4**

The cost and the contribution to human society of carriers of different genotypes. Further explanation in text. (After Wright)

Wright (1960) illustrates this relationship with the scheme in Fig. 6.4, where the dashed line symbolizes approximate equality of contribution and cost. The meanings of the subdivisions are as follows:

1-2. The bulk of the population (the adaptive norm): approximate balance of contribution and cost at modest levels.

3-4. The genetic elite: high to extraordinary contribution at moderate to high cost.

5. Contribution less than cost (e.g., unearned wealth).

6. Contribution much less than cost (criminals, charlatans, etc.)

7-10. Genetic load: subnormal health, low intelligence, early physical breakdown, major psychoses.

11-13. Genetic load: complete incapacity throughout lifetime, death before maturity, and death before birth.

Fraser (1962) rightly points out that the concept of genetic load "might be more realistic if the average rather than the optimum fitness (of a population) were considered." If one wishes to adhere to Crow's definition of a genetic load as given above, another term, such as "genetic burden" (Dobzhansky 1964a,b), might be more apt to evaluate the biological consequences of genetic variation on the overall adaptedness of a population or a species.

The mean adaptedness of a population is a meaningful and operationally accessible yardstick. One may distinguish further the adaptive norm, genetic burden or load, and genetic elite. The fact that the boundaries between these categories can be established only by convention is an advantage rather than a disadvantage. Consider, for example, classes 5 and 6 in Wright's classification. For some purposes these classes may be considered a part of the social and, by extension, the genetic burden, whereas from the more technical standpoint of public health they belong to the adaptive norm.

Perhaps the most serious drawback of the genetic load and, for that matter, genetic burden concepts is their failure to consider genetic variability in relation to the ecological factors that determine the death rates and population sizes in nature. As pointed out by Wallace (1968a,b).

Novel sources of premature death need not be met by a corresponding increase in the number of progeny produced. Population size, not progeny size, takes up the immediate shock of both genetic and nongenetic deaths. . . . The important point that emerges is that both genetic and nongenetic loads are absorbed not only by progeny size but by population size as well. Furthermore, with changing population size, the distinction between genetic and environmental loads is to a large extent removed; one type of load can be exchanged for another.

We shall return to a consideration of the ecological aspects of selection in Chapter 7.

### Lethal Equivalents and B : A Ratios

Morton, Crow, and Muller (1956) and Morton (1960) proposed to measure the genetic loads of different populations and even of species by expressing them in terms of "lethal equivalents." At the same time, they suggested a method to estimate the relative weights of the two components of the genetic loads—that kept up by mutation pressure and that maintained by heterotic balancing selection. These works can be esteemed as seminal, because of the great amount of experimentation, observation, and theoretical thought that they have evoked. On the other hand, doubts about the validity of the measures and the methods proposed may make it difficult to justify such an accolade.

A lethal equivalent is defined as "a group of mutant genes of such number that, if dispersed in different individuals, they would cause on the average one death, e.g., one lethal mutant, or two mutants each with 50 percent probability of causing death, etc. . . . The total mutational damage per gamete is the average number of lethal equivalents in the zygote that would result from doubling the chromosomes of this gamete." The probability of survival of a zygote, considering a single gene with a "normal" and a deleterious allele, is:

$$1 - qFs - q^2(1 - F)s - 2q(1 - q)(1 - F)sh$$

where $q$ is the frequency of the deleterious allele, $s$ the selection coefficient, and $h$ the coefficient of dominance. $F$ is the coefficient of inbreeding, which equals 0.25 for children of siblings, 0.0625 for children of first cousins, 0.0156 for children of second cousins, etc. Also, $qFs$ is the probability of death due to homozygosis from inbreeding (consanguinity), $q^2(1 - F)s$ the probability of death due to homozygosis under random mating, and $2q(1 - q)(1 - F)sh$ the probability of death due to deleterious effects in the heterozygotes.

A population carries deleterious mutant alleles of many genes. Furthermore, some deaths are due to environmental accidents ($x$). Morton, Crow, and Muller have assumed that all the genetic and environmental causes of death act independently of one another. The probability ($S$) of survival of a zygote in a population is then:

$$S = e^{-\Sigma x - F\Sigma qs - (1-F)\Sigma q^2 s - 2(1-F)\Sigma q(1-q)sh}$$

This expression can be conveniently written as:

$$-\ln S = A + BF$$

where $A$ is the mortality from genetic causes and environmental accidents in the population under random mating ($F = 0$), and $B$ is the concealed genetic load that would be expressed under complete homozygosis ($F = 1$). The values of $A$ and $B$ separately are:

$$A = \Sigma x + \Sigma q^2 s + 2\Sigma q(1-q)sh$$
$$B = \Sigma qs - \Sigma q^2 s - 2\Sigma q(1-q)sh$$

The total genetic load, expressed under this interpretation in lethal equivalents, is $B$ plus the genetic components of $A$ (i.e., excluding the environmental accidents, $\Sigma x$). The relative magnitudes of $A$ and $B$, that is, of the mortality or loss of fitness under random mating and with inbreeding, may give us an insight into the nature of the genetic load.

Consider as before (Chapter 5) a polymorphism for two alleles of a gene maintained by heterotic balancing selection, with selection coefficients $s$ and $t$ acting against the homozygotes. At equilibrium, the loss of viability or fitness will be $A = st/(s + t)$. If the population were to become completely homozygous (i.e., if the heterotic heterozygotes disappeared), the loss of viability or fitness would be $B = 2st/(s + t)$. The $B : A$ ratio is, then, 2 (with three alleles giving equally heterotic heterozygotes it would be 3, and with $n$ alleles it would be $n$). By contrast, with deleterious genes maintained by mutation pressure and opposed by normalizing selection, the $B : A$ ratio may be much larger. We have seen that, at equilibrium, the heterozygous carriers of deleterious recessives far outnumber the homozygotes. Even if recessivity is incomplete and the heterozygotes are opposed by a selection $sh$, the $B : A$ ratio will be approximately ½$h$. If the coefficients of dominance, $h$, are assumed to lie between 1 and 5 percent, the $B : A$ ratios will be between 10 and 50.

Accurate measurements of inbreeding effects in normally outbreeding species, such as man, were scarce before the work of Morton, Crow, and Muller gave impetus for the collection of such data. These authors utilized whatever observations were available on mortality and morbidity in the progenies of parents not known to be relatives, and among children of relatives, mostly cousin marriages. The average genetic load that a person carries was estimated as between 3 and 5 lethal equivalents (or between 1.5 and 2.5 per gamete). The $B : A$ ratios in different samples ranged from 7.94 to 24.41. This was taken as evidence that genetic loads in human populations are due chiefly to recurrent mutations; polymorphisms maintained by heterotic balancing selection were deemed rare and unimportant.

These conclusions were soon challenged on several grounds. A detailed and critical review of data on human populations has been given by Schull and Neel (1965). Data most carefully collected and analyzed by these investigators themselves for two Japanese cities have yielded the following estimates of lethal equivalents per gamete:

| City | Stillbirths | Neonatal Deaths | Infantile and Juvenile Deaths | Total |
|------|-------------|-----------------|-------------------------------|-------|
| Hiroshima | 0.14 | 0.29 | 0.63 | 1.06 |
| Nagasaki | − 0.02 | 0.20 | 0.15 | 0.33 |

Not only does the genetic load of the Hiroshima population seem to be three times heavier than that of Nagasaki, but also the $B : A$ ratios for these populations turn out to be 6.08 and 1.08, respectively. Taken at face value, these figures indicate a predominance of mutational load in Hiroshima and of balanced load in Nagasaki. Neel and Schull (1962) pointed out, however, that the same $B : A$ ratio (10 in their theoretical example) may arise under various conditions, with predominance of either the mutational or the balanced component of the genetic load.

By definition (see above), the lethal equivalents measure the genetic load that would be expressed at complete homozygosis ($F = 1$). In reality, the estimates can be obtained only by extrapolation from observations on much lower degrees of inbreeding. In man, marriages of first cousins ($F = 0.0625$) furnish the greater part of the data. Epistatic interactions between the components of the genetic loads could make the extrapolations seriously faulty. Suppose, for example, that the survival rate from disease A is 60 percent, and from disease B is 40 percent. If the survival and mortality from the two diseases are independent, 24 percent of those contracting both diseases simultaneously can be expected to survive. However, it may be that a double insult will leave few or no survivors (positive synergism); conversely, one disease may somehow counteract the other (negative synergism).

This problem is more easily approached in experimental animals or plants than in human materials. Dobzhansky, Spassky, and Tidwell (1963), Stone, Wilson, and Gerstenberg (1963), Torroja (1964), Mettler, Moyer, and Kojima (1966), and Spassky, Dobzhansky, and Anderson (1965) worked with *Drosophila pseudoobscura*; Nicoletti and Giardina (1964), Crow (1968), and Temin, Meyer, et al. (1969) with *D. melanogaster*; Malogolowkin-Cohen, Levene, et al. (1964) with *D. willistoni*; and Levene, Lerner, et al. (1965) with *Tribolium castaneum* and *T. confusum*. In almost all cases evidence of appreciable interactions was found.

The estimates of the numbers of lethal equivalents ($B$) derived from the publications just cited vary from $0.490 \pm 0.094$ to $0.876 \pm 0.247$ for *Drosophila pseudoobscura* and from $0.828 \pm 0.129$ to $1.435 \pm 0.160$ for *D. willistoni*. The $B : A$ ratios range from $3.30 \pm 1.59$ to $7.39 \pm 2.67$ in *D. pseudoobscura* and from $4.84 \pm 0.86$ to $14.97 \pm 6.67$ in *D. willistoni*. The experiments on Tribolium were made on two species (*T. castaneum* and *T. confusum*), in two environments that differ in humidity, and in a variety of outbred and inbred strains. The mortalities were recorded separately at each stage of the life cycle. The mean estimate of $B$ is 0.75 for outbred strains of *T. castaneum* and 0.44 for *T. confusum*. The mean $B : A$ ratios are 3.7 for outbred *T. castaneum* and 1.7 for *T. confusum*.

An overview of the available data leads, then, to a conclusion that could not be (or at least has not been) anticipated on theoretical grounds. The genetic loads in human populations, judged by the criteria used, are of the same order of magnitude as those in the lowly flies and beetles, Drosophila and Tribolium. On the other hand, Sorensen (1969) estimates the load in the Douglas fir. *Pseudotsuga menziesii*, to be between 3 and 27 lethal equivalents, with a median value of about 10. Actually, the genetic loads have not yet been measured with any precision in any of these species. Furthermore, the hope that the $B : A$ ratio may permit one to discriminate between the mutational and the balanced components of the loads has not been realized (see Levene 1963 and Levene, Lerner, et al. 1965).

## Balance and Classical Models Contrasted

In Chapter 4 we discussed the classical model of the genetic population structure, which assumes that there exists a "normal type" of each species or population, carrying the "normal genes." Evidence delineated in Chapters 5 and 6 places the validity of this model in doubt. Many genes in natural populations are not represented by homozygous "normal" alleles. Heterozygosis is common, because polymorphisms maintained by various forms of balancing selection are widespread or even ubiquitous. The balance model of the genetic population structure acknowledges genetic diversity as a fundamental phenomenon of nature. The gene pool of a population is envisaged as an array of alleles at many, perhaps at most, gene loci. None of these alleles may be the universally "normal" ones; the fitness conferred by many of these gene alleles on their carriers depends on what other alleles at the same and at other loci are present in the genotype and, of course, on the environment in which the carriers develop and live. There is no "normal type," only an adaptive norm composed of an array of genotypes, the common property of which is that they yield a satisfactory fitness in most of the environments which the population frequently encounters. The adaptive norm is not sharply delimited from the genetic load on one side and the genetic elite on the other. Many genotypes pass from one of these arbitrary classes to the others when the environment is altered.

Following Wallace (1968a), it is convenient to contrast the classical and the balance models by considering the extreme but perhaps not entirely unrealistic situations depicted in Fig. 6.5. In classical Dro-

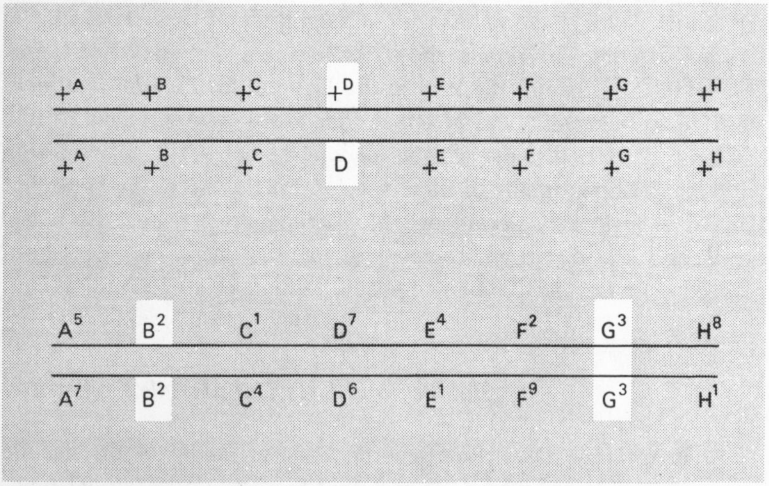

**FIGURE 6.5**

The classical (above) and the balance (below) models of the genetic population structure. In the former only a single gene locus is heterozygous $(D/+^D)$; in the latter only two loci are shown to be homozygous. $(B^2/B^2$ and $G^3/G^3$, after Wallace)

sophila genetics it has been customary to symbolize the normal, or wild-type, allele of each gene by a + (plus). The ideal normal type of the classical model would be then homozygous for all + alleles. This ideal is not always realized, however, because of mutation pressure. Many, perhaps all, individuals will have here and there a mutant allele at some locus or loci (Fig. 6.5, upper part). The balance model envisages a greater or lesser proportion of the gene loci being in the heterozygous state, frequently though not invariably for pairs of interacting alleles that give heterosis. How great this proportion is likely to be will be discussed in the next chapter. Some inbreeding occurs in all populations; in the lower part of Fig. 6.5 three-quarters of the loci are represented as heterozygous, and none of the alleles is symbolized by a +.

# CHAPTER SEVEN

# DIRECTIONAL SELECTION

## *Sieve and Beanbag Analogies*

The action of natural selection has often been compared to that of a sieve. Selection allegedly creates nothing new; it merely allows relatively ill-adapted genetic variants to be lost, and retains the better adapted ones. A related analogy is dubbed "beanbag genetics." According to Mayr (1963):

The procedure of the classical Mendelian genetics, of studying each gene locus separately and independently, was a simplification necessary to permit the determination of the laws of inheritance and to obtain basic information on the physiology of the gene. . . . The Mendelian was apt to compare the genetic contents of a population to a bag full of colored beans. Mutation was the exchange of one kind of bean for another.

Haldane (1964) promptly made a spirited defense of "beanbag genetics;" it has furnished many useful models of genetic processes, expressed in rigorous mathematical language.

The disagreement is illusory. The sieve analogy does apply in some circumstances. When a bacterial culture of many millions of cells is exposed to a sufficient concentration of an antibiotic, there is perhaps a single mutant cell, a differently colored "bean" in a very large bag, that survives and gives a culture of a resistant variety. The same thing may well occur in a population of an insect pest treated with DDT or another insecticide. On the other hand, Mayr rightly stresses that genes not only act but also interact, a fact of which Haldane was fully aware. Darwinian fitness is a property not of a gene but of a genotype and of the phenotypes conditioned by this genotype. Selection favors, or discriminates against, genotypes, that is, gene patterns. The coadaptation of supergenes, discussed in Chapter 5, and frequency-dependent selection, dealt with in Chapter 6, go beyond individual genotypes and operate in gene pools of populations. To sustain the sieve analogy, one would have to imagine an extraordinary "sieve," in which the loss or retention of a particle would depend on the other particles it contains.

Consider the emergence of man from his Australopithecus-like ancestors. This was hardly a matter of the superposition of a few lucky mutations; major evolutionary advances probably always involve reconstructions of the genetic system. That selection can work only with raw materials arisen ultimately by mutation is manifestly true. But it is also true that populations, particularly those of diploid outbreeding species, have stored in them a profusion of genetic variability. A temporary suppression of the mutation process, even if it could be brought about, would have no immediate effect on evolutionary plasticity. Rapidly evolving groups need not have high mutation rates, nor should evolutionary stasis be taken as evidence of insufficient mutability. Polymorphisms maintained by various forms of balancing selection provide strikingly sensitive genetic systems that can react to changes in the environment without waiting for new mutations to appear. In Drosophila even seasonal changes in the environment evoke genetic alterations (Chapter 5). These alterations are, of course, cyclic and reversible. The gene pool is in constant motion; if a simile is desired, a stormy sea is more appropriate than a beanbag.

## The Efficacy of Artificial Selection

Darwin used artificial selection as a model of the natural process; a mathematical theory of selection must almost necessarily be derived from experiments on artificial selection. Perhaps the longest (50 years) selection experiment reported in detail is that of Woodworth, Leng, and Jugenheimer (1952). Selection for high and low protein and oil contents in corn gave results summarized in Table 7.1. Not only was the selection highly effective, but also no "plateau" seems to have been reached even after 50 generations.

An equally spectacular selection experiment, increasing the egg production in a White Leghorn flock between the years 1933 and 1965, has been reported by Lerner (1958, 1968). Spring-hatched pullets of the foundation stock laid on the average 125.6 eggs a year, of which only 24.1 eggs were laid before January 1. In 1965 the average annual production was 249.6 eggs, and the number laid by January 1 almost quintupled compared to the 1933 record.

**TABLE 7.1**

Progress of selection for protein and oil contents in corn (in percentages) (After Woodworth, Leng, and Jugenheimer 1952)

| Generation | High | | Low | |
|---|---|---|---|---|
| | Protein | Oil | Protein | Oil |
| Initial | 10.9 | 4.7 | 10.9 | 4.7 |
| 5 | 13.8 | 6.2 | 9.6 | 3.4 |
| 10 | 14.3 | 7.4 | 8.6 | 2.7 |
| 15 | 13.8 | 7.5 | 7.9 | 2.1 |
| 20 | 15.7 | 8.5 | 8.7 | 2.1 |
| 25 | 16.7 | 9.9 | 9.1 | 1.7 |
| 30 | 18.2 | 10.2 | 6.5 | 1.4 |
| 35 | 20.1 | 11.8 | 2.1 | 1.2 |
| 40 | 22.9 | 10.2 | 8.0 | 1.2 |
| 45 | 17.8 | 13.7 | 5.8 | 1.0 |
| 50 | 19.4 | 15.4 | 4.9 | 1.0 |

A summary of the history of improvement of the mold *Penicillium chrysogenum*, a producer of penicillin, is given by Dubinin (1961). The productivity of the original strain is taken as 100; selection of a spontaneous mutant increased it to 250. A mutant induced by X-ray almost doubled the productivity to 500, and an ultraviolet-induced mutant further raised it to 900. Another mutant, also induced by ultraviolet, decreased the productivity to 675, but freed the strain from an undesirable yellow pigment. A sequence of further mutations induced by ultraviolet and nitrogen mustard raised the productivity to 2000, 2500, 3000, and finally to 5000 units.

Insect strains can be selected for resistance to DDT and other insecticides (see below) or to poisons such as copper sulfate (Yanagishima 1961). One may wonder whence the genetic variance selectable for such resistances comes. Has nature equipped insect pests with genes for resistance in anticipation of chemists inventing ever new insecticides? Of course, this is not so; resistance to insecticides is achieved by modifications of physiological processes that originally served quite different functions. For example, houseflies resistant to DDT contain dehydrochlorinase, an enzyme that is also present, though in much lower quantities, in nonresistant strains (review in Bender and Gaensslen 1967).

How successful a selection program will prove to be is not easily predictable. Indeed, "no geneticist has succeeded, despite several efforts, in producing rat-sized mice, while dog fanciers, not in the least versed in genetics, have produced a fifty-fold range of variability, stretching from the four-pound Chihuahua to the St. Bernard weighing 200 pounds" (Lerner and Donald 1966). Waddington (1960) selected a strain of *Drosophila melanogaster* that survived feeding on a medium with up to 7 percent sodium chloride; by contrast, *D. pseudoobscura*, after 30 generations of selection for salt resistance, rarely survived on a medium with 3 percent sodium chloride (Dobzhansky and Spassky 1967b). Yet, it is remarkable that almost any trait, at least in sexually reproducing organisms, is changeable by artificial selection if applied systematically and for many generations.

## The Heritability and Prediction
## of Selection Gains

Consider a continuously varying trait, such as size of the body or of its parts, rate of growth, productivity, or Darwinian fitness. The selection of such traits has been practiced for several millennia and studied scientifically for more than a century. Modern genetic theory derives from the works of Wright (1921), Fisher (1930), and Mather and Harrison (1949).

Usually, though not always, continuously varying traits have a polygenic basis. The genes concerned have individually small phenotypic effects, and as a rule give intermediate heterozygotes instead of dominance or recessiveness. Again as a rule, these genes cannot be isolated and studied one by one, although Thoday and his colleagues (Spickett and Thoday 1966, Thoday 1967, and references therein) have achieved just such a feat.

The observed phenotypic variance ($\sigma_P^2$, the average squared deviation from the mean) usually has a component due to environmental modifications ($\sigma_E^2$) and also a genotypic component ($\sigma_G^2$). The latter is, in turn, a composite. The additive or genetic variance ($\sigma_A^2$) is "traceable to the differences between the average values of the different alleles in all genetic combinations in which they appear" (Lerner 1958). The remainder of the genotypic variance is due to dominance, recessiveness, or overdominance ($\sigma_D^2$), and to the epistatic interaction of genes at different loci ($\sigma_I^2$). Fisher's (1930) so-called fundamental theorem of natural selection states that "rate of increase in fitness of any organism at any time is equal to its additive genetic variance in fitness at that time."

An important statistic is the heritability, $h^2$, which is the ratio of the additive to the phenotypic variance, $\sigma_A^2/\sigma_P^2$. Several methods for the estimation of heritability have been devised. They are alike in principle; the expression of the trait concerned is compared in the population submitted to the selection, in the individuals selected, and in the progeny of these individuals. Heritability of 1.00, or 100 percent, means that the progeny is exactly like the selected parents; zero heritability means absence of correlation between the parents and their offspring. In reality, the heritabilities usually fall between these limits. Examples of heritabilities compiled from Falconer (1960a) and Brewbaker (1964) are as follows:

| | | | |
|---|---|---|---|
| Amount of white spotting in Friesian cattle | 0.95 | Ovary response to gonadotrophic horomone in rats | 0.35 |
| Slaughter weight in cattle | 0.85 | Milk production in cattle | 0.30 |
| Plant height in corn | 0.70 | Yield in corn | 0.25 |
| Root length in radishes | 0.65 | Egg production in poultry | 0.20 |
| Egg weight in poultry | 0.60 | Egg production in Drosophila | 0.20 |
| Thickness of back fat in pigs | 0.55 | Ear length in corn | 0.17 |
| | | Litter size in mice | 0.15 |
| Weight of fleece in sheep | 0.40 | Conception rate in cattle | 0.05 |

Heritability is not an immutable property of a trait. For environmentally labile traits heritability increases as the environment in which the population lives becomes more uniform, and decreases in heterogeneous environments. Inbreeding may lower heritability, and hybridization and mutation may increase it. Furthermore, the heritability measured in a single generation may not be the same as the heritability realized over several consecutive generations of selection. A great deal of experimental and theoretical work has been carried out, especially by the Edinburgh school of geneticists, to test the predictive value of the genetic theory of selection (F. W. Robertson 1955, 1957; Clayton, Morris, and A. Robertson 1957; A. Robertson 1960; Falconer 1960a, also Lerner 1958, and references therein). Can selection gains for a given trait be predicted if the heritability of the trait is known? The answer generally is that such predictions are borne out fairly well for several initial generations of selection. As the selection progresses, however, the gains are less and less in accord with expectation, being generally below those anticipated. Eventually the selection brings no response, and a "plateau" or "ceiling" is reached.

The simplest (and often the valid) explanation of selection plateaus is depletion of the store of genetic variation. The limiting case would occur if the selection favored a single genotype among many present in the original population, and this genotype were established to the exclusion of all others. One would then expect that in a population reaching a plateau for a given trait the heritability of this trait would be zero. One would also expect that relaxation (suspension) of the selection would leave the selection gains intact in the generations that followed. These expectations are in fact realized in some experiments; but in others heritability continues to be present, and when the selection is discontinued the selected trait gradually relapses toward the original population mean. Lerner (1954) defined "the property of the population to equilibrate its genetic composition and to resist sudden changes" as genetic homeostasis.

## *Mutability and Selection Advances*

It has been mentioned above that outbred sexual diploid populations generally have sufficient stores of genetic variability to respond to challenges of selection. As pointed out particularly by Mather (1953 and earlier works), the entire contents of these stores are not immediately available for selection to work with. If a trait is influenced by many genes, several genes modifying this trait in plus and minus directions may be linked in the same chromosomes. This variability can be "released" gradually, as crossing over generates chromosomes with only plus or only minus modifiers. In a population that has reached a selection plateau, the selection may suddenly become effective again, and then a new plateau is achieved. Such resumption of the activity of selection may be due to either or both of two causes: recombination of tightly linked genes, and the origin of new mutations. It is often difficult to discriminate between these possibilities.

The induction of useful mutants by X-ray or other mutagens was described in Chapter 3. Attempts to augment the supply of genetic variance by similar means have repeatedly been made. The most successful of these was reported by Scossirolli (1954, 1965). His starting material was a population of *Drosophila melanogaster*, which was previously selected for increased numbers of sternopleural bristles and had reached a plateau. Irradiation of this population ushered in a spectacular spurt of selection effectiveness. On the other hand, the attempt of Abplanalp, Lowry, et al. (1964) to achieve a similar enhancement of selection effectiveness for egg production in poultry gave a negative result.

The experiments of Ayala (1966, 1967, and references therein) are particularly interesting because the traits selected in them are closely affiliated to the adaptedness of the populations for living in stressful environments—to be sure, artificial. Populations of two related species, *Drosophila serrata* and *D. birchii*, were maintained by a serial transfer technique. Adult flies were introduced into regular culture bottles and transferred three times a week to fresh bottles; when the eggs deposited developed into new adults, these were counted, weighed, and added to the surviving older adults. Once in 2 weeks the adult populations were etherized, weighed, and counted. The productivity and the longevity, as well as the total population size, were thus recorded. The culture bottles were crowded, and the competition was intense. The resulting natural selection effected a steady improvement in the above parameters of adaptedness. Some populations received 2000 r of X-rays, while others served as unirradiated controls. In Table 7.2 it can be seen that the improvements were noticeably greater in the irradiated than in the control populations. It is hardly necessary to add that this result should be viewed in the perspective of the severity

**TABLE 7.2**

Productivity achieved by natural selection in unirradiated control and irradiated Drosophila populations (After Ayala 1966, 1967)

| | Number of Individuals | | Biomass, mg | |
| Population | Total Population | Produces per Week | Total Population | Produces per Week |
| --- | --- | --- | --- | --- |
| D. serrata | | | | |
| Control | $1294 \pm 50$ | $595 \pm 21$ | $868 \pm 32$ | $316 \pm 27$ |
| Irradiated I | $1955 \pm 65$ | $941 \pm 30$ | $1309 \pm 48$ | $527 \pm 22$ |
| Irradiated II | $2558 \pm 98$ | $1133 \pm 27$ | $1676 \pm 60$ | $614 \pm 20$ |
| D. birchii | | | | |
| Control | $992 \pm 67$ | $533 \pm 22$ | $651 \pm 39$ | $275 \pm 15$ |
| Irradiated I | $1800 \pm 167$ | $933 \pm 32$ | $1223 \pm 81$ | $497 \pm 36$ |
| Irradiated II | $1756 \pm 103$ | $833 \pm 31$ | $1149 \pm 70$ | $457 \pm 31$ |

of the selection to which these populations were exposed; the relatively few favorable mutants induced were doubtless far outnumbered by the unfavorable ones that were selected out.

### *Genetic Homeostasis*

Selection of *Drosophila pseudoobscura* for positive and for negative response to light (phototaxis) has given results represented in Fig. 7.1. In every generation, batches of 300 females and 300 males are forced to run through a maze, in which a fly must make 15 choices of light or dark passages. A fly that always chooses light is given a score of 16, and one choosing darkness a score of 1. The population was originally neutral to light, with an average score of almost exactly 8.5. To select for negative phototaxis 25 pairs of flies with lowest scores, and for positive phototaxis 25 pairs with highest scores, are chosen to be parents of the next generation. The realized heritability of behavior with respect to light is quite low, 0.09. Nevertheless, as the figure shows, genetically photopositive and photonegative populations have

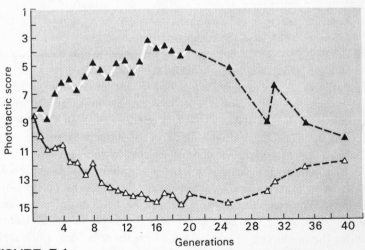

**FIGURE 7.1**

Selection for positive (light triangles) and negative (dark triangles) phototaxis Drosophila pseudoobscura. After the twentieth generation the selection was relaxed (dashed lines). (After Dobzhansky and Spassky)

been obtained (Dobzhansky and Spassky 1967a, 1969). After 20 generations of selection, very few flies were making equal numbers of light and dark choices.

Starting in the twentieth generation, the selection was relaxed. The parents of the following generations were taken regardless of their phototactic response. In about every fifth generation thereafter the populations were tested for their responses to light. It can be seen (dashed lines in Fig. 7.1) that the divergence in the phototactic response achieved by selection was almost obliterated by the fortieth generation. In point of fact, the population selected for negative phototaxis ended by being slightly photopositive. Very similar results have been obtained with selection for reaction to gravity (geotaxis).

Animal and plant breeders have found, sometimes to their displeasure, that relaxation of selection is quite often, though not invariably, followed by a gradual loss of what the selection had previously accomplished. Moreover, the deceleration of selection gains and the reaching of a "plateau" may occur without depletion of genetic variance. Lerner (1954) has analyzed this situation in a brilliant book. Genetic homostasis may be brought about by several mechanisms that are not mutually exclusive alternatives. The mean values of some characters in a population may be established and preserved by natural selection. For example, the mean size or weight of an animal, the rate of its development, and the mean number of progeny produced are those that yield the best achievable adaptedness in the environments in which the population lives. Artificial selection imposed on a population displaces these characters from their optima and is at loggerheads with natural selection; unless complete homozygosis for the genes concerned is reached, natural selection operates to undo the damage wrought by artificial selection as soon as the latter is relaxed.

A genotype that gives an optimal expression of a particular trait may be a heterozygote for one or more genes, and it will beget less fit homozygotes in the progeny. Lerner quotes the statement of a poultry breeder: "What one bird does, flocks can be bred to do," and comments, "Presumably the assumption is that the physiological factors limiting the production of any individual are the only ones which limit the production of a group. However, the laws governing the physiology of populations transcend those governing the physiology of individuals."

It is not necessary to suppose that the trait artificially selected for, in itself, conflicts with natural selection. Even if it is important in nature for a Drosophila population to be on the average photo- and geotactically neutral, it is not evident that such neutrality is also imperative for populations in laboratory bottles or cages. However, selection for one trait often produces correlated effects on other traits (see the next section). We have used above, as a paradigm of selection processes, the selection in bacterial cultures of mutants resistant to antibiotics or to the attacks of bacteriophages. In populations of diploid and outbreeding forms selection may be a more complex operation. Selection for one trait may unintentionally induce alterations elsewhere in the genetic system. Such alterations may be expected often to conflict with the exigencies of general adaptedness to the environment. Lerner (1954) has stressed particularly that high adaptedness of a population may depend on a certain "level of obligate heterozygosity," that is, on most of the component individuals being heterozygous for many gene alleles maintained, as we would now say, by the heterotic form of balancing natural selection. The level "for each species and probably for each less inclusive Mendelian population is determined by its evolutionary history." This obligate level may be interfered with by rapid changes imposed by artificial or natural selection.

## Correlated Responses to Selection

Darwin stressed that "the whole organism is so tied together during its growth and development, that when slight variations in any one part occur, and are accumulated through natural selection, other parts become modified. This is a very important subject, most imperfectly understood." Our present, still imperfect, understanding of such correlations derives mainly from works of Mather and Harrison (1949), Clayton, Knight, et al. (1957), Lerner (1958), and Falconer (1960a,b and references therein). The simplest cause is the pleiotropism of many genetic variants (see Chapter 2). For example, mutants in Drosophila that arrest the formation of the brown pigment in the eyes have pale or colorless testicular envelopes. Tight linkage of genes carried in the same chromosomes is a less simple but quite frequent cause.

The character selected for by Mather and Harrison (1949) was the number of abdominal bristles in *Drosophila melanogaster*; correlated responses included sterility and the numbers of spermathecae. Berg

(1960) studied "pleiades" of correlated characters in several plant species; Belyaev and Evsikov (1967) found the pelage colors in mink to be correlated with fertility and other physiological traits of these animals. Selection in Tribolium for modifications of the development rate also changes the body size, productivity, and viability of the beetles (Dawson 1966). Dobzhansky and Spassky (1967b) found in *D. pseudoobscura* that selection for the ability of larvae to develop on food with increased concentrations of sodium chloride interferes with the progress of simultaneous selection for geotaxis.

The literature dealing with correlated responses to selection for desirable traits in domesticated animals and agricultural plants is extensive and scattered; there are some useful references, in addition to those cited above, in Schwanitz (1967). Correlated responses due to pleiotropisms (physiological correlations) may make it impossible to endow a breed of domestic animals or plants with combinations of characteristics that would be desirable to man but are physiologically incompatible (see Lerner and Donald 1966). Correlations due to linkage can be overcome more easily, if desired crossovers are obtained; nevertheless, they may seriously slow down a selection program (Shultz 1953). Under natural selection, correlated responses may help to explain the combinations, found in many living species, of high adaptedness in some respects with other apparently maladapted traits.

Transference of the gains achieved by selection in one environment to other environments is a kindred problem. Falconer (1960a) selected mice, and Park, Hansen, et al. (1966) bred rats, kept on abundant and on meager diets, for large and for small body sizes. The selection was effective in both directions in both environments. Mice selected for large size on meager diet were bigger than those similarly selected on abundant diet when raised on a low plane of nutrition. Mice selected on either type of diet for small size were equally small when given a meager diet; those selected for small size on low diet were larger when grown on abundant diet.

In analogous experiments of Druger (1967), *Drosophila pseudoobscura* was selected at two temperatures, 25°C and 16°C, for long and for short wings (and large and small body size correlated with wing length). Control flies are larger when grown at low than at high temperature. Selection responses were obtained in both directions at both temperatures. When the selection was made in the same direction as the environmental modification, however, the carry-over of the selection gains to the other environment was incomplete. Results similar in principle were obtained also by Frahm and Kojima (1966) and by Tantawy and El-Helw (1966).

Canalizing selection (Chapter 4) tends to stabilize the development pattern of a species, to make certain traits develop similarly in most environments that this species encounters in its habitats. The result is eventually that some traits show little or no variation, being uniform in all representatives of the species. Are such traits genetically frozen, or can they be altered by selection? To consider a specific case, the number of secondary vibrissae (whiskers) in the house mouse is fixed at 19. However, a mutant gene Tabby reduces this number and makes it variable. Selection on the genetic background of Tabby permits genetic changes in positive as well as negative directions. Eventually, normal (i.e., non-Tabby) mice obtained from the selected strains have numbers of vibrissae deviating from 19 (Dun and Fraser 1959, and Kindred 1967). The constancy of the vibrissae number is evidently a result of developmental buffering, and not of lack of genotypic variance.

Waddington's (1953) so-called "genetic assimilation of an acquired character" is a similar tour de force, but achieved by manipulation of the external rather than of the genetic environment. Certain strains of *Drosophila melangogaster* exposed to 40°C for some hours during the pupal stage show a break in a particular wing vein, giving them a resemblance to the mutant crossveinless. Selection for and against the induction of this phenocopy (Chapter 2) was successful. Eventually the strain giving a strongly expressed phenocopy after the heat treatment showed some breaks in the crossvein at normal temperature as well. The analogy with alleged Lamarckian inheritance is superficial, at best, as Waddington clearly realizes. In a series of most careful studies Milkman (1962, 1965, 1966) demonstrated that polygenic variation modifying the crossveins in Drosophila is widespread in natural populations.

## *Industrial Melanism*

Darwin argued that natural selection must be genetically altering the living species. He did not claim to have observed the alterations; he supposed that the changes are too slow to be noticeable in a human lifetime. In general this remains true; yet some instances are on record in which changes wrought by natural selection have been witnessed. Changes in the chromosomal constitution of Drosophila populations were discussed in Chapter 5. Industrial melanism in moths, however, provides the most striking example, outside the realm of microorganisms.

A melanic, black variant of the moth *Biston betularia* was recorded in Manchester, England, as far back as 1848. The original form of this insect, light gray peppered with black dots, was until then the only one known. By 1895, however, about 98 percent of these moths in Manchester were black, and the melanic variants spread and became common or predominant in most of the industrial districts of England. The appearance and the spread in industrial districts of melanic forms are by now recorded for roughly 100 species of moths, mostly in Britain but also on the European continent and in North America. So spectacular a phenomenon could not fail to bring forth speculations, some of which were, it is now evident, on the wrong track. It was surmised, for example, that melanic mutations were produced by salts of heavy metals (lead and manganese) on the foliage of the vegetation polluted with industrial fumes. This would require mutation rates some orders of magnitude greater than are known to be induced by strong mutagens.

The modern understanding is derived chiefly from the splendid works of Kettlewell (1955, 1961, 1965), Clarke and Sheppard (1966), and Ford (1964, 1965, and references therein). In brief, the melanic variants are colored protectively where they rest on vegetation blackened by industrial pollutants, whereas the light-colored ancestral forms are better camouflaged on light backgrounds. Natural selection favors the variants best protected from predators by being inconspicuous because their colors match the most frequent backgrounds. The chief predators are birds, which hunt by sight and which were observed to pick moths resting on tree trunks.

Kettlewell has given an experimental demonstration that the color camouflage is really effective. He released equal numbers of melanic and light variants of *Biston betularia* in two woods; in one wood the bark of the trees was free of soot and overgrown with light lichens, and in the other the trees were blackened by soot and lichens were absent. In the first wood 12.5 percent of the light and 6.3 percent of the melanic specimens were recaptured alive; in the second wood there were 13.1 percent of lights and 27.5 percent of melanics among those recaptured. Among 190 moths observed to be seized by birds in the unpolluted wood, 164 were melanics and only 26 were light-colored. In the polluted area, 43 light and 15 of the equally numerous melanics fell victims to birds.

With few exceptions, the melanic variants were shown by breeding experiments to differ from the original light forms in single genes, and the dark colorations proved to be dominant over the light ones. Before the nineteenth century mutations from light to melanic forms were doubtless appearing spontaneously in *Biston betularia* and in other species, and were constantly eliminated by natural selection because their carriers were not camouflaged and were exposed to predators. The Industrial Revolution, however, caused widespread pollution of the countryside. The direction of the selection became reversed: the melanics are now protectively colored, whereas the formerly "normal" light forms are at a disadvantage in industrial districts. Here, then, is natural selection modifying a wild species toward better adaptedness in man-made environments.

Substitution of the melanic for the light alleles is, however, not the whole story. Since the alleles for melanism are dominant, the melanics in nature are mostly heterozygotes, at least until they become more frequent than the original form. It appears that during the half century between 1900 and 1950 the heterozygotes evolved heterosis, which they did not possess formerly. Records have been preserved of crosses of melanic to light *Biston betularia* made at the beginning of the century. The progeny showed a 1 : 1 segregation of the dark and the light. Similar crosses made by Kettlewell in 1953, however, gave a significant excess of melanics. Furthermore, the heterozygotes preserved in old collections are appreciably less darkly pigmented than those found in nature now. The advantage of melanism in polluted areas is evidently so great that natural selection promotes the spread of more extreme alleles as well as of some darkening modifying genes, in addition to the major gene for melanism. Hence the genetic difference between the melanic and the nonmelanic forms, as they occur in Britain, involves at present not a single gene but a gene complex. This has been proved by outcrossing the British melanics to a race or a closely related species of Biston from North America. The result was a breakdown of the dominance; instead of clear-cut melanic and nonmelanic segregation, a continuous series of individuals ranging from pale to black was obtained.

## Resistance to Insecticides

Fairly numerous species of animals and plants are pests. Some of them injure man directly, as parasites or vectors of disease; many more damage crops and other food sources or cause harm in various additional ways. Pest control is a stern necessity; it aims to restrict the abundance of such species as much as possible or even to exterminate them entirely. Most control techniques utilize various chemicals, insecticides and fungicides, some of them of remarkable potency. Pest populations have responded to these ingenious human inventions, however, by evolving strains resistant to the particular chemical substances that achieved satisfactory measures of control in previous generations. The sequel is what appears to be an endless race between novel means of control and the evolutionary versatility of the pests.

The red scale (*Aonidiella aurantiae*) yielded the first well-established instance of insecticide resistance. Fumigation of citrus trees attacked by these insects with hydrocyanic gas was an effective control technique until 1914, when a resistant population was observed in an orchard near Corona, California. The resistance then gradually spread to other citrus-producing areas of the state, although in some localities fumigation continued to give satisfactory results. Quayle (1938) and Dickson (1940) isolated resistant and nonresistant strains, and showed that $F_1$ hybrids between them are intermediate in resistance. A segregation is observed in the $F_2$ generation; the resistance appears to be caused by a single gene without dominance. Cyanide-resistant strains appeared also in other species of scale insects.

The invention of DDT and other highly potent insecticides was followed by their widespread use and misuse. One of the foremost problems in pest control became the emergence of strains resistant to these insecticides. The literature accumulated on this subject is immense. The early work was reviewed by Crow (1957) and Olenov (1958). Brown (1967) has published an excellent review of genetic studies on the resistance of insect vectors of disease. Strains of houseflies resistant to DDT appeared apparently independently in many countries, as have strains resistant to dieldrin, to organophosphorus compounds such as malathion, to carbamates, and to nicotine sulfate. Strains resistant to DDT and dieldrin have been found and studied genetically in several species of anopheline mosquitoes, in *Culex fatigans* and *Aedes aegypti*, in the cockroach *Blatella germanica*, in the cattle tick *Boophilus microplus*, in bedbugs, and in body lice. A variety of genetic situations was found in these organisms, as well as in species of Drosophila used for pilot experiments. The resistance may be due to a single gene, or it may be polygenic. Oshima and Hiroyoshi (1956) succeeded in locating the genes for DDT and for nicotine resistance on different chromosomes of *Drosophila melanogaster* and *D. virilis*. Usually the alleles for resistance show no dominance, although examples of dominant and of recessive alleles are also known.

Some authors looked for evidence as to whether mutations that confer resistance are present in pest populations before the insecticide is applied, or arise after the application. This question is usually insoluble, and it is of no particular importance anyway. The numbers of individuals in the populations of some pests are so great that even rare mutants are likely to be present in many localities. More important, from both the practical and the theoretical standpoint, is whether natural selection completely replaces the alleles that make the insect population sensitive with those that make it resistant to a given insecticide. If it is true, as almost certainly is the case, that the resistant variants are at least slightly lower in fitness than the nonresistant ones in the absence of insecticide treatments, then some of the latter may well be preserved in populations. When the application of a given insecticide is discontinued because it is no longer effective, the selection pressure that favored the alleles for resistance is relaxed, and in fact may be reversed in favor of the original alleles for sensitivity. Hence, after some generations of reversed selection the population may become sensitive again. Pertinent evidence in this connection is reviewed by Keiding (1967). It appears that in at least some cases the relaxation is indeed followed by a weakening of the resistance, but full sensitivity is not restored.

## Host-Parasite Coevolution

A biotic community includes usually several, and sometimes many, species, which stand to each other in relations of more or less close mutual dependence. Host-parasite, prey-predator, carrier-symbiont, flowering plant-pollinating insect are obvious examples. Ecologically related or interdependent species may undergo coevolution (Ehrlich and Raven 1964), making their interactions mutually advantageous, or at least minimizing the damage that one or both associates may suffer. The spread and transformation of the myxomatosis disease in rabbits in Australia constitutes a fascinating instance of coevolution, the main stages of which have been observed and recorded (Fenner 1959, 1965).

The rabbit (*Oryctolagus cuniculus*) population in Australia is descended almost exclusively from some two dozen individuals brought from England in 1859. By 1950, the population was estimated in hundreds of millions. Myxomatosis, a virus disease, was introduced as a control measure in 1950. It occurs naturally in the Brazilian rabbit, *Sylvilagus brasiliensis,* in which it causes a relatively benign infection. Transferred to European or Australian rabbits, it gives a lethal disease with gross lesions. The virus spread in Australia and within a few years reduced the rabbit population to about 1 percent of its former strength. However, in 1955 it was noticed that the disease was becoming less virulent. By 1958, only 54 percent of artificially inoculated rabbits showed "severe" symptoms, the rest having "moderate" or "mild" ones (in 1953, 95 percent had "severe" symptoms), and the rabbit population began increasing again. The rabbits have developed genetic resistance, while the virus is becoming less virulent.

Selective processes are taking place both in the host and in the parasite. The virus, which is transferred from rabbit to rabbit by mosquito bites, does not multiply in the mosquitoes; the insects serve merely as "flying needles." The selection favoring more resistant genetic variants among the rabbits is easily understood. The selection for reduced virulence in the virus is no less real. The virus can be transferred only from a living to another living rabbit; death of the host results in death of the virus. Hence the less virulent virus strains that do not kill their hosts, or at least leave them alive longer, have an advantage in transmission. The low virulence of the virus in the Brazilian rabbit species is probably an outcome of such coevolution for mutual accommodation.

Abundant data are available on populations of the stem rust of wheat, *Puccinia graminis tritici*. The wheat rust has what phytopathologists call "races," of which at least 189 are known. The races are identified by their ability to infect, and by the lesions produced on certain wheat varieties; each wheat variety is immune to some but susceptible to other races of the rust (Stakman 1947). A census of the frequencies of the races has been taken in the United States and other countries for some decades (Stakman, Loegering, et al. 1943), and during this period the rust populations have changed (Table 7.3). Breeders select and introduce new varieties of wheat, which are more or less resistant to rust "races" prevalent at the time and in the geographic regions where the selective breeding is practiced. Thus, rust race 56 was first found in the United States in 1928, soon after the susceptible variety Ceres was planted on a large scale. The rapid increase of No. 56 caused a drastic reduction first of the yield, and then of the plantings, of the Ceres variety. Races 36 and 49 were prevalent until 1933, but later became uncommon. No. 56 was rare until 1934 but became widespread after that; No. 34 was common between 1933 and 1935, etc. Here, then, is a competition between artificial selection by man of the wheat plant, and natural selection in the rust fungus.

Attempts to find blight-resistant American chestnuts were reported by Nienstaedt and Graves (1955).

**TABLE 7.3**

Percentage frequencies of "physiologic races" of the rust Puccinia graminis tritici in the United States in different years (After Stakman, Loegering, et al. 1943)

| Year | | | | | Race | | | | |
|------|-----|-----|-----|-----|------|-----|------|-----|-----|
|      | 11  | 17  | 19  | 21  | 34   | 36  | 38   | 49  | 56  |
| 1930 | 4.0 | 0.3 | 0.6 | 6.7 | 0.6  | 36  | 30   | 20  | 0.2 |
| 1931 | 22  | 0.6 | 1.3 | 4.0 | 2.1  | 28  | 15   | 25  | 1.0 |
| 1932 | 4.9 | 1.4 | 4.9 | 1.6 | 0.9  | 9.6 | 46   | 27  | 2.1 |
| 1933 | 1.7 | 1.4 | 1.4 | 4.5 | 7.1  | 3.7 | 33   | 37  | 3.7 |
| 1934 | 0.6 | 0.6 | 0.3 | 1.8 | 22   | 21  | 2.8  | 1.3 | 33  |
| 1935 | 19  | 1.5 | 1.3 | 7.4 | 18   | 6.1 | 4.6  | 1.4 | 44  |
| 1936 | 12  | 4.4 | 1.2 | 0.8 | 4.2  | 3.0 | 22   | 1.2 | 47  |
| 1937 | 8.4 | 6.1 | 3.1 | 0.6 | 1.1  | 6.0 | 8.7  | 7.4 | 56  |
| 1938 | 2.0 | 3.0 | 6.4 | 1.0 | 0.8  | 1.2 | 16   | 0.9 | 66  |
| 1939 | 3.2 | 10  | 3.3 | 0.4 | 0.6  | 0.8 | 24   | 0.6 | 56  |
| 1940 | 4.2 | 34  | 2.2 | 0   | 0.5  | 1.8 | 10   | 1.2 | 44  |
| 1941 | 1.3 | 51  | 3.8 | 0   | 0    | 2.5 | 6.0  | 2.4 | 32  |
| 1942 | 0.3 | 27  | 6.2 | 0   | 0.2  | 2.3 | 27.3 | 3.9 | 31  |
| 1943 | 0.1 | 23  | 1.9 | 0   | 0.1  | 0.4 | 24.4 | 0.3 | 49  |
| 1944 | 0   | 21  | 6.6 | 0   | 0    | 0.2 | 26.1 | 0.2 | 43  |

### Natural Selection in Plant Populations

Human activities have altered, sometimes radically, the environments of many living species. These species had either to respond by adaptive genetic changes or to die out. Bradshaw and his colleagues have made a series of studies on races of some common species of British plants that became adapted to live in harsh man-made environments (Bradshaw, McNeilly, and Gregory 1965, Jain and Bradshaw 1966, McNeilly and Bradshaw 1968, and McNeilly 1968). The soils near lead, copper, and zinc mines contain the salts of these metals in amounts that are highly toxic to plants. Nevertheless, some species of plants grow successfully on these soils. In particular, the grass *Agrostis tenuis* growing on soils contaminated with lead or copper, and *Anthoxanthum odoratum* (sweet vernal) on zinc-contaminated soil, have been investigated. The heavy metal tolerance of the plants on contaminated soils is genetic rather than due to acclimatization. It is absent in populations of the same species growing only a short distance away from the mines.

What is remarkable is the precise localization of the metal-tolerant genotypes on the contaminated soils. Copper-tolerant *Agrostis tenuis* grows on copper mine workings over an area about $400 \times 100$ meters in size. The surrounding grassland has little copper in the soil, and the Agrostis there is intolerant. The transition from full tolerance to intolerance may occur over a distance of only a few meters. The sharpness of the transition depends, however, on the gene exchange between the tolerant and the intolerant colonies. Where the prevailing winds carry the pollen of the tolerant plants toward the normally intolerant populations, the transition is more gradual than where the prevailing wind direction is the opposite. The selection against the intolerant genotypes on the contaminated soils is very severe; the tolerant genotypes are selected against on uncontaminated soils rather less rigidly.

A parallel situation, but one involving selection by natural rather than man-made environments, is described by Aston and Bradshaw (1966). *Agrostis stolonifera* grows both in locations exposed to winds from the sea and in nearby locations protected from these winds. The plants from wind-exposed locations have much shorter stolons than those growing in protected places, and this difference is also genetic. The sharpness of the transition is again dependent on the wind direction and the consequent pollen transport and gene flow. The selection evidently favors plants with short or long stolons, respectively, in the habitats exposed and protected from winds.

## Haldane's Dilemma and Load "Space"

Haldane (1957) pointed out in a seminal paper that evolution entails a "cost." If certain assumptions are granted, the substitution of one gene allele for another or of one chromosomal variant for another can be said to result in some genetic deaths. Moreover, this cost may be so great as either to slow down the evolutionary process or to seriously depress the vigor of the population on which the selection acts. If the substitution of alleles at many gene loci is involved, the change may require too many generations and too long a time to be realized. Kimura (1960, 1961) reaffirmed Haldane's inferences and introduced the concept of substitutional genetic load. This is a measure of the lowering of the Darwinian fitness in a population undergoing selection, compared to the supposedly optimal fitness reached when the substitution is completed.

Haldane considers as a model the substitution of the dominant allele for melanism in *Biston betularia* for the recessive light allele (see above). In his words, "It is convenient to think of natural selection provisionally in terms of juvenile deaths. If it acts in this way, by killing the less fit genotypes, we shall calculate how many must be killed while a new gene is spreading through a population." The total number of deaths, $D$, needed for the substitution is

$$D = -\ln p_0$$

where $p_0$ is the initial frequency of the favored dominant. For a gene without dominance $D = -2 \ln p_0$, and for a recessive gene $D = p_0^{-1} - \ln p_0 + O(k)$, where $k$ is the selection coefficient in favor of the optimal genotype, $O$. Since genes that are favored by selection but were previously unfavorable are initially rare, and so are favorable genes first arising by mutations, the frequency $p_0$ is usually small. Taking it to be of the order of $5 \times 10^{-5}$, Haldane calculates that the values of $D$ will lie between 10 and 100, and takes 30 as representative. He notes that, unless the selection is very strong, $D$ is nearly independent of the selection coefficients.

In biological terms, the value $D = 30$ means that 30 times the average number of individuals comprising the population in a generation must die to achieve the substitution. If the deaths due to the selection remove, on the average, 10 percent of the individuals, about 300 generations will be needed to accomplish the substitution at a single gene locus. In reality, evolutionary changes involve the substitution of many genes. The ravages of death necessary to substitute favored alleles at many independently acting genes will be so enormous that either the population must become extinct, or else unwieldy lengths of time and numbers of generations will be required for it to become improved by the selection. If species differ in hundreds or even thousands of genes, it is hard to understand how new species can ever be formed. Haldane was too good a biologist not to see that the result he reached creates a dilemma. He concluded his paper thus: "I am quite aware that my conclusions will probably need drastic revision. But I am convinced that quantitative arguments of the kind here put forward should play a part in all future discussions of evolution."

A cognate predicament arises if we consider the "costs," in terms of deaths (or reduction of fertility), of maintaining heterotic balanced polymorphisms (Chapter 6). Suppose that the three genotypes $A_1A_1$, $A_1A_2$, and $A_2A_2$ have fitness 0.9, 1, and 0.9. The mean fitness of the population at equilibrium is, then, 0.95. A population that consists of the "optimum genotype" $A_1A_2$, that is, of heterozygotes alone, would have a fitness of 1.00. Such a population cannot exist for more than a single generation in a sexual outbreeding species. Sacrificing 5 percent of the zygotes to maintain heterotic balance is not a prohibitively large cost under most circumstances.

We have seen, however, that there are valid reasons to suppose that many natural populations maintain many unfixed gene alleles balanced by heterosis. Suppose that there are 100 polymorphic genes like the above; if the reductions of fitness they produce are independent and multiplicative, the average fitness of a population containing them will be only $0.95^{100}$, or about 0.006. In other words, only 6 zygotes out of every thousand produced will survive, and 994 will suffer genetic death. The calculation does not take into account deaths due to environmental accidents, which befall presumably almost every population. If environmental and genetic deaths are also independent, very few if any organisms are fecund enough to withstand such devastations. Higher vertebrates and man certainly do not possess enough "load space" to maintain more than a very few balanced polymorphs.

## What Proportions of Genes Are Polymorphic and Heterozygous?

Evidence reviewed in the foregoing chapters shows, conclusively in my opinion, that much of the genetic variability in natural populations of outbreeding sexual species is maintained by several forms of balancing selection. This evidence upholds the balance model, rather than the classical model, of the genetic population structure. The "normal" species genotype is a will-o'-the-wisp, like Plato's *eidos*. With many gene loci, no single allele can be regarded as "normal"; the adaptive norm of a species or a population is an array of heterozygotes at many loci. A representative genotype in natural population is more like the one in Fig. 6.5B than that in 6.5A.

One is now naturally led to inquire just what proportion of the gene loci are polymorphic, and what is the approximate number of genes for which an average individual of a species is heterozygous. A path toward such explicit quantification of our models of the genetic population structure has been opened by the brilliant work of Hubby and Lewontin (1966 and Lewontin and Hubby 1966). They strove to find a technique that satisfies the following criteria: "(1) Phenotypic differences caused by allelic substitution at single loci must be detectable in single individuals. (2) Allelic substitutions at one locus must be distinguishable from substitutions at other loci. (3) A substantial portion of (ideally all) allelic substitutions must be distinguishable from each other. (4) Loci studied must be an unbiased sample of the genome with respect to physiological effects and degree of variation."

Studies of the electrophoretic mobility of enzymes and other proteins offer the best available approach to fulfilling these requirements. We have seen in Chapter 2 that gene mutations come from the substitution, loss, or addition of a single or several nucleotides in a DNA chain in a chromosome. In turn, this results in the substitution of one or more amino acids in the protein coded by the altered part of the DNA chain. A certain proportion, which Lewontin and Hubby estimate as approximately one-half, of the amino acid substitutions change the electric charge of an altered protein, and make it move more rapidly or more slowly in the electric field. It is evidently important to detect genes represented in a population by more than a single allele, as well as fixed, invariant genes. Yet Mendelian genetics is concerned with gene differences; the operation employed to discover a gene is hybridization: parents differing in some trait are crossed, and the distribution of the trait in the hybrid progeny is observed. The technique of electrophoresis also detects proteins that are uniform in all individuals studied; it allows, "as a first order of approximation, to equate a protein without any detectable variation to a gene without detectable variation" (Hubby and Lewontin 1966). To avoid bias, an enzyme or other protein is chosen for the study when chemical techniques for its detection are available, without prior knowledge of its variability or fixity.

Prakash, Lewontin, and Hubby (1969) have examined 24 gene-loci-controlling enzymes or larval proteins. Samples of natural populations of *Drosophila pseudoobscura* were taken in three localities in the western United States and in one locality in Colombia, South America. Among these genes, approximately 40 percent are polymorphic, that is, are represented by more than a single distinguishable allele in at least one population (Table 7.4). In the populations of separate localities, only that of Colombia has a lower polymorphism; this population is isolated from the main body of the species by a distribution gap of some 2400 kilometers. From the detected frequencies of homozygotes and heterozygotes at different loci, including those exhibiting no polymorphisms, the percentages of genes heterozygous in an average individual can easily be computed. As shown in Table 7.4, this average, considering all the populations, is 12.3 percent.

It must be emphasized that the above values are patently underestimates; if only one-half of the variant proteins are discriminated by the technique of electrophoresis, the percentages must be approximately doubled. Evidently the crucial problem is whether the genes studied are indeed a fair sample of at least the structural genes composing the hereditary endowment of the species. Since care was taken to avoid preferential choice of variable genes, there seems to be no valid reason to suspect a bias. A problem no less urgent is whether these spectacularly high proportions of polymorphic and heterozygous genes occur in organisms other than *Drosophila pseudoobscura*. Johnson, Kanapi, et al. (1968) in *D. ananassae*, Stone, Johnson, et al. (1968) in *D. nasuta*, O'Brien and MacIntyre (1969) in *D. melanogaster* and *D. simulans*, and my colleagues Ayala, Richmond, Perez, and Mourão (unpublished) in four species of *D. willistoni* groups have obtained results very similar to those in *D. pseudoobscura*.

What about man? Harris (1966) studied ten enzymes in the blood

## TABLE 7.4

Percentages of polymorphic genes, and estimated percentages of genes heterozygous in an average individual, in populations of Drosophila pseudoobscura (After Prakash, Lewontin, and Hubby 1969)

| Population | Number of Genes | Percent Polymorphic | Percent Heterozygous |
|---|---|---|---|
| California | 11 | 46 | 14.0 |
| Colorado | 10 | 42 | 11.0 |
| Texas | 9 | 38 | 12.0 |
| Colombia | 6 | 25 | 4.4 |
| Mean | 9 | 38 | 12.3 |

## TABLE 7.5

Enzyme polymorphisms in a human population (After Harris 1967)

| Enzyme | Number of Alleles | Frequency of Commonest Phenotype |
|---|---|---|
| Red-cell acid phosphatase | 3 | 0.43 |
| Phosphoglucomatase | | |
| $PGM_1$ | 2 | 0.58 |
| $PGM_3$ | 2 | 0.53 |
| Placental alkaline phosphatase | 3 | 0.41 |
| Acetyl transferase | 2 | 0.50 |
| Adenylate kinase | 2 | 0.90 |
| Serum cholinesterase | | |
| $E_1$ | 2 | 0.96 |
| $E_2$ | 2 | 0.96 |
| 6-Phosphogluconate dehydrogenase | 2 | 0.90 |

serum and placentae in the population of England. Four of the ten (red-cell acid phosphatase, two phosphoglucomutases, adenylate kinase) proved polymorphic. The average proportion of genes for which an individual is expected to be heterozygous may also be estimated from blood group polymorphisms and is about 16 percent (Lewontin 1967a). Table 7.5 lists nine gene loci responsible for enzyme polymorphisms, each with two or more alleles, the rarest of which has a gametic frequency greater than 0.01 (Harris 1967). Very rare alleles may be mutants controlled by normalizing selection, and 1 percent frequency is arbitrarily taken as a minimum for polymorphism maintained presumably by balancing selection. In five of the nine the frequency of the commonest phenotype (either a homozygote for the commonest allele or a heterozygote for two alleles) is between 40 and 60 percent. If all the genes in Table 7.5 are considered, the probability of two individuals taken at random having the same enzyme phenotype is only 7 per 1000. The only mammal other than man for which comparable data are available is the house mouse. Selander, Hunt, and Yang (1969) have analyzed 41 genes in Danish populations, and found 41 per cent of them polymorphic. The estimated proportion of the genes heterozygous in an average individual is 8.5 percent.

Suppose that a Drosophila zygote has 10,000 gene pairs, and a human zygote 20,000. Both figures are underestimates (see Chapter 3). The figures for the estimated proportions of the genes that are polymorphic in populations or heterozygous per individual are also, in all probability, underestimates. It then turns out that natural populations of Drosophila are polymorphic for at least 3000, and human populations for 6000, genes; an individual Drosophila is heterozygous on the average for some 1150 genes, and an individual human being for 3200.

The experimental findings in Drosophila and in man are clearly in accord with the balance rather than the classical model of the genetic population structure. The maintenance of the abundant polymorphism and heterozygosity in populations demands, however, an explanation. Several possibilities may be considered. If the heterozygotes for pairs of alleles that yield variant enzymes are superior in fitness to the homozygotes, the polymorphisms can, theoretically, be maintained by the heterotic form of balancing selection. The difficulty is, as we have seen, that if the effects on fitness of the polymorphisms of different genes are assumed to be independent and multiplicative, the genetic load becomes too heavy to carry. Suppose that each of the 3000 polymorphisms in Drosophila, and each of the 6000 in man, reduce the fitness of the population by as little as 1 percent. The aggregate reduction would be $0.99^{3000}$ and $0.99^{6000}$, or $10^{-13}$ and $10^{-26}$, respectively, of the optimal fitness. No organism, let alone the human species, could withstand such an eclipse of its reproductive potential.

Some forms of frequency-dependent balancing selection impose no genetic load when equilibrium frequencies are reached. Suppose, for example, that the carriers of genes for some variant enzymes have an advantage in mating when they are rare in the population, but a disadvantage when they are too common (see Chapter 6). Selection will tend toward an equilibrium when the mating success of the different genotypes is uniform. Although Yarbrough and Kojima (1967) obtained an indication of such selection for the esterase-6 gene in *Drosophila melanogaster*, it seems far-fetched to assume a similar selection for all of the thousands of polymorphic loci. Diversifying selection can also maintain polymorphisms if the various genotypes have superior fitness in different ecological niches or subenvironments. This might impose no genetic load if each genotype could unfailingly choose the environment to which it is best adapted, but more and more load results as environmental misplacement becomes frequent.

The easiest way to cut the Gordian knot is, of course, to assume that a great majority of the polymorphisms observed involve gene variants that are selectively neutral, that is, have no appreciable effects on the fitness of their carriers. This option has in fact been taken by Kimura and Crow (Kimura 1968, Kimura and Crow 1969, and Crow 1969). The problem of adaptively neutral genetic variants will be taken up in Chapter 8.

### Rigid versus Flexible Selection

In a scientific theory simplicity is evidently a desirable trait. In a sense, all science is an attempt to simplify the world in order to make it comprehensible. Yet simplicity is no warrant of validity; some brilliant scientists have been deluded into imagining that nature must have adopted the simplest solution that their minds were able to devise for her problems. Our strategy must be to try out simple hypotheses and theories first, but be ready for more complex ones if evidence indicates the need for them. Haldane's dilemma is a product of a theoretical study; the load-space dilemma arises from a series of experimental investigations climaxing in the research of Lewontin, Hubby, Harris, and others. These dilemmas are, hopefully, blessings in disguise, since they are forcing geneticists and evolutionists to look for paradigms of the natural selection process other than the classical one of "genetic death." Although no generally compelling new paradigms have yet emerged, the search for them is an inspiring intellectual adventure.

Defining the genetic load as the decrease of fitness in comparison with that of the optimum genotype leads to predicaments some of which have been discussed in Chapter 6. Wright, Wallace, the present writer, and others attempted to escape these predicaments by using the mean fitness, rather than the elusive optimal fitness, as an operationally meaningful standard to distinguish the adaptive norm from the genetic burden and the genetic elite. Li (1963) has exposed another paradox: "If we calculate the genetic load in terms of the highest fitness value, the population will never have any gain no matter how beneficial the mutation is. In fact, the more beneficial the mutation, the greater the genetic load, implying that the population is suffering from a greater amount of genetic elimination and is worse off from an 'optimum' genotype." Brues (1964) presented arguments essentially similar to those of Li, and contrasted the "cost of evolution with the cost of not evolving," the latter being much the greater.

In science, as in everyday life, it is possible to have before one's eyes all the components of a pattern and still fail to see the pattern. Feller (1967) the mathematician and Wallace (1968a,b) the biologist pointed out that this is in effect what has been happening to evolutionary geneticists, who have thought in terms of relative fitnesses and of relative frequencies of genes, and neglected the absolute population sizes and the factors controlling them in nature. Darwin, in deriving his theory of natural selection, used the quite general observation that only a fraction, and often a small fraction, of the progeny brought into being survive and become the parents of the next generation. For a bisexual population to be numerically stable, each of the breeding females must leave, on the average, one daughter, who will survive and reproduce. If the average is more than one daughter per mother, the population will expand; if less than one, it will contract. Most of the progeny die out or fail to reproduce because of environmental and genetic causes. The key question is, Are these causes always independent? Actually, both independence and interdependence occur in nature.

Consider a population that produces 1,000,000 fertilized eggs or seeds. Because of a limited food supply, restricted space, and other density-dependent factors, in a certain generation only 10,000 individuals reach maturity. In another generation the environment becomes more permissive, and 100,000 individuals mature. Suppose further that this population carries a burden of recessive lethal genes, such that 5 percent of the fertilized eggs are homozygous for these lethals. These 5 percent will die, regardless of whether only 10,000 or 100,000 individuals are able to reach maturity. Wallace calls this hard (I prefer to call it rigid) selection. By contrast, suppose that 5 percent of the zygotes have a genotype that enables them to survive under conditions such that a total of 100,000 individuals mature, but that makes them die where only 10,000 reach maturity. This is soft (according to Wallace) or flexible selection.

In what sense can a genotype subject to flexible selection be considered a part of the genetic load or burden of the population? The carriers of this genotype are among the zygotes eliminated when only 10,000 individuals survive, but when 100,000 individuals mature this genotype is included among the survivors. The genotype is not responsible for "genetic deaths," and it does not affect the size of the population. It will endanger the population only if it becomes very frequent in a succession of generations in a benign environment, after which the population is exposed to more stringent environmental conditions.

Unambiguous examples of flexible selection operating in nature are not easy to come by. This means, not that such selection is rare or unimportant, but only that interactions of genetic selection and ecological variables are little known. Consider again the relative fitnesses of the heterokaryotypes and homokaryotypes in *Drosophila pseudoobscura* described in Chapter 5. If the fitness of the best karyotype is taken to be 1.00, some other karyotypes are found to have much lower fitnesses. The homozygotes for the CH gene arrangement have a fitness of only 0.26, far down in the semilethal range. Does this mean that populations monomorphic for CH chromosomes cannot survive? Quite the contrary—such populations have been maintained in laboratory population cages, and at first sight they seem to be as flourishing as polymorphic populations, in which a majority of the individuals have fitness close to unity. To be sure, more detailed studies have disclosed that polymorphic populations usually have higher intrinsic rates of increase and produce more individuals from the same amount of food than monomorphic ones (see Chapter 5). All these observations are mutually consistent. Here the selection is flexible. Monomorphic CH populations have, under the conditions of the laboratory population cages, an adaptedness quite sufficient to survive and even flourish; yet when the populations are made chromosomally polymorphic, the comparatively low Darwinian fitness of the carriers of CH chromosomes depresses their relative frequency or even eliminates them entirely.

### Selection Thresholds

Sved, Reed, and Bodmer (1967), King (1967), Sved (1968), Maynard-Smith (1968a), and others have devised mathematical models of the operation of natural selection. Although these models are not identical, we may discuss them conjointly, since they postulate various forms of flexibility of selection. Consider a population with a fairly large number, such as 1000, of polymorphic genes maintained by a heterotic balancing selection. Suppose that the fitness of the heterozygote for each gene is 1 percent higher than that of the homozygotes (selection coefficients $s = t = 0.01$). With random mating, the numbers of genes for which individuals in this population will be heterozygous will form a probability distribution with a mean of 500. Individuals heterozygous and homozygous for most or for all of these genes will seldom or never be produced. Assume now that all genotypes with a number of heterozygous genes above a certain minimum have similar fitness, or at any rate that the fitness does not grow or decrease in a direct proportion to the number of heterozygous or homozygous loci.

Such a selection threshold has in fact been inferred by Lerner (1954), chiefly from experiments on the genetics of poultry, and called by him the obligate level of heterozygosity. The selection does not act on each gene independently from the others; it discriminates against individuals that carry more than a certain number of unfavorable genes. Each "genetic death," if one wishes to continue using this expression, removes from the population not a single such gene but an array of them. King (1967) concludes, "One thousand or more polymorphisms can be maintained through an average heterozygote superiority of about 1 percent per locus, with a very small total effect on the variance of fitness in the population." Sved, Reed, and Bodmer (1967) say cautiously that this number "could not be much greater than 1000." The reason for this caveat is that the theory leads one to expect losses of fitness on inbreeding that are perhaps greater than those observed in experiments.

In discussing Haldane's dilemma, Sved (1968) makes the following point:

The only condition required for a gene to be selectively advantageous is that individuals possessing the gene be on the average fitter than those not possessing it. If the population size is controlled in some density-dependent manner, then the increase in the numbers of individuals possessing the gene could be purely at the expense of those not possessing it. This could, for example, be due to inherited differences in ability to compete for some limiting resource. The mean fitness of the population, as measured by the immediate change in the population size, might be raised, conceivably lowered, or very likely left undamaged as a result of the gene substitution.

Sved then proceeds to show that, with selection working as he has stated, there is no obvious upper limit to the number of loci or the rate at which the allelic substitution may take place.

The arguments of Maynard-Smith (1968a) are essentially similar to those of Sved, but he discusses briefly the possibility that gene substitutions not controlled by density-dependent factors are free of any "cost" of genetic deaths. Suppose that the distribution area of a species or a population is limited by a boundary beyond which it is unable to stand the climatic conditions, such as cold or dryness. Mutations in one or more genes that confer such an ability will make possible a spread into previously uninhabitable territories. In such a case the total species population expands and does not suffer losses on account of a substitutional load.

In summary, the problems of the maintenance of genetic variability in natural populations, and of the ways in which natural selection acts, are as yet far from solved. These are basic problems of any causal theory of evolution. Both theoretical and experimental studies in this field, however, have resulted in gratifying or even spectacular advances in recent years. Moreover, it is probable that the state of the knowledge as outlined above will be surpassed in the near future.

# CHAPTER EIGHT

# RANDOM DRIFT AND FOUNDER PRINCIPLE

*ᴗᴖᴗ*

## *Directed and Random Processes*

The elementary components of evolutionary changes are alterations of the frequencies of gene alleles or chromosomal variants in the
gene pool of a population. Consider the simplest case of a single gene;
the change can be symbolized as a movement of a point on a frequency
scale in either direction from 0 (absence of an allele) to 1 (its fixation).
If two, three, or n genes are considered, the point must be envisaged
as moving in a two-, three-, or *n*-dimensional space. Gene frequency
changes may be brought about by deterministic (directed) or stochastic
(random) causes. With the former, the gene frequency in any generation is predictable, provided that the pressures impelling the change
are known; with the latter, the frequency is indeterminate, and only
the variance of the possible frequencies can be anticipated. Wright's
(1955) classification of the "modes of change in gene frequency" is
as follows:

1. *Directed processes*    a. Recurrent mutation
                                      b. Recurrent migration and crossbreeding
                                      c. Selection
2. *Random processes*    a. Fluctuations in mutation rate
                                      b. Fluctuations in migration
                                      c. Fluctuations in selection
                                      d. Accidents of sampling
3. *Unique events*         a. Novel favorable mutation
                                      b. Unique hybridization
                                    c. Swamping by mass immigration
                                      d. Unique selective incident
                                    e. Unique reduction in numbers.

For didactic reasons, the operation of each of the above "modes"
can be studied in isolation from the others. Only rarely, however, are

evolutionary changes in nature due exclusively to one mode; far more often, the interaction of several modes is involved. This simple consideration has been emphasized repeatedly by Wright, because its disregard has led to some unenlightening and at times acrimonious polemics. An evolutionary change need not be due either to directed or to random processes; quite probably it is the result of a combination of both types. The theoretically desirable and rarely achieved aim of investigation is to quantify the respective contributions of the different factors of gene frequency change, as well as their interactions.

## Random Genetic Drift

The idea of genetic drift was adumbrated by Brooks (1899) and by A. L. Hagedoorn and A. C. Hagedoorn (1921). It was developed independently by Fisher (1928, 1930), Dubinin and Romaschov (1932 and Dubinin 1931), and especially Wright (1921, 1931, 1932) and Malécot (1948, 1959). Sometimes referred to as the "Sewall Wright principle," it has been misused in a way Wright himself never intended, namely, as a spurious "explanation" of evolutionary changes that seem to be devoid of adaptive significance, and therefore hard to explain by natural selection. In the absence of mutation, selection, and migration, the frequencies of genetic variants in a population remain, in accord with the Hardy-Weinberg principle (Chapter 4), constant generation after generation. This is strictly true, however, only in ideal, infinitely large populations. In reality, no population is infinite and many are small.

Consider sexual diploid populations of 500,000, 5000, and 50 individuals, respectively. If the population sizes remain constant, the next generation will come from samples of 1,000,000, 10,000, and 100 gametes from the gene pools of the previous generation. Suppose that two alleles, $A$ and $a$, are in some generation equally frequent in these populations ($p = q = 0.5$). The sampling process introduces a variance of $pq/N$ and a standard deviation $\sqrt{pq/N}$, where $N$ is the number of gametes sampled. The frequencies of alleles $A$ and $a$ in the next generation will, therefore, be $0.5000 \pm 0.0005$, $0.500 \pm 0.005$, and $0.50 \pm 0.05$, respectively, in the three populations. This means that in about 95 of 100 samples the gene frequencies will be between 0.4990 and 0.5010 in the large, between 0.490 and 0.510 in the intermediate, and between

0.40 and 0.60 in the small population. The variation in gene frequency may be considered negligible in the large, small in the intermediate, but appreciable in the small population.

Evidently the gamete sampling process occurs in every generation, and the variance $pq/N$ grows in proportion to the number of generations elapsed. Imagine many isolated colonies of a species, all of which start with equal frequencies, $p = q = 0.5$, of two alleles of some gene. The average frequency of the alleles, even after many generations, will still be 0.5. If the populations of the colonies are large, the spread of the frequencies among individual colonies will be small, following a high-peaked bell-shaped curve with a mode at 0.5. However, in small colonies one of the alleles may be lost or fixed ($p = 0$ and $q = 1$, or vice versa). A lost allele can be reintroduced only by mutation or migration. On the assumption that neither occurs, the frequencies of the colonies with different proportions of $A$ and $a$ will reach a U-shaped distribution, as shown in Figs. 8.1A and 8.1B. In other words, more and more colonies will contain only allele $A$ or only allele $a$, and intermediate allele frequencies will be progressively infrequent. Given enough time, the colonies will be of two kinds, some monomorphic for $A$ and others monomorphic for $a$. This result will be achieved sooner if the colonies are small than if they are large.

## Interactions of Random Drift, Selection, Mutation, and Migration

These interactions have been examined especially by Wright (1931, 1940, 1948, 1966). His mathematics are too abstruse to be presented here, but his premises and conclusions are admirably simple and clear. The smaller the population size, the greater are random variations in gene frequencies, and the less effective become weak selection pressures. In small populations, alleles favored by selection may be lost and less favored ones may reach fixation. In large populations even very small selective advantages and disadvantages will eventually be effective, but a more rigorous selection is needed to overcome the random drift in small populations.

The relations between population size and selection intensity are illustrated in the diagrams in Fig. 8.1. The abscissae indicate the gene frequencies from 0 (loss) to 1 (fixation). The ordinates may be inter-

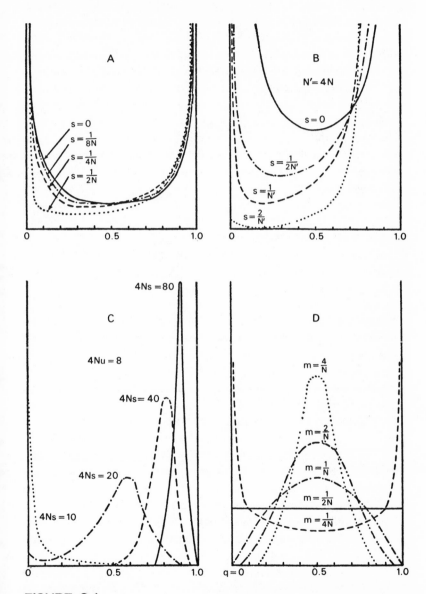

**FIGURE 8.1**

Distribution of gene frequencies in populations of different size under different selection, mutation, and migration pressures. (From Wright)

preted in any one of three ways. First, one may consider the fate of the different genes in a single population, for natural populations vary with respect to many genes. Some of these genes may reach fixation, others may be lost, and still others remain unfixed, represented by two or more alleles with different frequencies $(0<q<1)$. The ordinates indicate, then, the frequencies of the different genes in a population. Second, one may follow the fate of the same gene in different populations, in the colonies into which a species is broken up. The ordinates refer then to the frequencies of the subgroups in which a given gene frequency is reached. Third, the ordinates may show how often, in the long run, any one gene comes to possess a given frequency.

In small populations (Fig. 8.1A) the gene frequency curves are U-shaped. A majority of variable genes are either fixed or lost most of the time. The effectiveness of weak selection is low in small populations. With small selection coefficients, of the order $s = 1/8N$ to $s = 1/2N$, the shape of the curves is little modified. Genes are lost or fixed at random, with little reference to the selection pressure. Figure 8.1B represents the action of a selection of the same intensity as in Fig. 8.1A, but in a population that is four times larger $(N' = 4N)$. Here a selection of the order $s = 2/N'$ is rather effective; the curve no longer is U-shaped but has a maximum at the right, indicating that the gene alleles favored by selection largely supplant the less favored ones.

The interaction of mutation pressure with selection and the population size factor is even more complex. If the selection pressure is of the same order as the mutation rate, and both are small, the random variations of the gene frequencies in small populations become important. The curve is U-shaped, indicating that gene alleles reach fixation or loss largely irrespective of the mutation and selection pressures. Mutation and selection rates that may be regarded as small are such as make the products $4Nu$ and $4Ns$ less than unity. The greater the mutation and selection pressures, the greater is their effectiveness.

An example borrowed from Wright (1931) is reproduced in Fig. 8.1C. It refers to a population of intermediate size with a moderate mutation rate $(4Nu = 8)$ opposed by a selection of varying intensity. With selection of the order $4Ns = 10$, the mutation pressure gets the upper hand, and the allele favored by selection is largely lost. A doubling of the selection intensity $(4Ns = 20)$ changes the situation. The gene frequencies fluctuate over a great range of values. In a species segregated into numerous isolated colonies this means a differentiation into local races, some of which will possess characteristics favored by selection and others relatively unfavorable ones. With selection becoming more stringent ($4Ns = 40$ and $4Ns = 80$), the amplitude of variation is gradually restricted, the gene frequencies being kept within rather narrow limits centered on the equilibrium values.

In the three models just described, it was assumed that the colonies into which a species is subdivided are completely isolated from each other. In reality this rarely if ever happens. Even populations of oceanic islands receive occasional migrants from the mainland or from other islands. Wright's Fig. 8.1D shows the effects of migration. If the migration coefficient is $m = 1/4N$ (one migrant individual on the average in four generations), the isolation is effective and the curve of gene frequencies becomes U-shaped. With $m = 1/2N$ (one migrant in alternate generations) the fixation of alleles is slowed down. With more frequent migration the distribution of the gene frequencies shows less and less variance. This may seem to make random drift inconsequential as an evolutionary agent. It should be noted, however, that Wright's $m$ coefficient really means that the migrants to the various colonies come at random from all the colonies into which a species is divided. In reality, this is not so; the exchange of migrants occurs mainly between adjacent colonies, which are likely to have rather more similar gene frequencies than colonies remote in space.

Small population sizes are not the only factors making random drift possible. Fluctuations of selection and mutation rates are other random processes that may lead to interesting results (Kimura 1954). Assume that there are genes each with two alleles, $A_1$ and $A_2$, $B_1$ and $B_2$, etc., which are adaptively neutral on the average, that is, over a long series of generations. The mean selection coefficients are then, zero: $s = 0$. However, from time to time one or the other of the alternatives alleles becomes slightly advantageous or disadvantageous, so that there is a variance of selection coefficients, $V_s$.

Kimura gives an example of a population numerically so large that sampling variations can be neglected, in which the alternative alleles are initially equally frequent ($p = q = 0.5$), and in which the variance of the selection coefficients is $V_s = 0.0483$. For about 27 generations the distribution curve of the gene frequencies remains unimodal and thereafter becomes U-shaped. After 100 generations most genes reach "quasi-fixation," the most probable frequencies of the alternative alleles being 0.0007 and 0.9993.

In another example, one allele is, on the average, favored by a mean selection coefficient $s = 0.1$, but the selection has a variance $V_s = 0.0025$. One may then assume either many genes in the same population, with the favored alleles being initially rare, or many populations in which the favored allele of a certain gene is initially rare. The frequencies of the favored allele or alleles will, of course, gradually increase. However, whereas with constant selection all frequencies will be predictable and alike in a given generation, with variable selection the frequency distributions will become more and more changeable.

### *The Biological Meaning of the Value N*

The genetically effective population size, $N$, is not identical with the census size, that is, the total number of individuals in a colony. The simplest model is that of a colony isolated from the rest of the species by secular barriers, within which the population is panmictic and remains stationary in numbers from generation to generation. For such a colony, $N$ is equal to the number of individuals of the generation now living that will be the actual progenitors of the following generation, or to the number of the actual parents of the generation now living. In reality, the surviving progeny of some parents is large, that of others is small, and that of still others has been destroyed entirely. If $N_0$ is the number of parents, and $K$ that of their gametes giving rise to the surviving offspring $(K = 2$ on the average), the effective population can be expressed as
$$N = \frac{4N_0 - 2}{2 + \sigma_K^2}$$

(Wright 1940). Populations of most species vary in numbers, often within an enormous range, from generation to generation. Such variations are connected either with seasonal cycles (as in insects that produce several generations per year), with climate, or with fluctuations in the abundance of parasites, enemies, or prey. Wright has shown that the effective $N$ is much closer to the number of individuals attained at the maximum contraction of the population than to that attained at the maximum expansion. For example, a population may increase tenfold in each of the succeeding generations and then return to its initial size, its minimum being $N_0$ and its maximum $N_0 \times 10^8$. The effective size is then $N = 6.3 N_0$ (Wright 1940).

Crow and Morton (1955) and Kimura and Crow (1963) have

defined the effective $N$ in two ways, which are usually though not always equivalent. First, in a finite population, two alleles of the same gene inherited by an individual have a certain probability of being identical by virtue of descent from the same ancestor. Second, random drift owing to the sampling variance in the process of gene transmission from generation to generation leads eventually to random loss or fixation of some gene alleles. The effective number may then be defined "as the size of an idealized population that would have the same amount of inbreeding or of random gene frequency drift as the population under consideration." Kimura and Crow give formulae for effective $N$'s in populations with different kinds of reproductive biology—monoecious and with separate sexes, constant and changing census numbers, etc. The variables in these formulae are census numbers (numbers of individuals in different generations), mean numbers of progeny per parent, variance of these mean numbers, and a measure of departure from the Hardy-Weinberg proportions.

The relationships between the census and the genetically effective population numbers are exceedingly complex. They are determined by ecological variables and by the reproductive biology of the species. The customary way of representing the distribution area of a species on a geographic map as a continuous territory is misleading. Rarely if ever is the population density uniform throughout the gross distribution area. Almost always one finds a mosaic of more or less discrete colonies separated by tracts where the species is rare or absent. The genetically effective sizes may vary greatly in different colonies. In this case the determining variables are not only the numbers of individuals per colony but also the rates of dispersal and migration, and the consequent gene flow between colonies. The dispersal is, in turn, a function of the vagility (mobility) of the species in different development stages.

Although the literature on territorial differentiation and vagility is extensive, most of the data have not been collected and, to my knowledge, not reviewed from the evolutionary point of view (see, however, the discussions in Andrewartha and Birch 1954, Mayr 1963, and Grant 1963). The most important fact to keep in mind is that animals capable of moving hundreds and even thousands of miles may nevertheless breed in close proximity to the places where they were born. It is well known that many migratory birds return to their old nesting places for breeding year after year. Some fishes, such as salmon, are born in streams in the headwaters of rivers; migrate to the ocean, where they grow to maturity; and then return to the exact stream in which they were born (Foerster 1968 and references therein). Twitty and his colleagues (Twitty 1959 and Twitty, Grant, and Anderson 1967) have described a remarkable homing ability in the newt, *Taricha rivularis*. It should be kept in mind, however, that the degree of precision of this homing migration differs from species to species. Mayr (1942) contrasts the behavior of geese (species of Anser and Branta) with that of ducks (Anas, Spatula). Mated pairs of geese migrate together to their winter quarters and return together to their nesting places; among the ducks the pair formation takes place in the winter quarters, and the mates are often natives of places remote from each other. The result is formation of many distinct races in geese and little race differentiation among ducks.

Tinkle (1965) and Merrell (1968) compared the absolute and the effective population numbers in the lizard *Uta stansburiana* and in the frog *Rana pipiens*, respectively. In the lizard the numbers of breeding adults were generally similar to the total numbers in the study areas. By contrast, in the frog the numbers of the egg masses counted were only fractions of the numbers of available females, so that the effective size was much smaller than the census size.

Colwell (1951) examined the dispersal of pine pollen by wind; most of the pollen is transported only 10–30 feet downwind from the source, although some pollen grains were found at distances of 150 and more feet. The seeds of a pine tree usually come from a male parent in the immediate neighborhood. The distance over which the pollen of Phlox is transported by insects is, on the average, only 1.1 meters; the maximum is 3.6 meters (Levin and Kerster 1968). Kerster and Levin (1968) estimate the genetically effective size of "neighborhood" colonies of *Lithospermum carolinense* as between 3.9 and 4.6.

## Random Drift in Experimental Populations

Interactions of random drift and natural selection were studied by Kerr and Wright (1954) in small laboratory populations of *Drosophila melanogaster*. The populations were propagated by 4 females and 4 males, taken to serve as progenitors of the next generation. Although 4 pairs of flies can produce hundreds of offspring, only 4 new pairs were taken at random in each progeny. The sex-linked recessive mutant forked bristles ($f$), the dominant Bar eye ($B$), and the autosomal recessives spineless ($ss$) and aristapedia ($ss^a$) were used as markers.

In the first experiment, 96 populations were started, each with 1 $f/f$, 2 $f/+$, and 1 $+/+$ females and 2 $f$ and 2 $+$ males. The initial frequencies of $f$ and of its wild type allele were, hence, 0.5. Because of the random choice of the parents in the following generations, however, the frequencies of $f$ rose in some populations and of $+$ in others. After 16 generations, only $f$ was present in 29 populations and only $+$ in 41 populations, while 26 populations had both $+$ and $f$. This result is expected if the effective population size was about 83 percent of the actual number, that is, 6.64 rather than the actual 8 individuals. Since the number of the populations in which $f$ was fixed was not much smaller than that of the populations in which the $+$ allele achieved fixation, the gene $f$ was not greatly discriminated against by natural selection.

In contrast, the second experiment showed that the Bar eye condition was distinctly disadvantageous. Here 108 experimental populations were started, each with 4 females heterozygous for Bar ($B/+$), 2 $B$ males and 2 $+$ males. The initial frequencies of $B$ and of $+$ were, then, equal at 0.5. After 10 generations, $B$ was lost in 95 populations and normal eyes in only 3 populations, while 10 populations continued to have flies both with Bar and with normal eyes. The observed rates of loss and fixation were as expected if the genetically effective population size was about 72 percent of the actual one.

In the third experiment, 113 populations were started, each with 4 females and 4 males heterozygous for spineless and for aristapedia ($ss/ss^a$). The heterozygotes for these two alleles of the same locus are heterotic, that is, more viable than either homozygous $ss/ss$ or $ss^a/ss^a$. As a consequence, the $ss$ allele reached fixation in only 8 populations and the $ss^a$ allele in no population after 10 generations. In 105 populations the $ss$ and $ss^a$ alleles continued to occur, the mean frequency of $ss^a$ being 38.8 percent, and the highest frequency 87.5 percent. The ratio of fitnesses of the three genotypes was approximately 0.40 $ss/ss$ : 1 $ss/ss^a$ : 0.14 $ss^a/ss^a$. The three experiments show the interactions of drift and selection with diagrammatic clarity.

The experiments of Buri (1956) were similar in principle. He used two alleles of brown (eye color) in *Drosophila melanogaster*, and the populations were perpetuated by groups of 16 individuals in each generation. From an initial frequency of 0.5 for each allele, the gene frequency distribution spread over the range of values from 0 to 1, and the frequencies in the neighborhood of 0.5 occurred no more often than the higher and lower ones after about 10 generations.

Prout (1954) approached the problem in a different way. Three populations of *Drosophila melanogaster* were kept by Bruce Wallace for many generations in laboratory population cages; two of them were "large," containing about 10,000 flies, and one "small," with about 1000 adult flies. The small and one of the large populations were irradiated with gamma rays of radium. A considerable proportion of the second chromosomes in these populations were lethal in double dose, and Prout studied the frequencies of allelic lethals among the lethal second chromosomes. Random drift in small populations may decrease the number of different lethal genes present, and therefore increase the frequencies of allelic lethals among the lethals that remain (see below). This is what was actually observed. The data were consistent with an estimate that the effective population size was about 256 in the population containing approximately 1000 flies. In the populations with 10,000 flies, the effective size could not be distinguished from infinite.

### *Isolation by Distance*

The model of the population structure considered above was that of a species subdivided into partially or completely isolated colonies. Wright (1943a, b, and Dobzhansky and Wright 1943, 1947) and Malécot (1948, 1959) envisaged also a population distributed uniformly over a large territory. This territory may be two-dimensional (continuous forest, steppe, surface waters in large lakes or seas) or unidimensional (a river or a shoreline for water-dwelling forms, river banks or coasts for terrestrial ones). There are, then, no impediments to migration, except for the isolation by distance; this is due to the limited locomotor abilities (vagility) of the organism concerned, which may be several orders of magnitude smaller than the total distribution area of the species.

Kimura and Weiss (1964) proposed a "stepping-stone" model, which is a compromise between the isolated-colonies and the isolation-by-distance types. This third model assumes that a species is distributed discontinuously, forming numerous colonies in a two-dimensional space or in one dimension, and that in any one generation the individuals born in any colony can migrate at most one step, to the adjacent colonies.

The papers cited above must be consulted by those who wish to follow in detail the mathematical treatment of the various models. The situations encountered are quite complex, especially if the interactions of natural selection with isolation by distance and other factors are to be analyzed. In point of fact, more mathematical work in this field is needed to clarify the situation.

Here again, however, the basic postulates and at least the main conclusions are simple enough. Wright considers that, in a population distributed uniformly over a two-dimensional territory, the parents of an individual are drawn from a certain average area. It may be assumed that this average area is a circle with a diameter $D$ and a population of $N$ breeding individuals. The grandparents come from a larger territory with a greater population, $\sqrt{2}\,D$ and $2N$, respectively. For $n$ generations the territory becomes $\sqrt{n}\,D$, and the population $nN$. The amount of local differentiation of the populations due to genetic drift is much less in a continuously inhabited territory than is expected in isolated colonies. With fewer than 100 breeding individuals within a circle of diameter $D$, ($N<100$), considerable differentiation will occur, provided that mutation and selection do not overpower the random drift. With $N$ greater than 1000 there will be little differentiation, and with $N$ greater than 10,000 substantially no differentiation. Genetic differentiation of the colonies may occur also under the stepping-stone model, more easily with a unidimensional distribution than with two-dimensional ones.

## Drift and Migration in Local Populations of Drosophila

Isolation-by-distance, stepping stone, and isolated-colonies models describe, more or less realistically, the breeding structures of natural populations of different organisms. All these models predict that local populations (sometimes called demes) may become genetically differentiated by random drift. This will happen provided that the vagility (migratory power) of the organism is so limited in relation to its population density that the genetically effective population size, $N$, of the colonies, demes, or neighborhoods is more or less small. With the same population densities, the effective $N$'s will evidently be smaller in animals that move little, or in plants whose seeds or spores are not widely dispersed, than in those that traverse on the average greater distances between their birthplaces and the places where they leave their offspring. With constant vagility, the effective $N$'s will be greater for species building dense populations per unit area than for species continuously or at least periodically rare.

Wright, Dobzhansky, Hovanitz (1942), Robertson (1962), Kimura, Maruyama, and Crow (1963), and Wallace (1968a) all pointed out that small effective population sizes may lead to experimentally detectable genetic phenomena. We know (Chapter 4) that natural populations of Drosophila carry many recessive or quasi-recessive autosomal lethals. In populations of effectively infinite size, the equilibrium value for a recessive autosomal lethal equals the square root of the mutation rate giving rise to the lethal. In populations of small effective sizes the gene frequencies vary within a range that is inversely related to the population size $(N)$. In a small colony some of the lethals will be altogether absent, others may be as common as their mutation rates would permit them to be in large populations, and still others may occur even more frequently. Wright showed that in a species segregated into small colonies each lethal will at any given time be present in a certain proportion of the colonies, but absent in others. In other words, each colony will contain only some of the lethals that exist in the species. Moreover, the average equilibrium frequencies of all lethals in a species as a whole will be smaller if the species is subdivided into small colonies than if it represents a very large undivided population. For a lethal that arises by mutation once in 100,000 gametes the situation will be as follows:

| Population Size, N | Equilibrium Frequency, q | Percentage of Colonies Free of the Lethal |
|---|---|---|
| 1,000,000 or more | 0.0032 | 0 |
| 100,000 | 0.0030 | 0 |
| 10,000 | 0.0020 | 15 |
| 1,000 | 0.0008 | 87 |
| 100 | 0.00026 | 99 |
| 10 | 0.00008 | 99.9 |
| Self-fertilization | 0.00002 | 99.996 |

If a species is a large panmictic population, or if it is subdivided into sizable breeding units, there should be no differentiation with respect either to kind or to frequencies of recessive lethals. The frequencies of the lethals should everywhere equal the square roots of their mutation rates. This situation is approached in the tropical species, *Drosophila willistoni*. Pavan, Cordeiro, et al. (1951) examined the incidence of lethals, semilethals, and sterility genes in populations of this species from diverse regions of Brazil. Although some variations were encountered, no systematic differences between the populations were brought to light. *Drosophila willistoni* is very common and widespread throughout Brazil, and its breeding populations are large. Pavan and Knapp (1954) found that among lethal second chromosomes extracted from populations of remote localities the frequency of allelic lethals was 0.00157. Lethals from remote localities are independent in origin by mutations. Among lethals from the same populations, some of which might have been identical by descent, the rate of allelism (0.00169) was not significantly higher. Interesting and meaningful exceptions were the populations of small isolated islands of Angra dos Reis, where a higher frequency (0.00514) of allelic lethals was found. Here a significant proportion of the lethals were doubtless identical by descent.

Spencer (1947a) found very high frequencies of heterozygotes for the recessive mutant stubble bristles in the population of *Drosophila immigrans* in a certain locality in Pennsylvania, but not in other populations of the same species. Such an accumulation of mutant heterozygotes in one population may well have been due to smallness of the genetically effective size of the population.

Dobzhansky and Wright 1941, 1943 and Wright, Dobzhansky, and Hovanitz 1942 found different sets of recessive lethal third chromosomes in *Drosophila pseudoobscura* populations from different localities. Population samples were taken at intervals of about one month during the breeding season, at nine stations on Mount San Jacinto, California. A "station" was a territory at most a hundred yards square, in which traps were exposed always in the same positions. The nine stations were in three groups or "localities." The distances between the localities were from 10 to 15 miles, and the distances between the stations within a locality varied from ¼ mile to 2 miles. There were no barriers to migration from station to station or from locality to locality. Some lethal-carrying third chromosomes were detected in every sample. The strains containing these lethals were then inter-crossed to determine which of the lethals were allelic (mutations of the same gene loci) and which were not allelic (mutants at different loci). The rates of allelism, expressed in percentages of the inter-crosses with allelic lethals, were as follows:

| | | |
|---|---|---|
| Within a station | Collected simultaneously | 2.53 |
| | 1–11 months apart | 1.97 |
| Within a locality | Collected simultaneously | 1.30 |
| | 1–11 months apart | 0.69 |
| Between localities | | 0.57 |
| Between regions | | 0.44 |

Lethals found in populations within territories less than 2 miles apart are alleles more frequently than those found 10-15 miles apart. In fact, no significant difference in the chances of allelism was observed among lethals collected in different localities on San Jacinto and those collected on San Jacinto and in the Death Valley regions (a distance of 200 miles or more apart).

The most refined studies on the rates of allelism of recessive lethals in relation to distance have been made in *Drosophila melanogaster* by Wallace, Zouros, and Krimbas (1966) and Wallace 1966b. The rates of allelism, in percentages were as follows:

| | |
|---|---|
| Within a collecting site | 4.61 |
| Sites 30 meters apart | 3.65 |
| Sites 60 meters apart | 3.24 |
| Sites 90 meters apart | 2.75 |

On the assumption that allelic lethals in geographically remote populations arose independently by similar mutations, the rates of their allelism permit estimation of the minimum numbers of genes that produce lethals in a given chromosome of a certain species. Such a minimum estimate for the third chromosome of *Drosophila pseudoobscura* is 289 (Dobzhansky and Wright 1941). From laboratory experiments we know that the gross mutation rate producing recessive lethals and semilethals in the third chromosome of *D. pseudoobscura* (i.e., the sum of the mutation rates at all loci) is 0.307 ± 0.036 percent, or about 3 new lethals per 1000 gametes per generation. With 289 loci producing the lethals, the mutation rate per locus is u = 0.000,0106 (i.e., 0.003,07 ÷ 289). In an infinitely large population the equilibrium frequency of a lethal is $q = \sqrt{u} = 0.003,209$. Yet only about 15 percent of the chromosomes in the California populations carry lethals. The concentration per locus is, then,

$$q = 0.15 \div 298 = 0.000,519$$

Taken at face value, the discrepancy between the observed and the computed equilibrium frequencies of the lethals indicates low effective sizes of the populations. The assumption here, however, is that the lethals are completely recessive, and we saw in Chapter 6 that this is not always the case. Furthermore, a discrepancy could arise also as the result of very local inbreeding, such as matings of siblings soon after their emergence from the pupae. These so far undefined variables do not explain, however, the well-established fact that lethals found within a population of a small territory are alleles more frequently than those from distant localities. This finding strongly indicates that the genetically effective size of the populations sampled was limited. Using the isolation-by-distance model, Wright (in Dobzhansky and Wright 1943) has computed from these data on the frequencies of allelism of the lethals that the parents of an individual of *D. pseudoobscura* in the localities studied are drawn from a population of some 500–1000 individuals.

The genetically effective sizes of at least some natural populations of Drosophila are small enough to make possible some differentiation by random drift. This conclusion does not rest on inferences from genetic data alone; it is supported also by ecological evidence. Timofeeff-Ressovsky (1939), Dobzhansky and Wright (1943, 1947), Dubinin and Tiniakov (1946), Burla, da Cunha, et al. (1950), Burla and Greuter (1959), and Wallace (1966a) b, 1968a) released in natural habitats of their species known numbers of Drosophila flies marked with easily visible mutant genes that do not incapacitate their carriers. At intervals after the release, baits that attract the flies were exposed at various distances from the point of the release; the numbers of marked and wild flies that came to the baits were recorded.

The rates of dispersal are greater in *Drosophila pseudoobscura* and *D. funebris* than in *D. willistoni or D. melanogaster* and are more rapid in each species at higher than at lower temperatures. One year after the release of mutant flies of *D. pseudoobscura* in a locality in the Sierra Nevada of California, about half of the progeny of these flies were found within a circle with a radius of approximately 0.86 kilometer from the point of release. About 95 percent of the progeny were estimated to be located within a circle having a radius of 1.76 kilometers, and 99 percent within a circle of 2.2 kilometers. *Drosophila melanogaster* has considerably lower vagility than *D. pseudoobscura* (Wallace 1966a, b). In both species, the population densities are low in many places, especially at unfavorable seasons. The slow migration, owing to random wanderings of the flies in search of food and oviposition sites is, however, not the only means of dispersal. Some individuals are occasionally transported involuntarily by winds over much greater distances (a review in Carlquist 1966). How frequent such long-distance transport is, and how much gene flow results from it, are not known. It may be more important historically, enabling the species to spread to new territories, than in determining the composition of the gene pools of local colonies. Genetic differentiation of partially isolated colonies by random drift is probably a widespread phenomenon.

## Drift and Migration in Human Populations

This is a controversial subject, owing, at least in part, to sheer misapprehension. Gene frequency differences observed between human populations need not be produced by selection alone or by drift alone; as indicated previously, they may be due to the interaction of both forces. Random drift is not limited to traits that are adaptively neutral; as shown above, a genetic trait that fluctuates from being advantageous in some generations to disadvantageous in others may also be subject to drift. To discover that some genetic variants differ in fitness under some circumstances does not rule out the possibility of drift. Moreover, although limitation of effective population size favors drift, the latter can also occur in large populations.

Glass, et al. (1952) and Glass (1954) made an elegant study of the Dunkers, a religious sect the members of which only rarely marry outside the community. The Dunkers, who now number about 3000 people in Franklin County, Pennsylvania, are descended from some 50 families that migrated from Western Germany to the United States between 1719 and 1729. The incidence of some blood group alleles among the Dunkers is significantly different both from that in the part of Germany from which their ancestors came, and from that of

the surrounding American population. For the "classical" O A B blood
system, the following allele frequencies have been found:

|                 | $i$ | $I^A$ | $I^B$ |
|-----------------|-----|-------|-------|
| Dunkers         | 60  | 38    | 2     |
| Western Germany | 64  | 29    | 7     |
| United States   | 70  | 26    | 4     |

The frequencies for these alleles among the Dunkers are not like
those among Germans or among Americans, nor are they intermediate
between the two. The MN blood types have frequencies of about 30
percent MM, 50 percent MN, and 20 percent NN, nearly equal among
Germans and among Americans. Yet among the Dunkers 44.5 percent MM and 13.5 percent NN have been found.

Steinberg, Bleibtreu, et al. (1967) observed even greater variations
in the M and N frequencies among colonies of another religious isolate
—the Hutterites, living in the northern United States (Montana and
South Dakota) and Canada (Alberta, Saskatchewan, and Manitoba).
In point of fact, the frequencies of the $M$ allele varied from 0.49 to
0.90, which is not far from the total frequency range of this allele in
mankind as a whole.

Birdsell (1950), studying aboriginal tribes in Australia, and Giles,
Walsh, and Bradley (1966) in New Guinea, found significant gene
frequency differences between neighboring populations. In the
Pitjandjara tribe in south-central Australia the frequency of the $I^A$
allele reaches 49 percent, whereas the adjacent tribe of Ngadadjara
has only 28 percent. The Nangatadjara and the Ngadadjara have 96
percent of the $M^N$ allele, whereas the Aranda, living not far away,
have only 62 percent.

It is well known that the recessive gene for albinism reaches high
frequencies in some isolated human populations, such as the San
Blas Indians of Panama, where about 7 persons per 1000 are albinos.
In Europe the frequencies of albinos are of the order of 1 : 10,000 to
1 : 30,000. Woolf and Dukepoo (1969 and Woolf 1965) found 26
albinos in a population of about 5000 in a group of villages of Hopi
Indians in Arizona, a frequency of 1 : 192. The authors suggest
"cultural selection" as a possible (though in my opinion not very
likely) explanation of this high frequency. Although many albinos
in Hopi communities never marry, male albinos stay in the villages

while normally pigmented individuals work in the fields, and thus have opportunities to beget children.

Cavalli-Sforza and Edwards (1964 and Cavalli-Sforza 1969) put forward as an "admitted oversimplification" the working hypothesis "that genetic diversity among present-day populations has been largely caused by random processes (both random genetic drift and the random variation of selective values)." Analysis of blood group polymorphisms in 37 mountain villages in the valley of Parma, Italy, revealed significant heterogeneities for 8 out of the 9 gene alleles studied (the OAB, MN, and Rh blood group systems). Most of the villages existed as early as the eleventh century, and the rate of immigration from the outside to the Parma valley was very low. The populations of the different villages in the valley do not intermarry freely; examination of marriage licenses shows that the probability of marriage is a function of the distance between the birthplaces of the persons concerned. In Fig. 8.2 the logarithm of the probability of

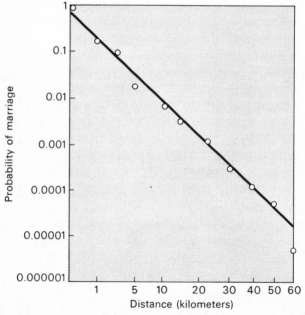

**FIGURE 8.2**

Probability of marriage and distance between the birthplaces of marriage partners. (After Cavalli-Sforza from Wallace)

marriage is plotted against the square root of the distance between the birthplaces of the marriage partners (prepared by Wallace 1968a, from Cavalli-Sforza's data). The observed points fit a straight line. Using Wright's isolation-by-distance model (see above) Cavalli Sforza, Barrai, and Edwards (1964) estimated the effective population sizes in the Parma valley as between 214 and 266. Alström and Lindelius (1966 and references therein) have made similar studies in Sweden.

A more ambitious extension of the work by Cavalli-Sforza et al. is the construction of evolutionary trees of the populations of the world. The points of branching and the lengths of the branches reflect the genetic "distances" between the populations, measured in terms of the gene frequency differences or differences in anthropometric characters. A sample of 15 populations, 3 from each continent, were chosen because of the availability from these populations of frequency data regarding 18 alleles (OAB, MN, Rh, Diego, and Duffy blood groups). The "tree" obtained (Fig. 8.3) is, as the authors say, "probably acceptable to many anthropologists."

## The Founder Principle

The term founder principle was proposed by Mayr (see 1963) for "the establishment of a new population by a few original founders (in an extreme case, by a single fertilized female) which carry only a small fraction of the total genetic variation of the parental population." This may be regarded as a special case of Wright's random drift (2d) or a unique event (3e in Wright's classification; see the first section of this chapter). Populations of many species on oceanic islands, though they may now number in millions, are descendants of single migrants or small groups of migrants, introduced long ago by accidental long-distance dispersal. The same may be true of inhabitants of isolated bodies of water and of various kinds of ecological "islands," such as forests isolated on the tops of mountain ranges or surrounded by treeless plains. Isolated colonies are also formed often on the peripheries of species distribution ranges, where a species reaches the limits of its ecological tolerance. Such colonies are exposed to the risk of extinction, because the environment may occasionally become vigorous beyond their tolerance limits; the colonies are repop-

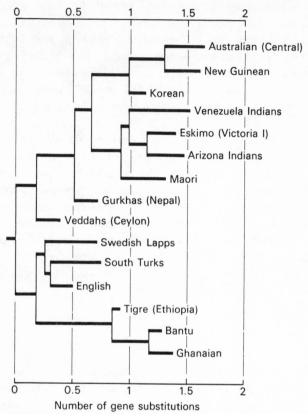

**FIGURE 8.3**

A phylogenetic tree of human population inferred from comparisons of the frequencies of certain genes in these populations. (After Cavalli-Sforza and Edwards)

ulated by new migrant founders from other parts of the distribution area. In primitive mankind, whole tribes were probably destroyed by various calamities and re-established from a few survivors or migrants from other tribes.

The immediate and obvious result of a population being reduced to very small numbers of individuals is, in normally outbred species, close inbreeding and loss of vigor. The ultimate result may be extinction (Voipio 1950, Suomalainen 1958, Andrewartha and Birch 1954, and references therein). If a colony escapes extinction, natural selection will work to restore its adaptedness. The selection must operate, however, barring new mutations, with the genetic variability that happens to be introduced or that is preserved in the founders. In the new, depauperate gene pool many gene alleles will find themselves in new genetic environments. Mayr (1954) dubbed this situation "genetic revolution." Both Mayr (1963 and references therein) and Carson (1959, 1965) surmised that such revolutionary reorganizations may initiate the formation of new species. This aspect will be considered in Chapter 11; here we shall examine some experimental studies of the operation of the founder principle.

We saw in Chapter 5 that chromosomal polymorphisms in the natural populations of some species of Drosophila are maintained by heterotic balancing selection. Heterokaryotypes, which have two chromosomes of a pair with different gene arrangements, are, as a rule, superior in fitness to homokaryotypes, which have the same gene arrangements in both members of a chromosome pair. This difference can be demonstrated also in experimental populations, maintained in laboratory population cages. Natural selection in such artificial populations establishes balanced equilibria, at which the different kinds of chromosomes achieve stable frequencies, determined by the relative fitnesses of the homo- and the heterokaryotypes (see Chapter 5 for more detail).

The rule of superior fitness of heterokaryotypes holds, however, chiefly in populations in which all the chromosomes are descended from ancestors collected together in the same natural locality. Such populations are said to be of uniform geographic origin.

Experimental populations can also be made with chromosomes of diverse geographic origins, derived from different populations. The outcome of selection in populations of mixed origin is remarkably erratic (Dobzhansky and Pavlovsky 1957 and references therein). The contrasting behaviors of populations of uniform and of mixed origins can be seen in Fig. 8.4. Eight experimental populations of *Drosophila pseudoobscura* have been made polymorphic for third chromosomes, some of which had the gene arrangement called Standard (ST) and others the Chiricahua (CH). All populations were started with 20 percent ST and 80 percent CH chromosomes. The four populations in Fig. 8.4A were of uniform geographic origin; their ancestors came from a certain locality in California. The four populations in Fig. 8.4B were of mixed origin—their ST chromosomes were

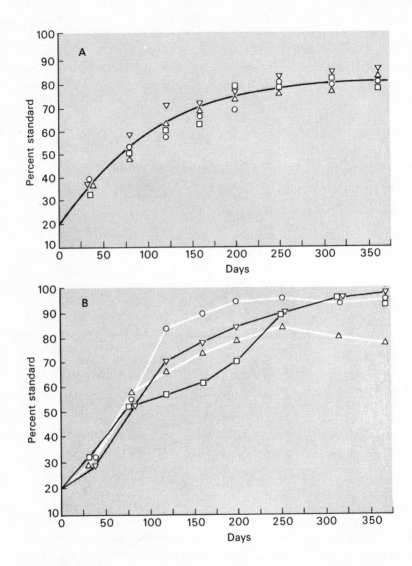

**FIGURE 8.4**

Natural selection in experimental populations of Drosophila pseudoobscura polymorphic for ST and CH gene arrangements in third chromosomes. Chromosomes of uniform geographic origin (A) and of different geographic origins (B). (After Dobzhansky and Pavlovsky)

derived from a population in California, and their CH chromosomes from a population in Mexico.

The changes observed in the geographically uniform populations were similar, within the limits of sampling errors. The fitnesses of the karyotypes, computed from the data in Fig. 8.4A, are as follows:

| ST/ST | ST/CH | CH/CH |
|-------|-------|-------|
| 0.895 | 1 | 0.413 |

The populations of different geographic origins (Fig. 8.4B) behaved quite similarly at first, but after the 100th day a divergence was observed. In no two populations were the changes quite similar. Only in one population was an apparently stable, balanced equilibrium eventually reached. In three others the CH chromosomes were on the way to elimination.

Why should there be so striking a difference between the behaviors of populations of uniform and mixed origins? In the former, the changes are repeatable and predictable, and in the latter indeterminate. As a working hypothesis, we can assume that the fitness of the homo- and heterokaryotypes for third chromosomes with ST and CH gene arrangements depends not only on these chromosomes themselves but also on the rest of the genetic system, that is, on the genes in all other chromosomes. Now, the gene contents of the ST and CH chromosomes in any natural population where they occur together are coadapted, fitted to each other and to the genes in other chromosomes by long-continued natural selection to yield highly fit heterokaryotypes. The populations of California and Mexico need not have their chromosomes coadapted, because hybrids between these populations are produced only in laboratory experiments. In how many genes the populations of California differ from those of Mexico we do not know, but it is reasonable to suppose that the number is fairly high, to make these populations adapted to their respective climatic and other environments. Experimental populations obtained by hybridization of natural populations of diverse geographic origins may thus undergo Mayr's "genetic revolutions" (see above).

Natural selection works in experimental populations, of uniform as well as of mixed origins. In the former it simply establishes the most favorable frequencies of the chromosomes on a relatively uniform genetic background. Gene recombination in mixed populations generates a great variety of genetic backgrounds. If we suppose that the parental populations differ in 100 genes, $3^{100}$ genotypes are potentially possible. The number of flies produced per generation in the experimental populations is between 1000 and 4000—infinitesimally small compared to the potentially possible numbers of genotypes. It is a matter of chance which ones of the possible genotypes appear in which population, or do not arise at all. Natural selection must, however, work with what is available, and it finds different genetic materials on hand in different populations. The result is the apparent indeterminacy of the outcomes in different populations.

It is possible, fortunately, to test the validity of this hypothesis experimentally. The variability of the outcome of selection in populations of mixed origin should be greater if they are started with few founders, and less if the founders are numerous. It is impossible to arrange populations with $3^{100}$ founders, which would give entirely uniform results. Dobzhansky and Pavlovsky (1957) made 10 populations with 4000 founders, and 10 with only 20 founders. The founders in all populations were $F_2$ hybrids of *Drosophila pseudoobscura* from California and from Texas, and all populations contained originally 50 percent of their third chromosomes with the Arrowhead (AR) gene arrangement from California, and 50 percent with Pikes Peak (PP) chromosomes from Texas. The results are shown in Fig. 8.5. "Large" and "small" refer exclusively to the numbers of founders; because of the high fertility of Drosophila, all population cages will come to contain about the same number of flies. It can be seen in the figure that the diversity of selection outcomes was greater among the small than among the large populations. This is statistically significant.

The same hypothesis was verified by Dobzhansky and Spassky (1962) in a still different way. In their experiments, 10 populations were started, each with 20 founders. The founders were hybrids of California strains with AR, and Texas strains with PP, chromosomes. In 5 populations, however, the founders were "multichromosomal," that is, hybrids of flies from 10 different California and 10 Texas strains. In the other 5 populations the founders were only "bichromosomal," descended from a single California and a single Texas individual. All the populations were put through several cycles of expansion in numbers, and new starts from 20 founders each. Multichromosomal populations should have considerably more genetic variability in their gene pools than bichromosomal ones and, therefore, are

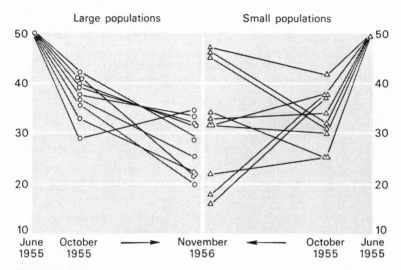

**FIGURE 8.5**

Experimental demonstration of the operation of the founder effect. Further explanation in text. (After Dobzhansky and Pavlovsky)

expected to show a greater diversity of selection outcomes. The evidence of the experiments was, indeed, in accord with this expectation.

Solima-Simmons (1966) added a still different corroboration. She outcrossed the two populations that diverged most among the multichromosomal ones described above, and used the $F_2$ hybrids to make 5 new populations, starting with 20 founders each; 5 other populations, which served as controls, were also started with 20 founders each, taken, however, from only one of the populations, without intercrossing. The populations were then put through 9 cycles of alternating expansions and reductions to 20 founders. The hybrid populations developed significant genetic divergence, whereas the nonhybrid ones showed no divergence.

The experiments of Dawson and Lerner (1966) were made with the beetles *Tribolium castaneum* and *T. confusum* competing in the same cultures. Under the experimental conditions used, *T. castaneum* outbreeds and eventually eliminates *T. confusum*. The authors made 10 populations with 10 pairs of each species as founders, and another 10 populations with 2 pairs as founders. The outcomes were much more variable in the populations started with fewer founders.

### The Decay of Genetic Variability

We saw in Chapter 4 that the pre-Mendelian concept of blending, or "blood heredity," created a quandary for the theory of evolution by natural selection, or for that matter any evolution theory. Indeed, the blending of parental heredities in the offspring would cause a decay of the hereditary variability in a sexual population far more rapidly than any known process could restore it. The demonstration by Hardy and Weinberg that the mechanism of Mendelian segregation averts the blending of parental heredities eliminated this quandary. Only in an ideal, infinite population, however, could hereditary variation be preserved indefinitely by the Mendelian mechanism alone. In finite populations this variation is subject to slow decay.

In a numerically stationary Mendelian population a pair of parents gives, on the average, two surviving offspring. Suppose that a gene $A_1$ mutates to $A_2$, and gives a single heterozygous individual $A_1A_2$. The individual must mate with a nonmutant, $A_1A_1 \times A_1A_2$. The offspring is expected to consist of equal numbers of $A_1A_1$ and $A_1A_2$. Because of chance, however, the number of survivors may be 0, 1, 2, 3, or more individuals, forming a Poisson series. If there are no survivors, the mutant allele is lost; if 1 survives, the probability of loss is 0.5; with 2 individuals surviving the probability of loss is 0.25, and with $r$ survivors it is $2^{-r}$. The aggregate probability is 0.3679 that a single mutant will be lost in a stationary population in every generation, 0.3679 that it will be represented in the next generation also by a single individual, 0.1839 that it will be represented by 2 individuals, 0.0613 by 3, 0.0153 by 4, etc. If the mutant is not lost in the first generation, it is exposed to the risk of extinction in the next one and in the following generations. To be sure, some mutants will, owing to chance, be represented by 2, 3, or more individuals. But since the loss of a gene is irreversible, most mutants are not preserved in the populations. As shown by Fisher (1930), this is true not only for neutral and harmful but even for advantageous mutants (see Table 8.1).

The decay of the variability may be visualized in another way. Imagine a population in which every gene is represented only once, that is to say, every individual carries 2 different alleles neither of which is present in any other individual. If the population is numerically stationary, 36.79 percent of the alleles will be lost in the next

**TABLE 8.1**

Probability of extinction and of survival of a mutation appearing in a single individual (After Fisher)

| Genera-tion | Probability of Extinction | | Probability of Survival | |
|---|---|---|---|---|
| | No Advantage | 1% Advantage | No Advantage | 1% Advantage |
| 1 | 0.3679 | 0.3642 | 0.6321 | 0.6358 |
| 3 | 0.6259 | 0.6197 | 0.3741 | 0.3803 |
| 7 | 0.7905 | 0.7825 | 0.2095 | 0.2175 |
| 15 | 0.8873 | 0.8783 | 0.1127 | 0.1217 |
| 31 | 0.9411 | 0.9313 | 0.0589 | 0.0687 |
| 63 | 0.9698 | 0.9591 | 0.0302 | 0.0409 |
| 127 | 0.9847 | 0.9729 | 0.0153 | 0.0271 |
| Limit | 1.0000 | 0.9803 | 0.0000 | 0.0197 |

generation, some will be represented once, and others twice, thrice, and more times. The loss of some and the increase in frequency of other alleles will continue in subsequent generations as well. If no mutation occurs, the population will ultimately become homozygous for a single allele.

Wright (1931) and later Kojima and Kelleher (1962) studied the process of decay of variability in populations that are stable and those that are fluctuating in numbers. In a stable population of $N$ breeding individuals, $1/2N$ genes either reach fixation or are lost in every generation. Suppose that in a population each of many genes is represented by 2 alleles that are equivalent with respect to selection, and that the frequency of each allele is 50 percent ($q = 0.5$). With no mutations, the frequencies of the alleles will fluctuate up and down from 50 percent, some becoming more and others less frequent. Eventually, gene frequencies from 0 to 100 percent will become equally numerous, and $1/4N$ of the genes will reach fixation and $1/4N$ will be lost in every generation. Wright's formula describing this process is

$$L_T = L_0 e^{-T/2N}$$

where $L_0$ and $L_T$ are the numbers of the unfixed genes in the initial and in the $T$ generation of breeding, respectively, $N$ is the effective population number, and $e$ is the base of natural logarithms.

If the population size fluctuates from generation to generation, the chance that a mutant allele will be retained is greater if the mutation occurs when the population is expanding than if it occurs during the contraction phase.

## The Opposition of Drift and Mutation

Random drift and mutation may now be envisaged as opposing forces, tending toward loss and replenishment, respectively, of the genetic variability. Kimura and Crow (1964) and Wright (1966) made a theoretical study of the variety of alleles that can be maintained in populations of various effective sizes. A gene can give rise to many different alleles by substitutions of single nucleotides in the DNA chain. The accumulation of variant alleles in the gene pool of the population will be counteracted, however, by their loss because of drift, until a steady state is reached at which equal numbers of alleles are added and lost (see Li 1955a). Suppose now that the alleles are all neutral, that is, do not modify the Darwinian fitness of their carriers. The effective number of the alleles maintained is then simply $4Nu + 1$, where $N$ is the effective population size and $u$ the mutation rate. Table 8.2 shows that this number depends greatly on the second parameter, as well as on the population size. It should be noted that the "effective" number is less than the "actual" or total number, the latter being swelled by very rare alleles that have not reached the steady state. Even so, with gene loci numbering in tens or hundreds of thousands, the genetic variety will be impressively large, except in very small populations.

If the mutant alleles are deleterious, their variety will of course be reduced. More interesting is the situation in which alleles produce

**TABLE 8.2**

Numbers of alleles per gene maintained in populations of various effective sizes by different mutation rates, when the alleles are neutral ($s = 0$) or heterotic ($s = 0.1$) (After Wright 1966)

| Population Size ($N$) | Mutation Rate ($u$) | Neutral | Heterotic | Population Size ($N$) | Mutation Rate ($u$) | Neutral | Heterotic |
|---|---|---|---|---|---|---|---|
| $10^3$ | $10^{-7}$ | 1.0 | 4.6 | $10^5$ | $10^{-7}$ | 1.0 | 51 |
| | $10^{-6}$ | 1.0 | 5.3 | | $10^{-6}$ | 1.4 | 62 |
| | $10^{-5}$ | 1.0 | 6.3 | | $10^{-5}$ | 5.0 | 81 |
| | $10^{-4}$ | 1.4 | 11.2 | | $10^{-4}$ | 41 | 137 |
| $10^4$ | $10^{-7}$ | 1.0 | 15.3 | $10^6$ | $10^{-7}$ | 1.4 | 176 |
| | $10^{-6}$ | 1.0 | 17.7 | | $10^{-6}$ | 5 | 219 |
| | $10^{-5}$ | 1.4 | 22.0 | | $10^{-5}$ | 41 | 323 |
| | $10^{-4}$ | 5.0 | 31.9 | | $10^{-4}$ | 401 | 689 |

heterozygotes of superior fitness and thus can be assisted by heterotic balancing selection. Wright (1966) makes the simplifying assumptions that all combinations of alleles induce a similar degree of heterosis, all homozygotes having a fitness of 0.99 and all heterozygotes of 1.00, and that the mutation rates at all loci are the same. The numbers of alleles that can be maintained even in small populations and with low mutation rates are then impressively large.

## Evolution by Random Walk

In Chapter 7 we reviewed some of the rapidly accumulating evidence that high proportions of genes are polymorphic in populations of Drosophila, man, and presumably other sexually reproducing species. We have also seen that these findings raise difficult theoretical problems. How are the multitudinous polymorphisms maintained? How is it possible for an average individual to be heterozygous for thousands of genes? The simplest explanation is that polymorphisms are maintained by balancing selection. This explanation contravenes the classical theory of genetic population structure, which would force us to conclude that numerous polymorphisms impose on the population a genetic burden too heavy to carry. King (1967), Sved, Reed, and Bodmer (1967); Wallace (1968a,b), and others have pointed out that the difficulty really stems from an oversimplified view of natural selection adopted by the classical theory. It ignores the ecologic factors regulating population size, the different modes of operation of rigid and flexible selection, and the importance of selection thresholds (see Chapter 7).

A quite different way to escape difficulty is advocated by King and Jukes (1969), Kimura and Crow (1969 and Crow 1969), and Arnheim and Taylor (1969). King and Jukes call their theory "non-Darwinian" evolution. This term is equivocal; if one restricts "Darwinian" to evolution by natural selection, there are many and diverse "non-Darwinian" theories (Lamarckism, autogenesis, nomogenesis, etc.). What King and Jukes actually postulate is evolution by random walk: given many genetic variants that are selectively neutral or very nearly so, their frequencies in populations will drift at random until some of them are lost and others reach fixation.

Consider an idealized diploid population of genetically effective size $N$. Suppose that a gene in this population has in some generation $2N$

alleles, no two of them identical, and yet all exactly equivalent in their effects on fitness. In the next and the following generations more and more alleles will be lost by chance (Table 8.1), but other alleles, also by chance, will be multiplied and represented by more and more copies. If there are enough generations of such random walk, only a single allele will remain, all $2N$ copies descended from one original gene. The chances of any one of the $2N$ originally different but selectively equivalent alleles being ultimately victorious and reaching fixation are equal, or $1/2N$. The average number of generations until fixation occurs in a population is $4N$ (Kimura and Ohta 1969). In a small isolated population, with effective $N$ of the order of tens or hundreds, this is not unrealistic. To have an allele fixed in an entire species, such as man, however, the time required may be too long, even on a geological scale.

Suppose now that mutations occur in the population, but that all mutant alleles are adaptively equivalent to the original one and to each other. The chances of any one of the mutant alleles being eventually fixed are still $1/2N$. Let the mutation rate yielding new but adaptively neutral alleles be $u$. The number of mutant alleles appearing in every generation will then be $2Nu$, and among them $2Nu/2N = u$ will eventually reach fixation. In other words, the number of alleles reaching fixation in every generation will, on the average, be equal, in an idealized equilibrium population, to that of new alleles arising by mutation.

Kimura (1969) considers, not mutant gene alleles, but nucleotide sites, some of which undergo substitution and produce mutations, all of them assumed to be adaptively neutral. A haploid gene complement in a mammal is estimated to contain 3–4 billion nucleotide pairs, enough to code for some 2 million polypeptide chains of 500 amino acids on the average. Assuming an effective population size of 10,000, and a rate of nucleotide substitution equal to 2 per gamete per generation, Kimura arrives at an impressively large figure of some 80 thousand heterozygous nucleotide sites per individual.

In another paper (1968) Kimura gives estimates of the average numbers of gene alleles maintained in populations of different sizes $(N)$. The number of gene alleles depends on the product of the mutation rate $(u)$ and the genetically effective population size $(N_e)$, always assuming that the alleles are neutral with respect to fitness. Some of the estimates are shown in Table 8.3.

**TABLE 8.3**

Average numbers of gene alleles expected in populations of different actual and genetically effective ($N_e$) sizes and different mutation rates ($u$) (After Kimura 1968)

| | Population Size | | | |
|---|---|---|---|---|
| $N_e u$ | $10^3$ | $10^4$ | $10^5$ | $10^6$ |
| 0.01 | 1.30 | 1.39 | 1.49 | 1.58 |
| 0.10 | 3.83 | 4.75 | 5.68 | 6.60 |
| 1.00 | 23.1 | 32.3 | 41.5 | 50.7 |
| 10.00 | 134.7 | 226.1 | 318.1 | 410.2 |

On the assumption that many or most mutational changes that arise are adaptively neutral, evolution by random walk must be regarded as an important, or even as the prevalent, evolutionary mode. The ubiquity of polymorphisms and the high heterozygosity found in natural populations are then no longer difficult to explain. It is the validity of the basic assumption that is very much in doubt.

### The Problem of Adaptively Neutral Traits

Anyone who compares the species of some large genus of animal or plants finds that many, and indeed most, of the traits in which the species differ seem to be trivial and to play no role in the survival or reproduction of the creatures involved. Why, for example, are the anterior scutellar bristles in many species of Drosophila always convergent and in other species invariably divergent? Or what adaptive significance can be ascribed to minor differences in the shape of the acorns in related species of oaks, Quercus? Or, for that matter, what is the selective value of facial differences among persons, provided, at least, that they are equivalent from the standpoint of sexual and social acceptability?

To concede that the above and many other traits are selectively neutral is to surrender before even starting on a quest to discover their significance. A visible "trait" may, indeed, be of no importance in itself, but it may be an outward manifestation, a part of the pleiotropic effects, of a variant gene contributing significantly to the organism's welfare (for examples, see Chapter 2). A "trait" is really an abstraction, a semantic device employed by a biologist to facilitate the description

of a kind of organism that he studies; the importance of a trait depends
on the developmental nexus of which it is a part (Dobzhansky 1956a).
What appears to be the adaptive neutrality of a trait may, then, be
simply a measure of our ignorance. On the other hand, to assert that
no trait and no genetic change can be selectively neutral is to create a
dogma, not to say a superstition. The adaptive role of a character must
be demonstrated; it cannot be assumed a priori.

The theory of evolution by natural selection was held in low esteem,
even by some pioneers of genetics, during, roughly, the first quarter of
the current century. Many evolutionists of that time assumed that evolutionary changes stem from some unknown internal "law" (e.g., Berg
1969). Many of these changes neither help nor hinder the organism's
survival—they are adaptively irrelevant. In the nineteen thirties,
Wright's random drift idea appeared to offer a ready explanation of
adaptively neutral changes, although, as pointed out at the beginning
of this chapter, Wright himself stressed the interactions of deterministic
and stochastic processes, and not drift alone. For about a quarter of a
century thereafter, a hyperselectionism became fashionable. All differences between populations and species were assumed to be products
of natural selection. Even so judicious an author as Mayr (1963) wrote,
"Selective neutrality can be excluded almost automatically wherever
polymorphism or character clines (gradients) are found in natural
populations," and "For these reasons, it appears probable that random
fixation is of negligible evolutionary importance."

Theories of non-Darwinian evolution by random walk have started
a new swing of the pendulum in the opposite direction (see, however, a
critique by Richmond 1970). King and Jukes (1969), perhaps to some
extent playing the role of devil's advocates, state, "Evolutionary change
is not imposed upon DNA from without; it arises from within. Natural
selection is the editor, rather than the composer, of the genetic message. One thing the editor does not do is to remove changes which it
is unable to perceive." But can one really believe that at least the general sense and the form of the genetic message have not been composed during the billions of years of evolution controlled by natural
selection?

Perhaps the strongest theoretical argument for the neutrality of
some mutants is based on the degeneracy of the genetic code. As we
have seen, six nucleotide triplets code for each leucine, serine, and
arginine (Table 1.2). Mutations that change a triplet to its synonym,

for example, CUU to CUC or CUA or CUG, should not be "perceived" by natural selection, because the protein formed will have the same amino acid in the same position. Almost one-fourth of the 549 possible nucleotide substitutions will yield synonymous codons. Even this argument, however, is not quite convincing. Because the synonymous codons often require different transfer RNA's for their translation, "synonymous" mutants need not be selectively equivalent. Transfer RNA's are not equally abundant in different tissues and different species (see, e.g., Holland, Taylor, and Buck 1967 and Caskey, Beaudet, and Nirenberg 1968).

The different amino acids are also not equally abundant in proteins. King and Jukes (1969) reasoned that, if many of the mutational substitutions are selectively neutral, the abundance of the amino acids may be correlated with the number of triplets coding for them. Indeed, they find such a correlation in 53 vertebrate proteins for which the amino acid composition is known. The commonest amino acids are serine and leucine, each coded by six synonymous triplets. Methionine and tryptophan, each with a single triplet, are least frequent. To be sure, the correlation is not perfect; for example, arginine is comparatively rare even though it is coded by six triplets. The argument is, however, ambiguous. King and Jukes themselves point out that the causal relationships may be the reverse of that assumed above: some amino acids may be common and others rare, not because they have more or fewer triplets, but because the genetic code may have evolved, in remote ancestors of the organisms now living, to match the abundance of the amino acids favored by natural selection.

The problem of neutral mutational changes will eventually be solved by relevant experimental evidence rather than by theoretical arguments. One source of such evidence is comparison of amino acid sequences in homologous proteins in different organisms. Cytochrome c is an enzyme performing similar functions in cellular respiration in most diverse organisms. Margoliash and his colleagues (Margoliash 1963, Margoliash and Smith 1965, Fitch and Margoliash 1967a,b, and references therein) compared the amino acid sequences in the cytochromes c in a variety of organisms—man, horse, pig, rabbit, chicken, tuna fish, a moth (Samia), a fungus (Neurospora), and a yeast. The cytochromes c of the vertebrates are chains of 104 amino acids, with a prosthetic heme group attached at positions 14 and 17. The yeast cytochrome c is a chain of 108 amino acids. In all these cytochromes 55, or 53 percent, of the positions are invariant, that is, occupied by the same amino acids. So great a similarity has a negligible probability of being due to chance; all the cytochromes are homologous (i.e., evolved from the cytochrome in a remote common ancestor).

Amino acids at other positions are variable. Organisms relatively close in the biological system (e.g., different mammals) have more similar cytochrome c's than do remote forms, such as mammals and yeasts. The invariant portions of the cytochrome c molecules are assumed to be essential for the function that the enzyme performs. The variable parts are, in Margoliash's words, "undoubtedly compatible with a variety of sequences." The hypothesis that the amino acid substitutions in the variable parts are due to chance was submitted by King and Jukes (1969) to the following test. By using the Poisson distribution formula, the numbers of substitutions expected by chance can be calculated and compared with the numbers actually observed. The two sets of values are in remarkably good agreement:

| Changes per site | 0 | 1 | 2 | 3 | 4 | 5 | 6 | 7 | 8 | 9 |
|---|---|---|---|---|---|---|---|---|---|---|
| Expected | 6 | 16 | 20 | 18 | 12 | 6 | 3 | 1 | 0.3 | 0.1 |
| Observed | 6 | 17 | 18 | 19 | 10 | 6 | 3 | 1 | 1 | 0 |

*In vitro* experiments appear to show that the cytochrome c's of various organisms are fully interchangeable. Does it follow that the amino acid replacements in the evolutionary process were merely the "noise" of adaptively neutral mutations? It is by no means certain that man would enjoy normal health if his cytochrome c were replaced by horse or yeast cytochrome, or vice versa.

Comparative studies on hemoglobins, particularly in vertebrates, reveal an interesting, but equally ambiguous, situation. Reference was made in Chapter 2 to variant hemoglobins found in some human families or individuals. A majority of the approximately 100 hemoglobins discovered differ from the ubiquitous hemoglobin in single amino acid replacements. Some of the variants are known to cause ill health, whereas for others the evidence is inconclusive. The hemoglobins of other animals differ in more numerous substitutions, as shown in Table 8.4. The alpha chain of human hemoglobin is identical with that in the chimpanzee, and differs by a single amino acid substitution from that in the gorilla (glutamic in man, and aspartic acid in gorilla at position 23), by 17–25 substitutions from that of the other

**TABLE 8.4**

Numbers of amino acid differences between the hemoglobin alpha chains of some animals. (After Dayhoff and Eck 1968)

|        | Gorilla | Horse | Donkey | Cattle | Sheep | Llama | Pig | Rabbit | Mouse | Carp |
|--------|---------|-------|--------|--------|-------|-------|-----|--------|-------|------|
| Human  | 1       | 18    | 20     | 17     | 20    | 20    | 18  | 25     | 17    | 71   |
| Gorilla| 0       | 19    | 21     | 18     | 20    | 19    | 19  | 26     | 18    | 70   |
| Horse  |         | 0     | 2      | 18     | 18    | 16    | 17  | 25     | 23    | 70   |
| Donkey |         |       | 0      | 20     | 19    | 18    | 18  | 27     | 25    | 70   |
| Cattle |         |       |        | 0      | 13    | 22    | 17  | 26     | 20    | 68   |
| Sheep  |         |       |        |        | 0     | 23    | 18  | 29     | 24    | 70   |
| Llama  |         |       |        |        |       | 0     | 20  | 23     | 18    | 60   |
| Pig    |         |       |        |        |       |       | 0   | 26     | 24    | 70   |
| Rabbit |         |       |        |        |       |       |     | 0      | 28    | 75   |
| Mouse  |         |       |        |        |       |       |     |        | 0     | 71   |

mammals in the table, and by 71 substitutions from that of the fish (carp). According to Perutz and Lehman (1968), if one compares the known sequences in the hemoglobins and myoglobins of various mammals, only 7 out of more than 140 amino acid sites have remained invariant. These invariant sites include the attachments of the heme groups and the points of contact between the different chains. Can man get along with gorilla hemoglobin and vice versa? This is not an unfair question, since, as pointed out above, many mutants with amino acid substitutions have been observed in man. Perhaps a gorilla-like human variant will some day be discovered.

Prakash, Lewontin, and Hubby (1969) argue most persuasively that the allozyme polymorphisms in natural populations of Drosophila are maintained by some forms of balancing natural selection, rather than by random drift. Let us recall that it was the discovery of the hitherto unperceived abundance of polymorphisms and heterozygosity in populations (see Chapter 7) that stimulated the revival of random drift or random walk theories. Yet Prakash et al. find identical frequencies of allozyme polymorphs maintained in remote parts of the distribution area of *Drosophila pseudoobscura*. Genetic drift should have diversified these frequencies unless the flies migrate freely over large distances. The migration rates are known, however, to be small (Dobzhansky and Wright 1943, 1947). Prakash et al. conclude, "The hypothesis of widespread balancing selection at most of the polymorphic loci fits most easily all of the observations on the central, marginal and isolated populations, although we cannot exclude, for some loci, a model of selectively neutral isoalleles." The problem of evolution by random walk invites further studies.

# CHAPTER NINE

# POPULATIONS, RACES, AND SUBSPECIES

*ᘐᘐ*

## *Individual and Group Variability*

Immanuel Kant, who was a naturalist before he became the prince of philosophers, wrote in 1775 the following remarkably perceptive lines:

Negroes and whites are not different species of humans (they belong presumably to one stock), but they are different races, for each perpetuates itself in every area, and they generate between them children that are necessarily hybrid, or blending (mulattoes). On the other hand, blonds or brunettes are not different races of whites, for a blond man can also get from a brunette woman altogether blond children, even though each of these deviations maintains itself throughout protracted generations under any and all transplantations.

It appears that Kant had a clearer idea about the distinction between individual variability and the variability of populations than many authors writing today.

In outbreeding sexual species—man, of course, included—no two individuals (identical twins excepted) have the same genotype. Parents differ genetically from each other and from their children, as do the latter among themselves. In asexual and some parthenogenetic species, on the contrary, there may be clones numbering thousands or even millions of individuals with identical genotypes. Clones are "pure races," two or more of which may occur sympatrically, that is, in the same territory. In sexual species, arrays of genetically identical individuals that could be considered pure races do not exist and never existed (although some anthropologists and biologists fancied their existence, usually in the past since they could not find them at present). Races are neither individuals nor particular genotypes; they are genetically distinct Mendelian populations. As a general rule, races are allopatric, living in different territories. Genetic differences between geographic races are maintained, at least in part, by their geographic separation.

Mankind is one of the exceptions to this rule. Before the advent of civilization, human races were allopatric, separated in space, like races of most other sexually reproducing animals and plants. Civilization created a variety of social forces that make possible, at least for a time, the sympatric coexistence of human races. Races or breeds of domesticated animals and plants are also often sympatric, their separation being maintained by the more or less deliberate effort of husbandmen.

A race is a Mendelian population, not a single genotype; it consists of individuals who differ genetically among themselves. It is important to realize that similar genetic elements are involved in individual and in race differences. For example, blonds and brunettes occur as individual variants, polymorphs, in many human populations, and races differ in the incidence of these variants. Some populations are polymorphic for blue and brown eye colors, whereas in others only brown eyes are found. Blue-eyed individuals are not a race distinct from brown-eyed ones, yet eye color is one of the traits distinguishing races. Blood groups are classic examples of intrapopulational polymorphisms and also of interpopulation variability. Individuals with O blood type are not racially distinct from those with A or B blood; however, races do differ in the incidence of these blood groups.

Some race differences, though by no means all, are qualitative: the frequency of a gene allele may be zero in one race and unity in another. If one examines phenotypic traits rather than genes, qualitative differences are more common. Natives of central Africa all have darker skins than do natives of Europe. Skin color, however, is a trait determined polygenically. Dark and light pigmentation alleles occur as polymorphs in most populations, and some populations are intermediate in phenotype, and presumably also in genotype, between the "blacks" and the "whites."

The recognition of the similarity of the genetic basis of individual and of group variability is one of the achievements of genetics. The classical race concept was typological. Thus, Hooton in 1926 (quoted after Count 1950) defined race as "a great division of mankind, the members of which, though individually varying, are characterized as a group by a certain combination of morphological and metrical features, principally non-adaptive, which have been derived from their common descent," and said, "One must conceive of race not as the combination of features which gives to each person his individual appearance, but rather a vague physical background, usually more or less obscured or overlaid by individual variations in single subjects, and realized best in a composite picture."

Some anthropologists claimed an almost preternatural ability to see Celtic, Nordic, Dinaric, Armenoid, Lapponoid, Cromanoid, Oriental, Berberic, etc., "types," all living together and interbreeding in populations of Ireland, Poland, and other countries. Criminals were a "race" different from law-abiding "races" living next door or even in the same families. Typology is at the bottom of the vulgar notion that any so-called Negro in the United States (though actually a majority of his genes may be derived from his white ancestors) has a basic and unremediable negroid nature, just as any Jew partakes of some Jewishness, etc. There are no Platonic types of Negroidness or Jewishness or of every race of squirrels or butterflies. Individuals are not mere reflections of their racial types; individual differences are fundamental biological realities, from which race differences are derived.

Curiously enough, whereas typological thinking leads some people to believe in indelible racial nature, it leads others to deny that races exist. A flurry of polemics among systematic zoologists was started by Wilson and Brown's (1953) critique of the practice of describing and naming subspecies of animals. (A subspecies is a race to which a Latin name has been given.) Some anthropologists rejected the existence of races in mankind (several critical articles are reprinted in the volume edited by Montagu 1964). Now, two issues are involved here: first, under what conditions races should be named; and, second, whether a biological phenomenon called race really exists. Races and species are given names in order that those who study them can tell each other what they are talking and writing about. But it is a typological fallacy to think that all individuals given the same group name are identical. As stated above, races are Mendelian populations in which no two individuals are identical. Furthermore, these populations are by no means always separated by geographic or other boundaries, and they are frequently connected by gradual transitions. The obvious fact is, however, that members of the same species who inhabit different parts of the world are often visibly and genetically different. This, in the simplest terms possible, is what race is as a biological phenomenon.

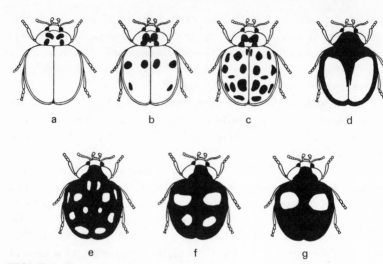

**FIGURE 9.1**

Color patterns in Harmonia axyridis. The form succinea a–c, aulica d, axyridis e, spectabilis f, and conspicua g.

### Gene Frequency Gradients in Harmonia

We consider first an example of racial variation due to frequency differences of alleles of a single gene. This is a paradigm of race variation in general. More complex situations will be considered later.

Variant color patterns in the Asiatic beetle *Harmonia axyridis* (Fig. 9.1) are so striking that some of them were originally described as separate species and even genera. Hosino (1940) and Tan (1946) showed, however, that the variation is caused by five alleles of a single gene; one of the alleles gives the yellow and the yellow black-spotted forms (*succinea, firgida, 19-signata*), another the black yellow-spotted *axyridis*, a third the yellow black-rimmed *aulica,* and the other two the black orange-spotted *spectabilis* and *conspicua* (Fig. 9.1). The alleles exhibit "mosaic dominance"—a heterozygote for any two alleles has black pigment in all parts of the wing covers (elytra) which are black in the carriers of either allele.

Table 9.1, compiled from data of Dobzhansky (1933) and of Komai, Chino, and Hosino (1950), shows the geographic distribution of the color variants. In Siberia west of Lake Baikal the populations consist almost entirely of the black yellow-spotted *axyridis*. From Baikal east-ward the population is mostly yellow or yellow black-spotted. On the Pacific Coast (Khabarovsk and Vladivostok) there appear also the black *spectabilis* and *conspicua*. In Japan (the localities in Table 9.1 are arranged from north to south) the frequencies of *succinea* decrease and those of *conspicua* increase as one goes southward. The black-rimmed *aulica* is found in eastern Siberia, China, and Japan, but always in low frequencies.

The variant color patterns are not only sharply distinct but also discrete; there are no intermediates between them. Yet it would not do to call them races, since they interbreed freely and the progeny of a pair may segregate into two or more variants. By contrast, the populations of different territories are racially distinct, because their gene pools contains different frequencies of the alleles responsible for the color forms (Table 9.1). If we are presented with a single speci-men of *Harmonia axyridis,* we shall only occasionally be able to tell from which population it came. For example, any form other than the black yellow-spotted *axyridis* is unlikely to have been found in the

## TABLE 9.1

Geographic variation of the frequencies of color pattern (in percentages) in Harmonia axyridis

| Region | succinea | axyridis | spectabilis | conspicua | Number Examined |
|---|---|---|---|---|---|
| Altai Mountains | 0.05 | 99.95 | . . . | . . . | 4,013 |
| Yeniseihk Province | 0.9 | 99.1 | . . . | . . . | 116 |
| Irkutsk Province | 15.1 | 84.9 | . . . | . . . | 73 |
| West Transbaikalia | 50.8 | 49.2 | . . . | . . . | 61 |
| Amur Province | 100.0 | . . . | . . . | . . . | 41 |
| Khabarovsk | 74.5 | 0.2 | 13.4 | 10.7 | 597 |
| Vladivostok | 85.6 | 0.8 | 6.0 | 6.8 | 765 |
| Korea | 81.5 | . . . | 6.2 | 12.5 | 64 |
| Mukden, China | 90.7 | . . . | 4.5 | 4.6 | 1,865 |
| Peking, China | 83.3 | . . . | 8.9 | 7.3 | 9,635 |
| Szechwan, China | 42.6 | 0.01 | 28.8 | 25.1 | 1,074 |
| Soochow, China | 66.6 | . . . | 16.5 | 16.1 | 6,231 |
| Sapporo, Japan | 42.9 | 1.0 | 21.6 | 34.3 | 1,184 |
| Akita, Japan | 60.0 | 2.2 | 9.6 | 28.2 | 135 |
| Takasino, Japan | 36.9 | 3.5 | 11.8 | 47.7 | 5,758 |
| Sanage, Japan | 23.1 | 14.5 | 25.9 | 36.2 | 24,443 |
| Kyoto, Japan | 15.3 | 5.1 | 15.8 | 63.7 | 2,494 |
| Matuyama, Japan | 10.7 | 5.8 | 19.1 | 64.1 | 534 |
| Fukuoka, Japan | 2.3 | 2.2 | 11.1 | 83.6 | 995 |

Altai Mountains, while a specimen of *axyridis* probably does not come from Peking, China. One would prefer to have a sample of as many individuals as possible, taken at random in the same neighborhood. The frequencies of the color patterns in such a sample will define its geographic origin, and generally the more precisely the larger is the sample.

What causes brought about the racial variation in *Harmonia* is unknown. Komai and Hosino (1951) and Komai (1954) presented evidence that natural selection must be at work. Population samples from Suwa, Japan, collected from 1912 to 1954, show a gradual decline in the frequency of *succinea* from above 40 to below 30 percent, and an increase of *conspicua* from 42 to 56 percent. In 1948–1950 samples were collected on different trees and crops; *axyridis* was more frequent on pine trees than on wheat, whereas *conspicua* showed the opposite preference.

## Chromosomal Races in Drosophila Pseudoobscura

The example of racial variation that we are about to consider is analogous to that of the color patterns in Harmonia. However, instead of alleles of a single gene it is concerned with a series of supergenes—coadapted combinations of several or many genes locked in inverted sections of chromosomes and therefore inherited as single units. In Chapters 5 and 8 the inversion polymorphism in the third chromosome of *Drosophila pseudoobscura* was described. The distribution area of this species extends from British Columbia to Guatemala, and from the Pacific to Texas (an isolated colony in the Andes of Colombia may or may not have been introduced by man.) Not counting very rare or local ones, eight gene arrangements are found over more or less extensive territories (Fig. 5.2), but not one of these is species-wide in distribution.

A typical situation is illustrated in Fig. 9.2; one observes gradients (clines) of frequencies of the various gene arrangements in traveling across the species distribution area. On the Pacific Coast of California the commonest gene arrangement is Standard (ST), followed by Arrowhead (AR) and Chiricahua (CH). Eastward from California, in Arizona and New Mexico, ST dwindles and AR increases in fre-

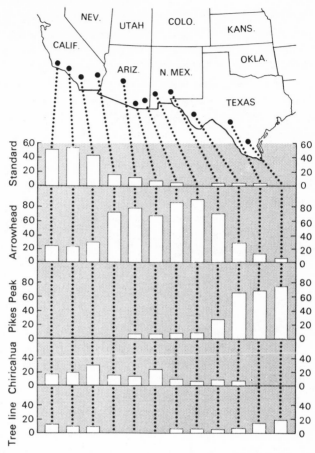

**FIGURE 9.2**

Frequencies of different gene arrangements in third chromosomes of Drosophila pseudoobscura in southwestern United
States.

quencies. Pikes Peak (PP) chromosomes also become more frequent
eastward, and are predominant along the eastern face of the Rocky
Mountains and in Texas. In North Mexico CH is the most frequent
chromosome, while in Central Mexico there appear chromosomes not
found at all in the United States (Dobzhansky and Epling 1944).

Where climatic and ecological conditions change rapidly, chromosome frequency gradients can be observed over distances much shorter
than those in Fig. 9.2. For example, as one ascends the slope of the

Sierra Nevada range in California, ST chromosomes change from about 45 percent at an elevation of 850 feet to only 10 percent at 10,000 feet, while AR chromosomes increase along the same transect from about 25 to 50 percent of the total (Dobzhansky 1948). This strongly suggests that the frequency gradient reflects in this case a response of the populations to natural selection. The same conclusion is compelled by the evidence of the frequency changes observed in some localities, mentioned briefly in Chapter 5. These changes are cyclic, following the seasons. Thus, in some localities on Mount San Jacinto, in California, ST chromosomes wane and CH wax in frequencies during spring months, whereas the reverse changes occur during the hot summer months.

The changes taking place in summer are easily reproduced in experiments in laboratory population cages (see Chapter 5) kept at 25°C. At this temperature, the ST/ST homokaryotype has a higher fitness than the CH/CH homokaryotype. It proved to be more difficult to reproduce the changes that occur in nature in spring, when CH/CH must have a fitness greater than that of ST/ST. This was achieved, however, by Birch (1955), who used experimental populations in which larval crowding was minimized. This condition makes sense—food is abundant in the habitats of the San Jacinto populations in spring, when these populations expand in number; they contract during the hot season (Dobzhansky 1956b).

Thus far, a satisfactory explanation has not emerged for the changes of longer duration, observed in the populations of *Drosophila pseudoobscura* in the western United States between 1940 and the present (Dobzhansky, Anderson, and Pavlovsky 1966, and references therein). In 1940, PP chromosomes were exceedingly rare along the Pacific Coast, from California to British Columbia (only 4 such chromosomes were found among more than 20,000 studied). By 1957–1963 they were present in all localities where adequate samples were made, their overall incidence in California having been between 6 and 8 percent. They have apparently slightly declined since then, although they remain the dominant chromosomal type in the Rocky Mountains and Texas. As shown in Fig. 9.3, the frequencies of CH have declined almost everywhere in the Pacific Coast states, as did the incidence of another gene arrangement, called Santa Cruz. The frequencies of ST and AR also underwent considerable changes, the former generally increasing and the latter decreasing in frequency.

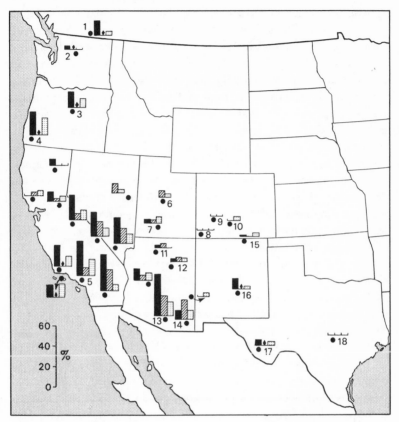

**FIGURE 9.3**

Changes in the frequencies of the CH gene arrangement in third chromosomes of Drosophila pseudoobscura in western United States. Black columns—samples taken around 1940; hatched columns—1957; stippled columns—1963-1965; black diamonds—absence of samples. (After Dobzhansky, Anderson, and Pavlovsky)

Many changes take place in the natural habitats of the flies; for example, droughts and rainy years occur, or some related and probably competing species of Drosophila become relatively more or less abundant. No correlations between these environmental changes and the genetic changes in *Drosophila pseudoobscura* have thus far been detected. By analogy with industrial melanism in British moths (Chapter 7), it seemed possible that contamination of the natural habitats with traces of DDT and other insecticides may have brought about genetic alterations in Drosophila populations. To date, however, experiments made to test this possibility have given negative results (Anderson, Oshima, et al. 1968). This increases the attractiveness of a hypothesis that is difficult to test experimentally, namely, that, by recombination or by mutation, new and better coadapted chromosomes emerge from time to time and spread in natural populations. Suppose, for example, that a "new" PP chromosome has arisen, the carriers of which have high fitness in Pacific Coast localities where the "old" chromosomes were not well adapted. Balancing natural selection will then favor the spread and increase in frequency of these chromosomes, until they reach their equilibrium frequencies. This is not an ad hoc hypothesis; we know that chromosomes with the same gene arrangement contain different supergenes in geographically more or less remote populations, as shown by the experiments on populations of geographically uniform and mixed origins reviewed in Chapter 8.

The existence of genetically different but cytologically identical chromosomes is instructive also in another respect. We have seen above that environmentally very different though spatially close localities are inhabited by populations with clearly distinct chromosome frequencies. These chromosome frequency differences can reasonably be interpreted, by analogy with the seasonal changes in natural and the changes in experimental populations, as selective responses to the habitats. Is this interpretation equally applicable to macrogeographic frequency differences, such as those shown in Fig. 9.2? For example, is the very high frequency of AR chromosomes in Arizona and other Great Basin states due to greater prevalence there of the habitats in which these chromosomes occur than in California and in Texas, where they are much less frequent? Such an interpretation is not called for; the AR chromosomes in these ecogeographic regions are most probably genetically adjusted in different ways to their respective habitats. This may be a situation analogous to the so-called area effect found among colonies of land snails (see below).

### Diversity of Chromosomes and of Environments

We have seen in Chapter 5 that some species of Drosophila are chromosomally monomorphic and others polymorphic; in some the polymorphism is not differentiated geographically, so that one cannot speak of chromosomal races, whereas in others the geographic differentiation is very clear. In certain species of this last category, an interesting relation is revealed between the racial characteristics and the environments in which these races live. *Drosophila willistoni* (da Cunha, Dobzhansky, et al. 1959 and references therein) inhabits an extensive territory, from Florida to Argentina. About 50 different inverted sections have been recorded in all chromosomes of this species; some of the inversions are rare and local, but at least 4 are almost species-wide in distribution. The point of major interest is that near the center of the geographic distribution, in central Brazil, many different inversions occur, and most individuals in natural populations are heterozygous for many inversions. The mean number of inversions per individual in these populations is about 9, and one individual was found heterozygous for 16 inversions, probably the record high for an individual that is not a species hybrid. As one proceeds from the center toward the periphery of the distribution area, the inversion heterozygosis decreases; in Argentina, southernmost Brazil, the West Indies, Florida, Guatemala, and also coastal Equador and northeastern Brazil, the inversion means are between 2 and 1, and even lower. Carson (1959, 1965) and Carson and Heed (1964) found a similar situation in *Drosophila robusta* in the eastern United States—high polymorphism in central and low polymorphism in peripheral parts of the geographic area.

Two different, though complementary rather than exclusive, interpretations of the above findings have been suggested by da Cunha and Dobzhansky and by Carson. As suggested long ago by Vavilov (1926), the center of the distribution area of a species is the territory in which the latter is, by and large, most "at home," and in which it has mastered the greatest variety of environmental opportunities or of available ecological niches. For a species of Drosophila, this may mean that it can subsist on many kinds of fruits and other fermenting substances, that its adaptedness is both wider and greater than that of related competing species, and that it withstands all seasonal vicissitudes and microclimatic contingencies. At the periphery of the distribution, except where an absolute barrier, such as a sea coast, prevents migration, the species has mastered perhaps only a few places in which to live. Genetic diversity—in the species under consideration, the chromosomal diversity—may be the means whereby the mastery of diversified environments is achieved. Of course, if it happens that the geographic center of the species distribution area is ecologically more confining than some more peripheral territory, the genetic diversity may actually be low at the center. This seems to be the case in *Drosophila pseudoobscura.*

Carson (1959) emphasizes that geographically or ecologically peripheral populations are often small and inbred and are dominated by "homoselection," which tends to evolve largely homozygous genotypes specialized to overcome the difficulties of marginal existence. Central populations, on the other hand, are dominated by "heteroselection," which leads to high heterozygosis, heterotic buffering, evolution of supergenes locked in chromosomal inversions, and wider but less plastic genetic adaptive capabilities. Carson supposes further that, although central populations possess a greater immediate adaptive flexibility, the peripheral ones are a more prolific field of genetic experimentation and may give rise to adaptive divergence and to the initiation of new species.

### Microgeographic Races in Cepaea Snails

Every living species has the means for active or passive dispersal of its progeny. Because of walking, flying, swimming, and the scattering of seeds, pollen, spores, etc., the birthplaces of the parents and their offspring are separated by some average distance. Individuals within this distance are called sympatric, and those at greater distances allopatric. The distinction between sympatric and allopatric populations, especially in a continuously inhabited territory, is not well defined. It is nevertheless of considerable interest in evolutionary biology; as stated above, races are usually allopatric populations, while polymorphs are variations within a sympatric population. Because the dispersal proficiencies of different living forms vary within a very wide range, races also vary from microgeographic to major geographic.

Since land snails are mostly slow-moving animals, it is not unexpected that populations of the same species living a few steps apart are sometimes genetically different. The extensive studies of Gulick (1905 and earlier) and Welch (1938) on Achatinella in Hawaii, of Crampton (1916, 1932) on Partula in Tahiti and Moorea, and of Diver (1940 and earlier) on Cepaea brought to light numerous examples of geographically very close but phenotypically quite distinctive populations of snails. Since the environments inhabited by these populations appear to be very much the same, it was assumed that the differentiation of the populations is not a result of differential adjustment to the living conditions by natural selection. Random genetic drift seemed a more plausible explanation.

The works of Cain and Sheppard (1950, 1954) and of their numerous disciples in Britain (see Currey, Arnold, and Carter 1964 and Cain, Sheppard, et al. 1968 for references), and of Schnetter (1950) and Sedlmair (1956) in Germany changed the situation (see also Ford 1964 for a review). The common European snail *Cepaea nemoralis* is highly polymorphic. The shell may be yellow (recessive) or brown (dominant). The outside surface of the shell may have five black bands (recessive) or may be unbanded (dominant); some of the bands may be missing or fused together. Working in the neighborhood of Oxford, England, Cain and Sheppard discovered that the incidence of shells of different colors varies, depending on the type of habitat. Figure 9.4 shows that in beechwoods most of the shells are brown and unbanded, whereas on rough herbage and in hedgerows the shells are predominantly yellow and banded. Cain and Sheppard were also able to demonstrate that one of the selective factors responsible for this regularity is predation of the snails by birds, particularly the thrush *Turdus ericetorum*. This bird has the habit of carrying the snails that it finds to "anvils," that is, to nearest convenient stones, where it breaks the shell and consumes the animal inside. The broken shells accumulate near the anvils, and their characteristics can be compared with those of living snails in the vicinity. This permitted Cain and Sheppard to prove that the predation is indeed selective—among the broken shells the proportion of those judged not protectively colored is greater than in the surrounding territory. Thus, in one locality the proportion of banded shells was 264 among 560 living snails, and 486 among 863 predated individuals—a statistically significant difference.

Although the evidence adduced by Cain and Sheppard and their school has established beyond doubt that natural selection is involved in the formation of local races of Cepaea, it does not rule out the possibility that some of the differences may also be due to random drift and to the operation of the founder principle. Lamotte (1951, 1959) in France and Goodhart (1962, 1963) in England did not find the same correlation between the characteristics of the local populations and their habitats that was observed by Cain and Sheppard. Lamotte

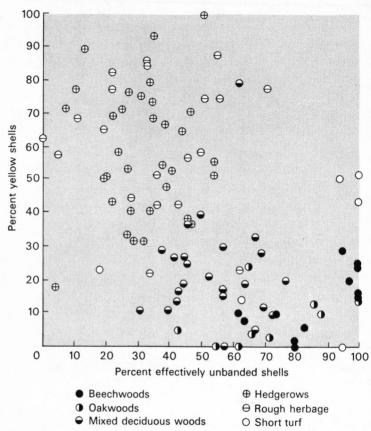

**FIGURE 9.4**

Shell color and banding in the snail Cepaea nemoralis in different environments. (After Cain and Sheppard)

observed a suggestive relationship between the sizes of the colonies and their diversities, the diversity of small colonies being greater than that of large ones. This is what one would expect if intercolonial diversity is due to random genetic drift in small populations. On the other hand, Lamotte found that snails with differently colored shells differ in temperature preferences and tolerances, so that some selection in addition to drift is probably involved.

Cain and his colleagues (Cain and Currey 1963 and Cain, Sheppard, et al. 1968) also found, in the chalk district of Marlborough Downs not far from Oxford, that the incidence of the color variants of the snails remains uniform over areas vastly larger than that of a panmictic snail population, irrespective of the character of the habitat and the color of the background. This phenomenon, which they have named the "area effect," they believe to be also a product of natural selection, though they have no clue to what factors are responsible for this selection. They observe that "the abruptness of change of gene frequencies in both color and banding might be caused by the change-over from one balanced gene complex to another requiring very different frequencies." If I understand them correctly, this can refer only to epistatic interactions between the genes, or supergenes, which govern the shell color and the rest of the genotype, the latter being different in different populations. If so, their area effect is closely related to the variety of coadaptive relationships observed in chromosomal races of *Drosophila pseudoobscura* (see above).

### Stability and Change in Races
### of Maniola jurtina

*Maniola jurtina* is a common European butterfly, which has been the subject of brilliant studies by Ford and his collaborators (Ford 1964 and references therein, Creed, Ford, and McWhirter 1964, and Dowdeswell and McWhirter 1967). An inconspicuous but most useful character is the number of spots, varying from none to five, on the underside of the hind wings, particularly in females. A large territory, extending from most of England to southern France, Finland, and Bulgaria, is inhabited by populations with a unimodal spot distribution in females, zero spots being the most frequent class. This "general European stabilization" is maintained despite the pronounced diversity of the habitats where the butterflies occur.

Suddenly in western Devon and Cornwall (southwest England) and on the nearby islands of Scilly, this "stabilization" gives way to remarkable variation. The Cornish race has a bimodal spot distribution in females, zero and two spots being common, and one, three, and more spots rare. On three "large" Scilly islands (682 acres or more) the classes with zero, one, and two spots are about equally common; on "small" islands (40 acres or less) there is a variety of populations with bimodal (zero and two) and with unimodal (zero or two) spot distributions.

The most striking fact (which, owing to the kindness of Professor E. B. Ford, I had the opportunity to observe personally) is that the boundary between the Cornish and the English (general European) races is quite abrupt, a matter of a few meters. Moreover, this boundary often shifts from year to year by several kilometers eastward or westward. The location of the boundary on a given year coincides with no perceptible environmental barriers. The insect concerned is a good flier and can cross the boundary easily. Such sharp boundaries are not unknown elsewhere; for example, White, Carson, and Cheney (1964) found an abrupt border between the chromosomal races of the grasshopper *Moraba viatica* in Australia. Ford and his colleagues have adduced indirect but convincing evidence that the spot distribution in populations of *Maniola jurtina* is subject to strong natural selection. Just what is the selective agency in operation is unknown; it is presumably not the number of spots as such but some pleiotropic effects of the genes responsible for the spotting.

The maintenance of several distinct island races on the Scilly archipelago is explained easily, since the butterfly does not fly across the intervening stretches of sea. The origin of these races poses a more difficult problem. Ford rejects the hypothesis that the racial differences between the islands might have arisen because of the islands having been originally populated by small numbers of founders (the founder principle; see Chapter 8). Ford's argument is that the spotting in some of the island populations has been observed to undergo changes from year to year, provoked by man's interference with the habitats or by weather fluctuations. Thus, the removal of cattle from the small island of Tean has altered its vegetation, and this was followed by changes in the spotting patterns of its population of *Maniola jurtina*. The genetic flexibility of the island populations contrasts, then, with the "stabilization" of the general European race, seemingly impervious to environmental variations.

It is tempting to compare this situation with flexible chromosomal polymorphisms in some populations and species of Drosophila, contrasting with rigid polymorphisms in other populations and species (Dobzhansky 1962). For example, clear-cut seasonal changes in the frequencies of the gene arrangements are observed in some populations of *Drosophila pseudoobscura,* whereas other populations of the same species show no such changes. The gene pool of some populations has reached a degree of adaptedness that makes superfluous genetic reconstructions in response to recurring environmental changes.

## Racial Variation of Blood Groups in Man

At the turn of the century, Landsteiner discovered that, when the red blood cells of some persons are placed in the blood sera of some other persons, the cells are clumped or agglutinated. By means of this reaction, people can be divided into four "classical" blood groups: O, A, B, and AB, which are inherited by means of three alleles of a single gene locus—$i$, $I^A$, and $I^B$. The incidence of these blood groups, and of the alleles determining them, varies in populations of different countries. Additional loci, determining immunochemical characteristics of the red blood cells, some of them comprising "systems" of alleles, have been discovered since, and still more are being added almost annually. Some of these are "private" blood groups, so-called because variant antigens have been found only in single families or in single persons, and a vast majority of people test alike with the immunological reagents employed. In addition to the classical OAB system, the following variations of red blood cells give polymorphisms in some or in all human populations:

| | | | |
|---|---|---|---|
| Rh | at least 15 alleles | Lutheran | 2 alleles |
| MNSs | 4 alleles | Kell | 2 alleles |
| Lewis | 4 alleles | Duffy | 3 alleles |
| P | 2 alleles | Kidd | 2 alleles |
| Diego | 2 alleles | | |

Mourant and his collaborators (Mourant 1954 and Mourant, Kopec, and Domaniewska-Sobzak 1958, and Race and Sanger 1968) have published excellent reviews of the enormous literature dealing with blood groups in man; Mourant's book has 1705 bibliographic references, and numerous works have appeared since 1954. The distribution of the classical blood groups is known best. With the exceptions indicated below, human populations contain persons of the four groups, but in different proportions. The Indians of Central and South America, where they are unmixed with people of European and African descents, are all homozygous for the gene $i$ (O blood group). Blood group O predominates also among the Indians of North America, with the exception of some tribes (such as the Blackfeet) which may have the highest known incidence of A. In the Old World, the gene $I^B$ is, as shown in Fig. 9.5, most frequent in central Asia, Mongolia, Tibet, northern India, and also in a part of Madagascar. Geographic gradients of declining frequencies go westward, eastward, and southward. The allele $I^B$ is rare in Australia and Polynesia. The allele $I^A$ is common in western Europe, South Australia, and, as stated above, in some Indian tribes in North America.

The Rhesus locus is most complex. In fact, there has been much inconclusive controversy between those who believe that only a single gene with many alleles is involved, and those who assume three closely linked genes ($C$, $D$, and $E$) which by rare recombination give rise to a variety of supergenes and of serological phenotypes. This issue need not concern us here; the $CDE$ notation is more convenient, and we use it in Table 9.2. The allele, or supergene, $CDe$ is common in Asia, among Australian aborigines, and also in Europe; it is infrequent among the Negroid populations of Africa. Conversely, $cDe$ is most frequent in Africa, but it occurs in low frequencies throughout the rest of the world. The allele $cde$ (Rh-negative) is predominately European,

**TABLE 9.2**

Percentage frequencies of the Rh blood group alleles in some human populations (After Mourant 1954)

| Population | CDE | CDe | CdE | Cde | cDE | cdE | cDe | cde | Tested |
|-----------|-----|-----|-----|-----|-----|-----|-----|-----|--------|
| English | 0.1 | 43.1 | 0 | 0.7 | 13.6 | 0.8 | 2.8 | 38.9 | 1038 |
| French | 0 | 41.0 | 0 | 0.9 | 13.0 | 0.4 | 3.9 | 40.8 | 1672 |
| Germans | 0.4 | 43.9 | 0 | 0.6 | 13.7 | 1.0 | 2.6 | 37.8 | 2472 |
| Spaniards | 1.0 | 43.0 | 0 | 1.3 | 12.4 | 0.5 | 5.4 | 36.4 | 2000 |
| Basques | 0.9 | 43.3 | 0 | 1.1 | 4.3 | 0.2 | 7.8 | 42.5 | 547 |
| Egyptians | 0 | 49.5 | 0 | 0 | 9.0 | 0 | 17.3 | 24.3 | 184 |
| Nigerians | 0 | 9.9 | 0 | 2.2 | 9.1 | 0 | 65.1 | 13.6 | 165 |
| Bantus | 0 | 4.7 | 0 | 5.8 | 8.5 | 0 | 59.6 | 21.4 | 600 |
| Australia (aboriginal) | 2.1 | 56.4 | 0 | 12.9 | 20.1 | 0 | 8.5 | 0 | 234 |
| Indonesians | 1.2 | 83.4 | 0 | 0 | 10.6 | 0 | 4.8 | 0 | 247 |
| Bengali | 1.6 | 63.3 | 0 | 6.5 | 7.6 | 0 | 3.9 | 17.7 | 236 |
| South Chinese | 0.5 | 75.9 | 0 | 0 | 19.5 | 0 | 4.1 | 0 | 250 |
| Eskimos | 3.4 | 72.5 | 0 | 0 | 22.0 | 0 | 2.1 | 0 | 158 |
| Navajo | 5.8 | 32.6 | 0 | 17.2 | 35.6 | 1.6 | 6.9 | 0 | 305 |

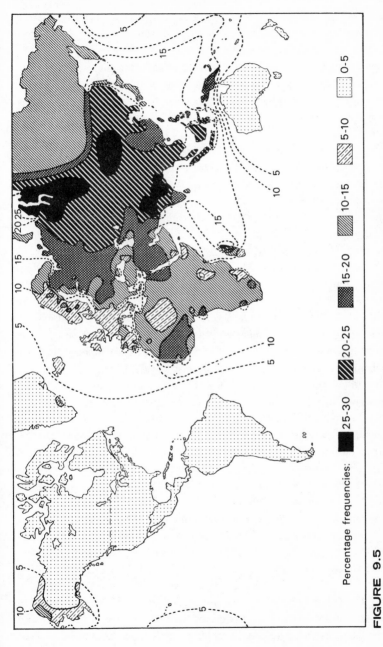

Percentage frequencies:

**FIGURE 9.5**

Frequencies of blood group gene B in aboriginal populations of the world. (After Mourant)

reaching the highest known frequency among the Basques. *Cde* is found mainly among Australian aborigines, and in some, but not in all, American Indians. Thus we have an instructive example of polymorphs that can be used as racial characters: the allele *cDe* is characteristic of Africans, but it occurs also, more or less as a rarity, among Europeans and Asiatics. There is no need to suppose that the Europeans and Asiatics who carry this allele always have some remote Negroid ancestry.

The MN blood group system is geographically less variable than the OAB or the Rh system, since most populations show fairly uniform frequencies of *M* and *N* genes, usually with a slight predominance of the former. However, *M* reaches high frequencies among American Indians, and *N* among Australian aborigines. The other blood group systems are as yet insufficiently studied. The Diego locus polymorphism was discovered originally among South American Indians and has since been found also in Mexico and in North America, as well as among Chinese and Japanese. Race and Sanger (1968) call one of the two Diego alleles "essentially a Mongolian character." One of the alleles of the Duffy system seems to be very frequent (above 90 percent) among west African Negroes, but rare (about 3 percent) in Europeans. An allele in the Kidd system is prevalent among Negroes, less common among Europeans, and least known among Chinese.

The development of methods for the separation of proteins by electrophoresis in starch and other gels made possible exploration of genetic variations of human blood sera (Smithies and Connell 1959). Two serum proteins, haptoglobins and transferrins, have attracted the most attention. Haptoglobins are detected by adding free hemoglobin to aliquots of a blood serum, and subjecting the mixtures to electrophoresis. Haptoglobin-hemoglobin complexes are formed that move in the electric field, depending on the kind of haptoglobin present. Two common gene alleles, *Hp¹ and Hp²*, give three haptoglobin phenotypes on starch electrophoresis, one of the homozygotes ($Hp^1Hp^1$) producing a single band, the other ($Hp^2Hp^2$) three bands at a different position, and the heterozygote ($Hp^1Hp^2$) all four bands (Giblett 1961). The allele $Hp^2$ is most frequent in India (up to 90 percent), while the frequencies of $Hp^1$ show ascending gradients westward to Europe, southwestward to Africa, as well as eastward in Asia, and particularly in the Americas, reaching frequencies above 70 percent in Peru and Chile (See Buettner-Janusch 1966). Giblett (1964) and others discovered at least eleven more haptoglobin phenotypes, which occur in very low frequencies, at least in the populations studied.

Transferrin is an iron-binding protein that plays an important role in the iron metabolism of the body. Smithies and Connell (1959) and Giblett (1961) discovered 3 kinds of transferrins: C, which is the commonest, and B and D, which are less common. About 15 kinds have since been described, some of them apparently restricted to certain human populations. The mode of inheritance is not known precisely, but apparently multiple alleles of one locus are involved.

The technically as well as genetically most complex, yet potentially most interesting, polymorphism has been found by Grubb, Podliachouk, Ropartz, Steinberg, and others (see Steinberg 1962, 1967, and Buettner-Janusch 1966 for reviews) in human gamma globulins. The testing procedure requires using (1) red blood cells from a donor of group O who is homozygous for the allele giving the D antigen of the Rh system (see above), (2) an anti-D serum, and (3) an agglutinating serum, most readily obtained from patients with rheumatoid arthritis. The possibility of detecting various antigens, of which about 20 have been found, depends, of course, on the availability of proper sera, a restriction that makes the data obtained by different authors not always comparable. The inheritance of the variant antigens is best interpreted as due to two genes or supergenes, $Gm$ and $Inv$, the former giving rise to at least 17, and the latter to 4, different antigens.

Table 9.3 reproduces Steinberg's list of $Gm$ alleles found in populations tested with a battery of antigens: Nos. 1, 2, 3, 5, 6, 13, and 14.

**TABLE 9.3**

Gn alleles commonly found in certain populations

| Population | Alleles Found | Population | Alleles Found |
|---|---|---|---|
| Caucasoid | $Gm^1$, $Gm^{1, 2}$, $Gm^{3, 5, 13, 14}$ | Bushmen | $Gm^1$, $Gm^{1, 5}$, $Gm^{1, 13}$, $Gm^{1, 5, 13, 14}$ |
| Negroid | $Gm^{1, 5, 13, 14}$ $Gm^{1, 5, 14}$, $Gm^{1, 5, 6}$ | Pygmy | $Gm^{1, 5, 13, 14}$, $Gm^{1, 5, 6}$ |
| | | Micronesian | $Gm^1$, $Gm^{1, 3, 5, 13, 14}$ |
| Mongoloid | $Gm^1$, $Gm^{1, 2}$, $Gm^{1, 13}$, $Gm^{1, 3, 5, 13, 14}$ | Melanesian | $Gm^1$, $Gm^{1, 2}$, $Gm^{1, 3, 5, 13, 14}$, |
| Ainu | $Gm^1$, $Gm^{1, 2}$, $Gm^{1, 13}$, $Gm^2$ | | $Gm^{1, 5, 13, 14}$ |

Some alleles (or supergenes) give rise to combinations of several detectable antigens. According to Muir and Steinberg (1967), the common alleles found among Negroes are $Gm^{1, 5, 13, 14}$, $Gm^{1, 5, 14}$, $Gm^{1, 5, 6}$, and $Gm^{1, 5, 6, 14}$. In Mongoloids (including the Amerindians) the common alleles are $Gm^1$, $Gm^{1, 2}$, and $Gm^{1, 5}$, which are the same as among Caucasoids. African Bushmen have the same alleles as Negroes and also $Gm^1$, $Gm^{1, 13}$, and an edemic allele, $Gm^{1, 5}$. Among the Melanesians, an interesting difference is found between the speakers of two groups of languages—the allele $Gm^{1, 2}$ is absent among those who use so-called MN languages but present in speakers of NAN languages.

Polymorphism in red blood cell and serum antigens is certainly not confined to the human species. Nonhuman primates have been examined for the antigens of the OAB, MN, Rh, and certain other systems (review in Wiener 1965 and Sullivan and Nute 1968). Chimpanzees are polymorphic for O and A, and orangs, gibbons, and baboons for A, B, and AB or very similar antigens. Antigens related to M and N are both found in chimpanzees, while chimpanzees and gibbons seem to differ with respect to their antigens of the Rh system. Transferrin polymorphisms have been observed in chimpanzees (7 phenotypes), gorillas (4), and gibbons (2), as well as in monkeys of the genus Macaca (11 alleles, a review in Buettner-Janusch 1966).

An impressive variety of red blood cell antigens has been revealed in domestic cattle (Stormont 1959) and sheep (Stansfield, Bradford, et al. 1964). Breeds are often recognizable by the alleles they carry. Protein polymorphisms (hemoglobins, transferrins, lactoglobulins, albumins, esterases, amilases) have been found in cattle, sheep, goats, pigs, horses, and poultry (bibliography in Ashton, Gilmour, et al. 1967). Blood groups and enzyme polymorphisms have been utilized in studies of the genetic population structure in domestic mice (Petras 1967) and in the deer mice, *Peromyscus maniculatus* (Rasmussen 1962). Briles and his colleagues (Briles, Allen, and Mullen 1957 and Briles 1964) have obtained data on blood group polymorphisms in chickens, indicating heterotic superiority in heterozygotes. Ferrell (1966) found significant differences in blood group frequencies in colonies of song sparrows (*Melospiza melodia*) living in various localities around San Francisco Bay in California. The enzyme polymorphisms found in Drosophila, discussed in Chapter 7, are phenomena analogous to the blood polymorphisms considered in the present chapter.

*Races of Mankind*

Boyd (1950) was the first to utilize the data then available on blood group polymorphisms to characterize human races. His classification was as follows:

1. Hypothetical Early European: the highest known incidence of Rh negative (*cde* in Table 9.2), probably no $I^B$. Basques are the modern descendants of this race.
2. European or Caucasoid: the next highest incidence of *cde*, a relatively high incidence of *CDe*.
3. African or Negroid: very high frequencies of *cDe*, moderate ones of *cde*.
4. Asiatic or Mongoloid: high frequencies of $I^B$, little if any *cde*.
5. Amerindian: zero to very high incidence of $I^A$, probably no $I^B$ or *cde*, low incidence of *N*.
6. Australoid: high incidence of $I^A$ and *N*, no *cde*.

Except for the Hypothetical Early European race, this classification represents no radical departure from the classificatory schemes of anthropologists who use externally visible traits, such as skin color, hair shape, or facial features. Nevertheless, some conservative anthropologists objected to Boyd's essay. Why substitute invisible blood traits for easily visible morphological ones? This objection misses the point. The advantage of blood antigens is that their inheritance is relatively simple, diagnosis by competent technicians is accurate, and differences between populations can be expressed in terms of gene frequencies rather than of visual impressions or at best as means of measurements. Skin and hair colors and shapes are polygenic traits; the mode of their inheritance is uncertain, and they are modifiable by environmental circumstances. As pointed out above, genetically simple traits make it possible to gain an insight into the nature of racial variation. This is not to deny that a racial classification should ideally take cognizance of all genetically variable traits, oligogenic as well as polygenic.

Garn (1965), fully conversant with the evidence of classical anthropology and of genetics, proposes the following classification of 9 "geographical races," some of them further subdivided into "local races":

1. Amerindian, with 4 local races.
2. Australian, with 2 local races.
3. African, with 4 local races.
4. European, with 5 local races.
5. Indian, with 2 local races.
6. Asiatic, with 5 local races.
7. Polynesian.
8. Micronesian.
9. Melanesian.

In addition, he recognizes "puzzling, isolated, numerically small local races": Lapp, Pacific Negrito, African Pygmy, and Eskimo; "long-isolated marginal" local races: Ainu, Bushmen, and Hottentots; and "hybrid, local races of recent origin": North American Colored, South African Colored, Ladino, and Neo-Hawaiian. Since there is no substantial difference between "geographical" and "local" races, this classification may as well be presented as comprising 35 races, some including many millions and others only thousands of persons, some expanding and others in the process of being submerged by hybridization with their more numerous neighbors.

Coon (1965) divides mankind into 5 "subspecies"—Caucasoid (more or less corresponding to Garn's European), Mongoloid (Garn's Asiatic plus Amerindian), Congoid (African), Capoid (Bushmen), and Australoid (Australian plus Melanesian). The Pygmies in Africa and the Negritoes in Australasia he considers, somewhat ambiguously, to be "races."

It should be made unequivocally clear that the number of races or subspecies which one chooses to recognize by giving them vernacular or formal Latin names is largely, though not completely, arbitrary. Every local population of human beings, or of any other sexual species, probably differs from other populations in the incidence of some gene alleles in its gene pool. Every population is, then, racially distinct from every other. But it would serve no useful purpose to give every population a name as a separate race. In a continuously inhabited territory populations have no boundaries; they merge into each other. The incidence of some blood group alleles has repeatedly been shown to be significantly different in the possessors of different surnames (Hatt and Parsons 1965 is a recent example). Possessors of the same surname do not constitute separate Mendelian populations, but the inhabitants of districts in which a given surname is particularly common may be such populations. Moreover, one should not confuse race differences and race names. The former are objectively ascertainable biological phenomena; the latter are matters of convenience. For some purposes it may be expedient to divide mankind into 35, or 9, races; for others, into only 5 named races.

There will always be some populations intermediate between, and failing to fit into, any of the races; some of the inhabitants of western Siberia and Turkestan are examples of the former type, while European Lapps are examples of the latter. Intermediate populations have traditionally been regarded as mixtures, that is, hybrids of the populations between which they are intermediate. To some extent this view is, of course, correct; gene diffusion within a species is normal and ubiquitous, unless geographic barriers intervene. The great plains of Europe and western Asia have few such barriers, the Caucasoid and Mongoloid races or subspecies are connected by many transitional populations, and the gene frequencies (see Fig. 9.5 for an example) show regular gradients. It is unnecessary, however, to suppose that in all cases there was a time in the past when the races were unmixed and the gene frequency gradients were absent.

By contrast, geographic barriers that impede travel also impede gene diffusion and make gene frequency gradients steeper or steplike at the barriers. Examples of this situation in respect to man are the Sahara Desert, separating African and European races, and the Himalaya range, separating Mongoloid from Indian races. It is evidently both an acknowledgment of the objectively ascertainable biological situation and a matter of convenience that race boundaries are drawn, whenever possible, at the breaks or steepenings of the gene frequency gradients. The number and the magnitude of the gene frequency differences impose other restrictions on the arbitrariness whereby populations are included in the same race or are given different racial names. Thus, Mongoloid and Amerindian populations are frequently placed together in a single race, but it would hardly occur to anybody to combine Amerindian and African populations and to contrast them with the Mongoloids. Although some separations and combinations are debatable, others are clearly reasonable, and still others obviously impossible.

### *Plant Races or Ecotypes*

Turesson (1922, 1925, 1930) pioneered experimental studies on the genetic adaptedness of local populations to their habitats. Working with as many as 31 different plant species, he demonstrated

that local populations found in different environments are often genetically different, and argued that the distinctions are adaptive in the
respective environments. His method was to transplant individuals
from different local populations and to grow them under uniform
conditions in his experimental garden. The transplants, though often
modified as compared to their appearance in their native habitats,
nevertheless did not become identical, proving that they were genetically distinct. Thus, the hawkweed *Hieracium umbellatum* transplanted
from populations on sandy seashores in southern Sweden was prostrate,
with long shoots and narrow, hairy leaves; from rocky localities it had
short shoots and broader, shiny leaves; and plants from inland localities
were tall and erect. Turesson regarded species (or ecospecies, as he
called them) as mosaics of local populations, which evolve different
ecotypes in different habitats. He defined an ecotype as "the product
arising as a result of the genotypical response of an ecospecies to a
particular habitat."

Clausen, Keck, and Hiesey (1940, 1948), Clausen (1951), and
Clausen and Hiesey (1958) carried the experimental study of ecotypes much further. Using species in which an individual can be cut
into several parts, they replanted the parts in different environments
in three transplant gardens in California—one close to sea level at Stanford, and the others at 4600- and 10,000-foot elevations in the Sierra
Nevada Mountains. Their most extensively studied materials were
species of yarrow (Achillea) and cinquefoil (Potentilla), and their
ecotypes were geographic races from various altitudinal and climatic
zones in California and from foreign countries. The findings were not
only that the races were genetically distinct, but also that their norms
of reaction (Chapter 2) were adaptively circumscribed to fit the
environments to which they were native. Individuals of different races
planted together, and also parts of the same individual replanted in
different environments, were distinguishable.

Yarrows (*Achillea lanulosa*), native to different elevations in the
Sierra Nevada and transplanted into the garden at Stanford, can be
seen in Fig. 9.6. Frequency distributions and the mean heights of
about 60 plants from each locality as they develop at Stanford are
shown. There are clear gradients of diminishing plant heights, as well
as changes in the foliage, as one moves from lower to higher elevations.
In addition, many plants native to high elevations failed to produce
flowers at Stanford. Races from higher elevations showed winter

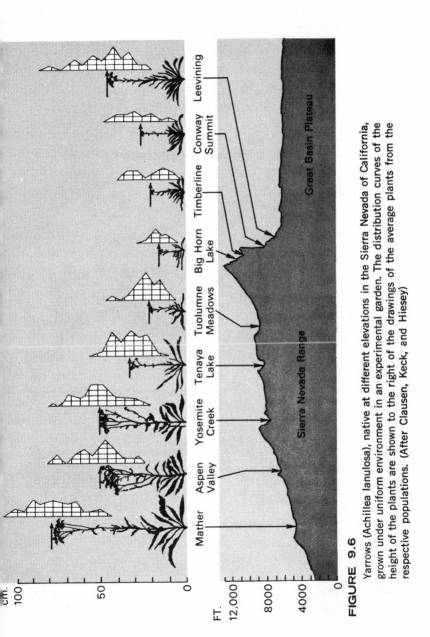

**FIGURE 9.6**

Yarrows (Achillea lanulosa), native at different elevations in the Sierra Nevada of California, grown under uniform environment in an experimental garden. The distribution curves of the height of the plants are shown to the right of the drawings of the average plants from the respective populations. (After Clausen, Keck, and Hiesey)

dormancy (i.e., did not grow in winter) at Stanford, whereas races from low elevations either had no dormancy or had summer dormancy. The climatic conditions at high elevations make winter dormancy essential for survival, but at Stanford winter dormancy is unadaptive.

Specimens of *Potentilla glandulosa* from different elevations were planted in the three experimental gardens. The race native at low elevations developed best in the Stanford garden, did reasonably well in the garden at 4600 feet, but was killed at 10,000 feet. The mid-elevation race was robust and abundantly flowering at 4600 feet; at Stanford it was less tall, was winter dormant, and produced few flowers; it hardly survived and seldom matured seed at 10,000 feet. The alpine race is a dwarf, but it was the only one that consistently matured seed at 10,000 feet; at 4600 feet it grew somewhat taller than in its native habitat; at Stanford it was winter dormant, very weak and hardly surviving.

Very interesting hybridization experiments on the altitudinal races of *Pontentilla glandulosa* have been carried out by Clausen and Hiesey (1958). Three generations ($F_1$–$F_3$) were raised of hybrids between an alpine and a low-elevation race. For a total of 19 distinguishing traits, the authors estimate that at least 100 gene differences are involved; some trait differences are due to a single pair or to two pairs of alleles, while others are polygenic. With so many gene differences, hardly any two individuals in the $F_2$ generation are identical in appearance or in physiological properties. Some of the $F_2$ segregants were "cloned," that is, cut into three parts, which were replanted in the three experimental gardens at different elevations in California. Among the 542 segregants so treated, some survived for the duration of the experimental period (5–9 years) at one or more transplant gardens (long survival), whereas others were weak and died usually within 1 or 2 years (short survival). As expected, some individuals survived long in one garden but soon died in others. The numbers of plants with different survival records are shown in Table 9.4.

Some of the segregants survived well only at the low, others at the low and the intermediate, or at the intermediate and the high, or only at the high, transplant station. Some recombination products of the genotypes of the parental races were ill adapted at all three stations—a phenomenon of hybrid breakdown that will be discussed in the next chapter. However, the class most abundantly represented

**TABLE 9.4**
Duration of survival (long or short) of cloned $F_2$ segregants from a cross of an alpine and a low-altitude race of Potentilla glandulosa (After Clausen and Hiesey 1958)

| Elevation (feet) of Transplant Garden | | | Number of Segregants | Elevation (feet) of Transplant Garden | | | Number of Segregants |
|---|---|---|---|---|---|---|---|
| 90 | 4600 | 10,000 | gants | 90 | 4600 | 10,000 | gants |
| Short | Short | Long | 26 | Long | Long | Long | 148 |
| Short | Long | Long | 56 | Long | Short | Long | 25 |
| Short | Long | Short | 68 | Long | Long | Short | 97 |
| Short | Short | Short | 58 | Long | Short | Short | 64 |

among the segregants consisted of plants that survived at all three stations, perhaps indicating the formation of genotypes with a norm of reaction more permissive than the norms in the parental races crossed. As might have been expected, most of the plants that survived best at 10,000 feet resembled the native alpine race also in their structural traits, and the plants surviving best at the lowermost station resembled the low-altitude race. But, interestingly enough, there were exceptions; some of the "synthetic alpines" contained a number of traits inherited from the foothill parental race. The six segregants that were notably successful at all three stations tended morphologically to resemble the foothill parent. A caveat must be entered at this point: since the segregants were transplanted artificially into well-tended experimental gardens and were not exposed to competition with native vegetation, their degree of adaptedness in the various environments is probably overestimated rather than underestimated.

Is there a difference between a geographic race and an ecotype? To a large extent the two terms are synonymous. Zoologists, however, seldom speak of ecotypes, and Mayr (1963) concludes, "It would appear safer to describe the result of studies in experimental taxonomy in less rigorous terms, such as climatic race or edaphic race, than in terms of the ecotype with its typological implications." The outstanding botanist and evolutionist Grant (1963) does not mention ecotypes in his book. It may be advisable to restrict the term ecotype to races that occur mosaic-fashion in a quasi-continuously inhabited territory, wherever a certain type of environment (e.g., sand, clay, or calcareous soils) appears. If so, the correlation between the colors and patterns of Cepaea snails and their habitats discovered by Cain, Sheppard, and their colleagues (see above) may be an example of ecotypic variation in an animal species. In any case, the experiments of Clausen and his colleagues can be regarded as shedding much needed light on the genetics of racial variation.

## *The Possible Adaptive Significance of Racial Variation in Man*

One might think that the adaptive significance of the race differences in man, as well as of the intrapopulational polymorphisms, would be comprehensively investigated and known in detail. On the contrary, at best only more or less plausible speculations exist concerning some characteristics, and not even conjectures concerning the rest. Reference was made above to the opinion of Hooton, a leading anthropologist of a generation ago, that race differences are "principally non-adaptive." This view has probably been shared by a majority of anthropologists. At the opposite pole is the dictum that neutral genetic traits are nonexistent or extremely rare, so that if some trait seems to be neutral it means only that its adaptive significance has not yet been discovered.

In the particular case of the human species the difficulty is compounded. The environments in which people now live are radically different from those in which their ancestors lived 1000, or even 100 or fewer, generations ago. Therefore, the adaptive function of a genetic difference at our time level may be entirely unlike its function in the past, when the human species and its subdivisions were in the process of formation. A best-seller has called man "The Naked Ape," but he usually goes clothed and is not an ape. Hairiness or lack of hair, skin pigmentation, or visual acuity may have been important for survival in the past; at present these traits may be nearly neutral or may affect fitness via differential mating success rather than differential survival.

The frequent mention of blood groups as examples of adaptively neutral traits goaded many investigators to discover physiological correlates of the blood groups that are not neutral. Starting with the pioneering work of Aird, Bentall, and Roberts (1953), the burgeoning literature has been ably summarized by, among others, Clarke (1961) and Reed (1961). A relationship between the classical O, A, B, and

AB blood groups and duodenal and gastric ulcers is probably the most thoroughly established. The percentages of persons with different blood groups among patients with these ulcers and in a control population are as follows:

|  | Blood group | | | |
|  | O | A | B | AB |
|---|---|---|---|---|
| Duodenal ulcer | 58.7 | 30.6 | 7.2 | 3.5 |
| Gastric ulcer | 49.1 | 40.0 | 8.2 | 2.7 |
| Controls | 49.0 | 39.1 | 9.4 | 2.5 |

The incidence of the O group is higher than in the controls among sufferers from duodenal but not from gastric ulcers, while among patients with gastric ulcers (and with cancers of the stomach) a higher frequency of blood group A is sometimes observed. Pernicious anemia has shown a statistically significant association with blood group A in some populations but not in others.

When the blood group of a fetus is unlike that of its mother, an immunological incompatibility may arise, and a statistically significant excess of fetal or neonatal death may be observed. This is established beyond doubt for Rh-positive children of Rh-negative mothers (i.e., $D$ versus $d$; see above). Similar incompatibilities for OAB and MN blood systems are less securely verified. Another association that has been claimed is that between blood group A and carcinoma of the cervix.

The taste threshold for solutions of phenylthiocarbamide (PTC) is determined largely by a single gene; specific solutions of this substance taste intensely bitter to some, and seem to have no taste at all to other persons. Only a minority of people are intermediate in their taste thresholds. The incidence of the dominant allele for tasting this substance, and of the recessive allele for taste-blindness to it, are racially variable. Several investigators (Kitchin, Evans, et al. 1959) found that among patients with adenomatous goiters nontasters are significantly more frequent than they are in the control population.

The above observations have shown that polymorphisms like those for blood group genes or for PTC tasting are not neutral, in the sense that they are significantly correlated with certain pathological conditions. Only a small percentage of persons with blood group O have duodenal ulcers, but among those who have such ulcers people with O blood are more frequent than among those who do not. Whether this explains the race differences in the incidence of the blood groups is a quite different question. It happens that the associations thus far discovered are with diseases affecting mainly people of postreproductive ages, so that the Darwinian fitness is but little changed. Moreover, it is not evident how these associations explain the observed racial differences. Do the American Indian tribes that have only O blood suffer from duodenal ulcers more frequently than do the inhabitants of the interior of Asia, among whom O blood is less prevalent? Or are we to suppose that environments in America are less ulcerogenic than those in Asia? There are no data for or against either conjecture.

A very different hypothesis—and one which, if confirmed, might explain the racial differences in the incidence of O, A, and B blood groups—was advanced by Vogel, Pettenkofer, and Helmbold (1961). They attempted to correlate the prevalence of these blood groups with epidemic diseases that ravaged the populations of various countries. Thus, blood group B is common in parts of the world subjected to epidemics of plague, while A and O may possibly be related to the prevalence of smallpox and syphilis. The evidence that these diseases are less dangerous to the carriers of some than of other blood groups is, however, far from convincing (a detailed and critical review in Otten 1967).

Although the rule is not without exceptions, dark-skinned populations live most in countries with abundant sunshine, and light-skinned ones where sunshine is at least seasonally deficient. The notion that dark pigmentation is protective against sunburn is very old; the idea that light skin may facilitate synthesis of vitamin D is more recent. Both notions are plausible, but the supporting evidence is not nearly as complete as could be wished. A summary of the extensive literature has been provided by Blum (1959, 1961). There is no doubt that ultraviolet wavelengths shorter than 3200 Ångstrom units cause erythema (reddening) and sunburn of unpigmented skin, but an acquired tan in otherwise light-skinned races gives protection as effective as the pigmentation of darker races. There is good evidence of higher incidence of skin cancers in lightly pigmented than in darker individuals, with presumably comparable amounts of sun exposure. Loomis (1967) argues that, whereas light pigmentation is adaptive because it facilitates the formation of vitamin D, dark pigmentation is protective against excessive and toxic doses of the substance.

Hamilton and Heppner (1967) found that zebra finches exposed to artificial sunlight used almost 23 percent less metabolic energy after they were dyed black; the authors conjecture that "dark human skin coloration may maximize the absorption of solar radiation in situations where energy must be expended to maintain body temperature, as at dawn and dusk in otherwise hot climates." It has also been surmised that dark skin may function as protective coloration for an individual stalking game or escaping from predators.

Body size, body build, and pigmentation vary widely in different countries (maps in Lundman 1967). It is very probable that these variations help (or helped in the past) human populations to adapt to climatic and other conditions in the countries they inhabit. The evidence in favor of this hypothesis is neither as complete nor as convincing, however, as could be wished. Heat conservation is assisted by minimizing the body surface in relation to mass, whereas heat dissipation, on the contrary, is helped by maximizing the radiating body surface. According to Allen's rule (see the next section), one expects cold-dwelling populations to be as nearly globular as possible—thickset, with relatively short arms and legs. Conversely, inhabitants of hot countries profit by a linear body build, with relatively long arms and legs. Bergmann's rule (see the next section) states that races of the same species of animal that live in cold climates are, on the average, larger than those in hot climates.

Attempts to apply these rules to human races have revealed a general agreement and also not a few exceptions (Hulse 1963, Schreider 1964b, Garn 1965). Scholander, Walters, et al. (1950) challenged the applicability of these rules to man on the ground that human beings deal with cold and heat stress by appropriate clothing and types of dwellings, rather than by body build. This is doubtless so, but in evolution several different adaptive contrivances are often used convergently to respond to an environmental challenge. Summaries and reviews of pertinent literature may be found in Barnicot (1959), Harrison (1961), Schreider (1963), and Baker and Weiner (1966).

Riggs and Sargent (1964) investigated "simulated survival" under conditions of humid heat in 19 matched pairs of white and Negro young male volunteers. Twenty-two "heat casualties" were observed—irregular pulse, anhidrosis, hypohidrosis, heat exhaustion; only one was a Negro. In other studies Baker and his colleagues (Baker 1966 and Baker, Buskirk, et al. 1967) compared physiological reactions to cold on the Andean Altiplano in native Quechua Indians and in partially acclimatized whites. During exposures for 2 hours to a temperature of

10°C, the Quechuas had higher rectal temperatures, skin temperatures, and toe temperatures, but lower mean oxygen consumption and lower cumulative heat exchange than the whites. To what extent this situation could be changed by lifelong cold acclimatization of the whites is difficult to tell. A similar question arises in connection with the findings by Mason, Jacob, and Balakrishnan (1964) that basal metabolic rates are lower among Indian than among European women living in Bombay.

It would be unprofitable to attempt here even a cursory review of the confused and confusing literature on alleged genetic differences between races of man in intelligence and other psychic traits (see Berelson and Steiner 1964, Pettigrew 1964, and Jensen 1969 for references). It is frequently found that the mean IQ scores for Negroes tend to be lower than those of whites living in the same cities or states, but what part of this difference is conditioned genetically and what part is due to social discrimination and inequality of opportunity cannot readily be determined. Even if some portion were shown to be genetic, this would still not justify racist attempts to deprive certain races and social classes of their human rights and dignity. Indeed not even a racist, unless he is wholly ignorant or dishonest, can deny that human races overlap so broadly in measurable psychic traits that every race contains many individuals who score both higher and lower than the means of other races. Schreider (1964a) found a positive correlation between stature and intelligence in the French population. Here, again, it is uncertain to what extent this correlation is genetically or environmentally caused. Whatever the answer may be, would anybody be prepared to argue that tall people are entitled to social preferment over short ones?

### Ecogeographical Rules

Adaptive significance of some traits can be inferred from indirect but still convincing evidence. Structural and physiological peculiarities of desert, alpine, prairie, tundra, tropical forest, and other types of vegetation have been known since pre-Darwinian times. Reduction of the evaporating leaf surface, transformation of leaves into spines, development of pubescence or waxy covering on the epidermis, presence of chlorophyll in the surface layers of the bark, and fleshiness of the leaves, twigs, and stems are well-known examples of the adaptations in desert plants. Astonishing resemblances between American cacti and African euphorbias provide spectacular illustrations of evolutionary convergence.

When the distribution area of a species extends over territories with different climatic, edaphic, and other environmental conditions, the races inhabiting these territories often reflect their differential adaptedness in their structural and physiological traits. Some rules, statistically valid but admitting of exceptions caused by special conditions, were noted by nineteenth-century naturalists. The modern formulation and statistical verification of these rules are due chiefly to the work of Rensch and his numerous students (critical reviews in Rensch 1929, 1960a, b, and Mayr 1942, 1963).

*Gloger's rule* states that, in mammals and birds, races inhabiting warm and humid regions have more melanin pigmentation than races of the same species in cooler and drier regions; arid regions are characterized by the accumulation of yellow and reddish brown phaeomelanin pigmentation. Among insects, the pigmentation increases in humid and cool and decreases in dry and hot climates, the humidity being apparently more effective than temperature (Zimmerman 1931 in wasps, Dobzhansky 1933 in ladybird beetles, and Watt 1968 in Colias butterflies). For the ladybirds, eastern Asia (Siberia and Japan) is the center of heavily pigmented races; to the southwest and southeast of this region, lighter and lighter races are encountered, until centers of very pale races are reached in California in the Western, and in Turkestan in the Eastern, hemisphere.

In mammals and birds, races that live in cooler climates are larger in body size than races of the same species in warmer climates (*Bergmann's rule*). Petersen (1949) finds, however, that in Scandinavian butterflies the wing length decreases northward. In warm-blooded animals, races inhabiting cooler regions have relatively shorter tails, legs, ears, and beaks than those from warmer climates (*Allen's rule*). Petersen finds this rule to apply to some, although not to all, European butterfly races. According to Rensch, Mediterranean races of species of Carabus beetles tend to be smaller and more elongate and to have relatively longer antennae and legs than those from central and northern Europe. In birds, races with relatively narrower and more acuminate wings tend to occur in colder, and those with broader wings in warmer, climates (*Rensch's rule*). Also, the inhabitants of colder countries deposit more eggs per clutch than those of warm countries. In mammals, shorter but coarser hair and a decrease in the amount of down are observed in warm countries. Fish of cooler waters tend to have a larger number of vertebrae than do races of the same species living in warmer waters; an increase in salinity has the same effect as a decrease in temperature. Forms that inhabit swiftly flowing waters tend to be larger and to have more stream-lined body shapes than inhabitants of sluggish or stagnant waters; cyprinid fishes isolated in desert springs tend to lose their pelvic fins (Hubbs 1940).

The adaptive significance of some of the rules is evident; that of others, conjectural. The function of longer pelage and greater amount of wool in mammals of cold lands is heat conservation (Irving 1966). As pointed out above, Bergmann's and Allen's rules are also concerned with problems of temperature regulation. Larger body size means a relatively smaller body surface, and consequently lesser loss of heat. Protruding body parts, such as extremities, tails, and ears, are subject to rapid loss of heat. Increasing the body surface in relation to the mass is therefore unfavorable in cold and desirable in warm climates.

Strange as it may seem, the correlations between racial traits and the environment were used in the past as arguments against the natural selection theory. Racial differentiation was considered a result of direct modification by the environment, perpetuated by a gradual change of the germ plasm in the direction of the phenotypic alteration. This interpretation appeared to be borne out by experiments showing that changes analogous to those observed in a particular geographical race may also be effected in other races of the same species by exposure to environmental agents. Thus, in the classical experiments of Standfuss, exposure to heat treatment produced, from the pupae of central European races, butterflies that resembled varieties from Syria or southern Italy. On the other hand, treatment of the central European races with cold resulted in a resemblance to races from northern Scandinavia. Exposure of a mammal to cold or heat may produce, respectively, increase or decrease of the hair length, a change analogous to the difference distinguishing geographic races from high and low latitudes. Bergmann's, Allen's, and Gloger's rules (see above) have their counterparts among the changes that can be induced in animals by the application of appropriate environmental stimuli, namely, changes in temperature and humidity. The same is true for plants, in which the phenotypic changes wrought by external agents may simulate the characteristics of races and species existing in nature.

The parallelism between genotypic racial variability and phenotypic modifications has, however, a more subtle and significant meaning. As pointed out in Chapter 2, harmony between the organism and its environment involves the possession of genotypes with favorable norms of reaction. A norm of reaction is favorable if frequently recurring environmental stimuli evoke phenotypic modifications that enable the organism to survive and to reproduce. It is no accident, therefore, that mammals inhabiting lands with temperate climates react to temperature changes by growing warmer fur in winter and a lighter coat in summer. On the other hand, the genes for warm fur may be fixed in permanently cold regions and for light fur in permanently warm climates. As pointed out particularly by Schmalhausen (1949), Waddington (1957, 1960), and Levins (1968), development may be canalized to yield a fixed outcome or may be plastic to produce varying phenotypes adaptive in different environments. The term organic selection has been coined to describe the parallelism between racial genotypic and environmental phenotypic variability.

### Heterosis and Hybrid Breakdown in Race Crosses

The gene pool of a natural population is a genetic system adapted to the environments that the population inhabits. The genetic systems of different races are adapted to different environments. When these genetic systems diverge in the evolutionary process, the gene recombination in the progeny of race hybrids may yield some genotypes of low fitness in the environments of one or of both parental races. We have seen in this chapter an example of this situation. In the experiments of Clausen and Hiesey (1958), it will be recalled, alpine and foothill races of *Potentilla glandulosa* were crossed; some of the $F_2$ segregants (Table 9.4) were poorly viable when grown at low or at intermediate or at high elevations, or at all of these. To be sure, some segregants seemed to be able to grow in experimental gardens at all three elevations. If these results are taken at face value, the gene recombination produced well adapted as well as poorly adapted genotypes.

The classical work of Goldschmidt (summarized in 1934 and 1940) on the gypsy moth (*Lymantria dispar*) revealed that its geographical races differ, not only in externally visible traits, but also in response to temperature, in rates of development, and in the length of incubation period needed for the young caterpillars to hatch from the eggs in spring. Hybridization of the races in laboratory experiments leads in some cases to production of intersexual hybrids. Thus, the races from northern Japan (Hokkaido) and from Europe have "weak" sex-determining factors. The sex determiners in races from Turkestan, Manchuria, and southwest Japan are "half-weak" or "neutral." Those from central Japan are "strong." The cross weak ♀ × strong ♂ produces in the $F_1$ generation normal males and intersexual females. The reciprocal cross, strong ♀ × weak ♂, gives normal females and males in the $F_1$ generation, but in the $F_2$ half of the males are intersexual. Denoting the female determiners by $F$, the male determiners by $M$, and the weak and strong alleles by the subscripts $w$ and $s$, the above results have been interpreted by Goldschmidt thus:

$$F_w M_w \text{ (weak ♀)} \times M_s M_s \text{ (strong ♂)}$$
$$= F_w M_s \text{ (intersex) and } F_w M_s M_w \text{ (♂)}$$
$$F_s M_s \text{ (strong ♀)} \times M_w M_w \text{ (weak ♂)}$$
$$= F_s M_w \text{ (♀) and } F_s M_w M_s \text{ (♂)}$$

One $F$ is normally sufficient to suppress the effects of a single $M$ and to produce a female; an $F_w$, however, is not strong enough to overpower an $M_s$, and hence an $F_w M_s$ individual is an intersex. Likewise, individuals of the constitution $F_s M_w M_w$ that appear in the $F_2$ from the cross strong ♀ × weak ♂ are not males but intersexes. The degree of intersexuality varies greatly among different crosses. In crosses where the "strengths" of the sex determiners in the parental races differ only slightly, the intersexes are so much like normal females or males that they are fertile. Where the difference between the parental races is greater, however, the intersexes are sterile. Finally, crosses between extremely strong and weak races transform the intersexes into individuals of the sex opposite to that which they should have had according to their chromosomal constitution (XX instead of XY females, and XY instead of XX males).

Sympatric strains have sex determiners of similar "strength." Indeed, a mutation that would appreciably change the "strength" may make its carriers intersexual and may be eliminated by normalizing natural selection. Populations with sex genes different enough to produce sterile hybrids when crossed never inhabit contiguous territories. The "strength" of the sex genes shows geographic gradients. As indicated above, the island of Hokkaido is inhabited by the "weakest" race of *Lymantria dispar.* From there, through Manchuria, Korea, southwestern Japan, and central Japan, progressively "stronger" races are encountered. The "strongest" race lives in the northern parts of the main island of Japan, separated from the "weakest" one in Hokkaido only by the Tsugaru Strait, which is, however, broad enough to prevent mingling of the races living on its opposite shores.

Vetukhiv (1953, 1954, 1956) and Wallace (1955) studied $F_1$ and $F_2$ hybrids between populations of the same species of Drosophila having different geographic origins. Larval viability under crowded conditions, fecundity, and longevity were examined. Three species, *Drosophila pseudoobscura, D. willistoni,* and *D. melanogaster,* were utilized. The populations of the same species were outwardly indistinguishable and were not regarded as representing different "races." Nevertheless, the $F_1$ hybrids between the populations were, as a rule, significantly superior, and the $F_2$ hybrids inferior, to the parental populations.

A synopsis of Vetukhiv's results, prepared by Wallace (1968a), is shown in Table 9.5. In this table, the means of the two parental populations are taken to be unity, and the hybrids are characterized by ratios of their scores divided by the parental means.

The ratios for $F_1$ hybrids in Table 9.5 are all above unity, indicating that these hybrids are luxuriant or heterotic. Since the parental popu-

**TABLE 9.5**

Viability, fecundity, and longevity in $F_1$ and $F_2$ hybrids between geographic populations of the same species of Drosophila (The mean of the parental populations is taken as unity.) (After Vetukhiv and Wallace)

| Trait | $F_1$ | $F_2$ |
|---|---|---|
| Viability | | |
|   D. pseudoobscura | 1.18 | 0.83 |
|   D. willistoni | 1.14 | 0.90 |
| Eggs per female per day | | |
|   D. pseudoobscura | 1.27 | 0.94 |
| Longevity | | |
|   D. pseudoobscura | | |
|     At 16°C | 1.25 | 0.94 |
|     At 25°C | 1.13 | 0.78–0.95 |

lations were not inbred, the origin of this luxuriance is unclear. Perhaps it is due to heterozygosis for greater numbers of genes, and here a comparison with the experiments of Wallace and Mukai on newly induced mutations, described in Chapter 6, may be relevant. The ratios for $F_2$ hybrids are all below unity; the loss of fitness in the $F_2$, as compared to the parental, populations is easier to interpret: the gene pool of each population is an integrated system, which is disrupted by hybridization.

Concordant results have been obtained by Anderson (1968) in a study of the body size in populations of *Drosophila pseudoobscura* from different parts of the species distribution area and in their hybrids. The $F_1$ hybrids were not consistently larger than the mean of the two parents crossed, but the $F_2$ hybrids were significantly smaller than their $F_1$ parents. On the other hand, MacFarquhar and Robertson (1963) found neither a luxuriance in $F_1$ nor a breakdown in $F_2$ hybrids between geographic populations of a fairly closely related species, *D. subobscura*. The cause of this discrepancy is a matter of speculation.

Study of the integration of the gene pool of a population was carried a step further by Brncic (1954) and Kitagawa (1967) in *Drosophila pseudoobscura* and by Wallace (1955) in *D. melanogaster*. By means of rather complex series of crosses that need not be considered here in detail, the following four classes of flies were obtained under conditions such that their relative viabilities could be measured: (1) those with both chromosomes of a pair derived from the population of a single locality; (2) those with the two chromosomes of a pair from different localities; (3) those with one chromosome the result of recombination (crossing over) between chromosomes from different localities, and the other chromosome unrecombined from one locality; and (4) those with both chromosomes of a pair the products of recombination of chromosomes of different geographic origin. Although the results varied from cross to cross, the most common viability sequence was $2 > 1 > 3 > 4$. In addition to confirming the older findings of Vetukhiv (see above), these experiments suggest that integration of the genotype occurs on both the interchromosomal and the intrachromosomal level. A gamete transporting a haploid set of chromosomes from a given population contains a coadapted system of genes. The coadaptation is partly lost when the chromosomes of a set are of different geographic origins and is further decreased if some of the chromosomes are compounded of sections of different geographic origins.

The fitness of race hybrids in man has been a controversial subject for a long time. Partisans of "race purity" prophesy that the hybridization of races will have dire consequences, but critical reviews of the evidence by Trevor (1953) and Penrose (1955) show that, if anything, race hybrids exhibit traces of heterosis. Hulse (1957) found in the Swiss canton of Ticino that people whose parents came from different villages (the products of "exogamous" marriages) are slightly but significantly taller than those having parents from the same village ("endogamous" marriages). By far the most extensive and careful study in this connection is that of Morton, Chung, and Mi (1967) on interracial crosses in Hawaii. Here hybrids of people of Chinese, Japanese, European, and Polynesian extractions have been studied for prenatal and postnatal mortality, congenital malformations, and morbidity, as well as for anthropometric traits. The results can be summarized in the words of the authors:

First generation hybrids between races in man are intermediate in size, mortality, and morbidity between the parental groups. At the present time, human populations do not represent coadapted genetic combinations which are disrupted by outcrossing. It remains an untested hypothesis that outcrossing effects might be observed in a more rigorous environment.

### Do Races Exist?

This question may seem odd at the conclusion of a chapter on race. However, as stated earlier, some authors contend that races do not exist. A glimpse at history and a reconsideration of the issue may be a good way to summarize the chapter. Linnaeus was interested mainly in species, which he regarded as the primordial created entities. He was too good a naturalist, however, not to see that there are subdivisions within species, which he called varieties. Darwin paid considerable attention to varieties, because he held that species develop from varieties by gradual divergence.

As the years passed, the term variety was stretched to include phenomena as disparate as geographic races, breeds of domesticated animals and plants, and intrapopulational polymorphs. Buffon was among the first to employ "race" in a biological sense in 1749, and the word gradually came to be used in connection with "varieties" of mankind. The importance of geographic isolation, and hence of geographic races, for speciation was stressed by Moritz Wagner in 1868 and 1889, and in a more nearly modern form by Karl Jordan in 1896 and 1905. Esper in 1781 distinguished between "essential varieties," which he called subspecies, and "accidental varieties." The employment of subspecies as a taxonomic category goes back to Schlegel in 1844 (see Mayr 1963 for a more detailed historical account).

The race and subspecies concepts are utilized in anthropology and biology primarily for purposes of classification. It has been known since antiquity that different parts of the world are inhabited by different varieties of men. Geographic explorations from the sixteenth to the nineteenth century called this ineluctable fact to general attention. Mankind is a polytypic species, that is, a species including two or several races or subspecies. Over the years, zoologists and botanists discovered that many, in fact most, of their species are also polytypic. They also found that they had described too many species, since some so-called species can be treated more meaningfully as subspecies constituting polytypic species. Modern systematists, studying better known groups such as birds and mammals, have done important work in revising the older classifications in accord with the polytypic species concept.

Mayr (1963, 1969) gives many examples of the results of this reform. Thus, in 1909 a list of species of birds of the world gave 19,000 names; in 1951 the number was reduced to about 8600 species with some 28,500 subspecies, about 3.3 subspecies per species on the average. Mayr does not believe that this average will be increased materially by future studies. The pocket gophers *Thomomys bottae* and *T. umbrinus* have 213 subspecies in the southwestern United States and Mexico (Anderson 1966). This is probably the record, since not even mankind has been honored by so extensive a subdivision. The biology of these gophers, dependent as they are and isolated by soil and vegetation barriers, makes the extensive race differentiation understandable.

In less intensively studied groups of animals, most species are monotypic, that is, not subdivided into subspecies with Latin names. Botanists use the subspecies category less often than zoologists; the important book of Stebbins (1950) mentions subspecies briefly, and that of Grant (1963) not at all. A species may be or may seem monotypic for various reasons. It may be geographically undifferentiated into genetically distinct populations. Relictual species may be reduced to a single colony. In species with strong migratory propensities the gene exchange between populations may prevent genetic divergence. On the other hand, geographic differentiation may involve physiological, cytological, or biochemical, rather than externally visible, morphological traits, and systematists are disinclined to name subspecies that they cannot distinguish by inspection. Species of Drosophila are excellent examples of this situation. Chromosomal races are known in many species, and evidence is accumulating that racial variation in enzyme polymorphisms is at least as common (see above). The tropical American *Drosophila polymorpha* is, however, one of the very few species with a conspicuous color pattern polymorphism and racial variation (da Cunha 1949, Heed 1963, and Heed and Blake 1963). Racial variation in external morphology is so slight that it is detectable only by careful biometric studies (Zürcher 1963 and Cals-Usciati 1964 in *D. melanogaster*, Monclus 1953 in *D. subobscura*, Sokoloff 1966 and Anderson 1968 in *D. pseudoobscura* and *D. persimilis*).

We have seen that the number of races one recognizes in a polytypic species is to a certain extent arbitrary; mankind may be divided into 5, 9, 35, and other numbers of races. I am not convinced that the 213 subspecies named in western American and Mexican pocket gophers (see above) are so clear-cut that they could not be combined into fewer but more inclusive subspecies (Ingels 1950). It should be stressed that the arbitrariness is not always explainable by insufficient data or remediable by more study. Descriptive and anthropometric observations on human populations have already shown that the geographic distributions of different racial traits are often uncorrelated or weakly correlated (maps in Lundman 1967). Not all peoples with black skins have frizzly hair; both tall and short peoples may have prominent or flat noses. Studies on the geographic gradients of gene frequencies have accentuated this lack of rigorous correlations. Not only do the blood group frequencies not vary in parallel with pigmentation or hair shape, but also the frequency gradients in different blood group systems show no strong correlations.

Opponents of racial or subspecific classifications have argued that one should study the geographic distributions of genes and character frequencies, rather than attempt to delimit races or subspecies. The truth is that both kinds of studies are necessary. Gene and character geography is the basis of the biological phenomenon of racial variation; classification and naming are indispensable for information storage and communication. The fact that races are not always or even not

usually discrete, and that they are connected by transitional populations, is in itself biologically meaningful. It is evidence that gene flow
between races is not only possible but actually realized. Gene flow
between species, however, is limited or prevented altogether. To hold
that because races are not rigidly fixed units they do not exist is a
throwback to typological thinking of the most misleading kind.

Without endeavoring to produce a series of formal definitions, we
may summarize the explication of some of the concepts dealt with in
this chapter. A Mendelian population is a community of individuals
of a sexually reproducing species within which matings take place.
There is a hierarchy of Mendelian populations. The most inclusive
Mendelian population is the species. The lowermost member of the
hierarchy is a panmictic unit, within which matings take place at
random. In a continuously inhabited territory the panmictic units have
no boundaries and merge into each other. A local population, including
one or several panmictic units, is a deme. A race is a cluster of local
populations that differs from other clusters in the frequencies of some
gene alleles or chromosomal structures. A subspecies (following Mayr
1969) is a "geographically defined aggregate of local populations which
differ taxonomically from other such subdivisions of the species." A
subspecies is, then, a race that a taxonomist regards as sufficiently
different from other races to bestow upon it a Latin name.

# REPRODUCTIVE ISOLATION

⋰⋰⋰

## Realized and Potential Genotypes

Desmond (1964) estimates that the number of human beings who ever lived is of the order of 77 billion ($7.7 \times 10^{10}$), distributed in time as follows:

600,000 B.C. to 6000 B.C.: 12 billion
6000 B.C. to A.D. 1650: 42 billion
A.D. 1650 to A.D. 1962: 23 billion

On the assumption that a human individual is heterozygous, on the average, for some 3200 genes (cf. Chapter 7), the potentially possible number of gametes with different gene constellations is $2^{3200}$ or $10^{963}$. Because of linkage, some of these constellations are much less likely to arise than others. Nevertheless, the probability of two individuals, whether siblings or persons not closely related, having the same genotype is remote indeed. The array of genotypes composing mankind at present will be replaced by a new array in the next generation. Which genotypes will or will not be realized within a panmictic unit, and even within a species, is to a considerable extent a matter of chance. If genius has a genetic basis, a genius may or may not appear in a given generation, or ever.

Consider now the genes in different species. There is no way at present to recombine human genes with those of, for example, mice or Drosophila (see, however, the hybrids of tissue culture cells mentioned in a later section). It is known that the insemination of eggs of one species by the sperm of a remote species fails altogether or gives inviable zygotes (see below). It is also known that gene recombination in the progenies of viable and fertile hybrids between closely related species gives rise to genotypes some of which are of low fitness. The genotypes composing a species are arrays of gene constellations that enable their carriers to survive and reproduce in certain ecological niches. In terms of Wright's model (Chapter 1), most of the realized genotypes cluster on the adaptive peaks. The adaptive peaks are separated by adaptive valleys—a metaphor for the multitude of gene combinations that are not formed at all or are eliminated on account of the low fitness of their carriers.

It is advantageous for populations that occupy different adaptive peaks to steer clear of the production of gene combinations in the progeny that would fall in the adaptive valleys. To be sure, a minority of the gene combinations formed by the hybridization of species might be fit, perhaps fit enough to spread onto as yet unoccupied adaptive peaks (see Chapter 11). A majority, however, would be relatively ill adapted in any environment. If so, transpecific hybridization would weaken the reproductive potentials of the populations engaged in such hybridization and gene exchange. Here, then, is a challenge which the evolution of life has constantly had to face. The sexual process and the resulting gene recombination facilitate adaptation by creating genetic materials for natural selection to work with; yet, unrestricted gene exchange decreases fitness because it yields too many worthless genotypes. The challenge is very old—it has existed ever since the emergence in evolution of various methods of gene exchange: transformation, transduction, parasexuality, and finally sex and meiosis.

Many and varied solutions of the problem arising from this challenge are known. A radical but trivial solution is to do away with gene exchange altogether. Asexual reproduction, by fission or budding, is one such solution. Parthenogenesis (apogamy), which makes the entire progeny genetically identical with the mother, is another. Still a third is substitution of obligatory self-fertilization for outbreeding, observed in hermaphroditic forms, especially among plants. Most interesting, however, are the nontrivial solutions compatible with sexual reproduction and outbreeding.

How do sexual, and obligatorily or at least facultatively outbreeding, species avoid disruption of their genetic systems by interspecific hybridization? There is again a variety of methods, among which two classes are easily distinguishable: geographic and reproductive isolation. When races or species are allopatric, their representatives do not meet and hence do not mate. Geographic isolation alone would, however, offer an only partial solution to the problem of maintenance of organic diversity. In any locality, there could live only one kind of organism, only a single Mendelian population. In reality, there are many, often many thousands, of sympatric animal and plant species. Moreover, unless separated by uninhabitable terrain, the distribution areas of allopatric species may come into contact. Gene exchange and gene diffusion may occur in the contact or "suture" zones (Remington 1969). This, in fact, is what actually happens with races; the results may be geographically and genetically intermediate populations, gene frequency gradients, and finally a merging of the races into a single population.

Reproductive isolation limits or prevents this gene exchange by means intrinsic to the organisms themselves. In principle at least, geographically isolated populations may be genetically identical. Reproductively isolated populations are necessarily different genetically, although the converse is not true (races are genetically different populations that are not reproductively isolated). Sympatric populations of sexual and outbreeding organisms must be isolated reproductively, for otherwise they could not keep apart and would fuse into a single population. Many species may coexist sympatrically, and their sympatry is *prima facie* evidence of their reproductive isolation. Obvious exceptions to this rule are human races. They are in part sympatric, but they are kept genetically apart, at least to some extent, by social instead of reproductive isolation.

### Classification of Reproductive Isolating Mechanisms

Not only are there different kinds of reproductive isolation, but also the isolation of species in the same group of organisms is often achieved by different means. Moreover, the isolation of a given pair of related species may result from several isolating mechanisms reinforcing each other's actions. Considered physiologically, different isolating mechanisms have scarcely a common denominator; yet genetically their effect is the same, that is, limitation or prevention of the gene exchange between the populations of different species. Dobzhansky (1937a) proposed "physiological isolating mechanisms" as a general designation for all causes, other than geographic isolation, that impede gene exchange between populations. The word physiological in this context led to misunderstanding, however, and Mayr (1942) changed the term to "reproductive isolating mechanisms."

Several variant classifications of reproductive isolating mechanisms have been proposed (Dobzhansky 1937d, Mayr 1942, 1963, Stebbins 1950, Riley 1952, Grant 1963, and others). The following one seems convenient:

1. *Premating* or *prezygotic* mechanisms prevent the formation of hybrid zygotes.
   A. *Ecological* or *habitat isolation*. The populations concerned occur in different habitats in the same general region.
   B. *Seasonal* or *temporal isolation*. Mating or flowering times occur at different seasons.
   C. *Sexual* or *ethological isolation*. Mutual attraction between the sexes of different species is weak or absent.
   D. *Mechanical isolation*. Physical noncorrespondence of the genitalia or the flower parts prevents copulation or the transfer of pollen.
   E. *Isolation by different pollinators*. In flowering plants, related species may be specialized to attract different insects as pollinators.
   F. *Gametic isolation*. In organisms with external fertilization, female and male gametes may not be attracted to each other. In organisms with internal fertilization, the gametes or gametophytes of one species may be inviable in the sexual ducts or in the styles of other species.
2. *Postmating* or *zygotic* isolating mechanisms reduce the viability or fertility of hybrid zygotes.
   G. *Hybrid inviability*. Hybrid zygotes have reduced viability or are inviable.
   H. *Hybrid sterility*. The $F_1$ hybrids of one sex or of both sexes fail to produce functional gametes.
   I. *Hybrid breakdown*. The $F_2$ or backcross hybrids have reduced viability or fertility.

It may be useful to reiterate that any reproductive isolation is caused by genetic differences between populations, whereas with geographic isolation this is not necessarily so. Habitat isolation (see 1A, above) comes closest to bridging the gap, but even there the attachment of different species to different habitats is evidently due to their genetic constitutions.

*Habitat Isolation*

The literature on reproductive isolating mechanisms is so extensive that a whole book would be needed to review it exhaustively. The examples discussed below were chosen to illustrate the remarkable diversity of the situations encountered in nature. More examples can be found in the books of Stebbins (1950, 1958a), Clausen (1951), Patterson and Stone (1952), Linsley (1958), Grant (1963, 1964b), Mayr (1963), Ford (1964), and others.

Among plants, related species often differ in their soil, sun or shade, or elevation requirements. For several years I had the opportunity to observe *Arctostaphylos mariposa* and *A. patula* in the Yosemite region of the Sierra Nevada of California (Dobzhansky 1953). Both species are large bushes or small trees, but they differ in several clear-cut and easily visible traits. *Arctostaphylos mariposa* occurs at relatively low elevations, up to about 4800 feet, and *A. patula* at higher ones, from 4600 feet upward. In the narrow altitudinal belt where both species live, *A. mariposa* occupies drier and exposed situations, and *A. patula* more sheltered sites. Even in that belt at least 90 percent of the trees belong to either one or the other species, and in some localities the altitudinal replacement of the species occurs without any hybrids being produced. In other localities some hybrids can be identified. A great majority of them are $F_1$ hybrids, but Professor G. L. Stebbins assures me (private communication) that he can detect signs of introgression (cf. Chapter 11) where both species occur side by side.

Muller (1952) has studied instances of habitat isolation of several forms of related species of oaks (Quercus). *Quercus mohriana* grows in Mexico and Texas on limestone or in shallow soils overlying limestone, whereas *Q. havardi* is confined to sandy soils. In some places, however, limestone and sand are juxtaposed, and there hybrids between the two species frequently occur. A third species, *Q. grisea,* is an inhabitant of igneous outcrops. Sometimes it grows also on dolomitic limestones, where it meets *Q. mohriana* and hybridizes with the latter. These species are kept separate mainly by habitat isolation. On the other hand, Muller mentions the existence of numerous related species growing together in the same habitat that do not produce hybrids, evidently because of other forms of isolation.

A curious analogy to this situation in oaks is described by Mori and

Matutani (1953) in caddis flies in Japan. These insects engage in daily swarming during which matings occur; each species, however, has its swarming place in a different kind of habitat. The authors refer to this as a "habitat segregation."

The toads *Bufo americanus* and *B. fowleri* inhabit the eastern and central United States. Blair (1941, 1942), Volpe (1952), and Cory and Manion (1955) showed that where these species occur together viable and fertile hybrids are produced. In Indiana and Michigan, three toad populations are found. One breeds early in spring and is pure *B. americanus*; another breeds late and is *B. fowleri*; the breeding period of the third is intermediate, and it consists of individuals resembling the pure species and the experimentally produced hybrids between them. This temporal isolation is insufficient to keep the species apart; in some localities in New Jersey *B. americanus* is no longer found, and the population consists of *fowleri*-like and hybrid individuals. The best interpretation of the situation is that the hybridization is of recent origin. Initially, *B. americanus* and *B. fowleri* occurred in different natural habitats. Human activities, such as destruction of forests and damming of streams, created new habitats acceptable to both species of toad. The gene exchange and formation of hybrid populations are the consequences.

The three-spined stickleback (*Gasterosteus aculeatus*) is a common fish in cold and temperate parts of the Northern Hemisphere. It has attracted the attention of numerous investigators for more than a century, because it has three morphologically, physiologically, and behaviorally different forms (Heuts 1947, Münzing 1963, and Hagen 1967). The form *leiurus* is a fresh-water fish with 3–8 lateral bony plates and an osmoregulatory capacity that maintains the chlorine content of the blood at a constant level in waters of low salinity. *Trachurus* lives in the sea in winter but migrates to river estuaries to breed in spring and summer. It has 30–36 bony plates and a variable chlorine ion concentration. The third form, *semiarmatus,* is a hybrid between the first two, with a highly variable number of plates (8–29).

In Europe, only *trachurus* is found along the coasts of northern Russia, Norway, Scotland, Ireland, and also the Black Sea, and only *leiurus* in fresh waters of Mediterranean countries; all three forms are found along the coasts of the North Sea and the western Baltic, with *leiurus* rare in the estuaries but common uprivers. Hagen (1967) made a most careful study of the situation in the Little Campbell River in

British Columbia. In the headwaters only *leiurus* is found and is very common there; close to the estuary, where the salinity is still low, *trachurus* immigrates in spring and breeds in large numbers during the summer. Only a 1-mile-long section of the stream is the "hybrid zone," where *leiurus,* hybrids, and *trachurus* occur with frequencies of about 10 : 8 : 1. Hagen correctly regards the parental forms, *Gasterosteus aculeatus* (*leiurus*) and *G. trachurus,* as full species, despite the fact that neither sexual behavior nor sterility barriers between them seem to exist. The gene exchange between the species is nevertheless blocked within 1 mile, no introgression occurs, and the hybrids are severely selected against outside the confines of the hybrid zone with its intermediate habitats.

## Temporal Isolation

Gene exchange is impossible between species that breed at different times. Perhaps the most extreme instance of this kind of isolation has been recorded in three species of the orchid Dendrobium (Holttum 1953). Their flowers open at dawn and wither by nightfall. The flowering is brought about by a meteorological stimulus, such as a sudden storm on a hot day. However, one of the species flowers 8 days, another 9 days, and a third 10 or 11 days after receiving the stimulus. Many species and races of plants require long, and others short, days for flowering. This photoperiod dependence is under genetic control, as shown most clearly by Smith (1950).

Countless examples of related animal species that differ in breeding season abound in monographs on the systematics and ecology of particular zoological groups. Tretzel (1955) has published an especially detailed study of the temporal isolation, and also of habitat isolations, among cognate species of spiders in Germany. A perusal of the numerous instances recorded by this author suggests some negative correlation between these isolating mechanisms: species found in the same habitats have different breeding seasons more often than do species that live in different habitats. This correlation is, however, far from complete. There are also instances of species some of which are diurnal and others nocturnal in their activities.

Alexander and Moore (1962) have stated:

The periodical cicadas make up a truly amazing group of animals; since their discovery over 300 years ago, the origin and significance of their extended life cycles have been a continual source of puzzlement to biologists. Their incredible abilty to emerge by the million as noisy, flying, gregarious, photopositive adults within a matter of hours after having spent 13 or 17 years underground as silent, burrowing, solitary, sedentary juveniles is without parallel in the animal kingdom.

There are three pairs of very closely related (sibling) species of Magicicada in the United States, one member of each pair having a 17- and the other a 13-year development time:

|  | 17 Years | 13 Years |
|---|---|---|
| M. | septendecim | M. tredecim |
| M. | cassini | M. tredecassini |
| M. | septendecula | M. tredecula |

Geographically, the species with 17-year cycles occur together, sympatrically, and so do the species with 13-year cycles; the former have, however, a more northern and the latter a more southern distribution, and only in a few places do the two kinds coexist. In any one place a mass emergence of the cicadas occurs only once in 17 (or in 13) years, but in different places the "broods" emerge in different years. The geography of the broods is rather precisely mapped, and in some places the periodicity is known to have been maintained for over three centuries. There are 13 large broods with 17-year cycles and 5 with 13-year cycles. Remarkably enough, all three sibling species emerge together in a given locality. They differ clearly in their "songs" and, to some extent, in microhabitat preferences.

Alexander and Moore have never found a heterospecific mating pair in nature, although the species do mate in captivity. Such differences in the behavior of species in nature and in experimental environments have also been found in Drosophila (see below). It is not known whether the 13-year and the 17-year sibling species intercross in the localities where they may emerge together, an event that will occur presumably once in 221 years.

The spectacular abundance of the species of Magicicada in the years of mass emergence indicates that they are highly successful insects. Why, then, do they have so dilatory a development (related genera develop much faster), and why do they appear only once in 17 or 13 years in a given locality? Alexander and Moore (1962) and Lloyd and Dybas (1966) suggest that this may be a singular adaptation to escape parasites and predators. No parasite is known with a life cycle of this length, and the predators (chiefly birds) are rapidly satiated for a week or two in the years of mass emergence. The relatively very small numbers of stragglers, cicadas that emerge a year after the mass eruption, are quickly destroyed by predators. This explains why the three sympatric species always emerge together; getting out of step would be selectively disadvantageous. It is less easy to understand the origin of the brood of each species emerging in different years, and the appearance of the 17- and the 13-year cycles.

## Ethological Isolation

Ethological isolation is a widespread and probably the most effective kind of reproductive isolation between species of animals, particularly arthropods and higher vertebrates. For the maintenance of a species with separate sexes it is indispensable that its females and males encounter each other and perform the acts that lead to the union of their sex cells. This is achieved in different organisms by a great variety of means, many of them quite ingenious and some extravagantly bizarre. Ethological isolation is effected in correspondingly diverse and often curious ways.

Ethology, the study of animal behavior, has been one of the expanding areas of modern biology in recent years. Sexual behavior has attracted a great deal of attention. Every species uses its own courtship and mating techniques; in some animals these techniques become rituals of extraordinary complexity. Birds are, like human beings, predominantly visual animals, and their activities are easily observable. This is probably the reason why so much modern ethological research has been done on birds (one of the pioneering works was that of Lorenz 1941; for general accounts and references, see Thorpe 1963, Tinbergen 1965, 1966, and Marler and Hamilton 1966). Among birds, species-specific plumage, adornments, courtship displays, and pantomimes, as well as songs, play important roles in species recognition and the avoidance of interspecific matings. Analysis of some courtship rituals has shown them to be recognizable modifications of threat, attack, and appeasement behaviors in the same or related species. When the rituals of different species do not coincide, attempted courtship may result in a genuine attack.

The courtship behavior of bowerbirds (Ptilorhynchidae), about nineteen species of which live in Australia and New Guinea, is most remarkable (Marshall 1954). The males build "bowers," each species in its own way, which they decorate in various styles. For the adornment of the bowers some use brightly colored flowers or fruits, or construct approach avenues of bleached bones, stones, pieces of metal if they can get them, or meadows of moss. One species goes so far as to paint its bower with fruit pulp, for which purpose it uses a tool—a wad of dry grass or spongy bark. Females are enticed to enter the bower, where copulation takes place. Nests are built elsewhere, however, without particular adornments.

In frogs and toads, auditory stimuli play an important role in the congregation of females and males of the same species in their breeding places. During the breeding season, the calls of the males attract the females and also stimulate other males to come and to begin calling, so that "choruses" of conspecific individuals are formed. The response to the call is species specific. The role of auditory stimuli in the reproductive isolation of species has been studied particularly by W. F. Blair and his numerous disciples (see Blair 1958a and 1964 for references).

Table 10.1 gives examples of the characteristics of the calls in eleven species of hylid frogs occurring in Florida. The dominant frequency (in cycles per second) and the average duration (in seconds), as revealed by sound spectograms, are shown. Even in regard to only the three characteristics shown in Table 10.1, no two species have the same call. Actually the differences are more numerous—for example, the repetition rate for the trilling species varies from 9.7 notes per second for *Hyla phaeocrypta* to 50.0 for *H. ocularis*.

Direct experimental evidence that the different calls act as isolating mechanisms is not as ample as could be wished. Blair and Littlejohn (1960) exposed mature females of *Pseudacris streckeri* to recorded calls of males of their own species and of the related *P. ornata*, reproduced by a loudspeaker. The females were attracted by the conspecific calls more often than by the heterospecific ones. Littlejohn and Loftus-Hills (1968) made similar experiments on frogs of the *Hyla ewingi* complex. The specificity in the response of female tree crickets (*Oecanthus*) to the calling songs of their males has been demonstrated by a similar technique (Walker 1957).

Pheromones are chemical substances that serve as signals eliciting behavioral reactions in individuals of the same species. They are impor-

**TABLE 10.1**

Average values for dominant frequency and duration of call in eleven species of hylid frogs (After Blair 1958b)

| Species | Dominant frequency, cycles per second | Duration, seconds | Trilling |
|---|---|---|---|
| Hyla gratiosa | 435 | 0.16 | — |
| H. crucifer | 2467 | 0.14 | — |
| Pseudacris ornata | 2562 | 0.06 | — |
| Hyla cinerea | 3407 | 0.18 | — |
| H. squirella | 3457 | 0.24 | — |
| Acris gryllus | 3914 | 0.04 | — |
| Hyla versicolor | 2444 | 0.84 | + |
| Pseudacris nigrita | 3325 | 0.39 | + |
| Hyla phaeocrypta | 4500 | 1.99 | + |
| H. femoralis | 4800 | 2.35 | + |
| H. ocularis | 7125 | 0.16 | + |

tant in species recognition and hence in ethological isolation. Most of the relevant studies deal with insects and mammals, but sex phero- mones are widespread in the animal kingdom. The chemical nature of some of the pheromones is becoming known (Jacobson and Beroza 1963, Wilson and Bossert 1963, and Roelofs and Comeau 1969). They are mostly small molecules, with molecular weights in the range 80–300. They are not necessarily species specific, nor are they expected to be so—species that are allopatric, live in different habitats, or have dif- ferent breeding seasons may well use the same pheromone, or react in experiments to the pheromones of other species. Roelofs and Comeau found, however, that two sympatric sibling species of gelechiid moths are attracted, respectively, to *cis*-9-tetradecenyl acetate and to the *trans* isomer of this substance. Moore (1965a,b) tested olfactory dis- crimination in the deer mice *Peromyscus maniculatus* and *P. polio- notus*. The former species shows greater sexual discrimination than the latter, a difference that may be due to *P. polionotus* being geo- graphically "insular," whereas *P. maniculatus* shares its territory with other species.

Species of Drosophila have been widely used for observations and experiments on ethological isolation. Spieth (1968 and references therein) carried out several painstaking studies of the courtship and mating in some 200 species; Bastock and Manning (1955 and Manning 1959) described in detail the sexual behavior of *D. melanogaster* and *D. similans*, Brown (1964) of *D. pseudoobscura* and its relatives, and Koref-Santibañez (1964) of species related to *D. mesophragmatica*. The courtship patterns involve various permutations of the orientation of a male toward another individual: tapping the latter with his forelegs, circling the object of courtship, vibrating, flicking, waving, scissoring, or fluttering of one or both wings, licking the genitalia of the female, spreading her wings, curling the abdomen, mounting, and intromission, as well as rejection signals on the part of the courted female or another male of the same or different species.

Chemical, visual, tactile, and auditory (more precisely, vibrational) stimuli are involved, playing different roles in different species. Spieth and Hsu (1950) and Grossfield (1966) showed that, whereas some species mate equally efficiently with light and in the dark, others are unable to copulate without light, and still others are intermediate. Closely related species may be unlike in this respect; for example, *Drosophila pseudoobscura* is light independent, but *D. subobscura* fails to mate in the dark. Wallace and Dobzhansky (1947) found *D. subobscura* males to be responsible for this failure; the females of the same species confined in darkness with males of *D. pseudoobscura* are sometimes inseminated.

Some of the species endemic to the Hawaiian archipelago have evolved rituals quite novel for drosophilids, namely, "lek" behavior and defense of territory (Spieth 1968). Males of these species take up positions on a single frond of a fern or on the trunk of some tree, where they engage in sexual displays. Their females, who feed elsewhere, are attracted to come to be courted and inseminated, whereupon the females depart for oviposition. Each male defends a certain area against intrusion by other males, and occasionally by unreceptive females. Interestingly enough, males of some of the species that engage in defense of territory have evolved special modification of the structure of their organs, particularly the proboscis and front legs.

Three different techniques have been used in experiments on ethological isolation in Drosophila. In no-choice experiments, females of one species are confined with males of another, and after the lapse of a certain time the proportions of the females inseminated and left virgins are recorded. In double-choice experiments, two kinds of sexually receptive females and males are placed in an observation chamber, and the matings that take place are recorded by inspection. Finally, the two kinds of females are exposed to males of one of them, and the proportions of the inseminated and virgin females are recorded. This is called, rather misleadingly, the male-choice technique, although it is agreed by most investigators that it is really the female who accepts or rejects the advances of the males, who are well-nigh promiscuous. Bateman (1948) argued very cogently that "undiscriminating eagerness in males and discriminating passivity in females" should be induced by natural selection in all bisexual species, except where strict monogamy combined with a sex ratio of unity eliminates intrasexual selection. Indeed, an excess of male sex cells contrasts, in most organisms, with a relatively limited production of female ones. Female fertility is limited by egg production and by the capacity to feed and rear the young. Male fertility, on the other hand, is largely a question of the number of females an individual inseminates. The "eagerness" and "passivity" of males and females are, thus, consequences of the fact that females produce much fewer gametes than do males.

The three techniques outlined above generally give concordant results. When the species tested are not close relatives (as judged by their structural traits), only homogamic (between likes) and no heterogamic (between unlikes) matings take place. With closely related species or with races or strains of the same species, some heterogamic matings do occur, or the matings may be at random. As an illustration, the matings recorded in observation chambers with various combinations of species of the *obscura* group of the genus Drosophila are shown in Table 10.2. It can be seen that the homogamic matings outnumber the heterogamic ones in all combinations.

Malogolowkin, Solima, and Levene (1965) proposed an isolation coefficient to measure the degree of isolation. It is computed by subtracting the proportion of all matings that are heterogamic from the proportion of homogamic ones. This coefficient is plus one if the isolation is complete, zero if there is no isolation, and negative if the heterogamic matings outnumber the homogamic ones.

Several items of interest should be noted in Table 10.2. Although the isolation is quite pronounced in all combinations, some interspecific matings do occur. This does not necessarily mean that there is gene exchange between these populations in nature. Some of them are allopatric—the strains of *Drosophila bifasciata* and *D. imaii* are from Japan, *D. pseudoobscura, D. persimilis,* and *D. miranda* from North America, and *D. subobscura* from Europe. Most crosses produce no vi-

**TABLE 10.2**

Numbers of matings recorded and the coefficients of ethological isolation for different combinations of species of the Obscura Group of Drosophila. (After Dobzhansky, Ehrman, and Kastritsis 1968)

| Species A | Species B | A♀ × A♂ | B♀ × B♂ | A♀ × B♂ | B♀ × A♂ | Isolation |
|---|---|---|---|---|---|---|
| D. bifasciata | D. imaii | 229 | 375 | 13 | 9 | +0.94 ± 0.01 |
| | D. pseudoobscura | 112 | 198 | 1 | 17 | +0.89 ± 0.03 |
| | D. persimilis | 157 | 203 | 1 | 8 | +0.96 ± 0.01 |
| | D. miranda | 114 | 142 | 1 | 4 | +0.96 ± 0.02 |
| | D. subobscura | 166 | 156 | 10 | 11 | +0.88 ± 0.03 |
| D. imaii | D. pseudoobscura | 102 | 126 | 10 | 53 | +0.57 ± 0.05 |
| | D. persimilis | 136 | 112 | 0 | 6 | +0.96 ± 0.01 |
| | D. miranda | 90 | 94 | 2 | 4 | +0.94 ± 0.02 |
| | D. subobscura | 142 | 59 | 5 | 1 | +0.96 ± 0.02 |
| D. pseudoobscura | D. persimilis | 56 | 54 | 2 | 3 | +0.91 ± 0.04 |
| | D. miranda | 111 | 105 | 1 | 0 | +0.98 ± 0.01 |
| | D. subobscura | 80 | 52 | 3 | 2 | +0.92 ± 0.03 |
| D. persimilis | D. miranda | 89 | 97 | 0 | 0 | +1.00 |
| | D. subobscura | 73 | 43 | 1 | 0 | +0.98 ± 0.01 |
| D. miranda | D. subobscura | 49 | 43 | 4 | 1 | +0.90 ± 0.05 |

able hybrids. Moreover, the isolation in nature tends to be stronger than under laboratory conditions. Thus, although hybrids of *D. pseudoobscura* and *D. persimilis* are obtainable in the laboratory, not a single heterogamic mating was observed among 305 copulating pairs collected in nature in 1951 in a locality where both species were present (Dobzhansky 1951). The avoidance of heterogamic matings may be even less pronounced in combinations that produce no viable hybrids (e.g., *D. imaii* with *D. pseudoobscura*) than in those where such hybrids do appear (e.g., the crosses between *D. pseudoobscura, D. persimilis,* and *D. miranda,* Table 10.2). And, finally, the isolation is often greater in one direction than in the reciprocal; thus the females of *D. bifasciata* and *D. imaii* accept males of *D. pseudoobscura, D. persimilis,* and *D. miranda* less easily than the females of the last three species accept males of the first two.

Strains of the same species of different geographic origins may mate at random. For example, Anderson and Ehrman (1969) tested strains of *Drosophila pseudoobscura* derived from places as remote as British Columbia, California, Texas, and Sonora, Mexico. The isolation indices ranged from $+0.14 \pm 0.19$ to $-0.09 \pm 0.10$, none significantly different from zero. On the other hand, Baker (1947) in *D. arizonensis,* Patterson and Wheeler (1947) in *D. peninsularis,* Miller and Westphal (1967) in *D. athabasca,* Dobzhansky (1944) in *D. sturtevanti,* and Dobzhansky and Streisinger (1944) in *D. prosaltans* all found more or less pronounced preferences for homogamic matings among geographic races of the same species. Dobzhansky, Pavlovsky, and Ehrman (1969) tested 25 combinations of geographic strains of the Transitional race of *D. paulistorum;* they found isolation coefficients ranging from $+0.09 \pm 0.09$, which is not significantly different from zero, to a high value of $+0.84 \pm 0.05$. The existence of such intraspecific variations is important; genetic materials are present within species from which ethological barriers separating them can be built.

## Mechanical Isolation

The complex structure of the genitalia in many animals, especially insects, has attracted the attention of morphologists and systematists, because closely related species can often be accurately classified by their genitalia. The "lock-and-key" theory was propounded by Leon Dufour in pre-Darwinian days and later elaborated, especially by K. Jordan (1905). According to Dufour, the female and the male genitalia are so exactly fitted to each other that even slight deviations in the structure of either make copulation impossible. The genitalia of each species are "a lock that can be opened by one key only." Different species are isolated from each other by the noncorrespondence of their genitalia.

Experimental evidence on mechanical isolation is scanty. In laboratory cultures *Drosophila melanogaster* males may attempt copulation with *D. pseudoobscura* females, and their genitalia occasionally become locked together. Variations of body size within a species do not seem to hinder copulation. In Drosophila giant and dwarf mutants, and large- and small-bodied flies produced from well-fed and from starved larvae, cross easily and give offspring. The usefulness of genitalia for distinguishing species does not necessarily mean that they are important in mechanical isolation. The reason for their usefulness is that the complexity of genitalic structures is often so great that species differences are more likely to be manifested in these structures than in the relatively simple external ones.

## Pollination Barriers

Since the Cretaceous period, a prime factor in the evolution of the angiosperms, the flowering plants, has been mutualistic relationships with animals that effect the transfer of pollen and hence cross-fertilization. Differences in the flower structure in related species may hinder or prevent interspecific pollen transfer. This is an analogue of mechanical isolation through noncorrespondence of the genitalia among animals. In plants there is an additional variable—flowers of different species, because of their particular odors, structures, or colors, may attract different animals as pollinators. There is voluminous literature on pollination mechanisms and floral and pollination ecology; the outstanding recent studies of the genetic aspects of the situation are those of V. Grant (1963; see also V. Grant and K. A. Grant 1965, and K. A. Grant and V. Grant 1968) and of Ehrlich and Raven (1964).

Some plants have flowers of simple structure and are pollinated "promiscuously" by many different pollen carriers. Others have complex flowers and are specialized for pollination by one or several species of insects, birds, or bats. An excellent example is the species pair of columbines *Aquilegia formosa* and *A. pubescens* (Grant 1963). The former has nodding flowers with relatively short upward-directed spurs; it is pollinated by hummingbirds hovering below the flowers. *Aquilegia pubescens* has erect flowers with long spurs, pollinated by hawk moths inserting their probosces from above. Three species of Penstemon sympatric in California are crossable in experiments, but rarely cross in nature because one of them is pollinated by Xylocopa bees, another by hummingbirds, and a third by wasps (Straw 1956). *Salvia apiana* and *S. mellifera* are incompletely isolated by a difference in flowering seasons, and in addition by attracting pollinating bees of different body size (K. A. Grant and V. Grant 1964).

Probably the extreme of specialization of pollination mechanisms is reached in some orchids. Certain species of orchids attract males of definite species of wasps, apparently by copying the sex-attractant odors and, to some extent, the shapes of the females of the latter. The wasps then engage in "pseudocopulation" with the flower, and in the process effect the transfer of pollen (Ames 1937, Kullenberg 1951, Dodson 1967, and references therein).

The phenomenon of flower constancy has been observed in pollinators as diverse as bees, hawk moths, and hummingbirds. An individual pollinator may visit preferentially, one after another, flowers of a certain species, or even of the same color variety if more than one variety is available. Other individuals "work" preferentially on flowers of different colors or different species (Bateman 1951). This factor may not make the reproductive isolation complete, but it will at least diminish the frequency of contamination (Levin and Kerster 1967a, b, 1968). The advantage conferred by flower-constant behavior has been described as follows: "A flower-feeding animal, once it has learned how to work a given flower mechanism, can thereafter obtain more food in less time by continuing to visit other flowers of the same type" (Grant 1963).

## Gametic Isolation

Copulation in animals with internal fertilization, the release of eggs and spermatozoa in forms with external fertilization, or pollen deposition on the stigma of a flower in plants is followed by a chain of reactions that bring about the actual union of the gametes, the fertilization proper. These reactions may be out of harmony in different species, resulting in a hindrance or prevention of the formation of hybrid zygotes.

It has been known since the classical work of Lillie (1921) that, if eggs of the two species of sea urchins, *Strongylocentrotus purpuratus* and *S. franciscanus,* are exposed to mixtures of sperm of both species, homogamic fertilizations greatly outnumber heterogamic ones. The same is true of fishes, in species that discharge their sexual products in water, as well as in forms with internal fertilization (e.g., Zander 1962).

The environment that spermatozoa encounter in the reproductive tracts of females of foreign species may be unfavorable. Patterson and his colleagues have done much work on such phenomena in species of Drosophila (Patterson and Stone 1952, and references therein). For example, cross-insemination between the related species *Drosophila virilis, D. americana, D. montana,* and *D. lacicola* is followed by a rather rapid loss of the mobility of the sperm in the sperm receptacles of foreign species, whereas in conspecific inseminations the mobility is conserved for a long time. A similar situation is found by Koref-Santibañez in *D. pavani* and *D. gaucha* (1964). In some species there is a so-called insemination reaction. A rapid secretion of a fluid into the cavity of the vagina takes place after copulation, causing a swelling of the organ. This swelling persists for some hours after intraspecific copulations, whereupon the vagina returns to its normal condition. Insemination by a male of a foreign species, however, gives a more violent reaction. The vagina remains swollen for days, and sometimes the secretion solidifies and obstructs the passage of eggs, making the female sterile. This does not occur in all Drosophila species: some species and species groups show no insemination reaction either after normal or after interspecific copulations.

Nor does a loss of viability of foreign sperm occur in all species. However, the number of offspring that result from one interspecific copulation between *D. pseudoobscura* and *D. persimilis* is, on the average, less than from one intraspecific mating, although the viability of the sperm in foreign sperm receptacles appears to be unaffected. Interspecific copulation results in the delivery of fewer spermatozoa than intraspecific insemination (Dobzhansky 1947). Also, in crosses of *D. pseudoobscura* with *D. imaii* foreign sperm may be inactivated

and expelled from the vagina (Dobzhansky, Ehrman, and Kastritsis 1968).

Species and geographic races of mosquitoes of the *Culex pipiens*
group exhibit some remarkable crossing relationships (Laven 1967
and references therein). Crosses may be successful in both directions
(i.e., strains A♀ × B♂ and B♀ × A♂), in one direction only, or in neither
direction. Thus, female mosquitoes from Hamburg produce hybrids
when crossed to males from Oggelshausen (Germany), but the cross
Oggelshausen ♀ × Hamburg ♂ gives no progeny. Laven showed that
what is involved here is an incompatibility of the Oggelshausen egg
cytoplasm with spermatozoa of the Hamburg race. The female hybrids
from the compatible cross were outcrossed for fifty generations to
Oggelshausen males, thus obtaining a strain with Hamburg cytoplasm
and Oggelshausen chromosomal genes. The crossing behavior of this
gene substitution strain remained, nevertheless, that of the Hamburg race.

Most impressive studies on reproductive isolation between sibling
species of ciliate Protozoa have been made by Sonneborn and his
school (Sonneborn 1957 and references therein). As many as sixteen
sibling species (which Sonneborn calls "varieties") are lumped under
the name *Paramecium aurelia*. Each species has at least two "mating
types," which function as different sexes, since conjugation occurs
between the mating types and does not ordinarily happen within a
mating type. Strains of these infusoria can be propagated asexually
by cell fission; the resulting clones may be tested for their ability to
form sexual unions. Different strains of the same species can be crossed,
and the progenies of the exconjugants sometimes exhibit heterosis
(Siegel 1958). By contrast, strains belonging to different species do
not, as a rule, conjugate. Some do form pairs, however, which adhere
to each other briefly and then fall apart without conjugation. Only a
small minority of the species combinations tested can undergo a conjugation process, which rarely if ever results in fit progeny. Death
may occur even in the $F_1$ generation, which then exhibits hybrid
inviability. Other species crosses give a viable $F_1$, but the $F_2$ generation and the backcrosses are completely or nearly completely inviable.
This may be regarded as a hybrid breakdown (see below). *Paramecium caudatum, P. bursaria, Tetrahymena pyriformis,* and *Euplotes
patella* are other names applied to groups of sibling species that
exhibit reproductive isolation more or less similar to that in *P. aurelia*.

In flowering plants a complex sequence of processes intervenes between the deposition of pollen on the stigma and the formation of a zygote. The pollen must germinate, the pollen tube grow down the style, and the pollen nuclei fuse with the nuclei in the ovules to form the embryo and the endosperm nuclei. This sequence may be disrupted at any point in hybrid crosses.

Crosses of different species of Datura were studied by Blakeslee and his collaborators (review and references in Avery, Satina, and Rietsema 1959). The speed of pollen tube growth is frequently greater in the style of its own species than in that of a foreign species. Moreover, the pollen tubes may burst in the styles of a foreign species before they reach the ovary. Table 10.3 shows the results of 174 attempted crosses between races and species of Gilia (phlox family). Grant (1963) summarizes the results as follows:

The incompatability barrier in the cobwebby gilias is manifested at different stages of flowering and fruiting. A flower pollinated with foreign pollen may fail to set a capsule; the capsule may ripen but contain only or mainly shriveled seeds; a reduced number of plump seeds may develop; or numerous plump seeds may form in the capsule but fail to germinate. From the developmental standpoint, there is evidently not one incompatability barrier but several.

It can only be added that in some instances the incompatibility could be overcome in experiments by the application of certain chemical substances, such as growth hormones (Emsweller and Stuart 1948). The pollen abortion may be under a simple genetic control; for example, Cameron and Moav (1957) found in a species of Nicotiana a gene that causes abortion of pollen not carrying it in hybrids with another species.

**TABLE 10.3**

Average number of normal seeds per flower, percentage of the crosses that produced any offspring, and number of hybrid individuals per ten flowers pollinated in Gilia (After Grant 1963)

| Cross | Seeds per Flower | Percentage of Successful Crosses | Hybrids per Ten Flowers |
|---|---|---|---|
| Within a population | 17.8 | 100 | 22 |
| Between races | 15.2 | 73 | 12 |
| Between species of a section | 3.7 | 43 | 3 |
| Between species of different sections | 0.004 | 2 | 0.038 |

*The Inviability of Hybrids*

Fantastic tales of most disparate animals mating and bringing forth offspring found ready credence in ancient, medieval, and even more recent times. Perhaps the ultimate fable of this type was that the ostrich came from hybridization of a camel and a sparrow. A critical reaction against such absurdities led some biologists to postulate that only crosses within a species produce viable and fertile hybrids. The truth lies in between the two extremes—some closely related species do hybridize in nature to a certain extent, and additional hybrids can be obtained in experiments.

Cells in tissue cultures can be induced to coalesce, and hybrid cells have been obtained carrying chromosomes of mouse and rat, mouse and hamster, and even mouse and man (Ephrussi and Weiss 1965, Weiss and Ephrussi 1966, and Weiss and Green 1967). Of course, a union of cells or gametes of different species does not necessarily lead to adult hybrid progeny; the life of a hybrid zygote may be cut short at any stage. In animals with external fertilization, spermatozoa may enter eggs of representatives of different classes and phyla (echinoderms × mollusks, echinoderms × annelids), but the sperm nucleus or its chromosomes may be eliminated from the cleavage spindle. Eggs of species of fish can be inseminated by sperm of different species, genera, or even families. All sorts of disturbances may, however, occur in the zygotes, from chromosome elimination during cleavage, through arrest of gastrulation or of organ formation, to death of the embryos in advanced stages.

In some instances the weakness of the hybrid can be overcome in experiments. Laibach's (1925) hybrids between species of flax constitute a classical example. In the cross *Linum perenne* ♀ × *L. austriacum* ♂ hybrid seeds fail to germinate if left to their own devices. If the embryos are freed from the seed coat (the seed coat being a maternal tissue), however, germination takes place, and the seedlings give rise to luxuriant hybrid plants that are fertile and produce normal seeds in the $F_2$ generation. Still greater is the suppression of seed development in the cross *L. austriacum* ♀ × *L. perenne* ♂, and yet if the diminutive embryos are extracted from the seeds and placed in a nutrient solution they continue to grow. After some days they may be transferred to moist paper and allowed to grow. The seedlings are then planted in soil.

Moore's (1949a,b, 1950) studies on isolating mechanisms in North American species of frogs (Rana) are another classic. Table 10.4 summarizes some of the information Moore obtained. The distribution areas of all these species overlap, making them sympatric in parts of their ranges. Because of preferences for different habitats during the breeding season, the species are to some extent, but never completely, isolated ecologically. Some species, however, show complete seasonal isolation. After artificial insemination of the eggs, from 0 to 100 percent of the hybrid embryos develop normally to the adult stage. Moore's estimates of the efficacies of the isolating mechanisms taken separately are shown in Table 10.4. In conjunction, they seem to give complete or nearly complete isolation in all cases.

**TABLE 10.4**

Estimates of the potency of geographic isolation (G), ecological isolation (E), seasonal isolation (S), and hybrid inviability (D) in species of frogs (After Moore 1949)

Complete isolation = 100; Absence of isolation = 0

| Males / Females | Rana sylvatica | Rana pipiens | Rana palustris | Rana clamitans | Rana catesbeiana | Rana septentrionalis |
|---|---|---|---|---|---|---|
| Rana sylvatica | | G 29<br>E 70<br>S 60<br>D 100 | G 61<br>E 40<br>S 100<br>D 100 | G 59<br>E 30<br>S 100<br>D 100 | G 68<br>E 70<br>S 100<br>D 100 | G 80<br>E 60<br>S 100<br>D ? |
| Rana pipiens | G 59<br>E 70<br>S 60<br>D 100 | | G 74<br>E 70<br>S 40<br>D 0 | G 67<br>E 70<br>S 100<br>D 100 | G 62<br>E 85<br>S 100<br>D 100 | G 88<br>E 80<br>S 100<br>D 100 |
| Rana palustris | G 13<br>E 40<br>S 95<br>D 100 | G 0<br>E 70<br>S 40<br>D 0 | | G 3<br>E 60<br>S 95<br>D 100 | G 23<br>E 70<br>S 100<br>D 100 | G 72<br>E 50<br>S 100<br>D ? |
| Rana clamitans | G 28<br>E 30<br>S 100<br>D 100 | G 0<br>E 70<br>S 100<br>D 100 | G 24<br>E 60<br>S 95<br>D 100 | | G 18<br>E 30<br>S 50<br>D 100 | G 22<br>E 20<br>S 0<br>D 100 |
| Rana catesbeiana | G 51<br>E 70<br>S 100<br>D 100 | G 0<br>E 85<br>S 100<br>D 100 | G 47<br>E 70<br>S 100<br>D 100 | G 29<br>E 30<br>S 50<br>D 100 | | G 93<br>E 30<br>S 50<br>D ? |
| Rana septentrionalis | G 0<br>E 60<br>S 100<br>D ? | G 0<br>E 80<br>S 100<br>D 100 | G 37<br>E 50<br>S 100<br>D 100 | G 36<br>E 20<br>S 0<br>D 100 | G 79<br>E 30<br>S 50<br>D 95 | |

*Rana pipiens* is a complex of races or closely related species. Its distribution ranges from southern Canada to Mexico and Costa Rica. Northern races have lower minimum and maximum temperature limits for normal embryonic development than do southern races. Thus, strains from Canada and Vermont have tolerance limits of about 5–28°C, while those from Florida have a range from 11 to 35°C. It should be noted, however, that in Canada this species breeds in May or June, in northern New York in mid-April, and near New York City in early April. These differences in breeding dates provide a "northern environment" for the developing eggs. The breeding season in North Carolina is February-March, while in Georgia and Florida the frogs may breed in any month of the year. Northern frogs develop more rapidly than southern ones at low temperatures, but at high temperatures the difference is diminished or even inverted.

The viability of hybrids between the races of *Rana pipiens* appears to be correlated with their adaptedness to different climatic conditions. Thus, the eggs of the Vermont race give normal development when fertilized with Wisconsin sperm. Fertilization of Vermont eggs by the sperm of New Jersey or Oklahoma races results in normal or slightly retarded development rates and a slight enlargement of the head of the embryo. With Louisiana sperm, the retardation is slight and the head enlargement moderate. With Florida or Texas sperm, a marked retardation and a strong enlargement of the head are observed. With eggs of southern and sperm of northern races, the embryos have markedly reduced heads and retarded developments. In either case, the hybrids between geographically extreme members of the series are inviable. Situations similar to those found by Moore in frogs have also been described by Minamori (1957) in species and races of the fishes *Misgurnus anguillicaudatus* and *Cobitis taenia,* and much earlier by Goldschmidt (1934) in the gypsy moth (*Lymantria dispar*) in northern Eurasia.

Some species crosses produce hybrids of one sex only; either male or female zygotes die, while the viability of the other sex is affected little or not at all. Haldane's rule (1922) states, "When in the $F_1$ offspring of two different animal races one sex is absent, rare or sterile, that sex is the heterozygous sex." In mammals and most insects, males are heterogametic, and male hybrids are defective more frequently than females. In birds, butterflies, and moths, females are heterogametic, and female hybrids are less viable than males.

A possible mechanism underlying Haldane's rule is as follows (Dobzhansky 1937b). *Drosophila pseudoobscura* and *D. miranda* differ in their gene arrangements, and some genes that lie in one species in the X chromosome lie in the other in the autosomes, and vice versa. The cross *D. miranda* ♀ × *D. pseudoobscura* ♂ produces viable female and abnormal male hybrids; the reciprocal cross gives rise to viable females, but the males die off. Suppose that *D. pseudoobscura* has in its X chromosome a group of genes *A* that lie in the autosomes of *D. miranda*, and that a group of genes *B*, which in *D. miranda* lie in the X chromosome, are located in the autosomes of *D. pseudoobscura;* with respect to these genes, the constitution of the females of both species and also of the female hybrids is alike, *AABB*. Males of *D. pseudoobscura* and the male hybrids from the cross *D. miranda* ♀ × *D. pseudoobscura* ♂ are *ABB*; *D. miranda* males and the male offspring from the cross *D. pseudoobscura* ♀ × *D. miranda* ♂ are *AAB*. The genotypes of the pure species are so adjusted that the constitution *ABB* in *D. pseudoobscura* and *AAB* in *D. miranda* permit the development of "normal" males. The constitution *AABB* is normal for females of either parent and for hybrid females as well. The constitution *ABB* is incompatible with the genotype of *D. miranda*, and *AAB* with that of *D. pseudoobscura*. The hybrid males are poorly viable or lethal because of disruption of the gene balance.

## Varieties of Hybrid Sterility

The sterility of hybrids between species has interested people since Aristotle, who discussed at length the sterility of mules. As stated previously, some biologists have attempted to define species as arrays of individuals that fail to produce viable and fertile offspring when crossed. Such definitions are invalid, however, because gene exchange between species may be prevented by any one of the reproductive isolating mechanisms or by a combination of several of them. Viable and fertile hybrids may be obtained in experiments between undoubtedly distinct species that are completely isolated reproductively in nature.

Hybrid sterility is not a result of a general weakness of a hybrid organism, as some authors have surmised. Many hybrids with reduced viability are nevertheless fertile, and some sterile hybrids (e.g., mules) are somatically vigorous. The cause of the sterility typically resides in the reproductive organs, not in the body. Dobzhansky and Beadle (1936) transplanted larval testes of hybrids between *Drosophila pseudoobscura* and *D. persimilis* into larvae of the parental species, and vice versa. Male hybrids between these species have grossly abnormal spermatogenesis and are sterile. If a transplanted testis of a pure species becomes attached to the sexual ducts of a hybrid, the latter becomes fertile, the functional sperm coming, of course, from the implanted testis. Hybrid testes do not develop functional spermatozoa in the bodies of pure species, however, and the gonads of the host are not affected by the presence of a hybrid testis.

In 1913, Federley made the discovery that the chromosomes fail to pair at meiosis in the sterile hybrids between species of the moth Pygaera. The disruption of the chromosome pairing is followed by various abnormalities in the chromosome distribution during the meiotic divisions and by irregularities in spermiogenesis. No functional spermatozoa are formed, and the hybrid males are sterile. Failures of the chromosome pairing at meiosis have since been observed in numerous other sterile hybrids, animals as well as plants (reviews in White 1954 and Stebbins 1958a). A plausible inference is that the disruption of the chromosome pairing at meiosis is the cause of the sterility. As we shall see, this inference is indeed warranted for some, though not for all, forms of sterility.

Some hybrids are sterile despite normal meiosis. The primroses *Primula verticillata* and *P. floribunda* both have nine chromosomes in the haploid set. Their hybrid forms nine bivalents at meiosis, but is nevertheless sterile (Upcott 1939). As stated above, male hybrids between *Drosophila pseudoobscura* and *D. persimilis* are completely sterile, although the chromosome pairing at meiosis varies from completely normal to none at all (Dobzhansky 1934). Within each species, strains are encountered that produce hybrids in which no bivalents are formed at meiosis, and other strains that produce hybrids with bivalents only and no univalents. The meiotic divisions are, however, abnormal in either case: the first division spindle elongates enormously and bends into a ring, the cell body fails to divide, the second meiotic division is absent, and the giant binucleate spermatids degenerate.

In other hybrids, such as those between *Drosophila melanogaster* and *simulans*, the gonads are rudimentary, and, as shown by Kerkis (1933), spermatogenesis and oogenesis do not advance beyond spermatogonia and oogonia. In many sterile hybrids between species of mammals (horse × ass, horse × zebra, domestic cow × yak), as well as of birds and fishes, the degenerative changes in the gametogenesis set in before meiotic pairing should normally begin (see Stebbins 1958a for references). Among some 150 hybrids between species of the plant genus Geum, Gajewski (1957, 1959) found completely sterile, partially fertile, and nearly normally fertile examples. Hybrids between some species fail to flower; others have disturbances in the development of the floral parts, failures of the meiotic chromosome pairing, or, finally, normal chromosome pairing followed by breakdowns in gametophyte development.

Meiosis, like any other physiological process, is controlled by the genotype of the organism. The normal course of meiosis involves a succession of events so delicately balanced that the failure of any one of them, or simply altered timing, causes disruptive changes. Genetic disharmonies brought about by the hybridization of species or of varieties that do not normally cross in nature may alter the process of meiosis at any stage. Chromosome pairing may fail despite the presence of pairs of chromosomes with similar genes arranged in identical linear series. The resulting sterility will be due to the genetic constitution of the organism. This is *genic sterility*. On the other hand, chromosomes may fail to pair and to form bivalents because they have no structurally similar partners. Chromosomes may contain identical genes, but they may be differently arranged. Sterility due to such structural dissimilarities is *chromosomal sterility*.

Müntzing (1961 and earlier), Stebbins (1958a), and Grant (1963) distinguish haplontic and diplontic sterilities. The former occur in plants when the haplonts, that is, the pollen grains and the embryo sacs, "are killed by their own genetic constitution." In the latter, "the constitution of the plant conditions a reduced or inhibited capacity to form progeny through sexual reproduction" (Müntzing 1961). On the basis of these criteria, all hybrid sterility in animals must be diplontic, because animal sex cells, which are haploid, generally function even if they carry grossly abnormal chromosome complements (see the next section). It remains to be added that the chromosomal and genic or the haplontic and diplontic, sterilities are not mutually exclusive and occur together in some hybrids. Furthermore, any one of these mechanisms may cause any degree of sterility, from barely noticeable to complete.

## Chromosomal Sterility

Suppose that two chromosomes carry the genes *ABCD* and *EFGHI*. A translocation gives two "new" chromosomes, *ABFE* and *DCGHI*. Meiosis in homozygous normals and in translocation homozygotes produces sex cells that carry every gene once and only once. In a translocation heterozygote six classes of sex cells can be produced: (1) *ABFE, DCGHI*; (2) *ABCD, EFGHI*; (3) *ABFE, EFGHI*; (4) *ABCD, DCGHI*; (5) *ABFE, ABCD*; and (6) *DCGHI, EFGHI*. Classes 1 and 2 carry balanced gene complements, but in classes 3–6 certain genes are deficient and others are present in duplicate; 1 and 2 are termed regular or orthoploid, and 3–6 exceptional or heteroploid gametes.

The fate of heteroploid gametes is different in animals and in plants. In animals, sex cells with grossly unbalanced gene complements retain their functional ability. If a translocation heterozygote is crossed either to a homozygous normal or to a translocation homozygote, however, the part of the progeny coming from the heteroploid gametes will suffer from deficiencies of some genes and duplications of others and will be inviable or crippled. In Drosophila, females heterozygous for a translocation crossed to normal males, or normal females crossed to males heterozygous for a translocation, deposit numerous eggs many of which contain "dominant lethals" and fail to develop. That the heteroploid sex cells nevertheless function can be demonstrated by having the chromosomes involved in the translocation marked with appropriate mutant genes. Females and males heterozygous for the same translocation are then intercrossed. Some heteroploid gametes are complementary, in the sense that one of them is deficient for the genes which the other carries in duplicate, and vice versa (gametes 3 and 4, and 5 and 6, above). The union of complementary gametes gives viable zygotes, which can then be identified by the mutant markers they carry.

In plants, meiotic divisions give rise to gametophytes that undergo several cell divisions before the generative cells, the gametes proper, are produced. Gametophytes with deficiencies and duplications are usually aborted. Only small duplications and, even more rarely, deficiencies pass through the gametophytes in nonpolyploid species. Translocation heterozygotes in plants produce mixtures of good and aborted pollen grains and embryo sacs; they are "semisterile," but the seeds that they mature are viable.

The degree of sterility depends on the proportions of orthoploid and heteroploid gametes; if the six classes of gametes shown above are equally frequent, the translocation heterozygote will produce 66.7 percent inviable progeny (in animals) or aborted pollen (in plants). A heterozygote for two, three, or more translocations may then produce few viable progeny and will be effectively sterile. In reality the proportions of heteroploid gametes vary, depending on the relative sizes of the chromosome sections exchanged and on other factors. In structurally homozygous individuals every chromosome has one and only one homologue with an identical gene arrangement. In translocation heterozygotes, some chromosomes consist of sections that are homologous to parts of two or more chromosomes. In inversion heterozygotes, chromosomes have homologues with the same genes arranged in different linear sequences. Meiotic pairing is due to a mutual attraction between homologous genes rather than between chromosomes as such. In structural heterozygotes, parts of the same chromosome may be pulled in different directions simultaneously. Pairing of some chromosome sections may be delayed or not attained at all. The more extensive the differences in gene arrangement between the chromosomes of the parents, the greater is the competition for pairing at meiosis, and the more frequent are the failures of pairing and disjunction.

A special case of chromosomal sterility is that of cryptic structural hybridity (Stebbins 1950, 1958a, Stephens 1950, and Grant 1963). Translocation of small blocks of genes may give rise to chromosomes that are homologous except for some small segments (e.g., chromosomes $ABCDEF$ and $GHIJKLM$ giving rise to $ABCDLF$ and $GHIJKEM$). A hybrid with such chromosomes is, of course, a translocation heterozygote. And yet, because of the competition for pairing, this hybrid will have apparently normal bivalents at meiosis ($ABCDEF/ABCDLF$ and $GHIJKLM/GHIJKEM$). Fifty percent of the gametes of such a hybrid will contain duplications and deficiencies. Accumulation of cryptic structural differences in several, or in all, chromosomes of a set may perhaps give virtually complete sterility, despite regular chromosome pairing at meiosis in the hybrid. The sterility of the primrose hybrids mentioned previously may well be of this kind.

Allopolyploidy as a mode of species formation will be discussed in Chapter 11. Here we are interested in one aspect of the story, since the best available evidence that the sterility of some species hybrids is, in fact, chromosomal comes from studies on allopolyploid plants. The pioneering work of Karpechenko (1928) may still be used as a paradigm, although similar results have since been obtained with many plant species. Radish (*Raphanus sativus*), cabbage (*Brassica oleracea*), and their $F_1$ hybrids have the same number of chromosomes, namely 18. In the parental species, 9 bivalents are formed regularly at meiosis; pollen and ovules contain 9 chromosomes. Little or no meiotic pairing takes place in the $F_1$ hybrids; the 18 univalents are distributed at random to the daughter cells at the first meiotic division, these cells come to contain varying numbers of chromosomes, mostly 6–12, no viable pollen and ovules are formed, and the hybrids are sterile. In some cells, however, the first meiotic division is abortive, viable pollen and ovules with 18 chromosomes are produced, and their union gives rise to $F_2$ plants with 36 chromosomes. These tetraploid plants, called radocabbage or Raphanobrassica, are quite vigorous, combine in their appearance the traits of both radish and cabbage, and, what is most interesting, are fully fertile.

The lack of chromosome pairing at meiosis in the diploid hybrid may be caused either by differences in the gene arrangements in the chromosomes of raddish and cabbage, or by disharmonies in the hybrid genetic constitution. The first possibility is upheld and the second refuted by the normal chromosome pairing and bivalent formation in the tetraploid Raphanobrassica. In this tetraploid hybrid every chromosome has one and only one partner with a similar gene arrangement. The sterility of the diploid hybrid is chromosomal, and fertility is restored in the tetraploid.

Genic sterility is not relieved by chromosome doubling. A genetic constitution that causes disruption of the meiotic pairing in a diploid has the same effect in a tetraploid hybrid. This is demonstrated by observations on tetraploid spermatocytes occasionally found in the testes of the sterile hybrids between *Drosophila pseudoobscura* and *D. persimilis* (see the next section). The meiotic chromosome pairing is no different in the tetraploid from that in the diploid spermatocytes; the meiotic divisions are equally abnormal, and the hybrids with tetraploid cells in their testes are completely sterile.

Comparative studies of chromosome behavior in fairly numerous diploid plant hybrids, and in the tetraploids obtained from them, led Darlington (1937) to formulate the following rule, applicable to hybrids whose sterility is chromosomal: Sterile diploid hybrids with little or no chromosome pairing at meiosis give allopolyploids that are fertile and display mostly or only bivalents at meiotic division. Conversely, the allopolyploids derived from diploids with many bivalents show an irregular chromosome pairing. The fertility of allopolyploids tends to be inversely proportional to that of their diploid ancestors. Chromosome pairing in a diploid hybrid shows that the gene arrangement in the chromosomes of the parents is similar enough for some or all chromosomes of one species to find approximate homologues among those of the other. The doubling of the chromosome complement gives to each chromosome three potential mates more or less similar to it. In the competition for pairing, the pairing of the chromosomes of the same species is disrupted by the presence of the partial homologues. As a result, bivalents, trivalents, quadrivalents, and univalents are formed in varying proportions; gametes with unbalanced chromosome complements are produced; and the hybrid is more or less sterile. When the chromosomes of the parental species fail to pair in the diploid because of extensive dissimilarities in the gene arrangement, however, every chromosome in the allotetradiploid has only one mate, with which it can pair with little or no interference from the chromosomes of the other species. Hence, only bivalents are produced, meiosis is regular, and fertility is restored.

## Genic Sterility in the Hybrids of Drosophila pseudoobscura × D. persimilis

*Drosophila pseudoobscura* and *D. persimilis* are sibling species. The cross *D. persimilis* ♀ × *D. pseudoobscura* ♂ gives $F_1$ hybrid males with small testes; the reciprocal cross, *D. pseudoobscura* ♀ × *D. persimilis* ♂, produces hybrid males with testes of normal size; in either case the males are completely sterile (Lancefield 1929). Backcrosses of the $F_1$ hybrid females to *D. persimilis* or *D. pseudoobscura* males give sons with testes of variable size, ranging from normal to very small. Males with small testes are always sterile; those with large ones are sometimes fertile. The sterility is due to a profound modification of the process of spermatogenesis. The meiotic chromosome pairing is variable; no univalents, some univalents, or only univalents may be present at the first meiotic division. Irrespective of the numbers of bivalents and univalents formed, only a single, very abnormal meiotic division takes place. The spermatids degenerate (Dobzhansky 1934). The disturbances in spermatogenesis are, in general, greater the smaller are the testes in a hybrid. Testis size is, therefore, a measure of the degree of departure from the normal course of the spermatogenesis. The disturbances in the hybrids are confined to the gonads; the rest of the reproductive system (the sexual ducts and external genitalia) is normal.

The hypothesis that the sterility of hybrids between *D. pseudoobscura* and *D. persimilis* is genic was tested and verified (Dobzhansky 1936). Backcrosses were made of the $F_1$ hybrid females to males of both parental species. In the progenies of such backcrosses individuals appear that carry all possible combinations of the chromosomes of the parents (Figs. 10.1 and 10.2). Experiments were so arranged that, by having the parental chromosomes marked by mutant genes with easily visible external effects, the combination of the chromosomes present in a given male was recognizable by his phenotype.

The mean sizes of the testes in the backcross males with different chromosomes are shown in Figs. 10.1 and 10.2. Backcross males with an X chromosome and the autosomes of the same species have testes as large as the males of the parental species. Such males are usually fertile, whereas the males with small testes are all sterile. The more dissimilar the X chromosome and the autosomes become in species origin, the smaller is the testis size. The smallest testes are observed in males with the X chromosome of one species and all autosomes of the other. With a single exception, all chromosomes act alike, and their action is additive. Thus, individuals carrying the *D. pseudoobscura* X chromosome and *D. persimilis* autosomes have very small testes (class 16, Fig. 10.1). The introduction of one fourth or one third or one second chromosome of *D. pseudoobscura* increases the testis size (classes 13–15, Fig. 10.1). Simultaneous introduction of the fourth and third (class 12), or the second and third (class 10), or the second and fourth (class 11), or the second, third, and fourth (class 9) chromosomes of *D. pseudoobscura* increases the testis size more than does each of these chromosomes alone. Males having all chromosomes of the same species or having one third or one fourth chromosome of the other species are sometimes fertile (classes 1, 2,

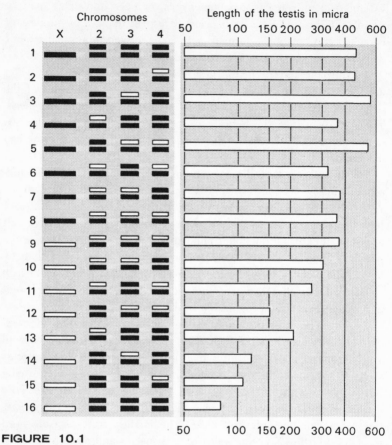

**FIGURE 10.1**

Testis size in backcross hybrids of Drosophila pseudoobscura and D. persimilis. The chromosomes of the former species are represented white and of the latter species black.

and 3). If both the third and the fourth chromosomes disagree in origin with the rest of the complement, the male is sterile. The exception mentioned above is that, in backcrosses to *D. persimilis* males, sons having the *D. pseudoobscura* third chromosome and the *D. persimilis* X chromosome have larger testes than their brothers homozygous for the *D. persimilis* third chromosome.

We can conclude that all the tested chromosomes of *D. pseudoobscura* and *D. persimilis* carry genes concerned with the fertility of

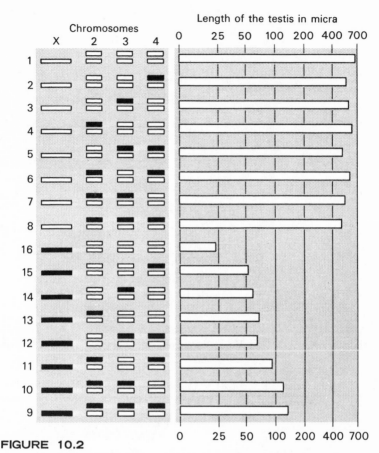

**FIGURE 10.2**

Testis size in backcross hybrids of Drosophila pseudoobscura and D. persimilis. The chromosomes of the former species are represented white and of the latter species black.

males of the same species and the sterility of hybrid males. Moreover, the X, the second, the third, and the fourth chromosomes have at least two such genes apiece. The minimum number of genes concerned with the sterility is, therefore, eight, but the actual number is almost certainly greater. The sterility of hybrids between animal species is most often genic, whereas chromosomal sterility seems prevalent in the plant kingdom, at least among flowering plants. However, Stebbins (1958a) lists several botanical examples of interspecific hybrids, the sterility of which may plausibly be ascribed to their genetic constitution.

### Genic Sterility in the Hybrids
### Drosophila virilis × D. americana

The sterility in the hybrids between the Oriental species *Drosophila virilis* and its American analogues *D. americana* and *D. texana* has been analyzed by Patterson and his colleagues (review in Patterson and Stone 1952). Crosses between *D. virilis* and *D. americana* or *D. texana* produce hybrids of both sexes; the fertility of these hybrids varies, depending on the strains of the parental species used, but on the whole it is lower than that of pure species. Hybrids in the $F_2$ and in the backcrosses are likewise semisterile. If *D. virilis* females are crossed to *D. texana* males, and the male hybrids are backcrossed to *D. virilis* females, only about 25 percent of the male progeny are fertile; if the initial cross is made using *D. texana* females, however, some 82 percent of the backcross males are fertile. The two series of crosses may be represented schematically as follows ($X^v$ and $X^t$, and $Y^v$ and $Y^t$, being X and Y chromosomes of *D. virilis* and *D. texana*, respectively):

$$\text{P: } \textit{virilis } (X^vX^v)♀ \times \textit{texana } (X^tY^t)♂$$
$$\text{Backcross: } \textit{virilis } (X^vX^v)♀ \times X^vY^t♂$$
$$X^vY^t \text{ males } (25\% \text{ fertile})$$
$$\text{P: } \textit{texana } (X^tX^t)♀ \times \textit{virilis } X^vY^v♂$$
$$\text{Backcross: } \textit{virilis } (X^vX^v)♀ \times (X^tY^v)♂$$
$$X^vY^v \text{ males } (82.5\% \text{ fertile})$$

The backcross males in both series are similar in that they carry the *Drosophila virilis* X chromosome, but in the series represented first they have the *D. texana* Y, and in the second series the *D. virilis* Y chromosome. Since the chromosomes of *D. virilis* and *D. texana* are distinguishable cytologically because of inversions and translocations, it has been possible to identify the constitution of the fertile backcross males by examining the chromosomes in their offspring. The fertile males with the *D. texana* Y chromosome invariably also possess the second and the fifth chromosomes of the same species. The Y, second, and fifth chromosomes of *D. texana* carry complementary genes that must be simultaneously present to enable a male to be fertile. Whether a single gene or several genes in each of these chromosomes are concerned is not known.

## Sterility and Nucleo-Cytoplasmic Imbalance

A hybrid inherits its chromosomes from both parents, but its cytoplasm chiefly or entirely from its mother. Although the genetic information is transmitted mainly through the nuclei and their chromosomes, some of it is also carried in the cytoplasm. The genome and the plasmon of a hybrid can be distinguished. The sterility of some hybrids, especially among plants, is due to genome-plasmon incompatibilities.

Michaelis (1954 and references therein) made most painstaking studies on hybrids between species of Epilobium. The cross *E. luteum* ♀ × *E. hirsutum* ♂ (i.e., flowers of the former species pollinated by the latter) gives healthy hybrid plants, with normal flowers and 15–20 percent good pollen. The reciprocal cross (*E. hirsutum* ♀ × *E. luteum* ♂) yields dwarfish plants, with underdeveloped flowers and no good pollen. The hybrids (*E. luteum* ♀ × *E. hirsutum* ♂) were pollinated by *E. hirsutum* pollen in several successive generations. In this way, plants were obtained that have acquired the *E. hirsutum* genes but have retained the *E. luteum* plasmon. Do such plants behave in crosses to *E. luteum* as the pure *E. hirsutum* did? The answer is no—the hybrids produced develop normally and have some 20 percent good pollen. The plasmon of *E. luteum* has retained its properties despite having carried an *E. hirsutum* genome for several generations.

Much work has been done by Japanese investigators (Kihara 1959, 1967, and references therein) on cytoplasmic male sterility in crosses between some species of wheat, Triticum, and of the related genus Aegilops. For example, hybrids between the bread wheat, *T. vulgare,* and *Ae. caudata* produce no good pollen but their ovules function normally. By a series of backcrosses to *T. vulgare* it is possible to obtain "substitution lines" having Triticum nuclei in Aegilops cytoplasm; they are female fertile but male sterile. Some strains of wheat, however, carry "fertility restorer genes," which make plants with Aegilops cytoplasm and Triticum genomes male fertile. These fertility restorers are specific for the cytoplasms of each species of Aegilops that induces sterility. Grun and Aubertin (1965) described cytoplasmic male sterilities in crosses between species of Solanum that closely resemble those in wheats.

The properties of an egg cell cytoplasm may be determined by its own self-replicating constituents, or by the chromosomes that were present in the egg before meiosis and fertilization. The former mechanism is cytoplasmic inheritance in the strict sense; the latter is known as maternal effect or predetermination of the cytoplasm by the maternal chromosomes. The elegant studies of Ehrman (1960, 1962) brought to light remarkably diverse sterility mechanisms in *Drosophila paulistorum*. This superspecies consists of at least five semispecies (see above and Chapter 11) which yield, when crossed, fertile $F_1$ females and sterile males with grossly abnormal spermatogenesis. The $F_1$ females, backcrossed to males of either parental semispecies, give progenies consisting again of fertile females and males all of which are sterile.

The absence of any fertile males in the backcross progenies seemed puzzling, since some of them should carry the genes of only one semispecies. (*Drosophila paulistorum* has three pairs of chromosomes, which in the hybrids between the semispecies tend to be inherited as units, on account of heterozygosis for inverted sections. Therefore, one might expect about one-eighth of the males resulting from the first backcross to have all their chromosomes like their fathers, and consequently to be fertile.) Making use of mutant gene markers, Ehrman showed that all males coming from the eggs deposited by a hybrid female are sterile, regardless of their own chromosomal constitution. In the particular crosses that she studied, any one of the three semispecies-foreign chromosomes present in a female makes all her male progeny sterile. However, in the backcrosses some females appear that no longer carry "foreign" chromosomes; when crossed to males of the same semispecies, they produce sons all of which are fertile. The chromosomal constitution of a mother, then, influences her sons but not necessarily her grandsons.

The hybrid sterility in *D. paulistorum* is, thus, of two kinds: that of the $F_1$ hybrid males, due to their own genetic constitution, and that of the backcross males, induced by the genetic constitution of their mothers. Williamson and Ehrman (1967 and Ehrman and Williamson 1969) found a third kind of sterility, possibly related to the second. Certain strains, which we may denote as A and B, give sterile $F_1$ males when crossed. These sterile males were ground and centrifuged, and the supernatant injected into A females, which were then crossed to A males. The progeny is evidently genetically identical with the A strain and is not hybrid at all; nevertheless the males coming from the eggs deposited by these females a week or longer after the injection are sterile. Neither A nor B males injected with the same supernatant nor their pure-bred male progenies, however, are sterile. The "infectious sterility" is induced in the eggs of the injected mothers, when these eggs develop into male individuals.

These results suggest that one or both of the strains crossed carry some symbiotic microorganisms, to which these strains are genetically adjusted, and the presence of which does not interfere with fertility. Hybridization has a disruptive effect on this adjustment, and the sterility is a consequence. Kernaghan and Ehrman (1970) have described what appears to be Mycoplasma-like symbionts in the testes of sterile males.

## Hybrid Breakdown

Consider species that are sympatric, between which matings or cross-pollinations occasionally occur and result in viable and fertile hybrids. Nevertheless, no gene exchange may take place between the populations of these species if the recombination products of their genotypes are discriminated against by natural selection. Moreover, as will be argued in the next chapter, the loss of fitness resulting from hybridization of genetically diverging populations may well be a challenge to which these populations could respond by developing reproductive isolation.

The often cited sibling species *Drosophila pseudoobscura* and *D. persimilis* are crossable in laboratory experiments, although no hybrids have been found in nature. The $F_1$ hybrids appear to be as vigorous as the parental species; the hybrid males are sterile, but the females produce numerous eggs when backcrossed to males of either parent. The viability of the backcross progenies, however, is dramatically reduced, as the following data clearly show (Dobzhansky 1936 and Weisbrot 1963).

*Drosophila pseudoobscura* females homozygous for the sex-linked genes beaded (*bd*), yellow (*y*), short (*s*), Bare (*Ba*, second chromosome), and purple (*pr*, third chromosome) were crossed to *D. persimilis* males homozygous for the recessive orange (*or*, third chromosome) and heterozygous for the dominant Curly (*Cy*, fourth chromosome). The $F_1$ generation was as follows:

$$\left.\begin{array}{ll} Ba\ ♀♀ & 432 \\ Ba\ Cy\ ♀♀\ 413 \end{array}\right\}\ 845 \qquad\qquad \left.\begin{array}{ll} bd\ y\ s\ Ba\ ♂♂ & 401 \\ bd\ y\ s\ Ba\ Cy\ ♂♂\ 385 \end{array}\right\}\ 786$$

Males are somewhat less numerous than females, the discrepancy being due to a decrease of viability caused by the mutants *bd*, *y*, and *s*. The *Ba Cy* hybrid females were backcrossed to *D. pseudoobscura* males homozygous for purple (*pr*) and orange (*or*). The females have, then, every chromosome, except the small fifth, marked with at least one mutant gene. In the backcross progeny the genetic constitution of every male may be ascertained from its appearance. If the crossing over in the X and in the third chromosomes is disregarded, sixteen classes of males are expected to appear in equal numbers, carrying the combinations of the chromosomes of the parental species represented diagrammatically in Figs. 10.1 and 10.2. Only eight classes of females are distinguishable (since the sex-linked recessive genes do not manifest themselves in the heterozygous females).

The results actually obtained are summarized in Table 10.5; the column headed "Class Number" refers to the Figs. 10.1 and 10.2. Table 10.5 shows that males are fewer than females, and that representatives of the different classes are far from equally numerous. The yield of adult backcross individuals per mother is very small; a majority of the backcross individuals evidently die. A feature at first sight paradoxical is that class 1 of the males, which consists of individuals having only *Drosophila pseudoobscura* chromosomes, is almost obliterated. If the decrease in viability were due only to mixing the chromosomes of the two species, class 1 would be expected to be the most viable category. A closer examination of Table 10.5 shows that the number of individuals of a given class recovered in this backcross is inversely proportional to the number of mutant genes this class carries. All the classes carrying *bd*, *y*, and *s* have few survivors. The gene *Ba* also depresses viability greatly, *pr* follows next, while *or* and *Cy* are relatively innocuous. The same mutant genes produce no drastic effects on the viability of pure species and of $F_1$ hybrids. The results indicate that the eggs deposited by $F_1$ hybrid females give individuals

**TABLE  10.5**

(See explanation in text.)

| Class Number | Males Phenotype | Males Observed | Females Phenotype | Females Observed |
|---|---|---|---|---|
| 1 | bd y s Ba pr | 2 | Ba pr | 41 |
| 2 | bd y s Ba pr Cy | . . . | Ba pr Cy | 32 |
| 3 | bd y s Ba or | 4 | Ba or | 92 |
| 4 | bd y s pr | 7 | pr | 190 |
| 5 | bd y s Ba or Cy | 1 | Ba or Cy | 89 |
| 6 | bd y s pr Cy | 7 | pr Cy | 372 |
| 7 | bd y s or | 14 | or | 140 |
| 8 | bd y s or Cy | 13 | or Cy | 336 |
| 9 | or Cy | 147 | | |
| 10 | or | 143 | | |
| 11 | pr Cy | 62 | | |
| 12 | Ba or Cy | 17 | | |
| 13 | pr | 58 | | |
| 14 | Ba or | 21 | | |
| 15 | Ba pr Cy | 14 | | |
| 16 | Ba pr | 6 | | |
| | Crossovers 121 | | Crossovers 311 | |
| | Total       637 | | Total         1603 | |

afflicted with a general constitutional weakness. Mutant genes that do not impair greatly the viability of pure species or of $F_1$ hybrids are semilethal in individuals developing from the eggs deposited by hybrid females.

To test this hypothesis further, experiments were so arranged that the class of backcross progeny identical in constitution with *D. pseudoobscura* (corresponding to class 1 in Table 10.5) was free from mutant genes, and the class having hybrid autosomes (corresponding to class 9 in Table 10.5) carried several mutants. The result was the opposite of that observed in the first experiment: class 9 was depressed in frequency, whereas individuals in class 1 survived.

Some diagrammatically clear cases of hybrid breakdown have also been described in species of cottons (Stephens 1949, 1950, and references therein). *Gossypium hirsutum, G. barbadense,* and *G. tomentosum* intercross easily and give fertile and vigorous $F_1$ hybrids. Only in the $F_2$ generation do types of low viability make their appearance. For example, among 110 $F_2$ seeds from the cross *G. hirsutum* var. *punctatum* × *G. tomentosum,* there were found:

 7 seeds with small embryos that failed to germinate.

36 seeds with apparently normal embryos that failed to germinate.

 9 seedlings that failed to expand their cotyledons.

22 seedlings that died within 3 weeks.

16 unthrifty seedlings at 3 weeks old.

20 strong seedlings at 3 weeks old.

Among many further examples that could be cited are the hybrids between *Zauschneria cana* and *Z. septentrionalis, Layia gaillardioides* and *L. hieracioides* (Clausen 1951), and *Lycopersicon esculentum* and *L. chilense* (Rick 1963a). The hybrids of Zauschneria and of Layia species are vigorous, perhaps even heterotic, show normal meiotic chromosome pairing, and are quite fertile. Yet among 2100 Zauschneria $F_2$ hybrids planted, only 250 survived, and even these were attacked by mildew and rust. Among the $F_2$ hybrids between Layia species many died early, and the survivors grew less rapidly than the parental species. This slow development is unadaptive in the environments of the parental species. In Clausen's words:

In *Layia*, lack of resistance against the drought of the California summer is compensated for by speedy development which enables the species to bloom early during the moist spring. The interchange of genes in the hybrid of *gaillardiodes* and *hieracioides* resulted in the development of lateness, a new character for *Layia* but an undesirable one for survival in the California climate, because lateness was not accompanied by development of protection against drought, as it is in other genera of the *Madiinae*.

# CHAPTER ELEVEN

# PATTERNS OF SPECIES FORMATION

*Historical and Philosophical Antecedents*

Man's reactions to the endless diversity and changeability of what he perceives are ambivalent. On the one hand, the diversity is esthetically enthralling. On the other, it overtaxes his memory and impedes setting his experience in order. The oldest and universal means for bridling the runaway multiformity of nature is human language. A word, a name, applies not to a single object but to an array of individually distinct entities. A need is felt, however, to reconcile the variegated experience with the semantic simplification. Parmenides (around 500 B.C.) made the earliest known and the most radical proposal—all variety and change are mere illusions, the true existence is one and immutable. Plato, a century later, erected a more sophisticated theory of immutable essences or archetypes (*Éidos*). As mentioned in Chapter 1 and elsewhere, what is real according to Plato are the eternal and changeless ideal Man, Horse, Pine, and Drosophila; the men, horses, pines and drosophilae that we actually see are only pale shadows of their perfect and ineffably beautiful *Éidos*.

Aristotle (fourth century B.C.) thought that the essences are not stored somewhere in heaven beyond human reach. They are embodied and expressed in the things we see and in the individuals we meet. It should be obvious, however, that to grasp the essence is a greater achievement than to behold its evanescent expression. Platonic and Aristotelian doctrines of archetypes or essences have strongly influenced medieval as well as some modern philosophies. Typological thinking has become habitual, not only among biologists and other scientists, but among the general public as well. Learned treatises are written about the one essential, unitary, and uniform Human Nature, which men always and everywhere are supposed to possess (a specimen of this genre is Jonas 1966). Opinions about this Nature are expressed casually in everyday conversation. Now, if there is an archetype for

Man, is every biological species also the embodiment of its own *Eidos*? The problem of species became embroiled in the philosophical dispute between the so-called realists and the nominalists; the former affirmed and the latter denied the reality of universal essences of Man, Horse, Dog, and other species. To a nominalist only individuals are real. A name applied to a group of individuals does not imply the existence of any supraindividual entity so designated.

In the eighteenth century, Linnaeus classified all living things (and minerals as well) into species, which he grouped into genera, orders, and classes. Linnaeus was an Aristotelian realist, and he maintained that biological species are real entities, whose essences were created by God. "There are," he stated, "as many species as produced in the beginning by the Infinite Being." Linnaeus was just as firmly convinced that genera are also primordial entities: "Every genus is natural, directly created at the beginning. Hence, it cannot be subdivided or combined gratuitously, or according to some theory." In contrast, he put no store in varieties: "A botanist need not bother about varieties. . . . There are as many varieties as are different plans grown from the seeds of the same species." This implies that the archetypes are more real than individual "varieties," which are, after all, only more or less successful imitations of the archetypes. According to this view, a biologist tries to descry the essence of a species or a genus through the murky exterior of individual variation. Probably no biologist will at present subscribe to these statements, and yet typology is implicit in the thinking of many practitioners of our science.

Darwin's goal was to demonstrate that "species are only strongly marked and permanent varieties, and that each species first existed as a variety." It is not surprising that at times he seemed to take a nominalist stance, seemingly denying the reality of species. Thus, in the concluding pages of "Origin of Species" we read: "In short, we shall have to treat species in the same manner as those naturalists treat genera, who admit that genera are merely artificial combinations made for convenience." Yet, on the very next page, Darwin states, "Our classifications will come to be, as far as they can be so made, genealogies; and will then truly give what may be called the plan of creation." Now, genealogies cannot be "made for convenience"; Darwin evidently does not argue that biological classifications are arbitrary; they reflect the objectively ascertainable clusters of organic forms, which Darwin ascribes to a community of descent. Classification by descent cannot be invented by biologists; it can only be discovered.

Taxonomic categories are arbitrary in a quite different sense. The number of supraspecific categories now used is fairly large: subgenus, genus, section, tribe, subfamily, family, superfamily, etc. The recognition that the units comprising a given complex of living forms are related by propinquity of descent is not arbitrary. The evaluation of a complex as a subgenus, genus, tribe, or family is a matter of convenience. Most of the Linnaean genera of insects are now treated as families. A classifier can exercise his choice, within the bounds of convenience and consistency. For example, a decade ago the genus Drosophila had some 750 described species in 8 subgenera (Wheeler 1959). One could just as well make these full genera and raise the species groups within them to the status of subgenera.

As another example, some paleoanthropologists have seen fit to give specific and generic names to every scrap of bone of fossil hominids discovered. The only telling argument against this practice is, however, that littering the scientific nomenclature with useless names breeds confusion. Many authors now assume only two hominid genera: Australopithecus with two species, *Australopithecus africanus* and *A. robustus*, and Homo also with two species, *Homo erectus* and *H. sapiens* (e.g., Campbell 1966). Yet Robinson (1967) puts the species *africanus* in the genus Homo, and *robustus* in the genus Paranthropus. What kind of evidence will decide which genera are the valid ones? Perhaps finding more fossils will indicate which classification is more convenient.

## Emergence of the Biological Species Concept

A taxon is defined by Mayr (1969) as "a taxonomic group of any rank that is sufficiently distinct to be worthy of being assigned to a definite category." We have seen that Linnaeus regarded his taxa, species as well as genera, as primordially created entities. Darwin preferred to view species and genera as "artificial combinations made for convenience." At present, species are considered biologically more meaningful entities than genera. A species is, of course, a taxon, like a genus or a family; but, more importantly, a species is a supraindividual biological system. In the latter sense, a species is more than a group concept. A species is composed of individuals as an individual is composed of cells, or as a termite or an ant colony is composed of fertile and sterile members. A biological species is an inclusive Mendelian population; it is integrated by the bonds of sexual reproduction and parentage. By contrast, the species of a genus or the genera of a family or the components of other taxa have no such bonds, although they are related by common descent, usually many generations back.

The biological species concept is a product of modern understanding of the genetic structure of Mendelian populations. Nevertheless, it was foreshadowed before Darwin and even before Linnaeus. Thus John Ray wrote in 1686:

After a long and considerable investigation, no surer criterion for determining species has occurred to me than the distinguishing features that perpetuate themselves in propagation from seed. Thus, no matter what variations occur in the individual or the species, if they spring from the seed of one and the same plant, they are accidental variations and not such as to distinguish a species . . . (quoted in Mayr 1963).

Cuvier in 1815 defined a species as "the reunion of individuals descended from one another, or from common parents, or from such as resemble them as strongly as they resemble each other." Similar ideas were expressed by several other early authors who were not evolutionists (see Mayr 1957, 1969, Greene 1961, and Zavadsky 1968 for references). Recognition that a species is not only a taxon but also a reproductive community is not incompatible with a belief that it is a manifestation of its unchanging *Éidos*.

Perhaps the most compelling evidence that species evolve from races or "varieties" was obtained in studies on the variation of species in space. Although Linnaeus had in his collections some animals and plants from remote countries, most of his materials came from his native Sweden. He worked mainly on sympatric rather than allopatric forms of life. Now, sympatric species of sexually reproducing organisms are discrete breeding communities, and usually these are also discrete in their outward characteristics. A student of the fauna or the flora of a single reasonably small territory generally encounters few difficulties in delimiting species.

With allopatric forms, however, problems arise. The eighteenth and nineteenth centuries saw rapid progress in the geographic exploration of the world. Biological museums received materials from diverse countries, and zoologists and botanists had to describe and to classify them. The problem of how to distinguish divergent races from closely related species sometimes defied solution, since races that inhabit remote territories may be about as distinct as sympatric species. Imagine an extraterrestrial zoologist who has seen two specimens each of Swedes, Bushmen, and Eskimos. He might well conclude that they represent three different species of primates. We know that this is not so, because we are familiar with numerous geographically and structurally intermediate populations, all of which exchange genes freely with at least their geographic neighbors. In any case, the typological and nonevolutionary species concept of the pioneer taxonomists floundered when it had to face the phenomenon of geographic races. The discomfiture of the taxonomists proved, however, a boon to the biologists.

Lamarck, who had ample experience in classifying plants and animals, saw that new evidence called for a new explanation. By the time of Darwin the evidence had grown to be overwhelming. The new paradigm was an ancestral species transforming into a derived one, or splitting into two or more derived ones. Darwin, although he was quite familiar with the phenomenon of geographic races, did not differentiate them from nongeographic "varieties" and polymorphisms. It remained for Wagner (1889), K. Jordan (1905), D. S. Jordan (1905), Semenov-Tian-Shansky (1910), Rensch (1929, 1960a), and Mayr (1942, 1963) to develop the theory of allopatric species formation and of polytypic species. Geographic isolation of allopatric races or subspecies is a usual, or even necessary, antecedent of species formation. The views of the early authors (up to Rensch 1929, but not Rensch 1960a!) were tinged with Lamarckism: allopatric populations become genetically different because they are changed by the different environments in the countries they inhabit. It is only fair to note that, while genetics was only groping for its fundamental concepts, the view that organisms are changed by their environments represented no more than a restatement in ambiguous terms of the observed facts.

We saw in Chapter 9 that most animal and plant species are complexes of local populations which differ from each other genetically to some extent (see Mayr 1963 and Grant 1963 for a more thorough treatment of this topic). Only some relictual species confined to very small territories are likely to be single panmictic populations. The difference between the populations may be sufficiently large to make most individuals recognizable as belonging to a certain population or to a group of populations. A taxonomist may then give them racial or subspecific names. Species that comprise two or more subspecies are polytypic; mankind is a prime example of a polytypic species. No race or subspecies of a polytypic species represents the essence or the archetype of that species (although the subspecies named first is technically known as the typical or the nominate subspecies).

The realization that many or most species are polytypic led to a better understanding of the biological nature of species, as well as to considerable simplification of taxonomy. At the beginning of the current century, some taxonomists succumbed to the temptation of assigning species names to every local race distinct enough for most specimens of it to receive determination labels. This occurred mainly in well studied groups, such as mammals, birds, and some genera of insects, in which most species had already been described, prompting specialists to overestimate intraspecific differences. The pandemonium of specific and generic splitting in paleoanthropology has been mentioned. A salutary reaction set in with the introduction of the polytypic species concept (see Mayr 1942, 1963, and 1969 for particulars). For example, the check list of birds had in 1910 some 19,000 species; although some additional ones have been described since, the number of recognized species has been reduced to about 8600.

Races of sexual and normally outbreeding organisms remain genetically distinct because they are usually allopatric; geographic isolation keeps the gene exchange infrequent enough to prevent swamping of the interpopulational differences. The example of human races attests to what happens when races become sympatric—they tend to merge into a single, variable population. In contrast to races, species are able to maintain their genetic integrity despite sympatric coexistence. For a long time biologists groped for an explanation of this fact.

Reference was made in Chapter 10 to the widespread but erroneous belief that viable and fertile hybrids result only from intraspecific, not from interspecific, crosses. Also, some entomologists assumed that differences in the genitalia mark species but not races. There are so many exceptions to these rules that they cannot be used as definitions of species. Lotsy (1931) regarded the "synagameon," which he defined as "a habitually interbreeding community of individuals," as the fundamental unit. This view has the merit of directing attention to Mendelian populations as biological realities, but the definition does not differentiate between local populations or demes and species.

Dobzhansky (1937a) pointed out that the process of species formation, in contrast to race formation, involves the development of reproductive isolating mechanisms. An ancestral species is transformed into two or more derived species when an array of interbreeding Mendelian populations becomes segregated into two or more reproductively isolated arrays. Species are, accordingly, systems of populations; the gene exchange between these systems is limited or prevented in nature by a reproductive isolating mechanism or perhaps by a combination of several such mechanisms. In short, a species is the most inclusive Mendelian population. Mayr (1969) has rephrased the definition thus: "Species are groups of interbreeding natural populations that are reproductively isolated from other such groups." Grant's (1963) definition is as follows: "The sum total of the races that interbreed frequently or occasionally with one another, and that intergrade more or less continuously in their phenotypic characters, is the species."

## *Some Difficulties of the Biological Species Concept*

The biological species concept expressed in these variant definitions is accepted by many biologists and criticized by others. The perennial controversy about species continues. Consideration of some of the objections is in order here.

First of all, it is sheer miscomprehension to allege that our species criterion is "intersterility." This term is an ambiguous locution, which may mean hybrid inviability, hybrid sterility, or both. Reproductive isolation subsumes these as well as the other isolating mechanisms discussed in Chapter 10. What is more, lack of "intersterility" in captivity or in an experimental garden does not rule out the possibility that reproductive isolation may be present in nature.

Another objection raised is that to talk about reproductive isolation is meaningless in asexual, parthenogenetic, or obligatorily self-pollinating forms, and yet systematists name species everywhere. Of course, the criterion of reproductive isolation is applicable only where there are Mendelian populations. Rejection of the species criterion on this ground, however, overlooks the duality of the species concept.

Species is not only a category of classification but also a form of supra-individual biological integration. In the former sense, any taxon may be called a species if it is convenient to use this designation. Species then become as arbitrary as subgenera, genera, and other categories. The virtue of the biological species concept is precisely that it makes the species a category that betokens a biologically highly significant fact. Having achieved reproductive isolation, a Mendelian population henceforth becomes a biological system evolving independently from other such systems.

Some logicians (e.g., Gregg 1954) see no difference between biological taxonomy and the classification of inanimate objects. This is a refusal to take evolution seriously; organisms resemble each other because they are descendants of common ancestors. This statement is not applicable to books or automobiles, except as a loose metaphor. When applied to species of sexually reproducing forms of life, extreme nominalism becomes ludicrous. The species mankind is not an invention of a taxonomist but a biological (as well as sociological and existential) reality. The development in recent years of phenetic, numerical, or computer taxonomies has led to lively disputes, some of which are tangential to the species problem (Sokal and Sneath 1963, Sokal 1965, Sokal and Camin 1965, Mayr 1965a,b, 1969, and others). In brief, phenetic taxonomists classify organisms according to their overall similarities rather than their descent (phylogeny). Modern computers permit what otherwise would be prohibitively laborious calculations of the degree of similarity of taxa with respect to as many of their characteristics as possible. The resulting "phenograms" look like classical phylogenetic trees, but show statistical estimates of the numbers of similarities and differences in the selected characters between any two taxa chosen for study. Critics have pointed out that treating randomly selected characters as equivalent is liable to result in misestimating the genetic similarities of the organisms classified. As Mayr (1969) caustically remarks, "Some users of electronic data processing have suggested that thinking and theory become unnecessary if we merely entrust our fate to the computer." Moreover, sibling species (see the next section) are not perceived by numerical taxonomies, whereas some race differences may loom unduly large.

It is not true that species defined as reproductively isolated Mendelian populations are operationally unusable because working taxonomists can only rarely obtain the pertinent information. Examination of the morphology and the geographic origin of an adequate sample of specimens of a given kind of animals or plants yields indirect but usually reliable evidence concerning the genetic limits of species populations. Classical taxonomists have grasped the existence of biological species intuitively, but correctly in a majority of cases. Moreover, the kinds of animals and plants that some preliterate peoples recognize as distinct, and on which they bestow names, quite often correspond to what zoologists and botanists recognize as species (trees in Amazonian forests, according to Pires, Dobzhansky, and Black 1953, and vertebrates in New Guinea, according to Diamond 1966). To be sure, other primitive peoples are less perspicacious taxonomists (Berlin, Breedlove, and Raven 1966).

The definition of species as reproductively isolated groups of populations is not intended to provide an infallible yardstick, which would always indicate whether two samples of specimens represent one or more species or only races. Rather, the value of this definition lies in its substitution of analytical judgments for less communicable intuitions. The incipient species, the species in *statu nascendi*, will always involve a residue of borderline cases for which the decision will be arbitrary (see below). This difficulty comes from the species being not fixed but evolving. The nonexistence of borderline cases could mean only that evolution has run its course and is no longer happening.

The approaches to recognition of sympatric species are different from those used with allopatric ones, as discussed in detail by Mayr (1942, 1963), Stebbins (1950), and Grant (1963). Two or more Mendelian populations can be sympatric, and can coexist indefinitely in the same territory, only if they are reproductively isolated, at least to the extent that the gene exchange between them is kept under control by natural selection. The genetic gaps between sympatric species are, as a rule, absolute. Since genetic differences are usually reflected in the morphology, greater or lesser morphological hiatus is usually found between species. "If a taxonomist receives a series of specimens from a particular locality, he is almost never in doubt as to whether they belong to one or to several species."

By contrast, "the gaps between allopatric species are often gradual and relative, as they should be, on the basis of the principle of geographic speciation" (Mayr). Allopatric populations do not directly exchange genes, simply because they are allopatric. Whether such populations are also isolated reproductively, so that they could maintain their genetic differences if they were to become sympatric, is sometimes a moot point. The problem can often be resolved by observing that the populations in question are united by a continuous chain of intermediate populations in the geographically intervening localities. The presence of such a chain of intermediate populations is prima facie evidence that gene exchange is possible between the populations by diffusion through the intervening space. This is clearly the case with races of the human species.

Is the criterion of reproductive isolation applicable to forms that were not contemporaneous? Obviously, nobody can make hybridization experiments of *Australopithecus africanus* with *Homo erectus*, and of *H. erectus* with *H. sapiens*. Simpson (1943, 1961) has rightly called this "only a pseudoproblem." His admirably lucid analysis can best be stated in his own words: "A taxonomic species is an inference as to the most probable limits of the morphological species from which a given series of specimens has been drawn." A morphological species, which in turn is an inference as to the most probable limits of the biological (genetic) species, is "a group of individuals that resemble each other in most of their visible characters, sex for sex and variety for variety, and such that adjacent local populations within the group differ only in variable characters that intergrade marginally." Species succeeding each other in time "should be so defined as to make the morphological difference between them at least as great as sequential differences among contemporaneous species of the same group or closely allied groups."

It is not true that the interbreeding versus reproductive isolation criteria are never applicable to fossil forms. We are reasonably certain that the Neanderthal man was a race of *Homo sapiens,* and not a separate species. One reason for this belief is that *H. sapiens neanderthalensis* varied in space as well as in time, and some variants were intermediate between the "classic" Neanderthal and *H. sapiens sapiens.* Also the population that left its remains on Mount Carmel in Palestine is like populations regularly formed in modern species where the territory of one subspecies abuts on that of another. It is rather misleading to call such populations hybrids between subspecies (see Mayr 1963 for a discussion of primary and secondary intergradation).

## Gene Differences between Species

De Vries, the founder of the mutation theory, believed that a simple mutation gives rise to a new species (see Chapter 2). Goldschmidt claimed a special category, systemic mutations, which generate not only species but genera and families as well; Lamprecht maintained that there exist special genes differentiating species, and others responsible for intraspecific variation (see Chapter 3). These views have few or no adherents at present. The only known kind of mutation that may at once bring a new species into being is a doubling of the chromosomal complement in a hybrid of two pre-existing species (allopolyploidy; see below). Otherwise genetic differences between species are compounded gradually of many genic and chromosomal alterations, each change having arisen ultimately by mutation.

Just how many gene and chromosome changes differentiate species is difficult to determine. The classical Mendelian method of observing segregation in progenies of crosses has its applicability severely limited by the inviability or sterility of most interspecific hybrids. Where $F_2$ hybrids between species can be obtained, the variability may be so great that any two individuals are visibly different. For example, Baur (1930) studied the hybrids between species of snapdragons *Antirrhinum majus* and *A. molle*. The $F_1$ hybrids are, on the whole, intermediate between the parents and no more variable than the latter. In the $F_2$, however, the variability is spectacular. Most individuals show various recombinations of the parental traits, but few or none can be mistaken for pure *A. majus* or pure *A. molle*. Some individuals possess characteristics present in neither parent, but found in other species of Antirrhinum or other genera of the family Scrophulariaceae. One such segregant was described as a "new species"—*A. rhinanthoides*, because it had certain attributes of the genus Rhinanthus. Baur estimated the number of gene differences between *A. majus* and *A. molle* as more than one hundred. Results similar in principle were obtained by Honing in species of Canna, Wickler in carnations (Dianthus), East in tobacco (Nicotiana), and Clausen in violets (Viola).

The early literature has been reviewed by Renner (1929). Among the more recent works on the genetic analysis of segregations in $F_2$ of sterile interspecific hybrids in plants, those of Gajewski (1957) on

Geum, Grant (1946) on Gilia, Harland (1936) on cottons (Gossypium), Stubbe (1940) and Mather and Vines (1951) on Antirrihinum, and Rick and Smith (1953) and Tal (1967) on Lycopersicum and Solanum, must be mentioned. The species differences are more or less highly polygenic.

By and large, morphologically distinct species give fertile hybrids less often in animals than in plants. Perhaps this is the reason why animal species proved rather more refractory to genetic analysis. Morgan (1919) wrote, "The slightest familiarity with wild species will suffice to convince any one that they differ from each other generally, not by a single Mendelian difference, but by a number of small differences." Nevertheless, Drosophila geneticists liked to assume that "in general, related species have essentially the same complements of genes" (Sturtevant 1948). The evidence against this assumption accumulated only gradually. *Drosophila melanogaster* is outwardly very close to *D. simulans.* Nevertheless, their hybrids are sterile, and one or the other sex, depending on the direction of the cross, is inviable (Sturtevant 1920–21). Using a sophisticated genetic technique, Pontecorvo (1943) estimated that no fewer than nine genes must be responsible for this inviability. Similarly, *D. pseudoobscura* and *D. persimilis* are morphologically almost indistinguishable, and yet the $F_1$ hybrid males are sterile and the backcross progenies suffer hybrid breakdown (see Chapter 10). It is evident that the outward similarity of these species pairs is underpinned by rather different systems of genes. This is what Harland (1936) meant by his dictum, "The modifiers really constitute the species."

Irwin and his colleagues have made notable studies of the genetic differences between species of pigeons and doves (Columbidae) in regard to the cellular antigens of their blood corpuscles (Irwin 1953, Irwin and Cumley 1943, Stimpfling and Irwin 1960, and references therein). Some of the species can be crossed and produce fertile hybrids. Comparison of the parental species and their $F_1$ hybrids shows that a certain proportion of the antigens are shared by both parents, whereas others occur in one species only. The $F_1$ hybrids usually have all the antigens present in both parents, and rarely new hybrid antigens, the latter being interaction products of the parental ones (Irwin 1966). By backcrossing the hybrids to the parental species, it is possible to isolate and identify the antigens that differentiate the species. It is not possible to determine by this technique how many antigenic substances are shared by the different species, since the genes determining these substances do not segregate in the hybrid offspring. However, fairly large numbers of differences are detected. Thus, nine antigenic characters distinguish the pearneck and ring doves (*Streptopelia chinensis* and *S. risoria*). Only rarely have any of these antigens been found in the other 23 species studied.

The genetic study of species differences entered a new phase when the technique of protein discrimination by electrophoretic mobilities became available (see Chapter 7). This overcomes, at least to some extent, the most serious limitation of the methodology of Mendelian genetics—the taxa compared need not be crossable and capable of giving fertile hybrids. With this technique, Duke and Glassman (1968) compared the enzyme xanthine dehydrogenase in 29 species belonging to 9 species group of the genus Drosophila. The electrophoretic mobilities of the enzyme are distinguishably different in most species; if the mobility in *D. melanogaster* is taken as 100, the enzyme mobilities in other species vary from 57 to 102. What is most remarkable is that the species considered to be related on morphological grounds had enzyme mobilities more similar than the less closely related ones.

The usefulness of protein discrimination studies by means of the relatively simple technique of electrophoresis can be pushed even further. If certain assumptions stated in Chapter 7 are granted, the proportions of the genes represented by similar and by different alleles in the forms examined can be estimated. Hubby and Throckmorton (1965) used this technique to compare 10 species of the *virilis* group of Drosophila. This is a compact array of related species in which, on the basis of cytological evidence (Stone, Guest, and Wilson 1960), two "phylads" of, respectively, 4 and 6 still more closely related species can be distinguished. A summary of the results is shown in Table 11.1. On the average, some 36 proteins have been examined per species. From 2.6 to 28 percent of these were "unique," that is, found in only a single species. The average proportion of such unique proteins in the species studied was about 14 percent. Between 17 and 38 percent of the proteins in a species are shared with the other species of the same phylad, but not with those of the other phylad. And, finally, 43–76 percent are "ancestral" proteins, which are present in species of both phylads.

In a more recent paper, Hubby and Throckmorton (1968) analyzed 9 groups of 3 species each, that is, 27 species, of Drosophila. In each

**TABLE 11.1**

Numbers of proteins studied in ten species of the virilis group of Drosophila, and percentages of these proteins unique to a given species, restricted to the phylad, and common to the species group (After Hubby and Throckmorton 1965)

| Phylad and Species | Number Studied | Percentage Unique to Species | Percentage Common to Phylad | Percentage Common to Group |
|---|---|---|---|---|
| Virilis phylad | | | | |
| D. americana | 38 | 5.3 | 23.7 | 71.1 |
| D. texana | 42 | 21.4 | 16.7 | 61.9 |
| D. novamexicana | 38 | 7.9 | 21.1 | 71.1 |
| D. virilis | 38 | 2.6 | 21.1 | 76.3 |
| Average for phylad | 39.0 | 9.3 | 20.7 | 70.1 |
| Montana phylad | | | | |
| D. littoralis | 39 | 28.2 | 25.6 | 46.2 |
| D. ezoana | 35 | 8.6 | 29.7 | 65.7 |
| D. montana | 37 | 18.9 | 37.8 | 43.2 |
| D. lacicola | 29 | 20.7 | 20.7 | 58.6 |
| D. borealis | 42 | 19.0 | 28.6 | 52.4 |
| D. flavomontana | 29 | 10.3 | 37.9 | 51.7 |
| Average for phylad | 35.2 | 17.6 | 29.4 | 53.0 |
| Grand average | 36.6 | 14.3 | 25.9 | 59.8 |

triplet of species, two are morphologically scarcely distinguishable sibling species, and the third is clearly different but still a relative of the first two. The members of the different triplets are still more distinct; in fact, some of them belong to different subgenera of Drosophila. Remarkably enough, the pairs of sibling species have, on the average, only about 50 percent of their proteins in common, despite their external similarities being so great that a museum taxonomist would find it difficult to distinguish them at all. Moreover, the percentages of proteins shared in pairs of sibling species range from a high of 86 (*D. victoria* and *D. lebanonensis*) to a low of only 23 (*D. willistoni* and *D. paulistorum*). The members of a triplet (i.e., the two siblings and the related nonsibling) share, on the average, about 11.6 percent of the proteins. The authors "interpret these results to indicate that speciation does not *require* a change in a large number of loci."

I believe that their findings warrant the opposite conclusion. On the assumptions that a Drosophila has at least 10,000 gene pairs (Chapter 3), and that the genetic differences detected in the proteins are a fair sample of all gene differences (Chapter 7), the sibling species must differ in thousands of genes. Whether there are distinct reproductively isolated species differing in really small numbers of loci remains to be discovered; certainly the sibling species studied by Hubby and Throckmorton could have been regarded as candidates for such close genic similarity, and yet they proved to have many different genes.

### Species as Genetic Systems

There are two ways of looking at the genetic architecture of species differences. First, the genes in which species differ may act in development largely independently of one another. The species difference is then an aggregate or a conglomeration of gene differences. Second, the genes may also interact and cooperate in such ways that development is an emergent product of their actions. The genotypes of different species are, then, organized systems or patterns. In the first case, it is tempting to compare the genes with solo players, and in the second with members of a symphonic orchestra. The two possibilities are evidently not mutually exclusive. The first may be realized more often in lower organisms and the second in higher ones, or the first in plants and the second in animals. Finally, there may be all gradations between gene aggregations and gene systems. Some evidence of gene patterning has already been mentioned. Members of sibling species pairs, such as *Drosophila melanogaster* and *D. simulans,* or *D. pseudoobscura* and *D. persimilis,* seem to be much the same in their morphological and physiological phenotypes. Yet recombinations of their genes produces hybrid breakdown and developmental disharmonies. On the other hand, the hybrid swarms found where some plant species hybridize sometimes consist of individuals apparently as fit as the parental species. Of course, it is possible that the unfavorable combinations of parental genes have been eliminated.

Hollingshead showed as early as 1930 that some strains of *Crepis tectorum* carry a dominant gene that produces no visible effects in the pure species; if, however, a hybrid between *C. tectorum* and *C. capillaris* carries this gene, it does not develop beyond the cotyledon stage. Accordingly, the crosses in which the *C. tectorum* parent is homozygous for the gene in question produce no viable seedlings, whereas 50 percent, or 100 percent, of such seedlings occur in cultures in which the gene is heterozygous or absent. The same gene is lethal for seedlings of the hybrids *C. tectorum* × *C. leontodontoides* and *C. tectorum* × *C.*

*bursifolia,* but not in the crosses *C. tectorum* × *C. setosa* and *C. tectorum* × *C. taraxacifolia.* The isolation between *C. tectorum* and certain of its congeners would become complete if *C. tectorum* were homozygous for the gene that is lethal in the hybrids.

A remarkably parallel situation, but one that occurs in animal rather than plant species, has been extensively studied by Gordon (1948, 1951, and Gordon and Rosen 1951). Natural populations of the platyfish, *Xiphophorus maculatus,* are often polymorphic. The dominant gene *Sp* produces a spotted pattern consisting of macromelanophores; *N* gives a broad black band on the flanks of the fish; *Sr* forms a series of horizontal lines; *Sd* gives dark spots on the dorsal fin; *Sb* causes a darkening of the ventral parts. If, however, strains of *X. maculatus* carrying any of these genes are crossed to the swordtail, *X. helleri,* the effects of the genes in the hybrids are greatly hypertrophied. The gene *Sp* initiates the development of cutaneous melanomas; *N* gives melanotic tumors anywhere along the black band on the side of the body; *Sd* causes melanotic tumors on the dorsal fin; *Sb* gives melanomas along the midventral line. The effects of *Sr* are exaggerated in $F_1$ hybrids but no tumors appear; if, however, the $F_1$ is backcrossed to the swordtail, some individuals in the backcross progeny develop tumors along the flanks. It is evident that the swordtail carries genes which interact with certain apparently useful platyfish genes in such a manner as to make the latter semilethal in the hybrids.

When certain strains of the cotton *Gossypium barbadense* are crossed to some strains of *G. hirsutum,* the $F_1$ hybrids are weak, have shortened internodes, and have the stem, petiole, and leaf midribs covered with a layer of cork. Hybrids between other strains of the same species, however, are vigorous and free from the "Corky" syndrome. Stephens (1946) has shown that the strains producing Corky hybrids carry complementary alleles, or complementary genes, $ck^x$ (in *G. hirsutum*) and $ck^y$ (in *G. barbadense*). The Corky syndrome is due to the simultaneous presence in the genotype of a plant of these complementary genes. The geographic distribution of the $ck^x$ and $ck^y$ alleles is very interesting. The species areas of *G. barbadense* and *G. hirsutum* overlap in the West Indies and on the northern fringe of South America. The genes that give the Corky syndrome occur almost exclusively in strains of the two species in the zone of the overlap. The Corky hybrids are poorly viable and rarely give $F_2$ generations in nature. When an $F_2$ generation is obtained from non-Corky $F_1$ hybrids, the $F_2$ hybrids are

**TABLE 11.2**

Percentages of germinable seeds that developed into vigorous individuals, and of vigorous individuals that were fertile, in different generations of hybrids of Gilia malior and G. modocensis (After Grant 1966a)

| Generation | Seeds Giving Vigorous Individuals | Fertility Among Vigorous Individuals |
|---|---|---|
| $F_1$ | 100 | $\pm 0$ |
| $F_2$ | 18 | $\pm 0$ |
| $F_3$ | 24 | 45 |
| $F_4$ | 25 | 83 |
| $F_5$ | 22 | 66 |
| $F_6$ | 37 | 71 |
| $F_7$ | 80 | 96 |
| $F_8$ | 97 | 100 |
| $F_9$ | 100 | 100 |

deficient in vigor. Thus, the Corky condition eliminates the $F_1$ hybrids and prevents the production of a degenerate $F_2$. Gerstel (1954) found a "red lethal" gene, $Rl_a$, which is viable in G. *hirsutum* but lethal in hybrids with another species, G. *arboreum*.

Rick (1963a) found what he calls "differential zygote lethality" in hybrids of tomato species *Lycopersicon esculentum* and *L. chilense*. The hybrid of these species is fertile, so that $F_2$ and backcross progenies are obtained. In these progenies, a pronounced differential survival is observed, which favors the constellations of the genes of the parental species and discriminates against mixtures and recombinations.

Grant (1966a, b) combined natural and artificial selection for vigor and fertility in the hybrids between two normally self-pollinating species of desert plants, *Gilia malior* and G. *modocensis*. The artificially obtained $F_1$ hybrids were somatically vigorous but almost completely sterile. The progress of the selection is shown in Table 11-2. Although the selection was quite successful, it is evident that only a minority of the recombinations of the parental genes gave rise to reasonably harmonious genetic systems.

## Incipient Species and the Borderline between Race and Species

Species evolve from races by the accumulation of genetic changes. If the foregoing statement is true, and if the divergence due to accumulation of the gene differences is a gradual process, then instances must be found (and they are found) in which two or more races have diverged so much as to approach, but not to attain completely, the status of reproductively isolated species. The gradualness of the divergence could not be postulated a priori. Goldschmidt (1940) believed that species do not evolve from races but arise through sudden "systemic" mutations. Once the process of speciation is fully consummated, species can no longer be mistaken for races. Groups of Mendelian populations can be recognized as distinct species, or as subspecies of one species, usually without hesitation, provided that sufficient material for study is available. It is for this reason that the category of species has shown a remarkable stability from the time of Linnaeus to our day. The cat and the lion, the horse and the ass, the Norway rat and the black rat belong to different species. The Siamese and the alley cat, the Arabian charger and the draft horse, the maize of Iowa and that of Mexico are distinct races and not distinct species. The same is true of the human races. The claim that there is more than a single living species of Homo can be treated only as an eccentricity or the manifestation of race prejudice.

The reason why biologists spend more time discussing doubtful borderline cases than undoubted species and undoubted races is not that the former are very common. It is rather that borderline cases are interesting to evolutionists: the relative rarity of such instances indicates that, although the process of divergence is a gradual one, speciation in the strict sense, that is, the development of reproductive isolation, is a crisis that is passed relatively rapidly.

The borderline cases recorded in the literature have been so thoroughly examined by Mayr (1963, particularly Chapters 11-16) for animals, and by Grant (1963, Chapters 12-16) for plants, that an attempt to review them here would be supererogatory. Perhaps the most striking are the "rings of races." Sympatric populations that share the same territory without gene exchange or intergradation are distinct species. Yet in some cases they are found to be united by a chain of allopatric races that grade into each other and into the extreme members of the series. Although the terminal links of the chain behave as reproductively isolated species, a gene flow through the connecting links is at least potentially possible.

The salamander *Ensatina eschscholtzi* lives in the mountains encircling the central valley of California, but not in the valley itself.

Six subspecies replace each other along the ring. Although some of these differ quite strikingly in coloration and other traits, the transitions between the subspecies in the intermediate localities are quite gradual. The genes of one subspecies obviously diffuse into the neighboring ones. In the mountains of southern California, however, the most distinct subspecies (*eschscholtzi, croceator,* and *klauberi*) meet without intergradation. The populations behave in southern California as full-fledged species, and yet they are connected by the populations living to the north. They could exchange genes, though not directly but via a circuitous route through the northern subspecies (Stebbins 1949, 1957).

### Superspecies and Semispecies

Mayr (1963, 1969) and Amadon (1966) define a superspecies as "a monophyletic group of closely related and largely or entirely allopatric species" or as "a group of entirely or essentially allopatric taxa that were once races of a single species but which now have achieved species status." The components of a superspecies are semispecies or allospecies. Semispecies are "populations which have part way completed the process of speciation. Gene exchange is still possible among semispecies, but not as freely as among conspecific populations" (Mayr 1963). One of the examples of superspecies and semispecies given by Mayr consists of the paradise magpies (Astrapia) of New Guinea; the semispecies of these magnificently colored birds differ strikingly from one another, and yet hybridize where their distribution areas come in contact.

The superspecies *Drosophila paulistorum,* mentioned in Chapter 10, presents a situation different from Astrapia in interesting ways. Dobzhansky and Spassky (1959) first noticed that strains classified as *D. paulistorum* from different parts of South America belong to several groups, which are now considered incipient species or semispecies (Dobzhansky and Pavlovsky 1967 and Dobzhansky, Pavlovsky, and Ehrman 1969 for further references). Crosses between the semispecies occur with difficulty, because of more or less strong ethological isolation; even when the females have no "choice," being confined with males of a different semispecies, most of them remain virgins until they die of old age, although the males continue to court them diligently. The few females that are inseminated produce, however, vigorous hybrid progeny of fertile females and sterile males. As mentioned in Chapter 10, the sterility, at least in the backcrosses, is caused by peculiar predetermination of the cytoplasm by the maternal chromosome complement before meiosis (Ehrman 1960). The genetic basis of the ethological isolation is quite different and not so unusual (Ehrman 1961). Apparently numerous polygenes are involved; the sexual acceptability of an individual, whether female or male, is a function of what semispecies most of its genes came from, and after repeated backcrosses to a particular semispecies the hybrid progeny behaves like this semispecies.

All semispecies are chromosomally highly polymorphic; Kastritsis (1967, 1969b) found 89 different inversions among 115 strains studied. Some inversion polymorphisms are shared by more than a single semispecies, whereas others are restricted to only one. Some inversions are homozygous in, and hence diagnostic of, a given semispecies.

The geographic distribution of the semispecies is shown in Fig. 11.1. Each inhabits an area of its own, but in some places their areas overlap. When two or even three semispecies are sympatric (and they have been attracted to the same banana bait), they rarely if ever cross, and thus behave like full-fledged species. Probably the best evidence of this has been adduced by Malogolowkin, Solima, and Levene (1965) and by Ehrman (1965). The map in Fig. 11.1 shows that the Andean-Brazilian semispecies occupies the most extensive territory in which no other semispecies occurs. On the contrary, the Amazonian and Orinocan semispecies more often occur together, and also with the Andean-Brazilian. One may expect (and the expectation is experimentally verified) that the Andean-Brazilian females will be inseminated by Amazonian and Orinocan males more easily than will the Amazonian or Orinocan females by Andean-Brazilian males.

Ehrman recorded the coefficients of ethological isolation obtained when sympatric strains of two semispecies are placed together; she compared them with the isolation observed between strains of the same semispecies but of allopatric origin. The average isolation coefficient for sympatric strains turned out to be 0.85, and between allopatric strains of the same semispecies 0.67. This can mean only that the pressure of natural selection maintaining the isolation is greater where the populations are exposed to the risk of hybridization than where they are not.

**FIGURE 11.1**

Known geographic distribution of the semispecies that compose the superspecies Drosophila paulistorum.

In western Colombia and northern Venezuela "Transitional" populations are found (Fig. 11.1.). Different strains, even from the same locality, exhibit a variety of behaviors; some of them, but not all, cross easily and give fertile hybrids with Centro-American or with Andean-Brazilian strains. On the other hand, some Transitional strains show appreciable ethological isolation from each other, and some crosses produce sterile $F_1$ hybrid males. Both genetical (Dobzhansky, Pavlovsky, and Ehrman 1969) and cytological (Kastritsis 1969b) evidence militates against the supposition that the Transitional is a hybrid of other semispecies; it is more likely to be the survivor of the primitive or ancestral *Drosophila paulistorum*. Because of the fertility of the hybrid females, the possibility of some gene flow between the semispecies nevertheless cannot be ruled out entirely. Furthermore, the findings of Ehrman and Williamson referred to in Chapter 10 suggest that the sterility of the male hybrids may, in a sense, be extraneous to the genotypes of these flies and due, in part, to different symbiotic microorganisms. The same can be inferred from the spontaneous origin of sterility of hybrid males in strains that were formerly fertile (Dobzhansky and Pavlovsky 1967). *Drosophila paulistorum* is, then, an example of a group of species still in *statu nascendi*.

### Sibling Species

It is probably a general rule that species differ in numerous genes. Some of these gene differences manifest themselves outwardly in such traits as colors and patterns, proportions and sizes, of various body parts. Others change the physiological, ecological, and behavioral characters of their carriers. Some mutational changes may, perhaps, involve nucleotide substitutions the gene products of which have identical effects in development. What proportions of the gene differences belong to these various classes we do not know. What we do know is that in some groups of organisms (such as pheasants, birds of paradise, and some butterflies) apparently closely related species are spectacularly heterogeneous to our eyes. The judgment of close relationship rests here on the facility with which these species hybridize in experiments or in nature, or on the species having geographic distributions that suggest a subspecific or semispecific (see the preceding section) status. At the opposite extreme, there are species that differ only in some recondite details (such as minor differences in the genitalia among insect species) or that appear altogether identical. These are sibling species—reproductively isolated arrays of populations that show little or no morphological distinctions. Sibling species are not necessarily the same as semispecies or incipient species. Some siblings may have completed the process of speciation and become reproductively isolated without acquiring differences easily apprehended by outward appearance.

Only the recognition of sibling species resolved the longstanding puzzle of why malaria is endemic in some European and Mediterranean countries and yet absent in others where the proven vector, *Anopheles maculipennis,* is commonly found. The simple solution is that at least six sibling species were confused under the name *A. maculipennis*. Whereas some of them feed by preference, or at least occasionally, on man, others are "zoophilous," feeding on other animals. Careful investigation disclosed that, although the adult insects are very hard to distinguish as to species, there are fairly reliable diagnostic traits in the color patterns of the eggs and in the manner in which the eggs are put together in the "egg floats." In addition, the various species differ in ecological preferences—fresh or brackish, flowing or stagnant waters—as well as in the gene arrangements in their chromosomes, in mating habits, and in geographic distribution. A similar complex of six sibling species of Anopheles is found in North America. Sibling species have been discovered also in such important disease vectors as *Anopheles gambiae* and *Aedes* (references to the extensive literature in Bates 1949, Kitzmiller, Frizzi, and Baker 1967, Davidson, Patterson, et al. 1967, and McClelland 1967).

Several complexes of sibling species have been studied in detail in the genus Drosophila. The siblings *D. pseudoobscura* and *D. persimilis* have repeatedly been mentioned in this book, and here we need only briefly summarize the information. The two were believed to be quite indistinguishable morphologically until Rizki (1951) found slight differences in the male genitalia, which make possible determination of the species of single males. Single females cannot be told apart by inspection. The distribution area of *D. pseudoobscura* extends from British Columbia to the highlands of Mexico, Guatemala, and the vicinity of Bogota, Colombia. The area of *D. persimilis* is much smaller and is included within that of its sibling. Where the species are sympatric, they differ in ecological preferences, *D. pseudoobscura* being more abundant in warmer and drier regions and *D. persimilis* in cooler, more humid localities.

The ethological isolation was described in Chapter 10; this is probably the key isolating mechanism preventing gene exchange between the populations of the siblings in nature. The sterility of hybrid males and the viability breakdown in backcross progenies were also discussed in Chapter 10. The most conclusive evidence of lack of gene diffusion between the species is that each of them has its own set of chromosomal polymorphs, not encountered even as exceptions in the other sibling (Dobzhansky and Epling 1944).

The superspecies *Drosophila paulistorum* described in the preceding section is a member of a group of six sibling species—*D. willistoni*,

*D. tropicalis, D. insularis, D. equinoxialis, D. paulistorum,* and *D. pavlovskiana.* Although the evidence here is not as conclusive as it is for *D. pseudoobscura* and *D. persimilis,* the *willistoni* group of siblings seem also to be reproductively isolated from each other. The claims of fertile hybrids between these species (Winge 1965) could not be confirmed in the very careful experiments of Ehrman and Petit (1968). Excellent recent studies of sibling species of the *D. ananassae* group have been published by Futch (1966), and of the *D. auraria* group by Kurokawa (1960).

In Diptera other than mosquitoes and Drosophila, much work has been done on sibling species of houseflies, Musca (a review in Saccà 1967), on black flies, Simuliidae (Rothfels 1956, and Landau 1962), and on Ceratopogonidae (Nielsen 1951). Examples in other animals are crickets (Fulton 1952, Ohmachi and Mazaki 1964, and Alexander 1968), shrimps Artemia (Halfer-Cervini, Piccinelli, et al., 1968), sea cucumbers Thyonella (Manwell and Baker 1963), oysters (Ostrea, Urosalpinx), and finally infusoria (Sonneborn 1957). For more examples, see Mayr 1963.

The description and classification of species has traditionally been, and to a large extent continues to be, the province of systematists working in museums and herbaria. Sibling species cannot be distinguished, however, by classical museum techniques. A museum taxonomist dislikes being unable to write a species determination label. For example, a pinned and dried female of *Drosophila paulistorum* can only be determined as belonging to the *willistoni* group of siblings. Not unexpectedly, some taxonomists contend that only forms which can be distinguished by their time-honored methods should be considered species. Less understandably, this contention has won support from some geneticists. Species are, however, phenomena of nature that exist regardless of our ability to distinguish them. The techniques of species investigation change with time, and cultural and biochemical tests are now used routinely to classify some microorganisms. Is it really necessary to have Drosophila pinned, dried, and shriveled before classifying them? To demand that modern taxonomists use only the techniques of Linnaeus is about as logical as to direct modern medicine to eschew any methods not utilized in Linnaeus' time.

We saw in Chapter 10 that sibling species in ciliate protozoans are referred to not as species but as "varieties." Sonneborn (1957) proposed the term syngen "for the potentially common gene pool, for organisms capable of 'generating together.'" "Syngen" is a synonym of "species."

## *The Multiple-Gene Hypothesis of the Origin of Reproductive Isolation*

Reproductive isolation has two aspects: (1) the interbreeding of species A with species B is difficult or impossible, whereas (2) individuals of A as well as of B are fully able to breed inter se. The reproductive biology of any species is organized to insure the procreation of a sufficient number of offspring. At the same time, it militates against gene exchange with other species. It is important to visualize how this state of affairs develops. Mutations that alter the sexual behavior, the breeding time, or the structure of the genitalia may occur in any species, but such mutations are not workable isolating mechanisms. Genetic changes that engender reproductive isolation must not only prevent cross-breeding between the mutant and the original type, but also must simultaneously insure normal reproduction of the mutants. Where isolation involves incapacitation of the hybrids, this effect must be restricted to the hybrids and must leave the parental populations unaffected.

Reproductive isolation arising in a single step can hardly become established in sexual and outbreeding forms. Mutants appear in populations at first as heterozygotes, and inviable or sterile heterozygotes will be eliminated by normalizing natural selection, regardless of how fit the corresponding homozygotes might be. This initial disadvantage is mitigated in hermaphrodites capable of self-fertilization and in parthenogenetic and asexual forms. The mutant, if viable, may reproduce and establish a small colony. Cross-fertilization and outbreeding may then be resumed.

In sexual and obligatory cross-fertilizing forms the formation of isolating mechanisms entails, not single mutational steps, but building systems of complementary genes. Assume that a population has the genetic constitution *aabb*, where *a* and *b* are single genes or groups of genes, and that this population is broken up into two allopatric, geographically isolated parts. In one part, *a* mutates to *A* and a local race *AAbb* is formed. In the other part, *b* mutates to *B*, giving rise to a race *aaBB*. Since individuals having constitutions *aabb*, *Aabb*, and *AAbb* interbreed freely, there is no difficulty in establishing the gene *A* in the population. The same is true for the gene or genes *B*, since *aabb*, *aabB*, and *aaBB* also interbreed freely. But the cross *AAbb* × *aaBB* is at a disadvantage, because the interaction of *A* and *B* produces one of the reproductive isolating mechanisms. If the carriers of genotypes *AAbb* and *aaBB* surmount the extrinsic barriers separating them, they are then able to become sympatric, since interbreeding is no longer possible.

## *Reproductive Isolation as a Product of Genetic Divergence and Natural Selection*

To state that races are incipient species is not tantamount to saying that every race is a future species. Race differentiation is reversible; race divergence may be superseded by convergence. This is, in fact, what is happening to the human species. To become species, races must evolve reproductive isolation. The question naturally presents itself, what causes bring about the development of reproductive isolating mechanisms? Two hypothetical answers have been proposed. First, reproductive isolation is a by-product of the accumulation of genetic differences between the diverging races. The same genes that make the races diverge in morphological and physiological traits render them reproductively isolated. Second, the isolation is built up by natural selection, when and if the gene exchange between the diverging populations generates recombination products of low fitness. The establishment of reproductive isolation is a special kind of genetic divergence. These two hypotheses are not mutually exclusive. Needless disputes have arisen because they were mistakenly treated as alternatives.

The first hypothesis has long been implicit in the thinking of systematists (discussion and references in Mayr 1942 and Rensch 1960a), but its genetic formulation is due to Muller (1940, 1942). The gene pool of a population is an integrated system of genes; evolutionary changes are not mere additions or subtractions of unrelated gene elements. The initial advantage of most mutations that arise and become established in a species is slight. As the accumulation of gene differences continues, genes that at one time might have been easily dispensed with become essential constituents of the genotype (Harland 1936 and Schmalhausen 1949). In the course of evolution, the functions of a gene in the development may undergo changes. If in two or more races or species the gene functions diverge, the gene systems may no longer be compatible in hybrids. In Muller's opinion, all isolating mechanisms may arise in this manner:

> Which kind of character becomes affected earliest, and to what degree . . . will depend in part upon its general complexity (which is correlated with the number of genes affecting it), in part on the nicety or instability of the equilibria of processes necessary for its proper functioning, and in part on the accidental circumstances that determined just which incompatible mutations happened to become established first.

The second hypothesis was, according to Grant (1963), suggested as far back as 1889 by A. R. Wallace, and later by Fisher (1930) and Dobzhansky (1940). It starts from the same premise as that of Muller (see above), namely, that the genotype of a species is an integrated system adapted to the ecological niches in which the species lives. Gene recombination in the offspring of species hybrids may lead to the formation of discordant gene patterns that decrease the reproductive potentials of both interbreeding populations. Suppose that incipient species, A and B, are in contact in a certain territory. Mutations arise in either or in both species that make their carriers averse to mating with the other species. The nonmutant individuals of A that cross to B will produce a progeny inferior to the pure species. Since the mutants breed only or mostly within the species, their progeny will be superior in fitness to that of the nonmutants. Consequently, natural selection will favor the spread and establishment of the mutant condition.

Sturtevant (1938) and Bruce Wallace (1968a) have pointed out one of the possible causes that might initiate such a process. Suppose that the gene arrangement *ABCDEFGH* in a chromosome is modified in one race to *AFEDCBGH* and in another race to *ABGFEDCH*. Heterozygotes carrying the ancestral and either of the modified arrangements will produce few or no inviable offspring. In a hybrid carrying the two modified arrangements, crossing over in the section *CDEF* will give chromosomes *AFEDCH* and *ABGFEDCBGH*. Such chromosomes may be inviable. Hence prevention of the interbreeding of carriers of *AFEDCBGH* and *ABGFEDCH* will have a selective advantage.

There is good experimental evidence that selection can build up reproductive isolation. Koopman (1950) made use of the observation that the ethological isolation between *Drosophila pseudoobscura* and *D. persimilis* is weaker at a low (16°c) than at a higher (25°c) temperature. He placed in population cages equal numbers of females and males of the two species, marked by two different recessive mutants. The offspring of matings within and between species are distinguishable by inspection; if the two species are *aaBB* and *AAbb*, the hybrids are wild-type, *AaBb*. In every generation, the hybrids were destroyed, and the populations were continued with equal numbers of the pure species. Therefore, the flies that mated with representatives of their own species had their progenies included among the parents of the next generation, whereas those mating with the other species suffered "genetic death." After only five generations of selection, the proportions of hybrids among the offspring fell to a fraction of the former value.

Working with the same two species as Koopman, Kessler (1966) used a superior technique, observing the matings directly. He selected both for weaker and for stronger ethological isolation. To weaken the isolation, he selected the females and males that mated soonest with individuals of the opposite sex of the foreign species, and subsequently mated them conspecifically. Since the species were marked by recessive mutant genes, the progenies of conspecific and heterospecific matings were distinguishable. To strengthen the isolation, individuals were selected that failed to mate with the other species, and then mated conspecifically. In eighteen generations of selection, Kessler obtained populations with both weaker and stronger isolation, in *D. pseudoobscura* and in *D. persimilis* alike. Although Manning (1961) was able to select *D. melanogaster* for increased and decreased mating speed, Kessler's results were due to changed behavioral responses to individuals of another species, and not simply to greater or lesser eagerness of the flies to mate.

In the experiments of Koopman and Kessler, pre-existing isolating mechanisms were enhanced or reduced. Wallace (1954) and Knight, Robertson, and Waddington (1956) initiated ethological isolation between two strains of *Drosophila melanogaster* that were marked by different recessive genes and that previously showed no mating discrimination. As in Koopman's experiments, the selection was made by discarding the progenies of heterogamic matings. A weak but statistically significant preference for homogamic matings developed over some thirty generations.

In order that natural selection may promote reproductive isolation, there must be a challenge of loss of fitness owing to gene flow between populations. Reduced viability or fertility of hybrid offspring provides such a challenge. This is another way of saying that postmating isolating mechanisms may act as stimuli for the development of premating isolation (cf. Chapter 10). Postmating isolating mechanisms (i.e., hybrid inviability, sterility, breakdown, or combinations of these) are, then, consequences of differential adaptedness of races or species to the conditions of life in their respective distribution areas. They are by-products of genetic divergence, although in experiments they can be enhanced or weakened by selection. Haley, Abplanalp, and Enya (1966) successfully selected strains of the domesticated Japanese quail (Coturnix) to produce viable offspring when artificially inseminated with the sperm of jungle fowl (*Gallus bankiva*) or domestic chickens. The experiments of Grant (1966a,b) on selection for viability and fertility in species hybrids of Gilia have already been mentioned.

Rick (1963b) has studied the wild tomato (*Lycopersicon peruvianum*), which grows in stream valleys along the coast of Peru. Intercrosses of northern strains with southern ones give few viable seeds. Nevertheless, geographically intermediate populations form a "compatibility bridge," and the genetic unity of the species is maintained. Rick states:

It is not difficult to understand how such barriers might arise gradually in races that have been isolated for long periods of time. Different reaction norms for rates of embryo and endosperm development, osmotic values, and other developmental characteristics might have become fixed by selection while races were adapting to the new environments into which they were migrating.

Similar situations have been observed by, among others, Grant (1954) in Gilia, Stebbins (1957) in Elymus, Kruckeberg (1957) in Streptanthus, Vickery (1959, 1964, 1966) in species of monkey flowers (Mimulus), and Levin and Kerster (1967b) in Phlox.

Hoenigsberg and Koref-Santibañez (1960) found differences in courtship patterns between some laboratory strains of *Drosophila melanogaster,* which result in a preference for homogamic matings. Similar preferences exist, as pointed out previously, in Transitional populations of *D. paulistorum* (Dobzhansky, Pavlovsky, and Ehrman 1969b) and in geographic strains of *D. birchii* (Ayala 1965). It is unlikely that these rudiments of ethological isolation were built by natural selection for their function as isolating mechanisms; on the other hand, they are genetic raw materials from which reproductive isolation may be compounded by natural selection. It is appropriate to mention at this point that not all genetic divergence leads to changed mating preferences. Robertson (1966) selected a population of *D. melanogaster* for adaptedness to a modified diet. Although the adaptation involved multiple, polygenic gene differences, no trace of ethological isolation between the original and the changed strains was found.

There is ample, though of necessity indirect, evidence that selection builds isolating mechanisms in nature. At least the premating isolating mechanisms between closely related species should be enhanced in the geographic areas where hybridization is most likely to occur. The observations of Ehrman (1965) on sympatric and allopatric strains of *Drosophila paulistorum* are among the most elegant verifications of this prediction. The ethological isolation is greater among sympatric than among allopatric strains of the same pairs of semispecies.

In a series of papers Grant (1954b, 1958, 1965, 1966d, a general discussion in 1963) has supplied a demonstration that mechanisms preventing the hybridization of species of Gilia arise by selection under conditions of sympatry. Five related species occur in the foothills and valleys of California and are often found growing side by side. Four other species occur in coastal localities in North and South America; they are completely allopatric with respect to one another, and largely so with respect to the five inland species. Experimentally obtained species hybrids are highly sterile in all combinations tried. Yet the allopatric species can be crossed quite easily, giving 18.1 hybrid seeds per flower on the average. In contrast, the sympatric species are separated by crossability barriers and yield only 0.2 seeds per flower when cross-pollinated artificially.

We saw in Chapter 10 that mating call differences are important isolating factors between related species of anuran amphibians. Littlejohn (1965) has analyzed the mating calls of allopatric and sympatric populations of two species of Australian frogs:

Whereas mating calls of remote allopatric populations of *Hyla ewingi* and *H. verreauxi* are very similar, those of the sympatric populations are quite distinct. . . . It is suggested that the marked differences between sympatric populations have resulted from the direct action of selection for increased reproductive efficiency, i.e., the slight differences present in the allopatric populations have been reinforced in the sympatric populations.

Some evidence of sympatric reinforcement of species differences in mating calls has also been recorded by Blair (1955) in *Microhyla olivacea* and *M. carolinensis* and by Ball and Jameson (1966) in *Hyla regilla* and *H. californiae*. No such reinforcement was found, however, by Michaud (1964) in *Pseudacris clarki* and *P. nigrita,* or by Blair and Littlejohn (1960) in *P. ornata* and *P. streckeri*. Hubbs and Delco (1960, 1962), working with four species of the fish Gambusia, found that males of sympatric species are better able to distinguish females of their own and foreign species than are males of allopatric species. A similar difference has been recorded by Smith (1965) for sympatric and allopatric strains of mice, *Peromyscus eremicus* and *P. californicus*.

The examples just cited of the reinforcement of premating isolating mechanisms may be viewed as instances of character displacement, which Brown and Wilson (1956) defined as "the situation in which, when two species of animals overlap geographically, the differences between them are accentuated in the zone of sympatry and weakened or lost entirely in the parts of their ranges outside this zone." Habitat, temporal, and ethological isolations are particularly likely to arise in this manner. In addition to the examples mentioned by Brown and Wilson and by Mayr (1963), reference may be made to the works of Brower (1959) on butterflies of the *Papilio glaucus* group, of Schoener (1965) on bill size differences among sympatric species of birds, and of Levin and Kerster (1967b) on Phlox.

Instances of the lack or the weakness of premating isolating mechanisms, where the populations of related species are wholly or largely allopatric, are perhaps as significant as their presence where the species are sympatric. Thus Zaslavsky (1966, 1967) found that hybrids between the ladybird beetle species (or semispecies) *Chilocorus bipustulatus* and *Ch. geminus* are sterile, but detected no ethological isolation at all, at least under experimental conditions. Hybrid belts, formed where the geographic areas of two species come into contact, have been studied to find whether premating isolating mechanisms may be formed there. The most thoroughly investigated cases are those of two species of crows (Corvus) in Europe, and of grackles (Quiscalus) in the United States. The evidence is ambiguous (Mayr 1963, Yang and Selander 1968, and Johnsgard 1967).

Whether postmating isolating mechanisms can be reinforced by natural selection is also an open problem. If the progeny of hybrids is inferior in fitness, it would seem advantageous to the species concerned to prevent hybridization, either by premating isolation or, failing that, by such postmating mechanisms as inviability or sterility of $F_1$ hybrids. Group selection (see Chapter 12) could, theoretically, bring such a result about. However, because the efficiency of group selection is low relative to the selection of individual genotypes, it is doubtful that isolating mechanisms frequently arise in this way.

## Polyploid Species in Plants

We have seen that differences between species involve many genes, and often also chromosomal changes. The transformation of one species into another in time, or the splitting of an ancestral species into two or several derived ones, is, therefore, a slow process. Yet, alongside this gradual method of species formation, new species may also emerge in a single generation, by polyploidy. This may occur, it will be recalled, either through doubling of the chromosome complement in the hybrid between two previously existing species (allopolyploidy), or through multiplication of the chromosomes of a single species (autopolyploidy). In either case, the polyploid possesses, at least initially, all the genes that were present in its ancestors and no new ones. However, the ancestral species may continue to exist side by side with the polyploid; the organic diversity is, therefore, augmented.

Species formation through polyploidy has occurred in all major groups of plants, with the possible exception of fungi, but only rarely in animals. Excellent reviews of the state of the knowledge about plant polyploids can be found in Stebbins (1950), Grant (1963), and Schwanitz (1967). Only a brief consideration is needed here.

Grant (1963) estimates that as many as 47 percent of species of angiosperms are recent or ancient polyploids; the frequency is higher among monocotyledons (58 percent) than among dicotyledons (43 percent). Polyploidy is rare among the gymnosperms, although the redwood (*Sequoia sempervirens*) is a polyploid. Manton (1950) and Klekowski and Baker (1966) found polyploidy very common among ferns. Some of the most important cultivated plants, such as wheat, oat, cotton, tobacco, potato, banana, sugar cane, and coffee, are polyploid.

Since most individuals in sexual and outbreeding plants are more or less complex heterozygotes, no sharp distinction can be drawn between auto- and allopolyploids (Stebbins 1950). As a convention, one may take the doubling of the chromosomes within a Mendelian population to produce autopolyploids, while hybrids between reproductively isolated populations are allopolyploids. Müntzing (1961) argues that autopolyploidy is an evolutionary factor of some consequence, and so it is among cultivated plants. Schwanitz (1967) lists tetraploid varieties of the clovers *Trifolium pratense* and *T. hybridum* and *Brassica rapa*, as well as of the ornamental plants *Cyclamen, Primula, Hyacinthus, Petunia, Crocus,* and *Antirrhinum,* that are superior to their diploid ancestors. Most of the wild species believed to be autopolyploid were later shown to be probably or certainly allopolyploid. Mosquin (1967) believes that a subspecies of *Epilobium angustifolium* is tetraploid or hexaploid. That allopolyploidy is a far more widespread method of species formation is, however, generally admitted.

Since allopolyploids possess gene complements of two or even three species, their reaction norms may be intermediate between those of the parents or may combine the properties of both. Sometimes, though not always, an allopolyploid possesses the environmental tolerances of both parents; such allopolyploids are likely to have high adaptive values. There is a considerable and still growing literature concerning the geographic regularities in the distribution of polyploids (Clausen, Keck, and Hiesey 1945, Gustafsson 1947, Stebbins 1950, Löve 1951, 1964, Johnson and Packer 1965, and references therein). The floras of arctic, subarctic, and recently glaciated territories have proportionately more polyploid species than do warmer and geologically more ancient lands. Löve and Löve (1949) give the list of percentages of polyploid species in different floras (arranged from south to north) shown in Table 11.3.

The formation of species through polyploidy is a process vastly more rapid than the more ubiquitous race divergence; polyploids are therefore most likely to colonize newly opened lands, such as those recently freed from the continental ice sheets (Babcock and Stebbins 1938 and Stebbins 1950). Also, the floras of high latitudes include

**TABLE 11.3**
Percentages of polyploid species of angiosperms

| Area | Latitude, °N | Polyploids | Area | Latitude, °N | Polyploids |
|------|------|------|------|------|------|
| Timbuctoo | 17 | 37 | Iceland | 63–66 | 64 |
| Cyclades | 37 | 34 | Sweden | 55–69 | 56 |
| Sicily | 37 | 37 | Kolguev | 69 | 64 |
| Hungary | 46–49 | 47 | Finland | 60–70 | 57 |
| Schleswig-Holstein | 54 | 50 | Norway | 58–71 | 58 |
| Denmark | 54–58 | 53 | South Greenland | 60–71 | 72 |
| Great Britain | 50–61 | 57 | Spitzbergen | 77–81 | 74 |
| Faroes | 62 | 61 | | | |

many perennial herbs and relatively few woody species; the incidence of polyploidy is known to be higher among the former than among the latter.

The hypothesis of Babcock and Stebbins is questioned by Löve (1951, 1964), who postulates instead that polyploids possess a selective superiority because of their greater genetic variability. Hutchinson, Silow, and Stephens (1947) pointed out that polyploids may show a greater variety of phenotypes than diploids because of dominant and semidominant genes. A diploid may carry either one or two dominant alleles, while genotypes with one, two, three, and four dominants may be formed in a tetraploid. Since genetic changes that affect polygenic traits are usually neither dominant nor recessive, Hutchinson et al. are of the opinion that the "evolutionary potentialities of a young polyploid will rapidly approach those of a diploid." Löve sees a confirmation of his view in the findings of S. Mangenot and G. Mangenot (1962) that the flora of tropical Africa contains a high proportion of very old polyploids, though a low percentage of young ones.

What makes polyploids of outstanding interest to evolutionists is the possibility, not only of creating new species experimentally, but also of tracing the phylogeny of existing polyploid species, and sometimes of re-creating them. Karpechenko's classical work on "radocabbage" (Raphanobrassica) was discussed in Chapter 10. Radocabbage not only is fully fertile with itself, but also produces sterile triploid hybrids when crossed to its ancestors, radish and cabbage. Another classic in this field is Müntzing's (1932) synthesis of the tetraploid ($2n = 32$) mint species *Galeopsis tetrahit* from its diploid ($2n = 16$) parents, *G. pubescens* and *G. speciosa*. The cross of the two diploid species gives a highly sterile $F_1$ hybrid with disturbed chromosome pairing at meiosis. Müntzing found a single plant in the $F_2$ generation, which proved to be triploid (24 chromosomes); this he outcrossed to *G. pubescens*. A single seed in the resulting progeny was a tetraploid (32 chromosomes), which gave rise to a strain of fertile "artificial *tetrahit*," identical in all essentials to the *G. tetrahit* found in nature. The hybrids of artificial and natural *tetrahit* have normal meiosis with 16 bivalents, and at least some of these are fully fertile.

The unraveling of the phylogeny of species of wheat (Triticum) and related grasses (Aegilops, Secale, Agropyron) constitutes one of the greatest success stories of cytogenetics, made possible by the work of many scientists in several countries (for references to the voluminous literature, see Sears 1948, 1956, Unrau 1959, and Kihara 1965). Diploid ($2n = 14$), tetraploid ($4n = 28$), hexaploid ($6n = 42$), and artificially produced octoploid ($8n = 56$) species are known. The analysis is made in terms of "genomes," that is, sets of 7 chromosomes each, differing in gene contents and gene arrangements, derived from different diploid ancestors. To oversimplify the story, if a hexaploid wheat, such as *Triticum vulgare* or *T. spelta*, with 42 chromosomes, is crossed to a tetraploid, such as *T. durum*, with 28 chromosomes, the hybrids have at meiosis up to 14 bivalents and 7 univalents. The inference is that *T. vulgare* has 2 genomes, or a total of 14 chromosomes in its gamete, sufficiently similar to the 2 genomes of *T. durum* to pair and to form bivalents. A cross of *T. durum* to the diploid einkorn wheat, *T. monococcum*, with 14 chromosomes, gives up to 7 bivalents and 7 univalents in the hybrid. Finally, *T. vulgare* crossed to *T. monococcum* gives up to 7 bivalents and 14 univalents. If the genome of *T. monococcum* is denoted as *A*, then the tetraploid wheats have also genome *A* and some other genome, *B*. The hexaploid wheats have genomes *A* and *B*, and also some third genome, *D*.

Genome *D* comes from the diploid grass, *Aegilops squarrosa*, with 14 chromosomes. The hypothesis suggests itself that the hexaploid wheats arose by a doubling of the chromosomes in a hybrid between some tetraploid wheat, and *Ae. squarrosa* or its close relative. This was verified independently by Sears and McFadden in America and by Kihara in Japan. A tetraploid wheat, *Triticum dicoccoides*, was crossed to *Ae. squarrosa*; by doubling the chromosomes in the resulting triploid hybrid, a hexaploid was obtained that proved to be strikingly similar to the existing hexaploid, *T. spelta*.

As so often happens, further studies have disclosed some complications. Presumably all of the seven chromosome genomes have descended in some remote past from some primordial genome, and subsequently became differentiated by gene mutations and rearrangements. Not surprisingly, some genomes still remain so similar that some of their chromosomes became paired at meiosis in the hybrids. One tetraploid wheat species, *Triticum timopheevi*, has the genomes *AG*, instead of *AB* as in *T. durum* and other tetrapoloids. Among the Aegilops species there is a diploid, *Aegilops caudata*, carrying genome *C*; a tetraploid, *Ae. cylindrica*, with genomes *C* and *D*; a diploid, *Ae. comosa*, with genome *M*; and several tetraploid and hexaploid species combining *DM*, *CM*, *DCM*, and their derivatives $C^uM^o$, $DC^uM^o$, $C^uM^t$, etc. Genome *B* may have been derived from a species of the grass Agropyron; an allotetraploid hybrid of this with *T. aegilopoides* (a relative of the neolithic cultivated *T. monococcum*) gave the tetraploid *T. dicoccoides*, the ancestor of the modern hard wheat, *T. durum*. In the Neolithic or Bronze Age there arose the hexaploid *T. spelta*, and later the modern cultivated bread wheat, *T. vulgare*. Similar analyses of the allopolyploid descent have been made for species of cottons (Hutchinson, Silow, and Stephens 1947), tobaccos, and some other plants.

## Animal Polyploids

The prevalence of polyploids among plants and their scarcity among animals constitute a striking difference between evolutionary patterns in the two kingdoms. Muller (1925) surmised that this is due to the preponderance of hermaphroditism (monoecy) among plants, and the separation of sexes (dioecy) among animals. Where sex is determined by a mechanism like that in Drosophila, polyploidy may result in the production of intersexes and other abnormal and sterile types. If the ratio of the numbers of X chromosomes and of sets of autosomes is intermediate between that in females (1 : 1) and that in males (1 : 2), the individual is a sterile intersex. A tetraploid individual arising by mutation in nature will cross to a normal diploid of the opposite sex, and the progeny will consist of triploid females and intersexes. A part of the progeny of a triploid female crossed to a normal male is also intersexual.

Muller's argument lost its force with the discovery that both in dioecious plants and in mammals the male determining genes are carried in the Y chromosome, and the female determiners in the X. In the plant *Melandrium album,* triploid individuals with two X's and a Y chromosome are fertile males, and not intersexes as they are in Drosophila (Warmke and Blakeslee 1940 and Westergaard 1948). In mice, diploid individuals with a single X and no Y are fertile females, and not sterile males as in Drosophila (Welshons and Russell 1959).

Natural polyploid species in animals occur among hermaphrodites, such as earthworms (Omodeo 1952) and planarians (Aeppli 1952), or in forms with parthenogenetic females, for example, some beetles, moths, sow bugs, shrimps, goldfish, and salamanders (Suomalainen 1947a, 1962, Seiler 1946, Vandel 1941, Cherfas 1966, Uzzell and Goldblatt 1967, and others). Astaurov (1969) obtained fertile allotetraploid hybrids of *Bombyx mori* (the silkworm moth) and the closely related *B. mandarina.* In his experiments Astaurov utilized the technique of artificial induction of parthenogenesis by heat treatment. He obtained triploid hybrids with two chromosome sets of *B. mori* and one of *B. mandarina.* Such hybrids are sterile, but artificial parthenogenesis leads to the development of some mosaic individuals, with triploid and hexaploid tissues, the latter having four sets of *B. mori* and two sets of *B. mandarina* chromosomes. These individuals are weakly fertile; crossed to the ordinary diploid *B. mandarina,* they yield more fertile allotetraploid moths (two chromosome sets from each parental species).

Wide variations in the chromosome numbers in related species of certain groups of animals led some authors to infer that polyploidy has played an evolutionary role in the animal kingdom comparable to that among plants. A critical analysis of these claims (see White 1954 and Matthey 1952, 1964a,b) showed that what is actually involved is either chromosome fusion and fragmentation in forms with diffuse centromeres (see Chapter 5), or changes owing to frequent translocations. This simpler interpretation has been borne out by measurements of the DNA contents in the nuclei of the alleged polyploids. In the fish family Salmonidae the chromosome numbers vary from 58 to 104; Rees (1964) nevertheless found similar amounts of DNA in *Salmo salar* (60 chromosomes) and *S. trutta* (80 chromosomes). Suomalainen (1965) also found uniform DNA contents in species of the geometrid moths Cidaria with chromosome numbers ranging from 12 to 32 (haploid). In polyploids, the amounts of DNA would be expected to form a series of multiples of some basic amount.

A much bolder claim in favor of polyploidy in animal evolution has been advanced by Ohno and Atkin (1966, Atkin and Ohno 1967) and by Taylor (1967). The amounts of DNA per nucleus vary greatly in different vertebrates and prochordates, being generally small in lower forms, which may be surmised to reflect the conditions in the ancestors of the vertebrate phylum. Thus, the ascidian Ciona has approximately 6 percent, the cephalochordate Amphioxus 17 percent, and the cyclostome fishes Lampetra and Eptatretus 38 and 76 percent, respectively, of the amounts in the nuclei of man and most mammals. At the opposite extreme, the lungfish Lepidosiren and some urodele amphibians have very high amounts, up to 35 times the mammalian value. Ohno and his colleagues ascribe these wide variations to a series of polyploidizations having occurred in the evolution of vertebrates and their ancestors. However, since polyploidy cannot be easily established in species with separate sexes and regular outcrossing, they see themselves as forced to relegate the hypothetical polyploidization to great antiquity, 300 million years ago, when "fishes ancestral to the terrestrial vertebrates of today did not have a firmly established chromosomal sex-determining mechanism, and there was no barrier against polyploid evolution then."

All that need be said concerning this highly imaginative speculation is that polyploidy is by no means the only known process whereby the amount of genetic material in the nucleus is changed. That duplications of chromosome sections occur in evolution is amply attested by the presence of numerous "repeat" areas in the salivary gland chromosomes of Drosophila and other polytene chromosomes.

### Sympatric, Stasipatric, and Saltational Species Formation

The essence of the process of species formation is the establishment of reproductive isolation between arrays of Mendelian populations. Most often this process occurs gradually, while the genetically diverging races are allopatric, that is, live in different territories. The geographic isolation is antecedent to reproductive isolation. One of the recurrently debated issues is, however, how often the speciation is not gradual but saltational, and occurs while the diverging populations are not allopatric but sympatric. Speciation by way of allopolyploidy is evidently saltational, and no less evidently it occurs sympatrically, since the species ancestral to the allopolyploid must occur in close proximity in order to produce hybrids.

Whether populations can diverge gradually while living in the same territory is a different issue. Mayr (1963 and earlier) has expertly marshaled arguments showing that this is unlikely to occur except under very special circumstances. The hypothesis of sympatric speciation, he states, "is neither necessary nor supported by irrefutable facts. It overlooks the fact that speciation is a problem of populations, not of individuals, and it minimizes the difficulties raised by dispersal and recombination of genes during sexual reproduction." Several authors, most recently Maynard-Smith (1966), Bush (1969), and Pimentel, Smith, and Soans (1967), have nevertheless devised plausible genetic models of how sympatric speciation could occur.

The findings of Lewis and Raven (1958 and Lewis 1966) and of Kyhos (1965) are in a different category. Reference has been made to the work of Grant (1966a,b) who, in nine generations, selected viable and fertile recombination products among poorly viable and semisterile hybrids between *Gilia malior* and *G. modocensis*. According to Lewis and Raven, *Clarkia franciscana* is a narrow endemic growing within the distribution area of *C. rubicunda*, from which it is reproductively isolated, and not far from the distribution margin of *C. amoena*. The authors infer that *C. franciscana* arose "*in situ*" from *C. rubicunda* "as a consequence of a rapid reorganization of the chromosomes due to the presence, at some time, of a genotype conducive to extensive chromosome breakage." Similarly, Kyhos finds that "*Chaenactis glabriuscula* is the living ancestor of *Ch. fremontii* and *Ch. stevioides*," from which it differs in chromosome number ($n = 6$ in the first species and $n = 5$ in *Ch. fremontii* and *Ch. stevioides*), as well as in a series of translocations.

White (1968) and his colleagues have studied the chromosomes in some 160 species and semispecies of flightless Australian grasshoppers of the subfamily Morabinae. At least 34 translocations resulting in chromosome fusion and 20 resulting in dissociation of chromosomes have taken place in the phylogeny of this group. Particularly interesting are the superspecies *Moraba viatica* and *M. scurra*. Semispecies with different karyotypes occupy adjacent territories; hybrids, which are often translocation heterozygotes, are found, nevertheless, only in very narrow zones of overlap, sometimes some hundred meters wide. The translocation heterozygosis reduces the fitness of its carriers. How, then, have the species and semispecies with different chromosome complements established themselves in the first place? White suggests that this may have happened "stasipatrically." A translocation establishes itself at first in a small local colony, either at the periphery of the distribution area of the ancestral species or inside it, by a process of random genetic drift (Chapter 8). If members of this colony possess high fitness, they subsequently spread and displace the ancestral form in a certain area. White believes that the allopatric and stasipatric models of species formation "seem essentially different" but are nevertheless "not entirely antithetical." Perhaps the stasipatric may be regarded as a special case of the allopatric model (Key 1968).

# CHAPTER TWELVE

# PATTERNS OF EVOLUTION

## Concepts of Progressive Evolution

Teilhard de Chardin (1959) saw in organic evolution "only one event, the grand orthogenesis of everything living toward a higher degree of immanent spontaneity." He was using, or misusing, the word orthogenesis in an unusual sense; the theory of orthogenesis proposes that "evolution is in a great measure an unfolding of preexisting rudiments" (Berg 1969). This is at variance with everything that modern biology has learned about evolution. Teilhard de Chardin himself supposed, on the contrary, that the evolutionary process proceeds by "groping"—a term that, to him, meant "pervading everything so as to find everything." This is a splendid, though somewhat impressionistic, characterization of evolution molded by natural selection. The groping leads to evolutionary progress in some lines of descent, extinction in many more lines, and evolutionary stasis in the rest.

That there has been progress in evolution is intuitively evident (Stebbins 1969). In Barbour's (1966) words, "By almost any standard man represents a higher level than primeval mud." And yet attempts to define what constitutes progress have met with only mediocre success. Mere change is not necessarily progress; in fact, the evolution of many parasitic groups can be regarded as regressive. The simplest and most primitive existing forms of life, microorganisms and viruses, show an adaptedness to their ecological niches not manifestly inferior to that of the most complex and advanced forms, including man.

Simpson (1949) finds only one really universal trend in evolution: "a tendency for life to expand, to fill in all the available spaces in the livable environments, including those created by the process of that expansion itself." Now, the "expansion" of life can occur by various means. One is cladogenesis (Rensch 1947) or splitting (Simpson 1953), which leads to diversification of phylogenetic lineages, adaptation to a greater variety of ecological niches, and, as a rule, growth of the biomass taken up by representatives of a lineage. Speciation, the appearance in time of two, several, or many contemporaneous species descended from a single ancestral one, is the most thoroughly studied kind of cladogenesis and is discussed in Chapters 10 and 11. Some evolutionists argue that the emphasis on speciation, started in Darwin's "Origin of Species" and continued in modern genetics, may have gone too far. The proliferation of more and more species may be a sign of the biological success or ascendancy of a lineage, but hundreds or thousands of species of a genus (such as Drosophila) or a family or superfamily (such as parasitic wasps, Ichneumonoidea) may be merely so many variations on the same theme.

The emergence of new organs, the development of novel ways of dealing with the environment, and advances into new adaptive zones are earmarks of anagenesis (Rensch 1947), phyletic evolution (Simpson 1949), or arogenesis (Takhtajan 1966). An anagenetic line may be represented by a single species or by the same number of species at different time levels. Anagenesis and cladogenesis are often mixed in various proportions. Human evolution is an excellent example of anagenesis. There were apparently only two hominid species (*Australopithecus africanus* and *A. robustus*) in the early Pleistocene, and there has been only one from the middle Pleistocene to the present (*Homo erectus* followed by *H. sapiens*). The cladogenetic element was confined to the formation of races or subspecies; some of these may have died out, but most races of *H. erectus* were eventually transformed into races of *H. sapiens*.

Huxley (1942) and Rensch (1947, 1968) arrived independently at fairly similar lists of characteristics of anagenesis or progressive evolution. These are increased complexity and rationalization of structures and functions, especially complexity and rationalization of central nervous systems; open-ended improvement, permitting further improvement, and increasing independence of the environment, making for greater autonomy of the organism. Simpson (1949) pointed out that none of these criteria can be taken as a valid touchstone of progress. There is no denying, however, that each one is applicable to some evolutionary developments that we may choose to call progressive. For example, the transition from unicellular to multicellular organisms clearly involved a structural complication. Consider, however, the evolutionary sequence fish → amphibian → reptile → mammal → man. The sequence is usually taken to be progressive, yet "it would be a brave anatomist who would attempt to prove that recent man is more complicated than a Devonian ostracoderm." Although the development of a variety of sense organs is generally taken as progress, mammals and man lack certain kinds of senses present in other vertebrates—the lateral line organs of fishes, which perceive variations in pressure, or the directional receptors for heat radiation present in pit vipers.

Thoday (1953) defined biological progress as increase in fitness. In his usage, however, "fitness" includes the capacity of species or of other units of evolution not only for immediate but also for future survival in future environments. "The probability that a unit of evolution will survive for a given long period of time, such as $10^8$ years, that is to say, will leave descendants after the lapse of that time, is the fitness of the unit." This definition leads to at least two difficulties. First, it is impossible to predict which of the existing organisms will have descendants not only after $10^8$ years, but even after periods some orders of magnitude shorter. Simpson (1969) goes so far as to say, "No known actions of man can guarantee or even make probable the *indefinite* survival of our species, which will almost certainly become extinct in due course, whatever we do now." Yet it is our cherished idea that man is the most progressive and fittest product of evolution! Second, if we use retrodiction instead of prediction, the primordial organism from which all the rest have descended must have been the fittest (Ayala 1969c).

There is, nevertheless, no denying that fitness in Thoday's sense, which may perhaps be designated as the durability of a unit of evolution, is a highly significant consideration. Slobodkin (1964, 1968) rightly says, "The animals that are now alive are successful players at the evolutionary game in that . . . extinction represents a kind of losing." The difficulty that a biologist encounters is that "the applicability of the concept of an existential game to evolution in any interesting way is contingent on the logical possibility of a non-intelligent player or an automation being able to be effective in an existential game, without being explicitly programmed with information about the future." Slobodkin then argues that success in the "game" depends on the interaction of behavioral, physiological, ecological, and genetic mechanisms. Their interaction with each other and with the environment should conserve or maximize the "homeostatic ability" of the population. This occurs when organisms "respond to environmental perturbations in such a way that they not only minimize the departure from steady state conditions caused by the perturbation but also maximize their ability to withstand further perturbations."

Kimura (1961) has made an interesting attempt to envisage progressive evolution as an increase in the amount of genetic information. We saw in Chapter 1 that the DNA content of a human chromosome set is about three orders of magnitude greater than that in a bacterial cell. It is reasonable to infer that the amount of genetic information is also greater in man than in a bacterium. Kimura is on less secure ground when he chooses to assume that man's ancestors who lived 500 million years ago, in Cambrian times, carried much smaller amounts of genetic information. However, having made this assumption, and proceeding also on the premise that evolution has occurred at a constant rate during this very long time, he computes the rate of accumulation of genetic information as approximately 0.29 bit per generation. The total amount of genetic information accumulated since the Cambrian in the lineage leading to mammals and man is estimated to be of the order of $10^8$ bits. The maximum amount of information that can be stored in the DNA of a human chromosome set is inferred to be about $10^{10}$ bits. This difference means, according to Kimura, that "either the amount of genetic information which has been accumulated is a small fraction of what can actually be stored in the chromosome set or, more probably, the DNA code itself is highly redundant." Although these numerical estimates can hardly be relied upon, even to the order of magnitude, Kimura's approach may lead to important developments if methods are found to actually measure the amount of accumulated genetic information.

One may well concede that each of the above concepts of evolutionary progress is meaningful, and yet agree with Simpson (1949) that "within the framework of the evolutionary history of life there have been not one but many different sorts of progress." Except in the new (1967) edition of his 1949 book, Simpson eschewed the topic of progressive evolution under this name in his later books (1953, 1961, 1964b, 1969). I feel that a biologist may reasonably speak of evolutionary progress, provided only that he makes clear what kind of progress is meant. My colleague F. J. Ayala has pointed out (unpublished) that the concept of progress, including biological progress, necessarily is axiological, that is, refers to some kind of value in reference to which we choose to consider objects or events. Our choice of values may or may not be determined by whether the valuation can be measured exactly.

The approach of evolution to man is almost inevitably in one's mind in considering the evolutionary history of life on earth. If made explicit (as Teilhard de Chardin 1959 has done), this emphasis is legitimate, although totally inapplicable to the evolution of the plant kingdom. The increase of individuation is another feasible criterion. Clones of billions of individuals, genetically identical except for newly arisen mutations, are easily obtained in many microorganisms. In sexually reproducing and outbreeding species, on the other hand, no two individuals have the same genotype. Moreover, an individual mammal may remain alive for years or even decades, during which it accumulates information about its environment. Cultural transmission in man makes this accumulation different in kind as well as in quantity from that characteristic of other living species. The destruction of billions of individuals is easily supported among bacteria, whereas in vertebrates an individual's life is hedged and sheltered by many physiological and developmental homeostatic mechanisms.

## Sex and Genetic Recombination

Sexual reproduction is the most widespread and successful of the mechanisms of recombination of genetic materials. The origin and development of these mechanisms constituted an outstanding achievement of progressive evolution, because it facilitated further progress. This achievement must have been made early in the history of life. The number of organisms in which no gene recombination is known to occur is steadily dwindling; at least some of these organisms are descendants of forms in which gene recombination did exist.

The diversity of organs that serve the functions of mating, pollination, and fertilization in animals and plants is immense. The variety of behavior patterns underpinning these functions is no less impressive. Some of the most fascinating chapters of zoology and botany are concerned with this diversity. The cellular mechanisms of meiosis, indispensable for sexual reproduction, are more standardized, but even these display interesting and sometimes bizarre variations (an excellent review in White 1954). The role of sex in evolution attracted the attention of evolutionists, beginning with Darwin. It was Weismann, however, who pointed out in 1891 that sexual reproduction results in the formation of ever new combinations of hereditary determinants, later called genes. Weismann's idea was developed in genetic terms in the early nineteen thirties by Fisher, Morgan, Muller, and Wright. Among recent authors, Muller (1964), Crow and Kimura (1965), Maynard-Smith (1968b), and Bodmer (1970) endeavored to place the arguments on a quantitative basis.

Just how greatly evolution is speeded up by sex is controversial. The conclusions of various authors differ, depending on what assumptions they choose as plausible in their calculations. The basic consideration is, however, simple and straightforward. Suppose that substitution of alleles $A_2$, $B_2$, $C_2$, etc., for $A_1$, $B_1$, $C_1$, etc., is an adaptive improvement. Mutations from $A_1$ to $A_2$, $B_1$ to $B_2$, etc., occur infrequently. Under strictly asexual reproduction, these mutations must happen among the descendants of a single individual. With gene recombination, the mutations may occur in different individuals and in different places, and be subsequently joined together. Bodmer (1970) considers a simple model of two genes in a haploid organism. The combination of the favorable mutant alleles $A_2$ and $B_2$ in a single individual will be achieved, on the average, in less than one-half as many generations in sexual as in asexual populations. Moreover, the advantage of recombination is strongly dependent on population size. According to Bodmer, the advantage is greater in small than in large populations. Crow and Kimura (1965), using a different model, found that, on the contrary, recombination is more important in large than in small populations.

Full-fledged sexual reproduction involves the union of the nuclei of two cells, gametes, followed sooner or later by meiosis and the formation of new gametes that contain half as many chromosomes as the zygote did. This occurs in eukaryotes, from protozoans to man. A remarkable variety of phenomena of gene recombination exists also, however, in prokaryotes, which lack discrete nuclei. One of the mechanisms is DNA-mediated transformation, described in Chapter 2. First discovered in pneumococci, it has been found in several other microorganisms, among them *Bacillus subtilis* and *Hemophilus influenzae*. How widespread gene recombination by transformation may be in nature is, however, an open question.

The already classical work of Lederberg and Tatum showed that certain strains of *Escherichia coli* containing so-called fertility or *F* factors undergo conjugation, that is, pairwise union of cells, followed by recombination of genetic materials. The conjugating bacterial cells do not fuse, however, to form zygotes. Moreover, the exchange of genetic materials is not equal and mutual, as it is in some eukaryotic protozoans, such as paramecia. Instead, one of the conjugating cells ($F^+$) is the donor of a chromosome, which is transferred as a whole or in part to the recipient ($F^-$) cell. Thereupon, recombination of the indigenous and the transferred chromosomes takes place (Jacob and Wollman 1961). Escherichia and probably other bacteria have a single chromosome, which is a closed circle.

Apparently the most widespread and important gene recombination mechanism in prokaryotes is transduction, first studied in Salmonella and Escherichia. This involves the transfer of genetic materials from one cell to another by means of a temperate phage serving as a vector. A temperate phage does not normally cause lysis of the bacterial cell in which it occurs, but reproduces at the same rate as the cell containing it. It may migrate, however, from one cell to another, doing this without the cells coming into physical contact, as in conjugation. The phage carries a part of the genetic material of the bacterial cell, and this material may undergo recombination with the chromosome of the recipient cell. In specialized transduction, a phage transfers only some particular section of the host chromosome, rather than any part of it. Different strains of bacteriophages may also undergo recombination with each other if two or more of them infect simultaneously the same host bacterial cells.

It must be understood, of course, that in prokaryotes, and also in some eukaryotes, gene exchange occurs by no means in every generation. Several or many asexual generations are interposed between the recurrent recombination events. This evolutionary pattern makes sense. Indeed, gene recombination is just as efficient in making new gene constellations as in breaking them. Suppose that a highly fit gene combination $A_2B_2$ has arisen in a population predominantly $A_1B_1$. If the genes $A$ and $B$ are not linked, meiosis in an $A_1A_2B_1B_2$ heterozygote will produce only one-quarter of $A_2B_2$ gametes. By contrast, asexual reproduction of $A_2B_2$ individuals will yield (barring mutation) all $A_2B_2$ offspring. By the time the next sexual generation occurs, the fitter genotype is likely to have multiplied in comparison to its frequency in the generation in which it arose.

### The Retrogression of Sexuality—Selfing

Viewed in the aspect of the adaptation of a species to its environment, gene recombination amounts to evolutionary experimentation. It produces swarms of new genotypes, some of which may be advantageous in some environments. By the same token, genotypes will arise that will be disadvantageous and will be discriminated against by natural selection. The life cycle of a mammal or a tree may be longer than that of a bacterium by four or more orders of magnitude. In more complex organisms, especially higher animals, fertilization, meiosis, and gene recombination occur in every generation.

Asexual reproduction is found predominantly in microorganisms. As Stebbins (1950) has stated:

Organisms like bacteria, fungi, and the smaller algae are usually small in size, are destroyed in huge numbers by their enemies, and depend for their survival chiefly on their ability to build up large populations rapidly in favorable medium. During the periods of increase the production of any organism not adapted to this medium is a wasted effort on the part of a population whose very life depends on reproductive efficiency. Such a growing population cannot experiment with new gene combinations; it must sacrifice flexibility to immediate fitness.

The necessity of such sacrifice under some circumstances explains why sexuality, as well as gene recombination, which is its corollary, went into eclipse in many evolutionary lines.

Some invertebrate animals and most higher plants are hermaphrodites. The production of both female and male gametes in the same individual makes self-fertilization possible but by no means necessary. There is a great diversity of contrivances that increase the probability of cross-fertilization in hermaphrodites or even ensure that it will occur. The most radical one is self-sterility, which makes the male gametes unable to fertilize the female gametes of the same individual. Selfing is rare or absent in most hermaphroditic snails and oligochaete worms, but it seems to be the rule in the remarkable hermaphroditic fish, *Rivulus marmoratus* (Harrington and Kallman 1968). Elsewhere self- and cross-pollination or insemination are both possible, and their relative frequencies vary all the way from zero to 100 percent. Self-pollination is obligatory, however, in so-called cleistogamous flowers, which are so constructed that foreign pollen is excluded (e.g., subterranean clover, Morley and Katznelson 1965).

Stebbins (1950, 1957), Grant (1958), Allard (1965), and others have sought to relate the reproductive biology to the ecological characteristics of higher plants. Among 101 species of grasses examined by Stebbins, 26 species are self-incompatible and hence cross-pollinated. All of them are perennial in growth habit, half of them being rhizomatous (underground stems or runners) and the other half cespitose (matted). Among 32 self-pollinating species, 27 are annuals and 5 cespitose perennial. The intermediate group of 43 species, in which both selfing and crossing are frequent, contains 39 cespitose perennials, 1 rhizomatous perennial, and 3 annuals. One of the advantages of selfing is that formation of seeds is assured regardless of possible shortage of insect pollinators and unfavorable weather conditions. This is evidently more important for annual than for perennial plants. Another possible advantage is that a self-pollinating population can withstand occasional reduction to very small size (Moore and Lewis 1965), and that new colonies may start from a single seed.

Selfing is a form of evolutionary opportunism, which sacrifices the evolutionary plasticity given by gene recombination for immediate, and perhaps ephemeral, adaptive advantages. According to Stebbins (1957), it leads into an evolutionary "blind alley," because "it apparently closes the door to the elaboration of radically new adaptive devices. On the other hand, a group of species may travel a long way down this 'alley' by evolving new variations on the theme laid down for them by their cross-fertilizing ancestors."

The studies of Allard and his school (Allard 1965, Harding, Allard, and Smeltzer 1966; Jain and Marshall 1967; Jain 1969, and references therein) have disclosed that the genetic system in at least some self-pollinators preserves more genetic variability than was formerly thought possible. Thus, despite more than 95 percent frequency of selfing in populations of lima beans (*Phaseolus lunatus*), the populations maintain a balanced polymorphism for the alleles S and s of a certain gene, the heterozygotes Ss having a fitness higher than the homozygotes SS and ss. Furthermore, the heterotic advantage is frequency-dependent; it is greatest when the heterozygotes are rare in a population. A parallel situation has been found in barley.

The two wild oats species, *Avena fatua* and *A. barbata*, are introduced weeds that are highly successful in California. The former species has only 3–5 percent of outcrossing by cross-pollination, whereas in the latter outcrossing is even less frequent. The wild populations of both show considerable variability, the nature of which is interestingly different in the two species. The variability in *A. barbata* is to a large extent due to a reaction norm permitting adaptive phenotypic plasticity; that in *A. fatua* shows genetic polymorphisms maintained by heterotic balancing selection.

*Festuca microstachys* is an array of many genetically different lines, reproducing almost exclusively by selfing. Allard and Kannenberg (1968) found no evidence of cross-pollination in some 20,000 individuals. Individual plants here appear to be homozygous, and yet the natural populations are genetically highly diversified, because they are complex mixtures of numerous selfing pure lines. Systematists have subdivided *F. microstachys* into eight named "species." Since they are aggregations of noninterbreeding pure lines, rather than Mendelian populations, giving them one or eight or some other number of Latin names is an arbitrary procedure.

Such arbitrariness has plagued the systematics of other selfing plants as well (Mansfield 1951 and Schwanitz 1967). For example, the name *Triticum aestivum* (or *T. vulgare*) applies to at least 404 varieties of soft wheats. They represent mostly different combinations of a smaller number of genetic characteristics and preserve their distinctiveness when propagated by self-pollination.

## The Retrogression of Sexuality—Apomixis

Selfing conserves the outer appearances and the underlying basic processes of sexual reproduction—flowers or genitalia, meiosis, female and male gametes. Only fertilization is, in a sense, frustrated; the uniting gametes are formed in the same individual. Selfing and crossing are often facultative, and both may occur with varying frequencies in the populations of the same species (Rick, 1947, 1950).

Apomixis dispenses with the union of gametes. The variety of apomictic phenomena is quite impressive (see Gustafsson 1947, Stebbins 1950, White 1954, Carson 1967, and Suomalainen 1969). The opportunism of biological evolution is displayed in full view: the sexuality has been allowed to break down in many different ways.

In parthenogenesis, an egg cell develops into an embryo and ultimately an adult without fertilization. In some plants, the embryo sac develops normally, but the meiosis is suppressed, giving rise to an ovule with the diploid chromosome number, which develops without fertilization (diplospory). Instead, the embryo sac may be pushed aside, and the embryo develops from the diploid somatic tissue (apospory, adventitious embryony). Curiously enough, in some apomictic plants (Citrus, Rubus, and others) pollination of the flowers is necessary for the production of germinable seed, although the ovule does not unite with the male gamete (pseudogamy). Still other apomicts no longer flower or mature seeds; they reproduce entirely by bulbs, bulbils, runners, stolons, etc. (e.g., the water weed *Elodea canadensis* in Europe).

Arrhenotokous parthenogenesis is found in hymenopteran and in a few representatives of other insect orders (such as scolytid beetles, Takenouchi and Takagi 1967). The females are diploid and come from eggs fertilized by spermatozoa; the males are haploid and develop from unfertilized eggs. Here the evolutionary advantages of sex are preserved, because gene recombination occurs regularly at meiosis in females. Hymenoptera are perhaps the most progressive order of insects. Thelytokous parthenogenesis is a very different phenomenon, resembling diplospory in plants. Meiosis is usually suppressed, and unfertilized eggs yield only or mostly females so that the populations are then unisexual. An outlandish situation has been discovered, however, in the amazon molly, *Mollienesia formosa* (C. P. Haskins, E. F. Haskins, and Hewitt 1960, Kallman 1962, and Hubbs 1964). Populations of this fish consist of females, which are "sexual parasites." They attract males of related species (*M. latipinna* and *M. sphenops*) to inseminate them; their eggs require for development stimulation by spermatozoa, but the sperm nuclei are eliminated. Hence the progeny of a female is identical with the mother in genotype. In a colony of *M. formosa* studied by Kallman, roughly 80 percent of the individuals belonged to only two clones.

Several, though mostly short-range, evolutionary advantages explain the sacrifice of sex in favor of apomixis. In contrast to self-fertilization, apomixis facilitates the maintenance of heterozygosity and of the resulting hybrid vigor. We saw in Chapters 5 and 7 that the polymorphism maintained by heterotic balancing selection entails a "price"; homozygotes whose fitness is lower than that of the heterozygotes are inevitably produced in every generation. With many polymorphisms the "price" is likely to be too high. Apogamy offers an escape, if all of the offspring have (barring mutation) the same genotype as their mother.

Where apomixis has not displaced fertilization entirely, the high heterozygosity of apomictic strains can be brought to light. Thus, in the blue grass Poa apomictic progenies are usually uniform, whereas sexual progenies evince great variability, sometimes no two individuals being alike. This explains one of the sad pages in the history of genetics. Mendel's experiments on the crossing of hawkweeds (Hieracium) appeared to him to give results contradictory to those he obtained in his classical work on peas. Mendel did not know that most hawkweeds are highly heterozygous apomicts.

Apomixis facilitates the establishment of polyploids, particularly those with odd numbers of chromosome complements, triploids, pentaploids, etc. We saw in Chapter 11 that polyploids are rare in nature in bisexual animals; polyploidy in animals is usually combined with parthenogenesis and unisexual populations. Triploid and tetraploid races and species have long been known, however, in the brine shrimp Artemia, wood lice (Trichoniscus, moth Solenobia, and earthworms Eisenia and Allolobophora (review in White 1954). The extensive studies of Suomalainen (1962, 1969) brought to light many parthenogenetic triploid and tetraploid species and races of weevils (Curculionidae), closely related to species that are bisexual, diploid, and presumably ancestral. Parthenogenetic triploid strains have been discovered even in vertebrates, such as a goldfish (Cherfas 1966) and a lizard (Darevsky 1966).

Apomixis, like polyploidy, is more widespread in the plant than in the animal kingdom. Apomictic species are found in many families, together with sexual ones. Many plants can reproduce both by apomixis and by cross-pollination, thus exploiting the advantages of both types of reproductive biology—generating ever new genotypes by recombination, and guarding the genotypes of proven fitness by the prevention of recombination. Some genetic systems are inherently unstable, however, and can be perpetuated only by asexual means. In this category are polyploidy with odd numbers of chromosome sets (triploids, pentaploids), and aneuploidy with some of the chromosomes triplicated whereas others are diploid. Such bizarre genotypes have, nevertheless, high fitness in some wild and especially in cultivated plants, and are conserved by apomixis (including artificial grafting and propagation by cutting and replanting in cultivated forms). Some garden plants (e.g., bananas) have lost sexual reproduction entirely, although their wild relatives mature seeds.

The transition from normal bisexual crossing to parthenogenesis has been studied experimentally in Drosophila by Stalker (1954) and Carson (1967a,b). In several species of Drosophila a small proportion of eggs can develop without fertilization, and at least one species, *Drosophila mangabeirai,* has parthenogenesis as the normal method of reproduction. In *D. mercatorum,* Carson was able, by selection, to increase the proportion of parthenogenetic eggs from about 0.1 to 6.4 percent. In nature, the selective stimulus comes from the presence of chromosomal structural heterozygosis, which would cause semisterility under cross-fertilization. Such structural heterozygosis has been found in the parthenogenetic fly *Lonchoptera dubia* (Stalker 1956), in parthenogenetic Drosophila (the works of Stalker and Carson, cited above), in grasshoppers (White, Cheney, and Key 1963), and in many plant apomicts.

When apomixis and selfing become the predominant or exclusive methods of reproduction, they make the delimitation of species a perplexing problem. Botanists have long regarded such genera as Rubus, Crataegus, and Hieracium as notoriously "difficult" (Gustafsson 1947, Stebbins 1950, and Hedberg 1955; see also Maslin 1968 on parthenogenetic vertebrates). The opinions of different authorities on what constitutes a species in these genera vary so widely that it is not uncommon to find one investigator uniting under a single specific name a complex of forms divided by other botanists into numerous "species." The subdivision of the mass of clones into the species *Escherichia coli, Salmonella typhosa,* and S. *enteritidis* is also a matter of taste; one might just as well regard all of them as a single species.

This does not mean that the diversity in asexual groups is continuous. On the contrary, aggregations of many more or less clearly distinct genotypes, each of which reproduces its like, are found. Although the carriers of these genotypes are sometimes called elementary species, they are not integrated groups, like the species in the cross-fertilizing forms. The term elementary species is, therefore, misleading and should be discarded. The existing genotypes do not embody all the combinations of genes potentially possible. As in cross-fertilizing organisms, the genotypes in the asexual ones are clustered on "adaptive peaks," while "adaptive valleys" remain uninhabited. Furthermore, the clusters are arranged in an hierarchical order, in a way again analogous to that in sexual forms. Some of the clusters may, then, be designated as species, others as subgenera, still others as genera, and so on. Which one of these ranks is ascribed to a given cluster is, however, a matter only of convenience, and the decision is in this sense arbitrary. The species, as a category less arbitrary than the rest, is lacking in asexual and obligatory self-fertilizing organisms.

### A Genetic Tour de Force—Oenothera

Two plant genera, Hieracium and Oenothera, have played curiously opposite roles in the history of genetics. Mendel, as stated in the preceding section, was frustrated by the results of his experiments on Hieracium, which he was unable to interpret since he did not know that these plants are apogamic. Some years later, de Vries developed his mutation theory on the basis of his work on *Oenothera lamarckiana,* also unaware of the peculiarities of the genetic system in his object. Some of his "mutations" were not mutations at all, but rare recombination products. Many ingenious studies by Renner, Cleland, Emerson, Darlington, Catcheside, Oehlkers, and others were needed to decipher the peculiarities of this genetic system (reviews in Cleland 1950, Stebbins 1950, and Grant 1964a).

Species of Oenothera are widespread in North America; some of them (including *Oenothera lamarckiana*) have become successful weeds when introduced into Europe. *Oenothera hookeri* in California and adjacent states is large-flowered and mostly cross-pollinated, and its 14 chromosomes form 7 bivalents at meiosis. A swarm of other "species," especially in the eastern United States, are permanent translocation heterozygotes, exhibiting at meiosis rings of from 4 to all 14 chromosomes, and from 5 to 0 bivalents. *Oenothera lamarckiana* forms a ring of 12 chromosomes and a single bivalent. The meiotic disjunction of the chromosomes is generally regular, with adjacent chromosomes in the ring going to opposite poles and alternate chromosomes to the same pole; the formation of aneuploid gametes is thus avoided (see Chapter 5). The chromosomes involved in the ring form two "complexes"; the members of each complex are transmitted together, as effectively as though they were a single chromosome and the genes contained in them a single linkage group. The ring-forming oenotheras are mostly small-flowered and self-pollinated. Permanent heterozygosity for the two complexes is tenaciously conserved, and the production of homozygous seeds is obviated by a peculiar mechanism of two different nonallelic lethals, one being included in each complex. Either these lethals may act in early zygotes, or else one of them eliminates the pollen and the other the embryo sac that carries it.

What is the evolutionary meaning of this eccentric genetic system? It combines the advantages of heterosis with the assured seed set from selfing. Chromosomal inversions in Drosophila protect from recombination the supergenes contained in these chromosomes, which yield heterosis in the inversion heterozygotes (Chapter 5). *Oenothera lamarckiana* has, in effect, two grand supergenes in the complexes of the chromosomes forming the ring, and merely a single pair of chromosomes left to form a bivalent at meiosis. The occurrence of new translocations or of rare recombinations between the supergenes produces some of the "mutants" that de Vries observed in his classical work.

In addition to Oenothera, some other plants have attempted the same genetic tour de force. *Rhoeo discolor* has all of its 12 chromosomes forming a single ring at meiosis; it belongs to a monotypic genus of the family Commelinaceae. Some species of Clarkia (Onagraceae, the family to which Oenothera also belongs), Trillium (Liliaceae), Paeonia (Paeoniaceae), and others have gone a part of the way in the same direction.

## Rudimentation and Regressive Evolution

Evolution is opportunistic; genetic changes are favored by natural selection if they increase the Darwinian fitness of their carriers at a given time and place, regardless of whether they might be favorable or otherwise in the long run. Any adaptive peak, however temporary, is occupied by a population, if it is at all accessible. Adaptation to new environments may decrease the importance of some organs and functions that were vital in past environments; such organs and functions may then become vestigial and disappear. Zoology and botany provide an abundance of examples of the rudimentation and disappearance of organs, especially among obligatory parasites. Thus many internal parasites have lost the alimentary canal and sense organs, such as eyes, that were doubtless present in their free-living ancestors. Some parasitic plants have lost the chlorophyll. If the acquisition of these organs and substances was a result of progressive evolution, then their disappearance can only be designated as regressive evolution.

Some of the best examples of rudimentation are encountered among cave inhabitants. Reduction and disappearance of the eyes and of the pigmentation of the body, as well as development of organs with tactile functions and of specialized behavior patterns, are observed in cave animals, from vertebrates to insects, crustaceans, and flatworms. Excellent reviews of the pertinent evidence are those of Vandel (1964), Barr (1968), and Poulson and White (1969). Instances in which the same or closely related species occur in the caves, as well as out of them, are particularly enlightening, since here the processes of adaptation to subterranean life may be studied. The variability in the structure of such organs as the eyes within the population of a single cave may be striking. Some individuals have fully developed eyes, whereas in others only rudiments are present; some individuals are fully pigmented, and others colorless. Aberrant individuals resembling the cave forms in certain particulars may be found in the surface populations as well, but their frequency outside the caves is small.

Although some of these variations have been proved to be hereditary, no less important is the extraordinary phenotypic plasticity of certain characters of cave animals. Many years ago Kammerer showed that the salamander *Proteus anguinus,* which, when kept in the dark, has vestigial eyes and little or no pigment, develops eyes and a black pigmentation when grown under light. The genotype of an organism is, in general, adjusted to ensure the development of vital organs and functions in the environments likely to be encountered; a deterioration of this adjustment may be one of the first steps of the rudimentation process.

The phenomena of rudimentation were happy hunting grounds for those who believed that acquired modifications are heritable. If such a Lamarckian explanation is ruled out, two hypotheses need be considered. First, mutation pressure may lead to rudimentation if not opposed by natural selection. Mutations that weaken or destroy an organ are more frequent than those that strengthen it; so long as the functioning of an organ is vital to its possessors, selection will discriminate against such mutations. When an organ ceases to be vital, selection is relaxed and the organ may regress. There is little evidence, however, that this actually happens. Post (1962, 1964, 1965) and Wolpoff (1969) compiled data suggesting that relaxation of the selection in human populations against such traits as color blindness and lessened hearing acuity may lead to increases in their frequencies. Wright (1964a) and Prout (1964) noted the extreme improbability of mutation alone causing the disappearance of an organ in a species, although such a view has been urged by Brace (1963).

Second, natural selection may favor the rudimentation of functionless organs. Weismann introduced the idea of a struggle of parts of the body; since it takes energy to build an organ, genetic changes that remove a superfluous organ save energy and thereby acquire positive adaptive value (Barr 1968 traces this idea back to Darwin, St. Hilaire, and Goethe). Evidence in favor of this view has been summarized by, among others, Rensch (1960), Barr (1968), and Byers (1969). In the nature of things, a direct test of the hypothesis is hardly possible; perhaps the best that can be said in its favor is that it does not encounter objections of the kind Wright and Prout raised against the mutation theory.

## Reticulate Evolution

Reproductive isolation and gene recombination resulting from sexual processes stand in mutual opposition. Sex generates a diversity of genotypes, among which there may arise some highly fit ones, which will be promoted by natural selection. Reproductive isolation, on the other hand, hinders or prevents gene exchange between populations that occupy different adaptive peaks. It wards off the origination of swarms of disharmonious gene patterns, and thus conserves the historically evolved arrays of genotypes that constitute the biological species. The conflict is resolved by a compromise. The frequency of gene exchange between Mendelian populations is regulated, so that genetic adaptability is maintained at the price of elimination of the smallest possible numbers of genotypes of low fitness. As could be expected, the compromise is reached in different organisms at different points in the gene exchange-reproductive isolation continuum. By and large, the reproductive isolation of animal species is more rigid than that of plant species. In stable environments, gene recombination is less likely to produce improved genotypes than in natural, and especially in man-made, environments that are in flux.

Infiltration of the genes of one species into another is termed introgression (Anderson 1949). There has been some controversy concerning how widespread and how important in evolution introgressive hybridization is. That it sometimes occurs is undeniable, but some authors have succumbed to the temptation of attributing universality to their special discoveries. Judicious reviews of botanical evidence can be found in Stebbins (1950, 1958b), Grant (1963), and Ehrendorfer (1963), and of zoological results in Mayr (1963) and Remington (1968). Some examples of introgression in both animals and plants were given in Chapters 10 and 11, in connection with the discussion of isolating mechanisms.

Riley (1952 and earlier) described a particularly clear example of introgression in the populations of *Iris fulva* and *I. hexagona* var. *gigantocaerulea*, which inhabit the Mississippi Delta region. The former species grows by preference on clay soils and in shade, whereas the latter prefers tidal marshes and full sun. This ecological isolation has suffered a breakdown because of the destruction of the forests and the drainage of the swamps for pastures. It is especially in such man-made habitats that hybrids between these Iris species are found; the $F_1$ hybrids are partially sterile, but backcrosses to the parental species give rise to populations of *I. hexagona* with some genes derived from *I. fulva*.

An equally convincing case of introgression is that between the sunflowers *Helianthus annuus, H. bolanderi,* and *H. petiolaris* (Heiser 1947). Many sunflower populations are now weeds growing on disturbed soils, and they have arisen by introgressive hybridization of two or more ancestral species. Some species of Eucalyptus in Australia have formed hybrid swarms (for examples, see Clifford and Binet 1954), and so have some species of oaks (Muller 1952 and Forde 1962), Liatris (Levin 1968), and certain other plants. Viemeyer (1958) states that species of Penstemon may amalgamate to a common gene pool by hybridization, and similar claims have been made for other plants (e.g., blueberries, Vaccinium) by other authors. The elegant work of Ownbey (1950) has shown that three species of Tragopogon in the northwestern United States have formed hybrids, which by doubling the chromosome complements gave rise to three derived allopolyploid species.

Some of the alleged cases of introgressive hybridization in animals need critical re-examination. According to Mayr (1963), secondary intergradation occurs when populations that were allopatric in the past come into contact again. Remington (1968), has stated, "From a study of the geographic occurrences of contemporary hybridization among North American animals, it has become apparent that most of the hybrids are produced in a few relatively localized zones, with little hybridizing in the vast areas between these zones of mixing." He records six major and seven minor mixing zones, which he calls suture zones, in the United States and Canada.

The hybridization of formerly ecologically isolated species in new habitats disturbed by human activities belongs in a different category. The two toad species, *Bufo americanus* and *B. fowleri,* discussed in Chapter 10, exemplify this situation. Other likely examples are the hybrids of fish species Notropis (Hubbs and Strawn 1956), turtles Pseudemys (Crenshaw 1965a), and birds—red-eyed towhees (Sibley 1954), orioles (Sibley and Short 1964), and flickers (Short 1965). Inferential but fairly convincing evidence of hybridization exists also for butterflies Pieris (Petersen 1955), leafhoppers (Ross 1958), coccinellid beetles Chilocorus in America (Smith 1962, 1966) and in central Asia (Zaslavsky 1966, 1967), and two species of Drosophila (Pipkin 1968). On the other hand, what appeared to be hybridization in nature of two species of the fruit fly Dacus has been rendered questionable by the study of Gibbs (1968).

Why introgression is more frequent in plants than in animals, and in some groups than in others, is not completely clear. Stebbins (1950, 1958b) and Grant (1958, 1963, 1966c) have advanced some interesting hypotheses. Many plants are perennial, long lived, or capable of asexual reproduction. An individual or a clone may persist for centuries or even millennia. Sexual reproduction by seeds serves in such plants to maintain genetic adaptability and evolutionary plasticity. This gives more freedom for wide outcrossing than exists in animals, where sexual union and gene recombination are obligatory in every generation. Furthermore, the open system of growth and the relative simplicity of plant tissues, as contrasted with the closed system of growth and the great complexity of tissues and organ systems in animals, are also relevant. The fitness of an animal genotype depends on the entire constellation of its genes, as an integrated whole, whereas in plants the genes may affect fitness more nearly independently.

## DNA Hybridization

The discovery of the so-called *in vitro* DNA hybridization has opened new possibilities for assessing the genetic similarities and differences between organisms that cannot be hybridized. The double-helical structure of DNA in solution is denatured by heating to nearly 100°C. The resulting single strands of DNA can be renatured, made to come together in pairs, when the solution is cooled. The pairing is specific, that is, the new pairs formed consist of strands that have wholly or at least largely complementary sequences of nucleotides. The amount of pairing between DNA strands of different species decreases as the nucleotide sequences become more and more unlike.

There are several techniques to make the assessment quantitative. Suppose that one wishes to compare the DNA's of species A and B. The DNA from species A is heated to separate the polynucleotide strands, mixed with a solution of agar, and cooled quickly to prevent reunion of the strands. The single strands of A are now immobilized in the agar gel. The DNA of species B is marked with a radioactive tracer, broken by mechanical shearing into fragments of some hundreds of nucleotides, and heated to separate the strands. The single-stranded fragments of B are then incubated at 60°C with A strands entrapped in the agar. The fragments are small enough to penetrate the agar gel and to form duplex structures with the immobilized strands, provided that they find sufficiently similar mates. The amounts of reassociated and of left-over DNA are assayed by measurement of the radioactivity.

McCarthy and Bolton (1963) compared the amounts of binding of DNA fragments of *Escherichia coli* with agar-bound DNA's of certain other bacteria and other organisms. If the amount of binding of the *E. coli* fragments with the conspecific DNA in agar is taken as 100, the binding with other DNA's is estimated as follows:

| | | | |
|---|---|---|---|
| *Salmonella typhimurium* | 71 | *Serratia marcescens* | 7 |
| *Shigella dysenteriae* | 71 | *Pseudomonas aeroginosa* | 1 |
| *Aerobacter aerogenes* | 51 | T2 bacteriophage | 1 |

Hoyer, McCarthy, and Bolton (1964) and Hoyer, Bolton, et al. (1965) made extensive experiments comparing the hybridizing abilities of DNA's from man, chimpanzee, Old World and New World monkeys, prosimians, mouse, hamster, guinea pig, chicken, and salmon. As expected, the DNA's of animals belonging to the same family are more similar than those of different families of the same order, of the same order more similar than of different orders, and of the same class more similar than of different classes. An attempt was made to correlate the similarity of the DNA's to the amounts of time elapsed since the separation of the phylogenetic branches to which the animals belong, as estimated by paleontologists. The result is shown in Fig. 12.1. A tolerably good linear relationship is obtained between the logarithms of the DNA similarity and the times of divergence.

A somewhat different technique was used by Laird and McCarthy (1968a) to compare the DNA's of three species of Drosophila. Denatured DNA of one species was entrapped on a nitrocellulose mem-

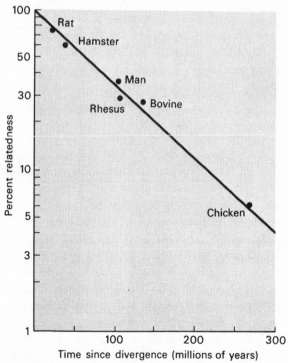

**FIGURE 12.1**

The relatedness, measured by the reaction of DNA fragments of different vertebrates with those of the house mouse, and its correlation with the time elapsed since the presumed separation of the respective evolutionary lines. (From Hoyer, McCarthy, and Bolton)

brane filter. The DNA of two species, labeled with a hydrogen isotope, was fragmented by shearing and denatured by heating to 95°C. The fragments of the DNA's were then made to compete for reunion with the DNA strands of one of them immobilized in the filter. The more similar are the DNA's, the greater proportions of the fragments find their homologues among the strands in the filter.

The magnitude of the differences found between species of the same genus is considered surprising by the authors. *Drosophila simulans* and *D. melanogaster* have about 80 percent of DNA sequences in common, and 20 percent "too distantly related to form stable duplexes." These species are related closely enough to give some viable, though completely sterile, hybrids. On the other hand, *D. funebris,* which belongs to a different subgenus and is not crossable to the other two, has only about 25 percent of common sequences. Contrary to the opinions of some geneticists (see Chapter 11), species formation entails genotypic reconstructions more profound than the substitution of a few "lucky" mutant alleles.

## Redundancy in Genetic Materials

To interpret correctly the evolutionary implications of the results just described, it must be kept in mind that the "common" sequences in the DNA fragments do not necessarily contain identical genes. Gene alleles that differ in several mutational stages by nucleotide substitutions may well be carried in "common" sequences. The proportions of the gene differences between the species arrived at from DNA hybridization experiments are more likely, therefore, to be underestimates than overestimates. On the other hand, the genetic endowment of the same species and individual may contain redundancies, that is, some genes may be represented by numerous copies. This fact was mentioned in Chapter 1. Britten and Kohne (1968) found that in eukaryotic, though apparently not in prokaryotic, organisms, from 15 to 80 percent of the DNA consists of sequences repeated from 100 to 1,000,000 times. The remaining 85 to 20 percent appears to be unique sequences, although the technique used would probably not distinguish between unique sequences and those repeated two or even several times.

The estimates are deduced from the speed of the reassociation of the DNA fragments with DNA strands immobilized in agar or on filters.

The more copies of a sequence that are available, the sooner a fragment is likely to encounter its mate. Conversely, unique sequences may only come into contact with similar ones after a considerable lapse of time, or may never chance to encounter them. In some animals (calf) Britten and Kohne found an apparent discontinuity between a fraction of some 40 percent of DNA, which reassociates rapidly, and one that does so very slowly. By contrast, many degrees of repetition are present in the DNA of a fish (salmon sperm), varying continuously from perhaps 100 to 100,000 copies. In *Drosophila melanogaster* the estimated proportion of partially redundant sequences is only 10 percent (Laird and McCarthy 1968b).

Reduplication of genes has long been recognized as an important evolutionary process. On the assumption that primordial life was represented by a single gene, the thousands of different genes now found in the same gamete in most organisms must be the diverged descendants of the primordial gene. Visible evidence of gene multiplication in the phylogeny can be seen under the microscope in the giant chromosomes of the salivary glands of Drosophila and other flies. The so-called repeats are groups of from two to ten similar stainable discs, which are constantly present at different locations in the same chromosome set. Their genetic homologies are attested to not only by a visible similarity but also by a tendency to somatic pairing. The repeats consist of genes homologous because of common descent. These homologous genes may gradually diverge in structure, however, as a result of the occurrence and fixation of different mutations. Fitch and Margoliash (1970) distinguish two kinds of homologous genes: orthologous genes remain similar in function, as the different hemoglobin genes of the vertebrates; paralogous genes diverge to assume different functions, as the hemoglobin and myoglobin genes.

Redundant and unique genes within the same genotypes may, however, play different roles. Wallace (1963a), Stebbins (1969), and Britten and Davidson (1969) have independently arrived at similar hypotheses that are relevant at this point. Their substance is that most structural genes are found among the unique genetic materials, while the redundant fraction of the genetic endowment may consist mainly of regulatory or controlling genetic elements. The highly complex developmental processes in higher organisms may require a minority of relatively stable structural genes, outnumbered by more labile controlling genes.

According to Wallace, his hypothetical model

does not require variation of structural genes; the stability of DNA and of the amino acid sequences this material encodes does not conflict with our model in any way. This remarkable stability is entirely compatible, however, with genetic variation and with the series of isoalleles revealed by experiments of population geneticists. This variation lies in what may be called the "physiological" as opposed to the "structural" gene and its controlling element.

Britten and Davidson point out that repeated DNA sequences are interspersed with unique sequences, and state, "This is precisely the pattern required in our model if repeated sequences are usually or often regulatory in function." The above authors, as well as Stebbins, surmise that in the evolution of higher organisms genetic changes in the regulatory mechanisms, rather than in the structural genes, play the leading role. Stebbins, in particular, sees here a likely genetic matrix of progressive evolution. It is probably premature to attempt to transform these interesting hypotheses into a more elaborate theoretical structure. Further studies in this field must be awaited with intense interest.

## Protein Phylogenies

In the fullness of time, the sequences of the genetic "letters," the nucleotides, in all genes of all organisms may imaginably, become known. It would then be possible to quantify the similarities and the differences between organisms and to erect a classification of living things, based on precise information about their genetic endowments. Although this utopia is very remote, it is becoming possible to determine and to compare the amino acid sequences in the orthologous and paralogous (see the preceding section) proteins of the same and of different species. Different amino acids are often found in similar positions in these linear sequences. Each amino acid in a protein, as we have seen, corresponds to a triplet of nucleotides in the DNA of the gene that codes for this protein. Consequently, it is possible to compute the mutation distances between homologous proteins; the mutation distance is defined "as the minimal number of nucleotides that would need to be altered in order for the gene for one protein to code for the other" (Fitch and Margoliash 1967b). Mutation distances between cytochromes c of organisms ranging from man to yeasts are shown in Table 12.1. A single mutation could transform human cytochrome c into that of a monkey, or vice versa. Some 66 mutations are needed, however, to effect a transformation of human and a yeast (Candida) cytochrome into each other.

Some aspects of protein evolution were considered in Chapters 2 and 8. The point that is essential for us here is that the amino acid sequences in certain proteins of different organisms are far too similar for these likenesses to be ascribed to chance. It is only reasonable to suppose that these proteins are homologous, and that the genes coding for them have descended by gradual accumulation of mutational changes from the same gene in a common ancestor (Ingram 1963, Zuckerkandl and Pauling 1965, Jukes 1966, Margoliash 1963, and others). Fig. 2.2 shows that most of the sites in different hemoglobins are occupied by the same amino acids, and even the sequence of amino acids in the myoglobin is too close to be attributed to chance. In most vertebrate animals, the alpha chains of the hemoglobins consist of 141 amino acids. In Table 8.4 it can be seen that related species (man and gorilla, horse and donkey) differ in 1 or 2 amino acids, representatives of different mammalian orders in about 20, and mammals and fish (carp) in 60–75. In addition to the hemoglobins, the most extensive comparative studies have been made on cytochrome c. The cytochromes c of representatives of different orders of mammals or birds differ in 2–17 amino acids, classes of vertebrates in 7–38, vertebrates and insects in 23–41, and animals and molds and yeasts in 56–72 (Table 12.1).

The mutation distances between homologous proteins have been used by Fitch and Margoliash (1967a,b, 1970) to construct phylogenetic trees of these proteins. Figure 12.2 shows a phylogeny of the cytochromes c. In superficial appearance, this phylogeny looks like classical phylogenetic trees of animal or plant groups constructed on the basis of morphological and paleontological information. The branches of the protein phylogenies show, however, estimates of the mutation distances between the proteins, in the present instance the cytochromes c, of any two species of organisms studied. These estimates are arrived at by statistical techniques that are simple in principle but involve calculations necessitating the use of electronic computers. Somewhat comparable, but not identical, statistical techniques were used by Cavalli-Sforza 1969, Cavalli-Sforza, Barrai, and Edwards 1964, and Cavalli-Sforza and Edwards 1964; to study the relationships

**TABLE 12.1**

Minimum numbers of mutations required to interrelate pairs of cytochromes c in the organisms studied (After Fitch and Margoliash)

| Organism | No. | Number of Mutations Required for Transformation |||||||||||||||||||
|---|---|---|---|---|---|---|---|---|---|---|---|---|---|---|---|---|---|---|---|---|
| | | 1 | 2 | 3 | 4 | 5 | 6 | 7 | 8 | 9 | 10 | 11 | 12 | 13 | 14 | 15 | 16 | 17 | 18 | 19 |
| Man | 1 | | | | | | | | | | | | | | | | | | | |
| Monkey (Macaca) | 2 | 1 | | | | | | | | | | | | | | | | | | |
| Dog | 3 | 13 | 12 | | | | | | | | | | | | | | | | | |
| Horse | 4 | 17 | 16 | 10 | | | | | | | | | | | | | | | | |
| Donkey | 5 | 16 | 15 | 8 | 1 | | | | | | | | | | | | | | | |
| Pig | 6 | 13 | 12 | 4 | 5 | 4 | | | | | | | | | | | | | | |
| Rabbit | 7 | 12 | 11 | 6 | 11 | 10 | 6 | | | | | | | | | | | | | |
| Kangaroo | 8 | 12 | 13 | 7 | 11 | 12 | 7 | 7 | | | | | | | | | | | | |
| Duck | 9 | 17 | 16 | 12 | 16 | 15 | 13 | 10 | 14 | | | | | | | | | | | |
| Pigeon | 10 | 16 | 15 | 12 | 16 | 15 | 13 | 8 | 14 | 3 | | | | | | | | | | |
| Chicken | 11 | 18 | 17 | 14 | 16 | 15 | 13 | 11 | 15 | 3 | 4 | | | | | | | | | |
| Penguin (Aptenodytes) | 12 | 18 | 17 | 14 | 17 | 16 | 14 | 11 | 13 | 3 | 4 | 2 | | | | | | | | |
| Turtle (Chelydra) | 13 | 19 | 18 | 13 | 16 | 15 | 13 | 11 | 14 | 7 | 8 | 8 | 8 | | | | | | | |
| Rattlesnake (Crotalus) | 14 | 20 | 21 | 30 | 32 | 31 | 30 | 25 | 30 | 24 | 24 | 28 | 28 | 30 | | | | | | |
| Fish (Tuna) | 15 | 31 | 32 | 29 | 27 | 26 | 25 | 26 | 27 | 26 | 27 | 26 | 27 | 27 | 38 | | | | | |
| Fly (Haematobia) | 16 | 33 | 32 | 24 | 24 | 25 | 26 | 23 | 26 | 25 | 26 | 26 | 28 | 30 | 40 | 34 | | | | |
| Moth (Samia) | 17 | 36 | 35 | 28 | 33 | 32 | 31 | 29 | 31 | 29 | 30 | 31 | 30 | 33 | 41 | 41 | 16 | | | |
| Mold (Neurospora) | 18 | 63 | 62 | 64 | 64 | 64 | 64 | 62 | 66 | 61 | 59 | 61 | 62 | 65 | 61 | 72 | 58 | 59 | | |
| Yeast (Saccharomyces) | 19 | 56 | 57 | 61 | 60 | 59 | 59 | 59 | 58 | 62 | 62 | 62 | 61 | 64 | 61 | 66 | 63 | 60 | 57 | |
| Yeast (Candida) | 20 | 66 | 65 | 66 | 68 | 67 | 67 | 67 | 68 | 66 | 66 | 66 | 65 | 67 | 69 | 69 | 65 | 61 | 61 | 41 |

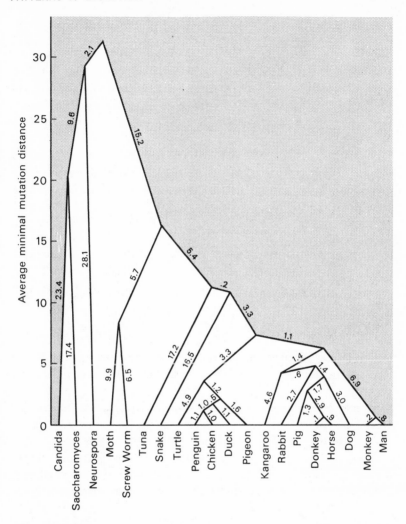

**FIGURE 12.2**

Phylogenetic relationships of the cytochromes c of different organisms. Further explanation in text. (From Fitch and Margoliash)

of human populations examined genetically and morphologically (see Chapter 8).

Without in the least underestimating the ingenuity and the promise of the method, some inconsistencies in the phylogeny in Fig. 12.2 must be indicated (they are recognized by Fitch and Margoliash 1970, themselves). The turtle turns out to be one of the birds, and quite remote from the only other reptile studied, the rattlesnake. The primates (man and monkey) branch off from the mammalian stem before the marsupial (kangaroo) does. Such inconsistencies cause no surprise to students of phylogenies; they are bound to occur if only a single trait is examined, even so sophisticated a one as the structure of a kind of protein.

A phylogeny of the protein chains composing the hemoglobins and the myoglobins has been constructed with the aid of similar methods (Zuckerkandl 1965 and Fitch and Margoliash 1967b). The kind of hemoglobin found most abundantly in the human adult consists of two alpha and two beta chains, of 141 and 146 amino acids, respectively. In the embryo and in the newborn, however, the prevalent hemoglobin consists of two alpha and two gamma chains. In addition, in the adult there is a relatively small amount of hemoglobin with beta replaced by delta chains. Myoglobin molecules are single chains of 153 amino acids each. All these kinds of molecules (or, rather, the genes coding for them) are descendants of a common gene that was present in a remote ancestor, perhaps a primitive vertebrate or an even earlier form. This gene underwent four duplications, giving rise to five genes, which diverged by accumulating different mutational changes. The earliest duplication, dated conjecturally about 650 million years ago, gave rise to genes coding for myoglobins, on the one hand, and to those coding for hemoglobins, on the other. The second duplication happened in the hemoglobin gene, perhaps 380 million years ago, and differentiated the genes that code for alpha chains from those for the other chains. The third duplication, say 150 million years ago, differentiated the embryonic gamma from the adult beta and delta chains. The last-named ones are the most similar in the amino acid alignments, and their genes may have started to diverge only 35 million years ago (Zuckerkandl and Pauling 1965 and Zuckerkandl 1965).

## Rates of Evolution and Evolutionary "Clocks"

If genetic differences were to accumulate at identical rates in all phylogenetic lines, the amount of genetic differentiation observed would be directly proportional to the time elapsed since the separation of any two lines. It is well known that this is not the case; the paleontological record shows that some groups evolve rapidly and others slowly. The assessment of the evolutionary rates is based, of course, on comparative morphological studies. The morphological, as well as the physiological and ethological, differentiation may, however, be taken to reflect, at least roughly, the amount of genetic differences. Exceptions, such as sibling species and convergent evolutionary lines, do not invalidate the general rule.

Paleontologists, most notably Simpson (1949, 1953, 1961, and other works), have firmly established that the rates of origination and extinction (in other words the "longevity") of species, genera, and families are much higher in some groups than in others. Thus, according to Simpson, the mean "survivorship" of a genus of bivalve molluscs is 78 million years, whereas for a genus of carnivore mammals it is only about 8 million years, approximately one order of magnitude difference. The extremes differ, of course, far more than the averages. The oldest, or at any rate one of the oldest, surviving species is the crustacean *Triops cancriformes*, known from the Jurassic period, some 170 million years ago. The brachiopod genus Lingula existed in the Ordovician, 400 million years ago, but the living Lingula is supposed to be specifically distinct from its fossil predecessor. Among mammals, opossums lived in the Cretaceous, 60 million years ago. Another case of extremely slow, bradytelic evolution (or of evolution arrested) is the coelacanth fish, Latimeria, the survivor of a once widespread and abundant group. Among plants, a species of Plantago has endured for about 20 million years (Stebbins and Day 1967). Man, on the contrary, is an example of very rapid, tachytelic evolution. *Homo habilis* (also classified as *Australopithecus africanus habilis*) lived only some 1.75 million years ago (Tobias 1965). *Homo sapiens presapiens* is perhaps 200,000 years old.

The cause of the differences between evolutionary rates is a matter of speculation (Simpson 1949, Schmalhausen 1949, and Rensch 1960a). Although very little is known about the mutation rates in bradytelic and tachytelic groups, mutation is quite unlikely to be the limiting factor in evolutionary transformations. Drosophila is, compared to man, evolving slowly, and yet the best estimates of the average mutation rates per generation are about the same. The mutation rates per unit of time are consequently lower in the rapidly developing hominid line. The evolutionary rate is a complex phenomenon, having to do more with selectional than with mutational processes. Environmental changes generally speed up evolution, and constancy slows it down. As a creative process (see below), evolution has an unpredictable element (at least at the present level of our knowledge).

The term quantum evolution (Simpson 1953) refers to evolutionary events that involve all-or-none transitions: "They are changes of adaptive zone such that transitional forms between the old zone and the new cannot, or at any rate do not, persist." What is involved is the adoption of novel ways of life, and hence of novel adaptive needs and possibilities. The emergence of man from his animal ancestors is a prime example of quantum evolution. Man adapts primarily by culture and to culture, and culture does not exist, except as minuscule rudiments, in nonhuman animals.

Studies on the evolution of proteins have led to new approaches to the problem of evolutionary rates. Given the numbers of amino acid differences in a group of homologous proteins, one can estimate the mutation distances between them (see the preceding section). These estimates can then be compared to those of the times elapsed since the separation of the phyletic lines, as appraised by paleontologists. King and Jukes (1969) give the following average rates of evolution of nine kinds of proteins in mammals, expressed in terms of $10^{-10}$ substitution per triplet codon of DNA per year:

| | | | |
|---|---|---|---|
| Insulin A and B | 3.3 | Immunoglobulin light chain | 33.2 |
| Cytochrome c | 4.2 | Fibrinopeptide A | 42.9 |
| Hemoglobin alpha | 9.9 | Bovine hemoglobin fetal | |
| Hemoglobin beta | 10.3 | chain | 22.9 |
| Ribonuclease | 25.3 | Guinea pig insulin | 53.1 |

Different proteins in the same group of animals evolve at clearly different rates. We saw in Chapter 8, however, that the amino acids at some positions within a protein chain are rigidly conserved throughout the evolutionary transformations, whereas other portions of the same chains vary more or less freely. It is reasonable to infer that the amino acids in the conservative portions are indispensable for the function which the protein serves. Mutations are probably as frequent in the conservative codons as in the variable ones. The mutants in the former act as lethals or at least as subvitals, and are eliminated by the normalizing natural selection. By contrast, the mutants in the variable codons are close to neutral. If so, they are tolerated by natural selection and are allowed to drift in the gene pool of a population. Most of them are eventually lost, but some reach fixation by random walk processes. The variable portions of the proteins are, then, assumed to evolve mainly by drift, while the constant ones change very slowly, if at all, by natural selection. The assumption of a dichotomy of constant versus variable parts is alleged to be confirmed by statistical tests. The numbers of the substitutions in the variable codons fit the expectations calculated with the aid of the Poisson distribution formula (see Chapter 8). A possible source of bias in such calculations is the deliberate exclusion from consideration of codons that do not fit the assumption of randomness.

A logical next step, made by Zuckerkandl and Pauling (1965), is to suppose that substitutions of the amino acids in protein chains, or at least in the adaptively neutral parts of these chains, occur at uniform rates in time. If so, comparative studies of the protein structure in different organisms can be used as an evolutionary "clock." Knowing the mutational distances between the proteins of representatives of two or several groups of organisms, and having an estimate of the substitution rates, one can arrive at an approximate date for the separation of the ancestral phylogenetic lines of these organisms.

Perhaps the boldest essay to read this "clock" is that of Sarich and Wilson (1967, and Wilson and Sarich 1969). The phylogeny of the higher primates, including man, has several incertitudes. One of these concerns the time of divergence of the three lines, those leading to the now living great apes, to man, and to the Old World monkeys (Cercopithecidae). There is apparently good paleontological evidence which leads some authors to conclude that the three lines separated more or less simultaneously, perhaps as long as 30 million years ago. Other authorities suppose that the separation of the human and the ape stems is much more recent, perhaps 4–5 million years ago, while the divergence of these two lines from the monkeys stem occurred in greater antiquity.

The gist of Sarich and Wilson's arguments is that the serum albumins and transferrins (studied by immunological techniques), the hemoglobins (studied by amino acid sequencing), and the DNA's (studied by "hybridization"; see above) are more similar in man and the apes (chimpanzee and gorilla) than in either of these and the monkeys. The mutational distance between man and chimpanzee hemoglobins is zero, man and gorilla 2, and monkey and man or monkey and ape 15–17. The average rate of amino acid replacement in mammalian hemoglobins is 1 per some 3.5 million years. Therefore, Sarich and Wilson state, "If the probability model of protein evolution . . . is applied to this case, then it can be calculated with the Poisson distribution that there is less than one chance in $10^5$ that a sequence difference of zero to two residues could result when the divergence time was 30 million years ago. . . ." The evidence adduced by these authors is certainly impressive, but their argumentation skirts close to the edge of circularity.

## Adaptive Radiation and Group Selection

At the beginning of this chapter reference was made to the two evolutionary modes: cladogenesis or splitting, and anagenesis or phyletic evolution. These two modes are not mutually exclusive and, in fact, are combined in various proportions in most lines of descent. Simpson (1953) has said, "It is strikingly noticeable from the fossil record and from its results in the world around us that some time after a rather distinctive new adaptive type has developed it often becomes highly diversified." Anagenesis and cladogenesis together result in adaptive radiation, that is, occupation and subdivision of more and more numerous adaptive zones and ecological niches. "There has been tremendous increase in the number of broad adaptive zones and in the fineness and multiplicity of subdivision of these in the course of geologic time" (Simpson 1953).

Comparison of the diversity of species and genera in different geographic regions and different ecological circumstances is one of the possible approaches to the analytic study of adaptive radiation. It has been known for a long time that there is a greater diversity of both plants and animals in the tropics than in temperate climates, and in the latter than in cold climates. Although one does not find many species of penguins or polar bears on the Equator, the rule has considerable generality. Moreover, it applies to recent as well as to fossil, and marine as well as to land, organisms (Stehli 1968 and Stehli, Douglas, and Newell 1969). Fig. 12.3 shows that the greatest diversity of mosquito genera is found in tropical America, Asia, and Africa, and the least diversity in subarctic and subantarctic lands. It must be understood, of course, that the diversity of taxa may be the reverse of the

**423**

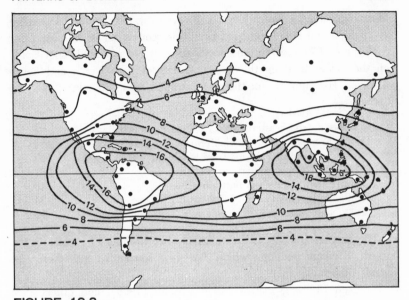

**FIGURE 12.3**

Numbers of genera of mosquitoes found in different territories. The places sampled indicated by dots. (From Stehli)

abundance of individuals. Although there may be clouds of mosquitoes in summer in northern Canada, Alaska, and Siberia, they are likely to belong to a single or a few species. In Amazonia, on the other hand, each mosquito you see is often specifically different from the last one.

Simpson (1964c) has produced probably the most careful and detailed study of the species diversity of mammals in North and Central America. He subdivided the continental area (ignoring islands) into squares 150 miles on each side and counted the numbers of species recorded in each square. An interesting and complex picture emerged. Species densities varied from 13 on the Melville peninsula (latitude 70°) to 163 in southern Costa Rica (latitude 10°). The north-south gradient is, however, far from regular. The species numbers increase from the extreme north to about the Canada-United States border, and then the diversity stays approximately constant down to the latitude 30°. The increasing trend is then resumed through Mexico to the climax in Costa Rica. A strong dependence on the topography emerges clearly. In the eastern United States the greatest diversity is found in the Appalachians, and in the West in the Rocky

Mountains and the Sierra Nevada. By contrast, the region of low relief in Yucatan and Honduras has low species counts for its latitude.

Baker (1967) records the species diversity of mammals specifically on the lowlands along the Pacific Coasts of both North and South America. His numbers for the zones studied are as follows:

| | |
|---|---:|
| Tundran (Alaska) | 25 |
| Coniferan (southeastern Alaska to San Francisco Bay) | 92 |
| North Eremian (southern California to Sonora) | 114 |
| North Subtropical (Mexico from Sinaloa to Tehuantepec) | 109 |
| Tropical (Chiapas to northern Peru) | 267 |
| South Eremian (Peru to northern Chile) | 18 |
| Nothofagian (middle and southern Chile) | 35 |
| Patagonian (southern Patagonia and Tierra del Fuego) | 10 |

The only irregularity is the relatively low number of species in the South Eremian section, which has few lowlands, and these are harsh deserts.

Simpson (1964c), Pianka (1966), Stehli (1968), and others (see the papers just mentioned for further references) have attempted to formulate hypothetical explanations of the above observations. Pianka lists six such explanations, most of which are not mutually exclusive, and all of which may be true in some situations.

1. All biotic communities diversify as time goes on; older communities have more species than younger ones. Because of glaciations, the cold-temperate and cold zone communities are the newest whereas the tropical and subtropical ones are the most ancient.

2. The environmental complexity grows as one proceeds toward the tropics. It also increases from lowlands to territories with complex topographic relief. Life responds to environmental complexity by increasing adaptive diversity.

3. Natural selection in the temperate and cold zones depends mainly on physical factors, and in the subtropics and tropics on biotic factors. There are more ecological niches in the tropics, and they are more finely subdivided there.

4. There are more predators and parasites in the tropics. This supposedly holds the prey populations to lower density levels, decreases the competition, and makes genetic changes more permissive.

5. Regions with stable climates allow the evolution of more specialized adaptedness.

6. Territories with greater energy production support a greater diversity of inhabitants.

Wright (1931, 1932) in his classical papers expounded the view that territorial subdivision of a species into numerous semiisolated colonies, especially colonies with moderate to small genetically effective population sizes, gives the most favorable conditions for evolutionary progress. A species so subdivided has, at it were, numerous scouting parties which "explore" the field of gene combinations. One or more of these parties may "discover" new, previously unoccupied, adaptive peaks (see Chapter 1), or superior genetic endowments for the higher levels of the old adaptive peak. A great majority of the parties, of course, discover nothing new. They eventually die out or become swamped by migrants from the more successful parties. This is interpopulational or group selection, natural selection that promotes the perpetuation and spread of genetically better endowed populations. Differential reproduction, the spread or the extinction, of competing species is a form of group selection. Species are reproductively, rather than only territorially, isolated Mendelian populations.

The effectiveness of group selection and its role in evolution are controversial matters. Among recent authors, Wynne-Edwards (1962) believes that group selection is responsible for the evolution of physiological and behavioral mechanisms that lower the reproductive rates of populations reaching or exceeding optimal densities. These mechanisms prevent the populations from overtaxing and eventually destroying the resources of their habitats.

At the opposite extreme, Williams (1966) uses the principle of Occam's razor to argue that group selection should not be assumed to exist if a form of adaptedness can conceivably be ascribed to intrapopulational selection. He wields this razor with some abandon, leaving only the polymorphism at the $t$ locus in the house mouse (Dunn 1964 and Lewontin 1962) plausibly ascribed to group selection. Several mutant alleles at this locus distort the segregation in heterozygous males; a considerable majority of the functional spermatozoa carry the mutant, and only a minority the normal allele. This confers upon the mutant alleles sizable selective advantages, which cause them to spread in mice populations. The mutant alleles are, however, lethal or cause sterility when homozygous, so that a population evidently cannot be homozygous for them. This case, by the way, is a diagrammatically clear demonstration that natural selection does not necessarily increase the adaptedness of a population. Group selection solves this predicament. Mouse colonies with high frequencies of lethal *t* alleles are replaced by migrants from colonies where *t* is absent or infrequent. Levin, Petras, and Rasmussen (1963) have questioned, however, whether group selection is a valid explanation of this situation.

It is easy to see that interpopulational or group selection per se is a process much less efficient than intrapopulational selection. The turnover of generations within a colony is obviously much more rapid than the extinction and replacement of colonies or of species. A 10 percent advantage of the carriers of an allele, $A_1$, over the carriers of $A_2$ would increase the frequency of $A_1$ in a population within a a number of generations much smaller than would be required for the extinction and replacement of colonies. Suppose that a genetic variant decreases the reproductive rate of its carriers when a population has outgrown the resources of its environment. How can such a variant spread in a species? Since natural selection has no foresight, it cannot avoid overpopulation, ending in a catastrophe of extinction. Selection cannot sacrifice the immediate for long-range benefits. One possibility is group selection: most populations commit suicide by excessive growth and destruction of their resources; only the populations that restrain their reproductive potentials survive. I agree with Williams (1966) that a more probable course is selection favoring individual variants within populations which "act on the assumption that reproduction is not worth the effort in crowded situations." In other words, selection favors individual variants that reproduce only when the environment is favorable for the survival of their offspring.

A closely related problem is the development in evolution of various forms of "altruistic" behavior. Individuals may expose themselves to risks of injury or death for the benefit of conspecific individuals. Human altruism presupposes conscious and free choice between alternative courses of action and is seemingly confined to a single species, man. There are, however, countless examples not only of parents defending their progeny, but also of some members of a herd or a flock (such as the strongest adult males) interposing themselves between a predator and the weaker, particularly the immature, members. For our purposes, altruism may be defined as behavior that is likely to bring injury or death to individuals so behaving but that benefits other members of the species.

Haldane long ago (1932) and Wright more recently (1949) discussed the possibility of genes for altruism being promoted by natural selection. This is possible in a large undivided population only if the individuals who benefit are close relatives of the altruist, and therefore are likely to be carriers of the same genes. To say the same thing in another way, the number of genes preserved in the relatives should exceed that lost in the altruist if he perishes. Assuming a single dominant gene, the self-sacrifice of an altruist should save more than two of his children or siblings, or even greater numbers of cousins or more remote relatives. The requirements are progressively relaxed, of course, if the altruist is part of the way through his reproductive age. Postreproductive individuals should be altruists even if they save only a single relative. With group selection, tribes containing many altruists may well have an advantage over those the members of which fend only for themselves.

The converse is true for genes predisposing toward egotism, aggression, or "criminal" behavior, which benefit the individuals behaving in these ways but injure conspecific individuals. Without group selection such genes will be favored, unless they do much damage to close relatives. Neel and Schull (1968) discuss, however, a model of frequency-dependent selection for such genes:

A primitive, polygynous society in which each male was highly aggressive might so decimate itself in the struggle for leadership that it was non-viable. At high frequencies of aggressiveness, the non-aggressive male who could keep aloof from the sanguine struggle might stand a better chance of survival and reproduction than the more aggressive, with his chance a function of the amount of aggressiveness in the group. But at low frequencies of the same traits, the aggressive male who assumed leadership (and multiple wives) would be the object of positive selection, and the more passive the group, the greater his reproductive potential. There would thus be an intermediate frequency at which this phenotype (and its genetic basis) would tend to be stabilized.

That natural selection can bring about sacrifice of individuals for the benefit of the species is incontestably shown by social insects. Termite, ant, bee, and wasp societies consist of numerous "workers" that do not reproduce, and a minority, often a single pair that belong to a reproductive caste. Natural selection acts to make the workers serve most efficiently the welfare of this reproductive caste. It is the group, the society, that is the unit of selection. The reproductive caste is analogous to the sex cells, and the workers to the somatic cells of a multicellular body. The origin of the situation need not be envisaged as group selection in the sense of Wynne-Edwards (see above). In a colony, the workers are siblings of the individuals of the reproductive caste that will be the founders of the next generation of colonies. Therefore, the workers are serving to transmit genes identical with their own, although borne in other individuals. The process is selection promoting the survival and perpetuation of groups of genetically related individuals.

## *The Irreversibility of Evolution*

There is considerable literature, much of it polemical, concerning the so-called Dollo's "law" of irreversibility of evolution, first formulated in 1896 or even earlier (for discussions, see Simpson 1953 and Rensch 1960a). Simply stated, the law (or rule) asserts that evolution does not double back on itself to return to ancestral states. Irrevocability of evolution is a complementary principle: the influence of ancestral conditions is not wholly lost in descendent groups.

The validity of these propositions obviously depends on the level of the evolutionary changes considered. A mutation is, in principle, reversible; a substitution of a nucleotide somewhere in a DNA chain may be reversed by restoration of the old nucleotide. A bacterial strain made resistant to an antibiotic by a mutation may revert to sensitivity by another mutation. Mutations restoring an old phenotype do not always restore the old genotype as well; suppressor mutations are by no means rare, and the apparent revertant may actually differ from the ancestral condition not in a single gene change but in two. Starting with a Drosophila population that is, on the average, neutral to light and to gravity, one can select photo-and geopositive and negative strains (see Chapter 7). Relaxation of the artificial selection, or selection in the opposite direction, causes reversion to photo- and geo-neutrality. Whether the reverted neutrals are really genetically identical to the original population is an open question.

More and more genetic changes accumulate as evolution proceeds;

a reversal grows less and less probable, and soon it becomes impossible. An evolutionary event, such as a mutation that is temporarily favored by selection, is reversible; an evolutionary history of many successive gene substitutions is practically irreversible. An analogy with human history suggests itself—an electoral victory of a political party may be reversed at the next election, but the Roman Empire as it was under Augustus cannot possibly be restored, even if this were desirable. Land-dwelling vertebrates are descendants of water-living ancestors; dolphins and whales returned to live in water, but they have not become fishes again.

A loose distinction is often drawn between microevolution and macroevolution, according to the magnitude of the morphological, physiological, or genetic changes. One may say that microevolutionary changes are possibly reversible, whereas macroevolutionary ones are not. This does not mean that there are two kinds of evolution, micro- and macro-, as was contended by some authors, principally believers in orthogenetic "evolution from within." The distinction is quantitative, and any boundary can only be arbitrary.

Certain microevolutionary events can be induced, or reproduced, in experiments. The origin of allopolyploid species is an example (Chapter 11). Some beginnings of macroevolutionary (or, if one prefers, mesoevolutionary) changes are, however, on record. The operation of the founder principle in chromosomally polymorphic experimental populations of *Drosophila pseudoobscura* was described in Chapter 8. An interesting variability, verging on the indeterminacy of the selection results, was observed. Intimations of the irreversibility, or the irrevocability, of evolution can be seen also in the experiments of Strickberger (1963) on chromosomal polymorphism in the same species. The environments in which Drosophila is cultured in labora-tories are patently different from the outdoor environments. Not un-expectedly, natural selection, unpremeditated by the experimenter, tends to increase the genetic adaptedness of laboratory populations to the particular environments in which they are kept.

Strikeberger began his experiments with two kinds of populations of *D. pseudoobscura* homokaryotypic for AR and for CH gene arrange-ments in their third chromosomes (see Chapter 5); some populations had been maintained for many generations in laboratory culture bottles, and others in laboratory population cages. They diverged genetically in response to these different environments, each becoming more efficient in its own environment. Strickberger then set up new polymorphic experimental populations with chromosomes that had different selectional histories. All populations were started by founders with 20 percent AR and 80 percent CH chromosomes. Within about a year (some 10-12 generations) the populations reached new equilibrium frequencies of the chromosomes. The equilibrium depended, however, on the previous selectional histories of the chromosomes. When AR chromosomes came from culture bottles and CH chromosomes from cages, the equilibrium was between 53 and 58 percent AR. In the reverse combination, AR from cages and CH from bottles, the equilibrium was 90–97 percent AR. Most remarkably, these populations showed no trend toward convergence to a common equilibrium level; 1065 days (some 32 generations) from the start, the high equilibrium populations had 92 percent AR chromosomes.

### Evolution as a Creative Process

Evolution is a creative process, in precisely the same sense in which composing a poem or a symphony, carving a statue, or painting a picture are creative acts. An art work is novel, unique, and unrepeatable; a copy of a painting, however exact, is only a reproduction of somebody's creation. Some creativity is possible, however, in playing music, the performer adding his own to that of the composer. The evolution of every phyletic line yields a novelty that never existed before and is a unique, unrepeatable, and irreversible proceeding. As we have seen above, only a most elementary component of the evolutionary process, a mutation followed by selection of a single gene allele, may be recurrent. An evolutionary history is a unique chain of events.

The objection has been raised that, after all, different biological species are only different combinations of a more limited assortment of mutational gene variants, something like different figures in the same kaleidoscope. This misses the point entirely. Following this line of reasoning, one would have to say that mosaic pictures have nothing new in them, because they consist of different combinations of the same kinds of colored stones. The stones are the raw materials; the creative act occurs when the stones are put together to compose a picture. Nucleotide substitutions in DNA chains provide gene variants, which are components of the genetic endowments of organisms. Mutation is a chemical (or, if you wish a molecular) process; selection is a biological or "compositionist" process (Simpson 1964a, b; see also Chapter 1).

How can selection, a process devoid of foresight, be the composer of biological symphonies? This idea is preposterous if selection is misrepresented as only a preserver of a lucky minority of random mutations. Selection is, however, much more than a sieve retaining the lucky and losing the unlucky mutants (see Chapter 7). The meaning of the adjective random as applied to mutations was explained in Chapter 3. Colors may be mixed at random in a pile of stones, but the artist composing a mosaic picture does not use them at random. Selection also creates order out of randomness. It renders possible formation of living systems that would otherwise be infinitely improbable. Nothing can be simpler and more ingenious than its mode of operation: gene constellations that fit the environment survive better and reproduce more often than those that fit less well. As the aesthetic satisfaction of the artist and the beholder is the guide in artistic creation (except, perhaps, in some forms of modern "art"), so the supremacy of life over death is the guiding principle of biological creation.

Unfortunately, a creative process is liable to end in frustration and failure. Extinction is the commonest fate of phyletic lines. The present inhabitants of the globe are the descendants of a minority of the denizens of past epochs, and of smaller and smaller minorities as we look further and further back. The extinct forms are miscarriages of natural selection, consequences of its lack of foresight. Man's foresight has not, however, enabled him to avoid miscarriages of his social and political history! Anyway, the living world not only persists but also contains a greater variety of forms and more complex, sophisticated, or "progressive" ones than in the past. Teilhard de Chardin (1959) has said that evolution is "pervading everything so as to find everything." This is an overstatement, since the potentially possible variety of gene patterns is vastly greater than the variety ever realized. Yet he is right in essence: natural selection has tried out an immense number of possibilities and has discovered many wonderful ones. Among which, to date, the most wonderful is man.

# BIBLIOGRAPHY

The following abbreviations of the names of periodicals are used:

| | |
|---|---|
| *A.N.* | *American Naturalist* |
| *Ch.* | *Chromosoma* (Berlin) |
| *C.S.H.* | *Cold Spring Harbor Symposia on Quantitative Biology* |
| *E.* | *Evolution* |
| *E.B.* | *Evolutionary Biology* (Th. Dobzhansky, M. K. Hecht, and Wm. C. Steere, Eds.), Appleton-Century-Crofts, New York |
| *Ga.* | *Genetika* (Moscow) |
| *G.R.* | *Genetical Research* (Cambridge) |
| *Gs.* | *Genetics* |
| *Hs.* | *Hereditas* |
| *Hy.* | *Heredity* |
| *N.* | *Nature* |
| *P.N.A.S.* | *Proceedings of the National Academy of Sciences (U.S.A.)* |
| *P. No.I.C.G.* | *Proceedings of the Nth International Congress of Genetics* |
| *Q.R.B.* | *Quarterly Review of Biology* |
| *S.* | *Science* |
| *S.Z.* | *Systematic Zoology* |
| *U.T.P.* | *University of Texas Publications* |
| *Z.i.A.V.* | *Zeitschrift für induktive Abstammungs- und Vererbungslehre* |

Abbott, U. K., V. S. Asmundson, and K. R. Shortridge. 1962. Nutritional studies with scaleless chickens. I. The sulphur-containing amino acids. *G.R.*, 3:181-195.

Abplanalp, H., D. C. Lowry, I. M. Lerner, and E. R. Dempster. 1964. Selection for egg number with X-ray induced variation. *Gs.*, 50:1083-1100.

Aeppli, E. 1952. Natürliche Polyploidie beiden Planarien *Dendrocoelum lacteum* (Müller) und *Dendrocoelum infernale* (Steinman). *Z.i.A.V.*, 84:182-212.

Aird, I., H. H. Bentall, and J. A. F. Roberts. 1953. A relationship between cancer of the stomach and the ABO blood groups. *Brit. Med. J.*, 1:799-801.

Alexander, R. D. 1968. Life cycle origins, speciation, and related phenomena in crickets (*Orthoptera, Gryllidae*). *Q.R.B.*, 43:1-41.

Alexander, R. D., and Th. E. Moore. 1962. The evolutionary relationship of 17-year and 13-year cicadas, and three new species. *Misc. Publ. Museum Zool. Univ. Mich.*, 121:1-57.

Ali, M. A. K. 1950. Genetics of resistance to common bean mosaic virus (bean virus 1) in the bean (*Phaseolus vulgaris L.*). *Phytopathology*, 40:69-79.

Allard, R. W. 1965. Genetic systems associated with colonizing ability in predominantly self-pollinating species. Pp. 50-76 in: H. G. Baker and G. L. Stebbins (Eds.), "The Genetics of Colonizing Species," Academic Press, New York.

——, and L. W. Kannenberg. 1968. Population studies in predominantly self-pollinating species. XI. Genetic divergence among the members of the *Festuca microstachys* complex. *E.*, 22:517-528.

Allen, A. C. 1966. The effects of recombination on quasi-normal second and third chromosomes of *Drosophila melanogaster* from a natural population. *Gs.*, 54: 1409-1422.

Allfrey, V. G., V. C. Littau, and A. E. Mirsky. 1963. On the role of histories in regulating ribonucleic acid synthesis in cell nucleus. *P.N.A.S.*, 49:414-421.

Allison, A. C. 1955. Aspects of polymorphism in man. *C.S.H.*, 20: 239-255.

——. 1964. Polymorphism and natural selection in human populations. *C.S.H.*, 29:137-150.

Alström, C. H., and R. Lindelius. 1966. A study of the population movement in nine Swedish populations in 1800-1849 from the genetic statistical viewpoint. *Acta Gen. Stat. Medica*, 16:1-44.

Amadon, D. 1966. The superspecies concept. *S.Z.*, 15:245-249.

Ames, O. 1937. Pollination of orchid through pseudo-copulation. *Harvard Univ. Bot. Museum Leaflet* 5.

Anders, G. 1955. Untersuchungen über das pleiotrope Manifestations-muster der Mutante lozenge-clawless ($l_z{}^{cl}$) von *Drosophila melanogaster*. *Z.i.A.V.*, 87: 113-186.

Anderson, E. 1949. Introgressive Hybridization. John Wiley, New York.

Anderson, S. 1966. Taxonomy of gophers, especially *Thomomys* in Chihuahua, Mexico. *'S.Z.*, 15:189-198.

Anderson, W. W. 1968. Further evidence for coadaptation in crosses between geographic populations of *Drosophila pseudoobscura*. *G.R.*, 12:317-330.

——, and L. Ehrman. 1969. Mating choice in crosses between geographic populations of *Drosophila pseudoobscura*. *Amer. Midland Natur.*, 81:47-53.

——, C. Oshima, T. Watanabe, Th. Dobzhansky, and O. Pavlovsky. 1968. Genetics of natural populations. XXXIX. A test of the possible influence of two insecticides on the chromosomal polymorphism in *Drosophila pseudoobscura*. *Gs.*, 58:423-434.

Andrewartha, H. G. 1952. Diapause in relation to the ecology of insects. *Biol. Rev.* 27:50-107.

——, and L. C. Birch. 1954. The Distribution and Abundance of Animals. Univ. Chicago Press, Chicago.

Anonymous. 1965. The Use of Induced Mutations in Plant Breeding. Report of the Meeting of FAO of the United Nations and the IAEA. Pergamon Press, New York.

Arnheim, N., and C. E. Taylor. 1969. Non-Darwinian evolution consequences for neutral allelic variation. *N.*, 223:900-903.

Ashton, G. C., D. G. Gilmour, C. A. Kiddy, and F. K. Kristjansson. 1967. Proposals on nomenclature of protein polymorphism in farm livestock. *Gs.*, 56: 353-362.

Astaurov, B. L. 1969. Experimental polyploidy in animals with special reference to the hypothesis of an indirect origin of natural polyploidy in bisexual animals. *Ga.*, 5, No. 7:129-149.

Aston, J. L., and A. D. Bradshaw. 1966. Evolution in closely adjacent plant populations. II. *Agrostis stolonifera* in maritime habitats. *Hy.*, 21:649-664.

Atkin, N. B., and S. Ohno. 1967. DNA values of four primitive chordates. *Ch.*, 23:10-13.

Auerbach, Ch. 1949. Chemical mutagenesis. *Biol. Rev.*, 24:355-391.

———. 1965. Past achievements and future tasks of research in chemical mutagenesis. *P. XI I.C.G.*, 2:275-284.

Auerbach, C., and D. Ramsay. 1968. The influence of treatment conditions on the selective mutagenic action of diepoxybutane in Neurospora. *Japan. J. Genetics*, 43:1-8.

Avery, A. G., S. Satina, and J. Rietsema, 1959. The Genus Datura. Ronald Press, New York.

Aya, T., Y. Kuroki, T. Kajii, K. Oikawa, and T. Miki. 1967. A familial survey of a B/C chromosome translocation. *J. Fac. Sci. Hokkaido Univ. Zool.*, 16:148-157.

Ayala, F. J. 1965. Sibling species of the *Drosophila serrata* group. *E.*, 19:538-545.

———. 1966. Evolution of fitness. I. Improvement in the productivity and site of irradiated populations of *Drosophila serrata* and *Drosophila birchii*. *Gs.*, 53: 883-895.

———. 1967. Evolution of fitness. III. Improvement of fitness in irradiated populations of *Drosophila serrata*. *P.N.A.S.*, 58:1919-1923.

———. 1968. Biology as an autonomous science. *Amer. Scientist*, 56:207-221.

———. 1969a. Genetic polymorphism and interspecific competitive ability in Drosophila. *G.R.*, 14:95-102.

———. 1969b. Evoluton of fitness. V. Rate of evolution of irradiated populations of Drosophila. *P.N.A.S.*, 63:790-793.

———. 1969c. An evolutionary dilemma: Fitness of genotypes versus fitness of populations. *Canad. J. Gen. Cytol.*, 11:439-456.

Babcock, E. B., and G. L. Stebbins, Jr. 1938. The American species of *Crepis*. *Carnegie Inst. Washington Publ.* 504.

Baglioni, C. 1967. Molecular evolution in man. Pp. 317-337 *in:* J. F. Crow and J. V. Neel (Eds.), "Proceedings of the 3rd International Congress on Human Genetics," Johns Hopkins Press, Baltimore.

Bailey, D. W. 1959. Rates of subline divergence in highly inbred strains of mice. *J. Heredity*, 50:26-30.

Baker, H. G. 1965. Characteristics and modes of origin of weeds. Pp. 147-172 *in:* H. G. Baker and G. L. Stebbins (Eds.), "The Genetics of Colonizing Species," Academic Press, New York.

Baker, P. T. 1966. Human biological variation as an adaptive response to the environment. *Eugen. Quart.*, 13:81-91.

Baker, P. T., G. R. Buskirk, J. Kollias, and R. B. Mazess. 1967. Temperature regulation at high altitude. Quechua Indians and U. S. whites during total body cold exposure. *Human Biol.*, 39:155-169.

Baker, P., and J. Weiner. 1966. Biology of Human Adaptability, Oxford Univ. Press, New York.

Baker, R. H. 1967. Distribution of recent mammals along the Pacific coastal lowlands of the Western Hemisphere. *S.Z.*, 16:28-37.

Baker, W. 1947. A study of isolating mechanisms found in *Drosophila arisonensis* and *Drosophila mojavensis*. *U.T.P.*, 4720:126-136.

Ball, R. W., and D. L. Jameson. 1966. Premating isolating mechanisms in sympatric and allopatric *Hyla regilla* and *Hyla californiae*. *E.*, 20:533-551.

Band, H. T. 1963. Genetic structure of populations. II. Viabilities and variances of heterozygotes in constant and fluctuating environments. *E.*, 17:198-215.

———. 1964. Genetic structure of populations. III. Natural selection and concealed genetic variability in a natural population of *Drosophila melanogaster*. *E.*, 18: 384-404.

——, and P. T. Ives. 1963. Genetic structure of populations. I. On the nature of the genetic load in the South Amherst population of *Drosophila melanogaster*. *E.*, 17:198-215.

——, and P. T. Ives. 1968. Genetic structure of populations. IV. Summer environmental variables and lethal and semilethal frequencies in a natural population of *Drosophila melanogaster*. *E.*, 22:633-641.

Bandlow, G. 1951. Mutationsversuche an Kulturpflanzen. II. Züchterisch wertvolle Mutanten bei Sommer- und Wintergersten. *Der Züchter*, 21:357-363.

Barbour, I. G. 1966. Issues in Science and Religion. Prentice-Hall, Englewood Cliffs.

Barnicot, N. A. 1959. Climatic factors in the evolution of human populations. *C.S.H.*, 24:115-129.

Barr, Th. C. 1968. Cave ecology and evolution of troglobites *E.B.*, 2:35-102.

Bartolos, M., and Th. Baramki. 1967. Medical Cytogenetics. Williams & Wilkins, Baltimore.

Bastock, M. 1956 A gene mutation which changes a behavior pattern. *E.*, 10: 421-439.

——, and A. Manning. 1955. The courtship of *Drosophila melanogaster*. *Behaviour*, 8:85-111.

Bateman, A. J. 1948. Intra-sexual selection in Drosophila. *Hy.*, 2:349-368.

——. 1951. The taxonomic discrimination of bees. *Hy.*, 5:271-278.

Bates, Marston. 1949. The Natural History of Mosquitoes. Macmillan, New York.

Bateson, W. 1894. Materials for the Study of Variation. Macmillan, London.

Battaglia, B. 1958. Balanced polymorphism in *Tisbe reticulata*, a marine copepod. *E.*, 12:358-364.

——. 1964. Advances and problems of ecological genetics of marine animals. *P. XI I.C.G.*, 2:451-463.

——, Lazzaretto, I., and L. Malesani-Tajoli. 1966. Attivita sessuale degli omo ed eterozigoti per i geni delle pigmentazione nel copepode marino *Tisbe reticulata*. *Arch. Oceanogr. Limnol.*, 14:359-364.

——, and H. Smith. 1961. The Darwinian fitness of polymorphic and monomorphic populations of *Drosophila pseudoobscura* at 16°C. *Hy.*, 16:475-484.

Baur, E. 1924. Untersuchungen über das Wesen, die Entstehung und die Vererbung von Rassenunterschieden bei *Antirrhinum majus*. *Bibliotheca Genetica*, 4:1-170.

——. 1930. Einführung in die Verenbungslehre. Borntraeger, Berlin.

Beadle, G. W., and M. Beadle. 1966. The Language of Life. Doubleday, New York.

Beardmore, J. A., Th. Dobzhansky, and O. Pavlovsky. 1960. An attempt to compare the fitness of polymorphic and monomorphic experimental populations of *Drosophila pseudoobscura*. *Hy.*, 14:19-33.

Beermann, W. 1955a. Cytologische Analyse eines *Camptochironomus* Artbastards. I. *Ch.*, 7:198-259.

——. 1955b. Geschlechtsbestimmung und Evolution der genetischen Y Chromosomen bei *Chironomus*. *Biol. Zentral.*, 74:525-544.

——. 1956. Inversion-Heterozygotie und Fertilität der Männchen von *Chironomus*. *Ch.*, 8:1-11.

Bell, G. 1969. I-DNA: Its packaging into I-somes and its relation to protein synthesis during differentiation. *N.*, 224:326-328.

Belyaev, D. R., and V. I. Evsikov. 1967. Genetics of fertility of animals. The effect of the fur color on the fertility of mink (*Lutreola vison* Brisson). *Ga.*, 1967, No. 2:21-34.

Bender, H. A., and R. E. Gaensslen. 1967. Physiological genetics. Pp. 487-504 *in:* J. W. Wright and R. Pal (Eds.), "Genetics of Insect Vectors of Disease," Elsevier, Amsterdam.

Benoit, J., P. Leroy, R. Vendrely, and C. Vendrely. 1960. Experiments on Pekin ducks treated with DNA from Khaki Campbell ducks. XXIX *Trans. New York Acad. Sci.*, 22:494-503.

Benzer, S. 1957. The elementary units of heredity. Pp. 70-93 *in:* W. D. McElroy and B. Glass (Eds.), "A Symposium on the Chemical Basis of Heredity," Johns Hopkins Press, Baltimore.

Berelson, B., and G. A. Steiner. 1964. Human Behavior: An Inventory of Scientific Findings. Harcourt, Brace, & World, New York.

Berg, L. S. (1922) 1969. Nomogenesis, or Evolution Determined by Law. M.I.T. Press, Cambridge, Mass.

Berg, R. L. 1960. The ecological significance of correlation pleiades. *E.*, 14:171-180.

Berlin, B., D. E. Breedlove, and P. H. Raven. 1966. Folk taxonomies and biological classification. *S.*, 154:273-275.

Bernal, J. D. 1967. The Origin of Life. Weidenfeld & Nicholson, London.

Bianchi, N. O., and O. Molina. 1966. Autosomal polymorphism in a laboratory strain of rat. *J. Heredity*, 57:231-232.

Birch, L. C. 1955. Selection in *Drosophila pseudoobscura* in relation to crowding. *E.*, 9:389-399.

Birdsell, J. B. 1950. Some implications of the genetical concept of race in terms of spatial analysis. *C.S.H.*, 15:259-314.

Blair, A. P. 1941. Variation, isolating mechanisms, and hybridization in certain toads. *Gs.*, 26:398-417.

——. 1942. Isolating mechanisms in a complex of four toad species. *Biol. Symposia*, 6:235-249.

Blair, W. F. 1955. Mating call and stage of speciation in the *Microhyla olivacea-M. carolinensis* complex. *E.*, 9:469-480.

——. 1958a. Mating call in the speciation of anuran amphibians. *A.N.*, 92:27-51.

——. 1958b. Call differences as an isolating mechanism in Florida species of hylid frogs. *Quart. J. Florida Acad. Sci.*, 21:32-48.

——. 1964. Isolating mechanisms and interspecies interactions in anuran amphibians. *Q.R.B.*, 39:334-344.

——, and M. J. Littlejohn. 1960. Stage of speciation of two allopatric populations of chorus frogs (*Pseudacris*). *E.*, 14:82-87.

Blakeslee, A. F., A. D. Bergner, and A. G. Avery. 1937. Geographical distribution of chromosomal prime types in *Datura stramonium. Cytologia,* Jubilee Volume: 1070-1093.

Blaylock, B. G. 1966. Chromosomal polymorphism in irradiated natural populations of *Chironomus. Gs.*, 53:131-136.

Bloom, B S. 1964. Stability and Change in Human Characteristics. John Wiley, New York.

Blum, H. F. 1959. Cancerogenesis by Ultraviolet Light. Princeton Univ. Press, Princeton.

——. 1961. Does the melanin pigment of human skin have adaptive value? *Q.R.B.*, 36:50-63.

Böcher, T. W. 1951. Studies on morphological progression and evolution in the vegetable kingdom. *Dan. Biol. Medd.*, 18, No. 13: 1-51.

Bodmer, W. F. 1970. The evolutionary significance of recombination in prokaryotes. *In* 20th Symposium of the Society for General Microbiology (in press).

Bodmer, W. F., and J. Felsenstein. 1967. Linkage and selection: Theoretical analysis of the deterministic two locus random mating model. *Gs.*, 57:237-265.

Boesiger, E. 1958. Influence de l'hétérosis sur la vigueur des mâles de *Drosophila melanogaster*. *C. R. Acad. Sci.*, 246:489-491.

——. 1962. Sur le degré d'hétérozygotie des populations naturelles de *Drosophila melanogaster* et son maintien par la sélection sexuelle. *Bull. Biol. France Belgique*, 96:3-122.

Bonner, J. 1950. The role of toxic substances in the interactions of higher plants. *Botan. Rev.*, 1950:51-65.

——. 1965. The Molecular Biology of Development, Oxford Univ. Press, New York.

Bonnier, G., and U. B. Jonsson. 1957. Studies on X-ray induced detrimentals in the second chromosome of *Drosophila melanogaster*. *Hs.*, 43:441-461.

Böök, J. H. 1953. A genetic and neuropsychiatric investigation of a North-Swedish population. *Acta Gen. Stat. Medica*, 4:1-139, 345-414.

Borisov A. I. 1969. The adaptive significance of the chromosomal polymorphism. *Ga.*, 5, No. 5:119-122.

Boyd, W. C. 1950. Genetics and the Races of Man. Little, Brown, Boston.

Boynton, J. E. 1966. Chlorophyll-deficient mutants in tomato requiring vitamin $B_1$. *Hs.*, 56:171-199, 238-254.

Brace, C. L. 1963. Structural reduction in evolution. *A.N.*, 97:39-49.

Bradshaw, A. D. 1965. Evolutionary significance of phenotypic plasticity in plants. *Adv. Genetics*, 13:115-155.

Bradshaw, A. D., T. S. McNeilly, and R. P. G. Gregory. 1965. Industrialization, evolution, and the development of heavy metal tolerance in plants. *Brit. Ecol. Soc. Symposium*, 5:327-343.

Brenner, S., L. Barnett, F. H. C. Crick, and A. Orgel. 1961. The theory of mutagenesis. *J. Mol. Biol.*, 3:121-124.

Bretscher, M. S. 1968. How repressor molecules function. *N.*, 127:509-511.

Brewbaker, J. L. 1964. Agricultural Genetics. Prentice-Hall, Englewood Cliffs.

Briles, W. E. 1964. Current status of blood groups in domestic birds. *Zeit. Tierzucht. Züchtungsbiol.*, 79:377-391.

——, C. P. Allen, and T. W. Mullen. 1957. The B blood group system of chickens. I. Heterozygosity in closed populations. *Gs.*, 42:631-648.

Britten, R. J., and E. H. Davidson. 1969. Gene regulation for higher cells; a theory. *S.*, 165:349-357.

——, and D. E. Kohne. 1968. Repeated sequences in DNA. *S.* 161:529-540.

Brncic, D. 1954. Heterosis and the integration of the genotype in geographic populations of *Drosophila pseudoobscura*. *Gs.*, 39:77-88.

——. 1961. Non-random association of inversions in *Drosophila pavani*. *Gs.*, 46:401-406.

——. 1966. Ecological and cytogenetic studies of *Drosophila flavopilosa*, a neotropical species living in *Cestrum* flowers. *E.*, 20:16-29.

——, and S. Koref-Santibañez. 1964. Mating activity of homo- and heterokaryotypes in *Drosophila pavani*. *Gs.*, 49:585-591.

——, and S. Koref-Santibañez. 1965. Geographical variation of chromosomal structure in *Drosophila gasici*. *Ch.*, 16:47-57.

——, S. Koref-Santibañez, M. Budnik, and M. Lamborot. 1969. Rate of development and inversion polymorphism in Drosophila pavani. Gs., 61:471-478.

Brooks, W. K. 1899. The Foundations of Zoology. Columbia Univ. Press, New York.

Brower, L. P. 1959. Speciation in butterflies of the Papilio glaucus group. II. Ecological relationships and interspecific sexual behavior. E., 13:212-228.

Brown, A. W. A. 1967. Genetics of insecticide resistance in insect vectors. Pp. 505-552 in: J. W. Wright and R. Pal (Eds.), "Genetics of Insect Vectors of Disease," Elsevier, Amsterdam.

Brown, R. G. B. 1964. Courtship behaviour in the Drosophila obscura group. I. D. pseudoobscura. Behaviour, 23:61-106.

——. 1965. Courtship behaviour in the Drosophila obscura group. II. Comparative studies. Behaviour, 25:281-323.

Brown, W. L., and E. O. Wilson. 1956. Character displacement. S.Z., 5:49-64.

Brues, A. M. 1964. The cost of evolution vs. the cost of not evolving. E., 18: 379-383.

Brust, R. A., and W. R. Horsfall. 1965. Thermal stress and anomalous development of mosquitoes (Diptera:Culicidae). IV. Aedes communis. Canad. J. Zool., 43:17-53.

Buettner-Janusch, J. 1966. Origins of Man. John Wiley, New York.

Buri, P. 1956. Gene frequency in small populations of mutant Drosophila. E., 10:367-402.

Burla, H., A. B. da Cunha, A. G. L. Cavalcanti, Th. Dobzhansky, and C. Pavan. 1950. Population density and dispersal rates in Brazilian Drosophila willistoni. Ecology, 31:393-404.

——, and M. Greuter 1959. Vergleich der Migrationsverhalten von Drosophila subobscura und Drosophila obscura. Rev. Suisse Zool., 66:272-279.

Burnet, B. 1962. Manifestation of eight lethals in Coelopa frigida. G.R., 3:405-416.

Bush, G L. 1969. Sympatric host race formation and speciation in frugivorous flies of the genus Rhagoletis. E., 23:237-251.

Bushland, R. C., and D. E. Hopkins. 1951. Experiments with screw-worm flies sterilized by X-rays. J. Econ. Entom., 44:725-731.

Byers, G. W. 1969. Evolution of wing reduction in crane flies (Diptera:Tipulidae). E., 23:346-354.

Cain, A. J., and J. D. Currey. 1963. Area effects in Cepaea. Phil. Trans., B, 246: 1-81.

——, and P. M. Sheppard 1950. Selection in the polymorphic land snail Cepaea nemoralis. Hy., 4:275-294.

——, and P. M. Sheppard. 1954. Natural selection in Cepaea. Gs., 39:89-116.

——, P. M. Sheppard, J. M. B. King, M. A. Carter, J. D. Currey, B. Clarke, C. Diver, J. Murray, and R. W. Arnold. 1968. Studies on Cepaea. Phil. Trans., B, 253:383-595.

Cals-Usciati, J. 1964. Étude comparative de caractères biométriques en fonction de l'origine géographique de diverses souches de Drosophila melanogaster. Ann. Genetique, 7:56-66.

Cameron, D. R., and R. M. Moav. 1957. Inheritance in Nicotiana tabacum. XXVII. Pollen killer, an alien genetic locus inducing abortion of microspores not carrying it. Gs., 42:326-335.

Campbell, B. G. 1966. Human Evolution. Aldine, Chicago.

Cannon, W. B. 1932. The Wisdom of the Body. Norton, New York.

Carlquist, S. 1966. The biota of long-distance dispersal. I. Principles of dispersal and evolution. *Q.R.B*, 41:247-270.

Carlson, E. A., R. Sederoff, and M. Cogan. 1967. Evidence favoring a frame-shift mechanism for ICR-170 induced mutations in *Drosophila melanogaster*. *Gs.*, 55:295-313.

Carson, H. L. 1951. Breeding sites of *Drosophila pseudoobscura* and *Drosophila persimilis* in the Transition Zone of the Sierra Nevada. *E.*, 5:91-96.

———. 1959. Genetic conditions which promote or retard the formation of species. *C.S.H.*, 24:87-105.

———. 1965. Chromosomal morphism in geographically widespread species of *Drosophila*. Pp. 508-531 *in:* H. G. Baker and G. L. Stebbins (Eds.), "The Genetics of Colonizing Species," Academic Press, New York.

———. 1967a. Selection for parthenogenesis in *Drosophila mercatorum*. *Gs.*, 55: 157-171.

———. 1967b. Permanent heterozygosity. *E.B.*, 1:143-168.

———, F. E. Clayton, and H. D. Stalker. 1967. Karyotypic stability and speciation in Hawaiian *Drosophila*. *P.N.A.S.*, 57:1280-1285.

———, and W. B. Heed. 1964. Structural homozygosity in marginal populations of neoarctic and neotropical species of *Drosophila* in Florida. *P.N.A.S.*, 52:427-430.

———, and H. D. Stalker. 1968. Polytene chromosome relationships in Hawaiian species of *Drosophila*. I. The *D. grimshawi* subgroup. *U.T.P.*, 6818::335-354.

Caskey, C. T., A. Beaudet, and M. Nierenberg. 1968. RNA codons and protein synthesis. 15. Dissimilar response of mammalian and bacterial transfer. RNA fractions to messenger RNA codons. J. Mol. Biol., 37:99-118.

Cattell, R. B., H. Boutourline Young, and J. D. Hundleby. 1964. Blood groups and personality traits. *Amer. J. Human Genetics*, 16:397-402.

Cavalli-Sforza, L. L. 1969. "Genetic drift" in an Italian population. *Sci. American*, 221:30-37.

———, I. Barrai, and A. W. F. Edwards. 1964. Analysis of human evolution under random genetic drift. *C.S.H.*, 29:9-20.

———, and A. W. F. Edwards. 1964. Analysis of human evolution. *P.* XI *I.C.G.*: 923-933.

Cherfas, N. B. 1966. Natural triploidy in females of the unisexual form of the goldfish (*Carassius auratus gibelio* Bloch). *Ga.*, 5:16-24.

Clarke, B. 1962. Balanced polymorphism and the diversity of sympatric species. *Systematics Assoc. Publ.*, 4:47-70.

Clarke, C. A. 1961. Blood group and disease. *Progr. Med. Genetics*, 1:81-119.

———, and P. M. Sheppard. 1960. The evolution of mimicry in the butterfly *Papilio dardanus*. *Hy.*, 14:163-173.

———, and P. M. Sheppard. 1962. Disruptive selection and its effects on a metric character in the butterfly *Papilio dardanus*. *E.*, 16:214-226.

———, and P. M. Sheppard. 1966. A local survey of the distribution of industrial melanic forms in the moth *Biston betularia* and estimates of the selective values of these in an industrial environment. *Proc. Royal Soc.*, B, 165:424-439.

———, P. M. Sheppard, and I. W. B. Thornton. 1968. The genetics of the mimetic butterfly *Papilio memnon* L. *Phil. Trans. Royal Soc. London*, B, 254:37-89.

Clausen, J. 1951. Stages in the Evolution of Plant Species. Cornell Univ. Press, Ithaca.

———, and W. M. Hiesey. 1958. Experimental studies on the nature of species. IV. Genetic structure of ecological races. *Carnegie Inst. Washington Publ.* 615: 1-312.

———, D. D. Keck, and W. M. Hiesey. 1940. Experimental studies on the nature of species. I. Effects of varied environments on western North American plants. *Carnegie Inst. Washington Publ.* 520:1-452.

———, D. D. Keck, and W. M. Hiesey. 1945. Experimental studies on the nature of species. II. Plant evolution through amphiploidy and autoploidy, with examples from the *Madiinae. Carnegie Inst. Washington Publ.* 564.

———, D. D. Keck, and W. M. Hiesey. 1948. Experimental studies on the nature of species. III. Environmental responses of climatic races of *Achillea. Carnegie Inst. Washington Publ.* 581:1-129.

Clayton, G. A., G. R. Knight, J. A. Morris, and A. Robertson. 1957. An experimental check on quantitative genetical theory. III. Correlated responses. *J. Genetics,* 55:171-180.

———, J. A. Morris, and A. Robertson. 1957. An experimental check on quantitative genetical theory. I. Short-term responses to selection. *J. Genetics,* 55:131-151.

Cleland, R. E. 1950. Studies on *Oenothera* cytogenetics and phylogeny. *Indiana Univ. Publ. Sci.* 16:1-348.

Clifford, H T., and F. E. Binet. 1954. A quantitative study of a presumed hybrid swarm between *Eucalyptus elaeophora* and *E. goniocalyx. Austral. J. Bot.,* 2:325-336.

Cloud, P. E. 1968. Premetazoan evolution and the origins of the metazoa. Pp. 1-72 *in:* E. T. Drake (Ed.), "Evolution and Environment," Yale Univ. Press, New Haven.

Cohen, M. M., M. W. Shaw, and J. W. MacCluer. 1966. Racial differences in the length of the human Y chromosome. *Cytogenetics* 5:34-52.

Colwell, R. N. 1951. The use of radioactive isotopes in determining spore distribution patterns. *Amer. J. Bot.,* 38:511-523.

Commoner, B. 1964. Deoxyribonucleic acid and the molecular basis of self-duplication. *N.,* 203:486-491.

Coon, C. S. 1965. The Living Races of Man. Knopf, New York.

Cordeiro, A. R. 1952. Experiments on the effects in heterozygous condition of second chromosomes for natural populations of *Drosophila willistoni. P.N.A.S.,* 38:471-478.

Correns, C. 1909. Vererbungsversuche mit blass (gelb) grünen und buntblättrigen Sippen bei *Mirabilis, Urtica,* und *Linaria. Z.i.A.V.,* 1:291-329.

Corrigan, J. J. 1969. D-amino acids in animals. *S.,* 164:142-149.

Cory, L., and J. J. Manion. 1955. Ecology and hybridization in the genus *Bufo* in the Michigan-Indiana region. *E.,* 9:42-51.

Cotter, W. B. 1967. Mating behavior and fitness as a function of single allele differences in *Ephestia kühniella* Z. *E.,* 21:275-284.

Count, G. W. 1950. This is Race. Henry Schuman, New York.

Court-Brown, W. M. 1967. Human Population Cytogenetics. North-Holland, Amsterdam.

Craig, G. B., and W. A. Hickey. 1967. Genetics of *Aedes aegypti.* Pp. 67-131 *in:* J. W. Wright and R. Pal (Eds.), "Genetics of Insect Vectors of Disease," Elsevier, Amsterdam.

Crampton, H. E. 1916. Studies on the variation, distribution, and evolution of the genus *Partula.* The species inhabiting Tahiti. *Carnegie Inst. Washington Publ.* 228:1-311.

———. 1932. Studies on the variation, distribution and evolution of the genus *Partula.* The species inhabiting Moorea. *Carnegie Inst. Washington Publ.* 410:1-335.

Creed, E. R., E. B. Ford, and K. McWhirter. 1964. Evolutionary studies on *Maniola jurtina:* the isles of Scilly 1958-1959. *Hy.,* 19:471-488.

Crenshaw, J. W. 1965a. Serum protein variation in an interspecies hybrid swarm of turtles of the genus *Pseudemys. E.,* 19:1-15.

——. 1965b. Radiation-induced increase in fitness in the flour beetle *Tribolium confusum. S.,* 149:426-427.

Crick, F. H. C. 1967. The genetic code. *Proc. Royal Soc.,* B, 167:331-347.

Crow, J. F. 1957. Genetics of insect resistance to chemicals. *Ann. Review Entom.,* 2:227-246.

——. 1958. Some possibilities for measuring selection intensities in man. Pp. 1-13 *in:* J. N. Spuhler (Ed.), "Natural Selection in Man," Wayne Univ. Press, Detroit.

——. 1968. Some analysis of hidden variability in *Drosophila populations.* Pp. 71-86 *in:* R. C. Lewontin (Ed.), "Population Biology and Evolution," Syracuse Univ. Press, Syracuse.

——. 1969. Molecular genetics and population genetics. *P. XII I.C.G.,* 3:105-113.

——, and M. Kimura. 1963. The theory of genetic loads. *P. XI I.C.G.,* 3:495-506.

——, and M. Kimura. 1965. Evolution in sexual and asexual populations. *A.N.,* 99:439-450.

——, and N. E. Morton. 1955. Measurement of gene frequency drift in small populations. *E.,* 9:202-214.

——, and R. G. Temin. 1964. Evidence for the partial dominance of recessive lethal genes in natural populations of *Drosophila. A.N.,* 98:21-33.

Crumpacker, D. W. 1967. Genetic loads in maize (*Zea mays* L.) and other cross-fertilized plants and animals. *E.B.,* 1:306-424.

Cunha, A. B. da. 1949. Genetic analysis of the polymorphism of color pattern in *Drosophila polymorpha. E.,* 3:239-251.

——. 1955. Chromosomal polymorphism in the *Diptera. Adv. Genetics,* 7:93-138.

——, Th. Dobzhansky, O. Pavlovsky, and B. Spassky. 1959. Genetics of natural populations. XXVIII. Supplementary data on the chromosomal polymorphism in *Drosophila willistoni* in its relation to its environment. *E.,* 13:389-404.

Currey, J. D., R. W. Arnold, and M. A. Carter. 1964. Further examples of variation of populations of *Cepaea nemoralis* with habitat. *E.,* 18:111-117.

Darevsky, I. S. 1966. Natural parthenogenesis in a polymorphic group of Caucasian rock lizards related to *Lacerta saxicola* Eversmann. *J. Ohio Herpet. Soc.,* 5:115-152.

Darlington, C. D. 1937. Recent Advances in Cytology. 2nd Ed. Blakiston, Philadelphia.

Davidson, E. H. 1968. Gene Activity in Early Development. Academic Press, New York.

——, M. Crippa, and A. E. Mirsky. 1968. Evidence for the appearance of novel gene products during amphibian blastulation. *P.N.A.S.,* 60:152-159.

Davidson, G., H. E. Patterson, M. Coluzzi, G. F. Mason, and D. W. Micks. 1967. The *Anopheles gambiae* complex. Pp. 211-250 *in:* J. W. Wright and R. Pal Eds.), "Genetics of Insect Vectors of Disease," Elsevier, Amsterdam.

Dawood, M. M., and M. W. Strickberger. 1964. The effect of larval interaction in viability in *Drosophila melanogaster.* I. Changes in heterozygosity. *Gs.,* 50: 999-1007.

Dawson, P. S. 1966. Correlated responses to selection for developmental rate in *Tribolium. Ga.,* 37:63-77.

——, and I. M. Lerner. 1966. The founder principle and competitive ability of *Tribolium. P.N.A.S.,* 55:1114-1117.

Dayhoff, M. O., and R. V. Eck. 1968. Atlas of Protein Sequence and Structure 1967-68. National Biomedical Research Foundation, Silver Spring, Maryland.

Demerec, M. 1936. Frequency of "cell-lethals" among lethals obtained at random in the X chromosome of *Drosophila melanogaster*. *P.N.A.S.*, 22:350-354.

——. 1948. Origin of bacterial resistance to antibiotics. J. Bacteriology, 56:63-74.

——. 1955. What is a gene? Twenty years later. *A.N.*, 89:5-20.

——, and U. Fano. 1945. Bacteriophage resistant mutants in *Escherichia coli*. *Gs.*, 30:119-136.

Dempster, E. R. 1955. Maintenance of genetic heterogeneity. *C.S.H.*, 20:25-32.

Desmond, A. 1964. How many people have ever lived on earth? Pp. 27-46 *in:* S. Mudd (Ed.), "The Population Crisis and the Use of World Resources," Indiana Univ. Press, Bloomington.

Diamond, J. D. 1966. Zoological classification system of a primitive people. *S.*, 151:1102-1104.

Dickson, R. C. 1940. Inheritance of resistance to hydrocyanic acid fumigation in the California red scale. *Hilgardia:* 515-522.

Diver, C. 1939. Aspects of the study of variation in snails. *J. Conchol.*, 21:91-141.

——. 1940. The problem of closely related species living in the same area. Pg. 303-328 *in:* J. S. Huxley, "New Systematics," Clarendon, Oxford.

Dobzhansky, Th. 1927. Studies on manifold effect of certain genes in *Drosophila melanogaster*. *Z.i.A.V.*, 43:330-388.

——. 1933. Geographical variation in lady-beetles. *A.N.*, 67:97-126.

——. 1934. Studies on hybrid sterility. I. Spermatogenesis in pure and hybrid *Drosophila pseudoobscura*. *Zeit. Zef. mikr. Anat.*, 21:169-223.

——. 1936. Studies on hybrid sterility. II. Localization of sterility factors in *Drosophila pseudoobscura* hybrids. *Gs.*, 21:113-135.

——. 1937a. Genetic nature of species differences. *A.N.*, 71:404-420.

——. 1937b. Further data on *Drosophila miranda* and its hybrid with *Drosophila pseudoobscura*. *J. Genetics*, 34:135-151.

——. 1937c. Further data on the variation of the Y chromosome in *Drosophila pseudoobscura*. *Gs.*, 22:340-346.

——. 1937d, 1941, 1951. Genetics and the Origin of Species. 1st, 2nd, and 3rd Eds. Columbia Univ. Press, New York.

——. 1940. Speciation as a stage in evolutionary divergence. *A.N.*, 74:312-321.

——. 1944. Experiments on sexual isolation in *Drosophila*. *P.N.A.S.*, 30:335-339.

——. 1946. Genetics of natural populations. XIII. Recombination and variability in population of *Drosophila pseudoobscura*. *Gs.*, 31:269-290.

——. 1947. Genetics of natural populations. XIV. A response of certain gene arrangements in the third chromosome of *Drosophila pseudoobscura* to natural selection. *Gs.*, 32:142-160.

——. 1948. Genetics of natural populations. XVI. Altitudinal and seasonal changes produced by natural selection in certain populations of *Drosophila pseudoobscura* and *Drosophila persimilis*. *Gs.*, 33:158-176.

——. 1951. Experiments on sexual isolation in *Drosophila*. X. Reproductive isolation between *Drosophila pseudoobscura* and *D. persimilis* under natural and under laboratory conditions. *P.N.A.S.*, 37:792-796.

——. 1953. Natural hybrids of two species of *Arctostaphylos* in the Yosemite region of California. *Hy.*, 7:73-79.

——. 1956a. What is an adaptive trait? *A.N.*, 90:337-347.

——. 1956b. Genetics of natural populations. XXV. Genetic changes in popula-

444                                                                    BIBLIOGRAPHY

tions of *Drosophila pseudoobscura* and *Drosophila persimilis* in some locations in California. *E.*, 10:82-92.

——. 1960. Evolution and environment. Pp. 403-428 *in:* Sol Tax (Ed.), "Evolution after Darwin," Vol. 1, Chicago Univ. Press, Chicago.

——. 1961. On the dynamics of chromosomal polymorphism in *Drosophila*. Pp. 30-42 *in:* J. S. Kennedy (Ed.), "Insect Polymorphism," Royal Entomological Society, London.

——. 1962. Rigid vs. flexible chromosomal polymorphisms in *Drosophila*. *A.N.*, 96:321-328.

——. 1964a. How do the genetic loads affect the fitness of their carriers in *Drosophila* population? *A.N.*, 98:151-166.

——. 1964b. Genetic diversity and fitness. *P. XI I.C.G.*, 3:541-552.

——. 1968a. On some fundamental concepts of Darwinian biology. *E.B.*, 2:1-34.

——. 1968b. Adaptedness and fitness. Pp. 109-121 *in:* R. C. Lewontin (Ed.), "Population Biology and Evolution," Syracuse Univ. Press, Syracuse.

——, W. W. Anderson, and O. Pavlovsky. 1966. Genetics of natural populations. XXXVIII. Continuity and change in populations of *Drosophila pseudoobscura* in western United States. *E.*, 20:418-427.

——, and G. W. Beadle. 1936. Studies on hybrid sterility. IV. Transplanted testes in *Drosophila pseudoobscura*. *Gs.*, 21:832-840.

——, L. Ehrman, and P. A. Kastritsis. 1968. Ethological isolation between sympatric and allopatric species of the *obscura* group of *Drosophila*. *Animal Behaviour*, 16:79-87.

——, and C. Epling. 1944. Contributions to the genetics, taxonomy, and ecology of *Drosophila pseudoobscura* and its relatives. *Carnegie Inst. Washington Publ.* 554:1-183.

——, and A. M. Holz. 1943. A re-examination of the problem of manifold effects of genes in *Drosophila melanogaster*. *Gs.*, 28:295-303.

——, and H. Levene. 1948. Genetics of natural populations. XVII. Proof of operation of natural selection in wild populations of *Drosophila pseudoobscura*. *Gs.*, 33:537-547.

——, H. Levene, B. Spassky, and N. Spassky. 1959. Release of genetic variability through recombination. III. *Drosophila prosaltans*. *Gs.*, 44:75-92.

——, R. C. Lewontin, and O. Pavlovsky. 1964. The capacity for increase in chromosomally polymorphic and monomorphic populations of *Drosophila pseudoobscura*. *Hy.*, 19:597-614.

——, and O. Pavlovsky. 1953. Indeterminate outcome of certain experiments on *Drosophila* populations. *E.*, 7:198-210.

——, and O. Pavlovsky. 1957. An experimental study of interaction between genetic drift and natural selection. *E.*, 11:311-319.

——, and O. Pavlovsky. 1958. Interracial hybridization and breakdown of coadapted gene complexes in *Drosophila paulistorum* and *Drosophila willistoni*. *P.N.A.S.*, 44:622-629.

——, and O. Pavlovsky. 1967. Experiments on the incipient species of the *Drosophila paulistorum* complex. *Gs.*, 55:141-156.

——, O. Pavlovsky, and L. Ehrman. 1969. Transitional populations of *Drosophila paulistorum*. *E.*, 23:482-492.

——, and B. Spassky. 1941. Intersexes in *Drosophila pseudoobscura*. *P.N.A.S.*, 27:556-562.

——, and B. Spassky. 1947. Evolutionary changes in laboratory cultures of *Drosophila pseudoobscura*. *E.*, 1:191-216.

——, and B. Spassky. 1953. Genetics of natural populations. XXI. Concealed variability in two sympatric species of *Drosophila*. *Gs.*, 38:471-484.

——, and B. Spassky. 1959. *Drosophila paulistorum*, a cluster of species in *statu nascendi*. *P.N.A.S.*, 45:419-428.

——, and B. Spassky. 1960. Release of genetic variability through recombination. V. Breakup of synthetic lethals by crossing over in *Drosophila pseudoobscura*. *Zool. Jahrb. Abt. Syst.*, 88:57-66.

——, and B. Spassky. 1963. Genetics of natural populations. XXXIV. Adaptive norm, genetic load and genetic elite in *Drosophila pseudoobscura*. *Gs.*, 48:1467-1485.

——, and B. Spassky. 1967a. Effects of selection and migration on geotactic and phototactic behaviour of *Drosophila*. I. *Proc. Royal Soc.*, B, 168:27-47.

——, and B. Spassky. 1967b. An experiment on migration and simultaneous selection for several traits in *Drosophila pseudoobscura*. *Gs.*, 55:723-734.

——, and B. Spassky. 1968. Genetics of natural populations. XL. Heterotic and deleterious effect of recessive lethals in populations of *Drosophila pseudoobscura*. *Gs.*, 59:411-425.

——, and B. Spassky. 1969. Artificial and natural selection for two behavioral traits in *Drosophila pseudoobscura*. *P.N.A.S.*, 62:75-80.

——, B. Spassky, and N. Spassky. 1952. A comparative study of mutation rates in two ecologically diverse species of *Drosophila*. *Gs.*, 39:472-487.

——, B. Spassky, and N. Spassky. 1954. Rates of spontaneous mutation in the second chromosomes of the sibling species, *Drosophila pseudoobscura* and *Drosophila persimilis*. *Gs.*, 39:899-907.

——, B, Spassky, and Γ. Tidwell. 1963. Genetics of natural populations. XXXII. Inbreeding and the mutational and balanced genetic loads in natural populations of *Drosophila pseudoobscura*. *Gs.*, 48:361-373.

——, and N. P. Spassky. 1962. Genetic drift and natural selection in experimental populations of *Drosophila pseudoobscura*. *P.N.A.S.*, 48:148-156.

——, and G. Streisinger. 1944. Experiments on sexual isolation in *Drosophila*. II. *P.N.A.S.*, 30:340-345.

——, and A. H. Sturtevant. 1938. Inversions in the chromosomes of *Drosophila pseudoobscura*. *Gs.*, 23:28-64.

——, and C. C. Tan. 1936. Studies on hybrid sterility. III. A comparison of the gene arrangement in two species, *Drosophila pseudoobscura* and *Drosophila miranda*. *Z.i.A.V.*, 72:88-114.

——, and S. Wright. 1941. Genetics of natural populations. V. Relations between mutation rate and accumulation of lethals in populations of *Drosophila pseudoobscura*. *Gs.*, 26:23-51.

——, and S. Wright. 1943. Genetics of natural populations. X. Dispersion rates in *Drosophila pseudoobscura*. *Gs.*, 28:304-340.

——, and S. Wright. 1947. Genetics of natural populations. XV. Rate of diffusion of a mutant gene through a population of *Drosophila pseudoobscura*. *Gs.*, 32:303-324.

Dodson, C. H. 1967. Relationships between pollinators and orchid flowers. *Atlas Simp. Biota Amazonica*, 5:1-72 (Rio de Janeiro).

Dowdeswell, W. H., and K. McWhirter. 1967. Stability of spot-distribution in *Maniola jurtina* throughout its range. *Hy.*, 22:187-210.

Drescher, W. 1964. The sex-limited genetic load in natural populations of *Drosophila melanogaster*. *A.N.*, 98:167-171.

Druger, M. 1967. Selection and the effect of temperature on scutallar bristle number in *Drosophila*. *Gs.*, 56:39-47.

Dubinin, N. P. 1931. Genetico-automatical processes and their bearing on the mechanism of organic evolution. *J. Exp. Biol.*, 7:463-479. (Russian).

——. 1961. Problems of Radiation Genetics. Gosatomizdat, Moscow.

——. 1964. Problems of Radiation Genetics. Oliver and Boyd, Edinburgh.

——. 1966. Evolution of Populations and Radiation. Atomizdat, Moscow.

——, and D. D. Romaschoff. 1932. Die genetische Struktur der Art und ihre Evolution. *Biol. Zhurnal*, 1:52-95.

——, D. D. Romashov [Romaschoff], M. A. Heptner, and Z. A. Demidova. 1937. Aberrant polymorphism in *Drosophila fasciata* Meig (Syn. - *melanogaster Meig*). *Biol. Zhurnal*, 6:311-354.

——, and G. G. Tiniakov. 1946. Inversion gradients and natural selection in ecological races of *Drosophila funebris*. *Gs.*, 31:537-545.

——, and fourteen collaborators. 1934. Experimental study of the ecogenotypes of *Drosophila melanogaster*. *Biol. Zhurnal*, 3:166-216

Dubos, R. 1965. Man Adapting. Yale Univ. Press, New Haven.

Duke, E. J., and E. Glassman. 1968. Evolution of xanthine dehydrogenase in *Drosophila*. *Gs.*, 58:101-112.

Dun, R. B., and A. S. Fraser. 1959. Selection for an invariant character, vibrissa number, in the house mouse. *Austral. J. Biol. Sci.*, 12:506-523.

Dunn, L. C. 1964. Abnormalities associated with a chromosome region in the mouse. *S.*, 144:260-263.

Edwards, A. J., and J. F. Cauley (Eds.) 1964. Physiological determinants of behavior. *Kansas Studies in Education*, 14: No. 3.

Ehrendorfer, F. 1963. Cytologie, Taxonomie und Evolution bei Samenpflanzen. *Vistas Bot.*, 4:99-186.

Ehrlich, P. R., and P. H. Raven. 1964. Butterflies and plants, a study in coevolution. *E.*, 18:586-608.

Ehrman, L. 1960. The genetics of hybrid sterility in *Drosophila paulistorum*. *E.*, 14:212-223.

——. 1961. The genetics of sexual isolation in *Drosophila paulistorum*. *Gs.*, 46: 1025-1038.

——. 1962. Hybrid sterility as an isolating mechanism in the genus *Drosophila*. *Q.R.B.*, 37:279-302.

——. 1965. Direct observation of sexual isolation between allopatric and between sympatric strains of the different *Drosophila paulistorum* races. *E.*, 19:459-464.

——. 1967. Further studies on genotype frequency and mating success in *Drosophila*. *A.N.*, 101:415-424.

——, and C. Petit. 1968. Genotype frequency and mating success in the *willistoni* species group of *Drosophila*. *E.*, 22:649-658.

——, B. Spassky, O. Pavlovsky, and Th. Dobzhansky. 1965. Sexual selection, geotaxis, and chromosomal polymorphism in experimental populations of *Drosophila pseudoobscura*. *E.*, 19:337-346.

——, and D. L. Williamson. 1969. On the etiology of the sterility of hybrids between certain strains of *Drosophila paulistorum*. *Gs.*, 62:193-199.

Eibl-Eibesfeldt, I. 1965. Angeborenes und Erworbenes in Verhalten einiger Säuger. *Zeit. Tierpsychol.*, 20:705-754.

Eiche, V. 1955. Spontaneous chlorophyll mutations in Scots pine (*Pinus silvestris* L.). *Medd. Stat. Skogsforskningsinst.*, 45, No. 13:1-69.

Eiseley, L. 1959. Charles Darwin, Edward Blyth, and the theory of natural selection. Proc. Amer. Philos. Soc., 103:94-158.

Emerson, S. 1939. A preliminary survey of the *Oenothera organensis* population. *Gs.*, 24:524-537.

Emsweller, S. L., and N. W. Stuart. 1948. Use of growth regulating substances to overcome incompatibilities. in *Lilium. Proc. Amer. Soc. Hort. Sci.*, 51:581-589.

Ephrussi, B., and M. C. Weiss. 1965. Interspecific hybridization of somatic cells. *P.N.A.S.*, 53:1040-1042.

Ergene, S. 1951. Wählen Heuschrecken ein homochromes Milieu? *Deutsche Zool. Zeit.*, 1:123-133, 187-195.

Erlenmeyer-Kimling, L., and W. Paradowski. 1966. Selection and schizophrenia. *A.N.*, 100:651-665.

Falconer, D. S. 1960a. Introduction to Quantitative Genetics. Ronald Press, New York.

———. 1960b. Selection of mice for growth on high and low planes of nutrition. *G.R.*, 1:91-113.

Falk, R. 1961. Are induced mutations in *Drosophila* overdominant? II. Experimental results. *Gs.*, 46:737-757.

———, and N. Ben-Zeev. 1966. Viability of heterozygotes for induced mutations in *Drosophila melanogaster*. II. Mean effects in irradiated autosomes. *Gs.*, 53:65-77.

Feller, W. 1967. On fitness and the cost of natural selection. *G.R.*, 9:1-15.

Fenner, F. 1959. Myxomatosis in Australian wild rabbit—evolutionary changes in an infectious disease. *Harvey Lectures, 1957-58:* 25-55.

———. 1965. Myxoma virus and *Oryctolagus cuniculus*, two colonizing species. Pp. 485-501 *in:* H. G. Baker and G. L. Stebbins (Eds.), "The Genetics of Colonizing Species," Academic Press, New York.

Ferguson, C. W. 1968. Bristlecone pine: science and esthetics. *S.*, 159:839-846.

Ferrell, G. T. 1966. Variation in blood group frequencies in populations of song sparrows of the San Francisco bay region. *E.*, 20:369-382.

Fisher, R. A. 1928. The possible modification of the response of the wild type to recurrent mutations. *A.N.*, 62:115-126.

———. 1930. The Genetical Theory of Natural Selection. Clarendon Press, Oxford.

Fitch, W. M., and E. Margoliash. 1967a. Construction of phylogenetic trees. *S.*, 155:279-284.

———, and E. Margoliash. 1967b. A method for estimating the number of invariant amino acid coding positions in a gene using cytochrome c as a model case. *Biochem. Genetics*, 1:65-71.

———, and E. Margoliash. 1970. The usefulness of amino acid and nucleotid sequences in evolutionary studies. *E.B.*, 4: (in press).

Foerster, R. E. 1968. The sockeye salmon *Oncorhynchus nerka. Fisheries Res. Canada Publ.* 162, Ottawa.

Ford, E. B. 1964. Ecological Genetics. Methuen, London.

———. 1965. Genetic Polymorphism. M.I.T. Press, Cambridge.

Forde, M. M. 1962. Effect of introgression on the serpentine endemism of *Quercus durata. E.*, 16:338-347.

Fox, A. S., and S. B. Yoon. 1966. Specific genetic effects of DNA in *Drosophila melanogaster. Gs.*, 53:897-911.

Fox, S. W. (Ed.). 1965. The Origin of Prebiological Systems. Academic Press, New York.

Fraenkel-Conrat, H., and B. Singer. 1957. Virus reconstruction. II. Combination of protein and nucleic acid from different strains. *Biochem. Biophys. Acta,* 24: 540-548.

——, and R. C. Williams. 1955. Reconstitution of active tobacco mosaic virus from its inactive protein and nucleic acid components. *P.N.A.S.,* 41:690-698.

Frahm, R. R., and K. I. Kojima. 1966. Comparison of selection responses of body weight under divergent larval density conditions in *Drosophila pseudoobscura. Gs.,* 54:625-637.

Fraser, A., and D. Burnell. 1967. Simulation of genetic systems. XII. Models of inversion polymorphisms. *Gs.,* 57:267-282.

Fraser, G. R. 1962. Our genetical "load." A review of some aspects of genetical variation. *Ann. Human Genetics,* 25:387-415.

Freese, E. 1965. The influence of DNA structure and base composition on mutagenesis. *P.* XI *I.C.G.,* 2:297-306.

Friedman, L. D. 1964. X-ray induced sex-linked lethal and detrimental mutations and their effects on the viability of *Drosophila melanogaster. Gs.,* 49:689-699.

Fulton, B. B. 1952. Speciation in the field cricket. *E.,* 6:283-295.

Futch, D. G. 1966. A study of speciation in South Pacific populations of *Drosophila ananassae. U.T.P.* 6615:79-120.

Gajewski, W. 1957. A cytogenetic study on the genus *Geum* L. *Monogr. Botanicae (Warszawa),* 4:1-415.

——. 1959. Evolution in the genus *Geum. E.,* 13:378-388.

Garen, A. 1968. Sense and nonsense in the genetic code. *S.,* 160:149-159.

Garn, S. M. 1965. Human Races. 2nd Ed. Charles C Thomas, Springfield, Ill.

Garnjobst, L., and E. L. Tatum. 1967. A survey of new morphological mutants in *Neurospora crassa. Gs.,* 57:579-604.

Gause, G. F. 1941. Optical Activity and Living Matter. Biodynamica, Normandy, Mo.

Geitler, L. 1938. Weitere cytogenetische Untersuchungen an natürlichen Populationen von *Paris quadrifolia. Z.i.A.V.,* 75:161-190.

Gerassimova, H. 1939. New experimentally produced strains of *Crepis tectorum* which are physiologically isolated from the original form owing to reciprocal translocation. *C. R. Acad. Sci. URSS,* 25:148-154.

Gerstel, D. U. 1954. A new lethal combination in interspecific cotton hybrids. *Gs.,* 39:628-639.

Gibbs, G. W. 1968. The frequency of interbreeding between two sibling species of *Dacus (Diptera)* in wild populations. *E.,* 22:667-683.

Giblett, G. 1961. Haptoglobins and transferrins. Pp. 132-158 *in:* B. S. Blumberg (Ed.), "Proceedings of the Conference on Genetic Polymorphisms and Geographic Variations in Disease," Grune & Stratton, New York.

——. 1964. Variant haptoglobin phenotypes. *C.S.H.,* 29:321-326.

Gibson, J. B., and J. M. Thoday. 1962. Effects of disruptive selection. VI. A second chromosome polymorphism. *Hy.,* 17:1-26.

——, and J. M. Thoday. 1963. Effects of disruptive selection. VIII. Imposed quasi-random mating. *Hy.,* 18:513-524.

Gilbert, J. J. 1966. Rotifer ecology and embryological induction. *S.,* 151:1234-1237.

Giles, E., R. J. Walsh, and M. A. Bradley. 1966. Micro-evolution in New Guinea: The role of genetic drift. *Ann. New York Acad. Sci.,* 134:655-665. *Service,* 38:33.

Gill, K. S. 1963. A mutation causing abnormal mating behavior. *Drosophila Inf.*

Glass, B. 1954. Genetic changes in human populations, especially those due to gene flow and genetic drift. *Adv. Genetics,* 6:95-139.

——. 1955. A comparative study of induced mutation in the oocytes and spermatozoa of *Drosophila melanogaster. Gs.,* 40:252-267, 281-296.

——, M. S. Sacks, E. J. Jahn, and C. Hess. 1952. Genetic drift in a religious isolate. An analysis of the causes of variation in blood group and other gene frequencies in a small population. *A.N.,* 86:145-160.

Goldschmidt, R. 1934. *Lymantria. Bibliogr. Genetica,* 11:1-186.

——. 1938. Physiological Genetics. McGraw-Hill, New York.

——. 1940. The Material Basis of Evolution. Yale Univ. Press, New Haven.

Golubovsky, M. D. 1969. The viability of heterozygotes for lethal mutations characterized by different concentrations in a natural population of *Drosophila melanogaster. Ga.,* 5, No. 8:116-126.

Goodhart, C. B. 1962. Variation in a colony of the snail *Cepaea nemoralis* (L.). *J. Animal Ecol.,* 31:207-237.

——. 1963. "Area effects" and non-adaptive variation between populations of *Cepaea. Hy.,* 18:459-465.

Gordon, M. 1948. Effects of five primary genes on the site of melanomas in fishes and the influence of two color genes on their pigmentation. *In:* "The Biology of Melanomas," *Spec. Publ. New York Acad. Sci.,* 4:216-268.

——. 1951. Genetic and correlated studies of normal and atypical pigment cell growth. *Growth Symposium,* 10:153-219.

——, and D. E. Rosen. 1951. Genetics of species differences in the morphology of the male genitalia of xiphophorin fishes. *Bull. Amer. Museum Nat. Hist.,* 95:409-464.

Gottesman, I.I. 1968. A sampler of human behavioral genetics. *E.B.,* 2:276-320.

Grant, K. A., and V. Grant. 1964. Mechanical isolation of *Salvia apiana* and *Salvia mellifera (Labiatae). E.,* 18:196-212.

——, and V. Grant. 1968. Hummingbirds and Their Flowers. Columbia Univ. Press, New York.

Grant, V. 1954a. Genetics and taxonomic studies in *Gilia.* VI. Interspecific relationships in the leafy-stemmed *Gilias. El Aliso,* 3:35-49.

——. 1954b. Genetic and taxonomic studies in *Gilia.* VII. The woodland *Gilias. El Aliso,* 3:59-91.

——. 1958. The regulation of recombination in plants. *C.S.H.,* 23:337-363.

——. 1963. The Origin of Adaptations. Columbia Univ. Press, New York.

——. 1964a. The Architecture of Germplasm. John Wiley, New York.

——. 1964b. The biological composition of a taxonomic species in *Gilia. Adv. Genetics,* 12:281-328.

——. 1965. Evidence for the selective origin of incompatibility barriers in the leafy-stemmed *Gilias. P.N.A.S.,* 54:1567-1571.

——. 1966a. Selection for vigor and fertility in the progeny of a highly sterile species hybrid in *Gilia. Gs.,* 53:757-775.

——. 1966b. Linkage between viability and fertility in a species cross in *Gilia. Gs.,* 54:867-880.

——. 1966c. The selective origin of incompatibility barriers in the plant genus *Gilia. A.N.,* 100:99-118.

——, and K. A. Grant. 1965. Pollination in the Phlox Family. Columbia Univ. Press, New York.

Greenberg, J. 1964. A locus for radiation resistance in *Escherichia coli. Gs.,* 49:771-778.

Greenberg, R., and J. F. Crow. 1960. Comparison of the effect of lethal and detrimental chromosomes from *Drosophila* populations. *Gs.*, 45:1153-1168.

Greene, J. C. 1961. The Death of Adam. New American Library, New York.

Gregg, J. R. 1954. The Language of Taxonomy. Columbia Univ. Press, New York.

Grinchuk, P. M. 1967. A study of the polymorphism of polytene chromosomes of the black fly *Prosimulium hirtipes (Diptera, Simulidae)* indigenous to the Leningrad region. *Ga.*, 1967, 165-172.

Gripenberg, U. 1964. Size variation and orientation of the human Y chromosome. *Ch.*, 15:618-629.

Grossfield, J. 1966. The influence of light on the mating behavior of Drosophila. *U.T.P.*, 6615:147-176.

Grun, P., and M. Aubertin. 1965. Evolutionary pathways of cytoplasmic male sterility in *Solanum*. *Gs.*, 51:399-409.

Grüneberg, H. 1938. An analysis of the "pleiotropic" effects of a new lethal mutation in the rat (*Mus norvegicus*). *Proc. Royal Soc.*, B, 125:123-144.

———. 1943. Congenital hydrocephaly in the mouse, a case of spurious pleiotropism. *J. Genetics*, 45:1-21.

Gulick, J. T. 1905. Evolution, racial and habitudinal. *Carnegie Inst. Washington Publ.* 25:1-269.

Gunn, D. L., and Ph. Hunter-Jones. 1952. Laboratory experiments on phase differences in locusts. *Anti-Locust Bull.* (London), 12.

Gustafsson, Å. 1941. Preliminary yield experiments with ten induced mutations in barley. *Hs.*, 27:337-359.

———. 1946. The effect of heterozygosity on viability and vigour. *Hs.*, 32:263-286.

———. 1947. Apomixis in higher plants. *Lunds Univ. Arsskrift*, N.F., 43:71-178.

———. 1951. Induction of changes in genes and chromosomes. II. Mutations, environment and evolution. *C.S.H.*, 16:263-281.

———. 1953. The cooperation of genotypes in barley. *Hs.*, 39:1-18.

———. 1963a. Productive mutations induced in barley by ionizing radiations and chemical mutagens. *Hs.*, 50:211-263.

———. 1963b. Mutations and the concept of viability. Pp. 89-104 *in:* E. Akerberg, A. Hagberg, et. al. (Eds.), Recent Plant Breeding Research, John Wiley, New York.

———, and N. Nybom. 1950. The viability reaction of some induced and spontaneous mutations in barley. *Hs.*, 36:113-133.

———, N. Nybom, and U. Wettstein. 1950. Chlorophyll factors and heterosis in barley. *Hs.*, 36:383-392.

Guthrie, G. D., and R. L. Sinsheimer. 1960. Infection of protoplasts of *Escherichia coli* by subviral particles of bacteriophage $\phi\chi$ 174. *J. Mol. Biol.*, 2:297-305.

Hadorn, E. 1951. Developmental action of lethal factors in Drosophila. *Adv. Genetics*, 4:53-85.

———. 1956. Patterns of biochemical and developmental pleiotropy. *C.S.H.*, 21:363-373.

———. 1961. Developmental Genetics and Lethal Factors. Methuen, London.

———, and H. Niggli. 1946. Mutations in *Drosophila* after chemical treatment of gonads *in vitro*. *N.*, 157-162.

———, S. Rosin, and G. Bertani. 1949. Ergebnisse der Mutationsversuche mit chemischer Behandlung von *Drosophila in vitro*. *P.* VIII *I.C.G.*:256-266.

Haga, T. 1956. Genome and polyploidy in the genus *Trillium*. VI. Hybridization and speciation by chromosome doubling in nature. *Hy.*, 10:85-98.

——, and M. Kurabayashi. 1954. Chromosomal variation in natural populations of *Trillium kamtschaticum* Pall. *Mem. Fac. Sci. Kyushu Univ.*, E, 1:159-185.

Hagedoorn, A. L., and A. C. Hagedoorn. 1921. The Relative Value of the Processes Causing Evolution. Martius Nijhoff, The Hague.

Hagen, D. W. 1967. Isolating mechanisms in three-spine sticklebacks. (*Gasterosteus*). *J. Fish. Res. Bd. Canada*, 24:1637-1692.

Håkansson, A. 1942. Zytologische Studien an Rassen und Rassenbastarden von *Godetia whitneyi* und verwandten Arten. *Lunds Univ. Arsskrift*, N.F., 38, No. 5:1-70.

Haldane, J. B. S. 1932. The Causes of Evolution. Harper, London and New York.

——. 1933. The part played by recurrent mutation in evolution. *A.N.*, 67:5-19.

——. 1937. The effect of variation on fitness. *A.N.*, 71:337-349.

——. 1957. The cost of natural selection. *J. Genetics*, 55:511-524. Reprinted *in*: E. B. Spiess (Ed.), "Papers in Animal Population Genetics," Little, Brown, Boston (1962).

——. 1964. A defense of beanbag genetics. *Persp. Biol. Med.*, 7:343-359.

——, and S. D. Jayakar. 1963a. Polymorphism due to selection of varying direction. *J. Genetics*, 58:237-242.

——, and S. D. Jayakar. 1963b. Polymorphism due to selection depending on the composition of a population. *J. Genetics*, 58:318-323.

Haley, L. E., H. Abplanalp, and K. Eyna. 1966. Selection for increased fertility of female quail when mated to male chickens. *E.*, 20:72-81.

Halfer-Cervini, A. M., M. Piccinelli, P. Prosdocimi, and L. Baratelli-Zambruni. 1968. Sibling species in *Artemia (Crustacea: Branchiopoda)*. *E.*, 22:373-381.

Hamilton, W. J., and F. Heppner. 1967. Radiant solar energy and the function of black homeotherm pigmentation: an hypothesis. *S.*, 155:196-197.

Harding, J., R. W. Allard, and D. G. Smeltzer. 1966. Population studies in predominantly self-pollinated species. IX. Frequency-dependent selection in *Phaseolus lunatus*. *P.N.A.S.*, 56:99-104.

Hardy, G. H. 1908. Mendelian proportions in a mixed population. *S.*, 28:49-50.

Harland, S. C. 1936. The genetical conception of the species. *Biol. Rev.*, 11:83-112.

Harrington, R. W., and K. D. Kallman. 1968. The homozygosity of clones of the self-fertilizing hermaphroditic fish *Rivulus marmoratus* Poey (*Cyprinodontidae, Atheriniformes*). *A.N.*, 102:337-343.

Harris, H. 1966. Enzyme polymorphisms in man. *Proc. Royal Soc.*, B, 164:298-316.

——. 1967. Enzyme variation in man: some general aspects. Pp. 207-214 *in*: J. F. Crow and J. V. Neel (Eds.), "Proceedings of the 3rd International Congress on Human Genetics," Johns Hopkins Press, Baltimore.

Harrison, G. A. (Ed.). 1961. Genetical Variation in Human Populations. Pergamon Press, Oxford.

Haskins, C. P., E. F. Haskins, and R. E. Hewitt. 1960. Pseudogamy as an evolutionary factor in the poeciliid fish *Mollienesia formosa*. *E.*, 14:473-483.

Hatt, D., and P. A. Parsons. 1965. Association between surnames and blood groups in the Australian population. *Acta Genetica*, 15:309-318.

Hauschteck, E., G. Mürset, A. Prader and E. Bühler. 1966. Siblings with different types of chromosomal aberrations due to D/E translocation of the mother. *Cytogenetics*, 5:281-294.

Hayes, C. 1951. The Ape in Our House. Harper & Row, New York.

Hedberg, O. 1955. Some taxonomic problems concerning the Afro-alpine flora. *Webbia*, 11:471-487.

Heed, W. B. 1963. Density and distribution of *Drosophila polymorpha* and its color alleles in South America. *E.*, 17:502-518.

———, and P. R. Blake. 1963. A new color allele at the *e* locus of *Drosophila polymorpha* from northern South America. *Gs.*, 48:217-234.

Heiser, C. B. 1947. Hybridization between the sunflower species *Helianthus annus* and *H. petiolaris*. *E.*, 1:249-262.

Helfer, R. G. 1941. A comparison of X-ray induced and naturally occurring chromosomal variations in *Drosophila pseudoobscura*. *Gs.*, 26:1-22.

Héritier, Ph. L'., and G. Teissier. 1934. Une experience de sélection naturelle. Courbe d'élimination du gene "Bar" dans une population de *Drosophiles* en équilibre. *C. R. Soc. Biol.*, 117:1049-1051.

Herskowitz, I. 1949a. Hexaptera, a homoeotic mutant in *Drosophila melanogaster*. *Gs.*, 34:10-25.

———. 1949. Tests for chemical mutagens in Drosophila. *Proc. Soc. Exp. Biol.*, 70:601-607.

Heuts, M. J. 1947. Experimental studies in adaptive evolution in *Gasterosteus aculeatus* L. *E.*, 1:89-102.

Hildreth, P. E. 1956. The problem of synthetic lethals in *Drosophila melanogaster*. *Gs.*, 41:729-742.

———. 1965. Doublesex, a recessive gene that transforms both males and females of *Drosophila* into intersexes. *Gs.*, 51:659-678.

Hiraizumi, Y., and J. F. Crow. 1960. Heterozygous effects on viability, fertility, rate of development and longevity of *Drosophila* chromosomes that are lethal when homozygous. *Gs.*, 45:1071-1083.

Hochman, B. 1961. On fourth chromosome lethals from a natural population of *Drosophila melanogaster*. *A.N.*, 95:375-382.

Hoenigsberg, H. F., and S. Koref-Santibañez. 1960. Courtship and sensory preferences in inbred lines of *Drosophila melanogaster*. *E.*, 14:1-7.

Holland, J. J., M. W. Taylor, and C. A. Buck. 1967. Chromatographic differences between tyrosyl transfer RNA from different mammalian cells. *P.N.A.S.*, 58:2437-2444.

Hollingshead, L. 1930. A lethal factor in *Crepis* effective only in interspecific hybrids. *Gs.*, 15:114-140.

Holttum, R. E. 1953. Evolutionary trends in an equatorial climate. *Symposia Soc. Exp. Biol.*, 7:159-173.

Horton, I. H. 1939. A comparison of the salivary gland chromosomes of *Drosophila melanogaster* and *D. simulans*. *Gs.*, 24:234-243.

Hosino, Y. 1940. Genetical studies on the pattern types of the lady bird beetle, *Harmonia axyridis* Pallas. *J. Genetics*, 40:215-228.

Hoyer, B. H., E. T. Bolton, B. J. McCarthy, and R. B. Roberts. 1965. The evolution of polynucleotides. Pp. 581-590 *in:* V. Bryson and H. J. Vogel (Eds.), "Evolving Genes and Proteins," Academic Press, New York.

———, B. J. McCarthy and E. T. Bolton. 1964. A molecular approach in the systematics of higher organisms. *S.*, 144:959-967.

Hrishi, N. J., and A. Müntzing. 1960. Structural heterozygosity in *Secale kuprijanovii*. *Hs.*, 46:745-752.

Hubbs, C. 1964. Interactions between a bisexual fish species and its gynogenetic sexual parasite. *Bull. Texas Mem. Museum*, 8:1-72.

———, and E. A. Delco. 1960. Mate preference in males of four species of gambusiine fishes. *E.*, 14:145-152.

——, and E. A. Delco. 1962. Courtship preferences of *Gambusia affinis* associated with the sympatry of the parental populations. *Copeia*, 1962:396-400.

——, and K. Strawn. 1956. Interfertility between two sympatric fishes, *Notropis lutrensis* and *Notropis venustus*. E., 10:341-344.

Hubbs, C. L. 1940. Speciation of fishes. A.N. 74:198-211.

Hubby, J. L., and R. C. Lewontin. 1966. A molecular approach to the study of genic heterozygosity in natural populations. I. The number of alleles at different loci in *Drosophila pseudoobscura*. Gs., 54:577-594.

——, and L H. Throckmorton. 1965. Protein differences in *Drosophila*. II. Comparative species genetics and evolutionary problems. Gs., 52:203-215.

——, and L. H. Throckmorton. 1968. Protein differences in *Drosophila*. IV. A study of sibling species. A.N., 102:193-205.

Hulse, F. S. 1957. Exogamie et hétérosis. *Arch. Suisse Anthrop. Gén.* 22:103-125.

——. 1963. The Human Species. Random House, New York.

Hutchinson, J. B., J. B. Silow, and J. G. Stephens. 1947. The evolution of *Gossypium*. Oxford Univ. Press, Oxford.

Huxley, J. S. (1942) 1963. Evolution, the Modern Synthesis. Rev. Ed. Harper, New York.

Ingels, L. G. 1950. Pigmental variations in populations of pocket gophers. E., 4:353-357.

Ingram, V. M. 1963. The Hemoglobins in Genetics and Evolution. Columbia Univ. Press, New York.

Irving, L. 1966. Adaptation to cold. *Sci. American*, 214:94-101.

Irwin, M. R. 1953. Evolutionary patterns of antigenic substances of the blood corpuscles in *Columbidae*. E., 7:31-50.

——. 1966. Interaction of nonallelic genes on cellular antigens in species hybrids of *Columbidae*. II. Identification of interacting genes. P.N.A.S., 55:34-40.

——, and R. W. Cumley. 1943. Interrelationships of the cellular characters of several species of *Columba*. Gs., 28:9-28.

Ives, P. T. 1945. The genetic structure of American populations of *Drosophila melanogaster*. Gs., 30:167-196.

——. 1950. The importance of mutation rate genes in evolution. E., 4:236-252.

Jacob, F., and J. Monod. 1961. Genetic regulatory mechanisms in the synthesis of proteins. *J. Mol. Biol.*, 3:318-356.

——, and E. L. Wollman. 1961. Sexuality and Genetics of Bacteria. Academic Press, New York.

Jacobson, M., and M. Beroza. 1963. Chemical insect attractants. S., 140:1367-1372.

Jain, S. K. 1969. Comparative ecogenetics of two *Avena* species occurring in central California. E.B., 3:73-118.

——, and A. D. Bradshaw. 1966. Evolutionary divergence among adjacent populations. I. The evidence and its theoretical analysis. Hy., 21:407-441.

——, and D. R. Marshall. 1967. Population studies on predominantly self-pollinating species. X. Variation in natural populations of *Avena fatua* and *A. barbata*. A.N., 101:19-33.

Jenkins, J. B. 1967. Mutagenesis at a complex locus in *Drosophila* with the monofunctional alkylating agent, ethyl methanesulfonate. Gs., 57:783-793.

Jensen, A. R. 1969. How much can we boost I.Q. and scholastic achievement? *Harvard Educ. Rev.*, 39:1-123.

Jensen, N. 1965. Multiple superiority in cereals. *Crop. Sci.*, 5:566-568.

Jinks, J. L. 1964. Extrachromosomal Inheritance. Prentice-Hall, Englewood Cliffs.

Johannsen, W. 1909 (1926). Elemente der exakten Erblichkeitslehre. Gustav Fischer, Jena.

John, B., and K. R. Lewis. 1958. Studies on *Periplaneta americana*. III. Selection for heterozygosity. *Hy.*, 12:185-197.

———, and K. R. Lewis. Selection for interchange heterozygosity in an inbred culture of *Blaberus discoidalis* (Serv.) *Gs.*, 44: 251-267.

Johnsgard, P. A. 1967. Sympatry changes and hybridization incidence in mallards and black ducks. *Amer. Midland Natur.*, 77:51-63.

Johnson, A. W., and J. G. Packer. 1965. Polyploidy and environment in arctic Alaska. *S.*, 148:237-239.

Johnson, F. M., C. G. Kanapi, R. H. Richardson, M. R. Wheeler, and W. S. Stone. 1968. An analysis of polymorphisms among isozyme loci in dark and light *Drosophila ananassae* strains from American and Western Samoa. *P.N.A.S.*, 56:119-125.

Johnson, M. P., L. G. Mason, and P. H. Raven. 1968. Ecological parameters and plant species diversity. *A.N.*, 102:297-306.

Jonas, H. 1966. The Phenomenon of Life. Harper & Row, New York.

Jones, H. A., J. C. Walker, T. M. Little, and R. M. Larson. 1946. Relation of color-inhibiting factor to smudge resistance in onion. *J. Agr. Res.*, 72:259-264.

Jordan, D. S. 1905. The origin of species through isolation. *S.*, 22:545-562.

Jordan, K. 1905. Der Gegensatz zwischen geographischer und nichtgeographischer Variation. *Zeit. wiss. Zool.*, 83:151-210.

Jukes, Th. H. 1966. Molecules and Evolution. Columbia Univ. Press, New York.

Käfer, E. 1952. Vitalitätsmutationen, ausgelöst durch Röntgenstrahlen beim *Drosophila melanogaster*. *Z.i.A.V.*, 84:508-535.

Kallman, K. D. 1962. Population genetics of the gynogenetic teleost, *Mollienesia formosa* (Girard). *E.*, 16:497-504.

Kaplan, W. D. 1948. Formaldehyde as a mutagen in *Drosophila*. *S.*, 108:43.

Karpechenko, G. D. 1928. Polyploid hybrids of *Raphanus sativus* L. × *Brassica oleracea* L. *Z.i.A.V.*, 48:1-85.

Kastritsis, C. D. 1966. Cytological studies on some species of the *tripunctata* group of *Drosophila*. *U.T.P.*, 6615:413-474.

———. 1967. A comparative study of the chromosomal polymorphs in the incipient species of the *Drosophila paulistorum* complex. *Ch.*, 23:180-202.

———. 1969a. The chromosomes of some species of the *guarani* group of *Drosophila*. *J. Heredity*, 60:51-57.

———. 1969b. A cytological study of some recently collected strains of *Drosophila paulistorum*. *E.*, 23:663-675.

Kaul, D., and P. A. Parsons. 1965. The genotype control of mating speed and duration of copulation in *Drosophila pseudoobscura*. *Hy.*, 20:381-392.

Keiding, J. 1967. Persistence of resistant populations after the relaxation of the selection pressure. *World Rev. Pest Control*, 6:115-130.

Kennedy, W. P. 1967. Epidemiologic aspects of the problem of congenital malformations. Birth Defects Original Series, Vol. 3, No. 2.

Kerkis, J. 1933. Development of gonads in hybrids between *Drosophila melanogaster* and *Drosophila simulans*. *J. Exp. Zool.*, 66:477-509.

———. 1936. Chromosome configuration in hybrids between *Drosophila melanogaster* and *Drosophila simulans*. *A.N.*, 70:81-86.

———. 1938. The frequency of mutations affecting viability. *Bull. Acad. Sci. USSR* (*Biol.*), 1938:75-96.

Kernaghan, R. P., and L. Ehrman. 1970. An electron microscopic study of the etiology of hybrid sterility in *Drosophila paulistorum*. I. Mycoplasma-like inclusions in the testes of sterile males. Chromosoma 29:291-304.

Kerr, W. E., and L. Kerr. 1952. Concealed variabilty in the X chromosome. *A.N.*, 96:405-407.

——, and S. Wright. 1954. Experimental studies of the distribution of gene frequencies in very small populations of *Drosophila melanogaster*. *E.*, 8:172-177, 225-240, 293-302.

Kerster, H. W., and D. A. Levin. 1968. Neighborhood size in *Lithospermum carolinense*. *Gs.*, 60:577-583.

Kessler, S. 1966. Selection for and against ethological isolation between *Drosophila pseudoobscura* and *Drosophila persimilis*. *E.*, 20:634-645.

Kettlewell, H. B. D. 1955. Selection experiments on industrial melanism in the *Lepidoptera*. *Hy.*, 9:323-342.

——. 1961. The phenomenon of industrial melanism in the *Lepidoptera*. *Ann. Rev. Entom.*, 6:245-262.

——. 1965. Insect survival and selection for pattern. *S.*, 148:1290-1296.

Key, K. H. L. 1950. A critique of the phase theory of locusts. *Q.R.B.*, 25:363-407.

——. 1957. Kentromorphic phases in three species of *Phasmatodea*. *Austral. J. Zool.*, 5:247-284.

——. 1968. The concept of stasipatric speciation. *S.Z.*, 17:14-22.

Keyl, H. G. 1961. Chromosomenevolution bei *Chironomus*. I. Strukturabwandlungen an Speicheldrüsen Chromosomen. *Ch.*, 12:26-47.

——. 1962. Chromosomenevolution bei *Chironomus*. II. Chromosomenumbauten und phylogenetische Beziehung der Arten. *Ch.*, 13:464-514.

——. 1965. Duplikationen von Untereinheiten der chromosomalen DNS während der Evolution von *Chironomus thummi*. *Ch.*, 17:139-180.

Kihara, H. 1959. Fertility and morphological variation in the substitution and restoration backcrosses of the hybrids, *Triticum vulgare* × *Aegilops caudata*. *P. X I.C.G.*, 1:142-171.

——. 1965. The origin of wheat in the light of comparative genetics. *Japan. J. Genetics*, 40:45-54.

——. 1967. Cytoplasmic male sterility in relation to hybrid wheat breeding. *Der Züchter*, 37:86-93.

Kimura, M. 1954. Process leading to quasi-fixation of genes in natural populations due to random fluctuations of selection intensities. *Gs.*, 39:280-295.

——. 1960. Optimum mutation rate and degree of dominance as determined by the principle of minimum genetic load. *J. Genetics*, 57:21-34.

——. 1961. Natural selection as the process of accumulating genetic information in adaptive evolution. *G.R.*, 2:127-140.

——. 1968. Genetic variability maintained in a finite population due to mutational production of neutral and nearly neutral isoalleles. *G. R.*, 11:246-269.

——. 1969. The number of heterozygous nucleotide sites maintained in a finite population due to steady flux of mutations. *Gs.*, 61:893-903.

——, and J. F. Crow. 1963. The measurement of effective population number. *E.*, 17:279-288.

——, and J. F. Crow. 1964. The number of alleles that can be maintained in a finite population. *Gs.*, 49:725-738.

——, and J. F. Crow. 1969. Natural selection and gene substitution. *G.R.*, 13:127-141.

——, T. Maruyama, and J. F. Crow. 1963. The mutation load in small populations. *Gs.*, 48:1303-1312.

——, and T. Ohta. 1969. The average number of generations until fixation of a mutant gene in a finite population. *Gs.*, 61:763-771.

——, and G. H. Weiss. 1964. The stepping-stone model of population structure and the decrease of genetic correlation with distance. *Gs.*, 49:561-576.

Kindred, B. 1967. Selection for an invariant character, vibrissa number in the house mouse. V. Selection on non-Tabby segregants from Tabby selection lines. *Gs.*, 55:365-373.

King, J. L. 1966. The gene interaction component of the genetic load. *Gs.*, 53:403-413.

——. 1967. Continuously distributed factors affecting fitness. *Gs.*, 55:483-492.

——, and Th. H. Jukes. 1969. Non-Darwinian evolution. *S.*, 164:788-798.

Kitagawa, O. 1967. Genetic divergence in M. Vetukhiv's experimental populations of *Drosophila pseudoobscura. G.R.*, 10:303-312.

Kitchin, F. D., W. H. Evans, C. A. Clarke, R. B. McConnell, and P. M. Sheppard. 1959. PTC taste response and thyroid disease. *Brit. Med. J.*, 1:1069-1074.

Kitzmiller, J. B. 1967. Mosquito cytogenetics. Pp. 133-150 *in*: J. W. Wright and R. Pal (Eds.), "Genetics of Insect Vectors of Disease," Elsevier, Amsterdam.

——, G. Frizzi, and R. H. Baker. 1967. Evolution and speciation within the *maculipennis* complex of the genus *Anopheles*. Pp. 151-210 *in*: J. W. Wright and R. Pal (Eds.), "Genetics of Insect Vectors of Disease," Elsevier, Amsterdam.

Klekowski, E. J., and H. G. Baker. 1966. Evolutionary significance of polyploidy in *Pteridophyta. S.*, 153:305-307.

Knight, G. R., A. Robertson, and C. H. Waddington. 1956. Selection for sexual isolation within a species. *E.*, 10:14-22.

Knipling, E. F. 1955. Possibilities of insect control or eradication through the use of sexually sterile males. *J. Econ. Entom.*, 48:459-462.

——. 1967. Sterile technique—principles involved, current application, limitations, and future application. Pp. 587-616 *in*: J. W. Wright and R. Pal (Eds.), "Genetics of Insect Vectors of Disease," Elsevier, Amsterdam.

Koestler, A. 1967. The Ghost in the Machine. Macmillan, New York.

Kojima, R. I., and T. M. Kelleher. 1962. Survival of mutant genes. *A.N.*, 96:329-346.

——, and T. M. Kelleher. 1963. Selection studies of quantitative traits with laboratory animals. *Stat. Genetics Plant Breeding NAS-NRC*, 982:395-422.

Komai, T. 1954. An actual instance of microevolution observed in an insect population. *Proc. Japan Acad.*, 30:970-975.

——, M. Chino, and Y. Hosino. 1950. Contributions to the evolutionary genetics of the lady bettle, Harmonia. I. *Gs.*, 35:589-601.

——, and Y. Hosino. 1951. Contributions to the evolutionary genetics of the lady beetle, Harmonia. II. Microgeographic variations. *Gs.*, 36:382-390.

Kondakova, A. A. 1935. Einfluss des Jods auf das Auftreten letaler mutationen im III. Chromosom von *Drosophila melanogaster. Biol. Zhurnal*, 4:721-726.

Konigsberg, W., R. G. Huntsman, F. Wadia, and H. Lehmann. 1965. Haemoglobin $D_{\beta Punjab}$ in an East Anglian Family. *J. Royal Anthrop. Inst.*, 95:295-306.

Koopman, K. F. 1950. Natural selection for reproductive isolation between *Drosophila pseudoobscura* and *Drosophila persimilis. E.*, 4:135-145.

Koref-Santibañez, S. 1964. Reproductive isolation between the sibling species *Drosophila pavani* and *Drosophila gaucha. E.*, 18:245-251.

Kornberg, A. 1962 Enzymatic Synthesis of DNA. John Wiley, New York.

Korzhinsky, S. I. 1899. Heterogenesis and Evolution. Academy of Science, St. Petersburg (Russian).

Kosiupa, D. E. 1936. The effect of sublimate on the occurrence of lethal mutations in *Drosophila melanogaster*. *Bull. Biol. Med. Exp. URSS*, 2:87-89.

Kozhevnikov, B. Th. 1936. Experimentally produced karyotypical isolation. *Biol. Zhurnal*, 5:727-752.

Kraczkiewicz, Z. 1950. Recherches cytologiques sur les chromosomes de *Lasioptera rubi* Heeg. (*Cecidomyidae*). *Zool. Poloniae*, 5:73-115.

Krimbas, C. B. 1960. Synthetic sterility in *Drosophila willistoni*. *P.N.A.S.*, 46: 832-833.

——. 1961. Release of genetic variability through recombination. VI. *Drosophila willistoni*. *Gs.*, 46:1323-1334.

——. 1964. The genetics of *Drosophila subobscura* populations. I. Inversion polymorphism in populations of southern Greece. *E.*, 18:541-552.

Kruckeberg, A. R. 1957. Variation in fertility of hybrids between isolated populations of serpentine species, *Streptanthus glandulosus* Hook. *E.*, 11:185-211.

Kullenberg, B. 1951. *Ophrys insectifera* L. et les insects. *Oikos*, 3:53-70.

Kurokawa, H. 1960. Sexual isolation among the three races, A, B, and C of *Drosophila auraria*. *Japan. J. Genetics*, 35:161-166.

Kyhos, D. W. 1965. The independent aneuplod origin of two species of *Chaenactis* (*Compositae*) from a common ancestor. *E.*, 19:26-43.

LaChance, L. E. 1967. The induction of dominant lethal mutations in insects by ionizing radiation and chemicals as related to the sterile-male technique of insect control. Pp. 617-650 *in:* J. W. Wright and R. Pal (Eds.), "Genetics of Insect Vectors of Disease," Elsevier, Amsterdam.

Laibach, F. 1925. Das Taubwerden von Bastardsamen und die Künstliche Aufzucht früh absterbender Bastardembryonen. *Zeit. Botanik*, 17:417-459.

Laidlaw, H. H., E. P. Gomes, and W. E. Kerr. 1956. Estimation of the number of lethal alleles in a panmictic population of *Apis mellifera* L. *Gs.*, 41:179-188.

——, J. G. Reiman, and D. E. Hopkins. 1964. A reciprocal translocation in *Cochliomyia hominivorax* (Diptera, *Calliphoridae*). *Gs.*, 49:959-972.

Laird, Ch. D., and B. J. McCarthy. 1968a. Magnitude of interspecific nucleotide sequence variability in *Drosophila*. *Gs.*, 60:303-322.

——, and B. J. McCarthy. 1968b. Nucleotide sequence homology within the genome of *Drosophila melanogaster*. *Gs.*, 60:323-334.

Lamotte, M. 1951. Recherches sur la structure génétique des populations naturelles de *Cepaea nemoralis* L. *Bull. Biol. France*, Suppl., 35:1-239.

——. 1959. Polymorphism of natural populations of *Cepaea nemoralis*. *C.S.H.*, 24:65-84.

Lamprecht, H. 1964. Species concept and the origin of species. The two categories of genes—intra- and interspecific ones. *Agri Hortique Genetica*, 22:272-280.

——. 1966. Die Entstehung der Arten und höheren Kategorien. Springer, Vienna and New York.

Lancefield, D. E. 1929. A genetic study of two races or physiological species in *Drosophila obscura*. *Z.i.A.V.*, 52:287-317.

Landau, R. 1962. Four forms of *Simulium tuberosum* Lundstr. in southern Ontario: Salivary gland chromosome study. *Canad. J. Zool.*, 40:921-939.

Landauer, W. 1948. Hereditary abnormalities and their chemically induced phenocopies. *Growth Symposia*, 12:171-200.

Larson, C. A. 1961. Phenylketonuria. *Genetica Medica*, 4:121-140.

Laugé, G. 1966. Étude comparative des effets d'un traitement thermique sur le développement des gonades et de divers charactères sexuels primaires chez les intersexués triploides de *Drosophila melanogaster*. *Bull. Soc. Zool. France*, 91: 661-686.

Laven, H. 1967. Speciation and evolution in *Culex pipiens*. Pp. 251-275 *in:* J. W. Wright and R. Pal (Eds.), "Genetics of Insect Vectors of Disease," Elsevier, Amsterdam.

Law, L. W. 1938. The effects of chemicals on the lethal mutation rate in *Drosophila melanogaster*. *P.N.A.S.*, 24:546-550.

Lea, A. J. 1955. Association of susceptibility to poliomyelitis with eye and hair color. *S.*, 121:608.

Lea, D. E. 1955. Action of Radiations on Living Cells. 2nd Ed. Cambridge Univ. Press, Cambridge.

Lécher, P. 1967. Cytogénétique de l'hybridation expérimentale et naturelle chez l'isopode *Jaera albifrons syei* Bocquet. *Arch. Zool. Exp. Gen.*, 108:633-698.

Lederberg, J. 1965. Signs of life. Criterion-system of exobiology. *N.*, 207:9-13.

Lejeune, J. 1969. Human cytogenetics. *P.* XII *I.C.G.*, 3:379-387.

——, R. Turpin, and M. Gautier. 1959. Le mongolisme, premier example d'aberration autosomique humaine. *Ann. Génét. Hum.*, 1:41-49.

Lerner, I. M. 1950. Population Genetics and Animal Improvement. Cambridge Univ. Press, Cambridge.

——. 1954. Genetic Homeostasis. Oliver & Boyd, Edinburgh.

——. 1958. The Genetic Basis of Selection. John Wiley, New York.

——. 1968. Heredity, Evolution and Society. Freeman, San Francisco.

——, and H. P. Donald. 1966. Modern Developments in Animal Breeding. Academic Press, London and New York.

Levene, H. 1953. Genetic equilibrium when more than one ecological niche is available. *A.N.*, 87:331-333.

——. 1963. Inbred genetic loads and the determination of population structure. *P.N.A.S.*, 50:587-592.

——, I. M. Lerner, A. Sokoloff, F. K. Ho, and I. R. Franklin. 1965. Genetic loads in *Tribolium*. *P.N.A.S.*, 53:1042-1050.

——, O. Pavlovsky, and Th. Dobzhansky. 1958. Dependence of the adaptive values of certain genotypes of *Drosophila pseudoobscura* on the composition of the gene pool. *E.*, 12:18-23.

Levin, B. R., M. L. Petras, and D. I. Rasmussen. 1969. The effect of migration on the maintenance of a lethal polymorphism in the house mouse. *A.N.*, 103: 647-661.

Levin, D. A. 1968. The structure of a polyspecies hybrid swarm in *Liatris*. *E.*, 22:352-372.

——, and H. W. Kerster. 1967a. An analysis of interspecific pollen exchange in *Phlox*. *A.N.*, 101:387-399.

——, and H. W. Kerster. 1967b. Natural selection for reproductive isolation in *Phlox*. *E.*, 21:679-687.

——, and H. W. Kerster. 1968. Local gene dispersal in *Phlox*. *E.*, 22:130-139.

Levins, R. 1968. Evolution in Changing Environments. Princeton Univ. Press, Princeton.

——, and R. MacArthur. 1966. The maintenance of genetic polymorphism in a spatially heterogeneous environment: variations on a theme by Howard Levene. *A.N.*, 100:585-589.

Levisohn, R., and S. Spiegelman. 1969. Further extracellular Darwinian experiments with replicating RNA molecules. Diverse variants isolated under different selective conditions. *P.N.A.S.*, 63:805-811.

Levitan, M., H. L. Carson, and H. D. Stalker 1954. Triads of overlapping inversions in *Drosophila robusta*. *A.N.*, 88:113-114.

Lewis, E. B. 1967. Genes and gene complexes. Pp. 17-47 *in:* R. A. Brink and E. D. Styles (Eds.), "Heritage from Mendel," Univ. Wisconsin Press, Madison.

Lewis, H. 1966. Speciation in flowering plants. *S.*, 152:167-172.

——, and P. H. Raven. 1958. Rapid evolution in *Clarkia*. *E.*, 12:319-336.

Lewis, K. R., and B. John. 1964. Spontaneous interchange in *Chorthippus brunneus*. *Ch.*, 14:618-637.

Lewontin, R. C. 1955. The effects of population density and composition on viability in *Drosophila melanogaster*. *E.*, 9:27-41.

——. 1962. Interdeme selection controlling a polymorphism in the house mouse. *A.N.*, 96:65-78.

——. 1967a. An estimate of average heterozygosity in man. *Amer. J. Human Genetics*, 19:681-685.

——. 1967b. The genetics of complex systems. *Proc. 5th Berkeley Symposium Math. Stat. Probability*, 4:439-455.

——. 1968. The concept of evolution. Pp. 202-210 *in:* D. L. Sills (Ed.), International Encyclopedia of Social Science, Vol. 5.

——, and J. L. Hubby. 1966. A molecular approach to the study of genic heterozygosity in natural populations. II. Amount of variation and degree of heterozygosity in natural populations of *Drosophila pseudoobscura*. *Gs.*, 54:595-609.

——, and Y. Matsuo. 1963. Interaction of genotypes determining viability in *Drosophila busckii*. *P.N.A.S.*, 49:270-278.

——, and M. J. D. White. 1960. Interaction between inversion polymorphisms of two chromosome pairs in the grasshopper *Moraba scurra*. *E.*, 14:116-129.

Li, C. C. 1955a. Population Genetics. Univ. Chicago Press, Chicago.

——. 1955b. The stability of an equilibrium and the average fitness of a population. *A.N.*, 89:281-296.

——. 1963. The way the load ratio works. *Amer. J. Human Genetics*, 15:315-321.

Lillie, F. R. 1921. Studies of fertilization. VIII. *Biol Bull.*, 40:1-22.

Lindsley, D. L., C. W. Edington, and E. S. von Halle. 1960. Sex-linked recessive lethals in *Drosophila* whose expression is suppressed by the Y chromosome. *Gs.*, 45:1649-70.

——, and E. H. Grell. 1968. Genetic variations of *Drosophila melanogaster*. *Carnegie Inst. Washington Publ.* 627:1-472.

Linsley, E. G. 1958. The ecology of solitary bees. *Hilgardia*, 27:543-599.

Littlejohn, M. J. 1965. Premating isolation in the *Hyla ewingi* complex (*Anura: Hylidae*). *E.*, 19:234-243.

——, and J. J. Loftus-Hills. 1968. An experimental evaluation of premating isolation in the *Hyla ewingi* complex. *E.*, 22:659-663.

Livingstone, F. B. 1964. The distribution of the abnormal hemoglobin genes and their significance for human evolution. *E.*, 18:685-699.

——. 1967. Abnormal Hemoglobins in Human Populations. Aldine, Chicago.

Lloyd, M., and H. S. Dybas. 1966. The periodical cicada problem. II. Evolution. *E.*, 20:466-505.

Lobashov, M. E. 1935. Uber die Natur der Einwirkung der chemischen Agentien auf den Mutationsprocess bei *Drosophila melanogaster*, *Ga.*, 19:200-241.

——, and F. Smirnov. 1934. On the nature of the action of chemical agents on the mutational process in *Drosophila melanogaster*. II. The effect of ammonia on the occurrence of lethal transgenations. *C. R. Acad. Sci. URSS*, 3:174-176.

Loomis, W. F. 1967. Skin-pigment regulation of vitamin-D biosynthesis in man. *S.*, 157:501-506.

Lorenz, K. 1941. Vergleichende Bewegungsstudien an Anatinen. *J. Ornithol.*, 89: 194-294.

Lotsy J. P. 1931. On the species of the taxonomist in its relation to evolution. *Ga.*, 13:1-16.

Löve, A. 1951. Taxonomical evaluation of polyploids. *Caryologia*, 3:263-284.

——. 1964. The biological species concept and its evolutionary structure. *Taxon*, 13:33-45.

——, and D. Löve. 1949. The geobotanical significance of polyploidy. I. Polyploidy and latitude. *Portugeliae Acta Biol.*, Goldschmidt Volumen:273-352.

Lucchesi, J. C. 1968. Synthetic lethality and semi-lethality among functionally related mutants of *Drosophila melanogaster*. *Gs.*, 59:37-44.

Ludwig, W. 1950. Zur Theorie der Konkurrenz. Die Annidation (Einnischung) als fünfter Evolutionsfaktor. *Neue Ergeb. Probleme Zool.*, Klatt-Festschrift 1950:516-537.

Lundman, B. 1967. Geographische Anthropologie. Gustav Fischer, Stuttgart.

Luria, S. E., and M. Delbrück. 1943. Mutations of bacteria from virus sensitivity to virus resistance. *Gs.*, 28:491-511.

McCarthy B. J., and E. T. Bolton. 1963. An approach to the measurement of genetic relatedness among organisms. *P.N.A.S.*, 50:156-164.

McClelland, G. A. H. 1967. Speciation and evolution in *Aedes*. Pp. 277-311 *in:* J. W. Wright and R. Pal (Eds.), "Genetics of Insect Vectors of Disease," Elsevier, Amsterdam.

MacFarquhar, A. M., and F. W. Robertson. 1963. The lack of evidence for coadaptation in crosses between geographical races of *Drosophila subobscura* Coll. *G.R.*, 4:104-131.

McKusick, V. A. 1966. Mendelian Inheritance in Man. Johns Hopkins Press, Baltimore.

McNeilly, T. 1968. Evolution in closely adjacent plant populations. III. *Agrostis tenuis* on a small copper mine. *Hy.*, 23:99-108.

——, and A. D. Bradshaw. 1968. Evolutionary processes in populations of copper tolerant *Agrostis tenuis*. *E.*, 22:108-118.

Magalhães, L. E., A. B. da Cunha, J. S. de Toledo, S. P. de Toledo, H. L. Souza, H. J. Targa, V. Setzer, and C. Pavan. 1965. On lethals and their suppressors in experimental populations of *Drosophila willistoni*. *Mutation Res.*, 2:45-54.

Magalhães, L. E., J. S. de Toledo, and A. B. da Cunha. 1965. The nature of lethals in *Drosophila willistoni*. *Gs.*, 52:599-608.

Magrzhikovskaja, K. V. 1938. The effect of $CuSO_4$ on the mutation process in *Drosophila melanogaster*. *Biol. Zhurnal*, 7:635-642.

Mainx, F., J. Fiala, and E. V. Kogerer. 1956. Die geographische Verbreitung der chromosomalen Strukturtypen von *Liriomyza urophorina* Mill. *Ch.*, 8:18-29.

Makino, S. 1951. An Atlas of the Chromosome Number in Animals. Iowa State College Press, Ames.

——, M. S. Sasaki, K. Yamada, and T. Kajii. 1963. A long Y chromosome in man. *Ch.*, 14:154-161.

——, and N. Takagi. 1965. Some morphological aspects of the abnormal human Y chromosome. *Cytologia*, 30:274-292.

Malécot, G. 1948. Les mathématiques de l'hérédité. Masson, Paris.

——. 1959. Les modèles stochastiques en génétique des populations. *Publ. Inst. Statistique Univ. Paris*, 8:173-210.

Malogolowkin-Cohen, Ch., H. Levene, N. P. Dobzhansky, and A. S. Simmons. 1964. Inbreeding and the mutational and balanced loads in natural populations of *Drosophila willistoni. Gs.*, 50:1299-1311.

———, A. S. Solima, and H. Levene. 1965. A study of sexual isolation between certain strains of *Drosophila paulistorum. E.*, 19:95-103.

Maly, R. 1951. Cytomorphologische Studien an strahleninduzierten, konstant abweichenden Plastidenfermen bei Farnprothalien. *Z.i.A.V.*, 33:447-478.

Mangenot, S., and G. Mangenot. 1962. Enquête sur les nombres chromosomiques dans une collection d'espèces tropicales. *Rev. Cytol. Biol. Végét.*, 25:411-447.

Manna, G. R., and S. G. Smith. 1959. Chromosomal polymorphism and interrelationships among bark weevils of genus *Pissodes* Germar. *Nucleus*, 2:179-208.

Manning, A. 1959. The sexual behavior of two sibling *Drosophila* species. *Behaviour*, 15:123-145.

———. 1961. The effects of artificial selection for mating speed in *Drosophila melanogaster. Animal Behavior*, 9:82-92.

Mansfeld, R. 1951. Das morphologische System des Saatweizens, *Triticum aestivum* L. *Der Züchter*, 21-41-66.

Manton, I. 1950. Problems of Cytology and Evolution in the *Pteridophyta*. Cambridge Univ. Press, Cambridge.

Manwell, C., and C. M. Ann Baker. 1963. A sibling species of sea cucumber discovered by starch gel electrophoresis. *Comp. Biochem. Physiol.*, 10:39-53.

Margoliash, E. 1963. Primary structure and evolution of cytochrome c. *P.N.A.S.*, 50:672-679.

———, and E. L. Smith. 1965. Structural and functional aspects of cytochrome c in relation to evolution. Pp. 221-242 *in:* V. Bryson and H. J. Vogel (Eds.), "Evolving Genes and Proteins," Academic Press, New York.

Marien, D. 1958. Selection for developmental rate in *Drosophila pseudoobscura. Gs.*, 43:3-15.

Marinkovic, D. 1967. Genetic loads affecting fertility in natural populations of *Drosophila pseudoobscura. Gs.*, 57:701-709.

Marler, P. R., and W. J. Hamilton. 1966. Mechanisms of Animal Behavior. John Wiley, New York.

Marquardt, H. 1952. Uber die spontanen Aberrationen in der Anaphase der Meiosis von *Paeonia tenuifolia. Ch.*, 5:81-112.

Marshall, A. J. 1954. Bowerbirds, Their Displays and Breeding Cycles. Clarendon, Oxford.

Marshall, R. E., C. T. Caskey, and M. Nirenberg. 1967. Fine structure of RNA code words recognized by bacterial, amphibian and mammalian transfer RNA. *S.*, 155:820-826.

Martin, J. 1965. Interrelation of inversion systems in the midge *Chironomus intertinctus.* II. A nonrandom association of linked inversions. *Gs.*, 52:371-383.

Maslin, T. P. 1968. Taxonomic problems in parthenogenetic vertebrates. *S.Z.*, 17:219-231.

Mason, E. D., M. Jacob, and V. Balakrishnan. 1964. Racial group differences in the basal metabolism and body composition of Indian and European women in Bombay. *Human Biol.*, 36:374-396.

Mather, K. 1941. Variation and selection of polygenic characters. *J. Genetics*, 41:159-193.

———. 1953. The genetical structure of populations. *Symposium Soc. Exp. Biol.*, 7:66-95.

———. 1955. Polymorphism as an outcome of disruptive selection. *E.*, 9:52-61.

——, and B. J. Harrison. 1949. The manifold effect of selection. *Hy.*, 3:1-52, 131-162.

——, and A. Vines. 1951. Species crosses in *Antirrhinum*. *Hy.*, 5:195-214.

Matthey, R. 1952. Chromosomes de *Muridae*. *Ch.*, 5:113-138.

——. 1963. Cytologie comparée et polymorphisme chromosomique chez des *Mus* africains appartenant aux groupes *bufotriton* et *minutoides*. *Cytogenetics*, 2:290-322.

——. 1964a. La signification des mutations chromosomiques dans les processus de spéciation. Etude cytogénétique du sous-genre *Leggada* Gray. *Arch. Biol.*, 75:169-206.

——. 1964b. Evolution chromosomique et spéciation chez les *Mus* du sous-genre *Leggada* Gray 1837. *Experientia*, 20:1-9.

——. 1966a. Le polymorphisme chromotomique des *Mus* africains du sous-genre *Leggada*. *Rev. Suisse Zool.*, 73:585-607.

——. 1966b. Une inversion péricentrique à l'origine d'un polymorphisme chromosomique non-robertsonien dans une population de *Mastomys* (*Rodentia-Murinae*). *Ch.*, 18:188-200.

Maynard-Smith, J. 1966. Sympatric speciation. *A.N.*, 100:637-650.

——. 1968a. "Haldane's dilemma" and the rate of evolution. *N.*, 219:1114-1116.

——. 1968b. Evolution in sexual and asexual populations. *A.N.*, 102:469-473.

Mayr, E. 1942. Systematics and the Origin of Species. Columbia Univ. Press, New York.

——. 1954. Change of genetic environment and evolution. Pp. 157-180. *In:* Huxley, J., and others, "Evolution as a Process," Macmillan, New York.

——. 1957. Species concepts and definitions. Pp. 1-22 *in:* E. Mayr (Ed.), "The Species Problem," American Associaton for the Advancement of Science, Washington.

——. 1963. Animal Species and Evolution. Belknap, Cambridge.

——. 1965a. Classification and phylogeny. *Amer. Zoologist*, 5:165-174.

——. 1965b. Numerical phenetics and taxonomic theory. *S.Z.*, 14:73-97.

——. 1969. Principles of Systematic Zoology. McGraw-Hill, New York.

Menzel, M. Y. 1964. Preferential chromosome pairing in allotetraploid *Lycopersicon esculentum-Solanum lycopersicoides*. *Gs.*, 50:855-862.

Merrell, D. J. 1968. A comparison of the estimated size and the "effective size" of breeding populations of the leopard frog, *Rana pipiens*. *E.*, 22:274-283.

——, and Ch. F. Rodell. 1968. Seasonal selection in the leopard frog, *Rana pipiens*. *E.*, 22:284-288.

Meselson, M., and F. W. Stahl. 1958. The replication of DNA in *Escherichia coli*. *P.N.A.S.*, 44:671-682.

Mettler, L. E., S. E. Moyer, and K. Kojima. 1966. Genetic loads in cage populations of *Drosophila*. *Gs.*, 54:887-898.

Michaud, T. C. 1964. Vocal variation in two species of chorus frogs, *Pseudacris nigrita* and *Pseudacris clarki* in Texas. *E.*, 18:498-506.

Michaelis, P. 1954. Cytoplasmic inheritance in *Epilobium* and its theoretical significance. *Adv. Genetics*, 6:287-401.

Milani, R. 1967. The genetics of *Musca domestica* and of other muscoid flies. Pp. 315-369 *in:* J. W. Wright and R. Pal (Eds.), "Genetics of Insect Vectors of Disease," Elsevier, Amsterdam.

Milkman, R. D. 1962. The genetic basis of natural variation. IV. On the natural distribution of *cve* polygenes of *Drosophila melanogaster*. *Gs.*, 47:261-272.

——. 1965. The genetic basis of natural variation. VII. The individuality of polygenic combinations in *Drosophila*. *Gs.*, 52:789-799.

——. 1966. The genetic basis of natural variation. VIII. Synthesis of *cve* polygenic combinations from laboratory strains of *Drosophila melanogaster*. *Gs.*, 53:863-874.

Miller, D. D., and R. A. Voelker. 1968. Salivary gland chromosome variation in the *Drosophila affinis* subgroup. *J. Heredity*, 59:86-98.

——, and N. J. Westphal. 1967. Further evidence on sexual isolation within *Drosophila athabasca*. *E.*, 21:479-492.

Millicent, E., and J. M. Thoday. 1961. Effects of disruptive selection. *Hy.*, 16:199-217.

Minamori, S. 1957. Physiological isolation in *Cobitidae*. VI. Temperature adaptation and hybrid inviability. *J. Sci. Hiroshima Univ.*, B, 17:65-119.

——, and Y. Saito. 1964. Local and seasonal variations of lethal frequencies in natural populations of *Drosophila melanogaster*. *Japan. J. Genetics*, 38:290-304.

Mirsky, A. E., and H. Ris. 1951. The desoxyribonucleic and acid content of animal cells and its evolutionary significance. *J. Gen. Physiol.*, 34:451-462.

Monclus, M. 1953. Variacion geographica de los peines tarsales de los machos de *D. subobscura*. *Genetica Iberica*, 5:101-114.

Montagu, A. (Ed.). 1964. The Concept of Race. Free Press, Glencoe.

Montalenti, G. 1965. Human population genetics. Synthesis. *Genetics Today*. P. XI *I.C.G.*, 3:965-972.

Moore, D. M., and H. Lewis. 1965. The evolution of self-pollination in *Clarkia xantiana*. *E.*, 19:104-114.

Moore, J. A. 1949a. Geographic variation of adaptive characters in *Rana pipiens* Schreber. *E.*, 3:1-24.

——. 1949b. Patterns of evolution in the genus *Rana*. *Genetics, Paleon., Evolution:* 315-338.

——. 1950. Further studies on *Rana pipiens* racial hybrids. *A.N.*, 84:247-254.

Moore, R. E. 1965a. Olfactory discrimination as an isolating mechanism between *Peromyscus maniculatus* and *Peromyscus polionotus*. *Amer. Midland Natur.*, 73:85-100.

——. 1965b. Ethological isolation between *Peromyscus maniculatus* and *Peromyscus polionotus*. *Amer. Midland Natur.*, 74:341-349.

Mooring, J. 1958. A cytogentic study of *Clarkia unguiculata*. I. Translocations. *Amer. J. Botany*, 45:233-242.

——. 1961. The evolutionary role of translocations in *Clarkia unguiculata* (*Onagraceae*). *Recent Adv. Botany, Biosystem.*:853-858.

Moos, J. R. 1955. Comparative physiology of some chromosomal types in *Drosophila pseudoobscura*. *E.*, 9:141-151.

Morgan, T. H. 1911. The origin of five mutations in eye color in *Drosophila* and their modes of inheritance. *S.*, 33:534-537.

——. 1919. The Physical Basis of Heredity. Lippincott, Philadelphia.

——, A. H. Sturtevant, H. J. Muller, and C. B. Bridges. 1915. The Mechanism of Mendelian Heredity. Holt, New York.

Mori, S., and Matutani, K. 1953. Daily swarming of some caddis fly adults and their habitat segregations. *Dobutsugaku Zasshi*, 62:191-198.

Morley, F. H. W., and J. Katznelson. 1965. Colonization in Australia by *Trifolium subterraneum* L. Pp. 269-285 *in:* H. G. Baker and G. L. Stebbins (Eds.), "The Genetics of Colonization Species," Academic Press, New York.

Morris, D. 1952. Homosexuality in the ten-spined stickleback (*Pygosteus pungitius* L.). *Behavior*, 4:233-261.

Morton, N. E. 1960. The mutational load due to detrimental genes in man. *Amer. J. Human Genetics*, 12:348-364.

———. 1964. Models and evidence in human population genetics. *P. XI I.C.G.*:935-951.

———, and C. S. Chung. 1959. Are the MN blood groups maintained by selection? *Amer. J. Human Genetics*, 11:237-251.

———, C. S. Chung, and L. D. Friedman. 1968. Relation between homozygous viability and average dominance in *Drosophila melanogaster*. *Gs.*, 60:601-614.

———, C. S. Chung, and M. P. Mi. 1967. Genetics of Interracial Crosses in Hawaii. Karger, Basel and New York.

———, J. F. Crow, and H. J. Muller. 1956. An estimate of the mutational damage in man from data on consanguineous marriages. *P.N.A.S.*, 42:855-863.

———, H. Krieger, and M. P. Mi. 1966. Natural selection on polymorphisms in northeastern Brazil. *Amer. J. Human Genetics*, 18:153-171.

Mosquin, Th. 1967. Evidence for autopolyploidy in *Epilobium angustifolium* (*Onagraceae*). *E.*, 21:713-719.

Mourad, A. K. 1964. Lethal and semilethal chromosomes in irradiated experimental populations of *Drosophila pseudoobscura*. *Gs.*, 50:1279-1287.

Mourant, A. E. 1954. The Distribution of the Human Blood Groups. Blackwell, Oxford.

———, A. C. Kopec, and K. Domaniewska-Sobczak. 1958. The ABO Blood Groups. Charles C Thomas, Springfield, Ill.

Muir, A., and A. G. Steinberg. 1967. On the genetics of the human allotypes, *Gm* and *Inv*. *Seminars Hematol.*, 4:156-173.

Mukai, T. 1964. The genetic structure of natural populations of *Drosophila melanogaster*. I. Spontaneous mutation rate of polygenes controlling viability. *Gs.*, 50:1-19.

———. 1967. A study of the genetic structure of natural populations in *Drosophila melanogaster* by means of spontaneous polygenic mutation rates. I and II. *Proc. Japan Acad.*, 38:741-746, 747-752.

———. 1969a. The genetic structure of natural populations of *Drosophila melanogaster*. VI. Further studies on the optimum heterozygosity hypothesis. *Gs.*, 61:479-495.

———. 1969b. Maintenance of polygenic and isoallelic variation in populations. *P. XII I.C.G.*, 3:293-308.

———, and A. B. Burdick. 1959. Single gene heterosis associated with a second chromosome recessive lethal in *Drosophila melanogaster*. *Gs.*, 44:211-232.

———, and A. B. Burdick. 1961. Examination of the closely linked dominant adaptive gene heterosis as an alternative to single gene heterosis associated with l (2) 55i in *Drosophila melanogaster*. *Japan. J. Genetics*, 36:97-104.

———, S. Chigusa, and I. Yoshikawa. 1964. The genetic structure of natural populations of *Drosophila melanogaster*. II. Overdominance of spontaneous mutant polygenes controlling viability in homozygous genetic background. *Gs.*, 50:711-715.

———, S. Chigusa, and I. Yoshikawa. 1965. The genetic structure of natural populations of *Drosophila melanogaster*. III. Dominance effect of spontaneous mutant polygenes controlling viability in heterozygous genetic backgrounds. *Gs.*, 52:493-501.

——, and T. Yamazaki. 1964. Position effect of spontaneous mutant polygenes controlling viability in Drosophila melanogaster. Proc. Japan Acad., 40:840-845.

——, and T. Yamazaki. 1968. The genetic structure of natural populations of Drosophila melanogaster. V. Coupling-repulsion effect of spontaneous mutant polygenes controlling viability. Gs., 59:513-535.

——, I. Yoshikawa, and K. Sano. 1966. The genetic structure of natural populations of Drosophila melanogaster. IV. Heterozygous effects of radiation-induced mutations on viability in various genetic backgrounds. Gs., 53:513-527.

Muller, C. H. 1952. Ecological control of hybridization in Quercus: A factor in the mechanism of evolution. E., 6:147-161.

Muller, H. J. 1925. Why polyploidy is rarer in animals than in plants. A.N., 59:346-353.

——. 1927. Artificial transmutation of the gene. S., 66:84-87.

——. 1928a. The problem of genic modification. Verh. V Intern. Kongr., 1:234-260.

——. 1928b. The measurement of gene mutation rate in Drosophila, its high variability, and its dependence upon temperature. Gs., 13:279-357.

——. 1940. Bearing of the "Drosophila" work on systematics. Pp. 185-268 in: J. S. Huxley, "New Systematics," Clarendon, Oxford.

——. 1942. Isolating mechanisms, evolution, and temperature. Biol. Symposia, 6:71-125.

——. 1950. Our load of mutations. Amer. J. Human Genetics, 2:111-176.

——. 1964. The relation of recombination to mutational advance. Mutation Res., 1:2-19.

——. 1965. Means and aims in human genetic betterment. Pp. 100-122 in: T. M. Sonneborn (Ed.), "The Control of Human Heredity and Evolution," Macmillan, New York.

——. 1967. What genetic course will man steer? Pp. 521-543 in: J. F. Crow and J. V. Neel (Eds.), "Proceedings of the International Congress on Human Genetics," Johns Hopkins Press, Baltimore.

——, and W. D. Kaplan. 1966. The dosage compensation of Drosophila and mammals as showing the accuracy of the normal type. G. R., 8:41-59.

Müntzing, A. 1932. Cytogenetic investigations on synthetic Galeopsis tetrahit. Hs., 16:105-154.

——. 1961. Genetics, Basic and Applied. LTs Förlag, Stockholm.

——. 1963. A case of preserved heterozygosity in rye in spite of long-continued inbreeding. Hs., 50:377-413.

Münzing, J. 1963. The evolution of variation and distributional patterns in European populations of the three-spined stickleback, Gasterosteus aculeatus. E., 17:320-332.

Myrianthopoulos, N. C., and S. M. Aronson. 1966. Population dynamics of Tay-Sachs disease. I. Reproductive fitness and selection. Amer. J. Human Genetics, 18:313-327.

Nagel, G. 1961. The Structure of Science. Harcourt, Brace, & World, New York.

Naumenko, V. A. 1936. Lethal mutations in Drosophila melanogaster induced by potassium permanganate. Bull. Biol. Med. Exp. USSR, 1:204-206.

Neel, J. V. 1958. A study of major congenital defects in Japanese infants. Amer. J. Human Genetics, 10:398-445.

——, S. S. Fajans, J. W. Conn, and R. T. Davidson. 1965. Diabetes mellitus. Pp. 105-132 in: J. V. Neel, M. W. Shaw, and W. J. Schull (Eds.), "Genetics and Epidemiology of Chronic Diseases," Government Printing Office, Washington.

——, and W. J. Schull. 1962. The effects of inbreeding on mortality and morbidity in two Japanese cities. *P.N.A.S.*, 48:573-582.

——, and W. J. Schull. 1968. On some trends in understanding the genetics of men. *Persp. Biol. Med.*, 11:565-602.

Newman, L. J. 1966. Bridge and fragment aberrations in *Podophyllum peltatum*. *Gs.*, 53:55-63.

Nicoletti, B., and C. Giardina. 1964. Genetic load and reproductive efficiency in natural and laboratory populations of *Drosophila melanogaster*. *Riv. Biol.* 57:209-236.

Nielsen, A. 1951. Contributions to the metamorphosis and biology of the genus *Atrichopogon* Kieffer (*Diptera, Ceratopogonidae*). *Biol. Skrift. Kongr. Dan. Viden. Selskab*, 6, No. 6:1-95.

Nienstaedt, H., and A. H. Graves. 1955. Blight-resistant chestnuts. *Conn. Agr. Exp. Stat. Circ.* 192.

Nilsson, S. E. 1962. Genetic and Constitutional Aspects of Diabetes Mellitus. Almquist & Wiksell, Stockholm.

Nirenberg, M. W., and J. H. Matthei. 1961. The dependence of cell-free protein synthesis in *E. coli* upon naturally occurring or synthetic polyribonucleotides. *P.N.A.S.*,47:1588-1602.

O'Brien, S. J., and R. J. MacIntyre. 1969. An analysis of gene-enzyme variability in natural populations of *Drosophila melanogaster and D. simulans*. *A.N.*, 103: 97-113.

Ohba, Sh. 1967. Chromosomal polymorphism and capacity for increase under near optimal conditions. *Hy.*, 22:169-189.

Ohmachi, F., and S. Mazaki. 1964. Interspecific crossing and development of hybrids between the Japanese species of *Teleogryllus* (*Orthoptera, Gryllidae*).*E.*, 18:405-416.

Ohno, S., and N. B. Atkin. 1966. Comparative DNA values and chromosome complements of eight species of fishes. *Ch.*, 18:455-466.

——, C. Weiler, J. Poole, L. Christian, and C. Steinus. 1966. Autosomal polymorphism due to pericentric inversions in the deer mouse (*Peromyscus maniculatus*) and some evidence of somatic segregation. *Ch.*, 18:177-183.

Oldroyd, H. 1964. The Natural History of Flies. Norton, New York.

Olenov, J. M. 1958. On the increase of the resistance of insects to the action of DDT. *Rev. Entom. URSS.*, 37:520-537.

Omodeo, P. 1952. Cariologia dei *Lumbricidae*. *Caryologia*, 4:173-275.

Oparin, A. I. 1964. The Chemical Origin of Life. Charles C Thomas, Springfield.

Oshima, C. 1967. Persistence of some recessive lethal genes in natural populations of *Drosophila melanogaster*. *Ciencia e Cultura*, 19:102-110.

——, and T. Hiroyoshi. 1956. Genetic studies of resistance to DDT and nicotine sulphate in *Drosophila virilis*. *Botyu Kagaku*, 21:65-70.

Otten, Ch. M. 1967. On pestilence, diet, natural selection, and the distribution of microbial and human blood group antigens and antibodies. *Current Anthrop.*, 8:209-226.

Ownbey, M. 1950. Natural hybridization and amphiploidy in the genus *Tragopogon*. *Amer. J. Bot.*, 37:487-499.

Paik, Y. K. 1960. Genetic variability in Korean populations. *E.*, 14:293-303.

Park, Y. I., C. T. Hansen, C. S. Chung, and A. B. Chapman. 1966. Influence of feeding regime on the effects of selection for postweaning gain in the rat. *Gs.*, 54:1315-1327.

Parsons, P. A., and M. M. Green. 1959. Pleiotropy and competition at the vermilion locus in Drosophila melanogaster. P.N.A.S., 45:993-996

Pasternak, J. 1964. Chromosome polymorphism in the blackfly Simulium vittatum (Zett). Canad. J. Zool., 42:135-158.

Pätau, K. 1935. Chromosomenmorphologie bei Drosophila melanogaster und Drosophila simulans und ihre genetische Bedeutung. Naturwiss., 23:537-543.

Patterson, J. T., and W. S. Stone. 1952. Evolution in the Genus Drosophila. Macmillan, New York.

——, and M. R. Wheeler. 1947. Two strains of Drosophila peninsularis with incipient reproductive isolation. U.T.P., 4720:116-125.

Pauling, L., H. A. Itano, S. J. Singer, and I. C. Wells. 1949. Sickle cell anemia, a molecular disease. S., 110:543-548.

Pavan, C., A. R. Cordeiro, N. Dobzhansky, Th. Dobzhansky, C. Malogolowkin, B. Spassky, and M. Wedel. 1951. Concealed genic variability in Brazilian populations of Drosophila willistoni. Gs., 36:13-30.

——, and E. N. Knapp. 1954. The genetic population structure of Brazilian Drosophila willistoni. E., 8:303-313.

Pavlovsky, O., and Th. Dobzhansky. 1966. Genetics of natural populations. XXXVII. The coadapted system of chromosomal variants in a population of Drosophila pseudoobscura. Gs., 53:843-854.

Paxman, G. J. 1957. A study of spontaneous mutation in Drosophila melanogaster. Ga., 29:39-57.

Penrose, L. S. 1955. Evidence of heterosis in man. Proc. Royal Soc., B, 144:203-213.

Pentzos, A. D., E. Boesiger, and A. Kanellis. 1967. Frequences de genes mutants dans plusieurs populations naturelles de Drosophila subobscura de Grèce. Ann. Fac. Sci. Univ. Thessaloniki, 10:133-152.

Perutz, M. F., and H. Lehman. 1968. Molecular pathology of human haemoglobin. N., 219-902-909.

Petersen, B. 1949. Studies on geographic variation of allometry in some European Lepidoptera. Zool. Bidrag. Uppsala, 29:1-38.

——, 1955. Geographische Variation von Pieris (napi)bryoniae durch Bastardierung mit Pieris napi. Zool. Bidrag Uppsala, 30:355-397.

Petit, C. 1958. Le déterminisme génétique et psycho-physiologique de la compétition sexuelle chez Drosophila melanogaster. Bull. Biol. France Belgique, 92:248-329.

——, and L. Ehrman. 1969. Sexual selection in Drosophila. E. B., 3:177-223.

Petras, J. W., and J. E. Curtis. 1968. The current literature on social class and mental disease in America. Critique and bibliography. Behav. Sci., 13:382-398.

Petras, M. L. 1967. Studies of natural populations of Mus. I. Biochemical polymorphisms and their bearing on breeding structure. E., 21:259-274.

Pettigrew, Th. F. 1964. Race, mental illness, and intelligence: A social psychological view. Eugen. Quart., 11:189-215.

Philiptschenko, J. 1927. Variabilität und Variation. Borntraeger, Berlin.

Pianka, E. R. 1966. Latitudinal gradients in species diversity: A review of concepts. A.N., 100:33-46.

Pimental, D., G. J. C. Smith, and J. Soans. 1967. A population model of sympatric speciation. A.N., 101:493-504.

Pipkin, S. B. 1968. Introgression between closely related species of Drosophila in Panama. E., 22:140-156.

Pires, J. M., Th. Dobzhansky, and G. A. Black. 1953. An estimate of the number of species of trees in an Amazonian forest community. *Bot. Gazette*, 114:467-477.

Polani, P. E. 1969. Abnormal sex chromosomes and mental disorder. *N.*, 223:680-686.

Polanyi, N. 1968. Life's irreducible structure. *S.*, 160:1308-1312.

Polivanov, S. 1964. Selection in experimental populations of *Drosophila melanogaster* with different genetic backgrounds. *Gs.*, 50:81-100.

Pollard, E. C. 1965. The fine structure of the bacterial cell and the possibility of its artificial synthesis. *Amer. Scientist*, 53:437-463.

Ponomarev, V. P. 1937-1938. The effect of lead nitrate on mutation in *Drosophila melanogaster*. *Biol. Zhurnal*, 7:619-634.

Pontecorvo, G. 1943. Viability interactions between chromosomes of *Drosophila melanogaster* and *Drosophila simulans*. *J. Genetics*, 43:51-66.

Post, R. H. 1962. Population differences in red and green color vision deficiency: A review and a query on selection relaxation. *Eugen. Quart.*, 9:131-146.

——. 1964. Hearing acuity variation among negroes and whites. *Eugen. Quart.*, 11:65-81.

——. 1965. Notes on relaxed selection in man. *Anthrop. Anz.*, 29:186-195.

Poulson, Th. L., and W. B. White. 1969. The cave environment. *S.*, 165:971-981.

Prakash, S., and R. C. Lewontin. 1968. A molecular approach to the study of genic heterozygosity in natural populations. III. Direct evidence of coadaptation in gene arrangements of *Drosophila*. *P.N.A.S.*, 59:398-405.

——, R. C. Lewontin, and J. L. Hubby. 1969. A molecular approach to the study of genic heterozygosity in natural populations. IV. Patterns of genic variation in central, marginal and isolated populations of *Drosophila pseudoobscura*. *Gs.*, 61:841-858.

Pratt, R. T. C. 1967. The Genetics of Neurological Disorders. Oxford Univ. Press, London.

Prevosti, A. 1964. Chromosomal polymorphism in *Drosophila subobscura* populations from Barcelona. *G.R.* 5:27-38.

Prout, T. 1954. Genetic drift in irradiated experimental populations of *Drosophila melanogaster*. *Gs.*, 39:529-545.

——. 1962. The effects of stabilizing selection on the time of development in *Drosophila melanogaster*. *G.R.*, 3:364-382.

——. 1964. Observations on structural reduction in evolution. *A.N.*, 98:239-249.

——. 1968. Sufficient conditions for multiple niche polymorphism. *A.N.*, 102:493-496.

Purdom, C. E. 1963. Genetic Effects of Radiations. Academic Press, New York.

Quayle, H. J. 1938. The development of resistance in certain scale insects to hydrocyanic gas. *Hilgardia*, 11:183-225.

Race, R. R., and R. Sanger. 1968. Blood Groups in Man. 5th Ed. Davis, Philadelphia.

Rana, R. S. 1965. Induced interchange heterozygosity in diploid *Chrysanthemum*. *Ch.*, 16:477-485.

——, and H. K. Jain. 1965. Adaptive role of interchange heterozygosity in the annual *Chrysanthemum*. *Hy.*, 20:21-29.

Rapoport, J. A. 1939. Specific morphoses induced in *Drosophila* by chemicals. *Bull. Exp. Biol. Med. (Moscow)*, 7:424-426.

——. 1946. Carbonyl compounds and the chemical mechanism of mutation. *C. R. Acad. Sci. URSS*, 54:65-67.

Rasmussen, D. I. 1962. Blood group polymorphism and inbreeding in natural populations of the deer mouse *Peromyscus maniculatus gracilis*. *E.*, 18:219-229.

Reed, T. E. 1961. Polymorphism and natural selection in blood groups. Pp. 80-101 *in:* B. S. Blumberg (Ed.), "Genetic Polymorphisms and Geographic Variation in Disease," Grune & Stratton, New York.

Rees, H. 1961. The consequences of interchange. *E.*, 15:145-152.

———. 1964. The question of polyploidy in the *Salmonidae*. *Ch.*, 15:275-279.

———, and S. Sun. 1965. Chiasma frequency and the disjunction of interchange associations in rye. *Ch.*, 16:500-510.

Reitalu, J. 1968. Chromosome studies in connection with sex chromosomal deviations in man. *Hs.*, 59:1-48.

Remington, Ch. L. 1968. Suture-zones of hybrid interaction between recently joined biotas, *E.B.*, 2:321-438.

Renner, O. 1929. Artbastarde bei Pflanzen. Borntraeger, Berlin.

Rensch, B. 1929. Das Prinzip geographischer Rassenkreise und das Problem der Artbildung. Borntraeger, Berlin.

———. 1947 (1960a). Evolution above the Species Level. Columbia Univ. Press, New York.

———. 1960b. The laws of evolution. Pp. 95-116 *in:* S. Tax (Ed.), "Evolution after Darwin," Chicago Univ. Press, Chicago.

———. 1968. Biophilosophie. Gustav Fischer, Stuttgart.

Rhoades, M. M. 1946. Plastid mutations. *C.S.H.*, 11:202-207.

Richardson, R. H., and K. I. Kojima. 1965. The kinds of genetic variability in relation to selection responses in *Drosophila* fecundity. *Gs.*, 52:583-598.

Richmond, R. C. 1970. Non-Darwinian evolution: a critique. *N.* (in press).

Rick, C. M. 1947. Partial suppression of hair development indirectly affecting fruitfulness and the proportion of cross-pollination in a tomato mutant. *A.N.*, 81:185-202.

———. 1950. Pollination in relation of *Lycopersicon esculentum* in native and foreign habitats. *E.*, 4:110-122.

———. 1963a. Differential zygotic lethality in a tomato species hybrid. *Gs.*, 48:1497-1507.

———. 1963b. Barriers to interbreeding in *Lycopersicon peruvianum*. *E.*, 17:216-232.

———, and P G. Smith. 1953. Novel variation in tomato species hybrids. *A.N.*, 87:359-373.

Riggs, S. K., and F. Sargent. 1964. Physiological regulation in moist heat by young American Negro and white males. *Human Biol.*, 36:339-353.

Riley, H. P. 1952. Ecological barriers. *A.N.*, 86:23-32.

Rizki, M. T. M. 1951. Morphological differences between two sibling species, *Drosophila pseudoobscura* and *Drosophila persimilis*. *P.N.A.S.*, 156-159.

———. 1952. Ontogenetic distribution of genetic lethality in *Drosophila willistoni*. *J. Exp. Zool.*, 121:327-350.

Robertson, A. 1960. A theory of limits in artificial selection. *Proc. Royal Soc.*, B, 153:234-249.

———. 1962. Selection for heterozygotes in small populations. *Gs.*, 47:1291-1300.

Robertson, F. W. 1955. Selection response and the properties of genetic variation. *C.S.H.*, 20:166-177.

———. 1957. Studies in quantitative inheritance. XI. Genic and environmental correlation between body size and egg production in *Drosophila melanogaster*. *J. Genetics*, 55:428-443.

——. 1966. A test of sexual isolation in *Drosophila*. *G.R.*, 8:181-187.

Robinson, J. T. 1967. Variation and the taxonomy of the early hominids. *E.B.*, 1:69-100.

Roelofs, W. L., and A. Comeau. 1969. Sex pheromone specificity: Taxonomic and evolutionary aspects in *Lepidoptera*. *S.*, 165:398-399.

Ross, H. H. 1958. Evidence suggesting a hybrid origin for certain leafhopper species. *E.*, 12:337-346.

Rothe, H. 1951. Morphologisch-Entwicklungsgeschichtliche und genetische Analyse einer sich variabel manifestierenden Mutation von *Antirrhinum majus* L. *Z.i.A.V.*, 84:74-132.

Rothfels, K. H. 1956. Black flies: sibling, sex, and species grouping. *J. Heredity*, 47:113-122.

Roy, S. K. 1960. Interaction between rice varieties. *J. Genetics*, 57:137-152.

Sabrosky, C. W. 1952. How many insects are there? Yearbook of Agriculture, Separate No. 2290, Washington.

Saccà, G. 1967. Speciation in *Musca*. Pp. 385-415 *in:* J. W. Wright and R. Pal (Eds.), "Genetics of Insect Vectors of Disease," Elsevier, Amsterdam.

Sacharov, W. W. 1936. Iod als chemischer Factor, der auf den Mutationsprozess von *Drosophila melanogaster* wirkt. *Ga.*, 18:193-216.

Salceda, V. M. 1967. Recessive lethals in second chromosomes of *Drosophila melanogaster* with radiation histories. *Gs.*, 57:691-699.

Samjatina, N. D., and O. T. Popova. 1934. Der Einfluss von Iod auf die Entstehung von Mutationen bei *Drosophila melanogaster*. *Biol. Zhurnal*, 3:679-693.

Sankaranarayanan, R. 1964. Genetic loads in irradiated experimental populations of *Drosophila melanogaster*. *Gs.*, 50:131-150.

——. 1965. Further data on the genetic loads in irradiated experimental populations of *Drosophila melanogaster*. *Gs.*, 52:153-164.

——. 1966. Some components of the genetic loads in irradiated experimental populations of *Drosophila melanogaster*. *Gs.*, 54:121-130.

Sarich, V. M., and A. C. Wilson. 1967. Rates of albumin evolution in primates. *P.N.A.S.*, 58:142-148.

Sarkar, I. 1955. A translocation heterozygote in the grasshopper *Gesonula punctifrons*. *J. Heredity*, 46:157-160.

Scharloo, W. 1964. The effect of disruptive and stabilizing selection on the expression of a cubitus interruptus mutant in *Drosophila*. *Gs.*, 50:553-562.

Schatz, G. 1951. Über die Formbildung des Flügel bei Hitzemodificationen und Mutationen von *Drosophila melanogaster*. *Biol. Zentral.*, 70:305-353.

Schlager, G., and M. M. Dickie. 1966. Spontaneous mutation rates at five coat-color loci in mice. *S.*, 151:205-206.

Schmalhausen, I. I. 1949. Factors of Evolution. Blakiston, Philadelphia.

Schnetter, M. 1950. Veränderungen der genetischen Konstitution in natürlichen Populationen der polymorphen Bänderschnecken. *Verh. Deutsch. Zool. Marburg*, 1950, 192-206.

Schoener, Th. W. 1965. The evolution of bill size differences among sympatric congeneric species of birds. *E.*, 19:189-213.

Scholander, P. F., V. Walters, R. Hock, and L. Irving. 1950. Heat regulation *Biol. Bull.*, 99:225-271.

Scholz, F., and Ch. O. Lehmann. 1962. Die Gaterslebener Mutanten der Saatgerste in Berziehung zur Formenmannigfaltigkeit der Art *Hordeum vulgare* L. *Kulturpflanze*, 10:312-334.

Schreider, E. 1963. Physiological anthropology and climatic variations. Pp. 37-73 *in:* "Proceedings of the Lucknow Symposium (UNESCO) on Environmental Physiology and Psychology in Arid Conditions."

———. 1964a. Recherches sur la stratification sociale des charactères biologiques. *Biotypologie,* 26:105-135.

———. 1964b. Ecological rules, body-heat regulation, and human evolution. *E.,* 18:1-9.

———. 1967. Un mécanisme sélectif possible de la différenciation sociale des caractères biologiques. *Biom. Humaine,* 11:67-83.

Schull, W. J., and J. V. Neel. 1965. The Effects of Inbreeding on Japanese Children. Harper & Row, New York.

———, and J. V. Neel. 1966. Some further observations on the effect of inbreeding on mortality in Kure, Japan. *Amer. J. Human Genetics,* 18:144-152.

Schwab, J. J. 1940. A study of the effects of a random group of genes on shape of spermatheca in *Drosophila melanogaster. Gs.,* 25:157-177.

Schwanitz, F. 1967. Die Evolution der Kulturpflanzen. Bayerischer Landwirt-schaftsverlag, München.

Scossiroli, R. E. 1954. Effectiveness of artificial selection under irradiation of plateaued populations of *Drosophila melanogaster. IUBS Symposium Genetics Population Structure,* B15:42-66.

———. 1965. Value of induced mutations for quantitative characters in plant breeding. Pp. 443-450 *in:* "The Use of Induced Mutations in Plant Breeding," Pergamon Press, Oxford.

Scott, J. P. 1967. The evolution of social behavior in dogs and wolves. *Amer. Zoologist,* 7:373-381.

———. 1968. Evolution and domestication of the dog. *E.B.,* 2:243-275.

———, and J. L. Fuller. 1965. Genetics and the Social Behavior of the Dog. Univ. Chicago Press, Chicago.

Scriver, Ch. R. 1967. Treatment in medical genetics. Pp. 45-56 *in:* J. F. Crow and J. V. Neel (Eds.), "Proceedings of the 3rd International Congress on Human Genetics," Johns Hopkins Press, Baltimore.

Sears, E. R. 1948. The cytology and genetics of the wheats and their relatives. *Adv. Genetics,* 2:240-270.

———. 1956. The systematics cytology and genetics of wheat. *Handbuch Pflanzen-züchtung,* 2:164-187.

Sedlmair, H. 1956. Verhaltens-, Resistenz-, und Gehäuseunterschiede bei den polymorphen Bänderschnecken *Cepaea hortensis* (Müll.) und *Cepaea nemoralis* (L.). *Biol. Zentral.,* 75:281-313.

Selander, R. K., W. G. Hunt, and S. Y. Yang. 1969. Protein polymorphism and genic heterozygosity in two European subspecies of the house mouse. *E.,* 23:379-390.

Semenov-Tian-Shansky, A. P. 1910. Die taxonomische grenzen der Art und ihrer Unterabfteilungen. Friedlander, Berlin.

de Serres, F. J. 1964. Mutagenesis and chromosome structure. *J. Cell. Comp. Physiol.,* 64 (Suppl.):33-42.

Sheppard, P. M. 1969. Evolutionary genetics of animal populations; the study of natural populations. *P.* XII *I.C.G.,* 3:261-279.

Shields, J. 1968. Summary of the genetic evidence for the transmission of schizophrenia. *J. Psychiat. Res.,* 6 (Suppl.): 95-126.

Shkvarnikov, P. K. 1966. Modern research problems of utilization of experimentally induced mutations in plants. *Ga.,* No. 2:7-19.

Short, L. L. 1965. Hybridization in the flickers (*Colaptes*) of North America. *Bull. Amer. Museum Nat. Hist.*, 129:307-428.

Shultz, F. T. 1953. Concurrent inbreeding and selection in the domestic fowl. *Hy.*, 7:1-21.

Sibley, C. G. 1954. Hybridization in the red-eyed towhees of Mexico. *E.*, 8:252-290.

——, and L. L. Short. 1964. Hybridization in the orioles of the Great Plains. *Condor*, 66:130-150.

Siegel, R. W. 1958. Hybrid vigor, heterosis, and evolution in *Paramecium aurelia*. *E.*, 12:402-416.

Siegel, S. M., and C. Giumarro. 1966. On the culture of a microorganism similar to the precambrian microfossil *Kakabekia umbellata* Barghoorn in $NH_3$-rich atmospheres. *P.N.A.S.*, 55:349-353.

Sinsheimer, R. L. 1959. A single-stranded deoxyribonucleic acid from bacteriophage 174. *J. Mol. Biol.*, 1:43-53.

Simpson, G. G. 1943. Criteria for genera, species, and subspecies in zoology and paleontology. *Ann. New York Acad. Sci.*, 44:145-178.

——. 1949 (1967). The Meaning of Evolution. Rev. Ed. Yale Univ. Press, New Haven.

——. 1953. The Major Features of Evolution. Columbia Univ. Press, New York.

——. 1961. Principles of Animal Taxonomy. Columbia Univ. Press, New York.

——. 1964a. Organisms and molecules in evolution. *S.*, 146:1535-1538.

——. 1964b. This View of Life. Harcourt, Brace, & World, New York.

——. 1964c. Species density of North American recent mammals. *S.Z.*, 13:57-73.

——. 1969. Biology and Man. Harcourt, Brace, & World, New York.

Singleton, R. 1951. Inheritance of corn grass, a macromutation in maize, and its possible significance as an ancestral type. *A.N.*, 85:81-96.

Skinner, F. A. 1968. The limits of microbial existence. *Proc. Royal Soc.*, B, 171:77-89.

Slobodkin, L. B. 1964. The strategy of evolution. *Amer. Scientist*, 52:342-557.

——. 1968. Towards a predictive theory of evolution. Pp. 187-205 *in:* R. C. Lewontin (Ed.), "Population Biology and Evolution," Syracuse Univ. Press, Syracuse.

Smith, H. H. 1950. Differential photoperiod response from interspecific gene transfers. *J. Heredity*, 41:199-203.

Smith, M. H. 1965. Behavioral discrimination shown by allopatric and sympatric males of *Peromyscus eremicus* and *Peromyscus californicus* between females of the same two species. *E.*, 19:430-435.

Smith, S. G. 1962. Cytogenetic pathways in beetle speciation. *Canad. Entom.*, 94:941-955.

——. 1966. Natural hybridization in the coccinellid genus *Chilocorus*. *Ch.*, 18:380-406.

Smithies, O., and G. E. Connell. 1959. Biochemical Aspects of the Inherited Variations in Human Serum Haptoglobins and Transferrins. Ciba Foundation Symposium, Biochemistry of Human Genetics, Churchill, London.

Snow, R., and M. P. Dunford. 1961. A study of interchange heterozygosity in a population of *Datura meteloides*. *Gs.*, 46:1097-1110.

Sokal, R. R. 1965. Statistical methods in systematics. *Biol. Rev.*, 40:337-391.

——, and J. H. Camin. 1965. The two taxonomies: areas of agreement and conflict. *S.Z.*, 14:176-195.

——, and I. Huber. 1963. Competition among genotypes in *Tribolium castaneum* at varying densities and gene frequencies (the sooty locus). *A.N.*, 97:169-184.

——, and P. H. A. Sneath. 1963. Principles of Numerical Taxonomy. Freeman, San Francisco and London.

Sokoloff, A. 1964. A dominant synthetic lethal in *Tribolium castaneum* Herbst. *A.N.*, 98:127-128.

——. 1966. Morphological variation in natural and experimental populations of *Drosophila pseudoobscura* and *Drosophila persimilis*. *E.*, 20:49-71.

——, and I. M. Lerner. 1967. Laboratory ecology and mutual predation of *Tribolium* species. *A.N.*, 101:261-276.

——, I. M. Lerner, and F. K. Ho. 1965. Self-elimination of *Tribolium castaneum* following xenocide of *T. confusum*. *A.N.*, 99:399-404.

Solima-Simmons, A. 1966. Experiments on random genetic drift and natural selection in *Drosophila pseudoobscura*. *E.*, 20:100-103.

Sonneborn, T. M. 1957. Breeding systems, reproductive methods, and species problems in Protozoa. Pp. 155-324 *in:* E. Mayr (Ed.), "The Species Problem," American Association for the Advancement of Science, Washington.

Sorensen, F. 1969. Embryonic genetic load in coastal Douglas fir. *Pseudotsuga menziesii* var. *menziesii*. *A.N.*, 103:389-398.

Spassky, B., Th. Dobzhansky, and W. W. Anderson. 1965. Genetics of natural populations. XXXVI. Epistatic interactions of the components of the genetic load in *Drosophila pseudoobscura*. *Gs.*, 52:623-664.

——, N. Spassky, H. Levene, and Th. Dobzhansky. 1958. Release of genetic variability through recombination. I. *Drosophila pseudoobscura*. *Gs.*, 43:845-867.

Spencer, W. P. 1947a. Genetic drift in a population of *Drosophila immigrans*. *E.*, 1:103-110.

——. 1947b. Mutations in wild populations of *Drosophila*. *Adv. Genetics*, 1:359-402.

Sperlich, D. 1958. Modellversuche zur Selektionswirkung verschiedener chromosomaler Strukturtypen von *Drosophila subobscura* Coll. *Z.i.A.V.*, 89:422-436.

——. 1966a. Equilibria for inversions induced by X-rays in isogenic strains of *Drosophila pseudoobscura*. *Gs.*, 53:835-842.

——. 1966b. Unterschiedliche Paarungsaktivität innerhalb und zwischen verschiedenen geographischen Stämmen von *Drosophila subobscura*. *Z.i.A.V.*, 98:10-15.

——, and H. Feuerbach. 1966. Ist der chromosomale Strukturpolymorphisms von *Drosophila subobscura* stabil oder flexibel? *Z.i.A.V.*, 98:16-24.

Spickett, S. G., and J. M. Thoday. 1966. Regular responses to selection. 3. Interaction between located polygenes. *G.R.*, 7:96-121.

Spiegelman, S., N. R. Pace, D. R. Mills, R. Levisohn, T. S. Eikhom, M. M. Taylor, R. L. Petersen, and D. H. L. Bishop. 1969. Chemical and mutational studies of a replicating RNA molecule. *P. XII I.C.G.*, 3:127-154.

Spiess, E. B. 1957. Relation between frequency and adaptive values of chromosomal arrangements in *Drosophila persimilis*. *E.*, 11:84-93.

——. 1959. Release of genetic variability through recombination. II. *Drosophila persimilis*. *Gs.*, 44:43-58.

——. 1968. Low frequency advantage in mating of *Drosophila pseudoobscura* karyotypes. *A.N.*, 102:363-379.

——, and A. C. Allen. 1961. Release of genetic variability through recombination. VII. Second and third chromosomes of *Drosophila melanogaster*. *Gs.*, 46:1531-1553.

——, and B. Langer. 1964a. Mating speed control by gene arrangement in *Drosophila pseudoobscura* homokaryotypes. *P.N.A.S.*, 51:1015-1019.

——, and B. Langer. 1964b. Mating speed control by gene arrangement carriers in *Drosophila persimilis. E.*, 18:430-444.

——, B. Langer, and L. D. Spiess. 1966. Mating control by gene arrangements in *Drosophila pseudoobscura. Gs.*, 54:1139-1149.

——, and L. D. Spiess. 1967. Mating propensity, chromosomal polymorphism and dependent conditions in *Drosophila persimilis. E.*, 21:672-688.

Spiess, L. D., and E. B. Spiess. 1969. Minority advantage in interpopulational matings of *Drosophila persimilis. A.N.*, 103:155-172.

Spieth, H. T. 1966. Mating behavior of *Drosophila ananassae* and *ananassae*-like flies from the Pacific. *U.T.P.*, 6615:133-145.

——. 1968. Evolutionary implications of sexual behavior in *Drosophila. E. B.*, 2:157-193.

——, and T. C. Hsu. 1950. The influence of light on the mating behavior of seven species of the *Drosophila melanogaster* group. *E.*, 4:316-325.

Sprague, G. F., W. A. Russell, and L. H. Penny. 1960. Mutations affecting quantitative traits in the selfed progeny of doubled monoploid maize stocks. *Gs.*, 45:855-866.

Stadler, L. J. 1954. The gene. *S.*, 120:1811-1819.

Staiger, H. 1954. Der Chromosomendimorphismus beim Prosobranchier *Purpura lapillus* in Beziehung zur Ökologie der Art. *Ch.*, 6:419-478.

——. 1955. Reciproke Translocationen in natürlichen Populationen von *Purpura lapillus. Ch.*, 7:181-197.

Stakman, E. C. 1947. Plant diseases are shifty enemies. *Sci. Progr.*, 5:235-279.

——, W. Q. Loegering, R. C. Cassell, and L. Hines. 1943. Population trends of physiologic races of *Puccinia graminis tritici* in the United States for the period 1930-1941. *Phytopathology*, 33:884-898.

Stalker, H. D. 1954. Parthenogenesis in *Drosophila. Gs.*, 39:4-34.

——. 1956. On the evolution of parthenogenesis in *Lonchoptera (Diptera). E.*, 10:345-359.

——. 1960. Chromosomal polymorphism in *Drosophila paramelanica* Patterson. *Gs.*, 45:95-114.

——. 1964a. Chromosomal polymorphism in *Drosophila euronotus. Gs.*, 49:669-682.

——. 1964b. The salivary gland chromosomes of *Drosophila nigromelanica. Gs.*, 49:883-893.

——. 1965. The salivary gland chromosomes of *Drosophila micromelanica* and *Drosophila melanica. Gs.*, 51:487-507.

——. 1966. The phylogenetic relationships of the species in *Drosophila melanica* group. *Gs.*, 53:327-342.

Stansfield, W. D., G. E. Bradford, C. Stormont, and R. J. Blackwell. 1964. Blood groups and their associations with production and reproduction in sheep. *Gs.*, 50:1357-1367.

Stauber, L. A. 1950. The problem of physiological species with special reference to oysters and oyster drills. *Ecology*, 31:109-118.

Stebbins, G. L. 1939. Structural hybridity in *Paeonia californica* and *P. brownii. J. Genetics*, 38:1-36.

——. 1950. Variation and Evolution in Plants. Columbia Univ. Press, New York.

——. 1957a. Self-fertilization and population variability in the higher plants. *A.N.*, 91:337-354.

——. 1957b. The hybrid origin of microspecies in the *Elymus glaucus* complex. *Cytologia*, Suppl. Vol.:336-340.

——. 1958a. The inviability, weakness, and sterility of interspecific hybrids. *Adv. Genetics*, 9:147-215.

——. 1958b. Longevity, habitat, and release of genetic variability in the higher plants. *C.S.H.*, 23:365-378.

——. 1969. The Basis of Progressive Evolution. Univ. North Carolina Press, Chapel Hill.

——, and A. Day. 1967. Cytogenetic evidence for long continued stability in the genus *Plantago*. *E.*, 21:409-428.

——, and E. Yagil. 1966. The morphogenetic effects of the hooded gene in barley. I. The course of development in hooded and awned genotypes. *Gs.*, 54:727-741.

Stebbins, R. C. 1949. Speciation in salamanders of the plethodontid genus *Ensatina*. *Univ. California Publ. Zool.*, 48:377-526.

——. 1957. Intraspecific sympatry in the lungless salamander *Ensatina eschscholtzi*. *E.*, 11:265-270.

Stehli, F. G. 1968. Taxonomic diversity gradients in pole location. The recent model. Pp. 163-227 *in:* E. T. Drake (Ed.), "Evolution and Environment," Yale Univ. Press, New Haven.

——, R. G. Douglas, and N. D. Newell. 1969. Generation and maintenance of gradients in taxonomic diversity. *S.*, 164:947-949.

Steinberg, A. G. 1959. The genetics of diabetes. A review. *Ann. New York Acad. Sci.*, 82:197-207.

——. 1962. Progress in the study of genetically determined human gamma globulin types (the *Gm* and *Inv* groups). Pp. 1-33 *in:* A. G. Steinberg and A. G. Bearn (Eds.), "Progress in Medical Genetics," Vol. 2, Grune & Stratton, London.

——. 1967. Genetic variations in human immunoglobulins: the *Gm* and *Inv*. types. Pp. 75-98 *in:* F. J. Greenwalt (Ed.), "Advances in Immunogenetics," Lippincott, Philadelphia.

——. 1969. Globulin polymorphisms in man. *Ann. Rev. Genetics*, 3:25-52.

——, H. K. Bleibtreu, Th. W. Kurczynski, A. O. Martin, and A. M. Kurczynski. 1967. Genetic studies on an inbred human isolate. Pp. 267-289 *in:* J. F. Crow and J. V. Neel (Eds.), "Proceedings of the 3rd International Congress on Human Genetics," Johns Hopkins Press, Baltimore.

Stephens, S. G. 1946. The genetics of "corky." *J. Genetics,* 47:150-161.

——. 1949. The cytogenetics of speciation in *Gossypium*. I. Selective elimination of the donor parent genotype in interspecific backcrosses. *Gs.*, 34:627-637.

——. 1950. The internal mechanism of speciation in *Gossypium*. *Bot. Rev.*, 16:115-149.

Stern, C. 1960. Principles of Human Genetics. 2nd Ed. Freeman, San Francisco.

——, G. Carson, M. Kinst, E. Novitski, and D. Uphoff. 1952. The viability of heterozygotes for lethals. *Gs.*, 37:413-450.

——, and C. Tokunaga. 1968. Autonomous pleiotropy in *Drosophila*. *P.N.A.S.*, 60:1252-1259.

Stevenson, A. C. 1959. The load of hereditary defect in human populations. *Radiation Res.*, Suppl. 1:306-325.

——. 1961. Frequency of congenital and hereditary disease. *Brit. Med. Bull.*, 17:254-259.

——, H. A. Johnston, M. I. P. Stewart, and D. R. Golding. 1966. Congenital Malformations. World Health Organization, Geneva.

Stimpfling, J. H., and M. R. Irwin. 1960. Evolution of cellular antigens in *Columbidae. E.*, 14:417-426.

Stone, W. S., W. C. Guest, and F. D. Wilson. 1960. The evolutionary implications of the cytological polymorphism and phylogeny of the *virilis* group of *Drosophila. P.N.A.S.*, 46:350-361.

——, F. M. Johnson, K. Kojima, and M. R. Wheeler. 1968. Isozyme variation in island populations of *Drosophila*. I. An analysis of a species of the *nasuta* complex in Samoa and Fiji. *U.T.P.*, 6818:157-170.

——, F. D. Wilson, and V. L. Gerstenberg. 1963. Genetic studies of natural populations of *Drosophila: Drosophila pseudoobscura*, a large dominant population. *Gs.*, 48:1089-1106.

Stormont, C. 1959. On the application of blood groups in animal breeding. *P. X I.C.G.*, I:206-224.

Strauss, B. S. 1964. Chemical mutagens and the genetic code. *Progr. Med. Genetics*, 3:1-48.

Straw, R. M. 1956. Floral isolation in *Penstemon. A.N.*, 90:47-53.

Streisinger, G., Y. Okada, J. Emrich, J. Newton, A. Tsugita, E. Terzagi, and M. Inouye. 1966. Frameshift mutations and the genetic code. *C.S.H.*, 31:77-84.

Strickberger, M. W. 1963. Evolution of fitness in experimental populations of *Drosophila pseudoobscura. Gs.*, 17:40-55.

——. 1968. Genetics. Macmillan, New York.

Stubbe, H. 1940. Kritische Bemerkungen zu *Antirrhinum rhinantoides* Lotsy. *Biol. Zentral.*, 60:590-597.

——. 1950. Über den Selektionswert von Mutanten. Sitzungsber. *Deutsch. Akad. Wissen. Berlin*, Landwirtshafliche Klasse, No. 1:1-42.

Sturtevant, A. H. 1920-21. Genetic studies on *Drosophila simulans. Gs.*, 5:488-500; 6:179-207.

——. 1926. A crossover reducer in *Drosophila melanogaster* due to inversion of a section of the third chromosome. *Biol. Zentral.*, 46:697-702.

——. 1929. The genetics of *Drosophila simulans. Carnegie Inst. Washington Publ.* 399:1-62.

——. 1948. The evolution and function of genes. *Amer. Scientist*, 36:225-236.

——, and E. Novitski. 1941. The homologies of the chromosome elements in the genus Drosophila. *Gs.*, 26:517-541.

Sullivan, B., and P. E. Nute. 1968. Structural and functional properties of polymorphic hemoglobins from orangutans. *Gs.*, 58:113-124.

Sullivan, W. 1964. We Are Not Alone. McGraw-Hill, New York.

Sun, S., and H. Rees. 1967. Genotypic control of chromosome behaviour in rye. IX. The effect of selection on the disjunction frequency of interchange associations. *Hy.*, 22:249-254.

Suomalainen, E. 1947a. Parthenogenese und Polyploidie bei Russelkäfern (*Curculionidae*). *Hs.*, 33:425-456.

——. 1947b. On the cytology of the genus *Polygonatum* group *alterniflora. Ann. Acad. Sci. Fennicae*, A, 13:1-66.

——. 1958. Über das Vorkommen und spätere Verschwinden von *Epinephele lycaon* Rott. (*Lep. Satyridae*) in Finland. *Ann. Entom. Fennici*, 24:168-181.

——. 1962. Significance of parthenogenesis in the evolution of insects. *Ann. Rev. Entom.*, 7:349-366.

——. 1965. On the chromosomes of the geometrid moth genus *Cidaria. Ch.*, 16:166-184.

——. 1966. Achiasmatische Oogenese bei trichopteren. *Ch.*, 18:201-207.

——. 1969. Evolution in parthenogenetic *Curculionidae*. *E.B.*, 3:261-296.

Sved, J. A. 1968. Possible rates of gene substitution in evolution. *A.N.*, 102:283-293.

——, T. E. Reed, and W. F. Bodmer. 1967. The number of balanced polymorphisms that can be maintained in a natural population. *Gs.*, 55:469-481.

Takahashi, E. 1966. Growth and environmental factors in Japan. *Human Biol.*, 38:112-130.

Takenouchi, Y., and Takagi, R. 1967. A chromosome study of two parthenogenetic scolytid beetles. *Annot. Zool. Japon.*, 40:105-110.

Takhtajan, A. 1966. Systema et Phylogenia Magnoliophytorum. Nauka, Moscow-Leningrad (Russian).

Tal, M. 1967. Genetic differentiation and stability of some characters that distinguish *Lycopersicon esculentum* Mill. from *Solanum pennellis* Cor. *E.*, 21:316-333.

Tan, C. C. 1935. Salivary gland chromosomes in the two races of *Drosophila pseudoobscura*. *Gs.*, 20:392-402.

——. 1946. Mosaic dominance in the inheritance of color patterns in the ladybird beetle *Harmonia axyridis*. *Gs.*, 31:195-210.

Tanner, J. M. 1962. Growth at Adolescence. 2nd Ed. Blackwell, Oxford.

Tano, S., and A. B. Burdick. 1965. Female fecundity of *Drosophila melanogaster* second chromosome recessive lethal heterozygotes in homozygous and heterozygous genetic background. *Gs.*, 51:121-135.

Tantawy, A. O., and M. R. El-Helw. 1966. Studies on natural populations of *Drosophila*. V. Correlated response to selection in *Drosophila melanogaster*. *Gs.*, 53:97-110.

Taylor, J. H. 1969. Replication and organization of chromosomes. *P. XII I.C.G.*, 3:177-189.

Taylor, K. M. 1967. The chromosomes of some lower chordates. *Ch.*, 21:181-188.

Teilhard de Chardin, P. 1959. The Phenomenon of Man. Harper & Row, New York.

Temin, R. G. 1966. Homozygous viability and fertility loads in *Drosophila melanogaster*. *Gs.*, 53:27-46.

——, H. U. Meyer, P. S. Dawson, and J. F. Crow. 1969. The influence of epistasis on homozygous viability depression in *Drosophila melanogaster*. *Gs.*, 61:497-519.

Thoday, J. M. 1953. Components of fitness. *Symposium Soc. Exp. Biol.*, 7:96-113.

——. 1959. Effects of disruptive selection. I. Genetic flexibility. *Hy.*, 13:187-203.

——. 1967. New insights into continuous variation. Pp. 339-350 *in:* J. F. Crow and J. V. Neel (Eds.), "Proceedings of the 3rd International Congress on Human Genetics," Johns Hopkins Press, Baltimore.

——, and T. B. Boam. 1959. Effects of disruptive selection. II. Polymorphism and divergence without isolation. *Hy.*, 13:205-218.

——, J. B. Gibson, and S. G. Spickett. 1964. Regular responses to selection. 2. Recombination and accelerated response. *G.R.*, 5:1-19.

Thomas, R. E., and P. A. Roberts. 1966. Comparative frequency of X-ray induced crossover suppressing aberrations recovered from oocytes and sperm of *Drosophila melanogaster*. *Gs.*, 53:855-862.

Thompson, J. B. 1956. Genetic control of chromosome behaviour in rye. II. Disjunction at meiosis in interchange heterozygotes. *Hy.*, 10:99-108.

Thompson, P. E. 1962. Asynapsis and mutability in *Drosophila melanogaster*. *Gs.*, 47:337-349.

Thorpe, W. H. 1930. The biology of the petroleum fly (*Psilofa petrolei* Cog.). *Trans. Entom. Soc. London*, 78:331-343.

——. 1963. Learning and Instinct of Animals. 2nd Ed. Harvard Univ. Press, Cambridge.

Timofeeff-Ressovsky, H. 1934. Über den Einfluss des genotypischen Milieus und der Ausenbedingungen auf die Realisation des Genotyps. *Nachr. Ges. Wiss. Göttingen, Biol.,* N. F. 1:53-106.

——. 1935. Auslösung von Vitalitätsmutationen durch Röntgenbestrahlung bei *Drosophila melanogaster. Nachr. Ges. Wiss. Göttingen, Biol.,* N. F., 1:163-180.

——. 1937. Experimentelle Mutationsforschung in der Vererbungslehre. Theodor Steinkopff, Dresden and Leipzig.

——. 1939. Genetik und Evolution. *Z.i.A.V.,* 76:158-218.

——, and N. W. Timofeeff-Ressovsky. 1927. Genetische Analyse einer freilebenden *Drosophila melanogaster* Population. *Arch. Entwicklungsmech. Organ.,* 109: 70-109.

Tinbergen, N. 1965. Some recent studies of the evolution of sexual behavior. Pp. 1-33 *in:* F. A. Beach, "Sex and Behavior," John Wiley, New York.

——. 1966. Social Behavior in Animals. 2nd Ed. Methuen, London.

Tinkle, D. W. 1965. Population structure and effective size of a lizard population. *E.,* 19:569-573.

Tjio, J. H., and A. Levan. 1956. The chromosome number in man. *Hs.,* 42:1-6.

Tobari, I. 1966. Effects of temperature on the viabilities of homozygotes and heterozygotes for second chromosomes of *Drosophila melanogaster. Gs.,* 54: 783-791.

——, and K. I. Kojima. 1967. Selective modes associated with inversion karyotypes in *Drosophila ananassae.* I. Frequency-dependent selection. *Gs.,* 57:179-188.

Tobias, Ph. V. 1965. Early man in Africa. *S.,* 149:22-33.

Torroja, E. 1964. Genetic loads in irradiated experimental populations of *Drosophila pseudoobscura. Gs.,* 50:1289-1298.

——. 1966. An experiment on the effects of sex-linked lethals in heterozygous condition in *Drosophila melanogaster. A.N.,* 100:77-80.

Tretzel, E. 1955. Intragenerische Isolation und interspecifische Konkurrenz bei Spinnen. *Zeit. Morph. Ökol. Tiere,* 44:43-162.

Trevor, J. C. 1953. Race crossing in man. *Eugenics Lab. Mem.* 36, Univ. London.

Tshetverikov, S. S. 1926 (1959). On certain aspects of the evolutionary process from the standpoint of genetics. *Zhurnal Exp. Biol.,* 1:3-54 (Russian); English translation: *Proc. Amer. Phil. Soc.* 105:167-195.

Turesson, G. 1922. The genotypical response of the plant species to the habitat. *Hs.,* 3:211-350.

——. 1925. The plant species in relation to habitat and climate. *Hs.,* 3:147-236.

——. 1930. The selective effect of climate upon the plant species. *Hs.,* 14:99-152.

Turpin, R., and J. Lejeune. 1965. Les chromosomes humains. Gauthier-Villars, Paris.

Twitty, V. 1959. Migration and speciation in newts. *S.,* 130:1735-1743.

——, D. Grant, and O. Anderson. 1967. Home range in relation to homing in the newt *Taricha rivularis. Copeia,* 1967:649-653.

Unrau, J. 1959. Cytogenetics and wheat breeding. *P.* X *I.C.G.,* 1:129-141.

Upcott, M. 1939. The nature of tetraploidy in *Primula kewensis. J. Genetics,* 39: 79-100.

Uvarov, B. P. 1928. Locusts and Grasshoppers. Imperial Bureau of Entomology, London.

——, and J. G. Thomas. 1942. The probable mechanism of phase variation in the pronotum of locusts. *Proc. Royal Soc.,* A, 17:113-118.

Uzzell, Th. M., and S. M. Goldblatt. 1967. Serum protein of salamanders of the *Ambystoma jeffersonianum* complex, and the origin of the triploid species of this group. *E.,* 21:345-354.

Vandel, A. 1941. Étude des garniture chromosomiques de quelques crustacés isopodes terrestres et d'eau douce européens. *Cytologia,* 12:44-65.

——. 1964. Biospéologie. Gauthier-Villars, Paris.

Vann, E. 1966. The fate of X-ray induced chromosomal rearrangements introduced into laboratory populations of *Drosophila melanogaster. A.N.,* 100:425-449.

Vanyushin, B. F., A. N. Belozersky, N. A. Kokurina, and D. X. Kadirova. 1968. 5-methylcytosine and 6-methylaminopurine in bacterial DNA. *N.,* 218:1066.

Vavilov, N. I. 1926. Studies on the Origin of Cultivated Plants. *Bull. Applied Botany.* Leningrad.

Vernadsky, V. I. 1965. Chemical Structure of the Biosphere of the Earth and Its Environs. Nauka, Moscow (Russian).

Vetukhiv, M. 1953. Viability of hybrids between local populations of *Drosophila pseudoobscura. P.N.A.S.,* 39:30-34.

——. 1954. Integration of the genotype in local populations of three species of *Drosophila. E.,* 8:241-251.

——. 1956. Fecundity of hybrids between geographic populations of *Drosophila pseudoobscura. E.,* 10:139-146.

Vickery, R. R. 1959. Barriers to gene exchange within *Mimulus guttatus (Scrophulariaceae). E.,* 13:300-310.

——. 1964. Barriers to gene exchange between members of the *Mimulus guttatus (Scrophulariaceae). E.,* 18:52-69.

——. 1966. Speciation and isolation in section *Simiolus* of the genus *Mimulus. Taxon,* 15:55-63.

Viemeyer, G. 1958. Reversal of evolution in the genus *Penstemon. A.N.,* 92:129-137.

Vogel, F., H. J. Pettenkofer, and W. Helmbold. 1961. Über die Populationsgenetik der ABO Blutgruppen. *Acta Gen. Stat. Med.,* 10:267-294.

Vogt, M. 1950. Analyse durch Athylurethan bei *Drosophila* induzirter Mutationen. *Z.i.A.V.,* 83:324-340.

Voipio, P. 1950. Evolution at the Population Level with Special Reference to Game Animals and Practical Game Management. Finnish Fdn. for Game Preservation. Helsinki.

Volpe, E. P. 1952. Physiological evidence for natural hybridization of *Bufo americanus* and *Bufo fowleri. E.,* 6:393-406.

Vries, Hugo de. 1901. Die Mutationstheorie. Veit, Leipzig.

Waagen, W. 1869. Die Formenreihe des *Ammonites subradiatus. Benecke geognostischpaläontol. Beitr.,* 2:179-257.

Waddington, C. H. 1953. Genetic assimilation of an acquired character. *E.,* 7:118-126.

——. 1957. The Strategy of the Genes. Allen & Unwin, London.

——. 1960. Evolutionary adaptation. Pp. 381-402 *in:* S. Tax (Ed.), "Evolution after Darwin," Univ. Chicago Press, Chicago.

Wagner, M. 1889. Die Entstehung der Arten durch räumliche Sonderung. Schwalbe, Basel.

Walker, J. C. 1951. Genetics and plant pathology. *In:* L. C. Dunn, "Genetics in the Twentieth Century," Macmillan, New York.

Walker, T. J. 1957. Specificity in the response of female tree crickets to calling songs of the males. *Ann. Entom. Soc. Amer.,* 50:626-636.

Wallace, B. 1953. On coadaptation in *Drosophila*. *A.N.*, 87:343-358.

——. 1954. Genetic divergence of isolated populations of *Drosophila melanogaster*. *P. IX I.C.G., Caryologia*, 6 (Suppl.): 761-764.

——. 1955. Interpopulation hybrids in *Drosophila melanogaster*. *E.*, 9:302-316.

——. 1958. The average effect of radiation-induced mutations on viability in *Drosophila melanogaster*. *E.*, 12:532-556.

——. 1962. Temporal changes in the roles of lethal and semilethal chromosomes within populations of *Drosophila melanogaster*. *A.N.*, 96:247-256.

——. 1963a. Genetic diversity, genetic uniformity, and heterosis. *Canad. J. Gen. Cytol.*, 5:239-253.

——. 1963b. Further data on the overdominance of induced mutations. *Gs.*, 48: 633-651.

——. 1965. The viability effects of spontaneous mutations in *Drosophila melanogaster*. *A.N.*, 99:335-348.

——. 1966a. On the dispersal of *Drosophila*. *A.N.*, 100:551-563.

——. 1966b. Distance and allelism of lethals in a tropical population of *Drosophila melanogaster*. *A.N.*, 100:565-578.

——. 1966c. Natural and radiation-induced chromosomal polymorphism in *Drosophila*. *Mutation Res.*, 3:194-200.

——. 1968a. Topics in Population Genetics. Norton, New York.

——. 1968b. Polymorphism, population size, and genetic load. Pp. 87-108 *in:* R. C. Lewontin (Ed.), "Population Biology and Evolution," Syracuse Univ. Press, Syracuse.

——, and Th. Dobzhansky. 1947. Experiments on sexual isolation in *Drosophila*. VIII. Influence of light on the mating behavior of *Drosophila subobscura*, *D. persimilis*, and *D. pseudoobscura*. *P.N.A.S.*, 32:226-234.

——, and Th. Dobzhansky. 1962. Experimental proof of balanced genetic loads in *Drosophila*. *Gs.*, 47:1027-1042.

——, J. C. King, C. V. Madden, B. Kaufmann, and E. C. McGunnigle. 1953. An analysis of variability arising through recombination. *Gs.*, 38:272-308.

——, and C. Madden. 1953. The frequencies of sub- and supervitals in experimental populations of *Drosophila melanogaster*. *Gs.*, 38:456-470.

——, and C. Madden. 1965. Studies on inbred strains of *Drosophila melanogaster*. *A.N.*, 99:495-510.

——, E. Zouros, and C. B. Krimbas. 1966. Frequencies of second and third chromosome lethals in a tropical population of *Drosophila melanogaster*. *A.N.*, 100: 245-251.

Wallace, M. E. 1965. How homozygous are our inbred lines and closed colony stocks? *Fd. Cosmet. Toxicol.*, 3:165-175.

Walles, B. 1963. Macromolecular physiology of plastids. IV. On amino acid requirements of lethal chloroplast mutants in barley. *Hereditas*, 50:317-344.

Walters, J. L. 1942. Distribution of structural hybrids in *Paeonia californica*. *Amer. J. Bot.*, 29:270-275.

Wasserman, M. 1960. Cytological and phylogenetic relationships in the *repleta* group of the genus *Drosophila*. *P.N.A.S.*, 46:842-859.

——. 1963. Cytology and phylogeny of *Drosophila*. *A.N.*, 97:333-352.

Watanabe, T. K., 1969a. Persistence of a visible mutant in natural populations of *Drosophila melanogaster*. *Japan. J. Genetics*, 44:15-22.

——. 1969b. Frequency of deleterious chromosomes and allelism between lethal genes in Japanese natural populations of *Drosophila melanogaster*. *Japan. J. Genetics*, 44:171-187.

Watson, J. D. 1965. The Molecular Biology of the Gene. Benjamin, New York.

——, and F. C. Crick. 1953. Genetical implication of the structure of deoxyribose nucleic acid. *N.*, 171:964.

Watt, W. B. 1968. Adaptive significance of pigment polymorphisms in *Colias* butterflies. I. Variation of melanin pigment in relation to thermoregulation. *E.*, 22: 437-458.

Weinberg, W. 1908. Über den Nachweis der Vererbung beim Menschen. *Jahreshefte Verein, Naturk. Würtemberg*, 64:368-382.

Welch, D'Alte A. 1938. Distribution and variation of *Achatinella mustellina* Michels in the Waianae Mountains, Oahu. *Bull. Bishop Museum*, 152:1-164.

Weisbrot, D. R. 1963. Studies on differences in the genetic architecture of related species of *Drosophila. Gs.*, 48:1121-1139.

——. 1966. Genotypic interactions among competing strains and species of *Drosophila. Gs.*, 53:427-435.

Weiss, M. C., and B. Ephrussi. 1966. Studies of interspecific (rat × mouse) somatic hybrids. I. Isolation, growth and evolution of the karyotype. *Gs.*, 54:1095-1109.

——, and H. Green. 1967. Human-mouse hybrid cell lines containing partial complements of human chromosomes and functioning human genes. *P.N.A.S.*, 58: 1104-1111.

Welshons, W. J. 1965. Analysis of a gene in *Drosophila. S.*, 150:1122-1129.

——, and L. B. Russell. 1959. The Y chromosome as the bearer of male determining factors in the mouse. *P.N.A.S.*, 45:560-566.

Wheeler, M. R. 1959. A nomenclatorial study of the genus *Drosophila. U.T.P.*, 5914:181-205.

White, M. J. D. 1949. A cytological survey of wild populations of *Trimetotripis* and *Circotettix* (*Orthoptera, Acrididae*). I. The chromosomes of twelve species. *Gs.*, 34:537-563.

——. 1954. Animal Cytology and Evolution. 2nd Ed. Cambridge Univ. Press, Cambridge.

——. 1957. Cytogenetics of the grasshopper *Moraba scurra*. II. Heterotic systems and their interaction. *Austral. J. Zool.*, 5:305-337.

——. 1966. Further studies on the cytology and distribution of the Australian parthenogenetic grasshopper *Moraba virgo. Rev. Suisse Zool.*, 73:383-398.

——. 1968. Models of speciation. *S.*, 159:1065-1070.

——, H. L. Carson, and Y. Cheney. 1964. Chromosomal races in the Australian grasshopper *Moraba viatica* in a zone of geographic overlap. *E.*, 18:417-429.

——, J. Cheney, and K. H. L. Key. 1963. A parthenogenetic species of grasshopper with complex structure heterozygosity (*Orthoptera, Acridoidea*). *Austral. J. Zool.*, 11:1-19.

——, R. C. Lewontin, and L. E. Andrew. 1963. Cytogenetics of the grasshopper *Moraba scurra*. VII. Geographic variation of adaptive properties of inversions. *E.*, 17:147-162.

——, and N. H. Nickerson. 1951. Structural heterozygosity in a very rare species of grasshopper. *A.N.*, 85:239-246.

Wiener, A. S. 1965. Blood groups of chimpanzees and other nonhuman primates. *Trans. New York Acad. Sci.*, 27:488-504.

Wilkie J. S. 1959. Buffon, Lamarck and Darwin, the originality of Darwin's theory of evolution. Pp. 262-307 *in:* P. R. Bell (Ed.), "Darwin's Biological Work," Cambridge Univ. Press, Cambridge.

Williams, C. B. 1960. The range and pattern of insect abundance. *A.N.*, 94:137-151.

Williams, G. C. 1966. Adaptation and Natural Selection. Princeton Univ. Press, Princeton.

Williamson, D. L., and L. Ehrman. 1967. Induction of hybrid sterility in non-hybrid males of Drosophila paulistorum. Gs., 55:131-140.

Wills, C. 1966. The mutational load in two natural populations of Drosophila pseudoobscura. Gs., 53:281-294.

——. 1968. Three kinds of genetic variability in yeast populations. P.N.A.S., 61:937-944.

Wilson, A. C., and V. M. Sarich. 1969. A molecular time scale for human evolution. P.N.A.S., 63:1088-1093.

Wilson, E. O., and W. H. Bossert. 1963. Chemical communication among animals. Recent Progr. Hormone Res., 19:673-716.

——, and W. L. Brown. 1953. The subspecies concept and its taxonomic application. S.Z., 2:97-111.

Winge, H. 1965. Interspecific hybridizaton between the six cryptic species of Drosophila willistoni group. Hy., 20:9-19.

Witkin, E. M. 1947. Genetics of resistance to radiation in Escherichia coli. Gs., 32:221-248.

——. 1966. Radiation-induced mutations and their repair. S., 152:1345-1353.

Wittmann-Liebold, B., and H. G. Wittmann. 1963. Die primäre Proteinstruktur von Stämmen des Tabakmosaikvirus. Z.i.A.V., 9::427-435.

Wolf, B. E. 1968. Adaptiver chromosomaler Polymorphismus und flexible Kontrolle der Rekombination bei Phryne cincta (Diptera, Nematocera). Zool. Beitr., 14:125-153.

Wolpoff, M. H. 1969. The effect of mutations under conditions of reduced selection. Social Biol., 16:11-23.

Wolstenholme, G. E. W., and C. M. O'Connor (Eds.). 1957. Drug Resistance in Microorganisms. CIBA Foundation Symposium, Little, Brown, Boston.

Woodson, R E. 1964. The geography of flower color in butterfly weed. E., 18:143-163.

Woodworth, C. M., E. R. Leng, and R. W. Jugenheimer. 1952. Fifty generations of selection for protein and oil in corn. Agron. J., 44:60-66.

Woolf, Ch. M. 1965. Albinism among Indians in Arizona and New Mexico. Amer. J. Human Genetics, 17:23-35.

——, and F. C. Dukepoo. 1969. Hopi Indians, inbreeding and albinism. S., 164:30-37.

Woolpy, J. H., and B. E. Ginsburg. 1967. Wolf socialization: a study of temperament in a wild social species. Amer. Zoologist, 7:357-363.

Wright, S. 1921. Systems of mating. Gs., 6:111-178.

——. 1931. Evolution in Mendelian populations. Gs., 16:97-159.

——. 1932. The roles of mutation, inbreeding, crossbreeding, and selection in evolution. P. VI I.C.G., I:356-366.

——. 1940. Breeding structure of populations in relation to speciation. A.N., 84:232-248.

——. 1943a. Isolation by distance. Gs., 28:114-138.

——. 1943b. An analysis of local variability of flower color in Linanthus parryae. Gs., 28:139-156.

——. 1948. On the roles of directed and random changes in gene frequency in the genetics of natural populations. E., 2:279-294.

——. 1949. Adaptation and selection. Pp. 365-389 in: G. L. Jepsen, G. G. Simpson, and E. Mayr (Eds.), "Genetics, Paleontology and Evolution," Princeton Univ. Press, Princeton.

———. 1955. Classification of factors of evolution. *C.S.H.*, 20:16-24.

———. 1960. On the appraisal of genetic effects of radiation in Man. Pp. 18-24 *in:* "The Biological Effects of Atomic Radiations," National Academy of Science, Washington.

———. 1964a. Pleiotropy in the evolution of structural reduction and of dominance. *A.N.*, 98:65-69.

———. 1964b. The distribution of self-incompatibility alleles in populations, *E.*, 18:609-619.

———. 1966. Polyallelic random drift in relation to evolution. *P.N.A.S.*, 55:1074-1081.

———, and Th. Dobzhansky. 1946. Genetics of natural populations. XII. Experimental reproduction of some of the changes caused by natural selection in certain populations of *Drosophila pseudoobscura*. *Gs.*, 31:125-150.

———, Th. Dobzhansky, and W. Hovanitz. 1942. Genetics of natural populations. VII. The allelism of lethals in the third chromosome of *Drosophila pseudoobscura*. *Gs.*, 27:373-394.

Wynne-Edwards, V. C. 1962. Animal Dispersion in Relation to Social Behaviour. Oliver & Boyd, Edinburgh and London.

Yanagishima, S. 1961. CuSO4 resistance in *Drosophila melanogaster*. III and IV. *Mem. College Sci. Univ. Kyoto*, B, 28:1-52.

Yang, S. Y., and R. K. Selander. 1968. Hybridization in the grackle *Quiscalus quiscula* in Louisiana. *S.Z.*, 17:107-143.

Yanofsky, Ch., H. Berger, and W. J. Brammar. 1969. *In vivo* studies on the genetic code. *P.* XII *I.C.G.*, 3:155-165.

———, G. R. Drapeau, J. R. Guest, and B. C. Carlton. 1967. The complete amino acid sequence of the tryptophan synthetase. A protein ($\alpha$ subunit) and its colinear relationship with the genetic map of the A gene. *P.N.A.S.*, 57:296-298.

Yarbrough, K., and K. I. Kojima. 1967. The model of selection at the polymorphic esterase 6 locus in cage populations of *Drosophila melanogaster*. *Gs.*, 57:677-686.

Yosida, T. H., and K. Amano. 1965. Autosomal polymorphism in laboratory bred and wild Norway rats, *Rattus norvegicus*, found in Misima. *Ch.*, 16:658-667.

———, A. Nakamura, and T. Fukaya. 1965. Chromosomal polymorphism in *Rattus rattus* (L) collected in Kusudomari and Misima. *Ch.*, 16:70-78.

Zander, C. D. 1962. Untersuchungen über einen arttrennenden Mechanismus bei lebendgebärenden Zahnkarpfen aus der Tribus *Xiphophorini*. *Mitt. Hamburg Zool. Mus. Inst.*, 60:205-264.

Zaslavsky, V. A. 1966. Isolating mechanism and its role in the ecology of two allied *Chilocorus* species. *Zool. Zhurnal*, 45:203-212. (Russian).

———. 1967. Reproductive self-destruction as an ecological factor. *J. Gen. Biol.*, 28:3-11. (Russian).

Zavadsky, K. M. 1968. Species and Species Formation. Nauka, Leningrad. (Russian).

Zimmerman, K. 1931. Studien über individuelle und geographische Variabilitat paläarktischer *Polistes* und verwandter Vespiden. *Zeit. Morph. Ökol. Tiere*, 22:173-230.

Zuckerkandl, E. 1964. Controller-gene diseases. *J. Mol. Biol.*, 8:128-147.

———. 1965. The evolution of hemoglobin. *Sci. American*, 212(5):110-118.

——, and L. Pauling. 1965. Evolutionary divergence and convergence in proteins. Pp. 97-166 *in:* V. Bryson and H. J. Vogel (Eds.), "Evolving Genes and Proteins," Academic Press, New York.

Zürcher, C. 1963. Der Faktor e$^{ug}$ bei *Drosophila melanogaster. Ga.*, 34:1-33.